Lady Sale

Staffordshire
Portrait Figures

Colour Plate 1
Turkey-England-France. Napoleon III, Queen Victoria and Abd-ul-Medjid. *Fig.* 75, *pl.* C-32. See pages 54 and 240.

STAFFORDSHIRE PORTRAIT FIGURES

and Allied Subjects of the Victorian Era

including the Definitive Catalogue

P.D. Gordon Pugh

Fellow of the Royal Society of Arts

Antique Collectors' Club

© P.D.G. Pugh 1970

First published in 1970 by Barrie & Jenkins Ltd.
Reprinted with corrections and additions in 1981.

New and revised edition 1987 published by the
Antique Collectors' Club

ISBN 1 85149 010 8

Pugh, P.D. Gordon
    Staffordshire portrait figures and allied
    subjects of the Victoria era. — 2nd,
    rev. ed.
    I. Pottery figures, Victorian —   England
    — Staffordshire
    I. Title
    738.8'2   NK4660

    ISBN 1 85149 010 8

Re-designed by John and Griselda Lewis

Printed in England by
Antique Collectors' Club Ltd.,
Woodbridge, Suffolk.

TO MARGERY

CONTENTS

COLOUR PLATES

INTRODUCTORY &
ACKNOWLEDGEMENTS

In Victorian times a new type of Staffordshire figure emerged. In its classical form it is known as the *flat-back*, but it was preceded by a more sophisticated and highly coloured type which attempted to imitate porcelain. All these figures were the work of artisans with no special original talent, who obtained their inspiration from whatever source they could, modifying it as fancy or necessity dictated. Those models which represent known persons are referred to as *portrait figures*.

There is a 'Madame Tussaud' fascination about portrait figures. One can never be quite certain, apart from members of royalty, for whom the potters no doubt saw steady patriotic sales, which contemporary, historical or legendary figures would take their fancy. In the main, however, an attempt seems to have been made to provide the 'news of the day' by means of portrait figures in much the same way as pictorial dailies provide this service today; for this reason the figures had a broad appeal throughout the land. Many would regard the Crimean War period as the heyday of portrait figures. Among nearly two hundred known figures there are portraits enough to show that every action throughout that war was recorded by a model of its commander; everyone that is to say except the most tragic and best remembered of all – the charge of the Light Brigade. That calamitous event silenced the potters.

Victorian Staffordshire portrait figures may be found with or without titles. If untitled the identification is often obvious. Sometimes, however, the likeness is so poor, or the person portrayed so little known, that the figure poses a major problem solved only when the potter's *source* comes to light. This may be an illustration in a contemporary periodical or a painting or similar treasure, as often as not, located in one of the great public collections.

Figures were made in varying degrees of excellence. Some are of outstanding quality, others mediocre and a few frankly hideous, but all are historically interesting and many pose unsolved problems that can be an unending source of entertainment. The discovery of a hitherto unrecorded figure or the identification of a hitherto unrecognized figure are thrills which are still available to the collector of today, and the final solution of all the problems is unlikely to be achieved for many decades.

My own concern in the subject began in the late forties and received impetus in 1953 with the publication of Mr Bryan Latham's pioneer work *Victorian Staffordshire Portrait Figures*. This book provoked widespread interest. From then onwards, collectors and dealers alike scoured the country from John o' Groats to Land's End in the hunt for these, hitherto unappreciated, comparatively cheap examples of one of the last folk arts. A further stimulus to collectors was provided in 1958 when the late Mr Thomas Balston published his classic catalogue *Staffordshire Portrait Figures of the Victorian Age*.

One of the attractions of Staffordshire figure hunting is the number of variations in the type of collection that can be built up. Other than those few who have amassed large general collections, ranging from two or three hundred figures to upwards of a thousand figures, there are more specialized collectors who have restricted their examples to royalty or to sporting figures, or to theatre, ballet and circus figures or to politicians, criminals or divines. There are also those who collect nothing but equestrian figures and those who simply collect figures that take their fancy. The whole joy of collecting Staffordshire figures is, in fact, that the enthusiast can collect just what he likes in just that quantity that suits his particular circumstance.

In 1963, by which time my own collection had reached somewhere in the region of four hundred and fifty figures, I determined to try and obtain photographs of all known portraits and allied subjects. The latter include castles, Crimean fortresses, murder houses and illustrious quadrupeds, such as 'Jumbo' and

the greyhound 'Master M'Grath'. Had I realized the problems ahead, it is doubtful if I would ever have started such a project; however, the fantastic enthusiasm with which the project was greeted and the help I received from collectors as the work progressed made it impossible for me to even consider turning back. Here it must be stated that I have failed in my original intention for unrecorded figures continue to come to light. Moreover, because of the known existence of a number of figures which must have pairs, it can be confidently predicted that this state of affairs will continue for many years to come.

The problems of photography were tremendous. There is no collection in the country that is anything like complete; moreover, to obtain the best effect, it was desirable to photograph many figures in groups, pairs or in series. A special feature of the volume is the illustration of as many figures as possible beside their sources. This too posed problems, for on occasions the source would be available and not the figure and vice versa. A special mobile stage was constructed for uniformity, and after first photographing my collection, Mr and Mrs Denys Bowns (who have undertaken much of the photography in this work) and myself travelled many hundreds of miles over a period of four years visiting other collectors, often taking figures with us to make up sets or pairs. As more and more hitherto unknown figures came to light, it became necessary to rearrange the grouping in many photographs already taken, so that in all nearly three thousand different photographs were involved. Difficulties occasionally arose when a collection had been dispersed by the time the need for an adjustment to a group became apparent. The final outcome exceeds eight hundred photographs covering over one thousand five hundred figures.

From the beginning, the enthusiasm, generosity and hospitality of other collectors made the task enthralling. I wish to extend my warmest thanks to all these friends, not only those who hold the largest collections, but also those with just the one or two pieces that had so far eluded me.

I have been privileged to obtain photographs of figures in the private collections of the following:

Mr Geoffrey Allen
Miss Jean Anderson
Mr H. T. Appleton
Mr Anthony Baer
The late Mr Thomas Balston, OBE, MC
Mrs Constance Chiswell
Rear-Admiral J. Dent, CB, OBE
Mr George Dermody
Mr Robert Eddison
Mr Joe Fairhurst
Mr Patrick Gibson
Mrs Thornley Gibson
Mr Geoffrey A. Godden, FRSA
Miss E. M. Groves
Mrs H. de C. Hastings
Mr Jack Hawkins, CBE
Dr S. J. Howard
Mr and Mrs E. H. Joyce
Mr Anthony D. Kerman
Lt Colonel A. C. W. Kimpton
Mr Bryan Latham, CBE
Wing Commander T. H. Lucas, RAF (rtd.)
Messrs Raymond Mander and Joe Mitchenson
Mr D. P. M. Michael, MA
Mr Anthony Oliver
Mrs Margaret Power
The Countess of Ranfurly
Mr George H. Rayner
Mr P. Redmayne

Mr David Robinson
Mr Bert Shevlov
Mr Ian N. R. Shield
Mr Ronald Shockledge
M. Marc de Smedt
Lady Snedden
Mr F. J. Stephens
Mrs Paul Stockman
Mr A. Guy Stringer
Dr T. D. V. Swinscow
Mr A. T. Thornton
The Hon. Mrs C. Wildman
Mrs Cecil Woodham-Smith, CBE

I have had invaluable help in obtaining rare figures and advice from many friends in the antique trade, but in particular I would like to mention:

Mr and Mrs R. Bonnett of 582, Kings Road, London, S.W.6.
Miss M. M. Frame of Adversane, Billingshurst, Sussex.
The late Mr T. E. Gascoigne.
Mr Hugo Morley-Fletcher of Messrs Christie, Manson & Woods.
Mr Anthony Oliver and Mr Peter Sutton of Oliver Sutton Antiques, 34c, Kensington Church Street, London, W.8.
Mr David Robinson of Highfields, Coggeshall, Essex.
Mr and Mrs W. W. Warner of 226, Brompton Road, London, S.W.3.

I must also acknowledge my indebtedness for help and advice and, on occasions, photographs from the Directors or their Assistants of:

The British Museum; the Victoria and Albert Museum; the National Portrait Gallery; the London Library; the London Museum; British Transport Historical Records, London; the Photographic Library, Ministry of Public Buildings and Works; the Zoological Society of London; the Dicken's House Museum, London; the Finsbury Public Library, London; the Ashmolean Museum, Oxford; the Fitzwilliam Museum, Cambridge; the Brighton Art Gallery and Museum; the Castle Museum, York; the Norwich Castle Museum; the City of Portsmouth Libraries and Museum Department; the Royal Marine Museum, Eastney Barracks; the City Museum and Art Gallery, Hanley, Stoke-on-Trent; the Central Library, Hanley, Stoke-on-Trent; Mintons Ltd., Stoke-on-Trent; the Laing Art Gallery and Museum, Newcastle upon Tyne; the Gloucester City Library; the National Library of Wales; the National Museum of Wales; the United States Information Service, American Embassy, London; the Metropolitan Museum of Art, New York; the Musée de La Dynastie, Brussels; the Bibliothèque Nationale, Paris; the Mozart Museum, Salzburg; the Lahore Museum, West Pakistan.

Among many others who have helped or advised in the production I would like to thank: The Most Hon. the Marquess of Anglesey; Mr R. S. Belcher; Colonel Mary Booth, CBE; Mr R. Gillies Cole; Mr Robert Graves, MA, B Litt; The Lord Gretton, OBE; Mr Disley Jones; Mr R. S. Lambert; Viscount Lambton, MP; Messrs D. M. and P. Manheim; Mr W. H. Paynter; Mr Geoffrey Wilson; Mr P. C. Withers; Mr Robert Wood.

I am particularly grateful to Mr and Mrs Eric Joyce who, from the start, have extended to me encouragement and hospitality, and advice which has proved invaluable; to Mr John Hall for his generous help in so many fields; to Messrs Raymond Mander and Joe Mitchenson for so much valuable information about 'theatrical figures'; to Mr Anthony Oliver for his painstaking researches on my behalf; to Mr H. S. Barnes of Barker Bros. Limited, Longton, who kindly allowed me to visit the site of the old Sampson Smith works and inspect the original moulds; to Mr Geoffrey Godden for allowing me to make so much use of his researches into the manufacture of these figures; to Mr and Mrs Bowns for their excellent photography; to my secretary, Mrs F. R. Watson who has been so accurate in her transcription from tape to paper; to my publishers for their co-operation in the production of such an attractive volume and finally, but not least, to my wife for her practical assistance and encouragement.

P.D.G.P., 1970

In this second impression, all known errors have been corrected. My text is otherwise unaltered except in the following respects. I should like to express my gratitude to Mr Paul Barthaud of Christie's South Kensington for supplying the Postscript to Chapter 7 and the Appendix 'Selected Auction Prices, 1978–80'; and to Mr Anthony Oliver for adding some new items to the Bibliography.

P.D.G.P., 1981

Publisher's note to the 1987 edition

P.D. Gordon Pugh's definitive catalogue of Victorian Staffordshire Portrait figures was first published in 1970. In 1981 it was reprinted with corrections and additions including an Appendix with up-dated prices.

The Antique Collectors' Club edition is based on the 1981 publication but with a completely new layout. Previously the plates were grouped separately from the text describing the figures. Now the text has been placed as near as possible to the plates, usually on the same page, and we hope that the book is now easier to use. New colour plates have been incorporated and we trust they are an improvement on the originals. In addition the number of colour plates has been increased from thirty-seven to sixty-two, and these have been spread throughout the book so that wherever possible they fall within the appropriate section. The Appendix on prices has been brought up to date.

We are confident that this new edition will be welcomed both by those who already possess the 1970 or 1981 versions, and by new collectors in this field who have been unable to obtain this essential reference book while it has been out of print.

'BUY MY IMAGES'

Written & Sung by
MR. *THOMAS HUDSON.*

1

Will you buy Images? I Images cry,
Very fine very pretty, very cheap will you buy?
Poor *Italiano* him never in de glooms
All sort Images beautiful your rooms.
First one *Prima* LORD BYRON head,
BYRON live longtimes after him dead
Loves tales *Poeta*—all very true one,
Every body's knows him call DON JUAN,
Will you buy Images? I Images cry
Very fine very pretty-cheap-will you buy?
Poor *Italiano* better laugh as cry,
Will you buy Images? very cheap, will you buy?

2

Dis Image one is MISTER SHAKISPEAR
Any prices charge you not pays dear
He go to High Park and steal a de Deer
Him work Play live more as Two hundred year
Every bodys know as take a de pains
To goes to Common Gardens and Drury Lanes
He make a you laugh and he make a you cry
Oftens dey murder him yet he never die.
   Buy my Images.

3

Nex' Image here dere come in de lot
Very great Noveltist—name WALER SCOTT
In prosa—in rima—never got greater
Him SCOTT too by names and by nature
So fas' make *Libro*—all write his own
Fus't was call him de Large not known
When discover himself—all delighted
Jus' fore he die he was be Knighted.
   Buy my Images.

4

Dis Image here was nobody spurn
Nother Scotch Poet you read ROBERT BURN
Poeta la Natura 'stonishing how
Him write and song wis follow de Plough
Him when alive Scotch clever confess
So leave him starve and die on distress
Now Scotch says wis national glows
BURN! greatest genius world ever knows!!!
   Buy my Images.

5

Dis de GREAT MILTON wis a bad wife cross
So compose himself for PARADISE LOSS
When wife dies dat ease some pains
So sit down to wrote PARADISE REGAINS
Him great scholars wis wonderful mind
And see very clears wis eyes all blir d
No let him daughters learn Latin stuff
One tongues for womans him says tis enough
   Buy my Images.

6

Here LORD NELSON *Inglese* man o'war
Him beat Spain France all both Trafalgar
When him right arm de battle bereft
Take sword tother and fight wis left
Defend *Inghilterra* wis wooden wall
Die wis Victory bury him Saint Paul
Fortys year afters dey finds him loss
Make de grand monument up Charing Cross
   Buy my Images.

7

Look a dis Images dis nex' one
Capitano Generale de LORD WELLINGTON
Him fight Buonaparté beat him too
And make fas' run 'way from Waterloo
Great as a Roman was he to de foes
Every bodys knows him well by's nose
Every body trues what every body says
De greatest man livings alive dis days
   Buy my Images.

8

Dis PRINCE ALBERT and try all you cans
You shall never found such a nice young mans
Queen fall in Loves wis him make stir
Him *Amantissimo* fall in Loves Her
Soon *Maritato* den he kneel down
Queen give Prince Albert wis Half a Crown
Wis Thirtys Thousand a years besides
For nothing but out wis Queen to rides
   Buy my Images.

9

Now *Finitissimo* nex' one seen
Dis FAIR VICTORIA Old England Queen
Got two Royal Babies ready for store
Every years mean haves one little more
Best Lady for Queen ever could known
Reign Peoples heart and grace *Inglese* Throne
Buy dis Images be *Lealta* seen
You not want Sovereign God save de Queen.
   Buy my Images.

c. 1842

1
Victorian Portrait Figures from their Evolution to their Decline

Introduction – The beginning, 1837-1840 – The early forties – The late forties to the early fifties – The Crimean period, 1854-1856 – The late fifties to the sixties – The seventies – The end of the reign, 1880-1901 – The early post-Victorian era, 1901-1905 – Reflections.

INTRODUCTION

During the nineteenth century a number of distinctive types of chimney ornaments emerged. Figures characteristic of the Victorian era began to appear in the 1840's. They may be distinguished from earlier Staffordshire figures by the greater whiteness of their clay. They are made generally from a three-piece mould. If subsidiary parts were necessary they, too, were moulded and not hand-made. Characteristically, the base is a smooth, flattened oval. Figures issued between the accession of Victoria and the early sixties are generally rich in colouring, particular advantage being taken of the remarkable brilliance exhibited by cobalt blue applied under the glaze. For later pieces the potters tended to be more sparing in applying colours, making effective use of the white undecorated glazed earthenware and confining decoration to flesh tints for the face and hands, black for hair and shoes and occasional touches of gold in appropriate places to enhance the general effect. During the early period designers tended to imitate porcelain, but later adopted the larger, simpler and more characteristic design of the period known as the *flat-back*, it being one that could be most efficiently reproduced in earthenware. The development of the flat-back was therefore probably a sequel to the need to simplify productive technique and lower costs in the face of increasing competition as the demand for chimney ornaments rose.

Although the overwhelming majority of portrait figures belong to this class, there are others. One distinctive type is that mounted on a rather elaborate four-legged table base associated with the name of Obadiah Sherratt. Most of these figures date from about 1815 until 1850, and the figure titled 'Her Majesty, Queen Victoria' (*fig. 2, pl.* A-2) is an example of this.

Many late eighteenth-century potters used a plinth base. This was continued well into the nineteenth century. The figure of William Shakespeare (*fig. 2, pl.* H-1) is a typical example.

As types which are generally considered to be pre-Victorian were undoubtedly produced, although in small numbers, during Victoria's reign, it is extremely difficult to be dogmatic in some cases as to whether a figure is Victorian or pre-Victorian. I have made no attempt to do so, including in my catalogue many portrait figures which although probably Victorian, might conceivably be pre-Victorian and even a few instructive pieces which are certainly pre-Victorian. Exactly the same position appertains at the end of the century when the art was dying. There are a number of figures which were almost certainly made several years after the death of Victoria which might, on superficial study, be dated to about 1880, the best example being the figure of Evan Roberts (*fig. 54, pl.* D-27).

THE BEGINNING (1837-1840)

It is fitting that the earliest datable Victorian portrait figure be of the Queen herself, even though, for reasons which will soon become apparent, it is neither made in the style for which the period is noted, nor is it strictly speaking, a true portrait of the young monarch. Reference has been made already to this figure; it is that modelled in the style of Obadiah Sherratt and titled 'Her Majesty, Queen Victoria' (*fig. 2, pl.* A-2). It portrays a young woman seated bare-headed on a sofa, a large double-arched crown to her right. It derives from a slightly earlier figure titled 'Malibran' (*fig. 308, pl.* E-149), otherwise identical except that there is no crown. This latter figure, in turn, was inspired by an engraving, by J. Rogers after A. M. Huffam, of the much loved opera singer Maria Malibran, who died on September 23rd, 1836, some weeks after a fall from a horse (*see pl.* A-3). The figure of the young songstress was 'adjusted' to represent the Queen when the requirement arose nine months later. There is no doubt that the potters were alive to expediences of this sort when urgent public demand justified them. The position of the crown suggests that the figure was sold from shortly after the Queen's accession on June 20th, 1837, until her coronation a year later.

The two figures of T. D. Rice in the character of 'Jim Crow' (*figs. 72 and 73, pl.* E-37), which he first played at the Royal Surrey Theatre in 1836, must have been issued either just before or soon after the Queen's accession.

The figure of Van Amburgh (*fig. 200, pl.* E-100) is of a pre-Victorian style, in so far that its many subsidiary parts are modelled by hand, but is undoubtedly Victorian for he first appeared at Astley's during the season of 1838. The two figures of the heroine Grace Darling (*figs. 39 and 40, pl.* 1-18) and the single figure of Lord Melbourne, adviser to the young Queen (*fig. 3, pl.* B-1) are also likely to date to about 1838.

THE EARLY FORTIES

Thereafter there came a flood of figures in the new style commencing with the seated pairs of the Queen and Prince Albert, such as *figs. 45 and 46, pl.* A-17 which celebrate the wedding of the young Queen in February 1840. Seated pairs of the Queen and Albert, in which she is holding a baby on her lap, such as *figs. 59 and 60, pl.* A-22, were probably issued about November 1840 when the Princess Royal was born. The Prince of Wales was born in November 1841, and it is possible that the same figures were issued to commemorate his birth. The seated pair of the Queen with the Princess and Albert with the Prince, each as small children (*figs. 56 and 57, pl.* A-20), is likely to date from 1843.

For the next few years countless figures were issued of the royal children, both with and without their parents, including some mounted or riding in pony carts. Only relatively few of these are titled or have other features which leave no room for doubt about their identification. The figures of Leopold, King of the Belgians (*fig. 248, pl.* A-87), uncle of Queen Victoria, and his consort, Louise-Marie (*fig. 249, pl.* A-87), also date to the early forties. The figure of Louis-Philippe, King of the French and father of Louise-Marie (*fig. 247, pl.* A-86), dates either to 1843 when Queen Victoria visited him at Château d'Eu, the first occasion on which she had trodden foreign soil, or to the following year when he returned the visit.

Victorian Portrait Figures

The first datable non-royal figures were those of Sir Robert and Lady Sale in 1842 (*figs.* 66 and 67, *pl.* C-26). There followed figures of Clarke, Pilch and Box, members of the *All England XI* in 1843 (*figs.* 1, 2 and 3, *pl.* F-1), George Hudson (*fig.* 29, *pl.* G-12), probably made at the time of *The Railway Plunder Bill* in 1844 and Ben Caunt, the pugilist in the same year (*fig.* 27, *pl.* F-13) together with four figures of Jemmy Wood (*figs.* 30-33, *pls.* G-15 and 16), which date from 1840-45. The figures of Rajah Gholab Singh and his son, Ranbir Singh (*figs.* 68 and 69, *pl.* C-27), can be dated to the period of the *First Sikh War* in 1846.

Surprisingly enough, it was not until 1839 that work was commenced on the first national monument to Nelson, sited in Trafalgar Square, and the statue itself was not raised until 1843. Many figures of Nelson seem to date to this period and were perhaps due to the public's interest in the progress of the monument; however, there is no figure known whose source is the statue, probably because of the complexities involved in its manufacture; and none that exactly match up to the sculptured relief of the death of Nelson at the foot of the column, although *fig.* 8, *pl.* C-9 is very similar.

THE LATE FORTIES TO THE EARLY FIFTIES

There seems to have been a falling off in demand for figures of the royal children during this period, only two of the Prince of Wales being known (*fig.* 182, *pl.* A-58 and *fig.* 187, *pl.* A-60). The former, based on the Winterhalter portrait of 1847, was probably not issued until 1852 (*see chapter two*), which would also be the approximate date of issue of the latter. Some of the larger single figures of the Queen and Albert may belong to this period, and the very elaborate figure of the Queen sitting on a sofa with Prince Albert on her right (*fig.* 3, *pl.* A-4) is of such outstanding quality that it may well have been made for the *Great Exhibition* in 1851.

It was during this period that the potters devoted most attention to the production of figures of non-royal persons in many walks of life. Some of these figures are amongst the finest produced in the whole period. Well over a score of figures were produced of the Duke of Wellington, including the magnificent figure of the Duke on his charger, 'Copenhagen', inscribed 'Up Guards and At Them' (*fig.* 21, *pl.* B-3) and the memorial piece (*fig.* 22, *pl.* B-3) which can be confidently dated to 1852. This latter is often found in purple lustre, and it may be that some of these figures emanate from the Sunderland potteries. Most of the figures of the Duke however, depict him in his role of elder statesman. There are ten figures of Peel, famous for his re-organization of the London Police Force, six of O'Connell, the Irish patriot, two of Cobden, famed for the Repeal of the Corn Laws in 1846 (*figs.* 5 and 6, *pl.* B-1), one each of Franklin, the Arctic explorer and his wife (*figs.* 70 and 71, *pl.* C-28), two probably of Shaftesbury, the philanthropist and advocate of the 'ragged schools' (*figs.* 7 and 9, *pl.* B-1), and one each of the chartist Thomas Duncombe (*fig.* 4, *pl.* B-1), and the poetess Eliza Cook, famous for *Eliza Cook's Journal* (*fig.* 36, *pl.* H-10).

There are a large number of theatrical figures which can be confidently attributed to this period, including the seven models based on engravings in Tallis' *Shakespeare Gallery* of 1852-3 (*see chapter two*). These figures, which are all titled, are 'Alas Poor Yorick' (*fig.* 6, *pl.* E-1A), depicting Kemble as 'Hamlet'; James Henry Hackett as 'Falstaff' (*fig.* 3, *pl.* E-1B); Macready as 'Shylock' (*fig.* 4, *pl.* E-1B) and as 'Macbeth' (*fig.* 8, *pl.* E-1B); Isabella Glyn as 'Lady Macbeth' (*fig.* 7, *pl.* E-1B); the Cushman sisters as 'Romeo' and 'Juliet' (*fig.* 1, *pl.* E-1A) and Jenny Marston and Frederick Robinson as 'Perdita' and 'Florizel' in *Winter's Tale* (*fig.* 2, *pl.* E-1A). Other than these, there are at least eighteen figures of the 'Swedish Nightingale' Jenny Lind (*pls.* E-80-91) and one of Jullien, the French conductor, who did much to establish promenade concerts in London (*fig.* 162, *pl.* E-81).

The crime wave of 1848-9 inspired one figure of J. B. Rush (*fig.* 48, *pl.* G-23) and two of his mistress, Emily Sandford (*figs.* 47 and 50, *pls.* G-23 and 24) together with models of Stanfield Hall, the site of the murder; Potash Farm where Rush lived and Norwich Castle where he was executed (*figs.* 44, 45 and 46, *pl.* G-20). Figures were also issued of F. G. and Maria Manning

(*figs.* 40 and 41, *pl.* G-18) and William Smith O'Brien and his wife (*figs.* 36 and 37, *pl.* G-17).

The visit to England, in 1851, of Kossuth, the Hungarian patriot inspired four figures (*figs.* 61-64, *pls.* B-19 and 20); and the advent of *Bloomerism*, in the same year, at least nine (*see pls.* E-63-67). Probably none of the latter figures portray Amelia Bloomer herself but merely a model in 'Bloomer costume', or, in a few instances, an actress in the role of a 'Bloomer girl' in one of the many 'Bloomer farces' that swept the country.

Many figures of illustrious persons of the past were made during this period. The figures of Archbishop Cranmer and of Bishops Ridley and Latimer (*figs.* 1 and 2, *pl.* D-1) can be dated to 1851 on account of the violent 'No Popery' agitation of that year. The single figure of Admiral Blake (*fig.* 1, *pl.* C-1) and the single figure of the explorer Captain Cook (*fig.* 4, *pl.* C-5) also date to this period, together with many of the figures of Napoleon Bonaparte. The latter appears to have been the commonest portrait produced in Staffordshire (*see chapter five*).

The reader will note that the majority of the figures so far described are examples of attempts by the potters to imitate porcelain. It has already been noted that after a few years they gradually relaxed their efforts and developed the broader, simpler designs. Some of these, such as the larger figures of Victoria and Albert, the figures of Leopold, King of the Belgians and his consort and figures of the Mannings appeared during this period, and in subsequent years only very few appeared in any other style.

THE CRIMEAN PERIOD (1854-1856)

In October 1853, Turkey declared war on Russia and in March 1854, Britain intervened on the side of Turkey. Subsequently, France and later Sardinia joined Britain and Turkey. The landing of the allied forces in the Crimea in September constituted a new phase in the war. At the same time there was an intense popular enthusiasm and interest, and an unprecedented demand for portrait figures of the allied leaders and their war commanders (*see figs.* 72-263, *pls.* C-31-88).

Figures were made of the Queen and Albert, Napoleon III and the Empress Eugénie, the Sultan and the King of Sardinia.

On the naval side, figures were made of four English admirals: Admiral Sir Deans Dundas, Admiral Sir Charles Napier, Admiral Sir Richard Dundas and Admiral Sir Edmund Lyons.

On the military side, figures were made of ten English commanders: the Duke of Cambridge, Field-Marshal Lord Raglan, General Sir George Brown, General Sir Colin Campbell, General Sir George Cathcart, General Sir William Codrington, General Sir James Simpson, General Sir William Fenwick Williams, General Sir Charles Windham, and Colonel Sir George De Lacy Evans.

There were figures of four French commanders: Prince Napoleon, Marshal Saint-Arnaud, General Canrobert and General Pelissier and of one Turkish general, Omar Pasha. In addition, there were four figures of Florence Nightingale and figures of three of the Russian fortresses, together with numerous figures of British and allied soldiers and sailors.

All these figures with the exception of Omar Pasha and its pair, Lord Raglan (*figs.* 163 and 380, *pls.* C-62A and 63) are in the larger and simpler designs and the majority are flat-backs. The period constitutes the heyday of this form of design, and all these figures are much sought after by collectors.

THE LATE FIFTIES TO THE SIXTIES

The *Indian Mutiny* of 1857 led to the production of further figures of General Sir Colin Campbell and of figures of General Sir Henry Havelock and Highland Jessie (*pls.* C-89-92B).

In 1860, Napoleon III annexed Savoy and Nice and, in so doing, aroused suspicions of his intentions. There was a revival of the *Volunteer Rifles*, 21,000 of whom were reviewed by the Queen in Hyde Park. The figure titled 'Volunteer Rifles' and the pair of figures of the British Lion couched on top of a French officer, presumed to be Napoleon III, commemorate this event (*figs.* 276 and 277, *pl.* C-93) as may that of the figure of the Queen with a lion (*fig.* 77, *pl.* A-28A).

The *American Civil War* of 1861-5 produced portraits of John Brown, the abolitionist, who was hanged in 1859 (*fig.* 77, *pl.* B-26) and of President Lincoln, assassinated in 1865 (*fig.* 73, *pl.* B-25). There is also an 'Off for the War' figure and numerous figures of the chief characters in Harriet Beecher Stowe's novel *Uncle Tom's Cabin*, many of which may of course date to as early as 1852, the date of publication, and signify intense public sympathy for the North (*pls.* B-26-30). The late Albert Lee has referred to *a coloured and gilt figure of Mrs Stowe* but I have never seen this figure myself (*Connoisseur:* November 1935).

Figures of royalty, during this period, to which dates can be assigned are confined almost entirely to the royal children. Thus, there were three each of the Prince of Wales and Prince Alfred when they received their first commissions in the army and navy in 1858 (*pls.* A-61-62). Figures were made also in connection with the royal marriages of this period, that of the Princess Royal and Prince Frederick William in 1858, that of Princess Alice and Prince Louis of Hesse in 1862 (*figs.* 217 and 218, *pl.* A-70), that of the Prince of Wales and Princess Alexandra in 1863 (*fig.* 219, *pl.* A-72) and possibly also for that of Princess Helena to Prince Christian of Schleswig-Holstein in 1866 (*fig.* 224, *pl.* A-75). We can date most of these figures to the engagement periods with a certain amount of accuracy because of their manner of titling, thus so far as those of the Prince of Wales and Princess Alexandra of Denmark are concerned, examples are titled either 'Prince of Wales and Princess' or alternatively, 'Prince and Princess'. If of a later period, it is reasonable to assume that the titling would have been 'Prince and Princess of Wales' (*see also figs.* 204 and 204(a), *pl.* A-66).

James Braidwood, Superintendent of the London Fire-engine Establishment, was killed by a falling wall in the *Great Fire of Tooley Street* in June 1861. The disaster was marked by the production of a standing figure of Braidwood (*fig.* 1, *pl.* I-1).

There are at least fifteen figures of Garibaldi. An engraving of the meeting of Garibaldi and Victor Emmanuel near Teano in October 1860, published in *The Illustrated London News* on December 29th of that year, is a source of a pair of figures which probably date to 1861, the year in which Victor Emmanuel was proclaimed King of Italy (*figs.* 302 and 303, *pl.* C-103). The nineteen-inch standing figure which pairs Shakespeare was probably issued in April 1864 when Shakespeare's tercentenary was being celebrated and Garibaldi first came to London (*see pl.* H-2). Several figures of Garibaldi pair with the mercenary Colonel Peard, otherwise known as 'Garibaldi's Englishman'. In 1859 he joined Garibaldi's forces, distinguishing himself at the Battle of Melazzo in 1860. Later he commanded the English Legion during Garibaldi's advance on Naples. Garibaldi visited him in England in 1864.

The *Abyssinian Expedition* of 1867 was commemorated by a figure of Lord Napier of Magdala. For this purpose the potters used a mirror-image (with minor modifications) of a figure of Garibaldi produced some years earlier, probably 1861. The figures form a matching pair. It is for this reason that Napier's sword is suspended from the right (*figs.* 282 and 283, *pl.* C-104).

Other figures which can be dated to this period include those of Doctor Palmer, the Rugeley poisoner in 1856, a figure of both local as well as national interest (*fig.* 42, *pl.* G-18A); J. S. Rarey, the American horse-tamer who came to England in 1857 (*figs.* 148 and 149, *pl.* E-77); Heenan and Sayers, the boxers who fought to a draw in April 1860 (*fig.* 15, *pl.* F-7); Charles Spurgeon, the Baptist preacher who first came to London in 1854 but whose figures probably date to the late fifties or early sixties (*pls.* D-20-22); E. A. Sothern, the actor who appeared as 'Lord Dundreary' at the Haymarket in 1861 (*fig.* 41, *pl.* E-18) and possibly Frank Gardiner, the Australian bushranger, sentenced to thirty-two years imprisonment for gold robbery in 1864, whose premature release in 1874 caused a public outcry (*fig.* 27, *pl.* G-10).

In this period, too, all of the figures are of the broader style other than those of Garibaldi, one of Victor Emmanuel, and one of Lord Napier of Magdala. There was however, a general tendency for highly-coloured figures to give way to figures coloured much more sparsely. Paint was applied only to the hair, faces, hands and shoes, although there was gilt decoration to the white parts. Many figures of this period can be found both in the coloured and paler states, and it seems that the potters made both types simultaneously whilst the public taste was changing. Towards the end of the century it will be noted that, with few exceptions, only paler pieces were produced.

THE SEVENTIES

The *Franco-Prussian War* of 1870 produced a spate of figures (*pls.* C-106-113). On the Prussian side figures were produced of the King, Queen, Crown Prince and Prince Frederick Charles, together with Von Moltke, Bismarck and General Von der Tann. On the French side there were figures of Napoleon III, Marshal MacMahon and Marshal Bazaine. The war started with pro-German feeling in this country, and it is likely that the figures of Prussian personalities were made between July 15th when the war began, and September 19th when Paris was invested and sympathy went over to France.

Two royal marriages occurred during this period and were commemorated by figures; that of the Princess Louise to the Marquess of Lorne in 1871 (*pls.* A-77 and 78) and that of the Duke of Edinburgh (Prince Alfred) to the Grand Duchess Marie of Russia in 1874 (*pls.* A-79 and 80).

The celebrated greyhound 'Master M'Grath', who won the Waterloo Cup three times, the last occasion being when he beat 'Pretender' in 1871, inspired a pair of figures (*figs.* 20 and 21, *pl.* F-7). In 1873, figures were issued both in connection with the visit to England of the American evangelists Moody and Sankey (*figs.* 9 and 10, *pl.* D-4), and also in celebration of the state visit of the Shah of Persia (*figs.* 252 and 253, *pl.* A-92). In 1873 also, Arthur Orton, 'The Tichborne Claimant', was brought to trial and a figure was produced of him (*fig.* 34, *pl.* G-16). In addition, figures were made of Captain Webb, the first man to swim the Channel, a feat he accomplished in 1875 (*fig.* 19, *pl.* F-7), of Pope Pius IX and Cardinal Manning, the latter was promoted Cardinal in 1875 (*figs.* 7 and 8, *pl.* D-4), and of Gladstone and Beaconsfield (*figs.* 47 and 48, *pl.* B-14). Disraeli was created Earl of Beaconsfield in 1876.

The *Russo-Turkish War* of 1877-78 was commemorated with figures of Alexander II of Russia (father of the Duchess of Edinburgh) and Sultan Abdul-Hamid II of Turkey (*figs.* 326 and 327, *pl.* C-114).

The outstanding feature of this decade was the virtual disappearance of underglaze blue. Paler figures now monopolized the market, the majority of the figures being predominantly white. Towards the end of the period underglaze black was much used in the clothing of civilian figures such as those of Moody and Sankey, and Gladstone and Beaconsfield, but the only figure found entirely painted, and at that generally crudely, is the coloured version of Arthur Orton.

The other salient feature of the period is the appearance of the monumental figures. Clearly those of Garibaldi and Shakespeare, produced in the preceding decade, had met with public approval, and now over a dozen monumental figures appeared both of royalty and distinguished civilians.

THE END OF THE REIGN (1880-1901)

The *Kilmainham Treaty* of 1882, in which agreement was reached between Gladstone and Parnell, resulted in the release from gaol of the latter. It was commemorated by the issue of figures of Gladstone and Parnell and a central figure inscribed 'Peace on earth goodwill towards men' (*figs.* 54, 55 and 56, *pl.* B-16).

Although by the beginning of this decade the art was beginning to die, a number of figures of interest appeared. In 1882 'Jumbo', the African elephant, a popular favourite at the London Zoo, was sold to Barnum, the American showman. 'Jumbo's' export to America provoked a public outcry and the two titled figures of him were produced probably at this time (*figs.* 211 and 212, *pl.* E-103).

In 1885 General Gordon was killed in Khartoum. Probably three of the four figures known of Gordon, including *fig.* 338, *pl.* C-119, a particularly fine example of the period, were produced at this time. The fourth figure, that of Gordon on a camel (*fig.* 337, *pl.* C-119), after the statue by Onslow Ford RA, could not have been produced before 1890 when the monument was unveiled by the Prince of Wales at Gillingham. The defeat of Arabi Pasha in 1882 and the abortive attempt to relieve

Gordon in 1884-5 are commemorated by three figures of Wolseley, two of which pair figures of the Duke of Connaught, who commanded the Guards Brigade, and the other Gordon. There are also figures of Major-General Sir Herbert Stewart and Colonel F. G. Burnaby, both of whom were killed in the campaign to relieve Gordon (*see pls.* C-115-118).

The *Golden Jubilee* of 1887 was commemorated by monumental figures of the Queen and the Prince of Wales, clearly debased copies of superior figures issued first early in the 1870's (*figs.* 235 and 236, *pl.* A-81). In 1891 a pair of figures were issued to commemorate the ill-fated betrothal of the Duke of Clarence and the Princess May (*figs.* 237 and 238, *pl.* A-82). For the *Diamond Jubilee* of 1897, the two figures of the Queen and the Prince of Wales, used in the preceding jubilee, were again produced with an appropriate adjustment to the title of the Queen's figure.

There is a pair of figures of Lord Kitchener and Sir Hector Macdonald which can be dated indisputably to the *Battle of Omdurman* in 1898 (*figs.* 341 and 342, *pl.* C-121). There is also a pair of figures inscribed '21st Lancers'. These latter figures commemorate the famous charge at Omdurman in which Winston Churchill partook (*figs.* 343 and 344, *pl.* C-123). There are five series of equestrian figures issued at the time of the *South African War*; subjects include Kitchener, Macdonald, Buller, Roberts, French, Baden-Powell and Dundonald (*see pls.* C-124-135). Although a number of these figures are often described as 'horrible' there are others, particularly the 11-inch (28 cm.) series, which have a grace and simplicity reminiscent of the best figures of the Crimean period. Two earlier figures were adjusted for use during the Boer War period, that of the now deceased Duke of Clarence was modified and retitled 'Baden-Powell' or 'De Wet', according to taste (*pls.* C-133-134), and the 'Peace' figure celebrating the Kilmainham Treaty was modified to celebrate the declaration of peace in 1902 (*fig.* 377, *pl.* C-140).

THE EARLY POST-VICTORIAN ERA (1901-1905)

After the Queen's death in January 1901 a few figures were made of King Edward and Queen Alexandra to celebrate their accession and their coronation, but none possess any real artistic merit (*pls.* A-84 and 85). A figure of Evan Roberts, the evangelist, which could not have been issued prior to 1905 confirms that the art, whilst moribund, had not finally expired (*fig.* 54, *pl.* D-27). However, with the possible exception of those of General Booth (*figs.* 55 and 56, *pl.* D-28), no other portrait figures are known to have been manufactured until the *First World War*. Although the majority of the figures issued then were of a different and more sophisticated kind, a few reminiscent of Victorian times, such as those of Edith Cavell, are known (*figs.* 378 and 379, *pl.* C-141).

REFLECTIONS

Some surprising and some understandable facts emerge from a review of this chapter. It is clear that there was great public interest in the royal family at least until the early seventies. Only one new figure is known to have been made of the Queen during the last twenty-five years of her reign (*fig.* 239, *pl.* A-83).

There was a demand for figures in connection with every major war in which this country was engaged, in particular the Crimean and South African Wars. There was also a demand for figures in connection with wars in which this country had an interest, such as the American Civil War, the Franco-Prussian War and the Russo-Turkish War.

Apart from these two main groups, there was also a demand for figures in connection with politics and religion. With regard to the former, there was a strong left-wing bias. Whilst there are only two figures of Beaconsfield, and at that only pairs to Gladstone, there are numerous figures not only of Gladstone but also of Peel and Cobden. There are also figures of Gurney and Shaftesbury, the philanthropists, and Duncombe, the chartist. Irish nationalism is represented by figures of O'Connell, Parnell, Sexton and O'Brien and, in addition, portraits were made of Lord Edward Fitzgerald, Wolfe Tone and McCracken which commemorate the centenary of the Irish Rebellion of 1798. There was a profusion of figures in connection with the Italian patriot Garibaldi and the Hungarian patriot Kossuth, but perhaps the most surprising manifestation of these left-wing sympathies was the fantastic output of figures of Napoleon I, which included the tallest and most magnificent figure to have emanated from Staffordshire, the twenty-four-inch figure illustrated on *pl.* C-23.

The religious figures are even more surprising, there being at least fifteen Nonconformist preachers and only one Church of England clergyman, the Reverend Goulburn. Even the identity of this figure is in some doubt (*fig.* 38, *pl.* D-18).

The last major group of figures, that of theatrical personalities, also poses a number of questions which cannot easily be answered, and these are discussed in chapter three.

There are also some extraordinary omissions. No figure is known of Charles Dickens whose works were extremely popular throughout the Queen's reign, although a number of figures have been found depicting characters in his novels, some of which are undoubtedly 'theatrical'. Likewise, no figures have been found of Palmerston, the nation's leader during the Crimean War, nor of Doctor Grace, the famous cricketer, nor of David Livingstone, the missionary and explorer, nor of Tennyson, the Poet Laureate. There seems to be no satisfactory explanation for these curious omissions, for if figures had been made they would certainly have been sold in such large numbers that copies would have survived today.

2
The Staffordshire Image Makers

Introduction–John (& Rebecca) Lloyd, Shelton, Hanley–Obadiah & Martha Sherratt, Burslem–H. Bentley, Hanley–Ridgway & Robey, Hanley–The 'Alpha' factory–The Rockingham myth–Minton, Stoke-on-Trent–John Carr–George Baguley, Hanley–Lockett Baguley & Cooper, Shelton, Hanley–Sampson Smith, Longton–The Parr and Kent Group of Potters, Burslem–Lancaster & Sons (Ltd.), Hanley; James Sadler & Sons (Ltd.), Burslem–Joseph Unwin (& Co.), Longton.

INTRODUCTION

The city of Stoke-on-Trent, which spreads over what was formerly thirty square miles of North Staffordshire moorland rich in quick-burning coals, clays and marls, has developed over the course of two centuries through the skill and business acumen of the community of potters, whose reputation has for long been world-wide.

The series of villages originally separated by what, in those days, would be considered great distances had, by the beginning of the nineteenth century, become towns. As they continued to grow the problems of local government increased, so that by the end of the nineteenth century it became clear that as the inhabitants of this compact area were predominantly engaged in a common industry they should be treated for the purposes of local government as a single unit. In 1910 following a long period of negotiation, the six main towns became united as the one County Borough of Stoke-on-Trent.

The six towns were *Tunstall* in the extreme north, *Burslem* which lay to its immediate south, *Hanley which included Shelton* which lay south of Burslem, *Stoke-on-Trent* which lay to the south-west of Hanley, *Fenton* which lay to the east of Stoke and *Longton* which lay to the south-east of Fenton. There have been some further extensions to the boundary of the County Borough since the federation in 1910.

The vast majority of so-called Staffordshire figures and many figures which dealers still delight to call Rockingham were, in fact, manufactured in the Staffordshire potteries. There is, however, little doubt that a minority of these figures were made in other parts of England, also probably in Wales and almost certainly in Scotland. A major difficulty has been that of the hundreds and thousands of earthenware figures produced from the accession of Queen Victoria to the turn of the century, only a few bear any clear factory mark and only one manufacturer–Sampson Smith of Longton–to whom these marks relate, can be shown to have been responsible for the production of large numbers of Staffordshire portrait figures. After exhaustive examination of many hundreds of these figures the late Mr Thomas Balston attributed certain pieces with very individual characteristics to two firms which, for convenience, were called the *Alpha factory* and the *Tallis factory*, but he made no serious effort to attribute these figures to a known manufacturer.

JOHN (& REBECCA) LLOYD, SHELTON, HANLEY

The earliest known portrait figures which can be attributed to a definite manufacturer, are those of 'Albert' and 'Victoria and

Princess Royal' (*figs. 59 and 60, pl. A-22*), the backs of which are impressed 'LLOYD/SHELTON' (*see ch. 2, pl. 1*). John and then Rebecca Lloyd worked at the Shelton factory from 1834-52, and the figures probably date to early in 1841. It will be recalled that the Princess Royal was born in November of the preceding year.

Another figure, that of a female musician in Middle-Eastern garb, which is probably 'theatrical', has been found with the same mark impressed on the base (*see fig. 296, pl. E-141*). At least some marked Lloyd figures are porcelain, not earthenware.

OBADIAH & MARTHA SHERRATT, BURSLEM

The figure of Queen Victoria (*c.* 1837) with an elaborate four-legged base (*fig. 2, pl. A-2*), is in the style of Obadiah Sherratt. It is derived from a figure of the singer Maria Malibran manufactured a year or two earlier. Obadiah Sherratt was born in 1775 and commenced making earthenware chimney ornaments about 1810, whilst living in Hot Lane, Burslem. He was assisted by his second wife, Martha. In 1829 he moved to Waterloo Road, where he was still potting in 1834. Between 1834 and 1846 he died, and his business passed to his son, Hamlet Sherratt. The firm was no longer in existence in 1860. A number of other Victorian figures in the same style, the majority of which are derived from earlier figures, are known.

H. BENTLEY, HANLEY

The figure of Ben Caunt (*fig. 27, pl. F-13*) which may be found in biscuit form or coloured has impressed at the back 'BY H. BENTLEY + MODELED FROM LIFE + 1844' [*sic*] (*see ch. 2, pl. 4*). There is a photograph in the *Connoisseur*, February 1919, number CCX, page XXIII, which forms part of an advertisement by Mortlocks Ltd., Orchard Street, London, W.1. This photograph illustrates a number of figures, one of which appears to be identical to *fig. 9, pl. A-7*. The caption to the photograph states: *No. 2 (Biscuit). H.R.H. PRINCE ALBERT, impressed at back. 'Modelled and manufactured by H. Bentley, Hanley, 1845'.*

Despite a search of directories and other sources, no mention can be found of this individual. *White's Directory* (1834) lists a William Bentley, modeller, as living at Glebe Street, Stoke-upon-Trent.

RIDGWAY & ROBEY, HANLEY

A group of figures which may well turn out to be theatrical portraits but are not yet proven as such, are those depicting characters from Dickens's *Nicholas Nickleby*. This novel was serialised from 1838-9 and dramatized on the London stage before the final instalment had been published. To date, only three figures have been recorded. They are 'Ralph Nickleby', 'Kate Nickleby' and 'Wackford Squeers' (*figs. 74, 75, 76, pls. E-38, 39*). No doubt others will come to light. Each figure is titled on the front in black transfer capitals, and on the back is the printed mark 'PUBLISHED June 15, 1839,/BY RIDGWAY & ROBEY/HANLEY./Staffordshire Potteries' (*see ch. 2, pl. 5*). The short-lived partnership of William Ridgway and Ralph Mayer Robey is mentioned in *Hanley Rate Records* of 1837-1839.

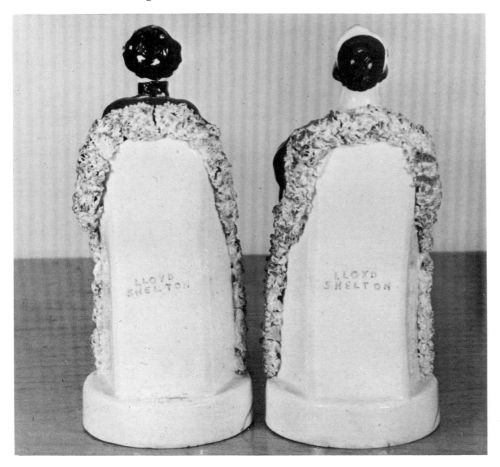

Plate 1
John (& Rebecca) Lloyd, Shelton, Hanley
Fig. 59 (Albert) and *fig.* 60 (Victoria and Princess Royal) *pl.* A-22.
Each is impressed at the back LLOYD/SHELTON and dates to *c.* 1841.
These are the earliest known Victorian portrait figures which can be attributed to a definite manufacturer.

Plate 2 (Below left)
L: *Fig.* 44 (Napoleon) *pl.* C-14. An earthenware figure.
R: *Fig.* 44(a) (Napoleon) *pl.* C-14. A porcelain figure.

Plate 3 (Below right, upper)
A few early models, particularly of royalty, were produced both in earthenware and porcelain. Some of the porcelain figures were left with open bottoms; only very rarely are pressed-earthenware figures found with open bottoms.
L: Bottom of *fig.* 44 (Napoleon) *pl.* C-14. Earthenware.
R: Bottom of *fig.* 44(a) (Napoleon) *pl.* C-14. Porcelain.
The significance of the impressed letter 'F' is unknown.

Plate 4 (Below right, lower)
H. Bentley, Hanley
Fig. 27 (Caunt) *pl.* F-13. Impresed at the back:
BY H. BENTLEY + MODELED FROM LIFE + 1844.

Plate 4A
George Baguley, Hanley
Fig. 18(a) (Wellington) *pl.* B-2A. Facsimile of factory mark printed in black on the rear of the base.
By courtesy of Wing Commander T.H. Lucas, RAF (rtd)

UNDER ROYAL PATRONAGE
Published by
GEORGE BAGULEY
HANLEY STAFFS
Oct. 1st 1852

Colour Plate 2
Charles I and Henrietta Maria. *Fig.* 286, *pl.* A-110. See pages 42 and 178.

Colour Plate 3
The Prince of Wales. *Fig.* 182, *pl.* A-58.
See pages 38-9 and 152.

Colour Plate 4
Ranbir Singh. *Fig.* 69, *pl.* C-27. See pages 52-3 and 237.

Colour Plate 5
Napoleon, on Le Vizir. *Fig.* 26, *pl.* C-11. See pages 49, 224 and 226.

Plate 4B
Lithograph music-front by H.G. Maguire for
the ballad *Buy Image!* sung by Madame Vestris.
Note:
The figure in the vendor's left hand and a
similar figure on the tray are almost certainly
'images' of Madame Vestris as 'A Broom Girl',
one of her most famous roles.

The Staffordshire Image Makers

THE 'ALPHA' FACTORY

There is an important group of figures, all sitting or standing, which can be recognized as emanating from one factory, referred to, by Balston, as the *Alpha factory*. These include Victoria, Prince of Wales and Princess Royal (*figs.* 130, 131 and 132, *pl.* A-46); Peel, Cobden and Shaftesbury (*figs.* 1, 6 and 7, *pl.* B-1); Sir John and Lady Franklin (*figs.* 70 and 71, *pl.* C-28); Jenny Lind and Jullien (*figs.* 160 and 162, *pl.* E-81); W. S. O'Brien and Mrs O'Brien (*figs.* 36 and 37, *pl.* G-17); Eliza Cook (*fig.* 36, *pl.* H-10); Bloomers (*figs.* 125 and 126, *pl.* E-66); Captain Cook (*fig.* 4, *pl.* C-5); Kossuth (*fig.* 64, *pl.* B-20); Byron and Burns (*figs.* 17 and 56, *pls.* H-7 and 18); and Uncle Tom's Cabin (*fig.* 88, *pl.* B-29). There are, also, six religious figures, Jesus Christ and the Virgin Mary and the apostles Matthew, Mark, Luke and John.

All the contemporary figures can be dated from 1845-1851, and the historical figures are so similar that they almost certainly belong to the same period. All the figures are modelled and painted all round, and each required at least three moulds. Captain Cook, the most complicated, and incidentally the most attractive, required eight. The majority are titled with indented capitals with a gilt leaf or three strokes of gold paint at each end of the lettering. The others have a gilt line halfway up across the front of the base and descending to the bottom of the base on each side. A few are titled with gilt script between, three gilt strokes. All, except 'Kossuth' and the two 'Franklins', are found with underglaze blue. All are of white porcelaneous clay and are so well modelled and painted as to be frequently offered for sale as 'Rockingham' (see below). No maker's marks have ever been found on these figures, and there is no evidence at all from which factory they emanated.

THE ROCKINGHAM MYTH

As a proportion of Staffordshire portrait figures are porcelaneous and of very fine quality, confusion has arisen with figures emanating from the Rockingham factory. It is now generally accepted that it is a myth to suppose that Rockingham porcelain is plentiful. In reality it is extremely rare, a fact which is not altogether surprising for, although earthenware was produced at Swinton from the middle of the eighteenth century, production of porcelain was confined to about sixteen years (1826-41), a fair proportion of which period saw times of difficulty and restricted output. Genuine Rockingham figures are of exceptionally high quality and by no means all bear an impressed factory mark.

Among figures that have caused confusion are a number of high quality whose sources are to be found in theatrical prints of the 1820's-1830's, for example Mrs Vining in the character of 'Peter Wilkins' (*see ch.* 3, *pl.* 40). The date of the print is 1827. This class of figure is almost invariably offered as Rockingham. All, or rather nearly all, have open bottoms; the majority are porcelain but some are found both in porcelain and earthenware. Many are marked with a blue dash inside the base and many are richly coloured in underglaze blue, typical of the period 1840-60 (*see chapter one*). They all appear to come from the same pottery and differ so much in colour, form and material from figures known to be pre-Victorian, that it is possible that the majority are Victorian. The two figures of Madame Vestris (*ch.* 3, *pl.* 68) as 'Paul' in *Paul and Virginia* were said to show the striking contrast between the true Rockingham figure and a Victorian Staffordshire figure, but the modern view is that both emanate from Staffordshire, the finer figure possibly being rather earlier and, in this case, pre-Victorian.

MINTON, STOKE-ON-TRENT

It has been noted that a proportion of Staffordshire portrait figures are porcelaneous, and also that identically modelled figures are occasionally found both in earthenware and porcelain (*see ch.* 2, *pls.* 2 and 3).

Porcelaneous figures can usually be identified because they often have open bottoms and because they transmit light. Only very occasionally are pressed-earthenware figures found with open bottoms. Victorian earthenware figures with open bottoms, in any event, are unusual, and the overwhelming majority were cast from slip-moulds, for instance, the figures of Mr and Mrs Gladstone (*figs.* 39 and 40, *pls.* B-12, 13).

Apparently it was rare for one pottery to make both earthenware and porcelain; the techniques differ and the majority of the factories were only small concerns. The tendency was to make either pottery or porcelain. Some of the larger manufacturers, for instance Minton, did have two separate plants run entirely independently. There is however, no evidence that Minton made any of the figures dealt with in this volume either in porcelain or earthenware. Mr Geoffrey Godden, whose researches on Minton are well known, has examined a number of pieces in my collection, particularly porcelain pieces, and confirms that none are 'Minton'. In most cases the same pieces occurring in both earthenware and porcelain are also decorated identically. This adds weight to the argument that they were made by the same, so far unidentified, concern. If they were not made by the same factory then a possible explanation lies in the existence of journeyman modellers, travelling from one factory to another, selling models and making moulds. Identical models may well have been sold to several concerns, which might have been manufacturers of either porcelain or earthenware. This would apply to the multitudes of tiny factories where only a few potters were employed; only the very big factories had their own modellers and mould makers. Alternatively, large factories that employed modellers are known to have sold models or moulds to other factories. Finally, frank copying may well have occurred.

Although Minton are not known to have made any portrait figures of the type herein catalogued, similar, although never identical, figures were manufactured by them in Parian and in white biscuit (unglazed china). Models similar to *fig.* 182 (Prince of Wales) *pl.* A-58, and *fig.* 13 (Shakespeare) *pl.* H-5 are known to have been manufactured by Minton in Parian (*see ch.* 3, *pls.* 4 and 56). Minton's first figure design book contains drawings of figures of Rowland Hill, Charles Wesley and John Wesley which enable us to identify with confidence similar untitled figures made by other factories (*see pls.* D-13, 15).

JOHN CARR

A very fine figure of Admiral Sir Charles Napier in my collection (*fig.* 102, *pl.* C-42) is incised on its base 'John Carr/1857' (*see ch.* 2, *pl.* 6). This may be the signature of the potter or designer. Mr Geoffrey Godden, who has kindly looked into the matter for me, points out that although there is no trace of a John Carr in Staffordshire, there was a *John Carr (& Co.) (& Son), Low Lights Pottery, North Shields, Northumberland, c.* 1845-1900, formerly *Carr & Patton*. It may be that this figure came from that factory and not from Staffordshire. However, in the absence of more definite information, I have felt it right to include it in this work, particularly as it seems to me unlikely that the same mould would have been used in potteries so far apart. There can be no doubt that most, if not all, 'Napier' figures were made in Staffordshire.

GEORGE BAGULEY, HANLEY

The fine porcelain figure of Wellington (*fig.* 18 (a), *pl.* B-2A) has inscribed on the rear of the base in black lettering 'Published by/GEORGE BAGULEY/HANLEY STAFF?/Oct? 1st 1852', and above this, a crown and the words 'UNDER ROYAL PATRONAGE' (*see ch.* 2, *pl.* 4A).

There are many ways of spelling the name. The following entry occurs on *p.* 118 of Mr Haggar's *Staffordshire Chimney Ornaments*:

BAGGALEY, GEORGE, High-street, Hanley. Flourished c. 1851. Manufacturer of toys and ornaments. (In 1864 GEORGE BAGULEY is listed as a manufacturer of china and earthenware, at Victoria Works, Broad-street, Hanley).

Probably Haggar's George Baggaley is our Baguley, the date and Hanley address fit.

Mr Geoffrey Godden has kindly pointed out that this figure

Plate 5 (Top left)
Ridgway & Robey Hanley
Fig. 76 (Ralph Nickleby) *pl.* E-39.
Printed in black on the back is:
PUBLISHED June 15 1839
BY RIDGWAY & ROBEY
HANLEY.
Staffordshire Potteries.

Plate 5A (Centre left)
L to R: *Fig.* 1 (Peel) *pl.* B-1
Fig. 8 (? Fry) *pl.* B-1
Fig. 7 (Shaftesbury) *pl.* B-1
Fig. 162 (Jullien) *pl.* E-81
Examples of the produce of the
'Alpha' factory.

Plate 5B (Right)
Fig. 102 (Napier) *pl.* C-42. This
figure is particularly well modelled.
Its base is incised 'John Carr/1857'
(*see plate 6*). It has every appearance
of emanating from Staffordshire but
there is no trace of a John Carr in
the appropriate directories.

Plate 6
John Carr
Fig. 102 (Napier) *pl.* C-42. In this
unique copy, the base is incised:
John Carr
1857

is most important, as it is, as far as is known, the only portrait figure written-up at the period. It is described in the *Art Journal* of November 1852, page 355.

LOCKETT BAGULEY & COOPER, SHELTON, HANLEY
The porcelain Crimean memorial obelisk (*fig.* 263, *pl.* C-88) has inscribed on its base in red lettering 'PUBLISHED BY/ LOCKETT BAGULEY/& COOPER/SHELTON, STAFFS. /June 25th 1856' (*see ch.* 2, *pl.* 7).

Lockett Baguley & Cooper were at the Victoria Works, Shelton, Hanley, from 1855-60.

SAMPSON SMITH, LONGTON
According to Haggar the exact date when Sampson Smith started up in business in Longton is not known. An old, but unverifiable, tradition gives the date as 1846. *White's Gazetteer* for 1851, which may well have been compiled in 1849 or 1850, lists Sampson Smith under the general heading of china and earthenware manufacturers as an 'ornamenter', and gives his address as Upper Hill Street, Longton. Sampson Smith is known to have produced portrait figures at the Garfield Pottery, High Street, Longton, from 1853-58. In 1859-60 he moved from the Garfield Pottery to the Sutherland Works, Barker Street,

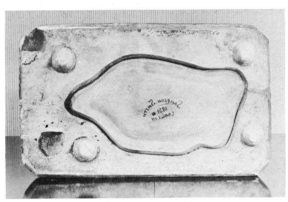

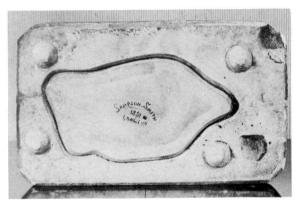

Plate 7 (Top Left)
Lockett Baguley & Cooper, Shelton
Fig. 263 (Crimean memorial obelisk) *pl.* C-88.
Printed in red on the base is:
PUBLISHED BY
LOCKETT BAGULEY
& COOPER
SHELTON, STAFFS.
JUNE 25th 1856.

Plate 8 (Top Right)
Sampson Smith, Longton
Fig. 16 (King) *pl.* G-4. The base of the figure is
marked in relief:

S. SMITH
LONGTON
1851

Plates 9(a) and **(b)** (Centre)
Sampson Smith, Longton
(a) The base of a three-piece press-mould for a
dog with maker's mark impressed thereon.
(b) The same printed in mirror-image to clarify
the mark:

SAMPSON SMITH
1851
LONGTON
The mould was one of those found in 1948 in a
disused part of the Sampson Smith factory.

Plate 10 (Below)
Sampson Smith, Longton
L: *Fig.* 363 (Roberts) *pl.* C-132.
R: *Fig.* 362 (Kitchener) *pl.* C-132.
The base of each of these figures is marked, in
relief, with a St. Andrew's cross and the mirror-
image of a letter; 'R' for Roberts and 'K' for
Kitchener. The style of lettering is identical to
the 'gilt script' used for titling the figures. The
presumption is that the base of the mould was
marked with the appropriate initial to remind
the potter whom he was potting.

Longton, where he produced a great variety of figures as a specialized line. In the *Post Office Directory*, 1860, he appears as a manufacturer of figures for home and exportation, and in the *Mercantile Directory of the Pottery District of Staffordshire*, 1864, he advertised that he made *figures in great variety*. Sampson Smith died on December 26th, 1878, aged sixty-five, but the firm of Sampson Smith remained in production at the old works, renamed Wetley Works, for many years. After his death the business was carried on under the same name by his executors until 1888, when it passed into the hands of Messrs. Adderley and Tams until 1912. From 1912 until 1918 the business was owned by John Adderley and W. H. Davies. About this time 'Ltd' was added to the title. Various owners carried on the same title, and it was only in 1963 that the present firm, Barker Bros. Limited, ceased to operate under that name. Figure making was not finally abandoned until at least 1926, as evidenced by the following advertisement by the firm in the *Pottery Gazette*:

A large assortment of Earthenware figures and Dogs in assorted sizes, nicely decorated in Colours and Gold. . . .

In 1910 G. Woolliscroft Rhead noted in his *British Pottery Marks*:

The works of 'Sampy Smith' are continued under the same style by Mr Adderley and the figures have had a wide circulation in country districts both in England and abroad. The 'Sampy Smith' figures are of importance to collectors both on account of their modernity and their frequent resemblance to old Staffordshire figures of the less artistic type. We have seen many 'Sampson Smiths' not six months old, offered and bought as genuine old Staffordshire figures. The firm, of course, are quite free from complicity, as they make them very cheaply in great quantities in the ordinary way of trade.

During the First World War the firm discontinued figure making, confining its activities to 'useful' wares such as teapots, etc.

Although there is no evidence that figure making continued after 1926 on the scale described above, it was in fact revived again for a short period in 1948 following the discovery of a number of old moulds in a disused part of the factory (see below).

Figures with *factory marks* include:
Fig. 52 (Burns) *pl.* H-15. Inscribed on the base is:
'Sampson Smith
Longton, Staff
England
1882'

Figs. 258 and 259 (Charles I and Cromwell) *pl.* A-96. In relief on the base of each is:

'SAMPSON SMITH
1851
LONGTON'

Fig. 47 (Burns and Mary) *pl.* H-12. In relief on the base is:
'S. SMITH
LONGTON
1851'

Figs. 15 and 16 (Turpin and King) *pl.* G-4. As above, in relief on the base of each (*see ch.* 2, *pl.* 8).
Fig. 63 (Tam o'Shanter and Souter Johnny) *pl.* H-20. In relief on the base is:

either 'SAMPSON SMITH   *or* 'SAMPSON SMITH
1851   LONGTON, STAFF
LONGTON'   ENGLAND
                         1892'
Fig. 12 (King) *pl.* G-4 has been found with the following mark in relief on the base:

It is undoubtedly a Sampson Smith figure for its mould was one of those found in 1948 (*see ch.* 4, *pl.* 4).

The significance of the various dates is obscure, as also the reason why so few of so many of these figures were marked at all. The style of the figures marked '1851' makes it clear that they were made much later. This date possibly refers to Sampson Smith's year of establishment and is unlikely to have any connection with the Great Exhibition.

The word 'England' occurring on a piece is usually said to signify a date after 1891. The inscribed mark on the base of the Burns figure (*fig.* 52, *pl.* H-15) is extremely difficult to read, and it may be that the date should be 1892 and not 1882, in which case that date may be the real date of manufacture of the piece or of its original mould. Support is added to this argument by the discovery of a dated press-mould of a figure of Burns very closely resembling *fig.* 52, *pl.* H-15, the date in this case being *May the* 2, *1892* (*see ch.* 4, *pl.* 2). However, Mr Godden informs me that the word 'England' does occasionally occur in figures produced prior to 1891 and is not incompatible with the date of 1882.

In 1948 about sixty old press-moulds were discovered in a disused part of the Sampson Smith factory. Most of them were single two-part moulds, and the majority were of dogs, cottages, jockeys, etc. However, there were seven moulds of portrait figures, those of Dick Turpin and Tom King (*figs.* 11 and 12, *pl.* G-4); Moody (*fig.* 9, *pl.* D-4); Burns and Mary (*fig.* 47, *pl.* H-12); Wellington and Napoleon (*figs.* 64 and 65, *pl.* C-25) and Burns (*fig.* 53, *pl.* H-16).

This discovery has proved to be of major importance. Firstly, none of the last three figures mentioned were at that time known to collectors. In fact, only one of the figures, that of Wellington, has been found subsequently in contemporary state. Secondly, the discovery of the Moody mould and of the existence of the Napoleon and Wellington figures has enabled us to confidently attribute a large number of other figures to the Sampson Smith factory.

The following monumental standing figures ranging in height from 16 in. (40.5 cm.) to 17½ in. (43.5 cm.) bear so close a resemblance to that of Moody, that there can be no doubt that they, too, are products of the Sampson Smith factory:

1. *Religious and Political*
Sankey, the pair to Moody (*fig.* 10, *pl.* D-4).
Pope Pius IX, and Cardinal Manning (*figs.* 7 and 8, *pl.* D-4).
O'Connell, and its variant (*figs.* 15 and 14, *pl.* B-2).
Beaconsfield, and the pair, Gladstone (*figs.* 47 and 48, *pl.* B-14).

I have come across smaller versions of all these figures, but care must be taken in ascribing them all to the Sampson Smith factory, for the 12 in. (30.5 cm.) figure titled 'Gladstone' and its pair 'Beaconsfield' (*figs.* 45 and 46, *pl.* B-14) are mentioned in a catalogue issued by William Kent in the early years of the present century (*c.* 1901) and the 11½ in. (29 cm.) versions of 'Moody' and 'Sankey' (*figs.* 9 and 10, *pl.* D-4) appear in a somewhat later catalogue of the same firm (*see chapter five*). These figures are titled in raised capitals and are not characteristic of the Kent factory. Mr Godden tells me that he has no knowledge of one factory selling moulds to another whilst in production. A possible explanation is that Sampson Smith may have 'farmed out' an order for the smaller models to the Kent factory.

All the larger versions are made from single two-part moulds except that of the Pope, a subsidiary mould being needed for the arm raised in blessing. Rare variants of the smaller versions of Sankey and Moody are known in which one leg is free and required a subsidiary mould (*see pl.* D-5).

2. *English and Foreign Royalty*
Queen Victoria and Prince of Wales (*figs.* 235 and 236, *pl.* A-81).
Duke and Duchess of Edinburgh (*figs.* 231 and 232, *pl.* A-79).
King and Queen of Prussia (*figs.* 306 and 307, *pl.* C-106).

The Royal figures can be shown to date from 1870-74 for the

following reasons: The King and Queen of Prussia became Emperor and Empress of Germany in January 1871. The figures are unlikely to have been made earlier than July 1870, the commencement of the Franco-Prussian War, at which time the German cause was extremely popular in England. The Duke of Edinburgh became betrothed to the Grand Duchess Marie of Russia in May 1873, the marriage taking place in January 1874. The figure of Queen Victoria titled 'Queen of England' and its pair 'Prince of Wales', closely resemble these figures, although obviously later, poorly modelled versions of the former are found with inscriptions commemorating the Jubilees of 1887 and 1897 and the death of the Queen in 1901. The other figures probably date from 1873 when Moody and Sankey first came to England until 1881, the year in which Beaconsfield died.

The contemporary copy of Wellington (*fig.* 64, *pl.* C-25), enables us to attribute a vast group of equestrian figures to the Sampson Smith factory. In the case of coloured versions, the style of decoration is so characteristic as to leave no room for doubt (*see chapter four*), but the design of the figures alone, particularly with regard to the saddle and saddle-cloths, is usually unmistakable. The following figures come into this category:

1. *Franco-Prussian Generals* (*see pls.* C-108 and 109). G. V. D. Tann, P. F. Charles, G: Moltke, G: Bismark [*sic*], also King of Prussia and Crown Prince.
2. *Late Victorian War Commanders, Series I* (*see pls.* C-121-126). The Sirdar, Col[11] Mac Donald [*sic*], 21st Lancers, General Buller, Lord Dundonald, Lord Kitchener, Lord Roberts, General French, Major Macdonald [*sic*].
3. *Late Victorian War Commanders, Series III* (*see pls.* C-130-132). General Buller, Lord Kitchener, Major Macdonald, Lord Dundonald, Lord Roberts, General French.
   (Although the style of this series is a little different, the manner of titling is very similar to series I, and some of the portraits virtually identical. The same celebrities have been selected for each series.)
4. *Various*
   'Have you seen the Shah' (*see pl.* A-92); William III and Sarsfield (*see pls.* A-101-102); Alexander II and Abdul Hamid II (*see pl.* C-114); Sir G. Wolseley and Duke of Connaught (*see pl.* C-115) and G. Stewart and C. Burnaby (*see pl.* C-118).

The period covered by the foregoing figures is from the Franco-Prussian War of 1870 to the end of the South African War in 1902.

A number of these figures, particularly those of the late Victorian war commanders, series III, have unusual marks underneath. Each consists of a St. Andrew's cross and one letter in 'mirror-image script'–both in relief (*see ch.* 2, *pl.* 10). The style of the lettering is identical to the 'gilt script' used for titling the figures of series III. Examples so far recorded are *D*, *F*, *K* and *R* on the bottoms of the figures of Dundonald, French, Kitchener and Roberts. There is no doubt that these marks were indented in the moulds to indicate to the decorator what title was to be applied to the figures.

Mr Godden has in his collection an example of *fig.* 220 (Prince & Princess) *pl.* A-73, on the base of which the letters 'AD' are to be found in relief, in mirror-image, thus: 'ᗡA'. It has been suggested that this stands for 'Alexandra of Denmark'.

Although no contemporary catalogues of Sampson Smith are known, J. F. Blacker in *The A.B.C. of XIXth Century English Ceramic Art*, published by Stanley Paul & Co. about 1910, illustrated what appears to be a sample page from an old Sampson Smith list showing typical specimens amongst which are George Rignold (*fig.* 190, *pl.* E-97) and Tam o'Shanter and Souter Johnny (*fig.* 63, *pl.* H-20), *see ch.* 2, *pl.* 11.

THE PORRIDGE SCHOOL: Figures are found with no paint on them, their body yellowish with some brown stains on it and their glaze with blue specks in it. They much resemble salt glaze. There are other figures that are similar but with a good bluish glaze and with very little brown stain. The faces and hands are uncoloured but boots, swords, horses' eyes, manes and tails are coloured black and bridles and reins brown. Mr

and Mrs Eric Joyce once described these figures as coming from the 'Porridge School', an extremely apt description. They are:
   1866: Princess Helena and Prince Christian (*fig.* 224, *pl.* A-75).
   1868: I O G T (*fig.* 60, *pl.* D-30).
   1870: King and Queen of Prussia (*figs.* 309 and 308, *pls.* C-107 and 106).
   1870: King of Prussia (*fig.* 320, *pl.* C-111).
   1870: G: Moltke, G: Bismark [*sic*], Napoleon III and Bazaine (*figs.* 316-319, *pl.* C-110).
   1873: 'Have you seen the Shah' (*fig.* 252, *pl.* A-92).
   1873: Sir R. Tichborne (*fig.* 34, *pl.* G-16).

The figures of the King and Queen of Prussia and the equestrian figures of the Franco-Prussian War clearly emanate from the Sampson Smith factory, although differing from the standard type of figure. It seems therefore very likely that all figures of the 'porridge school' come from Sampson Smith. Only the figures titled 'Sir R. Titchborne' and 'I O G T' are known to exist as highly-coloured lead glaze figures made from the same moulds, so it seems probable that the majority of these figures were designed to be issued in the 'porridge' state and are not figures that were thought too defective to be worth painting but which might be saleable at reject prices. None of these figures dates earlier than 1866 (marriage of Princess Helena and Prince Christian) or later than 1873 (the year of the trial of Arthur Orton the 'Tichborne claimant', and the visit of the Shah of Persia to England).

It will be seen that figures can be ascribed to the Sampson Smith factory from the 1860's to the turn of the century, but there are many figures of the forties and fifties, both large and small, standing and mounted, on plain, generally oval bases, titled with gilt script or raised capitals which may well have emanated from the factory. In particular, attention should be drawn to the six matching equestrian figures–the 'long' series, which date to the Crimean War and the Indian Mutiny, 1854-59. They bear a striking resemblance to the late Victorian war commanders, series I, and in my opinion, were almost certainly made by Sampson Smith (*see pl.* C-67).

THE PARR AND KENT GROUP OF POTTERS, BURSLEM

We must now consider the very difficult problem of the *Tallis* factory. The term 'Tallis' figure was first applied by Messrs Mander and Mitchenson to seven models which they found to be based on engravings in Tallis' *Shakespeare Gallery* of 1852-53 (*see ch.* 3, *pl.* 26-32). These figures, which are variously titled, are:
   Charlotte and Susan Cushman as 'Romeo' and 'Juliet' (*fig.* 1, *pl.* E-1A).
   Jenny Marston and Frederick Robinson as 'Perdita' and 'Florizel' in *Winter's Tale* (*fig.* 2, *pl.* E-1A).
   John Philip Kemble as 'Hamlet' (*fig.* 6, *pl.* E-1A).
   James Henry Hackett as 'Falstaff' (*fig.* 3, *pl.* E-1B).
   William Charles Macready as 'Shylock' (*fig.* 4, *pl.* E-1B).
   Isabella Glyn as 'Lady Macbeth' (*fig.* 7, *pl.* E-1B).
   William Charles Macready as 'Macbeth' (*fig.* 8, *pl.* E-1B).
Mr John Hall tells me that he has seen an untitled figure of Miss Vandenhoff as 'Juliet' based on the engraving in Tallis' *Shakespeare Gallery* and decorated in a manner similar to the preceding figures (*see pl.* E-1C). Unfortunately the figure is in America and I have been unable to obtain a photograph of it.

Other figures were found which clearly belonged to the same family. These were given the broad title of 'Tallis' figures by the late Mr Thomas Balston, although they had, in fact, no connection with Tallis' *Shakespeare Gallery*. Those which can be approximately dated are detailed below. In each case the earliest possible date is given.

c. 1847: Prince of Wales after Winterhalter (*fig.* 182, *pl.* A-58).
c. 1851: Archbishop Cranmer and Bishops Ridley and Latimer (*figs.* 1 and 2, *pl.* D-1).
   (This date was suggested by the late Mr Balston on account of the 'No Popery' agitation of that year.)
c. 1854: Omar Pasha ('Success to Turkey') and Lord Raglan (*figs.* 163 and 380, *pls.* C-62A and 63).

The Staffordshire Image Makers

Plate 11 (Left)

Sampson Smith Catalogue
No contemporary catalogues of
Victorian portrait figures are known.
However, this illustration is believed
to be a sample page from an old
Sampson Smith catalogue. It was
published *c.* 1910 in *The A.B.C. of
XIX Century English Ceramic Art* by
J.F. Blacker.
BL: *Fig.* 190 (Rignold) *pl.* E-97.
BC: *Fig.* 63 (Tam o'Shanter and
Souter Johnny) *pl.* H-20.
BR: *Fig.* 9 (Gordon-Cumming) *pl. I-4.*
*By courtesy of the Trustees of the British
Museum*

Plate 11B (Right)

L to R: *Fig.* 8 (Macready) *pl.* E-1B.
Fig. 7 (Glyn) *pl.* E-1B.
This superb pair is based on
engravings in Tallis' *Shakespeare Gallery*
(1852-3). The figures portray
Macready in the character of
'Macbeth' and Isabella Glyn as 'Lady
Macbeth'. Messrs Raymond Mander
and Joe Mitchenson have shown that
seven models, each obviously
emanating from the same factory,
were based on these engravings. They
termed them 'Tallis' figures. Recent
work suggests that they were made by
Thomas Parr.
In the Thomas Balston collection

Plate 11A

L to R: *Fig.* 15 (Turpin) *pl.* G-4.
Fig. 9 (Moody) *pl.* D-4.
Fig. 16 (King) *pl.* G-4.
All these figures were made by
Sampson Smith. The figures of
Turpin and King both have S.
SMITH/LONGTON/1851 in relief
on their bases and the original mould
of the Moody figure was found in
1948 in a disused part of the
Sampson Smith factory.

26

Plate 11C
Fig. 22 (Garrick) *pl.* E-7.
This figure of David Garrick as 'Richard III' in the
'Nightmare Scene' is based on Hogarth's painting *David
Garrick as Richard III* (1745), now in the Walker Art Gallery,
Liverpool. Although an engraving of this painting appears
in Tallis' *Shakespeare Gallery*, the figure has none of the
features of 'Tallis' figures and emanates from another, to
date unidentified, factory.
By courtesy of Mr and Mrs Eric Joyce

c. 1861: Garibaldi and Victor Emmanuel (*figs.* 302 and 303,
pl. C-103).
c. 1861: Garibaldi (*fig.* 282, *pl.* C-97).
c. 1863: Prince and Princess of Wales (*figs.* 204 and 205,
pl. A-66).
c. 1864: Garibaldi (*fig.* 288, *pl.* C-99).
Garibaldi at Home and Garibaldi (*figs.* 289 and 290,
pl. C-100).
c. 1867: Napier (*fig.* 283, *pl.* C-104).
c. 1885: Gordon (*fig.* 338, *pl.* C-119).

The *characteristics* listed for 'Tallis' figures are as follows:
1. They are made of an exceptionally hard and very heavy body.
2. They are modelled and are also painted all round (most
figures of the period have flat undecorated backs).
3. The bases are coloured with brown and green (occasionally
with a little pale orange) 'combed' in long, thin strokes.
4. All colours are overglaze enamels; underglaze blue does not
occur.
5. The titles or quotations are often transfer printed, which may
be regarded as almost unique to this class. Other titles are in
indented capital letters. No titles are in gilt script nor in
raised moulded letters.
The Prince of Wales (*fig.* 182, *pl.* A-58) is unusual because
it has neither title nor quotation. All, with the possible exception of the very late figures, are of excellent quality and moulded
in an unusually complicated manner. They are certainly far
better than the general run of earthenware figures of the period,
and in their case the term 'cottage ornaments' almost seems
inappropriate.

Mr Geoffrey A. Godden of *The Mark Research and Dating
Service* has conducted a fascinating enquiry to discover the
possible maker(s) of these figures, and I am most indebted to
him for allowing me to make use of much of his work. Mr
Godden prepared a list of 'Toy' or figure manufacturers mentioned in Staffordshire directories of the 1849-51 period, and to
this list added the working period of each potter or firm as indicated by rate records and subsequent directories. The list included thirty-three figure makers but only two entries covered
the whole period from *c.* 1847 to at least 1885; these were
James Dudson (1838-88) and William Stubbs (*c.* 1847-50 and
1853-97). An exhaustive enquiry did not produce satisfactory
evidence that either of these could have been the manufacturers
of the 'Tallis' figures.
Mr Balston noted in his *Staffordshire Portrait Figures* (1958):
*The moulds of very many 'Tallis' figures, not only portraits, are
now in the possession of William Kent (Porcelains) Ltd, by whom many
of them are still employed. This firm was not founded until 1878, and
therefore cannot be the original makers of the portrait figures except
Gordon, since the others all date from 1849-67.*
This is followed by a footnote:
*William Kent Ltd have kindly informed me that they do not know
how they acquired the moulds. At some date they brought moulds from
William Machin of Hanley, but he, according to Mr Haggar, flourished
from 1875 to 1889, too late to have originated them . . .*
Records confirm that William Machin commenced at the
Percy Street Works, Hanley, in 1875 but he continued at the
Dresden Works, George Street, up to *c.* 1911 and, until at least
1906, he was engaged in the production of earthenware figures.
This fact is confirmed not only by contemporary lists of potters,
but by William Scarratt in his interesting book *Old times in the
Potteries* (1906), for under William Machin there is the observation *Foreign competition has driven out of this locality nearly all, except
the last-named house. The firm still continues, having some rare models.*
These 'rare models' may well go back to a period before William
Machin's commencement in 1875, for there was reputedly a
connection (which it has not proved possible to substantiate)
between Machin and Messrs Livesley Powell & Co. of Hanley;
this latter firm traded between 1851 and *c.* 1865 and was
variously described as 'Toy' or china figure manufacturers.
Study of one of Kent's more recent catalogues (*Kent List C:
1955*) shows clearly that their vast stock of moulds were acquired
from a variety of sources. Some models date back to the 18th
century and many others of the Victorian era are obviously not
of the same class as the 'Tallis' figures; some, indeed, appear to
have come from the Sampson Smith factory. There is no proof
that the moulds acquired from William Machin were the
'Tallis' moulds, although the possibility exists.
It is of interest to trace back the history of the firm of William
Kent (Porcelains) Ltd. who, as has been seen, possess many of
the moulds from which the 'Tallis' figures were produced.
Previous to 1894 there was the partnership of Kent and Parr
(*c.* 1880-94). A contemporary advertisement reads:

*KENT & PARR,
Wellington Street, Burslem,
Manufacturers of all kinds of Earthenware Figures and orna-
ments comprising Centrepieces, Dogs, white and gold, black and
white, red and white, Hounds . . . Poodle Dogs, all in several sizes,
Watchstands, Hens and a very large assortment of Gross figures.*

Before this partnership, directories list John Parr as also at
Wellington Street, Burslem, *c.* 1870-79 and then several
different 'Toy' makers named Parr at Church Street, Burslem
(Edwin, Richard, Thomas and William Parr). The most
interesting from our point of view is Thomas Parr of 34, Church
Street, Burslem, who worked from 1852-70. Bearing in mind
that the earliest 'Tallis' portrait figure, that of the Prince of
Wales after Winterhalter, need not have been produced in 1847
(this is only the earliest possible date), and could very well have
been produced together with the figures and groups of Shakspearian actors in 1852-3, or later, it is possible to trace a line of
potters from 1852 to the present owners of the moulds. The line
is made up of Thomas Parr (*c. 1852-70*), John Parr (*1870-79*),
Kent & Parr (*1880-94*), William Kent (*1894-1944*) and William

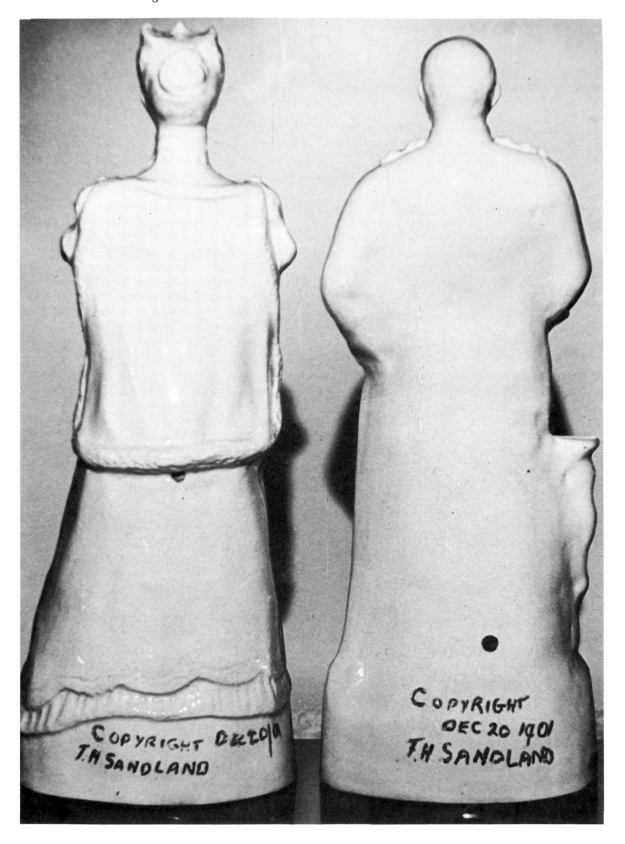

Plate 12

Lancaster & Sons Ltd
L: *Fig.* 243 (Alexandra) *pl.* A-85. Impressed on the back of
the figure is:

    COPYRIGHT DEC 20/01
       T.H. SANDLAND

R: *Fig.* 242 (Edward VII) *pl.* A-85. Impressed on the back
of the figure is:

    COPYRIGHT DEC 20 1901
       T.H. SANDLAND

Thomas Henry Sandland joined the firm of Lancaster &
Sons (Ltd.) in 1899. In 1944 his name was incorporated in
the partnership, the name of the firm becoming Lancaster
and Sandland Ltd.

Colour Plate 6
Admiral Sir Deans Dundas and Admiral Sir Charles Napier. *Figs.* 103 and 102, *pl.* C-42. See pages 21, 22, 246 and 250.

Plate 13
Lancaster & Sons Ltd
Fig. 240 (Edward VII) *pl.* A-84. Impressed on the back of
the figure is:
> COPYRIGHT
> DEC to 1901
> T.H. SANDLAND

See also pl. 12
In the collection of Mr Geoffrey Allen

Kent (Porcelains) Ltd. (*c. 1944 . . .*). Production of figures using
the original moulds ceased at the end of 1962.

The workmanship and general style of decoration of the
'Tallis' figures would indicate that they were produced by one
potter or at least by a continuous succession of potters closely
connected.

Although 'Gordon' 1884/5 (*fig.* 338, *pl.* C-119) is the latest
known figure typical of the 'Tallis' group, there is a set of
figures which I have called *Late Victorian War Commanders,
Series II*, which are worthy of the closest scrutiny (*see pls.* C-127
and 128). These figures are 14½ in. (36.75 cm.) and titled with
indented capitals. They comprise:

Gordon	Wolseley
French	Macdonald
Kitchener	Roberts
Buller	Baden-Powell

Figures can be found sparingly coloured, decoration being
confined to flesh tints for the hands and faces, black for the
horses' eyes and horsemen's boots, grey for the horses' nostrils
and the horsemen's hair with a few touches of gold which pick
up highlights including the title. More rarely, they are found
with the horse coloured deep cream, the reins and some of the
saddlery in maroon and the base in pale green. This latter style
is identical to that found in late untitled versions of the 'Tallis'
figure of Wellington 'Up guards and at them' (*fig.* 21, *pl.* B-3)
and in all but the very rare contemporary versions of *figs.* 302
and 303, *pl.* C-103 – Garibaldi and Victor Emmanuel on horseback. Equestrian figures of Gordon, Wolseley, Macdonald and
French are mentioned in *Kent List A* (*c.* 1901), together with the
preceding three figures. Curiously enough I have been unable
to find mention of the equestrian figures of Kitchener, Roberts,
Buller and Baden-Powell in any available Kent catalogue,

including *Kent List B* (*see chapter five*) in which Gordon, Wolseley,
Macdonald and French appear and have subsequently been
deleted in red ink as 'discontinued lines' – one in which it seems
reasonable to expect the entire series would receive mention.
This class of figure together with reproductions of 'Tallis'
figures are generally referred to in the trade as 'Kent'. Although
it cannot be proved, it seems almost certain that Gordon and
Wolseley were issued in 1884/5, the date of Wolseley's campaign
to relieve Gordon in Khartoum and at least possible that
Kitchener (wearing a fez) and Macdonald commemorate the
Battle of Omdurman (1898), although the Kent catalogue
suggests they are not a pair. The four remaining figures can be
dated *c.* 1900 and relate to the Boer War. If all the figures had
been made at the same time, namely during the Boer War, it
would be unlikely that Kitchener would be portrayed wearing
a fez and even more improbable that figures of Gordon and
Wolseley would have been made at all. It seems likely that the
production of these figures was also in the hands of a succession
of potters closely connected, a condition that can only be met
by the Parr and Kent group of potters. My personal view is that
the evidence is strong enough for the general term *Parr and Kent
group* to be substituted for the terms *Tallis* and *Kent*. Where
indicated the more specific details can be given, such as *Thomas
Parr* for the group of figures of Shakspearian actors described
by Manders and Mitchenson, *Kent and Parr* for figures of Gordon,
William Kent for the Boer War figures of French, Roberts, Buller
and Baden-Powell and for reproductions of some of the earlier
figures (*see chapter six*).

LANCASTER & SONS (LTD.), HANLEY
JAMES SADLER & SONS (LTD.), BURSLEM

There are a pair of standing figures of King Edward VII and
Queen Alexandra (*figs.* 242 and 243, *pl.* A-85), the former
inscribed:

> 'COPYRIGHT
> DEC 20 1901
> T. H. SANDLAND'

and the latter:

> 'COPYRIGHT DEC 20/01
> T. H. SANDLAND'

and a pair of similar equestrian figures (*figs.* 240 and 241,
pl. A-84), each inscribed:

> 'COPYRIGHT
> DEC 10 1901
> T. H. SANDLAND'

(*see ch.* 2, *pls.* 12 and 13).

T. H. Sandland does not appear in the directories as a manufacturer. When the word 'copyright' is added it usually refers
to the designer. I am grateful to Mr K. D. Miller, City Librarian
of the City of Stoke-on-Trent, for the following information:

*Although I have not been able to establish the position absolutely
beyond doubt, I suspect that the figures marked with the name 'T. H.
Sandland' were made or designed by Thomas Henry Sandland. According to the obituary in 'Pottery and Glass,' September 1956 and 'The
Pottery Gazette' for October 1956, he joined the firm of Lancaster &
Sons Ltd. in 1899 and in later years his name was incorporated in the
partnership, the name of the firm becoming Lancaster & Sandland. T. H.
Sandland eventually became chairman and managing director of the firm
and he was the last surviving member of the original board of directors.*

One must suppose that Sandland joined the firm *c.* 1899 as
a modeller/designer (perhaps having worked for them before
joining the firm) and was later taken on as a partner *c.* 1944.

Mr Balston referred to a figure of Lord Roberts [belonging
to the *Late Victorian War Commanders, Series IV (see pl.* C-135)]
having been found with the mark 'HANLEY/LANCASTERS
LIMITED/ENGLAND', but he did not state whether the
figure was from a press-mould or from the slip (*see chapter four*).
This is important as both varieties are known. As figures from
the slip have been found with the factory mark of James Sadler

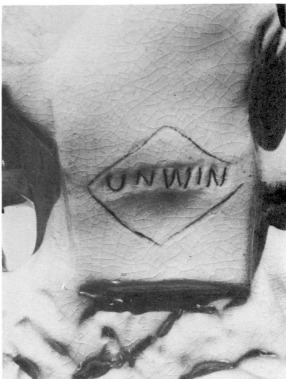

Plate 14
James Sadler & Sons (Ltd.). Burslem
Fig. 369(a) (Kitchener) *pl.* C-135. On the base is printed:
SADLER
BURSLEM
ENGLAND
Note the large hold in the base. This figure has been made
by casting. See chapter four for the use of slip-moulds.

Plate 15
Joseph Unwin (& Co.). Market Lane, Longton
Staffordshire earthenware group of two harvesters with the
moulded name-mark UNWIN within a diamond-shaped
outline.
By courtesy of Mr and Mrs Eric Joyce

& Sons (Ltd.) (*see below*) it would seem likely that Mr Balston's figure was one of the press-mould variety. These are very similar to the pair of equestrian figures of King Edward VII and Queen Alexandra referred to above, and add weight to the theory that all were manufactured by Lancaster & Sons (Ltd.). According to Mr Godden, although the firm was established in 1899 it did not become a limited liability company before 1906. Any figures with a form of mark recorded by Mr Balston must have been produced subsequent to 1906. The firm is continued today as Lancaster & Sandland Limited, a title it adopted in 1944.

I have in my collection a figure belonging to the *Late Victorian War Commanders, Series IV*, made from a slip-mould, *fig.* 369 (a) (Lord Kitchener) *pl.* C-135. This figure has the printed mark 'SADLER/BURSLEM/ENGLAND' on its base (*see ch. 2, pl.* 14). Mr Godden has recorded both this and its companion figure Gen. French (*fig.* 370 (a), *pl.* C-135) similarly marked. If Mr Balston was not mistaken, then we must accept that those figures from the series made from slip-moulds are likely to have been made by a different manufacturer from those produced from press-moulds. The slip-mould series may also be dated *c.* 1900, being produced by James Sadler of the Wellington and Central Potteries, Burslem. This factory, formerly Sadler & Co.,

began production in 1899 and is still in existence. It advertised *Cottage Figures in Great Variety.*

JOSEPH UNWIN (& CO.), LONGTON

An advertisement in the *Pottery Gazette*, June 1881, reads: *Joseph Unwin & Co., Manufacturers of Earthenware figures etc. for home and export, Cornhill Works, Longton.*

Joseph Unwin started on his own account *c.* 1877, being formerly in partnership as Poole & Unwin (1871-6). In 1891 the firm became Joseph Unwin (& Co.) and as such continued to *c.* 1926. The moulded name-mark 'UNWIN' within a diamond-shaped outline occurs on a Staffordshire earthenware group of two harvesters, *c.* 1877-90 (*see ch. 2, pl.* 15). A similar figure bears the initial mark 'P. & U.' of Poole & Unwin, and it is probable that the Unwin mark relates to Joseph Unwin. No portrait figures have come to light so far.

The aforementioned potters and firms represent only the better known manufacturers – the Staffordshire potteries of the period abounded in 'Toy' manufactories producing unmarked 'images' at low cost.

Colour Plate 7
Sir Robert Peel on his favourite mare. *Fig.* 31, *pl.* B-7. See pages 191-192.

3

The Potters' Sources
of Inspiration;
Identification of Figures

Introduction – Tallis' 'Shakespeare Gallery' – 'The Illustrated London News' and 'Punch' – Music-fronts and playbills – Baxter and Le Blond prints – Penny plain and tuppence coloured prints – The influence of the theatre – Celebrated statues, buildings and paintings – Figures derived from pre-Victorian examples – How sure can we be that the right source has been found? – Double titling – Why are so few theatre figures tilted? – Some anecdotes on collecting – Examples of the potters' sources.

INTRODUCTION

Who designed these figures and from whom or what did they gain their inspiration? Virtually nothing is known of the designers, for practically no records have come to light. H. Bentley, of Hanley, modelled the figure of Ben Caunt (*fig.* 27, *pl.* F-13) and also that of Albert (*fig.* 9, *pl.* A-7), but little is known of him. The incised mark 'John Carr/1857', found on the bottom of the figure of Admiral Sir Charles Napier (*fig.* 102, *pl.* C-42), to which reference is made in chapter two, is possibly the signature of the designer. Even if this is so, nothing is known of him. The impressed mark 'T. H. Sandland' found on the back of figures of Edward VII and Queen Alexandra (*figs.* 242 and 243, *pl.* A-85) almost certainly refers to Thomas Henry Sandland who joined the firm of Lancaster & Sons (Ltd.) in 1899. He probably designed these figures. In later years his name was incorporated in the partnership. No other names of designers are known.

Probably each pottery of any size employed artisans capable of any casual designing required, but it is unlikely that they would have any training in the arts such as would be necessary today. The problem facing the designers would be immense. If the source was a solitary engraving then the difficulties of producing a three-dimensional model from it are not difficult to imagine. As Thomas Balston so aptly remarked *Bernini required three Van Dyck portraits of Charles I and Henrietta Maria before he would attempt their busts.*

The fact that a single painting or engraving was the sole source of inspiration on many occasions, means that it is sometimes possible to identify an untitled figure by finding its source. It is this fascinating feature that provides one of the highlights for the collector of Staffordshire portrait figures. One reference has been found in contemporary literature to confirm the foregoing. In *The Illustrated London News* of October 14th, 1848, there appears an engraving of a Parian statuette of H.R.H. the Prince of Wales (*ch.* 3, *pl.* 4). This same statuette is also found in Staffordshire pottery (*fig.* 182, *pl.* A-58). The inscription states that:

This beautiful Portrait of the young Sailor Prince has been modelled, by permission of his Royal Highness Prince Albert, from the picture painted by Winterhalter, of which a print has been published by Alderman Moon. The statuette is from the establishment of Messrs. Minton and Co., of Stoke-upon-Trent.

In this case the potters' source seems to have been a print of a painting.

TALLIS' SHAKESPEARE GALLERY

The first real break-through in this field came in 1944 when Messrs Raymond Mander and Joe Mitchenson, who have together amassed a vast collection of theatrical material, discovered that seven figures with Shakspearian titles were based on engravings in Tallis' *Shakespeare Gallery* (1852-3). These figures all had similar characteristics and clearly emanated from the same factory. This discovery meant that, in these instances, the potter had portrayed, intentionally or otherwise, not merely a character in a play, but the actual actor in the role, for example, John Philip Kemble as 'Hamlet'. No one who has studied the figures beside the engravings can doubt that the potters in the 'Tallis' factory actually used Tallis' *Shakespeare Gallery* as their source (*see ch.* 3, *pls.* 26-32).

Study of the characteristics of the 'Tallis' Shakspearian figures has led to the attribution of many other figures to the same factory. All figures believed to have been made in this factory were subsequently termed 'Tallis' figures by Balston (*see chapter two*). There are, however, figures of a different style which obviously come from another factory, but which might also be thought to be based on engravings in Tallis' *Shakespeare Gallery*. An example is David Garrick as 'Richard III' (*fig.* 22, *pl.* E-7). This figure is based on Hogarth's painting of *David Garrick as Richard III* (1745), now in the Walker Art Gallery, Liverpool. As this is not a 'Tallis' figure, the actual source used by the potter may have been the engraving of Hogarth's work in Tallis' *Shakespeare Gallery*, or equally the large engraving which is illustrated in *ch.* 3, *pl.* 35, or possibly but less likely the actual painting itself.

'THE ILLUSTRATED LONDON NEWS' AND 'PUNCH'

During the fifties Mrs Eric Joyce, who together with her husband had amassed one of the finest collections of Staffordshire figures in the country, conducted a painstaking research through contemporary copies of *The Illustrated London News* and *Punch*. She discovered the sources of a number of figures, all of which I have been able to reproduce in this volume. Her finds included the engraving of Sir Robert Peel on horseback which appeared in *The Illustrated London News* on July 6th, 1850, the source of *fig.* 31, *pl.* B-7; the engraving of the medal by A. A. Caque, struck at the Paris Mint, in 1854, to commemorate the Anglo-French alliance, the source of *fig.* 75, *pl.* C-32 (*see ch.* 3, *pl.* 20), and the 'No Popery' cartoon which appeared in *Punch* in March 1851, the source of *fig.* 5, *pl.* D-2 (*see ch.* 3, *pl.* 23). A number of other collectors have undertaken similar research and the list of discoveries is now quite impressive.

Other periodicals have also proved fruitful. Thus Mr Anthony Oliver recently spotted an engraving of the landing of the invalided and the wounded from the Crimea in *Cassell's Illustrated Family Paper* for April 7th, 1855 (*see pl.* C-71A). It is the source of *fig.* 194, *pl.* C-71.

The Potters' Sources of Inspiration

MUSIC-FRONTS AND PLAYBILLS

Lithograph music-fronts of Victorian times have proved a most valuable field for investigation. Many identifications, particularly of theatrical figures, have been made by the painstaking perusal of collections of these and similar items. The figure of Miss Adelaide Kemble as 'Semiramide' and Mrs Alfred Shaw as 'Arsace' (*fig.* 181, *pl.* E-91) was identified in this way by Mr John Hall, it being the mirror-image of the portraits of these actresses in a lithograph music-front by John Brandard (*see ch.* 3, *pl.* 50). Information on the theatrical production and hence accurate dating of figures can often be achieved by the discovery of the appropriate playbill, as is well demonstrated by that for *Semiramide* (*see ch.* 3, *pl.* 51).

Where can we hope to make further discoveries? The answer is almost anywhere. As however, the majority of untitled figures so far unidentified almost certainly belong to the theatre, it is there that we are most likely to have a lucky strike. Many London museums are rich in theatrical material. The *Enthoven Theatre Collection* in the Victoria and Albert Museum includes innumerable engravings, playbills, music-fronts, prints, books, and newspaper cuttings covering the history of theatre production in London from the eighteenth century onwards. The solutions to many of the problems confronting the collector are almost certainly to be found there.

BAXTER AND LE BLOND PRINTS

Surprisingly the beautiful coloured prints produced in mid-Victorian times by George Baxter and later by Le Blond, many of which had the brilliance of oil paintings, do not seem to have inspired the potters very much. A figure of a lady walking, hanging on the arm of her cavalier, who carries his plumed hat in his hand, for long thought to portray Charles I and his consort, Henrietta Maria, and to be probably 'theatrical' has now been shown to be based on a Le Blond print inscribed 'Courtship' (*ch.* 3, *pl.* 6A). The scene is probably a figment of the artist's imagination. No other figures inspired by Baxter or Le Blond prints are known.

PENNY PLAIN, TUPPENCE COLOURED PRINTS

Mention must now be made of penny plain, tuppence coloured prints, of which there are good collections in the print room of the British Museum and in the London Museum. These prints may be either juvenile drama, combat prints or theatrical portraits. The origin of this class of print dates back to 1811 when Mr William West, who kept a small stationer's shop off the Strand, published sheets of theatrical characters copied from the latest productions at Covent Garden, Drury Lane, and many other theatres. Each plate of figures contained about eight small drawings depicting the various characters in their most dramatic moments. Later, scenery consisting of backdrops and side-wings, was also included. Each play consisted of about fifteen sheets usually sold at a penny plain or tuppence coloured; the colouring was done by hand in vivid hues that have remained fresh to this day. These toy theatre plays originally intended as theatrical souvenirs soon became immensely popular as childrens' playthings.

By the time Victoria came to the throne, *juvenile drama* was a thriving industry with at least fifty different publishers engaged in it. The child would stick the sheets on cardboard and carefully cut out the various figures, so that eventually the drama could be re-enacted. Juvenile drama has preserved with astonishing accuracy the appearance of the early nineteenth-century theatre and the gestures and mannerisms of its actors, including such famous persons as T. P. Cooke, Edmund Kean and Madame Vestris. Although only one figure (*fig.* 219, *pl.* E-109) has so far been found which *exactly* corresponds with an illustration in a juvenile drama sheet, it is occasionally possible to identify a figure with a reasonable degree of certainty by this means. It is fair comment to say that in most instances both print and figure are alike only because both portray the same dramatic moment in the same play. There is not the same likeness to be seen as that between the seven Shakspearian figures and the seven engravings in Tallis' *Shakespeare Gallery* (*see*

chapter two). The conclusion must be drawn that apart from the rare exceptions, juvenile drama sheets were not used by the potter as a source, although today they are proving of immense value in putting the enquiring collector on to the right track. It is possible that in some cases the potters did exactly what the early publishers of juvenile drama sheets did and worked from sketches made in the theatre during a performance, selecting a highlight of the drama; alternatively, and more probably, the explanation lies in the exact contemporary print used for the figure not having been found.

Combat prints each show a single actor in combat. They were issued in pairs, for instance Edmund Kean as 'Richard III' (*see ch.* 3, *pl.* 39) and Thomas Cooper as 'Richmond'. *Theatrical portraits* are similar prints showing the actor in characteristic pose during a highlight of the play. As with juvenile drama, both combat prints and theatrical portraits were sold penny plain or tuppence coloured. The child could colour the plain one himself, or alternatively apply tinsel, thereby transforming the print into what has become known as a *tinsel portrait* (*see pls.* E-75 and 76). In fact by about 1840 the rage for tinselling was so popular that theatrical portraits ceased to be in any way realistic representations of actual actors in costume but became merely conventional backgrounds for tinsel decoration. The characteristics of a tuppence coloured portrait can be readily recognized. The character is portrayed in full length, often in profile, striking a dramatic pose, and between his legs there is an indication of distant scenery. At the foot of the print the name of the actor, his role, and usually the name of the play are inscribed, and finally come the name and address of the publisher. Only occasionally is the name of the artist given. There is no doubt that theatrical portraits were used by the potters as sources of inspiration. A superb example of this is the pair of figures of Mr Macready as 'Rob Roy Macgregor' and Mrs Egerton as 'Helen Macgregor' (*figs.* 146 and 147, *pl.* E-74) which are without doubt based on the pair of tinsel portraits published by A. Park, illustrated on *pls.* E-75 and 76.

A knowledge of the approximate dates during which the main toy theatre publishers carried on business is important in dating figures derived from this source.

William West (1811-1831)	J. K. Green (1832-1860)
J. H. Jameson (1811-1827)	A. Park (1835-1863)
Hodgson & Co (1822-1830)	M. Skelt (1835-1872)
Dyer (1827-1835)	J. Redington (1850-1876)
J. Fairburn (1828-1840)	W. Webb (1844-1890)
Orlando Hodgson (1831-1834)	

Few new theatrical portraits were published after 1860 and probably not many portraits were tinselled after the 1870's. With the invention of photography the days of the 'tuppence coloured' portrait and tinsel picture were numbered.

THE INFLUENCE OF THE THEATRE

The minor theatre productions in particular and the theatre in general had a profound influence in inspiring figures. Figures such as those of Dick Turpin, Tom King and Will Watch tend to be accepted as the potters' versions of famous criminals and so indeed they are, but it is more than probable that the potters would never have thought of making them had it not been for the fact that the theatres reminded them of them. After all, Turpin and King operated in the early eighteenth century (Turpin: 1705-39), whereas *Dick Turpin's Ride to York* by H. M. Milner was put on at the Surrey on August 30th, 1841; *Dick Turpin and Tom King* by Morris Barnett at the Strand on July 5th, 1847, and *Dick Turpin* by William E. Suter at the Britannia on July 22nd, 1861. *Will Watch* by J. H. Amherst was produced at the Royalty on January 3rd, 1825. These figures may in fact more truly be considered 'theatre' than 'crime'.

CELEBRATED STATUES, BUILDINGS AND PAINTINGS

A number of figures have been found to be based on statues. Examples are Napoleon, Gordon and Wesley (*ch.* 3, *pls.* 17, 22 and 24). No doubt the potters had access to engravings of the monuments. There is a fine figure based on an engraving of a statue of Mozart unveiled in Salzburg in 1842 (*fig.* 79, *pl.* H-28). The monument, by Ludwig Schwanthaler, has much merit, but although the figure is a very accurate copy of the engraving, the engraving is a bad copy of the monument. Engravings have been found, and in this respect *The Illustrated London News* has been particularly rewarding, that correspond in all essential details with some of the 'murder houses', for instance Potash Farm, Stanfield Hall (*pls.* G-21 and 25) and Palmer's House (*pl.* G-18B).

There are several instances of the potters' use of celebrated paintings such as *Napoleon crossing the Alps* by David, *The Eagle's Nest* by George Dawes and *Master Lambton* by Sir Thomas Lawrence (*see ch.* 3, *pls.* 15 and 62, and *pl.* I-20).

FIGURES DERIVED FROM PRE-VICTORIAN EXAMPLES

Some pieces have been found that were probably based on earlier, sometimes pre-Victorian, Staffordshire portrait figures. The earlier portraits may themselves have been based on engravings. This point is well demonstrated on *pl.* E-17 where there are grouped the original engraving, the probable pre-Victorian portrait figure and the Victorian portrait figure of the actress Maria Foote. Victorian figures are usually simplified versions of the earlier figures, the modifications being made to suit the new methods of manufacture.

Some figures, for instance those of Cribb and Madame Vestris (*see ch.* 3, *pl.* 68), may have been re-issued to commemorate the death of these persons. Alternatively, a re-issue may have been made because the potter judged it a likely 'seller' on decorative grounds alone.

A classic case, already quoted (*p.* 1), is the use of a modified example of a pre-Victorian figure of the singer Maria Malibran to commemorate the accession to the throne of the young Princess Victoria.

HOW SURE CAN WE BE THAT THE RIGHT SOURCE HAS BEEN FOUND?

When the actual source of a portrait figure is discovered, there is seldom any room for doubt, although minor modifications may have been necessary simply to facilitate manufacture. The reader will find many examples amongst the figures illustrated that confirm this fact. Generally too, some little feature will be apparent that, so to speak, removes any lingering doubts, and I am grateful to Messrs Mander and Mitchenson for pointing out to me what I consider one of the best examples of this. The engraving of Mrs Vining as 'Peter Wilkins' (*ch.* 3, *pl.* 40) shows a broad hem around Peter's jacket and this is faithfully reproduced in the figure. When the reader studies this he can surely be left in no doubt that the piece is indeed a portrait of Mrs Vining.

Sometimes there may be little room for doubt even though the potter has modified the figure for practical considerations; or, the exact source has not been found. This particularly applies to juvenile drama sheets, a point already made, but it also applies to some of the 'news' engravings of the day. The best example of this is the engraving of 'Gholab Singh, his son and body guard' [*sic*] which appeared in *The Illustrated London News* of April 4th, 1846, in connection with a report on the First Sikh War. Careful comparison of the 'blow-up' of the engraving with the pair of figures illustrated reveals such a multiplicity of similarities as to render their identity beyond doubt (*see ch.* 3, *pls.* 18 and 19, also *figs.* 68 and 69, *pl.* C-27).

An example in which an engraving may be found to help and yet not provide the final answer is shown in *pl.* E-26. Here is illustrated a 'West' theatrical portrait of Mr Johnston as 'Giaffier' in the dramatized version of Byron's *The Bride of Abydos*. There is little doubt that the figure shown beside the engraving portrays an actor playing the same part at the same dramatic moment, yet the differences in costume are such that the figure is obviously a likeness of a different actor in a different production, and the source is likely to be another engraving that has not yet come to light.

Only rarely, once the source has been discovered, has later research thrown doubt on the findings. The figure now identified as the singer Maria Malibran (*fig.* 307, *pl.* E-148) was formerly identified first as the authoress Letitia Elizabeth Landon and later as the young Queen Victoria (*see p.* 1). The problem concerning the identity of *fig.* 1, *pl.* F-1, whether it be the captain of *The All England XI*, William Clarke or the bowler Frederick Lillywhite (*see pls.* F-1, 2, 3 and *text, p.* 537), is never likely to be resolved with certainty. The poster for *Mazeppa* (*pl.* E-107A) led some collectors to the erroneous conclusion that *fig.* 213, *pl.* E-107 was a portrait of Miss Adah Isaacs Menken in the title role, until research by Messrs Mander and Mitchenson showed conclusively that this could not be so (*see pl.* E-107B and *text, p.* 514). We are never likely to be certain whether *fig.* 40, *pl.* D-18 titled 'Revd. J. Fletcher' is intended to represent the same person as *fig.* 36, *pl.* D-16 titled 'John Fletcher', or another cleric with the same name.

By and large, and of course there are exceptions to the general run of things, the designers succeeded in producing a likeness which although often crude, left no real room for doubt as to whom it was intended to represent, and because of the circumstances of manufacture each figure has an individuality and charm which is quite unique. This applies not only to well-known persons such as Prince Albert, Wellington and Peel, but also to those less in the public eye. The identification of Thomas Jefferson (*fig.* 65, *pl.* B-21), for instance, is largely based on the striking facial resemblance between the figure and the portrait of Jefferson illustrated on *pl.* B-20B.

Additional items were often added which give a clue to the identity of a figure. Thus cannons are found frequently beside generals and anchors beside admirals; politicians and clerics have black coats; poets and authors books; composers and conductors music; royalty and actors portraying royalty have ermine cloaks and opera singers scrolls.

DOUBLE TITLING

In some cases it is obvious that no attempt has been made to capture a likeness. This must be so when the same figure is found with two titles, such as 'Dr Raffles' and 'Revd J. Fletcher' (*pl.* D-18) and 'Wallace' and 'Bruce' (*pl.* I-6). This was probably done for reasons of economy and it is not always possible to say, which, if either, figure represents a true likeness of its subject.

Fig. 80, *pl.* C-34 titled 'Eugenie and Napoleon' is also found titled 'Queen and Albert'. Likewise, *fig.* 232, *pl.* A-79 titled 'Duke of Edinburgh' is also found titled 'Prince of Wales'; and *fig.* 342, *pl.* C-121 titled 'The Sirdar' is found titled 'Lord Roberts'. In each case it seems certain that the former title is correct and the latter title was probably what might be termed a potter's error.

There are at least three other extraordinary anomalies. *Fig.* 182 (Prince of Wales) *pl.* A-58, although untitled, has been identified beyond doubt, it being based on the famous Winterhalter painting. Despite this a late Victorian version occasionally turns up titled 'Prince Alfred' in indented capitals (*see fig.* 185, *pl.* A-59). *Fig.* 12 (Cooke) *pl.* D-6 is a titled figure portraying the divine in a Gothic niche, in trousers (no cassock) and gown. Although I have only seen one copy of this very rare figure, I have now come across two identically titled with a figure of Wesley, in cassock and gown, instead of Cooke, in the niche. Finally it should be noted that with one solitary exception (*fig.* 69, *pl.* B-22) all recorded Victorian figures of Washington are in fact misnamed figures of Franklin. This is small wonder, for a demand for images of these two men who were allied in thought, word and action would be likely to have arisen at the same time (*see pls.* B-21, 23A, 23B, 24 and 24A).

Conclusive proof that the potters did economize with their figures as far as was practicable is not only illustrated by the Malibran/Victoria figures discussed on page one, but by *fig.* 238, *pl.* A-82 titled 'Duke of Clarence'. This figure was issued to commemorate the betrothal of the Duke to Princess May, later Queen Mary. Unfortunately, the Duke died shortly after the announcement of the engagement. There is no doubt that the potters took the mould and modified it in time for use to commemorate the ascendency into the public eye of Baden-Powell. The figures are compared in *pl.* C-133. It will be seen that the only adjustments required were to remove the title and substitute another in gilt script, to remove the head and substitute another with the typical slouch hat, and finally to make minor adjustments to the jacket, such as removing the sash and applying a bandoleer. The revised figure is found titled not only 'Baden-Powell' but also 'De Wet' (*see pl.* C-134). It seems figures were prepared for clients on both sides of the fence—in fact it has been suggested that if the figure bears a resemblance to anyone it is more likely to portray De Wet than Baden-Powell for the latter would be unlikely to wear a bandoleer.

The same principle has been used with regard to *fig.* 11, *pl.* G-4 which is titled 'Dick/Turpin' in raised capitals; for in *fig.* 27, *pl.* G-10 titled 'Frank Gardiner' in gilt script we find the identical figure has been used except that the raised capitals have been removed and the gilt script applied. Again, we find *fig.* 270, *pl.* A-101, titled 'William III, 1690', etc., also titled 'Sarsfield' (*see pl.* A-102) and *fig.* 3, *pl.* C-3, titled 'Will Watch' also titled 'Jean Bart' (*see pl.* C-2). Yet again, we find *fig.* 101, *pl.* C-42, titled 'Sir Charles Napier', also titled 'Sir E. Lyons' (*see pl.* C-42A). The last examples differ from that of Wallace and Bruce in that only one copy each has so far come to light of Frank Gardiner, Sarsfield, Jean Bart and Sir E. Lyons. In these circumstances it seems reasonable to assume that the figures were originally intended to portray Dick Turpin, William III, Will Watch and Sir Charles Napier, but that alternative titles were applied when the potter saw the possibility of opening up a new market.

Other examples will be found in the catalogue of figures being used, with or without minor adjustments, to portray a second person, particularly in the Boer War section. It is worth noting that 'double titling' seems to feature in a number of figures known to have been made by Sampson Smith.

One quite extraordinary series, which to the best of my knowledge is unique, consists of a set of three pairs of equestrian figures, Campbell and Canrobert, Brown and De Lacy Evans and Brown and Raglan (*see pls.* C-48, 49 and 50). It will be noted that these pairs of figures are all identical in every respect, excepting in size (each pair is of a different size) and the fact that in the case of Lord Raglan, the right forearm has been amputated in accordance with historical fact.

WHY ARE SO FEW THEATRE FIGURES TITLED?

It has already been emphasized that it is the absence of titles, particularly in theatrical portraits, that has stimulated research. It is really quite extraordinary that the only titled figures of persons who appeared on the stage are those of Jenny Lind, Macready and T. D. Rice (Jim Crow), although in addition, figures are found of circus personalities such as Van Amburgh and Rarey and of the conductor Louis Jullien. What is the explanation for this? Various theories have been put forward. It has been suggested that the actors of the day were so well known to the public that there was no necessity to add a title to the figures. All the evidence suggests that this is extremely unlikely. Titled figures can be quoted of persons who were every bit as well-known, namely Victoria herself, the Prince of Wales, Wellington, Peel and many others.

Another theory is that the figures were sold at each performance. To what extent this practice was carried on is not known, but it has been recorded that Van Amburgh was a great publicist and had both jugs and mugs made on which he and his animals were shown, either in transfer or relief. These articles were sold for his benefit at each performance. The majority of them are, however, found inscribed with his name. The only known figure of Van Amburgh also happens to be one of the few known titled figures of theatrical persons.

Mr Anthony Oliver has suggested that as so many of these Staffordshire figures or groups represent a dramatic highlight in the play, they probably functioned in much the same way as the photographs outside the theatre do today, and he thinks it probable that they would have been on sale at street traders' stalls outside the theatre. After careful research he has been unable to find any documentary evidence that they were sold either inside or outside any of the leading theatres but he has found some evidence that 'image sellers' were part of the 'scene' in the *Royal Gardens, Vauxhall* which were used extensively for concerts, fireworks and the occasional dramatic show and operetta until their closure in 1859. A pantomime *Harlequin and Mother Shipton; or Riquet with the tuft*, first performed on December 26th, 1826, has a scene portraying Vauxhall Gardens. The following is the cast list.

Lambs to Sell	...	...	...	...	...	...	Mr Fuller
Tiddy Doll Man	...	...	...	...	...	...	Mr Crumpton
Scarlett Garters	...	...	...	...	...	...	Mr Robinson
Cherry Woman	...	...	...	...	...	...	Mrs Wilson
Lavender Girl	...	...	...	...	...	...	Miss Appleton
Flower Girl	...	...	...	...	...	...	Mrs Brown
Watercress Woman	...	...	...	...	...	...	Miss Smith
Image Man	...	...	...	...	...	...	Mr Miers

Yet another theory is that the figures were issued primarily to depict characters in books or plays rather than the actual actors who were, so to speak, portrayed incidentally. This theory is supported by a number of pieces which, although portrait figures, are titled with the names of characters from the works of Shakespeare, Dickens, Byron, etc.

The last, and to me most plausible theory, is that the majority of the figures were made by the potters for purely decorative purposes. Engravings were used which were thought attractive and which happened to be portraits of actors of the day. The potters themselves were totally unaware that their figures would, in the years to come, cease to be regarded as decorative pieces, or even possibly, as representations of characters in popular plays or books, but would be looked upon rather as portraits of actual actors of the day in characteristic pose.

There is, in fact, strong evidence that certain figures were purely 'decorative', being manufactured solely to balance others, thereby making 'chimney-piece' pairs. Luigi Lablache (*fig.* 113, *pl.* E-62) is paired by an unidentified female (*fig.* 114, *pl.* E-62). This latter figure is undoubtedly derived from a figure of Eliza Cook (*fig.* 36, *pl.* H-10), being a modified mirror-image, and is therefore unlikely to portray anyone but intended simply to make up a pair.

There are a number of other pairs in which only one figure has been identified with certainty. The other may or may not portray an actual person. Among them are:

Fig. 9 (Kemble) and *fig.* 10 (? Siddons) : *pl.* E-2.
Fig. 20 (Macready) and *fig.* 21 (Unidentified actress) : *pl.* E-62.
Fig. 115 (Reeves) and *fig.* 116 (? Gras) : *pl.* E-62.
Fig. 160 (Lind) and *fig.* 161 (Unidentified male opera singer) : *pl.* E-82.

SOME ANECDOTES ON COLLECTING

The fun and interest to be derived from collecting Staffordshire portrait figures is often only just beginning at the time the figure is acquired. Early in 1965 I purchased *fig.* 255, *pl.* A-94 which it seemed to me was possibly a portrait of Leopold, King of the Belgians. I sent a photograph of this figure to M. Marc de Smedt in Belgium and asked him whether he knew of any possible source in the Belgian art galleries. This set into play an extraordinary chain of events. M. Marc de Smedt visited *Le Musée de la Dynastie* in Brussels and there discovered not a source of my figure but the pair of figures shown on *pl.* A-87, 'Leopold, King of Belgium' and 'Maria, Queen of Belgium', the latter being unknown to collectors in this country.

When he wrote to tell me of his find, M. Marc de Smedt kindly invited me to spend a few days with him at his home near Brussels. During the visit he took me to *Le Musée de la Dynastie*, where we were taken to inspect the figures by the President, Chevalier Albert de Selliers de Moranville. After examining the figures we looked at the various portraits of the Belgian Royal Family adorning the walls of the museum, and there, not ten feet away from the case containing the two figures, were the two sources of these figures (*see pls.* A-88 and 89). Thus, a new figure and two new sources were added to our knowledge so to speak by accident, and the identity of the figure which began it all still remains obscure.

Identification of Figures

There are a surprising number of figures like that of 'Maria, Queen of Belgium', of which only one is known. This strange feature remains unexplained, but because of it I have found the use of photographs invaluable for furthering research. Mr Anthony Oliver, an authority on theatre history, was perusing my photographs a few years ago when he remarked that he felt certain not only that the pair to *fig.* 147, *pl.* E-74 was in a London antique shop but also that the sources of both figures (a pair of tinsel portraits) were in the establishment of another London dealer. His surprising photographic memory made it possible to establish that *figs.* 146 and 147, *pl.* E-74 were a pair and that they portrayed Mr Macready as 'Rob Roy Mac-Gregor' and Mrs Egerton as 'Helen MacGregor' (*see pls.* E-75 and 76). At that time only one of each of these figures was known, and neither by itself would be likely to attract attention as a possible portrait figure. Almost certainly they were originally sold as purely decorative pieces, or possibly as representing Rob Roy and Helen MacGregor.

EXAMPLES OF THE POTTERS' SOURCES

Plate 1
L: *Fig.* 162 (Albert) *pl.* A-55
R: Music-front *Prince Albert's Band March.*
There is also a close similarity between the figure and the statue of Prince Albert at Holborn Circus, believed unique, since it shows a soldier in uniform with a raised cocked hat.
By courtesy of Mr John Hall

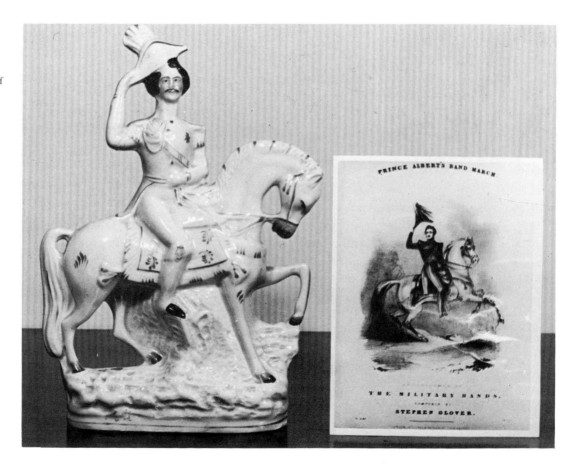

Plate 1

PRINCE ALBERT. The lithograph music-front *Prince Albert's Band March* has striking similarities to *fig.* 162, *pl.* A-55. This or a similar illustration was undoubtedly the potter's inspiration.

Plate 1A
L: *Fig.* 164 (? The Princess Royal with the Prince of Wales) *pl.* A-55
R: Engraving by G. Dawe *The Guardian Angel.*
By courtesy of Mr David Robinson

Plate 1A

THE GUARDIAN ANGEL. The engraving illustrated on the right is inscribed 'THE GUARDIAN ANGEL–*G. Dawe, Eng & Print*'., *9, Southampton Pl, New Rd*'. There seems little doubt that it inspired the potter to produce *fig.* 164, *pl.* A-55. This figure is generally thought to portray the Princess Royal with the Prince of Wales. It will be noted that the potter has substituted crowns for the floral devices above the children's heads. There is no evidence to suggest that the original engraving was intended to portray royal children.

Plates 2, 3, 4 and 4A

EDWARD VII as PRINCE OF WALES. The painting illustrated on *pl.* 3 is by F. X. Winterhalter (1805-73). It was painted in 1846 as a Christmas present for the Prince Consort. The little Prince is seen in the sailor's suit made for him by a tailor on board the Royal Yacht in the autumn of 1846. The painting is the source of *fig.* 182, *pl.* A-58. *Pl.* 4 is of an engraving taken from *The Illustrated London News* of October 14th, 1848. The text accompanying the engraving is as follows:

STATUETTE OF THE PRINCE OF WALES
This beautiful Portrait of the young Sailor Prince has been modelled, by permission of His Royal Highness Prince Albert, from the picture painted by Winterhalter, of which a print has been published by Alderman Moon. The statuette is from the establishment of Messrs. Minton and Co., of Stoke-upon-Trent. The material is Parian. The likeness is very striking, and the characteristic accessories of the nautical costume very nicely executed.

This is certainly one of the most interesting presentments of the youthful Royal Family yet published. It may be seen at Mr Cundall's, 12, Old-Bond street.

The sketch for the statuette in Minton's first figure design book is reproduced on *pl.* 4A.

Plate 2
Fig. 182 (Prince of Wales) *pl.* A-58
By courtesy of Mr R. Bonnett

Plate 3
Edward VII as Prince of Wales in a sailor suit, by Xaver Winterhalter (1805-73).
Reproduced by gracious permission of Her Majesty the Queen

Plate 4
Statuette of the Prince of Wales in Parian by Messrs Minton & Co., *The Illustrated London News,* October 14th, 1848.

Plate 4A
Sketch for the Parian statuette of the Prince of Wales. (From Minton's first figure design book.)
By courtesy of Mintons Ltd.

Plate 5
L: *Fig.* 191 (Prince of
Wales) *pl.* A-62
R: Lithograph music-front
by J. Brandard *The
Coldstream Guards March.*

Plate 5

THE PRINCE OF WALES. The lithograph music-front by J.
Brandard titled '*The Coldstream Guards March*' *composed and
respectfully inscribed to Colonel H.R.H. Prince of Wales by Stephen
Glover* is the source of *fig.* 191, *pl.* A-62. It is probable, although
I have not yet been able to confirm it, that the lithograph is after
a painting by Winterhalter. Although titled *The Coldstream
Guards March*, the Prince was not attached to either of the regi-
ments of the Household Brigade

Plate 6
R: *Fig.* 193 (Prince of Wales) *pl.* A-62
L: The Prince of Wales: An engraving after a
photograph by Mayall, which appeared in *The
Illustrated London News,* December 11th, 1858.

Plate 6

HIS ROYAL HIGHNESS the PRINCE OF WALES in his
uniform as Colonel in the Army from a photograph by Mayall.
This engraving appeared in *The Illustrated London News* of
December 11th, 1858. The accompanying narrative states that
*the Prince is not attached to either of the regiments of the Household
Brigade, but has merely the rank of an Unattached Colonel in the Army
. . . he wears only the ribbon and star of the Order of the Garter . . . a
simple unsophisticated uniform.* This photograph by Mayall is
almost certainly the source of *fig. 193, pl.* A-62.

Plate 6A
L: *Fig.* 286 (? Charles I and Henrietta Maria) *pl.* A-110
R: Le Blond print titled *Courtship.*

Plate 6A

COURTSHIP. *Fig.* 286, *pl.* A-110 has long been thought, on no positive evidence, to portray Charles I and his consort, Henrietta Maria. Recently, the source of the figure, a Le Blond print titled *Courtship* has come to light. It is an illustration to *Renshaw's Ladies' Pocket-book* (1851).

Identification of Figures

Plate 7

LEOPOLD, KING OF BELGIUM. The lithograph by F. Judenne illustrated on the left of the plate is titled *Leopold Premier, Roi des Belges, née Le 16 Decembre 1790*. It may be seen in the *Musée de la Dynastie* in Brussels and is undoubtedly the source of *fig.* 248, *pl.* A-87.

Plate 8

MARIA, QUEEN OF BELGIUM. The lithograph by F. Judenne illustrated on the right of the plate is titled *Louise Marie d'Orleans, Reine des Belges, née Le 3 Avril 1812*. It may be seen in the *Musée de la Dynastie* in Brussels and is undoubtedly the source of *fig.* 249, *pl.* A-87.

Plate 9
Fig. 3 (Lord Melbourne) *pl.* B-1

Plate 9A
Engraving of Lord Melbourne.

Plate 10
Earl of Shaftesbury: Portrait by Sir Francis
Grant (1803-78).
*'Crown Copyright', by permission of the Rt. Hon.
Mr Speaker, House of Commons*

Plates 9 and 9A

LORD MELBOURNE. *Fig.* 3, *pl.* B-1 has puzzled collectors
for many years. It has been variously identified as Palmerston
and Peel. It has, however, a very close resemblance to the
engraving of Lord Melbourne illustrated immediately underneath, and this is particularly apparent when the figure is held
beside the engraving and rotated. It is not a positive identification – but a likely one, for the figure dates to the early 1840's and
Lord Melbourne was Prime Minister at the accession of Queen
Victoria in 1837 and acted as adviser to the young Queen until
his resignation in 1841.

Plate 11
L: *Fig.* 8 (? Fry) *pl.* B-1
C: *Fig.* 9 (Shaftesbury) *pl.* B-1
R: *Fig.* 7 (Shaftesbury) *pl.* B-1

Plates 10 and 11

EARL OF SHAFTESBURY. Balston remarked on the close resemblance both as regards shape of head, hair style and clothes between *figs.* 7 and 9, *pl.* B-1 and the painting of the Earl of Shaftesbury by Sir Francis Grant, now in the House of Commons. Whilst not a positive identification, it is certainly a possibility.

Plate 12
L: *Fig.* 12 (O'Connell) *pl.* B-1
R: Engraving of O'Connell which
appeared in *The Illustrated London
News* of November 25th, 1843.

Plate 12

DANIEL O'CONNELL. The head and shoulders of *fig.* 12,
pl. B-1 are virtually identical to the engraving of Daniel
O'Connell which appeared in *The Illustrated London News* of
November 25th, 1843. This identification is beyond doubt.

Plate 12A
Fig. 29 (Wellington) *pl.* B-5
In the Thomas Balston collection

Plate 12B
Lithograph music-front by Louisa Corbaux for the song *Wellington* by
Charles Jefferys.
The song was published by Stannard and Dixon on September 16th,
1852 — two days after the death of the Duke at Walmer Castle.

Plates 12A and 12B

THE DUKE OF WELLINGTON. The lithograph music-
front by Louisa Corbaux for the song, *Wellington* by Charles
Jefferys, first published by Stannard and Dixon on September
16th, 1852, two days after the death of the Duke at Walmer
Castle, is the undoubted source of *fig.* 29, *pl.* B-5. The Duke is
portrayed as *a huddled figure in a high-backed chair.*

Plate 13 (Left)
Fig. 61 (Kossuth) *pl.* B-19

Plate 13A (Right)
An engraving from a daguerreotype by Claudet of Kossuth which appeared in *The Illustrated London News* of November 15th, 1851.

Plate 14 (Left)
Fig. 84 (Topsy and Eva) *pl.* B-26

Plate 14A (Right)
Lithograph music-front of *Topsy's Song.*

Plates 13 and 13A

M. KOSSUTH. This engraving appeared in *The Illustrated London News* of November 15th, 1851, and is inscribed *M. Kossuth:— From a daguerreotype by Claudet.* It is the source of *fig.* 61, *pl.* B-19 and probably of *figs.* 63 and 64, *pl.* B-20, and *fig.* 62, *pl.* B-19. The periodical contained, in addition, a detailed account of Kossuth's life. It will be recalled that after the defeat at Temesvár on August 9th, 1849, Kossuth had fled to Turkey, where he was made a prisoner, but not extradited. In September 1851, he was liberated through British and American influence, and came to England where he was received with respect and sympathy.

Plates 14 and 14A

EVA & TOPSY. The music-front illustrated is titled:

TOPSY'S SONG
Eva and Topsy
'I love you because you haven't had any Father, or Mother, or Friends because you have been a poor abused child!'

Vide Uncle Tom's Cabin.

Written by Charles Jefferys, composed by Stephen Glover.

The lithograph of Eva and Topsy is the undoubted source of *fig.* 84, *pl.* B-26 and may well be a theatrical portrait, although definite proof of this is still lacking.

Plate 15
L: *Fig.* 26 (Napoleon)
pl. C-11
R: Coloured lithograph
music-front after a
painting by David — *The
Emperor Napoleon's March
Across the Alps.*

Plate 15

NAPOLEON BONAPARTE, Ier Consul. The coloured lithograph music-front is after a painting (*c.* 1800) by Napoleon's court painter, Jacques-Louis David (1748-1825). The original is at the *Musée de Versailles.* Although it depicts Napoleon crossing the Great Saint Bernard Pass in the Alps on a fiery white charger which is rearing on the edge of a precipice, the true story is that the First Consul travelled in a coach from Martigny to Bourg-Saint-Pierre where he modestly mounted a mule to make the crossing.

Several Staffordshire figures are likely to be derived from this painting, but the one illustrated (*fig.* 26, *pl.* C-11) is probably the closest.

The music-front is inscribed:
'The Emperor Napoleon's March Across the Alps.'
For the pianoforte, composed by Adolphe Schubert.
It was published by Leoni Lee & Coxhead, music sellers to Her Majesty Queen Victoria, 48, Albemarle Street.

Plate 16
L: Lithograph of Marin-Lavigne inscribed *Napoleon at St. Helena.*
R: *Fig.* 38 (Napoleon) *pl.* C-12
Note: Napoleon's sword is found in two sizes. Compare that in the above
figure with that in *pl.* C-12. Both are original.
*By courtesy of Le Conservateur, Cabinet des Estampes, Bibliothèque Nationale, Paris
and of M. Marc de Smedt*

Plate 16

NAPOLEON AT ST. HELENA. There is a painting on rice
paper of Napoleon in uniform reclining on rocks to be found at
Caillou Farm, the headquarters of Napoleon at Waterloo. The
farm is now a museum and nothing is known there of the artist,
nor is the painting titled. Napoleon is portrayed, bareheaded,
with a book titled 'France' in his left hand, his sword to his
left and his hat on the rocks to his right. There are palm trees to
his right and a waterfall to his left. It is clear that *fig.* 38, *pl.* C-12
is derived from this or a similar painting, being identical in all
important respects except that the hat lies to Napoleon's left;
also, I have not yet come across a figure in which the book
in his left hand has been titled.

Mr P. C. Withers, who kindly examined a photograph of the
Caillou Farm painting for me, in the hope that he might be
able to throw some further light on its source, pointed out that
there is an engraving by Marin-Lavigne, an example of which
is in the *Cabinet des Estampes* at the *Bibliothèque Nationale, Paris,*

which is obviously the source from which the rice paper picture
is taken. The posture and surroundings are identical, with the
single exception that the little waterfall is not shown in the
engraving. I am indebted to M. Nicole Villa, the conservateur
of the *Cabinet des Estampes*, for supplying me with the following
information:

*In 1830 Engelmann brought to the Cabinet des Estampes a litho-
graph of Marin-Lavigne titled 'Napoleon at St. Helena' (Ref.A.A.3).
An entry in the register of the Legal Department on April 8th, 1830
suggests that the lithograph is by Horace Vernet. This is not surprising
as Marin-Lavigne was a pupil of Horace Vernet. I have been unable to
determine if the lithograph was from a drawing or a painting of Vernet's.
The lithograph was revised with a few differences of detail in 1850. The
new one appeared in the Vincel collection, vol. 75, no. 9788 (printed by
A. Bés and F. Dubreuil, in Paris).*

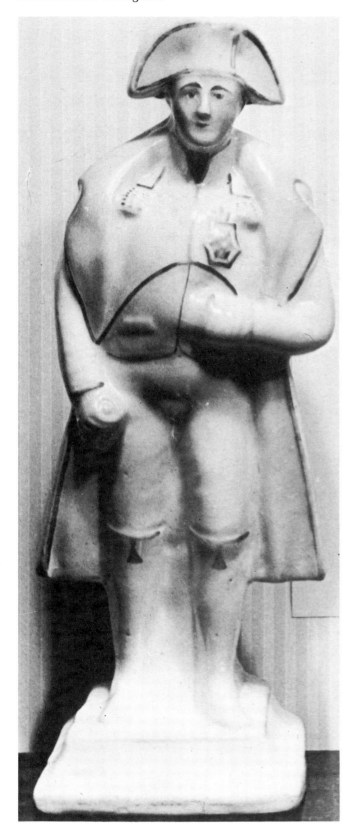

Plate 17
L: *Fig.* 52 (Napoleon) *pl.* C-17
R: Engraving of two pieces of statuary which have crowned La Colonne Vendôme, Paris.

Plate 17

LA COLONNE VENDÔME, Paris. The engraving shown to the right of the plate illustrates two pieces of statuary which have crowned La Colonne Vendôme, Paris. That on the left depicts Napoleon as the 'Little Corporal' and is by E. Seure; that on the right shows Napoleon as 'Caesar' and is by Chaudet.

The history of the column which has gone through various fortunes in different regimes is as follows:

1810. Inauguration of the column and Chaudet's statue of Napoleon as Caesar, the latter cast from the bronze of 1,200 cannons captured from the enemy.

1814. Replacement of the statue by a white flag to the cries of 'Vive Louis XVIII'.

1818. Melting down of the statue to permit the casting of another of Henry IV for erection on the Pont Neuf. Replacement of the statue by an enormous Fleur de lys.

July 28th, 1833. The erection of the statue of Napoleon as the 'Little Corporal' by E. Seure.

November 4th, 1863. Seure's statue was taken to Courbevoie and replaced on the order of Napoleon III by the present statue of Napoleon as Caesar by Dumont.

1871. Courbet ordered the destruction of the column and the statue.

1873. Restoration of the column and the statue at Courbet's expense.

September 17th, 1870. Versailles taken by the Prussians; the Seure statue taken from Courbevoie by order of the Government of the Third Republic. It was thrown into the Seine near Neuille Bridge. It was recovered on January 23rd, 1871, by the architect Le Fuel. In 1911 it was erected in the Hall of Honour at Les Invalides.

Fig. 52, *pl.* C-17 appears to be based on the Seure statue which it will be noted crowned La Colonne Vendôme between 1833 and 1863. Several other figures of Napoleon are probably based on this statue. However, the one illustrated is the best example because of the nature of its base, although it must be admitted that there are no cannon-balls between the feet, nor is there a sword.

Plate 18
L: *Fig.* 69 (Ranbir Singh) *pl.* C-27
R: *Fig.* 68 (Gholab Singh) *pl.* C-27

Plates 18 and 19

GHOLAB SINGH AND HIS SON, RANBIR SINGH. The engraving illustrated on *pl.* C-27 appeared in *The Illustrated London News* of April 4th, 1846. It is inscribed *Gholab Singh, his son and body guard–from a highly finished native drawing in the possession of G. T. Vigne, Esq.* Details of this engraving are illustrated on *ch.* 3, *pl.* 19. *Figs.* 68 and 69, *pl.* C-27 have been identified beyond doubt through this engraving. This may well be regarded as the most astonishing identification so far reported. The faces of the figures are brown; that of Gholab Singh is bearded and that of his son clean-shaven. Gholab Singh is wearing a jacket with an open collar and a cummerbund, and his son a simple shirt and wristlets. These characteristics are also found in the engraving. The sabres likewise are of identical design, and the horses have a similar stance. The ornate bridles are identical, as also the saddles and saddle-cloths. There are, in short, too many identical features to allow for coincidence.

Plate 19
Details of the engraving inscribed *Gholab Singh, his son and body guard* which appeared in *The Illustrated London News* on April 4th, 1846.

Plate 20
L: Engraving of the obverse and reverse of a medal, by A.A. Caque, struck at the Paris Mint in 1854, to commemorate the Anglo-French alliance. Reproduced from *The Illustrated London News* of September 9th 1854.
R: *Fig.* 75 (Turkey-England-France) *pl.* C-32

Plate 20

VICTORIA WITH NAPOLEON III AND THE SULTAN. The engraving illustrated to the left of the plate was reproduced in *The Illustrated London News* of September 9th, 1854, and is of a medal by A. A. Caque struck at the Paris Mint to commemorate the Anglo-French alliance. In the same edition, it is recorded that *Prince Albert and the King of the Belgians paid a friendly visit to the French Emperor at Boulogne and visited along with him the Camp of the North, then forming between St. Omer and Boulogne . . . this significant fact will not tend greatly to comfort the Czar, or the King of Prussia, under their present gloomy aspect of affairs.*

The medal inspired the potters to produce *fig.* 75 (Turkey-England-France) *pl.* C-32.

Plate 21
L: Engraving of Abdu'l Medjid, Sultan of Turkey, proceeding to the feast of the Bairam — from a picture in the Palace at Constantinople, which appeared in *The Ilustrated London News* on September 17th, 1853.
R: *Fig.* 167 (Abd-ul-Medjid) *pl.* C-64
By courtesy of Mr and Mrs Eric Joyce

Plate 21A
Lithograph music-front, by Corbetta, of Giuseppe Garibaldi. Based on an original photograph.

Plate 21B
Fig. 285 (Garibaldi) *pl.* C-98

Plate 21

ABD-UL-MEDJID, SULTAN OF TURKEY. This engraving appeared in *The Illustrated London News* of September 17th, 1853, with the following inscription:

Abdu'l Medjid, Sultan of Turkey, Proceeding to the Feast of the Bairam – From a picture in the Palace at Constantinople.

Overleaf the information is given that *the portrait is from a daguerreotype of a picture in the Palace at Constantinople* and adds that the Sultan is *usually dressed in a plain European blue frock and trousers and wears a dark blue coat, fastened by a blazing diamond clasp upon his breast.* There is little doubt that *fig.* 167, *pl.* C-64 is based on this engraving.

Plates 21A and 21B

GIUSEPPE GARIBALDI. The lithograph music-front illustrated on *pl.* 21A is by Corbetta and based on an original photograph. It is the source of *fig.* 285, *pl.* C-98.

A contemporary description of Garibaldi represents him as follows: *Of middle height, well-made with broad shoulders and square chest. He had light chestnut brown hair falling over his shoulders, a heavy moustache, and light blond beard ending in two points. His nose had an exceedingly broad root; hence his nickname 'Leone'. He was dressed in a red tunic with short flaps and on his head he had a little black felt sugar-loaf hat with two black ostrich feathers. In his left hand he held a light plain horseman's sabre and a cavalry cartridge bag hung down by the left shoulder.*

Plate 22
L: The Gordon Statue at the Gordon
Boys' School, Woking
R: *Fig.* 337 (Gordon) *pl.* C-119
In the collection of Lady Ranfurly

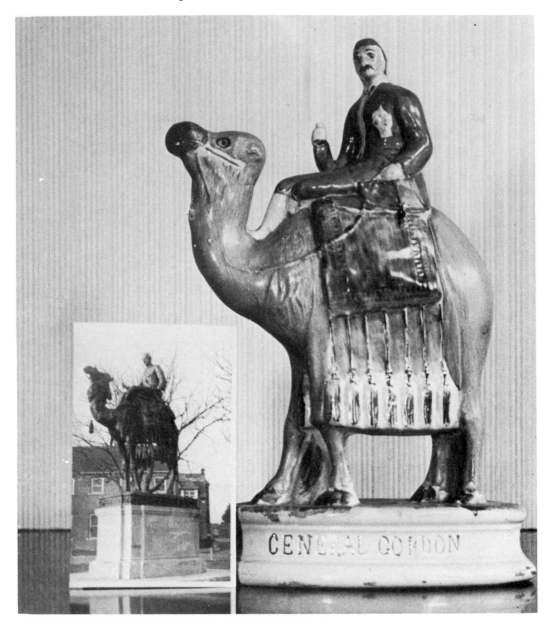

Plate 22

THE GORDON STATUE. The statue of Major-General Charles G. Gordon CB, riding a camel, and wearing the 'dress of honour' bestowed on him by the Khedive, which stands outside the main building of the School of Military Engineering, Gillingham, was commissioned by a group of regular and volunteer officers in his memory. The sculptor selected was Onslow Ford RA. The statue was exhibited in the Royal Academy before being unveiled in its present site by Edward, Prince of Wales on May 19th, 1890. It is the source of *fig.* 337, *pl.* C-119.

A replica of this statue produced from the original cast, was unveiled by the Duke of Cambridge in July 1902, in St. Martin's Place, London, on the site now occupied by the memorial to Nurse Cavell. In October of that year, largely due to the instigation of Lord Kitchener and Lord Glenesk of *The Morning Post*, the statue was moved to the Sudan. It had an adventurous journey. It was initially shipped in the S.S. *Cedardine* for Australia. She collided with another vessel and the statue was submerged for twenty-four hours in the River Thames before being transferred to another ship. In November 1903, after a long and arduous journey by rail and barge from Alexandria, including another submersion in the River Nile, the statue was placed on a pedestal in Gordon Avenue behind the Palace in Khartoum. Its tribulations were, however, not complete. Shortly after the statue was set up, the foundation of the pedestal subsided. Fifty-five years later and almost seventy-four years after

Gordon's death, the statue was covered with a canvas shroud and lowered from its pedestal. It was conveyed to its present resting place, the Gordon Boys' School, West End, Woking. It is this statue which is illustrated beside the figure of Gordon.

(I am grateful to Messrs Raymond Mander and Joe Mitchenson for supplying me with this information, which they had obtained from Brigadier J. H. S. Lácey CBE.)

Plate 23

£10,000. This cartoon appeared in *Punch* in March 1851 in connection with the 'No Popery' agitation aroused by the Pope giving English territorial titles to bishops. The cartoon is inscribed:

THE KIDNAPPER:— A CASE FOR THE POLICE.
Kidnapper: 'There's a Be-autiful Veil!!!
Give me your parcel, my dear, while you put it on.'

Fig 5, *pl.* D-2 in which the girl carries a bundle labelled £10,000 has exactly the same theme as this cartoon, which portrays a monk holding out a veil to a girl carrying a bundle labelled £. *s. d.* It enables the figure to be dated with confidence to 1851.

Plate 24

MONUMENT TO JOHN WESLEY. This engraving appeared in *The Illustrated London News* of May 24th, 1856, with

Identification of Figures

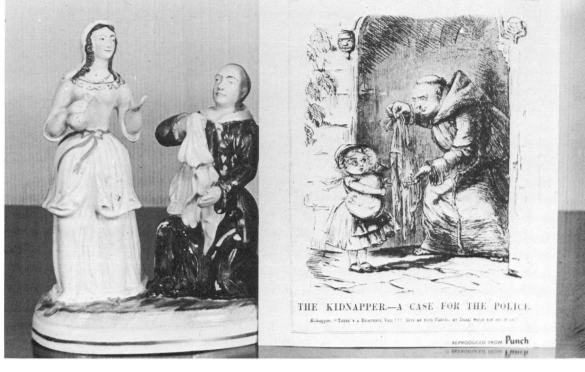

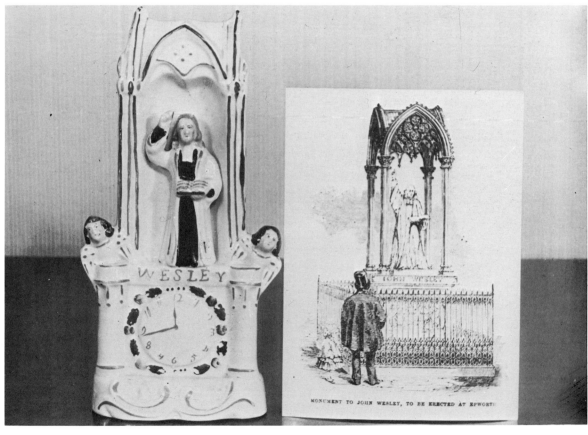

the inscription *Monument to John Wesley, to be erected at Epworth*.

The accompanying account referred to the proposed erection of the monument to be paid for by a National Penny Subscription. It went on to relate that Wesley was born on June 17th, 1703, at the Old Rectory House at Epworth. He was rescued from the flames when six years old by two courageous and humane inhabitants of the town. He brought about the revival of religion in the eighteenth century. The writer remarked that there was not a lasting monument to perpetuate his (Wesley's)

memory and that Mr Tilbury had designed the intended monument which consisted of a statue 7 feet 9 inches high placed upon a square stone basement 9 feet high. Upon this basement rose a Gothic floriated baldachino, or canopy, underneath which was the figure. He was represented holding a bible in one hand, exhorting the people with that earnestness and truth which so distinguished his life. *Fig.* 13, *pl.* D-6A is probably based on the design of the intended monument.

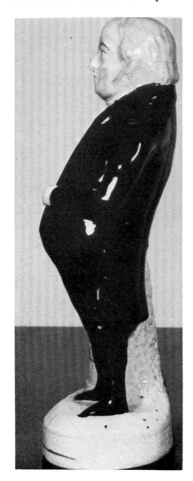

Plate 25B
L: *Fig.* 51 (Mathew) *pl.* D-25
R: Engraving of *The Very Revd. Theobald Mathew, administering the Temperance Pledge.*
Note: The right arm of this figure — the only one known to me — has been incorrectly restored.

Plate 25 (Above)
Fig. 46 (Bryan) *pl.* D-23
In the collection of Mrs Cecil Woodham-Smith

Plate 25A (Below)
Lithograph of the Rev. John Bryan.
Signed: *Eich Serchog* (Your sincere),
J. Bryan.
By courtesy of The Librarian, National Library of Wales, Aberystwyth

Plates 25 and 25A

J. BRYAN. The lithograph of the Reverend John Bryan is in the National Library of Wales. It is signed:
Eich Serchog (Your sincere)
J. Bryan
Fig. 46, *pl.* D-23 corresponds in all essential details with this lithograph.

Plate 25B

FATHER THEOBALD MATHEW. The identities of the 'untitled' *figs.* 52 and 53, *pl.* D-26 were established from engravings similar to this, *before* the discovery of the 'titled' *fig.* 51, *pl.* D-25. It seems likely that the design of the latter was based on the exact engraving illustrated.

Plate 26
L: *Fig.* 1 (Cushman sisters) *pl.* E-1A
R: Engraving from Tallis' *Shakespeare Gallery* of Charlotte and Susan Cushman as 'Romeo' and 'Juliet'.
In the collection of Messrs Raymond Mander and Joe Mitchenson

FIGURES BASED ON ENGRAVINGS IN TALLIS'
SHAKESPEARE GALLERY (1852-3)

(Plates 26-32 inclusive)

In 1944 Messrs Raymond Mander and Joe Mitchenson made the important discovery that seven Shakspearian figures were based on engravings in Tallis' *Shakespeare Gallery* (1852-3), and from the lettering on the engravings showed that these figures were not imaginary representations of Shakspearian characters, but portraits of actual actors. These figures, which became known as 'Tallis' figures, are now thought to have been made by the Parr and Kent group of potters (*see p. 15*). They were made in various sizes, and many were still being made from the original moulds continually, except for short gaps due to the wars, until December 1962. It is however, simple on acquaintance to distinguish the different periods, and in particular the more recent examples.

Plate 26

ROMEO AND JULIET. This engraving from Tallis' *Shakespeare Gallery* is inscribed :

CHARLOTTE AND SUSAN CUSHMAN
AS
ROMEO AND JULIET

Act 3, Scene 5

Engraved from a painting (1845) by Margaret Gillies.

Fig. 1, *pl.* E-1A is based on this engraving. Charlotte and Susan Cushman came to England in 1845 and appeared on December 29th as 'Romeo' and 'Juliet' at the Haymarket Theatre, and subsequently in the country. The figure is titled:

Jul: 'O think'st thou we shall ever meet again?'
Rom: 'I doubt it not; and all these woes shall serve
For sweet discourses in our time to come.'

The scene is Juliet's chamber.

Plate 27
L: *Fig.* 2 (Marston and Robinson) *pl.* E-1A
R: Engraving from Tallis' *Shakespeare Gallery* of Miss Jenny Marston and Mr F. Robinson as 'Perdita' and 'Florizel'. *In the collection of Messrs Raymond Mander and Joe Mitchenson*

Plate 27

FLORIZEL AND PERDITA. This engraving from Tallis' *Shakespeare Gallery* is inscribed:

MISS JENNY MARSTON AND MR. F. ROBINSON
AS FLORIZEL AND PERDITA

Flor: 'Thou dearest Perdita,
 With these forced thoughts I pry thee darken not
 The myrth o' the feast.'
Winter's Tale, Act 4, Sc. 3
Engraved by Sherratt from a Daguerreotype by Paine of Islington.

Fig. 2, *pl.* E-1A is derived from this engraving. Jenny Marston and Frederick Robinson appeared as 'Perdita' and 'Florizel' in Phelps's revival of *The Winter's Tale* at Sadler's Wells on July 28th, 1851.

The scene is Bohemia. A Lawn before the Shepherd's Cottage.

[OPHELIA *(fig.* 5, *pl.* E-1A) does not occur in the 'Tallis' series. The modellers rectified this omission by using the figure of 'Perdita', with minor modifications, and titling the piece

'Ophelia'. The figure of 'Ophelia' therefore does not portray an actress in the role.]

Plate 28

HAMLET. This engraving from Tallis' *Shakespeare Gallery* is inscribed:

JOHN PHILIP KEMBLE AS HAMLET

'Alas! Poor Yorick.'
Act 5, Scene 1.

From an engraving after Lawrence's portrait.

The figures illustrated are as follows:

Fig. 6, *pl.* E-1A titled 'ALAS! POOR YORICK' in gilt or black transfer; *fig.* 32, *pl.* E-13 titled 'HAMLET' in indented capitals and the small version of *fig.* 6, which is untitled (I have never seen a titled copy). There are several minor variants of *fig.* 6, *pl.* E-1A. The example of *fig.* 32, illustrated in this chapter

Identification of Figures

Plate 28
L: *Fig.* 6 (Kemble) *pl.*
E-1A
Fig. 6 (Kemble) *pl.* E-4
(small version)
Fig. 32 (Kemble) *pl.* E-13
(late copy)
R: Engraving from
Tallis' *Shakespeare Gallery*
of John Philip Kemble as
'Hamlet'.
*In the collection of Messrs
Raymond Mander and Joe
Mitchenson*

is a late copy. A contemporary copy of the figure may be seen on *pl.* E-13. Either this figure or *fig.* 6, *pl.* E-1A pairs with 'Ophelia' (*fig.* 5, *pl.* E-1A). The latter is a 10½ in. (26.5 cm.) version but the Kent catalogue also lists a 6 in. (15.25 cm.) version to pair with the smaller 'Hamlet'.

Kemble's first success was as 'Hamlet' in Dublin in 1781. His

first appearance in London was at Drury Lane in 1783, again as 'Hamlet'.

The scene is a churchyard. Hamlet has taken the skull. Yorick was the King's jester and known to Hamlet.

Hamlet : 'I knew him Horatio; a fellow of infinite jest.'

Plate 29A
Engraving from Tallis' *Shakespeare Gallery* of Mr Hackett as 'Falstaff'.
In the collection of Messrs Raymond Mander and Joe Mitchenson

Plate 29
Fig. 3 (Hackett) *pl.* E-1B (late copy of small version).

Plates 29 and 29A

FALSTAFF. This engraving taken from Tallis' *Shakespeare Gallery* is inscribed:

   MR. HACKETT AS FALSTAFF

Fal : 'There's but a shirt and a half in all my company: and the half shirt is two
   napkins tacked together, and thrown over the shoulders like a herald's coat
   without sleeves: and the shirt to say the truth, stolen from my host at St. Albans.'
      King Henry IV
      Part I, Act 4, Sc. 2.

Engraved by C. Jeens from a Daguerreotype by P. Haas, New York.

Fig. 3, *pl.* E-1B is derived from this engraving.

The piece was made in two sizes, 7¼ in. (18.25 cm.) and 9½ in. (24 cm.). The figure illustrated is the smaller figure and is of relatively recent production. Note, in particular, the generally crude appearance and also the style of lettering. Compare this with the larger figure illustrated on *pl.* E-1B which is contemporary with the engraving. The two sizes are of virtually identical design.

Plate 30A
Fig. 4 (Macready) *pl.* E-1B

Plate 31
L: *Fig.* 7 (Glyn) *pl.* E-1B
R: Engraving from Tallis' *Shakespeare Gallery* of Miss Glyn as 'Lady Macbeth'.
In the Thomas Balston collection

Plate 30
Engraving from Tallis' *Shakespeare Gallery* of
Mr Macready as 'Shylock'.
By courtesy of Mr and Mrs Eric Joyce

Plates 30 and 30A

SHYLOCK. This engraving is also from Tallis' *Shakespeare Gallery*. It is inscribed:

MR. MACREADY AS SHYLOCK
MERCHANT OF VENICE
Act I, Scene 3
From a Daguerreotype by Paine of Islington.

Fig. 4, *pl.* E-1B titled 'Shylock' is derived from this engraving.
Macready played 'Shylock' in *The Merchant of Venice* at the
Haymarket Theatre on September 30th, 1839.
The scene is a public place in Venice.

Plate 32
L: *Fig.* 8 (Macready) *pl.* E-1B
R: Engraving from Tallis'
Shakespeare Gallery of Mr Macready
as 'Macbeth'.
In the Thomas Balston collection

Plate 31

LADY MACBETH. This engraving is from Tallis' *Shakespeare Gallery* and is inscribed:

MISS GLYN AS LADY MACBETH

'Glamis thou art, and Cawder; and shalt be
what thou art promised.'
MACBETH
Act I, Scene 5.

From a Daguerreotype by Paine of Islington.

Fig. 7, pl. E-1B is based on this engraving. It is known in two sizes. The smaller 8 in. (20.5 cm.) version is illustrated on *pl.* E-2, and it will be seen to approximate slightly more closely to the engraving than the 10 in. (25 cm.) version illustrated here. Both the illustrated versions are contemporary copies.

The scene is Inverness, Macbeth's castle. Enter Lady Macbeth reading a letter.

Plate 32

MACBETH. The engraving from Tallis' *Shakespeare Gallery* illustrated here is inscribed:

MR. MACREADY AS MACBETH

Macb: 'Two truths are told, as happy prologues to
the swelling act of the imperial theme.'
Act I, Sc. 3.

Engraved by Sherratt after a painting by Tracey.

Fig. 8, pl. E-1B is derived from this engraving. The 10½ in. (26.5 cm.) version illustrated here is rather closer to the engraving than the smaller 8¼ in. (21 cm.) version illustrated on *pl.* E-2, in particular the shield is held rather more centrally.

The scene is a heath in Scotland.

Plate 33
L: *Fig.* 17 (Kemble)
pl. E-7
C: Engraving by H. Dawe
of a painting by Sir
Thomas Lawrence PRA
inscribed:
*To Mrs Siddons
This Print of Her Brother
John Philip Kemble Esq as
Hamlet
Is with permission most
respectfully dedicated by her
obedt Servant James Bulcock*
R: *Fig.* 9 (Kemble) *pl.* E-2
*In the collection of Messrs
Raymond Mander and Joe
Mitchenson*

Plate 33

HAMLET. The engraving is of the painting by Sir Thomas Lawrence now in the National Portrait Gallery. It is inscribed *John Philip Kemble Esq. as Hamlet. Fig.* 9, *pl.* E-2 and *fig.* 17, *pl.* E-7 show none of the characteristics of the Parr and Kent group, i.e. they are not 'Tallis' figures. The assumption must be that their source was not the engraving of Lawrence's painting to be found in Tallis' *Shakespeare Gallery* but rather the engraving illustrated or the painting itself. Very possibly they preceded the 'Tallis' figures and were manufactured in the 1840's. In many respects they are closer to the original than the 'Tallis' figures. Note the broad ribbon passing from his right shoulder across his tunic, also the cloak over both shoulders.

Plates 34 and 34A

WILLIAM CHARLES MACREADY. The engraving on the right appeared in *The Illustrated London News* on May 23rd, 1846, and is inscribed 'Scene from the new play of *The King of the Commons* at the Princess' Theatre'. The engraving depicts Macready in the role of 'James V of Scotland'; another engraving appeared in the *Theatrical Times* of June 1846. Study of the actor's dress leaves little room for doubt that *fig.* 20, *pl.* E-7 portrays Macready in this role.

Plate 35

MR GARRICK in the Character of Richard the 3^d. This

Colour Plate 8
James Henry Hackett as Falstaff, William Charles Macready as Shylock and
Isabella Glyn as Lady Macbeth. *Figs.* 3, 4 and 7, *pl.* E-1B. See pages 362-4.

Colour Plate 9
Jenny Lind as Alice. *Fig.* 158, *pl.* E-80. See pages 76 and 410.

Plate 34 (Left)
Fig. 20 (Macready) *pl.* E-7
*By courtesy of Mr and Mrs
Eric Joyce*

Plate 34A (Right)
Engraving from *The
Illustrated London News* of
May 23rd, 1846 of a
scene from *The King of the
Commons* at the Princess'
Theatre with Macready
in the role of 'James V of
Scotland'.

Plate 35
L: *Fig.* 22 (Garrick) *pl.* E-7
R: Engraving of Hogarth's
painting *David Garrick as
Richard III* (1745), now in
the Walker Art Gallery,
Liverpool.
*In the collection of Messrs
Raymond Mander and Joe
Mitchenson*

engraving is of Hogarth's painting *David Garrick as Richard III*
(1745), now in the Walker Art Gallery, Liverpool.

It is the source both of *fig.* 22, *pl.* E-7, which is occasionally
found titled 'Richard the Third' (gilt script), and also of the
small version, *fig.* 37, *pl.* E-13, which has never been found
titled.

Another engraving by Portbury of the same painting appears
in Tallis' *Shakespeare Gallery* (1852-3). The scene depicted is, of
course, Bosworth Field. King Richard in his tent starts out of
his dream as the Ghosts vanish. The Tallis engraving is inscribed:

GARRICK AS RICHARD 3RD.

'Give me another horse.
Bind up my wounds.'
Act 5, Scene 3.

The style of the two figures is however, quite different from
the style of other figures whose source is known to be Tallis'
Shakespeare Gallery and which are thought to have been manufactured by the Parr and Kent group (*see p. 15*).

Plate 36
L: *Fig.* 30. (Shylock) *pl.*
E-13
R: Engraving of Mr
Charles Kean in the role
of 'Shylock' in 'the trial
scene' in *The Merchant of
Venice* from a drawing by
E.H. Wehnert, which
appeared in *The Illustrated
London News* on January
6th, 1849.

Plate 37 (Left)
Fig. 31 (Othello and
Iago) *pl.* E-13
*By courtesy of Mr and Mrs
Eric Joyce*

Plate 38 (Right)
Engraving of a
watercolour by S.A. Hart
RA (1806 81) titled
Othello and Iago, which
appeared in *The National
Magazine* in 1858.
*By courtesy of the British
Museum*

Plate 36

THE MERCHANT OF VENICE. The engraving illustrated appeared in *The Illustrated London News* of January 6th, 1849, and is inscribed *Plays at Windsor Castle: Shakespeare's 'Merchant of Venice', performed before Her Majesty: produced under the direction of Mr. Charles Kean.*

An article on the subject headed *Theatrical performances at Windsor Castle* recorded that:

'Shakespeare's play "The Merchant of Venice" was performed, by

command, in the Castle, on Thursday evening, December 28th 1848. The stage for the performance was erected in the Rubens Room. . . .

Her Majesty and Prince Albert and the Duchess of Kent and the ladies and gentlemen of the Royal suite in waiting, sat on a raised platform in the centre of the apartment. . . .

The cast included Shylock (a Jew), Mr. Charles Kean, Portia (a rich Heiress), Mrs. Charles Kean, Antonio (the Merchant of Venice), Mr. Rogers and Jessica (Daughter of Shylock), Mrs. Compton.'

At the conclusion of the article it is noted that *the illustration*

Colour Plate 10
General Gordon (Left). *Fig.* 337, *pl.* C-119. See pages 56 and 309. Shah Nasr-ed-Din (Right). *Fig.* 252, *pl.* A-92. See page 170.

Plate 39
L: *Fig.* 34 (Edmund Kean) *pl.* E-14
R: Theatrical 'combat' print inscribed *Mr KEAN as RICHARD the THIRD.*

is of '*the trial scene*' in the '*Merchant of Venice*' *from a drawing by Mr. E. H. Wehnert.*

The scene is Act IV, Scene I. Venice. A Court of Justice.

Shylock : 'The pound of flesh which I demand of him,
Is dearly bought; 'tis mine and I will have it.'

Fig. 30, *pl.* E-13 indubitably depicts Shylock in this scene for he is carrying both knife and scales. To date however, the actor has not been positively identified, although it is almost certainly Mr Charles Kean. The figure is very similar to the engraving, but it is not close enough for a positive identification.

Plates 37 and 38

OTHELLO AND IAGO. *Fig.* 31, *pl.* E-13 is undoubtedly based on the watercolour of *Othello and Iago* by S. A. Hart RA (1806-81) which is in the Victoria and Albert Museum. The engraving of the painting which is illustrated on *pl.* 38 was published on *p.* 243 of the *National Magazine* in 1858.

Plate 39

RICHARD THE THIRD. This penny plain, tuppence coloured theatrical 'combat' print is inscribed:
Mr. KEAN as RICHARD the THIRD
Clarke's Theatrical Portraits from Original Drawings No. 12
London published as the Act commands August 12th 1821.

Fig. 34, *pl.* E-14 is obviously derived from this portrait. The costume is typical of that worn by Edmund Kean.

Fig. 35, *pl.* E-14, its pair, is more controversial. Whilst it undoubtedly represents Henry, Earl of Richmond (*afterwards,* King Henry the Seventh) the actor playing the part has not been positively identified. It may well be T. A. Cooper (1776-1849).

The dramatic moment in *Richard III* commemorated by these two figures is Act 5, Scene 4: *Another part of Bosworth Field.*

Alarums: Enter from opposite sides King Richard
and Richmond, and exeunt fighting.

Plate 40
L: *Fig.* 48 (Vining) *pl.* E-24
R: Engraving published
by Thos. McLean,
Haymarket, 1827,
inscribed: *Mrs Vining in
the Character of Peter Wilkins
'The Castanet Dance'
Act I, Scene 5.
In the collection of
Messrs Raymond Mander
and Joe Mitchenson*

Plate 40

PETER WILKINS, or THE FLYING INDIANS, a melo-romantic spectacle (*Easterpiece*) produced at the Theatre Royal, Covent Garden, April 16th, 1827.

The engraving illustrated was published by Thos. McLean, Haymarket, 1827, and is inscribed: *Mrs. Vining in the Character of Peter Wilkins – The Castanet Dance – Act I, Scene 5.*

The ultimate source of *fig.* 48, *pl.* E-24 is undoubtedly this engraving, although the opinion is held by some authorities that the figure dates from 1837 or later (*see p. 11*).

It has been remarked that the potters often include something which enables the source to be determined with near certainty. This is well illustrated by the hem on the jacket of 'Peter Wilkins', which is a salient feature both of the engraving and the figure.

There is a pair to this figure of a girl dancing (*fig.* 47, *pl.* E-24). This is probably Miss Mary Glover playing the part of 'Yourawkee'. 'Yourawkee' sings whilst 'Peter' dances. However, no print has been traced of Miss Glover in this character so the figure may be just a 'fictitious' pair.

Identification of Figures

Plate 40A (Left)
Fig. 88 (Perrot and Grahn) *pl.* E-51

Plate 40B (Right)
Coloured lithograph music-front by John Brandard of Jules Perrot in the role of 'Diavolino' and Lucille Grahn as ' 'Catarina' in Act 1, Scene 1 of the ballet *Catarina, ou La Fille du Brigand.*
In the collection of Messrs Raymond Mander and Joe Mitchenson

Plate 41
L: *Fig.* 103 (Wood) *pl.* E-60
R: Lithograph music-front by Endicott of New York inscribed:
'On yonder Rock Reclining.'
From *Auber's Grand Opera*
Of
Fra Diavolo
As sung by
Mr and Mrs Wood.

Fig. 49, *pl.* E-24, probably of 'Peter Wilkins' and 'Your-awkee', is a centrepiece. It has also been suggested that *fig.* 50, *pl.* E-133 may be derived from the same production. However, no small boy appears in the list of characters. It is just possible that the child is 'Hallycarnie'.

An extract from the playbill (*pl.* E-25) reads:

Peter Wilkins, the navigator ...   .   Mrs. Vining
      (wrecked on the load stone rock)
Yourawkee ...   .   Miss M. Glover
Hallycarnie ...   .   Miss J. Scott
   (daughters of the chief of the Flying Islanders)

The play was published as '*Peter Wilkins; or The Flying Islanders*', a melodramatic spectacle in two acts.

Plates 40A and 40B

CATARINA, ou LA FILLE DU BRIGAND, a ballet in 3 Acts by Jules Perrot, first performed at Her Majesty's Theatre in 1846. The coloured lithograph music-front by John Brandard, illustrated on *pl.* 40B, of Jules Perrot in the role of 'Diavolino' and Lucille Grahn as 'Catarina' in Act I, Scene 1 of the ballet is the source of *fig.* 88, *pl.* E-51.

Plate 42
L: *Fig.* 113 (Lablache) *pl.* E-62
R: Coloured lithograph music-front by John Brandard to *Operatic Celebrities* (a series of six selections), published in 1848. Note that Luigi Lablache in the role of 'Dr Dulcamara', is holding a philtre (love-potion) in the lithograph and a piece of music in the figure.
In the collection of Messrs Raymond Mander and Joe Mitchenson

Plate 41

FRA DIAVOLO, the popular name of an Italian brigand Michele Pezza (1771-1806). His story was the subject of an Opéra Comique in three Acts by Auber, first produced in Paris in 1830 and in English (adapted by R. Lacy) at Drury Lane, November 3rd, 1831.

The source of *fig.* 103, *pl.* E-60 is the lithograph music-front by Endicott of New York inscribed:

'On Yonder Rock Reclining',
From Auber's Grand Opera
of
Fra Diavolo
As sung by
Mr. and Mrs. Wood.

The figure may be a portrait of William Burke Wood (1779-1861) in the title role. *Fig.* 102, *pl.* E-59 which is very similar, except that there is a child behind the brigand, cannot be connected with the opera because no child appears in the script.

Several similar figures are known, none of which can be definitely placed.

Plate 42

DR DULCAMARA in Donizetti's *L'Elisir d'Amore*. Fig. 113, *pl.* E-62 is derived from a coloured lithograph music-front by John Brandard to *Operatic Celebrities* (a series of six selections), published in 1848, in which Luigi Lablache, in the title role, holds a philtre (*love-potion*) instead of a piece of music.

The pair to this figure (*fig.* 114, *pl.* E-62) is similar to *fig.* 36 (Eliza Cook) *pl.* H-10, except that it is reversed; she wears no jacket over her bodice and in her left hand she holds a scroll instead of a book; the base is rococo. This suggests that the figure may not represent any particular person, but rather that the potter has borrowed another figure and modified it simply to make a pair.

Plate 43
Music-front:
L: *Musical Bouquet* music-front with 'borrowed' lithograph of Mr Sims Reeves as 'Edgardo' in *Lucia di Lammermoor.*
R: Music-front inscribed *The Ravenswood Waltzes* portraying Madame Dorus Gras and Mr Sims Reeves.
Figures:
L: *Fig.* 115 (Reeves) *pl.* E-62
R: *Fig.* 116 (? Gras) *pl.* E-62

Plate 44
Music-fronts:
L: Coloured lithograph music-front by T. Coventry inscribed *I want to be a Bloomer!* sung by Miss Rebecca Isaacs, the words by Henry Abrahams, the music by W.H. Montgomery.
R: Coloured lithograph by unidentified artist of two girls in bloomers.
Figures:
L: *Fig.* 124 (?Rebecca Isaacs) *pl.* E-66
R: *Fig.* 119 (Girl in bloomers) *pl.* E-63
In the collection of Mrs Constance Chiswell and the author

Plate 43

MR SIMS REEVES. *Fig.* 115, *pl.* E-62 is based on a coloured lithograph of Mr Sims Reeves as 'Edgardo' in *Lucia di Lammermoor* on a music-front for Popular Airs sung by Mr Sims Reeves, arranged for the pianoforte by C. W. Glover. The same lithograph has been borrowed for the *Musical Bouquet* music-front illustrated on the left of this plate. Another music-front, illustrated on the right, inscribed *The Ravenswood Waltzes*, depicts Madame Gras in the role of 'Lucia' in addition to Mr Sims Reeves as 'Edgardo'. *Fig.* 116, *pl.* E-62 (the pair to Mr Sims Reeves) may well be intended to represent Madame Gras, but to date there is no proof of this. Unfortunately the dress worn by Madame Gras both in the music-front illustrated and in two

engravings in *The Illustrated London News* of December 11th, 1847, is dissimilar to the dress portrayed on the figure. Another engraving must surely exist which will prove whether or not this is in fact Madame Gras or someone else.

Plate 44

REBECCA ISAACS AND A GIRL IN BLOOMERS. The music-front illustrated on the left of this plate is for the song *I want to be a Bloomer!* sung by Miss Rebecca Isaacs, the words by Henry Abrahams, the music by W. H. Montgomery. The coloured lithograph is by T. Coventry. Both *fig.* 123, *pl.* E-65

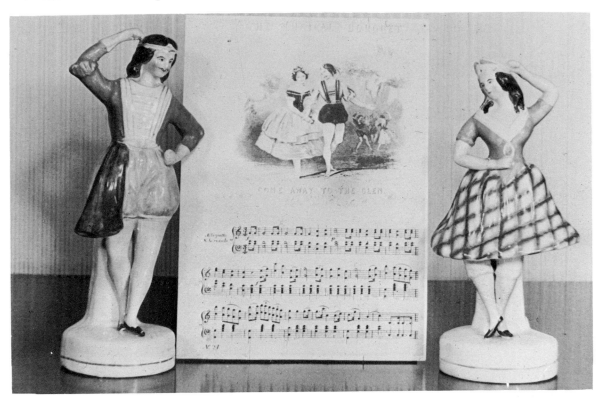

Plate 45
L: *Fig.* 132 (Perrot) *pl.*
E-68
C: Music-front in the
Musical Bouquet series,
No. 24, inscribed *Gone
away to the glen,* illustrating
Carlotta Grisi as 'Giselle'
and Jules Perrot in the
role of 'Albrecht'. Note
the two figures in the
right background are in
the same stance as *figs.*
132 and 133.
R: *Fig.* 133 (? Grisi) *pl.*
E-68
*By courtesy of Mr and Mrs
Eric Joyce*

and *fig.* 124, *pl.* E-66 are derived from this lithograph. It is very probable that the woman portrayed on the music-front is intended to be Rebecca Isaacs. The only authentic portrait of Amelia Bloomer herself in her costume is the one reproduced on *pl.* E-64.

The coloured lithograph illustrated on the right of the plate is by an unknown artist and depicts two girls in bloomers. *Fig.* 119, *pl.* E-63 incorporates features from the costumes worn by each girl. It is possibly based on this lithograph, or alternatively, upon another lithograph which has so far not been identified.

Plate 45

GISELLE. *Fig.* 132, *pl.* E-68 has been identified as Jules Perrot playing 'Albrecht' in *Giselle.* The original source of this figure is so far untraced, but the music-front in the *Musical Bouquet* series *No.* 24 shows him in the same costume. This engraving is a montage (combination of pictures) as the figure of Carlotta Grisi as 'Giselle' is copied from the engraving of her in the *Beauties of the Opera and Ballet* (1844-5) from a painting by A. E. Chalon.

The pair to 'Albrecht' is a female dancer (not 'Giselle') with skirt shortened to show 'modesty panties' (*fig.* 133, *pl.* E-68). The dress looks like gypsy costume. It is possibly Carlotta Grisi, Perrot's wife, but so far no picture has been found by which it may be identified.

Two figures in the right background of the *Musical Bouquet* engraving are in the same stance as *figs.* 132 and 133.

There are three versions of this pair, *figs.* 132 and 133 with the legs from separate moulds, *figs.* 132 (a) and 133 (a) with the legs incorporated in the column (not illustrated) and *figs.* 134 and 135, *pl.* E-68. The last two figures, which have a scarf placed behind the hands and across the back of each, seem to be the last phase, as they are always crude.

Plate 46

PIZARRO. The moment in the tragedy is readily identifiable as occurring in Act V, Scene II:

The Out-post of the Spanish Camp – The background wild and rocky, with the Torrent falling down the Precipice, over which a Bridge is formed. A fell'd Tree.

Rolla has been captured by soldiers and is brought in, in chains. Almagro, Pizarro's lieutenant, refers to him as having been caught spying. Pizarro enters and suggests to Rolla that they cease to be foes. He orders Rolla's release and offers him a sword. Davillo, another of Pizarro's associates, enters with soldiers and a child they have caught escaping from the Peruvian stronghold. It is the child of Alonzo (*see p. 414*). Pizarro, who hates Alonzo, decides to hold the child as a hostage. Rolla seizes the child and escapes.

Rolla: 'Then with this sword Heaven's gift, not thine! (*seizes the child*). Who moves one step to follow me dies upon the spot' (*exit with child. Later he is seen crossing the wooden bridge over the cataract pursued by soldiers. He tears from the rock the tree that supports the bridge, and retreats by the background bearing off the child*).

When the play was first produced at Drury Lane on May 24th, 1799, John Philip Kemble played the part of 'Rolla' and Mrs Siddons that of 'Elvira'; but the success of the production was not only due to their performance but also to the magnificence of the scenery, preparations for which caused the theatre to cancel its performance on the eve of the first night. Later actors who played the part of 'Rolla' included Wallack, Young, Macready and Charles Kean. There are a number of prints of these actors playing the role.

The penny plain, tuppence coloured theatrical portrait published c. 1856, by A. Park and inscribed *Mr. C. Kean as Rolla* illustrated on *pl.* 46 is undoubtedly the source of *fig.* 152, *pl.* E-78. The tragedy was revived at the Princess' Theatre on September 1st, 1856, with Charles Kean (1811-68) in the part of 'Rolla'.

Fig. 153, *pl.* E-80 titled 'Rolla' is also probably a theatrical portrait but its source has not yet come to light, so that the actor remains unidentified.

Plates 47 and 47A

T. P. COOKE (1786-1864) was an actor specializing in sailor parts who had been an authentic serving sailor. He danced the genuine hornpipe in most of his sailor roles and if by any chance he played a part which did not include the dance, the audience yelled until he obliged. He toured and was equally famous in

Plate 46
L: *Fig.* 152 (Charles Kean) *pl.* E-78
R: Penny plain, tuppence coloured
theatrical portrait published by A. Park
c. 1856 and inscribed *Mr C. KEAN as
ROLLA.*
*In the collection of Messrs Raymond Mander and
Joe Mitchenson*

Plate 47A
Photograph of T. P. Cooke in *The Pilot (Guy Little collection)*. This is the
only existing photograph of the actor and was taken late in his career.
By courtesy of the Victoria and Albert Museum

Plate 47
L: Penny plain, tuppence coloured plate:
Skelt's Characters in The Red Rover, by
G. Skelt, Saint Helier, Jersey. The third
character from the left on the bottom row
is 'Dick Fid'.
R: *Fig.* 155 (T.P. Cooke) *pl.* E-80
In the collection of Mr Anthony Oliver

the provinces as in London, so that Staffordshire figures of him
would have had a ready sale all over England.

Fig. 155, *pl.* E-80 is a fine porcelaneous figure modelled in
the round and presenting a good likeness of Cooke, who lived
long enough to be photographed and whose features were
distinctive (*see pl.* 47A). It portrays him dancing the hornpipe
and could represent anyone of a number of his famous roles
from 'William' in *Black Eyed Susan* (1829) to 'Harry Halyard' in

Polly my Partner Joe (1857). It does so happen, however, that
Cooke played the character of 'Dick Fid' in the Fitzball play
The Red Rover, which was adapted from the Cooper novel and
performed at the Adelphi Theatre in 1829. One of the theatrical
prints of this play is the penny plain, tuppence coloured sheet
Skelt's Characters in The Red Rover, Pl. 6 which is illustrated
to the left of *pl.* 47. It will be noted that the portrait of 'Dick Fid'
(*third from the left on the bottom row*), is very similar to the figure

Plate 48
L: *Fig.* 158 (Lind) *pl.* E-80
R: Coloured lithograph by and after T. Packer of *Jenny Lind as 'Alice' in Meyerbeer's opera of ROBERTO IL DIAVOLO.*
In the collection of Messrs Raymond Mander and Joe Mitchenson

except that no gun is carried. It is not possible to be dogmatic that the figure portrays T. P. Cooke in *The Red Rover*, but there is no doubt that it does portray Cooke.

Plate 48

JENNY LIND. This coloured lithograph by and after T. Packer is of Jenny Lind as 'Alice' in Meyerbeer's opera of *Roberto il Diavolo*. It is the source of *fig.* 158, *pl.* E-80 and a number of similar figures. See also *pl.* E-85A.

Plate 49

JENNY LIND. This coloured lithograph music-front by John Brandard is from Jullien's *Celebrated Polkas, No. 16*. It is inscribed *MLLE. JENNY LIND in the character of MARIA in Donizetti's opera LA FIGLIA DEL REGGIMENTO.*

The *Vivandiere* scene in Act I of the opera is performed in military costume. The lithograph is the source of *fig.* 164, *pl.* E-83, the smaller – 6¾ in. (17 cm.) version of which is illustrated.

Plate 49A

JENNY LIND. The lithograph music-front by John Brandard for *La Vivandiere Quadrille* depicts Miss Jenny Lind in the role of 'Marie' in *La Figlia del Reggimento*. It is the source of *fig.* 177, *pl.* E-91.

Plates 50 and 51

SEMIRAMIDE. Opera by Rossini, based on Voltaire's tragedy. The opera was translated especially for the Theatre Royal, Covent Garden, by T. H. Reynoldson and adapted to the English stage by Jules Benedict, being produced on October 1st, 1842, with Miss Adelaide Kemble in the title role, together with Mrs Alfred Shaw (Mary Shaw) making her English début as 'Arsace'.

Fig. 181, *pl.* E-91 is almost certainly derived from the lithograph music-front by Brandard of Miss Adelaide Kemble and Mrs Alfred Shaw singing the duet *Thy smile is joy indeed!* The potter has produced his figure as a mirror-image, but in every other important respect it is identical to the lithograph (*see pl.* 50).

Plate 49
L: *Fig.* 164 (Lind) *pl.* E-83.
R: Coloured lithograph music-front by John Brandard for Jullien's *Celebrated Polka's, No. 16*. It is inscribed *JENNY LIND in the character of MARIA in Donizetti's opera LA FIGLIA DEL REGGIMENTO.*
In the collections of Mr David Robinson and the author

Plate 49A
L: *Fig.* 177 (Lind) *pl.* E-91
R: Lithograph music-front by John Brandard for *La Vivandiere Quadrille*. It portrays Miss Jenny Lind in the role of 'Marie' in *La Figlia del Reggimento*.
In the collections of Messrs Raymond Mander and Joe Mitchenson, and the author

Plate 50
L: *Fig.* 181 (Kemble and Shaw) *pl.* E-91
R: Lithograph music-front by J.
Brandard of Miss Adelaide Kemble and
Mrs Alfred Shaw singing the duet *Thy
smile is joy indeed!* from *Semiramide,* an
opera by Rossini translated especially for
the Theatre Royal, Covent Garden by
T.H. Reynoldson.

Plate 51
Playbill for Theatre Royal, Covent
Garden advertising the tenth
performance of *Semiramide,* on Saturday,
October 22nd, 1842.

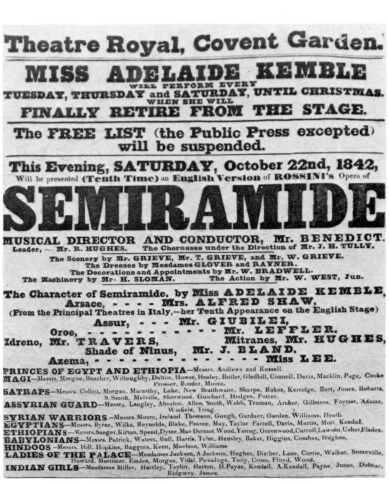

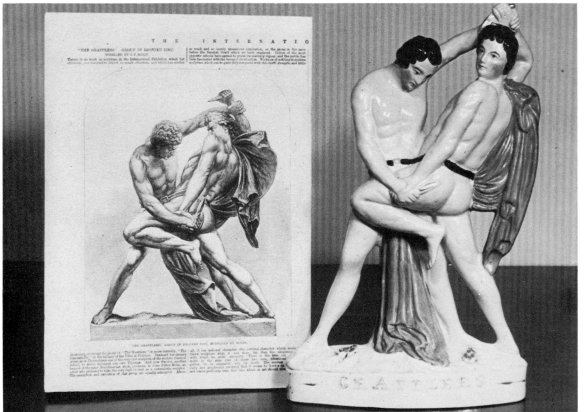

Plate 52 (Above left)
L: *Fig.* 190 (Rignold)
pl. E-97
R: Untitled Parian figure
of George Rignold in the
character of 'Henry V'.
'Once more unto the
breach, dear friends, once
more...'
*Henry V, Act III, Scene 1.
In the collection of Messrs
Raymond Mander and Joe
Mitchenson*

Plate 53 (Above right)
L: *Fig.* 193 (Joan of Arc)
pl. E-97
R: Coloured lithograph
music-front by John
Brandard for the 'Joan of
Arc' waltz by Chas.
d'Albert.
*By courtesy of Mr and Mrs
Eric Joyce*

Plate 54
L: An engraving
inscribed *'The Grapplers',
Group in Bronzed Zinc,
Modelled by Molin* which
appeared in *The Illustrated
London News* on
November 1st, 1862.
R: *Fig.* 17 (Grapplers)
pl. F-7

Plate 52

GEORGE RIGNOLD. On the right of the plate is a Parian
figure untitled but known from a contemporary advertisement
to be George Rignold in the character of 'Henry V'. The design
is close enough to *fig.* 190, *pl.* E-97 to leave little room for doubt
that this figure too is intended to portray the same actor. The
dramatic moment is Act III, Sc. 1 : *France. Before Harfleur.*

   K. Hen: 'Once more unto the breach, dear friends,
       once more . . .'

Plate 53

JOAN OF ARC. *Fig.* 193, *pl.* E-97 is obviously based on the
coloured lithograph music-front by John Brandard of Joan of
Arc. Likewise there is no doubt that this lithograph portrays
an actress in the title role, but she has so far escaped identification.

Plate 54

THE GRAPPLERS. A group in bronzed-zinc modelled by J. P. Molin. An engraving of this group which appeared in *The Illustrated London News* in connection with the International Exhibition on November 1st, 1862, is illustrated here. The writer says:

There is no work in sculpture in the International Exhibition which has attracted, and deserved to attract, so much attention, and which has elicited so much and so nearly unanimous admiration, as the group in the nave before the Swedish Court which we have engraved. Critics of the most opposite schools have agreed to praise its masterly vigour, and the public has been fascinated with the terror of its situation. We know of nothing in modern sculpture which can be quite fitly compared with this death struggle, and little in ancient art except the group of 'The Wrestlers', or, more accurately, 'The Pancratiasts', in the tribune of the Uffizi at Florence. Denmark has already given us in Thorwaldsen one of the very first sculptors of the modern classical school, to which belonged our own Flaxman. And now Sweden, another branch of the same Scandinavian stock, produces, in Jean Petter Molin, an artist who promises to take the very highest rank as a naturalistic sculptor. The conception and execution of this group are equally admirable. Above all, it has national character—the national character which made the old Greek sculptor what it was more, far, than the idealising theories with which we credit antiquity. There is the true old fiery Norse-spirit in the grim duel of these two men, relentlessly belted together, to be separated only by death. The combat is so vigorously and graphically rendered that it seems to border on exaggeration, and comes perilously near that line which in art should always be drawn betwixt terror and horror.

This group is the source of *fig.* 17, *pl.* F-7. The original statue now stands in front of the National Museum, Stockholm.

Plate 55

MASTER M'GRATH. This engraving appeared in *The Illustrated London News* on March 11th, 1871, and is inscribed *Lord Lurgan's greyhound, Master M'Grath.* Fig. 20, *pl.* F-7 is probably based on this engraving. The report states:
By carrying off the Waterloo Cup for the third time, a feat which coursing writers unanimously pronounced him incapable of, Master M'Grath has stamped himself as the most remarkable greyhound ever put into the slips.

Plate 55A

JEMMY WOOD. This woodcut portrait in *Life and Anecdotes of Jemmy Wood* (Kent & Co. n.d.), probably published in 1845, was almost certainly the inspiration of all four of the Jemmy Wood figures (*figs.* 30–33, *pls.* G-15 and 16).

Plate 55
L: *Fig.* 20 (M'Grath) *pl.* F-7
R: Engraving of *Lord Lurgan's greyhound, Master M'Grath* which appeared in *The Illustrated London News* on March 11th, 1871.
In the collection of Mrs Cecil Woodham-Smith

Plate 55A
L: *Fig.* 33 (Wood) *pl.* G-16
R: Woodcut portrait of Jemmy Wood in *Life and Anecdotes of Jemmy Wood* (Kent & Co., n.d.), probably published in 1845.

Plate 56

THE SHAKESPEARE CLOCK. The engraving illustrated appeared in *The Illustrated London News* of March 18th, 1848, and is titled *The Shakespeare Clock: designed by Bell*. This clock was exhibited at the Society of Arts Exhibition of British Manufacturers in 1848. Of it *The Illustrated London News* said:

. . . we have several novelties which have not yet found their way into the shops; indeed, those in the Exhibition are but specimens. One of the most original is THE SHAKESPEARE CLOCK, designed and modelled by Bell, and made in Parian by the Mintons; the works to be furnished by Vulliamy; the Dial by Drayton's silvering process, already mentioned. The Dial is placed between two figures representing Tragedy and Comedy, as typical of Time passing between Joy and Grief:

'Joy absent, grief is present for that time.'*—Richard II.*

'the time of life is short:
To spend that shortness basely were too long,
If life did ride upon a dial's point,
Still ending at th'arrival of an hour.'*—First part of Henry IV.*

The composition is surmounted by a statuette of Shakespeare, the likeness founded upon the Poet's bust in the chancel of Stratford Church. A full-length statue of the same figure has been exhibited by the sculptor in Westminster Hall.

Fig. 13, *pl.* H-5 is based on this engraving, but it will be noted that the likeness of Shakespeare used by the potter is not the same as that used for the statuette which surmounts the clock.

Plate 57

SHAKESPEARE'S HOUSE. *Fig.* 23 (Shakspeare's House [*sic*]) *pl.* H-7, probably dates from the period of the house's reconstruction in 1857-64. It will be noted that it is very similar to the house as we find it today.

Plate 58

ROBERT BURNS. The engraving shown appeared in *The Illustrated London News* of August 10th, 1844, in connection with the Burns Festival at Ayr on August 6th. It will be noted that the engraving is the source of *fig.* 59, *pl.* H-18A.

Plate 59
L: *Fig.* 2 (Morgan) *pl.* I-2
R: Undated lithograph by E. Walker and J.C. Rowland of Edward Morgan.
By courtesy of the Librarian, National Library of Wales, Aberystwyth

Plate 59

EDWARD MORGAN. The undated lithograph by E. Walker and J. C. Rowland published by T. Catherall of Chester and inscribed *Edward Morgan* illustrated here is undoubtedly the source of *fig.* 2, *pl.* I-2 and *fig.* 188, *pl.* C-70.

In 1825 Charles James Mathews wrote *A song of Jenny Jones and Ned Morgan.* Edward Morgan and Jenny Jones were ploughman and dairymaid at Pontblyddin Farm, near Llangollen. Morgan, after serving for twenty years in the navy, had returned to marry Jenny, his childhood sweetheart. In 1836 Mathews produced a one-act farce *He would be an actor* at the Olympic Theatre and included in it the aforementioned song. The song was extremely popular for the next twenty years. The verse on the music-front runs:

> *And we'll live on our cheese and our ale in contentment,*
> *And long thro' our dear native valley we'll rove;*
> *For indeed in our hearts we both love that Llangollen,*
> *And sweet Jenny Morgan with truth will I love.*

Plate 60
L: *Fig.* 3 (Jones) *pl.* I-2
R: Undated lithograph by E. Walker and J.C. Rowland of Jenny Jones.
By courtesy of The Librarian, National Library of Wales, Aberystwyth.

Plate 60

JENNY JONES. The lithograph by E. Walker and J. C. Rowland published by T. Catherall of Chester and titled *Jenny Jones* illustrated here is undoubtedly the source of *fig.* 3, *pl.* I-2. The caption to the music reads *The Words by Charles Mathews. The Music by John Parry.* It will be noted that in this lithograph Edward Morgan can be seen in the background seated at a table with a mug of beer raised in his right hand. In the right foreground there is a milestone inscribed 'LANGOLEN/1/Mile' [*sic*]. This milestone is the inspiration for *fig.* 4, *pl.* I-2 in which Edward Morgan appears on the left and Jenny Jones on the right with a milestone with the same inscription on it between them.

Plates 61 and 61A

MARY ANNE TALBOT *otherwise* JOHN TAYLOR. The engraving illustrated here is by G. Scott after James Green and appeared in Robert Kirby's *Wonderful Museum* (2, 160). The face of Mary Anne, although clean shaven, is remarkably like that of *fig.* 7, *pl.* I-4 titled 'Sportsman: Mary Taylor'. Although no engraving has been found that could be the source of this figure there can be little doubt that it does portray Mary Anne Talbot. The title appears to derive from her real name and her male pseudonym. The prefix 'Sportsman' can be considered as adding weight to this theory.

Plate 62

MASTER LAMBTON (*The Red Boy*). The painting illustrated here is by Sir Thomas Lawrence PRA and portrays Charles William Lambton (1818-31), eldest son of John George Lambton, later first Earl of Durham. The painting was executed in 1825 and is undoubtedly the source of *fig.* 35, *pl.* I-17 and *fig.* 35 (a), illustrated here. All known examples of this somewhat rare figure have the jacket coloured in underglaze blue.

[The Lawrence painting was featured on the 4d. stamp of a special issue illustrating English art (July 10th, 1967).]

Plate 63
L: *Fig.* 41 (Alphington
Ponies) *pl.* I-18
R: Coloured lithograph
music-front for the
Torquay Polka.
In the collection of Dr. S.J.
Howard

Plate 63

THE ALPHINGTON PONIES. The lithograph music-front
illustrated here is inscribed:

Torquay Polka
Pour le
Piano Forte
Par
E. Carpentier de Selvier

and was published by O. Angel, 94, Fore Street, Exeter. That
the persons portrayed are the Alphington Ponies is proved by
three lithographs that appear in S. Baring-Gould's *Devonshire
Characters*, *pp.* 16-21. *Fig.* 41, *pl.* I-18 is undoubtedly derived
from these lithographs. It has occasionally been found titled 'A
Present from Torquay', in gilt script. An example of this is
illustrated on *pl.* I-18.

Plate 64 (Left)
L: *Fig.* 42 (Parr) *pl.* I-18
R: Engraving by R. Page
of likeness by Rubens
who saw Thomas Parr
when he was about 140
years of age and painted
him.
*In the collection of
Lt-Col. A.C.W. Kimpton*

Plate 66 (Right)
The Nubian Giraffe
by Laurent Agasse.
*Reproduced by gracious
permission of
Her Majesty the Queen*

Plate 65
L: *Fig.* 44 (Giraffe and
keeper) *pl.* I-18
R: *Fig.* 45 (Giraffe and
keeper)
*By courtesy of
Mr and Mrs Eric Joyce*

Plate 64

OLD PARR. The engraving illustrated is by R. Page of a likeness taken by Rubens who saw Thomas Parr when he was about 140 years of age and painted him. This may well have been used by the potter when designing *fig.* 42, *pl.* I-18, for it will be noted that they are very similar.

Plates 65 and 66

THE NUBIAN GIRAFFE. The painting illustrated on *pl.* 66 portrays the first giraffe to be seen in England, together with his two Arab keepers. The giraffe was given to King George IV by Mehemet Ali, Pasha of Egypt. It was provided with a special paddock at Windsor. The painting by Laurent Agasse, the distinguished French animal painter, was commissioned by the King. The inspiration of *figs.* 44 and 45, *pl.* I-18 may well be this painting. The dress of the Arab keeper is very similar and the size of the giraffe suggests that the potter intended to make it clear to his clientele that the animal was a calf.

Identification of Figures

Plate 67
L: *Fig.* 100 (Trinity
College) *pl.* I-51
R: The east front of the
Great Gate, Trinity
College as it is today.
By courtesy of Mr John Hall

Plate 68
L: Pre-Victorian
Staffordshire figure of
Tom Cribb.
LC: *Fig.* 25 (Cribb)
pl. F-12
RC: Pre-Victorian
Staffordshire porcelaneous
figure of Madame Vestris.
R: *Fig.* 224 (Vestris)
pl. E-113
*By courtesy of Mr John Hall
and in the collections of
Mr Anthony Oliver and the
author*

Plate 67

TRINITY COLLEGE, CAMBRIDGE. It will be noted that the photograph of the east front of the Great Gate as it is today shows *fig.* 100, *pl.* I-51 to be roughly based on it.

Plate 68

TOM CRIBB AND MADAME VESTRIS. The figure of Tom Cribb shown on the *extreme left* has all the features of 'early' Staffordshire. It pairs with Molineaux and probably dates to 1811, the year of their classic encounters. That shown *left-centre* is suggestive of Victorian Staffordshire. No pair has yet been recorded. It may well have been issued at the time of Cribb's death in 1848 (*fig.* 25, *pl.* F-12).

The figure of Madame Vestris, as she appeared at the final curtain, playing 'Paul' in *Paul and Virginia* at Drury Lane Theatre in 1822, shown *right-centre*, is a fine porcelaneous figure which whilst undoubtedly 'Staffordshire' would, in the past, have been termed 'Rockingham'. Vestris played the role in 1822 and the figure is likely to be contemporary. The similar earthenware copy on the *extreme right* is cruder and more robust. It is likely to be later; again, it may have been issued in connection with the death of the actress in 1856 (*fig.* 224, *pl.* E-113).

4
The Manufacture of and Methods of Colouring Portrait Figures

Historical – Glossary of ceramic terms – Processes of manufacture by press-moulds – Processes of manufacture by casting; the use of slip-moulds – The colouring of Staffordshire portrait figures – The use of gold in decoration – Methods of titling.

HISTORICAL

The number of Staffordshire potters engaged in the manufacture of figures in the nineteenth century is much greater than is generally realized. Many, however, were small concerns which did not last for very long. In his article *Victorian Earthenware Chimney-Ornaments* (*Apollo*, Nov. 1965) Mr Geoffrey Godden gives an interesting first-hand contemporary account of one such 'toy manufactory', that of George Hood of Burslem (*c.* 1822-64), handed down by an employee of the firm, C. Shaw:

> . . . *The toy manufactory itself was a curiosity in structure and management. It was rusty and grim. As for form, it might have been brought in cartloads from the broken-down cottages on the opposite side of the street. The workshops were neither square, nor round, nor oblong. They were a jumble of the oddest imaginable kind, and if there had been the ordinary number of workshops on an average size pot-works, placed as these were placed, it would have been impossible to have found the way in and the way out. . . . Only about a dozen people were employed on the 'bank,' and if we all turned out together we were thronged in the narrow spaces outside the shops.*
>
> *I remember the figure of Napoleon Bonaparte was the leading article of our industry at this toy factory. . . . He had a dark blue coat on, tightly buttoned, a buff waistcoat and white breeches. There were touches of gold on his coat and on his large black hat, with flat sides and point, with a high peak. These Napoleons must have been in large demand somewhere, for shoals of them were made at this time. . . . We made cats, too, on box-lids, representing cushions. We made dogs of all sizes, from 'Dignity' to 'Impudence.' We made the gentlest of swains and the sweetest of maids, nearly always standing under the shade of a tree. . . .*

According to Mr Godden, if Shaw may be compared with other child-workers engaged in the toy trade in the 1840's, he would have been paid about two shillings per week and could have produced over 400 small images during one working day; figures such as these were quoted in an official report of 1842 for a boy aged nine.

The overwhelming majority of Victorian Staffordshire portrait figures were produced in press-moulds made of plaster of Paris. Thin bats of moist clay were carefully pressed by hand into the contours of the moulds and subsequently built up into the complete article.

It has already been noted that a number of original moulds are still in existence. In 1948 over fifty were discovered in an old disused part of the Sampson Smith factory. It was thought at first that they would be quite useless, but, as they had been stored on a second-storey floor which was built around an intermittent biscuit oven, it was found that the normal damp atmosphere of the old building, alternating with the hot, dry atmosphere created when the oven was firing, had preserved the plaster excellently over a period of some seventy or eighty years. In modern times figures are generally produced by pouring thin liquid clay into a plaster mould; the plaster absorbs the surplus moisture leaving a thin wall of clay after the remaining liquid clay termed 'slip' has been poured from the mould. This method is quicker and cheaper and results in a thin, even-walled figure outwardly similar to the nineteenth-century hand-pressed figure except that it has an open base or a hole in the base through which the smooth, even walls can be seen (*see ch. 6, pl. 4*). Some of the Sampson Smith moulds were converted from the old press-mould type into suitable casting moulds, and a number of figures satisfactorily produced (*see ch. 4, pl. 1 and ch. 6, pl. 3*). The majority of the moulds were in three parts, although some were more complicated and involved assembly of a number of separate portions and 'sticking up'. A typical three-piece mould is that for Burns illustrated in *ch. 4, pls. 2 and 3*. The front of the mould is inscribed *B/May the 2/1892*. The letter *B* is found on a number of these old moulds and probably signifies that this is an original 'block-mould'. Moulds that have been modified in recent times for use by casting usually have a channel cut into each side, as has happened in the case of the Moody mould (*ch. 4, pl. 1*). The majority of the moulds have nothing written on the outside, but occasionally the name of the portrait is inscribed, for instance *Tom King* (*see ch. 4, pl. 4*).

GLOSSARY OF CERAMIC TERMS

Definitions of a few of the terms to be used in subsequent sections may be found helpful at this stage.

BISCUIT: The biscuit or bisque state is a stage in the production of glazed earthenware.

There are three states incidental to the production of glazed pottery:

(*a*) *Clay state:* before firing.
(*b*) *Biscuit state:* when the ware has been passed through the biscuit oven and fired once.
(*c*) *Glazed* or '*glost*' *state:* after the ware has been glazed and fired in the 'glost' oven.

BODY OR PASTE: Ceramic term for the clay or mixture of materials of which the ware is made.

COLOURS: Pottery colours are derived from those few mineral substances capable of withstanding the enormous heat required for firing. Enamel colours are the pure bases mixed with abundant flux. This enables them to fuse (*blend*) over the glaze at a relatively low heat in the enamel kiln.

EARTHENWARE: Consists of flint, ball clay, china stone and china clay. It is generally cream coloured but can be stained by colouring oxides. Victorian Staffordshire figures are distinguished from earlier Staffordshire figures by the greater whiteness of their clay. In the biscuit state earthenware is brittle and semi-porous, but it becomes impervious to liquids after glazing. It does not transilluminate.

FLUX: A glassy substance introduced into the colour bases to enable them to fuse with the glaze at relatively low temperatures. The commonest materials used for fluxes are felspar, borax, alkaline carbonates and bismuth.

GLAZE: The vitreous or glass-like substance applied to the ware in the biscuit state which after firing renders it impervious to fluids. The two chief glazes which have been used are lead-glaze (*a liquid lead-glaze was used for Victorian portrait figures*) and salt-glaze.

  (*a*) *Over-glaze colouring*: Painting on the glazed surface of the ware.

  (*b*) *Under-glaze colouring*: Painting on the unglazed surface of the ware.

KILN: The brickwork chamber used for firing pieces decorated in enamel colours. Built in various sizes, it may be high enough for a man to stand up in. It is provided with an iron-door with a peep-hole at the top. The heat generated varies from 700-900°C.

OVEN: A much larger chamber than the kiln. It is used for bringing the ware to the biscuit state – 1100°C (*biscuit oven*) – and 'glost' state – 950°C ('*glost*' oven).

PORCELAIN: A vitreous or glass-like, semi-translucent body, originally made from a mixture of white clay, felspathic stone and silica, e.g. Chinese, Dresden, Plymouth and Bristol. 'Soft' porcelain contains similar ingredients with additional materials which when fired give the 'paste' greater translucency, e.g. Chelsea, Bow, Nantgarw, etc.

The chief characteristic of porcelain is that it is to varying degrees translucent, whereas earthenware is opaque.

THE PROCESSES OF MANUFACTURE BY PRESS-MOULDS

1. The original model was made by the designer in an oily clay and thereafter encased in a mould of plaster of Paris, which was divided into two or three parts, for instance a front, back and bottom piece. The parts were removed from the original model (which was generally damaged in the process) and constituted the master-mould, otherwise called the 'block-mould'.

2. The master-mould, or to be more correct, the front and back pieces of the master-mould, were put together and the hollow filled with liquid plaster of Paris. When the plaster had set, the pieces of the master-mould were again removed, leaving a solid replica (referred to as the 'block') of the original clay model. The 'block' was preserved for emergencies.

3. Each piece of the master-mould was separately encased in a further mould of plaster of Paris, and each of these moulds were detached in two pieces. The two pieces were then put together again and filled with liquid plaster of Paris. When the plaster had set they were detached, leaving an exact replica of that piece of the master-mould which they had encased. The master-mould was preserved for future use, and the replicas of the pieces of the master-mould were put together again to become the first working-mould. Each working-mould could be used for the manufacture of up to 200 figures without serious deterioration, but not more than two to three figures could be made from one mould in a working day, because of the time needed for it to dry out after each usage. If only a very few figures were required, then working-moulds were not made but the figures manufactured directly from the master-mould. If a large number of figures were required, then a number of working-moulds were made.

4. A flat sheet of damp clay known as a 'bat' was laid upon each part of the working-mould and pressed into it with a sponge or other implement, the surplus around the edges being trimmed with a knife. After each piece of the mould had been so treated, the trimmed edges were painted with clay diluted to the consistency of cream, known as 'slip', and fitted together and tied tightly with string. Thin rolls of clay were pressed into the seams by fingers inserted through the bottom of the mould, in order to join together the pieces of the figure. The moisture from the clay was quickly absorbed by the porous plaster of

Paris, and as the clay dried it would shrink and become detached from the plaster, so as to become firm enough to be handled. At this stage the pieces of the mould were removed and the figure could be stood on a flat surface without sagging.

5. The open bottom of the figure was then closed by pressing it on to the bottom piece of the working-mould, whose convex side had been covered with a body of bat. When this had dried, the mould was detached, leaving the figure with a concave bottom. Very rarely pressed-earthenware figures were left with open bottoms, but generally those figures found with open bottoms have been produced in porcelain.

6. The repairer now scraped away the seams produced by the parts of the mould and filled in any cracks or depressions by dabbing on slip and filling with clay. He would also stick on any subsidiary parts made from other moulds by applying a little slip, or produce effects such as 'ermine-edging' by pressing clay through a sieve and applying the shreds to the figure with a knife. He might also cut small holes in the figure which could not be made in the modelling, such as a gap between the horse's tail and his rump, or between the arm and the chest wall when the hand had been placed on the hip. Generally too, a small hole was cut into the bottom of the figure to enable air to escape when the figure was fired.

7. The figure now received the first firing at about 1100°C. The condition after this firing was known as 'biscuit' because although not really brittle, the figure was still in a matt and porous state.

8. Any underglaze colour, viz, cobalt blue or black, was now applied and hardened on by a further firing at 700°C. This was necessary to prevent colours coming off when dipped in the glaze. The need for this firing could be averted if the colour had been applied with gum arabic, but this was a more expensive process and was seldom used.

9. The porous 'biscuit' figure was dipped into liquid lead-glaze and re-fired in the 'glost' oven at 950°C. This process transformed the glaze into a thin film of glass enveloping the whole figure. Care was taken to use a glaze which in cooling contracted uniformly with the 'body' of the figure, for if the glaze shrank more, little cracks known as 'crazing' would tend to appear either immediately or later.

10. The overglaze or enamel colours mixed with a vitreous flux were now applied and the figure re-fired at about 800°C in the kiln, this temperature being sufficient to allow the glaze to soften and fuse with the flux of the enamels. When it was taken from the kiln the figure was now complete.[1]

It will be noted that a sharp figure may be of more recent manufacture than a poor one, for obviously it may have been produced from a later working-mould. Similarly, the very process of their manufacture ensures that no two figures will ever be found which are exactly similar, for there will inevitably be at least some minor variations which could occur, either during the application of subsidiary parts, during the correcting of any faults, or during the application of the colours.

PROCESSES OF MANUFACTURE BY CASTING; THE USE OF SLIP-MOULDS

Very few Victorian earthenware figures were produced by slip-casting, although this system was used for the contemporary but more complicated figures and groups in white Parian china. Among the few on record are the bust of Havelock, *fig.* 273, *pl.* C-92A (*c.* 1857), Jumbo, *fig.* 212, *pl.* E-103 (*c.* 1882) and Mr and Mrs Gladstone, *figs.* 39 and 40, *pls.* B-12 and 13 (*c.* 1890).

The working slip-mould was made in exactly the same manner as the working press-mould. The front and back pieces of the slip-mould were tied together and slip (*clay diluted to the consistency of cream*) was poured in through the opening until the mould was full. The porous plaster absorbed water from the slip, and after half an hour a layer of clay of suitable thickness would have formed against the mould. At this stage the rest of the slip was poured away. The remaining clay then gradually dried and became detached, so that it was possible to remove the two pieces

---

[1] Some figures were not complete, of course, until gold had been applied, fired and burnished.

of the mould. The figure was usually left with an open bottom or a large hole in the bottom, and the processes of firing and colouring were the same as detailed for the press-mould method.

The disadvantage of casting and the reason why it was not commonly used, was that the working-moulds deteriorated rapidly and could not be employed satisfactorily for the production of more than twenty figures, hence a popular model would require the manufacture of a large number of working-moulds.

THE COLOURING OF STAFFORDSHIRE PORTRAIT FIGURES

UNDERGLAZE COLOURING means that after the application of the paint, the figure was glazed and refired at a great heat. Only very few paints which were commercially worthwhile could withstand the enormous heat of the glost-oven, which was unfortunate because colours are seen to great advantage through the glaze, exhibiting a remarkable and lasting brilliance. The only practical colours were, in fact, cobalt blue and a black made of cobalt, manganese and iron.

OVERGLAZE COLOURING (enamelling) means that because colours often tended to fade badly in the extreme heat of the glost-oven they were mixed with a vitreous flux and applied later over the glaze, either by brush or by means of transfers or rubber stamps. The figures were then fired again at a much lower heat so that colours retained their brilliance and the glazing remained unaffected. When the amount of flux added was small in proportion to the colouring material as in deeper colours, then the surface tended to be matt and liable to flake. Conversely, if the proportion of flux was greater as in paler colours, then the surface had a glazed appearance and was more durable.

Colouring followed definite fashion trends. The earliest Victorian portrait figures are distinguished for their *underglaze blue* passages (c. 1840-60), and their appearance coincides with the availability to the potteries of a compound devised in 1802, by the French chemist Thénard, which contained only thirty parts of cobalt to 100 parts of alumina. Thénard's blue, in which the rich brilliance of cobalt oxide was unaffected, was available at 1s. 3d. per lb as compared with 6s. per lb for the cheapest grades of the pure substance. During this period cobalt blue became a great standby, particularly for uniforms.

However, theatrical figures from engravings of 1820-30 decorated in cobalt blue do exist (*see chapter two*). Some are found both in porcelain and in earthenware. Mr Balston was of the opinion that as most have Victorian characteristics (other than open bottoms) and differ so much in colour and material from figures known to be pre-Victorian that they were probably made after 1837. Many collectors would now agree with Mr Anthony Oliver's view (*Antique Dealer and Collectors Guide*: Nov. 1967) that *the only safe thing to say about the early years of the century is that Staffordshire potters used a much whiter clay than before, more gold decoration, and that the underglaze blue appears earlier than has sometimes been thought, round about 1820.*

The virtual abandonment of underglaze blue after 1860 may be attributed to a change in public taste or, more probably, to reasons of economy, for an extra firing was required before glazing. With the exception of General Booth (*fig. 55, pl.* D-28), which cannot date earlier than the 1890's and about whose provenance there is doubt, the last datable underglaze blue passages occur in the figure of the Prince of Wales and his betrothed, Princess Alexandra of Denmark (*fig. 220, pl.* A-73) which is not later than 1863. However, underglaze blue is occasionally seen in figures of Pope Pius IX, Cardinal Manning (*figs.* 7 and 8, *pl.* D-4) and O'Connell (*fig.* 15, *pl.* B-2), of the 1870's, although it has been suggested that in these cases the blues are enamels.

Underglaze black was not used commonly, although more effective than enamel black. It has been stated already that the latter tends to have a matt surface and is liable to flake. The reason for the infrequent use of underglaze black was the difficulty in making a compound which did not show a brown or bluish tinge, especially when thinly applied. Examples in which underglaze black passages occur are Jemmy Wood (*pl.* G-16); Christmas Evans, Rev John Elias and Rev J. Bryan (*pl.* D-23); Dr Raffles and Rev J. Fletcher (*pl.* D-18); Father Mathew

(*pl.* D-25) and certain figures of Wesley, all of which date to the 1840's. It was used for most of the figures of Dick Turpin in which not only his hat, boots and hair, but also 'Black Bess' are decorated (*pls.* G-3-8). The majority of these figures probably date from 1840-70. In the seventies also, the monumental figures of O'Connell (*pl.* B-2); Gladstone and Beaconsfield (*pl.* B-14) and Moody and Sankey (*pl.* D-4) are also decorated in underglaze black.

In the earlier period too, apart from underglaze blue, extensive use was made of enamel colours, in particular light and dark green and bright red or orange and brown. After the 1860's figures were coloured much more sparingly, decoration being confined to flesh tints for the face and hands, black for the hair and shoes. The undecorated glazed earthenware body which was white, was effectively decorated with occasional touches of gold. In the transitional period, in particular, the same figures are found both in the highly coloured state and also in the paler state.

Certain Crimean equestrian figures have been found in which the same horse is either white and virtually undecorated or coloured grey, chestnut, or as a piebald (having white and black in irregular patches), skewbald (having patches of white and some colour other than black), or dapple grey (grey dappled with darker spots).

The Sampson Smith equestrian figures of the Franco-Prussian War of the 1870's may be found in white, grey, skewbald or in a form resembling salt-glaze known as the 'porridge state' (*see chapter two*). The equestrian figures of the Parr and Kent group which commemorate Wolseley's attempted relief of Gordon of the early eighties and certain Boer War heroes of the turn of the century are found with the horse either white or occasionally pale cream.

The manner of colouring of the saddle-cloths of the Franco-Prussian War and certain other Sampson Smith figures is of particular interest. The main cloths may be coloured blue, purple, orange or yellow and the edgings always a different colour again, either blue, purple, orange or yellow. In a true matching pair it appears that the colours are generally, although not invariably, reversed. Thus if one figure has a blue saddle-cloth with purple edgings, then its pair will have a purple saddle-cloth with blue edgings. If a pair of figures is found in which this is not so, it is suggestive, although not confirmatory evidence, that it is not a 'matching' pair.

The colouring of figures produced by the Parr and Kent group of potters, has already been described in detail (*see chapter two*). It will be recalled that there is no underglaze colouring, that the decoration is carried all round and that the bases are coloured with a characteristic brown and green with the occasional addition of a little pale orange, the whole 'combed' in long thin strokes.

THE USE OF GOLD IN DECORATION

Gold overglaze painting was used throughout the period for titling and incidental decoration; on top of underglaze blue passages in figures prior to 1860 and later, on the extensive white areas which had been glazed but not painted. Gold was virtually never used over enamel colours, for this would necessitate a further firing. Up to 1880 the type of gold used was known as 'Best Gold' (*mercuric gold*) which was a mixture of gold and mercury with a flux. After firing it was so dull that it required burnishing either with agate stone or with a special sand. It tended to rub off, and this was particularly so over protuberances such as raised capitals or buttons, etc.

In the 1880's 'Bright Gold', a liquid preparation, was introduced. It was applied by means of an artist's brush to the glazed surface of the ware. After firing, a bright surface was maintained, thus eliminating the expense of burnishing. Also, it was more stable although harsher in appearance and far less attractive. Because of this 'Best Gold' was still employed for the most expensive types of pottery. There is little difficulty in distinguishing between burnished 'Best Gold' and 'Bright Gold', and this is often important in assessing the age of a figure.

'Best Gold' has been used to 'pick out' the epaulettes in

certain figures in a very particular manner : ◯——

All figures decorated in this way obviously come from the same factory. Those which I have so far come across are:

R. S. Dundas and Pelissier (*figs.* 137 and 138, *pl.* C-54);
Duke of Cambridge (*fig.* 158, *pl.* C-59);
Princess Royal and Prince Frederick William (*fig.* 217, *pl.* A-70);
Louis Napoleon (*fig.* 93, *pl.* C-38);
Vivandiere (*fig.* 237, *pl.* C-83) and
C. Napier and J. W. D. Dundas (*figs.* 102 and 103, *pl.* C-42).

METHODS OF TITLING

Many portrait figures are invariably 'untitled', some are found both 'titled' and 'untitled', and others are found either with titles which differ or with the same title applied differently. The means by which 'untitled' figures may sometimes be identified have been described in chapter three.

Figures may be found 'titled' by one or other of the following methods:

RAISED CAPITALS: These may be made in a number of ways:

(*a*) By outline on the original clay model, and thus reproduced in the mould.

(*b*) By the application of a clay plaque upon which the title has already been reproduced, before the first firing.

(*c*) By being impressed by a roller on which the letters have been engraved in 'mirror-image'.

Method (*a*) is the most economical and thus most generally used. It ensures that *every* figure is 'titled', and 'untitled' versions are not found. Several examples are known in which it has been necessary to tamper with the master-mould in order to alter the title. Thus 'BEGGING SAILOR' was first adjusted to 'XXXXXXX SAILOR', and then 'SAILOR' (*see pls.* C-81-83). Method (*b*), the second commonest, allows for the same figure to be found both 'titled' and 'untitled'.

Raised capitals were generally gilded or, after 1854, occasionally enamelled black, in either case the colouring may be so worn as to be hardly perceptible.

INDENTED CAPITALS: These were invariably applied by stamping each figure individually before its first firing. Sometimes the indentations are barely noticeable because the clay had become too dry before it was stamped. This particularly applies to small figures. Figures so marked may be found 'titled', 'untitled' or 'titled' in some other manner, viz gilt-script (*see below*). 'Alpha' figures and figures made by the Parr and Kent group of potters are commonly titled in this manner. Again, they were generally painted in gold or black. The delicate colouring and clear indentations of early 'Shakspearian figures' attributable to Thomas Parr contrast vividly with the crude colouring and shallow indentations of reproductions of the same figures attributable to William Kent (*see chapter six*).

GILT SCRIPT: This may be hand-painted in early examples such as Van Amburgh (*fig.* 200, *pl.* E-100) and Lord and Lady Sale (*figs.* 66 and 67, *pl.* C-26) and by means of transfer in later examples, particularly those emanating from the Sampson Smith factory, *viz.* the Boer War generals illustrated on *pl.* C-132.

GILT CAPITALS: The only certain example of hand-painted gilt capitals is 'Jimmy, Wood' [*sic*] (*fig.* 33, *pl.* G-16). This figure dates to no later than 1845. Painted gilt capitals using 'Bright Gold' may be found on some modern reproductions of models which originally had indented capitals, or on frank forgeries or fakes (*see ch.* 6, *pl.* 2).

BLACK OR GREY SCRIPT: Both are uncommon and generally were applied by transfer. They date to the latter part of the nineteenth century. Examples of the former are Princess Louise and the Marquess of Lorne (*figs.* 229 and 230, *pl.* A-78) and of the latter, T. Sexton MP (*fig.* 58, *pl.* B-17A).

BLACK CAPITALS: Black capitals are used in the titling of the figures of characters from *Nicholas Nickleby* (*pls.* E-38 and 39). They are probably hand-painted, although they may be transfers. These figures date to 1839. Black capitals are also found on Kent reproductions of earlier figures.

TRANSFERS: Printing from transfers and possibly metal or rubber stamps was much used, particularly by the Parr and Kent group of potters and Sampson Smith, both for titles (*in capitals or script*) and for inscriptions (*in upper and lower case*). They are generally in black, but not infrequently in gold. On Gordon (*fig.* 338, *pl.* C-119), a product of Kent and Parr, the title is in crimson transfer.

Plate 1
Press-mould of *fig.* 9 (Moody) *pl.* D-4, discovered in a disused part of the Sampson Smith factory in 1948, together with a modern figure 'cast' from the original mould. The height of the mould is 20in (50cm); the height of the figure 17in (42.5cm). The discovery of this mould was of particular importance as it made possible the confident attribution of a number of other figures to the Sampson Smith factory.

Plate 2
Three-piece press-mould for a figure of Burns (*fig.* 53, *pl.* H-16). The mould is 20in (50cm) in height.
The front of the mould is inscribed:
B *May the* 2 1892
The letter *B* has been found on a number of old moulds and probably signifies that this is an original Block Mould.

Plate 3
The three-piece press-mould of *fig.* 53 Burns (*illustrated assembled on the preceding plate*) taken apart.
Although a figure taken from this mould would be similar to *fig.* 52 (Burns) *pl.* H-15 it would not be identical; the pedestal would be square, not circular. No figure from this mould has, to date, been recorded and no modern copies have been cast. *Fig.* 53 has been tentatively reserved for it.

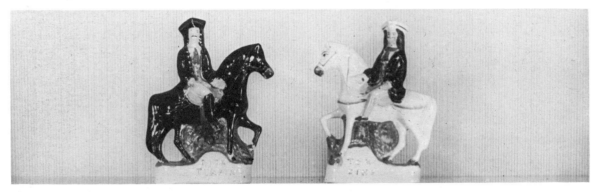

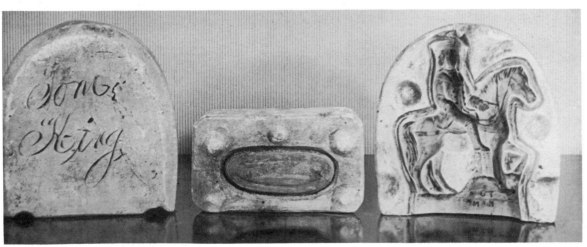

Plate 4
T: On the right may be seen a contemporary copy of *fig.* 12 (King) *pl.* G-4, and on the left, its pair *fig.* 11 (Turpin) *pl.* G-4.
B: A three-piece mould of Tom King (*fig.* 12) found in a disused part of the Sampson Smith factory in 1948. No modern examples of the King figure have been cast from this mould.

The Manufacture and Colouring of Portrait Figures

Plate 4A
Fig. 4 (Cook) *pl.* C-5
This fine figure of the explorer Captain James Cook is based on a portrait by Nathaniel Dance now in the National Maritime Museum. It provides an excellent example of the sparkling appearance of figures decorated with cobalt blue.
In the Thomas Balston collection

Plate 4B
Fig. 17 (Wellington) *pl.* B-2
Although some figures are invariably coloured in the same manner, others were decorated in a variety of ways. Wellington, for instance, is found with his coat coloured black, in addition to the blue, white and orange shown here. All are authentic contemporary pieces.
By courtesy of Mr and Mrs Eric Joyce

Plate 4C
Fig. 61 (Napoleon) *pl.* C-23
Certainly the tallest (24 in, 61 cm) and widely regarded as the finest Staffordshire portrait figure.

Plate 4D
L to R: *Fig.* 68 (Washington) *pl.* B-21
Fig. 65 (Jefferson) *pl.* B-21
Fig. 66 (Franklin) *pl.* B-21
All the evidence goes to show that although many portrait figures were made of Americans, they were intended primarily for the home market.

Plate 5
Mini-figures
The *raison d'être* for these figures is not clear. It has been said that they are traveller's samples, but if this is so they provide very little indication of the excellence or otherwise of the larger versions. Maybe they are just children's toys.
L to R:
1 Sailor and bollard (3½ in, 9cm)
(mini-version of *fig.* 250, *pl.* C-85).

2 Girl and bollard (3½ in, 9cm)
(*fig.* 251, *pl.* C-85).
3 ? Florence Nightingale (4¼ in, 10.75cm)
4 Unidentified priest (4½ in, 11.5cm)
5 Unidentified clown (3in, 9.25cm)
[*See also fig.* 202 (Unidentified clown) *pl.* E-101]
6 Jemmy Wood (2¾ in, 7cm)
(mini-version of *fig.* 31, *pl.* G-16).

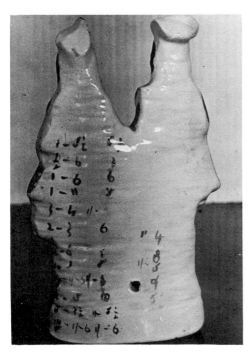

Plate 6
This extraordinary model has a number of figures written on its back under the glaze. Their significance is unknown.

Plate 9
Fig. 165 (Lind and ? Lablache) *pl.* E-83
Note the inscription *Present from the Thames Tunnel.* The tunnel was opened as a thoroughfare for foot passengers on March 25th, 1843, the carriageway being completed later. It is known that there were booths in the tunnel, each with an individual address, viz. 43, *Thames Tunnel.* Presumably it was from one of these that the piece was originally sold.
In the collection of Mr F.J. Stephens

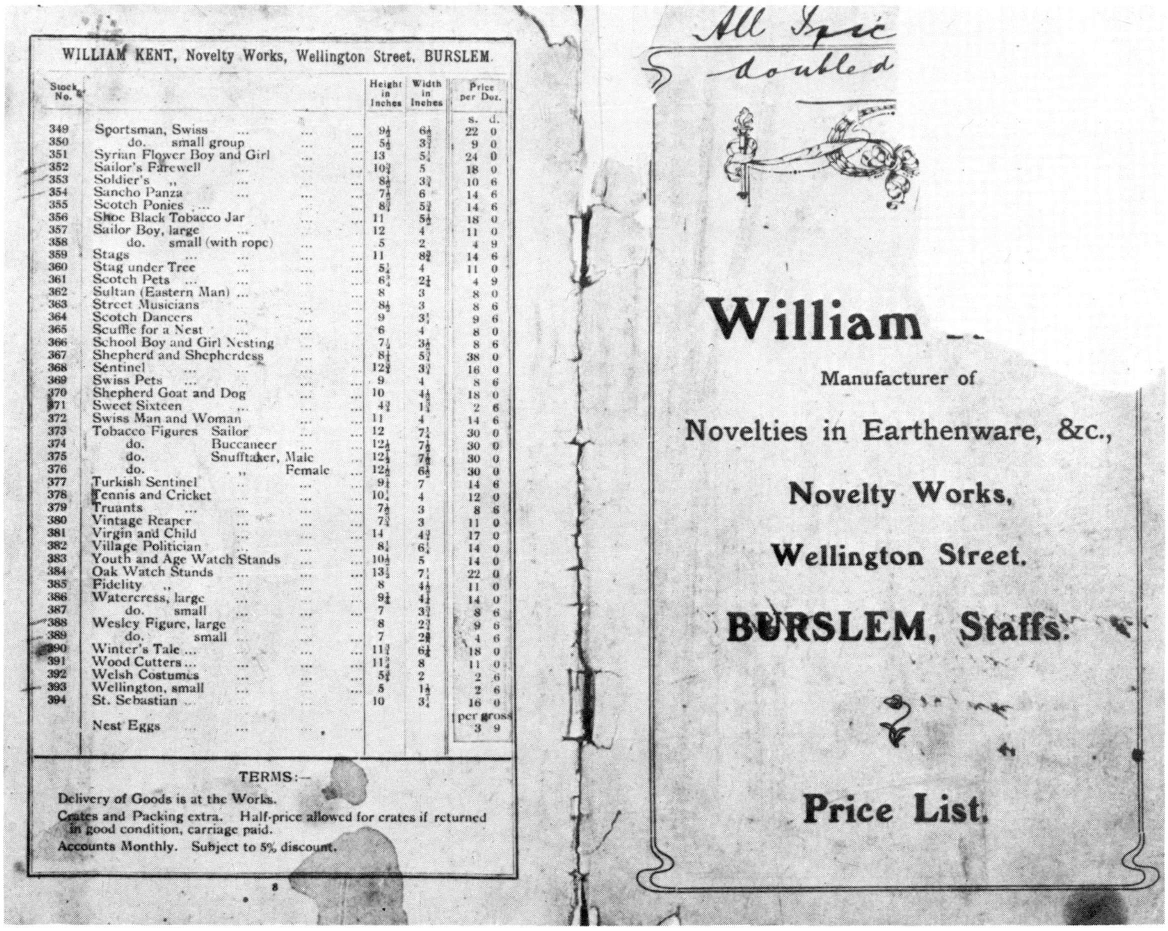

WILLIAM KENT, Novelty Works, Wellington Street, BURSLEM.

Stock No.		Height in Inches	Width in Inches	Price per Doz. s.	d.
349	Sportsman, Swiss	9½	6¼	22	0
350	do. small group	5½	3¾	9	0
351	Syrian Flower Boy and Girl	13	5¼	24	0
352	Sailor's Farewell	10¾	5	18	0
353	Soldier's ,,	8½	3¾	10	6
354	Sancho Panza	7¼	6	14	6
355	Scotch Ponies	8¾	5½	14	6
356	Shoe Black Tobacco Jar	11	5½	18	0
357	Sailor Boy, large	12	4	11	0
358	do. small (with rope)	5	2	4	9
359	Stags	11	8¾	14	6
360	Stag under Tree	5¼	4	11	0
361	Scotch Pets	6¾	2¼	4	9
362	Sultan (Eastern Man)	8	3	8	0
363	Street Musicians	8½	3	8	6
364	Scotch Dancers	9	3¼	9	6
365	Scuffle for a Nest	6	4	8	0
366	School Boy and Girl Nesting	7¼	3½	8	6
367	Shepherd and Shepherdess	8¼	5¾	38	0
368	Sentinel	12¾	3¾	16	0
369	Swiss Pets	9	4	8	6
370	Shepherd Goat and Dog	10	4½	18	0
371	Sweet Sixteen	4¾	1¾	2	6
372	Swiss Man and Woman	11	4	14	6
373	Tobacco Figures Sailor	12	7¼	30	0
374	do. Buccaneer	12½	7½	30	0
375	do. Snufftaker, Male	12½	7½	30	0
376	do. ,, Female	12½	6½	30	0
377	Turkish Sentinel	9¼	7	14	6
378	Tennis and Cricket	10¼	4	12	0
379	Truants	7½	3	8	6
380	Vintage Reaper	7¾	3	11	0
381	Virgin and Child	14	4¾	17	0
382	Village Politician	8¼	6¼	14	0
383	Youth and Age Watch Stands	10½	5	14	0
384	Oak Watch Stands	13½	7¼	22	0
385	Fidelity ,,	8	4½	11	0
386	Watercress, large	9½	4½	14	0
387	do. small	7	3¾	8	6
388	Wesley Figure, large	8	2¾	9	6
389	do. small	7	2¾	4	6
390	Winter's Tale	11¾	6½	18	0
391	Wood Cutters	11¾	8	11	0
392	Welsh Costumes	5¾	2	2	6
393	Wellington, small	5	1½	2	6
394	St. Sebastian	10	3¼	16	0
	Nest Eggs			per gross 3	9

TERMS:—

Delivery of Goods is at the Works.

Crates and Packing extra. Half-price allowed for crates if returned in good condition, carriage paid.

Accounts Monthly. Subject to 5% discount.

8

All Spic doubled

William ...

Manufacturer of

Novelties in Earthenware, &c.,

Novelty Works,

Wellington Street,

BURSLEM, Staffs.

Price List.

Plate 7
William Kent Price List, c. 1901 (Referred to in the text as *Kent List A.*) Note that the 'price per dozen' column has had a 20% increase pasted over the original prices. The catalogue is undated but the assumption is that it was issued about 1901-02. There is no indication in the catalogue of either the date of, or the reason for the increase in prices.
By courtesy of Mr John Hall

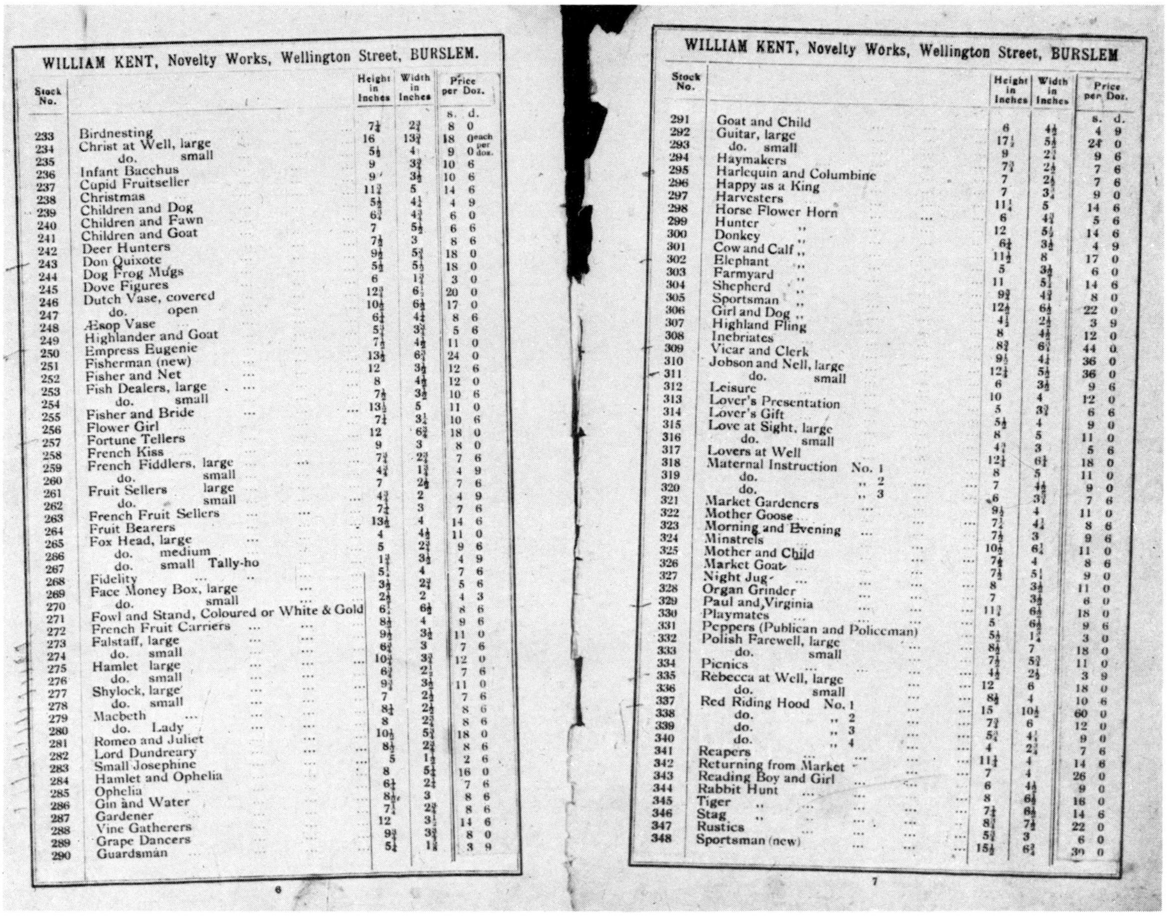

WILLIAM KENT, Novelty Works, Wellington Street, BURSLEM.

Stock No.		Height in Inches	Width in Inches	Price per Doz. s.	d.
233	Birdnesting	7¼	2¾	8	0
234	Christ at Well, large	16	13¾	18	0 each
235	do. small	5½	4	9	0 per doz.
236	Infant Bacchus	9	3¾	10	6
237	Cupid Fruitseller	9	3½	10	6
238	Christmas	11¾	5	14	6
239	Children and Dog	5½	4¼	4	9
240	Children and Fawn	6¾	4¾	6	0
241	Children and Goat	7	5½	6	6
242	Deer Hunters	7½	3	8	6
243	Don Quixote	9½	5¾	18	0
244	Dog Frog Mugs	5½	5½	18	0
245	Dove Figures	6	1¾	3	0
246	Dutch Vase, covered	12¾	6½	20	0
247	do. open	10½	6½	17	0
248	Æsop Vase	6¼	4¼	8	6
249	Highlander and Goat	5¾	3¾	5	6
250	Empress Eugenie	7½	4½	11	0
251	Fisherman (new)	13½	6¾	24	0
252	Fisher and Net	12	3½	12	6
253	Fish Dealers, large	8	4½	12	0
254	do. small	7½	3½	10	6
255	Fisher and Bride	13½	5	11	0
256	Flower Girl	7¼	3¼	10	6
257	Fortune Tellers	12	6¾	18	0
258	French Kiss	9	3	8	0
259	French Fiddlers, large	7¾	2¾	7	6
260	do. small	4¾	1¾	4	9
261	Fruit Sellers large	7	2½	7	6
262	do. small	4¾	2	4	9
263	French Fruit Sellers	7¼	3	7	6
264	Fruit Bearers	13½	4	14	6
265	Fox Head, large	4	4½	11	0
266	do. medium	5	2¾	9	6
267	do. small Tally-ho	1¾	3½	4	9
268	Fidelity	5¼	4	7	6
269	Face Money Box, large	3½	2¾	5	6
270	do. small	2½	2	4	3
271	Fowl and Stand, Coloured or White & Gold	6¼	6½	8	6
272	French Fruit Carriers	8½	4	9	6
273	Falstaff, large	9½	3½	11	0
274	do. small	6¾	3	7	6
275	Hamlet large	10¼	3¾	12	0
276	do. small	6¾	2½	7	6
277	Shylock, large	9¾	3½	11	0
278	do. small	7	2½	7	6
279	Macbeth	8¼	2½	8	6
280	do. Lady	8	2¾	8	6
281	Romeo and Juliet	10½	5¾	18	0
282	Lord Dundreary	8½	2¾	8	6
283	Small Josephine	5	1½	2	6
284	Hamlet and Ophelia	8	5¼	16	0
285	Ophelia	6¼	2¼	7	6
286	Gin and Water	8½	3	8	6
287	Gardener	7¼	2¾	8	6
288	Vine Gatherers	12	3½	14	6
289	Grape Dancers	9¾	3¾	8	0
290	Guardsman	5¼	1⅛	3	9

6

WILLIAM KENT, Novelty Works, Wellington Street, BURSLEM

Stock No.		Height in Inches	Width in Inches	Price per Doz. s.	d.
291	Goat and Child	6	4½	4	9
292	Guitar, large	17½	5½	24	0
293	do. small	9	2¼	9	6
294	Haymakers	7¾	2½	7	6
295	Harlequin and Columbine	7	2½	7	6
296	Happy as a King	7	3¼	9	0
297	Harvesters	11¼	5	14	6
298	Horse Flower Horn	6	4¾	5	6
299	Hunter ,,	12	5½	14	6
300	Donkey ,,	6¼	3½	4	9
301	Cow and Calf ,,	11½	8	17	0
302	Elephant ,,	5	3½	6	0
303	Farmyard ,,	11	5¼	14	6
304	Shepherd ,,	9¾	4¾	8	0
305	Sportsman ,,	12½	6½	22	0
306	Girl and Dog ,,	4½	2½	3	9
307	Highland Fling	8	4½	12	0
308	Inebriates	8¾	6¼	44	0
309	Vicar and Clerk	9½	4¼	36	0
310	Jobson and Nell, large	12¼	5½	36	0
311	do. small	6	3½	9	6
312	Leisure	10	4	12	0
313	Lover's Presentation	5	3¾	6	6
314	Lover's Gift	5½	4	9	0
315	Love at Sight, large	8	5	11	0
316	do. small	4¾	3	5	6
317	Lovers at Well	12¼	6½	18	0
318	Maternal Instruction No. 1	8	5	11	0
319	do. ,, 2	7	4½	9	0
320	do. ,, 3	6	3¾	7	6
321	Market Gardeners	9½	4	11	0
322	Mother Goose	7¼	4¼	8	6
323	Morning and Evening	7½	3	9	6
324	Minstrels	10½	6¼	11	0
325	Mother and Child	7½	4	8	6
326	Market Goat	7½	5¼	9	0
327	Night Jug	8	3½	11	0
328	Organ Grinder	7	3½	6	0
329	Paul and Virginia	11¾	6½	18	0
330	Playmates	5	6½	9	6
331	Peppers (Publican and Policeman)	5½	1¼	3	0
332	Polish Farewell, large	8½	7	18	0
333	do. small	7½	5¾	11	0
334	Picnics	4½	2½	3	9
335	Rebecca at Well, large	12	6	18	0
336	do. small	8½	4	10	6
337	Red Riding Hood No. 1	15	10½	60	0
338	do. ,, 2	7¾	6	12	0
339	do. ,, 3	5¾	4¼	9	0
340	do. ,, 4	4	2¼	7	6
341	Reapers	11½	4	14	6
342	Returning from Market	7	4	26	0
343	Reading Boy and Girl	6	4½	9	0
344	Rabbit Hunt	8	6½	16	0
345	Tiger ,,	7½	6½	14	6
346	Stag ,,	8¾	7½	22	0
347	Rustics	5¾	3	6	0
348	Sportsman (new)	15½	6¾	30	0

7

Plate 8
William Kent Price List, c. 1901 (Referred to in the text as *Kent List A.*)
By courtesy of Mr John Hall

5
The Home and Overseas Markets for Staffordshire Figures

Historical – Figures for the French market – Napoleon's popularity in England – Portrait figures of Americans – The home market – On contemporary prices – The purposes for which these figures were made.

HISTORICAL

Little is known about the marketing of Staffordshire figures in the Victorian era, and most of the information which is available has been gleaned from contemporary advertisements.

A rare contemporary reference noted by Mr Geoffrey Godden (*Apollo*, Nov. 1965) is contained in *The Leisure Hour, a family journal of instruction and recreation*. In the issue of June 2nd, 1853, under the heading 'A visit to the Staffordshire Potteries' and to Longton in particular, the writer notes:

. . . An immense quantity of the low-priced English china, as well for exportation as for home consumption is here manufactured weekly, as well as earthenwares of all kinds, and toys consisting of images in gold and colours of men and women, and rustic groups, and dogs and cats, and Swiss cottages, and Bonapartes, Victorias, Great Moguls, Dukes of Wellington, Tom Thumbs, Shepherds, Dairymaids, Cows, John Bulls and John Wesleys, etc., etc., as the advertisements say, 'too numerous to mention'.

Mr Godden goes on to note that the only firms of toy manufacturers at Longton in 1853 were those of Thomas Cooper (*working period c.* 1846-64), Sampson Smith (*c.* 1851-1963) and George Townsend (*c.* 1850-64). All three must have been large scale producers, although today the collector remembers only Sampson Smith.

A. F. Tschiffely, in *This Way Southward* (1940), records the discovery of Staffordshire figures in the homesteads of Welsh settlers in Patagonia. In particular, he mentions that the base of one was inscribed 'Made by Sampson Smith, Loughton [*sic*], 1851'.

FIGURES FOR THE FRENCH MARKET

It is clear that the figures were intended for exportation as well as for the home market. A good example of this is the figure of Will Watch (*fig.* 3, *pl.* C-3). Mr Bryan Latham has the same figure inscribed 'Jean Bart' in gilt script on the base (*fig.* 2, *pl.* C-2). The latter was a French naval hero born at Dunkirk in 1651. Mr Bryan Latham's comments on this are:

The provenance of the Will Watch figures (and the solitary Jean Bart) is intriguing. My researches lead me to believe that there are two facial types:
(1) The straight, upstanding figure, where the face with a fringed beard has a typical Nelsonic nautical look, (2) the more striking attitude usually accompanied by pistols and a barrel, where the face with its little spade beard – although the figure is labelled Will Watch – has a definite French look. In other words, this second figure if it is labelled Jean Bart seems to be entirely fitting with its Frenchified appearance. On the other hand when, as commonly, it is labelled Will Watch, it seems to be out of place.

All this lends support to the belief that there was a considerable export business done in Staffordshire Victorian portrait figures and that potters were astute enough to adapt their figures to the market they were supplying.

Figures of Napoleon Bonaparte were made in profusion, and many of these must have been intended for the French market. The figure titled 'Napoleon Buonaparte' in gilt script (*fig.* 61, *pl.* C-23), which is 24 in. (61 cm.) in height and the tallest and finest Staffordshire portrait figure ever made, is unlikely, as was first thought, to have been made for the Paris Exhibition. I am grateful to Mr P. C. Withers for the following comments in this connection:

With regard to the Staffordshire figure of Napoleon BUONA-PARTE, this can scarcely have been made for the French market since only the opponents of Napoleon made use of the 'U' in his name as a kind of insult. Only the French Royalists and the hostile governments used the letter 'U' to designate the great Emperor, not wishing to recognise him Emperor of the French. I should therefore imagine that it was for distribution on the English market.

NAPOLEON'S POPULARITY IN ENGLAND

We have seen that more figures were made of Napoleon by Victorian potters, than of anyone else; moreover, the finest figure to come out of the potteries was also of Napoleon. There is evidence that some of these figures were made for the French market, but doubtless the majority were intended for home consumption. Why was this? M. Théo Fleischman has probed the problem in considerable depth (*Bulletin de Société Belge d'Études Napoléoniennes*, March 1966).

If the English government never ceased to attack Napoleon, an imposing number among the élite of society and among the common people had a sympathy and admiration for him which manifested itself on many occasions, sometimes in an impressive way. These attitudes were evidenced during the Consulate, and lasted through the Empire period and beyond, stimulated by a liberal tradition which was very definitely pro-French. Mention was made in a previous Bulletin *of the study by the historian Jules Dechamps of accounts by English travellers in Belgium after Waterloo. He has described the same state of mind in two other works,* The British Isles and the French Revolution *and* Napoleon's Supporters in Great Britain from 1815-1830. *He says 'Napoleon was never without partisans and admirers across the Channel', and 'His legend lives on in England from the beginning of the nineteenth century until today', and again 'In Great Britain Napoleon supporters are as eager as his adversaries, and his legend has been nourished and embellished'.*

The historian Hallam, although an anti-democrat, admitted 'the intense admiration for this man, shown by so many people'. One is surprised to read in accounts of debates in the House of Commons words such as these about the Emperor: '. . . the greatest man of this century, and of all time . . . this extraordinary man' (General Torleton, 1810). Hobhouse, later Lord Broughton, wrote Letters on the Hundred Days *which were remarkable for their enthusiasm, and his friend Lord Byron in* Childe Harold *paid tribute to Napoleon.*

Certain English soldiers felt the same. A Lieutenant Woodbery, in his journal, recounts a happening of 6th June, a few days before Waterloo. At Grammont, the Hussars, having regaled themselves, followed their feasting by rushing across the fields to give the French peasants a fine impression of the English Hussars by crying 'Long Live Napoleon!' The same Lieutenant, hearing of the Emperor's discourse at the Champ de Mai noted 'The Emperor's speech was good and everyone is well pleased'. In his Journal of the Waterloo Campaign *artillery officer Cavalié Mercer described a moment of intense emotion. On 17th June between Quatre-Bras and Mont-Saint-Jean he suddenly saw Napoleon appear riding across the field. 'I had always wanted to see Napoleon, this great man of war, this incredible genius whose fame was world-wide. Now I saw him, and there was something sublime, unequalled in this moment'.*

The English public manifested a curiosity and admiration on many occasions. In his Mémorial de Sainte-Hélène *Las Cases recounts that the* Bellerophon *with Napoleon onboard dropped anchor at Torbay. 'The water was full of small boats manned by the curious. From a beautiful house nearby, the owner sent Napoleon a present of fruit'. A few days later in Plymouth waters 'The Emperor's arrival had produced a feverish curiosity. Public notices informed us of the decision (the transfer to St. Helena), condemning it. All England arrived at Plymouth. . . . So it happened among the crew of his ship who said 'Speak what ill one may of this man, if in England he were known as we know him, not a hair of his head would be touched . . .'*

George Home in his memoirs of Napoleon wrote 'You will forgive my fastidious attention to detail, since he is the most remarkable man born in the last four thousand years'.

It seems hardly necessary to call to mind the indignant shame with which the population and certain areas of the political world heard the news of his deportation. Also we know how numerous were the recommendations to the Government in favour of the prisoner of Longwood. In 1823 the French diplomat (and royalist) Comte de La Ferronnays wrote 'I do not know what has taken hold of the English since the Battle of Waterloo. England has become Bonapartist and revolutionary, even into the upper classes'. In 1828 General Sir William Napier declared 'He is the greatest man in history, the most marvellous chief in battle, the wisest politician, the most profound of statesmen'.

There are other curious illustrations of the popularity enjoyed among the English people by he who they called with familiarity 'Bony'. A writer of the times says 'The lower classes have formed a habit of calling Bonaparte by a nickname more affectionate than derogatory'. General Lejeune in his memoirs In Prison and in War *recounts that on his return from England where he was imprisoned he said to Napoleon 'I have not entered a cottage nor a castle in England without finding an image or picture of "Bony". . . It is the name by which they call you, Your Majesty'. . .*

PORTRAIT FIGURES OF AMERICANS

Although many portrait figures were made of Americans, they seem to have been intended primarily for the home market. They include Washington, Franklin, Lincoln, Jefferson, John Brown, Hackett, the Cushman sisters, Van Amburgh, Heenan, Rarey, Moody and Sankey and, of course, the 'Bloomer' figures. There are also a number of figures of Uncle Tom, Little Eva and other characters in Mrs Harriet Beecher Stowe's novel *Uncle Tom's Cabin* which seized the imagination of English readers as it had that of those in its native land.

The late Mr Albert Lee (*Connoisseur*, Nov. 1935) recorded that *While the Staffordshire potters glutted the American market with table-ware, they apparently did not export many figures–possibly owing to the bulkiness of these and the cost of packing and shipping. . . .* Comparatively few, even of those which from patriotic motives alone should have appealed to Americans, seem to have been exported at the time. *The majority,* he said, *of Staffordshire figures which are now included in public and private American collections are not there because of the initiative of the Staffordshire potters and their sales agents, but because the American traveller and the American collector, went to England and were captivated by the charm and quality of these products. . . . It was not until the mid-Victorian era, and after the close of the Civil War in America, that Americans began to visit Europe in any numbers. . . . Figures of national heroes or otherwise– although in most cases perhaps artistically inferior to the products of the best of the earlier potters, nevertheless possess a certain virility, quaintness and even individuality which are recognized today–perhaps more so in America than in England. . . . Examples of almost all the Staffordshire pieces representing American subjects, which perhaps might be designated as 'Americana', have been gathered into American collections, whenever Americans could obtain them.*

THE HOME MARKET

At home, the figures were sold in markets, fairs and shops in most districts of the British Isles, and possibly also inside or outside theatres (*see p. 28*). *Fig.* 165, *pl.* E-83 which probably portrays Jenny Lind and Luigi Lablache in a scene from *The Daughter of the Regiment* has been found inscribed 'Present from the Thames Tunnel' (*ch 4, pl.* 9). The tunnel was opened as a thoroughfare for foot passengers on March 25th, 1843, the carriage-way being completed later. Jenny Lind first appeared in London in 1847. It is known that there were booths either in, or in the vicinity of the tunnel, and that each had its own address, viz., *43, Thames Tunnel*. Presumably it was from one of these booths that the piece was originally sold. There are a number of pieces similarly inscribed, for instance *fig.* 41 (Alphington Ponies) *pl.* I-18, found marked 'A present from Torquay', and *fig.* 105 (Unidentified house) *pl.* I-55 which is marked 'A present from Scarborough'. I have also seen a pair of swans similarly marked; and coursing hounds, one inscribed 'A present from Blackpool' and another 'A present from Rhyl', Mr Parry Michael has told me of an old lady of eighty in the antique business in Aberystwyth who told him that she had heard from her grandmother that there was a marine-store dealer near the bridge in Aberystwyth who, in return for 'rags and bones' collected from the locals, gave them Staffordshire figures.

Many figures were doubtless sold by street vendors, often itinerant Italians. The frontispiece of this volume is a lithograph music-front by H. C. Maguire for the ballad *Buy Image!* sung by Madame Vestris. It is one of the few contemporary illustrations of an image vendor. A comic song titled *Buy My Images*, written and sung by Mr Thomas Hudson, possibly throws some light on the 'cries' of these itinerant salesmen of the early Victorian era (*see p. x*).

There is more than a hint that the manufacturers were intent on something other than a purely local trade, for with the exception of a few Welsh preachers, few figures are found of local worthies unknown elsewhere in the British Isles. Whilst there were many 'pot-boilers' such as Wellington and Napoleon, other figures were produced to satisfy the ever-growing demand for likenesses of persons in the news. This demand went far beyond the Royal Family, politicians, clerics and war heroes, and extended from heroines, such as Grace Darling, to criminals, such as Arthur Orton, the Tichborne claimant; from cricketers, such as Clarke, Pilch and Box, to operatic stars, such as Jenny Lind and Sims Reeves. The full catalogue is reminiscent of a nineteenth-century *Dictionary of National Biography*. Staffordshire portrait figures provided the 'news of the day' in much the same way as the pictorial dailies of the twentieth century and for this reason had just as broad an appeal throughout the land.

Most authorities would agree with Mr Balston that Sir Herbert Read's statement that *the pottery figure was never meant to be more than a cheerful ornament in a farm-house or a labourer's cottage* can hardly be correct and that although until recently many farmhouses and cottages had at least one figure on a mantelpiece, there are many figures, especially those of theatrical characters, which must have been intended for a more sophisticated and urbane public.

It has already been remarked that only a handful of figures are found of local celebrities little known elsewhere in the British Isles. Those that come to mind include Christmas Evans (*fig.* 48, *pl.* D-23), chief minister of all the Baptist Churches in Anglesey; John Elias (*fig.* 45, *pl.* D-23), Welsh Calvinistic Methodist preacher in Anglesey and Caernarvonshire, John Bryan (*fig.* 46, *pl.* D-23), Wesleyan minister, much of whose life was spent as grocer and local preacher at Caernarvon, and Evan Roberts (*fig.* 54, *pl.* D-27), who launched a revivalist movement at Loughor, near Llanelly, which soon grew to massive proportions. This latter portrait, although strictly speaking after our period (1905), is very similar to figures known to have been made by Sampson Smith and lends support to Mr Balston's conclusion that none of these figures were made in Wales but that the demand among the Welsh for portraits of these worthies was such that it paid the Staffordshire potters to make them. Moreover, there is another group of figures which include Beaumaris and Caernarvon Castles (*figs.* 92 and 93, *pl.* I-49), and Edward Morgan and Jenny Jones (*figs.* 2 and 3, *pl.* I-2), as well as numerous untitled figures of Welsh women and Welsh men in national costume obviously attractive to English souvenir hunters as well as having local appeal. These figures, too, were made in Staffordshire. Mr Balston quotes Miss Dorothy Hartley, of Llangollen, as stating that at that period there was much traffic between Staffordshire and North Wales, and to this day gypsies follow old pack-horse routes from Stafford with pottery which they sell in the local markets.

Whereas it seems certain that all the Welsh 'portraits' were made in Staffordshire, it is less easy to be dogmatic about figures of Scottish national heroes. Scottish earthenware figures are extremely difficult to distinguish from English, having been manufactured during the period in question very largely by potters, painters, and gilders imported from Staffordshire. There is no evidence to attribute figures such as Prince Charles (*fig.* 261, *pl.* A-97), Bruce and Wallace (*figs.* 12 and 13, *pl.* I-6) to Scottish potteries, and certainly the tartan pattern on a figure was almost equally popular in England as in Scotland.

Two figures of Burns and one of Tam o'Shanter and Souter Johnnie are known by factory marks to have been made by Sampson Smith (*see chapter two*). The great popularity of the works not only of Burns, but also of Scott, provoked wide public interest in Scotland and her heroes. There seems every reason to suppose that the majority of figures of Burns and Scott as well as those of characters from their works were made in Staffordshire.

ON CONTEMPORARY PRICES

The prices commanded by portrait figures in Victorian times are not known with certainty, for no contemporary price-list has come to light. However, I have been able to examine two lists of William Kent from which it is possible to hazard a reasonable guess as to what these prices were likely to have been, for included in the lists are the wholesale prices per dozen of many nineteenth-century figures of which Kent still had moulds. Neither catalogue is dated but from the figures listed it can be deduced that the earliest (hereafter referred to as *Kent List A*) was issued about 1901-2, and the second (hereafter referred to as *Kent List B*), perhaps ten or even twenty years later.

Kent List A is of interest in that no reference is made to the manufacture of reproductions of old Staffordshire ware; also, the *price per dozen* column has had a 20 per cent increase pasted over the original prices (*see ch.* 4, *pls.* 7 and 8). The hidden prices, which were in force when the catalogue was first issued, are unlikely to differ much from those of the original makers, for prices remained fairly constant from 1850-1902 for those products in which there was no great change in the process of manufacture. When and why the 20 per cent increase was imposed is uncertain.

Kent List B is of interest in that it refers to the manufacture of earthenware figures, etc., *including reproductions of old Staffordshire ware*. New stock numbers appear in this catalogue, a number of figures catalogued in *Kent List A* are omitted and others are to be found deleted in red ink as *discontinued lines*. There has been a further price increase of over 100 per cent.

EXAMPLES TAKEN FROM *KENT LIST A* (*circa 1901-2*)

PARR AND KENT GROUP OF POTTERS

Stock No.	*My Figure No.*	*Height*		*Price* per Doz.* s.	d.
40	*356, 353, pls.* C-128 and 127	15 in. (38 cm.)	Generals Macdonald and French on Horse.......	18	0
41	*352, 351, pl.* C-127	15 in. (38 cm.)	Generals Gordon and Wolseley on Horse.....	18	0
42	*303, pl.* C-103	15 in. (38 cm.)	Garibaldi on Horse	30	0
43	*302, pl.* C-103	15 in. (38 cm.)	Victor Emmanuel on Horse.................	30	0
44	*21, pl.* B-3	11½ in. (29 cm.)	Wellington on Horse ...	20	0
45	*375, pl.* C-138	10½ in. (26.5 cm.)	Huzzar on Horse	13	0
46	*205, 204, pl.* A-66	7¾ in. (20 cm.)	Prince and Princess on Horse................	9	0
47	*282, pl.* C-97	14 in. (35.5 cm.)	Large Garibaldi and Horse................	48	0
48	*282, pl.* C-104	8¾ in. (22 cm.)	Small Garibaldi and Horse................	16	0
49	*283, pl.* C-104	8½ in. (21.5 cm.)	Small Napier and Horse	16	0
51	*288, pl.* C-99	9¼ in. (23.5 cm.)	Garibaldi at War.......	8	0
127	*338, pl.* C-119	16 in. (40.5 cm.)	General Gordon	16	0
128	*163*(a), *pl.* C-63	4½ in. (11.5 cm.)	Emin Pasha on Horse [*sic*]	5	0
207	*19, pl.* A-11	7¼ in. (18.25 cm.)	Queen Box	7	0
243	*77, pl.* H-26	9½ in. (24 cm.)	Don Quixote..........	15	0
250	*79*(a), *pl.* C-36	7½ in. (19 cm.)	Empress Eugenie	9	0
273	*3, pl.* E-1B	9½ in. (24 cm.)	Falstaff, large	9	0
274	*3, pl.* E-1B	6¾ in. (17 cm.)	do. small.........	6	0
275	*6, pl.* E-1A	10¾ in. (27 cm.)	Hamlet, large	10	0
276	*6, pl.* E-4	6¾ in. (17 cm.)	do. small.........	6	0
277	*4, pl.* E-1B	9¾ in. (24.5 cm.)	Shylock, large.........	9	0
278	*4, pl.* E-1B	7 in. (17.5 cm.)	do. small.........	6	0
279	*8, pl.* E-2	8¼ in. (21 cm.)	Macbeth	7	0
280	*7, pl.* E-2	8 in. (20.5 cm.)	do. Lady	7	0
281	*1, pl.* E-1A	10½ in. (26.5 cm.)	Romeo and Juliet......	15	0
282	*41, pl.* E-18	8½ in. (21.5 cm.)	Lord Dundreary.......	7	0
284	*19, pl.* E-7	8 in. (20.5 cm.)	Hamlet and Ophelia ...	13	0
285	*5, pl.* E-1A	6¼ in. (16 cm.)	Ophelia..............	6	0
295	*248, 249, pl.* E-126	7 in. (17.5 cm.)	Harlequin and Columbine	6	0
337	*245, pl.* E-124	15 in. (38 cm.)	Red Riding Hood No. 1	48	0
354	*76, pl.* H-26	7½ in. (19 cm.)	Sancho Panza.........	12	6
378	*8, pl.* F-4	10¼ in. (25.75 cm.)	Tennis and Cricket.....	10	0
390	*2, pl.* E-1A	11¾ in. (29.75 cm.)	Winter's Tale	15	0

OTHER FIGURES

Stock No.	*My Figure No.*	*Height*		*Price* per Doz.* s.	d.
60	*211, pl.* E-103	10¾ in. (27 cm.)	Elephant (Jumbo)	16	0
125	*334, pl.* C-119	14 in. (35.5 cm.)	Lord Roberts	12	0
126	*335, pl.* C-119	14 in. (35.5 cm.)	Lord Kitchener	12	0
129	*45, pl.* B-14	11½ in. (29 cm.)	Gladstone	8	0
130	*46, pl.* B-14	11½ in. (29 cm.)	Beaconsfield	8	0
133	*244, pl.* A-85	14 in. (35.5 cm.)	King Edward VII	15	0
134	*245, pl.* A-85	14 in. (35.5 cm.)	Queen Alexandra......	15	0
137	*34, pl.* C-12	11½ in. (29 cm.)	Toby Jugs, Nelson	18	0
229	*49, pl.* H-12	12 in. (30.5 cm.)	Burns and Mary.......	15	0

*Note the prices given are the original 'hidden' prices (*see text*). They are approximately 20 per cent less than figures given by the late Mr Thomas Balston.

Prices given are wholesale prices. The retail prices would probably be about 50 per cent higher. Thus the 'Large Garibaldi and Horse', the most complex and expensive of these figures, would cost the retailer 4s. each and be sold for about 6s. A similar figure, well executed but restored, was sold at Christie's as long ago as 1965 for 44 guineas (*see chapter eight*). The small Macbeth and Lady Macbeth cost the retailer 1s. 2d. the pair, and would be sold for about 1s 9d. Contemporary versions are so rare that they have not yet been tested at auction but would be likely to fetch over 400 guineas today. Even a pair of reproductions, actually referred to by the auctioneer as being 'later' fetched 18 guineas at Christie's back in 1966, although they might well have been made and sold for £4 5s. within the preceding ten years (*see over*).

Prices in Kent lists show a steady increase over the years. A copy of the 1939 list in the possession of Messrs Mander and Mitchenson shows King Edward VII to have risen from 15s. in 1901 to 80s. per dozen, i.e. to be over five times as expensive.

In response to an enquiry made of a London supplier[1] of William Kent (Porcelains) Ltd in February 1958, the following prices were quoted for single copies of 'Old Staffordshire Pottery'[2]:

[1]A. Grohmann Ltd., 48, Britton St., Clerkenwell, London, E.C.1.

[2]This is the last price list known to me to have been issued before cessation of production on December 31st, 1962. At that time, delivery of items not held in stock was about three months. As an example of the price changes since 1900 note that the large Falstaffs then cost about 1s. 1½d. each retail!

	Height	£	s.	d.
Falstaff	9½ in. (24 cm.)	2	10	0
do.	6¾ in. (17 cm.)	1	15	0
Garibaldi & Horse	14 in. (35.5 cm.)		*Not made*	
do.	8¾ in. (22 cm.)		*Not made*	
Garibaldi on Horse	15 in. (38 cm.)		*Not made*	
Harlequin & Columbine	7 in. (17.5 cm.) *pair*	3	10	0
Hamlet & Ophelia	8 in. (20.5 cm.)	3	10	0
Hamlet	10¾ in. (27 cm.)	2	10	0
Hamlet	6¾ in. (17 cm.)	1	15	0
Macbeth	8¼ in. (21 cm.)			
Lady Macbeth	8 in. (20.5 cm.) *pair*	4	5	0
Ophelia	6¼ in. (16 cm.)	1	5	0
Romeo & Juliet	10¼ in. (25.75 cm.)	3	15	0
Shylock	9¾ in. (24.5 cm.)	2	10	0
Shylock	7 in. (17.5 cm.)	1	15	0

THE PURPOSES FOR WHICH THESE FIGURES WERE MADE

Apart from those figures which were purely decorative, commemorative, patriotic, or issued for purposes of 'news' or propaganda, and those which portrayed persons either well-known nationally, or occasionally only locally, albeit because they were famous or infamous, some figures had an additional specific purpose.

EXAMPLES MAY BE QUOTED OF:

Candle snuffers, viz. *fig.* 79 (Albert) *pl.* A-30.

Candlesticks, viz. *fig.* 165 (Victoria, Albert and Prince of Wales) *pl.* A-55.

Inkwells, viz. *fig.* 35(a) (Lambton) *pl.* I-17 (*ch.* 3, *pl.* 62).

Jugs, viz. *fig.* 34 (Nelson) *pl.* C-12.

Money-boxes, viz. *fig.* 105 (Unidentified house) *pl.* I-55.

Pastille-burners, viz. *fig.* 121 (Windsor Lodge) *pl.* A-42.

Spill-holders, viz. *fig.* 2 (Marston and Robinson) *pl.* E-1A. (Some examples catalogued as spill-holders have trumpet-like openings and were perhaps intended as *flower holders*.)

Tobacco jars, viz. *fig.* 376 (British Lion) *pl.* C-139.

Trinket boxes, viz. *fig.* 19 (Victoria) *pl.* A-11.

Watch-holders, viz. *fig.* 16 (Milton and Shakespeare) *pl.* H-6. (It is not clear whether these so-called watch-holders were intended to hold a real watch or an imitation watch, *see fig.* 241 [The Three Graces] *pl.* E-122.)

There is also an item probably intended to hold seed or water for a bird-cage (*fig.* 82 [Albert] *pl.* A-30) and another, probably intended to hold a sample of tea (*fig.* 43 [Monkey porter] *pl.* I-18).

6

Forgeries, Fakes, Reproductions, Restorations and Repairs

Introduction – Forgeries – Fakes – Reproductions – Restorations and repairs.

INTRODUCTION

Forgeries are copies of works of art, in our case portrait figures, made for fraudulent purposes. The term must be used with care, for it is the 'intention' that is all important. To prove a forgery it is necessary not only to show the intention to reproduce the appearance of the original, but also the intention to sell it as the original at a high price. Although, only a handful of Staffordshire portrait figures have been forged to date, forgeries of other types of pottery and porcelain exist in fair profusion. They are commonly found with chips and scratches, and some have even been purposely broken and restored. There is little doubt that the forger not infrequently inclines to the view that if the buyer's mind can be occupied in assessing the extent of the restoration and its effect on the value of the piece, he will be less inclined to focus his attention on such basic things as the nature of the body, the type of glaze and style of decoration, all three of which must agree with the same features in other figures known to be genuine. The problem facing the would-be forger of a Staffordshire portrait figure is that unless he draws on the original sources for his materials–which in this case, for a variety of reasons, he cannot–he can only imitate the figure in other substances.

Fakes are genuine figures which have been restored, altered in character, added to, or otherwise tampered with for the purposes of deception and enhancement of value.

Reproductions are copies of contemporary figures, sold as such. Although made for an honest purpose, a reproduction may subsequently fall into dishonest hands. If sold, later, as a genuine contemporary piece, the reproduction assumes the mantle of a forgery. This is especially so if it has been tampered with– artificially 'crazed', chipped or otherwise defaced to give it a false appearance of age, or if any factory mark applied by the copyist has been erased. The recognition of a reproduction of a portrait figure is usually by no means difficult, even to the relatively inexperienced. However, occasionally figures turn up which puzzle even the expert. In such an event, a reproduction may be sold by an honest dealer or auctioneer under the genuine impression that it is a contemporary copy. Reproductions may themselves date from the late Victorian era.

Victorian portrait figures only rarely have a factory mark (*see chapter two*). It follows that if a forgery or fake is marked at all it will bear a copy of the original mark, whereas a reproduction if marked will bear the mark of the copyist (*see ch. 6, pl. 4*).

FORGERIES

The reader may be surprised to learn that until very recently only one pair of figures was known to have been made with the indisputable intent to deceive. These forgeries are of the 'small cricketers' (*figs.* 11 and 12, *pl.* F-6) and are particularly well executed. In 1962 a student working in the ceramic section of a well-known college of art, was given the task of reproducing one pair of figures from a contemporary pair as an exercise. He found a ready market for this pair and subsequently produced

further copies. When a leading London dealer was offered a second pair of these relatively rare figures within a week, he became suspicious. By comparing the figures with known contemporary pieces his worst fears were confirmed. By the time the matter had been sorted out and further production stopped, a fair number of forgeries were in circulation. So good are they that the collector is advised to purchase the smaller versions only from an established dealer with experience of the problem, or alternatively, to limit himself to the larger 14 in. (35.5 cm.) figures of which neither forgeries nor reproductions are to date known.

I have now examined a number of both genuine figures and forgeries (*see ch.* 6, *pl.* 1). The most important single feature is that the genuine figures are slightly shorter than the forgeries. The bowler is 10⅛ in. (25.4 cm.) in the genuine figure; 11 in. (28 cm.) in the forgery. The batsman is 10¼ in. (25.75 cm.) in the genuine figure and 10⅝ in. (27.75 cm.) in the forgery. Other points are that the genuine figures are heavier; the faces are better modelled; the sash knot, both in the bowler and the batsman, is a separate item and not just painted in; the blue of the coats is a more mellow colour and the colouring of the shirts is in finer detail. A number of forgeries have been found to be warped, but I have not found this feature in any genuine figure. The first batch of forgeries were not crazed, but later ones were. A pair of forgeries is shown on the left of *ch.* 6, *pl.* 1; the bowler is an example of the first issue (being uncrazed), but the batsman is a later production and heavily crazed. To the right of this pair is a pair, although not a matching pair, of genuine figures. Similar forgeries to those illustrated in this volume, unrecognized as such by the auctioneers, were sold to a private buyer for just over fifty pounds in a London auction room a few years ago. The under-bidder was a dealer. The low price, seventy pounds might have been expected then, in itself invited suspicion, particularly as I understand the same pair had appeared at another auction room in the preceding month and had been withdrawn at just under twenty pounds.

In 1967, a number of other forgeries were reported for the first time. It was said that the perpetrators in return for being allowed to borrow a figure from which the copies were made, allowed the donor one copy in payment. Whether this is so I do not know, but certainly I have seen forgeries of the small versions of Potash Farm and Stanfield Hall (*figs.* 44a and 46a, *pls.* G-23 and 24) which were apparent immediately because of the inability of the forger to gild in the manner of the Victorian craftsmen. Forgeries have also been reported of the Duke and Duchess of Cambridge (*figs.* 155 and 156, *pl.* C-59), Turpin and King, Garibaldi and Peard and several other figures.

To complete a successful prosecution for forgery may be by no means easy. It is necessary first to prove beyond all reasonable doubt that the object is spurious, and then to connect it with the perpetrator. In so far as the sale of a forged figure is concerned, although the vendor might be compelled to return the money, it would be necessary to prove not only that he knew he was offering a forgery, but also that he had described it inaccurately, before he could be successfully prosecuted for fraud. In the case of a specialist dealer who sold an obvious

Plate 1
The Small Cricketers
Forgeries:
L to R: *Fig.* 11 (Unidentified bowler) *pl.* F-6
Height 11 in (28 cm)
Fig. 12 (Unidentified batsman) *pl.* F-6
Height 10⅝ in (27.75 cm)
Fig. 11 in uncrazed and *fig.* 12 crazed. The former is from

the first batch of forgeries and the latter from a later issue.
Contemporary versions:
Fig. 11 (Unidentified bowler) *pl.* F-6
Height 10⅛ in (25.4 cm)
Fig. 12 (Unidentified batsman) *pl.* F-6
Height 10¼ in (25.75 cm)
The differing levels of the gilt lines indicate that this is not a 'matching' pair.

forgery–an unlikely occurrence–this might not present too much difficulty; but if the figure were unusually deceptive, a defence that he, also, was deceived would very probably succeed.

FAKES

Fig. 138 (Princess Royal) *pl.* A-47 is, as far as I am aware, never found with a contemporary title. The version illustrated in *ch.* 6, *pl.* 2 is particularly badly modelled and poorly coloured. In an attempt to add interest to the figure and thereby enhance its value it has been 'faked up' by applying the title 'Princess' in gold paint. This is a deliberate, although crude, attempt to deceive and one which we are likely to see more of in the future.

The most brazen fake, to date, is the piece illustrated in *ch.* 6, *pl.* 2A. It turned up in a leading London auction room, early in 1969, and was sold for just under sixty pounds. I understand that the sale was cancelled later. A man with a peg leg stands beside a pillar playing a concertina. He is wearing a blue cloak and yellow breeches. The piece, 7¼ in. (18.25 cm.) in height, is titled 'Whaler', in black painted capitals on the base, which is green. Naturally, it is unique! Comparison with *pl.* H-7 reveals, however, that it is probably nothing other than a genuine figure of Shakespeare, badly broken. The missing hands, one of which carried a manuscript, have been replaced by new hands holding a concertina. The broken left leg has been replaced by a peg leg, and a cloth cap has been applied to the head. Only on close examination is it possible to unravel these secrets. Latterly, I have heard of a similar figure inscribed 'Ahab'.

REPRODUCTIONS

This is a much more difficult subject. Reproductions have been made both of figures of the Parr and Kent group of potters and of figures from the Sampson Smith factory.

In 1955 William Kent (Porcelains) Ltd. published a brochure by Mr Douglas C. Hall titled *The Story of 'Old Staffordshire' Pottery by Kent of Burslem.* In it the author stated that although the Kent factory was now a highly mechanized concern making, in the main, porcelain fittings, the Kent family had retained a small portion of the factory wherein 'Old Staffordshire' style

pottery was still made from moulds produced from the original master-moulds. Craftsmen made each piece of pottery by the old method of 'pressing' entirely by hand from plastic clay. After firing, each was decorated by brush work, which was applied by craftswomen, so that each piece carried a personal touch of the artist. It was also remarked in the handbook that Kent's 'Old Staffordshire' pottery was not 'reproduction' in the strictest sense of the word, because except for a period during wartime, the pottery had been produced continuously from the early days.

There followed a list of pottery made by William Kent (Porcelains) Ltd., henceforth referred to as *Kent List C*. A footnote to the list states that: *The list of articles, although comprehensive, cannot be finalised as further old moulds are continually being discovered from our stock of ancient moulds. Nor can we guarantee to make all the pieces listed. . . .* No prices are quoted in *Kent List C*. Production of 'Olde Staffordshire Ware' by William Kent (Porcelains) Ltd. ceased on December 31st, 1962.

Of the figures referred to in *Kent List A (see p. 97)* the following still appear either in *Kent List B* or *C* or both.

PARR AND KENT GROUP OF POTTERS	KENT LIST A Stock No. (c. 1901)	KENT LIST B Stock No. (c. 1910-20)	Deleted as 'discontinued lines' (c. 1920)	KENT LIST C Ref. No. (1955)
Generals Macdonald and French on Horse	40	—	265	—
Generals Gordon and Wolseley on Horse	41	—	266	—
Garibaldi on Horse	42	263	—	263
Victor Emmanuel on Horse	43	397	—	397
Wellington on Horse	44	398	—	398
Huzzar on Horse	45	276	—	276
Prince and Princess on Horse	46	316	—	316
Large Garibaldi and Horse	47	261	—	261
Small Garibaldi and Horse	48	262	—	262
Small Napier and Horse	49	306	—	306
Garibaldi at War	51	260	—	—
General Gordon	127	—	264	—
Emin Pasha on Horse [sic]	128	214	—	214
Queen Box	207	166	—	166
Don Quixote	243	210	—	210

Plate 2
The Faked Princess
Fig. 138, *pl.* A-47, as far as I am aware, is never found with
a contemporary title. The version illustrated is particularly
badly modelled and poorly coloured. It has been 'faked-up'
by applying the title 'Princess' in gold paint in an attempt to
deceive the collector into believing he has found a rarity.

Plate 2A
A broken figure of Shakespeare (see *fig.* 24, *pl.* H-7). It has
been 'restored' and inscribed *WHALER*. The figure is 7¼ in
(18.25 cm) in height. A cap has been applied to the bard's
head, a concertina substituted for the manuscript in his left
hand and a peg leg used to replace his left leg. This 'unique
piece' fetched just under £60 in a leading London auction
room but fortunately its secrets were unravelled before it was
too late.

	KENT LIST A Stock No. (c. 1901)	KENT LIST B Stock No. (c. 1910-20)	Deleted as 'discontinued lines' (c. 1920)	KENT LIST C Ref. No. (1955)
Empress Eugenie	250	212	—	212
Falstaff, large	273	215	—	215
do. small	274	216	—	216
Hamlet, large	275	273	—	273
do. small	276	274	—	274
Shylock, large	277	355	—	355
do. small	278	356	—	356
Macbeth	279	302	—	302
do. Lady	280	303	—	303
Romeo and Juliet	281	329	—	329
Lord Dundreary	282	—	290	—
Hamlet and Ophelia	284	272	—	272
Ophelia	285	308	—	308
Harlequin and Columbine	295	270	—	270
Red Riding Hood, No. 1	337	323	—	323
Sancho Panza	354	347	—	347
Tennis and Cricket	378	—	359	—
Winter's Tale	390	405	—	—

OTHER FIGURES

Elephant (Jumbo)	60	—	—	—
Lord Roberts	125	—	292	—
Lord Kitchener	126	—	291	—
Gladstone	129	—	259	259

	KENT LIST A Stock No. (c. 1901)	KENT LIST B Stock No. (c. 1910-20)	Deleted as 'discontinued lines' (c. 1920)	KENT LIST C Ref. No. (1955)
Beaconsfield	130	—	177	—
King Edward VII	133	—	283	—
Queen Alexandra	134	—	283	—
Toby Jugs, Nelson	137	372	—	372
Burns and Mary	229	121	—	121

In what way do reproductions differ from contemporary
versions? Later examples, almost without exception, have no
spontaneous charm in their decoration. They are often too
meticulous and lack the spirit of their forerunners. In Victorian
times *to work quickly was profitable* and the skill thus acquired
gave to much of the work the directness and sleight of hand of
a sketch. The almost total absence of this 'sureness of eye' and
'lightness of touch' is the most marked defect of the reproduction. Over the years the reproduction became more and more
lifeless until eventually it was not decorated at all but coated
all over with coarse colours as a substitute for the old skill. This
coarseness extends to the touch in many cases. Not only is the
colouring cruder, but in many instances it is entirely different.
I have been told that this is because of factory laws that have
prohibited the use of certain paints since mid-Victorian times,

but have not been able to substantiate this. The typical delicate green of the early figures of the Parr and Kent group of potters, those attributed to Thomas Parr, has never been reproduced. The original figures have their bases coloured with brown and green 'combed' in long, thin strokes sometimes with a little pale orange added. Kent reproductions are never 'combed', and the green is cruder and brighter and the brown 'splodged' on.

In late figures the modelling is seldom sharp. Thus, in figures titled with indented capitals, such as the Shakspearian figures of the Parr and Kent group, the indentations are never more than faintly perceptible and are crudely outlined in black (see ch. 6, pl. 7) instead of being well-defined and picked out delicately in black, as in the contemporary versions also illustrated. This difference in the manner of titling can easily be perceived even in a black and white photograph.

The style of titling by transfer, also, is quite different in contemporary as compared with later, albeit Victorian, examples. Comparison may be made of early and late examples of Garibaldi and Victor Emmanuel (pl. C-103) and of Garibaldi and Napier (pls. C-104 and 105). The figure of 'Romeo' and 'Juliet' (fig. 1, pl. E-1A) is usually found titled in transfer in upper and lower case letters:

Jul: 'O think'st thou we shall ever meet again?'
Rom: 'I doubt it not; and all these woes shall serve
For sweet discourses in our time to come.'

Figures made, I have been told, only *after* 1939, occasionally turn up. They are titled in gilt script 'Romeo & Juliet' and a good example was illustrated in an article by Mr Bryan Latham which appeared in *The Lady*, **141**, 50, 1955. A similar figure is known to have changed hands with the buyer under the impression that he had secured a Victorian version.

A band of white was left at the base in earlier figures. When the familiar dull gold line through this band, commonly seen in untitled figures, has been replaced by a crude yellow, maroon or black line it may be taken as an indication of comparatively late origin.

As reproductions have been made over a long period, many show ageing in the form of chips, crazing, discoloration or other natural signs of usage.

Some reproductions are probably Victorian. One example of this is the figure of the actor Edward Sothern as 'Lord Dundreary' (fig. 41, pl. E-18), first produced in 1861. A contemporary version of this figure will be found decorated in the style of Thomas Parr (see p. 16); but later figures from the identical mould are coloured with the dark maroon seen in Boer War figures produced by William Kent. 'Lord Dundreary' is marked as a 'discontinued line' in *Kent List B* (see above). It seems likely that the figure was reproduced in 1890 when *Our American Cousin* was revived at the Novelty Theatre; that production was continued for a few more years, and then finally stopped, probably not later than 1920. Even the most recent of these figures is unlikely to be much less than fifty years old today.

The figure of the Empress Eugénie with the Prince Imperial (fig. 79, pl. C-34) can be dated to the latter's birth in 1856. Contemporary figures are *invariably* untitled. The pair to the figure is Napoleon III (fig. 78, pl. C-34), likewise never found titled. However, a 'late' example of the Eugénie figure is found titled 'Empress Eugenie' in black script and this figure is listed in all three of the Kent lists (see fig. 79(a), pl. C-36). As a 'late' example of the figure of Napoleon III (d. 1873) to pair with this figure is not listed, nor has one been found, and as the style of titling is similar to that found on figures of Princess Louise and the Marquess of Lorne (see pl. A-78) which can be dated to the 1870's, and as many of the figures seem to have some age, it seems possible, if not probable, that they were reproduced in 1879, a time of intense public sympathy for Empress Eugénie who was in exile in this country and for the Prince Imperial who was killed in the Zulu War.

Many figures of 'Wellington on Horse' ('Up guards and at them'; fig. 21, pl. B-3) are decorated in an identical manner to those coloured figures of the late Victorian war commanders, series II and probably were reproduced during the same period,

i.e. at some time between 1884 and 1902. 'Wellington on Horse' does, however, appear in *Kent List C* (1955). Only contemporary versions of the figure are found titled, but I have seen one which was not. Unsullied reproductions have *never* been found titled. It follows that a titled figure is likely to be either genuine or a reproduction which has been tampered with. Contemporary titling is always in transfer; up to now 'faked' titling has been crudely applied by hand, and easy to recognize.

Many modern reproductions have been artificially crazed, to give an impression of age, by immersion in hot fat or by some similar method. Because of this, crazing as a criterion of age, is the least important factor. We must remember first that the early figures are relatively rare and sometimes extremely rare and that modern reproductions are relatively common, although it is true that they are becoming less common. This applies, in particular, to Shakspearian characters. Figures of 'Falstaff' are still to be found in antique shops. They are usually crazed but only very rarely contemporary. No 'Falstaff', so far as I am aware, is contemporary if his long coat is green, and in particular, if iron-red – the hall-mark of reproductions – has been applied to the waistcoat. A period 'Falstaff' is usually 'white and gilt' or his long coat is of a delicate lilac hue. The knee-length frock of Macbeth is always an iron-red in the reproduction and usually a pale colour in the contemporary copy (see ch. 6, pl. 7). The Nelson toby jugs (fig. 34, pl. C-12) are only rarely found in contemporary state and then, as far as I know, never titled. Toby jugs titled 'Nelson' in black script date from a period towards the end of the nineteenth century to very recently. This also applies to figures titled 'Mr Pickwick' (fig. 81, pl. E-44), some of which appear to be old while others are clearly of recent manufacture. It may well be that the earliest examples of these date from the production of *Pickwick* at the Lyceum in 1871, or possibly from a later production at the Comedy in 1889.

G. Woolliscroft Rhead records in *British Pottery Marks* (1910) that nineteenth-century figures from Sampson Smith's works were being reissued in the twentieth century:

The figures have had a wide circulation in country districts both in England and abroad. . . . We have seen many 'Sampson Smiths' not six months old offered and bought as genuine 'Olde Staffordshire' figures. . . . I know of no way of identifying these reproductions today.

Mention has already been made of the discovery in 1948, in an old disused part of the Sampson Smith factory, of press-moulds used for the manufacture of Victorian portrait figures. The moulds were converted into suitable casting moulds, and a number of figures satisfactorily produced. The only portrait figures reproduced were Wellington on Horse, Moody, Burns and his Mary and Napoleon on Horse (see ch. 6, pl. 3); also, a toby jug of Mr Gladstone, seated holding an axe (fig. 50, pl. B-15). The base of each figure has a large hole, the figure having been made by the slip method, and the factory mark applied by transfer, for example:

Sampson Smith
est. 1846
Olde Staffordshire figures
from Original Moulds
No. 7. Burns & Mary
Made in England

These marks alone, render identification simple (see ch. 6, pl. 4), although no doubt in the future many will be erased for nefarious purposes. Many of these reproductions were released in the white glost state, others have been rather crudely coloured. The manufacture of these figures lasted for only a short time, and the moulds have now been disposed of. The figure of 'Napoleon on Horse' is of interest, as no contemporary copy has yet been found.

There is another figure, which must be considered, which is neither 'Kent' nor 'Sampson Smith'. It is of Grace Darling (fig. 40, pl. I-18). The contemporary figure is 6½ in. (16.5 cm.) in height and the reproduction 5½ in. (14 cm.). There are minor differences in the modelling. The reproduction has the impressed mark '18' on the bottom, no title and the base is painted in green. In general, it is a poor sort of figure and the collector

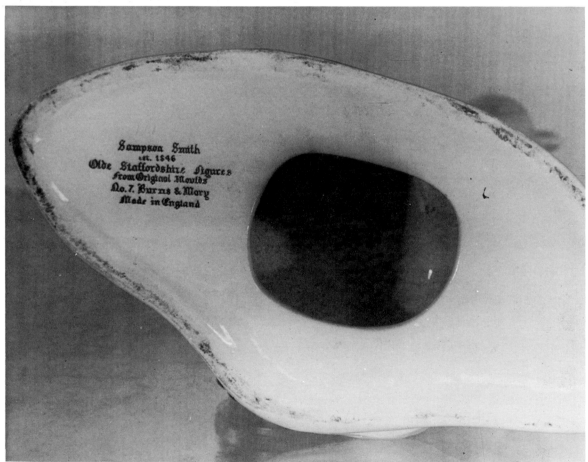

Plate 3 (Above)
Modern cast figures made from old press-moulds found in the Sampson Smith Factory in 1948. These represent the only portrait figures to have been reproduced from the old moulds.
L to R: *Fig.* 64 (Wellington) *pl.* C-25
Fig. 9 (Moody) *pl.* D-4
Fig. 47 (Burns and Mary) *pl.* H-12
Fig. 65 (Napoleon) *pl.* C-25
(No contemporary version of the latter figure has been reported.)

Plate 4 (Below)
Base of 'cast' reproduction of *fig.* 47 (Burns and Mary) *pl.* H-12.
In black transfer on the base is written:
> *Sampson Smith*
> *est. 1846*
> *Olde Staffordshire figures*
> *from Original Moulds*
> *No. 7. Burns & Mary*
> *Made in England*

should have no difficulty in recognizing it. If this figure began as a forgery it would be unlikely to have any mark, for by this it obviously differs from a contemporary copy, nevertheless either through malice or sheer ignorance it has, to my knowledge, been sold as the genuine article.

RESTORATIONS AND REPAIRS

The term *restoration* means that a missing part, such as a hand, has been restored; a *repair* means that a broken part has been fixed back and that nothing of the original figure is missing.

In recent years there have been vast improvements in the techniques of restoring and repairing both porcelain and earthenware, with the result that it is now often extremely difficult to detect the restorer's work. This means that many restored figures may be justifiably termed 'fakes', when, *as is not uncommon*, they are offered for sale by the unscrupulous dealer without mention of the defect, often with the intention to deceive. Commonly, when the figure is examined in an antique shop, not only is it very dirty, having been purposely left so by the dealer, but the lighting may leave a lot to be desired. A restoration is of particular gravity if it involves such a salient part of a figure as the head. It is not uncommon to see either the head of a totally different figure applied, or alternatively, for a new head to be made up. Either is a grievous example of dishonesty if the customer is not told, *see fig. 2 (King) pl.* G-4.

THE FOLLOWING TESTS MAY BE USED TO DETECT DAMAGE TO THE PIECE:

1. Pick it up and shake it. If there is a rattle such as may be caused by a loose piece of pottery inside, the collector may be quite certain that the chances weigh heavily that the piece is damaged. In fact, I would go so far as to say that I have never yet come across a piece that rattles that did not eventually turn out to be damaged, although on a number of occasions I have been unable to detect the damage at the time. The rattle is caused either by a small fragment of pottery which got in at the time of the original fracture, or by a piece of loose plaster or similar material used in the repair. The unscrupulous dealer may tell the collector, and I have heard this on several occasions, that the potters occasionally left coins inside the figures and that was the cause of the rattle. I have never yet found this to be so, nor is it likely when one considers that the figures originally cost only a few pence each.

2. If the figure is lightly tapped with the knuckles and emits the characteristic 'crackpot' sound, then it is assuredly cracked, even though the crack may not be obvious at first. Sometimes cracks have been sprayed with enamel. I am told that on occasions restorers have been successful in getting rid of the crackpot sound.

3. In picking up the figure, if surprised by the weight, that is to say if it feels heavier than one would expect for a figure of that particular size, then one should be on one's guard, for it may have been filled with plaster of Paris by the restorer, in order to bolster up his repairs. One must bear in mind, of course, that figures made by the Parr and Kent group of potters *always feel rather heavier* than one would expect.

4. If the fingers are passed over the figure, particularly at places which are suspect, for instance the neck or hands, it is very often possible to detect a different texture should there have been a restoration. Some experts place more reliance on their teeth (gently applied!) for this purpose. What might be described as 'a sticky feeling' is usually present to a greater or lesser extent and this seems to be so even in the best restorations.

5. If a knife is passed over the surface of the figure, it will glide until it reaches the restored surface, when it will tend to dig in.

6. The use of a magnifying glass is very often a great help, particularly in examinations around the neck or at the junction of hand and forearm. Here, minor restorations which are not visible to the unaided eye may become apparent, particularly if the restorer has not 'crazed' the area which he has painted over.

7. *Acetone* applied to a restored surface, even one which has been refired, will invariably take off both the glazing and the paint. This test is virtually infallible but it destroys the work of the restorer. If the restoration was satisfactory, it means incurring unnecessary expense in 'restoring' the restoration.

8. Some of the leading dealers, auction houses and even private collectors make use of *ultra-violet light radiation*. The ultra-violet lamp provides a swift and accurate method of examination and is a guide to condition, state of restoration and a means of assessing fakes and forgeries.

Fluorescence is the emission of visible light rays (generally coloured) by an object when placed under the invisible rays of an ultra-violet lamp. The colours seen vary from purple and indigo through yellow to blue and mauve. Many materials fluoresce; different materials fluoresce in different ways; while new material is distinguishable from old.

Restorations, fine cracks, insertions and retouching of glazes both in pottery and porcelain, not visible in ordinary light, show clearly and distinctly. In this field the use of the light does not require a great deal of specialized knowledge. Examination should be carried out in a darkened room, although complete darkness is not required. Restorations in paint and plaster glow brightly but *care should be taken that the object under examination is free of any traces of soap or detergents, which fluoresce bright yellow or blue*.

A portable light-weight hand lamp, in carrying case, is available. The light is cool, requires no time for 'warm up', and is safe for operator and object (*see ch. 6, pls. 5 and 6(a) and (b)*).

The advances in techniques of restoration and repair include 'spraying', so that the repaired parts blend with the original, and 'refiring'. This latter term, often used by dealers in praising the work of their restorers, is worthy of closer examination. Although most restorers are very secretive about their methods, it seems that for 'repairs' it is common practice to employ one of the modern synthetic adhesives whose adherent properties are increased by the application of heat. For 'restorations' plaster of Paris is often used, but again, it is becoming common practice to use a modern modelling material based on P.V.C. In its 'uncured' state it has the appearance of putty but after submission to heat, as in an electric cooking oven set at $325\,°F.\,(163\,°C.)$; it becomes practically indestructible and can be painted. The amount of heat employed in these manoeuvres is far less than that which was used in the original processes of manufacture, nor is it repeated. The term 'firing' therefore, is hardly appropriate to the case, and it seems only reasonable to suppose that as the methods involve rolling several steps into one that the permanence of the colours must be suspect. Nowadays too, the figures are liable to be submitted to the hazards of central heating. The best that can be said of the most skilful restoration today, is that the colour is less likely to alter, and the broken parts far less likely to separate when the figure is exposed to heat or damp, than hitherto.

A number of collectors are reticent about allowing their figures to be repaired or restored by methods involving so-called 'firing'. They take the view that the repaired part should be fixed in place by one of the modern adhesives and simply painted and glazed. When the colour changes, as it usually will over the course of years, the glaze and paint can be removed quite easily and then renewed. It is claimed that if the repair has been 'fired', that a future repair or restoration may be prejudiced. I am uncertain whether or not this is correct, but to date, I have not come across a piece which has been allegedly 'refired', that could not be adequately cleaned by one or other of the available methods, so permitting further repair or restoration.

Restorations tend to discolour much more easily than repairs, and for this reason they have a far more serious effect on the value of a piece (*see chapter seven*).

Gilding always seems to be a weak point in restoration. It tends to be harsh and granular compared with the warm and mellow contemporary 'mercuric gold' which after firing was burnished, usually with agate stone – an art too time-consuming and expensive for these days.

Occasionally, pieces are found which have been wrongly restored from photographs or from ignorance. A good example of this is that of the figures 'Popery' and 'Protestantism' (*see*

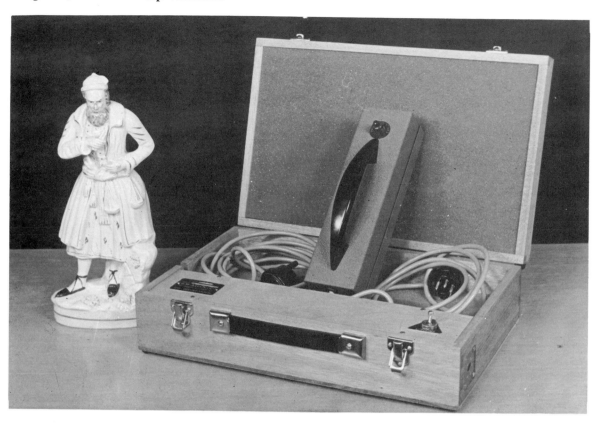

Plate 5 (Above)
R: Portable ultra-violet hand lamp with carrying case
containing control gear and cables. The lamp is of particular
value in detecting restorations, fine cracks and retouching of
glazes and is claimed to be safe for both operator and object.
L: *Fig.* 30 (Shylock) *pl.* E-13. Restoration to the figure is
barely visible to the naked eye, but see plates 6(a) and (b).

Plates 6(a) and (b) (Below)
Fig. 30 (Shylock) *pl.* E-13. The same figure illustrated on
the preceding plate is now illuminated by ultra-violet
light. Restorations in paint and plaster, both to nose and
waist (it has at one time been in half), fluoresce brightly.

Plate 7
Shakespearian figures of the Parr and Kent group.
T: Reproductions.
B: Contemporary versions.
L to R: *Fig.* 8 (Macready as 'Macbeth') *pl.* E-2
Fig. 3 (Hackett as 'Falstaff') *pl.* E-1B
Fig. 7 (Isabella Glyn as 'Lady Macbeth') *pl.* E-2

Production of 'Olde Staffordshire Ware' by William
Kent (Porcelains) Ltd., ceased on December 31st, 1962.
The collector should have no difficulty in
distinguishing a contemporary copy from a reproduction. Note, in particular, the difference in the
manner of titling. The crude iron-red seen in
Falstaff's waistcoat and Macbeth's knee-length frock
is never seen in early pieces.

Plate 8
L to R: *Fig.* 21 (Wellington) *pl.* B-3
Contemporary version
Fig. 21 (Wellington) *pl.* B-3
Reproduction
This figure is referred to as 'Wellington on
Horse' in the Kent lists. It still appears in *Kent
List C* (1955). As reproductions have been made
over a long period, many show ageing and are
difficult to date. The 'reproduction' illustrated
here might well have been manufactured at the
'turn of the century'.

pl. D-2). The priest portrayed in the figure inscribed 'Popery'
should be carrying a *chained bible* in his right hand, and the
young woman in the figure titled 'Protestantism' should be
carrying an *open book* inscribed 'Holy Bible' in her left hand. Both
hands are apparently very susceptible to damage. At all events,
I have come across many examples in which the priest is carrying a scroll in his right hand and the young woman a scroll in
her left. Apparently they have been restored by someone basing
his information on the photograph of these figures (*both incorrectly restored*) in the late Mr Balston's book.

Occasionally figures are found, pairs of figures in particular,
which were originally white and gilt and which have subsequently been painted over. The fact that they have been over-
painted is usually obvious because of the choice of colours; this
may not, of course, be so apparent to the inexperienced. The
reason for overpainting white and gilt figures is usually that one
or both of them have been damaged, and this fact must always
be borne in mind. A few years ago I purchased a pair of figures
of Lord Dundonald and Major Macdonald. Both these figures
had been heavily overpainted, and I realized that one at least
was damaged. When, however, the paint was cleaned off, the
damage was confined to a break through the neck of one figure,
the other figure being absolutely perfect. Again, a relatively
rare figure of General Brown came up at a sale at one of the
leading auction rooms, and being over-painted was thought by
the trade to have been damaged and restored. It was neglected
and went very cheaply, but when the paint was cleaned off it
was found to be absolutely perfect. The probable explanation
was that initially its pair had been damaged. Both were painted
at the same time to 'match up', and later the pair was broken
again and this time disposed of.

7
Prices

Introduction – Factors that determine value – How the figures come on to the market – Auction prices.

INTRODUCTION

Many collectors have asked me to include a chapter on prices in this volume; it is perhaps the most difficult task I have to undertake. The reason is that the market is in such a state of uncertainty and flux at the moment, that it is not often possible to give a definite value to any particular figure. Moreover, there is a real risk that I will be accused of encouraging the speculator at the expense of the true collector. Such an argument is, however, superfluous, for if the former does not obtain his information here, he will obtain it elsewhere.

Before World War II, collectors of these figures were few and far between. The figures themselves were generally scorned and could be obtained for a matter of shillings in most antique shops. Nevertheless, one or two discerning people were quietly building up collections. In the immediate post-war era much the same position prevailed. In 1951, the late Mr Thomas Balston published a beautifully illustrated article in the *Country Life Annual* titled *Victorian Staffordshire Portraits*. Furthermore, in 1953, Mr Bryan Latham published his *Victorian Staffordshire Portrait Figures*, the first work devoted entirely to the subject. The writings of these pioneers provoked immediate interest, and prices began to rise as collectors multiplied. In 1958, Balston published his *Staffordshire Portrait Figures of the Victorian Age*. This classic volume included a catalogue of nearly 500 figures and led to a tremendous upsurge of interest. The whole country began to be scoured by an increasing number of collectors and dealers, and more and more figures hitherto unknown came to light. Prices once more rose steeply. In 1962, the first big collection, that of Mr Theodore Smythe, was put on the market, being sold by Mr and Mrs R. Bonnett at a special exhibition. Although the prices realized at this exhibition were considered to be good, it was not until Mr Bryan Latham's collection was sold at auction by Christie's on October 14th, 1963, that collectors and dealers had any real idea of the value of the wares they were handling. In 1963 too, Balston published a *Supplement* to his catalogue containing 108 new entries.

Important sales have been held in all the leading London auction houses since 1963. The general picture seems to be one of a steady increase in prices, particularly of the rarer and finer items. Most figures are now realizing at least twice what they might have fetched in 1963, and in the case of the more sought after pieces, up to twenty times as much. Details are given later in the chapter.

FACTORS THAT DETERMINE VALUE

It will be as well at this stage to discuss the factors which determine the value of a figure. They are:

1. *Rarity*. One of the most mystifying things that the collector discovers about Staffordshire portrait figures is that there are many of which only one or very few are known. I know of no adequate explanation for this phenomenon. It is certainly unconnected with the age of a figure, for there are, I believe, more figures of which less than five are recorded in the later periods, than there are in the earlier periods. At least a dozen Boer War figures are of extreme rarity. Several explanations have been offered for this. One is that the later figures are of such poor quality that they have been thrown away. I do not agree with this, because although some Boer War figures are ghastly, there are others that are attractive and of great interest. It is the latter that tend to be scarce. Another explanation is that many figures have yet to be released to the market, remaining in the possession of the immediate descendants of the persons who originally purchased them. This may well be so, but does not provide an explanation for the scarcity of certain earlier figures, such as those of Colonel Pestal and George Hudson (*figs.* 28 and 29, *pls.* G-11 and 12), of which only one of each is known; nor does it explain why although the figures of Stanfield Hall and Potash Farm are relatively common, only one example is known of their companion figure Norwich Castle (*see pl.* G-20). How well known the person portrayed was to the general public does not seem to be a factor either. Thus, only two examples are known of the 24 in. (61 cm.) figure titled 'Napoleon Buonaparte' (*fig.* 61, *pl.* C-23), the tallest recorded Staffordshire figure of the Victorian period. It seems quite extraordinary, too, that although the potters made figures of Leopold, King of the Belgians and his consort, Louise-Marie, only three figures of the former have come to light, and but one of the latter, which incidentally, is in Brussels (*figs.* 248 and 249, *pl.* A-87). There is only one example known of the figure titled 'Duke/Cambridge' and of its pair titled 'Prince/Napoleon' (*figs.* 159 and 160, *pls.* C-60 and 61). Finally, because of the known existence of figures which lack pairs, it can be confidently predicted that at least fifty figures are still to come to light.

2. *Desirability*. It seems to be a fact that there are certain figures that collectors 'go for' and others in which they have less interest. This has nothing to do with rarity, colouring or any of the other features which I will discuss later, but is simply concerned with the figure's inherent interest. The classic example is that of figures of Florence Nightingale. Those versions illustrated on *pl.* C-55 are not rare, although they appear to be so. It seems that they are difficult to obtain simply because they have a wide appeal and because people like them and keep them. For this reason they do not come on to the market very often, and when they do so, they fetch large sums. This applies also to the 'Boxers' (*fig.* 15, *pl.* F-7), to Captain Cook (*fig.* 4, *pl.* C-5) and to many other figures, including that of Wellington titled 'Up guards and at them' (*fig.* 21, *pl.* B-3). None of the figures mentioned can, under any stretch of imagination, be regarded as very rare; however, all are difficult to come by because they are 'desirable'.

3. *Modelling*. The first figures taken from moulds are generally the sharpest and cleanest. If the potter intended to colour the figures, he usually chose only the best available examples. There is all the difference in the world between a sharp, well-modelled figure and one 'late out of the mould'. If a figure is unique it must be taken as it comes, but if a figure is relatively common then only the finest example should be chosen. Obviously, the finer figures are those that command the higher prices.

4. *Colour*. In general, there is a preference among collectors for the highly-coloured figures, particularly those with underglaze blue. The majority of these date to before 1863 (*see chapter four*). If a figure is found either highly coloured, or in white and gilt, then the coloured example will usually command a higher price. Nevertheless, there are a number of collectors who specialize in white and gilt figures. Although it is

true that bright colours in a well-lit cabinet catch the eye; it is also true that the white and gilt figures have an attraction of their own.

5. *Size.* If figures were manufactured in more than one size, the larger size is usually the better, and hence the more likely to command the higher price. However, some collectors exclude really large figures, such as the monumental figures of Sampson Smith, from their collection, simply because they take up too much space.

6. *Design.* Figures of the earlier period are usually of better design than 'late' ones. The heyday of design was about the time of the Crimea. After 1880, the art was dying, and although there were pieces issued at the time of the Boer War which, in my opinion, are well worth collecting, the standard generally, was considerably lower than in the preceding period.

7. *Restoration and Repairs.* This has been dealt with in some detail in chapter six. The point to remember is that if a figure is rare, then a repair does not seem to materially affect the value; a minor restoration, for instance a new hand, would have rather more, although still not a great affect; a major restoration, such as a new head, a profound affect. Common figures which have been repaired or restored should be avoided. There are still some dealers, although they are becoming increasingly uncommon, who make substantial reductions for a damaged figure.

8. *Whether Titled.* Some figures are found either 'titled' or 'untitled'. In this case, the 'titled' figure is always worth substantially more than the 'untitled' one. If a figure is never found 'titled', then of course this factor does not arise, except that there are some collectors who only collect 'titled' figures. If the person portrayed by an 'untitled' figure be identified from a painting or engraving (*see chapter three*), then the value of the figure may be materially increased.

9. *The Type of Collection.* The value of 'theatre figures', when positively identified, seems to be out of all proportion to the value of all other figures. The only explanation I can offer for this phenomenon is that collectors of this type of figure have more money in their pockets than others! Needless to say, this is hotly denied.

HOW THE FIGURES COME ON TO THE MARKET

It seems that the price a collector has to pay for a figure is often determined by the stage at which it is intercepted on its journey from the home of the initial vendor. Thus at one extreme it may be purchased direct from the house, or at a small country auction or village antique shop and at the other, only after it has passed through many persons' hands, each of whom has had his cut. It is still possible, although unusual, for interception to take place at a relatively early stage and for a rare figure to be obtained for a comparatively small sum. Collecting Staffordshire figures is really a question of 'swings and round-abouts'.

Figures come on to the market in a number of different ways. There are, for instance, professional gentlemen, known in the trade as 'knockers', who visit houses in search of bargains. Needless to say, these 'visitors' usually offer the unsuspecting owner a price considerably less than the market value. It has been said that the most unscrupulous of them are not adverse to 'accidentally' knocking the head off a desirable figure, thereby rendering it apparently worthless and thus facilitating the sale. Whether these gentlemen are called 'knockers' because of this trait, or because they knock on the front door, is something I have not yet been able to determine. This phenomenon has been offered as a reason for so many figures being defective, but the more plausible explanation is that these fragile items have been 'at risk' from the very day they were made. It is only in recent times that they have been given accommodation in cabinets; for over 100 years they have added colour and charm to mantelpieces, open shelves and other exposed places. Most of today's survivors are likely to have spent a large proportion of their lives, unappreciated in cupboards or attics. A 'knocker' may take his prize either to a local antique shop or he may go direct to one of the London dealers.

A 'runner' is a gentleman who makes a livelihood by travelling round the country visiting antique shops. It is a hard life and he drives many thousands of miles during the course of the year. The professional runner will go through a cycle of trips. The local dealers will know when to expect him and will put particular pieces bought privately, or at auction, on one side. Dealers, not unreasonably, tend to do this because they know that they will be able to dispose of all their pieces in this way and not just the best pieces. Thus, a large proportion of pieces sold in the country never appear in the local shop windows at all but go straight to London.

There is also much dealing between dealers. A piece may pass through as many as half a dozen hands before being purchased by a private buyer. In 1965, I saw a pair of figures of William and Mary in Yorkshire which were, I thought *at the time*, overpriced at £12. The identical pair reached London ten weeks later and were eventually sold for £46 to a private buyer. Subsequently, I came across no less than four different dealers through whose hands these same figures had passed on their way to London.

Many collectors are not adverse to purchasing a piece which they know is rare even though they may already have it, either to sell to a London dealer or to swop with another collector. All these factors have tended to make it more and more difficult for other collectors to find anything worthwhile in country shops and have driven up prices throughout the land.

The fall in the purchasing power of the pound and recent tax laws, particularly those appertaining to death-duties and capital gains, have stimulated interest in those persons who otherwise might not have been expected to give a second thought to these hitherto despised objects. This unfortunate development has also tended to force prices up.

The scarcity of figures has led to new collectors being less discerning than old ones. Because of this the prices of inferior figures have also tended to rise. This applies not only to poorly moulded, damaged or otherwise defective contemporary figures but also to reproductions.

Although there are some unscrupulous dealers, the majority of dealers tend to pass on the benefit to their regular customers when selling pieces procured favourably. When buying directly from a dealer, the collector obviously has to depend very much on his integrity. There is all the difference in the world between a dealer who fixes a price realistic in terms of what can be acquired elsewhere, whilst at the same time making proper allowance for his own expertise or the advice he has acquired, and the dealer to whom profit is everything and whose extravagant claims will not stand the test of impartial examination.

Price tickets may be marked in code:

1	H	M	A
2	A	A	B
3	N	G	S
4	D	I	A
5	I	C	N
6	W	F	T
7	O	L	I
8	R	U	Q
9	K	T	U
0	S	E	E

Codes are based on ten-letter words. Examples given here are *Handiworks, Magic Flute* and *ABS–Antique* (the dealer's initials prefix the word 'antique'– in this example his name was A. B. Smith). There are obviously infinite variations. Some dealers use the convention of substituting 'Z' for the last letter of the code word, in order to make the breaking of the code even more difficult.

Thus, using the code-word 'handiworks', a ticket marked N/HS/- would mean that the piece had cost the dealer £3 10s.; alternatively, it might be marked OS/-, i.e. 70s. If the dealer has been known for some time and has periodically disclosed what he gave for the object, or this is known from attending the same auction, it is sometimes possible to break down the code. When the letter 'T' is found followed by a number, the latter signifies either the discount the dealer may expect, or the trade price.

Most dealers will take a pound or two off the marked price for the regular customer, but experience goes to show that in the Staffordshire field it does not pay to haggle. Such is the present-day market that those who argue over the price of rare pieces are just not offered them, or alternatively, a higher starting price will be set against the intended selling price.

AUCTION PRICES*

The most remarkable feature of the early auctions, was the enormous prices realized for quite common figures which could be obtained from London dealers at the same time for much less. Many figures similar to those that commanded such high prices had been on the dealers' shelves, to my knowledge, for some time. Figures were bought at auction at apparently inflated prices, not only by private buyers who might have been ignorant of the whereabouts of similar figures, but also by other dealers. No one has been able to offer a satisfactory explanation for this, but in the later auctions it has become apparent that purchasers are now more discriminating. The present position seems to be that the value of rare figures continues to increase dramatically, and that of indifferent figures modestly. The currency devaluation of 1967 brought a significant increase in prices and doubtless prices will continue to rise.

The prices obtained in major sales of Staffordshire portrait figures to date* are as follows:

*See also 'Postscript' overleaf and the Appendix: 'Selected Auction Prices, 1978-86'.

	Number of lots	Number of pieces	Price obtained	Average per piece
Latham collection sold at Christie's, October 1963	100	253	£3,107	£12.5.0
Joyce collection (part I) sold at Christie's, October 1964	107	233	£2,340	£10.0.0
The property of a Gentleman sold at Bonham's, March 1965	25	72	£590	£8.3.0
Thornton collection sold at Christie's, November 1965	93	219	£3,735	£17.1.0
Gilbert collection sold at Sotheby's, April 1966	31	75	£684	£9.2.4
Livock collection sold at Christie's, April 1966	49	87	£1,330	£15.5.0
Joyce collection (part II) sold at Christie's, October 1966	84	160	£2,187	£14.5.10
Howe collection and other properties sold at Christie's, December 1966	17	26	£489	£18.16.4
Fairhurst collection (part I) and other properties sold at Christie's, February 1967	114	324	£3,187	£9.16.8
Various properties sold at Sotheby's, February 1967	10	32	£349	£10.18.1
Fairhurst collection (part II) and other properties sold at Christie's, April 1967	83	261	£1,860	£7.2.1
Various properties sold at Sotheby's, December 1967	7	16	£308	£19.5.1
The property of Miss Jean Anderson sold at Christie's, February 1968	9	19	£190	£10.0.0
Jackson collection and other properties sold at Christie's, October 1968	42	82	£974	£11.17.7
Joyce collection (part III) and other properties sold at Christie's, January 1969	162	275	£6,791	£24.13.10
Various properties sold at Sotheby's, April 1969	11	15	£1,163	£77.10.8
Various properties sold at Christie's, June 1969	39	55	£2,312	£42.0.9

[To obtain a realistic estimate, lots not containing portrait figures or allied subjects have been omitted from the calculations.]

Some sales contained a higher percentage of fine figures than others, but of all the pieces quoted above, not more than 5 per cent were rare or very rare; at least 70 per cent had some damage or were poorly modelled, and not more than 30 per cent were sharp, well-coloured, fine examples of the output of the era. A surprising number of Kent reproductions crept in, and the prices realized by them were even more astonishing.

At the present time, although there has been some improvement since the *Trade Descriptions Act* became law, little reliance can be placed on descriptions of Staffordshire figures in auction catalogues. Auctioneers in their conditions of sale disclaim any responsibility for descriptions in their catalogues, but having covered themselves with a disclaimer they then seem quite prepared to describe the figures on hearsay evidence alone. Collectors must beware of this facility in christening every figure as someone or something, regardless of the evidence. Moreover, a habit has grown up of embellishing the descriptions of figures with fantasies. Two examples follow, and many others could be quoted:

A RARE FIGURE OF GARIBALDI, of the same model as the last but with the left leg amputated above the knee, his shirt in pink, with a blue coat under his arm, no title, 18½ in.

* This version is unrecorded by Balston but clearly commemorates the loss of his leg at the Battle of Aspromonte in 1862.

Comment: The left leg of the 'large' Garibaldi (*fig.* 280, section C., see *pl.* H-2), is made from a subsidiary mould. In the example quoted the potter had omitted to apply the leg, and the site at which it should have been stuck on had been glazed over. This type of 'potter's error' is not uncommon, and is one of which the auctioneer should, in my opinion, have been aware. Moreover, I cannot find that Garibaldi ever lost a leg at Aspromonte or anywhere else! No comment was made by the auctioneer at the time of the sale and the bidders showed their disbelief by going no further than £15, whereas the two-legged, 'less interesting' Garibaldi reached £16!

A RARE FIGURE OF PRINCE ALFRED, standing in a yellow hat and sailor suit, his name impressed in capitals–11 in. (28 cm.) high.

Unrecorded in these rooms or by Balston.

Comment: The following lot had appeared two months before in the same auction room:

. . . a figure of the Prince of Wales, standing, wearing a yellow straw hat and grey sailor suit after the painting by Winterhalter . . .

The figure titled 'Prince Alfred' (*fig.* 185, *pl.* A-59) was a late, poorly modelled, wrongly titled example of *fig.* 182 (Prince of Wales) *pl.* A-58. As the latter figure had been through their hands only two months previously, albeit unheralded in their catalogue by capital letters, the auctioneers had, in my view, a moral responsibility to point out to prospective buyers that the lot was not a figure of Prince Alfred (*portraits of whom are rare and much sought after*), but of the Prince of Wales, as proven by the Winterhalter portrait.

If current prices are maintained 'mixed' collections of the type that have already been tested at auction may be expected to realize well over twenty guineas per figure. The highest price obtained in the Latham sale was 115 guineas for the pair of figures of William Smith O'Brien MP and his wife, the latter had a restored hand. The highest price in the first Joyce sale was 52 guineas for a set of three figures of Lord Edward Fitz-Gerald, Theobald Wolfe Tone and Henry Joy McCracken. In the Thornton sale 105 guineas were obtained for the figures of Omar Pasha and Lord Raglan (*figs.* 130 and 132, *pl.* C-53). The 'Grapplers' (*fig.* 17, *pl.* F-7) fetched 140 guineas at Christie's in February 1967, £320 at Sotheby's in April 1969 and 350 guineas at Christie's in June 1969; and a pair of 'large cricketers' (*figs.* 13 and 14, *pl.* F-7) £200 at Puttick and Simpson in May 1968 and the same again at Sotheby's in April 1969.

Because each lot is usually made up of two or more pieces, it is still difficult to give a definite value to any one piece. Moreover, the majority of the rarest and finest pieces have yet to be tested at auction, but prices reached at the two sales held at Christie's in January and June 1969, give some indication of the present trend.

Grapplers (*fig.* 17, *pl.* F-7)	350 gns.
Othelo and Iago (*fig.* 31, *pl.* E-13)	190 gns.
Cranmer (*fig.* 2, *pl.* D-1)	180 gns.
Rarey (*fig.* 149, *pl.* E-77)	170 gns.
Palmer (*fig.* 42, *pl.* G-18A)	160 gns.
Lyons (*fig.* 101(a), *pl.* C-42A)	150 gns.
Lillywhite (*fig.* 1, *pl.* F-1)	140 gns.
Ridley and Latimer (*fig.* 1, *pl.* D-1)	130 gns.
Bloomers (*fig.* 125, *pl.* E-66)	100 gns.
Nelly Chapman (*fig.* 150, *pl.* E-78)	100 gns.

It is interesting to reflect that the highest price so far reached for a Victorian 'portrait', 350 guineas for the 'Grapplers', was for a relatively common figure which is not, strictly speaking, a portrait figure at all!

In my catalogue I have grouped pieces as either very rare (VR), rare (R), average (Av) or common (C). 'Very rare' figures are those of which I have seen or heard of only three or under. 'Rare' figures are those of which I have seen or heard of ten or under. Where appropriate, I have also indicated those figures which I believe to be generally considered desirable (D), attractive (A), or both. As already indicated, the scarcity, desirability and attractiveness of a figure have to be taken account of as well as whether it is well modelled and whether or not it has been damaged, when assessing its value.

POSTSCRIPT

The price rises which were so apparent in the 1960s have continued through the 1970s and all indications point to the trend continuing into the 80s.

The last ten years have brought many new collectors into the market and the resulting spiral of more people chasing after fewer items has led to a noticeable increase in the price of damaged and repaired figures. Certainly in 1980 one could conclude that the difference in price between a perfect item and a damaged one was considerably less than it was in 1960.

However, it is for the rarer figures, particularly those in fine condition, that the increase in prices over the last twenty years becomes particularly apparent. This was shown when a good figure of Colonel George de Lacy Evans fetched £680 in 1979

against a previously recorded value of 72 guineas in 1963, when it was sold with a figure of Pelissier.

The real strength of the market is indicated when a fine collection comes on the market. The recent two-part dispersal of the Kimpton collection at Christie's South Kensington seemed to draw collectors as well as dealers from throughout the United Kingdom and further afield, and the resulting prices were substantially above the auctioneer's estimates.

The Kimpton is one of two collections which have been offered since the end of 1979, the other being a section of the Owen collection, which contained many general Staffordshire as well as Portrait Figures:

	Number of lots	Number of pieces	Price Obtained	Average per piece
Kimpton collection sold at Christie's South Kensington, October and November 1979	401	453	£42,167	£93.08
Owen collection sold at Phillips Knowle, October 1980	291	331	£15,299	£46.22

P.B., 1981

The Appendix on p.547 shows examples of prices for figures between 1978 and 1980 and comparative figures for 1985-86.

A.C.C., 1987.

8

Catalogue of Figures

Introduction

The System of Cataloguing Used in this Book

Figures have been grouped, as far as is feasible, into *nine sections:*

> A—British and Foreign Royalty
> B—Statesmen and Politicians
> C—Naval, Military and Exploration
> D—Religious
> E—Theatre, Opera, Ballet and Circus
> F—Sport
> G—Crime
> H—Authors, Poets, Composers et cetera
> I—Miscellaneous

Plates in each of the preceding chapters are numbered from one upwards; in this chapter they are numbered from one upwards in each section. All figures shown in colour are also shown in the black and white plates. The colour plates are numbered separately but reference is given to the page on which a description of the figure may be found and the catalogue number given.

Plates located in this chapter are referred to throughout the volume in accordance with the section; plates found elsewhere are referred to in accordance with the chapter. *Examples:*

The fourth plate in chapter three is referred to as: *ch.* 3, *pl.* 4.

The sixty-second plate, in chapter eight, section A, is referred to as: *pl.* A-62.

Figures are numbered from one upwards in each section of the catalogue. *Example:*

A figure of Prince Albert is number eighteen, on plate eleven, in section A. It is referred to in full as:

Fig. 18 (Albert) *pl.* A-11; or, in certain circumstances, as *fig.* 18, *pl.* A-11, or *fig.* 18 (Albert).

Each section is divided into *two parts:*

1. *Short biographies of those persons portrayed.* The length of a biography will be found to bear no relation to the fame of the person. Details of the illustrious are easy to obtain from any of the standard reference books; therefore, more space is devoted to lesser known persons. Short historical notes are also given of plays, buildings, etc., where indicated. The number of the appropriate plate(s) is given at the end of each biography or historical note.
2. *Photographs and details of the figures.* A photograph is included of virtually every figure catalogued, with the exception of those for which provision has been made because of the known

existence of figures which must have pairs. Included here is all the authentic information about each figure, which it is felt may be of interest to the collector. Abbreviations include:

VR. (very rare): Three or under known to the author,
R. (rare): Ten or under known to the author,
Av. (average): Fifteen or under known to the author,
C. (common): Over fifteen known to the author,
D. (desirable): See *ch.* 7,
A. (attractive): See *ch.* 7.

Prices realized at auction* are noted where possible but it must be remembered that no sale-room distinguishes in its price-records between objects sold and objects withdrawn. A figure marked at £100 may not have attracted a serious bid at all. £100 may have been the reserve price that was never reached. Catalogue descriptions very rarely convey an adequate notion of quality. As quality and the presence or absence of repairs or restorations play so large a part in determining the market value, auction price-records are not a great help, for few catalogues indicate the presence of repairs and even when they do the extent is not recorded.

Victorian Staffordshire portrait figures may be viewed at:

City Museum and Art Gallery, Stoke-on-Trent.
The Gordon Pugh Collection

Stapleford Park, Melton Mowbray.
The Thomas Balston Collection

The Fitzwilliam Museum, Cambridge.
The Glaisher Collection (part of)

The Brighton Art Gallery and Museum.
The Willett Collection (part of)

The Laing Art Gallery, Newcastle upon Tyne.
The Lady Wise Collection

In most cases it is advisable to enquire before visiting.

*These prices are those given in the 1970 first edition. Some examples of recent prices are given in the Appendix.

Section A
British and Foreign Royalty
Biographies and Historical Notes

ADELAIDE, Queen of William IV (1792–1849). Daughter of George, duke of Saxe-Coburg Meiningen. In 1818 she married William, duke of Clarence who succeeded to the throne in 1830.
See **pl. A-**108.

ALBERT EDWARD, Prince of Wales (1841–1910). *See* **Edward VII.**

ALBERT FRANCIS CHARLES AUGUSTUS EMMANUEL, Prince-Consort of England (1819–61). Second son of Ernest, duke of Saxe-Coburg-Gotha. Became betrothed to Queen Victoria in 1839, the marriage taking place in 1840. Assisted the Queen in the performance of her political duties and offered advice to her ministers. Proposed and encouraged the idea of the Great Exhibition in 1851. Gave valuable advice throughout the Crimean campaign. It was his conciliatory attitude which averted war with the United States at the time of the Trent affair. He died of typhoid fever in 1861.
See **pls. A-**4, 5, 6, 7, 8, 11, 12, 13, 14, 15, 16, 17, 18, 19, 20, 22, 23, 24, 27, 28, 30, 31, 32, 33, 35, 35A, 36, 37, 38, 39, 40, 40A, 41, 44, 55, 56, 57,
pls. C-31, 35, 77, 78, 79.

ALBERT VICTOR CHRISTIAN EDWARD, Duke of Clarence (1864–92). Eldest son of the Prince of Wales, later Edward VII. Joined training ship *Britannia* at Portsmouth 1877. Betrothed to Princess Mary of Teck in 1891 but died before the wedding.
See **pl. A-**82.

ALEXANDER II, Tsar of Russia (1818–81).
For biography see **section C.**
See **pls. A-**90, 91,
pl. C-114.

ALEXANDRA of Denmark, Queen-Consort of Edward VII (1844–1925). Eldest daughter of Prince Christian, later King Christian IX of Denmark. Married Albert Edward, prince of Wales in 1863. Both as Princess of Wales and Queen, notable for her charities.
See **pls. A-**65, 66, 68, 72, 73, 74, 76, 84, 85.

ALFRED ERNEST ALBERT, Duke of Edinburgh (1844–1900). Second son of Queen Victoria. Educated for the Royal Navy and served in the Channel, North America, West Indies and Mediterranean stations. Created Duke of Edinburgh in 1866. In 1874 he married Grand-duchess Marie Alexandrovna, only daughter of Alexandra II, tsar of Russia. Rear-admiral 1878, admiral 1887, commander-in-chief at

Devonport 1890–3, admiral of the fleet 1893. Succeeded his father's brother as reigning Duke of Saxe-Coburg and Gotha in 1893, relinquishing his privileges as an English peer. Died at Rosenau, near Coburg in 1900.
See **pls. A-**58, 59, 61, 62, 79, 80.

ALICE MAUD MARY, Grand-duchess of Hesse (1843–78). Second daughter of Queen Victoria. In 1862 she married Prince Louis of Hesse who succeeded his uncle as grand-duke in 1877.
See **pls. A-**69, 70.

ANNE BOLEYN, second Queen of Henry VIII (1507–36).
See **section E.**

ARTHUR WILLIAM PATRICK ALBERT, Duke of Connaught (1850–1942).
See **section C.**

AUGUSTA, Queen of Prussia (1811–90).
See **section C.**

BALMORAL CASTLE. Balmoral House was leased by Queen Victoria in 1848 and purchased in 1852. At that time work was commenced on the castle which was completed in 1854. Here a part of every spring and autumn was spent during the remainder of the Queen's life. Telegraph communication was established between London and Balmoral in the 1860's.
See **pl. A-**41A.

BROWN, JOHN (1826–83). Born at Craithenaird, Balmoral, he was for many years the personal attendant of Queen Victoria. He died at Windsor Castle in 1883.
The following extract from the *Court Circular* is of interest:

Mr. John Brown who for many years has been the Queen's personal attendant, died somewhat suddenly at Windsor Castle on Tuesday night. Mr. Brown had taken a cold on Sunday week, and since Friday had remained in his apartment in the Castle. Erysipelas, which affected his head, set in on Monday. Sir William Jenner, Physician to the Queen, was in attendance, but his skill was unavailing. The patient became much worse on Tuesday, and was unable to recognize any of those around him. His two brothers were with him when he died, as was also Sir William Jenner.
The melancholy event has caused the deepest regret to the Queen, and all the members of the Royal Household. To Her Majesty the loss is irreparable and the death of this truly faithful and devoted servant has been a grievous shock to the Queen. In 1849 Mr. Brown entered the Queen's service as one of the Balmoral gillies, and by his careful attention, steadiness, and intelligence, he rose in 1858 to the position of the Queen's personal attendant in Scotland, which in 1864 was extended to that of constant personal attendance upon Her Majesty on all occasions. During the last eighteen and a half years he served Her Majesty constantly, and never once absented himself from duty for a single day. He has

accompanied the Queen in her daily walks and drives, and all her journeys and expeditions, as well as personally waiting on her at banquets, etc. An honest, faithful, and devoted follower, a trustworthy, discreet, and straightforward man, and possessed of strong sense, he filled a position of great and onerous responsibility, the duties of which he performed with such constant and unceasing care as to secure for himself the real friendship of the Queen.
Mr. Brown was a native of Aberdeenshire, having been born at Craithie in 1826. His father was a farmer at Bush on the estate of Colonel Farquharson, of Invercauld. There was a large family of sons and daughters, some of whom went abroad to seek their fortunes, but John remained at home helping his father, and afterwards entered the Royal service, with which he has been connected for over thirty years. A few years ago, in token of her appreciation of his long and valuable service, Her Majesty conferred on him the title of Esquire. Mr. Brown has endeared himself to all in his native parish and elsewhere in Scotland. His brother, Mr. Archibald Brown, is a gentleman usher to the Queen, and was former personal attendant to His Royal Highness the Duke of Albany.
See **pls. A-**48, 48B.

CAMBRIDGE, second Duke of (1819–1904).
See **section C.**

CAMPBELL, JOHN DOUGLAS SUTHERLAND, ninth Duke of Argyll (1845–1914). As Marquess of Lorne married Princess Louise, fourth daughter of Queen Victoria, in 1871. Governor-general of Canada 1878–83.
See **pls. A-**74, 77, 78.

CHARLES I, King of Great Britain and Ireland (1600–49). Second son of James VI of Scotland. Succeeded to the throne in 1625 and in the same year married Princess Henrietta Maria of France. Became involved by his policies in quarrels with his parliaments. Governed without a parliament from 1629–40 when he summoned two; the Short Parliament which lasted for three weeks and the Long, which outlasted him. In 1642 civil war broke out. At the battle of Naseby in 1645 he was utterly annihilated. He surrendered to the Scots at Newark in May, 1646 and was handed over by them to parliament in January, 1647. Brought to trial, condemned and eventually executed on January 30th, 1649.
See **pls. A-**95, 96, 97, 109, 110.

CHARLES EDWARD, the 'Young Pretender' (1720–88).
See **Stewart, Charles Edward.**

CHRISTIAN OF SCHLESWIG-HOLSTEIN, Prince (1831–1917). Married Princess Helena, third daughter of Queen Victoria, in 1866.
See **pl. A-**75.

Section A. British and Foreign Royalty

CLARENCE, Duke of (1864–92).
See **Albert Victor.**

CONNAUGHT, Duke of (1850–1942).
See **section C.**

CROMWELL, OLIVER, the Protector
(1599–1658). Educated at Cambridge and
subsequently went to London to study law.
Embraced Puritanism in its most enthusi-
astic form. Sat for Cambridge in the Short
and Long Parliaments (1640). When the
Civil War broke out in 1642 he vigorously
organized his district for the parliament and
as captain of a troop of horse, fought at
Edgehill. Formed unconquerable 'Ironsides'.
After leading his army to a decisive victory
at Naseby in June,. 1645 he marched on
London and coerced parliament. Charles
was made a prisoner and was brought to
trial, Cromwell signing the death warrant
(1649).
   The final victory which ended the Civil
War was gained at Worcester in 1651.
Declared Protector in 1653. He died in
1658.
See **pls. A**-95, 96, 97.

EDINBURGH, Duke of (1844–1900).
See **Alfred Ernest Albert.**

**EDWARD VII, King of Great Britain
and Ireland and of the British Domin-
ions beyond the Seas** (1841–1910). Eldest
son and second child of Queen Victoria
and Prince Albert. As Prince of Wales,
became betrothed to Princess Alexandra
of Denmark in September 1862, the
marriage taking place on March 10th,
1863. In 1901 succeeded as King Edward
VII.
See **pls. A**-12, 20, 42, 43, 44, 45, 46, 47, 48,
49, 50, 53, 54, 54A, 55, 56, 57, 58, 59, 60,
61, 62, 63, 64, 65, 66, 68, 72, 73, 74, 76, 81,
84, 85.

**FAIRBROTHER (FAREBROTHER),
LOUISA** (1816–90).
See **section C.**

FITZGEORGE, Mrs (1816–90).
See **section C (Fairbrother).**

FITZHERBERT, MARIA ANNE (1756–
1837). A Roman Catholic who, after the
death of her second husband, went through
a ceremony of marriage in secret with
George, prince of Wales, later George IV.
The marriage in 1785 was recognised by the
Royal Family although illegal, and therefore
invalid under the terms of the Royal
Marriage Act of 1772, because of the Roman
Catholic religion of Mrs Fitzherbert.
See **pl. A**-107.

FRANZ JOSEPH I (1830–1916). Emperor
of Austria 1848, King of Hungary 1867.
The son of Archduke Francis and nephew
of Ferdinand I, whom he succeeded. Sub-
dued the Hungarian revolt and rigorously
suppressed the various nationalities of the
Empire, being determined to fuse them into
one state. Reasserted his claim to rule as an
absolute sovereign. In 1859 Lombardy was
wrested from Austria by Sardinia. By the
war with Prussia in 1866, Austria was excluded from Germany and compelled to
cede Venetia to Sardinia, Prussia's ally.
Thereafter, the Emperor adopted a more
conciliatory policy towards the various

national groups within his Empire. His
attack on Serbia in 1914 precipitated
World War I.
See **pl. A**-93.

**FREDERICK III, second German Em-
peror and eighth King of Prussia** (1831–
88). Son of William I. As Prince Frederick
William married Victoria, Princess Royal of
England in 1858. Crown Prince of Prussia,
1861. Nicknamed 'Our Fritz' he commanded the third army during the Franco-
Prussian War in 1870. Succeeded William I
as Emperor on March 9th, 1888 but died of
cancer June 15th of the same year.
See **pls. A**-67, 68, 70, 71,
pls. C-108, 112.

**FREDERICK CHARLES, Prince of
Prussia** (1828–85).
See **section C.**

**FREDERICK WILLIAM, Crown Prince
of Prussia** (1831–88).
See **Frederick III.**

**GEORGE IV, King of Great Britain and
Ireland** (1762–1830). Eldest son of George
III. Owing to his father's mental illness,
became Prince Regent in 1810 and succeeded in 1820. In 1785 fell in love with and
married Mrs Maria Anne Fitzherbert but
denied marriage to conciliate parliament.
In 1795 married Caroline of Brunswick
(1768–1821) by whom his only child
Princess Charlotte was born in 1796. His
marriage was an unhappy one and he soon
returned to Mrs Fitzherbert, but broke with
her on his installation as Prince Regent in
1810. As King he sought to divorce Caroline,
but the scandal was terminated by her death
in 1821.
See **pl. A**-107.

**GEORGE WILLIAM FREDERICK
CHARLES, second Duke of Cambridge**
(1819–1904).
See **section C.**

**HELENA AUGUSTA VICTORIA,
Princess** (1846–1923), third daughter of
Queen Victoria. Married Prince Christian
of Schleswig-Holstein, in 1866.
See **pl. A**-75.

**HENRIETTA MARIA, Queen-Consort
of Charles I** (1609–69). Youngest daughter
of Henry IV and Marie de Mèdicis. She
married by proxy and came to England in
1625. A fiery and unhappy woman, her life
was a turmoil of assassination, exile and civil
war. She urged Charles on to decisive and
often rash actions, but when the 'Royal
Star' waned, she fled to France and never
saw her husband again.
See **pl. A**-110.

HENRY VIII, King of England (1491–
1547).
See **section E.**

JAMES II, King of England (1633–1701).
Second son of Charles I. As Duke of York
was Lord High Admiral in the second and
third Dutch wars. As a Roman Catholic he
resigned his office after the Test Act of 1673
and was nearly excluded from the succession. When he came to the throne in 1685 he
aroused strong and united opposition by his
attempts to obtain better conditions for his
co-religionists. The unsuccessful Mon-
mouth Rebellion, the Bloody Assize and a

number of other events marked a reign
which ended with the abdication and flight
of the King, who was succeeded in 1689 by
William III and Mary.
See **pl. A**-106.

**JANE SEYMOUR, third Queen of
Henry VIII** (? 1509–37).
See **section E.**

JOHN, King of England (1167–1216).
See **section E.**

LEOPOLD I, King of the Belgians
(1790–1865). Son of Francis, duke of Saxe-
Coburg and uncle of Queen Victoria.
General in the Russian army. In 1816 he
married the Princess Charlotte, only child of
George IV and Caroline of Brunswick, but
she died the following year after giving birth
to a still-born boy. In 1829 he married
morganatically the German actress Caroline
Bauer (1807–78). Their union was brief and
unhappy. In 1831 elected King of the
Belgians. In 1832 married Louise-Marie of
Orleans, daughter of Louis-Philippe, king
of the French. As first King of the Belgians
he conducted himself with prudence and
moderation. Was constant correspondent
and adviser to his niece Victoria and favoured her marriage to Prince Albert. He
was 'the uncle who held a father's place in
her affections'. He won for himself from
contemporary powers the name of 'Nestor of
Europe'.
See **pls. A**-87, 88.

LORNE, Marquess of (1845–1914).
See **Campbell, John Douglas Sutherland.**

**LOUIS, Grand-duke of Hesse-Darm-
stadt** (1837–92). As Prince Louis of Hesse
married Princess Alice, second daughter of
Queen Victoria in 1862.
See **pls. A**-69, 70.

LOUIS-PHILIPPE, King of the French
(1773–1850). Born in Paris, the eldest son of
the Duke of Orleans. Entered the National
Guard and fought in the wars of the
Republic, but after an order for his arrest,
escaped into Austria. In 1800, resided near
London. In 1809 he married Marie Amélie,
daughter of Ferdinand I of the Two Sicilies.
After the Revolution of 1830, he was
appointed Lieutenant-General and then
accepted the crown as the elect of the
sovereign people. Was known as the
'Citizen King'. In September 1843, Queen
Victoria visited Louis-Philippe at Château
d'Eu. This was the first occasion on which
the Queen had trodden foreign soil and,
the first time an English sovereign had
visited a French sovereign since Henry VIII
appeared on the Field of the Cloth of
Gold at the invitation of Francis I in 1520.
The visit was returned in October, 1844,
this being the first time a French monarch
voluntarily landed on English shores. Although a man of great ability, he was by
fear forced into paths of reactionary
violence. Newspapers were muzzled and
trial by jury interfered with. There was a
rising in Paris in February, 1848 as a sequel
to which he had to abdicate, escaping to
England as 'Mr Smith'. He died at
Claremont. His daughter Louise-Marie
married Leopold I, king of the Belgians.
See **pls. A**-15, 18, 19, 86.

**LOUISE CAROLINE ALBERTA,
Duchess of Argyll** (1848–1939). Fourth
daughter of Queen Victoria. As Princess

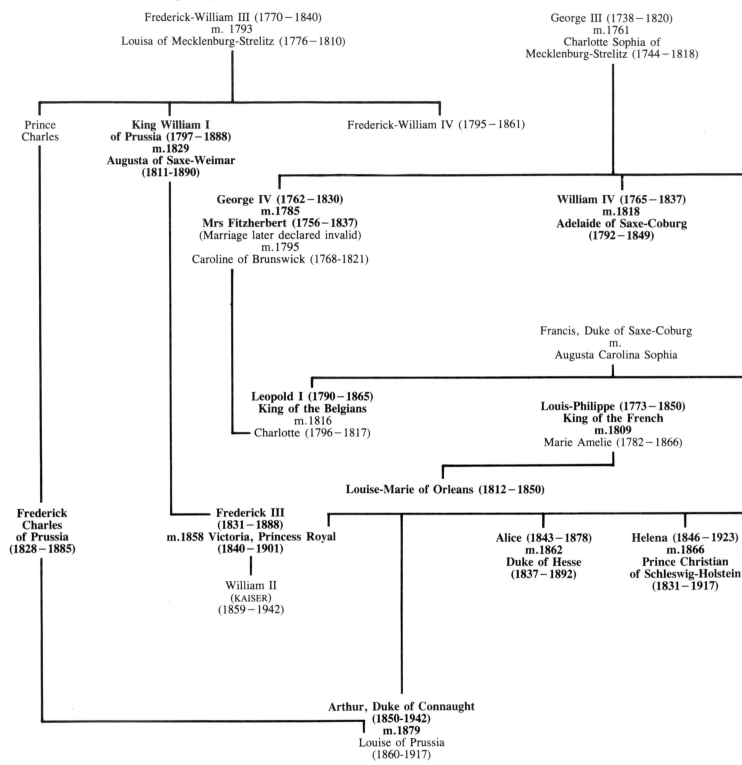

Frederick-William III (1770−1840)
m. 1793
Louisa of Mecklenburg-Strelitz (1776−1810)

George III (1738−1820)
m.1761
Charlotte Sophia of
Mecklenburg-Strelitz (1744−1818)

Prince Charles

**King William I
of Prussia (1797−1888)
m.1829
Augusta of Saxe-Weimar
(1811-1890)**

Frederick-William IV (1795−1861)

**George IV (1762−1830)
m.1785
Mrs Fitzherbert (1756−1837)**
(Marriage later declared invalid)
m.1795
Caroline of Brunswick (1768-1821)

**William IV (1765−1837)
m.1818
Adelaide of Saxe-Coburg
(1792−1849)**

Francis, Duke of Saxe-Coburg
m.
Augusta Carolina Sophia

**Leopold I (1790−1865)
King of the Belgians**
m.1816
Charlotte (1796−1817)

**Louis-Philippe (1773−1850)
King of the French
m.1809**
Marie Amelie (1782−1866)

Louise-Marie of Orleans (1812−1850)

**Frederick
Charles
of Prussia
(1828−1885)**

**Frederick III
(1831−1888)
m.1858 Victoria, Princess Royal
(1840−1901)**

William II
(KAISER)
(1859−1942)

**Alice (1843−1878)
m.1862
Duke of Hesse
(1837−1892)**

**Helena (1846−1923)
m.1866
Prince Christian
of Schleswig-Holstein
(1831−1917)**

**Arthur, Duke of Connaught
(1850-1942)
m.1879**
Louise of Prussia
(1860-1917)

Louise married (1871) the Marquess of Lorne, later ninth Duke of Argyll. A gifted sculptress.
See **pls. A**-74, 77, 78.

LOUISE-MARIE, Queen of the Belgians (1812–50). Daughter of Louis-Philippe, king of the French. As Louise-Marie of Orleans, she married Leopold I, king of the Belgians in 1832. Her eldest son became Leopold II. When reporting her death, at Ostend, from phthisis the correspondent for *The Illustrated London News* (October 19th, 1850) wrote:

Queen Victoria and Queen Louise were dear and intimate friends, they were frequently together and

when absent from each other, corresponded.
See **pls. A**-87, 89.

MACDONALD, FLORA (1722–90), Jacobite heroine, daughter of Ranald Macdonald, a farmer in South Uist (Hebrides). In 1746 whilst on a visit to the Clanranalds in Benbecula (Hebrides), she met Prince Charles Edward in flight after Culloden and helped him to reach Skye. She was imprisoned in the Tower of London but released by Act of Indemnity, 1747. Married Allan Macdonald, 1750.
See **pl. A**-98,
pl. I-33.

MALIBRAN, MARIA FELICITA (1808–36).
See **section E.**
See **pls. A**-2, 3,
pls. E-86, 87, 130, 148, 149.

MARIE ALEXANDROVNA, Duchess of Edinburgh (1853–1920). As the Grandduchess Marie, only daughter of Alexandra II, tsar of Russia, married Alfred, duke of Edinburgh in 1874.
See **pls. A**-79, 80.

MARIE-ALEXANDROWNA, Empress of Russia (1824–80). Daughter of the

The genealogical table of British and related European Royal Families.

Where Portrait Figures are known or thought to have been made, names are shown in bold type.

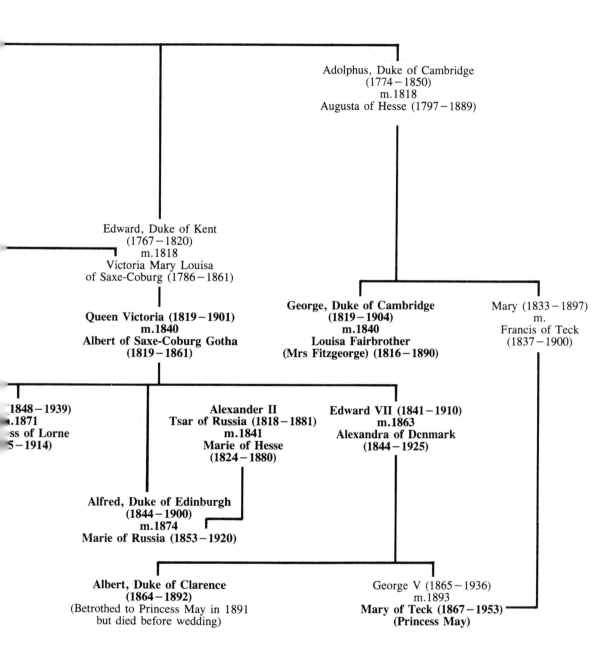

Grand-duke of Hesse. As Marie of Hesse married Alexander II, tsar of Russia in 1841. Crowned Empress of Russia at Moscow, September 7th, 1856. Mother of Marie of Russia (1853–1920), who married Alfred, duke of Edinburgh (1844–1900) in 1874.
See **pls. A**-90, 91.

MARY, Queen-Consort of King George V (1867–1953). Daughter of Francis of Teck and grand-daughter of Adolphus, duke of Cambridge. As Princess May of Teck was betrothed to Albert, duke of Clarence, eldest son of the Prince of Wales, but she died before marriage and she subsequently

married (1893) the second son, Prince George, later King George V. Much loved as a regal figure with a keen sense of duty. *See* **pl. A**-82.

MARY II, Queen of England, Scotland and Ireland (1662–94). Eldest child of James II and Anne Hyde. Brought up a protestant. Married William of Orange in 1677. Arrived in England in 1689 and accepted crown with William, having been obliged by fate to choose between father and husband. Died of small-pox in 1694. *See* **pls. A**-99, 103, 104.

NASR-ED-DIN, Shah of Persia (1829–96). Became Shah in 1848. In 1872 the Indo-European telegraph line from London to India through Teheran was inaugurated and in the following year the Shah visited England. His arrival caused considerable excitement and he was lavishly entertained, especially by the Prince of Wales. *Have you seen the Shah?*, the title of a song sung by the Great Vance, became a popular catchword. An able and cultured leader, he introduced European ideas into Persia. He visited England again in 1889. He was assassinated in Teheran in 1896. *See* **pl. A**-92.

PEEL, JOHN (1776–1854). The hero of the well-known hunting song *D'ye ken John Peel* composed by his friend John Woodcock Graves. Born at Caldbeck, Cumberland, John Peel ran the famous pack of hounds that bore his name for over 40 years.
See pl. A-40A.

RICHARD III, King of England (1452–85).
See **section E.**

SARSFIELD, PATRICK, Earl of Lucan (? 1645–93), Irish soldier. Born at Lucan and educated at a French military college. Lieutenant-colonel of Dover's horse, 1685. Received from James II command of Irish troops in England and was created Earl of Lucan. He followed the King to France and then to Ireland, 1689. He drove the English out of Sligo, was present at the Boyne, 1690, and commanded reserve at Aughrim, July 12th, 1691. Defended Limerick and on its capitulation sailed to France, joining the French service with many of his troops. Commanded the Irish soldiers intended for the invasion of England, 1692. Fought at Steenkirk, 1692; mortally wounded at Landen, 1693.
See pl. A-102.

STANHOPE, LADY HESTER LUCY (1776–1839).
For biography see **section I.**
See pl. A-40,
pl. C-95A,
pls. I-36, 37.

STEWART, CHARLES EDWARD, the 'Young Pretender' (1720–88). Also known as 'Bonny Prince Charlie', or alternatively, the 'Young Cavalier'. Elder son of James Francis Edward, the 'Old Pretender', and grandson of James II. Became the centre of Jacobite hopes. After an initial failure when leading a French invasion on England, he sailed from Nantes, landing in the Hebrides with seven followers in 1745. The clansmen flocked in and he marched on Edinburgh, subsequently defeating Sir John Cope at Prestonpans. He then began a march on London but was defeated at Culloden Moor by a force dispatched against him under the Duke of Cumberland (1746). He became a fugitive in the Highlands. He was helped at one stage in his escape by Flora Macdonald, being disguised as her maid 'Betty Burke'. He reached France but was expelled from there in 1848. Alienated the Jacobites by drunkenness. Died in Rome, 1788.
See pls. A-54A, 97, 98.

VICTORIA, Queen of the United Kingdom of Great Britain and Ireland and Empress of India (1819–1901). The only child of George III's fourth son, Edward, duke of Kent. Born at Kensington Palace May 24th, 1819. On June 20th, 1837 succeeded to the throne on the death of her uncle, William IV. She was instructed in the duties of her station by Lord Melbourne and received constant advice from her uncle, Leopold I, king of the Belgians. In 1840 she married her first cousin, Prince Albert of Saxe-Coburg-Gotha. Her first child, Princess Victoria, was born in November, 1840. Her second, Albert, prince of Wales (later Edward VII) was born in November, 1841. Princess Alice was born in April, 1843 and in September of that year the Queen visited Louis-Philippe, the king of the French at Château d'Eu, this being the first occasion on which an English sovereign had visited a French sovereign since Henry VIII appeared on the Field of the Cloth of Gold in 1520. Prince Alfred was born in August, 1844 and in that year also Louis-Philippe returned the Queen's visit. In 1849 the Queen paid her first visit to Ireland. Her third son, Arthur, was born in May, 1850. In 1851 she took a great interest in the arrangements for the Great Exhibition. In 1854 the Crimean War broke out, and the Queen initiated or supported many voluntary measures for the comfort of the troops. In 1855 Napoleon III visited the Queen at Windsor and was dissuaded from taking command, in person, of the French troops in the Crimea. In June, 1856 the Queen instituted the Victoria Cross for acts of conspicuous valour in war. In December, 1861 the Prince Consort died and the sense of desolation which the Queen experienced never wholly left her. For most of the remaining years of her reign she stayed in retirement and never ceased to wear mourning for him. At times there was a feeling throughout the country that the Queen's prolonged seclusion was contrary to the national interest. In 1887 she celebrated her Golden Jubilee and in 1897 her Diamond Jubilee. She died at Osborne on January 22nd, 1901.
See pls. A-2, 4, 5, 6, 7, 8, 9, 10, 11, 12, 13, 14, 15, 16, 17, 18, 19, 20, 21, 22, 23, 24, 25, 26, 27, 28, 28A, 29, 30, 31, 32, 33, 34, 35, 37, 38, 39, 40, 41, 44, 46, 48, 53, 55, 57, 81, 83, pls. C-32, 33, 38.

VICTORIA ADELAIDE MARY LOUISE, Princess Royal of Great Britain and German Empress (1840–1901). Eldest child of Queen Victoria. Devoted to eldest brother, the Prince of Wales. In 1858 she married Prince Frederick William of Prussia. Crown Princess of Prussia, 1861. Resented Bismarck's rise to power and repeatedly quarrelled with him. Nursed her husband during his illness from cancer, was present with him when William I died and continued nursing him during his subsequent short reign as emperor. Mother of Kaiser William II.
See pls. A-14, 16, 20, 22, 23, 24, 25, 29, 33, 44, 45, 46, 47, 48, 48A, 49, 50, 51, 52, 53, 54, 55, 56, 57, 58, 63, 64A, 65, 67, 68, 70, 71.

WILLIAM I, seventh King of Prussia and first German Emperor (1797–1888).
See **section C.**

WILLIAM III, King of England, Scotland and Ireland (1650–1702). Posthumous son of William II, prince of Orange and Mary, daughter of Charles I of England. On the murder of De Witt in 1672 he was chosen Stadholder of the United Provinces. By his wisdom the republic's apparently hopeless contest with France was terminated in 1678 by the advantageous treaty of Nijmegen. In 1677 he married his cousin Mary, daughter of James II of England. In 1688 the indignation of the people of England at the behaviour of the catholic James II was such that leading politicans formally solicited the interposition of the protestant Prince of Orange (James' son-in-law and nephew). William landed at Torbay in November, 1688 and marched on London. Parliament declared the throne vacant and in 1689 William and Mary were declared King and Queen. James escaped to France and in 1689, aided by a small body of French troops, invaded Ireland making an ineffectual attempt to regain his throne. He was defeated at the Battle of the Boyne (1690) and returned to France, where he resided until his death in 1701. William's reign saw the establishment of the Bank of England, the liberty of the press secured and the British Constitution established on a firm basis. He left no children and the crown passed to Anne, Mary's sister.
See pls. A-99, 100, 101, 103, 104, 105, 106.

WILLIAM IV, King of Great Britain and Ireland (1765–1837). Third son of George III. Known as the 'sailor king'. Entered the navy in 1779 reaching the rank of admiral of the fleet in 1811. In 1818 married Adelaide of Saxe-Coburg Meiningen who bore him two daughters who died in infancy. Succeeded to the throne on the death of his eldest brother, George IV, in 1830. Died in 1837, being succeeded by his niece, Victoria.
See pl. A-108.

WINDSOR CASTLE. The original castle was built about 1070, being designed by William the Conqueror and his barons to form a link in the chain of castles around London. In the centre of the castle was an artificial mound, or keep, surrounded by a deep ditch. It was crowned by a wooden building where the Round Tower now stands. During the reign of Henry II (1154–89) the Round Tower and the outer walls of the castle were built in stone to the north, east and south. The western wall was built during the reign of Henry III (1216–72). St. George's Chapel was built by King Edward IV (1461–83). After the death of King Charles I the castle entered a period of neglect until in 1778 George III (1760–1820) resolved to modernize it. A more elaborate reconstruction was undertaken by King George IV (1820–30). The work undertaken was so thorough that little has needed to be done to the castle since.
See pls. A-41A, 42.

WINDSOR LODGE. It has not proved possible to identify the figure titled 'Windsor Lodge'. No house is recorded that bears this name. The figure does not resemble either Royal Lodge or Queen's Lodge. The former, once a favourite residence of George IV, was remodelled in 1932 as the private residence of the Royal Family; the latter, a barrack-like building erected by George III during a period of reconditioning at Windsor Castle, was pulled down in 1824.
See pl. A-42.

Section A
British and Foreign Royalty
Details of the Figures

Plate 1
Fig. 1 Royal Coat-of-Arms

Plate 1
Figure 1
Subject: **Royal Coat-of-Arms**
Title: None
Height: 9½ in (24 cm)
Colour: White or coloured versions exist.
Rarity: Av. D. A.
Description: Clock-face surmounted by a crown. To the left is a lion and to the right a unicorn.
Observations: Commonly used by collectors as a centre-piece for a collection of royalty.

Plate 2
Fig. 2 Victoria
In the collection of Mr Jack Hawkins

Plate 2
Figure 2
Subject: **Victoria**
Title: HER   QUEEN (indented capitals
      MAJESTY VICTORIA on two plaques)
Date: 1837–8
Height: 10½ in (26.5 cm)
Colour: Well coloured.
Maker: In the style of Obadiah Sherratt
Rarity: VR. D. A.
Description: Sitting, bare-headed, on a sofa.
She is wearing a low-necked, full-sleeved
and full-skirted dress. She holds a small open
book in her right hand which rests on her
lap. There is a large double-arched crown
on the sofa to her right. The base of the
figure and its titling are in the style of
Obadiah Sherratt.
Observations: 1. The earliest dateable Victorian portrait figure.
2. This figure is a modified version of *fig.* 308
(Malibran) *pl.* E-149. Note that it is identical except for the addition of the crown and
alteration in title. The figure of Maria
Malibran is, in turn, based on the engraving
of the young opera singer by J. Rogers
after A. M. Haffam (see *pl.* A-3). Maria
Malibran died on September 23rd, 1836,
some weeks after a fall from a horse. After
the Queen's accession on June 20th, 1837,
the potters anticipated a big public demand
for a figure of the young monarch and rose
to the occasion by modifying the existing
figure of Maria Malibran. The position of
the crown suggests that the figure was sold
from shortly after the Queen's accession
until her coronation a year later.

Plate 3
Maria Felicita Malibran (1808-1836). An engraving for the
Dramatic Magazine after A.M. Huffam by J. Rogers inscribed
Mme MALIBRAN GARCIA. This engraving is the
ultimate source of *fig.* 2. *By courtesy of the Victoria and Albert
Museum*

Plate 4
Fig. 3 Victoria and Albert

Section A. British and Foreign Royalty

Plate 3

Maria Malibran

An engraving for the *Dramatic Magazine* by J. Rogers after A. M. Huffam inscribed: *MME MALIBRAN GARCIA*

This engraving is not only the source of the figure of Maria Malibran, illustrated on *pl.* E-149, but also, indirectly, the source of the figure titled 'Queen Victoria' illustrated on *pl.* A-2.

Plate 4

Figure 3
Subject: **Victoria and Albert**
Title: None
Date: *c.* 1851
Height: 6½ in (16.5 cm)
Colour: Very fine.
Rarity: VR. D. A.
Description: Sitting on a sofa. The Queen is seated on the left wearing a large double-arched crown with a long dress and under-skirt showing as an inverted 'V' from the waist downwards. Albert is seated on the right, bare-headed, in long jacket, waistcoat and trousers. He is looking upwards and tends to look more elderly than in other figures. The base of the figure, which is rococo, is decorated with a shamrock, rose and thistle.
Observations: A piece of such outstanding quality that it may well have been made for the Great Exhibition in 1851.

Plate 5
Figure 4
Subject: **Victoria**
Title: None
Height: 17½ in (43.5 cm)
Colour: Usually finely coloured, but sometimes garish.
Rarity: R.
Pair: Fig. 5 (Albert)
Description: Standing crowned on a high rocky plinth, wearing an ermine-edged cloak, long dress and sash over her left shoulder. Her left arm is by her side and her right arm across her waist. She holds a rose in her right hand. A porcelaneous figure, sometimes with a hollow and sometimes with a solid base.
Observations: A fine single figure fetched 28 gns at Christie's in 1963.

Figure 5
Subject: **Albert**
Title: None
Height: 18½ in (47.5 cm)
Colour: Usually finely coloured, but sometimes garish.
Rarity: R.
Pair: Fig. 4 (Victoria)
Description: Standing bare-headed in long cloak, and military uniform. His left hand holds the scabbard of his sword which is suspended from his belt. He stands on a rocky pedestal. A porcelaneous figure, some-

times with a hollow and sometimes with a solid base.
Observations: A pair of figures, of moderate quality fetched £28 at Sotheby's in 1967.

Plate 6
Figure 6
Subject: **Victoria**
Title: None
Date: *c.* 1845
Height: 11¼ in (28.5 cm)
Colour: Usually well coloured.
Rarity: Av.
Pair: Fig. 7 (Albert)
Description: Standing crowned, with necklace, short cloak, long dress, sash over her left shoulder.

Figure 7
Subject: **Albert**
Title: None
Date: *c.* 1845
Height: 11½ in (29 cm)
Colour: Usually well coloured.
Rarity: Av.
Pair: Fig. 6 (Victoria)
Description: Standing bare-headed, wearing a cloak and uniform with trousers. Both hands are gauntleted. His right hand is on his hip and he holds his sword in his left hand.
Observations: A similar figure was sold at Christie's for 38 gns in 1965.

Plate 5
Fig. 4 Victoria
Fig. 5 Albert
In the collection of Mrs Thornley Gibson

Plate 6
Fig. 6 Victoria
Fig. 7 Albert

Plate 7
Fig. 8 Victoria
Fig. 9 Albert

Plate 8
T: *Fig.* 10 Albert
Fig. 10 Victoria
B: *Fig.* 14 Albert
Fig. 12 Victoria
Fig. 13 Albert
*By courtesy of
Mr and Mrs Eric Joyce*

Plate 7
Figure 8
Subject: **Victoria**
Title: None
Date: c. 1845
Height: 9 in (23 cm)
Colour: Usually well coloured.
Maker: Possibly H. Bentley, Hanley
Rarity: Av.
Pair: *Fig.* 9 (Albert)
Description: Standing crowned, with large bun, short ermine-edged cloak and long dress.
Observations: See under *fig.* 9 (Albert).

Figure 9
Subject: **Albert**
Title: None
Date: c. 1845
Height: 9½ in (24 cm)
Colour: Usually well coloured.
Maker: Possibly H. Bentley, Hanley
Rarity: Av.
Pair: *Fig.* 8 (Victoria)
Description: Standing bare-headed, in long cloak and military uniform. Both hands are gauntleted. His right hand is on his hip, and his left hand holds the hilt of his sword.
Observations: In the *Connoisseur* February, 1919, *no.* ccx, *p.* xxiii there is an advertisement by Mortlocks Ltd., Orchard Street, London. Included in this advertisement is a photograph of a figure described as follows: 'No. 2 (Biscuit), H.R.H. Prince Albert, impressed at back. *Modelled and manufactured by H. Bentley, Hanley, 1845*'.

The photograph is not very clear, but the figure appears to be very similar if not identical to *fig.* 9. Note that *fig.* 27 (Caunt) *pl.* F-13, is also impressed 'H. Bentley'.

Plate 8
Figure 10
Subject: **Victoria**
Title: Queen Victoria (gilt script)
Date: 184-
Height: 11 in (28 cm)
Colour: Usually white and gilt.
Rarity: Av.
Pair: *Fig.* 11 (Albert)
Description: Standing crowned, wearing necklace, bodice and full-length dress. Her left hand is on her waist and in her right hand she holds a reticule.

Figure 11
Subject: **Albert**
Title: Prince Albert (gilt script)
Date: 184-
Height: 11½ in (29 cm)
Colour: Usually white and gilt.
Rarity: Av.
Pair: *Fig.* 10 (Victoria)
Description: Standing bare-headed, dressed in military uniform with trousers and long cloak. He holds his cocked hat by his side in his right hand, and his left hand is on his hip. Beside his left leg is a pedestal.

Figure 12
Subject: **Victoria**
Title: None
Date: 184-
Height: 12 in (30.5 cm)
Colour: White and gilt or sometimes rather beautiful pastel shades.
Rarity: R.
Pair: *Fig.* 13 (Albert)
Description: Standing crowned, wearing a two-tiered necklace, short cloak and full-length dress. To her left is a pedestal upon which is a book. Both hands rest on the book.
Observations: A similar figure and its pair fetched 45 gns at Christie's in 1969.

Figure 13
Subject: **Albert**
Title: None
Date: 184-
Height: 12 in (30.5 cm)
Colour: As for *fig.* 12 (Victoria).
Rarity: R.
Pair: *Fig.* 12 (Victoria)
Description: Standing bare-headed, in the robes of the Order of the Garter. He holds his hat in his right hand and to his right also is a pedestal.
Observations: 1. The only known figure of the Prince Consort in the robes of the Order of the Garter.
2. A similar figure and its pair fetched 45 gns at Christie's in 1969.

Figure 14
Subject: **Albert**
Title: None
Date: 184-
Height: 13½ in (34.25 cm)
Colour: Richly coloured.
Rarity: R.
Pair: There is almost certainly a pair to this figure, but it has not been described to date. *Fig.* 15 has been reserved for it.
Description: Standing bare-headed, in military uniform and trousers. His left hand is on his hip and his cloak is draped over his left forearm. His right hand is by his side holding his plumed cocked hat. There is a pedestal to his right.

Plate 9
Figure 16
Subject: **Victoria**
Title: None
Date: 184-
Height: 13½ in (34.25 cm)
Colour: Usually well coloured.
Rarity: Av.

Section A. British and Foreign Royalty

Pair: There is almost certainly a pair to this figure, but it has not been reported.
Description: Standing, wearing a crown, two-tiered necklace and short cloak, with full-length two-flounced dress. Her right hand is across her waist and in it she holds a flower. Her left hand is by her side.

Plate 10
Figure 17
Subject: **Victoria**
Title: None
Date: 184–
Height: 13¼ in (33.5 cm)
Colour: Usually well coloured.
Rarity: Av.
Pair: There is almost certainly a pair to this figure, but it has not been reported.
Description: Standing crowned, with single-tier necklace, a sash over her left shoulder, three-quarter length ermine-edged cloak and flounced full-length dress. Her left arm is by her side and her right hand in front of her waist.

Plate 11
Figure 18
Subject: **Albert**
Title: None
Date: 184–
Height: 11 in (28 cm)
Colour: Well coloured.
Rarity: R.
Pair: There is almost certainly a pair to this figure, but it has not been reported.
Description: Standing bare-headed, in military uniform and trousers. His right hand is by his side and in it he holds his cocked hat. His left hand holds a book which rests on another book lying on a pedestal. In the figure illustrated a sword hilt may be seen, but in other examples this has been omitted.

Figure 19
Subject: **Victoria (Queen Box)**
Title: None
Date: 185–
Height: 7¼ in (18.25 cm)
Colour: Well coloured, in the style of Thomas Parr, see *ch.* 2.
Maker: Thomas Parr
Rarity: Contemporary figures are rare
Description: Standing, wearing a crown, bodice and full-length multi-flounced skirt. Her hands are clasped in front of her skirt. In two pieces (trinket box).
Observations: 1. Catalogued as 'Queen Box' in Kent lists: no. 207 in *Kent List A* and no. 166 in *Kent Lists B* and *C*.
2. Many reproductions from the original mould exist; they are often difficult to distinguish. Contemporary figures seem to have the bodice coloured either in overglaze blue or mauve. The blue is much darker than that used in reproductions.

Figure 20
Subject: **Albert**
Title: None
Date: 184–
Height: 11½ in (29 cm)
Colour: Well coloured.
Rarity: R.
Pair: Almost certainly exists, but has not been reported to date.
Description: Standing bare-headed, in swallow-tailed coat, waistcoat and trousers, a sash over his left shoulder. His right hand is across his chest and his left hand rests on top of a draped pedestal.

Plate 9
Fig. 16 Victoria
In the Thomas Balston collection

Plate 10
Fig. 17 Victoria
In the collection of Mrs H. de C. Hastings

Plate 11
Fig. 18 Albert
Fig. 19 Victoria
Fig. 20 Albert

A121

Plate 12
Fig. 21 Albert
Fig. 22 Victoria with the Prince of Wales
In the collection of Mr H.T. Appleton

Plate 12
Figure 21
Subject: **Albert**
Title: None
Date: 1842
Height: 8½ in (21.5 cm)
Colour: Richly decorated.
Rarity: VR. D. A.
Pair: *Fig.* 22 (Victoria and Prince of Wales).
Description: Sitting bare-headed, in military uniform and trousers, on an ornate throne. A lion and unicorn beside his feet.
Observations: There are smaller versions of this figure (see *pls.* A-18 and 19).

A122

Figure 22
Subject: **Victoria and Prince of Wales**
Title: None
Date: 1842
Height: 8½ in (21.5 cm)
Colour: Richly decorated.
Rarity: VR. D. A.
Pair: *Fig.* 21 (Albert)
Description: Sitting on an ornate throne wearing a high double-arched crown, bodice and full-length flounced skirt. On her lap she holds the Prince of Wales, who wears a short frock and a three-feathered hat. A lion and a unicorn beside her feet.

Plate 13
Figure 23
Subject: **Victoria, Albert and child**
Title: None
Date: 184–
Height: 6¾ in (17 cm)
Colour: Coloured, often poorly.
Rarity: Av.
Description: The Queen sits on the left, wearing a full-length dress and garter sash. On her lap is a baby in long clothes. To the right stands Albert, bare-headed in military uniform. His right leg is crossed in front of his left leg.

Section A. British and Foreign Royalty

Plate 13
Fig. 23 Victoria, Albert
and child
Fig. 24 Victoria, Albert
and child
Fig. 25 Victoria and
Albert

Figure 24
Subject: **Victoria, Albert and child**
Title: None
Date: 184–
Height: 7¾ in (20 cm)
Colour: Both white and gilt, and coloured versions are recorded.
Rarity: Av.
Description: Victoria sits on the left on a high-backed throne surmounted by a crown. She wears a bodice and flounced skirt and on her lap she holds a baby, wearing a bonnet and long clothes. Albert stands to the right, bare-headed, in military uniform with a cloak over his left shoulder. His right leg is crossed in front of his left leg.
Observations: 1. A similar figure fetched 32 gns at Christie's in 1969.
2. A figure, identical in every respect, except that Albert wears a plumed cocked hat, has been noted (*fig.* 24(*a*)).

Figure 25
Subject: **Victoria and Albert**
Title: None
Date: 184–
Height: 7¼ in (18.25 cm)
Colour: Both white and gilt, and coloured versions are recorded.
Rarity: R.
Description: The Queen stands on the left, crowned, wearing an ermine-edged cloak and flounced skirt. Albert stands on the right, bare-headed, in military tunic, trousers and cloak.
Observations: Of the many royal figures, only two others were made of the Queen and Albert together (*fig.* 3, *pl.* A-4 and *fig.* 87, *pl.* A-32).

Plate 14
Figure 26
Subject: **Albert**
Title: None
Date: 184–

Height: 7¼ in (18.25 cm)
Colour: Well coloured.
Rarity: R.
Pair: *Fig.* 27 (Victoria and Princess Royal)
Description: Standing bare-headed, wearing a cloak, military uniform and trousers. He holds his cocked hat in his left hand.

Figure 27
Subject: **Victoria and Princess Royal**
Title: None
Date: 184–
Height: 7¼ in (18.25 cm)
Colour: Well coloured.
Rarity: R.
Pair: *Fig.* 26 (Albert)
Description: Standing, wearing a high double-arched crown, gown, bodice and flounced skirt. Her left arm is by her side and in her right arm she holds the Princess Royal who wears a bonnet and long clothes.

Plate 14
Fig. 26 Albert
Fig. 27 Victoria with the Princess Royal
Fig. 28 Victoria
Fig. 29 Albert
In the Thomas Balston collection

Plate 14 continued
Figure 28
Subject: **Victoria**
Title: None
Date: 184–
Height: 6 in (15.25 cm)
Colour: Well coloured.
Rarity: R.
Pair: Fig. 29 (Albert)
Description: Standing, wearing a head-dress with long streamers which fall over her skirt, bodice, and skirt with flounce. To her right is a chair with low arms and a high back surmounted by a large crown.

Figure 29
Subject: **Albert**
Title: None
Date: 184–
Height: 6 in (15.25 cm)
Colour: Well coloured.
Rarity: R.
Pair: Fig. 28 (Victoria)

Description: Standing bare-headed, in military uniform and trousers with a long cloak draped over both shoulders. In his left hand he holds his cocked hat which is resting on the seat of a chair with a high back and low arms.

Plate 15
Figure 29
Subject: **Albert**
Observations: See *pl.* A-14.

Figure 30
Subject: **Victoria**
Title: None
Date: 184–
Height: 8¼ in (21 cm)
Colour: Well coloured.
Rarity: Av.
Pair: Fig. 31 (Albert)
Description: Standing, wearing a high double-arched crown, bodice with sash over her left shoulder and full-length flounced skirt, a gown over both shoulders.

Figure 31
Subject: **Albert**
Title: None
Date: 184–
Height: 8¼ in (21 cm)
Colour: Well coloured.
Rarity: Av.
Pair: Fig. 30 (Victoria)
Description: Standing, wearing a plumed cocked hat, cloak, military jacket with epaulettes, a sash over his left shoulder, breeches and thigh-boots. His right hand is in front of his waist, and his left hand clutches the hilt of his sword.

Figure 32
Subject: **Victoria**
Title: None
Date: 184–
Height: 8¾ in (22 cm)
Colour: Well coloured.
Rarity: Av.
Pair: Fig. 33 (Albert)

Plate 15
T: *Fig.* 30 Victoria
   Fig. 31 Albert
   Fig. 32 Victoria
   Fig. 33 Albert

B: *Fig.* 29 Albert
   Fig. 34 Victoria
   Fig. 35 ? Louis-Philippe
   Fig. 36 Albert

Description: Standing crowned, wearing a short cloak, bodice, full-length flounced skirt, a sash over her left shoulder. Her left arm is by her side and in her right hand she holds a small flower in front of her waist.

Figure 33
Subject: **Albert**
Title: None
Date: 184–
Height: 8¾ in (22 cm)
Colour: Well coloured.
Rarity: Av.
Pair: Fig. 32 (Victoria)
Description: Standing bare-headed, wearing a cloak, military jacket with epaulettes and long trousers. His right hand is on his hip, and his left hand holds the hilt of his sword. To his left is a pedestal upon which is a manuscript.

Figure 34
Subject: **Victoria**
Title: None
Date: 184–
Height: 9 in (23 cm)
Colour: Well coloured.
Rarity: Av.
Pair: Fig. 35 (? Louis-Philippe)
Description: Standing crowned, wearing an ermine-edged cloak and full-length dress. To her right is a pedestal upon which is a book.
Observations: See fig. 35 (? Louis-Philippe).

Figure 35
Subject: **? Louis-Philippe, King of the French**
Title: None
Date: 184–
Height: 9 in (23 cm)
Colour: Well coloured.
Rarity: Av.
Pair: Fig. 34 (Victoria)
Description: Standing crowned, wearing a long ermine-edged cloak, military jacket, breeches and knee-boots. His left elbow rests on a pedestal and in his hands he clutches a manuscript.
Observations: This figure was catalogued as Albert by Balston, but this identification has been the subject of much controversy. If it is Albert, it is the only one of him wearing a crown, and it is well-known that Queen Victoria would never permit this. The knee-boots, too, are not in keeping, although in fig. 31, which is almost certainly Albert, he is seen to be wearing them. Among other suggestions are Napoleon I and George IV.

If the latter, then fig. 34 portrays Queen Adelaide. In my view it is almost certain that the figure portrays Louis-Phillipe, king of the French. It will be recalled that in September 1843, Queen Victoria visited Louis-Philippe at Château d'Eu. This was the first occasion on which the Queen had trodden foreign soil, and the first occasion in which an English sovereign had visited a French sovereign since Henry VIII appeared on the Field of the Cloth of Gold at the invitation of Francis I in 1520. The visit was returned in October 1844, this being the first time that a French monarch voluntarily landed on English shores (see also fig. 247, pl. A-86).

Figure 36
Subject: **Albert**
Title: None
Date: 1841
Height: 7½ in (19 cm)
Colour: Well coloured.
Rarity: Av.
Pair: Fig. 37 (Victoria and Princess Royal) pl. A-16.
Description: Standing bare-headed, in long cloak, military uniform with trousers. He holds his cocked hat in his left hand.

Plate 16
Figure 37
Subject: **Victoria and Princess Royal**
Title: None
Date: 1841
Height: 7 in (17.5 cm)
Colour: Well coloured.
Rarity: Av.
Pair: Fig. 36 (Albert) pl. A-15.
Description: Standing crowned, wearing a long dress, sash over her left shoulder. She holds the Princess Royal, who is wearing a long dress, on her right arm.

Figure 38
Subject: **Victoria**
Title: None
Date: c. 1837
Height: 5½ in (14 cm)
Colour: Well coloured.
Rarity: R.
Description: Standing bare-headed, wearing a bun. She is dressed in a blouse and long skirt, and has a shawl wrapped round her. Both hands are in a muff.
Observations: Mr Ronald Shockledge has suggested that this figure represents the

Princess Victoria receiving the news of her accession from the Lord Chamberlain and the Archbishop of Canterbury at Kensington Palace on June 20th, 1837.

Figure 39
Subject: **Victoria and child**
Title: None
Date: 184–
Height: 5½ in (14 cm)
Colour: Well coloured.
Rarity: Av.
Pair: Fig. 40 (Albert)
Description: Seated on a throne, wearing a crown and full-length dress. She cradles a child in her left arm on her lap. The child wears a bonnet and a long dress.

Figure 40
Subject: **Albert**
Title: None
Date: 184–
Height: 5½ in (14 cm)
Colour: Well coloured.
Rarity: Av.
Pair: Fig. 39 (Victoria and child)
Description: Seated bare-headed, wearing a long jacket with a high neck, belt but no insignia nor epaulettes. In his right hand he clutches a scroll.

Figure 41
Subject: **Victoria**
Title: Queen (raised capitals)
Date: 184–
Height: 11 in (28 cm)
Colour: Sometimes coloured, more often white and gilt.
Rarity: Av.
Pair: Fig. 42 (Albert)
Description: Standing crowned, wearing a long ermine-edged gown, full-length dress with a sash over her left shoulder.

Figure 42
Subject: **Albert**
Title: Albert (raised capitals)
Date: 184–
Height: 11 in (28 cm)
Colour: As for fig. 41 (Victoria).
Rarity: Av.
Pair: Fig. 41 (Victoria)
Description: Standing bare-headed, wearing a long cloak, military jacket, with a sash over the right shoulder and trousers. He holds the hilt of his sword against his left leg, and to his left is a pedestal.

Plate 16a
Fig. 38 Victoria
Fig. 45 Victoria
Fig. 47 Albert
Fig. 37 Victoria and child
Fig. 39 Victoria and child
Fig. 40 Albert

Plate 16 continued
Figure 43
Subject: **Victoria**
Title: None
Date: 184–
Height: 8¼ in (21 cm)
Colour: Largely white and gilt.
Rarity: VR. D.
Description: Standing crowned, wearing a bodice and full-length flounced skirt. Both hands are clasped in front of her waist clutching a handkerchief. She wears a long flowing gown which is decorated on her right with what appears to be the Garter insignia. A two-piece box.
Observations: A rare, and more sophisticated version of 'Queen Box'.

Figure 44
Subject: **Victoria**
Title: Victoria (raised capitals)
Date: 184–
Height: 9¾ in (24.5 cm)
Colour: Pale.
Rarity: VR.
Pair: There is almost certainly a pair to this figure, but it has not been described.
Description: Standing crowned, wearing a full-length flounced dress and ermine-edged cloak. Her left hand is by her side and in her right hand she holds an object, probably the Orb.

Figure 45
Subject: **Victoria**
Observations: See *pl.* A-17.

Figure 47
Subject: **Albert**
Observations: See *pl.* A-18.

Plate 17
Figure 45
Subject: **Victoria**
Title: None
Date: 1840
Height: 5¼ in (13.5 cm)
Colour: Usually sparingly coloured.
Rarity: Av.
Pair: *Fig.* 46 (Albert)
Description: Sitting on a throne crowned, wearing a full-length dress and garter sash, both hands on her lap.

Figure 46
Subject: **Albert**
Title: None
Date: 1840
Height: 5¼ in (13.5 cm)
Colour: Usually sparingly coloured.
Rarity: Av.
Pair: *Fig.* 45 (Victoria)
Description: Sitting on a throne bare-headed, wearing a long jacket with a high neck and belt but no insignia nor epaulettes. He holds a scroll in his right hand.
Observations: Seated pairs of Albert and Victoria when bought individually are sometimes difficult to match. What cannot be shown adequately photographically is that the back of the throne is often as great a help in matching as the front, showing an individuality for each pair, see *ch.* 2, *pl.* 1.

Plate 17
Fig. 46 Albert
Fig. 45 Victoria

Plate 18
Fig. 48 Victoria
Fig. 47 Albert
Fig. 49 ?Louis-Philippe
Fig. 50 Victoria

Plate 18
Figure 47
Subject: **Albert**
Title: None
Date: 184–
Height: 6¾ in (17 cm)
Colour: Well coloured.
Rarity: R.
Pair: Fig. 48 (Victoria)
Description: Standing bare-headed, wearing a frock-coat, neckerchief, waistcoat with insignia and trousers. His left hand is in the pocket of his coat and in his right hand he clutches a scroll or book.

Plate 19
T: *Fig.* 51 Albert
Fig. 52 Victoria
Fig. 49(a) ?Louis-Philippe
B: *Fig.* 53 Victoria
Fig. 54 Victoria

Figure 48
Subject: **Victoria**
Title: None
Date: 184–
Height: 6½ in (16.5 cm)
Colour: Well coloured.
Rarity: R.
Pair: Fig. 47 (Albert)
Description: Standing crowned, with a short cape and full-length ermine-edged dress, with short puffed sleeves. A triangle of underskirt protrudes below the waist.

Figure 49
Subject: **? Louis-Philippe, King of the French**
Title: None
Date: 184–
Height: 7½ in (19 cm)
Colour: Well coloured.
Rarity: Av.
Pair: Fig. 50 (Victoria)
Description: Sitting, wearing a plumed cocked hat athwartships, military uniform and trousers, a lion and unicorn beside his feet.
Observations: 1. There are several minor variants of this figure, an example is *fig.* 49(a), *pl.* A-19.
2. Although *figs.* 51 and 52, *pl.* A-19 are obviously smaller versions of *figs.* 21 and 22, *pl.* A-12, doubt remains about the identification of *fig.* 49, for the face portrayed (which is not adorned by a moustache) does not bear any resemblance to that of Albert; moreover, the potter has given his subject a plumed cocked hat athwartships. It would seem likely that he did this in order to convince himself, if no-one else, that he was attempting to portray a different character. It is quite possible that this figure is intended to represent Louis-Philippe, king of the French. It will be recalled that Queen Victoria paid a state visit to France in 1843 and that this visit was returned in 1844.

Figure 50
Subject: **Victoria**
Title: None
Date: 184–

Height: 7 in (17.5 cm)
Colour: Well coloured.
Rarity: Av.
Pair: Fig. 49 (? Louis-Philippe)
Description: Sitting, wearing a high double-arched crown. In her right hand she holds a sceptre, and at her feet are a lion and unicorn.
Observations: There are several minor variants of this figure which is almost identical to *fig.* 52 (Victoria) *pl.* A-19. Like *fig.* 52, the figure is a smaller version of *fig.* 22 (Victoria and the Prince of Wales) *pl.* A-12, only in this version the positions of the lion and unicorn are reversed, and the Queen holds a sceptre instead of the Prince of Wales.

Plate 19
Figure 49(a)
Subject: **? Louis-Philippe, King of the French**
Observations: A minor variant of *fig.* 49, *pl.* A-18.

Figure 51
Subject: **Albert**
Title: None
Date: 184–
Height: 6¾ in (17 cm)
Colour: Well coloured.
Rarity: Av.
Pair: Fig. 52 (Victoria)
Description: Sitting bare-headed and moustached, wearing military uniform and trousers. At his feet a lion and unicorn.
Observations: A small version of *fig.* 21 (Albert) *pl.* A-12. Note the position of the lion and unicorn have been reversed.

Figure 52
Subject: **Victoria**
Title: None
Date: 184–
Height: 6½ in (16.5 cm)
Colour: Well coloured.
Rarity: Av.
Pair: Fig. 51 (Albert)
Description: Sitting, wearing a high double-arched crown and full-length dress. She carries a sceptre in her right hand and at her feet are a lion and unicorn.

A127

Plate 19 continued
Observations: A small version of *fig.* 22 (Victoria) *pl.* A-12, but in this instance the Prince of Wales has been omitted and a sceptre substituted; also, the positions of the lion and unicorn have been reversed.

Figure 53
Subject: **Victoria**
Title: None
Date: 184–
Height: 8½ in (21.5 cm)
Colour: Very beautifully coloured.
Rarity: R.
Pair: There is possibly a pair to this figure, but it has not been recorded to date.
Description: Sitting on a throne wearing an open crown, ermine-edged cloak and long dress with large sleeves. On an irregular oval base.

Figure 54
Subject: **Victoria**
Title: None
Date: 184–
Height: 7 in (17.5 cm)
Colour: Well coloured.
Rarity: Av.
Pair: No pair has been recorded in this size, but to a smaller size of much inferior quality, viz *fig.* 54(*a*), *pl.* A-20 there is a pair, *fig.* 55 (Prince Albert) *pl.* A-20. This suggests that the figure was not made prior to the Queen's marriage in 1840.
Description: Sitting crowned, in ermine-edged cloak with large sleeves. On a square base with pinched-in sides.
Observations: 1. A similar figure fetched 10 gns at Christie's in 1964; and another, 28 gns in 1965.
2. It has been suggested that the source is the portrait by Sir George Hayter, painted when the Queen was nineteen.

Plate 20
Figure 54(a)
Subject: **Victoria**
Title: None
Date: 184–
Height: 6 in (15.25 cm)
Colour: Tends to be garish.
Rarity: C.
Pair: Fig. 55 (Albert)
Description: Sitting crowned, in ermine-edged cloak and long dress with large sleeves. Square base.
Observations: A smaller and inferior version of *fig.* 54, *pl.* A-19.

Figure 55
Subject: **Albert**
Title: None
Date: 184–
Height: 6 in (15.25 cm)
Colour: Tends to be garish.
Rarity: C.
Pair: Fig. 54(*a*) (Victoria)
Description: Sitting, wearing an ermine-edged cloak, jacket with a star on his left breast and a sash over his right shoulder and trousers.
Observations: See *fig.* 54 (Victoria) *pl.* A-19.

Figure 56
Subject: **Victoria and Princess Royal**
Title: None
Date: c. 1843
Height: 7 in (17.5 cm)
Colour: Well coloured.
Rarity: Av.
Pair: Fig. 57 (Albert and Prince of Wales)

Description: Sitting crowned, wearing an ermine-edged cloak and long dress. Her right arm is on the Princess's shoulder. The Princess is bare-headed, holds a posy in her hand and wears a skirt and pantalettes.

Figure 57
Subject: **Albert and Prince of Wales**
Title: None
Date: c. 1843
Height: 7½ in (19 cm)
Colour: Well coloured.
Rarity: Av.
Pair: Fig. 56 (Victoria and Princess Royal)
Description: Sitting bare-headed, wearing a neckerchief, frock-coat and trousers. His left hand rests on the Prince's shoulder. The Prince is wearing a plumed bonnet, kilt and pantalettes.
Observations: A similar figure and its pair fetched 40 gns at Christie's in 1965.

Plate 21
Figure 58
Subject: **Victoria**
Title: None
Date: 184–
Height: 7¼ in (18.25 cm)
Colour: Well coloured.
Rarity: R.
Pair: A pair to this figure possibly exists, but has not been recorded.
Description: Seated wearing a crown, ermine-edged cloak, full-length dress with large sleeves. Circular base.

Plate 22
Figure 59
Subject: **Albert**
Title: None
Date: c. 1841
Height: 6¾ in (17 cm)
Colour: Very fine.
Maker: John (& Rebecca) Lloyd, Shelton
Rarity: VR. D.
Pair: Fig. 60 (Victoria and Princess Royal)
Description: Seated bare-headed, wearing a jacket, waistcoat, neckerchief and trousers. In his right hand he holds a book. The sides of the throne are edged with ermine.
Observations: 1. The back of the figure illustrated is impressed LLOYD/SHELTON, see *ch.* 2, *pl.* 1.
2. This and its pair are the earliest known Victorian portrait figures which can be attributed to a definite manufacturer.

Figure 60
Subject: **Victoria and Princess Royal**
Title: None
Date: c. 1841
Height: 6¾ in (17 cm)
Colour: Very fine.
Maker: John (& Rebecca) Lloyd, Shelton
Rarity: VR. D.
Pair: Fig. 59 (Albert)
Description: Seated, wearing a shallow crown and full-length dress. She holds the Princess Royal in her left arm on her lap, the Princess being dressed in a bonnet and long clothes. The sides of the throne are edged with ermine.
Observations: 1. The back of the figure illustrated is impressed LLOYD/SHELTON, see *ch.* 2, *pl.* 1.
2. This figure and its pair fetched 95 gns at Christie's in 1967.

Plate 23
Figure 61
Subject: **Albert**
Title: None

Date: c. 1841
Height: 5¾ in (14.5 cm)
Colour: Well coloured.
Rarity: Av.
Pair: Possibly to *fig.* 62 (Victoria and Princess Royal), but there is some doubt.
Description: Seated bare-headed, wearing a long coat with a high collar, belted at the waist, no epaulettes nor sash, trousers. In his right hand he holds a manuscript.

Figure 62
Subject: **Victoria and Princess Royal**
Title: None
Date: c. 1841
Height: 6 in (15.25 cm)
Colour: Well coloured.
Rarity: Av.
Pair: Possibly to *fig.* 61 (Albert), but there is some doubt.
Description: Seated, wearing a coronet and long dress. She holds the Princess Royal in her left arm on her lap. The Princess Royal is wearing a bonnet and long dress.

Figure 63
Subject: **Albert**
Title: None
Date: c. 1841
Height: 5½ in (14 cm)
Colour: Well coloured.
Rarity: C.
Pair: Probably to *fig.* 64 (Victoria and Princess Royal), but there is a little doubt.
Description: Seated bare-headed, wearing a short jacket, low coat, waistcoat, neckerchief and trousers. In his right hand he holds a scroll.
Observations: Note in this figure his hand is right round the scroll, whereas in *fig.* 61 his hand only partially grips the scroll.

Figure 64
Subject: **Victoria and Princess Royal**
Title: None
Date: c. 1841
Height: 5¾ in (14.5 cm)
Colour: Well coloured.
Rarity: C.
Pair: Probably to *fig.* 63 (Albert), but there is a little doubt.
Description: Seated bare-headed, wearing a full-length dress. She holds the Princess Royal in her left arm on her lap. The Princess Royal is wearing a bonnet and a long dress.

Plate 20
T: *Fig.* 55 Albert
Fig. 54(a) Victoria
B: *Fig.* 56 Victoria and

Princess Royal
Fig. 57 Albert and the
Prince of Wales

Plate 22
Fig. 59 Albert
Fig. 60 Victoria and the Princess Royal
The reverses are impressed **LLOYD/**

SHELTON. They are the earliest
Victorian portrait figures whose
provenance is known with certainty.

Plate 21
Fig. 58 Victoria

Plate 23
Fig. 61 Albert
Fig. 62 Victoria and the Princess Royal
Fig. 63 Albert
Fig. 64 Victoria and the Princess Royal
When figures are purchased individually and not in
matching pairs, it is sometimes difficult to be certain

how they pair up. In seated figures of Victoria and
Albert the problem may often be solved by looking at
their backs, for the thrones of figures constituting a pair
match. If there are differences in the legs or backs of the
thrones, as viewed from the back, then the figures do
not form a true pair.

Plate 24
Above: *Fig.* 65 Victoria and the Princess Royal
Fig. 66 Albert
Right: *Fig.* 67 Albert
Fig. 68 Victoria

Plate 24
Figure 65
Subject: **Victoria and Princess Royal**
Title: None
Date: *c.* 1841
Height: 5¼ in (13.5 cm)
Colour: Well coloured.
Rarity: Av.
Pair: *Fig.* 66 (Albert)
Description: Seated wearing a crown, full-length dress, a sash over her left shoulder. She holds the Princess Royal in her right arm.
Observations: A seated version of *fig.* 37 (Victoria and Princess Royal) *pl.* A-16.

Figure 66
Subject: **Albert**
Title: None
Date: *c.* 1841
Height: 5¼ in (13.5 cm)
Colour: Well coloured.
Rarity: Av.
Pair: *Fig.* 65 (Victoria and Princess Royal)
Description: Seated bare-headed, in military jacket and trousers.
Observations: A seated version of *fig.* 36 (Albert) *pl.* A-15.

Figure 67
Subject: **Albert**
Title: None
Date: *c.* 1840
Height: 6½ in (16.5 cm)
Colour: Well coloured.
Rarity: C.
Pair: *Fig.* 68 (Victoria)
Description: Seated bare-headed, in long jacket with a star over his left breast. The jacket is belted at the waist, but there are no epaulettes, trousers. In his right hand he holds a paper.

Figure 68
Subject: **Victoria**
Title: None
Date: *c.* 1840

Height: 6½ in (16.5 cm)
Colour: Well coloured.
Rarity: C.
Pair: *Fig.* 67 (Albert)
Description: Seated crowned, wearing a full-length dress, sash over her right shoulder.
Observations: Seated figures of Victoria and Albert are generally supposed to date to 1840. Those of Victoria and Albert with the Princess Royal probably date to 1841 and those of Victoria and Albert, with the Princess Royal and the Prince of Wales to 1842–3.

Plate 25
Figure 69
Subject: **Victoria and Princess Royal**
Title: None
Date: *c.* 1841
Height: 6¼ in (16 cm)
Colour: Well coloured.
Rarity: R.
Pair: No pair has yet been described for this figure but probably one exists.
Description: Seated, wearing a floral bonnet and full-length dress. In her left arm she holds the Princess Royal on her lap, the child being robed in a bonnet with a long dress decorated with a crown. Square base with pinched-in sides.

Plate 26
Figure 70
Subject: **Victoria and child**
Title: None
Date: 184–
Height: 6¼ in (16 cm)
Colour: Well coloured.
Rarity: Av.
Pair: No pair has been found to this figure, but one probably exists.
Description: Seated, wearing a floral bonnet and gown displaying an inverted 'V' of underskirt. She holds a child in her left arm on her lap. Square base with pinched-in sides.
Observations: Clearly comes from the same

factory as *fig.* 69, *pl.* A-25, and on these grounds is likely to portray Victoria, although in this case there is not the positive evidence of a crown.

Plate 27
Figure 71
Subject: **Victoria**
Title: None
Date: 184–
Height: 8½ in (21.5 cm)
Colour: Well coloured.
Rarity: Av.
Pair: *Fig.* 72 (Albert)
Description: Standing crowned, wearing a half-length cloak, necklace, full-length dress with a single flounced skirt. There is a sash over her left shoulder and a star on her left breast.

Figure 72
Subject: **Albert**
Title: None
Date: 184–
Height: 8¼ in (21 cm)
Colour: Well coloured.
Rarity: Av.
Pair: *Fig.* 71 (Victoria)
Description: Standing bare-headed, in three-quarter length cloak, military uniform and trousers. Both hands are gauntleted. His right hand is on his hip and his left hand by his side clutching his cocked hat.

Figure 73
Subject: **Victoria**
Title: None
Date: 184–
Height: 8½ in (21.5 cm)
Colour: Well coloured.
Rarity: Av.
Pair: *Fig.* 74 (Albert)
Description: Standing crowned, wearing a half-length cloak, full-length dress, necklace, sash over her left shoulder.

Section A. British and Foreign Royalty

Plate 25 (Left)
Fig. 69 Victoria and
the Princess Royal
*By courtesy of Mr and
Mrs Eric Joyce*

Plate 26 (Right)
Fig. 70 Victoria and
child

Plate 27
Fig. 71 Victoria
Fig. 72 Albert
Fig. 73 Victoria
Fig. 74 Albert

Figure 74
Subject: **Albert**
Title: None
Date: 184–
Height: 8¼ in (21 cm)
Colour: Well coloured.
Rarity: Av.
Pair: *Fig.* 73 (Victoria)

Description: Standing bare-headed, wearing a military jacket and trousers, with a three-quarter length cloak. Both hands are gauntleted. His right hand is on his hip and his left hand by his side clutching the hilt of his sword.

Plate 28 (Left)
Fig. 75 Victoria
Fig. 76 Albert

Plate 29 (Right)
Fig. 78 Victoria and the
Princess Royal

Plate 28A
Fig. 77 Victoria
In the Thomas Balston collection

Plate 28
Figure 75
Subject: **Victoria**
Title: None
Date: 184–
Height: 7¾ in (20·cm)
Colour: Very fine.
Rarity: R.
Pair: Fig. 76 (Albert)
Description: Standing crowned, wearing a full-length dress and the Order of the Garter. In her right hand she holds a long scroll. Shaped base.

Figure 76
Subject: **Albert**
Title: None
Date: 184–
Height: 8¼ in (21 cm)
Colour: Very fine.
Rarity: R.
Pair: Fig. 75 (Victoria)
Description: Standing bare-headed, in cloak, military jacket and trousers. His right hand is on his hip and his left hand holds the hilt of his sword. Shaped base.

Plate 28A
Figure 77
Subject: **Victoria**
Title: None
Date: ? 1860
Height: 8½ in (21.5 cm)
Colour: Pale.
Rarity: R.

Description: Standing crowned, wearing a full-length dress. She holds a long scroll in her right hand and a flag in her left. To her left is a lion.
Observations: 1. Referring to the threat of a French invasion in 1860, Balston wrote: *It is possible that the single figure of the Queen with a lion synchronized with the Napoleon beneath a lion, see fig. 277, pl.* C-93.
2. A similar figure, together with *fig.* 122 (Prince of Wales) *pl.* A-42, fetched 40 gns at Christie's in 1965.

Plate 29
Figure 78
Subject: **Victoria and Princess Royal**
Title: None
Date: c. 1841
Height: 6¾ in (17 cm)
Colour: Fine.
Rarity: R.
Pair: There is almost certainly a pair to this figure, but it has not yet come to light.
Description: Standing crowned, wearing a cloak, full-length dress with flounced skirt, and holding the Princess in her right arm. The Princess is wearing a bonnet and long dress.

Plate 30
Figure 79
Subject: **Albert**
Title: None
Date: 184–
Height: 5¼ in (13.5 cm)

Colour Plate 11
Victoria and Albert. *Figs.* 75 and 76, *pl.* A-28. See opposite.

Colour Plate 12
Princess Louise and the Marquess of Lorne. *Figs.* 229 and 230, *pl.* A-78. See page 164.

Colour Plate 13
Duke and Duchess of Edinburgh. *Figs.* 233 and 234, *pl.* A-80. See page 164.

Plate 30
Fig. 79 Albert
Fig. 80 Victoria
Fig. 81 Albert
Fig. 82 Albert

Plate 30 continued
Colour: Well coloured.
Rarity: Av.
Pair: There is almost certainly a pair to this figure, but it has so far escaped detection.
Description: Standing bare-headed, in military frock-coat and trousers, a sash over his right arm. Candle snuffer.

Figure 80
Subject: **Victoria**
Title: None
Date: 184–
Height: 4½ in (11.5 cm)
Colour: Well coloured.
Rarity: Av.
Pair: *Fig.* 81 (Albert)
Description: Seated crowned, wearing a full-length dress. Hollow base.

Figure 81
Subject: **Albert**
Title: None
Date: 184–
Height: 4½ in (11.5 cm)
Colour: Well coloured.
Rarity: Av.
Pair: *Fig.* 80 (Victoria)
Description: Sitting bare-headed, wearing neckerchief, frock-coat, waistcoat and trousers, a scroll in his right hand. Hollow base.

Figure 82
Subject: **Albert**
Title: None
Date: 184–
Height: 5¾ in (14.5 cm)
Colour: Well coloured.
Rarity: VR.
Pair: There is probably a pair to this figure, but it has not been described.
Description: Seated wearing a cocked hat athwartships, military frock-coat and trousers. He holds a scroll in his right hand and behind there is a canister, presumably for bird seed.
Observations: This is the only figure of this type that I have ever seen. It was possibly modified by the potter for his child and not intended for the general market.

Plate 31
Figure 83
Subject: **Albert**

A134

Title: None
Date: 184–
Height: 5¾ in (14.5 cm)
Colour: Well coloured.
Rarity: Av.
Pair: *Fig.* 84 (Victoria)
Description: Standing bare-headed, in long cloak, military uniform with epaulettes and sash across the left shoulder, and trousers. Hollow base.
Observations: A mini-version of *fig.* 36 (Albert) *pl.* A-15.

Figure 84
Subject: **Victoria**
Title: None
Date: 184–
Height: 5½ in (14 cm)
Colour: Well coloured.

Rarity: Av.
Pair: *Fig.* 83 (Albert)
Description: Standing crowned, wearing bodice and full-length flounced skirt, a garter sash over her left shoulder. She holds the orb in her left hand. Hollow base.
Observations: A mini-version of *fig.* 37 (Victoria and Princess Royal) *pl.* A-16; the Princess Royal is omitted.

Figure 85
Subject: **? Albert**
Title: None
Date: 184–
Height: 5¾ in (14.5 cm)
Colour: Well coloured.
Rarity: Av.
Pair: No pair is known to this figure, but *fig.* 86 has been reserved for it.

Plate 31
Fig. 83 Albert   *Fig.* 85 ?Albert
Fig. 84 Victoria   *In the collection of Lt.-Col. A. Kimpton*

Description: Standing, wearing a beaver hat, cloak, neckerchief, low-cut waistcoat, coat and trousers. Hollow base.
Observations: Almost certainly Albert, especially as it is in the same style as the two preceding figures, but there is, of course, no positive proof.

Plate 32
Figure 87
Subject: **Victoria and Albert**
Title: None
Date: *c.* 1858
Height: 7 in (17.5 cm)
Colour: Well coloured.

Rarity: Av.
Description: The Queen stands on the right and Albert on the left. They are arm-in-arm. The Queen wears a poke bonnet, shawl, muff and full-length skirt. Albert wears a beaver hat, neckerchief, frock-coat and trousers.
Observations: The figure appears to be based on a mirror-image of a photograph of the Queen and Albert taken about 1858, the main difference being that the disparity in their height, so clearly demonstrated in the photograph, has not been portrayed by the potter. Nevertheless, the similarity between figure and photograph is very convincing.

Plate 33
Figure 88
Subject: **Victoria**
Title: None
Date: 184–
Height: 6 in (15.25 cm)
Colour: Well coloured.
Rarity: R.
Pair: *Fig.* 89 (Albert)
Description: Seated on a mound wearing a top hat draped with a short scarf, blouse, with a Garter star on the left breast and full-length skirt. She holds an unidentified object in her right hand. The base is three-sided in front and semi-circular behind.

Figure 89
Subject: **Albert**
Title: None
Date: 184–
Height: 6¼ in (16 cm)
Colour: Well coloured.
Rarity: R.
Pair: *Fig.* 88 (Victoria)
Description: Sitting on a mound, wearing a top hat, morning coat, low-cut waistcoat and trousers. He holds a book in his left hand. The base is three-sided in front and semi-circular behind.

Figure 90
Subject: **Victoria and Princess Royal**
Title: None
Date: *c.* 1841
Height: 6½ in (16.5 cm)
Colour: Well coloured.
Rarity: R.
Pair: *Fig.* 91 (Albert)
Description: Standing wearing a bonnet, cape, and ankle-length dress with a flounced skirt. She holds the Princess Royal in her left arm, and appears to be proffering her a sweetmeat with her right hand. The Princess is wearing a bonnet and long dress. Six-sided base.

Figure 91
Subject: **Albert**
Title: None
Date: 184–
Height: 6¾ in (17 cm)
Colour: Well coloured.

Plate 32 (Above)
Fig. 87 Victoria and Albert
In the collection of Mr D.P.M. Michael
The photograph of Queen Victoria and the Prince Consort was taken about 1858. It helps to confirm the identification of the figure and may even be its source, although the position of the couple has been reversed. The difference in their heights has been less clearly defined.

Plate 33
Fig. 88 Victoria
Fig. 89 Albert
Fig. 90 Victoria and the Princess Royal
Fig. 91 Albert

Colour Plate 14
Prince Frederick William of Prussia and the Princess Royal. *Figs.* 206 and 207, *pl.* A-67. See page 158.

Colour Plate 15
Prince of Wales and the Princess Royal. *Figs.* 194 and 195, *pl.* A-63. See page 155.

Plate 34 (Left)
Fig. 92 Victoria

Plate 35 (Right)
T: *Fig.* 94 Victoria
Fig. 95 Albert
B: *Fig.* 96 Victoria
Fig. 97 Albert

Plate 33 continued
Rarity: R.
Pair: *Fig.* 90 (Victoria and Princess Royal)
Description: Standing bare-headed, in skirted coat, neckerchief, low-cut waistcoat and trousers. His left hand is in his coat pocket and in his right hand he clutches what appears to be a biscuit or snuff-box. Six-sided base.
Observations: Two of the four figures I have seen had a firing crack across the left forearm repaired with 'parsley' by the potter, see *pl.* A-33. There was obviously a weakness in the design which may account for the relative scarcity of the figure.

Plate 34
Figure 92
Subject: **Victoria**
Title: None
Date: 184–
Height: 7¼ in (18.25 cm)
Colour: Well coloured.
Rarity: R.
Pair: There must be a pair to this figure, Albert, but it has so far escaped detection. *Fig.* 93 has been reserved for it.
Description: Standing, wearing a top hat draped with a scarf. Her riding skirt is looped up over her right wrist, thus displaying a triangle of underskirt. On an oval base.

Plate 35
Figure 94
Subject: **Victoria**
Title: None
Date: 184–
Height: 7 in (17.5 cm)
Colour: Well coloured.

Rarity: R.
Pair: *Fig.* 95 (Albert)
Description: Standing, in a top hat draped with a scarf which falls over her right shoulder. Her riding skirt is looped up over her right wrist, thus displaying a triangle of underskirt. On a square base with pinched-in sides.
Observations: Except for the base, the figure is virtually identical to *fig.* 92 (Victoria) *pl.* A-34.

Figure 95
Subject: **Albert**
Title: None
Date: 184–
Height: 7¾ in (20 cm)
Colour: Well coloured.
Rarity: R.
Pair: *Fig.* 94 (Victoria)
Description: Standing, wearing a broad-brimmed top hat, skirted coat, low-cut waistcoat and trousers. His left hand is in his coat pocket and his right hand is held forwards. Square base with pinched-in sides.
Observations: A similar figure and its pair were sold at Christie's for 72 gns in 1967.

Figure 96
Subject: **Victoria**
Title: None
Date: 184–
Height: 7¾ in (20 cm)
Colour: Well coloured.
Rarity: R.
Pair: *Fig.* 97 (Albert)
Description: She stands, wearing a high, broad-topped, peaked hat which is draped with a scarf falling over her right shoulder.

With her left hand she holds up a fold of the skirt of her riding habit, and her right hand is across her waist. Square base with pinched-in sides.
Observations: Mr Balston in his description of what appears to be the same figure, refers to a 'crop' in her right hand, but the figure illustrated on *pl.* A-35 has not and never has had a crop. It must be assumed therefore that two similar figures exist.

Figure 97
Subject: **Albert**
Title: None
Date: 184–
Height: 8 in (20.5 cm)
Colour: Well coloured.
Rarity: R.
Pair: *Fig.* 96 (Victoria)
Description: Virtually identical, other than for height, to *fig.* 95 (Albert).

Plate 35A
Figure 97(a)
Subject: **? Albert**
Title: None
Height: 8 in (20.5 cm)
Colour: Richly coloured and gilded. The blue of his cloak is distinctive and similar to that seen in some of the figures known to emanate from the factory of John (& Rebecca) Lloyd.
Maker: Possibly John (& Rebecca) Lloyd, Shelton.
Rarity: VR. A.
Pair: Not known but must exist, *fig.* 96(a) has been reserved for it.
Description: Standing in top hat, cloak, jacket and trousers. The cloak is open in

A137

Plate 35A (Left)
Fig. 97(a) ?Albert

Plate 36 (Right)
Fig. 98 Albert

Plate 35a continued

front and the lining is displayed. He is holding the lining in his left hand, and with his right hand he fingers a cord suspended from his neck at the end of which is a monocle, or possibly, a fob watch. Ornate base.

Observations: 1. This figure is very reminiscent of *figs*. 95 and 97, *pl.* A-35 but it has evolved into a flat-back.

2. The base of the figure is impressed '5' and has a blue cross under the glaze.

3. There is doubt about the identity of this figure. The person portrayed is cleanshaven and I can find no evidence that Albert ever wore a monocle. Nevertheless as already noted it is in the same spirit as *figs*. 95 and 97, *pl.* A-35.

Plate 36
Figure 98
Subject: **Albert**
Title: None
Date: 184–
Height: 8 in (20.5 cm)
Colour: Well coloured.
Rarity: R.
Pair: Fig. 99 (Victoria) *pl.* A-37.
Description: On a horse facing left, wearing a broad brimmed top-hat, skirted coat, low-cut waistcoat and trousers. He holds the reins in his left hand.

Plate 37
Figure 99
Subject: **Victoria**
Title: None
Date: 184–
Height: 8 in (20.5 cm)
Colour: Well coloured.
Rarity: R.
Pair: Fig. 98 (Albert) *pl.* A-36.
Description: On a horse facing right, wearing a top hat draped with a scarf, and riding habit. Her left hand is on the horse's mane, and she holds the reins in her right hand.

A138

Figure 100
Subject: **? Victoria**
Title: None
Date: 184–
Height: 8 in (20.5 cm)
Colour: Well coloured.
Rarity: R.
Pair: No pair has been recorded to date. If this figure is Victoria, then it is likely to pair Albert, for which *fig.* 101 has been reserved, but see *observations*.
Description: On a horse facing left, in top hat draped with a scarf which falls over her left shoulder. She is wearing a full riding habit and her right hand is on the horse's mane.
Observations: Probably Queen Victoria, but this figure does bear a striking likeness to a portrait painted in 1793 by George Stubbs of Laetitia, Lady Lade, a brilliant horsewoman and a raffish friend of George IV when Prince of Wales. This painting is in the Royal Collection. The similarity between the figure and the painting is not quite enough to justify dogmatism.

Figure 102
Subject: **Albert**
Title: Albert (gilt script)
Height: 11¾ in (29.75 cm)
Colour: Sparingly coloured, largely white and gilt.
Maker: Probably Sampson Smith
Rarity: R.
Pair: Fig. 103 (Victoria)
Description: On a horse facing right, in full military uniform. He is holding his cocked hat to his head with his right hand, and in his left hand he holds the reins.

Figure 103
Subject: **Victoria**
Title: Queen (gilt script)
Height: 10 in (25 cm)
Colour: As for *fig.* 102 (Albert).
Maker: Probably Sampson Smith
Rarity: R.
Pair: Fig. 102 (Albert)

Description: On a horse facing left, wearing a round hat with a scarf blowing out over her left shoulder. Dressed in a full riding habit. She holds the reins in both hands.

Plate 38
Figure 104
Subject: **Albert**
Title: None
Date: 184–
Height: 8½ in (21.5 cm)
Colour: Beautifully coloured.
Rarity: R.
Pair: Fig. 105 (Victoria)
Description: On a horse facing right, wearing a plumed cocked hat athwartships, military uniform with epaulettes, a sash across his right shoulder and a star on his right breast. He is holding the reins in his right hand and his left hand is on the horse's mane. There is a small flower on the base.
Observations: See *fig.* 105 (Victoria).

Figure 105
Subject: **Victoria**
Title: None
Date: 184–
Height: 8 in (20.5 cm)
Colour: Beautifully coloured.
Rarity: R.
Pair: Fig. 104 (Albert)
Description: On a horse facing left, wearing a round hat with a scarf flowing out over her left shoulder. There is a star on the left breast of her riding habit, and she is holding the reins in both hands. The base of the figure is decorated with one flower.
Observations: 1. In this case the figure and its pair undoubtedly portray Victoria and Albert, but there is a striking resemblance between this pair and Sir Robert and Lady Sale (*figs*. 66 and 67, *pl.* C-26).
2. A similar pair of figures fetched 28 gns at Christie's in 1965.

Plate 37
T: *Fig.* 99 Victoria
Fig. 100 ?Victoria
B: *Fig.* 102 Albert
Fig. 103 Victoria
In the collection of Lady Ranfurly

Plate 38
Fig. 104 Albert
Fig. 105 Victoria

Plate 39
T: *Fig.* 106 Victoria
Fig. 107 Albert
B: *Fig.* 108 Albert
Fig. 109 Victoria

Plate 39
Figure 106
Subject: **Victoria**
Title: None
Date: 184–
Height: 7½ in (19 cm)
Colour: Well coloured.
Rarity: Av.
Pair: Fig. 107 (Albert)
Description: On a horse facing right, wearing a round hat with a scarf flowing over her right shoulder. She is dressed in a full riding habit, with a sash over her left shoulder. She holds the reins in her right hand and her left hand is on the horse's mane.

Figure 107
Subject: **Albert**
Title: None
Date: 184–
Height: 8¼ in (21 cm)
Colour: Well coloured.
Rarity: Av.
Pair: Fig. 106 (Victoria)
Description: On a horse facing left, in full military uniform, wearing a plumed cocked hat, cape, military jacket with epaulettes and a star on his left breast. He holds the reins in his left hand and his right hand is on the horse's mane.

Figure 108
Subject: **Albert**
Title: Albert (raised capitals)
Date: 184–
Height: 9½ in (24 cm)
Colour: Well coloured.
Rarity: Av.
Pair: Fig. 109 (Victoria)
Description: On a horse facing right, in

cocked hat, military jacket with epaulettes, a sash over his right shoulder and trousers. His right hand is on the horse's rump, and he holds the reins in his left hand.

Figure 109
Subject: **Victoria**
Title: Queen (raised capitals)
Date: 184–
Height: 9 in (23 cm)
Colour: Well coloured.
Rarity: Av.
Pair: Fig. 108 (Albert)
Description: On a horse facing left, wearing a low round hat with a plume and a scarf flowing over her left shoulder. She is dressed in a full riding habit. Her left hand is on the horse's mane and she holds the reins in her right hand.
Observations: A similar figure and its pair fetched 18 gns at Christie's in 1964; another pair fetched 38 gns in the same rooms in 1969.

Plate 40
Figure 110
Subject: **? Albert**
Title: None
Date: 184–
Height: 7 in (17.5 cm)
Colour: Pale colouring.
Rarity: Av.
Pair: Fig. 111 (? Victoria)
Description: On a pony facing right, in plumed cocked hat and military uniform.

Figure 111
Subject: **? Victoria**
Title: None
Date: 184–

Plate 40
T: *Fig.* 110 ?Albert
Fig. 111 ?Victoria
B: *Fig.* 112 ?Albert
Fig. 113 ?Victoria
Fig. 114 ?Victoria
Fig. 115 ?Albert
In the collection of Lady Ranfurly

Plate 40A
Fig. 116 Albert
In the collection of Mrs Margaret Power

A140

Plate 40 continued
Height: 6½ in (16.5 cm)
Colour: Pale colouring.
Rarity: Av.
Pair: *Fig.* 110 (? Albert)
Description: On a pony facing left, wearing a plumed hat with a scarf draped down from it over her left shoulder. Dressed in full riding habit.
Observations: There are a number of figures rather similar to this figure and its pair. Probably the majority represent Victoria and Albert, although there is no positive proof of this.

Figure 112
Subject: **? Albert**
Title: None
Date: 184–
Height: 8 in (20.5 cm)
Colour: The horse is usually a piebald.
Rarity: Av.
Pair: *Fig.* 113 (Victoria)
Description: On a horse facing right, in plumed cocked hat, military uniform and knee-boots.

Figure 113
Subject: **? Victoria**
Title: None
Date: 184–
Height: 7 in (17.5 cm)
Colour: The horse is usually a piebald.
Rarity: Av.
Pair: *Fig.* 112 (? Albert)
Description: On a horse facing left, wearing a round hat or crown, cape blowing out to the right, and full riding habit.
Observations: This figure and its pair have been catalogued by Balston as Victoria and Albert, and it is likely that this is so. Collectors have, however, noted the close similarity between this pair of figures and other similar figures, to the figures of Sir Robert and Lady Sale. I understand from two different sources that *fig.* 113 has been found titled 'Lady Hester Stanhope', but I have never seen an example of this myself.

Figure 114
Subject: **? Victoria**
Title: None
Date: 184–
Height: 7½ in (19 cm)
Colour: Well coloured.
Rarity: R.
Pair: *Fig.* 115 (? Albert)
Description: On a horse facing right, wearing a round hat and riding habit, a sash over her left shoulder. Her left hand is on the horse's mane, and she holds the reins in her right hand.

Figure 115
Subject: **? Albert**
Title: None
Date: 184–
Height: 8 in (20.5 cm)
Colour: Well coloured.
Rarity: R.
Pair: *Fig.* 114 (? Victoria)
Description: On a horse facing left, wearing a plumed cocked hat athwartships, cloak, military uniform and thigh boots. His right hand is on the horse's mane and he holds the reins in his left hand.
Observations: The same difficulty of identification exists about this pair as with the preceding figures, although in this case the pair almost certainly represents Victoria and Albert.

Section A. British and Foreign Royalty

Plate 40A
Figure 116
Subject: **Albert**
Title: Royal stag hunt (gilt script)
Date: 184–
Height: 10 in (25 cm)
Colour: Well coloured.
Rarity: VR. A.
Description: Below, two hounds are seen chasing a stag uphill to the right. Above, Albert is seen galloping to the right. He wears a top hat and long coat. To the right, also, is a small bridge over a stream.
Observations: A figure exists which is very similar except that the horseman is clean-shaven and wears a huntsman's cap, and the hounds are chasing a fox instead of a stag. This figure is known in the trade as 'John Peel', but I know of no evidence to support the identification.

Plate 41
Figure 117
Subject: **Victoria, Albert and child**
Title: Pr. Albert & Queen (raised capitals)
Date: 184–
Height: 12½ in (31.75 cm)
Colour: Well coloured.
Rarity: R.
Description: Albert stands on the left, wearing a plumed bonnet and full Highland dress. Victoria stands in the centre bare-headed, and to her left stands a child wearing a plumed bonnet.

Plate 41A
Figure 118
Subject: **Balmoral Castle**
Title: Balmoral Castle (raised capitals on plaque)

Plate 41
Fig. 117 Victoria, Albert and child

Date: c. 1854
Height: 9½ in (24 cm)
Colour: Well coloured.
Rarity: R.
Description: A series of towers decreasing in height from left to right. The entrance to the castle is on the right.

Figure 118(a)
Subject: **Balmoral Castle**
Title: Balmoral Castle (gilt script)
Date: c. 1854
Height: 8⅛ in (20.75 cm)
Colour: Well coloured.
Rarity: VR.
Description: A series of towers decreasing in height from left to right. Two doorways, one on either side.
Observations: 1. The only example known to me is slightly damaged.
2. Apparently neither this nor the preceding figure bear any real resemblance to Balmoral Castle.

Figure 119
Subject: **Windsor Castle**
Title: None
Height: 6 in (15.25 cm)
Colour: Well coloured.
Rarity: Av.
Description: A flight of steps leads up to the arched entrance in the centre. On the left is a large three-storied tower, and to the right two smaller towers.
Observations: 1. Identified from the virtually identical, titled porcelaneous figure (*fig.* 120, *pl.* A-42).
2. It does not bear a close resemblance to any part of Windsor Castle, although it is probably meant to portray the Round Tower.

Plate 42
Figure 120
Subject: **Windsor Castle**
Title: Windsor Castle (gilt script)
Height: 5½ in (14 cm)
Colour: Well coloured.

Plate 41A
Fig. 118 Balmoral Castle
Fig. 118(a) Balmoral Castle
Fig. 119 Windsor Castle

Plate 42
Fig. 122 The Prince of Wales and Windsor Castle
Fig. 121 Windsor Lodge
Fig. 120 Windsor Castle

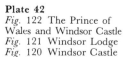

Plate 42 continued
Rarity: VR. A.
Description: A porcelaneous figure of the same design as *fig.* 119, *pl.* A-41A. A flight of stairs in the centre leads to an arched entrance above which is a clock. To the left is a large three-storied tower, and to the right two smaller towers. The figure is richly embellished with floral decoration.
Observations: 1. See *fig.* 119 (Windsor Castle) *pl.* A-41A.
2. This figure fetched 28 gns in Christie's in 1964.

Figure 121
Subject: **Windsor Lodge**
Title: Windsor Lodge (gilt script)
Height: 5¼ in (13.5 cm)
Colour: Largely white and gilt.
Rarity: R.
Description: A two-storied house, the entrance to which is reached by a flight of steps. There are two projecting windows and one chimney-stack. Pastille-burner.
Observations: In spite of the most intensive research, the identity of this building remains obscure. Mr Geoffrey de Bellaigue, Deputy Surveyor of the Queen's Works of Art, has kindly examined *pl.* A-42 for me and writes:

I must confess that I do not recognize any of the buildings represented. I have made enquiries among my colleagues and they too are of the opinion that these buildings are not identifiable. I do not know of a house called 'Windsor Lodge'. It might, however, be a variant on 'Royal Lodge'.

Even if the title 'Windsor Lodge' is a variant on 'Royal Lodge', the figure bears no similarity whatever to the building.
In the *Official Guide to Windsor Castle* it is remarked that:

. . . in 1778 King George III (1760–1820) resolved to bring it (Windsor Castle) once more into line with advancing standards of domestic comfort. For himself and his family during the work of reconditioning he erected a commonplace building known as Queen's Lodge, which was pulled down in 1824.

It appears that 'Queen's Lodge' was a barrack-like structure built by Sir William Chambers. It was reproduced by Benjamin West as a background to a portrait of Queen Charlotte which now hangs in the Queen's Ball Room at Windsor Castle. It, too, bears no relation to *fig.* 121.

Figure 122
Subject: **Prince of Wales and Windsor Castle**
Title: None
Date: c. 1849
Height: 6¾ in (17 cm)
Colour: Well coloured.
Rarity: Av.
Description: A boy dressed in a boater, jacket, shirt and trousers is paddling a skiff towards a bridge. A castle, which may be reached by steps to the left of the bridge, lies above. It consists of a large round tower to the left, which may be entered through a central door, and two smaller towers to the right. The general appearance bears some similarity to *fig.* 120 (Windsor Castle).
Observations: 1. This figure is generally believed to represent the Prince of Wales and Windsor Castle. The identification of the castle is, of course, based solely on its similarity to the titled version, for it bears no resemblance to Windsor Castle itself.
2. In *The Illustrated London News* of April 22nd, 1848 there appears an engraving of a skiff with the inscription *Boat for His Royal*

Highness the Prince of Wales, together with the following account:

BOAT FOR THE PRINCE OF WALES
The Prince of Wales is about to be initiated in the manly and healthful exercise of rowing; for which purpose a new and beautiful single-sculling boat is now being constructed for his Royal Highness, on the latest and most improved principles, by Messrs. Searle, her Majesty's boat-builders, of Stangate-street, near Westminster-bridge. The skiff is a complete model of the boats used by gentlemen on the Thames, and a fine specimen of workmanship. It is 20 feet in length, of proportionate breadth, and is built of the finest bird's-eye maple, with mahogany linings, sax-boards and thwarts. The spaces between the timbers are filled with a material said to be considerably more buoyant than cork; it is, in fact, a perfect life-boat in miniature. The cushion on which his Royal Highness will sit to pull his sculls is also stuffed with this material, and which, it is affirmed, will prevent the possibility of the little craft sinking.

The minor appointments are of an elegant and tasteful description, and in perfect keeping with the general appearance of the boat, which has been inspected at Messrs. Searle's upper premises, near Lambeth Palace, by most of the members of the Oxford and Cambridge and other aquatic clubs, who have expressed their admiration of its perfect build and equipments. It is stated to be intended as a present for his Royal Highness from the Institution of Civil Engineers, Great George-street, Westminster, or one of the members of that Society.

3. A similar figure, together with *fig.* 77 (Victoria) *pl.* A-28A, fetched 40 gns at Christie's in 1965; another, by itself, fetched 28 gns at Christie's in 1969.

Plate 43
Figure 123
Subject: **Prince of Wales**
Date: c. 1848
Height: 2¾ in (7 cm)
Colour: Well coloured.
Rarity: R.
Description: Sitting in a skiff facing left, wearing a boater, jacket, shirt and trousers. He holds a paddle in his left hand.
Observations: The identical figure to that used for *fig.* 122 (Prince of Wales and Windsor Castle) *pl.* A-42. The basis of identification is the same.

Figure 124
Subject: **? The Royal Children in a boat**
Title: None
Date: c. 1848
Height: 7½ in (19 cm)

Colour: Usually sparsely coloured.
Rarity: Av.
Description: In a gondolier-type boat. The Princess is sitting on the left, and the Prince stands on the right, wearing a sailor's hat, jacket, shirt and trousers. He carries a flag in his left hand; to his left is an anchor.
Observations: It is generally thought that this type of figure, of which there are several variants, represents the royal children, but I know of no definite evidence to support this view.

Plate 44
Figure 125
Subject: **Victoria**
Title: None
Date: 184–
Height: 6½ in (16.5 cm)
Colour: Well coloured.
Rarity: R.
Pair: *Fig.* 126 (Albert)
Description: Standing crowned, wearing a bodice and ankle-length skirt. Her left hand is on her hip and her right hand, which holds an orb, is held in front of her chest.

Figure 126
Subject: **Albert**
Title: None
Date: 184–
Height: 6½ in (16.5 cm)
Colour: Well coloured.
Rarity: R.
Pair: *Fig.* 125 (Victoria)
Description: Standing bare-headed, wearing a cloak, jacket, waistcoat and trousers. His left arm is held in front of his chest, and in his left hand he is carrying a sceptre. His right arm is by his side.

Figure 127
Subject: **Prince of Wales**
Title: None
Date: 184–
Height: 5 in (12.75 cm)
Colour: Beautifully coloured.
Rarity: VR. D. A.
Pair: *Fig.* 128 (Princess Royal)
Description: Sitting bare-headed, in a high-backed chair surmounted by a crown. He is wearing a kilt.

Plate 43
Fig. 124 ?The royal children in boat
Fig. 123 The Prince of Wales
In the collection of Mr Anthony Oliver

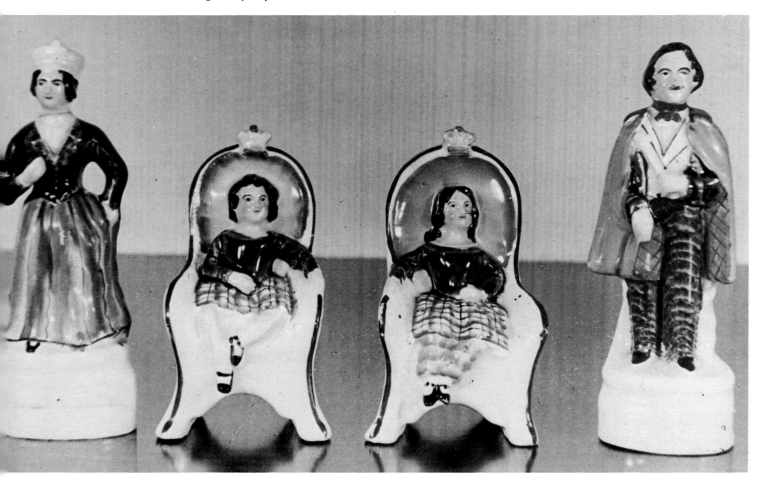

Plate 44
Fig. 125 Victoria   *Fig.* 127 The Prince of Wales   *Fig.* 128 The Princess Royal   *Fig.* 126 Albert
By courtesy of Mr and Mrs Eric Joyce

Figure 128
Subject: **Princess Royal**
Title: None
Date: 184–
Height: 5 in (12.75 cm)
Colour: Beautifully coloured.
Rarity: VR. D. A.
Pair: Fig. 127 (Prince of Wales)
Description: Sitting bare-headed, in a high-backed chair surmounted by a crown. She is wearing a short skirt and pantalettes.

Plate 45
Figure 129
Subject: **Prince of Wales and Princess Royal**
Title: None
Date: 184–
Height: 6½ in (16.5 cm)
Colour: Well coloured.
Rarity: R.
Description: The Princess with the Prince on her right is sitting on a long bench in an arbour. The Prince is bare-headed and wears a short jacket, waistcoat and trousers. The Princess is bare-headed and wears a full-length dress with a flounced skirt.

Plate 46
Figure 130
Subject: **Victoria**
Title: Queen (indented capitals)
Date: c. 1838–9
Height: 7 in (17.5 cm)
Colour: Very well coloured.
Maker: Alpha factory

Rarity: VR. D. A.
Pair: Not known
Description: Sitting crowned, wearing a full-length dress with Garter sash and holding a book in her right hand.
Observations: 1. Probably made after her coronation but before her marriage to Prince Albert in February, 1840.

2. It has been suggested that the inspiration for the figure is the painting of Queen Victoria's first Privy Council by Sir David Wilkie RA.
3. A similar figure fetched 40 gns at Christie's in 1965.

Plate 45
Fig. 129 The Prince of Wales and the Princess Royal

Plate 46
Fig. 131 The Princess Royal
Fig. 130 Victoria
Fig. 132 The Prince of Wales
By courtesy of Mr and Mrs Eric Joyce

Plate 46 continued
Figure 131
Subject: **Princess Royal**
Title: Princess (indented capitals)
Date: 184–
Height: 6¼ in (16 cm)
Colour: Well coloured.
Maker: Alpha factory
Rarity: VR. A.
Pair: Fig. 132 (Prince of Wales)
Description: Standing bare-headed, wearing a bodice, flounced skirt and pantalettes. She holds her hat in her left hand, and her right hand rests on a parrot standing on a round table. Base oval, concave in the front, with steps.

Figure 132
Subject: **Prince of Wales**
Title: Prince (indented capitals)
Date: 184–
Height: 6¼ in (16 cm)
Colour: Well coloured.
Maker: Alpha factory
Rarity: VR. A.
Pair: Fig. 131 (Princess Royal)
Description: Standing bare-headed, wearing a short jacket, waistcoat and trousers. He holds his hat in his right hand, and his left hand is holding a model ship which is resting on a round table. Base oval, concave in the front, with steps.

Plate 47
Figure 133
Subject: **Princess Royal**
Title: Princes (*sic*) Royal (gilt script)
Date: 184–
Height: 6¼ in (16 cm)
Colour: Very well coloured.
Maker: Probably the Alpha factory
Rarity: VR.
Pair: Fig. 134 (Prince of Wales)
Description: Similar to *fig.* 131 (Princess Royal) *pl.* A-46, except for the manner of titling and the shape of the base, which is plain oval.

Figure 134
Subject: **Prince of Wales**
Title: Prince of Wales (gilt script)
Date: 184–

A144

Height: 6½ in (16.5 cm)
Colour: Very well coloured.
Maker: Probably the Alpha factory.
Rarity: VR.
Pair: Fig. 133 (Princess Royal)
Description: Similar to *fig.* 132 (Prince of Wales) *pl.* A-46, except for the manner of titling and the shape of the base, which is plain oval.

Figure 135
Subject: **Princess Royal**
Title: None
Date: 184–
Height: 6 in (15.25 cm)
Colour: Well coloured.
Maker: Possibly the Alpha factory
Rarity: C.
Pair: Fig. 136 (Prince of Wales)
Description: Similar to *fig.* 131 (Princess Royal) *pl.* A-46, except that it is untitled. The base, although oval, is more obviously concave and stepped in front.
Observations: There are several variants of this figure. It will be noted that *figs.* 135 and 136 are not a 'matching' pair due to a minor variation in the shape of the base.

Figure 136
Subject: **Prince of Wales**
Title: None
Date: 184–
Height: 6½ ins (16.5 cm)
Colour: Well coloured.
Maker: Possibly the Alpha factory
Rarity: C.
Pair: Fig. 135 (Princess Royal)
Description: Similar to *fig.* 132 (Prince of Wales) *pl.* A-46, except that it is untitled. The base, although oval, is more obviously concave and stepped in front.
Observations: See *fig.* 135 (Princess Royal).

Figure 137
Subject: **Prince of Wales**
Title: None
Date: 184–
Height: 7 in (17.5 cm)
Colour: Well coloured.
Rarity: C.
Pair: Fig. 138 (Princess Royal)
Description: Standing on a throne, wearing a

plumed bonnet and Highland dress, a parrot perched on his left arm.
Observations: See *fig.* 138 (Princess Royal).

Figure 138
Subject: **Princess Royal**
Title: None
Date: 184–
Height: 7½ in (19 cm)
Colour: Well coloured.
Rarity: C.
Pair: Fig. 137 (Prince of Wales)
Description: Standing on a throne, wearing Highland dress, a parrot perched on her right arm.
Observations: I have never seen this figure with a contemporary title, but the poor version illustrated in *ch.* 6, *pl.* 2 has had the title 'Princess' added recently in an attempt to enhance its value. This class of fake is likely to become commoner as figures become scarcer.

Figure 139
Subject: **Prince of Wales**
Title: None
Height: 5¾ in (14.5 cm)
Colour: Chestnut, piebald and skewbald versions have been noted.
Rarity: Av.
Pair: Fig. 140 (Princess Royal) *pl.* A-48. Same series as *fig.* 141 (Victoria) and *fig.* 142 (Groom), *pl.* A-48.
Description: On a pony facing left, wearing a plumed bonnet, tunic and trousers. Hollow base.
Observations: 1. In pairing figures of children on horseback it is sometimes difficult, at first sight, to tell which is the boy and which the girl, for there is little difference in the appearances of the tunic and trousers of the former and the blouse, skirt and pantalettes worn by the latter. However, the potter invariably made clear which was intended by portraying the girl as riding side-saddle and the boy as riding astride. The reverse of *fig.* 139 (Prince of Wales) is shown on *pl.* A-48.
2. There are many pairing equestrian figures of children on ponies which may or may not represent the Prince of Wales and the Princess Royal. Probably most of them

Plate 47
T: *Fig.* 137 The Prince of Wales
Fig. 143 The Prince of Wales and the Princess Royal
Fig. 138 The Princess Royal

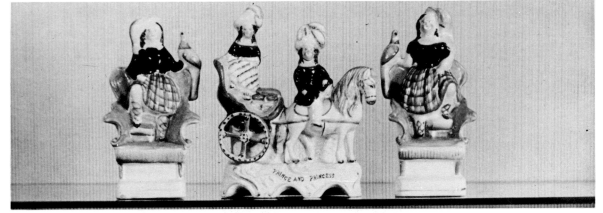

B: *Fig.* 135 The Princess Royal
Fig. 136 The Prince of Wales
Fig. 139 The Prince of Wales
Fig. 133 The Princess Royal
Fig. 134 The Prince of Wales

do. *Figs.* 139 and 140, *pls.* A-47 and 48 come as close as one is ever likely to get to a positive identification of untitled figures of this type. They are in exactly the same style and colouring as *figs.* 141 and 142, *pl.* A-48 which appear to portray Victoria and an unidentified groom, possibly John Brown (1826-83).

Figure 143
Subject: **Prince of Wales and Princess Royal**
Title: Prince and Princess (indented capitals)
Date: 184–
Height: 7½ in (19 cm)

Colour: Well coloured.
Rarity: Av.
Description: There is a pony carriage facing right. The Prince who wears a plumed hat, tunic and trousers is astride the pony, and the Princess wearing a plumed hat, bodice and full-length skirt is standing in the carriage. The wheel of the carriage is spoked and the base of the figure rococo.

Plate 48
Figure 139 (in reverse)
Subject: **Prince of Wales**
Observations: See *pl.* A-47.

Figure 140
Subject: **Princess Royal**
Title: None
Height: 5⅜ in. (13.75 cm)
Colour: Chestnut, piebald and skewbald versions have been noted.
Rarity: Av.
Pair: *Fig.* 139 (Prince of Wales) *pl.* A-47. Same series as *fig.* 141 (Victoria) and *fig.* 142 (Groom).
Description: On a pony facing right, wearing a plumed bonnet, bodice, skirt and pantalettes. Hollow base.

Plate 48
Fig. 140 The Princess Royal
Fig. 142 Unidentified groom
Fig. 141 ?Victoria
Fig. 139 (*reverse*) The Prince of Wales
These figures are all in the same manner, and although of two different sizes are thought to represent a family group. The potter was always very accurate with regard to his representation of children on ponies. Thus the boy is always portrayed riding astride and the girl riding side-saddle.

Plate 48 continued

Figure 141
Subject: **? Victoria**
Title: None
Height: 7½ in (19 cm)
Colour: Chestnut, piebald and skewbald versions have been noted.
Rarity: Av.
Pair: *Fig.* 142 (Unidentified groom)
Description: On a horse facing left, wearing a plumed hat and riding habit with ermine edging to the neck. A dog is at the horse's feet racing to the left. Solid base.
Observations: Generally thought to portray Queen Victoria but the identification must be guarded. However, the ermine edging round the neck does suggest royalty.

Figure 142
Subject: **Unidentified groom**
Title: None
Height: 7⅛ in (18 cm)
Colour: Chestnut, piebald and skewbald versions have been noted.
Rarity: Av.
Pair: *Fig.* 141 (? Victoria)
Description: On a horse facing right, wearing a round hat, jacket, waistcoat and trousers. A dog is at the horse's feet racing to the right. Solid base.
Observations: The figure portrayed is almost certainly a groom; compare with groom portrayed in *fig.* 175 (Princess Royal) *pl.* A-57. There is no evidence on which to base an identification but possibly the subject is John Brown who for thirty-four years was personal attendant to Queen Victoria.

Plate 48A
Figure 140(a)
Subject: **Princess Royal**
Title: Princes (*sic*) Royal (gilt script)
Date: 184–
Height: 6¾ in (17 cm)
Colour: Well coloured; underglaze black horse.
Rarity: VR.
Pair: A pair, the Prince of Wales, must exist but has not yet been recorded. *Fig.* 139(a) has been allocated.
Description: On a pony facing right, in plumed bonnet, calf-length frock and pantalettes. A star on her left breast.

Plate 48B
Figure 142(a)
Subject: **? John Brown**
Title: None
Height: 7 in (17.5 cm)
Colour: Well coloured.
Rarity: VR.
Description: Standing in Highland dress, wearing cap, open shirt, jacket with belt and strap over his right shoulder, kilt, sporran, stockings and shoes. He leans on a pedestal to his left. He holds the muzzle of a gun in his right hand, the butt of which rests on the ground.
Observations: 1. It has been suggested that this is a portrait of John Brown (1826–83), but I have been unable to confirm this. The nature of the figure suggests that there is a pair, in which case, it would be unlikely to be Brown.
2. The gun is missing in the piece illustrated.

Plate 49
Figure 144
Subject: **Prince of Wales and Princess Royal**
Title: Prince and Princess (indented capitals)

A146

Plate 48A (Above left)
Fig. 140(a) The Princess Royal
In the collection of Mrs Margaret Power

Plate 48B (Above)
Fig. 142(a) ?John Brown

Plate 49
Fig. 144 The Prince of Wales and the Princess Royal

Date: 184–
Height: 7½ in (19 cm)
Colour: Well coloured.
Rarity: Av.
Description: Identical to *fig.* 143, *pl.* A-47, except that the wheel is solid and not spoked, and the base is flat, although the rococo pattern is retained.

Plate 50
Figure 145
Subject: **Prince of Wales and Princess Royal**
Title: Prince and Princess (indented capitals)
Date: 184–
Height: 7¼ in (18.25 cm)

Colour: Well coloured.
Rarity: VR. A.
Description: In a goat carriage facing right. The Prince wearing a plumed bonnet, tunic and trousers sits sideways on the goat. The Princess wearing a plumed bonnet, bodice, skirt and pantalettes is standing in the carriage holding a basket of flowers. The base of the figure is rococo and the wheel of the carriage is solid.

Figure 146
Subject: **Prince of Wales**
Title: None
Date: 184–
Height: 10 in (25 cm)
Colour: In the manner of Thomas Parr.

Section A. British and Foreign Royalty

Maker: Thomas Parr
Rarity: Av.
Pair: Fig. 147 (Princess Royal)
Description: The Prince of Wales, wearing a Scottish bonnet and full Highland dress, is standing in front of a St. Bernard dog, holding the lead in his left hand.
Observations: Late Kent versions exist of this figure and its pair.

Figure 147
Subject: **Princess Royal**
Title: None
Date: 184–
Height: 9 in (23 cm)
Colour: In the manner of Thomas Parr.
Maker: Thomas Parr
Rarity: Av.
Pair: Fig. 146 (Prince of Wales)
Description: The Princess Royal, bare-headed in Highland dress, is standing in front of a St. Bernard dog, whose lead she holds in her right hand.

Plate 51
Figure 148
Subject: **Princess Royal**
Title: Princess (raised capitals)
Date: 184–
Height: 8 in (20.5 cm)
Colour: Delicately coloured. However, crude versions are known.
Rarity: VR.
Pair: No pair is known to this figure, but one must surely exist. If the figure is the Princess Royal, then the pair will be the Prince of Wales.
Description: Sitting, in a plumed hat, in a basket-like carriage on one pair of wheels which is drawn by a pony, facing left, between two long shafts.
Observations: It probably portrays the Princess Royal. However, the possibility that it represents either the Princess of Wales or Princess Louise cannot be excluded. The final identification can only be made when the pair, which must surely exist, comes to

light. *Fig.* 149 has been reserved for it.

Plate 52
Figure 150
Subject: **Princess Royal**
Title: None
Date: 184–
Height: 7½ in (19 cm)
Colour: Inclined to be crude.
Rarity: VR.
Pair: Fig. 151 (Prince of Wales) *pl.* A-53.
Description: Standing to the left of a throne. She is bare-headed and wears a bodice, knee-length skirt and pantalettes. In her left hand she holds what may be a windmill, and on the seat of the throne is a basket containing either flowers or, more probably, three dead birds.

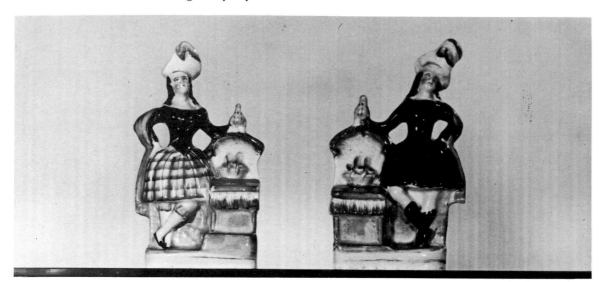

Plate 53
T: *Fig.* 152 The Princess Royal
Fig. 153 The Prince of Wales

B: *Fig.* 151 The Prince of Wales
Fig. 154 The Princess Royal
Fig. 156 ?Victoria and the Prince of Wales
In the collections of Mr Ronald Shockledge and the author

Plate 53

Figure 151
Subject: **Prince of Wales**
Title: None
Date: 184–
Height: 7½ in (19 cm)
Colour: Inclined to be crude.
Rarity: Av.
Pair: Fig. 150 (Princess Royal) *pl.* A-52.
Description: Standing to the right of a throne, wearing a straw hat and sailor suit. His left hand is raised to the brim of his hat, and in his right hand he holds a flag. There is a sailing ship on the throne and a furled anchor to the right of his left leg.
Observations: The significance of this figure and its pair *fig.* 150 (Princess Royal) is, as far as I know, not understood.

Figure 152
Subject: **Princess Royal**
Title: None
Date: 184–
Height: 6¼ in (16 cm)
Colour: Well coloured.
Rarity: Av.
Pair: Fig. 153 (Prince of Wales)

Description: Standing, wearing a plumed hat, bodice, knee-length skirt and pantalettes. Scarf over her right shoulder. Her right hand is on her hip and her left hand holds a falcon which is perched on the back of a chair. On the seat of the chair is a basket containing dead birds.
Observations: See *fig.* 153 (Prince of Wales).

Figure 153
Subject: **Prince of Wales**
Title: None
Date: 184–
Height: 6½ in (16.5 cm)
Colour: Well coloured.
Rarity: Av.
Pair: Fig. 152 (Princess Royal)
Description: Standing, wearing a plumed bonnet, tunic and calf-boots. His left hand is on his hip and his right hand holds a falcon which is perched on the back of a chair upon which is a basket containing dead birds. Scarf over his left shoulder.
Observations: There is no definite evidence that this figure and its pair portray the royal children, but it is likely that this is so. Alternatively, the figures may be 'theatrical'.

Figure 154
Subject: **Princess Royal**
Title: Princes (*sic*)/Royal (gilt script)
Date: 184–
Height: 7 in (17.5 cm)
Colour: Delicately coloured.
Rarity: VR. A.
Pair: Fig. 155 (Prince of Wales) *pl.* A-54.
Description: On a pony facing right, wearing a plumed bonnet, bodice and skirt. Rococo base.
Observations: An example of this figure and its pair fetched 55 gns at Christie's in 1968.

Figure 156
Subject: **? Victoria and Prince of Wales**
Title: None
Date: 184–
Height: 9¾ in (24.5 cm); 8 in (20.5 cm) version illustrated
Colour: Well coloured. Sometimes in authentic contemporary versions the base is coloured green.
Rarity: Av.

A148

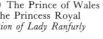

Plate 54A
The Young Cavalier
Engraving by John Cochran after a painting by William Salter
(1804-1875). It is the source of *fig.* 160 (The Prince of Wales)
pl. A-54.
By courtesy of Mr John Hall

Plate 54
T: *Fig.* 158 ?The Princess Royal   B: *Fig.* 160 The Prince of Wales
Fig. 155 The Prince of Wales   *Fig.* 161 The Princess Royal
Fig. 159 The Prince of Wales   *In the collection of Lady Ranfurly*

Pair: *Fig.* 157 (? Albert and Princess Royal)
pl. A-55.
Description: The Queen is standing, wearing
a plumed hat, bodice, knee-length two-
flounced skirt above pantalettes, long scarf
over her right shoulder. On her left is the
Prince of Wales wearing a tricorn hat, short
jacket and kilt. His right hand is in her left
hand.
Observations: The 9¾ in (24.5 cm) version of
this figure is catalogued in Mr Balston's
Supplement as 'Victoria with the Prince of
Wales'. In my view there is considerable
doubt about this. I know of no contemporary
portraits of the Queen showing her dressed
in this manner, and it is hard to conceive
that she ever would have done so. It seems
to me much more likely that this figure and
its pair are theatrical.

Plate 54
Figure 155
Subject: **Prince of Wales**
Title: Prince/of Wales (gilt script)
Date: 184–
Height: 7½ in (19 cm)
Colour: Delicately coloured.
Rarity: VR. A.
Pair: *Fig.* 154 (Princess Royal) *pl.* A-53.
Description: On a pony facing left, wearing a
plumed bonnet, shirt and trousers. Rococo
base.
Observations: An example of this figure and
its pair fetched 55 gns at Christie's
in 1968.

Figure 158
Subject: **? Princess Royal**
Title: None
Date: 184–
Height: 6¾ in (17 cm)
Colour: Well coloured.
Rarity: Av.
Pair: *Fig.* 159 (? Prince of Wales)
Description: On a pony facing right, wearing
plumed bonnet, bodice, skirt and panta-
lettes.

Figure 159
Subject: **? Prince of Wales**
Title: None
Date: 184–
Height: 7 in (17.5 cm)
Colour: Well coloured.
Rarity: Av.
Pair: *Fig.* 158 (? Princess Royal)
Description: On a pony facing left, wearing a
plumed hat, jacket, shirt and trousers.

Figure 160
Subject: **Prince of Wales**
Title: None
Date: 184–
Height: 9¼ in (23.5 cm)
Colour: In the manner of Thomas Parr.
Maker: Thomas Parr
Rarity: Contemporary figures are very rare.
Pair: *Fig.* 161 (Princess Royal)
Description: On a pony facing right, wearing
a Scottish bonnet and tunic with a tartan
sash round his waist.

Observations: Based on an undated engraving
The Young Cavalier by John Cochran after a
painting by William Salter (1804–75). See
pl. A-54A.

Figure 161
Subject: **Princess Royal**
Title: None
Date: 184–
Height: 8½ in (21.5 cm)
Colour: In the manner of Thomas Parr.
Maker: Thomas Parr
Rarity: Contemporary figures are very rare.
Pair: *Fig.* 160 (Prince of Wales)
Description: On a horse facing left, bare-
headed, holding her bonnet in her left hand
and the reins in her right. Wearing a calf-
length dress.
Observations: 1. A pair of similar figures
fetched 35 gns at Christie's in 1968.
2. Kent reproductions of this figure and its
pair are seen commonly. They are usually
poorly coloured and not difficult to distinguish from the finely coloured contemporary pair illustrated.

Plate 54A
The Young Cavalier
An undated engraving by John Cochran
after a painting by William Salter (1804–75),
published by Geo Virtue, 26, Ivy Lane,
London. It is recorded on the engraving
that the picture was *in the possession of
Colonel Grant, CB*. The engraving is the
source of *fig.* 160, *pl.* A-54, a piece always

A149

Plate 55
T: *Fig.* 162 Albert
Fig. 164 ?The Princess Royal with the Prince of Wales
Fig. 163 Victoria

B: *Fig.* 165 Victoria, Albert and the Prince of Wales
Fig. 166 ?Albert and the Princess Royal
Fig. 168 ?Victoria and the Princess Royal
Fig. 169 Victoria and the Princess Royal
Fig. 157 ?Albert with the Princess Royal

Plate 54 continued

assumed to portray the young Prince of Wales.

The Prince paid his first visit to Scotland in 1848, staying at Balmoral House, then a hired shooting lodge, thereafter he made annual visits. The title of the engraving, one of Bonnie Prince Charlie's nicknames, is almost certainly a 'tongue in the cheek' reference to the Prince of Wales.

The *D.N.B.* records that *Field-Marshal Sir Patrick Grant* (1804–94) was awarded the CB in 1846 and was promoted brevet colonel and aide-de-camp to Queen Victoria in 1849. If this is the Colonel Grant referred to in the engraving, then the details in the *D.N.B.* provide a very good reason for the colonel being in possession of the picture.

Plate 55
Figure 162
Subject: **Albert**
Title: None
Height: 13½ in (34.25 cm)
Colour: Usually white and gilt.
Rarity: Av.
Pair: Fig. 163 (Victoria)
Description: On a horse facing right, wearing military uniform and knee-boots. He is holding his cocked hat to his head with his right hand.
Observations: Possibly based on a lithograph of Prince Albert on horseback used to illustrate the music for *Prince Albert's Band*

March, see *ch.* 3 *pl.* 1. It is similar, also, to the statue of Prince Albert in Holborn Circus.

Figure 163
Subject: **Victoria**
Title: None
Height: 12¼ in (31 cm)
Colour: Usually white and gilt.
Rarity: Av.
Pair: Fig. 162 (Albert)
Description: On a horse facing left, wearing a plumed hat with her scarf blown out to the right, and full riding habit. Her right hand is holding the reins on her left forearm.

Figure 164
Subject: **? Princess Royal and Prince of Wales**
Title: None
Date: c. 1844
Height: 9¼ in (23.5 cm)
Colour: Well coloured.
Rarity: C.
Description: The two babies are asleep on a sofa. There is a crown above each head, and standing behind the sofa is a Guardian Angel.
Observations: Based on an engraving, *The Guardian Angel*, by G. Dawe (see *ch.* 3, *pl.* 1A). Note it is the potter who has added the crowns and given a royal connotation to the figure.

Figure 165
Subject: **Victoria with Albert and Prince of Wales**
Title: None
Date: c. 1848
Height: 9½ in (24 cm)
Colour: Well coloured.
Rarity: R.
Description: The Queen is sitting crowned, to the left of a tall pedestal surmounted by a vase (candlestick). Prince Albert is seated to the right. Below them in a small boat is the Prince of Wales sculling.
Observations: See *fig.* 122 (Prince of Wales and Windsor Castle) *pl.* A-42.

Figure 166
Subject: **? Albert and Princess Royal**
Title: None
Date: 184-
Height: 11¾ in (29.75 cm)
Colour: Well coloured.
Rarity: R.
Pair: There is said to be a pair to this figure (Victoria and Prince of Wales) for which *fig.* 167 has been reserved. I have never seen it.
Description: Albert, dressed in Tyrolese costume, is standing on some rocks. There is a gun to his right and at his feet is a dog, beside which is a dead bird. The Princess is to his left and below, bare-headed, holding her hat in her left hand.
Observations: 1. Maybe there is a pair, and

maybe the figure does portray Albert. However, although the gun in this figure is apparently genuine, I have twice seen figures identical in every respect except that the man carries a bow. A constant feature of every figure is a small knob on the child's head which could be intended for an apple; however, I have never seen it coloured as such. On balance I think the figure is probably intended to portray William Tell. 2. An example with the bow fetched 20 gns at Christie's in 1969.

Figure 168
Subject: **? Victoria and Princess Royal**
Title: None
Date: 184
Height: 7¼ in (18.25 cm)
Colour: Well coloured.
Maker: Alpha factory
Rarity: R.
Pair: So far no pair has been recorded.
Description: A lady is seated on what appears to be a throne. She is wearing a round hat with a ribbon attached, blouse and full-length tartan skirt. A small bareheaded child is standing on the right arm of the throne with her arms round her mother's neck.
Observations: There is no evidence that this figure is Victoria, but it could well be so. The matter should be solved if and when the pair comes to light.

Figure 169
Subject: **Victoria and Princess Royal**
Title: None
Date: 184–
Height: 8¾ in (22 cm)
Colour: Well coloured.
Rarity: R.
Pair: Fig. 170 (Albert and Prince of Wales) *pl.* A-57, but see *observations* under that figure.
Description: The Princess Royal, wearing a plumed bonnet, long ermine-edged coat, skirt and pantalettes, is riding side-saddle on a pony facing right. To her left, behind the pony, stands the Queen, wearing a plumed hat, jacket and single-flounced skirt.

Figure 157
Subject: **? Albert and Princess Royal**
Title: None
Date: 184–
Height: 9½ in (24 cm)
Colour: Well coloured. Sometimes in authentic contemporary versions the base is coloured green.
Rarity: Av.
Pair: Fig. 156 (? Victoria and Prince of Wales) *pl.* A-53.
Description: Standing, wearing a cocked hat with a high plume, military jacket, breeches and knee-boots. His left hand is on his hip, and his left foot infront of his right foot. His right hand is holding the Princess's left. She is wearing a tricorn hat, short skirt, pantalettes and calf-boots.
Observations: This figure has been catalogued by Mr Balston as 'Prince Albert with the Princess Royal'. However, there is considerable doubt about the identification of both it and its pair (See *observations fig.* 156, *pl.* A-53.) My own feelings are that the figures are probably theatrical.

Plate 56
Fig. 171 ?The Prince of Wales and the Princess Royal
Fig. 172 ?Albert and the Princess Royal
In the collection of Mr D.P.M. Michael

Plate 56
Figure 171
Subject: **? Princess Royal and Prince of Wales**
Title: None
Date: c. 1844
Height: 8½ in (21.5 cm)
Colour: Well coloured.
Rarity: C.
Description: The Prince and Princess are seated at the foot of a tree trunk (spill-holder) asleep. Behind them stands a Guardian Angel.
Observations: This identification is based on the close similarity of the figure to *fig.* 164, *pl.* A-55. Note, however, that in both instances the babies appear to be of the same age and 'royal children' is likely to be a more accurate description.

Figure 172
Subject: **? Albert and Princess Royal**
Title: None
Date: 184–
Height: 9¼ in (23.5 cm)
Colour: Well coloured.
Rarity: R.
Pair: There is almost certainly a pair to this figure, for which *fig.* 173 has been reserved. So far, however, it has not been reported.
Description: The man stands on the left. He is bare-headed, wearing a full-length cloak, military jacket with epaulettes, breeches and knee-boots. In his right hand he holds a parrot-like bird which may be a lory. His left arm rests on the head of a small child who is standing on the right, on a cushion, on a pedestal. The girl is bare-headed and wears a bodice, knee-length skirt and pantalettes. With her left hand she holds a bunch of grapes to her head, and her right hand rests on the man's shoulder.
Observations: The man bears some resemblance to Prince Albert, but the general tenor of the piece is theatrical. Doubtless the problem will be solved when the pair comes to light.

Plate 57
Figure 170
Subject: **Albert and Prince of Wales**
Title: None
Date: 184–
Height: 9 in (23 cm)
Colour: Well coloured.
Rarity: R.

Pair: Fig. 169 (Victoria and Princess Royal) *pl.* A-55.
Description: The Prince of Wales is seated on a chair on a pony facing left, wearing a plumed hat, bodice and skirt. To his right, behind the pony's front legs, stands Prince Albert, wearing a high plumed hat and military uniform. He holds the reins in his left hand.
Observations: This figure is catalogued in Mr Balston's *Supplement* as a pair to *fig.* 169, *pl.* A-55. I agree that this seems likely, but if it is so, it is a rare example of a pair of figures which are not strictly speaking 'matching'. The possibility cannot be excluded that two further figures exist, one to pair *fig.* 169 and the other to pair *fig.* 170.

Figure 174
Subject: **Prince of Wales and Groom**
Title: None
Date: 184–
Height: 9¼ in (23.5 cm)
Colour: Well coloured. Horse usually piebald.
Rarity: R.
Pair: Fig. 175 (Princess Royal and Groom)
Description: The Prince is sitting astride a prancing horse, facing right, which is being controlled by a groom on the right. There is a crown on the rear angle of the saddle-cloth.
Observations: See next figure.

Figure 175
Subject: **Princess Royal and Groom**
Title: None
Date: 184–
Height: 8½ in (21.5 cm)
Colour: Well coloured. Horse usually piebald.
Rarity: R.
Pair: Fig. 174 (Prince of Wales and Groom)
Description: The Princess is sitting side-saddle on a prancing horse, facing left, which is being controlled by a groom on the left. There is a crown on the rear angle of the saddle-cloth.
Observations: See *observations fig.* 142 (Unidentified groom) *pl.* A-48.

Figure 176
Subject: **Victoria**
Title: None
Date: 184–
Height: 6 in (15.25 cm)
Colour: Well coloured.

Plate 57
T: *Fig.* 174 The Prince of Wales and Groom
Fig. 176 Victoria
Fig. 175 The Princess Royal and Groom

B: *Fig.* 178 Albert and the Prince of Wales
Fig. 170 Albert and the Prince of Wales
Fig. 179 Victoria and the Princess Royal
By courtesy of Mr and Mrs Eric Joyce and in the collection of the author

Plate 58
T: *Fig.* 180 ?The Prince of Wales
Fig. 181 ?The Princess Royal

B: *Fig.* 182 The Prince of Wales
Fig. 183 ?The Prince of Wales
Fig. 184 ?Prince Alfred

Plate 57 continued
Rarity: R.
Pair: There is almost certainly a pair to this figure (Albert), for which *fig.* 177 has been reserved.
Description: On a horse facing left, wearing a top hat draped with a scarf and full riding habit.

Figure 178
Subject: **Albert and Prince of Wales**
Title: None
Date: 184–
Height: 10½ in (26.5 cm)
Colour: Well coloured.
Rarity: R.

A152

Pair: *Fig.* 179 (Victoria and Princess Royal)
Description: Albert is standing, wearing a plumed cocked hat and full military uniform. His left arm is round the waist of the Prince of Wales who is standing bare-headed on the back of a goat. A scarf links the two.

Figure 179
Subject: **Victoria and Princess Royal**
Title: None
Date: 184–
Height: 9¾ in (24.5 cm)
Colour: Well coloured.
Rarity: R.

Pair: *Fig.* 178 (Albert and Prince of Wales)
Description: Standing crowned, wearing a bodice and flounced skirt. Her right arm is round the Princess Royal, who is standing bare-headed on the back of a goat. A scarf links the two.

Plate 58
Figure 180
Subject: **? Prince of Wales**
Title: None
Date: 184–
Height: 11¼ in (28.5 cm)
Colour: Well coloured.
Rarity: Av.
Pair: *Fig.* 181 (? Princess Royal)
Description: Standing, wearing a bonnet with three feathers, short coat and trousers. A dog is jumping up on to his right leg.
Observations: See next figure.

Figure 181
Subject: **? Princess Royal**
Title: None
Date: 184–
Height: 10¾ in (27 cm)
Colour: Well coloured.
Rarity: Av.
Pair: *Fig.* 180 (? Prince of Wales)
Description: Standing, wearing a bonnet with three feathers, blouse, knee-length skirt and pantalettes. There is a sheep jumping up on to her left leg.
Observations: 1. This figure and its pair are sometimes thought to portray the Prince of Wales and the Princess Royal, but there is no real evidence to support this.
2. A similar but by no means identical pair of figures have been found impressed at the back: 'LLOYD/SHELTON'
3. There is yet another pair of similar figures each with a tree trunk (spill-holder).

Figure 182
Subject: **Prince of Wales**
Title: None
Date: Although the figure could have been made in 1847, there are arguments for supposing it was not made until 1852 or later (see *ch.* 2).
Height: 12¼ in (31 cm)
Colour: Well coloured in the manner of Thomas Parr.
Maker: Thomas Parr
Rarity: Contemporary versions are relatively uncommon. Late, poorly coloured versions are common.
Description: Standing, wearing a sailor suit, both hands in his pockets.
Observations: 1. Based on a portrait by Winterhalter, painted in 1846 as a Christmas present for the Prince Consort, see *ch.* 3, *pl.* 3.
2. This figure is of particular interest, for a similar figure manufactured in Parian ware by Minton, with the approval of Prince Albert, was illustrated in *The Illustrated London News* of October 14th, 1848, see *ch.* 3, *pl.* 4.
3. A late debased reproduction of this figure exists. It is titled erroneously 'Prince Alfred' (indented capitals), see *fig.* 185, *pl.* A-59.

Figure 183
Subject: **? Prince of Wales**
Title: None
Date: c. 1858
Height: 12 in. (30.5 cm)
Colour: Well coloured.

Plate 59
Fig. 185 Prince of Wales mistitled Prince Alfred

Plate 60
Fig. 186 The Prince of Wales
Fig. 187 The Prince of Wales

Maker: Thomas Parr
Rarity: R.
Pair: *Fig.* 184 (? Prince Alfred)
Description: Standing in military uniform. His right elbow and left hand on the muzzle of a rifle.
Observations: Generally supposed to portray the Prince of Wales who was gazetted as having been invested with the rank of a colonel in the army, in 1858. I know of no evidence in support of this.

Figure 184
Subject: **? Prince Alfred**
Title: None
Date: *c.* 1858
Height: 12 in (30.5 cm)
Colour: Well coloured.
Maker: Thomas Parr
Rarity: R.
Pair: *Fig.* 183 (? Prince of Wales)
Description: Standing in a sailor suit. His right hand on his hip, an anchor beside his left leg and a package behind.
Observations: Generally supposed to portray Prince Alfred who passed his examination as a naval cadet in 1858, and was appointed to the *Euryalus*. I know of no evidence in support of this. He looks young.

Plate 59
Figure 185
Subject: **Prince of Wales**
Title: Prince Alfred (indented capitals)
Date: *c.* 1890
Height: 12¼ in (31 cm)
Colour: Poor.
Maker: Kent and Parr

Rarity: VR.
Description: Identical, other than for title, to *fig.* 182 (Prince of Wales) *pl.* A-58.
Observations: 1. This figure is a late figure from the same mould as *fig.* 182 (Prince of Wales) *pl.* A-58. It is titled in indented capitals touched up with 'Bright Gold', and dates probably to about 1890. The reason why the old mould was taken out and the figure re-issued, wrongly titled, is obscure. Possibly the potter mistook the figure for that of Prince Alfred, because the Prince was a professional sailor, being commander-in-chief at Devonport in 1890. He was promoted to admiral of the fleet in 1893.
2. A similar figure was sold at Christie's for 24 gns in 1966.

Plate 60
Figure 186
Subject: **Prince of Wales**
Title: Prince of Wales (raised capitals)
Date: *c.* 1862
Height: 14¼ in (36.25 cm)
Colour: Well coloured or in pale state.
Rarity: C.
Description: Standing bare-headed in short jacket, waistcoat and trousers. His right hand is on a draped pedestal and with his left hand he strokes the head of a dog, which is rubbing against his knee.
Observations: Balston thought that this single figure may have been issued early in 1862 when plans for the Prince of Wales's marriage were first rumoured. It was followed by a spate of figures of him and the Princess Alexandra after their engagement was announced in September.

Figure 187
Subject: **Prince of Wales**
Title: Prince of Wales (raised capitals)
Date: *c.* 1852
Height: 14¾ in (37.5 cm)
Colour: Well coloured or in pale state.
Rarity: C.
Description: Standing bare-headed in Highland dress, a plaid over his left shoulder, his bonnet in his right hand. To his left a Dalmatian dog.
Observations: Probably portrays the Prince as a young lad at Balmoral.

Plate 61
Figure 188
Subject: **Prince Alfred**
Title: Pr. Alfred (raised capitals)
Date: 1858
Height: 10½ in (26.5 cm)
Colour: Well coloured.
Rarity: Av.
Pair: *Fig.* 189 (Prince of Wales)
Description: Standing to the left of a broad chair, bare-headed in naval costume and carrying his hat in his right hand.
Observations: See next figure.

Figure 189
Subject: **Prince of Wales**
Title: Pr. of Wales (raised capitals)
Date: 1858
Height: 10½ in (26.5 cm)
Colour: Well coloured.
Rarity: Av.
Pair: *Fig.* 188 (Prince Alfred)

A153

Plate 61
Fig. 188 Prince Alfred
Fig. 189 The Prince of Wales

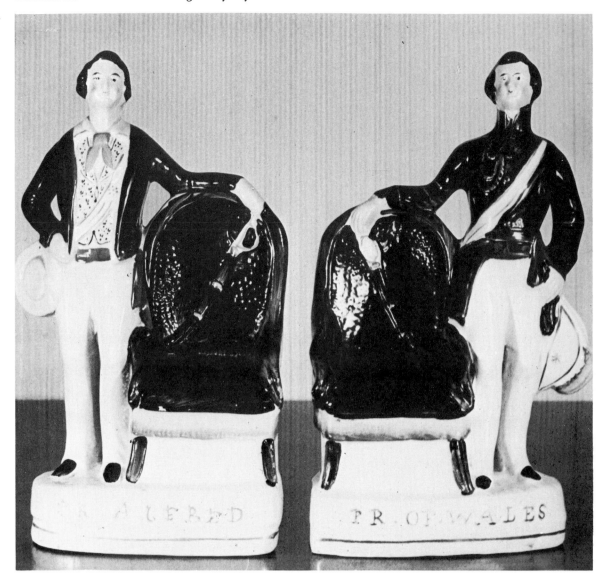

Plate 61 continued
Description: Standing bare-headed, in military uniform, to the right of a broad chair. He is holding his plumed cocked hat in his left hand.
Observations: 1. The Prince of Wales and Prince Alfred received their first commissions in 1858.
2. A fine pair of these figures fetched 82 gns at Christie's in 1965.

Plate 62
Figure 190
Subject: **Prince Alfred**
Title: P Alfred (raised capitals)
Date: 1858
Height: 8¼ in (21 cm)
Colour: Well coloured.
Rarity: R. D.
Pair: Fig. 191 (Prince of Wales)
Description: Standing bare-headed, in naval uniform. His right forearm rests on a capstan and he holds his hat in his left hand.
Observations: 1. Prince Alfred received his first commission in 1858.
2. A similar figure fetched 55 gns at Christie's in 1969.

Figure 191
Subject: **Prince of Wales**
Title: P of Wales (raised capitals)
A154

Date: 1858
Height: 9¼ in (23.5 cm)
Colour: Well coloured.
Rarity: R. D.
Pair: Fig. 190 (Prince Alfred)
Description: Standing bare-headed, in military tunic and trousers, sash over his left shoulder. His right hand is on his hip, his left arm by his side. To his left is a pedestal upon which is his plumed cocked hat and a cloak.
Observations: 1. From a coloured lithograph music-front by John Brandard '*The Coldstream Guards March*' *composed and respectfully inscribed to Col. H.R.H. the Prince of Wales by Stephen Glover, see ch. 3, pl. 5.*
2. The Prince of Wales received his first commission in 1858 holding the rank of an *Unattached Colonel in the Army.* He wore only the ribbon and star of the Order of the Garter.

Figure 192
Subject: **Prince Alfred**
Title: Prince Alfred (raised capitals)
Date: 1858
Height: 10¾ in (27 cm)
Colour: Well coloured.
Rarity: R. D. A.
Pair: Fig. 193 (Prince of Wales)
Description: Standing bare-headed, in naval

costume, his right hand on a capstan and his left hand holding his hat. There is a coil of rope near his left foot.
Observations: A similar figure together with *fig.* 191 (Prince of Wales) fetched 62 gns at Christie's in 1965; another, by itself, fetched 60 gns in the same rooms in 1969.

Figure 193
Subject: **Prince of Wales**
Title: Prince of Wales (raised capitals)
Date: 1858
Height: 10¾ in (27 cm)
Colour: Well coloured.
Rarity: VR. D. A.
Pair: Fig. 192 (Prince Alfred)
Description: Standing bare-headed, in military uniform, his left hand on a pedestal and his right hand holding his plumed cocked hat.
Observations: Based on a photograph by Mayall, an engraving of which appeared in *The Illustrated London News* of December 11th, 1858, see ch. 3 pl. 6.

Plate 63
Figure 194
Subject: **Prince of Wales**
Title: Prince of/Wales (raised capitals)

Section A. British and Foreign Royalty

Plate 62
Fig. 190 Prince Alfred
Fig. 192 Prince Alfred
Fig. 193 Prince of Wales
Fig. 191 Prince of Wales
By courtesy of Mr and Mrs
Eric Joyce and in the
collection of the author

Plate 63
Fig. 194 Prince of Wales
Fig. 195 Princess Royal
In the Thomas Balston
collection

Date: c. 1853
Height: 11¾ in (29.75 cm)
Colour: Well coloured.
Rarity: Av.
Pair: Fig. 195 (Princess Royal)
Description: On a horse facing right, wearing a high bonnet, plaid over his left shoulder, and kilt.
Observations: Balston has catalogued this figure and its pair (*fig.* 195) as the 'Prince of Wales' and 'Princess Alexandra', later Princess of Wales. He dates the figures to 1862, the year the couple became betrothed.

The figure of the Prince of Wales seems to be of a boy rather than of a young man, and that combined with the Highland dress suggests that this is a portrait of the young Prince at Balmoral. The castle was leased in 1848. If this were so, the Princess portrayed would be the Princess Royal. In all the circumstances, I have decided to identify the figures as the Prince of Wales and the Princess Royal and to date them to about 1853. This applies not only to this pair but also to *figs.* 196 and 197, and *figs.* 198 and 199, *pls.* A-64, 64A and 65.

Figure 195
Subject: **Princess Royal**
Title: Princess (raised capitals)
Date: c. 1853
Height: 10¾ in (27 cm)
Colour: Well coloured.
Rarity: Av.
Pair: Fig. 194 (Prince of Wales)
Description: On a horse facing left, wearing a plumed bonnet and riding habit. A scarf blows outwards from her left shoulder.
Observations: See *observations fig.* 194 (Prince of Wales).

A155

Section A. British and Foreign Royalty

Plate 64
Figure 196
Subject: **Prince of Wales**
Title: Prince of Wales (raised capitals on plaque)
Date: c. 1853
Height: 9¾ in (24.5 cm)
Colour: Poorly coloured.
Rarity: VR.
Pair: Fig. 197 (Princess Royal) *pl.* 64A.
Description: On a horse facing right, wearing a high bonnet, plaid over his left shoulder and kilt.
Observations: 1. See *observations fig.* 194 (Prince of Wales) *pl.* A-63.
2. A similar figure is illustrated in Mr Bryan Latham's *Victorian Staffordshire Portrait Figures* (*fig.* 8). Mr Latham describes it as *a charming child study showing the Prince of Wales when quite a small boy, dressed in Highland costume and riding a Shetland pony. The locality is undoubtedly Balmoral.* If this is accepted, and I agree, then *fig.* 197 which is titled 'Princess' must portray the Princess Royal and not Princess Alexandra of Denmark, later the Princess of Wales.

Plate 64A
Figure 197
Subject: **Princess Royal**
Title: Princess (raised capitals on plaque)
Date: c. 1853
Height: 9½ in (24 cm)
Colour: Poorly coloured.
Rarity: R.
Pair: Fig. 196 (Prince of Wales)
Description: On a horse facing left, wearing a plumed bonnet and riding habit. There is a scarf blowing out to the right from her left shoulder.
Observations: See *observations fig.* 196 (Prince of Wales) *pl.* A-64.

Plate 65
Figure 198
Subject: **Prince of Wales**
Title: Prince of Wales (raised capitals)
Date: c. 1853
Height: 11¼ in (28.5 cm)
Colour: Well coloured.
Rarity: R.
Pair: Fig. 199 (Princess Royal)
Description: Similar in all, except minor respects, and in the style of titling to *fig.* 194 (Prince of Wales) *pl.* A-63.
Observations: See *observations fig.* 194 (Prince of Wales) *pl.* A-63.

Figure 199
Subject: **Princess Royal**
Title: Princess (raised capitals)
Date: c. 1853
Height: 10½ in (26.5 cm)
Colour: Well coloured.
Rarity: R.
Pair: Fig. 198 (Prince of Wales)
Description: Similar, except for minor details, to *fig.* 195 (Princess Royal) *pl.* A-63.

Figure 200
Subject: **Prince of Wales**
Title: Prince of Wales (raised capitals)
Date: 1862
Height: 11 in (28 cm)
Colour: Well coloured.
Rarity: Av.
Pair: Fig. 201 (Princess of Wales)
Description: On a horse facing right, bareheaded in civilian dress. His right hand

A156

Plate 64
Fig. 196 Prince of Wales

Plate 64A
Fig. 197 Princess Royal

rests on the horse's rump, clutching his top hat, and his left hand holds the reins.

Figure 201
Subject: **Princess Alexandra of Denmark,** later Princess of Wales
Title: Princess (raised capitals)
Date: 1862
Height: 10½ in (26.5 cm)
Colour: Well coloured.
Rarity: Av.
Pair: Fig. 200 (Prince of Wales)
Description: On a horse facing left, in flat hat with a plume and veil and full riding habit.
Observations: This figure and its pair are two of a number of figures issued at the time of the announcement of the engagement of the Prince of Wales to Princess Alexandra of Denmark.

Figure 202
Subject: **Prince of Wales**
Title: None
Date: Uncertain, probably c. 1885
Height: 9 in (23 cm)
Colour: In the manner of later figures of the Parr and Kent group of potters (see *ch.* 2, *p.* 15).
Maker: Probably Kent and Parr
Rarity: Av.
Pair: Fig. 203 (Princess of Wales)

Description: Similar to *fig.* 200 except for height and minor details such as the manner of holding the top hat.
Observations: I have only seen this figure and its pair decorated in the manner of figures attributable to Kent and Parr (1880–94) or later. The two figures seem to be a rehash of *figs.* 200 and 201. Even so they have much merit.

Figure 203
Subject: **Princess Alexandra of Denmark,** later Princess of Wales
Title: None
Date: Uncertain, probably c. 1885
Height: 9 in (23 cm)
Colour: As for preceding figure.
Maker: Probably Kent and Parr
Rarity: Av.
Pair: Fig. 202 (Prince of Wales)
Description: Similar to *fig.* 201 (Princess of Wales) except for minor differences.
Observations: See preceding figure.

Plate 66
Figures 204 and *204(a)*
Subject: **Princess Alexandra of Denmark,** later Princess of Wales
Title: The Princess *or* Princess of Wales (indented capitals)
Date: 1862–3
Height: 7¾ in (20 cm)
Colour: In the manner of Thomas Parr (see *ch.* 2, *p.* 15).
Maker: Thomas Parr
Rarity: VR. D. A.
Pair: Fig. 205 (Prince of Wales)
Description: On a horse facing right, bareheaded and wearing riding habit. The design at the back of the centre support incorporates the Prince of Wales' feathers.
Observations: 1. Three contemporary figures titled 'The Princess' are known (*fig.* 204) and one inscribed 'Princess of Wales' (*fig.* 204(a)). The discovery of the latter confirms what had hitherto been believed, *i.e.* that these figures portray the Princess of Wales and *not* the Princess Royal. Presumably figures titled 'The Princess' were issued at the time of the betrothal of the Princess to the Prince of Wales in 1862, and figures titled 'Princess of Wales', immediately after their marriage in 1863.
2. The solitary figure titled 'Princess of Wales' is the only portrait figure bearing this title known to me.
3. Contemporary copies of this figure are very rare, but late reproductions, all titled 'The Princess', are quite common. This figure and its pair are in all the Kent lists, being no. 316 in *Kent List C* (1955).

Figure 205
Subject: **Prince of Wales**
Title: Prince of Wales (indented capitals)
Date: 1862
Height: 7¾ in (20 cm)
Colour: In the manner of Thomas Parr (see *ch.* 2, *p.* 15).
Maker: Thomas Parr
Rarity: VR. D. A.
Pair: Either *fig.* 204 or *fig.* 204(a) (Princess of Wales).
Description: On a horse facing left, bareheaded and in civilian clothes.
Observations: 1. Issued in celebration of the announcement of the engagement of the Prince of Wales to Princess Alexandra of Denmark in 1862.
2. Contemporary figures are very rare, but reproductions common. Note that the title

Plate 65
T: *Fig.* 198 Prince of Wales
Fig. 199 Princess Royal
B: *Fig.* 200 Prince of Wales
Fig. 201 Princess of Wales
Fig. 202 Prince of Wales
Fig. 203 Princess of Wales
In the collection of Lady Ranfurly

Plate 66
T: *Fig.* 204 Princess of Wales
(*reproduction*)
Fig. 205 Prince of Wales (*reproduction*)
B: *Fig.* 204(a) Princess of Wales
(*contemporary*)
Fig. 204 Princess of Wales (*contemporary*)
Fig. 205 Prince of Wales (*contemporary*)
Note page from *Kent List C* (1955)
illustrating the figure of the Prince of
Wales. Contemporary copies of these
figures are very rare but reproductions
are relatically common (see *ch.* 6). *Fig.*

204(a), which is only known in
contemporary form, differs from *fig.* 204
not only as regards title, being the only
figure inscribed 'Princess of Wales' but
also in several other minor particulars.

in the late example illustrated on *pl.* A-66
is not only cruder but differs from the
contemporary version ('The Prince' instead
of 'Prince of Wales'). The reproduction is
listed in all Kent lists. In *Kent List C* (1955)
there is also a coloured illustration.
3. A similar figure fetched 32 gns in
Christie's in 1966.

Plate 67
Figure 206
Subject: **Prince Frederick William of Prussia**
Title: Prince F. Prussia (raised capitals)
Date: 1857
Height: 10¼ in (25.75 cm)
Colour: Well coloured.
Rarity: VR.
Pair: Fig. 207 (Princess Royal)
Description: On a horse facing right, in plumed cocked hat athwartships, cloak and military uniform.
Observations: This figure and its pair probably date to the announcement of the betrothal of Prince Frederick William of Prussia to the Princess Royal in 1857.

Figure 207
Subject: **Princess Royal**
Title: Princess (raised capitals)
Date: 1857
Height: 9¼ in (23.5 cm)
Colour: Well coloured.
Rarity: VR.
Pair: Fig. 206 (Prince Frederick William)
Description: On a horse facing left, in flat hat with veil but no plume, and full riding habit.
Observations: Differs from all other figures titled in a similar manner but tends to escape detection if not accompanied by its pair.

Plate 68
Figure 208
Subject: **Prince Frederick William of Prussia**
Title: Prince Frederick W. (raised capitals)
Date: 1858
Height: 12¾ in (32.25 cm)

Colour: White and gilt.
Rarity: VR.
Pair: Fig. 209 (Princess Royal)
Description: On a horse facing right, in cocked hat, ermine-edged cloak and military uniform. His left hand holds the reins and his right hand is on his thigh.
Observations: See *fig.* 209 (Princess Royal).

Figure 209
Subject: **Princess Royal**
Title: Princess Royal of P. (raised capitals)
Date: 1858
Height: 11½ in (29 cm)
Colour: White and gilt.
Rarity: VR.
Pair: Fig. 208 (Prince Frederick William)
Description: On a horse facing left, in flat hat with plume and veil and full riding habit.
Observations: The title suggests that this figure, together with its pair, were issued soon after the royal marriage in 1858.

Figure 210
Subject: **Prince Frederick William of Prussia**
Title: Prince FR^K. W^M. (raised capitals)
Date: 1857
Height: 14¼ in (36.25 cm)
Colour: Well coloured or white and gilt copies exist.
Rarity: R.
Pair: Fig. 211 (Princess Royal)
Description: On a horse facing right, wearing a plumed cocked hat and military uniform and without cloak. His right hand is raised in the salute.
Observations: Probably dates to the announcement of the betrothal of Prince Frederick William to the Princess Royal in 1857.

Figure 211
Subject: **Princess Royal**
Title: Princess (raised capitals)
Date: 1857
Height: 13¾ in (35 cm)
Colour: Well coloured or white and gilt copies exist.
Rarity: Av.
Pair: Fig. 210 (Prince Frederick William)
Description: On a horse facing left, wearing plumed hat and veil, together with full riding habit.
Observations: This figure was first issued in 1857, being intended to portray the Princess Royal at the time of her engagement to Prince Frederick William of Prussia. The same figure (*fig.* 213, *pl.* A-68) was used again in 1862 to portray Princess Alexandra of Denmark at the time of her engagement to the Prince of Wales.

Figure 212
Subject: **Prince of Wales**
Title: Prince of Wales (raised capitals)
Date: 1862
Height: 13 in (33 cm)
Colour: Well coloured or white and gilt copies exist.
Rarity: Av.
Pair: Fig. 213 (Princess of Wales)
Description: On a horse facing right, bare-headed in civilian dress. In his right hand he holds a plumed hat, and in his left the horse's reins.
Observations: See *observations fig.* 213 (Princess of Wales).

Figure 213
Subject: **Princess Alexandra of Denmark,** later Princess of Wales
Title: Princess (raised capitals)

Plate 68
T: *Fig.* 208 Prince
Frederick William
Fig. 209 Princess Royal

B: *Fig.* 210 Prince
Frederick William
Fig. 211 Princess Royal or
Fig. 213 Princess of Wales
Fig. 212 Prince of Wales

Date: 1862
Height: 13¾ in (35 cm)
Colour: Well coloured or white and gilt copies exist.
Rarity: Av.
Pair: Fig. 212 (Prince of Wales)
Description: Identical in all respects to *fig.* 211 (Princess Royal).
Observations: This is a reissue of the model used in 1857 to portray the Princess Royal at the time of her engagement to Prince Frederick William of Prussia. It has been used again for a similar purpose, namely to portray the Princess Alexandra of Denmark, the future Princess of Wales, at the time of her engagement to the Prince of Wales in 1862.

Plate 69
Figure 214
Subject: **Prince Louis of Hesse**
Title: PL of Hesse (raised capitals)
Date: 1862
Height: 9½ in (24 cm)
Colour: Well coloured.
Rarity: VR. D.
Pair: Fig. 215 (Princess Alice)
Description: On a horse facing right, bare-

headed and in civilian dress, a star on his left breast. He carries a hat in his right hand and holds the reins in his left.

Figure 215
Subject: **Princess Alice**
Title: Pˢ Alice (raised capitals)
Date: 1862
Height: 9¼ in (23.5 cm)
Colour: Well coloured.
Rarity: VR. D.
Pair: Fig. 214 (Prince Louis of Hesse)
Description: On a horse facing left, in plumed pill-box hat and full riding habit, a sash over her left shoulder.
Observations: Princess Alice, second daughter of Queen Victoria, married Prince Louis of Hesse (later Grand-duke of Hesse-Darmstadt) in 1862.

Figure 216
Subject: **Princess Alice and Prince Louis of Hesse**
Title: None
Date: *c.* 1862
Height: 9 in (23 cm)
Colour: Poorly coloured, often a crude figure.
Rarity: R.

Pair: This figure may be intended to form the centre-piece for *fig.* 214 (Prince Louis of Hesse) and *fig.* 215 (Princess Alice).
Description: Prince Louis stands on her left, bare-headed and in civilian dress. The appearance of the face, jacket and trousers are similar to those of *fig.* 214, except that the star on the breast of the jacket noted on *fig.* 214 is portrayed as a pocket in *fig.* 216; also, he appears to be carrying a bonnet rather than a hat. The Princess is dressed in a low round plumed hat, hanging sleeves, looped-up overskirt, and large muff. Her appearance, particularly the top half, is very nearly identical to her appearance in *fig.* 218, *pl.* A-70.
Observations: The identification of this figure is based on reasons already given in the description, and seems almost definite.

Plate 69
Fig. 214 Prince Louis of Hesse
Fig. 216 Princess Alice and Prince Louis of Hesse
Fig. 215 Princess Alice
By courtesy of Mr and Mrs Eric Joyce and in the collection of the author

Plate 70
Fig. 217 Princess Royal with Prince Frederick William
Fig. 218 Princess Alice with Prince Louis of Hesse

Plate 70
Figure 217
Subject: **Princess Royal and Prince Frederick William of Prussia**
Title: Princess Royal & FR^K of Prussia (raised capitals)
Date: 1857
Height: 16 in (40.5 cm)
Colour: Well coloured or white and gilt versions are known.
Rarity: C.

A160

Description: Standing bare-headed, the Prince on the left, wearing military uniform with a sash over his left shoulder; the Princess on the right, wearing bodice and flounced skirt and holding a reticule in her left hand.
Observations: One curious modification of the titling of the figure is illustrated on *pl.* A-71. It will be noted that the original titling in raised capitals (in the mould) has been partially erased and the new title 'Pr. &

Prss. of Prusia' applied in gilt script [*fig.* 217(*a*)]. The difference in titling supports the theory that *fig.* 217 was produced about 1857 (the time of the announcement of the betrothal of the Princess Royal to Prince Frederick William of Prussia), being modified after their marriage in 1858.

Figure 218
Subject: **Princess Alice and Prince Louis of Hesse**

Section A. British and Foreign Royalty

Plate 71
Fig. 217(a) Princess
Royal with Prince
Frederick William (base
of figure).
Note the title 'Pr. & Prss.
of Prusia' has been
applied to the base of the
standard figure after the
erasure of the original
title 'Princess Royal and
FRk of Prussia'.
This figure was probably
issued after the marriage
of the Princess Royal to
Prince Frederick William
of Prussia in 1858,
whereas the former figure
was probably issued to
celebrate their betrothal
in 1857.
*Formerly in the collection of
the author*

Title: None
Date: 1862
Height: 14 in (35.5 cm)
Colour: Well coloured or white and gilt.
Rarity: R.
Description: Standing, the Prince on the
left and the Princess on the right. The
Prince is bare-headed and moustached
(in the mould). He wears a knee-length
jacket, waistcoat and strapped trousers and
carries a cloak over his right forearm. His
left arm is round the Princess's shoulders.
She wears a flat plumed hat, hanging
sleeves, looped-up overskirt displaying a
large expanse of underskirt and a large
muff.
Observations: Mr Balston dealt with the
evidence that this figure portrays Princess
Alice and Prince Louis in his *Supplement*
(1963). The couple were betrothed in
December, 1860 and married in July, 1862.
At that time (1861) the same factory
produced *fig.* 63 (Fountain) *pl.* D-30. It will
be noted that the young man is wearing
exactly the same clothes and that the
figure is painted with the same pink, red,
green and brown. That *fig.* 218 commemorates a royal engagement is corroborated
by the fact that when only two months after
Prince Louis's marriage, the Prince of
Wales became engaged to Princess Alexandra (the only other royal engagement of
this period), the same factory made very
similar large groups of the Prince and
Princess, see *pls.* A-72-74. In these the
Prince of Wales wears the same clothes as
Prince Louis, except that the collar of his
jacket is more open. The identification of
Prince Louis is further corroborated by his
moustache. He and Prince Albert were the
only princes connected with the English
royal family who wore moustaches, without
whiskers or beards. In *figs.* 214 and 216,
pl. A-69 the figures are moustached in the
mould, but the decorator has omitted to
paint them in.

Plate 71
Figure 217(*a*)
Subject: **Princess Royal and Prince
Frederick William of Prussia**
Observations: See *fig.* 217, *pl.* A-70.

Plate 72
Figure 219
Subject: **Prince of Wales and Princess
Alexandra of Denmark,** later Princess of
Wales
Title: Prince and Princess (raised capitals)
Date: 1862
Height: 9½ in (24 cm)
Colour: Usually white and gilt.
Rarity: VR.
Description: Standing, the Prince on the right.
He is wearing knee-length jacket, waistcoat
and strapped trousers. He carries his gloves
in his right hand and his top hat in his left.
The Princess, on the left, has her hair in a
snood, and carries her hat over her right
arm. She wears a bodice and full-length
skirt.
Observations: 1. Probably issued in 1862 to
commemorate the announcement of the
betrothal of the Prince of Wales to Princess
Alexandra of Denmark. The marriage took
place in March, 1863.
2. May have been intended as a centrepiece for *fig.* 226 (Prince of Wales) and *fig.*
225 (Princess of Wales), *pl.* A-76.

Plate 72
Fig. 219 Prince and Princess of Wales

Plate 73
Fig. 220 Prince and
Princess of Wales
Fig. 221 Prince and
Princess of Wales
*By courtesy of Mr and Mrs
Eric Joyce*

Plate 73

Figure 220

Subject: **Prince of Wales and Princess Alexandra of Denmark,** later Princess of Wales

Title: Prince & Princess (raised capitals)

Date: 1862

Height: 9½ in (24 cm)

Colour: Coloured with underglaze blue, or in white and gilt.

Rarity: C.

Description: Similar to *fig.* 219, *pl.* A-72 except that 1. the Princess does not wear a snood and 2. the manner of titling differs.

Observations: Mr Geoffrey Godden possesses a copy of this figure on the base of which are the letters 'AD' in relief, in mirror-image, thus: 'ꓷA'
It is just possible that these letters stand for 'Alexandra of Denmark', thus providing an indication to the potter of what figure he was decorating. Similar examples are known in Boer War figures, see *ch.* 2, *pl.* 10.

Figure 221

Subject: **Prince of Wales and Princess Alexandra of Denmark,** later Princess of Wales

Title: Prince & Princess (raised capitals)

Date: 1862

Height: 15½ in (39.25 cm)

Colour: Coloured with underglaze blue, or in white and gilt.

Rarity: C.

Description: Similar to *fig.* 220 except that the Princess has her hair in a snood and the ribbon of her hat is in the mould. The Prince has a slightly different neckerchief.

Observations: See *fig.* 219, *pl.* A-72.

Plate 74

Figure 222

Subject: **Prince of Wales and Princess Alexandra of Denmark,** later Princess of Wales

Title: Prince & Princess (raised capitals)

Date: 1862

Height: 10¾ in (27 cm)

Colour: Coloured in underglaze blue, or in white and gilt.

Rarity: C.

Description: Standing, on the left the Prince wearing knee-length jacket, waistcoat and strapped trousers, his top hat in his right hand; on the right the Princess, bare-headed wearing a full-length flounced skirt and her hat over her left arm, no snood.

Observations: An untitled version of this figure [14¼ in (36.25 cm)] is described in Mr Balston's catalogue.

Figure 223

Subject: **Princess Louise and Marquess of Lorne**

Title: None

Date: 1871

Height: 11¼ in (28.5 cm)

Colour: Usually well coloured, but with no underglaze blue.

Rarity: Av.

Description: The Princess is standing on the left arm-in-arm with Lord Lorne. She wears a plumed hat, bodice and flounced skirt, and he wears a plumed bonnet and Highland dress, with a plaid over his left shoulder.

Observations: The identification of this figure is based on its similarity to *figs.* 229 and 230, *pl.* A-78. It may well have been intended as a centre-piece for this pair.

Plate 75

Figure 224

Subject: **Princess Helena and Prince Christian of Schleswig-Holstein**

Title: None

Date: c. 1866

Height: 11¾ in (29.75 cm)

Colour: Not decorated—'porridge school' piece.

Maker: Sampson Smith

Rarity: R.

Description: She stands on the left, wearing a plumed round hat, bodice and flounced skirt. He stands on the right, in plumed helmet and military uniform.

Observations: I am grateful to Mr D. P. M.

Plate 74
Fig. 222 Prince and Princess of Wales
Fig. 223 Princess Louise with the Marquess of Lorne

By courtesy of Mr and Mrs Eric Joyce and in the collection of the author

Plate 75 (Left)
Fig. 224 Princess Helena
and Prince Christian
In the collection of
Mr D.P.M. Michael

Plate 76 (Right)
Fig. 225 Princess of Wales
Fig. 226 Prince of Wales

Michael for supplying me with the arguments for the identification of this figure as Princess Helena and Prince Christian.

GENERAL ARGUMENTS
1. It is a 'porridge school' piece and therefore made in the sixties or early seventies. The couple were married in 1866.
2. It is not a decorative piece and therefore commemorative.
3. The pose is typically that of betrothal or marriage (compare *figs.* 217 and 218, *pl.* A-70 and *figs.* 222 and 223, *pl.* A-74).
4. It is untitled, as were so many royal family pieces.

PARTICULAR ARGUMENTS
(*a*) Man.
1. He has a moustache and beard. See illustrations nos. 215 and 216 in *Queen Victoria: A Biography in Word and Picture*, by Helmut and Alison Gernsheim. Longmans, 1959.
   Prince Louis of Hesse had a moustache only, and the Marquis of Lorne (see illustration no. 230) had neither.
2. He is in military uniform with a hat plumed in front. Prince Louis of Hesse (see illustration no. 197) was married in civilian clothes. The Marquis of Lorne was a Scot. Prince Christian was married in military uniform and in the official wedding photograph (see illustration no. 215) he carried a plumed hat in his hand. Prince Christian had a very receding hairline (Queen Victoria commented on it) and the potter kindly hid it.
(*b*) Woman.
1. The costume and round hat with feather are typical of 1865–66. Compare the figure with the photograph of Princess Louise taken in 1865 (see illustration no. 210).
2. Princess Helena almost certainly had a similar outfit to Princess Louise. In every photograph illustrated in the work cited, where Princess Louise and Princess Helena appear together they are dressed alike, until Princess Helena's marriage in 1866 (see illustration nos. 133, 144, 146, 162, 165, 169 and 203).

Plate 76
Figure 225
Subject: **Princess Alexandra of Denmark,** later Princess of Wales
Title: Princess (raised capitals)
Date: 1862
Height: 9½ in (24 cm)
Colour: White and gilt.
Rarity: R.
Pair: *Fig.* 226 (Prince of Wales). *Fig.* 219 (Prince and Princess) *pl.* A-72 may have been intended to form a centrepiece.
Description: Standing wearing a snood, bodice and full-length dress, her hat on her right forearm.

Figure 226
Subject: **Prince of Wales**
Title: Prince (raised capitals)
Date: 1862
Height: 9½ in (24 cm)
Colour: White and gilt.
Rarity: R.
Pair: *Fig.* 225 (Princess of Wales). *Fig.* 219 (Prince and Princess) *pl.* A-72 may have been intended to form a centrepiece.
Description: Standing bare-headed, wearing a knee-length jacket, waistcoat and strapped trousers, his top hat in his left hand.
Observations: This and the preceding figure were, no doubt, issued at the time of the betrothal of the Prince of Wales to Princess Alexandra in 1862.

Plate 77
Figure 227
Subject: **Princess Louise**
Title: Princess Louise (raised capitals)
Date: c. 1871
Height: 12¾ in (32.25 cm)
Colour: White and gilt.
Rarity: VR. D.
Pair: *Fig.* 228 (Marquess of Lorne). *Fig.* 223 (Princess Louise and Marquess of Lorne) *pl.* A-74 may have been intended as a centrepiece.
Description: Standing in plumed hat, bodice and flounced skirt.

Figure 228
Subject: **Marquess of Lorne**
Title: Marquess of Lorne (raised capitals)
Date: c. 1871
Height: 12¾ in (32.25 cm)
Colour: White and gilt.
Rarity: VR. D.
Pair: *Fig.* 227 (Princess Louise). *Fig.* 223 (Princess Louise and Marquess of Lorne) *pl.* A-74 may have been intended as a centrepiece.
Description: Standing, wearing a plumed bonnet and full Highland dress, his right forearm rests on a pedestal.
Observations: 1. This and the preceding figures were, no doubt, issued in connection with the marriage of the Princess to the Marquess in 1871.
2. A similar pair of figures were sold at Christie's in 1963 for 32 gns; another pair fetched 90 gns in the same rooms in 1969.

Plate 77 (Far Left)
Fig. 227 Princess Louise
Fig. 228 Marquess of Lorne
By courtesy of Mr and Mrs Eric Joyce

Plate 78
Fig. 229 Princess Louise
Fig. 230 Marquess of Lorne

Plate 78

Figure 229
Subject: **Princess Louise**
Title: Princess Louise (black script underglaze transfer)
Date: *c.* 1871
Height: 10 in. (25 cm)
Colour: Rather crudely coloured.
Maker: In the style of John Parr
Rarity: VR. (titled); Av. (untitled)
Pair: Fig. 230 (Marquess of Lorne). Fig. 223 (Princess Louise and Marquess of Lorne) *pl.* A-74 may have been intended as a centrepiece.
Description: Wearing a low round plumed hat, bodice and multi-flounced skirt, a handkerchief in her left hand.

Figure 230
Subject: **Marquess of Lorne**
Title: Marquess of Lorne (black script underglaze transfer)
Date: *c.* 1871
Height: 10¼ in (25.75 cm)
Colour: Rather crudely coloured.
Maker: In the style of John Parr
Rarity: VR. (titled); Av. (untitled)
Pair: Fig. 229 (Princess Louise). Fig. 223 (Princess Louise and Marquess of Lorne) *pl.* A-74 may have been intended as a centrepiece.
Description: Wearing a plumed bonnet and Highland dress. To his right is a draped pedestal.
Observations: This and the preceding figures were doubtless issued in connection with the marriage of the Princess to the Marquess in 1871.

Plate 79
Figure 231
Subject: **Duchess of Edinburgh**
Title: Duchess of Edinburgh (gilt script)
Date: 1874
Height: 17 in (42.5 cm)
Colour: Pale state.
Maker: Sampson Smith
Rarity: R. D.

A164

Pair: Fig. 232 (Duke of Edinburgh)
Description: Standing, wearing a Russian tiara, bridal veil, bodice and multi-flounced skirt.
Observations: Issued in connection with the marriage of the Grand-duchess Marie Alexandrovna of Russia to the Duke of Edinburgh, formerly Prince Alfred in 1874.

Figure 232
Subject: **Duke of Edinburgh**
Title: Duke of Edinburgh (gilt script)
Date: 1874
Height: 17 in (42.5 cm)
Colour: Pale state.
Maker: Sampson Smith
Rarity: R. D.
Pair: Fig. 231 (Duchess of Edinburgh)
Description: Standing bare-headed and bearded, in uniform and trousers, his left hand on a draped pedestal.
Observations: 1. See *fig.* 231 (Duchess of Edinburgh).
2. This figure has been found erroneously titled 'Prince of Wales'.

Plate 80
Figure 233
Subject: **Duke of Edinburgh**
Title: None
Date: 1874
Height: 13½ in (34.25 cm)
Colour: Brightly coloured.
Rarity: VR. A.
Pair: Fig. 234 (Duchess of Edinburgh)
Description: Standing bare-headed and heavily bearded, in uniform with sashes over both shoulders. There is a bow (? love-knot) on his right shoulder. His left hand is on his hip and his right hand rests on a square pedestal to his right, and in it he holds his plumed cocked hat.
Observations: See next figure.

Figure 234
Subject: **Duchess of Edinburgh**

Title: None
Date: 1874
Height: 13 in (33 cm)
Colour: Brightly coloured.
Rarity: VR. A.
Pair: Fig. 233 (Duke of Edinburgh)
Description: Standing wearing a Russian tiara, and full-length dress with a bow (? love-knot) on each shoulder. In her right hand she holds a posy against her chest, and her left hand rests on a fluted pedestal to her left.
Observations: The bows are said to be 'love-knots' and signify a Royal wedding but I have been unable to substantiate this. 'Bright Gold', used in the decoration, enables this figure and its pair to be dated to the seventies or eighties. These facts, and the general appearance of the persons portrayed leave little room for doubt that the figures represent the Duke of Edinburgh and the Grand-duchess Marie Alexandrovna of Russia on their wedding day (1874).

Plate 81
Figure 235
Subject: **Victoria**
Title: Queen of England (gilt script)
Date: 187–
Height: 17½ in (43.5 cm)
Colour: Largely white and gilt.
Maker: Sampson Smith
Rarity: C.
Pair: Fig. 236 (Prince of Wales)
Description: Standing crowned, with veil, ermine-edged cloak, multi-flounced skirt and Garter sash.
Observations: 1. This figure is thought to date to the early 1870's. The reasons for this are discussed on *p.* 14.
2. The following later debased versions of this figure are known:
Fig. 235(*a*) 1887 16¾ in. (42.25 cm)
Title: Queen of England & Empress of India./Crowned June 20th 1837. Year of Jubilee 1887. (gilt script)
Fig. 235(*b*) 1897 16 in (40.5 cm)

Section A. British and Foreign Royalty

Plate 79
Fig. 231 Duchess of
Edinburgh
Fig. 232 Duke of
Edinburgh
*By courtesy of Mr and Mrs
Eric Joyce*

Plate 80 (Right)
Fig. 233 Duke of
Edinburgh
Fig. 234 Duchess of
Edinburgh

Plate 81
Fig. 235 Victoria
Fig. 236 Prince of Wales
Fig. 235(b) Victoria
*By courtesy of Mr and Mrs
Eric Joyce*

Title: Queen of England & Empress of
India./Crowned June 20th 1837. Year of
Jubilee 1897. (gilt script)
Fig. 235(*c*) 1901 15 in (38 cm)
Title: Queen Victoria crowned June 20th
1837./Years of Jubilee 1887–97./Died Jan.
22nd 1901. (gilt script)
3. *Fig.* 235 has been noted titled in green
script and in black script.

Figure 236
Subject: **Prince of Wales**
Title: Prince of Wales (gilt script)
Date: 187–
Height: 18 in (45.5 cm)
Colour: Largely white and gilt.
Maker: Sampson Smith
Rarity: C.
Pair: Fig. 235 (Victoria)

Description: Standing bearded and bare-
headed, in military uniform with trousers,
his left arm on a draped pedestal.
Observations: 1. A similar figure together with
fig. 235 fetched £13 at Sotheby's in 1966.
Another, together with *fig.* 235(*a*), fetched
£30 at Sotheby's in 1967.
2. See also *fig.* 235 (Victoria).

A165

Plate 82 (Left)
Fig. 237 Princess May
Fig. 238 Duke of Clarence

Plate 83 (Right)
Fig. 239 Victoria

Plate 84
Fig. 240 King Edward VII
Fig. 241 Queen Alexandra
In the Thomas Balston collection

Plate 82
Figure 237
Subject: **Princess May,** later Queen Mary
Title: Princess May (raised capitals)
Date: 1891
Height: 15¼ in (38.5 cm)
Colour: Largely white and gilt.
Maker: Probably Sampson Smith
Rarity: Av.
Pair: *Fig.* 238 (Duke of Clarence)

A166

Description: Standing bare-headed, in full-length dress, a reticule suspended from her right wrist, her left hand on a pedestal.

Figure 238
Subject: **Duke of Clarence**
Title: Duke of Clarence (raised capitals)
Date: 1891
Height: 15¾ in (39.75 cm)
Colour: Largely white and gilt.

Maker: Probably Sampson Smith
Rarity: VR. D.
Pair: *Fig.* 237 (Princess May)
Description: Standing bare-headed, in military uniform, his right hand on his hip and his left hand on a gun.
Observations: The Duke of Clarence was the eldest son of Edward VII. He was betrothed to Princess Mary (May) of Teck in 1891, but he died before the wedding. The

potters subsequently modified the mould to make *fig.* 365 (Baden-Powell) *pl.* C-133 and *fig.* 366 (De Wet) *pl.* C-134.

Plate 83
Figure 239
Subject: **Victoria**
Title: Victoria (raised capitals)
Date: 1890
Height: 10¾ in (27 cm)
Colour: White and gilt.
Maker: Probably Sampson Smith
Rarity: R.
Description: A bust of the Queen in later life wearing crown and veil. On a circular pedestal.
Observations: 1. I believe I saw the original mould for this figure in the disused part of the Sampson Smith factory when I visited it in 1964, but I cannot be certain.
2. The only recorded portrait of the Queen in the last twenty-five years of her reign other than those made from earlier moulds.

Plate 84
Figure 240
Subject: **Edward VII,** formerly Prince of Wales
Title: King Edward VII (raised capitals)
Date: 1901
Height: 13¼ in (33.5 cm)
Colour: Usually white and gilt; occasionally rather vivid colouring.
Maker: Lancaster & Sons Ltd.
Rarity: Av.
Pair: *Fig.* 241 (Alexandra)
Description: On a horse facing right, in cocked hat and military uniform with knee-boots. His right hand is on his hip; his left hand holds the horse's reins.
Observations: 1. The back of a number of these figures is impressed 'Copyright/Dec. 10 1901/T. H. Sandland' (*ch.* 2, *pl.* 13). See *p.* 17 for reasons for attributing this figure and its pair to Lancaster & Sons Ltd.
2. This figure and its pair were probably issued in connection with the Coronation (1902).

Figure 241
Subject: **Alexandra,** formerly Princess of Wales
Title: Queen Alexandra (raised capitals)
Date: 1901
Height: 12¾ in (32.25 cm)

Colour: Usually white and gilt; occasionally rather vivid colouring.
Maker: Lancaster & Sons Ltd.
Rarity: R.
Pair: *Fig.* 240 (Edward VII)
Description: On a horse facing left, in bowler hat, tight bodice and full-length skirt. Her left hand is on the horse's flank; her right hand holds the reins.
Observations: A number of these figures are impressed 'Copyright/Dec. 10 1901/T. H. Sandland'. The interpretation of this mark is discussed on *p.* 17.

Plate 85
Figure 242
Subject: **Edward VII,** formerly Prince of Wales
Title: King Edward VII (raised capitals)
Date: 1901
Height: 13 in (33 cm)
Colour: Usually white and gilt; occasionally rather vividly coloured.
Maker: Lancaster & Sons Ltd.
Rarity: C.
Pair: *Fig.* 243 (Alexandra)
Description: Standing bare-headed and nearly bald, in military uniform. He holds his plumed cocked hat in his right hand and his left hand rests on the hilt of a sword. To his right is a pedestal.
Observations: 1. A number of these figures are found impressed on the back 'Copyright/Dec. 20 1901/T. H. Sandland' (*ch.* 2, *pl.* 12). The interpretation of this mark is discussed on *p.* 17.
2. This figure and its pair were probably manufactured in connection with the Coronation (1902).

Figure 243
Subject: **Alexandra,** formerly Princess of Wales
Title: Queen Alexandra (raised capitals)
Date: 1901
Height: 13 in (33 cm)
Colour: Usually white and gilt; occasionally rather vividly coloured.
Maker: Lancaster & Sons Ltd.
Rarity: C.
Pair: *Fig.* 242 (Edward VII)
Description: Standing, wearing a low crown, full-length dress with Garter sash. She holds a fan in her left hand.

Observations: A number of these figures are impressed on the back 'Copyright Dec. 20/01/T. H. Sandland' (*ch.* 2, *pl.* 12). The interpretation of this mark is discussed on *p.* 17.

Figure 244
Subject: **Edward VII,** formerly Prince of Wales
Title: King Edward VII (indented capitals)
Date: 1901
Height: 14 in (35.5 cm)
Colour: White and gilt and/or black.
Maker: William Kent
Rarity: Av.
Pair: *Fig.* 245 (Alexandra)
Description: Standing, wearing a plumed cocked hat and Garter cloak over his uniform. He clutches his speech in his left hand.
Observations: 1. No. 133 in *Kent List A*; no. 283 in *Kent List B* but deleted as a 'discontinued' line, see *p.* 105.
2. This figure and its pair were probably manufactured in connection with the Coronation (1902).
3. A similar figure and its pair fetched 22 gns at Christie's in 1969.

Figure 245
Subject: **Alexandra,** formerly Princess of Wales
Title: Queen Alexandra (indented capitals)
Date: 1901
Height: 14 in (35.5 cm)
Colour: White and gilt and/or black.
Maker: William Kent
Rarity: Av.
Pair: *Fig.* 244 (Edward VII)
Description: Standing, wearing a small crown, long veil and a cloak over her full-length dress. Garter sash.
Observations: No. 134 in *Kent List A*; no. 283 in *Kent List B* but deleted as a 'discontinued line', see *p.* 105.

Figure 246
Subject: **Edward VII,** formerly Prince of Wales
Title: King of England (transfer gilt script)
Date: 1901
Height: 14½ in (36.75 cm)
Colour: White, black and gilt.
Maker: Uncertain. Possibly Sampson Smith

Plate 85
Fig. 242 King Edward VII
Fig. 243 Queen Alexandra
Fig. 244 King Edward VII
Fig. 245 Queen Alexandra
Fig. 246 King Edward VII
Fig. 246(a) Queen Alexandra

Plate 85 continued
Rarity: VR.
Pair: *Fig.* 246(*a*) (Alexandra)
Description: Standing, wearing a plumed cocked hat and Garter cloak over his uniform. He clutches his speech in his right hand.
Observations: This figure and its pair were probably manufactured in connection with the Coronation (1902).

Figure 246(a)
Subject: **Alexandra,** formerly Princess of Wales
Title: Queen of England (transfer gilt script)
Date: 1901
Height: 14½ in (36.75 cm)
Colour: White, black and gilt.
Maker: Uncertain. Possibly Sampson Smith
Rarity: R.
Pair: *Fig.* 246 (Edward VII)
Description: Standing, wearing a small crown and veil, long dress and ermine-edged cloak, a fan in her left hand.

Plate 86
Figure 247
Subject: **Louis-Philippe, King of the French**
Title: None
Date: c. 1843
Height: 7½ in (19 cm)
Colour: Well coloured with underglaze blue.
Rarity: VR.
A168

Pair: No pair has been described for this figure. If a pair does exist, and the identification is correct, then it would be likely to be Queen Victoria.
Description: Standing bare-headed, in military uniform and trousers. There is a sash over his right shoulder and two stars on his left breast. He holds his plumed cocked hat in his right hand beside his right leg, and his left hand is on the hilt of his sword. A porcelaneous figure with a hollow base.
Observations: There is a striking similarity between this figure and the portrait of **Louis-Philippe** by Winterhalter, in the Louvre.

Although the figure is not identical, I have little doubt that it was intended to represent Louis-Philippe, being manufactured probably in 1843–4. It will be recalled that in September, 1843 Queen Victoria visited Louis-Philippe at Château d'Eu. The visit was returned in October, 1844, it being the first time a French monarch had voluntarily landed on English shores, see also *fig.* 35, *pl.* A-15 and *fig.* 49, *pl.* A-18.

Plate 87
Figure 248
Subject: **Leopold I, King of the Belgians**
Title: Leopold King of Belgium (gilt script)
Date: 184–
Height: 9 in (23 cm)
Colour: Pale, largely white and gilt.

Rarity: VR. D.
Pair: *Fig.* 249 (Louise-Marie)
Description: Standing bare-headed, in uniform. He holds the hilt of his sword in his left hand, and his right hand rests on the orb and sceptre which lie on a draped pedestal.
Observations: After a lithograph by F. Judenne inscribed:
Leopold Premier, Roi des Belges. Née Le 16 *Decembre* 1790.
In Le Musée de la Dynastie, Bruxelles (See *pl.* A-88).

Figure 249
Subject: **Louise-Marie, Queen of the Belgians**
Title: Maria Queen of Belgium (gilt script)
Date: 184–
Height: 9 in (23 cm)
Colour: Pale; largely white and gilt.
Rarity: VR. D.
Pair: *Fig.* 248 (Leopold I)
Description: Standing wearing a plumed hat, necklace with a cross suspended therefrom, tight bodice with leg-of-mutton sleeves, full-length skirt showing a 'V' of underskirt and a sash round her waist with tassels in front. In her left hand she holds a posy of flowers, and in her right hand a handkerchief.
Observations: 1. After a lithograph by F. Judenne inscribed: *Louise Marie d'Orleans, Reine des Belges. Née Le 3 Avril 1812.*

Plate 87
Fig. 248 Leopold I, King of the Belgians
Fig. 249 Louise-Marie, Queen of the Belgians
By courtesy of Le Président of Le Musée de la Dynastie, Brussels

Plate 88
'Leopold Premier. Rio des Belges. Née Le 16 Decembre 1790'
A lithograph by F. Judenne in Le Musée de la Dynastie in Brussels. This engraving is the source of fig. 248 (Leopold I, King of the Belgians).
By courtesy of Le Président of Le Musée de la Dynastie, Brussels

Plate 89
'Louise Marie d'Orleans, Reine des Belges. Née Le 3 Avril 1812'
A lithograph by F. Judenne in Le Musée de la Dynastie in Brussels. This engraving is the source of fig. 249 (Louise-Marie, Queen of the Belgians).
By courtesy of Le Président of Le Musée de la Dynastie, Brussels

In Le Musée de la Dynastie, Bruxelles (See *pl.* A-89).
2. There is no explanation forthcoming as to why the potter elected to call Louise-Marie, 'Maria, Queen of Belgium'. I have been unable to ascertain that this was a nickname for her in this country, and I understand from M. Marc de Smedt that she was not known by that name in Belgium.

Plate 88
Leopold I, King of the Belgians
Lithograph by F. Judenne. The source of *fig.* 248, *pl.* A-87.

Plate 90
Fig. 250 ?Alexander II of Russia
Fig. 251 ?Marie-Alexandrowna of Russia
By courtesy of Mr Arthur Thornton

Plate 89
Louise-Marie, Queen of the Belgians
Lithograph by F. Judenne. The source of *fig.* 249, *pl.* A-87.

Plate 90
Figure 250
Subject: **? Alexander II, Tsar of Russia**
Title: None
Date: *c.* 1856
Height: 7½ in (19 cm)
Colour: Well coloured.
Rarity: Av. A.
Pair: Fig. 251 (? Marie-Alexandrowna)
Description: Standing bare-headed and moustached, in military uniform, trousers and calf-boots. His ermine-edged cloak is slung over his right shoulder and held together in front with his right hand. He has a sash over his right shoulder and his left breast is decorated with two stars. In his left hand he holds a book.
Observations: 1. This figure, together with its pair, were sold for 60 gns at Christie's in 1965. They were catalogued as *A pair of figures of Prince Charming and Cinderella, in 'La Cenerentola'*. I know of nothing to support this identification. The possibility that the figures portray Alexander II of Russia and his consort, Marie-Alexandrowna is put forward tentatively, although I think it may well turn out to be correct.
2. The identification is based on the closeness of *fig.* 250 to an engraving of Alexander II of Russia which appeared in *The Illustrated London News* on September 13th, 1856 following his coronation at Moscow on September 7th (see *pl.* A-91). There is an extremely close resemblance between the face of Alexander II portrayed in the engraving and the face portrayed in the figure. In both engraving and figure he is shown wearing a similar military jacket and ermine-edged cloak, and has a sash

over his right shoulder and two stars. The style of the figure is about right for the date, although it is perhaps more characteristic of a decade or so earlier. The difficulty is that the matching engraving of Marie-Alexandrowna does not bear any worthwhile resemblance to *fig.* 251, with the one important exception that the faces are very similar, both being pear-shaped. If the assumption is correct, then doubtless another engraving of Marie-Alexandrowna closer to the figure will come to light. It must be conceded, that if the identification is right, it is strange that both engravings in *The Illustrated London News* were not used. Possibly the potters used other sources for *both* figures. The same engraving of Alexander II, for instance, is used on the music-front for *The Emperor's Gallop*.

Figure 251
Subject: **? Marie-Alexandrowna of Russia**
Title: None
Date: *c.* 1856
Height: 7½ in (19 cm)
Colour: Well coloured.
Rarity: VR. A.
Pair: Fig. 250 (? Alexander II)
Description: Standing bare-headed, wearing a tight bodice with leg-of-mutton sleeves and a star on her left breast. Her ermine-edged skirt is open in front to display a 'V' of underskirt. Tasselled sash round her waist.
Observations: See *fig.* 250 (? Alexander II).

Plate 91
Alexander II and Marie-Alexandrowna
Engravings of Alexander II, emperor of Russia and of his consort Marie-Alexandrowna which appeared in *The Illustrated London News* of September 13th, 1856, following their Coronation.

Plate 92
Figure 252
Subject: **Shah Nasr-ed-Din**
Title: Have you seen the Shah (raised capitals)
Date: *c.* 1873
Height: 13½ in (34.25 cm)

Colour: A 'porridge' piece, usually un-coloured. Rarely, pairs are found quite nicely coloured in the tradition of Sampson Smith.
Maker: Sampson Smith
Rarity: R.
Pair: Figures are found, facing either right

HAVE·YOU·SEEN·THE·SHAH.

HAVE YOU SEEN THE SHAH

Plate 93
Fig. 254 ?Franz Joseph I

Plate 94
Fig. 255 Unidentified monarch

or left, with only minor differences.
Description: On a horse facing right or left, wearing a high fez-shaped hat with a jewelled plume and full military uniform. Sash over his left shoulder.
Observations: A 10 in (25 cm) untitled version exists for which *fig.* 252(*a*) has been allotted. The only example I have seen is on a horse facing left. This figure is in the same style as similar sized figures of Franco-Prussian War generals.

Figure 253
Subject: **Shah Nasr-ed-Din**
Title: Have you seen the Shah (raised capitals)
Date: *c.* 1873
Height: 15¼ in (38.5 cm)
Colour: A fine quality piece in white and gilt with the face darkened.
Maker: Sampson Smith
Rarity: R.
Pair: In the examples I have seen the horses face left, but doubtless 'matching' figures exist with the horses facing right.
Description: On a horse facing left. Similar except for minor details, particularly with regard to the position of the hands, to *fig.* 252.
Observations: Issued in connection with the visit of the Shah of Persia to England in 1873. *Have you seen the Shah?* was the title of a 'hit-tune' of the day, sung by the Great Vance. It became a popular catchword.

Plate 93
Figure 254
Subject: **? Franz Joseph I, Emperor of Austria**
Title: None
Date: *c.* 1855

Height: 16½ in (41.5 cm)
Colour: Well coloured.
Rarity: R.
Description: Standing, wearing a feathered hat, cloak over his right shoulder, loose coat, waistcoat, breeches and knee-boots. In his right hand he holds the muzzle of a gun and over his right shoulder is a lashing attached to the hind legs of a stag which lies in front of his left foot.
Observations: Bears a very close resemblance to an engraving which appeared in *The Illustrated London News* of June 9th, 1855 of the Emperor of Austria in the 'Jager' or Styrian costume in which he used to go capercailyelzie (*grouse*) shooting in the Styrian mountains.

Plate 94
Figure 255
Subject: **Unidentified monarch**
Title: None
Height: 10½ in (26.5 cm)
Colour: Well coloured.
Rarity: VR. A.
Pair: No pair has yet been recorded.
Description: Standing crowned, wearing a cloak over his left shoulder, military uniform with breeches and knee-boots, a sash over his right shoulder. His right hand is on his hip, his left hand over the front of his thigh. Behind him is a brick wall.
Observations: Has defied identification. It has been postulated that it may be a portrayal of Louis-Philippe, king of the French, or alternatively Leopold, king of the Belgians, but the real answer is not known. It may, of course, turn out to be a theatrical portrait.

Plate 95
Fig. 256 ?Charles I
Fig. 257 ?Cromwell
By courtesy of Mr John Hall

Plate 96
Fig. 258 Charles I
Fig. 259 Cromwell
By courtesy of Miss M.M. Frame

Plate 95
Figure 256
Subject: **? Charles I**
Title: None
Height: 10 in (25 cm)
Colour: Usually sparsely coloured, but some examples, well coloured in the manner of Thomas Parr, do exist.
Maker: Thomas Parr
Rarity: Av.
Pair: Fig. 257 (? Cromwell)
Description: Standing, wearing a round plumed hat and pointed beard, doublet, breeches and knee-boots. His left hand is on his hip and his right hand on a pedestal upon which is a manuscript.
Observations: Generally regarded as portraying Charles I, although there is no positive evidence of this. It may be theatrical for it almost certainly comes from the same factory which produced *figs.* 115 (Reeves) and 116 (? Gras), *pl.* E-62.

Figure 257
Subject: **? Cromwell**
Title: None
Height: 10 in (25 cm)
Colour: As for preceding figure.
Maker: Thomas Parr
Rarity: Av.
Pair: Fig. 256 (? Charles I)
Description: Standing, wearing a plumed hat, narrow moustache, doublet, breeches and thigh-boots. His right hand is tucked into his jacket, and his left hand rests on an upturned cannon.
Observations: This figure has been variously thought to be Oliver Cromwell (1599–1658) and Prince Rupert (1619–82). The latter, otherwise known as the 'mad cavalier', was the life and soul of the loyalist cause. In 1848 he accepted the command of that portion of the English fleet which had espoused King

Charles' cause. He acquitted himself with great daring, but in 1850, Blake attacked his squadron and burned or sank most of his vessels. The Prince escaped to the West Indies. Those who support the view that this figure is indeed Prince Rupert, base their identification on the fact that the cannon shown appears to be a naval cannon. A firm identification will have to await the discovery of an appropriate print. The figure may well be theatrical (see preceding figure).

Plate 96
Figure 258
Subject: **Charles I**
Title: None
Height: 13¼ in (33.5 cm)
Colour: White and gilt.
Maker: Sampson Smith
Rarity: Av.
Pair: Fig. 259 (Cromwell)
Description: On a horse facing right, wearing a round plumed hat, pointed beard, cloak, frilled lace collar and cuffs, doublet, breeches and calf-boots. He holds a scroll in his left hand and the reins in his right.
Observations: This figure has been found with the following factory mark in relief on its base:

SAMPSON SMITH
1851
LONGTON

Figure 259
Subject: **Cromwell**
Title: None
Height: 12¾ in (32.25 cm)
Colour: White and gilt.
Maker: Sampson Smith
Rarity: Av.
Pair: Fig. 258 (Charles I)
Description: On a horse facing left, clean-

shaven, wearing a round plumed hat, straight Puritan collar, cloak, doublet, breeches and knee-boots. His right hand holds the horse's reins and his left hand is on the horse's flank.
Observations: 1. The typical Carolean dress portrayed in *fig.* 258 compared with the Puritan dress portrayed in *fig.* 259 leaves little room for doubt that these figures are intended to portray Charles I and Cromwell. 2. This figure has also been found with the Sampson Smith factory mark, in relief, on the base (see preceding figure).

Plate 97
Figure 260
Subject: **Charles I and Cromwell**
Title: King Charles & Cromwell (gilt script) or K. Charles & Cromwell (gilt script)
Height: 15 in (38 cm)
Colour: Usually rather poorly coloured.
Rarity: C.
Description: King Charles sits to the left, and Cromwell stands to the right of a tree trunk (spill-holder). Both are similarly dressed in broad-brimmed plumed hats, short coats, breeches and knee-boots. Each holds a manuscript. Each is bearded.

Figure 261
Subject: **Charles Edward Stewart,** also known as 'Bonnie Prince Charlie', the 'Young Cavalier' and the 'Young Pretender'
Title: Prince Charles (gilt script)
Height: 14½ in (36.75 cm)
Colour: Usually sparsely coloured.
Rarity: R. (titled); Av. (untitled)
Description: Standing bare-headed in Highland dress, a plaid over his left shoulder, his bonnet in his right hand.
Observations: Bears a similarity, particularly with regard to style of decoration, to *figs.* 12 (Wallace) and 13 (Bruce), *pl.* I-6.

Section A. British and Foreign Royalty

Plate 97
Fig. 260 Charles I and Cromwell
Fig. 261 Charles Edward Stewart
In the collection of
Mr F. J. Stephens

Plate 98
Fig. 262 ?Charles Edward Stewart and Flora Macdonald

Plate 98
Figure 262
Subject: **? Charles Edward Stewart,** also known as 'Bonnie Prince Charlie', **and Flora Macdonald**
Title: None
Height: 6 in (15.25 cm)
Colour: Well coloured.
Rarity: R.
Description: Bonnie Prince Charlie, bare-headed in tunic and calf-boots, is being helped out of a boat by Flora Macdonald. She is standing on the left bare-headed,

in blouse and knee-length flounced skirt. Beside her is a dog.
Observations: Generally thought, without any positive evidence, to represent Bonnie Prince Charlie and Flora Macdonald. It may well be a theatre piece.

Plate 99
Figure 263
Subject: **Mary II**
Title: Queen Mary (raised capitals)
Height: 10¼ in (25.75 cm)
Colour: White and gilt or well-coloured.

Rarity: C.
Pair: Fig. 264 (William III)
Description: On a horse facing right, in plumed hat with long veil and full riding habit. She holds the reins in her right hand and her left hand is across her chest.

Figure 264
Subject: **William III**
Title: King William III
Height: 10¼ in (25.75 cm)
Colour: White and gilt or well coloured.
Rarity: C.

Plate 99
Fig. 263 Queen Mary II
Fig. 264 William III
Fig. 265 William III
In the collection of Lady Ranfurly

Plate 99 continued
Pair: *Fig.* 263 (Mary II)
Description: On a horse facing left, in plumed hat, long coat with ermine-edged sleeves, breeches and knee-boots. In his right hand he holds a scroll and in his left hand the reins. Long, tapering saddle-cloth.
Observations: A similar figure and its pair fetched 25 gns at Christie's in 1966.

Figure 265
Subject: **William III**
Title: None
Height: 9 in (23 cm)
Colour: Well coloured.
Rarity: Av.
Pair: There is almost certainly a pair to this figure, although it has not been reported so far, *fig.* 266 has been reserved for it.
Description: On a horse facing left, dressed similarly to *fig.* 264. The only major differences other than height and the absence of titling are 1. the position of the horse's forelegs is reversed and 2. the saddle-cloth is short.

Plate 100
Figure 267
Subject: **William III**
Title: King William (raised capitals)
Height: 12½ in (31.75 cm)
Colour: White and gilt or coloured.
Rarity: Av.
Pair: There is almost certainly a pair to this figure (Mary II), but it has not been reported so far, *fig.* 268 has been reserved for it.
Description: On a horse facing left, in plumed tricorn hat, long coat, breeches and knee-boots. Long squared-off saddle-cloth. He holds a manuscript in his right hand which rests on the horse's mane.

Plate 100
Fig. 267 William III
In the collection of Lady Ranfurly

Plate 101
Figure 269
Subject: **William III**
Title: William III 1690/Derry Aughrim Enniskillen/and the Boyne (gilt script)
Height: 14¾ in (37.5 cm)
Colour: White and gilt.
Maker: In the style of Sampson Smith
Rarity: Av.
Pair: *Fig.* 270 (William III)

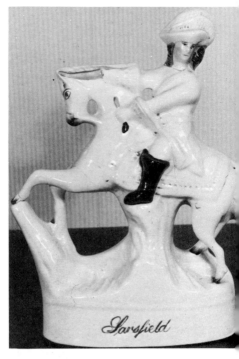

Plate 102
Fig. 271 Sarsfield

Description: On a horse facing right, in plumed hat, long coat, and knee-boots. In his left hand he holds his sword pointing forward over the horse's head, and in his right hand a pistol.

Figure 270
Subject: **William III**
Title: William III 1690/Derry Aughrim Enniskillen/ and the Boyne (gilt script)

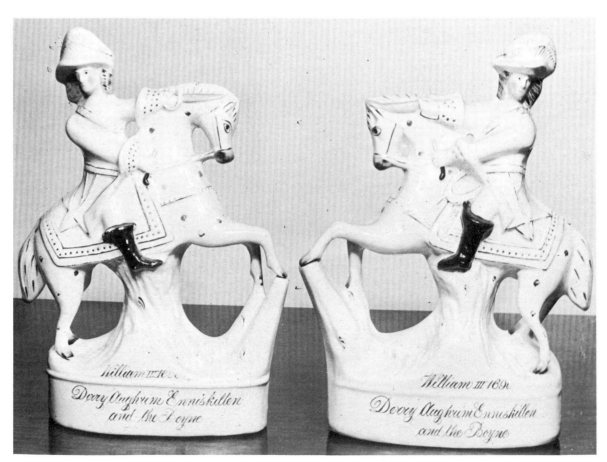

Plate 101
Fig. 269 William III
Fig. 270 William III
By courtesy of Mr John Hall

Plate 103
Fig. 272 Queen Mary II
Fig. 273 William III
By courtesy of
Miss M.M. Frame

Height: 14¾ in (37.5 cm)
Colour: White and gilt.
Maker: In the style of Sampson Smith
Rarity: Av.
Pair: Fig. 269 (William III)
Description: Virtually a mirror-image of *fig.* 269 (William III).
Observations: This figure has been found titled 'Sarsfield', see *pl.* A-102.

Plate 102

Figure 271
Subject: **Patrick Sarsfield, Earl of Lucan**
Title: Sarsfield (grey script)
Height: 14½ in (36.75 cm)
Colour: White and gilt.
Maker: In the style of Sampson Smith
Rarity: VR.

Pair: No pair has been described, unless it be *fig.* 269 (William III).

Description: Identical, other than in title, to *fig.* 270 (William III).

Observations: That the potter inscribed figures of William III, 'Sarsfield', is a typical example of catering for two markets at the same time. Sarsfield, created Earl of Lucan by James II, drove the English out of Sligo, was present at the Boyne and Aughrim, and defended Limerick. Figures so titled would appeal to certain Catholic elements in Ireland where, in fact, this figure was found. This is a very similar situation to that found during the Boer War when the same figure was produced titled either Baden-Powell or De Wet (see *pls.* C-133 and 134).

Plate 103

Figure 272
Subject: **Mary II**
Title: Mary (gilt script)
Height: 9⅛ in (23.25 cm)
Colour: White and gilt.
Rarity: Av.
Pair: Fig. 273 (William III)
Description: On a horse facing right, in plumed hat and long veil, and full riding habit.

Figure 273
Subject: **William III**
Title: King Wm 3 (gilt script)
Height: 9¼ in (23.5 cm)
Colour: White and gilt.
Rarity: Av.
Pair: Fig. 272 (Mary II)

Plate 104
Fig. 274 Queen Mary II
Fig. 276 William III
In the collection of
Mr Ronald Shockledge

Plate 103 continued
Description: On a horse facing left, in plumed hat, long coat and knee-boots.

Plate 104
Figure 274
Subject: **Mary II**
Title: Mary 2nd (gilt script)
Height: 9 in (23 cm)
Colour: White and gilt.
Rarity: Av.
Pair: No pair has been reported so far, but undoubtedly one exists, *fig.* 275 has been reserved for it.
Description: Similar to *fig.* 272 (Mary II) *pl.* A-103, except for minor differences.

Figure 276
Subject: **William III**
Title: King William 3rd (gilt script)
Height: 11 in (28 cm)
Colour: White and gilt.
Rarity: Av.
Pair: There is almost certainly a pair to this figure, for which *fig.* 277 has been reserved, but it has not been reported so far.
Description: On a horse facing left, in plumed hat, long coat and knee-boots. Short square saddle-cloth.

Plate 105
Figure 278
Subject: **William III**
Title: King Wm. 3rd (gilt script)
Height: 12 in (30.5 cm)
Colour: White and gilt.
Rarity: R.
Pair: There is almost certainly a pair to this figure, for which *fig.* 279 has been reserved.
Description: Virtually identical to *fig.* 276 (William III) *pl.* A-104 except for the titling and minor differences.

Plate 106
Figure 280
Subject: **? William III**

Title: None
Height: 10 in (25 cm)
Colour: Well coloured.
Rarity: Av.
Pair: Fig. 281 (? James II)
Description: On a prancing horse facing right, wearing plumed round hat. At the horse's feet are an upturned cannon and cannon balls.
Observations: 1. An 11¾ in (29.75 cm) version of this figure exists in which the upturned cannon is on a wheeled carriage.
2. This figure and its pair may portray William III and James II, but there is doubt.

Figure 281
Subject: **? James II**
Title: None
Height: 10 in (25 cm)
Colour: Well coloured.
Rarity: Av.
Pair: Fig. 280 (? William III)
Description: On a prancing horse facing left, wearing plumed cocked hat. At the horse's feet are an upturned cannon and cannon balls.
Observations: See preceding figure.

Plate 107
Figure 282
Subject: **? George IV (when Prince Regent) and Mrs Fitzherbert**
Title: None
Height: 6 in (15.25 cm)
Colour: Well coloured.
Rarity: R.
Description: Seated on a settee, the Prince Regent, on the left, is bare-headed in coat, waistcoat, breeches, stockings and shoes. He clutches a knob on the arm of the settee with his right hand and is playing with his cravat with his left hand. Mrs Fitzherbert sits on the right, bare-headed in bodice with leg-of-mutton sleeves, and full-length skirt.
Observations: 1. Generally supposed to portray the Prince Regent and Mrs Fitzherbert, but I know of no positive evidence.

Plate 105
Fig. 278 William III
By courtesy of Miss M.M. Frame

2. A figure similar to this was sold at Christie's on October 14th, 1963 as *The Prince Regent and Mrs Herbert* (sic). It, together with *fig.* 165 (Victoria, Albert and the Prince of Wales) *pl.* A-55, fetched 24 gns. Another figure, by itself, fetched 35 gns at Christie's in 1969.

Plate 106
Fig. 280 ?William III
Fig. 281 ?James II

Section A. British and Foreign Royalty

Plate 107
Fig. 282 ?Prince Regent
and Mrs Fitzherbert
*By courtesy of Mr and Mrs
Eric Joyce*

Plate 108 (Right)
Fig. 283 William IV
Fig. 284 Queen Adelaide

Plate 109
Fig. 285 ?Charles I
By courtesy of Mr John Hall

Plate 110 (Right)
Fig. 286 ?Charles I and
Henrietta Maria
Probably the persons
portrayed are imaginary,
see *ch.* 3, *pl.* 6A.

Plate 108
Figure 283
Subject: **William IV**
Title: None
Date: *c.* 1830
Height: 13½ in (34.25 cm)
Colour: White.
Rarity: VR.
Pair: Fig. 284 (Adelaide)
Description: Standing crowned, wearing
cloak, Garter sash, star over his left breast,
breeches and stockings. He holds the orb

in his right hand.
Observations: See *fig.* 284 (Adelaide).

Figure 284
Subject: **Adelaide**
Title: None
Date: *c.* 1830
Height: 13¼ in (33.5 cm)
Colour: White.
Rarity: VR.
Pair: Fig. 283 (William IV)
Description: Standing crowned, wearing a

cloak and ankle-length dress. She holds the
orb in her right hand.
Observations: These figures, which were
probably made about the time of the
coronation of William IV and Adelaide in
1830, are included to show the style of figure
immediately prior to our period. There is a
similar pair of figures included in the
Willett collection, nos. 71 and 71(a). They
are catalogued as 'White earthenware—
Staffordshire'.

A177

Plate 109
Figure 285
Subject: **? Charles I**
Title: None
Height: 13½ in (34.25 cm)
Colour: Well coloured.
Rarity: VR.
Description: Standing bearded, with wide-brimmed, plumed hat, cloak, doublet, breeches and loose boots. There is a sash over his right shoulder. He holds his sword against his chest in his right hand.
Observations: This figure has been said to portray Charles I in the act of surrendering his sword, but I know of nothing to substantiate this claim.

Plate 110
Figure 286
Subject: **? Charles I and Henrietta Maria**
Title: None
Height: 10½ in (26.5 cm)
Colour: Well coloured.
Rarity: R.
Description: He stands on the left, bare-headed and bearded, in mid-thigh length coat with lace collar, breeches and jack-boots. He has a sash across his right shoulder and holds his plumed hat in his right hand. She stands on the right, wearing a necklace, bodice and full-length dress. Her right arm is linked with his left arm and she holds a fan in her left hand.

Observations: This figure has for long been thought to portray Charles I and Henrietta Maria and possibly to be theatrical in origin. Recently, however, the source, a Le Blond print inscribed *Courtship*, has come to light (*ch.* 3, *pl.* 6A). It is not known whether the persons portrayed in the Le Blond print are real or imaginary but the title 'Courtship' would seem to preclude Charles I and Henrietta Maria, for they married by proxy.

Section B
Statesmen and Politicians
Biographies and Historical Notes

BEACONSFIELD, Earl of (1804–81). *See* **Disraeli, Benjamin**.

BROWN, JOHN (1800–59). American abolitionist, born in Connecticut of pilgrim descent. Successively tanner, land-surveyor and farmer. Became a strong abolitionist and wandered through the country on anti-slavery campaigns. Twice married and had twenty children. After various skirmishes, schemed to establish a stronghold in the mountains of Virginia, as a refuge for runaway slaves. 'To draw attention and secure recruits, he made a hair-brained attack on the United States armoury at Harper's Ferry in 1859. He broke into the armoury with eighteen men and took several citizens prisoner. Next day Colonel Robert E. Lee with a company of marines arrived from Washington. After a fight in which two of his sons were killed and he himself was severely wounded, Brown was captured. Subsequently he was tried by a Virginian court for insurrection and murder. He was convicted and hanged. The song *John Brown's body lies a-mouldering in the grave* commemorates the raid at Harper's Ferry and was a popular Republican song in the Civil War.
See **pl. B-26**.

COBDEN, RICHARD (1804–65). English economist and politician known as the 'Apostle of free-trade'. Commenced life as a commercial traveller. In 1831 set up an establishment for calico-printing in Lancashire. Visited the United States in 1835 and thereafter began to preach free-trade and non-intervention. In 1838 founded the Anti-Corn Law League. Member of Parliament for Stockport in 1841 and played a foremost part in bringing about the abolition of the Corn Laws in 1846. Opposed the Crimean War but spoke out strongly in favour of the North during the American Civil War. Except for an interval of two years, he remained in Parliament from 1841 until his death.
See **pls. B-1, 1A** (appendix).

COOPER, ANTHONY ASHLEY, seventh Earl of Shaftesbury (1801–85). Distinguished philanthropist. Member of Parliament from 1826 to 1851. Urged reform of the lunacy laws (1829) and fought for the protection of factory operatives (1834–44), colliery workers (1842) and chimney-sweeps. He advocated 'ragged schools' (1848). Identified himself with religious associations of many kinds.
See **pl. B-1**.

COPENHAGEN (1808–36), Wellington's famous chestnut charger, probably named after the battle of 1801. Grandson, on his sire's side, of the celebrated racehorse *Eclipse*, and his dam, *Lady Catherine*, was sired by *John Bull*, winner of the 1792 Derby. He possessed tremendous stamina and his manners on duty were superb, but like so many spirited blood horses, he had one frivolity which he indulged out of sheer joie de vivre. He seldom bit people but he much enjoyed taking a swipe at them with his hind hoofs.

At the Battle of Waterloo he behaved perfectly throughout the thunder of cannon and the turmoil, but when, after eighteen hours in the saddle, Wellington dismounted and incautiously patted his faithful charger's hindquarters in token of thanks, he lashed out, missing the Duke's head by a few inches. The Duke harboured no ill-feeling and indeed, refused to part with *Copenhagen*, who subsequently settled down to a well-earned retirement at the Wellington country residence *Strathfieldsaye*. Of him the Duke said: 'There may have been many faster horses, no doubt many handsomer, but for bottom and endurance I never saw his fellow.' When he died he was buried with military honours and a tomb was erected to his memory. On it was inscribed:

God's humble instrument through meaner clay,
Should share the glory of that glorious day.

See **pl. B-3,**
pl. C-11.

DISRAELI, BENJAMIN, first Earl of Beaconsfield (1804–81). Statesman and novelist. Exercised considerable influence on Conservative political theories. His first novel *Vivian Grey* was published when he was only 21. Two subsequent novels *Coningsby* and *Sybil* published twenty years later aroused the social conscience to the evils of industrial life and the deplorable relations between rich and poor. He entered Parliament in 1837 and was Prime Minister in 1868, and from 1874 to 1880. During his second period in office he negotiated the purchase of the Suez Canal shares. During this period, also, the Queen assumed the title of 'Empress of India.' He was a great orator and a rival and antithesis of Gladstone. Queen Victoria had a high regard for his policies, and created him Earl of Beaconsfield in 1876. He became an intimate friend and was known by her as 'Dizzy'.
See **pl. B-14**.

DUNCOMBE, THOMAS SLINGSBY (1796–1861). English politician, Member of Parliament for Hertford (1826, 1830 and 1831); radical MP for Finsbury 1834. In 1842 he presented the chartist petition to Parliament. He was known as 'the best-dressed man in the House'. He was concerned with the escape of Prince Louis Napoleon, later Napoleon III, from imprisonment in Ham in 1846, and also worked on behalf of Kossuth in 1861.
See **pl. B-1**.

FITZGERALD, LORD EDWARD (1763–98). Irish politician, born near Dublin, the younger son of the Duke of Leinster. Served with distinction in the American war. Member of Parliament in Ireland for Athy and Kildare. Attracted to Paris by the Revolution. Renounced his title, married and returned to Ireland in 1793. Joined 'United Irishmen' in 1796 and went to France to organize a French invasion of Ireland. His plot was betrayed and he was seized in Dublin. In the struggle with the police he received wounds from which he died.
See **pl. B-16**.

FRANKLIN, BENJAMIN (1706–90). American philanthropist, scholar, philosopher, scientist and statesman. He was born at Boston, his father having migrated from Banbury in 1685. Apprenticed at the age of twelve to his brother as a printer. First attracted public attention by publishing his *Poor Richard's Almanac* (1732). Commenced a series of scientific experiments which included the invention of the lightning-conductor (1746). Elected Fellow of the Royal Society. Was for ten years a member of the General Assembly. Resided in Britain for eighteen years as an agent for his state. On his return to America, played a part in the framing of the constitution of the United States which led to the Declaration of Independence (1776).
See **pls. B-20A, 21, 23, 23B, 25A**.

FRY, ELIZABETH (1780–1845). English Quaker prison reformer. Third daughter of John Gurney, the rich Quaker banker, and sister of Joseph John Gurney, the Quaker minister and philanthropist (*q.v.*). In 1800 she married Joseph Fry, a leading London Quaker merchant. In 1810, she visited Newgate prison and found 300 women, tried and untried, with their numerous children, herded together in filth and neglect. Thenceforth, she devoted her life to prison reform and also founded hospitals for the homeless and charity organization societies.
See **pl. B-1**.

GLADSTONE, CATHERINE (1813–1900). Daughter of Sir Stephen Glynne, Bt., she married Gladstone in 1839. *See* **pl. B-12**.

Section B. Statesmen and Politicians

GLADSTONE, WILLIAM EWART
(1809–98). Liberal statesman of the latter half of the nineteenth century, known as the 'Grand Old Man'. He entered Parliament in 1832 as a tory and held office under Peel as President of the Board of Trade. In 1844 after a battle with George Hudson, the 'Railway King', he pushed the first General Railway Bill through Parliament. He joined the Aberdeen coalition in 1852 and served as Chancellor of the Exchequer. Liberal Prime Minister from 1868–74, 1880–5, 1886 and 1892–4. His financial policy was able and very successful. His first ministry included the Education Act (1870) and the Irish Land Act (1873). His second ministry witnessed the defeat by the Boers at Majuba Hill and the death of General Gordon at Khartoum. The last two ministries were marked by the adoption of the policy of Home Rule for Ireland, which he was unable to carry through.
See pls. B-1, 12, 13, 14, 15, 16.

IRISH NATIONAL FORESTERS.
The following has been culled from H. B. L. Pollard's *Secret Societies of Ireland* (London 1922):

The 'Irish National Foresters' is an organization which must not be confused with the respectable body of similar name, which is an English Friendly Society. The order was established in Dublin in 1877, and is, technically, a Benefit Society (No. 504, Ireland) and registered under the Friendly Societies Act. Nominally, it provides for the relief of members and their wives and families in sickness, burial, insurance, relief and maintenance of widows and orphans, and general circumstances of distress . . .

The Society is generally held to be moderately non-political and respectable; but there is no doubt that some members who hold office in the Society use the Society as a cover for criminal societies with which they are personally connected. Many prominent members and brothers of the I.N.F. are also members of the I.R.A.; and the branches in the United Kingdom are peculiarly suspect . . . The Irish Forester's Hall in Dublin was raided in June, 1921 and found to contain a class of I.R.A. and Fianna practising signalling. The Irish National Forester's Hall at Liverpool was the centre of Irish criminal activity in that city, and some of the leading members of the organization were implicated in serious outrage. The chief function of the branch was, however, to make arrangements for smuggling wanted criminals from Ireland to the United States, by getting them engagements as workers or paying their passages on outward bound ships.

The two figures, each titled 'Irish National Forrester', illustrated on *pl.* B-18 were, incidentally, purchased in Birkenhead.
See pl. B-18.

JEFFERSON, THOMAS
(1743–1826), third President of the United States. Born at Shadwell, Virginia. Was admitted to the bar in 1767. Author of the celebrated Declaration of Independence, 1776. Governor of Virginia from 1779 to 1781. Secured the adoption of the decimal system of coinage in 1783. Elected president of the United States in 1801, doing two terms in office. Secured the prohibition of the slave-trade during his second term.
See pls. B-20B, 21.

KOSSUTH, LOUIS
(1802–94). Hungarian patriot. Initially practised law, but in 1832 was a deputy at the Diet of Presburg. In 1837 he issued a lithographed paper and this led to his imprisonment. He was freed in 1840 and became editor of the *Pesti Hirlap* which advocated extreme liberalism. In 1847 he became leader of the opposition, and after the French Revolution of 1848, demanded independence for Hungary. He prepared for carrying on war. In April, 1849, after declaring that the Hapsburg

dynasty had forfeited the throne, he was appointed provisional governor of Hungary. Finding dissension between himself and Görgei was damaging his cause, he resigned his dictatorship in favour of Görgei. In August, 1849 he fled to Turkey, where he was made prisoner but not extradited. In September, 1851 he came to England where he was received with respect and sympathy. He also visited the United States. From 1852 he resided mainly in England. When the Franco-Italian war with Austria broke out in 1859, he proposed to Napoleon that a Hungarian rising be arranged against Austria. Was bitterly disappointed by the peace of Villafranca and tried on several occasions to bring about a rising against Austria. When, in 1867, Deak effected the reconciliation of Hungary with the dynasty, he retired from active political life.
See pls. B-19, 20.

LAMB, WILLIAM, second Viscount Melbourne
(1779–1848). English statesman, who entered the House of Commons in 1805, under the auspices of the Whigs. Irish Secretary under Canning (1827) and under Wellington (1828). He succeeded to the title in 1829. Home Secretary (1830–4). Prime Minister for a few months in 1834 and again in 1835. He was still in office at the accession of Queen Victoria in 1837 and acted as adviser to the young Queen until his resignation in 1841. He showed remarkable tact and was universally approved for the manner in which he introduced the young sovereign to her duties. He was succeeded by Sir Robert Peel and thereafter took little part in politics.
See pl. B-1.

LINCOLN, ABRAHAM
(1809–65), sixteenth President of the United States. Born in Kentucky, began life as a lawyer. Returned to Congress in 1846 from Springfield, Illinois. Elected president of the United States in 1861 when he delivered his famous anti-slavery pronouncement which led to the Civil War of 1861–5. Re-elected president in 1864, but in the following year was assassinated by the actor John Wilkes Booth at Ford's Theatre, Washington. Famed as the saviour of his country and the liberator of a race.
See pl. B-25.

McCRACKEN, HENRY JOY
(1767–98). Helped to form the first society of 'United Irishmen' in Belfast in 1791. Was in command of the rebels in Co. Antrim in 1798, and as such was arrested, tried and executed.
See pl. B-16.

MELBOURNE, second Viscount
(1779–1848).
See Lamb, William.

O'CONNELL, DANIEL
(1775–1847). Irish political leader known as the 'Liberator'. Called to the Irish Bar in 1798 and built up a highly successful practice. Was a leader of the agitation for the rights of catholics. In 1828 elected Member of Parliament for Clare, but was prevented as a catholic from taking his seat. Re-elected in 1830 after passing of the Catholic Emancipation Bill. Denounced the ministries of Wellington and Peel. In 1841 elected Lord Mayor of Dublin. Throughout his life he advocated the cause of Ireland with courage and audacity. He died at Genoa in 1847 on

his way to Rome. His heart was buried in St. Agatha's, Rome and his body in the Glasnevin Cemetery, in Dublin.
See pls. B-1, 2, 17.

PARNELL, CHARLES STEWART
(1846–91). Irish politician. In 1875 he was returned as a Home Ruler for County Meath. In 1877 he gained great popularity by the use of deliberate obstruction in parliamentary tactics. In that year, also, he threw himself into the agrarian agitation and was elected president of the Irish National Land League. In 1880 he was returned for the city of Cork. In 1881 he refused to accept Gladstone's Land Bill as a final settlement to the question, and in October of that year Gladstone sent him to Kilmainham jail. He was released in May, 1882 soon after the agreement reached with Gladstone's government known as the Kilmainham Treaty. After enlisting Gladstone's support for the policy of Home Rule, he was accused by *The Times* of complicity in the crimes of the Land League. This accusation was on the basis of letters forged by Richard Pigott. A Royal Commission led to his complete vindication and he was awarded heavy damages. However, he appeared subsequently as co-respondent in a divorce case brought by Captain O'Shea against his wife, and a decree was granted with costs against Parnell in November, 1890. His career was ruined and as a result of pressure he retired from the leadership and died in 1891, five months after his marriage to Mrs O'Shea.
See pl. B-16.

PEEL, SIR ROBERT, second Baronet
(1788–1850). British statesman who entered Parliament at the age of 21 and immediately showed great ability. From 1812–8 he was Secretary for Ireland and in 1822 became Home Secretary, introducing the new police service, associated with his name— 'Bobbies', 'Peelers' etc. In 1834 he was Prime Minister for four months, and in 1841 he became Prime Minister for the second time. During this period Anti-Corn Law agitation became more intense. Peel abandoned his former policy and carried through the Repeal measure in 1846. He died in 1850 as a sequel to being thrown from his horse in Hyde Park. Of this calamity *The Illustrated London News* (July 6th, 1850) said:

In the noon-time of his fame, in the ripe vigour of his intellect . . . Sir Robert Peel has been snatched from his countrymen by a sudden and shocking death.

See pls. B-1, 7, 8, 9, 10, 12, 13, 13A.

SEXTON, THOMAS
(1848–1932). Irish politician, leader-writer in the *Nation* (1867). Parnellite Member of Parliament for various Irish constituents from 1880–92. In 1881 signed the 'No Rent' manifesto and was confined with Parnell for a time in Kilmainham jail. His speech on the second reading of the Home Rule Bill was described by Gladstone as the most elegant he had ever heard. He was also regarded as a skilful obstructionist. In 1891 Sexton, who was later Lord Mayor of Dublin, introduced a Bill in the British Parliament proposing the removal of the one hundred and thirty-four feet high Nelson Pillar which had been erected in 1807 in Dublin's main street. The Bill was hotly debated and finally defeated. The statue, which had been a sore point to Irish Republican Army members for many years, was eventually destroyed by an explosion in 1966. From 1892–6 Sexton sat as an anti-

Section B. Statesmen and Politicians

Parnellite Member of Parliament for North Kerry.
See **pl. B-**17A.

SHAFTESBURY, seventh Earl of (1801–85). *See* **Cooper, Anthony Ashley**.

TONE, THEOBALD WOLFE (1763–98). Irish Nationalist, born in Dublin, the son of a coach-maker. Called to the Irish bar in 1789. Acted as secretary to the Catholic Committee and helped to organize the 'United Irishmen'. He had to flee to America in 1795. Went to Paris in 1796. Tried to induce the Republican Government to invade Ireland and held a command in Hoche's expedition. In 1798 embarked in a small French squadron and was captured following a fierce fight, taken to Dublin and condemned to be hanged as a traitor, but cut his throat in prison.
See **pl. B-**16.

UNCLE TOM'S CABIN, an anti-slavery novel published in the *National Era* in 1851–52, and in book form in 1852. The authoress was Mrs Harriet Elizabeth Beecher Stowe (1811–96) of Connecticut who was a school teacher before her marriage. It aroused intense sympathy with the abolitionists throughout the world, and by its presentation of the sufferings imposed on the negroes by the system of slavery, the separation of husbands from wives and mothers from their children, and the brutality of some of the slave-owners, did much to hasten the American Civil War of 1861. The book was dramatized on many occasions in this country. It first appeared as a domestic drama in three Acts by E. Fitzball with the title *Uncle Tom's Cabin; or, the Horrors of Slavery* at Drury Lane on December 27th, 1852. Characters included Uncle Tom, Aunt Chloe, Eva, Topsy and George and Eliza Harris. Mrs Stowe described her work as 'a collection and arrangement of real incidents . . . grouped together with reference to a general result'.
See **pls. B-**26, 27, 28, 29, 30,
pl. C-71B.

WASHINGTON, GEORGE (1732–99), first President of the United States. Of English descent, he was living in his estate at Mount Vernon when the dispute arose between the British Home Government and the Colonists. He became a leader of the local opposition and was elected to the first Congress of Philadelphia. In 1775 he became commander-in-chief of the American army and from that time to the end of the struggle in 1783 he was the hero of the people. When the republic was founded in 1789 he became its first president, serving a second term from 1793.

See **pl. B-**20A, 21, 22, 23A, 23B, 24, 24A.

WELLESLEY, ARTHUR, first Duke of Wellington (1769–1852). Field-marshal and elder statesman. Educated at Eton and the Angers Military Academy. Lieutenant of Foot, 1787. He distinguished himself in India and successfully conducted the Peninsula War. In 1814 he was the British ambassador at Paris. There followed Napoleon's escape from Elba and the historic victory at Waterloo on June 18th, 1815 which led to the final overthrow of Napoleon. From 1828–30 he was Prime Minister. Thereafter, he assumed the roll of elder statesman. From 1842 to his death, he was commander-in-chief. He was the most famous British general of the nineteenth century and his funeral at St. Paul's was one of the great pageants of history.
See **pls. B-**2, 2A, 2B, 3, 3A, 3B, 4, 4A, 5, 6, 25,
pls. C-10, 11, 14, 16B, 16C, 20, 21, 25.

WELLINGTON, first Duke of (1769–1852). *See* **Wellesley, Arthur**.

WILBERFORCE, WILLIAM (1759–1833). *See* **section I**.

Section B
Statesmen and Politicians
Details of the Figures

Plate 1
Figure 1
Subject: **Sir Robert Peel**
Title: S. R. Peel (indented capitals)
Height: 7½ in (19 cm)
Colour: Well coloured; often striped trousers.
Maker: Alpha factory
Rarity: Av.
Description: Standing bare-headed, in frock-coat, waist-coat and trousers. In his right hand he holds a scroll (possibly a speech) and he grasps the edge of his lapel with his left hand. There is a low wall behind him.

Figure 2
Subject: **Sir Robert Peel**
Title: Sir R. Peel (gilt script)
Date: c. 1846
Height: 8¼ in (21 cm)
Colour: Well coloured.
Rarity: Av.
Pair: Probably to *fig.* 5 (Cobden)
Description: He stands bare-headed, in frock-coat, waistcoat and trousers. His left hand is on his hip, his right hand rests on the top of a pedestal, upon which lies a scroll inscribed in gilt script 'Repeal of the Corn Law'.
Observations: 1. The Corn Laws were repealed in 1846.
2. This figure and its pair fetched 42 gns at Christie's in 1965.

Figure 3
Subject: **Lord Melbourne** (William Lamb, second Viscount Melbourne)
Title: None
Date: c. 1840
Height: 8½ in (21.5 cm)
Colour: Well coloured.
Rarity: R.
Description: Standing bare-headed, in frock-coat, waistcoat and trousers. His left hand rests on a pedestal and his right hand on his hip.
Observations: No titled version of this figure has been found, nor any exact source. At one time it was suggested that it portrayed Palmerston. To my mind, there is little room for doubt that it is intended to represent Lord Melbourne (see *ch.* 3, *pl.* 9A), Prime Minister at the accession of the Queen in 1837 and her adviser until his resignation in 1841.

Figure 4
Subject: **Thomas Slingsby Duncombe**
Title: T. S. Duncombe (gilt script)
Date: c. 1848
Height: 9 in (23 cm)
Colour: Well coloured.
Rarity: VR. D.
Description: Standing bare-headed, in frock-coat, waistcoat and trousers; his left hand on his hip, his right hand on a pedestal upon which is a paper inscribed 'Presedent (*sic*)/ of the Trades' in gilt script.

Observations: In 1848, Duncombe presented the People's Petition, signed by over three millions, to the House of Commons.

Figure 5
Subject: **Richard Cobden**
Title: R. Cobden (gilt script)
Date: c. 1846
Height: 8½ in (21.5 cm)
Colour: Well coloured.
Rarity: Av.
Pair: Probably to *fig.* 2 (Peel)
Description: He stands bare-headed, in frock-coat, waistcoat and trousers. His right hand is on his hip and he clutches a scroll in his left hand. To his left is a pedestal.
Observations: 1. Cobden was one of the principal agitators for the repeal of the Corn Laws (1846).
2. This figure and its pair fetched 42 gns at Christie's in 1965; another, together with *fig.* 7 (? Shaftesbury) fetched 42 gns in the same rooms in 1969.

Figure 6
Subject: **Richard Cobden**
Title: R. Cobden (indented capitals)
Date: c. 1846
Height: 7½ in (19 cm)
Colour: Well coloured; often with striped trousers.
Maker: Alpha factory
Rarity: Av.
Description: Sitting bare-headed, in frock-coat, waistcoat and trousers. His right hand rests on his knee and grasps a scroll. There is a cornucopia (symbol of plenty) against his right leg.

Figure 7
Subject: **? Lord Shaftesbury** (Anthony Ashley Cooper, seventh Earl of Shaftesbury) **and child**
Title: None
Date: c. 1848
Height: 7½ in (19 cm)
Colour: Well coloured; jacket may be in blue or pink.
Maker: Alpha factory
Rarity: R.
Pair: Fig. 8 (? Elizabeth Fry)
Description: Seated bare-headed, a small boy standing between his knees. In his right hand he holds what appears to be a bible.
Observations: 1. A similar figure, together with *fig.* 5 (Cobden), fetched 42 gns at Christie's in 1969.
2. There has been much discussion as to whom this figure portrays, particularly since the discovery of its pair. Balston remarked on the close resemblance, particularly with regard to the shape of head, hair style and clothes, between the figure and the painting of Shaftesbury by Sir Francis Grant at present in the House of Commons (see *ch.* 3, *pl.* 10).

Figure 8
Subject: **? Elizabeth Fry and child**
Title: None
Date: c. 1848
Height: 7 in (17.5 cm)
Colour: Well coloured.
Maker: Alpha factory
Rarity: R.
Pair: Fig. 7 (? Shaftesbury)
Description: Seated bare-headed. In her right hand she holds what appears to be a bible. A small bare-headed girl is standing against her left knee.
Observations: No definite identification of this figure has been made. Balston (*personal communication*) suggested that it might be Elizabeth Fry.

Figure 9
Subject: **Lord Shaftesbury** (Anthony Ashley Cooper, seventh Earl of Shaftesbury) **and child**
Title: None
Date: 1848
Height: 7½ in (19 cm)
Colour: Well coloured.
Rarity: VR.
Description: He is standing bare-headed, in frock-coat, waistcoat and trousers. His right hand is on his hip and his left hand on the head of a small boy.
Observations: See *fig.* 7 (? Shaftesbury).

Figure 10
Subject: **William Ewart Gladstone**
Title: Turkish Extinguisher (black script)
Date: c. 1877
Height: 3⅛ in (8 cm)
Colour: Well coloured.
Maker: Probably German and not Staffordshire in origin
Rarity: Av.
Description: Candle snuffer. Gladstone stands bare-headed in a pulpit. His right hand rests on the turban of a Turk, who stands against its front.
Observations: 1. This figure appears as 28(g) in Balston's *Supplement to Staffordshire Portrait Figures of the Victorian Age*. It is shown here for completeness. Most collectors would, I think, agree with me that Mr Balston was mistaken in attributing the figure to Staffordshire. It is much more in keeping with German pottery of the period.
2. The Bulgarian atrocities of 1876 aroused Gladstone's anger against the Ottoman power in Europe.

Figure 11
Subject: **? Sir Robert Peel**
Title: None
Height: 7¾ in (20 cm)
Colour: Found with blue underglaze coat, or poorly coloured.
Rarity: R.
Description: Standing bare-headed, in frock-

Section B. Statesmen and Politicians

Plate 1
T: *Fig.* 1 Peel
Fig. 2 Peel
Fig. 3 Melbourne

Fig. 4 Duncombe
Fig. 5 Cobden
Fig. 6 Cobden

B: *Fig.* 7 ? Shaftesbury
Fig. 8 ? Fry
Fig. 9 ? Shaftesbury
Fig. 10 Gladstone

Fig. 11 ? Peel
Fig. 12 O'Connell
Fig. 13 O'Connell

coat, waistcoat and trousers. His left arm is across his chest and in his hand he clutches a scroll. His right arm is by his side with the wrist flexed and the palm upwards.
Observations: The face bears a close resemblance to that of Peel and I have classified the figure as such, although I have met some collectors who consider it to be a representation of O'Connell.

Figure 12
Subject: **Daniel O'Connell**
Title: None
Date: *c.* 1843
Height: 8 in (20.5 cm)
Colour: Well coloured.
Rarity: R.
Description: Standing in high broad-brimmed hat, frock-coat and trousers. His left forearm rests on a pedestal and he clasps a speech in his right hand. Angled, hollow base.
Observations: The portrait engraving in *The Illustrated London News* of November 25th, 1843 establishes the identity, see *ch.* 3, *pl.* 12.

Figure 13
Subject: **Daniel O'Connell**
Title: None
Height: 5½ in (14 cm)
Colour: Well coloured.
Rarity: R.
Description: He is standing bare-headed, in frock-coat, waistcoat and trousers. He holds a scroll in his left hand. His right hand is on his hip. Hollow base.
Observations: Almost certainly portrays O'Connell.

Section B. Statesmen and Politicians

Plate 2
T: *Fig.* 17 Wellington
Fig. 18 Wellington
Fig. 19 Wellington

B: *Fig.* 14 O'Connell
Fig. 15 O'Connell
Fig. 16 O'Connell

Colour Plate 16
Richard Cobden, Thomas Slingsby Duncombe and Sir Robert Peel. *Figs.* 5, 4 and 2, *pl.* B-1. See page 183.

Colour Plate 17
Duke of Wellington. *Fig.* 20, *pl.* B-3.
See page 187.

Colour Plate 18
William Ewart Gladstone and Benjamin Disraeli, first Earl of Beaconsfield. *Figs.* 47 and 48, *pl.* B-14.
See page 195.

Section B. Statesmen and Politicians

Plate 2
Figure 14
Subject: **Daniel O'Connell**
Title: Dan o'Connel (gilt script)
Date: 187–
Height: 13¾ in (35 cm)
Colour: Well coloured, underglaze black.
Maker: Probably Sampson Smith
Rarity: R.
Description: Standing bare-headed, right hand on hip, left hand on a draped pedestal.
Observations: 1. Appears to be a smaller, modified version of *fig.* 15 (O'Connell).
2. A similar figure fetched £22 at Sotheby's in 1966.

Figure 15
Subject: **Daniel O'Connell**
Title: Dan o'Connel (gilt script)
Date: 187–
Height: 17¾ in (44 cm)
Colour: Well coloured, underglaze black.
Maker: Sampson Smith
Rarity: R.
Description: He is standing bare-headed, right hand on hip, left hand on a draped pedestal.
Observations: 1. Similar to *fig.* 14 (O'Connell) except for differences in height and the manner in which the pedestal is draped.
2. A similar figure fetched 20 gns at Christie's in 1964; another 26 gns in 1967; and another 50 gns in 1969.

Figure 16
Subject: **Daniel O'Connell**
Title: D. O. Connell (raised capitals)
Height: 14 in (35.5 cm)

Colour: Very finely coloured.
Rarity: R. D. A.
Description: He stands bare-headed, in frock-coat, waistcoat and trousers. His right hand rests on his hip and his left on a draped pedestal to his left. On his right a low crown hat rests on another draped pedestal.
Observations: Generally regarded as one of the finest pieces made in the Potteries.

Figure 17
Subject: **Duke of Wellington**
Title: Wellington (raised capitals)
Height: 13 in (33 cm)
Colour: Well coloured. The coat has been found coloured blue, black, orange or white (see *ch.* 4, *pl.* 4B).
Rarity: C.
Description: He is standing facing half right, bare-headed in frock-coat, waistcoat and trousers. His right hand grasps the edge of his coat and his left hand rests on a draped pedestal.
Observations: A similar figure fetched 16 gns at Christie's in 1966.

Figure 18
Subject: **Duke of Wellington**
Title: Wellington (gilt script)
Height: 11 in (28 cm)
Colour: White and gilt.
Rarity: VR.
Description: Standing bare-headed, in military great coat. His plumed cocked hat is clasped in his right hand which rests by his side. In his left hand he holds a scroll.

Figure 19
Subject: **Duke of Wellington**
Title: Wellington (raised capitals)
Date: 1852
Height: 13½ in (34.25 cm)
Colour: White and gilt.
Rarity: R.
Description: He stands bare-headed, in military dress, a scroll in his right hand. The figure is mounted on a square two-tiered base, with no inscription at the back, see *fig.* 22 (Wellington) *pl.* B-3.
Observations: May well be a copy of one of the numerous statues of Wellington erected after his death, although so far I have not been able to find the original.

Plate 2A
Figure 18(a)
Subject: **Duke of Wellington**
Title: W (transfer capital)
Date: 1852
Height: 15½ in (39.25 cm)
Colour: Well coloured.
Maker: George Baguley, Hanley
Rarity: VR. A.
Description: Standing bare-headed, with right foot thrust slightly forward. In his right hand is a scroll or speech. His left arm is held behind his back. He is wearing a long, black frock-coat buttoned down the front with five buttons. The trousers are grey with lines and dashes in black by way of decoration. On the front of the base is a 'W' with sprays of laurel beneath. A porcelain figure.
Observations: 1. Printed in black on the rear of the base of the example illustrated is:
'*Published by*
GEORGE BAGULEY
HANLEY STAFFS
Oct. 1st 1852'.
Above is a crown and the words 'UNDER ROYAL PATRONAGE', see *ch.* 2, *pl.* 4A.
2. Mr Godden has kindly drawn my attention to *The Art-Journal*, November 1852, *p.* 355:
STATUETTE OF THE LATE DUKE OF WELLINGTON.—One of the most striking statuettes we have seen for some time is that produced by Mr. George Baguley, of Hanley, in Staffordshire, and modelled from drawings by Mr. Cust. It represents the late Duke of Wellington in full length attitude, habited in his ordinary private attire; the figure is in a somewhat stooping position, but the countenance shows more of the vigour and fulness of manhood than his grace's features latterly wore, and is remarkably intellectual. The execution of this statuette is most perfect; sharp and delicate in its details, especially about the head and neck, and yet not deficient in general boldness.
This seems to be the only Staffordshire portrait figure known to have been written up at the period.

Plate 2B
Figure 18(b)
Subject: **Duke of Wellington**
Title: Wellington (raised upper and lower case)
Height: 8½ in (21.5 cm)
Colour: Well coloured.
Rarity: VR. A.
Description: Standing bare-headed, wearing military frock-coat with epaulettes, medals and stars, and two sashes over his right shoulder, breeches and knee-boots. He holds his plumed cocked hat against his knee in his right hand, and his baton against his hip in his left hand. Hollow base.
Observations: This figure is of German manufacture and has been included inadvertently.

Plate 2A
Fig. 18(a) Wellington
By courtesy of Wing Commander T.H. Lucas, RAF (rtd.)

Plate 2B
Fig. 18(b) Wellington
By courtesy of Wing Commander T.H. Lucas, RAF (rtd.)

Plate 3
Fig. 20 Wellington
Fig. 21 Wellington
Fig. 22 (*reverse*) Wellington
Fig. 23 Wellington

Plate 3
Figure 20
Subject: **Duke of Wellington**
Title: Wellington (gilt script)
Height: 18½ in (47.5 cm)
Colour: Well coloured, underglaze blue coat.
Rarity: R.
Description: He stands facing half-right, bare-headed in frock-coat, waistcoat and trousers. His right hand is on his hip, and he holds a speech in his left.
Observations: 1. A similar figure fetched 14 gns at Christie's in 1964.
2. See also *pl.* B-3A for details of smaller version [*fig.* 20(*a*)].

Figure 21
Subject: **Duke of Wellington on Copenhagen**
Title: Up guards and at them (upper and lower case black transfer)
Height: 11½ in (29 cm)
Colour: Well decorated in tradition of Thomas Parr. *Copenhagen* is correctly coloured chestnut in contemporary figures.
Maker: Thomas Parr
Rarity: R. D. A. Reproductions are also quite uncommon.
Description: Wellington is astride a prancing chestnut horse facing right, in cocked hat and full military uniform. He holds a telescope in his right hand which points forwards.
Observations: 1. This figure is catalogued in the Kent lists as 'Wellington on Horse'. The reference is no. 44 in *Kent List A* and no. 398 in *Kent List C* (1955).
Some reproductions probably date to the late Victorian era, being manufactured by Kent and Parr, see *ch.* 6.
2. Whereas *Copenhagen* is correctly coloured chestnut in contemporary figures, he is cream coloured in reproductions.
3. There are several versions of Wellington's battle cry at Waterloo. According to his biographer, Sir Herbert Maxwell, his words were *Stand up, Guards*. In a Belgian guide-book *Excursions to the Lion at Waterloo* (1904),

this is embellished to *Upright guards! prepare for battle*.
4. A similar figure, somewhat damaged, fetched 36 gns at Christie's in 1963.

Figure 22
Subject: **Duke of Wellington**
Title: None
Date: 1852
Height: 13½ in (34.25 cm)
Colour: White and gilt with purple lustre base.
Rarity: R.
Description: Standing bare-headed, in military uniform on a square two-tiered base which is inscribed at the back 'To the/Memory of the/Duke of/Wellington' in indented capitals.
Observations: 1. This figure is identical to *fig.* 19 (Wellington) *pl.* B-2 except that it has no title on the front, but the above-mentioned inscription on the back. It is always found with a purple lustre base and was probably issued very shortly after the death of the Duke in 1852.
2. An example of this figure fetched 50 gns at Christie's in 1969.

Figure 23
Subject: **Duke of Wellington**
Title: Wellington (gilt script)
Date: c. 1850
Height: 12 in (30.5 cm)
Colour: Either highly coloured or in white and gilt.
Rarity: Av.
Description: He sits in a high-backed armchair, bare-headed, in frock-coat, waistcoat and trousers. His knees are crossed. His head is upright.
Observations: A similar figure with blue coat together with a coloured example of *fig.* 17 (Wellington) *pl.* B-2 fetched 36 gns at Christie's in 1963. A white and gilt example fetched 18 gns at Christie's in 1964. Another white and gilt example together with a coloured figure of the Duke in blue frock-coat and flowered waistcoat (*fig.* 17, *pl.* B-2) fetched 38 gns at Christie's in 1965.

Plate 3A
Figure 20(a)
Subject: **Duke of Wellington**
Title: Wellington (raised capitals on plaque)
Height: 16 in (40.5 cm)
Colour: Well coloured.
Rarity: Av.
Pair: Possibly to *fig.* 43 (Peel) *pl.* B-13.
Description: Same design as *fig.* 20, *pl.* B-3 other than for height and manner of titling.
Observations: See *fig.* 43 (Peel) *pl.* B-13.

Plate 3B
Figure 21(a)
Subject: **Duke of Wellington**
Title: None
Height: 6 in (15.25 cm)
Colour: Underglaze blue uniform, white charget.
Rarity: R.
Pair: No pair recorded, but one almost certainly exists.
Description: On a horse facing right, in uniform. He holds the reins in his left hand and points forwards with his right hand. Base may be hollow or solid.
Observations: Similar, although on a much smaller scale, to *fig.* 21, *pl.* B-3.

Plate 4
Figure 24
Subject: **Duke of Wellington**
Title: Wellington (gilt script)
Date: 184–
Height: 10 in (25 cm)
Colour: Well coloured.
Rarity: Av.
Description: He stands bare-headed, in uniform, with trousers. His left forearm rests on a vertical cannon, and he clasps his plumed cocked hat in his hand beside his right leg.
Observations: Mr Arthur Thornton has postulated that this figure has been taken from the painting by John Lucas commissioned by the Marquis of Anglesey and executed in 1841 (see *The Life and Letters of Henry William Paget, Marquis of Anglesey*

Colour Plate 19
Charles Stewart Parnell, Peace Group and William Ewart Gladstone. *Figs.* 55, 56 and 54, *pl.* B-16. See page 197.

Colour Plate 20
George Washington, Thomas Jefferson and Benjamin Franklin. *Figs.* 68, 65 and 66, *pl.* B-21. See pages 200-1.

Section B. Statesmen and Politicians

Plate 3A (Left)
Fig. 20(a) Wellington
*In the Thomas Balston
collection*

Plate 3B (Right)
Fig. 21(a) Wellington

Plate 4
Fig. 24 Wellington
Fig. 25 Wellington
Fig. 26 Wellington
*By courtesy of Mr and Mrs
Eric Joyce*

[*1768–1854*] written by the present Marquis of Anglesey and published by Jonathan Cape in 1961). In 1840 the Marquis of Anglesey asked 'a very great favour' of the Duke of Wellington. In his letter to the Duke, he pointed out that the Duke had a portrait of Anglesey by Lawrence, but Lawrence had died in 1830. The Duke responded immediately and selected John Lucas and in writing to him said, 'The sooner you make the design of this picture the better

. . . of course, I will give you any sittings that may be necessary'. The painting is illustrated in the biography referred to above. In Mr. Thornton's view the design of the painting is almost completely reversed in the figure, otherwise it is a straight forward copy with some simplification to help in the production. Although I agree that the figure undoubtedly portrays the Duke in uniform in later life, I do not think it is near enough to Lucas's painting to justify

the assertion that it is, in fact, derived from it, although the possibility exists.

2. A similar figure fetched 44 gns at Christie's in 1965.

Figure 25
Subject: **Duke of Wellington**
Title: Wellington (raised capitals)
Date: *c.* 1852
Height: 11½ in (29 cm)
Colour: White and gilt.

B189

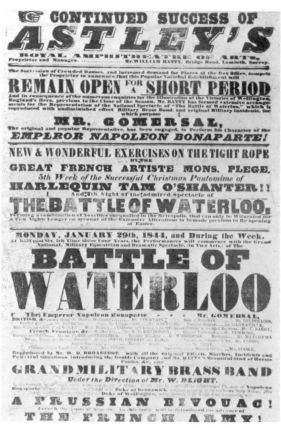

Plate 4A (Left)
Fig. 27 Wellington
By courtesy of
Wing Commander
T.H. Lucas, RAF (rtd.)

Plate 6 (Right)
Playbill issued by Astley's
Royal Amphitheatre of
Arts for Monday,
January 29th, 1844 and
During the Week.
The Battle of Waterloo
was quite commonly
performed at Astley's. It
is possible that some
figures of Wellington and
Napoleon are theatrical
portraits.

Plate 5
Fig. 28 Wellington
Fig. 29 Wellington
Fig. 30 Napoleon I and
Wellington
In the collection of
Mr Ronald Shockledge

Plate 4 continued

Rarity: VR.
Description: It is much the same design as
fig. 23 (Wellington) *pl.* B-3 except that:
1. His head leans to the right.
2. His right foot rests on a hassock instead
of a book.
3. He holds the book between the fingers of
his right hand instead of resting it on his
knee.

4. There are fenestrations in the back of the
chair.
Observations: 1. The general appearance is of
an old man lolling in semi-decrepitude.
2. Wellington died in an armchair in Wal
mer Castle, Kent.
3. This figure, together with *fig.* 16 (Nelson)
pl. C-10, fetched 120 gns at Christie's in
1969.
4. There is a similar figure, untitled, in
which the fenestrations in the back of the

chair are smaller. It is found with the head
erect [*fig.* 25(*a*)] or with the head lolling
over to the right [*fig.* 25(*b*)]. Both figures
are moderately rare.
Wing Commander Lucas, an authority on
the subject, has suggested to me that the
figure with the head erect was produced
shortly before he died; after his death it was
modified by bending the head over to the
right.

Section B. Statesmen and Politicians

Figure 26
Subject: **Duke of Wellington**
Title: None
Height: 12 in (30.5 cm)
Colour: Well coloured.
Rarity: VR.
Description: He stands bare-headed, in a tunic, breeches and Wellington boots. There is an ermine-edged cloak over both shoulders, part draped over his left forearm on to a pedestal. His plumed cocked hat is up-ended against his right leg and he holds a document in his right hand.
Observations: Probably portrays the Duke in later life.

Plate 4A
Figure 27
Subject: **Duke of Wellington**
Title: None
Height: 6½ in (16.5 cm)
Colour: White and gilt.
Rarity: VR. A.
Description: He sits in a high-backed armless chair facing to his left. His left hand is on the seat behind him, and he holds a speech in his right.
Observations: The piece illustrated, together with *fig.* 18(*a*), *pl.* B-2A, are in the collection of 'Wellingtoniana' amassed by Wing Commander T. H. Lucas, RAF (rtd.). This collection has now been given to the Nation and is at Walmer Castle in Kent where the Duke died in 1852.

Plate 5
Figure 28
Subject: **Duke of Wellington**
Title: None
Height: 9½ in (24 cm)
Colour: Well coloured.
Rarity: R.
Pair: *Fig.* 49 (Napoleon), *pl.* C-16.
Description: On a horse facing right, in plumed cocked hat, uniform and cloak. In his right hand he holds a baton against the saddle-cloth.

Figure 29
Subject: **Duke of Wellington**
Title: None
Date: 1852
Height: 8½ in (21.5 cm)
Colour: White and gilt.
Rarity: VR.
Description: He is sitting bare-headed, in a high-backed chair, with hands clasped over his crossed knees, the left knee above the right.
Observations: Corresponds with a lithograph music-front by Louisa Corbaux for the song *Wellington* by Charles Jefferys, published by Stannard & Dixon on September 16th, 1852 —two days after the Duke died at Walmer Castle—'a huddled figure in a high-backed chair' (see *ch.* 3, *pl.* 12B).

> Sweet Muse, aspire! the deeds admire
> Of Wellington the great:
> With golden lyre, celestial fire,
> Sing, Muse of Tippoo's fate,
> How the Duke's shield girt every field
> Of Portugal and Spain,
> What armies reel'd when he revealed
> His movements on the plain.
>
> How valour frees the Portugese,
> The rights of Spain restored;
> The Duke, with ease o'er Pyrenees
> Drove Joseph with his sword.
> At Waterloo his colour flew
> Amidst the lurid blaze,
> His soldiers true, like giants grew—
> Sad was Napoleon's gaze.
>
> March on! Advance! Come, conquer France,
> Said Wellington the Wise,
> Behold the chance of sword and lance,
> Proud Paris is our Prize.
> The French Guards fled o'er heaps of dead,
> And cried that all was lost;
> Confusion spread, battalions bled,
> And dear the victory cost.
>
> Glory shone around, and Britons crowned
> At sunsets rosy light:
> Shrill bugles sound, and Prussians frown'd
> And chased the French at night;
> Night's lovely queen illumed the scene
> With her pale silvery rays,
> And Blucher keen, in savage mien,
> Vowed Paris walls to raze.

> But on the earth, with lively mirth,
> Descended heavenly peace;
> Men hailed her birth, perceived her worth—
> The Duke said war must cease!
> Now Wellington his race has run:
> Through age the warrior dies;
> His work is done, and like the sun,
> He sets again to rise!

Figure 30
Subject: **Napoleon I and Duke of Wellington**
Title: None
Height: 6¼ in (16 cm)
Colour: Well coloured.
Rarity: R.
Description: On the left stands Napoleon, cocked hat athwartships. On the right stands Wellington, a scroll in his right hand and his cocked hat in his left hand beside his leg. Between them is a clock above which is a pair of crossed French flags and below which is a cannon.

Plate 6

Playbill

Playbill issued by Astley's Royal Amphitheatre of Arts for Monday, January 29th, 1844 and During the Week.

The Performance commenced with *the Grand National, Military Equestrian and Dramatic Spectacle, (in Two Acts,) of the Battle of Waterloo*. Note the leading role, played by Mr Gomersal, is that of 'The Emperor Napoleon Bonaparte'; 'His Grace the Duke of Wellington' is in much smaller type! See comments on Napoleon's popularity in England in *ch.* 5.

The Battle of Waterloo was quite commonly performed at Astley's and it is possible that some figures of Wellington and Napoleon are theatrical portraits.

Plate 7
Figure 31
Subject: **Sir Robert Peel on his favourite mare**

Plate 7
Fig. 31 Peel
The engraving illustrated to the left of the figure appeared on the front page of *The Illustrated London News* of July 6th, 1850, four days after the death of Sir Robert Peel following a riding accident. It portrays 'The late Baronet, on his favourite horse'. It is the source of *fig.* 31, and, more particularly, of *fig.* 31(a).
In the collection of Lady Ranfurly

Plate 8 (Left)
Fig. 32 Peel
Fig. 32(a) Peel

Plate 9 (Right)
Fig. 33 Peel

Plate 7 continued
Title: Sir Robert Peel (gilt script); alternatively, Sir R. Peel (gilt script).
Date: 1850
Height: 12¼ in (31 cm)
Colour: Well coloured, bay horse.
Rarity: R. D. A.
Description: On a horse with docked tail facing left, in top hat and civilian dress. A cloak over his right shoulder hides his right arm and forearm.
Observations: 1. A similar figure fetched 55 gns at Christie's in 1967, and another 70 gns in the same rooms in 1969.
2. See also *fig.* 31(a) (Peel).

Figure 31(a) (not illustrated)
Subject: **Sir Robert Peel on his favourite mare**
Title: Sir Robert Peel (gilt script)
Date: 1850
Height: 13 in (33 cm)
Colour: Well coloured, bay horse.
Rarity: VR. D. A.
Description: A very superior version of *fig.* 31. It is exactly the same design except that Peel is not wearing a cloak; the whole of his right arm and forearm show, with his hand on the near-side mane.
Observations: 1. The only recorded example of this figure was spotted by the late Mr Balston in a china menders in London. It was not for sale and not photographed.
2. Both *fig.* 31 and particularly *fig.* 31(a) are based on an engraving which appeared in *The Illustrated London News* on July 6th, 1850, four days after the death of Peel following a riding accident. It will be noted that he is not wearing a cloak. The engraving which was published on the front page was described as being 'copied, by permission from a characteristic portrait of the late Baronet, on his favourite horse, published by Mr M'Lean, Haymarket'. It appears that Peel rode the same favourite bay mare for many years. It having become old, he was advised

B192

to procure a more sure-footed animal. Whilst riding a new horse on trial up Constitutional Hill, after making a call at the Palace, the horse 'started' and threw its rider over its head on to his face with fatal consequences.

Plate 8
Figure 32
Subject: **Sir Robert Peel**
Title: Sir R. Peel (gilt script)
Date: *c.* 1850
Height: 8 in (20.5 cm)
Colour: Well coloured.
Rarity: VR.
Description: A bust (head, neck and shoulders) on a square base, one piece.
Observations: Its appearance suggests a memorial piece.

Figure 32(a)
Subject: **Sir Robert Peel**
Title: Sir R. Peel (indented capitals at back of bust)
Height: 7½ in (19 cm)
Colour: Well coloured.
Rarity: VR.
Description: A bust (head, neck and shoulders) on a circular base, one piece.

Plate 9
Figure 33
Subject: **Sir Robert Peel**
Title: None
Date: 184–
Height: 9¼ in (23.5 cm)
Colour: Well coloured. Underglaze blue. Striped trousers.
Maker: Alpha factory
Rarity: VR.
Pair: None recorded
Description: Bare-headed and seated, wearing cravat, morning coat, waistcoat and striped trousers. His right elbow rests on the arm of the chair and his left forearm rests on a book on a pedestal to his left. Shaped base.

Plate 10
Figure 34
Subject: **Sir Robert Peel**
Title: Sir R. Peel (gilt script)
Height: 8¼ in (21 cm)
Colour: Well coloured.
Maker: Alpha factory
Rarity: R.
Description: He stands bare-headed, in frock coat, waistcoat and trousers. In his right hand he holds an open speech near his hip. His left hand touches a closed book on a pedestal.
Observations: Similar to *fig.* 37 (Peel) *pl.* B-12. Minor differences are noted under that number.

Figure 35
Subject: **A Policeman**
Title: None
Height: 6 in (15.25 cm)
Colour: Well coloured.
Rarity: Av.
Description: A pepper castor. Helmet with perforations. In his right hand he holds a truncheon, and in his left a bull's eye lantern.

Plate 11
Figure 36
Subject: **A Policeman**
Title: Watching/the/Budget (raised capitals)
Date: A late figure
Height: 11¾ in (29.75 cm)
Colour: Crudely cast and coloured.
Rarity: R.
Description: The policeman has a lamp attached to his belt and a truncheon by his side. Between his legs is a bottle. A cast figure.
Observations: 1. The significance of this piece has so far eluded me.
2. A similar figure, together with an unimportant non-portrait group, fetched 38 gns at Christie's in 1967.

Section B. Statesmen and Politicians

Plate 10 (Left)
Fig. 35 A policeman
Fig. 34 Peel
In the collection of
Dr S.J. Howard

Plate 11 (Right)
Fig. 36 A policeman

Plate 12
Figure 37
Subject: **Sir Robert Peel**
Title: None
Height: 9¾ in (24.5 cm)
Colour: Well coloured.
Maker: Alpha factory
Rarity: R.
Description: Standing bare-headed, his right hand holding a closed speech near his hip; his left is touching a closed book on a pedestal.
Observations: Very similar to *fig.* 34 (Peel) *pl.* B-10, except that in this case the figure is untitled, slightly larger and the speech is closed.

Figure 38
Subject: **William Ewart Gladstone**
Title: None
Height: 12 in (30.5 cm)
Colour: Well coloured. Marble base.
Rarity: R.
Description: Standing bare-headed, in frock-coat, waistcoat and trousers. His left hand clasps the lapel of his coat and his right hand rests on two closed books on a square pedestal.
Observations: 1. A similar figure fetched 38 gns at Christie's in 1968; and another 40 gns, in the same rooms, in 1969.
2. I have seen one figure inscribed 'W.E.G.' in black, on the front of the pedestal. The lettering appeared to be contemporary.

Figure 39
Subject: **Mrs Gladstone**
Title: Mrs Gladstone (raised capitals)
Date: 189–
Height: 10½ in (26.5 cm)
Colour: Usually white and gilt.
Rarity: Av.
Pair: Fig. 40 (Gladstone) *pl.* B-13.
Description: Standing, wearing a cap and holding a fan in her left hand. A cast figure.

Plate 12
Fig. 38 Gladstone
Fig. 39 Mrs Gladstone
Fig. 37 Peel

Section B. Statesmen and Politicians

Plate 13
Fig. 42 Peel
Fig. 43 Peel
Fig. 41 Gladstone
Fig. 40 Gladstone
By courtesy of
Mr and Mrs Eric Joyce and
in the collection of the author

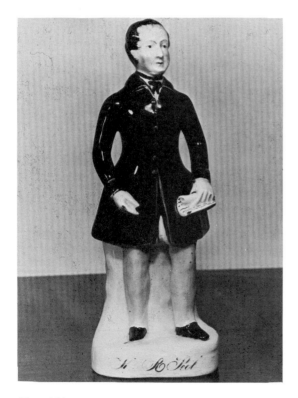

Plate 14
T: *Fig.* 45 Gladstone
Fig. 46 Beaconsfield

B: *Fig.* 47 Gladstone
Fig. 49 Gladstone
Fig. 48 Beaconsfield

Plate 13A
Fig. 44 Peel
In the Thomas Balston collection

Section B. Statesmen and Politicians

Plate 13
Figure 40
Subject: **William Ewart Gladstone**
Title: Mr Gladstone (raised capitals)
Date: 189–
Height: 10¾ in (27 cm)
Colour: Usually white and gilt.
Rarity: Av.
Pair: Fig. 39 (Mrs Gladstone) *pl.* B-12.
Description: Standing bare-headed, his left hand on a pedestal, his right hand clutching a speech against his waistcoat. A cast figure.
Observations: This figure and its pair fetched 44 gns in 1963 (together with *figs.* 54 and 55, *pl.* B-16); another pair fetched 30 gns in 1964 (together with *fig.* 54, *pl.* B-16); a third pair fetched 48 gns in 1966 (together with *fig.* 20(*a*), *pl.* B-3A).

Figure 41
Subject: **William Ewart Gladstone**
Title: None
Height: 12 in (30.5 cm)
Colour: White.
Rarity: R.
Description: Standing bare-headed in three-quarter length overcoat.

Figure 42
Subject: **Sir Robert Peel**
Title: Sir/R/Peel (gilt script)
Height: 10 in (25 cm)
Colour: Well coloured.
Rarity: R.
Description: He stands bare-headed, his right hand holding a speech against his leg, his left hand on his hip. The title is inscribed on the pedestal behind his right leg.

Figure 43
Subject: **Sir Robert Peel**
Title: Peel (raised capitals on plaque)
Height: 16½ in (41.5 cm)
Colour: Well coloured with blue coat. White and gilt versions also exist.
Rarity: R.
Pair: Possibly to *fig.* 20(*a*) (Wellington) *pl.* B-3A.
Description: He is standing bare-headed, in frock-coat, waistcoat and trousers. His right hand holds a speech against his waistcoat and his left hand is on his hip.
Observations: I have never seen a 'matching pair' of these figures but their height and style suggest that pairs do exist.

Plate 13A
Figure 44
Subject: **Sir Robert Peel**
Title: Sir R. Peel (gilt script)
Height: 11¼ in (28.5 cm)
Colour: Well coloured.
Rarity: VR.
Description: He stands bare-headed, in frock-coat, closely buttoned up to the neck. In his left hand he holds a speech against the skirt of his coat, and his right hand hangs down empty.

Plate 14
Figure 45
Subject: **William Ewart Gladstone**
Title: Gladstone (raised capitals)
Date: 187–
Height: 12 in (30.5 cm)
Colour: White and gilt with underglaze black.
Maker: See *observations*
Rarity: Av.
Pair: Fig. 46 (Beaconsfield)
Description: Standing bare-headed, in frock-coat, waistcoat and trousers, his right hand

on a speech resting on a pedestal, his left hand on his hip.
Observations: The provenance of this figure and its pair (*fig.* 46) poses a major problem. *Fig.* 45 (Gladstone) is catalogued in *Kent List A* as no. 129. In *Kent List B* it is deleted as a 'discontinued line', but it reappears in *Kent List C* (1955). *Fig.* 46 (Beaconsfield) is listed in *Kent List A* as no. 130. In *Kent List B* it is deleted as a 'discontinued line', and it is not listed in *Kent List C*.

Both figures appear to be smaller versions of *figs.* 47 and 48, which certainly emanate from the Sampson Smith factory (see *ch.* 2).

The explanation of all this is not clear but perhaps Sampson Smith 'farmed out' an order for the smaller models to the Kent factory.

Figure 46
Subject: **Benjamin Disraeli, first Earl of Beaconsfield**
Title: Beaconsfield (raised capitals)
Date: 187–
Height: 12 in (30.5 cm)
Colour: White and gilt with underglaze black.
Maker: See *observations* under preceding figure.
Rarity: Av.
Pair: Fig. 45 (Gladstone)
Description: Standing bare-headed, in frock-coat, waistcoat and trousers, his right hand on his hip, his left hand on a pedestal beside his left leg.
Observations: 1. See preceding figure.
2. Benjamin Disraeli was created Earl of Beaconsfield in 1876.

Figure 47
Subject: **William Ewart Gladstone**
Title: Gladstone (gilt script)
Date: 187–
Height: 16 in (40.5 cm)
Colour: White and gilt with underglaze black.
Maker: Sampson Smith
Rarity: Av.
Pair: Fig. 48 (Beaconsfield)
Description: Similar to *fig.* 45 (Gladstone)
Observations: The reasons why this figure and its pair *fig.* 48 (Beaconsfield) are considered to emanate from the Sampson Smith factory are given in *ch.* 2.

Figure 48
Subject: **Benjamin Disraeli, first Earl of Beaconsfield**
Title: Beaconsfield (gilt script)
Date: 187–
Height: 16½ in (41.5 cm)
Colour: White and gilt with underglaze black.
Maker: Sampson Smith
Rarity: Av.
Pair: Fig. 47 (Gladstone)
Description: Similar to *fig.* 46 (Beaconsfield).
Observations: 1. See *fig.* 45 (Gladstone).
2. A pair of similar figures fetched 24 gns at Christie's in 1963, and another 30 gns in 1967.

Figure 49
Subject: **William Ewart Gladstone**
Title: Gladstone (gilt script)
Height: 15¼ in (38.5 cm)
Colour: White and gilt.
Rarity: R.
Pair: Possibly *fig.* 58 (Sexton) *pl.* B-17A.
Description: He stands bare-headed, in frock-coat, waistcoat and trousers, his right hand clasping the lapel of his coat, the left hand holding a speech against a tree trunk.
Observations: A similar figure fetched 32 gns at Christie's in 1966.

Plate 15
Fig. 50 Gladstone

Plate 15
Figure 50
Subject: **William Ewart Gladstone**
Title: None
Date: c. 1868
Height: 8½ in (21.5 cm)
Colour: Well coloured.
Maker: Sampson Smith
Rarity: VR.
Description: A toby jug in the likeness of Mr Gladstone seated against the stump of a tree with a woodman's axe between his knees.
Observations: 1. Mr Haggar in *Staffordshire Chimney Ornaments* refers to Sampson Smith:

In politics he was a Liberal, and at the 1868 election voted for George Melly, the local Liberal candidate. It is not therefore surprising to find amongst the firm's original models a Toby jug in the likeness of Mr Gladstone . . . When this model was made is not clear, possibly after Gladstone's visit to Burslem in 1863 when he laid the foundation stone of the Wedgwood Institute; more probably after the formation of Mr Gladstone's first ministry.

2. The old press-mould of this toby jug was one of those found in a disused part of the Sampson Smith works in 1948 and some reproductions were made from it over a short period.

Plate 16
T: *Fig.* 51 Tone
Fig. 52 McCracken
Fig. 53 Fitzgerald

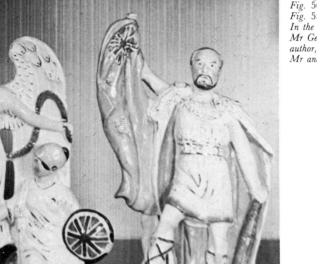

B: *Fig.* 54 Gladstone
Fig. 56 Peace
Fig. 55 Parnell
*In the collections of
Mr George Dermody and the
author, and by courtesy of
Mr and Mrs Eric Joyce*

Plate 16
Figure 51
Subject: **Theobald Wolfe Tone**
Title: Theobald Wolfe Tone (gilt script)
Date: 1898
Height: 14 in (35.5 cm)
Colour: White and gilt.
Maker: Probably Sampson Smith
Rarity: VR. D.
Series: Same series as *fig.* 52 (McCracken)
and *fig.* 53 (Fitzgerald).
Description: Standing bare-headed, in military jacket, breeches and stockings. In his
left hand he holds two flags across his chest.
To his right is a pedestal inscribed 'Who
fears to speak of '98/1798/1898' (transfer
capitals).
Observations: Helped to found the 'United
Irishmen' in Dublin in 1791. In 1796 was
adjutant-general in the French expedition
to Ireland which failed to land. A second

expedition surrendered at sea. He committed
suicide in 1798, after being sentenced to death.

Figure 52
Subject: **Henry Joy McCracken**
Title: Henry Joy McCracken (gilt script)
Date: 1898
Height: 13½ in (34.25 cm)
Colour: White and gilt.
Maker: Probably Sampson Smith
Rarity: R. D.
Series: Same series as *fig.* 51 (Tone) and
fig. 53 (Fitzgerald).
Description: He stands bare-headed, in short
coat, breeches and stockings. His right hand
holds the lapel of his coat and left hand rests
on a pedestal inscribed as in *fig.* 51 (Tone).
Observations: In 1798 he commanded the
rebels in Co. Antrim, and was arrested,
tried and executed.

Figure 53
Subject: **Lord Edward Fitzgerald**
Title: Lord Edward Fitzgerald (gilt script)
Date: 1898
Height: 14 in (35.5 cm)
Colour: White and gilt.
Maker: Probably Sampson Smith
Rarity: VR. D.
Series: Same series as *fig.* 51 (Tone) and
fig. 52 (McCracken).
Description: He stands bare-headed, in short
coat and trousers, his left hand on a pedestal
inscribed in the same manner as *fig.* 51
(Tone).
Observations: 1. Joined the 'United Irishmen'
in 1796. In 1798 he died of wounds received
whilst resisting arrest by the Dublin police.
2. A similar series of three figures fetched
52 gns at Christie's in 1964.

Plate 17
Fig. 57 O'Connell
In the collection of Mrs H. de C. Hastings

Plate 17A
Fig. 58 Sexton
In the Thomas Balston collection

Figure 54
Subject: **William Ewart Gladstone**
Title: W. E. Gladstone (raised capitals)
Date: 1882
Height: 12½ in (31.75 cm)
Colour: Poorly coloured.
Rarity: Av. D.
Pair: Fig. 55 (Parnell); *fig.* 56 (Peace) forms a centrepiece to the pair.
Description: He stands bare-headed, in coat, waistcoat and trousers, an axe in his right hand, a tree stump behind. A flag with a Union Jack in the corner flies above his left shoulder.
Observations: This figure, together with its pair *fig.* 55 (Parnell) and its centrepiece *fig.* 56 (Peace) were issued to commemorate the Kilmainham Treaty of 1882.

Figure 55
Subject: **Charles Stewart Parnell**
Title: C. S. Parnell (raised capitals)
Date: 1882
Height: 13¾ in (35 cm)
Colour: Poorly coloured.
Rarity: Av. D.
Pair: Fig. 54 (Gladstone); *fig.* 56 (Peace) forms a centrepiece to the pair.
Description: He stands bare-headed, in Greek dress with bare arms and legs, holding a shillelagh in his left hand. In his right hand he holds a flag with the Union Jack and the Irish harp embossed on it.
Observations: 1. This figure, together with its pair *fig.* 54 (Gladstone) and its centrepiece *fig.* 56 (Peace) were issued to com-

memorate the Kilmainham Treaty of 1882.
2. Balston considered that this figure was adapted from some figure of Hercules holding up the Nemean Lion.
3. A similar pair of figures fetched 44 gns at Christie's in 1963 (together with *figs.* 39 and 40, *pls.* B-12 and 13). Another pair, sold alone, fetched 75 gns at Christie's in 1969.

Figure 56
Subject: **An angel standing behind two seated women representing Ireland and Britannia**
Title: See *description*
Date: 1882
Height: 12½ in (31.75 cm)
Colour: Poorly coloured.
Rarity: R. D.
Centrepiece: It forms the centrepiece to the pair *fig.* 54 (Gladstone) and *fig.* 55 (Parnell).
Description: In front and to the left is a seated woman with a harp representing Ireland. In front and to the right sits Britannia. They are shaking hands. Behind them stands an angel holding a ribbon inscribed 'PEACE ON EARTH GOOD-WILL TOWARDS MEN' (indented capitals).
Observations: 1. This figure was issued in 1882 to commemorate the signing of the Kilmainham Peace Treaty between England and Ireland.
2. In modified form it was reissued in 1902 to commemorate the end of the Boer War (see *fig.* 377, *pl.* C-140).

Plate 17
Figure 57
Subject: **Daniel O'Connell**
Title: D. O'Connell (gilt script)
Height: 13½ in (34.25 cm)
Colour: White and gilt.
Rarity: VR.
Description: He stands bare-headed, with a three-quarter length overcoat. In his left hand he holds a speech. Behind his right foot is a small tree trunk.

Plate 17A
Figure 58
Subject: **Thomas Sexton**
Title: T Sexton MP (grey script)
Date: 188–
Height: 15¼ in (38.5 cm)
Colour: White and gilt.
Rarity: VR. (titled); R. (untitled)
Pair: Possibly *fig.* 49 (Gladstone) *pl.* B-14.
Description: Standing bare-headed and bearded, in low turned-down collar, knotted tie and overcoat. His left hand rests on a pedestal to his left and behind him is a brick wall. His right hand is across his chest.
Observations: Initially identified by Balston as Parnell because the beard and clothes agreed with the portraits of Parnell in *The Illustrated London News*, vol. 77 (1880) *p.* 493 and *vol.* 88 (1886) *p.* 383. The discovery, in 1962, of the titled copy, led to rethinking on the subject.

Section B. Statesmen and Politicians

Plate 18
Fig. 59 Irish National Forester
Fig. 60 Irish National Forester
In the collection of Mr D. P. M. Michael

Plate 19
Fig. 61 Kossuth
Fig. 62 Kossuth
By courtesy of Mr and Mrs Eric Joyce

Plate 20
Fig. 63 Kossuth
Fig. 64 Kossuth
In the collection of Mr Ronald Shockledge

Plate 20A
L: *George Washington:* From the original painting by Stuart.
C: *Statue of Franklin* erected on September 17th, 1856 in Boston, U.S. The statue bears a close likeness to the Staffordshire portraits.
From *The Illustrated London News* of October 25th, 1856.
R: *Franklin:* An engraving by J. Thompson from an original picture by J.A. Duplessis.

Plate 18
Figure 59
Subject: **Irish National Forester**
Title: Irish National Forrester (gilt script)
Date: *c.* 1877
Height: 13 in (33 cm)
Colour: White and gilt.
Maker: Probably Sampson Smith
Rarity: R.
Pair: Fig. 60 (Irish National Forester)
Description: Bearded, on a horse facing right, in high plumed hat, cloak, jacket with ermine cuffs, breeches, stockings and calf-boots. He wears a cravat and possibly a chain of office. A poorly moulded and sparsely coloured figure.

Figure 60
Subject: **Irish National Forester**
Title: Irish National Forrester (gilt script)
Date: *c.* 1877
Height: 13 in (33 cm)
Colour: White and gilt.
Maker: Probably Sampson Smith
Rarity: R.
Pair: Fig. 59 (Irish National Forester)
Description: Clean-shaven, on horse facing left, with plumed hat, cloak, jacket with ermine cuffs, breeches and knee-boots. A poorly moulded and sparsely coloured figure.
Observations: The Irish National Foresters is an organization established in Dublin in 1877. There is much information on it in H. B. L. Pollard's *Secret Societies of Ireland*, London (1922).

Plate 19
Figure 61
Subject: **Louis Kossuth**
Title: Kossuth (gilt script)
Date: *c.* 1851
Height: 10¾ in (27 cm)

Colour: Well coloured.
Rarity: Av. D.
Description: Standing, bearded, in a low, flat-brimmed plumed hat, thigh-length coat and strap-trousers, his right hand on a cloak draped over a wall.
Observations: 1. Kossuth first visited England in 1851.
2. A daguerreotype by Claudet, an engraving of which appeared in *The Illustrated London News* of November 15th, 1851, is the probable source of this and similar figures (see *ch. 3, pl.* 13A).

Figure 62
Subject: **Louis Kossuth**
Title: Kossuth (gilt script)
Date: *c.* 1851
Height: 10½ in (26.5 cm)
Colour: Usually sparsely coloured.
Rarity: R. D.
Description: Standing, in low plumed hat with curled-brim, his right hand on cloak draped over a wall. Angled base.
Observations: 1. An example of this figure fetched 48 gns at Christie's in 1969.
2. See *fig.* 61 (Kossuth)

Plate 20
Figure 63
Subject: **Louis Kossuth**
Title: None
Date: *c.* 1851
Height: 11 in (28 cm)
Colour: Well coloured.
Rarity: R. D.
Description: Standing, in high, flat-brimmed plumed hat, his left hand on his waist, his right hand on a draped pedestal.
Observations: See *fig.* 61 (Kossuth) *pl.* B-19.

Figure 64
Subject: **Louis Kossuth**
Title: Kossuth (indented capitals)
Date: 1851
Height: 9 in (23 cm)
Colour: Sparsely coloured. No figure yet reported with a blue coat.
Maker: Alpha factory
Rarity: VR. D.
Description: Standing, in high, flat-brimmed plumed hat, his left hand on his waist and his right hand on a cloak draped over and entirely covering a wall or pedestal.
Observations: See *fig.* 61 (Kossuth) *pl.* B-19.

Plate 20A
Washington and Franklin
Left: George Washington—From the original painting by Stuart.
Centre: Statue of Franklin erected on September 17th, 1856 in Boston. The statue bears a close likeness to the Staffordshire portraits.
(From *The Illustrated London News* of October 25th, 1856)
Right: Franklin—An engraving by J. Thomson from an original picture by J. A. Duplessis.
Walter H. Page when American ambassador in London in 1918 wrote:

I have on my mantelpiece a statuette of Benjamin Franklin, an excellent and unmistakable likeness which was made here during his lifetime; and the inscription burnt on its base is 'Washington'. It serves me many a good turn with my English friends. I use it as a measure of their ignorance of us.

B199

Plate 20B (Left)
Thomas Jefferson
(1743-1826).
By courtesy of the United States Information Service, American Embassy, London

Plate 22 (Right)
Fig. 69 Washington
This is the only figure to portray a true likeness of Washington.
The Metropolitan Museum of Art, Gift of William H. Huntington, 1883

Plate 21
Fig. 65 Jefferson
Fig. 68 Washington
Fig. 66 Franklin
Fig. 67 The Old English Gentleman
Figs. 67 and 68, in fact, portray Franklin and are erroneously titled.

Plate 20B
Jefferson
This portrait of Thomas Jefferson, by an unknown artist, shows such a similarity in features, hair style and dress as to leave little room for doubt that *fig.* 65, *pl.* B-21 does indeed portray him.

Plate 21
Figure 65
Subject: **Thomas Jefferson**
B200

Title: None
Date: 187–
Height: 15 in (38 cm)
Colour: Underglaze black coat. Dark maroon or gilt band round base, see *ch.* 4, *pl.* 4D.
Maker: John Parr or Kent & Parr
Rarity: VR. D. A.
Series: Same series as *fig.* 69 (Washington) and *fig.* 70 (Franklin), *pls.* B-22 and 23.
Description: He stands bare-headed, facing half-right, in long coat edged with fur,

floral waistcoat, breeches and stockings. He carries a tricorn hat in his left hand and the 'Declaration' in his right. Circular base.
Observations: 1. Similar in style and size to *fig.* 69 (Washington) and *fig.* 70 (Franklin). All three figures were made by the Parr and Kent group of potters and probably date to the 1870's.
2. There is such a striking similarity between the figure and the portrait of Thomas Jefferson illustrated on *pl.* B-20B, both as

regard to features, hair style and dress, as to leave little room for doubt regarding its identification. A portrait of Jefferson by the French artist, Charles Févret de Saint-Memin (1770–1852) is also very similar to the figure.

3. Thomas Jefferson drafted the 'Declaration of Independence' and became the third President of the United States.

Figure 66
Subject: **Benjamin Franklin**
Title: Franklin (raised capitals)
Date: 185–
Height: 14 in (35.5 cm)
Colour: Well coloured.
Rarity: Av. D.
Description: Standing bare-headed, in coat, long waistcoat, breeches, stockings and shoes. He holds a document in his right hand and a tricorn hat in his left. Angular base.
Observations: 1. A true likeness of Franklin. Compare with illustration on *pl*. B-20A. The same likeness was also used for figures of 'Washington' and 'The Old English Gentleman'.
2. A similar figure fetched 32 gns at Christie's in 1963.

Figure 67
Subject: **An old gentleman** (Franklin)
Title: The Old English Gentleman (gilt script)
Date: 185–
Height: 15½ in (39.25 cm)
Colour: Well coloured.
Rarity: Av.
Description: Apart from the base (which is circular), the height and the title, it is identical in all respects to *fig*. 66 (Franklin).
Observations: 1. A possible explanation of the 'change in country' is the unpopularity of the United States in the late fifties. Maybe the potter, still wishing to use the mould, looked around for another title. *The Old English Gentleman* was originally a traditional ballad. It was re-written by Charles H. Purday in 1826 and retained its popularity in the 1850's. The music-front carried a lithograph of an old gentleman whose costume bore a period resemblance to the 'Franklin-Washington' figure. This lithograph and its title doubtless gave the potter the idea for a new means of marketing the figure as of an English subject.
2. A similar figure, together with *fig*. 73 (Lincoln) *pl*. B-25, fetched 65 gns at Christie's in 1967.

Figure 68
Subject: **George Washington** (Franklin)
Title: Washington (gilt script)
Date: 185–
Height: 15¼ in (38.5 cm)
Colour: Well coloured.
Rarity: Av. D.
Description: Same design as *fig*. 66 (Franklin) except for the base (which is circular), the title and the height.
Observations: With one exception (*fig*. 69, *pl*. B-22), all recorded figures of Washington have Franklin's head, and *all* the figures have Franklin's body. The only known figure with a true likeness of Washington's head is untitled.
Figures of 'Washington' with Franklin's head and body may be variously titled:

> Washington
> G. Washington
> Gl. Washington
> Gnl. Washington
> General Washington

Plate 23
Fig. 70 Franklin
In the collection of Mr Ronald Shockledge

Plate 22
Figure 69
Subject: **George Washington**
Title: None
Date: 187–
Height: 14¾ in (37.5 cm)
Colour: Largely white and gilt; black shoes, greyish hair; natural colouring to hands and face. The band round the base is gilt in the only copy known to me.
Maker: John Parr or Kent & Parr.
Rarity: VR. D.
Series: Same series as *fig*. 65 (Jefferson) and *fig*. 70 (Franklin), *pls*. B-21 and 23.
Description: Standing bare-headed, a tricorn hat in his left hand and a document in his right, long coat, waistcoat, breeches and stockings.
Observations: 1. The only Victorian Staffordshire portrait figure known to me in which Washington's features are correctly portrayed (see illustration on *pl*. B-20A). It is in the Metropolitan Museum of Art, New York. All known figures titled 'Washington' have Franklin's features.
2. See *observations fig*. 65 (Jefferson) *pl*. B-21.

Plate 23
Figure 70
Subject: **Benjamin Franklin**
Title: None
Date: 187–
Height: 15 in (38 cm)
Colour: Underglaze black coat. Dark maroon or gilt band round base. Paler versions are known.
Maker: John Parr or Kent & Parr
Rarity: VR. D.
Series: Same series as *fig*. 65 (Jefferson) and *fig*. 69 (Washington), *pls*. B-21 and 22.
Description: Standing bare-headed, a tri-

Plate 23A
Fig. 70(a) Washington
The figure portrays Franklin and is erroneously titled.
The Metropolitan Museum of Art,
Gift of William H. Huntington, 1883

corn hat in his left hand, and a document in his right. He wears a long coat, waistcoat, breeches and stockings.
Observations: 1. The features are those of Franklin (see illustration on *pl*. B-20A) but all known titled versions are labelled 'General Washington' or some modification thereof.
2. See *observations fig*. 65 (Jefferson) *pl*. B-21.

Plate 23A
Figure 70(a)
Subject: **George Washington** (Franklin)
Title: General Washington (gilt script)
Date: 187–
Height: 15⅜ in (39 cm)
Colour: Both coloured and paler versions exist.
Maker: John Parr or Kent & Parr
Rarity: Av. D.
Description: A 'mistitled' version of *fig*. 70 (Franklin). It is very similar to *fig*. 68 (Washington) *pl*. B-21, but both arms are from separate moulds and the manuscript is held at a slightly different angle.
Observations: 1. Not infrequently the manuscript is inscribed 'Freedom'.
2. A similar figure (with inscribed manuscript) was sold at Christie's for 40 gns in 1963, and another (also inscribed) for 44 gns in 1966. This latter lot included a figure of Uncle Tom and Eva.

Plate 23B
Figure 70(b)
Subject: **George Washington** (Franklin)
Title: Gl. Washington (gilt script)
Height: 10 in (25 cm)
Colour: White and gilt.
Maker: John Parr or Kent and Parr
Rarity: R. D.
Description: Similar to *fig*. 70(a) (Washing-

Plate 23B
Fig. 70(b) Washington
Fig. 70(c) Franklin
Fig. 70(b) portrays Franklin and is erroneously titled.

Plate 24
Fig. 71 Washington
The figure portrays Franklin and is erroneously titled.
By courtesy of Mr and Mrs Eric Joyce

Plate 23B continued

ton) except that the arms are not separate, it is shorter and the title differs.
Observations: This figure, like *fig.* 70(a), is a product of the Parr and Kent group of potters. The figures are unusual in that they are titled in gilt script, a method not usually associated with the Parr and Kent group.

Figure 70(c)
Subject: **Benjamin Franklin**
Title: None
Height: 10¼ in (25.75 cm)
Colour: In glost state—uncoloured.
Maker: John Parr or Kent and Parr
Rarity: R. D.
Description: Similar to *fig.* 70 (Franklin) except that it is smaller.
Observations: In the glost state prior to the application of the enamels.

Plate 24
Figure 71
Subject: **George Washington** (Franklin)
Title: Washington (raised capitals)
Height: 16 in (40.5 cm)
Colour: Well coloured.
Rarity: R. D.
Description: Identical in all respects, other than for height and titling to *fig.* 66 (Franklin) *pl.* B-21.
Observations: See *fig.* 68 (Washington) *pl.* B-21.

B202

Plate 24A
Figure 71(a)
Subject: **George Washington** (Franklin)
Title: Washington (gilt script)
Height: 15½ in (39.25 cm)
Colour: Well coloured.
Rarity: R. D.
Description: Identical in all major respects to *fig.* 68 (Washington) *pl.* B-21, except for the base which is 'shaped' instead of circular.
Observations: See *fig.* 68 (Washington) *pl.* B-21.

Plate 25
Figure 72
Subject: **Duke of Wellington**
Title: Wellington (raised capitals)
Date: Uncertain
Height: 15 in (38 cm)
Colour: Largely white, black, and gilt.
Maker: In the style of Sampson Smith
Rarity: R.
Pair: Fig. 73 (Lincoln)
Description: On a horse facing right, bare-headed, in uniform with a cloak draped over both shoulders. He holds his plumed cocked hat in his right hand behind his right thigh.
Observation: See under next figure.

Figure 73
Subject: **Abraham Lincoln**
Title: A. Lincoln (raised capitals)
Date: 186–
Height: 15 in (38 cm)
Colour: As for preceding figure.
Maker: In the style of Sampson Smith
Rarity: Av.
Pair: Fig. 72 (Wellington)

Description: On a horse facing left, bare-headed, with cloak draped over both shoulders, coat, waistcoat and trousers. Hat behind his left hand against the horse's rump.
Observations: 1. This figure would not have been made prior to 1860 when Lincoln assumed the presidency of the United States. Its pair, *fig.* 72 (Wellington), could be a much earlier figure.
2. Both this figure and its pair tend to have a grey body.
3. A similar figure fetched 42 gns at Christie's in 1969.

Plate 25A
Figure 74
Subject: **? Benjamin Franklin**
Title: None
Height: 9¾ in (24.5 cm)
Colour: Well coloured, underglaze blue coat.
Maker: Alpha factory
Rarity: R.
Description: Standing bare-headed, in long coat, waistcoat, breeches and stockings. His left hand is plunged into the pocket of his waistcoat and his right forearm rests on a pile of books on a pedestal to his right.
Observations: 1. Both features and costume bare a striking resemblance to those portrayed in known figures of Franklin (see *pl.* B-21).
2. Balston listed the figure as Voltaire, but offered no evidence for this identification.
3. A photograph of the piece has been examined by the Director of the Institut et Musée Voltaire in Geneva who has commented that it is *certainly not Voltaire*.

Plate 24A
Fig. 71(a) Washington
The figure portrays Franklin and is erroneously titled.
In the Thomas Balston collection

Plate 25A
Fig. 74 ? Franklin
By courtesy of M. Marc de Smedt

Plate 25
Fig. 72 Wellington
Fig. 73 Lincoln
In the collection of Mr Ronald Shockledge

Section B. Statesmen and Politicians

Plate 26
Figure 75
Subject: **Uncle Tom and Eva**
Title: Five-line quotation of Eva and Tom's conversation, beginning: '*Eva.* O Uncle Tom! What funny things you are making there!' (black transfer; upper and lower case).
Date: *c.* 1852
Height: 7½ in (19 cm)
Colour: Well coloured.
Rarity: Av.
Description: Tom sits on a rock with a slate in both hands. To his left Eva stands. Both are bare-headed.
Observations: *Uncle Tom's Cabin* by Mrs Beecher Stowe was first published in 1852, nine years before the outbreak of the American Civil War. A play based on it aroused intense sympathy with the abolitionists. Numerous figures were manufactured of the chief characters in the story. It is probable that most of them were made before the war.

Figure 76
Subject: **Uncle Tom and Eva**
Title: Uncle Tom & Eva (raised capitals)
Date: *c.* 1852
Height: 8½ in (21.5 cm)
Colour: Largely black and white.
Rarity: Av.
Description: Tom is seated. He holds a book in his left hand and his right arm is round Eva who sits on his lap. She has a posy in her right hand. Tom's hat is on the ground.

Figure 77
Subject: **John Brown**
Title: John Brown (raised capitals)
Date: *c.* 1859
Height: 11½ in (29 cm)
Colour: Well coloured with blue coat, or in black, white and gilt.
Rarity: R. D.
Description: Standing bare-headed with long beard, morning coat, waistcoat and trousers, on either side a negro child.
Observations: 1. John Brown was hanged in 1859, two years before the outbreak of the American Civil War.
2. A similar figure fetched 46 gns at Christie's in 1967.

Figure 78
Subject: **Uncle Tom and Eva**
Title: Uncle Tom (raised capitals)
Date: *c.* 1852
Height: 11½ in (29 cm)
Colour: Largely black, white and gilt.
Rarity: Av.
Description: Similar to *fig.* 76, but Eva stands on Tom's right leg and there is a garland round his neck. He holds his hat instead of the book in his left hand.
Observations: A similar figure fetched 20 gns at Christie's in 1968.

Figure 79
Subject: **Uncle Tom and Eva**
Title: None
Date: *c.* 1852
Height: 6½ in (16.5 cm)
Colour: Well coloured.
Rarity: Av.
Description: Eva and Uncle Tom sit under an arbour. Eva has an open book on her lap.
Observations: It has been suggested that this figure is theatrical.
B204

Plate 26
T: *Fig.* 75 Uncle Tom and Eva
Fig. 76 Uncle Tom and Eva
Fig. 77 John Brown
Fig. 78 Uncle Tom and Eva
Fig. 79 Uncle Tom and Eva

B: *Fig.* 80 Uncle Tom and Eva
Fig. 82 Aunt Chloe
Fig. 83 George and Eliza Harris
Fig. 81 Uncle Tom
Fig. 84 Topsy and Eva
In the collection of Mr Ronald Shockledge

Figure 80
Subject: **Uncle Tom and Eva**
Title: Uncle Tom (raised capitals)
Date: *c.* 1852
Height: 12 in (30.5 cm)
Colour: Well coloured.
Rarity: Av.
Description: Tom and Eva stand in a boat. Tom (a white man in this case) stands forward with oar in his left hand and his right arm round Eva, who is standing aft on a package.
Observations: Figures of Uncle Tom are found occasionally with the face and hands white instead of coloured. Whether this was a 'potter's error' or intended for a particular market is unknown. A 'coloured' version may be seen on *pl.* B-27.

Figure 81
Subject: **Uncle Tom**
Title: Uncle Tom (gilt script)
Date: *c.* 1852
Height: 8¾ in (22 cm)
Colour: Well coloured.
Rarity: R.
Pair: *Fig.* 82 (Aunt Chloe)
Description: Standing bare-headed, his hat against his right foot. His right hand is on a book which rests on a corded package.

Figure 82
Subject: **Aunt Chloe**
Title: Aunt Chloe (gilt script)
Date: *c.* 1852
Height: 8½ in (21.5 cm)
Colour: Well coloured.
Rarity: R.

Pair: *Fig.* 81 (Uncle Tom)
Description: Standing with scarf over her head, a basket in her left hand.

Figure 83
Subject: **George and Eliza Harris and child**
Title: George & Eliza Harris (gilt script)
Date: *c.* 1852
Height: 14 in (35.5 cm)
Colour: Largely white and gilt.
Rarity: Av.
Description: Both stand bare-headed, George on the left, his hat in his right hand. Between them is a child in Eliza's arms.
Observations: 1. One example of this figure is known titled 'Sailor Return' (gilt script), see *pl.* C-71B.
2. George Harris was a young mulatto slave, *i.e.* half negro and half white; Eliza Harris was a quadroon, *i.e.* one-quarter negro and three-quarters white—neither are portrayed 'coloured' in the figures.

Figure 84
Subject: **Topsy and Eva**
Title: Topsy & Eva (gilt script)
Date: *c.* 1852
Height: 8¾ in (22 cm)
Colour: Well coloured.
Rarity: Av.
Description: Both are kneeling and bare-headed. Eva's right arm is on Topsy's shoulder and her left hand holds Topsy's right.
Observations: The lithograph music-front illustrated on *ch.* 3, *pl.* 14A titled *Topsy's*

Colour Plate 21
John Brown (Left). *Fig.* 77, *pl.* B-26. See opposite. Daniel O'Connell (Right). *Fig.* 16, *pl.* B-2. See page 186.

Colour Plate 22
Duke of Wellington and Abraham Lincoln. *Figs.* 72 and 73, *pl.* B-25. See page 202.

Plate 27
Fig. 85 Uncle Tom and Eva

Fig. 80 Uncle Tom and Eva

Fig. 78(a) Uncle Tom and Eva
By courtesy of Mr and Mrs Eric Joyce

Plate 26 continued
Song is without doubt the source of this
figure. It may well be a theatrical portrait,
although definite proof of this is lacking.

Plate 27
Figure 78(a)
Subject: **Uncle Tom and Eva**
Title: None
Date: *c.* 1852
Height: 10¼ in (25.75 cm)
Colour: Largely black, white and gilt
Rarity: Av.
Description: Similar to *fig.* 78, *pl.* B-26, except
for the absence of title, difference in height
and shape of base.

Figure 80
Subject: **Uncle Tom and Eva**
Observations: See *pl.* B-26.

Figure 85
Subject: **Uncle Tom and Eva**
Title: Eva & Uncle Tom (gilt script)
Date: *c.* 1852
Height: 8½ in (21.5 cm)
Colour: Sparsely coloured.
Rarity: Av.
Description: Tom sits bare-headed, on a
corded package. He has an open book on
his lap. To his right stands Eva, bare-headed
with her hat in her right hand. Her left
hand rests on Tom's right shoulder.
Observations: See *fig.* 75 (Uncle Tom and
Eva) *pl.* B-26.

Plate 28
Figure 86
Subject: **Aunt Chloe**
Title: None
Date: *c.* 1852
Height: 7 in (17.5 cm)
Colour: Well coloured.
Maker: Thomas Parr
Rarity: R.
Pair: *Fig.* 87 (Uncle Tom)
Description: Seated with a scarf over her

Plate 28
Fig. 86 Aunt Chloe
Fig. 87 Uncle Tom

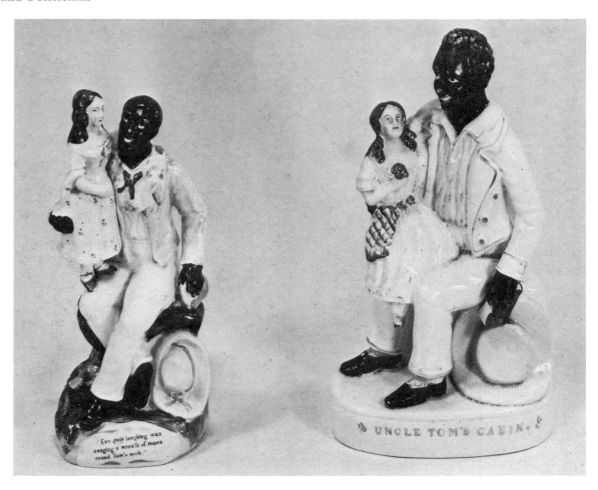

Plate 29
Fig. 89 Uncle Tom and Eva   *Fig.* 88 Uncle Tom's Cabin

head, a basket, probably containing cotton, to her right.

Observations: I have been told that this figure has been found titled in indented capitals but I have never seen this myself.

Figure 87
Subject: **Uncle Tom**
Title: None
Date: 1852
Height: 7 in (17.5 cm)
Colour: Well coloured.
Maker: Thomas Parr
Rarity: R.
Pair: *Fig.* 86 (Aunt Chloe)
Description: He sits bare-headed and with knees crossed, a book in his right hand and a basket, probably containing cotton, to his left.
Observations: See preceding figure.

Plate 29
Figure 88
Subject: **Uncle Tom and Eva**
Title: Uncle Tom's Cabin (indented capitals)
Date: *c.* 1852

Height: 9 in (23 cm)
Colour: Both well coloured versions with underglaze blue coat, and paler versions exist.
Maker: Alpha factory
Rarity: Av.
Description: Very similar to *fig.* 76 (Uncle Tom & Eva) *pl.* B-26.

Figure 89
Subject: **Uncle Tom and Eva**
Title: Three-line quotation: 'Eva gaily laughing was/ hanging a wreath of roses/ round Tom's neck' (black transfer; upper and lower case).
Date: *c.* 1852
Height: 8 in (20.5 cm)
Colour: Well coloured in the manner of Thomas Parr.
Maker: Thomas Parr
Rarity: Av.
Description: Tom is seated. He holds a book in his left hand and below is his hat. He has his right arm around Eva, who stands on his lap. She is hanging a wreath of roses round his neck. Below is a three-line quotation.

B207

Colour Plate 23
Jean Bart. *Fig.* 2, *pl.* C-2. See page 220.

Plate 30
Fig. 90 Uncle Tom and Eva
Fig. 91 Uncle Tom

Plate 31
Fig. 92 Private in American Civil War

Plate 30
Figure 90
Subject: **Uncle Tom and Eva**
Title: None
Date: *c.* 1852
Height: 8 in (20.5 cm)
Colour: Well coloured and pale versions exist.
Rarity: Av.
Description: Tom is seated on the right with a blackboard in his left hand. His right arm is around Eva who is bare-headed and holds a hat in her right hand. Behind her head is a scarf.

Figure 91
Subject: **Uncle Tom**
Title: Uncle Tom (indented capitals)
Date: 1852
Height: 5¼ in (13.5 cm)
Colour: Black and white.
Maker: Probably Thomas Parr
Rarity: Av.
Description: He stands bare-headed. His hands are manacled in front of him.
Observations: The title is always difficult to define but, I believe, invariably present.

Plate 31
Figure 92
Subject: **Non-portrait figure of a private in the American Civil War**
Title: None
Date: *c.* 1861
Height: 5¼ in (13.5 cm)
Colour: See *observations*.
Rarity: Av.
Pair: See *observations*
Description: He is wearing uniform, including a peaked cap, and carrying a rifle between his legs.
Observations: A private in the Union army (1861–5) wore a dark blue jacket; a private in the Confederate army (1861–5) wore a grey jacket. These figures are often found in pairs so coloured as to portray privates in each army.

Section C
Naval, Military and Exploration
Biographies and Historical Notes

ABD-UL-HAMID II, Sultan of Turkey (1842–1918), second son of Sultan Abd-ul-Medjid. Succeeded in 1876 on the deposition of his brother Murad V. So distrustful of other persons that he is said to have extracted his own teeth and prepared his own medicines. The oppression of the Christian subjects of the Sultan made hostilities between Turkey and Russia inevitable. Russia declared war on April 24th, 1877. Turkey was defeated and peace signed on January 31st, 1878. Domestic troubles culminated in the deposition and exile of the Sultan in 1909.
See **pl. C**-114.

ABD-UL-MEDJID, Sultan of Turkey (1823–61). Succeeded his father Mahmud II in 1839 and continued the reforms of the previous reign. In 1850 he refused to give up Kossuth. He played a difficult part well during the Crimean War (1854–6), but thereafter allowed affairs to drift. *The Illustrated London News* of September 17th, 1853 said of him:

The Sultan, who is only 30, looks at least ten years older. He has a black beard and a handsome well-bred face, of a French cast; his countenance and figure are marked by an indescribable air of languor and debility arising from his early initiation into the worst features of Oriental life . . . He is always surrounded and followed by a crowd of eunuchs, pachas, colonels, and officers of state.
See **pls. C**-30, 31, 32, 53, 62, 64, 65, 66, 68.

ALBERT FRANCIS CHARLES AUGUSTUS EMMANUEL, Prince-Consort of England (1819–61).
For biography see **section A.**
See **pls. A**-4, 5, 6, 7, 8, 11, 12, 13, 14, 15, 16, 17, 18, 19, 20, 22, 23, 24, 27, 28, 30, 31, 32, 33, 35, 35A, 36, 37, 38, 39, 40, 40A, 41, 44, 55, 56, 57,
pls. C-31, 35, 77, 78, 79.

ALEXANDER II, Tsar of Russia (1818–81). The term Tsar is a title given to Russian emperors. The son of Nicholas I, he was born at St. Petersburg. In 1841 he married the Princess Marie, daughter of the Grand-duke of Hesse. He succeeded to the throne in 1855, a year before the end of the Crimean War. Achieved emancipation of the serfs in 1861. In 1874, his only daughter Marie married Alfred, duke of Edinburgh, second son of Queen Victoria. He shared the national sympathy with the Slavonic races under Turkish rule, and took the field with the army during the victorious war between Russia and Turkey, in 1877–8. Although a liberal monarch, his government repressed revolutionists with great

cruelty. He died in 1881 from injuries sustained when a bomb was thrown at him near his palace.
See **pls. A**-90, 91,
pl. C-114.

ARNAUD, JACQUES LEROY DE SAINT (1796–1854). *See* **Saint-Arnaud, Jacques Leroy de.**

ARTHUR WILLIAM PATRICK ALBERT, Duke of Connaught (1850–1942), third son of Queen Victoria. Entered Royal Military Academy, Woolwich, 1866. Commissioned in Royal Engineers, 1868. Created Duke of Connaught, 1874. Married Princess Louise (1860–1917), daughter of Frederick Charles of Prussia, in 1879. In 1882, as a major-general, he commanded 1st Guards Brigade under the then, Sir Garnet Wolseley. Helped to crush the rebellion of the Egyptian army under Arabi Pasha at Tel-el-Kebir and occupied Cairo. Field-marshal, 1902; governor-general of Canada (1911–6).
See **pls. C**-115, 116.

AUGUSTA, Queen of Prussia, (1811–90). Daughter of the Grand-duke of Saxe-Weimar. In 1829 she married Prince William of Prussia, later King of Prussia and Emperor of Germany.
See **pl. C**-106.

BADEN-POWELL, ROBERT STEPHENSON SMYTH, first Baron Baden-Powell (1857–1941). Lieutenant-general and founder of the Boy Scouts and Girl Guides. Educated at Charterhouse. Gazetted to the 13th Hussars in India, in 1876. Sent to South Africa to raise two regiments in 1899. Held Mafeking during the siege of 217 days. Relieved May 17th, 1900. Major-general in 1900 and lieutenant-general in 1907. Retired in 1910 to devote himself to the Boy Scout movement, which together with the Girl Guide movement, was designed to promote good citizenship in the rising generation.
See **pls. C**-128, 129, 133, 135.

BART, JEAN (1651–1702). French naval hero born at Dunkirk. The son of a fisherman, served in the French navy under De Ruyter, but on the outbreak of the war with Holland, passed over to the French service. In 1691 he commanded a small squadron in the North Sea and destroyed many English vessels. In 1694 he was

involved in a desperate struggle with the Dutch fleet and recaptured a large number of corn ships bringing them safely back to Dunkirk. Soon after, he was taken prisoner and carried to Plymouth, but escaped in a fishing boat to France.
See **pls. C**-2, 4.

BAZAINE, FRANCOIS ACHILLE (1811–88), marshal of France. Entered the army in 1831 and served in the Crimea. In the Franco-Prussian War of 1870 he took over supreme command in August when the French army was already in retreat. He brought it back to Metz, where it surrendered on October 14th. Three marshals, six thousand officers and nearly two hundred thousand men were taken prisoners of war. In 1873 he was court-martialled and sentenced to degradation and death. This sentence was later commuted to twenty years imprisonment. The following year he escaped from the island fortress on which he was held. He died fourteen years later in Madrid.
See **pl. C**-110.

BEATTY, SIR WILLIAM (1773–1842), surgeon. Entered navy in 1791. Attended Nelson at Trafalgar, 1805, and subsequently published *Authentic Narrative of Death of Lord Nelson.* Licentiate of the Royal College of Physicians, 1817; FRS, 1818; Physician at Greenwich Hospital (1822–40). Knighted in 1831.
See **pl. C**-6.

HMS BELLEROPHON (74-guns). Launched in 1789, she played an important part in the Battle of the Nile in 1798. The climax of the battle was marked by the blowing up of Bruey's flag-ship *Orient*. Due to her close proximity, the *Bellerophon* sustained severe damage including the loss of all three masts. Her other claim to fame came in 1815, after Napoleon's defeat at Waterloo. After fleeing to Paris he abdicated on June 22nd and surrendered to Captain Fred L. Maitland of the *Bellerophon* at Rochefort on July 15th. On the 24th *Bellerophon* anchored at Torbay. Napoleon was not allowed to land. The vessel subsequently moved to Plymouth Harbour where, on July 31st, Napoleon was informed that his future home was to be St. Helena. He protested in vain. On August 4th, *Bellerophon* put to sea and on the 7th Napoleon was transferred to the *Northumberland*, which sailed on August 8th for St. Helena.
See **pl. C**-12.

BISMARCK, OTTO EDWARD LEOPOLD VON, Prince Bismarck, Duke of Lauenburg, (1815–98). Prusso-German statesman and chief architect of the German empire. Prussian ambassador at St. Petersburg (1859–62) and at Paris (1862). He was recalled to Germany by William I to head his government. The autocratic rule which proved so disastrous in the long term can be dated from this period. There followed the victory over Austria in 1866 and the humiliation of France in the Franco-Prussian War of 1870, culminating in William I being proclaimed Emperor of Germany at Versailles in 1871. From 1871 until the death of William I in 1888, the rule of the 'Iron Chancellor' dominated Europe. A struggle for supremacy developed between Bismarck and William II, which ended in the former's retirement in 1890, during which he spent most of his time criticizing the Emperor.
See **pls. C**-109, 110.

BLACK WATCH, the name of the first of the Highland Regiments, so-called because the uniform was a dark tartan, whilst the regular soldiers wore red. The regiment was formed from independent companies of Highlanders for service in Scotland in the seventeenth century. Included in its battle honours are Waterloo, the Crimea, the Indian Mutiny and the Egyptian campaign of 1882. The regiment also served with distinction in the South African War of 1899–1902.
See **pl. C**-137.

BLAKE, ROBERT (1599–1657). British admiral, second only to Nelson. The eldest of a merchant's twelve sons, he seems to have spent much of his time in his father's business or as a country gentleman until the age of 40. In 1640 he was returned for Bridgwater in the Short Parliament and threw in his lot with the parliamentarians. Became a member of the Long Parliament in 1645. He was an ardent republican and a man of blunt character, devoid of fear, much respected by Cromwell. As a parliamentary general he attracted notice at the siege of Bristol and by his defence at Lyme in 1644 against Prince Maurice. He defended Taunton for nearly a year against overwhelming odds and this proved a turning point in the Civil War. In 1649, appointed to command the Fleet, then in a state of disaffection and weakness. Within two years he had blockaded Lisbon, destroyed the squadron of Prince Rupert and forced the royalists to surrender. In 1652, he began the struggle with the Dutch for the supremacy of the seas and pitted himself against Tromp, De Ruyter and De Witt. He eventually shattered the naval supremacy of Holland. The highlight of his career was the destruction of the Spanish West Indies Fleet at Santa Cruz in 1657. He died of fever as his ship was entering Plymouth Harbour after the exploit.
See **pls. C**-1, 1A.

BONAPARTE, NAPOLEON JOSEPH CHARLES PAUL (1822–91), known as PRINCE NAPOLEON. Born at Trieste. Fought in the Crimea, commanding French troops at Alma and Inkerman, 1854–5. In 1859 he married the Princess Clotilde, daughter of Victor Emmanuel of Italy. After the fall of the Empire he took up residence in England, but returned to France in 1872. On the death of the Prince Imperial in 1879, Prince Napoleon's eldest son became heir of Bonapartist hopes and in 1886 father and son were exiled as pretenders to the throne. Died in Rome in 1891.
See **pls. C**-30, 61.

BROWN, SIR GEORGE (1790–1865), general. Served with distinction in the Peninsula. Lieutenant-general, 1851; KCB, 1852. Commanded the Light Division in the Crimea and the English contingent against Kertch, 1855.
See **pls. C**-49, 50, 56, 67.

BROWN, JESSIE (dates unknown), the wife of Corporal Brown of the 32nd regiment also known as 'Highland Jessie'. Present at the relief of Lucknow. According to a letter written by M. de Banneroi, a French physician in the service of Mussur Rajah, and published in *Le Pays* (a Paris newspaper) dated Calcutta, October 8th 1857, Jessie Brown, consumed by fever, awoke on the night of September 26th, 1857 when Lucknow was at its last gasp, stood upright and screamed 'Dinna ye hear it? Dinna ye hear it? Ay, I'm no dreamin', it's the slogan o' the Highlanders! We're saved, we're saved'. Then, flinging herself on her knees, she thanked God with passionate fervour. When there was no longer any doubt of the fact that it was the pibroch (a form of bagpipe music) of the Highlanders that Jessie had heard a cheer went up 'God save the Queen' to which the Highlanders replied by playing *Should auld acquaintance be forgot*, etc. Jessie was presented to General Sir Colin Campbell on his entrance into the fort, and at the officer's banquet her health was drunk by all present. Later writers have regarded Jessie Brown as a mythical figure. It has been said that among the many rumours current immediately before the relief, it was reported that bagpipes could be heard in the still watches of the night. It was known that a regiment of Highlanders formed part of the relief force, and doubtless the wish was father to the thought.
See **pl. C**-89.

BULLER, SIR REDVERS HENRY (1839–1908), general. Born at Crediton, educated at Eton. Commissioned in 1858, he served in the Red River expedition, 1870; and under Wolseley in Ashanti, 1873. Commanded the Frontier Light Horse in the sixth Kaffir War in South Africa, 1878–9. Awarded the Victoria Cross for gallant rescues, 1879. Chief-of-staff in Wolseley's campaign to relieve Gordon, 1884. KCB, 1885. General, 1896. In command at Aldershot, 1898. Was commander-in-chief in the South African War from October to December, 1899 when, after his defeat at Colenso, he was superseded by Lord Roberts. Relieved Ladysmith, February 28th, 1900. Returned to England, November 1900.
See **pls. C**-124, 128, 129, 132, 135.

BURNABY, FREDERICK GUSTAVUS (1842–85), lieutenant-colonel. Cavalry officer and traveller. Linguist, accomplished military balloonist, and author of narratives of his travels. Famous for his ride from Kazala to Khiva in 1875. Joined Wolseley's expedition in 1884. Killed in action in the attempt to relieve Khartoum in 1885.
See **pl. C**-118.

BURTON, LADY ISABEL (1831–96), wife of Sir Richard Burton whom she married in 1861. Shared as far as possible her husband's life in exploration and literature and after his death, prepared his biography.
See **pls. C**-95, 95A.

BURTON, SIR RICHARD FRANCIS (1821–90), explorer and scholar. In 1842 served in Sind under Sir Charles Napier. Made a pilgrimage to Mecca disguised as a Pathan, 1853. Served in the Crimea, 1855. In 1856 he set out with Speke to discover the Nile sources. Reached Lake Tanganyika in 1858. Speke then travelled alone and discovered Victoria Nyanza and gave information to Sir Samuel Baker which enabled him to discover the third lake, Albert Nyanza. Speke was about to defend his identification of the source of the Nile against Burton's doubts at a meeting of the British Association in 1864, when he accidentally shot himself partridge shooting. In 1861 Burton married Isabel Arundell (*see* Burton, Lady Isabel). She subsequently shared in his travels and writing. In 1861 he was appointed consul at Fernando Po. He held subsequently similar posts at Santos, Brazil, Damascus and at Trieste. Knighted in 1886. Wrote many books including *First footsteps in East Africa* (1856) and *Wanderings in West Africa* (1863).
See **pl. C**-94.

CAMBRIDGE, second Duke of (1819–1904).
See **George William Frederick Charles.**

CAMPBELL, SIR COLIN, Baron Clyde (1792–1863), field-marshal. Born in Glasgow, the son of a carpenter. Gazetted ensign in 1808. Twice wounded in the Peninsular War. The next thirty years were spent mainly in garrison duties at Gibraltar, Barbados, England etc. KCB for services in the second Sikh War, 1848–9. Appointed to the command of the Highland Brigade at the outbreak of the Crimean War in 1854. Was largely responsible for the victory at Alma and for the repulse of the Russians at Balaclava. At the outbreak of the Mutiny in July, 1857 he was offered the command of the forces in India by Lord Palmerston and effected the final relief of Lucknow in November. Created Baron Clyde in 1858.
See **pls. C**-47, 48, 56, 67, 89, 91, 92, 92B.

CANROBERT, FRANCOIS CERTAIN, (1809–95), marshal of France. Supported the coup d'état of 1851. Commanded in the Crimea in 1854 and was wounded at the Alma. He succeeded Saint-Arnaud as commander-in-chief on the latter's death in September, 1854 and served as such until May, 1855. In the Franco-Prussian War of 1870 he was shut up in Metz with Bazaine and became a prisoner-of-war.
See **pls. C**-48, 52, 53, 54.

CATHCART, SIR GEORGE (1794–1854), general. Younger son of William Schaw Cathcart, first Earl Cathcart. Aide-de-camp to Wellington at Waterloo and in France, 1815–8. Major-general, 1851. Commander-in-chief in South Africa, 1852–4. Commanded the Fourth Division in the Crimea. Urged in vain for an immediate

attack on Sebastopol, September 1854. Killed at Inkerman in a cavalry charge on November 5th, 1854.
See **pl. C-51.**

CAVELL, EDITH (1866–1915), nurse. She was trained at the London Hospital, 1895. Matron of the Berkendael medical institute at Brussels, 1907. In charge of the institute when it became a Red Cross hospital, 1914. She attended German, Belgian and allied wounded, but was arrested by the Germans on August 5th, 1915 for assisting allied soldiers to escape. She was placed in solitary confinement and when brought for trial confessed that her efforts had been successful. She was condemned to death by court-martial and shot on October 12th, 1915.
See **pl. C-141.**

COCHRANE, DOUGLAS MACKINNON BAILLIE HAMILTON, twelfth Earl of Dundonald (1852–1935), lieutenant-general. Entered the 2nd Lifeguards, 1870. His rides with despatches to announce the death of Gordon and the fall of Khartoum made him famous. Succeeded to the title in 1885. Commanded the 2nd Lifeguards, 1895–9. Fought in the South African War, 1899–1900. Lieutenant-general, 1906. KCVO, 1907.
See **pls. C-126, 129, 130.**

CODRINGTON, SIR WILLIAM JOHN (1804–84), general. In 1854 showed great courage at Alma and Inkerman whilst in command of the Light Division. In November, 1855 he succeeded Simpson as commander-in-chief of the British troops in the Crimea. Fought at Sebastopol. Member of Parliament for Greenwich, 1857. Governor of Gibraltar, 1859–65.
See **pls. C-43, 46, 47.**

CONNAUGHT, Duke of (1850–1942).
See **Arthur William Patrick Albert.**

COOK, JAMES (1728–79), English navigator. Born in Yorkshire, the son of an agricultural labourer. Apprenticed to Whitby ship owners and spent several years in the coasting and Baltic trade. Entered the navy as an able seaman in 1755. Master in 1759. Thereafter was engaged for several years in surveying part of the St. Lawrence river and Newfoundland. From 1768 to 1771 was in command of the *Endeavour* and conveyed to the Pacific the expedition for observing the transit of Venus. On the return, he circumnavigated New Zealand and surveyed the east coast of Australia, completing the voyage by way of Java and the Cape of Good Hope. Was given command of a second voyage of discovery in the *Resolution* and *Adventurer* from 1772 to 1775, with the task of discovering how far the Antarctic stretched northward. Promoted to captain in 1775. His third and final voyage from 1776 to 1779 was to discover a passage round the north coast of America from the Pacific and was by the way of the Cape, Tasmania, New Zealand, the Pacific islands, the Sandwich islands and the west coast of North America. He was murdered by natives in Hawaii in February, 1779 after turning back from Icy Cape in the Behring Strait.
See **pl. C-5.**

COPENHAGEN (1808–36).
For biography see **section B.**
See **pl. B-3,**
pl. C-11.

DE LACY EVANS, SIR GEORGE (1787–1870), British general. Served in India, the Peninsula and at Waterloo. Liberal MP for Rye, 1831–2; and for Westminster, 1833–65, with the exception of the period from 1841 to 1846. Commanded the 'Spanish Legion' for Queen Isabella against the Carlists, 1835–7. In 1854 he commanded the 2nd Division in the Crimea. He was engaged at Alma and repelled a fierce enemy sortie with great gallantry during the siege of Sebastopol. Invalided home February 1855, receiving the thanks of Parliament.
See **pls. C-49, 54.**

DE WET, CHRISTIAN (1854–1922), Boer general. Was a renowned hunter before distinguishing himself in the Transvaal War of 1880–1. In the South African War of 1899–1902 he was the most outstanding and audacious of all the Boer commanders. In 1907 he was appointed Minister for Agriculture of the Orange River Colony. In October 1914, he joined the South African insurrection. After capture, he was sentenced to six years imprisonment, but was released after a year in gaol.
See **pl. C-134.**

DUNDAS, SIR JAMES WHITLEY DEANS (1785–1862), admiral. Commander in the Baltic, 1807. Frequently sat for Greenwich after the passing of the Reform Bill. Promoted to vice-admiral in 1852 and appointed commander-in-chief of the Mediterranean in the same year. On the outbreak of the Crimean War in 1854, he proceeded to the Black Sea. He forced the powerful Russian fleet to retire into hiding and conveyed a huge unwieldy armada into its appointed place of disembarkation at Sebastopol, where it got ashore under the cover of his guns. Of his personal courage there could be no doubt, but he was sixty-nine years old and in poor health. He hauled down his flag in January 1855, and was relieved by Sir Edmund Lyons (*q.v.*). There was no hint of dissatisfaction with his services in correspondence between him and the Admiralty. GCB; admiral, 1857.
See **pls. C-41, 42, 42A.**

DUNDAS, SIR RICHARD SAUNDERS (1802–61), vice-admiral. Son of Robert Saunders Dundas, second Viscount Melville. Captain in the navy, 1842. Junior Lord of the Admiralty, 1853–61. Succeeded Sir Charles Napier as commander-in-chief of the Baltic fleet in February 1855. In command of the operations off Sweaborg. Appointed KCB at the close of the Crimean War in 1856 for his Baltic services. Promoted vice-admiral, 1858.
See **pl. C-54.**

DUNDONALD, twelfth Earl of (1852–1935). *See* **Cochrane, Douglas Mackinnon Baillie Hamilton.**

EUGENE LOUIS JEAN JOSEPH, Prince Imperial (1856–79). Son of Napoleon III. Was in the field with his father in 1870, but escaped to England where he entered Woolwich Academy. He was killed in the Zulu campaign of 1879.
See **pls. C-34, 35, 36, 38.**

EUGENIE, Empress of France (1826–1920). Daughter of the Count of Montigo, she married Napoleon III in 1853. As Empress she was acclaimed the beauty of Paris, but the marriage was not a success. She was unresponsive and the Emperor consoled himself elsewhere. With the birth of the Prince Imperial in 1856, she reached emotional maturity, and centred all her love upon her son. She came to England in 1870 at the fall of the French Empire. When the Prince Imperial was killed in the Zulu War of 1879 she was inconsolable.
See **pls. C-34, 35, 36, 37, 38, 39, 40.**

EVANS, SIR GEORGE DE LACY (1787–1870). *See* **De Lacy Evans.**

FAIRBROTHER (FAREBROTHER), LOUISA (1816–90). Born the daughter of a Bow Street painter. As a young girl she went on the stage, calling herself Lucy Farebrother or Fairbrother. She could both act and dance, an unusual combination for actresses of her day. She was extremely pretty and was a hit in *The Forty Thieves*, *Aladdin* and as 'Little John' in *Robin Hood*. She was one of the first to dance the polka. She contracted a morganatic marriage in 1840 with George, second Duke of Cambridge who, as a young soldier, saw her 'on the boards' at the Lyceum and fell in love with her. Thereafter she was known as **Mrs FitzGeorge.** She lived on the most affectionate terms with her husband and was devoted to her children. When her husband was wounded at Inkerman, Louisa rushed out to nurse him. This act of devotion weakened Victoria's prejudices, although officially the marriage continued to be non-existent. Nevertheless the Fitz-George coachmen and footmen wore royal livery and the Prince of Wales openly admired her. At her funeral her coffin was covered with flowers sent by every member of the royal family.

Figures of her are titled 'Duchess'. Either the potters thought she was a duchess or gave her this courtesy title in deference to her popularity.
See **pl. C-59.**

FITZGEORGE, Mrs LOUISA (1816–90). *See* **Fairbrother (Farebrother), Louisa.**

FRANKLIN, LADY JANE (1792–1875). Married Sir John Franklin in 1828. Travelled in Syria and Asia Minor with her husband. When her husband was Governor of Tasmania she gave much attention to female convicts. She fitted out, at her own expense, five ships to search for Franklin when he disappeared, while searching for the North-West passage. She received the founder's medal of the Geographical Society in 1860.
See **pl. C-28.**

FRANKLIN, SIR JOHN (1786–1847), English Arctic explorer born at Spilsby in Lincolnshire. He entered the navy at the age of 14 and was present at the battles of Copenhagen, 1801 and Trafalgar, 1805. From 1819 to 1822 and again from 1825 to 1827 he made extensive land journeys along the Coppermine river and the Canadian arctic coast. Knighted, 1829. Governor of Tasmania, 1834–45. In 1845, he commanded the *Erebus* and *Terror* in an attempt

to discover the North-West passage. He was last sighted at the entrance to Lancaster Sound on July 26th, 1845. From 1847 to 1857 thirty-nine expeditions were sent to find him. A number of these were financed by Lady Franklin. Traces of ships and provisions were found on Beechey Island in 1850. In 1854 Sir Leopold McClintock, in Lady Franklin's yacht *Fox* came upon a boat, skeletons and a paper stating that the ships had been deserted on April 22nd, 1848 after nineteen months in the ice. Franklin had died on June 11th, 1847. The 105 survivors under Captain Crozier died of starvation whilst attempting to reach one of the Hudson Bay Company's posts. Franklin has since been recognized as the discoverer of the North-West passage.
See **pls. C**-28, 29.

FREDERICK III, German Emperor and eighth King of Prussia (1831–88). *For biography see* **section A.**
See **pls. A**-67, 68, 70, 71,
pls. C-108, 112.

FREDERICK CHARLES, Prince of Prussia (1828–85), field-marshal, also known as the 'Red Prince' from his favourite Hussar uniform. Son of Prince Charles, the brother of Emperor William I. Commanded the second army in the Franco-Prussian War of 1870. Defeated Bazaine at Metz, captured Orleans and broke up the army of the Loire. His daughter, Princess Louise of Prussia married Arthur, Duke of Connaught in 1879.
See **pl. C**-109.

FREDERICK WILLIAM, Crown Prince of Prussia (1831–88).
See **Frederick III.**

FRENCH, JOHN DENTON PINK-STONE, first Earl of Ypres (1852–1925), field-marshal. Born in Ripple, Kent. Joined the navy in 1866 and the army in 1874. Served in Wolseley's expedition for relief of Gordon, 1884–5. On outbreak of South African War, was despatched to Natal to command mounted troops under Sir G. S. White. His record of success as a cavalry commander in South Africa was unbroken, 1899–1901. Lieutenant-general, 1902; field-marshal, 1913. Chief of Imperial General Staff, 1911–4. Was in supreme command of the British Expeditionary Force in France, 1914–5. Created Viscount and appointed commander-in-chief of home forces in 1916. Created Earl of Ypres in 1921.
See **pls. C**-126, 127, 131, 132, 135.

GARIBALDI, GIUSEPPE (1807–82), Italian soldier and patriot. Was condemned to death in 1834 for being concerned in a plot to seize a government vessel, but escaped to South America where he spent some years in various revolutionary activities. He returned to Italy in 1848 and joined the Roman republican movement, but was ultimately compelled to flee, emigrating to New York. In 1854 he again returned to Italy, and on the outbreak of war in 1859 rendered valuable service to Victor Emmanuel in the cause of Italian liberation. After the peace of Villafranca he helped annex various territories to Sardinia. On May 11th, 1860 Garibaldi and 'the thousand' landed at Marsala. The men, dressed in plain clothes or red shirts, were

armed with muskets fit for a scrap-heap. Nevertheless the 'Liberator' with the aid of the Sicilian populace took the capital from 24,000 regular troops armed with rifles. Within three months Sicily was freed. Later, they crossed the straits and entered Naples. In February, 1861 Victor Emmanuel was proclaimed King of Italy. Garibaldi refused all reward, but Rome still occupied his thoughts and in 1862 he embarked on an ill-considered expedition to the capital. The Italian government sent troops against him and he was taken prisoner at Aspromonte. In 1864 he visited England and was welcomed with great enthusiasm. Garibaldi and his 'Red Shirts' were the heroes in the story of Italian independence. Although a good commander of regulars, he sometimes showed an ignorance of politics that did his cause harm. In later years he was crippled by rheumatism.
See **pls. C**-96, 97, 98, 99, 100, 101, 102, 103, 104,
pl. H-2.

GEORGE WILLIAM FREDERICK CHARLES, second Duke of Cambridge (1819–1904), field-marshal and commander-in-chief of the army. Son of Adolphus, duke of Cambridge, seventh son of George III. In 1840 he contracted a morganatic marriage to the actress Louisa Fairbrother, afterwards known as Mrs FitzGeorge. Commanded a division in the Crimea and was present at Alma. Was 'grazed by a bullet' at Inkerman and subsequently fell ill. His devoted wife rushed out to nurse him. Promoted field-marshal in 1862. Commander-in-chief of the army from 1856 to 1895. He was known as 'The Umbrella Duke' on account of taking an umbrella on parade instead of a sword when the weather was bad.
See **pls. C**-30, 59, 60, 67.

GHOLAB SINGH, Maharaja (1792–1857), otherwise known as either **Gulab Singh** or **Goolab Singh**. Sikh chief who appears to have been a prime mover in the first Sikh War, both in the intrigues at Lahore as well as in the negotiations with the British. In August 1845 he sought 'British protection' on the strength of the help he had rendered in the Afghan War, placing his own services and those of his chiefs at the disposal of the British. He offered to attack the Sikhs and to so divide the Lahore government, the army, and the people, as to enable the British to march into the Punjab and occupy its capital with the minimum of violence. In return he was to receive as a reward the kingdom of Jammu and Kashmir. It has been said of him that:

Like a brazen-faced traitor he had forgotten all the patronage and favours he had received from Maharaja Ranjit Singh[1] and became an easy tool in the hands of the British for carrying out their designs on the Sikh kingdom.

Henry Hardinge, Governor-General of India, writing to Sir Charles Napier said:

Gulab Singh was the most thorough ruffian that ever was created—a villain from the kingdom down to a penny.

Henry Havelock wrote in 1846:

If a painter sought to employ all the smooth cunning of Asiatic intrigue in one face, he would throw away his sketches as soon as he saw that Gulab Singh, cease to draw on his imagination and limn (portray) the features of Rao Sahib, as the Lahore people call him, with fidelity.

On February 10th, 1846 the commander-in-chief, Sir Hugh Gough and a force of twenty thousand men attacked the Sikhs on

the British side of the Sutlej river at a place on the Sobraon and after a hard fought bloody engagement totally defeated them at all points. The Sikhs were compelled to submit. British troops reached Lahore on February 20th without further opposition. At the Treaty of Lahore, signed in March 1846, the Sikhs agreed to pay one and a half million pounds sterling to defray the expenses of war. Jammu and Kashmir were transferred to Gulab Singh in independent sovereignty in reward for his services to the British. On March 15th 1846, Gulab Singh was formally invested with the title of 'Maharaja'. The policy of rewarding this unscrupulous villain for treachery to the Lahore side was questioned at the time, but he was regarded as an able ruler, amenable to British influence. On his death in 1857 he was succeeded by his son, Ranbir Singh.

1. *Maharaja Ranjit Singh* (1780 1839), known as the 'Lion of the Punjab' was ruler of Lahore and directed all his energies to founding a kingdom which should unite all the Sikh provinces. He was suceeded by *Maharaja Duleep Singh* who was aged seven years and a half at the time of the first Sikh War. He was exiled by Britain and sent to England in 1846 after the Treaty of Lahore.

See **pl. C**-27.

GORDON, CHARLES GEORGE (1833–85), British soldier born at Woolwich. He entered Woolwich Academy in 1847 and the Royal Engineers in 1852. He was wounded in the trenches before Sebastopol in 1855 and took part in the attack on the Redan. In 1860 he went to China and took part in the capture of Peking. From 1863 to 1864 he was in command of a Chinese force that fought thirty-three actions against the Taipings, being known afterwards as 'Chinese Gordon'. In 1873 he was made governor of the equatorial provinces in Egypt. In 1877 he went out to the Sudan for the Egyptian government, and in 1884 revisited the territory on behalf of the English government, to deal once more with the difficulties which had arisen consequent on the Mahdi's rebellion. The Mahdi was a religious leader whose aim was to bring back the people of Egypt and the Sudan, ruled in his eyes by an alien prince who had departed from the injunctions of the Prophet, to a right way of life. He was also a leader with considerable political and military skill. On January 26th, 1885, whilst defending beleaguered Khartoum, Gordon was murdered by the Mahdi's forces on the palace staircase. The siege of Khartoum had lasted 317 days, the relief of Gordon having been delayed. The chicanery of Gladstone and the ineptitude of his cabinet provoked a public outcry at the time. In addition to being a distinguished soldier and administrator, Gordon was also an earnest Christian.
See **pls. C**-119, 127.

GORDON HIGHLANDERS, otherwise known as 'The Gay Gordons'. One of the most famous regiments of the British army. It now constitutes part of the Highland Brigade. The regiment was raised in 1794 by the Marquess of Huntly, afterwards fifth and last Duke of Gordon. Battle honours include India, the Kaffir War in South Africa, the Indian Mutiny and the Egyptian campaign of 1882. During the Boer War the regiment formed part of General Sir George White's force defending Ladysmith.
See **pl. C**-136.

GREENWICH HOSPITAL PENSIONERS. The Royal Hospital, Greenwich which first received pensioners in 1705, was a royal charity for seamen the main purpose of which was not clinical, but rather to provide a home for the care of the aged and infirm. Amongst the latter there were, of course, many amputees. Every seaman contributed to the upkeep of the hospital by being mulcted sixpence a month out of his wages. The rules laid down for pensioners included directives with regard to dress and behaviour. They were to wear a blue coat, a waistcoat and breeches of brown cloth, blue stockings and a black cocked hat. They were punished for drunkenness, uncleanness, theft, lying, begging outside the gates, smoking anywhere except in the Chalk Walk, keeping pigeons or selling their victuals outside, by wearing a yellow coat and a red collar, the blue coat being turned inside out to display the punishment colours. Pensioners were permitted to wander outside the hospital grounds to the alehouses and slums of Greenwich. They were given a ticket for free board and one shilling a week pocket money with an allowance for a wife, provided she was not employed as a nurse.
See **pl.** C-76.

HAVELOCK, SIR HENRY, first Baronet (1795–1857), major-general. Born in Sunderland and educated at Charterhouse and the Middle Temple. He entered the army a month after Waterloo. Fought in Afghanistan, 1840. Assisted Sir R. Sale in holding Jellalabad, 1841. Fought in the Sikh Wars, 1845–6. On the outbreak of the Indian Mutiny he organized a column of Highlanders at Allahabad with which to relieve Cawnpore and Lucknow. He engaged and broke the rebels at Fatehpur and entered Cawnpore, seeing the horrors of the massacre. He then crossed the Ganges, but after several victories had to retire to Cawnpore, owing to sickness in his army. In September, 1857 Outram arrived with reinforcements and Havelock again advanced, Outram waiving his superior rank. The relieving force engaged the enemy three miles from Lucknow and fought their way thence to the Residency, thus effecting the first relief of Lucknow. However, they in turn were besieged until November, when Sir Colin Campbell forced his way to their rescue. Havelock, who had already been created a KCB, died of dysentery on November 24th, 1857, a week after the second relief. At the foot of the monument, by William Behnes, erected to Havelock's memory in Trafalgar Square in 1861, is recorded his famous remark:

> Soldiers! Your Labours
> Your Privations Your Sufferings,
> Will not be Forgotten by a Grateful Country.

The rank of a baronet's widow and a pension were given to his widow, and the baronetcy was conferred on his son Sir Henry Havelock-Allan, VC (1830–97).
See **pls.** C-56, 57, 67, 89, 90, 91A, 92, 92A, 92B.

HIGHLAND JESSIE (dates unknown). *See* **Brown, Jessie.**

HUSSARS. Originally a name applied to Hungarian cavalry whose duties were scouting, reconnaissance and roving commissions. Speed being an essential feature, they had to travel light. At the beginning of the nineteenth century some Light Brigade regiments were converted into Hussars. The distinctive features of the dress are busby, ribbed short jacket, and pelisse, or hanging jacket, worn over the left shoulder. Their roll of honour includes Waterloo and the Crimea. The type of fighting in the South African War (1899–1902) was particularly suited to cavalry, and the Hussars had their full share of action.
See **pl.** C-138.

IMPERIAL, PRINCE (1856–79). *See* **Eugene Louis Jean Joseph.**

ITALY, King of (1820–78).
See **Victor Emmanuel II.**

KITCHENER, HORATIO HERBERT, first Earl Kitchener of Khartoum and of Broome (1850–1916), soldier and statesman. Born in Kerry. Commissioned in Royal Engineers, 1871. Took part in Wolseley's expedition for the relief of Gordon from 1884 to 1885. British commander-in-chief of the Egyptian Army (sirdar), 1892. Began to prepare for reconquest of the Sudan. As General Sir Herbert Kitchener, he executed the campaign that finally avenged the death of General Gordon. Proceeding up the Nile valley, he annihilated the Khalifa's army at Omdurman, with great loss of dervishes, and reoccupied Khartoum, 1898. Created baron in the same year. Churchill, who had been present at Omdurman, published an historical account of the reconquest of the Sudan, *The River War* (1899); his sharp criticism of Kitchener caused a sensation in military circles. Kitchener was in turn chief of the staff to Lord Roberts and commander-in-chief in South Africa, 1899–1902. At the conclusion of the Boer War he was created Viscount. Field-marshal, 1909. Secretary of State for War, 1914; reorganized the army. Disagreed with Churchill over conduct of Dardanelles operation and advised abandonment of Gallipoli campaign, 1915. Drowned when the *Hampshire* was sunk on the way to Russia in June, 1916.
See **pls.** C-119, 121, 122, 124, 128, 129, 132, 135.

21st LANCERS, famous for their charge at the Battle of Omdurman, September 2nd, 1898. Several VC's were won and in recognition of their courage they were given the title 'Empress of India's'. This was the last of the great cavalry charges in the tradition of that of the Light Brigade in the Crimea—the last flourish of nineteenth century warfare before the machine-gun took control. As a military operation it was not an unqualified success. Some three hundred lancers took part. Whilst riding to cut off a body of the enemy they stumbled suddenly into a shallow ravine containing several thousand Dervishes. Launching themselves at full gallop, they went straight through the solid mass which was about twenty deep. It was all over in under three minutes and when the Lancers regrouped, they found seventy of their number cut down and one hundred and nineteen horses killed, whilst but forty or fifty Dervishes lay dead. Sir Winston Churchill, at that time a lieutenant in the 4th Hussars, twenty-four years of age, was attached to the Lancers. Unable to hold a lance because of a recently dislocated shoulder, he carried a pistol. Finding himself alone among the Dervishes at the end of the charge, he managed to shoot his way back into the British lines. Of the charge he wrote:

> I am glad to have added the experience of a cavalry charge to my military repertoire . . . It was I suppose the most dangerous 2 minutes I shall live to see.

See **pl.** C-123.

LYONS, Edmund, first Baron Lyons (1790–1858), admiral and diplomat. Entered the navy, 1803. Saw active service in the East Indies, 1810–1. Post-captain, 1814. In 1828, while commanding the *Blonde*, he shared in blockade of Navarino. In 1835, appointed English minister in Athens. Created baronet in 1840. Minister to Swiss confederation, 1849–51. Promoted rear-admiral, 1850. Minister at Stockholm, 1851–3. In 1853, appointed second-in-command of the Black Sea fleet under Admiral Sir James Deans Dundas. The sinking by the Russians of their ships in the harbour of Sebastopol, did not allow him the opportunity of a great naval engagement, but he displayed the most signal bravery in the sea attack on the great forts. Appointed to the chief command of the fleet on the resignation of Admiral Dundas in January 1855, but was prevented by a strong gale from co-operating in the final and successful attack on Sebastopol in September of that year. In June, 1856 he was raised to the peerage.
See **pl.** C-42A.

MACDONALD, SIR HECTOR ARCHIBALD (1853–1903), major-general. Joined the army as a private in the Gordon Highlanders, 1870. Served with distinction in the second Afghan War, 1879–80. Won nickname of 'Fighting Mac'. Promoted second lieutenant in 1880. Shared in the Nile Expedition of 1885. Distinguished in the Sudan campaign of 1888–91. Displayed adroitness and courage at Omdurman, September 1898. Brigadier-general in Punjab, 1899–1900. Promoted to major-general in 1900. In South African War he prepared the way for the relief of Kimberley, February 1900. An unsavoury accusation prompted him to shoot himself in Paris in 1903.
See **pls.** C-121, 125, 128, 129, 130, 135.

MACMAHON, MARIE EDME PATRICE MAURICE (1808–93), French marshal descended from Irish Jacobite family. After entering the army he served in Algeria. Commanded at Malakoff in 1855. In 1859 was made marshal and Duke of Magenta. Governor-general of Algeria in 1864. In the Franco-Prussian War of 1870 he commanded the first army corps but was defeated at Wörth and captured at Sedan. In 1873 elected President of the Republic for seven years. Resigned in 1879 and died at Château la Forêt.
See **pl.** C-106.

MALAKOFF. An outwork of Sebastopol in the Crimea.
See **pl.** C-69.

MERYON, CHARLES LEWIS (1783–1877), physician and biographer of Lady Hester Stanhope (*q.v.*). Educated at Oxford and St. Thomas's Hospital. Accompanied Lady Hester Stanhope as medical attendant, 1810. Is known to have dressed as a

Bedouin. MD, 1817; FRCP, 1821. Revisited Lady Hester Stanhope in Syria in 1821. Published *Memoirs of Lady Hester Stanhope* (1845) and *Travels of Lady Hester Stanhope* (1846).
See **pl. C**-95A,
pl. I-36.

MOLTKE, HELMUTH, Count von
(1800–91), Prussian field-marshal. Entered Prussian service in 1822. Appointed to the staff in 1832. Between 1835 and 1839 he assisted the Sultan in remodelling the Turkish army. From 1858 to 1888 was chief of the general staff in Berlin and reorganized the Prussian army. He was a great strategist as was evident by the successful wars with Denmark in 1863-4, with Austria in 1866 and in the Franco-Prussian War of 1870-1. Known as 'The Silent', he was a man of great modesty and simplicity. In 1841, he married Marie von Burt (1825–68), his step-sister's daughter by an English father.
See **pls. C**-109, 110.

NAPIER, SIR CHARLES (1786–1860),
British admiral. Born near Falkirk, he was a cousin to Sir Charles James Napier (1782-1853), British general and hero of Sind. He went to sea at 13 and received his first command in 1808. He commanded the *Thames* in 1811, inflicting severe damage on the enemy in the Mediterranean. In 1814 he led the way in the ascent of the Potomac. In command of the fleet of the young Queen of Portugal, he defeated the Miguelite fleet and placed Donna Maria on the throne. Took part in the storming of Sidon in 1840. Created KCB, 1840. He commanded the Baltic fleet in the Crimean War, 1854. The public's expectations ran high:

> Don't you know the wrong you're doing?
> Mighty Czar! Mighty Czar!
> Don't you see there's mischief brewing?
> Mighty Czar!
> France and England in one council,
> Are impatient for the day,
> And are steaming to the Baltic
> Ripe and ready for the fray.
> We have hearts that never fail us,
> So look out for wounds and scars
> For there's Charlie Napier coming,
> With his gallant Jack Tars!
> For there's Charlie Napier coming,
> With his Jolly Jack Tars!

He captured Bomarsund; but because of lack of gun-boats was unable to accomplish anything against Cronstadt or Sweaborg. A public clamour was created against him; he quarrelled with Sir James Graham, the first Lord of the Admiralty and was in consequence dismissed from his command, being superseded by R. S. Dundas. He sat twice in Parliament and spent much of his life labouring to reform the naval administration. It has been said of him that he was 'a strange medley of naval skill and courage, eccentricity, slovenliness, shrewdness and imprudence. He was excitable, vain, choleric, frank, and truthful; fond of fun and frolic; self-confident, full of daring, ambition, energy and indomitable will'.
See **pls. C**-41, 42, 43.

NAPIER, ROBERT CORNELIS, first
Baron Napier of Magdala (1810–90), field-marshal. Born at Colombo, he entered the Bengal Engineers in 1826. He served in campaigns in India and distinguished himself at Lucknow during the Indian Mutiny. He received the thanks of Parliament for his services both in the Chinese War of 1860 and

for his conduct of the expedition in Abyssinia in 1868, for which he was created a baron. In 1870 he became commander-in-chief in India and was subsequently governor of Gibraltar, field-marshal and constable of the Tower.
See **pls. C**-104, 105.

NAPOLEON I, or NAPOLEON BONAPARTE
(1769–1821). Born in Corsica, he was sent to France to receive a military education, being commissioned second lieutenant of artillery in 1785. In 1794 he served in Italy with such distinction that he won a generalship, and on the following year was appointed commander-in-chief. There followed a series of astonishing successes. The Austrian forces were defeated in 1797. After conducting an expedition to Syria and Egypt in 1798, he returned in 1799 to find himself the most popular man in France. In November of that year he proclaimed himself 'First Consul'. In 1800 after crossing the Alps, via the St. Bernard Pass, he gained further victories in Italy. The defeat of the Austrians at Marengo on June 14th resulted in almost all Northern Italy passing into French hands. In 1804 he was proclaimed Emperor. In 1805, having abandoned his notion to invade England on account of her naval supremacy, he was again in the field against England, Russia, and Austria, achieving a series of victories at Austerlitz and elsewhere. He became dictator of Europe, distributing kingships amongst his brothers. Thus Joseph became King of Naples, Louis King of Holland, and Jérôme King of Westphalia. However, the tide began to turn and his invasion of Russia proved disastrous, the Peninsular War went against him, and in 1814 the allies entered Paris and forced him to abdicate. He was sent to the island of Elba and Louis XVIII was restored to the French throne. In 1815, he made his escape and gathering his old army, sallied forth to meet the English and Prussian armies. The result was his final defeat at Waterloo on June 18th 1815. He fled to Paris but abdicated on June 22nd and surrendered to Captain Maitland of the *Bellerophon* at Rochefort on July 15th. He was banished to St. Helena, where he died in 1821. His body was brought back and laid in the crypt of Les Invalides, Paris in 1840.
See **pl. B**-5,
pls. C-11, 12, 12A, 13, 14, 14A, 15, 16, 17 18, 19, 22, 23, 23A, 24, 25.

NAPOLEON III, CHARLES LOUIS
NAPOLEON BONAPARTE (1808–73). Born at Paris, the third son of Louis Bonaparte, king of Holland. After several unsuccessful attempts to secure the French throne and years of imprisonment, he took advantage of the revolution of 1848, in which Louis-Philippe was overthrown, to return to France. Following the coup d'état of December 2nd, 1851, he emerged as master of France. He was proclaimed Emperor the following year. In 1853, he married Eugénie d'Montijo, a Spanish countess of great beauty. He was Britain's ally during the Crimean War (1854-6) and had her support in the campaign against Austria (1859) and the expeditions to China (1857-60). He was dictatorial and discredited at home and his surrender at Sedan in the Franco-Prussian War of 1870 brought ruin to the Second Empire. France once again became a republic. He took refuge in

England in 1871 and died at Chislehurst in Kent.
See **pls. C**-32, 33, 34, 35, 37, 38, 39, 40, 77, 78, 78A, 79, 93, 110.

NAPOLEON, PRINCE (1822–91). *See*
Bonaparte, Napoleon Joseph Charles Paul.

NELSON, HORATIO, Viscount Nelson
(1758–1805), vice-admiral. Entered the navy, 1770. Much of his early life was spent in service in the West Indies. When captain of the *Boreas* frigate he met Fanny Nisbet, widow of Dr Nisbet of Nevis, and married her in 1787. Soon after, his health broke down, and he returned to England from the West Indies with his wife. He lived in retirement for five years at his birth-place, Burnham Thorpe, Norfolk. In 1793, he was given the 74-gun ship *Agamemnon* and sailed for the Mediterranean. In July, 1794 while engaged in the siege of Calvi in Corsica, his journal records that he was 'much bruised about the face and eyes by sand from the works struck by a shot.' However, he made light of the matter in a letter to his wife in which he referred to the wound as 'a very slight scratch towards my right eye which has not been the smallest inconvenience' and again, 'a blemish, not to be perceived unless told'. Nevertheless, it later appeared that he had lost the use of his right eye. It seems, however, that the eye was externally normal. It is possible that he suffered a detachment of the retina but the exact nature of the injury must remain uncertain. In later years he often wore a green shade to protect his left eye from the sun's glare. Because he strained this eye so much, it was the opinion of Beatty, the surgeon of the *Victory* that he would soon have become totally blind had he not been killed.

In 1797, at the Battle of Cape St Vincent he received an abdominal injury, but a more serious wound was sustained five months later at the unsuccessful landing at Santa Cruz, Teneriffe when a grape-shot shattered his right elbow. After being given the usual tot of rum and a leather pad to bite on, an amputation was carried out 'very high, near the shoulder' aboard the *Theseus*. Although the stump healed well in time, he suffered from phantom pains for the rest of his life.

At Aboukir Bay in 1798, he again narrowly escaped with his life, being struck on the forehead by a piece of langridge. A tremendous reception awaited him on his return to Naples. Here he fell in love with Lady Hamilton, wife of the English ambassador—a liaison which only death severed. The Battle of Copenhagen, 1801, the hardest fought of all Nelson's battles, was the only one in which he himself was not wounded. Between June 16th, 1803 and July 19th, 1805 when he landed at Gibraltar after chasing Villeneuve to the West Indies and back, Nelson did not set foot on shore. On October 21st, 1805 the French fleet was at last engaged off Cape Trafalgar. During the action Nelson insisted on standing on the quarter-deck wearing all his medals and orders, and was shot from the tops of the *Redoubtable* at a range of only fifteen yards. The ball struck the epaulette on the left shoulder and penetrated through the lung to the spine with some gold braid adhering to it. The dying admiral was carried to the cockpit, his face covered with a handkerchief. As he laid down he turned to his surgeon and said 'Ah Mr Beatty, you can do' nothing for me. I have but a short time to live . . . my back is shot through'. Beatty on Nelson's directive began to attend to the other wounded and left Revd Dr Scott, the chaplain and Mr Burke, the purser to support the admiral whilst he amputated the leg of a midshipman. Fifty minutes later the surgeon returned and at the same time, Captain Hardy appeared and gave Nelson the news of victory. He died moments later. According to Beatty:

There was no lead on board to make a coffin: a cask called a leaguer, which is of the largest size on shipboard, was therefore chosen for the reception of the Body; which, after the hair had been cut off, was stripped of the clothes except the shirt, and put into it, and the cask was then filled with brandy.

After arrival of the *Victory* at Spithead, the body was taken from the cask; an autopsy was performed and the fatal bullet extracted. Eventually the body was placed in a wooden coffin made from the mainmast of the *L'Orient*, after the battle of the Nile. After lying-in-state in the Painted Hall at Greenwich, he was interred at St. Paul's.
See **pls.** C-6, 7, 8, 9, 10, 11, 12, 14, 16, 16A.

NIGHTINGALE, FLORENCE (1820–1910). Reformer of hospital nursing. Born in Florence. Trained as a nurse at the Kaiserswerth Institute, 1851, and in Paris. Was engaged in hospital visiting and nursing both in London and abroad. Became the superintendent of the Hospital for Invalid Gentlewomen, Chandos Street, 1853. Soon after the outbreak of the Crimean War she was invited by the Secretary of War to take out nurses to the Crimea. She reached Scutari on November 4th, 1854, arriving in time to receive the wounded from Inkerman. By exerting her tremendous powers of organization and discipline she revolutionized the conditions at the army hospital. She established kitchen and laundry facilities and looked after the soldier's wives and children. She was christened by the wounded patients 'The Lady with the Lamp'. By instituting rigid sanitary reforms she reduced the cases of cholera, typhus and dysentery. She herself was attacked by fever when visiting the hospitals at Balaclava in May, 1855. She returned to England in 1856 and visited Queen Victoria at Balmoral. A fund of £50,000 was subscribed with which she formed an institution for the training of nurses at St Thomas's and at King's College Hospital. The remainder of her life was devoted to the question of army sanitary reform and to the improvement of nursing. Received the Order of Merit, 1907.
See **pls.** C-54, 54A, 54B, 55, 73.

OMAR PASHA, properly Michael Latas (1806–71), Turkish general. Born at Plasky in Croatia. Initially served in the Austrian army but in 1828 deserted, fled to Bosnia and embracing Mohammedanism, became writing-master to Abd-ul-Medjid. On the accession of the latter to the Ottoman throne in 1839, Omar Pasha was made colonel, and in 1842, governor of Lebanon. On the invasion of the Danubian Principalities by the Russians in 1853, Omar Pasha with an army of 60,000 men, crossed the Danube and defeated the Russians. He arrived in the Crimea in February, 1855 and repulsed 40,000 Russians at Eupatoria, but was sent too late to relieve Kars.

See **pls.** C-30, 53, 54, 62, 62A, 63, 64, 65, 66, 67A.

PEARD, JOHN WHITEHEAD (1811–80), 'Garibaldi's Englishman'. Said to have been of great stature and extraordinary muscular strength, he joined Garibaldi's forces in 1859. He distinguished himself at the battle of Melazzo in 1860 and commanded the English Legion during Garibaldi's advance on Naples. Awarded the Cross of the Order of Valour by Victor Emmanuel. He was so like Garibaldi that he impersonated him on one critical occasion. He was visited by Garibaldi in England in 1864.
See **pls.** C-98, 100, 101, 101A, 102.

PELISSIER, AIMABLE JEAN JACQUES, Duc de Malakoff (1794–1864), French marshal. Born near Rouen. Served in Spain in 1823, and in Algeria in 1830 and 1839. Commanded the First Corps in the Crimea in 1854 and succeeded Canrobert as commander-in-chief before Sebastopol. He was made Marshal and Duc de Malakoff for storming the fortress of Malakoff, an outwork of Sebastopol. French ambassador in London, 1858–9.
See **pls.** C-44, 46, 47, 51A, 54, 67.

PRINCE IMPERIAL (1856–79).
See **Eugene Louis Jean Joseph**.

PRINCE NAPOLEON (1822–91).
See **Bonaparte, Napoleon Joseph Charles Paul**.

RAFFET (1804–60), painter and engraver. Produced a host of lithographs of the Napoleonic era. He had an eye for the amusing side of warfare, yet he was anything but oblivious to the gruesome side of a campaign, as evidenced by the excellent prints illustrating Napoleon's ill-starred attempt to march into Russia.
See **pl.** C-18.

RAGLAN, FITZROY JAMES HENRY SOMERSET, first Baron (1788–1855), field-marshal. Entered the army in 1804. Was present at Waterloo and lost his 'sword' arm during the action. Thereafter sat in Parliament as MP for Truro and spent many years in the War Office. Elevated to the peerage in 1852. Promoted field-marshal in 1854, and nominated to head the expeditionary force against the Russians in the Crimea. Gained an initial victory at Alma on September, 20th, 1854. Censored Lucan for the blunder and loss of the Light Brigade at Balaclava, October 25th, 1854 and ordered his recall. Showed bravery at Inkerman on November 5th, for which he was thanked by Queen Victoria. There followed the weary months of siege warfare about Sebastopol during the terrible winter of 1854–5, during which he was made the scapegoat of mismanagement. Was deeply disturbed by the failure of the attack on Malakoff and the Redan on June 18th, 1855 and died ten days later 'an unprotesting victim of the cabinet's unpreparedness and inefficiency'.
See **pls.** C-30, 45, 50, 51, 53, 56, 58, 63, 64, 65, 66.

RANBIR SINGH, Maharaja (d. 1885). Son of Gholab Singh (Gulab Singh), he succeeded his father as maharaja of the state of Jammu and Kashmir in 1857. Because of his loyalty during the Indian Mutiny was granted the right of adoption in lieu of natural heirs.
See **pl.** C-27.

REDAN, THE. An outwork of Sebastopol in the Crimea.
See **pl.** C-70.

ROBERTS, FREDERICK SLEIGH, first Earl of Kandahar, Pretoria and Waterford (1832–1914), field-marshal. Born at Cawnpore and educated at Sandhurst. Served in the Indian Mutiny, 1857–8. Won VC in 1858. Accompanied Sir Robert Napier, later Lord Napier of Magdala, on Abyssinian expedition. Conducted the famous march from Kabul to Kandahar, resulting in the pacification of Afghanistan, 1880. Created baronet in 1880. Commander-in-chief in India, 1885–93. Baron, 1892; field-marshal, 1895. Appointed to supreme command in South Africa at the end of 1899. He at once increased the number of mounted troops, and with the help of Lord Kitchener remodelled transport. Returned to England after the annexation of Transvaal in October, 1900. He was created Earl, in 1901, for services in saving the situation in the South African War. Commander-in-chief from 1900 to 1905. Died in France when colonel-in-chief of the Indian Expeditionary Force, 1914.
See **pls.** C-119, 122, 124, 127, 129, 132, 135.

SAINT-ARNAUD, JACQUES LEROY DE (1796–1854), French marshal. Born at Bordeaux, made his reputation in Algeria. Recalled by Louis Napoleon, and as War Minister took an active part in the coup d'état of December 2nd, 1851. For this he was awarded the marshal's baton. Was commander-in-chief of the French army in the Crimea, and co-operated with Lord Raglan at Alma, but died nine days later on his way home to France.
See **pls.** C-30, 64, 65, 66.

SALE, LADY FLORENTIA (1790–1853). Married Sir Robert Henry Sale in 1809 and was in Kabul in 1842. She shared the horrors of the British retreat and was taken captive, but her party was subsequently rescued by Sir Richmond Shakespeare. Her *Journal of the Disasters in Afghanistan* (1843) is one of the authorities for the campaign. After galloping through a narrow pass under fire, she recorded dryly 'fortunately, I had only *one* ball in my arm'. She died at Cape Town in 1853.
See **pl.** C-26.

SALE, SIR ROBERT HENRY (1782–1845), British colonel. Commissioned in 1795, he fought at Seringapatam, 1799; the capture of Mauritius, 1810; and in the Burmese War, 1824–5. Commanded advanced brigade in the first Afghan campaign, 1838–40. Entered Kandahar, April 1839. Created KCB, 1839. In command of the British retreat from Kabul, 1842. Served in the Sikh War, 1845 and died from effects of wounds received at Mudki.
See **pl.** C-26.

SARDINIA, King of (1820–78).
See **Victor Emmanuel II**.

SARSFIELD, PATRICK, Earl of Lucan (? 1645–93).
See **section A.**

SEBASTOPOL. A Russian fortress in the Crimea which was besieged by the allies from October, 1854 until its fall in September, 1855.
See **pl. C**-69.

SIMPSON, SIR JAMES (1792–1868), general. Served with the Grenadier Guards in Peninsular War, 1812–3. Second in command to Sir Charles James Napier in Kacchi expedition, 1845. Chief of staff in the Crimea, 1854. Succeeded Lord Raglan as commander of the British troops on his death in July, 1855. Created GCB and promoted general after the capture of Sebastopol. Resigned, November 1855.
See **pls. C**-44, 56.

SOLDIER'S DREAM, THE. Poem by the Scottish poet Thomas Campbell (1777–1844). Campbell travelled in Germany and Denmark, 1800–1. At Ratisbon (Regensburg), where he stayed at a time of military stress and danger, he witnessed a skirmish, this being his only experience of active warfare. He was at Altona (Hamburg) at the time of the battle of Hohenlinden, December 1800. During this sojourn he produced *Ye Mariners of England* and *The Soldier's Dream*. The sudden appearance of the English fleet off the sound, March 1801, indicating the intention of punishing Denmark for her French bias, caused Campbell and other English residents to make an abrupt departure from Altona. He landed at Yarmouth on April 17th, 1801. Although *The Soldier's Dream* was a poem of the Napoleonic era, there is little doubt that the same theme was very much in the minds of the public at the time of the Crimean War, hence the appearance of several figures portraying this subject.

THE SOLDIER'S DREAM
(First three verses)
Our bugles sang truce, for the night-cloud had lower'd
    And the sentinel stars set their watch in the sky;
And thousands had sunk on the ground overpower'd,
    The weary to sleep, and the wounded to die.

When reposing that night on my pallet of straw,
    By the wolf-scaring faggot that guarded the slain;
At the dead of the night a sweet Vision I saw,
    And thrice ere the morning I dreamt it again.

Methought from the battle-field's dreadful array,
    Far, far I had roam'd on a desolate track;
'Twas Autumn,—and sunshine arose on the way
    To the home of my fathers, that welcomed me back.
                                        T. Campbell
See **pls. C**-72, 73.

STANHOPE, LADY HESTER LUCY (1776–1839).
For biography see **section I.**
See **pl. A**-40,
pl. C-95A,
pls. I-36, 37.

STEWART, SIR HERBERT (1843–85), major-general. Brigade-major of cavalry in the Zulu War of 1879. Military secretary to Wolseley, 1880. Created KCB for services in Suakim campaign, 1884. In Wolseley's expedition for relief of Gordon, 1884–5. Mortally wounded when in command of desert column proceeding to Metemmeh.
See **pl. C**-118.

SULTAN, THE.
See either **Abd-ul-Hamid II** (1842–1918) *or* **Abd-ul-Medjid** (1823–61).

TANN, Baron von der (1815–81), Bavarian general. Born at Darmstadt in Germany. He served in the Schleswig-Holstein War of 1848–50 and against Prussia in 1866. He was commander of the first Bavarian Army Corps in the Franco-Prussian War of 1870, commanding independently on the Loire. He occupied Orleans on October 11th, 1870 but was defeated and driven out on November 9th. Orleans was finally retaken early in December. He died at Merano in the Tyrol.
See **pl. C**-109.

VICTOR EMMANUEL II, King of Sardinia and first King of Italy (1820–78). Son of Charles Albert; ascended the throne of Sardinia in 1849 on the latter's abdication. In 1852, appointed Cavour as his chief minister. In January 1855, Sardinia joined the allies against Russia, ten thousand men being landed in the Crimea. At the Congress of Paris (1856) the Sardinian envoys drew the attention of France and England to the oppressive government of the states of Italy. In 1857, diplomatic relations were broken off with Austria. When in 1859, Austria demanded the disarmament of Sardinia, this was refused and the following day the Austrians crossed the Ticino. The Austrians were defeated at Montebello, Magenta, and Solferino with the help of the French army. By the Treaty of Villafranca, Lombardy was ceded to Sardinia. In 1860 Parma, Modena, and the Romagna, together with Tuscany were annexed to Sardinia, and Sicily and Naples were added by Garibaldi. A French force of occupation protected the papal territories from annexation. In February 1861, Victor Emmanuel was proclaimed King of Italy at Turin. After the fall of the Empire in 1870, the French occupation came to an end and Victor Emmanuel entered Rome, the province being added to his kingdom.
See **pls. C**-32, 33, 38, 38A, 102, 103.

VICTORIA, Queen of the United Kingdom of Great Britain and Ireland and Empress of India (1819–1901).
For biography see **section A.**
See **pls. A**-2, 4, 5, 6, 7, 8, 9, 10, 11, 12, 13, 14, 15, 16, 17, 18, 19, 20, 21, 22, 23, 24, 25, 26, 27, 28, 28A, 29, 30, 31, 32, 33, 34, 35, 37, 38, 39, 40, 41, 44, 46, 48, 53, 55, 57, 81, 83, **pls. C**-32, 33, 38.

HMS VICTORY (first-rate 104-guns). Laid down in July 1759, in Chatham Dockyard, after a decision had been taken to build a first-rate of the finest type. She was launched in 1765, over 3,000,000 cu. ft. of oak having been required for her construction. She was completed in 1778 and despatched from Chatham to Portsmouth to hoist the flag of Admiral the Hon. Augustus Keppel, commander-in-chief of the Channel Fleet. A succession of admirals included such famous names as Sir Charles Hardy, Hyde Parker, Kempenfelt, Howe, Hood and Sir John Jarvis, later Lord St Vincent. She was involved in many lesser known actions until she first became a household word as a flag-ship at the Battle of Cape St Vincent. In the same year she was relegated to be a prison hospital ship on the

Medway. Later, she underwent a major reconstruction and was ready for sea again in 1803, being chosen by Nelson to be his flag-ship on his appointment as commander-in-chief of the Mediterranean. She took part in the tedious blockade off Toulon, and later in the glorious victory at Trafalgar, 1805. In 1815, she became the flag-ship of the commander-in-chief, Portsmouth. In 1832, the then Princess Victoria persuaded her mother, the Duchess of Kent, to take her to visit the old ship. This awoke the public interest and it subsequently became a fashionable amusement to go over the *Victory*. However, interest faded and by 1922 the vessel was falling to pieces. A 'Save the Victory Fund' was launched, and Sir J. Caird, a patriotic ship owner, raised a large sum of money to restore the old vessel to the appearance she held in her finest days. She was placed in a dry dock, where she has remained to this day.
See **pls. C**-7, 9.

VIZIR, LE (dates unknown), Napoleon's favourite horse. A thoroughbred white Arab, *Le Vizir* was presented to the Emperor by the Sultan of Turkey in 1805. He accompanied his master into exile at St Helena and outlived him. Branded with the initial 'N' and the imperial crown, he stands stuffed in Les Invalides, Paris, near Napoleon's tomb.
See **pl. C**-11.

VOLUNTEER RIFLES. In 1859, Austria demanded the disarmament of Sardinia. This was refused and a French army advanced to aid the Sardinians. The Austrians were defeated and in 1860 Savoy and Nice were ceded to France. The annexation of these territories by Napoleon III, aroused a grave suspicion of his intentions and caused a revival of the Volunteers. By the summer of 1860, 130,000 had been enrolled, 21,000 of whom were reviewed by the Queen in Hyde Park.
See **pl. C**-93,
pls. F-5, 5A.

VON DER TANN (1815–81). *See* **Tann, Baron von der**.

WELLESLEY, ARTHUR, first Duke of Wellington (1769–1852).
For biography see **section B.**
See **pls. B**-2, 2A, 2B, 3, 3A, 3B, 4, 4A, 5, 6, 25,
pls. C-10, 11, 14, 16B, 16C, 20, 21, 25.

WELLINGTON, first Duke of (1769–1852). *See* **Wellesley, Arthur** (sections B and C).

WILL WATCH, legendary privateer and smuggler with a Sussex background. Features as a hero in a number of melodramas, the best known of which being *Will Watch and his Black-Eyed Sue*.

T'was one morn when the wind from
    the northward blew keenly,
And suddenly wav'd the big waves
    of the main,
A fam'd smuggler, Will Watch, kissed
    his Sue, then serenely,
Took helm, and to sea boldly steer'd
    out again.

See **pl. C**-3,
pls. I-14, 14A, 15.

WILLIAM I, seventh King of Prussia and first German Emperor (1797–1888).

Son of Frederick-William III. In 1829, married Princess Augusta of Saxe–Weimar. In 1840, on accession of his brother, Frederick-William IV, he became heir-presumptive. In 1844, he visited England and formed friendship with Queen Victoria and Prince Albert. Succeeded his brother on his death in 1861. The defeat of the French in the Franco-Prussian War of 1870, was followed by the proclamation of William as first German Emperor on January 18th, 1871. Father of Prince Frederick William.
See **pls. C**-106, 107, 108, 111.

WILLIAMS, SIR WILLIAM FENWICK, Baronet 'of Kars' (1800–83), general. Educated at Woolwich. British Commissioner for the settlement of the Turko-Persian boundary, 1848. In 1854, during the Crimean War, was appointed British military commissioner with the Turkish army in Asia. He arrived at Kars in September to find the Turks utterly demoralized. With tremendous energy he corrected abuses and got rid of corrupt officers, becoming idolized by the Turkish army. In June 1855, the Russians advanced on Kars. After a heroic defence he was compelled to capitulate on November 25th. He was kept prisoner by the Russians until the peace, when he was given a baronetcy and an annuity of £1,000.
See **pl. C**-67.

WINDHAM, SIR CHARLES ASH (1810–70), lieutenant-general. Educated at Sandhurst. Served in Canada (1838–42). Colonel, 1854. Assistant and quartermaster-general of the 4th Division of Army of the East in Crimea, 1854. Served at Alma, Balaclava and Inkerman. Created CB in 1855. Commanded the 2nd Brigade of the 2nd Division at the assault on the Redan in 1855. Major-general, 1855. Commanded the 4th Division; chief of staff to Sir William J. Codrington, 1855. Commanded troops at Cawnpore, 1857.
See **pls. C**-43, 44.

WOLSELEY, GARNET JOSEPH, Viscount (1833–1913), field-marshal. Born in County Dublin of an old Staffordshire line. Joined the army in 1852. Served with distinction in the Crimean War, 1854–6; Indian Mutiny, 1857–9; and China War, 1860. Commanded the Red River expedition in 1870. Created KCMG in 1870. Sent to retrieve the situation in the Zulu War of 1879. He was commander-in-chief of the expedition which crushed the rebellion of the Egyptian army under Arabi Pasha at Tel-el-Kebir and occupied Cairo, 1882. For this he received the thanks of Parliament and was gazetted Baron Wolseley of Cairo and of Wolseley in Stafford. Conducted the unsuccessful Nile campaign for the relief of General Gordon, 1884–5. Created Viscount in 1885. Commander-in-chief of the British army 1895–9 during which period many reforms were carried out.
See **pls. C**-115, 117, 127.

Section C
Naval, Military and Exploration
Details of the Figures

Plate 1
Fig. 1 Blake

Plate 1A
Fig. 1(a) Blake
In the collection of Mr R. Shockledge

Plate 1
Figure 1
Subject: **Robert Blake**
Title: Admiral Blake (gilt script)
Height: 10½ in (26.5 cm)
Colour: Well coloured, underglaze blue coat.
Rarity: VR. D. A.
Description: He stands bare-headed, wearing cloak, short coat, breeches and stockings. To his right is a barrel of a gun, and in his right hand, which is raised, he clasps a sword, the point of which rests on the barrel.
Observations: A similar figure, together with *fig.* 221 (Greenwich Hospital pensioner) *pl.* C-76 fetched 54 gns at Christie's in 1963.

Plate 1A
Figure 1(a)
Subject: **Robert Blake**
Title: Adm¹ Blake (gilt script)
Height: 10½ in (26.5 cm)
Colour: Well coloured, underglaze blue coat.
Rarity: VR. D. A.
Description: Identical to *fig.* 1, except for manner and site of titling (see *illustrations*).

Plate 2
Fig. 2 Bart
In the collection of Mr Bryan Latham

Plate 3
Fig. 3 Watch
In the collection of Mrs Constance Chiswell

Plate 4
Statue of John Bart at Dunkerque.
This engraving appeared in *The Illustrated London News* on October 4th, 1845.

Plate 2
Figure 2
Subject: **Jean Bart**
Title: Jean Bart (gilt script)
Date: *c.* 1845
Height: 13 in (33 cm)
Colour: Well coloured.
Rarity: VR.
Description: Seated on a rock, wearing low plumed hat, shirt, jacket, gauntlets, breeches and boots. He holds a pistol in his right hand and there is a barrel to the left of his right foot. A pistol is grasped in his left hand also.
Observations: An identical figure is found titled 'Will Watch', see *fig.* 3, *pl.* C-3. Mr Bryan Latham has concluded that the potters were astute enough to adapt their figures to the market they were supplying (see *ch.* 5). Certainly this figure is adequate for Will Watch or Jean Bart (see *pl.* C-4 for engraving of statue of Jean Bart).

Plate 3
Figure 3
Subject: **Will Watch**
Title: Will Watch (gilt script)
Height: 13 in (33 cm)
Colour: Well coloured.
Rarity: Av.
Description: Identical to *fig.* 2 (Jean Bart) except for title.
Observations: 1. See *fig.* 2 (Jean Bart) *pl.* C-2.
2. Other figures of Will Watch are listed in section I—pls. 14, 14A and 15.
3. 'Will Watch' (with his 'Black-eyed Susan') was the legendary hero of many ballads and melodramas. See appropriate *observations* in section I.

Plate 4
Jean Bart
Statue of Jean Bart at Dunkerque: This engraving appeared in *The Illustrated London News* on October 4th, 1845. In the accompanying text it was noted that Jean Bart was born at Dunkerque. The writer went on to say:

Precisely at 12, the veil on the statue dropt, and discovered the hero, in the costume of the time of Louis XIV, brandishing a sword in his right hand, a pistol in his left and wearing another in his belt. He is supposed to be engaged in boarding a ship, this was his usual and favourite mode of carrying on the fight, and which ensured to him much success: he succeeded in capturing and carrying into Dunkerque upwards of 200 Dutch merchant vessels, during the war with the Dutch States. The Statue is of bronze, 16 feet high, and executed in the first style of the celebrated David (d'Angers)—the Thorwaldsen of France.

Section C. Naval, Military and Exploration

Plate 5
Figure 4
Subject: **James Cook**
Title: None
Date: 184–
Height: 7½ in (19 cm)
Colour: Well coloured, underglaze blue coat. Seven variants of colour of waistcoat and breeches have been noted.
Maker: Alpha factory
Rarity: Av. D. A.
Description: Seated bare-headed, in a captain's full-dress uniform (1774–87). To his right is a round-topped table upon which is a manuscript.
Observations: 1. From the portrait executed in May 1776, by Nathaniel Dance (1735–1811), in the National Maritime Museum.
2. Although there is no doubt whatever regarding the identification of this figure, the uniform worn is not well portrayed and the 'manuscript' should be a map of the world.
3. This is a good example of a point already made. A not uncommon figure has become scarce because it is not only very attractive but there is a big demand for it in Australia and New Zealand.
4. A good example fetched 65 gns at Christie's in 1967.

Plate 6
Fig. 5 Nelson

Plate 7
Fig. 5(*reverse*) Nelson

Plate 6
Figure 5
Subject: **Death of Nelson**
Title: None
Date: 184–
Height: 7½ in (19 cm)
Colour: Well coloured, underglaze blue coats.
Rarity: VR. D. A.
Description: Seated, in cocked hat worn athwartships. To his right an officer, bare-headed, is seated. He is in the act of prof-

fering a mug in his right hand to Nelson. To his left another officer, bare-headed, is standing with his left hand about to clasp Nelson's left wrist. The outline of the *Victory* is moulded on the reverse of this figure (see *pl.* C-7).
Observations: 1. None of the several figures depicting the death of Nelson have been found to correspond exactly to any of the many paintings on this subject by A. W. Devis and others, nor with the bronze relief portraying the event at the foot of Nelson's

Column. Nevertheless, it is fair to assume that in this particular figure and possibly in others, the subjects portrayed are, on the *left* the Revd Dr Scott, the ship's chaplain in the act of offering lemonade to the dying Admiral; and on the *right* Mr Beatty, the ship's surgeon about to feel his pulse.
2. Probably the finest of all the 'Death of Nelson' figures.
3. A national monument to Nelson was discussed in Parliament in 1818, but it was not until 1838 that a Nelson Memorial

C221

Plate 8
Fig. 6 Nelson
In the collection of Rear-Admiral
J. Dent, CB, OBE

Plate 6 continued

Committee was formed to collect subscriptions and hold a competition for its design. Meanwhile the Charing Cross Act (1826) had been passed which had cleared the area now known as Trafalgar Square. It remained unnamed until about 1835 and even so the name seems to have arisen independently of any plan to put a Nelson monument there.

The Committee accepted William Railton's design for the memorial, but the proposed height of the column was reduced subsequently. The present site, described by Peel as 'the finest in Europe', was granted by the Government. Work was begun on the concrete foundations in 1839, and the statue, by E. H. Baily RA, was raised in 1843. By 1844, £20,000 had been collected towards the cost of the memorial, but it was not until 1852 that the last of the four bronze reliefs was in place. Landseer's lions, part of the original design, were not erected until 1867.

It was presumably due to the public interest in the memorial that such a large number of figures of Nelson were made in the 1840's. It may have been stimulated, too, by the Queen's visit to the *Victory* at Portsmouth on Trafalgar Day, 1844.

Plate 7
Figure 5 (in reverse)
Subject: **Death of Nelson**
Observations: The outline of the *Victory* is portrayed. See *fig.* 5, *pl.* C-6.

Fig. 8 Nelson   Fig. 9 Nelson and *Victory*   Fig. 7 Nelson

Plate 9
In the collections of
Mr Anthony Oliver and the
author

Plate 8
Figure 6
Subject: **Death of Nelson**
Title: None
Date: 184–
Height: 8 in (20.5 cm)
Colour: Well coloured.
Rarity: R.
Description: Similar in most respects to *fig.* 5, *pl.* C-6 except there is no model of the *Victory* moulded on the reverse.
Observations: See *fig.* 5 (Death of Nelson) *pl.* C-6.

Plate 9
Figure 7
Subject: **Death of Nelson**
Title: None
Date: 184–
Height: 8 in (20.5 cm)
Colour: Well coloured, base usually green.
Rarity: R.
Description: Similar apart from minor details to *fig.* 6, *pl.* C-8. In this figure, also, the *Victory* is not moulded on the reverse.
Observations: See *fig.* 5 (Death of Nelson) *pl.* C-6.

Figure 8
Subject: **Death of Nelson**
Title: Death of Nelson (gilt script)
Date: 184–
Height: 8¼ in (21 cm)
Colour: Well coloured.
Rarity: Av. D. A.
Description: He lies sprawled on the deck, his cocked hat athwartships. His head and shoulders rest on a civilian seated to his right, who is bare-headed and who holds a mug in his right hand. To his left an officer, bare-headed, kneels holding his left wrist in

his left hand. The ends of two lanyards with rings attached overhang the base.
Observations: See *fig*. 5 (Death of Nelson) *pl*. C-6.

Figure 9
Subject: **Nelson and the 'Victory'**
Title: None
Date: 184–
Height: 5⅝ in (14.3 cm)
Colour: Usually well coloured.
Rarity: R. A.
Pair: Fig. 10 (Napoleon and *Bellerophon*) *pl*. C-12.
Description: He stands, hat athwartships in tailcoat, breeches and shoes. To his right lies the *Victory* in full rig, 3¼ in (8.25 cm) in height, made from a separate mould. Both earthenware and porcelaneous versions exist.

Plate 10
Figure 11
Subject: **Horatio Nelson**
Title: None
Date: 184–
Height: 10½ in (26.5 cm)
Colour: Well coloured.
Rarity: R.
Series: Same series as *fig*. 12 (Wellington) *pl*. C-10 and *fig*. 40 (Napoleon) *pl*. C-12.
Description: He stands in cocked hat athwartships, a sword by his left side, an anchor behind his right leg. Solid base.
Observations: 1. It has now been shown that the majority of single figures of Nelson, Wellington, and Napoleon belong to one or other of the several sets of three 'matching' figures. All 'matching' sets are rare; individual figures, less so.
2. No standing figure of Nelson has yet been found that is identical to that surmounting Nelson's column.
3. Nelson is never portrayed with a patch over his eye because he *never* wore one; nor did he even lose an eye, only the sight in it.

Figure 12
Subject: **Duke of Wellington**
Title: None
Date: 184–
Height: 10 in (25 cm)
Colour: Well coloured.
Rarity: R.
Series: Same series as *fig*. 11 (Nelson) *pl*. C-10 and *fig*. 40 (Napoleon) *pl*. C-12.
Description: He stands bare-headed, in civilian dress, a cloak held together by both hands at waist level. Solid base.
Observations: See preceding figure.

Figure 13
Subject: **Duke of Wellington**
Title: None
Date: 184–
Height: 8 in (20.5 cm)
Colour: Well coloured.
Rarity: Av.
Series: Same series as *fig*. 14 (Nelson) *pl*. C-11 and *fig*. 15 (Napoleon) *pl*. C-17.
Description: He stands in cocked hat, cloak, military jacket and knee-boots, a star on his left breast, a scroll in his right hand. Hollow base.
Observations: See *fig*. 11 (Nelson) *pl*. C-10.

Figure 16
Subject: **Death of Nelson**
Title: None
Date: 184–
Height: 5½ in (14 cm)

Fig. 11 Nelson   Fig. 12 Wellington

Fig. 13 Wellington   Fig. 16 Nelson   Fig. 17 Wellington

Colour: Well coloured.
Rarity: VR. D. A.
Description: Nelson, wearing a cocked hat athwartships, is seated between (on his right) a civilian kneeling and bare-headed and (on his left) an officer also kneeling. A sail provides a background to the group.
Observations: 1. See *fig*. 5 (Death of Nelson) *pl*. C-6.
2. This figure, together with *fig*. 25 (Wellington) *pl*. B-4, fetched 120 gns at Christie's in 1969.

Figure 17
Subject: **Duke of Wellington**
Title: None
Date: 184–
Height: 9 in (23 cm)
Colour: Well coloured.
Rarity: Av.
Series: Neither a definite matching 'Napoleon' nor a 'Nelson' has yet been found but this figure may belong to the series: *fig*. 31 (Nelson) *pl*. C-12 and *fig*. 32 (Napoleon) *pl*. C-13.
Description: He stands with a plumed cocked hat athwartships, uniform jacket with epaulettes, a scroll or baton in his right hand, knee-boots. Solid base.

Plate 11
Figure 14
Subject: **Horatio Nelson**
Title: None
Date: 184–
Height: 7¾ in (20 cm)
Colour: Well coloured.
Rarity: Av.
Series: Same series as *fig*. 13 (Wellington) *pl*. C-10 and *fig*. 15 (Napoleon) *pl*. C-17.
Description: Standing with cocked hat athwartships, uniform jacket with epaulettes, and anchor beside his right leg. His left hand rests on the hilt of a sword. Hollow base.
Observations: See *fig*. 11 (Nelson) *pl*. C-10.

Figure 18
Subject: **Horatio Nelson**
Title: None
Date: 184–
Height: 7½ in (19 cm)
Colour: Well coloured.
Rarity: Av.
Series: Same series as *fig*. 19 (Napoleon) and *fig*. 20 (Wellington).
Description: He stands, in cocked hat athwartships, tail-tunic and trousers. He holds a scroll in his left hand and to his left is a square pedestal draped by a cloak.

Plate 11 (Left and below)

Fig. 18 Nelson   *Fig.* 19 Napoleon   *Fig.* 20 Wellington   *Fig.* 21 Nelson

Fig. 22 Nelson   *Fig.* 23 Wellington   *Fig.* 25 Wellington   *Fig.* 27 Wellington   *Fig.* 26 Napoleon   *Fig.* 14 Nelson   *Fig.* 30 Napolec

Plate 11 continued

Figure 19
Subject: **Napoleon**
Title: None
Date: 184–
Height: 7½ in (19 cm)
Colour: Well coloured.
Rarity: Av.
Series: Same series as *fig.* 18 (Nelson) and *fig.* 20 (Wellington).
Description: He stands wearing a cocked hat, long tailed uniform and knee-boots. His arms are crossed on his chest and a draped pedestal is beside his left leg.

Figure 20
Subject: **Duke of Wellington**
Title: None
Date: 184–
Height: 7¾ in (20 cm)
Colour: Well coloured.
Rarity: Av.
Series: Same series as *fig.* 18 (Nelson) and *fig.* 19 (Napoleon).
Description: He stands in cocked hat, tail-coat and knee-boots. In his right hand he holds a scroll and his left hand rests on his hip. To his right is a draped pedestal.

Figure 21
Subject: **Death of Nelson**
Title: Death of Nelson (gilt script)
Date: 184–

Height: 9 in (23 cm)
Colour: Well coloured.
Rarity: C.
Description: Nelson is seated, wearing a cocked hat athwartships. To the left a bare-headed civilian, also seated, proffers a mug to Nelson. To the right stands an officer, bare-headed. Viewed from infront, Nelson appears to be raised on a seat; viewed from behind the 'impressed' outline of the *Victory* may be discerned (see *pl.* C-12).
Observations: See *fig.* 5 (Death of Nelson) *pl.* C-6.

Figure 21(a) (not illustrated)
Subject: **Horatio Nelson**
Title: Death of Nelson (gilt script)
Date: 184–
Height: 8¼ in (21 cm)
Rarity: VR.
Description: Sitting bare-headed. Right, an officer standing; left, an officer sitting. Both officers in cocked hats.
Observations: Described by Balston [33(d)]. I have never seen this figure.

Figure 22
Subject: **Horatio Nelson**
Title: None
Date: 184–
Height: 7¾ in (20 cm)
Colour: Well coloured.
Rarity: Av..

Series: Same series as *fig.* 23 (Wellington) *pl.* C-11 and *fig.* 24 (Napoleon) *pl.* C-13.
Description: He stands, cocked hat athwartships, anchor to the left, sword to the right. Solid base.

Figure 23
Subject: **Duke of Wellington**
Title: None
Date: 184–
Height: 8¼ in (21 cm)
Colour: Well coloured.
Rarity: Av.
Series: Same series as *fig.* 22 (Nelson) *pl.* C-11 and *fig.* 24 (Napoleon) *pl.* C-13.
Description: Standing with tall cocked hat with spangles attached to either end; full uniform with epaulettes, a scroll in his right hand. His left hand rests on the hilt of his sword. A cloak lies on a pedestal beside his right leg.

Figure 25
Subject: **Duke of Wellington on Copenhagen**
Title: None
Date: 184–
Height: 7 in (17.5 cm)
Colour: Well coloured. Usually a piebald horse.
Rarity: R.
Pair: Fig. 26 (Napoleon)
Description: On horse rearing and facing

Colour Plate 24
Death of Nelson. *Fig.* 8, *pl.* C-9. See page 222.

Colour Plate 25
James Cook. *Fig.* 4, *pl.* C-5. See page 221.

Plate 12
T: *Fig.* 31 Nelson
Fig. 33 Nelson
Fig. 34(*reproduction*) Nelson
Fig. 21(*reverse*) Nelson
Fig. 35 Nelson

B: *Fig.* 10 Napoleon and
Bellerophon
Fig. 37 Napoleon
Fig. 38 Napoleon
Fig. 39 Napoleon
Fig. 40 Napoleon
Fig. 41 Napoleon

Plate 11 continued
right. He wears a cocked hat, uniform and a cloak fastened round his neck. His right hand is raised to his hat.
Observations: Copenhagen, Wellington's favourite charger, was a chestnut.

Figure 26
Subject: **Napoleon, on Le Vizir**
Title: None
Date: 184–
Height: 7 in (17.5 cm)
Colour: Well coloured. Usually a piebald horse.
Rarity: Av.
Pair: *Fig.* 25 (Wellington)
Description: On horse rearing and facing left. He wears a cocked hat, long coat and a cloak which is blown forwards over his right shoulder. His right arm is lifted against it.
Observations: 1. After the painting by Napoleon's court painter Jacques-Louis David (1748–1825) depicting Napoleon crossing the Alps. The original is at the Musée de Versailles, see *ch.* 3, *pl.* 15.
2. Possibly intended to portray Napoleon's favourite white Arab, *Le Vizir*, although in fact, Napoleon crossed the Alps on a mule.

Figure 27
Subject: **Duke of Wellington**
Title: None
Date: 184–
Height: 7 in (17.5 cm)
Colour: Well coloured.
Rarity: R.

Series: Same series as *fig.* 28 (Nelson) *pl.* C-14 and *fig.* 29 (Napoleon) *pl.* C-13.
Description: Standing, with cocked hat fore and aft, uniform jacket, scroll in his right hand. Hollow base.

Figure 30
Subject: **Napoleon**
Title: None
Date: 184–
Height: 7¾ in (20 cm)
Colour: Well coloured.
Rarity: Av.
Pair or series: None known
Description: He stands, wearing cocked hat athwartships, long cloak blown out to his right, a tricolour flag protruding from behind his left leg. Solid base.

Plate 12
Figure 10
Subject: **Napoleon and 'Bellerophon'**
Title: None
Date: 184–
Height: 5¾ in (14.5 cm)
Colour: Well coloured and poorly coloured examples have been noted.
Rarity: R.
Pair: *Fig.* 9 (Nelson and *Victory*) *pl.* C-9.
Description: He stands on a mound, cocked hat athwartships. To his left is a fully rigged man-o-war, presumably *Bellerophon*. It is made from a separate mould and is 3¼ in (8.25 cm) in height. Both earthenware and porcelaneous versions exist.

Figure 21 (in reverse)
Subject: **Death of Nelson**
Observations: The outline of the *Victory* is portrayed. See *fig.* 21, *pl.* C-11.

Figure 31
Subject: **Horatio Nelson**
Title: None
Date: 184–
Height: 8½ in (21.5 cm)
Colour: Well coloured.
Rarity: Av.
Series: Pair to *fig.* 32 (Napoleon) *pl.* C-13; also, *fig.* 17 (Wellington) *pl.* C-10 may belong to the series.
Description: Standing, in cocked hat athwartships, uniform jacket with epaulettes, breeches and stockings. His left forearm rests on a gun emplacement at the foot of which is a pile of shells. Earthenware and porcelaneous versions have been noted.

Figure 33
Subject: **Death of Nelson**
Title: Death of Nelson (gilt script)
Date: 184–
Height: 8¾ in (22 cm)
Colour: Well coloured.
Rarity: Av.
Description: Nelson sits bare-headed, with his hat at his feet. He is supported on each side by an officer, each standing in cocked hat worn fore and aft. Occasionally the back of this figure may be found impressed very faintly with an outline of the *Victory*.

Section C. Naval, Military and Exploration

Figure 34
Subject: **Horatio Nelson**
Title: None
Date: 184–
Height: 11½ in (29 cm)
Colour: In the manner of Thomas Parr.
Maker: Parr and Kent group of potters.
Rarity: Contemporary versions are VR. I have never seen one titled. Reproductions are C. They are titled 'Nelson' (black script).
Description: A jug with its handle behind. Nelson stands in a cocked hat, tailcoat with epaulettes, waistcoat, breeches, stockings and shoes. ? A telescope in his left hand which rests on a gun, the rope of which is against his left leg.
Observations: This figure appears in all Kent lists. In *Kent List A* it is no. 137; in *Kent List B* it is no. 372 and in *Kent List C (1955)* it is no. 372, also.

Figure 35
Subject: **Horatio Nelson**
Title: None
Date: 184–
Height: 6¼ in (16 cm)
Colour: Well coloured.
Rarity: R.
Pair: Fig. 35(a) (Napoleon) pl. C-12A.
Description: He stands, wearing a cocked hat athwartships, uniform jacket, waistcoat and trousers, a scroll in his left hand. A low brick wall behind.

Figure 37
Subject: **Napoleon**
Title: None
Date: 184–
Height: 10¼ in (25.75 cm)
Colour: Well coloured, but poorly coloured versions exist too.
Rarity: C.
Description: He stands, cocked hat athwartships, in uniform, overcoat and knee-boots. His right hand is thrust into his waistcoat and his left hand lies behind his back. To his left is an eagle.
Observations: Appears to be a smaller version of *fig. 61, pl. C-23*.

Figure 38
Subject: **Napoleon**
Title: None
Date: 184–
Height: 7¾ in (20 cm)
Colour: Well coloured.
Rarity: Av.
Description: He sits bare-headed on rocks. His right hand is thrust into his waistcoat and his left arm rests on the rocks. He clasps a book in his left hand. His sword lies to his left, as also his cocked hat.
Observations: 1. From a lithograph of Marin-Lavigne entitled *Napoleon at St. Helena* (see ch. 3, pl. 16).
2. Note that Napoleon's sword is found in two sizes. Both are contemporary.
3. Usually made from press-moulds but I have noted two examples made from slip-moulds.

Figure 39
Subject: **Napoleon**
Title: None
Date: 184–
Height: 8¾ in (22 cm)
Colour: Well coloured.

Rarity: Av.
Description: Sitting on rocks, in cocked hat, uniform and knee-boots. His cloak, which is over both shoulders, is blown out to his right and he holds a scroll or baton in his right hand.

Figure 40
Subject: **Napoleon**
Title: None
Date: 184–
Height: 10¼ in (25.75 cm)
Colour: Well coloured.
Rarity: R.
Series: Same series as *fig. 11* (Nelson) *pl.* C-10, and *fig. 12* (Wellington) *pl.* C-10.
Description: He stands bare-headed, in a long-tailed uniform, breeches and stockings. His right hand is thrust into his waistcoat and his left hand into the small of his back.
Observations: I have some reservations as to whether this figure does belong to the series.

Figure 41
Subject: **Napoleon**
Title: None
Date: 184–
Height: 7 in (17.5 cm)
Colour: Well coloured.
Rarity: R.
Pair or series: Not known
Description: He stands in cocked hat athwartships, his ermine-edged cloak blown out to his right, his right hand in his waistcoat, his left arm in the small of his back. Solid base.

Plate 12A
Figure 35(a)
Subject: **Napoleon**
Title: None
Date: 184–
Height: 6 in (15.25 cm)
Colour: Well coloured.
Rarity: R.
Pair: Fig. 35 (Nelson) *pl.* C-12.
Description: He stands, cocked hat athwartships, long military coat, jacket, waistcoat, breeches and knee-boots. His right hand is tucked into his waistcoat and left hand in the small of his back. A low brick wall behind. Solid base.

Plate 13
Figure 24
Subject: **Napoleon**
Title: None
Date: 184–
Height: 8¼ in (21 cm)
Colour: Well coloured.
Rarity: Av.
Series: Same series as *fig. 22* (Nelson) *pl.* C-11 and *fig. 23* (Wellington) *pl.* C-11.
Description: Standing with cocked hat athwartships, uniform, greatcoat and knee-boots. The skirts of his coat are blown out to his right. He carries a scroll in his right hand and his left arm is in the small of his back. Solid base.

Figure 24(a)
Subject: **Napoleon**
Title: None
Height: 6⅝ in (16.75 cm)
Colour: Well coloured.

Plate 12A
Fig. 35(a) Napoleon
In the collection of Mr F.J. Stephens

Rarity: R.
Pair or series: Not known
Description: Very similar to *fig. 24*, other than for size. Solid base.

Figure 29
Subject: **Napoleon**
Title: None
Date: 184–
Height: 7 in (17.5 cm)
Colour: Well coloured.
Rarity: R.
Series: Same series as *fig. 27* (Wellington) *pl.* C-11 and *fig. 28* (Nelson) *pl.* C-14.
Description: He stands, cocked hat athwartships, wearing uniform jacket, epaulettes, waistcoat, breeches and knee-boots, his arms crossed in front of him. Pedestal to his right. Hollow base.

Figure 32
Subject: **Napoleon**
Title: None
Date: 184–
Height: 7¾ in (20 cm)
Colour: Well coloured.
Rarity: Av.
Series: Pair to *fig. 31* (Nelson) *pl.* C-12; also *fig. 17* (Wellington) *pl.* C-10 may belong to this series.
Description: Standing with cocked hat

Colour Plate 26
Lady Franklin (Left) and Sir John Franklin (Right). *Figs.* 70, 71, *pl.* C-28. See page 238. Admiral Robert Blake (Centre). *Fig.* 1, *pl.* C-1.
See page 219.

Colour Plate 27
Sir Robert and Lady Sale. *Figs.* 66, 67, *pl.* C-26. See page 237.

Plate 13

Fig. 29 Napoleon　　　*Fig.* 24 Napoleon　　　*Fig.* 32 Napoleon　　　*Fig.* 24(a) Napoleon

Plate 13 continued
athwartships, uniform jacket, breeches, knee-boots and cloak, his left forearm resting on a gun emplacement. May be found with a solid or hollow base.

Plate 14
Figure 28
Subject: **Horatio Nelson**
Title: None

Date: 184–
Height: 6¾ in (17 cm)
Colour: Well coloured.
Rarity: R.

Pair or series: Same series as *fig.* 27 (Wellington) *pl.* C-11 and *fig.* 29 (Napoleon) *pl.* C-13.
Description· Standing with cocked hat athwartships, uniform jacket with epaulettes, waistcoat, breeches and stockings. There is an anchor behind his right leg, and a

pedestal with a cloak draped over it, to his right. He clasps a sword against his left leg. Hollow base.

Figure 42 (left)
Subject: **Napoleon**
Title: None
Date: 184–
Height: 4 in (10 cm)
Colour: Well coloured.

Plate 14
By courtesy of
Mr Arthur Thornton　　　*Fig.* 42 Napoleon　　　*Fig.* 43 Napoleon and Wellington　　　*Fig.* 28 Nelson

Section C. Naval, Military and Exploration

Plate 14 continued
Rarity: Av.
Pair: *Fig.* 42 (right) (Napoleon) *pl.* C-15.
Description: On horse facing left, in cocked hat, long coat, and a cloak over his right shoulder, blowing out in front of him. Hollow base.
Observations: 1. After a painting by Napoleon's court painter Jacques-Louis David (1748–1825), executed *c.* 1800. The original is at the Musée de Versailles, and depicts Napoleon crossing the Alps on a white charger, see *ch.* 3, *pl.* 15. In fact, he crossed the Alps on a mule.
2. See also *fig.* 26, *pl.* C-11.

Figure 43
Subject: **Napoleon and Wellington**
Title: None
Date: 184–
Height: 9 in (23 cm)
Colour: Well coloured.
Rarity: VR.
Description: Left: Napoleon wearing cocked hat athwartships, cloak, uniform jacket, waistcoat, breeches and long boots; a scroll in his right hand.
Right: Wellington with plumed cocked hat, uniform jacket, trousers and cloak; a sword in his left hand which rests against his left leg.
Between them a clock-face.

Plate 14A
Figure 42(a) (left)
Subject: **Napoleon**
Title: None
Date: 184–
Height: 5½ in (14 cm)
Colour: Well coloured.
Rarity: R.
Pair: Unknown, but almost certainly Napoleon, for which *fig.* 42(a) (right) has been reserved.

Plate 14A
Fig. 42(a) Napoleon
In the collection of M. Marc de Smedt

Description: The same as *fig.* 42 (left), *pl.* C-14 except for height, minor differences in design and solid base.
Observations: As for *fig.* 42 (left), *pl.* C-14.

Plate 15
Figure 42 (right)
Subject: **Napoleon**
Title: None
Date: 184–
Height: 4 in (10 cm)
Colour: Well coloured.
Rarity: Av.
Pair: *Fig.* 42 (left) (Napoleon) *pl.* C-14.
Description: Identical in all respects to *fig.* 42 (left) except that it is a mirror-image. Hollow base.

Figure 44
Subject: **Napoleon**
Title: None
Date: 184–
Height: 5⅛ in (13 cm)
Colour: Well coloured, underglaze blue coat.
Rarity: Av.
Pair or series: Unknown
Description: Standing with cocked hat athwartships, long coat, waistcoat, breeches and knee-boots. A scroll in his right hand his left hand tucked into his waistcoat. Solid base. An earthenware figure.
Observations: See *fig.* 44(a).

Figure 44(a)
Subject: **Napoleon**
Title: None
Date: 184–
Height: 4⅞ in (12.5 cm)
Colour: Well coloured, underglaze blue coat.
Pair or series: Unknown
Description: Identical to *fig.* 44, except for height; also it is a porcelaneous figure with a hollow base.
Observations: 1. The interior of this particular figure is impressed 'F'. The significance of the mark is unknown, but it is probably a potter's mark (see *ch.* 2, *pl.* 3).
2. There is no doubt that *fig.* 44(a) is porcelain, and little doubt that *fig.* 44 is earthenware. The two figures are decorated identically and would appear to come from the same factory. Very few manufacturers produced both porcelain and earthenware, but one of those that did was Minton (from two separate factories). Mr Geoffrey Godden has examined these figures and assures me that neither came from Minton. There is no doubt, also, that different factories sometimes produced the same figure. Maybe the explanation lies in journeyman modellers; maybe in one factory purchasing the mould from another; or, maybe in just frank copying.

Plate 15   *Fig.* 44 Napoleon   *Fig.* 42 Napoleon   *Fig.* 44(a) Napoleon

Plate 16

Fig. 45 Nelson   *Fig.* 46 Nelson   *Fig.* 48 Napoleon   *Fig.* 49 Napoleon

Plate 16
Figure 45
Subject: **Horatio Nelson**
Title: None
Height: 10¼ in (26.5 cm)
Colour: Pale colouring.
Rarity: Av.
Description: Nelson bust in jug form. The medals are correct and the lower medallion is often found inscribed 'Nile/1798.'
Observations: After earlier Lambeth stoneware jug which has also 'Nile/1798' inscribed on the lower medallion and, in addition, on its base in indented capitals, 'Trafalgar 1805/England expects every man to do his duty' (no. 219 in the Willett collection).

Figure 46
Subject: **Horatio Nelson**
Title: None
Date: 184–
Height: 11 in (28 cm)
Colour: Usually well coloured.
Rarity: Av.
Pair: *Fig.* 47 (Napoleon) *pl.* C-17.
Description: He stands, cocked hat athwartships, in uniform jacket with epaulettes, breeches and stockings. A cannon with a pile of shells to his left. Solid base.

Figure 48
Subject: **Napoleon**
Title: N.B. (yellow capitals)
Date: 184–
Height: 13⅛ in (33.25 cm)
Colour: Well coloured.
Rarity: R.
Description: He stands, cocked hat athwartships, in uniform jacket, waistcoat, breeches and knee-boots, his arms crossed in front. Behind his right leg is a cannon and to his left a pedestal with a cloak draped over it. The whole is mounted on a plinth on which is painted 'N.B.', surmounted by a floral device.

Figure 49
Subject: **Napoleon**
Title: None
Height: 9½ in (24 cm)
Colour: Well coloured.
Rarity: R.
Pair: *Fig.* 28 (Wellington) *pl.* B-5.
Description: On horse facing left, in cocked hat, long coat, breeches and knee-boots. A cloak over his right shoulder blows out behind.

Plate 16A
Figure 45(a)
Subject: **Horatio Nelson**
Title: Trafalgar, 1805 (indented capitals)
Height: 9⅛ in (23.25 cm)
Colour: Well coloured, underglaze blue.
Rarity: VR.
Description: A bust forming a jug. Wearing a cocked hat athwartships, jacket with epaulettes. The 'empty' right sleeve is pinned across his chest. The medals are correct and the lower medallion is impressed Nile/1798.

Plate 16A
*Fig.*45(a) Nelson

Plate 16B
Fig. 45(b) Wellington
By courtesy of the Brighton Art Gallery and Museum

Plate 16C
Fig. 45(c) Wellington
By courtesy of the Brighton Art Gallery and Museum

Plate 16B
Figure 45(b)
Subject: **Duke of Wellington**
Title: None
Height: 5 in (12.75 cm)
Colour: Well coloured, underglaze blue.
Rarity: Av.
Description: A bust of the Duke forming a tobacco jar and cover.
Observations: No. 144 in the Willett collection. Is dated *c.* 1815 in the catalogue, but is probably Victorian.

Plate 16C
Figure 45(c)
Subject: **Duke of Wellington**
Title: None
Height: 7¼ in (18.25 cm)
Colour: Well coloured, underglaze blue.
Rarity: Av.
Description: A bust of the Duke forming a jug.
Observations: No. 145 in the Willett collection. Is dated *c.* 1815 in the catalogue, but is probably Victorian.

Plate 17 (Above and below)

Plate 17
Figure 15
Subject: **Napoleon**
Title: None
Date: 184–
Height: 8¼ in (21 cm)
Colour: Well coloured.
Rarity: Av.
Series: Same series as *fig.* 13 (Wellington) *pl.* C-10 and *fig.* 14 (Nelson) *pl.* C-11.
Description: He stands, cocked hat athwartships, in greatcoat, uniform jacket, breeches and knee-boots. The skirts of the coat are blown out to his right. Hollow base.

Figure 36
Subject: **Napoleon**
Title: None
Date: 184–
Height: 6 in (15.25 cm)
Colour: Well coloured.
Rarity: Av.
Pair: Unknown.
Description: He stands, cocked hat athwartships, in uniform jacket with epaulettes, waistcoat, breeches and knee-boots. His arms are crossed in front of him; there is a pedestal to his right. Solid base.

Figure 47
Subject: **Napoleon**
Title: None
Date: 184–
Height: 10¾ in (27 cm)
Colour: Usually well coloured.
Rarity: Av.

Pair: *Fig.* 46 (Nelson) pl. C-16.
Description: He stands with cocked hat athwartships, in greatcoat, jacket, waistcoat, breeches and knee-boots; a scroll in his right hand, his left hand tucked into his waistcoat; a pile of shells between his legs. Solid base.

Figure 50
Subject: **Napoleon**
Title: None
Date: 184–
Height: 5¼ in (13.5 cm)
Colour: Well coloured.
Rarity: Av.
Description: He stands inside an embellished tent, cocked hat athwartships, in uniform jacket, breeches and knee-boots, his arms crossed in front of his chest. Inkwell.
Observations: 1. It has been suggested that this figure represents Tom Thumb in the character of Napoleon, but Tom Thumb would be portrayed in miniature relative to his surroundings, as in *fig.* 87, *pl.* E-50.
2. Several minor variants, both as regards size and design, exist.

Figure 51
Subject: **Napoleon**
Title: None
Date: 184–
Height: 8 in (20.5 cm)
Colour: White and gilt.
Rarity: Av.
Pair: Not known
Description: On prancing horse facing left,

Fig. 50 Napoleon   *Fig.* 51 Napoleon   *Fig.* 36 Napoleon

Fig. 15 Napoleon   *Fig.* 52 Napoleon   *Fig.* 47 Napoleon   *Fig.* 53 Napoleon   *Fig.* 54 Napoleon

Plate 18
Fig. 55 Napoleon
To the right of the figure
is an engraving by Raffet
(1804-60) titled *L'oeil du
maitre.* (The master's eye).
*In the collection of
M. Marc de Smedt*

wearing cocked hat athwartships, his cloak
blown out in front of him. The horse is
about to leap over a number of stakes.

Figure 52
Subject: **Napoleon**
Title: None
Date: 184–
Height: 10¼ in (25.75 cm)
Colour: Usually pale.
Rarity: Av.
Pair: Not known
Description: Standing in cocked hat, great-
coat, jacket, waistcoat, breeches and stock-
ings; his left hand in his waistcoat, his right
arm by his side. Square plinth.
Observations: This figure appears to be based
on the Seure statue which crowned La
Colonne Vendome between 1833 and 1863,
see *ch.* 3, *pl.* 17.

Figure 53
Subject: **Napoleon**
Title: N (gilt transfer)
Date: 184–
Height: 8½ in (21.5 cm)
Colour: Well coloured.
Rarity: VR.
Pair or series: Not known
Description: He stands, cocked hat athwart-
ships, in uniform jacket, waistcoat, breeches
and knee-boots, his arms crossed in front
of him; pedestal to his left with a cloak
draped over it.

Figure 54
Subject: **Napoleon**
Title: None
Date: 184–
Height: 7 in (17.5 cm)
Colour: Well coloured.
Rarity: R.
Pair or series: Not known
Description: Similar in all respects to *fig.* 53
(Napoleon) except that it is smaller and
untitled. Solid base.

Plate 18
Figure 55
Subject: **Napoleon**
Title: None
Date: 184–
Height: 7½ in (19 cm)
Colour: Well coloured.
Rarity: R.
Pair or series: Unknown but doubtless is
part of a series.
Description: Standing facing half-left, in
cocked hat, uniform, greatcoat, breeches
and knee-boots. The skirts of the coat are
blown out to his right. He holds a telescope
in his right hand and his left forearm is
thrust into the small of his back. Hollow
base.
Observations: 1. The example illustrated has
a '3' in underglaze blue inside the base. This
suggests it is part of a set of three (Nelson,
Wellington and Napoleon).
2. The engraving illustrated to the right of
the figure is titled *L'Oeil du Maitre* ('The
Master's Eye') and is an original of Raffet
(1804–60). It does not illustrate any
particular battle, but is purely an artistic
composition. There is little doubt that it
provides the source of *fig.* 55 which seems to
be identical in every respect.

Plate 19
Figure 56
Subject: **Napoleon**
Title: None
Date: 184–
Height: 6¼ in (16 cm)
Colour: Well coloured.
Rarity: R.
Pair or series: Unknown
Description: Standing, cocked hat athwart-
ships, in greatcoat, jacket, waistcoat, breeches
and knee-boots; his left arm in the small of
his back, his right hand tucked into his
waistcoat. Solid base.

Plate 19
Fig. 56 Napoleon
In the collection of Lt.-Col. A.C.W. Kimpton

Plate 20
Figure 57
Subject: **Wellington**
Title: None
Date: 184–
Height: 5½ in (14 cm)
Colour: Well coloured.
Rarity: Av.
Pair or series: Unknown
Description: Bare-headed, in uniform jacket with epaulettes, plumed cocked hat beside his right leg held in his right hand, sword beside his left leg held in his left hand. Hollow base.

Plate 21
Figure 58
Subject: **? Wellington**
Title: None
Date: 184–
Height: 6¾ in (17 cm)
Colour: Well coloured.
Rarity: R.
Pair or series: Unknown
Description: Bare-headed, in uniform jacket with high collar and epaulettes and trousers. His left hand is across his chest and in it he grasps a scroll. His right hand is by his right side and in it he grasps his plumed cocked hat. Solid base.

Plate 20
Fig. 57 Wellington

Plate 21
Fig. 58 ?Wellington
In the collection of Rear-Admiral J. Dent, CB, OBE

Plate 22
Figure 59
Subject: **Napoleon**
Title: None
Date: 184–
Height: 3¾ in (9.5 cm)
Colour: Reasonably coloured.
Rarity: R.
Description: He stands, cocked hat athwartships, arms crossed in front of his chest, flags behind his right leg and a cannon behind his left. Hollow base.
Observations: Possibly a candle snuffer.

Figure 60
Subject: **Napoleon**
Title: None
Date: 184–
Height: 7¼ in (18.25 cm)
Colour: Well coloured.
Rarity: R.
Description: A bust in the form of a vase. Napoleon wears a cocked hat, jacket with epaulettes and greatcoat.

Plate 23
Figure 61
Subject: **Napoleon**
Title: Napoleon Buonaparte (*sic*) (gilt script)
Date: Uncertain
Height: 24 in (61 cm)

Colour: Well coloured, underglaze blue.
Rarity: VR. D. A.
Pair: Not known
Description: Similar in all respects to *fig.* 37 (Napoleon) *pl.* C-12 except for size and in the absence of an eagle on the wall.
Observations: 1. The tallest and most magnificent Staffordshire portrait figure of the Victorian era.
2. For comments on the title see *ch.* 5.

Figure 62
Subject: **Napoleon**
Title: None
Date: 184–
Height: 2¾ in (7 cm)
Colour: Blue underglaze coat.
Rarity: Av.
Pair: Not known
Description: He stands, cocked hat athwartships, in uniform and great coat; the latter is blown out to his right and the tricolour lies behind his left leg.

Plate 23A
Figure 61(a)
Subject: **Napoleon**
Title: None
Date: Uncertain
Height: 21 in (52.5 cm)

Colour: Well coloured.
Rarity: VR. A.
Pair: Not known
Description: Standing, cocked hat athwartships, arms crossed and right foot slightly forward of left. He is wearing a jacket with epaulettes, waistcoat, breeches and knee-boots. There is a tree trunk behind his left boot. The base is an octagonal, stepped pedestal, 5½ in (14 cm) in height.
Observations: The second tallest recorded Victorian Staffordshire portrait figure.

Plate 24
Figure 63
Subject: **Napoleon**
Title: N (raised capital)
Date: Uncertain
Height: 13½ in (34.25 cm)
Colour: Black, white and gilt.
Rarity: VR.
Pair or series: Unknown
Description: He stands, dressed in cocked hat, uniform, greatcoat and knee-boots. His left hand is thrust into his waistcoat. There are cannon balls between his feet. The plinth is shaped like a tomb or casket and on the front is inscribed 'N'.
Observations: Fetched 55 gns at Christie's in 1966.

Plate 22
Fig. 59 Napoleon
Fig. 60 Napoleon

Plate 23
Fig. 61 Napoleon
Fig. 62 Napoleon
The giant and midget of Victorian
Staffordshire portrait figures!

Plate 23A
Fig. 61(a) Napoleon
The runner-up!
In the collection of Mr Anthony Kerman

Plate 24
Fig. 63 Napoleon
By courtesy of Mr and Mrs Eric Joyce

Plate 25
Fig. 64 Wellington
Behind this figure are two
parts of the old press-
mould of its pair, fig. 65
(Napoleon)
*In the collection of
Mr Ronald Shockledge*

Plate 26
Fig. 66 Sale
Fig. 67 Lady Sale

Plate 25
Figure 64
Subject: **Duke of Wellington**
Title: Wellington (raised capitals)
Date: 187–
Height: 16¾ in (42.25 cm)
Colour: Largely white and gilt, with some
additional colouring, especially for saddle-
cloth.

Maker: Sampson Smith
Rarity: VR.
Pair: Fig. 65 (Napoleon)
Description: On horse facing right, in cocked
hat and uniform. He holds a baton in his
right hand which rests on the saddle-cloth.
The plinth, which is 5½ in (14 cm) high, is
decorated with a clock-face, grapes and vine
leaves.

Observations: The original Sampson Smith
moulds of this figure and its pair still exist
and reproductions have been made of both
figures (see *ch.* 6, *pl.* 3).

Figure 65 (not illustrated, but see *ch.* 6, *pl.* 3
for photograph of reproduction)
Subject: **Napoleon**
Title: Napoleon (raised capitals)

Plate 27
Fig. 68 Gholab Singh

In the background is an engraving from *The Illustrated London News* of April 4th, 1846. The caption reads 'Gholab Singh, his son and bodyguard'.

Fig. 69 Ranbir Singh

Date: 187–
Height: 16¼ in (41 cm)
Colour: See preceding figure.
Maker: Sampson Smith
Rarity: VR.
Pair: *Fig.* 64 (Wellington)
Description: On horse facing left, in cocked hat, short overcoat and knee-boots. The plinth, which is 5½ in (14 cm) high, is decorated with a clock-face, grapes and vine leaves.
Observations: 1. No contemporary version has been found yet.
2. The original Sampson Smith moulds of this figure and its pair still exist and reproductions of each figure have been made (see *ch.* 6, *pl.* 3).

Plate 26
Figure 66
Subject: **Sir Robert Sale**
Title: Sir R. Sale (gilt script)
Date: *c.* 1842
Height: 8 in (20.5 cm)
Colour: Well coloured, blue tunic.
Rarity: R. D.
Pair: *Fig.* 67 (Lady Sale). Appears to be the same series as *fig.* 104 (Albert) and *fig.* 105 (Victoria), *pl.* A-38.
Description: On horse facing right, in cocked hat and uniform; his right hand on the saddle-cloth, his left arm on the horse's mane.
Observations: 1. Sir Robert Sale was in command of the British retreat from Kabul in 1842.
2. A similar pair of figures fetched 52 gns at Christie's in 1963, and another pair 90 gns in the same rooms in 1965.

Figure 67
Subject: **Lady Sale**
Title: Lady Sale (gilt script)
Date: *c.* 1842
Height: 7¼ in (18.25 cm)
Colour: Well coloured.
Rarity: R. D.
Pair: *Fig.* 66 (Sir R. Sale). Appears to be the same series as *fig.* 104 (Albert) and *fig.* 105 (Victoria), *pl.* A-38.
Description: On horse facing left, in high round hat and riding habit. She clasps the horse's reins with her left hand and her right hand is on the horse's mane.
Observations: A number of untitled figures occur which could be either Victoria and Albert or Lady Sale and Sir R. Sale. It may well be that all were intended to be Victoria and Albert and that *figs.* 66 and 67 were selected for titling in this manner when Sir Robert and Lady Sale 'hit the headlines', see *pls.* A-38–40 and *pl.* I-41.

Plate 27
Figure 68
Subject: **Gholab Singh**
Title: None
Date: *c.* 1846
Height: 9 in (23 cm)
Colour: Very delicately coloured; face of rider 'dark'.
Rarity: VR. D. A.
Pair: *Fig.* 69 (Ranbir Singh)
Description: On horse facing left, bearded, with plumed turban, vest, jacket, waist-sash, trousers and shoes; scimitar in left hand, his right hand on the horse's mane.

The horse's bridle is braided; saddle and saddle-cloth.
Observations: 1. The engraving illustrated on this plate appeared in *The Illustrated London News* on April 4th, 1846. The caption reads 'Gholab Singh, his son and bodyguard'. The engraving establishes the identity of both this figure and its pair, *fig.* 69 (Ranbir Singh). If any doubt remains in the reader's mind, he should study the 'blow up' of this engraving (see *ch.* 3, *pls.* 18 and 19). In the author's opinion this is one of the most spectacular and unexpected identifications so far recorded.
2. Havelock wrote of him:

. . . dress plain, even slovenly . . . the volume of his life is to be read in his astute and glazing (*sic*) countenance.

Figure 69
Subject: **Ranbir Singh**
Title: None
Date: *c.* 1846
Height: 9 in (23 cm)
Colour: Very delicately coloured; face of rider 'dark'.
Rarity: VR. D. A.
Pair: *Fig.* 68 (Gholab Singh)
Description: On horse facing right, clean-shaven, in plumed turban. A much younger looking person than that portrayed in preceding figure; he wears a vest, shirt, trousers and shoes. In his right hand he clasps a scimitar and his left hand is on the horse's mane. The horse's bridle is braided; saddle and saddle-cloth.
Observations: See *fig.* 68 (Gholab Singh).

Plate 28
Fig. 71 Franklin
Fig. 70 Lady Franklin
In the Thomas Balston collection

Plate 29
Sir John Franklin (1786-1847)
An engraving which appeared in *The Illustrated News* on
September 13th, 1851.
By courtesy of The Illustrated London News

Plate 28
Figure 70
Subject: **Lady Franklin**
Title: Lady Franklin (indented capitals)
Date: 184–
Height: 10½ in (26.5 cm)
Colour: Usually sparsely coloured; no figures known with underglaze blue.
Maker: Alpha factory
Rarity: VR. D. A.
Pair: *Fig.* 71 (Sir John Franklin)
Description: She stands bare-headed, except for a wreath-like object. She wears a necklace, a bodice with puffed sleeves and a wide skirt. A shawl is draped across her arms.
Observations: Sir John Franklin sailed in quest of the North-West Passage in 1845. When no news had been heard of him, thirty-nine searching expeditions were launched between 1847 and 1857. Between 1850 and 1857 Lady Franklin fitted out five ships at her own expense to find the missing explorer.

Figure 71
Subject: **Sir John Franklin**
Title: Sir John Franklin (indented capitals)
Date: 184–
Height: 10½ in (26.5 cm)
Colour: Usually sparsely coloured; no figure known with underglaze blue.

Maker: Alpha factory
Rarity: VR. D. A.
Pair: *Fig.* 70 (Lady Franklin)
Description: Standing in naval uniform. He holds a telescope in both hands.
Observations: 1. The figure portrays Franklin exceptionally well. Compare with engraving on *pl.* C-29.
2. A similar figure, together with *fig.* 49 (Napoleon) *pl.* C-16 and *fig.* 28 (Wellington) *pl.* B-5, fetched 52 gns at Christie's in 1963; another alone, fetched 105 gns in the same rooms in 1968.

Plate 29
    Sir John Franklin
An engraving which appeared in *The Illustrated London News* on September 13th, 1851.

Plate 30
Commanders of the Allied Armies in the East
An engraving which appeared in *The Illustrated London News* on July 15th, 1854.
From left to right: Lord Raglan, Duke of Cambridge, Omer Pacha, The Sultan, Achmet Pacha, Prince Napoleon, Marshal St. Arnaud.

Plate 31
Figure 72
Subject: **Albert**
Title: P. Albert (raised capitals)
Date: c. 1854
Height: 7½ in (19 cm)
Colour: Well coloured.
Rarity: VR.
Pair: *Fig.* 73 (Abd-ul-Medjid)
Description: On horse facing right, in plumed cocked hat and military uniform.
Observations: This figure and its pair were issued to commemorate the Anglo-Turkish alliance in the Crimean War (1854–6).
Figure 73
Subject: **Abd-ul-Medjid, Sultan of Turkey**
Title: Sultan (raised capitals)
Date: c. 1854
Height: 7½ in (19 cm)
Colour: Well coloured.
Rarity: VR.
Pair: *Fig.* 72 (Albert)
Description: On horse facing left, in round plumed hat and military uniform.
Observations: See preceding figure.

Plate 30
Commanders of the Allied Armies in the East
An engraving which appeared in *The Illustrated London News* on July 15th, 1854.

From left to right: Lord Raglan, Duke of Cambridge, Omer Pacha, The Sultan, Achmet Pacha, Prince Napoleon, Marshal St. Arnaud.

Plate 31
Fig. 72 Albert
Fig. 73 Abd-ul-Medjid
In the collection of Mr D.P.M. Michael

Plate 32

Fig. 74 The Allied Powers   Fig. 76 France-England Turkey[1]   Fig. 75 Turkey-England-France
[1]Small version (9 in, 23 cm)
illustrated

Plate 33   Fig. 77 Queen Emperor   Fig. 77 Queen Emperor (*small version*)
(7½ in, 19 cm)

Figure 75
Subject: **Abd-ul-Medjid, Victoria and Napoleon III**
Title: Turkey England France (raised capitals)
Date: *c*. 1854
Height: 10¼ in (25.75 cm)
Colour: Well coloured, underglaze blue coats.
Rarity: C.
Description: The Queen stands in the centre, crowned; to her right is Sultan Abd-ul-Medjid, wearing a turban; and to her left Napoleon III, bare-headed, in military uniform.
Observations: 1. The source of this figure is a medal by A. A. Caque struck at the Paris mint in 1854 to commemorate the Anglo-French alliance. An engraving of the medal appeared in *The Illustrated London News* of September 9th, 1854, see *ch*. 3, *pl*. 20.
2. A similar figure, together with *fig*. 74 (Allied Powers) fetched 85 gns at Christie's in 1969.

Figure 76
Subject: **Napoleon III, Victoria and Abd-ul-Medjid**
Title: France England Turkey (raised capitals on plaques)
Date: *c*. 1854
Height: 11¼ in (28.5 cm); the smaller [9 in (23 cm)] version is illustrated.
Colour: Sparingly coloured.
Rarity: R.
Description: Victoria stands, crowned; to her right is Napoleon, bare-headed and in military uniform; to her left the Sultan, wearing a turban.
Observations: Virtually a mirror-image of *fig*. 75 (Turkey England France).

Plate 33
Figure 77
Subject: **Victoria and ? Napoleon III**
Title: Queen Emperor (raised capitals)
Date: *c*. 1854
Height: 11 in (28 cm)
Colour: Well coloured.
Rarity: R.

Plate 32
Figure 74
Subject: **Napoleon III, Victoria and Victor Emmanuel II**
Title: The Allied Powers (raised capitals)
Date: *c*. 1854
Height: 12 in (30.5 cm)
Colour: Usually sparsely coloured.
Rarity: VR. D.

Description: Victoria stands in the centre, crowned; to her right is Napoleon III, wearing plumed cocked hat and military uniform; to her left is Victor Emmanuel II, king of Sardinia similarly attired.
Observations: A similar figure, together with *fig*. 75 (Turkey England France) fetched 85 gns at Christie's in 1969.

Section C. Naval, Military and Exploration

Description: To the left stands the Queen, crowned; to the right stands Napoleon III, bare-headed, in cloak and military uniform.
Observations: Balston has catalogued this figure as Victoria and Napoleon III. Support for this is provided by the title. Comparison with other figures suggests that the potter intended to portray the Queen and Victor Emmanuel II. A smaller untitled version is found occasionally [7½ in (19 cm)].

Plate 34
Figure 78
Subject: **Napoleon III**
Title: None
Date: c. 1856
Height: 8¼ in (21 cm)
Colour: Well coloured.
Maker: Probably Thomas Parr
Rarity: Av.
Pair: ? *Fig.* 79 (Eugénie and the Prince Imperial)
Description: Standing bare-headed, in military uniform, epaulettes and knee-boots. In his left hand he clutches the hilt of his sword and in his right hand his cocked hat.

Plate 34 (Above and below) *Fig.* 78 Napoleon III   *Fig.* 79 Eugénie and Prince Imperial

Fig. 80 Napoleon and Eugénie   *Fig.* 81 Napoleon, Eugénie and Prince Imperial   *Fig.* 80(a) Napoleon and Eugénie

Observations: 1. Behind him is a plinth constructed of stones of identical size and shape to those composing the wall upon which Empress Eugénie sits (see *figs.* 78 and 79 in reverse, *pl.* C-35). This strengthens the theory that the two figures are a pair. Stones of this sort are seen in a number of figures known to have been made by the Parr and Kent group of potters, see *pls.* C-127 and 128. *Fig.* 79 (Eugénie) appears in the Kent lists.
2. The possibility that a single standing figure can be a pair to a seated figure suggests that a number of figures of 'Victoria on throne' may have a standing figure of Albert as a pair. However, to date, no examples have come to light.

Figure 79
Subject: **Empress Eugenie and the Prince Imperial**
Title: None, but see *fig.* 79(*a*), *pl.* C-36.
Date: c. 1856
Height: 8 in (20.5 cm)
Colour: Sparingly coloured.
Maker: Thomas Parr
Rarity: Av.
Pair: ? *Fig.* 78 (Napoleon III)
Description: Sitting crowned, the Prince on her lap supported by her left arm. Her right hand rests on his chest.
Observations: 1. The stones upon which she is sitting are of the same size and shape as those forming the plinth of *fig.* 78 (Napoleon

III). This strengthens the view that the two figures are a pair (see *pl.* C-35).
2. The figure has been mistakenly referred to in the literature as 'Victoria and child'.
3. Further confirmation of the identity of the figure is provided by the existence of an identical 'late' figure inscribed 'Empress Eugenie' in transfer black script, see *fig.* 79(*a*), *pl.* C-36. The figure appears in all three Kent lists.

Figure 80
Subject: **Empress Eugenie and Napoleon III**
Title: Eugenie & Napoleon (gilt script)
Date: c. 1854

Plate 34 continued

Height: 12½ in (31.75 cm); figure illustrated is 9½ in (24 cm).
Colour: Usually white and gilt, but an exceptionally fine untitled version [11¾ in (28.5 cm)] occurs, see *ch. 1, pl.* 10.
Rarity: Av.
Description: Napoleon stands bare-headed, in uniform, his left hand on a plinth. Eugénie sits on a broad-backed chair, a veil on her head, and flounced skirt.
Observations: Sometimes found wrongly titled 'Queen and Albert' in gilt script (see below).

Figure 80(a)
Subject: **Empress Eugenie and Napoleon III**
Title: Queen & Albert (gilt script)
Date: 1854
Height: 9½ in (24 cm)
Colour: Usually white and gilt.
Rarity: Av.
Description: Identical to *fig.* 80 (Napoleon and Eugénie), except for title.
Observations: The figure is well modelled, leaving no room for doubt that the potter's intention was that it should portray Napoleon and Eugénie.

Figure 81
Subject: **Napoleon III, Empress Eugenie and the Prince Imperial**
Title: None
Date: c. 1856
Height: 8 in (20.5 cm)
Colour: Sparingly coloured.
Rarity: Av.
Description: Napoleon stands to her left, bare-headed in military uniform; to his left is a pedestal. Eugénie sits bare-headed in flounced skirt. She holds the Prince Imperial on her lap in both arms. A shawl covers both their heads.
Observations: A similar figure fetched 30 gns at Christie's in 1968.

Plate 35
Figure 78 (in reverse)
Subject: **Napoleon III**
Observations: See *pl.* C-34.

Figure 79 (in reverse)
Subject: **Empress Eugenie and Prince Imperial**
Observations: See *pl.* C-34.

Figure 82
Subject: **Napoleon III**
Title: Emperor (raised capitals)
Date: c. 1854
Height: 10⅛ in (25.4 cm)
Colour: Well coloured; white and gilt versions exist.
Rarity: R.
Pair: Fig. 83 (Eugénie)
Description: On horse facing right, in cocked hat athwartships and military uniform. His right hand is raised to his hat in salute. His left hand holds the reins on the horse's neck.

Figure 83
Subject: **Eugenie, Empress of France**
Title: Empress (raised capitals)
Date: c. 1854
Height: 10 in (25 cm)
Colour: Well coloured; white and gilt versions exist.
Rarity: R.
Pair: Fig. 82 (Napoleon III)
Description: On horse facing left, in round hat and veil that hangs to her right.

Observations: A similar figure fetched 18 gns at Christie's in 1969.

Figure 84
Subject: **Albert**
Title: None
Date: 1854
Height: 7½ in (19 cm)
Colour: Well coloured.
Rarity: Av.
Pair: Fig. 85 (Napoleon III)
Description: Identical in all respects to *fig.* 82 (Napoleon III) except for (*a*) absence of title, (*b*) size and (*c*) facial characteristics, which are clearly those of Albert rather than Napoleon III.
Observations: 1. This figure has often been thought to portray Napoleon III, but there is little doubt, in my mind, that the original larger model has been intentionally adjusted to portray Albert.
2. This figure and its pair, together with *fig.* 162 (Albert) *pl.* A-55 fetched 32 gns at Christie's in 1965.

Figure 85
Subject: **Napoleon III**
Title: None
Date: c. 1854
Height: 7½ in (19 cm)
Colour: Well coloured.
Rarity: Av.
Pair: Fig. 84 (Albert)
Description: On horse facing left, in cocked hat, fore and aft, and military uniform. His left hand is on his left thigh, and his right hand is on the horse's mane.
Observations: 1. The facial features leave little room for doubt that this figure portrays Napoleon III.
2. This figure and its pair probably commemorate Prince Albert's visit to Napoleon III at St. Omer on September 5th, 1854.

Figure 86
Subject: **Napoleon III**
Title: Louis Napoleon (raised capitals)
Date: 1854
Height: 12¾ in (32.25 cm)
Colour: Well coloured usually, but paler versions, such as that illustrated, are not uncommon.
Rarity: Av.
Pair: Fig. 87 (Eugénie)
Description: On horse facing right, in cocked hat and uniform, his left hand on the horse's head, his right hand resting on his right thigh.
Observations: Several sizes of this figure exist with minor variants both in title (which, although identical, may occur as raised capitals on a plaque) and in the figure itself.

Figure 87
Subject: **Eugenie, Empress of France**
Title: Empress of France (raised capitals)
Date: 1854
Height: 11¼ in (28.5 cm)
Colour: As for preceding figure.
Rarity: Av.
Pair: Fig. 86 (Napoleon III)
Description: On horse facing left, in round hat with a veil hanging over to her left.
Observations: 1. See preceding figure.
2. A similar pair of figures fetched 24 gns at Christie's in 1964; another 36 gns, in the same rooms, in 1968; and another 50 gns, in the same rooms, in 1969.

Plate 36
Figure 79(a)
Subject: **Empress Eugenie and the Prince Imperial**
Title: Empress Eugenie (transfer black script)
Date: c. 1879
Height: 8 in (20.5 cm)
Colour: Usually rather more colourful than *fig.* 79, *pl.* C-34, but tends to be garish.
Maker: Parr and Kent group of potters.
Rarity: Av.
Pair: No pair for this figure has been found.
Description: Identical in all respects to *fig.* 79, *pl.* C-34 except that it is obviously a later figure, being very crudely coloured, also, it is titled.
Observations: 1. The titling of this figure is in the same style, although somewhat cruder, as that of *fig.* 229 (Princess Louise) and *fig.* 230 (Marquess of Lorne), see *pl.* A-78. This pair was probably issued at the time of the marriage of the Princess Louise and the Marquess of Lorne in 1871. This gives support to the belief that *fig.* 79(a) was a reissue in the seventies or eighties of *fig.* 79, making use of the old mould. It may, for instance, have been issued at the time of the death, in the Zulu War in 1879, of the Prince Imperial. At that time the widowed and exiled Empress Eugénie was living in this country and there was great public sympathy.
2. The figure appears in all three Kent lists. There is no mention of a figure of Napoleon III. In *Kent List A* it is no.250; in *Kent List B*, no. 212, as also in *Kent List C*.

Plate 37
Figure 87 (smaller version of that illustrated on *pl.* C-35)
Subject: **Eugenie, Empress of France**
Title: Empress of France (raised capitals on plaque)
Date: c. 1854
Height: 9 in (23 cm)
Colour: Well coloured.
Rarity: Av.
Pair: Pair to either *fig.* 86 (Napoleon III) *pl.* C-35, 10 in (25 cm) version, or to *fig.* 88 (Lewis Nepolian).
Description: On horse facing left. Identical except for the style of titling, height and other minor points to the 11¼ in (28.5 cm) version of this figure (see *pl.* C-35).

Figure 88
Subject: **Napoleon III**
Title: Lewis Nepolian (raised capitals)
Date: c. 1854
Height: 10 in (25 cm)
Colour: Well coloured.
Rarity: R.
Pair: Fig. 87 (Eugénie), 9 in (23 cm) version.
Description: On horse facing right, in cocked hat and military uniform. Similar to *fig.* 86, *pl.* C-35 except for size, titling and minor details.
Observations: 1. The two figures illustrated on this plate are undoubtedly a pair in spite of the obvious differences in style of title. The 9 in (23 cm) version of *fig.* 87 may pair *fig.* 88 (Lewis Nepolian) or the 10 in (25 cm) version of *fig.* 86 (Napoleon III), *pl.* C-35.
2. It is possible that this version was intended for the Welsh market.
3. The same figure is found occasionally titled in raised capitals 'Lois Napoleon', [*fig.* 88(a)].

Plate 35
T: *Fig.* 84 Albert
Fig. 82 Napoleon III
Fig. 83 Empress Eugénie
Fig. 85 Napoleon III

B: *Fig.* 86 Napoleon III
Fig. 78(*reverse*) Napoleon III
Fig. 79(*reverse*) Empress Eugénie and
Prince Imperial
Fig. 87 Empress Eugénie

Plate 36
Fig. 79(a) Empress Eugénie and the
Prince Imperial
In the collection of Mr D.P.M. Michael

Plate 38A
Fig. 89(a) Victor Emmanuel II
By courtesy of Mr Arthur Thornton

Plate 38A
Figure 89(a)
Subject: **Victor Emmanuel II**
Title: King of Sardina (*sic*) (raised capitals)
Date: 1855
Height: 4¾ in (12.25 cm)
Colour: Poorly coloured.
Rarity: VR.
Description: A midget version of *fig.* 89, *pl.*
C-38, except that instead of both hands
being on his belt, his left hand clasps a
sword by his side and his right hand alone
clasps the belt.
Observations: The smallest known figure in
which the title has been incorporated in the
mould.

Plate 38
Figure 89
Subject: **Victor Emmanuel II**
Title: King of Sardinia (raised capitals on
plaque)
Date: *c.* 1855
Height: 15 in (38 cm)
Colour: Usually well coloured with underglaze blue coat; sometimes poorly coloured.
Rarity: R.
Description: Standing in cocked hat athwartships, cloak and uniform, both hands on
belt.
Observations: 1. Our ally in the Crimean War
(1854–6). Visited England in 1855. Proclaimed King of Italy in 1861.
2. See *pl.* C-38A for midget version of this
piece [*fig.* 89(*a*)].
3. A similar figure fetched 65 gns at Christie's
in 1969.

Plate 37
Fig. 88 Lewis Nepolian

Fig. 87 Empress Eugénie
In the collection of Mr George H. Rayner

Colour Plate 28
Field Marshal Lord Raglan (Left). *Fig.* 112, *pl.* C-45. General Pelissier (Right). *Fig.* 116, *pl.* C-47. See page 253.

Colour Plate 29
General Sir George Brown and Field Marshal Lord Raglan. *Figs.* 123, 124, *pl.* C-50. See page 257.

Plate 38

T: *Fig.* 89 Victor Emmanuel II
Fig. 90 Victor Emmanuel II
Fig. 91 Victoria and Victor Emmanuel II
Fig. 92 Victor and Emmanuel II and Victoria

B: *Fig.* 93 Napoleon III[1]
Fig. 94 Empress Eugénie
Fig. 96 Napoleon III
Fig. 97 Empress Eugénie and the Prince Imperial

Fig. 98 Napoleon III
[1]Small version illustrated
(12 in, 30.5 cm)

Plate 38 continued

Figure 90
Subject: **Victor Emmanuel II**
Title: King of/Sardinia (raised capitals)
Date: *c.* 1855
Height: 17 in (42.5 cm)
Colour: Usually sparsely coloured.
Rarity: R. D. A.
Description: Standing bare-headed, in uniform, his right hand on a draped pedestal, his left hand on his hip.
Observations: A fine figure.

Figure 91
Subject: **Victoria and Victor Emmanuel II**
Title: Queen & King of/Sardinia (raised capitals)
Date: *c.* 1855

Height: 14 in (35.5 cm)
Colour: Usually well coloured.
Rarity: C.
Description: The Queen, crowned, stands on the left. To the right stands the King of Sardinia, bare-headed and in military uniform. A dog peeps through the gap between his legs.

Figure 92
Subject: **Victor Emmanuel II and Victoria**
Title: None
Date: *c.* 1855
Height: 9 in (23 cm)
Colour: Well coloured and sparsely coloured versions exist.
Rarity: R.

Description: The Queen stands on the right of a clock-face. She is crowned. The King is on the left, bare-headed, wearing uniform with epaulettes, his hat in his right hand. Their hands are clasped over the clock.

Figure 93
Subject: **Napoleon III**
Title: Louis Napoleon (raised capitals)
Date: *c.* 1854
Height: 16 in (40.5 cm); 12 in (30.5 cm) version illustrated.
Colour: Usually well coloured.
Rarity: Av.
Pair: The 12 in (30.5 cm) version may be the pair to *fig.* 94 (Eugénie).
Description: Standing bare-headed, in military uniform, cocked hat in his right hand,

his left hand on his hip; to his right is a pedestal.

Observations: A similar figure fetched 16 gns at Christie's in 1969.

Figure 94
Subject: **Eugenie, Empress of France**
Title: Empress of France (raised capitals)
Date: c. 1854
Height: 10¼ in (25.75 cm)
Colour: Both pale and coloured versions exist.
Rarity: VR.
Pair: Possibly a pair to the 12 in (30.5 cm) version of *fig*. 93 (Napoleon III).
Description: She stands bare-headed, her hair reaching to her shoulders. Her left arm is by her side, her right hand across her waist. She wears a bodice, flounced skirt and an overskirt.

Figure 96
Subject: **Napoleon III**
Title: Em. Napoleon (raised capitals)
Date: 1854
Height: 16 in (40.5 cm)
Colour: Well coloured.
Rarity: C.
Description: He is sitting on a gun emplacement, in cocked hat athwartships, and full military uniform. His right arm rests on a cannon and at his feet are piles of shells.
Observations: A similar figure fetched 45 gns at Christie's in 1969; and another, 20 gns six months later.

Figure 97
Subject: **Empress Eugenie and the Prince Imperial**
Title: Empress of France (raised capitals on plaque)
Date: 1856
Height: 12¼ in (31 cm)
Colour: Pale and coloured versions exist.
Rarity: R.
Pair: Fig. 98 (Napoleon III)
Description: She sits, a fillet round her hair, with both arms around the Prince Imperial, who rests on her lap, a wreath of roses in his left hand. The throne has a high back which is surmounted by an eagle.
Observations: 1. The Prince Imperial was born in 1856.
2. A similar figure fetched 28 gns at Christie's in 1963; and another 40 gns, in the same rooms in 1969.

Figure 98
Subject: **Napoleon III**
Title: Emperor of France (raised capitals on plaque)
Date: 1856
Height: 12¼ in (31 cm)
Colour: Pale and coloured versions exist.
Rarity: R.
Pair: Fig. 97 (Eugénie)
Description: He sits, bare-headed, in uniform and cloak. He holds his cocked hat in his right hand, which rests on his knee. The throne has a high back and is surmounted by an eagle.

Plate 39
Figure 95
Subject: **Napoleon III and Empress Eugenie**
Title: Emperor Empress (raised capitals)
Date: c. 1854

Height: 11¾ in (29.75 cm)
Colour: Well coloured with blue underglaze.
Rarity: VR.
Description: Napoleon stands on the right, in plumed cocked hat, uniform and trousers. On the left stands Eugénie, bare-headed in low bodice, flounced skirt and overskirt. Her left hand is on his right forearm.

Plate 40
Figure 99
Subject: **Napoleon III**
Title: Emperor (raised capitals)
Date: c. 1856
Height: 8¼ in (21 cm)
Colour: Well coloured.
Rarity: VR. A.
Pair: Fig. 100 (Eugénie)
Description: He sits bare-headed, in uniform, in a high armchair with perforated back. He clasps his cocked hat in his right hand. His legs are crossed.
Observations: 1. The title of this figure and its pair seem to have been applied by being impressed by a roller on which the letters have been engraved in 'mirror-image' (see *ch*. 4). The resulting titles, in raised capitals, are:
'EMPER' for Emperor
and
'EMPRESS OE ERANCE' for Empress of France
In the two figures illustrated these titles have been left unaltered. In other figures I have seen, the correct titles have been applied by overpainting in black enamel.
2. A similar figure, with 'EMPEROR' in black enamel over the title 'EMPER' in raised capitals (no. 382 in the Willett collection at Brighton), is catalogued as Francis II, Emperor of Austria (1768–1835). The discovery of the pairing figure 'Empress of France' precludes this identification.

Figure 100
Subject: **Empress Eugenie and the Prince Imperial**
Title: Empress of France (raised capitals)
Date: c. 1856
Height: 7 in (17.5 cm)
Colour: Well coloured.
Rarity: VR. A.
Pair: Fig. 99 (Napoleon III)
Description: She sits in a high armchair, the back of which is not perforated. She is bare-headed, wears a long flounced dress and clasps the Prince Imperial in both arms on her lap.
Observations: See preceding figure.

Plate 41
Figure 102
Subject: **Admiral Sir Charles Napier**
Title: C. Napier (raised capitals)
Date: c. 1854
Height: 11¾ in (29.75 cm)
Colour: Well coloured and pale versions exist.
Rarity: C.
Pair: Fig. 103 (Deans Dundas)
Description: Standing bare-headed, in uniform, cocked hat in his right hand, a cloak in his left. To his right, a cannon with shells. Brickwork can be seen behind, between his legs.
Observations: 1. See *observations fig*. 101 (Napier) *pl*. C-42.
2. Considered to be a smaller version of *fig*. 102 (Napier) *pl*. C-42.

Figure 103
Subject: **Admiral Sir Deans Dundas**
Title: Dundas (raised capitals)
Date: c. 1854
Height: 11¾ in (29.75 cm)
Colour: Well coloured and pale versions exist.
Rarity: C.
Pair: Fig. 102 (Napier)
Description: Standing bare-headed, in uniform, to his left a cannon, shells, a wheel and brickwork; to his right a flag.
Observations: 1. See *observations fig*. 101 (Napier) *pl*. C-42.
2. Considered to be a smaller version of *fig*. 103 (Deans Dundas) *pl*. C-42.
3. A similar pair of figures fetched 26 gns at Christie's in 1964.

Plate 42
Figure 101
Subject: **Admiral Sir Charles Napier**
Title: Sir Charles Napier (gilt script)
Date: c. 1854
Height: 16¼ in (41 cm); figure illustrated 11 in (28 cm).
Colour: White and gilt, or coloured.
Rarity: VR.
Pair: Not known
Description: Standing bare-headed, in uniform with epaulettes and sword, cocked hat in his right hand, a cloak in his left. Beside his right leg is a cannon and shells.
Observations: 1. Figures are known which are titled 'Sir Charles Napier', 'Sir C. Napier' and 'C. Napier', also 'Dundas', 'Admiral Dundas' and 'R. S. Dundas'. With regard to the 'Napier' figures, the uniform is so indefinite that it could be either naval or military, so that on the face of it, the figures could represent either *Admiral Sir Charles Napier* (1786–1860), in command of the Baltic fleet in the Crimean War or *General Sir Charles James Napier* (1782–1853), the conqueror of Sind. However, at least one of the Napier figures pairs Dundas and there is, therefore, little doubt that all the figures portray the Admiral. The figures are typical Crimean portraits and less likely to have been manufactured in the early 1840's.

With regard to the figure titled 'Dundas', it would seem likely that this figure portrays *Admiral Sir Deans Dundas* (1785–1862), in command of the Mediterranean fleet (1853–4). This was much the same period that Admiral Sir Charles Napier was in command of the Baltic Fleet. The solitary figure titled 'Admiral Dundas', *fig*. 101(*b*), *pl*. C-42A is identical to *fig*. 101 (Napier). The figure titled 'R. S. Dundas' represents *Admiral Sir Richard Saunders Dundas* (1802–61) who commanded the Baltic fleet, in succession to Sir Charles Napier, from 1855–61. This figure, likely to be a little later than the figure titled 'Dundas', was titled with initials as well as surname to distinguish the one from the other.
2. See also *fig*. 101(*a*) (Lyons) and *fig*. 101(*b*) (Dundas), *pl*. C-42A.

Figure 102
Subject: **Admiral Sir Charles Napier**
Title: C. Napier (raised capitals)
Date: c. 1854
Height: 16 in (40.5 cm)
Colour: Usually well coloured with blue jacket, but paler versions exist.
Rarity: C.
Pair: Fig. 103 (Deans Dundas)—matching sizes exist.

Colour Plate 30
Victoria and Napoleon III. *Fig.* 77, *pl.* C-33. See pages 240-1.

Plate 39
Fig. 95 Napoleon III and Empress Eugénie
In the Thomas Balston collection

Plate 40
Fig. 99 Napoleon III
Fig. 100 Empress Eugénie
In the collection of Mr A. Guy Stringer

Plate 41
Fig. 102 Napier
Fig. 103 Deans Dundas
By courtesy of Miss M.M. Frame

Plate 42

Fig. 101 Napier   *Fig.* 102 Napier   *Fig.* 104 Napier   *Fig.* 103 Deans Dundas   *Fig.* 105 Napier

Plate 42A
Fig. 101(a) Lyons
By courtesy of Messrs Christie, Manson & Woods

Plate 42 continued
Description: He stands bare-headed, in uniform, cocked hat in his right hand, a cloak in his left; to his right a cannon with shells.
Observations: One example has been noted incised 'John Carr/1857', see *p.* 12.

Figure 103
Subject: **Admiral Sir Deans Dundas**
Title: Dundas (raised capitals)
Date: *c.* 1854
Height: 15½ in (39.25 cm)
Colour: Usually well coloured with blue jacket, but paler versions exist.
Rarity: C.
Pair: Pair to either *fig.* 102 (Napier) or *fig.* 104 (Napier).
Description: Standing bare-headed in uniform; to his left a cannon, shells and wheel; to his right a flag.
Observations: 1. A similar pair of figures fetched 28 gns at Christie's in 1963; and another pair 55 gns at Christie's in 1969.
2. See preceding plate for illustration of smaller version of this figure and its pair.

Figure 104
Subject: **Admiral Sir Charles Napier**
Title: C. Napier (raised capitals)
Date: *c.* 1854
Height: 16½ in (41.5 cm); figure illustrated 14½ in (36.75 cm).
Colour: Well coloured with blue jacket.
Rarity: Av.
Pair: Fig. 103 (Deans Dundas)—matching sizes exist.
Description: He stands bare-headed, in uniform, cocked hat in his right hand, a cloak in his left.
Observations: 1. The title of this figure is inscribed on a plaque which is not 'raised'. I have seen an otherwise identical figure in which there is no plaque and on which the title 'Sir C. Napier' is inscribed in gilt script [*fig.* 104(*a*)].

2. A similar figure and pair, fetched 55 gns at Christie's in 1969.

Figure 105
Subject: **Admiral Sir Charles Napier**
Title: Sir Charles Napier (gilt script)
Date: *c.* 1854
Height: 12¾ in (32.25 cm)
Colour: Both coloured and pale versions exist.
Rarity: R. D. A.
Description: He stands bare-headed, in uniform, a telescope in his right hand, his left foot on a cannon with a pile of shells close by.
Observations: No pair, such as Dundas, is known to this figure. Even so, it is probably a Crimean portrait of Admiral Sir Charles Napier. Alternatively, it may have been intended to portray the same Napier at the storming of Sidon in 1840, or his cousin, *General Sir Charles James Napier* (1782–1853), the conqueror of Sind (1843). See *observations fig.* 101.

Plate 42A
Figure 101(a)
Subject: **Admiral Sir Edmund Lyons**
Title: Sir E. Lyons (gilt script)
Date: *c.* 1855
Height: 11 in (28 cm)
Colour: Well coloured.
Rarity: VR.
Pair: Not known
Description: Standing bare-headed, in uniform with epaulettes and sword. He holds his cocked hat in his right hand, a cloak in his left. Beside his right leg are a cannon and shells.
Observations: 1. Identical, other than for title, to similar sized version of *fig.* 101 (Napier) *pl.* C-42. The only recorded example appears to be late out of the mould. The figure was originally intended to portray Napier. It was probably renamed when Lyons suc-

Plate 43
In the collection of
Mr D.P.M. Michael

Fig. 107 Codrington   *Fig.* 108 Windham   *Fig.* 106 Napier

ceeded Admiral Sir James Deans Dundas in command of the Mediterranean fleet early in 1855; by then, the Crimean War was nearly over. Conveniently for the potters, the moulds of the figure lay idle at that time, for Napier had been relieved of his command of the Baltic fleet early in 1855 also, and public interest in him had wained. No true portrait of Lyons is recorded.

2. The same figure fetched 150 gns at Christie's in 1969.

3. I have seen a solitary example of the same figure titled 'Admiral Dundas' (see below). This is the only instance known to me of one figure with three different identities.

Figure 101(b) (not illustrated)
Subject: **Admiral Sir Deans Dundas**
Title: Admiral Dundas (gilt script)
Date: *c.* 1854
Height: 11¼ in (28.5 cm)
Colour: White and gilt.
Rarity: VR.
Pair: Not known
Description: Standing bare-headed, in uniform with epaulettes and sword. He holds his cocked hat in his right hand, a cloak in his left. Beside his right leg are a cannon and shells.
Observations: 1. In absence of initials, can be assumed to be intended to be Admiral Sir Deans Dundas, but the figure was originally a portrait of Admiral Sir Charles Napier.

2. Identical, other than for title, to similar sized versions of *fig.* 101 (Napier) *pl.* C-42 and *fig.* 101(*a*) (Lyons). See also, under preceding figure.

Plate 43
Figure 106
Subject: **Admiral Sir Charles Napier**
Title: C. Napier (raised capitals)
Date: *c.* 1854
Height: 12¾ in (32.25 cm)
Colour: Pale.
Rarity: VR. D. A.
Description: Similar to *fig.* 105 (Napier) *pl.* C-42 except for the manner of titling and the addition of two sashes which dangle from his belt.
Observations: See *fig.* 105 (Napier) *pl.* C-42.

Figure 107
Subject: **General Sir William Codrington**
Title: G. Codrington (raised capitals on plaque)
Date: *c.* 1854
Height: 13 in (33 cm)
Colour: Well coloured and pale versions exist.
Rarity: R. A.
Description: He stands, in cocked hat with a plume hanging on either side, tailed tunic with high collar, epaulettes, and trousers. His left hand is on the hilt of a sword hanging

against his left leg and in his right hand he holds a speech. To his left is a cloak with ermine collar draped over a pedestal, and behind his right leg is a tilted cannon on a wall with a pile of shells below. Above this is a large flag.

Figure 108
Subject: **General Sir Charles Windham**
Title: G. Windham (raised capitals on plaque)
Date: *c.* 1854
Height: 18 in (45.5 cm)
Colour: Well coloured.
Rarity: VR. A.
Pair: No pair to this figure is known.
Description: He stands, in plumed cocked hat, uniform and cloak. He holds a sword against his right leg, and to his right is a gun emplacement with a pile of shells at its base, and a flag.
Observations: 1. Similar to *fig.* 110 (Windham) *pl.* C-44. This latter is one in a series of three figures, the other two being *fig.* 109 (Simpson) and *fig.* 111 (Pelissier). The only difference between the two Windham portraits is the presence or absence of a flag and the manner of titling.

2. A similar figure, and another similar to *fig.* 109 (Simpson) *pl.* C-44, fetched 48 gns at Christie's in 1963.

Plate 44
*In the Thomas Balston
collection*

Fig. 111 Pelissier   *Fig.* 110 Windham   *Fig.* 109 Simpson

Plate 45
Fig. 112 Raglan

Plate 46
In the collection of Lady Ranfurly
Fig. 114 Codrington

Fig. 115 Pelissier

Section C. Naval, Military and Exploration

Plate 44
Figure 109
Subject: **General Sir James Simpson**
Title: G. Simpson (raised capitals)
Date: *c.* 1854
Height: 17½ in (43.5 cm)
Colour: Well coloured or pale versions exist.
Rarity: R. D.
Series: Same series as *fig.* 110 (Windham)
and *fig.* 111 (Pelissier).
Description: Standing, in cocked hat and
military uniform, an ermine cloak over his
left arm, a manuscript in his right hand. To
his right a gun emplacement with shells at
its base and two flags.
Observations: A similar figure, together with
one similar to *fig.* 108 (Windham) *pl.* C-43,
fetched 48 gns at Christie's in 1963.

Figure 110
Subject: **General Sir Charles Windham**
Title: G. Windham (raised capitals)
Date: *c.* 1854
Height: 18 in (45.5 cm)
Colour: Pale version only seen.
Rarity: VR. D.
Series: Central figure of a set of three, the
other two being *fig.* 109 (Simpson) and *fig.*
111 (Pelissier).
Description: Standing, in cocked hat and
military uniform, a cloak draped over his
left shoulder. He holds a sword in his right
hand against his right leg, and to his right is
a gun emplacement with shells at its base.
There are no flags.
Observations: Similar, but not identical, to
fig. 108, *pl.* C-43.

Figure 111
Subject: **General Pelissier**
Title: G. Pelissier (raised capitals)
Date: *c.* 1854
Height: 17½ in (43.5 cm)
Colour: Well coloured or pale versions exist.
Rarity: R. D.
Series: Same series as *fig.* 109 (Simpson) and
fig. 110 (Windham).
Description: Standing, in kepi and military
uniform, a manuscript in his left hand and
an ermine cloak draped over his right
forearm. His right hand is on his waist. To
his left is a gun emplacement, with shells at
its base and two flags.

Plate 45
Figure 112
Subject: **F-M. Lord Raglan**
Title: Lord Raglan (raised capitals on
plaque)
Date: 1854
Height: 11¾ in (29.75 cm)
Colour: Well coloured.
Rarity: VR. A.
Pair: Unknown but must exist, *fig.* 113 has
been reserved. Same series as *fig.* 114
(Codrington) and *fig.* 115 (Pelissier).
Description: On prancing horse facing right.
in cocked hat and military uniform, his
right sleeve pinned upon his chest.

Plate 46
Figure 114
Subject: **General Sir William Codrington**
Title: Gnl. Codrington (raised capitals on
plaque)
Date: 1854
Height: 11½ in (29 cm)
Colour: Well coloured and pale versions
exist.
Rarity: R.

Plate 47 (continues overleaf)
Fig. 116 Pelissier

Pair: Fig. 115 (Pelissier). Same series as
fig. 112 (Raglan) *pl.* C-45.
Description: On horse facing right, wearing
round hat and military uniform. His left
hand is on the horse's mane.
Observations: A similar figure and its pair
fetched 50 gns at Christie's in 1969.

Figure 115
Subject: **General Pelissier**
Title: Gnl. Pelissier (raised capitals on
plaque)
Date: 1854
Height: 12½ in (31.75 cm)
Colour: Well coloured and pale versions
exist.
Rarity: R.
Pair: Fig. 114 (Codrington). Same series as
fig. 112 (Raglan) *pl.* C-45.
Description: On horse facing left, in cocked
hat, military uniform, cape and trousers.
His right arm is on the horse's mane.
Observations: A similar figure and its pair
fetched 50 gns at Christie's in 1969.

Plate 47
Figure 116
Subject: **General Pelissier**
Title: Gnl. Pelissier (raised capitals)
Date: *c.* 1854
Height: 12½ in (31.75 cm)
Colour: Well coloured.
Rarity: R. A.
Pair: Not known
Description: On prancing horse facing left,
in cocked hat and military uniform.
Rococo base with a cannon and shells.

Figure 117
Subject: **General Sir William Codrington**
Title: Gnl. Codrington (raised capitals on
plaque)
Date: *c.* 1854
Height: 10¾ in (27 cm)

Colour: Well coloured and pale versions
exist.
Rarity: R.
Series: Fig. 118 (Campbell), 12½ in (31.75
cm) version, and possibly *fig.* 127 (Pelissier)
pl. C-51A.
Description: Standing in round hat and
military uniform. His left leg is against a
cannon and his right hand is on a flag at
the base of which is a pile of shells.
Observations: This figure, together with a
damaged version of *fig.* 123 (Brown) *pl.*
C-50, fetched 40 gns at Christie's in 1963.

Figure 118
Subject: **General Sir Colin Campbell**
Title: Sir Colin Campbell (raised capitals
on plaque)
Date: *c.* 1854
Height: 12½ in (31.75 cm); a 14½ in (36.75
cm) version has been recorded, but no pair
to it is known, see below.
Colour: Well coloured.
Rarity: R.
Pair: Fig. 117 (Codrington), and possibly
fig. 127 (Pelissier) *pl.* C-51A.
Description: Standing, with moustache and
imperial, in plumed busby, short jacket
and trews. His left hand is on his hip and
behind his left leg is a cannon and shells.
His right hand is on a flag which appears
to be the French tricolour with a rough
representation of the Union Jack in the top
corner.
Observations: 1. Figures of Sir Colin Campbell were issued both in connection with the
Crimean War and the Indian Mutiny. That
this figure is a Crimean figure is suggested
by the French tricolour and confirmed by
the fact that it pairs *fig.* 117 (Codrington).
2. A 12½ in (31.75 cm) version of this figure,
together with a 9¼ in (23.5 cm) version of
fig. 102 (Napier) *pl.* C-41, fetched 62 gns at
Christie's in 1965.

Plate 47 continued   Fig. 117 Codrington   Fig. 118 Campbell

Plate 48
Figure 119
Subject: **General Sir Colin Campbell**
Title: C. Campell (*sic*) (raised capitals)
Date: c. 1854
Height: 11 in (28 cm)
Colour: Sparsely coloured, and gilt and white versions exist.
Rarity: R.
Pair: Fig. 120 (Canrobert)
Description: On horse facing right. Bare-headed, he holds a Scotch bonnet to his head with his right hand, military uniform.
Observations: Identical figure (other than in size and title) to *fig.* 121 (Brown) *pl.* C-49 and *fig.* 123 (Brown) *pl.* C-50.

Figure 120
Subject: **General Canrobert**
Title: Canrobert (raised capitals)
Date: c. 1854
Height: 11 in (28 cm)
Colour: White and gilt.
Rarity: VR. D.
Pair: Fig. 119 (Campbell)
Description: On horse facing left, in plumed cocked hat, swallow-tailed coat and trousers. The reins are held low in his left hand and his right forearm rests on a circular platform, with a tasselled border, on the horse's back.
Observations: Identical figure (other than in size and title) to *fig.* 122 (Evans) *pl.* C-49 and *fig.* 124 (Raglan) *pl.* C-50, except that in the latter case the right forearm is missing, and the sleeve empty. *Fig.* 126 (Raglan) *pl.* C-51 also bears some similarity to these figures.

C254

Plate 49
Figure 121
Subject: **General Sir George Brown**
Title: G. Brown (raised capitals)
Date: c. 1854
Height: 13½ in (34.25 cm)
Colour: Usually white and gilt.
Rarity: R.
Pair: Fig. 122 (Evans)
Description: On horse facing right. Bare-headed, he holds a bonnet to his head with his right hand.
Observations: The same design has been used for *fig.* 119 (Campbell) *pl.* C-48 and *fig.* 123 (Brown) *pl.* C-50.

Figure 122
Subject: **Col. Sir George de Lacy Evans**
Title: D. L. Evans (raised capitals)
Date: c. 1854
Height: 13¼ in (33.5 cm)
Colour: Usually white and gilt, but one finely coloured version has been seen.
Rarity: VR. D.
Pair: Fig. 121 (Brown)
Description: On horse facing left, in plumed cocked hat, swallow-tailed coat and trousers. The reins are in his left hand and his right forearm rests on a platform on the horse's back.
Observations: An identical figure in all respects (except for height and title) to *fig.* 120 (Canrobert) *pl.* C-48 and to *fig.* 124 (Raglan) *pl.* C-50, although in the latter instance the right forearm is missing, and the sleeve empty. *Fig.* 126 (Raglan) *pl.* C-51 also bears some similarity to these figures.

Plate 48
Fig. 119 Campbell
Fig. 120 Canrobert
In the collection of Lady Ranfurly

Plate 49
Fig. 121 Brown
Fig. 122 Evans
In the Thomas Balston collection

Plate 50
*In the collection of
Lady Ranfurly*

Fig. 123 Brown   *Fig.* 124 Raglan

Plate 51
*In the Thomas Balston
collection*

Fig. 125 Cathcart   *Fig.* 126 Raglan

Plate 51A
Fig. 127 Pelissier
In the Thomas Balston collection

Plate 52
Fig. 128 Canrobert
In the collection of Mr D.P.M. Michael

Plate 50
Figure 123
Subject: **General Sir George Brown**
Title: Sir George Brown (gilt script)
Date: *c.* 1854
Height: 14 in (35.5 cm)
Colour: White and gilt.
Rarity: R.
Pair: Fig. 124 (Raglan)
Description: On horse facing right. Bare-headed, he holds a bonnet to his head with his right hand.
Observations: The same design has been used in the case of *fig.* 119 (Campbell) *pl.* C-48 and *fig.* 121 (Brown) *pl.* C-49.

Figure 124
Subject: **F-M. Lord Raglan**
Title: Lord Raglan (gilt script)
Date: *c.* 1854
Height: 14½ in (36.75 cm)
Colour: White and gilt.
Rarity: VR.
Pair: Fig. 123 (Brown)
Description: On horse facing left, in plumed cocked hat, military tunic, epaulettes and trousers. The reins are held low in his left hand and his right sleeve has been pinned to his tunic.
Observations: The same figure has been used for *fig.* 120 (Canrobert) *pl.* C-48, only in this case the right forearm is present. It has also been used for *fig.* 122 (Evans) *pl.* C-49 and in this case also the right forearm is present.

Plate 51
Figure 125
Subject: **General Sir George Cathcart**
Title: G. Cathcart (raised capitals)
Date: *c.* 1854
Height: 12½ in (31.75 cm)
Colour: White and gilt.
Rarity: VR. D.
Pair: Fig. 126 (Raglan)
Description: On horse facing right, in plumed cocked hat, swallow-tailed coat and knee-boots. His left forearm rests on a circular smooth platform with tasselled borders.
Observations: See following figure.

Figure 126
Subject: **F-M. Lord Raglan**
Title: L. Raglan (raised capitals)
Date: *c.* 1854
Height: 12¾ in (32.25 cm)
Colour: Usually white and gilt, but one fine example with underglaze blue coat has been seen.
Rarity: VR.
Pair: Fig. 125 (Cathcart)
Description: On horse facing left, in plumed cocked hat, swallow-tailed coat, and knee-boots. His right sleeve, which is empty, is pinned to his jacket. A sword is suspended from his belt.
Observations: This figure is a mirror-image of *fig.* 125 (Cathcart) except for the sword behind his left leg, and the absence of his right forearm.

Plate 51A
Figure 127
Subject: **General Pelissier**
Title: Gnl. Pelissier (raised capitals on plaque)
Date: *c.* 1854
Height: 11½ in. (29 cm)
Colour: Well coloured.
Rarity: VR.
Series: Possibly same series as *fig.* 117 (Codrington) and *fig.* 118 (Campbell), *pl.* C-47.
Description: He stands, in cocked hat and military uniform. His left hand holds his sword against a heap of shells by his left leg.

Plate 52
Figure 128
Subject: **General Canrobert**
Title: General Canrobert (raised capitals)
Date: *c.* 1854
Height: 11 in (28 cm)
Colour: Well coloured.
Rarity: VR.
Pair: This figure clearly has a pair, but so far it has not come to light; *fig.* 129 has been reserved for it.
Description: On horse facing right. Bare-headed in military uniform. His left forearm rests on an oval smooth surface, with tasselled sides, on the horse's back, and his left hand holds the reins. His right hand, holding his hat, is on the horse's flank. He himself faces right and has a moustache and imperial.

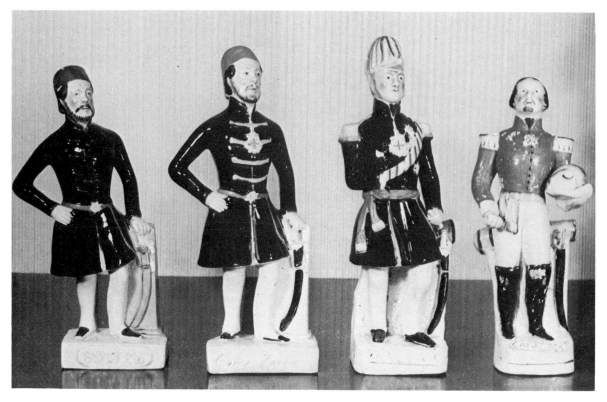

Fig. 131 Abd-ul-Medjid   *Fig.* 130 Omar Pasha   *Fig.* 132 Raglan   *Fig.* 133 Canrobert

Plate 53
Figure 130
Subject: **Omar Pasha**
Title: Omer Pacha (gilt script)
Date: *c.* 1854
Height: 13 in (33 cm)
Colour: Well coloured, blue coat.
Rarity: Av.
Series: Similar to *fig.* 131 (Abd-ul-Medjid),
fig. 132 (Raglan) and *fig.* 133 (Canrobert).
Although not a 'matching' series, all
emanate from the same factory and have
close similarities.
Description: Standing facing half-right, in fez,
military frock-coat and trousers; his right
hand on his hip and his left hand, by his side,
grasping a sabre.
Observations: 1. An identical figure has been
used for *fig.* 131 (Abd-ul-Medjid).
2. A similar figure, together with *fig.* 132
(Raglan), fetched 105 gns at Christie's in
1965.

Figure 131
Subject: **Abd-ul-Medjid, Sultan of Turkey**
Title: Sultan (raised capitals on lozenge
shaped plaque)
Date: *c.* 1854
Height: 13 in (33 cm)
Colour: Well coloured.
Rarity: R.
Series: Similar to *fig.* 130 (Omar Pasha),
fig. 132 (Raglan) and *fig.* 133 (Canrobert).
All have close similarities and clearly
emanate from the same factory.
Description: Identical in all respects, other
than title, to *fig.* 130 (Omar Pasha).
Observations: The same figure has been used
both for *fig.* 130 (Omar Pasha) and for *fig.*
131 (Abd-ul-Medjid).

Figure 132
Subject: **F-M. Lord Raglan**
Title: Raglan (raised capitals on plaque)
Date: *c.* 1854
Height: 13½ in (34.25 cm)

Colour: Well coloured.
Rarity: VR. D. A.
Series: Clearly emanates from the same
factory as *fig.* 130 (Omar Pasha), *fig.* 131
(Abd-ul-Medjid) and *fig.* 133 (Canrobert).
It has close similarities to all three, but
particularly to Canrobert.
Description: Standing half-right, in heavily
plumed cocked hat, and frock-coat with the
right sleeve empty. He carries a baton in his
left hand and behind him there is a gun
emplacement against which he leans his
sword.
Observations: A similar figure, together with
fig. 130 (Omar Pasha), fetched 105 gns at
Christie's in 1965.

Figure 133
Subject: **General Canrobert**
Title: Canrobert (raised capitals)
Date: *c.* 1854
Height: 11½ in (29 cm)
Colour: Well coloured.
Rarity: VR. D. A.
Series: Has close similarities to *fig.* 130
(Omar Pasha), *fig.* 131 (Abd-ul-Medjid)
and *fig.* 132 (Raglan).
Description: Standing bare-headed, in mili-
tary uniform. Cocked hat in his left hand,
a gun emplacement behind him.

Plate 54
Figure 102
Subject: **Admiral Sir Charles Napier**
Observations: See *pl.* C-41.

Figure 134
Subject: **Omar Pasha**
Title: Omar Pasha (gilt script)
Date: *c.* 1854
Height: 11 in (28 cm)
Colour: Well coloured.
Rarity: R.
Description: Standing in fez, cloak, short
tunic, trousers and knee-boots. His left hand
rests on a pedestal.

Figure 135
Subject: **Col. Sir George de Lacy Evans**
Title: Sir de Lacy/Evans (raised capitals)
Date: *c.* 1854
Height: 12½ in (31.75 cm)
Colour: Well coloured.
Rarity: VR. D. A.
Description: Standing bare-headed, in mili-
tary uniform. His plumed cocked hat is on a
table to his right, and his left hand rests on a
pedestal.
Observations: A similar figure and *fig.* 138
(Pelissier) fetched 72 gns at Christie's in
1963.

Figure 136
Subject: **General Canrobert**
Title: None
Date: *c.* 1854
Height: 9 in (23 cm)
Colour: Well coloured.
Rarity: R.
Description: Standing in cocked hat, tunic
with epaulettes, and trousers; sash over his
right shoulder. His right hand is on his hip,
and his left hand rests on a pedestal upon
which there appears to be a manuscript.
Rococo base.
Observations: 1. Although this piece has
never been positively identified, there is a
very close resemblance to General Can-
robert.
2. A similar figure together with *fig.* 181
(Sebastopol) *pl.* C-69 fetched 26 gns at
Christie's in 1964.

Figure 137
Subject: **Admiral Sir Richard Saunders
Dundas**
Title: R. S. Dundas (raised capitals)
Date: *c.* 1855
Height: 12½ in (31.75 cm)
Colour: Well coloured.
Rarity: R. D. A.
Description: Standing with cocked hat
athwartships, in full naval uniform. His left

Section C. Naval, Military and Exploration

Fig. 134 Omar Pasha   *Fig.* 135 Evans   *Fig.* 136 Canrobert

Fig. 137 R.S. Dundas   *Fig.* 102 Napier   *Fig.* 138 Pelissier   *Fig.* 139 Nightingale

hand rests on a sword. He holds a telescope at waist level in his right hand. There is a tilted flag beside each leg and cannon balls beside his right foot. Rococo base.
Observations: See *observations fig.* 101 (Napier) *pl.* C-42.

Figure 138
Subject: **General Pelissier**
Title: Gnl. Pelissier (raised capitals on plaque)
Date: *c.* 1854

Height: 12 in (30.5 cm)
Colour: Well coloured.
Rarity: VR. A.
Description: He is standing in cocked hat and military frock-coat. His left hand holds a sword, his right hand is on his hip, and there are shells against his right leg.
Observations: 1. Similar design to *fig.* 127 (Pelissier) *pl.* C-51A except that the shells are against his left leg in that figure.
2. This figure and one similar to *fig.* 135 (Evans) fetched 72 gns at Christie's in 1963.

Figure 139
Subject: **Florence Nightingale**
Title: Miss F. Nightingale (raised capitals)
Date: *c.* 1855
Height: 10½ in (26.5 cm)
Colour: Well coloured.
Rarity: R. D. A.
Description: She is standing bare-headed, in long-sleeved dress, a small tray with two cups in her right hand.
Observations: Very similar to *fig.* 140 (Nightingale) *pl.* C-54A.

Plate 54A
Fig. 140 Nightingale
In the collection of Lt.-Col. A.C.W. Kimpton

Plate 54B
Fig. 141 Nightingale
By courtesy of the Brighton Art Gallery and Museum

Plate 54A
Figure 140
Subject: **Florence Nightingale**
Title: Miss F. Nightingale (raised capitals)
Date: *c.* 1855
Height: 11 in (28 cm)
Colour: Well coloured.
Rarity: R. D. A.
Description: She stands bare-headed, with Zouave jacket and sash. Her forearms are exposed, the sleeves being open to the elbow; wide skirt. She carries a large tray with two cups in her right hand.
Observations: Similar apart from minor differences to *fig.* 139 (Nightingale) *pl.* C-54.

Plate 54B
Figure 141
Subject: **Florence Nightingale**
Title: None
Date: *c.* 1855
Height: 9 in (23 cm)
Colour: Well coloured.
Rarity: VR.
Description: Bust. Bare-headed. Circular base.
Observations: No. 160 in the Willett collection.

Plate 55
Figure 142
Subject: **Florence Nightingale**
Title: Miss / Nightingale (raised capitals)
Date: *c.* 1856
Height: 14¼ in (36.25 cm)
Colour: Well coloured and pale versions exist.
Rarity: Av. D. A.
Description: Standing with a veil on her head, long flowing dress and long sleeves.

Plate 55
In the collections of
Mr A Guy Stringer and the
author

Fig. 142(a) Nightingale   *Fig.* 142 Nightingale   *Fig.* 143 Nightingale and officer

C260

Plate 56 (Above and below)

Fig. 144 Campbell   *Fig.* 146 Campbell   *Fig.* 148 Havelock

Fig. 151 Campbell   *Fig.* 149 Brown   *Fig.* 150 Simpson   *Fig.* 152 Raglan

To her left is a pedestal upon which are three books, and her left hand rests on them. Her right forearm supports a shawl. From her neck is suspended a locket with a cross which had been given her by Queen Victoria in 1856.

Observations: 1. An untitled, virtually identical, midget figure exists, *fig.* 142(*a*), 5¼ in (13.5 cm). This figure is nearly always 'late'. Although the majority were produced in the present century, I have occasionally come across what has appeared to be a contemporary copy.

2. There is also another 'mini-figure' thought to portray Miss Nightingale, 4¼ in (10.75 cm), see *ch.* 4, *pl.* 5.

3. Although christened by wounded patients 'The Lady with the Lamp', no figure has yet come to light depicting Miss Nightingale thus.

Figure 143
Subject: **Florence Nightingale and wounded officer**
Title: Miss / Nightingale (raised capitals)
Date: c. 1855
Height: 9¾ in (24.5 cm)
Colour: Well coloured and pale versions exist.

Rarity: Av. D. A.
Description: Standing to the right, a veil on her head, wearing a long flowing dress with short sleeves. To her right sits an officer, bare-headed, his left arm in a sling.
Observations: 1. Mrs Cecil Woodham-Smith has told me that this figure would be unlikely to have a source, because Florence Nightingale devoted all her energies to the welfare of the men, and had little to do with wounded or sick officers.

2. A similar figure fetched 68 gns at Christie's in 1965. Another, poorly coloured, fetched 32 gns at Christie's in 1967. Another, with *fig.* 142, fetched 50 gns at Christie's in 1963. Another, with *fig.* 142, fetched 135 gns at Christie's in 1966; both were well coloured. Another, with *fig.* 142, fetched 110 gns at Christie's in 1967; both figures were poorly coloured. Another, state unknown, fetched 28 gns at Christie's in 1968; and another, 55 gns at Christie's in 1969.

Plate 56
Figure 144
Subject: **General Sir Colin Campbell**
Title: S. C. Campbell (raised capitals)
Date: 1857

Height: 10 in (25 cm)
Colour: Well coloured.
Rarity: VR.
Pair: Fig. 145 (Havelock) *pl.* C-57.
Description: He stands bare-headed, in jacket with high collar and no epaulettes. He holds a plumed bonnet above his head in his right hand. Behind and to his right is a cannon and a pile of shells. Behind his left leg are two flags.
Observations: Figures of Campbell were produced both in connection with the Crimean War and the Indian Mutiny. Before *fig.* 145 (Havelock) *pl.* C-57 was discovered this figure was thought likely to be Crimean. Now it is certain that it was produced in connection with the Indian Mutiny.

Figure 146
Subject: **General Sir Colin Campbell**
Title: Sir / Colin Campbell (raised capitals)
Date: 1857
Height: 11 in (28 cm)
Colour: White and gilt, or coloured, with cinnamon horse.
Rarity: Av.
Pair: Fig. 147 (Havelock) *pl.* C-89.
Description: On horse facing right, in

Plate 57
Fig. 145 Havelock
In the collection of Dr S.J. Howard

Plate 58
Fig. 153 Raglan
By courtesy of Mr and Mrs Eric Joyce

Plate 56 continued
plumed Scotch bonnet, high-necked long coat, sash over his left shoulder and trousers.
Observations: As this figure pairs *fig.* 147 (Havelock), it must have been produced in connection with the Indian Mutiny.

Figure 148
Subject: **General Sir Henry Havelock**
Title: Havelock (raised capitals)
Date: 1857
Height: 10¼ in (25.75 cm)
Colour: Well coloured.
Rarity: VR.
Pair: Not known
Description: He stands bare-headed, in military uniform. A cannon and heap of shells are beside his left leg. There is a flag behind his right shoulder and he holds a baton or telescope in his left hand.

Figure 149
Subject: **General Sir George Brown**
Title: G. Brown (raised capitals)
Date: c. 1854
Height: 13 in (33 cm)
Colour: Well coloured.
Rarity: Av.
Pair: Fig. 150 (Simpson)
Description: On horse facing right, in cocked hat and full military uniform. In his right hand he holds a flagstaff with the flag flying above his head.
Observations: See next figure.

Figure 150
Subject: **General Sir James Simpson**
Title: G. Simpson (raised capitals on plaque)
Date: c. 1854
Height: 13 in (33 cm)
Colour: Well coloured.
Rarity: Av.
Pair: Fig. 149 (Brown)

Description: On horse facing left, in cocked hat and uniform. In his left hand he holds a flagstaff with the flag flying above his head.
Observations: 1. This figure and its pair are unusual in that each is titled in a different manner—the one in raised capitals on the figure and the other in raised capitals on a plaque.
2. A similar pair of figures fetched 62 gns at Christie's in 1965.

Figure 151
Subject: **General Sir Colin Campbell**
Title: Sir Colin Campbell (gilt script)
Date: c. 1854
Height: 10½ in (26.5 cm)
Colour: Well coloured.
Rarity: VR.
Pair: Fig. 152 (Raglan)
Description: He stands bare-headed, in military jacket with epaulettes and trousers. To his left is a cannon and two flags. In his left hand he holds a plumed Scotch bonnet to his head, and to his right is a sword.
Observations: 1. No large version of this figure has been found, see *fig.* 153 (Raglan) *pl.* C-58.
2. Undoubtedly a Crimean figure as its pair is *fig.* 152 (Raglan).

Figure 152
Subject: **F-M. Lord Raglan**
Title: Lord Raglan (gilt script)
Date: c. 1854
Height: 9¾ in (24.5 cm)
Colour: Well coloured.
Rarity: R.
Pair: Fig. 151 (Campbell)
Description: He stands bare-headed, in military uniform. His right sleeve, which is empty, is pinned to his chest. To his left is

a pedestal, with a book on top, on which his left hand rests. To his right and behind is a cannon and two flags.
Observations: Similar in all respects, other than in height and title, to *fig.* 153 (Raglan) *pl.* C-58, although no pair for the latter figure is known.

Plate 57
Figure 145
Subject: **General Sir Henry Havelock**
Title: S. H. Havelock (raised capitals)
Date: 1857
Height: 9¼ in (23.5 cm)
Colour: Both well coloured and white and gilt versions exist.
Rarity: R.
Pair: Fig. 144 (Campbell) *pl.* C-56.
Description: Standing bare-headed, in military uniform. To his left is a cannon and a pile of shells. His left hand rests on a sword. To his right are two flags and in his right hand he clasps a plumed hat.
Observations: See *fig.* 144 (Campbell) *pl.* C-56.

Plate 58
Figure 153
Subject: **F-M. Lord Raglan**
Title: F M Lord Raglan (gilt script)
Date: c. 1854
Height: 15½ in (39.25 cm)
Colour: White and gilt.
Rarity: R.
Pair: No pair is known to this figure, but· *fig.* 154 has been reserved for it. It seems probable that a titled figure of Campbell will eventually be discovered [see *fig.* 151 (Campbell) and *fig.* 152 (Raglan), *pl.* C-56].
Description: Identical in all respects, other than in height and title, to *fig.* 152 (Raglan).
Observations: Sometimes titled 'Lord Raglan' (gilt script).

Section C. Naval, Military and Exploration

Plate 59
Figure 155
Subject: **George, second Duke of Cambridge**
Title: Duke/of Cambridge (raised capitals)
Date: *c.* 1854
Height: 9 in (23 cm)
Colour: Both coloured and white and gilt versions exist.
Rarity: Av.
Pair: *Fig.* 156 (Mrs FitzGeorge)
Description: On horse facing right, bareheaded in military uniform. He holds his plumed cocked hat in his left hand which rests on the horse's mane.

Figure 156
Subject: **Louisa Fairbrother (Mrs Fitz-George)**
Title: Duchess (raised capitals)
Date: *c.* 1854
Height: 9 in (23 cm)
Colour: Both coloured and white gilt versions exist.

Fig. 155 Duke of Cambridge   *Fig.* 156 Mrs FitzGeorge

Plate 59 (Above and below)

Fig. 157 Mrs FitzGeorge   *Fig.* 158 Duke of Cambridge

Rarity: Av.
Pair: *Fig.* 155 (Duke of Cambridge)
Description: On horse facing left, in plumed hat and riding habit.
Observations: 1. Figures titled 'Duchess' are generally thought to portray *Louisa Fairbrother* (1816–90) who contracted a morganatic marriage with George, second Duke of Cambridge in 1840, being known afterwards as *Mrs FitzGeorge*. The potters either thought she was a 'Duchess' or alternatively, gave her a courtesy title in deference to her popularity.
2. A similar figure and its pair fetched 35 gns at Christie's in 1969.

Figure 157
Subject: **Louisa Fairbrother (Mrs Fitz-George)**
Title: Duchess (raised capitals)
Date: *c.* 1854
Height: 14½ in (36.75 cm)
Colour: Both coloured and white and gilt versions exist.
Rarity: C. D. A.
Pair: *Fig.* 158 (Duke of Cambridge)
Description: On horse facing right, in plumed hat and riding habit. Very similar to, but the reverse of *fig.* 156 (Mrs FitzGeorge).
Observations: See preceding figure.

Figure 158
Subject: **George, second Duke of Cambridge**
Title: Duke/of Cambridge (raised capitals)
Date: *c.* 1854
Height: 14½ in (36.75 cm)
Colour: Both coloured and white and gilt versions exist.
Rarity: C. D. A.
Pair: *Fig.* 157 (Mrs FitzGeorge)
Description: On horse facing left, bareheaded in military uniform. He holds his plumed cocked hat in his right hand which rests on the horse's mane.
Observations: A similar pair of figures fetched 22 gns at Christie's in 1964.

Plate 60
Fig. 159 Duke of Cambridge
By courtesy of Mr and Mrs Eric Joyce

Plate 61
Fig. 160 Prince Napoleon
In the collection of Lady Ranfurly

Plate 60
Figure 159
Subject: **George, second Duke of Cambridge**
Title: Duke/Cambridge (raised capitals)
Date: c. 1854
Height: 8 in (20.5 cm)
Colour: Sparsely coloured.
Rarity: VR. D.
Pair: *Fig.* 160 (Prince Napoleon) *pl.* C-61. ·
Description: On horse facing right, in military uniform. He is holding his plumed cocked hat against the side of his head, with his right hand, as if in the act of doffing it to Prince Napoleon.

Plate 61
Figure 160
Subject: **Prince Napoleon**
Title: Prince/Napoleon (raised capitals)
Date: c. 1854
Height: 8 in (20.5 cm)
Colour: Sparsely coloured.
Rarity: VR. D.
Pair: *Fig.* 159 (Duke of Cambridge) *pl.* C-60.
Description: On horse facing left, in cocked hat athwartships and full military uniform. He holds both reins with his hands.

Plate 62
Figure 161
Subject: **Abd-ul-Medjid, Sultan of Turkey**
Title: Sultan (raised capitals on plaque)
Date: c. 1854
Height: 8¾ in (22 cm)
Colour: Both white and gilt, and coloured versions are known.
Rarity: R.

C264

Pair: *Fig.* 162 (Omar Pasha)
Description: On horse facing right, in turban, long coat and Turkish trousers, a sword in front of his right leg.
Observations: Although the style of titling of this figure is somewhat different from that of *fig.* 162 (Omar Pasha), I have little doubt that they are a pair. This is borne out, not only by the fact that on two occasions I have found them as pairs, but also by the fact that the shape of their heads, which are 'flattened sideways', is without parallel and has not been found in any other figure.

Figure 162
Subject: **Omar Pasha**
Title: Omer Pasha (raised capitals)
Date: c. 1854
Height: 9⅛ in (23.25 cm)
Colour: Both white and gilt, and coloured versions are known.
Rarity: R.
Pair: *Fig.* 161 (Abd-ul-Medjid)
Description: On horse facing left, in turban, long military coat and Turkish trousers. He carries a curved sword which lies behind his left leg.
Observations: See preceding figure.

Plate 62A
Figure 163
Subject: **Omar Pasha**
Title: Omar/Pasha (gilt script)
Date: c. 1854
Height: 10¾ in (27 cm)
Colour: Well coloured in the manner of Thomas Parr.

Maker: Thomas Parr
Rarity: VR. D. A.
Pair: *Fig.* 380 (Raglan) *pl.* C-63.
Description: On a horse facing left, in fez, military frock-coat and trousers.
Observations: See *fig.* 163(a) (Omar Pasha) *pl.* C-63.

Plate 63
Figure 163(a)
Subject: **Omar Pasha**
Title: Omer Pacha/Success to Turkey (type, black transfer, upper and lower case)
Date: c. 1854
Height: 10¾ in (27 cm)
Colour: Well coloured in the manner of Thomas Parr.
Maker: Thomas Parr
Rarity: Av. D. A.
Pair: None, but see observations.
Description: Identical to *fig.* 163, *pl.* C-62A, other than for title.
Observations: 1. Contemporary versions of this figure are in two sizes: In the *larger* [10¾ in (27 cm)] size the horse always faces left. In the *smaller* [6½ in (16.5 cm)] size one horse faces left and there is a pair, similarly titled (Omer Pacha/Success to Turkey), facing right.
2. A pair of the *smaller* [6½ in (16.5 cm)] version fetched 60 gns at Christie's in 1965. An example of the *larger* version [*fig.* 163(a)] together with *fig.* 201 (Turkish soldiers) *pl.* C-72, fetched 42 gns at the same sale; and another by itself, 60 gns in the same rooms in 1969.

Colour Plate 31
Duke of Wellington. *Fig.* 23, *pl.* B-3.
See page 187.

Colour Plate 32 (Top right)
Napoleon. *Fig.* 40, *pl.* C-12. See page 227.

Colour Plate 33
Florence Nightingale. *Fig.* 142, *pl.* C-55.
See pages 260-1.

Plate 62
Fig. 161 Abd-ul-Medjid

Fig. 162 Omar Pasha
In the collection of Mr D.P.M. Michael

Plate 62A
Fig. 163 Omar Pasha
By courtesy of Mr John Hall

Plate 63
Fig. 380 Raglan
Fig. 163(a) Omar Pasha
The 'matching pair' to
fig. 380 is *fig.* 163 (Omar
Pasha) *pl.* C-62A. It is
identical to *fig.* 163(a)
other than for title.
Note also the untitled
pair of figures of Omar
Pasha (4½ in, 11.5 cm).
This pair, as far as is
known, is always 'late'
being catalogued in *Kent
List A* as 'Emin Pasha on
Horse' (sic).
*In the Thomas Balston
collection*

Plate 63 continued

3. A 4½ in (11.5 cm) untitled pair is also known and appears in all three Kent lists. I have never seen early versions of this pair, which seem likely to have been made, for the first time, late in the nineteenth century. They are listed as 'Emin Pasha on Horse' (sic): *Kent List A*, no. 128; *Kent List B*, no. 214, as also in *Kent List C* (1955).

Figure 380
Subject: **F-M. Lord Raglan**
Title: Lord/Raglan (gilt script)
Date: *c.* 1854
Height: 11¾ in (29.75 cm)
Colour: Well coloured in the manner of Thomas Parr.
Maker: Thomas Parr.

Rarity: VR. D. A.
Pair: *Fig.* 163 (Omar Pasha) *pl.* C-62A.
Description: On a horse facing right, in cocked hat and uniform. His 'empty' right sleeve is pinned to his chest.
Observations: Reminiscent of *fig.* 21 (Wellington) *pl.* B-3 ('Up guards and at them'; 'Wellington on Horse').

Plate 64
T: *Fig.* 164 Arnaud
Fig. 165 Raglan

B: *Fig.* 166 Omar Pasha
Fig. 167 Abd-ul-Medjid
In the collection of Lady Ranfurly

Plate 65
T: *Fig.* 164(a) Arnaud
Fig. 167(a) Abd-ul-Medjid

B: *Fig.* 166(a) Omar Pasha
Fig. 165(a) Raglan
By courtesy of Mr and Mrs Eric Joyce

Plate 64
Figure 164
Subject: **Marshal Saint-Arnaud**
Title: Marshal/Arnaud (raised capitals on plaque)
Date: *c.* 1854
Height: 10 in (25 cm)
Colour: Well coloured. Horses have been found uncoloured, piebald, grey, cinnamon and brown.
Rarity: Av. D. A.
Pair or series: Fig. 165 (Raglan). Same series as *fig.* 166 (Omar Pasha) and *fig.* 167 (Abd-ul-Medjid).
Description: On horse facing right, bareheaded in military uniform. His right hand holds his cocked hat against the horse's flank.
Observations: 1. Figs. 164 (Arnaud), 165 (Raglan), 166 (Omar Pasha) and 167 (Abd-ul-Medjid) constitute the *Short Crimean Series I*.
2. A small version of the series is illustrated on *pl.* C-65.
3. 'Matching pairs' are coloured in a similar manner.

Figure 165
Subject: **F-M. Lord Raglan**
Title: Lord/Raglan (raised capitals on plaque)
Date: *c.* 1854
Height: 10½ in (26.5 cm)
Colour: Well coloured, as for *fig.* 164 (Arnaud).
Rarity: Av. D. A.
Pair or series: Fig. 164 (Arnaud). Same series as *fig.* 166 (Omar Pasha) and *fig.* 167 (Abd-ul-Medjid).
Description: On horse facing left, in cocked hat and full military uniform.
Observations: See *fig.* 164 (Arnaud).

Figure 166
Subject: **Omar Pasha**
Title: Omer/Pacha (raised capitals on plaque)
Date: *c.* 1854
Height: 10½ in (26.5 cm)
Colour: Well coloured, as for *fig.* 164 (Arnaud).
Rarity: Av. D. A.
Pair or series: Fig. 167 (Abd-ul-Medjid). Same series as *fig.* 164 (Arnaud) and *fig.* 165 (Raglan).
Description: On horse facing right, in fez, frock-coat and trousers.
Observations: See *fig.* 164 (Arnaud).

Figure 167
Subject: **Abd-ul-Medjid, Sultan of Turkey**
Title: The/Sultan (raised capitals on plaque)
Date: *c.* 1854
Height: 10¾ in (27 cm)
Colour: Well coloured, as for *fig.* 164 (Arnaud).
Rarity: Av. D. A.
Pair or series: Fig. 166 (Omar Pasha). Same series as *fig.* 164 (Arnaud) and *fig.* 165 (Raglan).
Description: On horse facing left, in plumed hat, long coat and Turkish trousers.
Observations: 1. Based on an engraving of Abd-ul-Medjid which appeared in *The Illustrated London News* on September 17th, 1853 (see *ch.* 3, *pl.* 21).
2. See *fig.* 164 (Arnaud).
3. A similar figure, together with *fig.* 164 (Arnaud), fetched 30 gns at Christie's in 1964.

Plate 65
Figure 164(a)
Subject: **Marshal Saint-Arnaud**
Title: Marshal / Arnaud (raised capitals on plaque)
Date: *c.* 1854
Height: 7½ in (19 cm)
Colour: Well coloured. Horses have been found uncoloured, piebald, skewbald, grey, cinnamon and brown.
Rarity: Av.
Pair or series: Fig. 165(a) (Raglan). Same series as *fig.* 166(a) (Omar Pasha) and *fig.* 167(a) (Abd-ul-Medjid).
Description: Identical in all respects to *fig.* 164 (Arnaud) *pl.* C-64, except with regard to height and certain differences in the modelling of the horse's legs.
Observations: 1. Figs. 164(a) (Arnaud), 165(a) (Raglan), 166(a) (Omar Pasha) and 167(a) (Abd-ul-Medjid) constitute a small version of the *Short Crimean Series I* (see *pl.* C-64 for large version).
2. 'Matching pairs' are coloured in a similar manner and the pattern of the horses' legs is identical. There are two versions of this series, one in which two legs are 'incorporated' and two are 'free' and the other, rather cruder version, in which three legs are 'incorporated' and only one is 'free'. This version is 7 in (17.5 cm) in height.
3. A similar figure fetched 18 gns at Christie's in 1968.

Figure 165(a)
Subject: **F-M. Lord Raglan**
Title: Lord/Raglan (raised capitals on plaque)
Date: *c.* 1854
Height: 7½ in (19 cm)

C267

Colour Plate 34
Louisa Fairbrother (Mrs Fitzgeorge) and George, second Duke of Cambridge. *Figs.* 157 and 158, *pl.* C-59. See page 263.

Colour Plate 35
General Sir Colin Campbell and General Sir Henry Havelock. *Figs.* 176 and 177, *pl.* C-67. See page 270.

Plate 66
T: *Fig.* 168 Arnaud
Fig. 171 Abd-ul-Medjid

B: *Fig.* 170 Omar Pasha
Fig. 169 Raglan
*In the collection of Lady Ranfurly
and the author*

Plate 65 continued
Colour: Well coloured, as for *fig.* 164(*a*)
(Arnaud).
Rarity: Av.
Pair or series: *Fig.* 164(*a*) (Arnaud). Same
series as *fig.* 166(*a*) (Omar Pasha) and *fig.*
167(*a*) (Abd-ul-Medjid).
Description: Identical in all respects to *fig.*
165 (Raglan) *pl.* C-64, except with regard to
size and to the modelling of the horse's legs.
Observations: See *fig.* 164(*a*) (Arnaud).

Figure 166(a)
Subject: **Omar Pasha**
Title: Omer/Pacha (raised capitals on
plaque)
Date: *c.* 1854
Height: 7½ in (19 cm)
Colour: Well coloured, as for *fig.* 164(*a*)
(Arnaud).
Rarity: Av.
Pair or series: *Fig.* 167(*a*) (Abd-ul-Medjid).
Same series as *fig.* 164(*a*) (Arnaud) and *fig.*
165(*a*) (Raglan).
Description: Identical in all respects to *fig.*
166 (Omar Pasha) *pl.* C-64, except with re-
gard to size and modelling of the horse's legs.
Observations: See *fig.* 164(*a*) (Arnaud).

Figure 167(a)
Subject: **Abd-ul-Medjid, Sultan of Turkey**
Title: The/Sultan (raised capitals on
plaque)
Date: *c.* 1854
Height: 7½ in (19 cm)
Colour: Well coloured, as for *fig.* 164(*a*)
(Arnaud).
Rarity: Av.
Pair or series: *Fig.* 166(*a*) (Omar Pasha).
Same series as *fig.* 164(*a*) (Arnaud) and
fig. 165(*a*) (Raglan).

Description: Identical in all respects to *fig.*
167 (Abd-ul-Medjid) *pl.* C-64, except with
regard to size and to the modelling of the
horse's legs.
Observations: See *fig.* 164(*a*) (Arnaud).

Plate 66
Figure 168
Subject: **Marshal Saint-Arnaud**
Title: Marshal Arnaud (raised capitals on
two plaques)
Date: *c.* 1854
Height: 8¼ in (21 cm)
Colour: White and gilt or coloured versions
are seen. The horse may be white or
cinnamon.
Rarity: VR.
Pair or series: *Fig.* 169 (Raglan). Same series
as *fig.* 170 (Omar Pasha) and *fig.* 171 (Abd-
ul-Medjid).
Description: On horse facing right, bare-
headed, in military uniform. His right hand
bearing his plumed cocked hat rests on the
horse's flank.
Observations: *Figs.* 168 (Arnaud), 169 (Raglan), 170 (Omar Pasha) and 171 (Abd-ul-
Medjid) constitute the *Short Crimean Series II*.
Apart from their height and their method of
titling, they are very similar to the figures
forming the *Long Crimean Series*, see *pl.* C-67.
They obviously come from the same factory
and may be considered as precursors of this
series, for it seems likely that they were the
first to be produced. Having proved satisfactory and popular, they were improved
upon when the later figures were issued.

Figure 169
Subject: **F-M. Lord Raglan**
Title: Lord Raglan (raised capitals on two
plaques)

Description: Identical in all respects to *fig.*
167 (Abd-ul-Medjid) *pl.* C-64, except with
regard to size and to the modelling of the
horse's legs.
Observations: See *fig.* 164(*a*) (Arnaud).

Date: *c.* 1854
Height: 8¼ in (21 cm)
Colour: As for *fig.* 168 (Arnaud).
Rarity: VR.
Pair or series: *Fig.* 168 (Arnaud). Same series
as *fig.* 170 (Omar Pasha) and *fig.* 171 (Abd-
ul-Medjid).
Description: On horse facing left, in plumed
cocked hat and full military uniform.
Observations: See *fig.* 168 (Arnaud).

Figure 170
Subject: **Omar Pasha**
Title: Omer Pacha (raised capitals on two
plaques)
Date: *c.* 1854
Height: 8¼ in (21 cm)
Colour: As for *fig.* 168 (Arnaud).
Rarity: VR.
Pair or series: *Fig.* 171 (Abd-ul-Medjid).
Same series as *fig.* 168 (Arnaud) and *fig.* 169
(Raglan).
Description: On horse facing right, in round
hat, frock-coat and Turkish trousers.
Observations: See *fig.* 168 (Arnaud).

Figure 171
Subject: **Abd-ul-Medjid, Sultan of Turkey**
Title: The Sultan (raised capitals on two
plaques)
Date: *c.* 1854
Height: 8¼ in (21 cm)
Colour: As for *fig.* 168 (Arnaud).
Rarity: VR.
Pair or series: *Fig.* 170 (Omar Pasha). Same
series as *fig.* 168 (Arnaud) and *fig.* 169
(Raglan).
Description: On horse facing left, in fez, frock-
coat and Turkish trousers.
Observations: See *fig.* 168 (Arnaud).

B: *Fig.* 172 Brown
Fig. 174 Williams
Fig. 176 Campbell
*By courtesy of Mr and Mrs Eric Joyce
and in the collection of the author*

Plate 67

Figure 172
Subject: **General Sir George Brown**
Title: Sir/George Brown (raised capitals)
Date: c. 1854 (*Crimean War*)
Height: 9 in (23 cm)
Colour: White and gilt, or coloured with blue jacket and cinnamon or brown horse.
Rarity: R. D. A.
Pair or series: *Fig.* 173 (Pelissier). Same series as *fig.* 174 (Williams) and *fig.* 175 (Duke of Cambridge); and *fig.* 176 (Campbell) and *fig.* 177 (Havelock)—the *Long Crimean Series*.
Description: On horse facing right, bareheaded in military uniform. His right hand holds his cocked hat against the saddle.
Observations: See next figure.

Figure 173
Subject: **General Pelissier**
Title: General/Pelissier (raised capitals)
Date: c. 1854 (*Crimean War*)
Height: 9 in (23 cm)
Colour: As for *fig.* 172 (Brown).
Rarity: R. D. A.
Pair or series: *Fig.* 172 (Brown). Same series as *fig.* 174 (Williams) and *fig.* 175 (Duke of Cambridge); and *fig.* 176 (Campbell) and *fig.* 177 (Havelock)—the *Long Crimean Series*.
Description: On horse facing left, bareheaded in full military uniform. He holds his plumed, cocked hat in his left hand.
Observations: 1. The proof that *fig.* 172 (Brown) and *fig.* 173 (Pelissier) are a pair lies not only in the fact that I have found them together on several occasions, but also because it is possible to note certain similarities not present in the other four figures. The most obvious is the plumed cocked hat held in the hands of the riders, each of which has a long plume extending almost to the ground. This feature is not present in any of the other figures.
2. It would seem likely that this pair was

released in 1854, shortly after the issue of the four precursors which are illustrated on *pl.* C-66.

Figure 174
Subject: **Sir William Fenwick Williams**
Title: Sir / W. F. Williams (raised capitals)
Date: c. 1855 (*Crimean War*)
Height: 9 in (23 cm)
Colour: White and gilt, or coloured with blue jacket and cinnamon or brown horse.
Rarity: R. D. A.
Pair or series: *Fig.* 175 (Duke of Cambridge). Same series as *fig.* 172 (Brown) and *fig.* 173 (Pelissier); and *fig.* 176 (Campbell) and *fig.* 177 (Havelock)—the *Long Crimean Series*.
Description: On horse facing right, bareheaded in military uniform. His right hand rests on the horse's flank.
Observations: See next figure.

Figure 175
Subject: **George, second Duke of Cambridge**
Title: Duke / of Cambridge (raised capitals)
Date: c. 1855 (*Crimean War*)
Height: 9 in (23 cm)
Colour: As for *fig.* 174 (Williams).
Rarity: R. D. A.
Pair or series: *Fig.* 174 (Williams). Same series as *fig.* 172 (Brown) and *fig.* 173 (Pelissier); and *fig.* 176 (Campbell) and *fig.* 177 (Havelock)—the *Long Crimean Series*.
Description: On horse facing left, bareheaded in full military uniform, his left hand on the horse's flank.
Observations: 1. The proof that *fig.* 174 (Williams) and *fig.* 175 (Duke of Cambridge) constitute a pair lies in the fact that they have similarities not present in the other four in this series. The most obvious is that Williams' right hand and the Duke's left hand rest on their horses' flanks.
2. This pair was probably issued in 1855 at

the time when Kars was being defended by Williams, against the Russians.

Figure 176
Subject: **General Sir Colin Campbell**
Title: Sir / C. Campbell (raised capitals)
Date: c. 1857 (*Indian Mutiny*)
Height: 9 in (23 cm)
Colour: White and gilt, or coloured with blue jacket and cinnamon or brown horse.
Rarity: R. D. A.
Pair or series: *Fig.* 177 (Havelock). Same series as *fig.* 172 (Brown) and *fig.* 173 (Pelissier); and *fig.* 174 (Williams) and *fig.* 175 (Duke of Cambridge)—the *Long Crimean Series*—extending into the Indian Mutiny.
Description: On horse facing right, bareheaded in military uniform. He holds a Scotch bonnet in his right hand.
Observations: See next figure.

Figure 177
Subject: **General Sir Henry Havelock**
Title: Sir / H. Havelock. CB. (raised capitals)
Date: c. 1857 (*Indian Mutiny*)
Height: 9 in (23 cm)
Colour: As for *fig.* 176 (Campbell).
Rarity: R. D. A.
Pair or series: *Fig.* 176 (Campbell). Same series as *fig.* 172 (Brown) and *fig.* 173 (Pelissier); and *fig.* 174 (Williams) and *fig.* 175 (Duke of Cambridge)—the *Long Crimean Series*—extending into the Indian Mutiny.
Description: On horse facing left, bareheaded and in military uniform. His left hand and his plumed cocked hat rest on the horse's flank.
Observations: This figure clearly pairs *fig.* 176 (Campbell). Note this is the only pair in which the riders wear white trousers, and shoes. In each of the other figures the riders wear knee-boots.

Section C. Naval, Military and Exploration

Summary: The *Long Crimean Series* is made up of three pairs of figures. The first pair, *fig.* 172 (Brown) and *fig.* 173 (Pelissier), was probably issued in 1854; the second, *fig.* 174 (Williams) and *fig.* 175 (Duke of Cambridge), was probably issued in 1855; and the final pair, *fig.* 176 (Campbell) and *fig.* 177 (Havelock), was issued in 1857-8, during the Indian Mutiny.

These three pairs of figures followed the successful appearance of the two pairs illustrated on *pl.* C-66: *Fig.* 168 (Arnaud) and *fig.* 169 (Raglan); and *fig.* 170 (Omar Pasha) and *fig.* 171 (Abd-ul-Medjid).

Plate 67A

Figure 178
Subject: **Omar Pasha**
Title: None
Date: *c.* 1854
Height: 9 in (23 cm)
Colour: Well coloured.
Rarity: VR.
Pair: *Fig.* 179 (Abd-ul-Medjid) *pl.* C-68.
Description: On horse facing right, in flat-topped turban with scarf hanging to his right shoulder, tunic with epaulettes. He wears Turkish trousers and low shoes and holds the reins against his belt with his left hand.

Plate 68

Figure 179
Subject: **Abd-ul-Medjid, Sultan of Turkey**
Title: None
Date: *c.* 1854
Height: 8½ in (21.5 cm)
Colour: Well coloured.
Rarity: VR.
Pair: *Fig.* 178 (Omar Pasha) *pl.* C-67A.
Description: On horse facing left, in flat-topped turban with scarf hanging down over his left shoulder, tunic, trousers and low shoes. His right arm rests on the horse's

mane, and he carries a scroll in his right hand. His left hand holds the reins against his belt. Sword behind his left leg.

Plate 69

Figure 180
Subject: **Malakoff**—an outwork of Sebastopol
Title: Malakoff (raised capitals)
Date: *c.* 1854
Height: 6¾ in (17 cm)
Colour: Well coloured.
Rarity: Av.
Description: A battlemented wall with a high central tower and a smaller tower on the right. The French tricolour flies from the central tower.
Observations: A similar figure, together with an example of *fig.* 181 (Sebastopol), fetched 22 gns at Christie's in 1963.

Figure 181
Subject: **Sebastopol**—Russian fortress in the Crimea
Title: Sebastopol (raised capitals)
Date: *c.* 1854
Height: 10 in (25 cm)
Colour: Well coloured.
Maker: See *observations*
Rarity: Av.
Description: Gateway, flanked by two large round towers. The French tricolour flies from the slightly lower tower on the right. A Turkish soldier stands to the left of the gate and an English soldier to the right.
Observations: 1. A similar figure fetched 20 gns at Christie's in 1969.
2. The original mould for a figure of Sebastopol was among those found in a disused part of the Sampson Smith factory in 1948. Unfortunately I did not see the mould, nor can I find any record as to whether it was the mould of *fig.* 181 or *fig.* 182.

Figure 182
Subject: **Sebastopol**—Russian fortress in the Crimea
Title: Sebastopol (raised capitals on plaque)
Date: *c.* 1854
Height: 7½ in (19 cm)
Colour: Well coloured.
Rarity: Av.
Description: Identical in all respects to *fig.* 181 (Sebastopol), except for height and for the absence of soldiers.
Observations: See preceding figure.

Figure 183
Subject: **English sailor**
Title: England (raised capitals)
Date: *c.* 1854
Height: 9½ in (24 cm)
Colour: Both well coloured and pale versions noted.
Rarity: Av.
Pair: *Fig.* 184 (Scotland)
Description: A sailor stands at the salute. His right foot rests on a cannon and behind his right leg are two flags.

Figure 184
Subject: **Highland soldier**
Title: Scotland (raised capitals)
Date: *c.* 1854
Height: 10¼ in (25.75 cm)
Colour: Both well coloured and pale versions noted.
Rarity: Av.
Pair: *Fig.* 183 (England)
Description: A soldier stands bare-headed, with Scotch bonnet raised in his left hand. His left foot rests on a cannon, and behind his left leg are two flags.
Observations: A similar pair of figures fetched 20 gns at Christie's in 1965; and another, 48 gns at Christie's in 1969.

Plate 69
T: *Fig.* 180 Malakoff
Fig. 181 Sebastopol
Fig. 182 Sebastopol

B: *Fig.* 183 England
Fig. 184 Scotland
Fig. 185 The Victory
Fig. 186 Britain's Glory
Fig. 187 Scotland's Pride

Plate 69 continued

Figure 185
Subject: **English sailor, French and Turkish soldier**
Title: The Victory (raised capitals)
Date: 1856
Height: 14¼ in (36.25 cm)
Colour: Well coloured.
Rarity: R. A.
Description: An English sailor sits on a cannon, raising a mug in his left hand To his left stands a French soldier and to his right a Turkish soldier. The sailor holds a flag, likewise the French soldier.
Observations: A similar figure fetched £26 at Sotheby's in 1966; and another, 65 gns at Christie's in 1969.

Figure 186
Subject: **English sailor**
Title: Britain's Glory (raised capitals)
Date: c. 1854
Height: 10½ in (26.5 cm)
Colour: Well coloured.
Rarity: C. A.
Pair: Fig. 187 (Scotland's Pride)
Description: A sailor wearing a jacket leans against a cannon.

Figure 187
Subject: **Highland soldier**
Title: Scotland's Pride (raised capitals)

Date: c. 1854
Height: 10½ in (26.5 cm)
Colour: Well coloured.
Rarity: C. A.
Pair: Fig. 186 (Britain's Glory)
Description: A Scottish soldier stands with plumed bonnet, his left foot on a cannon, his left arm supporting a flag.
Observations: A similar figure and its pair fetched 35 gns at Christie's in 1969.

Plate 70
Figure 188
Subject: **A sailor and his sweetheart**
Title: None
Date: ? 1854
Height: 10¾ in (27 cm)
Colour: Both well coloured and pale versions exist.
Rarity: Av.
Description: A sailor stands on the left. He wears a hat, neckcloth, shirt, jacket and trousers and has a gun in his belt. His right leg is on a chair and he holds a tankard in his right hand. His left arm is round a young lady who is wearing a bonnet. She is seated at a table upon which, on the left, is a cheese; and on the right, a loaf of bread. She is about to carve the loaf with a knife.
Observations: 1.Mr A. Oliver suggested recently that this figure may portray Ned Morgan

and Jenny Jones, see section I. Comparison with *ch.* 3, *pl.* 59 confirms his hypothesis. A gun was never any part of the issue to lower deck sailors in the navy. In a Staffordshire figure its presence is some indication that the piece is theatrical. The famous Victorian 'nautical' actor T. P. Cooke regularly appeared in an ordinary sailor's dress but with a brace of pistols. In Victorian melodramas, the participants got involved in gun-fights, usually sooner rather than later!
2. For a long time this figure was mistakenly thought to portray a female bilateral above-knee amputee seated on a chair!

Figure 189
Subject: **The Redan**—a fortress near Sebastopol
Title: The Redan (raised capitals on plaque)
Date: c. 1854
Height: 8¾ in (22 cm)
Colour: Well coloured.
Rarity: VR. D.
Description: A battlemented wall with a three-storied round central tower. The French tricolour flies from the tower.

Figure 190
Subject: **English soldier**
Title: Ready Willing (*sic*) (gilt script)
Date: c. 1854

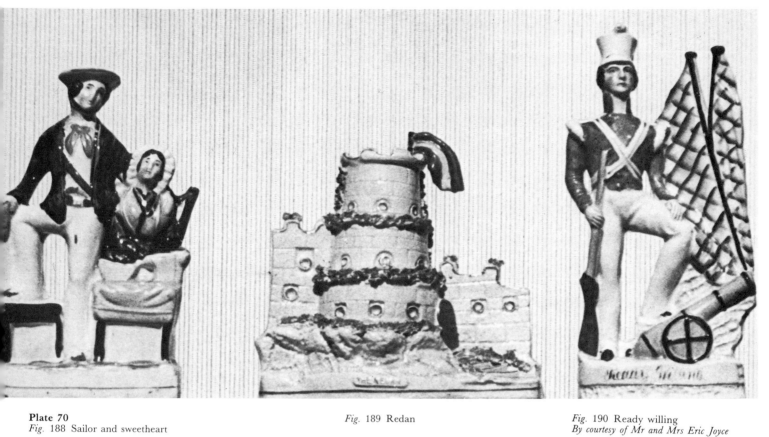

Plate 70
Fig. 188 Sailor and sweetheart

Fig. 189 Redan

Fig. 190 Ready willing
By courtesy of Mr and Mrs Eric Joyce

Height: 11¾ in (29.75 cm)
Colour: Well coloured.
Rarity: R.
Pair: Fig. 191 (Ready & Willing) *pl.* C-70A.
Description: A soldier is standing. He carries a rifle in his right hand, and has his left foot on a cannon. To his left are two flags.

Plate 70A
Figure 191
Subject: **English sailor**
Title: Ready & Willing (gilt script)

Date: *c.* 1854
Height: 12¼ in (31 cm)
Colour: Well coloured.
Rarity: R.
Pair: Fig. 190 (Ready Willing) *pl.* C-70.
Description: A sailor stands propped up against a gun. This figure is identical in design to *fig.* 186 (Britain's Glory) *pl.* C-69, except that in this case the sailor wears no jacket.
Observations: An untitled verison of this figure is illustrated on *pl.* C-72.

Plate 71
Figure 192
Subject: **English soldier and Highlander**
Title: Hears to the Lasses (*sic*) (raised capitals)
Date: *c.* 1854
Height: 10¼ in (25.75 cm)
Colour: Pale.
Rarity: VR.
Description: Two soldiers are seated on a drum. On the left is a Highlander with a mug in his left hand. To the right is an

Plate 70A
Fig. 191 Ready & willing
By coutesy of Mr and Mrs Eric Joyce

Plate 71 (Right)
T: *Fig.* 192 Hears to the Lasses
Fig. 193 *(obverse)* English sailor
Fig. 194 The wounded sailor
Fig. 195 *(obverse)* English sailor

B: *Fig.* 196 Soldier's return
Fig. 197 The sailor's return
Fig. 198 The soldier's farewell
Fig. 199 The soldier's return

Plate 71 continued
English soldier in trousers, carrying a bottle in his right hand.

Figure 193 (obverse)
Subject: **English sailor**/French soldier
Title: None
Date: *c.* 1854
Height: 13 in (33 cm)
Colour: Well coloured.
Rarity: R.
Description: An English sailor, a flag held in his left hand above his head, an anchor beside his right leg.
Observations: The reverse of this figure portrays a French soldier, see *pl.* C-72.

Figure 194
Subject: **English soldier and sailor**
Title: The Wounded/Soldier (raised capitals)
Date: *c.* 1855
Height: 12¾ in (32.25 cm)
Colour: Well coloured and pale versions exist.
Rarity: Av.
Series: Same series as *fig.* 197 (The / Sailor's Return), *fig.* 198 (The / Soldier's Farewell) and *fig.* 199 (The / Soldier's Return).
Description: On the left is a wounded soldier; his left arm round the shoulders of an English sailor.
Observations: 1. A similar figure, together with an example of *fig.* 197 (The / Sailor's Return), fetched 55 gns at Christie's in 1965; another by itself, fetched 38 gns in 1969.
2. Based on an engraving of the 'Landing of the invalided and the wounded from the Crimea' which appeared in *Cassell's Illustrated Family Paper* on April 7th, 1855. See *pl.* C-71A.

Figure 195 (obverse)
Subject: **English sailor** / French soldier
Title: None
Date: *c.* 1854
Height: 9 in (23 cm)
Colour: Pale colours.
Rarity: R.
Description: An English sailor stands clasping a flag in his right hand. To his left is another flag.
Observations: The reverse of this figure portrays a French soldier, see *pl.* C-72.

Figure 196
Subject: **Highlander and girl**
Title: Soldier's return (raised capitals on plaque)
Date: *c.* 1854
Height: 8½ in (21.5 cm)
Colour: Poorly coloured usually.
Rarity: R.
Description: To the right a soldier stands, bare-headed, in swallow-tailed coat, trousers, and tartan sash, a cap against his left foot. He holds his right arm around a girl, who stands bare-headed in a long skirt. Her left arm is round his neck.

Figure 197
Subject: **English sailor and girl**
Title: The / Sailor's Return (raised capitals)
Date: *c.* 1855
Height: 12½ in (31.75 cm)

Colour: Well coloured and pale versions exist.
Rarity: Av.
Series: Same series as *fig.* 194 (The Wounded / Soldier), *fig.* 198 (The / Soldier's Farewell) and *fig.* 199 (The / Soldier's Return).
Description: To the right stands a sailor, holding his hat above his head. His right arm is round the waist of a girl standing on the left.

Figure 198
Subject: **Highlander and girl**
Title: The / Soldier's Farewell (raised capitals)
Date: *c.* 1855
Height: 12½ in (31.75 cm)
Colour: Well coloured and pale versions exist.
Rarity: Av.
Series: Same series as *fig.* 194 (The Wounded/ Soldier), *fig.* 197 (The / Sailor's Return) and *fig.* 199 (The / Soldier's Return).
Description: To the right stands a Highlander, his right arm round the shoulders of a bare-headed girl with a long skirt. His left hand clasps her hand.

Figure 199
Subject: **Highlander and girl**
Title: The / Soldier's Return (raised capitals)
Date: *c.* 1855
Height: 12 in (30.5 cm)
Colour: Well coloured and pale versions exist.
Rarity: Av.
Series: Same series as *fig.* 194 (The Wounded / Soldier), *fig.* 197 (The / Sailor's Return) and *fig.* 198 (The / Soldier's Farewell).

Plate 71A
Landing of the invalided and the wounded from the Crimea.
Engraving which appeared in *Cassell's Illustrated Family Paper* on April 7th, 1855 (vol.II, p.105). It is the source of *fig.* 194 (The wounded soldier) *pl.* C-71.
By courtesy of the London Library

Plate 71B
Fig. 197(a) Sailor return
By courtesy of Mr John Hall

Description: To the right stands a Scots officer. He holds a bonnet above his head. To the left stands a girl, bare-headed, her left hand supported by his right forearm.

Plate 71A
English soldier and sailor
An engraving which appeared in *Cassell's Illustrated Family Paper* on April 7th, 1855 (vol. 11, p. 105) inscribed: 'Landing of the invalided and the wounded from the Crimea'. It is the probable source of *fig.* 194, *pl.* C-71, differing only, in pose and costume, in minor ways.

Plate 71B
Figure 197(a)
Subject: **Sailor, wife and child**
Title: Sailor Return (gilt script)
Height: 13¼ in (33.5 cm)
Colour: White, black and gilt.
Rarity: VR.
Description: The sailor stands on the left, bare-headed, and with hat in his right hand. His wife, also bare-headed, stands on the right holding a baby in her arms.
Observations: Identical, other than for title, to *fig.* 83 (George and Eliza Harris and child) *pl.* B-26.

Plate 72
Figure 191
Subject: **English sailor**
Title: None
Observations: See *pl.* 70A.

Figure 193 (reverse)
Subject: **French soldier** / English sailor
Title: None
Date: c. 1854
Height: 13 in (33 cm)
Colour: Well coloured.
Rarity: R.
Description: A French soldier stands holding a flagstaff in his right hand, the flag flying above his head and to his left. To his left, also, is a pile of cannon balls.
Observations: The obverse of this figure portrays an English sailor, see *pl.* C-71.

Figure 195 (reverse)
Subject: **French soldier** / English sailor
Title: None
Date: c. 1854
Height: 9 in (23 cm)
Colour: Pale colours.
Rarity: R.
Description: A French soldier stands clasping

a flag in his right hand. There is another flag to his left.
Observations: The obverse of this figure portrays an English sailor, see *pl.* C-71.

Figure 200
Subject: **A non-portrait Crimean figure**
Title: None
Date: c. 1854
Height: 11½ in (29 cm)
Colour: Well coloured.
Rarity: Av.
Description: To the right stands a sailor holding a flagstaff in his left hand, with a large Union Jack flying above his head. His right arm is around a girl wearing a plumed bonnet and carrying a fish-basket in her right hand.

Figure 201
Subject: **A non-portrait Crimean figure**
Title: None
Date: c. 1854
Height: 9 in (23 cm)
Colour: Well coloured.
Rarity: Av.

Plate 72 (Above and below)

Fig. 200 Sailor and girl Fig. 201 Turkish soldiers Fig. 193 *(reverse)* French soldier Fig. 202 Sailor and bear Fig. 195 *(reverse)* French soldier

Fig. 203 Soldier's dream Fig. 204 Fireside study Fig. 205 Soldier's dream Fig. 191 Ready & willing Fig. 206 Sailor and girl

Plate 72 continued
Description: Two Turkish soldiers are portrayed in front of a mosque. Each wears a fez. On the left, one stands, and on the right, the other sits smoking a long pipe.
Observations: This figure is found occasionally in the form of a watch-holder.

Figure 202
Subject: **English sailor and a Russian bear**
Title: None
Date: *c.* 1854
Height: 11½ in (29 cm)
Colour: Well coloured.
Rarity: R.
Description: A sailor stands bare-headed, his right leg raised on a gun. His left foot is couched on a muzzled Russian bear attached to a heavy chain. He holds a flag-staff in his right hand, and the flag, plain except for a small Union Jack moulded in its top left corner, flies above his head He holds his hat above his head in his left hand.

Figure 203
Subject: **Soldier's Dream**
Title: None
Date: *c.* 1854
Height: 11½ in (29 cm)
Colour: Usually white and gilt.
Rarity: C.
Description: A Highlander sleeps. His left forearm rests on a drum. There are flags to his left, and at his feet, a cannon.
Observations: This figure, together with *fig.* 205 and *figs.* 210 and 211, *pl.* C-73, illustrate the theme of *Soldier's Dream*, a poem by Thomas Campbell (1777–1844), written during the Napoleonic wars. Its popularity was revived during the period of the Crimea. Campbell also wrote about the dog *Tray* (see *pl.* I-21).

Figure 204
Subject: **A non-portrait Crimean figure**
Title: None
Date: *c.* 1854
Height: 7½ in (19 cm)
Colour: Well coloured.
Rarity: Av.
Description: A fireside study. There are three candles above the mantelpiece, and to the right sits an officer and on the left a girl.

Figure 205
Subject: **Soldier's Dream**
Title: None
Date: *c.* 1854
Height: 12¾ in (32.25 cm)
Colour: Well coloured.
Rarity: R.
Description: A soldier in Highland dress is standing, his left foot on a gun, his left elbow resting on a drum behind which are two flags.
Observations: See *fig.* 203 (Soldier's Dream).

Figure 206
Subject: **A non-portrait Crimean figure**
Title: None
Date: *c.* 1854
Height: 11 in (28 cm)
Colour: Well coloured.
Rarity: R.
Description: To the left stands a sailor. He supports the staff of a large flag in his right hand. To his left a girl is seated, her left arm around a wheat-sheaf.

Plate 73
Figure 207
Subject: **Peace**
Title: Peace (raised capitals)
Date: 1856
Height: 11¼ in (28.5 cm)

Colour: Well coloured.
Rarity: R.
Description: A watch-holder inscribed above in raised capitals 'Peace'. It is supported on the right by a sailor, and on the left by a girl in bonnet and wide-flounced skirt, a scarf draped over her right arm.

Figure 208
Subject: **Peace**
Title: Peace (raised capitals on plaque)
Date: 1856
Height: 11¼ in (28.5 cm)
Colour: Well coloured.
Rarity: Av.
Description: A clock-face is supported on a vine beneath which lies a lion. To the right is a seated lady, bare-headed, with a cornucopia in her right arm.
Observations: It has been suggested that the lady is Miss Florence Nightingale, but there is no evidence to support this.

Figure 209
Subject: **Sailor and girl**
Title: None
Height: 10 in (25 cm)
Colour: Well coloured.
Rarity: C.
Description: On the left is a sailor, bare-headed. He looks out to sea, shielding his eyes with his right hand. At his feet kneels a girl, bare-headed; her hands clasped in front of her breast.
Observations: This figure is almost certainly not a Crimean figure. It has been suggested that it portrays 'Paul' and 'Virginia', see *p.* 413.

Figure 210
Subject: **Soldier's Dream**
Title: Soldier's Dream (raised capitals on plaque)

Plate 73
T: *Fig.* 207 Peace
Fig. 209 Sailor and girl
Fig. 208 Peace
B: *Fig.* 210 Soldier's dream
Fig. 211 Soldier's dream
Fig. 212 Soldier and sailor
By courtesy of Mr and Mrs Eric Joyce and in the collection of the author

Plate 74
Fig. 213 Sailor
Fig. 214 Sailor and fishwife
Fig. 215 Sailor
In the collection of Rear-Admiral J. Dent, CB, OBE

Plate 75
Fig. 217 A mother's last gift
Fig. 218 Beggar and sailor
In the collections of Mr Anthony Oliver and the author

Plate 75A
Fig. 219 English sailor
Fig. 220 French girl
In the collection of M. Marc de Smedt

Date: *c.* 1854
Height: 13¾ in (35 cm)
Colour: Well coloured.
Rarity: R. A.
Description: A Highlander sits cross-legged. He is dozing, with his left elbow resting on a drum. Behind him is a flag, and at his feet a rifle and a pile of shells.
Observations: This figure, together with *figs.* 203 and 205, *pl.* C-72 and *fig.* 211 portray the theme of *Soldier's Dream*, a poem by Thomas Campbell (1777–1844), written during the Napoleonic wars. The popularity of the poem was revived during the period of the Crimean War. Campbell also wrote about the dog *Tray* (see *pl.* I-21).

Figure 211
Subject: **Soldier's Dream**
Title: Soldier's Dream (gilt script)
Date: *c.* 1854
Height: 10½ in (26.5 cm)
Colour: White and gilt.
Rarity: R.
Description: A seated soldier sleeps with his left elbow resting on a drum; at his feet is a cannon. There are flags to his left. The figure differs in only minor respects from *fig.* 203, *pl.* C-72.
Observations: See preceding figure.

Figure 212
Subject: **A non-portrait Crimean figure**
Title: None
Date: *c.* 1854
Height: 13½ in (34.25 cm)
Colour: Well coloured, and white and gilt versions are known.
Rarity: R.
Description: A French soldier carrying the tricolour stands on the left of a gun emplacement; to the right stands an English sailor with a white ensign.
Observations: *Fig.* 213 (Sailor) *pl.* C-74 is

virtually identical to this figure, except that the French soldier has been omitted.

Plate 74
Figure 213
Subject: **A non-portrait Crimean figure**
Title: None
Date: 1854
Height: 13¼ in (33.5 cm)
Colour: Well coloured.
Rarity: R.
Description: A sailor stands with a flagstaff in his left hand, the white ensign flying above his head. To his right is a gun-emplacement.
Observations: The right hand portion of *fig.* 212 (Soldier and sailor) *pl.* C-73.

Figure 214
Subject: **Sailor and fishwife**
Title: None
Date: Uncertain
Height: 15½ in (39.25 cm)
Colour: Both coloured, with underglaze blue coat, and poorly coloured versions are seen.
Rarity: Av.
Description: To the right is a sailor with his right forearm resting on a capstan. To the left is a bare-headed fishwife, her apron turned up to form a bag in which there are shells.
Observations: This figure is probably post-Crimean.

Figure 215
Subject: **Sailor**
Title: None
Date: Uncertain
Height: 11½ in (29 cm)
Colour: Pale.
Rarity: Av.
Pair: *Fig.* 216 (Sailor)
Description: A sailor stands with his left

elbow on a barrel. The barrel is resting on a coil of rope. In his right hand he holds a mug against his chest.
Observations: See *fig.* 216 (Sailor).

Figure 216 (not illustrated)
Subject: **Sailor**
Title: None
Date: Uncertain
Height: 11½ in (29 cm)
Colour: Pale.
Rarity: Av.
Pair: *Fig.* 215 (Sailor)
Description: A sailor in 'pirate's' attire is standing beside a barrel resting on a coil of rope, to his right.
Observations: This figure and its pair are difficult to date, but are probably post-Crimean and possibly theatrical.

Plate 75
Figure 217
Subject: **English sailor and his mother**
Title: A, Mothers. Last. Gift, (gilt script)
Date: *c.* 1854
Height: 10 in (25 cm)
Colour: Well coloured.
Rarity: VR. A.
Description: To the right stands a mother with a lace cap, apron, and bag in her left hand. In her right hand she holds a bible which she is handing over to her sailor son, who stands on her right.
Observations: Generally regarded as one of the most attractive of the non-portrait Crimean figures.

Figure 218
Subject: **A non-portrait Crimean figure**
Title: None
Date: *c.* 1854
Height: 8½ in (21.5 cm)

Plate 76
Fig. 221 Greenwich Hospital pensioner

Between the two figures is displayed an engraving from *The Illustrated London News* of April 13th, 1844. It portrays Greenwich Hospital pensioners. From left to right: Joseph Burgin, James Connell, George French.

Fig. 222 Greenwich Hospital pensioner

Plate 75 continued
Colour: Well coloured.
Rarity: VR.
Description: On the left an old man is seated in cocked hat, long jacket and trousers. The right trouser leg is rolled up above his peg leg. He is clearly a beggar but his hat and jacket are officer's kit, presumably given to him. With his right hand he salutes a sailor who holds a purse to his up-turned left hand.

Plate 75A
Figure 219
Subject: **English sailor**
Title: None
Date: *c.* 1854
Height: 10 in (25 cm)
Colour: Well coloured.
Rarity: R.
Pair: Fig. 220 (French girl)
Description: A sailor stands, left hand on his hip, right hand holding a white ensign, an anchor to his right.

Figure 220
Subject: **French girl, possibly a vivandiere**
Title: None
Date: *c.* 1854

Height: 10¼ in (25.75 cm)
Colour: Well coloured.
Rarity: R.
Pair: Fig. 219 (English sailor)
Description: A girl is standing, her right hand holding up her apron in which there are some shells, her left hand on a French tricolour, an anchor to her left.
Observations: The only pair of figures I have come across in which the decorator has gone to considerable trouble to accurately portray an English and a French flag.

Plate 76
Figure 221
Subject: **Greenwich Hospital pensioner**
Title: None
Date: *c.* 1844
Height: 8 in (20.5 cm)
Colour: Well coloured.
Maker: Alpha factory
Rarity: Av. A.
Pair: Fig. 222 (Greenwich Hospital pensioner)
Description: Seated, his right elbow resting on a table top. In his right hand he holds a jug and in his left hand a mug. He has a right peg leg and is dressed in the uniform

of a Greenwich Hospital pensioner, black cocked hat, coat, waistcoat, breeches and stocking.
Observations: This figure is sometimes referred to in the trade as 'Long John Silver', but *Treasure Island* was not published until 1881–3. The dress is that of a Greenwich Hospital pensioner, as will be seen by comparing the figure with the pensioners portrayed in the engraving taken from *The Illustrated London News* of April 13th, 1844.

Figure 222
Subject: **Greenwich Hospital pensioner**
Title: None
Date: *c.* 1844
Height: 7¼ in (18.25 cm)
Colour: Well coloured.
Maker: Alpha factory
Rarity: Av. A.
Pair: Fig. 221 (Greenwich Hospital pensioner)
Description: Seated, a table to his left. His left hand holds a mug which is on the table top. On the table top, also, is a manuscript and a churchwarden pipe. He is dressed in the uniform of a Greenwich Hospital pen-

Plate 77
T: *Fig.* 223 Napoleon III
and Albert
Fig. 223 Napoleon III
and Albert
Fig. 224 Napoleon III
and Albert

B: *Fig.* 225 Napoleon III
and Albert
Fig. 226 Napoleon III
and Albert

sioner with black cocked hat, coat, waistcoat, breeches and stockings.

Observations: Many attempts have been made to identify this figure, and, among others, it has been thought to be Dr Johnson. However, in spite of intensive enquiries, no firm attribution has been made. As it pairs *fig.* 221, it seems reasonable to assume that it, too, portrays a Greenwich Hospital pensioner and not a specific personality.

Plate 77
Figure 223
Subject: **Albert and Napoleon III**
Title: None
Date: *c.* 1854
Height: 12½ in (31.75 cm); 9 in (23 cm) version illustrated.
Colour: Well coloured.
Rarity: R.
Description: To the left stands Napoleon, in

kepi (French soldier's straight-peaked cap); to the right stands Albert, in cocked hat. Between them are two flags, a wall containing a gun emplacement and a heap of shells.

Figure 224
Subject: **Albert and Napoleon III**
Title: Napoleon/Albert (raised capitals)
Date: *c.* 1854

C279

Plate 78
Fig. 227 Napoleon III and Prince Albert
In the collection of Mr A. Guy Stringer

Plate 78A
Fig. 227(a) Brothers in Arms
By courtesy of Mr John Hall

Plate 77 continued
Height: 11 in (28 cm)
Colour: Well coloured, or largely white versions have been noted.
Rarity: Av.
Description: To the left stands Napoleon, in full military uniform with cocked hat athwartships. To the right stands Albert, in full military uniform with cocked hat fore and aft. They clasp hands. Between them is a brick wall with a pile of shells at its base. Above Napoleon's head is a Union Jack, and above Albert's the tricolour.
Observations: A similar figure fetched 38 gns at Christie's in 1969.

Figure 225
Subject: **Albert and Napoleon III**
Title: Napoleon Albert (raised capitals)
Date: c. 1854
Height: 13¼ in (33.5 cm)
Colour: Well coloured, or largely white versions, have been noted.
Rarity: Av.
Description: To the left stands Napoleon, in full military uniform with cocked hat athwartships. To the right stands Prince Albert, in full military uniform with cocked hat fore and aft. They clasp hands. Between them is a brick wall with a pile of shells at its base, and above them are two flags.
Observations: A similar figure, together with *fig.* 102 (Napier) *pl.* C-42, fetched 45 gns at Christie's in 1969.

Figure 226
Subject: **Albert and Napoleon III**
Title: Albert & Napoleon (gilt script)
Date: 1854
Height: 12 in (30.5 cm)
Colour: Well coloured.
Rarity: R.
Description: Virtually identical to *fig.* 225, except for title and size. Albert is portrayed on the right.
Observations: There seems to be no uniformity with regard to the flags in these figures. Sometimes it is not clear what the flag is intended to be; sometimes it is obviously a Union Jack and on other occasions obviously a tricolour. Sometimes the tricolour is above Napoleon and sometimes above Albert.

Plate 78
Figure 227
Subject: **Albert and Napoleon III**
Title: Napoleon & Albert or Napoleon & Prince Albert (gilt script)
Date: c. 1854
Height: 14 in (35.5 cm)
Colour: Well coloured or pale versions exist.
Rarity: Av.
Description: Virtually identical to *fig.* 225, *pl.* C-77, except for title and size.

Plate 78A
Figure 227(a)
Subject: **? Napoleon III and unidentified British officer**

Title: Brothers in Arms (raised capitals)
Date: Probably c. 1854
Height: 12 in (30.5 cm)
Colour: Well coloured.
Rarity: VR. A.
Description: On the left stands a British officer, with busby, tailed tunic with high collar and epaulettes, and trousers. On the right is a French officer, leaning heavily on the British officer, and being supported by him. Each has his arms around the other. The French officer wears an imperial, long military coat with epaulettes and high collar, and trousers. At their feet is a pile of shells.
Observations: The French officer resembles Napoleon III, nevertheless the figure is probably a non-portrait, Crimean figure.

Plate 79
Figure 228
Subject: **A non-portrait Crimean figure**
Title: None
Date: c. 1854
Height: 7 in (17.5 cm)
Colour: Well coloured.
Rarity: VR.
Description: To the left an officer stands, bare-headed with epaulettes. To his right is a flag. In his right hand he holds the right hand of a seated girl, and his left hand is over her hat. She holds his cocked hat in her left hand.
Observations: The figure is a version of 'Soldier's farewell'.

Plate 79

Fig. 228 Soldier's farewell   *Fig.* 229 Soldier and girl   *Fig.* 230 Napoleon III and Prince Albert   *Fig.* 231 Drummer boys

Figure 229
Subject: **A non-portrait Crimean figure**
Title: None
Date: *c.* 1854
Height: 10¼ in (25.75 cm)
Colour: Well coloured.
Rarity: R.
Description: A watch-holder. To the left stands a girl, with a plumed bonnet; to the right an officer, with peaked cap, military jacket, epaulettes and trousers. Behind them are two flags.

Figure 230
Subject: **Albert and Napoleon III**
Title: None
Date: *c.* 1854
Height: 10¼ in (25.75 cm)
Colour: Well coloured.
Rarity: VR.
Description: Identical in all respects, other than minor details, to *fig.* 223 (Albert and Napoleon III) *pl.* C-77, except that there is a drum to the left of Napoleon and another to the right of Albert.

Figure 231
Subject: **A non-portrait Crimean figure**
Title: None
Date: *c.* 1854
Height: 7 in (17.5 cm)
Colour: Well coloured.
Rarity: R.
Description: Two drummer boys are standing in Albert shakos (a form of military peaked cap), tunics and trousers. There is a Union Jack between their heads.

Plate 80
Figure 232
Subject: **A non-portrait Crimean figure**
Title: None
Date: *c.* 1854
Height: 15½ in (39.25 cm)
Colour: Well coloured.
Rarity: VR. A.
Description: A sailor is standing with a flag in

his left hand and with his right arm round the shoulders of a small boy, also dressed in sailor's uniform, but bare-headed. The boy is standing on a high mound to the sailor's right.
Observations: Amongst the finest of the non-portrait Crimean figures.

Figure 233
Subject: **A non-portrait Crimean figure**
Title: None
Date: *c.* 1854

Height: 10 in (25 cm)
Colour: Well coloured in the manner of Thomas Parr.
Maker: Thomas Parr
Rarity: R.
Description: To the right stands a sailor with his right hand raised to his hat, his left leg on a platform and his right foot raised on a gun. To the left a sailor kneels on his left knee, with his left arm resting on the gun and his right arm ramming a shell into its muzzle.

Plate 80
Fig. 232 Sailor and boy
Fig. 233 Two sailors and a gun

Plate 81
Figure 234
Subject: **Fat sailor**
Title: None
Date: Probably 1870's
Height: 13½ in (34.25 cm)
Colour: Usually sparsely.
Rarity: C.
Description: A fat sailor dressed in rig typical of the middle to the late nineteenth century.
Observations: It has been suggested that this and similar figures are theatrical.

Figure 235
Subject: **Fat sailor in boat**
Title: None
Date: Probably 1870's
Height: 13 in (33 cm)
Colour: Usually sparsely.
Rarity: Av.
Description: Similar in all respects to *fig.* 234, except that he holds a flag in his right hand and is standing in a boat.
Observations: See preceding figure.

Figure 236
Subject: **Sailor and boy**
Title: Begging sailor (raised capitals)
Date: c. 1854
Height: 16¼ in (41 cm)
Colour: Well coloured.
Rarity: R.
Pair: Possibly to *fig.* 238 (Highlander) *pl.* C-83.
Description: He stands, wearing a straw hat, with a sailing boat on his left shoulder. His right hand rests on the bare head of a small boy, who is also dressed in naval rig.
Observations: There is a problem about this figure which has so far remained unsolved.

On *pl.* C-82 we may see the base of a similar piece [*fig.* 236(a)] in which the word 'Begging' has been deleted. On *pl.* C-83 we may see *fig.* 236(b) in which the title has been amended to 'Sailor' alone, and this has been centred on the figure. Clearly, we are seeing an evolution from 'Begging sailor' to 'Sailor', but why this is so remains a mystery.

Plate 82
Figure 236(a) (Base of figure only illustrated)
Subject: **Sailor and boy**
Title: Sailor (raised capitals)
Date: c. 1854
Height: 16¼ in (41 cm)
Colour: Well coloured.
Rarity: VR.
Description: Identical to *fig.* 236 (Begging sailor) *pl.* C-81, except that the word 'Begging' has been erased and overprinted with a complex design in gilt.
Observations: See *fig.* 236, *pl.* C-81.

Plate 83
Figure 236(b)
Subject: **Sailor and boy**
Title: Sailor (raised capitals)
Date: c. 1854
Height: 16¼ in (41 cm)
Colour: Well coloured.
Rarity: Av.
Pair: Possibly to *fig.* 238 (Highlander).
Description: Identical in all respects to *fig.* 236 (Begging sailor) *pl.* C-81, except for the title.
Observations: See *fig.* 236, *pl.* C-81.

Figure 237
Subject: **French soldier and vivandiere**
Title: Vivandiere (raised capitals)

Date: c. 1854
Height: 14 in (35.5 cm)
Colour: Well coloured.
Rarity: Av.
Description: A woman stands in front of a French soldier who is mounted on a horse, facing right.
Observations: 1. Vivandière is, by definition, a woman who sold provisions to the French troops in the Crimea.
2. The soldier somewhat resembles Napoleon III.
3. This figure, together with two other unimportant groups, fetched 22 gns at Christie's in 1963. Another, with *fig.* 203 (Soldier's Dream) *pl.* C-72, fetched 32 gns at Christie's in 1965.

Figure 238
Subject: **Highlander**
Title: None
Date: c. 1854
Height: 16¼ in (41 cm)
Colour: Well coloured.
Rarity: Av.

Plate 83

Fig. 236(b) Sailor   Fig. 237 Vivandiere   Fig. 238 Highlander

Plate 83A
In the Thomas Balston collection

Fig. 239 England & France   Fig. 241 Zouave and English officer   Fig. 240 Kneeling soldier

Pair: Possibly to *fig*. 236 (Begging sailor) *pl*. C-81.
Description: A Highland soldier standing holding a flagstaff in his right hand with the flag billowing behind his bonnet. Beside his right leg is a drum, and beside his left a pile of shells.
Observations: It has never been found titled and *fig*. 236 has never been found untitled. It is doubtful therefore if they are a pair.

Plate 83A
Figure 239
Subject: **English and French officers**
Title: England & France (raised capitals)
Date: *c*. 1854
Height: 12 in (30.5 cm)
Colour: Pale.
Rarity: VR.
Description: To the left stands an English officer, clean-shaven and to the right a

French officer, bearded. Both are in full military uniform and each carries a rifle in his left hand. They are shaking hands.

Figure 240
Subject: **A non-portrait Crimean figure**
Title: None
Date: *c*. 1854
Height: 11¾ in (29.75 cm)

Plate 83A continued
Colour: Well coloured.
Rarity: VR.
Description: A soldier in the same dress as *fig.* 190 (Ready Willing) *pl.* C-70 is kneeling on his left knee. To his right, on high ground, is a gun surmounted by two large flags and below it a drum.

Figure 241
Subject: **A non-portrait Crimean figure**
Title: None
Date: c. 1854
Height: 8⅛ in (20.75 cm)
Colour: Well coloured.
Rarity: VR.
Description: To the left stands a Zouave officer, in round plumed hat, short jacket with epaulettes, sash, breeches, stockings and shoes. To the right stands an English officer, in peaked hat, tunic with epaulettes and trousers. Between them on the ground is a drum.

Plate 84
Figure 242
Subject: **Unidentified sailors in boat**
Title: None
Date: Uncertain
Height: 7¼ in (18.25 cm)
Colour: Sparsely coloured.
Rarity: Av.
Description: Two sailors are in a boat. The one on the left is standing and holds an oar in his left hand. The one on the right is seated on a barrel. There is a flag at either end of the boat.
Observations: Possibly theatrical.

Figure 243
Subject: **A non-portrait figure, probably Crimean**
Title: To the / memory / of a / soldier (indented capitals)
Date: c. 1854
Height: 7¾ in (20 cm)
Colour: Well coloured.
Rarity: Av.
Series: There are at least three others in this series depicting a sailor, soldier or girl beside a tombstone, each with appropriate inscription.
Description: A sailor stands to the right of a tombstone. His right elbow rests on it. The tombstone is inscribed as above, and embossed in the top left hand corner is a skull. At the foot of the tombstone are some flowers and a sword.

Figure 244
Subject: **Sailor**
Title: None
Date: Uncertain
Height: 6½ in (16.5 cm)
Colour: Well coloured.
Rarity: Av.
Pair: There is usually a pair to this class of figure, but so far it remains undetected.
Description: A sailor stands with his legs crossed and his left elbow resting on an anchor against which he leans.
Observations: This may be a Crimean figure or possibly a theatrical figure.

Figure 245
Subject: **A non-portrait figure, probably Crimean**
Title: None
Date: c. 1854
Height: 8½ in (21.5 cm)
Colour: Well coloured.
Rarity: R.
Description: On the left a 'lady' sits holding a mug in her right hand which she proffers to a sailor seated on her left. He holds a bottle in his left hand and a flag in the crook of his left arm.

Figure 246
Subject: **Sailor**
Title: None
Date: Uncertain
Height: 7 in (17.5 cm)
Colour: Sparsely.
Rarity: Av.
Pair: There is usually a pair to this class of figure, but so far it remains undetected.
Description: A sailor stands, bare-headed, with his hat held above his head in his right hand. To his left is an anchor.

Figure 247
Subject: **Sailor**
Title: None
Date: Uncertain
Height: 7½ in (19 cm)
Colour: Well coloured.
Rarity: Av.
Pair: There is usually a pair to this class of figure, but so far it remains undetected.
Description: A sailor stands with his right hand on his waist and his left hand resting on an anchor. His legs are crossed.

Plate 85
Figure 248
Subject: **A non-portrait figure, probably Crimean**
Title: None
Date: c. 1854
Height: 8¾ in (22 cm)
Colour: Well coloured.
Rarity: Av.
Pair: *Fig.* 249 (Girl with flag)
Description: A sailor stands with a flag-pole in his right hand. He holds the lapel of his jacket with his left hand.

Figure 249
Subject: **A non-portrait figure, probably Crimean**
Title: None
Date: c. 1854
Height: 8¾ in (22 cm)
Colour: Well coloured.
Rarity: Av.
Pair: *Fig.* 248 (Sailor with flag)
Description: A girl stands wearing a round hat, and carrying a flag in her right hand.

Figure 250
Subject: **Sailor leaning against a bollard**
Title: None
Date: Uncertain
Height: 8¼ in (21 cm)
Colour: Well coloured.
Rarity: R.
Pair: A pair is known to this figure (see *ch.* 4, *pl.* 5), to which *fig.* 251 has been allotted. It has, however, only been found as a 'midget' pair to the midget version of *fig.* 250. Each of these figures is 3½ in (9 cm).
Description: A sailor stands wearing a round hat, his left hand tucked into his shirt. He rests his right elbow on a bollard.
Observations: The 8¼ in (21 cm) version is a very fine figure and may well be a portrait, although to date it has not been identified. It has been postulated that it portrays Prince Alfred but there is no supporting evidence. Alternatively, it may turn out to be a theatrical figure.

Colour Plate 36
English sailor, French and Turkish soldier, 'The Victory'. *Fig.* 185, *pl.* C-69. See page 272.

Figure 252
Subject: **Sailor**
Title: None
Date: Uncertain
Height: 8½ in (21.5 cm)
Colour: Sparsely coloured.
Rarity: R.
Pair: Unknown
Description: A bearded sailor stands, his legs apart, both hands on his hips.
Observations: Very similar to *fig.* 234 (Fat sailor) *pl.* C-81, except that this sailor is not fat. The general appearance of the figure suggests that it may be theatrical.

Figure 253
Subject: **A non-portrait Crimean figure**
Title: None
Date: *c.* 1854
Height: 9¼ in (23.5 cm)
Colour: Well coloured and pale versions exist.
Rarity: Av.
Description: A sailor stands with his right hand to his head and his legs crossed; his left arm is round the waist of a bare-headed girl whose legs are likewise crossed. They may well be doing the polka.

Figure 254
Subject: **Sailor**
Title: None
Date: Uncertain
Height: 9¼ in (23.5 cm)

Colour: Well coloured.
Rarity: R.
Pair: There is probably a pair to this figure, although it has so far not been identified.
Description: A sailor stands with his legs crossed, his right elbow resting on a barrel, his left arm raised against his hat. He carries a bottle in his left hand.
Observations: This figure presents many similarities to *fig.* 217 (? T. P. Cooke) *pl.* E-108. It may well be theatrical.

Plate 86
Figure 255
Subject: **Girl with boarding-pike**
Title: None
Date: *c.* 1854
Height: 9½ in (24 cm)
Colour: Well coloured.
Rarity: C.
Pair: Fig. 256 (Sailor)
Description: A girl stands, wearing a round hat. She holds a flag-pole and flag in her right hand. To her left is a boarding-pike.
Observations: A boarding-pike was a long pole with a metal tip used to repel invaders. This seems to be the likely identification of the object portrayed in this figure.

Figure 256
Subject: **Sailor with flag**
Title: None
Date: *c.* 1854

Height: 9½ in (24 cm)
Colour: Well coloured.
Rarity: C.
Pair: Fig. 255 (Girl).
Description: A sailor stands bare-headed, a flagstaff and flag in his left hand. To his right is a cannon.

Figure 257
Subject: **Sailor and girl**
Title: None
Date: Uncertain
Height: 8 in (20.5 cm)
Colour: Well coloured.
Rarity: R.
Description: A woman wearing a round hat is seated to the left of a tree. She has a net, and at her feet is a basket of fish. To the right of the tree stands a sailor.

Figure 258
Subject: **Sailor**
Title: None
Height: 8 in (20.5 cm)
Colour: Sparsely coloured.
Rarity: R.
Pair: Unknown
Description: A sailor is dancing. He wears a broad-brimmed hat, striped jersey, neckcloth and trousers. His right hand is raised to the brim of his hat and his left hand is on his hip. He has a long pigtail behind.
Observations: Almost certainly a theatrical

Section C. Naval, Military and Exploration

Plate 87
Fig. 261 Soldier and girl
Fig. 87 Albert and
Victoria *pl.* A-32
Fig. 262 Sailor and girl

Plate 87A (Left)
Fig. 261(a) War
Fig. 262(a) Peace
By courtesy of Mr Disley Jones

Plate 88 (Right)
Fig. 263 Crimean
memorial obelisk

figure, although it has so far defied identification.

Figure 259
Subject: **Sailor and girl**
Title: None
Date: Uncertain
Height: 8¼ in (21 cm)
Colour: Often appears poorly decorated in a late style.
Rarity: Av.

Description: A woman is seated on the left; to her left stands a sailor, whose left elbow rests on a barrel. He holds a flagstaff and flag in his right hand.

Figure 260
Subject: **Sailor and girl**
Title: None
Date: Uncertain
Height: 5½ in (14 cm)
Colour: Well coloured.

Rarity: R.
Description: To the left stands a girl with a flag; to her right is a sailor with a flag. Between them is a clock-face.

Plate 87
Figure 261
Subject: **A non-portrait Crimean soldier and girl**
Title: None

Colour Plate 37
General Sir Garnet Wolseley and the Duke of Connaught.
Figs. 328 and 329, *pl.* C-115. See page 306.

Colour Plate 38
Omar Pasha. *Fig.* 163, *pl.* C-62A. See page 264.

Plate 87 continued
Date: *c.* 1854
Height: 8 in (20.5 cm)
Colour: Well coloured.
Rarity: Av.
Pair: *Fig.* 262 (Sailor and girl). The 'centre-piece', *fig.* 87 (Victoria and Albert) *pl.* A-32 is probably not part of this set, although it takes its place very suitably.
Description: To the left stands a soldier, his right hand grasping the hand of a girl, and his left hand round her shoulder. The girl wears a bonnet, necklace, long dress and apron.
Observations: Mr Anthony Oliver has suggested that this figure represents a scene from Act II of *La Figlia del Reggimento*. Jenny Lind wore a similar costume, including necklace, when playing 'Marie', see *fig.* 160, *pl.* E-81. The soldier would be her lover 'Tonio'. The objection to this theory is that the figure definitely pairs *fig.* 262.

Figure 262
Subject: **A non-portrait Crimean sailor and girl**
Title: None
Date: *c.* 1854
Height: 8 in (20.5 cm)
Colour: Well coloured.
Rarity: Av.
Pair: *Fig.* 261 (Soldier and girl). See also preceding figure.
Description: To the right stands a sailor, with a hat, jacket, neckcloth, shirt and trousers; his left hand on his hip, his right hand clasping the right hand of a girl, who has her left arm round his neck. She wears a hat, blouse, long skirt and apron.

Plate 87A
Figure 261(a)
Subject: **War**
Title: War (raised capitals on plaque)
Date: *c.* 1856
Height: 15 in (38 cm)
Colour: In the paler tradition.
Rarity: VR.
Pair: 262(a) (Peace)
Description: A Highlander stands with his left hand clutching a flagstaff and his right hand on his hip. His left foot is on a drum and there is a rifle and a heap of shells to his right.
Observations: See next figure.
Figure 262(a)
Subject: **Peace**
Title: Peace (raised capitals on plaque)
Date: *c.* 1856
Height: 14½ in (36.75 cm)
Colour: In the paler tradition.
Rarity: VR.
Pair: 261(a) (War)
Description: A farm-lad stands to the left of a tree trunk (spill-holder). He holds a sickle in his right hand and a sheaf of corn in his left.
Observations: This figure and its pair were probably issued in celebration of the end of the Crimean War.

Plate 88
Figure 263
Subject: **Crimean memorial obelisk**
Title: To / the / fallen / brave, on the front side of the memorial obelisk (gilt transfer capitals); Sebastopol / Alma / Balaklava / Inkermann, one on each side of the base of the obelisk (gilt transfer capitals).
Date: 1856

Plate 89
T: *Fig.* 264 Campbell
Fig. 147 Havelock

B: *Fig.* 265 Highland Jessie
Fig. 266 Highland Jessie

Height: 17 in (42.5 cm)
Colour: White and gilt.
Maker: Lockett Baguley & Cooper, Victoria Works, Shelton, Hanley. See *ch.* 2, *pl.* 7.
Rarity: VR.
Description: A conventional memorial obelisk of porcelain.
Observations: The base of this obelisk is inscribed in red lettering 'PUBLISHED BY / LOCKETT BAGULEY / & COOPER / SHELTON, STAFFS. / June 25th, 1856.'

Plate 89
Figure 147
Subject: **General Sir Henry Havelock**
Title: G. Havelock (raised capitals)
Date: *c.* 1857
Height: 10¾ in (27 cm)
Colour: White and gilt, or well coloured with cinnamon horse.
Rarity: Av.
Pair: Either *fig.* 146 (Campbell) *pl.* C-56 or *fig.* 264 (Campbell).
Description: On a horse facing left, wearing hat with sun-curtain.

Figure 264
Subject: **General Sir Colin Campbell**
Title: Sir / C. Campbell (raised capitals)
Date: *c.* 1857
Height: 10¾ in (27 cm)
Colour: White and gilt, or well coloured with cinnamon horse.
Rarity: Av.
Pair: *Fig.* 147 (Havelock)
Description: On horse facing right, bare-headed, in long coat and trousers, bonnet in his right hand which is held against the horse's flank.
Observations: All figures of Campbell which pair Havelock must date from 1857 to 1859, the time of the Indian Mutiny. Havelock

was unknown to the public at the time of the Crimean War. Figures of Campbell occurring singly or paired with someone other than Havelock are probably of Crimean War vintage.

Figure 265
Subject: **Highland Jessie and probably Corporal Brown**
Title: Highland / Jessie (raised capitals)
Date: *c.* 1857
Height: 9 in (23 cm)
Colour: Well coloured.
Rarity: Av.
Description: Jessie is standing on the right, beside a jug on a pedestal. To her right sits a soldier, holding a rifle on a barrel.
Observations: See next figure.

Figure 266
Subject: **Highland Jessie and probably Corporal Brown**
Title: Highland Jessie (raised capitals)
Date: *c.* 1857
Height: 14½ in (36.75 cm)
Colour: Well coloured.
Rarity: Av.
Description: Jessie stands wearing a plumed bonnet and holding a rifle in her right hand. To her left, with his right arm in hers, is a soldier with his left arm in a sling.
Observations: The soldier in this figure, and in the preceding figure, was probably intended to represent Corporal Brown. There is no mention of a wounded soldier in the story of Highland Jessie, see biography (Brown, Jessie).
A similar group, and another unimportant group, fetched 26 gns at Christie's in 1963; another fetched 28 gns in the same rooms 1966.

Section C. Naval, Military and Exploration

Plate 90
Fig. 267 Havelock
Fig. 268 Havelock
By courtesy of Mr and Mrs Eric Joyce

Plate 90
Figure 267
Subject: **General Sir Henry Havelock**
Title: M G. Havelock. K C B (raised capitals)
Date: *c.* 1857
Height: 13½ in (34.25 cm)
Colour: White and gilt.
Rarity: R.

Pair: Not known
Description: Standing bare-headed, in full military uniform. His right hand is on his hip, and in it he holds his plumed cocked hat. There is a cannon beside his right leg. His left hand rests on a pedestal.
Observations: 1. Sir Henry Havelock co-operated with Sir Colin Campbell in the second relief of Lucknow in November 1857;

he died of dysentery a week after its final relief. He was created KCB shortly before his death, and the rank of a baronet's widow, together with a pension, were given to his widow. This figure was almost certainly produced after his death.
2. A similar figure fetched 32 gns at Christie's in 1969.

Figure 268
Subject: **General Sir Henry Havelock**
Title: Havelock (gilt script)
Date: *c.* 1857
Height: 9¼ in (23.5 cm)
Colour: Well coloured.
Rarity: R.
Pair: Not known
Description: Standing bare-headed, in long military coat with epaulettes, and sash over left shoulder, trousers and shoes. He holds a sword in his left hand.

Plate 91
Figure 269
Subject: **General Sir Colin Campbell**
Title: Sir C. Campbell (raised capitals)
Date: *c.* 1857
Height: 11¾ in (29.75 cm)
Colour: White and gilt.
Rarity: VR.
Pair: *Fig.* 270 (Havelock) *pl.* C-91A.
Description: On prancing horse facing right, in plumed bonnet and full military uniform.

Plate 91A
Figure 270
Subject: **General Sir Henry Havelock**
Title: G. Havelock (raised capitals)
Date: *c.* 1857
Height: 11¼ in (28.5 cm)
Colour: White and gilt.
Rarity: VR.
Pair: *Fig.* 269 (Campbell) *pl.* C-91.
Description: On prancing horse facing left, wearing a hat with a sun-curtain, and full military uniform.

Plate 91
Fig. 269 Campbell
In the collection of Lady Ranfurly

Plate 91A
Fig. 270 Havelock
In the Thomas Balston collection

Section C. Naval, Military and Exploration

Plate 92
Fig. 271 Campbell
Fig. 272 Havelock
In the Thomas Balston collection

Plate 92
Figure 271
Subject: **General Sir Colin Campbell**
Title: Campbell (raised capitals)
Date: *c.* 1857
Height: 9¾ in (24.5 cm)
Colour: White and gilt, or coloured versions are known.
Rarity: C.
Pair: Fig. 272 (Havelock)
Description: On horse facing right, in plumed bonnet and full military uniform.

Figure 272
Subject: **General Sir Henry Havelock**
Title: Havelock (raised capitals)
Date: *c.* 1857
Height: 8¾ in (22 cm)
Colour: White and gilt, or coloured versions are known.
Rarity: C.
Pair: Fig. 271 (Campbell)
Description: On a horse facing left, wearing a hat with a sun-curtain, and military uniform.

Plate 92A
Figure 273
Subject: **General Sir Henry Havelock**
Title: Locknow. Havelock. Cawnpore. (raised capitals)
Date: *c.* 1857
Height: 9 in (23 cm)
Colour: Well coloured.
Rarity: VR. D. A.
Description: A bust. Bare-headed in tunic with high collar and epaulettes.
Observations: A cast figure.

Plate 92A (Left)
Fig. 273 Havelock
By courtesy of The Director, City Museum and Art Gallery, Hanley, Stoke-on-Trent

Plate 92B
Figure 274
Subject: **General Sir Henry Havelock**
Title: Havelock (raised capitals)
Date: c. 1857
Height: 12 in (30.5 cm)
Colour: Well coloured.
Rarity: VR. D. A.
Pair: Not known
Description: He is standing bare-headed, in civilian frock-coat, waistcoat and trousers. In his right hand he holds a paper against his waistcoat. His left hand is on a round pedestal. A sword and belt hang from the pedestal.
Observations: A similar figure, broken through the waist, fetched £85 at Bonham's in 1966.

Figure 275
Subject: **Sir Colin Campbell**
Title: Colin Campbell (raised capitals)
Date: c. 1857
Height: 12 in (30.5 cm)
Colour: In the paler manner.
Rarity: VR. D. A.
Pair: Not known
Description: He stands bare-headed, in jacket with epaulettes and trousers. There is a long scarf over his right shoulder. He leans to the right against a gun. A sword hangs from his right hand against a pile of shells, and with his left hand he holds a Scotch bonnet to his head.

Plate 93
Figure 276
Subject: **Volunteer Rifles**
Title: V. Rifles (raised capitals)
Date: 1860
Height: 12 in (30.5 cm)

Colour: In the paler manner.
Rarity: R.
Description: An officer stands to the right and a soldier to the left of a clock-face, on which stands a drum, bugle, and two flags.
Observations: 1. The Volunteer Rifles were revived in 1860 at the time of the Anglo-French war scare.
2. A similar figure fetched 38 gns at Christie's in 1968; and another 60 gns, in 1969.

Figure 277
Subject: **? Napoleon III, upon whom squats the British lion**
Title: None
Date: 1860
Height: 9 in (23 cm)
Colour: Well coloured.
Rarity: C.
Pair: This figure is produced with the lion facing either right or left.
Description: A large lion, facing right or left, squats on a French officer wearing an imperial.
Observations: The figure almost certainly represents the British lion and Napoleon III, and was probably produced at the time of the Anglo-French war scare of 1860.

Plate 94
Figure 278
Subject: **? Sir Richard Francis Burton**
Title: None
Date: c. 1861
Height: 8½ in (21.5 cm)
Colour: Well coloured.
Rarity: R.
Pair: Fig. 279 (Lady Isabel Burton) *pl.* C-95.
Description: On a camel, facing right. The man portrayed appears to be a European.

He wears a turban, cloak, jacket, shirt, necktie, and knee-boots.
Observations: See next figure.

Plate 95
Figure 279
Subject: **? Lady Isabel Burton**
Title: None
Date: c. 1861
Height: 8½ in (21.5 cm)
Colour: Well coloured.
Rarity: VR.
Pair: Fig. 278 (Sir Richard Burton) *pl.* C-94.
Description: On a camel facing left, riding side-saddle and dressed in quasi-European clothes.
Observations: 1. Lady Isabel Burton married in 1861 and accompanied her husband on many journeys of exploration in Africa and elsewhere. Both this and the preceding figure date to about that period, and although no engraving has been found to provide positive identification, it seems very likely that they represent Sir Richard and Lady Isabel Burton.
2. Alternatively, the figures portray Sir Samuel White Baker (1821–93), traveller and sportsman, and Lady Baker. In 1861, Baker accompanied by his young and beautiful Hungarian wife, undertook an expedition in search of the great Lake in Equatorial Africa and the source of the Nile. No white woman had ever entered these regions before. The story is recounted in Edwin Hodder's *Heroes of Britain in Peace and War* (c. 1880). It is accompanied by an engraving of Baker and his wife, mounted on camels, on their journey. Their dress is not dissimilar from that portrayed in the figures.

Section C. Naval, Military and Exploration

Plate 94 (Left)
Fig. 278 ? Sir Richard
Burton
*In the collection of
Lady Ranfurly*

Plate 95 (Right)
Fig. 279 ? Lady Isabel
Burton
*In the collection of
Dr S.J. Howard*

Plate 95A
Figure 279(a)
Subject: **? Lady Hester Stanhope and Dr Meryon**
Title: None
Height: Large version: 10¼ in (25.75 cm); small version: 7¼ in (18.25 cm).
Colour: Well coloured.
Rarity: VR.
Pair: Unknown in the large size, but in the small version is paired by its mirror-image.
Description: On a camel facing left, riding side-saddle, and dressed in quasi-European clothes. She is accepting a mug of water from an Arab with her left hand. The Arab, who is standing in front of the camel's rump, proffers the mug with his right hand

and holds a flask in his left. The camel looks round at what is going on. In the foreground is an oasis.
Observations: 1. The figure seems likely to portray either Lady Hester Stanhope and her physician Dr Meryon, who is known to have dressed as a Bedouin, while accompanying her on her journeys; or alternatively, the Hon. Jane Digby, later Lady Ellenborough. The latter, who married a camel driver, is referred to in Lady Isabel Burton's *Memoirs* as 'a worthy successor to Lady Hester Stanhope'.
2. The theme is reminiscent of that portrayed in *fig.* 72 (? Lady Hester Stanhope) *pl.* I-36, and the style of decoration suggests that it emanates from the same factory.

Plate 96
Figure 280 (see *pl.* H-2)
Subject: **Giuseppe Garibaldi**
Title: Garibaldi (gilt script)
Date: c. 1864
Height: 19 in (48 cm)
Colour: Well coloured, red shirt.
Maker: Sampson Smith
Rarity: Av.
Pair: Fig. 3 (Shakespeare) *pl.* H-2.
Description: He stands bare-headed, in shirt and trousers. His right hand rests on a sword hilt and he holds a paper in his left. There is a cloak over his left forearm which rests on a round pedestal.
Observations: 1. The pairing of figures of Garibaldi and Shakespeare can be explained

Plate 95A (Left)
Fig. 279(a) ?Lady Hester
Stanhope and Dr Meryon

Plate 96 (Right)
Fig. 281 Garibaldi
Fig. 4 (section H)
Shakespeare

Plate 97
Fig. 282 Garibaldi
Fig. 282 Garibaldi (*midget version*)
Fig. 282 Garibaldi
Behind these is displayed the coloured engraving 'General Garibaldi' which appeared in the *Supplement* to *The Illustrated London News* on January 26th, 1861.

Plate 96 continued
on the grounds that Garibaldi visited England in 1864, the year in which the tricentenary of the birth of Shakespeare was being celebrated.
2. A similar figure fetched 7 gns at Christie's in 1963; another £16 at Sotheby's in 1966; and another, 30 gns at Christie's in 1969.

Figure 281
Subject: **Giuseppe Garibaldi**
Title: Garibaldi (raised capitals)
Date: c. 1864
Height: 15 in (38 cm)
Colour: Well coloured, red shirt.
Maker: Probably Sampson Smith
Rarity: R.
Pair: Fig. 4 (Shakespeare) section H.
Description: Similar to *fig.* 280, see *pl.* H-2, except as regards size, method of titling and the fact that there is no cloak over his forearm nor paper in his hand. There is a cloak draped against his right leg and his legs are not crossed.
Observations: See preceding figure.

Figure 4 (section H.)
Subject: **William Shakespeare**
Title: Shakspeare (*sic*) (raised capitals)
Date: c. 1864
Height: 15 in (38 cm)
Colour: Well coloured.
Maker: Probably Sampson Smith
Pair: Fig. 281 (Garibaldi)
Description: See section H.

Plate 97
Figure 282
Subject: **Giuseppe Garibaldi**

Title: Garibaldi (transfer black capitals)
Date: c. 1861
Height: 14 in (35.5 cm)
Colour: Well coloured, in the tradition of Thomas Parr.
Maker: Thomas Parr
Rarity: Av.
Pair: Fig. 283 (Napier) *pl.* C-104 pairs 9 in (23 cm) version.
Description: He stands, beside a horse facing left, bare-headed in shirt and trousers, his right arm on the horse's shoulders.
Observations: 1. The most complex and expensive figure made by the Parr and Kent group of potters.
2. Identical in all respects to the coloured engraving which appeared in the *Supplement* to *The Illustrated London News* of January 26th, 1861.
3. This figure appears in all three Kent lists as follows:

	KENT LIST A Stock No.	KENT LIST B Stock No.	KENT LIST C Ref. No. (1955)
Large Garibaldi and Horse	47	261	261
Small Garibaldi and Horse	48	262	262

In general, contemporary copies of either figure are of average rarity, reproductions of the small figure are common, reproductions of the large figure are uncommon. Reproductions are easy to distinguish by the title alone. This is invariably crude, see *pl.* C-105.
4. Three sizes of this figure are known (see plate).
5. An example of the large version fetched 44 gns at Christie's in 1965; and another 48 gns, in the same rooms, in 1968.

Plate 98
Figure 284
Subject: **Giuseppe Garibaldi**
Title: Liberte (raised capitals)
Date: c. 1864
Height: 13¼ in (33.5 cm); 10¼ in (25.75 cm) version illustrated.
Colour: Well coloured with red shirt.
Rarity: Av.
Description: He stands bare-headed, in shirt and trousers. His left hand rests on a sword hilt and his right holds a pennon inscribed 'Liberte'.
Observations: A similar figure fetched 38 gns at Christie's in 1969.

Figure 285
Subject: **Giuseppe Garibaldi**
Title: None
Date: c. 1864
Height: 8½ in (21.5 cm)
Colour: Well coloured with red shirt.
Rarity: VR.
Description: He stands bare-headed, in shirt and trousers. His right hand rests on a sword hilt and his right forearm on a round pedestal. His left hand is on his belt and there is a pile of shells against his left leg.
Observations: The upper two-thirds of this figure are identical to an original photograph in the British Museum. There are a number of lithographs based on this photograph; one by W. Holt and another (illustrated in *ch.* 3, *pl.* 21A) by Corbetta.

Figure 286
Subject: **Giuseppe Garibaldi**
Title: Garibaldi (raised capitals)
Date: c. 1864
Height: 12½ in (31.75 cm)

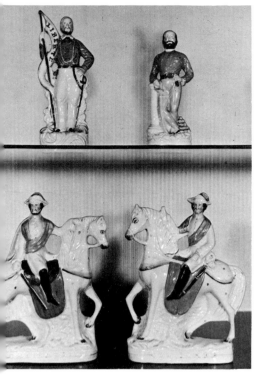

Plate 98
T: *Fig.* 284 Garibaldi
Fig. 285 Garibaldi
B: *Fig.* 286 Garibaldi
Fig. 287 Peard
In the collection of Mr R. Shockledge

Plate 100
T: *Fig.* 289 Garibaldi
Fig. 290 Garibaldi
B: *Fig.* 291 Peard
Fig. 293 Garibaldi and Peard
Fig. 292 Garibaldi

Plate 99
Fig. 288 Garibaldi
In the collection of Miss E.M. Groves

Colour: In the pale tradition.
Rarity: R.
Pair: *Fig.* 287 (Peard)
Description: On a horse facing right, in cocked hat, tunic, breeches and knee-boots.

Figure 287
Subject: **Colonel Peard**
Title: Col Peard
Date: c. 1864
Height: 12½ in (31.75 cm)
Colour: In the pale tradition.
Rarity: R.
Pair: *Fig.* 286 (Garibaldi)
Description: On a horse facing left, in cocked hat, tunic, breeches and knee-boots.

Plate 99
Figure 288
Subject: **Giuseppe Garibaldi**
Title: Garibaldi (indented capitals)
Date: c. 1864
Height: 9¾ in (24.5 cm)
Colour: Well coloured, in the tradition of Thomas Parr.
Maker: Thomas Parr.
Rarity: VR.
Description: Standing bare-headed, in shirt and trousers; with his right hand he grasps the hilt of his sword, which is to his left, while he holds the scabbard with his left hand.
Observations: 1. Almost certainly the figure referred to in the Kent lists as 'Garibaldi at War', 9¼ in (23.5 cm), although I have never seen a late version.
2. No. 51 in *Kent List A*, no. 260 in *Kent List B*, but does not appear in *Kent List C*.

Plate 100
Figure 289
Subject: **Giuseppe Garibaldi**
Title: Garibaldi/at Home (indented capitals)
Date: c. 1864
Height: 9½ in (24 cm)
Colour: In the tradition of Thomas Parr.
Maker: Thomas Parr
Rarity: Av.
Description: Sitting bare-headed, in shirt and trousers. He holds a spade between his legs with his left hand. There is a steeple hat beside his left foot.
Observations: This figure is not mentioned in any of the Kent lists. Apparently, it was not reproduced.

Figure 290
Subject: **Giuseppe Garibaldi**
Title: Garibaldi (indented capitals)
Date: c. 1864
Height: 12¼ in (31 cm)
Colour: In the tradition of Thomas Parr.
Maker: Thomas Parr
Rarity: Av.
Description: He is standing bare-headed, in shirt and trousers. His left hand is tucked into his shirt and right hand grips the muzzle of his rifle which is between his legs.
Observations: Balston noted that this may be a larger version of the 'Garibaldi at War', 9¼ in (23.5 cm) x 3½ in (8.75 cm), which appears in *Kent List A*. At that time *fig.* 288, *pl.* C-99 had not been recorded. It is now generally conceded that this latter figure is that referred to in the Kent lists.

Figure 291
Subject: **Colonel Peard**
Title: C Peard (raised capitals)

Date: c. 1864
Height: 13¼ in (33.5 cm)
Colour: Sparsely coloured.
Rarity: Av.
Pair: *Fig.* 292 (Garibaldi); *fig.* 293 (Garibaldi and Peard) forms a centrepiece to this pair.
Description: Standing bare-headed, in shirt, breeches and gaiters. There is a scarf over his shoulders, a flag to his right and a cannon to his left. Two piles of shells.

Figure 292
Subject: **Giuseppe Garibaldi**
Title: Garibaldi (raised capitals)
Date: c. 1864
Height: 13½ in (34.25 cm)
Colour: Sparsely coloured.
Rarity: Av.
Pair: *Fig.* 291 (Peard); *fig.* 293 (Garibaldi and Peard) forms a centrepiece to this pair.
Description: He stands bare-headed, in shirt, breeches and gaiters, a scarf over his shoulder. To his left is a flag and to his right a cannon. Two piles of shells at his feet.
Observations: This figure and its pair fetched 38 gns at Christie's in 1969.

Figure 293
Subject: **Giuseppe Garibaldi and Colonel Peard**
Title: Garibaldi (raised capitals)
Date: c. 1864
Height: 13 in (33 cm)
Colour: Sparsely coloured.
Rarity: Av.
Pair or series: Centrepiece to the pair *fig.* 291 (Peard) and *fig.* 292 (Garibaldi).
Description: In the centre is a watch-holder

Plate 100 continued

surmounted by two flags, and beneath it a cannon and a drum with a pile of shells. To the left of the clock-face stands Garibaldi, dressed as in *fig.* 292; to the right stands Peard, dressed as in *fig.* 291.

Observations: 1. It is not uncommon to find a centrepiece for a pair.

2. Garibaldi visited Peard in England in 1864.

3. A similar figure fetched 26 gns, and another 30 gns, at Christie's in 1969.

Plate 101
Figure 294
Subject: **Giuseppe Garibaldi**
Title: Garibaldi (raised capitals)
Date: *c.* 1864
Height: 15½ in (39.25 cm)
Colour: Usually sparsely coloured.
Rarity: Av.
Pair: Fig. 295 (Peard)
Description: On a horse facing right, in plumed cocked hat, tunic, breeches and knee-boots.

Figure 295
Subject: **Colonel Peard**
Title: C. Peard (raised capitals)
Date: *c.* 1864
Height: 15 in (38 cm)
Colour: Usually sparsely coloured.
Rarity: Av.
Pair: Fig. 294 (Garibaldi)
Description: On a horse facing left, in plumed cocked hat, tunic, breeches and knee-boots.

Plate 101A
Figure 295(a)

Subject: **Colonel Peard**
Title: Col Peard (raised capitals)
Date: *c.* 1864
Height: 9½ in (24 cm)
Colour: Sparsely coloured.
Rarity: VR.
Pair: Not recorded, but must exist. *Fig.* 294 (*a*) has been reserved for it.
Description: On a horse facing left, in plumed round hat, tunic, breeches and knee-boots.

Plate 102
Figure 296
Subject: **Giuseppe Garibaldi**
Title: Garibaldi (raised capitals)
Date: *c.* 1864
Height: 13 in (33 cm)
Colour: Well coloured, underglaze blue tunic.
Rarity: VR.
Pair: Fig. 297 (Peard)
Description: On a horse facing right, in cocked hat with flattened plume, tunic, breeches and knee-boots.
Observations: This is the only known example in which Garibaldi's tunic has been coloured blue. Usually it is red, occasionally uncoloured.

Figure 297
Subject: **Colonel Peard**
Title: Col. Peard (raised capitals)
Date: *c.* 1864
Height: 13 in (33 cm)
Colour: Well coloured, underglaze blue tunic.
Rarity: VR.
Pair: Fig. 296 (Garibaldi)
Description: On a horse facing left, in cocked hat with flattened plume, tunic, breeches and knee-boots.

Plate 101A
Fig. 295(a) Peard
In the collection of Mr A. Guy Stringer

Plate 102
T: *Fig.* 296 Garibaldi
Fig. 297 Peard

B: *Fig.* 298 Victor Emmanuel II
Fig. 300 Victor Emmanuel II
Fig. 299 Garibaldi
In the collection of Lady Ranfurly and the author

Figure 298
Subject: **Victor Emmanuel II**
Title: K. of Sardinia (raised capitals)
Date: c. 1860
Height: 11½ in (29 cm)
Colour: Well coloured, or white and gilt versions exist.
Rarity: R.
Pair: Fig. 299 (Garibaldi)
Description: On a horse facing right, in cocked hat and full military uniform, both hands on his right hip.
Observations: See *fig.* 302 (Victor Emmanuel 11) *pl.* C-103.

Figure 299
Subject: **Giuseppe Garibaldi**
Title: Garibaldi (raised capitals)
Date: c. 1860
Height: 10¾ in. (27 cm)
Colour: Well coloured, or white and gilt versions exist.
Rarity: R.
Pair: Fig. 298 (Victor Emmanuel 11)
Description: On a horse facing left, in full military uniform. He holds his peaked hat in his right hand against the horse's neck, and the reins in his left hand. He is portrayed as if he is in the act of greeting the King of Sardinia.
Observations: See *fig.* 302 (Victor Emmanuel 11) *pl.* C-103.

Figure 300
Subject: **Victor Emmanuel II**
Title: King. of / Sardinia (raised capitals)
Date: c. 1854
Height: 12¾ in. (32.25 cm)
Colour: Well coloured.

Rarity: R.
Pair: No pair is known, but *fig.* 301 has been reserved.
Description: On a horse facing left, in plumed cocked hat and full military uniform. His cloak hangs over his right arm and his left hand is on the back of the saddle-cloth.
Observations: Probably a Crimean figure.

Plate 103
Figure 302
Subject: **Victor Emmanuel II**
Title: Victor Emmanuel (transfer black capitals)
Date: c. 1861
Height: 15 in (38 cm)
Colour: White and gilt, or rather garishly coloured in the manner of Kent and Parr or William Kent.
Maker: Parr and Kent group of potters. The version illustrated is contemporary and dates to the period of Thomas Parr.
Rarity: VR.
Pair: Fig. 303 (Garibaldi)
Description: On a horse facing right, in kepi, tunic, cloak and trousers. He holds the reins about the horse's neck in his left hand, and his right hand is on the back of the saddle.
Observations: 1. Victor Emmanuel II, king of Sardinia was our ally in the Crimean War. He was proclaimed King of Italy in 1861. This figure is virtually identical to an engraving in *The Illustrated London News* of December 29th, 1860 inscribed 'The meeting of General Garibaldi and Victor Emmanuel on the 26th October, near Teano'. 2. Both this figure and its pair appear in all three Kent lists as follows:

Plate 103
Fig. 302 Victor
Emmanuel II
Fig. 303 Garibaldi
(1) Behind these two
figures is the engraving
which appeared in *The
Illustrated London News* of
December 29th, 1860
captioned 'The meeting
of General Garibaldi
and Victor Emmanuel
on the 26th October,
near Teano'.
(2) *Fig.* 302 is titled in
a manner which may be
confidently accepted as
contemporary, *Fig.* 303
is of later date.
*In the collection of
Lady Ranfurly*

Plate 104
Fig. 283 Napier
Fig. 282 Garibaldi
Both these figures are
decorated and titled in
the 'contemporary
manner' associated with
Thomas Parr.
*By courtesy of Mr and Mrs
Eric Joyce*

Plate 103 continued

	KENT LIST A Stock No.	KENT LIST B Stock No.	KENT LIST C Ref. No. (1955)
Garibaldi on Horse	42	263	263
Victor Emmanuel on Horse	43	397	397

Period versions of either figure are extremely rare but may be identified instantly by the style of titling—compare *figs.* 302 and 303 in this plate. Reproductions are also uncommon

and were probably made mainly in the late Victorian era.

Figure 303
Subject: **Giuseppe Garibaldi**
 Title: Garibaldi (transfer black capitals)
 Date: *c.* 1861
 Height: 15 in (38 cm)
 Colour: White and gilt, or rather garishly coloured in the manner of Kent and Parr or William Kent. No contemporary copy seen.

Maker: Parr and Kent group of potters. The version illustrated probably dates to the period of William Kent.
 Rarity: VR.
 Pair: Fig. 302 (Victor Emmanuel II)
 Description: On a horse facing left, bareheaded, in shirt and trousers. His right hand holds his hat and the reins of the horse, and his left hand is on the saddle-cloth. He is portrayed in the act of greeting Victor Emmanuel II.

Plate 105
Fig. 283 Napier
This figure is decorated and titled in the 'later' style associated with William Kent and is not a contemporary version.

Observations: 1. When Garibaldi met Victor Emmanuel on October 26th, 1860 he said, 'King of Italy!'. The latter replied, 'I thank you!'.
2. See preceding figure.

Plate 104
Figure 282
Subject: **Giuseppe Garibaldi**
Title: Garibaldi (transfer black capitals)
Date: *c.* 1861
Height: 14 in (35.5 cm); 9 in (23 cm) version illustrated
Observations: See *pl.* C-97.

Figure 283
Subject: **General Lord Napier of Magdala**
Title: Napier (transfer black capitals)
Date: *c.* 1867
Height: 9 in (23 cm)
Colour: Well coloured in the manner of Thomas Parr.
Maker: Thomas Parr
Rarity: VR.
Pair: *Fig.* 282 (Garibaldi), 9 in (23 cm) version. The figure of Napier was first produced at least three years after that of Garibaldi.
Description: Standing bare-headed, in tunic, breeches and knee-boots, beside his horse facing right, his left arm on its shoulder, his right hand on the hilt of his sword.
Observations: 1. This figure appears in all three Kent lists:

	KENT LIST A Stock No.	KENT LIST B Stock No.	KENT LIST C Ref. No. (1955)
Small Napier and Horse	49	306	306

Contemporary figures, which are very rare, may easily be distinguished, not only by their titling but also by their colouring. Kent versions tend to be garish. Compare *pls.* C-104 and 105.
2. Napier carries his sword in his right hand instead of his left because the potter has made the figure a true mirror-image of the earlier model of Garibaldi.
3. A pair of similar figures, both late, together with *fig.* 289 (Garibaldi) *pl.* C-100 fetched 42 gns at Christie's in 1963.

Plate 106
T: *Fig.* 304 MacMahon
Fig. 305 King William I of Prussia

B: *Fig.* 306 Queen Augusta of Prussia
Fig. 308 Queen Augusta of Prussia
Fig. 307 King William I of Prussia

Plate 105
Figure 283
Subject: **General Lord Napier of Magdala**
Title: Napier (crudely applied)
Date: A late version.
Height: 9 in (23 cm)
Colour: Garishly coloured and crudely titled.
Maker: William Kent
Rarity: Av.
Pair: *Fig.* 282 (Garibaldi)
Description: See preceding plate.

Plate 106
Figure 304
Subject: **Marshal MacMahon**
Title: Mac Mahon (raised capitals)
Date: *c.* 1870
Height: 11½ in (29 cm)
Colour: Sparsely coloured.
Maker: In the style of Sampson Smith.

Rarity: R.
Pair: *Fig.* 305 (King of Prussia)
Description: On a horse facing right, in plumed cocked hat, military tunic, cape and knee-boots.
Observations: 1. A similar figure fetched 24 gns at Christie's in 1963.
2. See next figure.

Figure 305
Subject: **William I, King of Prussia**
Title: King of Prussia (raised capitals and lower case)
Date: *c.* 1870
Height: 11½ in (29 cm)
Colour: Sparsely coloured.
Maker: In the style of Sampson Smith.
Rarity: R.
Pair: *Fig.* 304 (MacMahon)
Description: On a horse facing left, in helmet,

Plate 107
Fig. 309 King William I of Prussia
In the collection of Mr. R. Shockledge

Plate 106 continued

cape, military tunic and knee-boots. The base of the figure is decorated with a cannon.
Observations: This figure and the preceding figure were issued at the time of the Franco-Prussian War, 1870.

Figure 306
Subject: **Augusta, Queen of Prussia**
Title: Queen of Prussia (gilt script)
Date: c. 1870
Height: 16½ in (41.5 cm)
Colour: Sparsely coloured.
Maker: Sampson Smith
Rarity: Av.
Pair: *Fig.* 307 (King of Prussia)
Description: Standing bare-headed, with cape and long flounced skirt.
Observations: See next figure.

Figure 307
Subject: **William I, King of Prussia**
Title: King of Prussia (gilt script)
Date: c. 1870
Height: 15¾ in (39.75 cm)
Colour: Sparsely coloured.
Maker: Sampson Smith

Rarity: Av.
Pair: *Fig.* 306 (Queen of Prussia)
Description: Standing bare-headed, in full military uniform, his right hand on his hip, his left resting on a plinth which is draped with his cloak.
Observations: This figure and the preceding figure cannot date from later than January, 1871 when the King and Queen of Prussia became Emperor and Empress of Germany. They are unlikely to be earlier than July, 1870 when the Franco-Prussian War began. For a few months the German cause was very popular in England.

Figure 308
Subject: **Augusta, Queen of Prussia**
Title: Queen of Prussia (raised capitals)
Date: c. 1870
Height: 15 in (38 cm)
Colour: Virtually uncoloured; 'porridge' school.
Maker: Sampson Smith
Rarity: R.
Pair: *Fig.* 309 (King of Prussia) *pl.* C-107.
Description: Identical to *fig.* 306, except for (1) she wears a tiara, (2) size and (3) it is only found in the 'porridge' state.

Plate 108   *Fig.* 310 King William I of Prussia

Fig. 311 Prince Frederick William

Section C. Naval, Military and Exploration

Plate 107
Figure 309
Subject: **William I, King of Prussia**
Title: King of Prussia (raised capitals)
Date: *c.* 1870
Height: 15 in (38 cm)
Colour: Virtually uncoloured; 'porridge' school.
Maker: Sampson Smith
Rarity: R.
Pair: Fig. 308 (Queen of Prussia) *pl.* C-106.
Description: Identical in all respects to *fig.* 307, *pl.* C-106, other than for size, and that it is only found in the 'porridge' state.

Plate 108
Figure 310
Subject: **William I, King of Prussia**
Title: King of Prussia (gilt script)
Date: *c.* 1870
Height: 14½ in (36.75 cm)
Colour: Pale colours; horses may be white or grey.
Maker: Sampson Smith
Rarity: VR.
Pair: Fig. 311 (Prince Frederick William)
Description: On a horse facing right, in plumed helmet, military uniform, knee-boots.
Observations: See next figure.

Figure 311
Subject: **Prince Frederick William of Prussia**
Title: Crown Prince (gilt script)
Date: *c.* 1870
Height: 14½ in (36.75 cm)
Colour: Pale colours; horses may be white or grey.
Maker: Sampson Smith
Rarity: VR.
Pair: Fig. 310 (King of Prussia)
Description: On a horse facing left, in plumed helmet, military uniform, knee-boots. He is heavily bearded.
Observations: This figure and its pair are very similar to *figs.* 312–315, other than for the manner of titling. They are likely to have been the precursors of these figures.

Plate 109
Figure 312
Subject: **Count von Moltke**
Title: G: Moltke (raised capitals)
Date: *c.* 1870
Height: 14½ in (36.75 cm)
Colour: Pale colourings; the horses may be white, grey, piebald or skewbald.
Maker: Sampson Smith
Rarity: R.
Pair or series: Fig. 313 (Bismarck). Same series as *fig.* 314 (Von der Tann) and *fig.* 315 (Prince Frederick Charles).
Description: On a horse facing right, in plumed helmet, uniform and knee-boots. Single saddle-cloth.
Observations: 1. The four Prussians constituting this series can be 'paired' by their horses' saddle-cloths.
2. 11¾ in (29.75 cm) versions, identical in all respects other than height, have been noted of Von der Tann and Prince Frederick Charles; presumably similar models were made of Von Moltke and Bismarck.

Figure 313
Subject: **Prince Bismarck**
Title: G: Bismark (*sic*) (raised capitals)
Date: *c.* 1870
Height: 14¾ in (37.5 cm)

Colour: Pale colourings; the horses may be white, grey, piebald or skewbald.
Maker: Sampson Smith
Rarity: R.
Pair or series: Fig. 312 (Von Moltke). Same series as *fig.* 314 (Von der Tann) and *fig.* 315 (Prince Frederick Charles).
Description: On a horse facing left, in plumed helmet, military uniform and knee-boots. Single saddle-cloth.
Observations: See *fig.* 312 (Von Moltke).

Figure 314
Subject: **General von der Tann**
Title: G. V. D. Tann (raised capitals)
Date: *c.* 1870
Height: 14½ in (36.75 cm)
Colour: Pale colourings; the horses may be white, grey, piebald or skewbald.
Maker: Sampson Smith
Rarity: R.
Pair or series: Fig. 315 (Prince Frederick Charles). Same series as *fig.* 312 (Von Moltke) and *fig.* 313 (Bismarck).
Description: On a horse facing right, in plumed helmet, military uniform and knee-boots. Double saddle-cloth.
Observations: See *fig.* 312 (Von Moltke).

Figure 315
Subject: **Prince Frederick Charles of Prussia**
Title: P F Charles (raised capitals)
Date: *c.* 1870
Height: 14½ in (36.75 cm)
Colour: Pale colourings; the horses may be white, grey, piebald or skewbald.
Maker: Sampson Smith
Rarity: R.
Pair or series: Fig. 314 (Von der Tann). Same series as *fig.* 312 (Von Moltke) and *fig.* 313 (Bismarck).
Description: On a horse facing left, in plumed helmet, military uniform and knee-boots. Double saddle-cloth.
Observations: See *fig.* 312 (Von Moltke).

Plate 110
Figure 316
Subject: **Count von Moltke**
Title: G: Moltke (raised capitals)
Date: *c.* 1870
Height: 13 in (33 cm)
Colour: 'Porridge' school; virtually uncoloured.
Maker: Sampson Smith
Rarity: VR.
Pair: Fig. 317 (Bismarck). Same series as *fig.* 318 (Napoleon III), *fig.* 319 (Bazaine), *fig.* 320 (King of Prussia) *pl.* C-111, and *fig.* 321 (Prince Frederick William) *pl.* C-112.
Description: Identical in most respects to *fig.* 312 (Von Moltke) *pl.* C-109, except that it has only been found in the 'porridge' state, it is slightly smaller than *fig.* 312 and the arrangement of the horse's legs is quite different.
Observations: This series of six (four Prussians and two Frenchmen) can again be 'paired' by their horses' saddle-cloths.

Figure 317
Subject: **Prince Bismarck**
Title: G: Bismark (*sic*) (raised capitals)
Date: *c.* 1870
Height: 13¾ in (35 cm)
Colour: 'Porridge' school; virtually uncoloured.
Maker: Sampson Smith
Rarity: VR.

Pair: Fig. 316 (Von Moltke) Same series as *fig.* 318 (Napoleon III), *fig.* 319 (Bazaine), *fig.* 320 (King of Prussia) *pl.* C-111, and *fig.* 321 (Prince Frederick Charles) *pl.* C-112.
Description: On a horse facing left. Identical in all respects to *fig.* 313 (Bismarck) *pl.* C-109, except that it is only found in the 'porridge' state, it is somewhat smaller and the arrangement of the horse's legs is different.

Figure 318
Subject: **Napoleon III**
Title: Napoleon (raised capitals)
Date: *c.* 1870
Height: 14 in (35.5 cm)
Colour: 'Porridge' school; virtually uncoloured.
Maker: Sampson Smith
Rarity: VR.
Pair: Fig. 319 (Bazaine). Same series as *fig.* 316 (Von Moltke), *fig.* 317 (Bismarck), *fig.* 320 (King of Prussia) *pl.* C-111, and *fig.* 321 (Prince Frederick William) *pl.* C-112.
Description: On a horse facing right, in plumed cocked hat athwartships, military uniform with epaulettes. Double saddle-cloth.
Observations: This figure is not found in the preceding series, but it is similar, except for its head and in being found only in the 'porridge' state, to *fig.* 314 (Von der Tann) *pl.* C-109. It may be that it was issued later on in the war when the German cause was less popular.

Figure 319
Subject: **Marshal Bazaine**
Title: Bazaine (raised capitals)
Date: *c.* 1870
Height: 13½ in (34.25 cm)
Colour: 'Porridge' school; virtually uncoloured.
Maker: Sampson Smith
Rarity: VR.
Pair: Fig. 318 (Napoleon III). Same series as *fig.* 316 (Von Moltke), *fig.* 317 (Bismarck), *fig.* 320 (King of Prussia) *pl.* C-111, and *fig.* 321 (Prince Frederick William) *pl.* C-112.
Description: On a horse facing left, in plumed helmet, military uniform and knee-boots. Double saddle-cloth.
Observations: 1. This figure is not found in the preceding series, although it resembles *fig.* 315 (Prince Frederick Charles) *pl.* C-109 in all respects, other than height, the fact that it is only found in the 'porridge' state and in its titling.
2. A similar figure and its pair fetched 60 gns at Christie's in 1969.

Plate 111
Figure 320
Subject: **William I, King of Prussia**
Title: King : of : Prussia (raised capitals)
Date: *c.* 1870
Height: 13 in (33 cm)
Colour: 'Porridge' school; virtually uncoloured.
Maker: Sampson Smith
Rarity: VR.
Pair: Fig. 321 (Prince Frederick William) *pl.* C-112. Same series as *fig.* 316 (Von Moltke), *fig.* 317 (Bismarck), *fig.* 318 (Napoleon III), *fig.* 319 (Bazaine) *pl.* C-110.
Description: Identical in all respects to *fig.* 310 (King of Prussia) *pl.* C-108, except that it is smaller, that it is only found in the 'porridge' state, and the arrangement of the horse's legs and the style of titling is different.

Plate 109
T: *Fig.* 312 Von Moltke
Fig. 313 Bismarck

B: *Fig.* 314 Von der Tann
Fig. 315 P.F. Charles
In the collection of Lady Ranfurly

Plate 110
T: *Fig.* 316 Von Molke
Fig. 317 Bismarck

B: *Fig.* 318 Napoleon III
Fig. 319 Bazaine
By courtesy of Mr and Mrs Eric Joyce

Plate 111 (Above)
Fig. 320 King William I of Prussia

Plate 112 (Below)
Fig. 321 Prince Frederick William

Plate 112
Figure 321
Subject: **Prince Frederick William of Prussia**
Title: Crown : Prince (raised capitals)
Date: c. 1870
Height: 13 in (33 cm); 9½ in (24 cm) version illustrated.
Colour: 'Porridge' school; virtually uncoloured.
Maker: Sampson Smith
Rarity: VR.
Pair: Fig. 320 (King of Prussia) *pl.* C-111.
Same series as *fig.* 316 (Von Moltke), *fig.* 317 (Bismarck), *fig.* 318 (Napoleon III), *fig.* 319 (Bazaine) *pl.* C-110.
Description: Identical in all respects to *fig.* 311 (Prince Frederick William) *pl.* C-108, ex-

cept that it is smaller, that it is only found in the 'porridge' state, and the arrangement of the horse's legs and the style of titling is different.
Summary: Two series have emerged:
SERIES I consists of *fig.* 310 (King of Prussia), *fig.* 311 (Prince Frederick William), *fig.* 312 (Von Moltke), *fig.* 313 (Bismarck), *fig.* 314 (Von der Tann), *fig.* 315 (Prince Frederick Charles).
Notes: 1. *Figs.* 310 and 311 are titled in gilt script instead of raised capitals.
2. 10 in (25 cm) versions have been found of *figs.* 310 and 311, titled in gilt script; and 11¾ in (29.75 cm) versions have been found of *figs.* 314 and 315, titled in raised capitals.
SERIES II consists of *fig.* 316 (Von Moltke), *fig.* 317 (Bismarck), *fig.* 318 (Napoleon III),

fig. 319 (Bazaine), *fig.* 320 (King of Prussia) and *fig.* 321 (Prince Frederick William).
The two series are strikingly similar and clearly the one is evolved from the other. Marshal Bazaine did not take over supreme command of the French army until August, 1870 when it was already in retreat, and he brought it back to Metz where it surrendered on October 14th. It seems likely that the 'porridge' school series was a secondary series brought out at a time when public sympathy was veering from the Prussian to the French cause.
In the 'porridge' school series, smaller [9½ in (24 cm)] versions are known of *fig.* 316 (Von Moltke), *fig.* 317 (Bismarck), *fig.* 320 (King of Prussia) and *fig.* 321 (Prince Frederick William).

Section C. Naval, Military and Exploration

Plate 113

Figure 322
Subject: **Unidentified Prussian general**
Title: None
Date: *c.* 1870
Height: 11½ in (29 cm)
Colour: Well coloured.
Maker: Sampson Smith
Rarity: Av.
Pair: *Fig.* 323 (Unidentified Prussian general)
Description: On a horse facing right, bare-headed, in full military uniform, jacket with epaulettes, and knee-boots. In his right hand he holds a hat similar to that portrayed in *fig.* 326 (Alexander II) *pl.* C-114.
Observations: It has always been supposed that this figure, together with its pair, represent so far unidentified Prussian generals of the Franco-Prussian War era. However, the possibility does exist that it is Alexander II of Russia who is portrayed in this figure.

Figure 323
Subject: **Unidentified Prussian general**
Title: None
Date: *c.* 1870
Height: 11½ in (29 cm)
Colour: Well coloured.
Maker: Sampson Smith
Rarity: Av.
Pair: *Fig.* 322 (Unidentified Prussian general)
Description: On a horse facing left, bare-headed, in full military uniform, jacket with epaulettes and knee-boots. In his right hand he holds a plumed helmet.
Observations: Has so far defied identification.

Figure 324
Subject: **Unidentified Prussian general**
Title: None
Date: *c.* 1870
Height: 11¾ in (29.75 cm)
Colour: Well coloured.
Maker: Sampson Smith
Rarity: Av.
Pair: *Fig.* 325 (Unidentified Prussian general)
Description: On a horse facing right, in plumed helmet, jacket with epaulettes and knee-boots.
Observations: Has so far defied identification.

Figure 325
Subject: **Unidentified Prussian general**
Title: None
Date: *c.* 1870
Height: 11¾ in (29.75 cm)
Colour: Well coloured.
Maker: Sampson Smith
Rarity: Av.
Pair: *Fig.* 324 (Unidentified Prussian general)
Description: On a horse facing left, in plumed helmet, jacket with epaulettes, knee-boots.
Observations: Has so far defied identification.

Plate 113
T: *Fig.* 322 Unidentified Prussian general
Fig. 323 Unidentified Prussian general

B: *Fig.* 324 Unidentified Prussian general
Fig. 325 Unidentified Prussian general
In the collection of Lady Ranfurly

Plate 114
Fig. 326 Alexander II, Tsar of Russia
Fig. 327 Abd-ul-Hamid II, Sultan of Turkey
In the collection of Mr R. Shockledge

Plate 114
Figure 326
Subject: **Alexander II, Tsar of Russia**
Title: Emperor of Russia (gilt script)
Date: *c.* 1877
Height: 14½ in (36.75 cm)
Colour: Pale colouring; saddle-cloths in the style of Sampson Smith.
Maker: Sampson Smith
Rarity: VR. D. (titled and untitled)
Pair: Fig. 327 (Abd-ul-Hamid II)
Description: On a horse facing right, in plumed bonnet, tunic with epaulettes, waist sash. He holds the reins with his left hand and his right hand, clutching a manuscript, rests on the horse's flank. Long saddle-cloth.
Observations: See next figure.

Figure 327
Subject: **Abd-ul-Hamid II, Sultan of Turkey**
Title: Sultan of Turkey (gilt script)
Date: *c.* 1877
Height: 14 in (35.5 cm)
Colour: Pale colouring; saddle-cloths in the style of Sampson Smith.
Maker: Sampson Smith
Rarity: VR. D. (titled and untitled)
Pair: Fig. 326 (Alexander II)
Description: On a horse facing left, wearing tasselled fez and military jacket with epaulettes. He holds the reins in his right hand and clutches a scroll in his left. Long saddle-cloth; a sword by his side.

Observations: This figure and the preceding figure portray the principal opponents in the Russo-Turkish War (1877–8). In 1876 Europe was deeply disturbed by the 'Bulgarian atrocities', sparked off by the imposition of extra taxation by the Turks on the revolting Bulgarians. This led to widespread insurrection against the Turkish domination in the Balkans and endless international bickering, for Turkey, 'the sick man of Europe,' was always a grave anxiety to the Powers. Finally, in 1877, Russia declared war on Turkey. Britain, full of suspicion of everything Russian, because of that country's Eastern policy, instantly ranged all its sympathies on the side of Turkey. For a time the Turks gallantly checked the impetuous Russian advance at Plevna, but once that city was carried, there seemed nothing to stop the Russians from reaching Constantinople. Britain was roused. If the Russians took Constantinople their next step might be India. Led by the London music-halls everybody was carried away by 'jingoism'. The British battle-fleet steamed through the Dardanelles and army reservists were recalled. It seemed that war with Russia was inevitable. But it never came. Instead, the peace treaty signed at San Stefano was followed by the Treaty of Berlin. Lord Beaconsfield himself, represented and brought home, so he said, 'Peace with Honour'.

Plate 115
Fig. 328 Wolseley
Fig. 329 Duke of Connaught

Plate 115
Figure 328
Subject: **General Sir Garnet Wolseley**
Title: Sir / G. Wolseley (raised capitals)
Date: 1882
Height: 14 in (35.5 cm)
Colour: Sparsely coloured, saddle-cloth in style of Sampson Smith.
Maker: Sampson Smith
Rarity: Av.
Pair: Fig. 329 (Duke of Connaught)
Description: On a horse facing right, in helmet, uniform jacket and knee-boots.
Observations: 1. In 1882 Sir Garnet Wolseley crushed the rebellion of the Egyptian army under Arabi Pasha, and was made a baron. The Duke of Connaught commanded the Guards Brigade in Wolseley's Egyptian campaign.
2. A similar pair of figures, together with *fig.* 330 (Duke of Connaught) *pl.* C-116, fetched £38 at Sotheby's in 1966.

Figure 329
Subject: **Arthur, Duke of Connaught**
Title: Duke / of. Connaught (raised capitals)
Date: 1882
Height: 14 in (35.5 cm)
Colour: Sparsely coloured, saddle-cloth in style of Sampson Smith.
Maker: Sampson Smith
Rarity: Av.
Pair: Fig. 328 (Wolseley)
Description: On a horse facing left, in helmet, military uniform and knee-boots.
Observations: See preceding figure.

Plate 116
Figure 330
Subject: **Arthur, Duke of Connaught**
Title: Dᵉ. Connaught (raised capitals)
Date: c. 1882
Height: 12¼ in (31 cm)
Colour: Sparsely coloured.
Maker: Uncertain
Rarity: VR. D.
Pair: Fig. 331 (Wolseley) *pl.* C-117.
Description: On a horse facing right, in helmet, military uniform and knee-boots.
Observations: See *fig.* 328 (Wolseley) *pl.* C-115.

Plate 117
Figure 331
Subject: **General Sir Garnet Wolseley**
Title: Gᴸ. Wolseley (raised capitals)
Date: c. 1882
Height: 12½ in (31.75 cm)
Colour: Sparsely coloured.
Maker: Uncertain
Rarity: VR. D.
Pair: Fig. 330 (Duke of Connaught) *pl.* C-116.
Description: On a horse facing left, in helmet, military uniform and knee-boots.
Observations: See *fig.* 328 (Wolseley) *pl.* C-115.

Plate 118
Figure 332
Subject: **Major-General Sir Herbert Stewart**
Title: G. Stewart (raised capitals)
Date: c. 1885
Height: 14½ in (36.75 cm)
Colour: White and gilt, and sparsely coloured

versions with saddle-cloths in style of Sampson Smith, are known.
Maker: Sampson Smith
Rarity: Av.
Pair: Fig. 333 (Burnaby)
Description: On a horse facing right, in helmet, military jacket and knee-boots. Double saddle-cloth.
Observations: 1. He commanded the desert column in the 1884–5 campaign conducted by Wolseley for the relief of Gordon, and died of wounds.
2. This undoubted pair is unusual, in that the saddle-cloths do not match.

Figure 333
Subject: **Colonel F. G. Burnaby**
Title: C. Burnaby (raised capitals)
Date: c. 1885
Height: 14½ in (36.75 cm)
Colour: White and gilt, and sparsely coloured versions with saddle-cloths in style of Sampson Smith, are known.
Maker: Sampson Smith
Rarity: Av.
Pair: Fig. 332 (Stewart)
Description: On a horse facing left, in helmet, military jacket and knee-boots. Single saddle-cloth.
Observations: 1. Died of wounds in Wolseley's 1884–5 campaign conducted to relieve Gordon at Khartoum.
2. A similar figure and its pair fetched 28 gns at Christie's in 1969.

Plate 116
Fig. 330 Duke of Connaught

Plate 117
Fig. 331 Wolseley

Plate 118
Fig. 332 Stewart
Fig. 333 Burnaby

Plate 119
T: *Fig.* 334 Roberts
Fig. 337 Gordon
Fig. 335 Kitchener

Plate 119
Figure 334
Subject: **F-M. Lord Roberts**
Title: Roberts (raised capitals)
Date: c. 1900
Height: 14 in (35.5 cm)
Colour: White and gilt.
Maker: William Kent
Rarity: Av.
Pair: Fig. 335 (Kitchener)
Description: Standing in peaked cap and service dress, a sword in his right hand, a pile of shells beside his left foot.

C308

Observations: Appears in *Kent List A* under no. 125. Appears also in *Kent List B* under no. 292, but has been deleted as a 'discontinued line'.

Figure 335
Subject: **General Lord Kitchener**
Title: Kitchener (raised capitals)
Date: c. 1900
Height: 14 in (35.5 cm)
Colour: White and gilt.
Maker: William Kent
Rarity: Av.

Pair: Fig. 334 (Roberts)
Description: Standing in peaked cap, service dress and gaiters, a sword in his left hand.
Observations: Appears in *Kent List A* under no. 126. Appears also in *Kent List B* under no. 291, but has been deleted as a 'discontinued line'.

Figure 336
Subject: **General Lord Kitchener**
Title: Kitchener (raised capitals)
Date: c. 1900
Height: 14 in (35.5 cm)

Plate 120
Fig. 340 Soldier and sailor
In the collection of Mr Anthony Oliver

Colour: White and heavily gilded.
Rarity: R.
Pair: No pair is known.
Description: Standing bare-headed, in full military uniform with medals and orders. He holds the hilt of his sword in his left hand and a scroll in his right.

Figure 337
Subject: **General Gordon**
Title: General Gordon (indented capitals)
Date: c. 1890
Height: 13¼ in (33.5 cm)
Colour: Well coloured.
Description: On a camel facing left, with decorated saddle-cloth with tassels. He wears a fez, close-fitting dress and stockings.
Observations: 1. This figure is based on the statue of Gordon, in the 'dress of honour' bestowed upon him by the Khedive, riding a camel. It stands outside the main building of the School of Military Engineering, Chatham. The sculptor was Onslow Ford RA. The statue was exhibited in the Royal Academy before being unveiled in its present site by Edward, prince of Wales, on May 19th, 1890. A replica may be seen in the grounds of the Gordon Boys' School, Woking, see *ch. 3, pl. 22.*
2. A similar figure fetched 20 gns at Christie's in 1963.

Figure 338
Subject: **General Gordon**
Title: Gordon (transfer capitals in crimson)
Date: c. 1885
Height: 16 in (40.5 cm)
Colour: Well coloured in the manner of Kent and Parr.
Maker: Parr and Kent group of potters.
Rarity: VR. D. A. (titled); Av. (untitled).
Description: Standing in fez and full military uniform. His left hand rests on the muzzle of a cannon. His right hand holds a cane.
Observations: 1. This figure fetched 24 gns at Christie's in 1963. A similar, but untitled figure fetched 30 gns in the same rooms in 1969.
2. The majority of these figures are found untitled and may be of any date following Gordon's death. The occasional rare figure found with the crimson titling is likely to

have been issued shortly after his death.
3. Appears in *Kent List A* under no.127. Appears also in *Kent List B* under no. 264, but has been deleted as a 'discontinued line'.

Figure 339
Subject: **General Gordon**
Title: G. Gordon (raised capitals)
Date: c. 1885
Height: 17¾ in (44 cm)
Colour: Usually well coloured.
Rarity: Av.
Description: Standing in fez, uniform and trousers, his left hand on his hip, his right hand on the trunk of a tree.
Observations: A similar figure fetched 22 gns at Christie's in 1969.

Plate 120
Figure 340
Subject: **A non-portrait River War figure**
Title: None
Date: c. 1898
Height: 12 in (30.5 cm)
Colour: Well coloured.
Rarity: Av.
Description: On the left is a soldier (reputedly a 21st Lancer) and on the right a sailor. Each is dressed in the appropriate rig of the period, and each carries a cloth bag. The sailor is linked to the soldier with his right arm.

Plate 121
Figure 341
Subject: **Major-General Sir Hector Macdonald**
Title: Col^nl Mac Donald (*sic*) (gilt script)
Date: c. 1898
Height: 10⅝ in (26.75 cm)
Colour: White and gilt.
Maker: Sampson Smith
Rarity: VR. D.

Plate 121
Fig. 341 Col. Macdonald
Fig. 342 The Sirdar (Kitchener)

Plate 122
Fig. 342(a) Lord Roberts
This figure of 'The Sirdar' (Kitchener) has been incorrectly titled

Observations: The 21st Lancers were famous for their charge at the Battle of Omdurman, September 2nd, 1898.

Figure 344
Subject: **An officer of the 21st Lancers mounted**, facing left
Title: 21st Lancers (gilt script)
Date: *c.* 1898
Height: 10½ in (26.5 cm)
Colour: White and gilt.
Maker: Sampson Smith
Rarity: VR. D.
Pair: *Fig.* 343 (21st Lancers—*right*). Same series as *fig.* 341 (Macdonald), *fig.* 342 (Kitchener), *fig.* 345 (Roberts), *fig.* 346 (Kitchener), *fig.* 347 (Buller), *fig.* 348 (Macdonald), *fig.* 349 (Dundonald) and *fig.* 350 (French).
Description: On a horse facing left, in the uniform of an officer of the 21st Lancers.
Observations: See preceding figure.

Plate 124
Figure 345
Subject: **F-M. Lord Roberts**
Title: Lord Roberts (gilt script)
Date: *c.* 1900
Height: 11 in (28 cm)
Colour: White and gilt.

Maker: Sampson Smith
Rarity: VR.
Pair: *Fig.* 346 (Kitchener). Same series as *fig.* 341 (Macdonald), *fig.* 342 (Kitchener), *fig.* 343 (21st Lancers—*right*), *fig.* 344 (21st Lancers—*left*), *fig.* 347 (Buller), *fig.* 348 (Macdonald), *fig.* 349 (Dundonald) and *fig.* 350 (French).
Description: On a horse facing right, in cocked hat and full military uniform.

Plate 121 continued
Pair: *Fig.* 342 (Kitchener). Same series as *fig.* 343 (21st Lancers—*right*), *fig.* 344 (21st Lancers—*left*), *fig.* 345 (Roberts), *fig.* 346 (Kitchener), *fig.* 347 (Buller), *fig.* 348 (Macdonald), *fig.* 349 (Dundonald) and *fig.* 350 (French).
Description: On a horse facing right, in topee, military jacket and puttees.
Observations: This pair, together with the pair of figures of the 21st Lancers (*figs.* 343 and 344, *pl.* C-123) were issued to commemorate the Battle of Omdurman. Macdonald, who at that time was a colonel, commanded an Egyptian Brigade in the River War and by his tactics at Omdurman, turned a possible disaster into a victory.

Figure 342
Subject: **General Lord Kitchener**
Title: The Sirdar (gilt script)
Date: *c.* 1898
Height: 11 in (28 cm)
Colour: White and gilt.
Maker: Sampson Smith
Rarity: VR. D.
Pair: *Fig.* 341 (Macdonald). Same series as *fig.* 343 (21st Lancers—*right*), *fig.* 344 (21st Lancers—*left*), *fig.* 345 (Roberts), *fig.* 346 (Kitchener), *fig.* 347 (Buller), *fig.* 348 (Macdonald), *fig.* 349 (Dundonald) and *fig.* 350 (French).
Description: On a horse facing left, in topee, military jacket and puttees.
Observations: 1. 'The Sirdar' was the title given to the British commander-in-chief of the Egyptian army. The figure dates to the time of Omdurman, when Kitchener occupied this position.
2. This figure has been found incorrectly

titled 'Lord Roberts', see *fig.* 342(*a*), *pl.* C-122.
3. A figure of 'The Sirdar', together with *fig.* 277 (British lion and Napoleon III) *pl.* C-93, fetched 55 gns at Christie's in 1966.

Plate 122
Figure 342(a)
Subject: **F-M. Lord Roberts** (Kitchener)
Title: Lord Roberts (gilt script)
Date: *c.* 1900
Height: 11 in (28 cm)
Colour: White and gilt.
Maker: Sampson Smith
Rarity: VR.
Description: Identical to *fig.* 342 (Kitchener), other than for title.
Observations: This figure is obviously one of 'The Sirdar', incorrectly titled 'Lord Roberts'.

Plate 123
Figure 343
Subject: **An officer of the 21st Lancers mounted**, facing right
Title: 21st Lancers (gilt script)
Date: *c.* 1898
Height: 10½ in (26.5 cm)
Colour: White and gilt.
Maker: Sampson Smith
Rarity: VR. D.
Pair: *Fig.* 344 (21st Lancers—*left*). Same series as *fig.* 341 (Macdonald), *fig.* 342 (Kitchener), *fig.* 345 (Roberts), *fig.* 346 (Kitchener), *fig.* 347 (Buller), *fig.* 348 (Macdonald), *fig.* 349 (Dundonald) and *fig.* 350 (French).
Description: On a horse facing right, in the uniform of an officer of the 21st Lancers.

Figure 346
Subject: **General Lord Kitchener**
Title: Lord Kitchener (gilt script)
Date: *c.* 1900
Height: 11 in (28 cm)
Colour: White and gilt.
Maker: Sampson Smith
Rarity: VR.
Pair: *Fig.* 345 (Roberts). Same series as *fig.* 341 (Macdonald), *fig.* 342 (Kitchener), *fig.* 343 (21st Lancers—*right*), *fig.* 344 (21st Lancers—*left*), *fig.* 347 (Buller), *fig.* 348 (Macdonald), *fig.* 349 (Dundonald) and *fig.* 350 (French).
Description: On a horse facing left, in helmet and full military uniform.

Figure 347
Subject: **General Sir Redvers Buller**
Title: General Buller (gilt script)
Date: *c.* 1899
Height: 11 in (28 cm)
Colour: White and gilt.
Maker: Sampson Smith
Rarity: VR.
Pair: *Fig.* 348 (Macdonald), *pl.* C-125. Same series as *fig.* 341 (Macdonald), *fig.* 342 (Kitchener), *fig.* 343 (21st Lancers—*right*), *fig.* 344 (21st Lancers—*left*), *fig.* 345 (Roberts), *fig.* 346 (Kitchener), *fig.* 349 (Dundonald) and *fig.* 350 (French).
Description: On a horse facing right, in peaked cap and full military uniform.
Observations: Commander-in-chief in South Africa from October to December, 1899 when, as a sequel to his defeat at Colenso, he was superseded by Lord Roberts.

Plate 123
Fig. 343 21st Lancers (R)
Fig. 344 21st Lancers (L)
In the collection of Lady Ranfurly

Plate 124
Fig. 345 Lord Roberts
Fig. 347 General Buller
Fig. 346 Lord Kitchener
In the collections of Lady Ranfurly and the author

C311

Plate 125
Fig. 348 General Macdonald
In the collection of Mrs Cecil Woodham-Smith

Plate 126
Fig. 349 Lord Dundonald
Fig. 350 General French
In the collection of Mr George H. Rayner

Plate 125
Figure 348
Subject: **Major-General Sir Hector Macdonald**
Title: Major Macdonald (gilt script)
Date: c. 1900
Height: 11½ in (29 cm)
Colour: White and gilt.
Maker: Sampson Smith
Rarity: VR.
Pair: *Fig.* 347 (Buller) *pl.* C-124. Same series as *fig.* 341 (Macdonald), *fig.* 342 (Kitchener), *fig.* 343 (21st Lancers—*right*), *fig.* 344 (21st Lancers—*left*), *fig.* 345 (Roberts), *fig.* 346 (Kitchener), *fig.* 349 (Dundonald) and *fig.* 350 (French).
Description: On a horse facing left, in helmet and military uniform.
Observations: This figure has been noted as 'pairing' *fig.* 347 (Buller) *pl.* C-124, but it may have been intended to pair either *fig.* 345 (Roberts) *pl.* C-124, or *fig.* 349 (Dundonald) *pl.* C-126. Whichever is correct, there is no doubt that the figure was produced at the time of the Boer War, as distinct from *fig.* 341 (Macdonald) *pl.* C-121, which was produced at the time of Omdurman. 'Major' is an abbreviation for 'Major-General'. Sir Hector Macdonald was promoted major-general in 1900.

Plate 126
Figure 349
Subject: **Douglas, twelfth Earl of Dundonald**
Title: Lord Dundonald (gilt script)
Date: c. 1900
Height: 10½ in (26.5 cm)
Colour: White and gilt.
Maker: Sampson Smith
Rarity: VR.
Pair: *Fig.* 350 (French). Same series as *fig.*

341 (Macdonald), *fig.* 342 (Kitchener), *fig.* 343 (21st Lancers—*right*), *fig.* 344 (21st Lancers—*left*), *fig.* 345 (Roberts), *fig.* 346 (Kitchener), *fig.* 347 (Buller) and *fig.* 348 (Macdonald).
Description: On a horse facing right, in helmet and military uniform.
Observations: In 1900, he commanded the 2nd Cavalry Brigade in the relief of Ladysmith.

Figure 350
Subject: **Major-General Sir John French**
Title: General French (gilt script)
Date: c. 1900
Height: 11 in (28 cm)
Colour: White and gilt.
Maker: Sampson Smith
Rarity: VR.
Pair: *Fig.* 349 (Dundonald). Same series as *fig.* 341 (Macdonald), *fig.* 342 (Kitchener), *fig.* 343 (21st Lancers—*right*), *fig.* 344 (21st Lancers—*left*), *fig.* 345 (Roberts), *fig.* 346 (Kitchener), *fig.* 347 (Buller) and *fig.* 348 (Macdonald).
Description: On a horse facing left, in helmet and full military uniform.

Summary: LATE VICTORIAN WAR COMMANDERS, SERIES I
Figures belonging to this series, which was produced by Sampson Smith, are titled in gilt script and vary in size from 10½ in (26.5 cm) to 11½ in (29 cm) in height. It is the longest series of equestrian figures to come to light so far and is constituted as follows:

Battle of Omdurman, 1898

Fig.No.	Title	Fig.No.	Title
341.	Colnl. Mac Donald (*sic*.)	342.	The Sirdar
343.	21st Lancers (*R*)	344.	21st Lancers(*L*)

South African War, 1899–1902

345.	Lord Roberts	346.	Lord Kitchener
347.	General Buller	348.	Major Macdonald (*sic*)
349.	Lord Dundonald	350.	General French

All the figures of this series are very rare.

Plate 127
Figure 351
Subject: **General Sir Garnet Wolseley**
Title: Wolseley (indented capitals)
Date: c. 1885
Height: 15 in (38 cm)
Colour: Either white and gilt, or sparsely coloured in 'late' manner.
Maker: Kent and Parr.
Rarity: Av.
Pair: *Fig.* 352 (Gordon). Same series as *fig.* 353 (French), *fig.* 354 (Roberts), *fig.* 355 (Kitchener), *fig.* 356 (Macdonald), *fig.* 357 (Baden-Powell) and *fig.* 358 (Buller).
Description: On a horse facing right, in cocked hat, military uniform and knee-boots.
Observations: In 1884–5, Wolseley conducted the Nile campaign to relieve Gordon in Khartoum.

Figure 352
Subject: **General Gordon**
Title: Gordon (indented capitals)
Date: c. 1885
Height: 14½ in (36.75 cm)
Colour: Either white and gilt, or sparsely coloured in 'late' manner.
Maker: Kent and Parr
Rarity: Av.
Pair: *Fig.* 351 (Wolseley). Same series as *fig.*

Plate 127
T: *Fig.* 351 Wolseley
Fig. 352 Gordon

B: *Fig.* 353 French
Fig. 354 Roberts

353 (French), *fig.* 354 (Roberts), *fig.* 355 (Kitchener), *fig.* 356 (Macdonald), *fig.* 357 (Baden-Powell) and *fig.* 358 (Buller).
Description: On a horse facing left, in fez, military uniform and knee-boots.
Observations: Gordon was murdered in Khartoum in 1885.

Figure 353
Subject: **Major-General Sir John French**
Title: French (indented capitals)
Date: *c.* 1900
Height: 15 in (38 cm)
Colour: Either white and gilt, or sparsely coloured in 'late' manner.

Maker: William Kent
Rarity: Av.
Pair: *Fig.* 354 (Roberts). Same series as *fig.* 351 (Wolseley), *fig.* 352 (Gordon), *fig.* 355 (Kitchener), *fig.* 356 (Macdonald), *fig.* 357 (Baden-Powell) and *fig.* 358 (Buller).
Description: On a horse facing right, in cocked hat and full military uniform.
Observations: 1. Issued at the time of the South African War, 1899–1902.
2. See *fig.* 356 (Macdonald) *pl.* C-128.

Figure 354
Subject: **F-M. Lord Roberts**
Title: Roberts (indented capitals)

Date: *c.* 1900
Height: 14½ in (36.75 cm)
Colour: Either white and gilt, or sparsely coloured in 'late' manner.
Maker: William Kent
Rarity: Av.
Pair: *Fig.* 353 (French). Same series as *fig.* 351 (Wolseley), *fig.* 352 (Gordon), *fig.* 355 (Kitchener), *fig.* 356 (Macdonald), *fig.* 357 (Baden-Powell) and *fig.* 358 (Buller).
Description: On a horse facing left, in cocked hat and full military uniform.
Observations: Issued at the time of the South African War, 1899–1902.

Plate 128
T: *Fig.* 355 Kitchener
Fig. 356 Macdonald

Plate 128

Figure 355

Subject: **General Lord Kitchener**

Title: Kitchener (indented capitals)

Date: *c.* 1898

Height: 15 in (38 cm)

Colour: Either white and gilt, or sparsely coloured in 'late' manner.

Maker: William Kent

Rarity: Av.

Pair: Fig. 356 (Macdonald). Same series as *fig.* 351 (Wolseley), *fig.* 352 (Gordon), *fig.* 353 (French), *fig.* 354 (Roberts), *fig.* 357 (Baden-Powell) and *fig.* 358 (Buller).

Description: On a horse facing right, in fez, military uniform and knee-boots.

C314

Observations: As Kitchener is wearing a fez, there seems little doubt that this figure was issued at the time of the battle of Omdurman, 1898. However, see *fig.* 356 (Macdonald).

Figure 356

Subject: **Major-General Sir Hector Macdonald**

Title: Macdonald (indented capitals)

Date: *c.* 1898

Height: 15 in (38 cm)

Colour: Either white and gilt, or sparsely coloured in 'late' manner.

Maker: William Kent

Rarity: Av.

Pair: Fig. 355 (Kitchener). Same series as *fig.* 351 (Wolseley), *fig.* 352 (Gordon), *fig.* 353 (French), *fig.* 354 (Roberts), *fig.* 357 (Baden-Powell) and *fig.* 358 (Buller).

Description: On a horse facing left, in cocked hat and full military uniform.

Observations: Originally thought to pair *fig.* 355 (Kitchener) and to portray Macdonald at the time of Omdurman, 1898. However, there is some doubt about this, as in *Kent List A* Macdonald appears to pair *fig.* 353 (French). Kitchener, Roberts, Buller and Baden-Powell are not mentioned in any of the Kent lists.

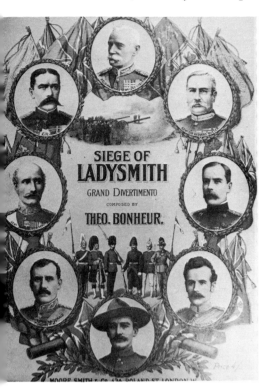

Figure 357
Subject: **Colonel R. S. S. Baden-Powell**
Title: Baden Powell (indented capitals)
Date: *c*. 1900
Height: 14½ in (36.75 cm)
Colour: White and gilt versions only seen.
Maker: William Kent
Rarity: Av.
Pair: Fig. 358 (Buller). Same series as *fig.* 351 (Wolseley), *fig.* 352 (Gordon), *fig.* 353 (French), *fig.* 354 (Roberts), *fig.* 355 (Kitchener) and *fig.* 356 (Macdonald).
Description: On a horse facing right, in slouch hat, military uniform and knee-boots.
Observations: Issued at the time of the South African War, 1899–1902.

Figure 358
Subject: **General Sir Redvers Buller**
Title: Buller (indented capitals)
Date: *c*. 1900
Height: 14¾ in (37.5 cm)
Colour: White and gilt, or sparsely coloured in 'late' manner.
Maker: William Kent
Rarity: Av.
Pair: Fig. 357 (Baden-Powell). Same series as *fig.* 351 (Wolseley), *fig.* 352 (Gordon), *fig.* 353 (French), *fig.* 354 (Roberts), *fig.* 355 (Kitchener) and *fig.* 356 (Macdonald).
Description: On a horse facing left, in peaked cap, military uniform and knee-boots.
Observations: Issued at the time of the South African War, 1899–1902.

Plate 129
Music-front titled 'Siege of Ladysmith'
Top-centre proceeding clockwise: Field-Marshal Lord Roberts, General Sir Redvers Buller, General Lord Methuen, Lord Dundonald, Colonel Baden-Powell, General Hector Macdonald ('Fighting Mac'), General Sir George White, Lord Kitchener.

Plate 130
Figure 359
Subject: **Douglas, twelfth Earl of Dundonald**
Title: Lord Dundonald (gilt script)
Date: *c*. 1900
Height: 14¾ in (37.5 cm)
Colour: White and gilt.
Maker: Sampson Smith
Rarity: R.
Pair: Fig. 360 (Macdonald). Same series as *fig.* 361 (French), *fig.* 362 (Kitchener), *fig.* 363 (Roberts) and *fig.* 364 (Buller).
Description: On a horse facing right, with long saddle-cloth. He wears helmet, military jacket, breeches and knee-boots.
Observations: See *fig.* 361 (French) *pl.* C-131.

Figure 360
Subject: **Major-General Sir Hector Macdonald**
Title: Major Macdonald (gilt script)
Date: *c*. 1900
Height: 14½ in (36.75 cm)
Colour: White and gilt.
Maker: Sampson Smith
Rarity: R.
Pair: Fig. 359 (Dundonald). Same series as *fig.* 361 (French), *fig.* 362 (Kitchener), *fig.* 363 (Roberts) and *fig.* 364 (Buller).
Description: On a horse facing left, with long saddle-cloth. He wears helmet, military jacket, breeches and knee-boots.
Observations: This figure pairs Lord Dundonald and may be dated, with confidence, to the period of the South African War.

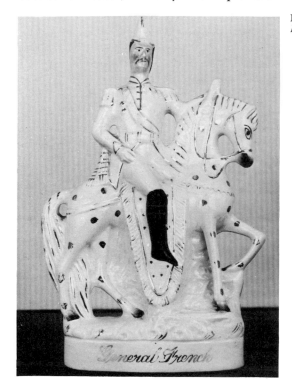

Plate 131
Fig. 361 General French

Summary: LATE VICTORIAN
WAR COMMANDERS, SERIES II
Figures belonging to this series, which was
produced by the Parr and Kent group of
potters, are titled in indented capitals and
vary in size from 14½ in (36.75 cm) to 15 in
(38 cm) in height. The series is constituted
as follows:

*Wolseley's campaign to relieve Gordon in
Khartoum*, 1885

Fig. No.	Title	Fig. No.	Title
351.	Wolseley	352.	Gordon

Battle of Omdurman, 1898

355.	Kitchener	356.	Macdonald

South African War, 1899–1902

353.	French	354.	Roberts
357.	Baden Powell	358.	Buller

It will be seen that this series was produced
over a period of nearly fifteen years. *Fig.* 351
(Wolseley) seems to have been used again
for *fig.* 353 (French) and *fig.* 356 (Macdonald) seems to have been used again for
fig. 354 (Roberts).

For some reason, which has defied explanation, only four of these figures appear in
the Kent lists, and even they have been
deleted as 'discontinued lines' in *Kent List B*
(*c.* 1920). They are 'Generals Macdonald
and French on Horse' and 'Generals Gordon
and Wolseley on Horse'. It will be noted
that French and Macdonald are paired.
This throws doubt on my suggested
grouping for the series, but I have retained
it in the absence of information regarding
the remaining four figures.

Plate 131
Figure 361
Subject: **Major-General Sir John French**
Title: General French (gilt script)
Date: *c.* 1900

Height: 14 in (35.5 cm)
Colour: White and gilt.
Maker: Sampson Smith
Rarity: R.
Pair: *Fig.* 362 (Kitchener) *pl.* C-132. Same
series as *fig.* 359 (Dundonald), *fig.* 360
(Macdonald), *fig.* 363 (Roberts) and *fig.* 364
(Buller).
Description: On a horse facing right, with
long saddle-cloth. He wears helmet, military jacket, breeches and knee-boots.
Observations: 1. This and other figures of the
series are occasionally found marked, in
relief on the base, with a St Andrew's cross
and the first letter of the surname of the
portrait concerned, in mirror-image. The
lettering is in an identical style to that
used for titling the figure; in this case an
'F' (see *ch.* 2, *pl.* 10). Presumably this was
done to remind the potter whom he was
'potting'.
2. The same figure is occasionally found
titled 'G. French'. To this *fig.* 361(*a*) has
been allotted, see *pl.* C-132.

Plate 132
Figure 361(a)
Subject: **Major-General Sir John French**
Title: G. French (gilt script).
Observations: See *fig.* 361, *pl.* C-131.

Figure 362
Subject: **General Lord Kitchener**
Title: Lord Kitchener (gilt script)
Date: *c.* 1900
Height: 14½ in (36.75 cm)
Colour: White and gilt.
Maker: Sampson Smith
Rarity: R.
Pair: *Fig.* 361 (French) *pl.* C-131. Same
series as *fig.* 359 (Dundonald), *fig.* 360
(Macdonald), *fig.* 363 (Roberts) and *fig.* 364
(Buller).

Description: On a horse facing left, with
long saddle-cloth, in helmet, military
jacket and knee-boots.
Observations: See *fig.* 361 (French) *pl.* C-131.

Figure 363
Subject: **F-M. Lord Roberts**
Title: Lord Roberts (gilt script)
Date: *c.* 1900
Height: 14½ in (36.75 cm)
Colour: White and gilt.
Maker: Sampson Smith
Rarity: R.
Pair: *Fig.* 364 (Buller). Same series as *fig.* 359
(Dundonald), *fig.* 360 (Macdonald), *fig.* 361
(French), *fig.* 362 (Kitchener).
Description: On a horse facing right, with
long saddle-cloth, wearing· helmet, mili-
tary jacket, breeches and knee-boots.
Observations: The identical figure is found
occasionally titled 'General Roberts', and
to this the *fig.* 363(*a*) has been allotted.
Roberts was, incidentally, created baron in
1892, and promoted field-marshal in 1895!

Figure 364
Subject: **General Sir Redvers Buller**
Title: General Buller (gilt script)
Date: *c.* 1900
Height: 14 in (35.5 cm)
Colour: White and gilt.
Maker: Sampson Smith
Rarity: R.
Pair: *Fig.* 363 (Roberts). Same series as *fig.*
359 (Dundonald), *fig.* 360 (Macdonald),
fig. 361 (French) and *fig.* 362 (Kitchener).
Description: On a horse facing left, with
long saddle-cloth, wearing peaked cap,
military jacket, breeches and knee-boots.

Plate 132
T: *Fig.* 361(a) G. French
Fig. 362 Lord Kitchener

B: *Fig.* 363(a) General
Roberts
Fig. 364 General Buller
Fig. 363 Lord Roberts

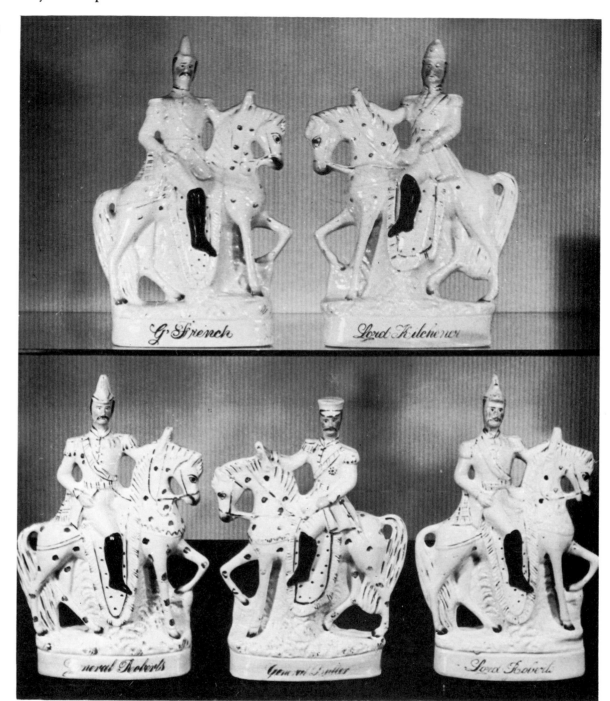

Summary: LATE VICTORIAN
WAR COMMANDERS, SERIES III
Figures belonging to this series, which was
produced by Sampson Smith, are titled in
gilt script and vary in size from 14 in
(35.5 cm) to 14¾ in (37.5 cm) in height.
Figures are sometimes found marked, in
relief on the base, with a St Andrews cross
and the mirror-image of the first letter of
the surname of the portrait, see *ch.* 2, *pl.* 10.

South African War, 1899–1902
Fig.No   Title   Fig.No.   Title
359. Lord Dundonald 360. Major Macdonald

361. General French 362. Lord Kitchener
363. Lord Roberts   364. General Buller

All these figures were produced during the
South African War, but it may be noted
that the same figure was used for *fig.* 361
(French) and *fig.* 363 (Roberts). Also, the
same figure, but with different heads, for
fig. 362 (Kitchener) and *fig.* 364 (Buller).
Fig. 359 (Dundonald) and *fig.* 360 (Macdonald) are derived from *fig.* 328 (Wolseley)
and *fig.* 329 (Duke of Connaught), compare
pl. C-115 with *pl.* C-130.

Plate 133
Fig. 365 Baden-Powell
Fig. 238 (section A) Duke of Clarence

Plate 134
Fig. 366 De Wet

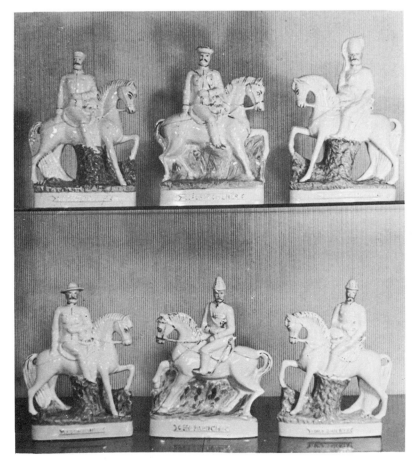

Plate 135
T: *Fig.* 367 Sir Redvers Buller
Fig. 369(a) Lord Kitchener
Fig. 372 Hector Macdonald

B: *Fig.* 371 Baden-Powell
Fig. 370(a) General French
Fig. 368 Lord Roberts

Plate 133
Figure 365
Subject: **Colonel R. S. S. Baden-Powell**
Title: Baden Powell (gilt script)
Date: *c.* 1900
Height: 16½ in (41.5 cm)
Colour: White and gilt.
Maker: Sampson Smith
Rarity: Av.
Description: He stands in a slouch hat, jacket and trousers. A sword hangs from his belt and he wears a bandoleer (shoulder-belt with cartridge-loops). His left hand rests on the barrel of a cannon.
Observations: 1. This figure bears a striking resemblance to *fig.* 238 (Duke of Clarence) *bl.* A-82. When the Duke died in 1892, the mould of his figure was presumably put on one side until the South African War, when it was taken out and modified. The modifications included a new head, minor adjustments to the jacket and the deletion of the title in raised capitals and application of the new title in gilt script.
2. *Fig.* 366 (De Wet), *pl.* C-134 is identical in all respects, other than title, to *fig.* 365. The figure is considerably rarer than that of Baden-Powell and was probably produced during the South African War for the pro-Boer faction in this country. Apparently the uniform is more in keeping with that which would have been worn by De Wet than that which would have been worn by Baden-Powell.

Plate 134
Figure 366
Subject: **General De Wet**
Title: De Wet (gilt script)
Date: *c.* 1900
Height: 16½ in (41.5 cm)
Colour: White and gilt.
Maker: Sampson Smith
Rarity: VR.
Description: Identical in all respects, other than title, to *fig.* 365 (Baden-Powell) *pl.* C-133.
Observations: See *fig.* 365 (Baden-Powell).

Section C. Naval, Military and Exploration

Plate 135
Figure 367
Subject: **General Sir Redvers Buller**
Title: Sir Redvers Buller (raised capitals on plaque)
Date: *c.* 1900
Height: 12 in (30.5 cm)
Colour: Largely white and gilt, crude green base.
Maker: Probably James Sadler, see *fig.* 369 (Kitchener).
Rarity: C.
Pair: *Fig.* 368 (Roberts). Same series as *fig.* 369 (Kitchener), *fig.* 370 (French), *fig.* 371 (Baden-Powell) and *fig.* 372 (Macdonald).
Description: On a horse facing right, in peaked cap and military uniform.
Observations: 1. *Fig.* 367 is from a press-mould. A similar cast figure exists for this and also others of the series. It is identical in every way except for the arrangement of the horse's feet and the fact that it has a large hole in its base. Cast figures are catalogued with a small (*a*) after the number.
2. A 'mixed' set of six of these figures fetched 24 gns at Christie's in 1963; but see also *figs.* 370 (French) and 372 (Macdonald).

Figure 368
Subject: **F-M. Lord Roberts**
Title: Lord Roberts (raised capitals on plaque)
Date: *c.* 1900
Height: 12¼ in (31 cm)
Colour: Largely white and gilt, crude green base.
Maker: Probably James Sadler, see *fig.* 369 (Kitchener).
Rarity: C.
Pair: *Fig.* 367 (Buller). Same series as *fig.* 369 (Kitchener), *fig.* 370 (French), *fig.* 371 (Baden-Powell) and *fig.* 372 (Macdonald).
Description: On a horse facing left, in low plumed helmet.
Observations: See *fig.* 367 (Buller).

Figure 369 (*fig.* 369(*a*) illustrated)
Subject: **General Lord Kitchener**
Title: Lord. Kitchener (raised capitals on plaque)
Date: *c.* 1900
Height: 12 in (30.5 cm)
Colour: Largely white and gilt, crude green base.
Maker: Probably James Sadler, see *observations*.
Rarity: C.
Pair: *Fig.* 370 (French). Same series as *fig.* 367 (Buller), *fig.* 368 (Roberts), *fig.* 371 (Baden-Powell) and *fig.* 372 (Macdonald).
Description: On a horse facing right, in peaked cap and military uniform.
Observations: 1. As in all other members of this series, this figure is found made either from a press-mould or by casting. It is a cast figure [*fig.* 369(*a*)] which is illustrated. Both this and *fig.* 370(*a*) have been found bearing the printed mark 'SADLER/BURSLEM/ENGLAND', see *ch.* 2, *pl.* 14.
2. Balston recorded a figure of Lord Roberts belonging to this series which had been found with 'HANLEY/LANCASTERS LIMITED/ENGLAND' stamped on its base. He did not record whether the figure was from a press-mould or cast. I have never seen a figure with this mark.

Figure 370 (*fig.* 370(*a*) illustrated)
Subject: **Major-General Sir John French**
Title: Gen. French (raised capitals on plaque)
Date: *c.* 1900
Height: 12 in (30.5 cm)
Colour: Largely white and gilt, crude green base.
Maker: Probably James Sadler, see *fig.* 369 (Kitchener).
Rarity: C.
Pair: *Fig.* 369 (Kitchener). Same series as *fig.* 367 (Buller), *fig.* 368 (Roberts), *fig.* 371 (Baden-Powell) and *fig.* 372 (Macdonald).
Description: On a horse facing left, in helmet and military uniform.
Observations: 1. See *fig.* 369 (Kitchener).
2. A similar figure and its pair fetched 35 gns at Christie's in 1969.

Figure 371
Subject: **Colonel R. S. S. Baden-Powell**
Title: Baden-Powell (raised capitals on plaque)
Date: *c.* 1900
Height: 12 in (30.5 cm)
Colour: Largely white and gilt, crude green base.
Maker: Probably James Sadler, see *fig.* 369 (Kitchener).
Rarity: C.
Pair: *Fig.* 372 (Macdonald). Same series as *fig.* 367 (Buller), *fig.* 368 (Roberts), *fig.* 369 (Kitchener) and *fig.* 370 (French).
Description: On a horse facing right, in slouch hat and military uniform.
Observations: See *fig.* 369 (Kitchener).

Figure 372
Subject: **Major-General Sir Hector Macdonald**
Title: Hector M^(ac)donald (raised capitals on plaque)
Date: *c.* 1900
Height: 12½ in (31.75 cm)
Colour: Largely white and gilt, crude green base.
Maker: Probably James Sadler, see *fig.* 369 (Kitchener).
Rarity: C.
Pair: *Fig.* 371 (Baden-Powell). Same series as *fig.* 367 (Buller), *fig.* 368 (Roberts), *fig.* 369 (Kitchener) and *fig.* 370 (French).
Description: On a horse facing left, in busby and military uniform.
Observations: 1. See *fig.* 369 (Kitchener).
2. A similar figure fetched 35 gns at Christie's in 1969.

Summary: LATE VICTORIAN WAR COMMANDERS, SERIES IV
Figures belonging to this series, which was produced by James Sadler, vary in size from 12 in (30.5 cm) to 12½ in (31.75 cm) in height. They are titled with raised capitals on a plaque. They occur in two forms.
(a) *Cast.* These were definitely manufactured by James Sadler.
(b) *Press-moulded.* These, also, were probably manufactured by James Sadler, but possibly manufactured by Lancasters Limited (*p.* 17).

South African War, 1899–1902

Fig. No.	Title	Fig. No.	Title
367.	Sir Redvers Buller	368.	Lord Roberts
369.	Lord Kitchener	370.	Gen. French
371.	Baden-Powell	372.	Hector Macdonald

It is not possible to be absolutely dogmatic about the pairing of these figures, but it was probably as given above.
Figures made from the slip, are catalogued with an additional '(*a*)' and may readily be recognized by the large hole in the base through which the slip was poured.

Plate 136
Figure 373
Subject: **A non-portrait South African War figure**
Title: Gordon/Highlander (raised capitals)
Date: *c.* 1900
Height: 12¾ in (32.25 cm)
Colour: Crude.
Maker: In the style of Sampson Smith.
Rarity: Av.
Pair: *Fig.* 374 (Black Watch) *pl.* C-137.
Description: Standing in the uniform of a Gordon Highlander, with a fixed bayonet to his right.
Observations: The Gordon Highlanders fought with distinction in the South African War.

Plate 136
Fig. 373 Gordon Highlander
By courtesy of Mr J. Fairhurst

Section C. Naval, Military and Exploration

Plate 137
Fig. 374 Black Watch

Plate 138
Fig. 375 Hussar on horse (R)

Plate 139
Fig. 376 British Lion
In the collection of The Hon. Mrs C. Wildman

Plate 140
Fig. 377 The Peace, 1902
In the collection of Mrs Cecil Woodham-Smith

Section C. Naval, Military and Exploration

Plate 141
Fig. 378 Cavell
Fig. 379 Cavell
By courtesy of Mrs W. W. Warner and in the collection of the author

Plate 137
Figure 374
Subject: **A non-portrait South African War figure**
Title: Black Watch (raised capitals)
Date: *c.* 1900
Height: 12¾ in (32.25 cm)
Colour: Crude.
Maker: In the style of Sampson Smith.
Rarity: Av.
Pair: *Fig.* 373 (Gordon Highlander) *pl.*C-136.
Description: Standing in the uniform of the Black Watch. His fixed bayonet is by his right side, but his hands are clasped above his sporran.
Observations: The Black Watch fought with distinction in the South African War.

Plate 138
Figure 375
Subject: **Hussar on horse—a non-portrait South African war figure**
Title: None
Date: *c.* 1900
Height: 10¾ in (27 cm)
Colour: Either white and gilt, or rather garishly coloured.
Maker: William Kent
Rarity: Av.
Pair: This figure appears facing both right and left.
Description: On a horse facing right or left, in the uniform of a Hussar.
Observations: 1. The figure appears in all the Kent lists:

	KENT LIST A Stock No.	KENT LIST B Stock No.	KENT LIST C Ref. No. (1955)
Huzzar on Horse (*sic*)	45	276	276

2. An example fetched 26 gns at Christie's in 1965.
3. It has been postulated that the figure represents the Prince of Wales, later King Edward VII. There is a bronze statuette of

the Prince of Wales by J. E. Boehn, dated 1872, in Osborne House, in which the Prince is portrayed mounted, in the uniform of the Xth Hussars. However, this figure and the Staffordshire figure have little in common.

Plate 139
Figure 376
Subject: **A lion**
Title: British/Lion (raised capitals)
Date: *c.* 1900
Height: 7 in (17.5 cm)
Colour: Well coloured.
Rarity: R.
Description: A lion, the head of which is detachable to form a tobacco jar. At its base, on the left, is a Union Jack and on the right a medallion with 'British/Lion' inscribed in raised capitals.
Observations: Almost certainly of South African War vintage.

Plate 140
Figure 377
Subject: **A Boer, John Bull and an angel**
Title: Boer War/Peace Declared/June 1st 1902 (raised capitals)
Date: 1902
Height: 12½ in (31.75 cm)
Colour: Largely white and gilt.
Rarity: VR.
Description: In front and to the left, is a bareheaded, bearded Boer. In front and to the right, is John Bull with a Union Jack inscribed on his waistcoat. Both are seated and shaking hands. Behind is an angel. She holds a ribbon inscribed 'Peace on earth goodwill towards men' (indented capitals).
Observations: This crude figure is derived from *fig.* 56 (Peace) *pl.* B-16, first issued in 1882 to celebrate the Kilmainham Treaty,

see *p.* 4. The two seated women representing Ireland and Britannia have had their heads amputated and the heads of a Boer and John Bull have been substituted. The bodies were presumably remoulded while the clay was still soft:

Plate 141
Figure 378
Subject: **? Edith Cavell**
Title: None
Date: *c.* 1915
Height: 9¾ in (24.5 cm)
Colour: Largely white.
Rarity: R.
Description: She is standing, in nurse's uniform, with a red cross over her apron. A pair of scissors is suspended from her left wrist and a bag from her right wrist. Made from the slip.
Observations: 1. This figure is almost certainly a crude representation of Miss Edith Cavell and is included to show how the art continued into the twentieth century in a debased form.
2. Edith Cavell was matron of the Berkendael medical institute in Brussels. This institute became a Red Cross hospital in 1914.

Figure 379
Subject: **Edith Cavell**
Title: None
Date: *c.* 1915
Height: 3¼ in (8.25 cm)
Colour: Largely uncoloured.
Rarity: R.
Description: In London Hospital uniform. A porcelaneous figure.
Observations: Edith Cavell was trained at the London Hospital in 1895.

Section D
Religious
Biographies and Historical Notes

BAND OF HOPE, THE.
See **Temperance and Teetotal Societies**.

BOOTH, WILLIAM (1829–1912), founder of the Salvation Army. Popularly known as 'General Booth'. Apprenticed to Nottingham pawnbroker. Itinerant preacher of Methodist New Connexion, 1852. Independent revivalist, 1861. Opened the Christian mission in Whitechapel, 1865, which became known as the Salvation Army, 1878. Championed the cause of the 'down and out' in the cities.
See **pl. D-28**.

BRYAN, JOHN (1770–1856), Wesleyan minister. Born at Llanfyllin; joined Calvinistic Methodists in 1798, but soon transferred to the Wesleyans. Minister of various Welsh and English circuits from 1801 to 1824. Subsequently set up as a grocer, first at Leeds and later at Caernarvon, where he continued to preach until his death. Made many converts by his brilliant preaching.
See **pl. D-23**.

COOKE, HENRY (1788–1868), Irish Presbyterian leader. Studied science and medicine at Glasgow, 1815–7. DD, Jefferson College, USA, 1829. Violently opposed the disestablishment of the Irish Episcopal Church. Published sermons, hymns and articles in periodicals. Considered one of the most effective of Irish preachers and debaters.
See **pls. D-6, 6A**.

CRANMER, THOMAS (1489–1556), Archbishop of Canterbury under Henry VIII and Edward VI. Played a leading part in the reformation. On the accession of Mary, he at first agreed to return to the old faith, but when called upon to make public avowal of his recantation, he refused and was burnt at the stake at Oxford. Was responsible for the English Bible, and Book of Common Prayer.
See **pl. D-1**.

ELIAS, JOHN, (1774–1841), Welsh Calvinistic Methodist who taught in the first Sunday school in Caernarvonshire. Itinerant preacher. He helped draw up the Methodists' articles of faith, 1823. Published religious tractates in Welsh.
See **pls. D-23, 23A**.

EVANS, CHRISTMAS (1766–1838), Welsh preacher. He began life as a farm labourer. Sustained an injury to his right eye in a religious brawl in 1788. From

1792 to 1826 was the autocratic Baptist minister in Anglesey. He was known as the 'Bunyan of Wales'. He published his sermons in Welsh.
See **pls. D-23, 23B**.

EVANS, ROBERT TROGWY (1824–1901), Welsh Congregationalist. Ministered at Manchester from 1853 to 1857 and at Greenfield, Flintshire from 1858 to 1870. He emigrated subsequently to the United States. He was a powerful force in the temperance movement.
See **pl. D-24**.

FLETCHER, JOHN WILLIAM (1729–85), properly De La Flechere, a theologian. Born at Nyon in Switzerland, he was educated for the Protestant church, but chose a military life and sought service in Portugal and Belgium. He was disappointed, and came on a visit to England in 1750, when he acquired the English language. He entered into the English Church in 1757. His only preferment was the vicarage of Madeley in Shropshire, which he received in 1760. He was a great friend and colleague of John Wesley and took an important part in the conferences of the Methodist preachers of that day. John Wesley wrote:

I was intimately connected with Mr Fletcher for 30 years. I never heard him speak an improper word, or do an improper action. In fourscore years I have known many excellent men, holy in heart and life, but one equal to him I have not known, one so uniformly devoted to God.

Bishop Ryle, the great evangelical bishop of Liverpool, at the close of the last century wrote of Fletcher:

I can find very few men of the 18th century, about whom there is so striking an agreement on all sides, that Fletcher was pre-eminently and peculiarly a most holy man, a saint indeed, a living epistle of Christ.

See **pls. D-16, 18**.

FLETCHER, JOSEPH, the elder (1784–1843), theological writer. Congregational minister of Blackburn, 1807–23, and afterwards at Stepney. DD, Glasgow, 1830. Author of the *Principles and Institutions of the Roman Catholic Religion* (1817).
See **pls. D-18, 19**.

FLETCHER, JOSEPH, the younger (1816–76), Congregational minister and son of Joseph Fletcher, the elder. Congregational minister at Hanley, 1839–49. Published *Memoirs of Rev. Joseph Fletcher, DD* (1846).
See **pls. D-18, 19**.

FOUNTAIN.
See **Temperance and Teetotal Societies**.

GOULBURN, EDWARD MEYRICK (1818–97), Dean of Norwich. Educated at Eton and Oxford. Ordained priest, 1843; DD, 1856. Headmaster of Rugby from 1849 to 1857. Dean of Norwich from 1866 to 1889. Between 1854 and 1862 published three popular devotional books.
See **pl. D-18**.

GURNEY, JOSEPH JOHN (1788–1847), Quaker philanthropist and writer. Brother of Daniel Gurney and Mrs Elizabeth Fry. Quaker minister, 1818. Played a leading part in prison reform, negro emancipation and the move towards the abolition of capital punishment.
See **pl. D-23**.

HALLAHAN, MARGARET MARY (1803–68). A poor Irish servant who, in 1844, founded a community of Dominican Tertians in Coventry, and in 1851, a further community in the Potteries at Longton, later transferred to Stone. Her purpose in Longton was to open schools for 'the poor', for 'young ladies' and a night school for the neglected and illiterate girls and women who worked such long hours in the Potteries. 'Sister Margaret and her wenches' as they were at first contemptuously called, were stared at in astonishment, no less so their chaplain Père Moulaert, a Belgian, for no Dominican in black and white robes had walked an English road for three hundred years. The figures of Moulaert and Hallahan were potted by those whose children they taught and whose sick they nursed and whose condition of whose lives they sought to ameliorate. See article by M. Littledale (*Antique Dealer and Collectors Guide*, Jan. 1954).
See **pl. D-12A**.

HILL, ROWLAND (1744–1833), preacher. Son of a Shropshire baronet. Educated at St John's College, Cambridge. Much influenced by Whitefield. From his ordination in 1773 until 1783, he was an itinerant preacher. Thereafter, he preached at the Surrey Chapel, Blackfriars Road, London, which he had built himself. Reputed to have started the first Sunday school in London.
See **pls. D-13, 14, 14A**.

HUNTINGTON, WILLIAM S. S. (1745–1813), eccentric preacher. After acquiring rudiments of knowledge at Cranbrook Grammar School, he went into service as

an errand-boy. He was afterwards successively gentleman's servant, gunmaker's apprentice, sawyer's pit-man, coachman, hearse-driver, tramp, gardener, coalheaver, and popular preacher. Having seduced a young woman, the daughter of a tailor in Kent, he decamped on the birth of a child and changed his name to Huntington to avoid identification, 1769. Later, formed association with a servant girl. At Sunbury, he underwent conversion. In anticipation that his past would come to light, he confided in his more devoted adherents and appended to his name the letters 'SS', i.e. 'Sinner Saved'. Joined Calvinistic Methodists in 1773. Built 'Providence Chapel', Titchfield Street, London and preached there from 1783 to 1811. Had controversies with Rowland Hill. Published *God the Guardian of the Poor*.
See **pls. D-**24A, 24B.

INDEPENDENT ORDER OF GOOD TEMPLARS (IOGT).
See **Temperance and Teetotal Societies.**

LATIMER, HUGH (c. 1485–1555), Bishop of Worcester under Henry VIII. Played a leading part in the reformation. On the accession of Mary he was condemned as a heretic and burnt at the stake together with Ridley.
See **pl. D-**1.

MANNING, HENRY EDWARD (1808–1892), English Roman Catholic cardinal. He was born at Totteridge, Hertfordshire; educated at Harrow and Balliol College, Oxford. An eloquent preacher and a high churchman, he became, in 1833, rector of Woollavington and Graffham, Sussex; and in 1840, Archdeacon of Chichester. In 1851, he joined the Church of Rome, and in 1865 became Archbishop of Westminster. Was a most zealous supporter of the infallibility dogma. Named cardinal in 1875. Took a prominent part in temperance and benevolent movements.
See **pl. D-**4.

MATHEW, THEOBALD (1790–1856), Roman Catholic priest and 'apostle of temperance'. Signed total abstinence pledge in 1838, and visited principal cities in Ireland with great success. A powerful speaker, his crusades in Ireland from 1838 to 1842, helped by worsening poverty in the country, cut consumption of spirits by half—although it still came to 5.29 million gallons a year at the end of his campaigns. In 1843, he came to England, and in August that year he reached London and held huge meetings at which thousands took the pledge. He was received into liberal society and Queen Victoria granted him a pension, but he did not enjoy success on the scale he had known in Ireland, and often it did not survive his departure. He visited the United States in 1849 and returned to Ireland in 1851. Had the backing of both Catholics and Protestants of all social grades and of all the temperance and teetotal societies in his campaign.
See **pls. D-**25, 26.

MOODY, DWIGHT LYMAN (1837–99), American evangelist. Born at Northfield, Mass. A shopkeeper in Boston, he moved in 1856, to Chicago, where he became engaged in missionary work. There he joined, in

1870, Ira David Sankey, and together they visited England as evangelists both in 1873 and 1883. Moody preached and Sankey sang. Subsequently they worked together in America.
See **pls. D-**4, 5.

MOULAERT, BERNARD (1808–70), Belgian Dominican. Père Moulaert was librarian of the Monastery at Tirlemont. About 1830 he worked at Longton with Sister Hallahan (*q.v.*).
See **pl. D-**12A.

NO POPERY AGITATION. In 1851 there was a violent 'No Popery' agitation aroused by the decision of Pope Pius IX to grant English territorial titles to bishops. It seems likely that the five anti-Catholic figures: 'Cranmer', 'Ridley and Latimer', 'Popery', 'Protestantism' and '£10,000' (see *pls.* D-1 and 2) were made during this period.
See **pls. D-**1, 2.

PENN, WILLIAM (1644–1718), Quaker and founder of Pennsylvania. Educated at Christ Church, Oxford; sent down for nonconformity. Became Quaker in 1667. Committed to the Tower of London in 1668 for publishing his *Sandy Foundation Shaken*. Whilst confined to the Tower, wrote treatise on the Christian duty of self-sacrifice, *No Cross, no Crown*. Released, 1669. Sailed for America, 1682, and founded colony of Pennsylvania as a refuge from persecution of his co-religionists.
See **pls. D-**3, 3A.

PIUS IX (1792–1878), named Giovanni Maria Mastai Ferretti. Born at Sinigaglia and took deacon's orders in 1818. In 1840, he became a cardinal, and on the death of Gregory XVI in 1846, was elected pope. He started on a series of reforms. In 1848, he published his *Statuto Fondamentale*, a scheme for the temporal government of the papal states by two chambers, one nominated by the pope and the other by the people. At first popular, the revolutionary fever of 1848 spread too fast for a reforming pope, and his refusal to make war upon the Austrians forfeited the affections of the Roman people. On November 15th, 1848, his first minister was murdered, and two days later a mob assembled in the square of the Quirinal. On the 24th he escaped to Gaeta, and a republic was proclaimed in Rome. Papal government was re-established in 1849, after a French expedition had taken Rome. Otherwise known as 'Pio Nono', he proved to be an unyielding conservative, closely allied with the Jesuits. His decision, in 1851, to grant English territorial titles to bishops, led to a violent 'No Popery' agitation in this country. Following the war between the French and Sardinians against the Austrians of 1859, and the popular vote of 1860, the greater part of the papal territory was incorporated in the Sardinian (Italian) kingdom, but the Pope refused to recognize the fact. The Vatican Council (1869–70) proclaimed the infallibility of the Pope. For the preceding ten years, the Pope's temporal power had been maintained only by the French garrison, and on its withdrawal in 1870, the soldiers of Victor Emmanuel entered Rome. For the remainder of his reign the Pope lived a voluntary 'prisoner' within the Vatican.
See **pl. D-**4.

RAFFLES, THOMAS (1788–1863), independent minister. Worked in Liverpool from 1811 to 1862. It was said of him that he was 'Tall and dignified, his voice and manner were suasive, and his power of anecdote suasive'. Chairman of the Congregational Union, 1839.
See **pls. D-**18, 19.

RIDLEY, NICHOLAS (1500–55). Bishop of Rochester in 1547 and Bishop of London in 1550. He played a leading role in the reformation. He was burnt at the stake together with Latimer.
See **pl. D-**1.

ROBERTS, EVAN (1878–1951), revivalist. Born at Bwlchymynydd, near Loughor. Son of a miner, he was educated at the local national school. Worked underground as a blacksmith. Attended preparatory school for ministers at Newcastle Emlyn. Underwent psychic experiences which led to him launching a revivalist movement at Loughor, near Llanelly, which soon grew to massive proportions. Throughout 1905, a rekindled religious fervour swept through Wales. Chapel membership, most marked in the Baptist denomination mounted rapidly. Rumours followed the revivalist around. His relationship with the young women who went with him on crusades was questioned, and some people frankly thought him insane. The strain undermined his health and he went into retirement at Leicester. In 1920, he sent a 'message' to the Welsh people and spoke at a convention at Cardiff. The revival, written off by some as mass hysteria, is generally regarded as one of the greatest features of Welsh life at the beginning of this century.
See **pls. D-**27, 27A.

SANKEY, IRA DAVID (1840–1908), American evangelist. Born at Edinburgh, Pennsylvania. Joined Moody in 1870. In 1873 and 1883 they visited England as evangelists. Sankey sang and Moody preached. Subsequently they worked together in America.
See **pls. D-**4, 5.

SPURGEON, CHARLES HADDEN (1834–92), English Baptist preacher. In 1854, he became pastor of the New Park Street Chapel, London. In 1859, the Metropolitan Tabernacle, with seating accommodation for six thousand, was erected for him. He withdrew from the Baptist Union in 1887, because no action was taken against persons charged with fundamental errors. The Metropolitan Tabernacle was burnt down in 1898. He was the author of many works.
See **pls. D-**20, 21, 22.

TEMPERANCE AND TEETOTAL SOCIETIES, ETC.
1. **THE BAND OF HOPE.** Founded in Leeds, in 1847, by an Irishwoman, Mrs Ann Jane Carlile, to save children before they were tempted. In 1851, local bands were amalgamated into a Band of Hope Union. The society is still in existence and the hymn they sang at their first festival at Leeds is still sung today.

> The Band of Hope shall be our name,
>   the temperance star our guide;
> We will not know the drunkard's
>   shame—the drunkard's drink avoid.

Section D. Religious

Cold water cannot do us harm, strong
    drink may bring us woe,
So we have signed the temperance
    pledge a short time ago.

See **pls. D**-29, 30.

2. THE INDEPENDENT ORDER OF GOOD TEMPLARS. Founded in 1851, by a group of abstainers at Utica in New York State, with the object of world-wide total abolition. Introduced into Great Britain in 1868.

See **pls. D**-30, 30A.

3. FOUNTAIN 1861: Temperance Societies were horrified and irritated by Gladstone's Refreshment House Act (1860), which authorized the granting of beer licences to eating-houses, and by his Revenue Act (1861), which reduced the duties on wine. There followed an upsurge in temperance propaganda and many public drinking fountains were installed. A number of untitled groups with fountains probably relate to this period.

See **pls. D**-30, 31.

VINCENT DE PAUL, SAINT (1576–1660), French priest and philanthropist. Admitted to the priest's orders in 1600. Captured by corsairs and sold into slavery at Tunis. Converted his master to the Christian faith and returned to France in 1607. Founded the Paris Foundling Hospital, the noble Sisterhood of Charity and other lay nursing organizations. Canonized, 1737. The St Vincent de Paul Charitable Society was founded in 1833, in France, by twelve young men. It extended its extremely beneficial operations into Britain. Its power excited the jealousy of the French government, which suppressed its central committee of Paris, in October, 1861.

See **pl. D**-5.

WESLEY, CHARLES (1707–1788), divine and hymn-writer. Youngest son of Samuel Wesley (1662–1735). Educated at Westminster School and Christ Church, Oxford. Joined fellow students in strict method of religious observance and study, whence they were nicknamed 'methodists'. Ordained in 1735. Did much evangelistic work in London, and later, Bristol, Wales and Cornwall. From 1747 to 1748, travelled in Ireland. Developed divergent views on doctrine of 'perfection' from his brother, John Wesley, 1762. Composed over six thousand hymns, of which five hundred are still in use. Some sermons and poetical pieces by him were published posthumously.

See **pls. D**-6A, 7, 8, 10, 11, 13, 15, 17.

WESLEY, JOHN (1703–91), evangelist and leader of Methodism. A younger son of Samuel Wesley, rector of Epworth. Educated at Charterhouse and Christ Church, Oxford. Ordained deacon, 1725. Fellow of Lincoln College, Oxford, 1726–51. MA, 1727. John Wesley became leader of a group which had gathered round his brother Charles, the hymn-writer and divine. This group had been nicknamed 'methodists', a name later adopted by John for the adherents of the great evangelical movement which was its outgrowth. Originally a rigid high churchman, he experienced a dramatic conversion in 1738, and Methodism in its true sense was born. He began open-air preaching, and opened the first Methodist chapel at Bristol in 1739. During half a century he travelled 250,000 miles and preached 40,000 sermons. He appealed mainly to working class neighbourhoods, and the mass of his converts were colliers, foundrymen, weavers, spinners and especially pottery workers. He also undertook a prodigious amount of literary work. In 1751, he married the widow Mary Vazeille, who deserted him following a quarrel in 1776.

See **pls. D**-6A, 7, 8, 9, 10, 12.

Plate 1
Fig. 1 Ridley and Latimer
Fig. 2 Cranmer
By courtesy of Mr and Mrs Eric Joyce

Section D
Religious
Details of the Figures

Plate 1
Figure 1
Subject: **Bishops Ridley and Latimer**
Title: Ridley and Latimer (transfer capitals)
Date: c. 1851
Height: 9½ in (24 cm)
Colour: Either white and gilt, or coloured in the manner of Thomas Parr.
Maker: Thomas Parr
Rarity: R. D.
Series: Fig. 2 (Cranmer); also, *figs.* 3 (Popery), 4 (Protestantism) and 5 (£10,000), *pl.* D-2.
Description: They stand, back to back, among burning faggots, a stake between them.

Underneath the title is the following inscription in u. & l. case transfer:
'Be of good comfort, Master Ridley, and play the man: we shall this day light such a candle, by God's grace, in England, as I trust shall never be put out'.
Observations: 1. See *fig.* 5 (£10,000) *pl.* D-2.
2. A similar figure fetched 130 gns at Christie's in 1969.

Figure 2
Subject: **Archbishop Cranmer**
Title: Archbishop Cranmer (transfer capitals)

Date: c. 1851
Height: 9 in (23 cm)
Colour: Either white and gilt, or coloured in the manner of Thomas Parr.
Maker: Thomas Parr
Rarity: VR. D.
Series: Fig. 1 (Ridley and Latimer); also, *figs.* 3 (Popery), 4 (Protestantism) and 5 (£10,000), *pl.* D-2.
Description: He stands, surrounded by burning faggots, his back to a stake, in prayer.

The following inscription in u. & l. case transfer appears underneath the title:
'Burnt at Oxford/March 21 1556'
Observations: 1. Cranmer's hands have been incorrectly restored. They should be more vertical.
2. See *fig.* 5 (£10,000) *pl.* D-2.
3. A similar figure fetched 180 gns at Christie's in 1969.

Plate 2
Figure 3
Subject: **Priest**
Title: Popery (transfer capitals)
Date: c. 1851
Height: 9½ in (24 cm)
Colour: Usually well coloured in the manner

of Thomas Parr; rarely white and gilt.
Maker: Thomas Parr
Rarity: Av. D.
Pair or series: Fig. 4 (Protestantism); same series as *figs.* 1 (Ridley and Latimer) and 2 (Cranmer), *pl.* D-1, and *fig.* 5 (£10,000).
Description: A young priest standing, bareheaded, in bands, soutane and cloak, holds a chained closed bible in his right hand. His left hand rests on a document inscribed, in u. & l. case transfer, 'Either we must root out the Bible or the Bible will root out us. The translators of the English Bible are to be abhorred to the depths of Hell. It would be better to be without God's law than without the Pope — Dr Troy, Archbishop of Dublin, 1816.'

Behind the document is a flag inscribed, in u. & l. case transfer, 'He that committeth his conscience to the keeping of another is no longer a free man. Freedom of conscience & freedom of thought are essential to the freedom of a nation. Therefore a nation of Catholics is a nation of Slaves'.
Observations: 1. In the late Mr Balston's book (*pl.* 38), this figure is illustrated with the right hand incorrectly restored; the priest is carrying a scroll instead of a chained bible. This mistake has been copied on

Plate 2
Fig. 3 Popery
Fig. 5 £10,000
Fig. 4 Protestantism
In the collection of
Lt.-Col. A.C.W. Kimpton

numerous occasions by restorers.
2. A similar figure fetched £50 at Sotheby's in 1969.
3. See *fig.* 5 (£10,000).

Figure 4
Subject: **Young woman**
Title: Protestantism (transfer capitals)
Date: c. 1851
Height: 9 in (23 cm)
Colour: Usually delicately coloured in the manner of Thomas Parr; rarely white and gilt.
Maker: Thomas Parr
Rarity: Av. D.
Pair or series: Fig. 3 (Popery); same series as figs. 1 (Ridley and Latimer) and 2 (Cranmer) *pl.* D-1, and *fig.* 5 (£10,000).
Description: A young woman stands, bare-headed, in long dress and bare feet. In her left hand she holds an open bible with the words 'Holy Bible' in transfer capitals. Her right hand rests on a document which is inscribed, in u. & l. case transfer, 'Search the Scriptures,' John 5.39. 'Prove all things,' Thes. 5.27. 'Let the word of Christ dwell in you richly', C. 3.16. 'To the Law and to the Testimony: if they speak not according to this word it is because there is no light in them', Isa. 8.26.
  At the back of the scroll a flag is inscribed, in u. & l. case transfer, 'The Bible, the open Bible, is the Religion of Protestants. It is like every thing else from God, free as the air we breathe. It spurns alike indulgences and Penance'.
Observations: 1. In the late Mr Balston's book (*pl.* 38), this figure is shown, incorrectly restored, with a scroll in the young woman's left hand. This illustration has been used on many occasions by restorers, and numerous figures similarly restored may be found.
2. A similar pair of figures, together with a titled version of *fig.* 39 (Raffles) *pl.* D-18, and *fig.* 18 (Wesley) *pl.* D-9, fetched 30 gns at Christie's in 1963.
3. See *fig.* 5 (£10,000).

Figure 5
Subject: **Young woman and priest**
Title: None
Date: c. 1851
Height: 9 in (23 cm)
Colour: Well coloured in the tradition of Thomas Parr.
Maker: Thomas Parr
Rarity: R. D.
Series: Same series as figs. 1 (Ridley and Latimer) and 2 (Cranmer), *pl.* D-1, and figs. 3 (Popery) and 4 (Protestantism).
Description: A young woman stands on the left, holding in her right hand a bag inscribed '£10,000'; to the right, a priest kneels, holding out a veil towards her.
Observations: 1. Balston noted that this figure and the preceding four figures, all had a somewhat pre-Victorian appearance; and furthermore, the inscription on 'Popery' was of a pronouncement made by the Archbishop of Dublin in 1816. This suggested that they belonged to the period of the agitation against Catholic emancipation. However, the figures all had the characteristics of the products of Thomas Parr, and a similar pre-Victorian style was apparent in the same potter's 'Winter's Tale' and 'Romeo and Juliet', each of which could not be earlier than 1852, see *pl.* E-1A. The recesses of the folds in Perdita's dress in 'Winter's

Plate 3
Fig. 6 Penn
In the collection of Mr Patrick Gibson

Plate 3A
Fig. 6(a) Unidentified quaker
By courtesy of Mr and Mrs Eric Joyce

Tale' showed touches of pink paint, while the projections were left white. This feature was also found in the painting of the girls' skirts in both 'Protestantism' and '£10,000'. It was Balston's view that all these facts provided proof that the figures were manufactured in 1851, the year of the violent 'No Popery' agitation, aroused by the granting of English territorial titles to bishops by the Pope.
2. The source of *fig.* 5 is an anti-catholic cartoon inscribed 'The Kidnapper' published in *Punch* in March, 1851, see *ch.* 3, *pl.* 23. The theme of a monk holding out a veil to a girl who carries a bundle labelled '£ s. d.' is identical to that of '£10,000'.
3. A similar figure, together with three other unimportant figures, fetched 42 gns at Christie's in 1967.

Plate 3
Figure 6
Subject: **William Penn**
Title: None
Height: 8¼ in (21 cm)
Colour: Well coloured in the manner of Thomas Parr.
Maker: Thomas Parr
Rarity: VR.
Description: Standing, wearing a broad-brimmed hat, long coat, waistcoat, breeches and stockings. In his right hand he holds a deed, with seal attached. It has been suggested that this represents the letters patent for his American lands.
Observations: There seems little doubt that this figure does portray William Penn, although there is no confirmatory evidence.

Plate 3A
Figure 6(a)
Subject: **Unidentified Quaker**
Title: None
Height: 9½ in (24 cm)
Colour: Largely white and gilt.
Rarity: VR.
Description: Standing, wearing a broad-brimmed hat, coat, waistcoat, breeches, stockings and shoes. His left hand is on his hip, and he holds a large loaf of bread against his right side with his right hand.
Observations: Clearly a quaker, and it is tempting to suppose it is William Penn, but there is no evidence to support this theory.

Plate 4
Figure 7
Subject: **Pope Pius IX**
Title: His Holiness the Pope (gilt script)
Date: 187–
Height: 18¼ in (46 cm)
Colour: Well coloured.
Maker: Sampson Smith
Rarity: R.
Pair: Fig. 8 (Manning)
Description: He stands in skull-cap, knee-length coat and trousers, his right hand raised in blessing. To his right, is a draped plinth with two books on it.
Observations: 1. It seems likely that the 'source' used by the potter was only half-length, otherwise he would not have ended the soutane above the knees and finished the job with trousers.
2. A similar figure fetched 30 gns at Christie's in 1964.

Plate 4
By courtesy of Mr and Mrs Eric Joyce

Fig. 7 Pius IX *Fig. 8* Manning *Fig. 9* Moody *Fig. 10* Sankey

Figure 8
Subject: **Cardinal Manning**
Title: Cardinal Manning (gilt script)
Date: *c.* 1875
Height: 18 in (45.5 cm)
Colour: Well coloured.
Maker: Sampson Smith
Rarity: VR.
Pair: *Fig.* 7 (Pius IX)
Description: He stands with his right hand on a draped pedestal. He wears a biretta, chasuble and soutane.
Observations: 1. Made cardinal in 1875.
2. A similar figure, together with a 13½ in (34.25 cm) version of *fig.* 7 (Pius IX), fetched 50 gns at Christie's in 1963.

Figure 9
Subject: **Dwight Lynam Moody**
Title: Moody (raised capitals)
Date: *c.* 1873
Height: 17 in (42.5 cm)
Colour: Well coloured, underglaze black.
Maker: Sampson Smith
Rarity: C.
Pair: *Fig.* 10 (Sankey)
Description: He stands bare-headed, with a long beard. He wears a frock-coat, waistcoat and trousers. His left hand is on his hip and his right hand rests on a book on a pedestal.
Observations: 1. The discovery, in 1948, of a mould of this figure, in a disused part of the old Sampson Smith factory, enabled a number of other similar monumental standing figures to be attributed to the same factory, see *ch.* 4, *pl.* 1.

2. Cast reproductions from the original press-mould were made for a short period.
3. The 11½ in (29 cm) version, illustrated on *pl.* D-5, is unusual in that the right leg is made from a separate mould. It has been given a special number [*fig.* 9(*a*)].
4. Although the large versions of this figure and its pair were undoubtedly made by Sampson Smith, doubt exists regarding the smaller versions because of the following entry in *Kent List B*:

Stock No.	Height in inches	Width in inches	Price per Doz. s. d.
414 Moody	11½	4¼	22 0
415 Sankey	11½	4¼	22 0

The figures are not catalogued in either of the other lists. Possibly the moulds were sold by Sampson Smith to Kent. The two listed figures may be the unusual versions referred to above.
5. Moody and Sankey made their first visit to England in 1873.
6. An example, 13¾ in (35 cm) in height, fetched 15 gns at Christie's in 1968; and another and pair, 28 gns at Christie's in 1969.

Figure 10
Subject: **Ira D. Sankey**
Title: Sankey (raised capitals)
Date: *c.* 1873
Height: 17 in (42.5 cm)
Colour: Well coloured, underglaze black.
Maker: Sampson Smith
Pair: *Fig.* 9 (Moody)

Description: Standing bare-headed, with moustache and whiskers. He wears a frock-coat, waistcoat and trousers. His right hand is on his hip, and his left hand rests on a book on a pedestal.
Observations: 1. The 11½ in (29 cm) version, illustrated on *pl.* D-5, is unusual in that the left leg is made from a separate mould. It has been given a special number [*fig.* 10(*a*)].
2. A similar, 17 in (42.5 cm), pair of figures fetched 16 gns at Christie's in 1966. Another pair fetched 28 gns in 1966; and another pair fetched 25 gns in the same rooms in 1967.
3. See *observations* for preceding figure.

Plate 5 (Left)
Fig. 9(a) Moody
Fig. 11 St Vincent Paul
Fig. 10(a) Sankey
Note: Moody's right leg and Sankey's left leg have been made from separate moulds. Compare with figures illustrated on preceeding plate.

Plate 6 (Right)
Fig. 12 Cooke
By courtesy of Mr and Mrs Eric Joyce

Plate 5
Figure 9(a)
Subject: **Dwight Lynam Moody**
Height: 11½ in (29 cm)
Observations: See *fig.* 9 (Moody) *pl.* D-4.

Figure 10(a)
Subject: **Ira D. Sankey**
Height: 11½ in (29 cm)
Observations: See *fig.* 10 (Sankey) *pl.* D-4.

Figure 11
Subject: **Vincent de Paul**
Title: St Vincent Paul (indented capitals)
Height: 14¾ in (37.5 cm)
Colour: Well coloured.

Rarity: VR. D. A.
Description: He is standing with a child in his arms. He wears a skull-cap, soutane and cloak.
Observations: Probably connected in some way with the St Vincent de Paul Charitable Society.

Plate 6
Figure 12
Subject: **Revd. Henry Cooke**
Title: Cooke DD (raised capitals)
Height: 10½ in (26.5 cm)
Colour: White, gilt and black.
Rarity: VR.
Description: He stands bare-headed, in a Gothic niche. He wears bands, surplice and trousers (*no* cassock). Clock-face below title.
Observations: I have seen only three examples of this very rare piece. Of these, only one had the figure illustrated on this plate in the niche, *i.e.* a priest wearing trousers but no cassock. Presumably, this is a true portrait of Henry Cooke. The other two pieces, see *fig.* 12(a), *pl.* D-6A, are the same as the former piece, except that the figure in the niche wears a cassock. This figure is identical to that used in the piece portraying Wesley, *fig.* 13, *pl.* D-6A.

Plate 6A
Figure 12(a)
Subject: **Revd. Henry Cooke** (Wesley)
Title: Cooke DD (raised capitals)
Height: 10½ in (26.5 cm)
Colour: White, gilt and black.
Rarity: VR.
Description: He stands bare-headed, in a Gothic niche. He wears bands, surplice and cassock.
Observations: See *fig.* 12 (Cooke) *pl.* D-6.

Figure 13
Subject: **Charles or John Wesley**
Title: Wesley (raised capitals)
Height: 11¼ in (28.5 cm)
Colour: White, gilt and black.
Rarity: C.
Description: Standing bare-headed, in a Gothic niche, wearing bands, surplice and cassock; right arm raised, an open bible in his left hand. Clock-face below title.
Observations: 1. The whole piece bears a striking resemblance to the engraving of the proposed monument to John Wesley, which appeared in *The Illustrated London News* on May 24th, 1856, see *ch.* 3, *pl.* 24. On the other hand, the figure is very similar to the drawing of Charles Wesley in the first Minton design book, see *pl.* D-15.
2. See *fig.* 14 (Wesley) *pl.* D-7 for prices.

Plate 6A
Fig. 12(a) Cooke
Fig. 13 Wesley

Section D. Religious

Plate 7 (Left)
Fig. 14 Wesley
In the collection of
Lt.-Col. A.C.W. Kimpton

Plate 8 (Right)
Fig. 15 John Wesley
Fig. 16 Charles Wesley

Plate 7
Figure 14
Subject: **? Revd. John Wesley**
Title: Wesley (raised capitals)
Height: $11\frac{1}{4}$ in (28.5 cm)
Colour: White, gilt and black.
Rarity: C.
Description: He is standing half-length in pulpit, bare-headed, in bands and surplice; an open bible in front of him, his right arm raised. Clock face in front of pulpit.
Observations: 1. Probably John Wesley, but it could be intended to portray Charles.
2. *Fig.* 13 (Wesley) *pl.* D-6A, *fig.* 14 (Wesley) and *fig.* 44 (Spurgeon) *pl.* D-22 fetched 12 gns at Christie's in 1963. A similar lot fetched 20 gns in the same rooms in 1964, and another similar lot fetched 28 gns in the same rooms in 1967.

Plate 8
Figure 15
Subject: **Revd. John Wesley**
Title: Rev⁴ J, Wesley (gilt script)
Date: c. 1850
Height: $10\frac{3}{4}$ in (27 cm)
Colour: White, gilt and black.
Rarity: VR.
Description: Bust on square plinth with circular base.
Observations: A very fine bust, clearly Victorian.

Figure 16
Subject: **Revd. Charles Wesley**
Title: None
Height: $5\frac{3}{4}$ in (14.5 cm)
Colour: White, gilt and black.
Rarity: Av.

Description: He stands bare-headed, with an open bible in his left hand and his right arm raised. He wears bands, surplice and cassock. The latter is short, and exposes stockings and shoes. Circular solid base.
Observations: 1. See *observations fig.* 35 (C. Wesley) *pl.* D-15, for reasons for supposing that *fig.* 16 portrays Charles Wesley.
2. Similar in all respects, other than size, to *fig.* 35, *pl.* D-15 and *fig.* 37, *pl.* D-17.

Plate 9
Figure 17
Subject: **Revd. John Wesley**
Title: None
Height: 5 in (12.75 cm)
Colour: Well coloured.
Rarity: Av.
Description: Standing bare-headed, in bands,

Plate 9
In the collections of
Lt.-Col. A.C.W. Kimpton
and the author

Fig. 17 John Wesley   *Fig.* 18 John Wesley   *Fig.* 19 John Wesley   *Fig.* 20 John Wesley   *Fig.* 21 John Wesley   *Fig.* 22 John Wesley

Plate 10
*In the collections of
Lt.-Col. A.C.W. Kimpton
and the author*

Fig. 23 Charles Wesley *Fig.* 24 John Wesley *Fig.* 25 John Wesley *Fig.* 26 John Wesley *Fig.* 27 John Wesley

Plate 9 continued

surplice and cassock. The latter is short, and exposes stockings and shoes; open bible in his left hand, his right hand turning over a page. Sloping circular hollow base.
Observations: This figure and all others illustrated on this plate are similar. In the light of the title applied to *fig.* 21, all may be assumed to portray John Wesley.
2. The standing figures of both Charles and John Wesley, can be very deceptive. Very often one or other hand has been restored, and as often as not, incorrectly restored. Possibly some of the figures illustrated fall into this category.

Figure 18
Subject: **Revd. John Wesley**
Title: Wesley (indented capitals)
Height: 7 in (17.5 cm)
Colour: White and black, occasionally gilt.
Rarity: C.
Description: Similar to *fig.* 17, except that the cassock is full-length, and for other minor differences. Solid base.
Observations: See *fig.* 17 (J. Wesley).

Figure 19
Subject: **Revd. John Wesley**
Title: Wesley (gilt transfer capitals)
Height: 6¾ in (17 cm)
Colour: White, gilt and black.
Rarity: Av.
Description: Similar to *fig.* 17, except for minor differences. Hollow base.
Observations: See *fig.* 17 (J. Wesley).

Figure 20
Subject: **Revd. John Wesley**
Title: Wesley (gilt script)
Height: 7 in (17.5 cm)
Colour: White, gilt and black.
Rarity: Av.
Description: Similar to *fig.* 17, except for minor differences. Solid base.
Observations: See *fig.* 17 (J. Wesley).

Figure 21
Subject: **Revd. John Wesley**
Title: Rev^d. J. Wesley (gilt script)
Height: 6½ in (16.5 cm)

Colour: White, gilt and black.
Rarity: VR.
Description: Similar to *fig.* 17, except for minor differences. Solid base.
Observations: Allows us to assume that all similar figures portray John rather than Charles Wesley.

Figure 22
Subject: **Revd. John Wesley**
Title: None
Height: 5¼ in (13.5 cm)
Colour: White, gilt and black.
Rarity: Av.
Description: Similar to *fig.* 17, except for minor differences. Solid base.
Observations: See *fig.* 17 (J. Wesley).

Plate 10
Figure 23
Subject: **Revd. Charles Wesley**
Title: None
Height: 6¾ in (17 cm)
Colour: White, gilt and black.
Rarity: VR.
Description: Similar to *fig.* 16 (C. Wesley) *pl.* D-8. Solid hexagonal base.
Observations: See *observations fig.* 35 (C. Wesley) *pl.* D-15, for reasons for supposing that *fig.* 16 portrays Charles Wesley.

Figure 24
Subject: **Revd. John Wesley**
Title: None
Height: 7½ in (19 cm)
Colour: White, gilt and black.
Rarity: Av.
Description: Similar to *fig.* 21 (J. Wesley) *pl.* D-9, other than for minor differences. Solid base.
Observations: See *fig.* 17 (J. Wesley) *pl.* D-9.

Figure 25
Subject: **Revd. John Wesley**
Title: J. Wesley, M.A. (gilt script)
Height: 8½ in (21.5 cm)
Colour: White, gilt and black.
Rarity: VR.
Description: Similar to *fig.* 24, except for

minor differences. The base is circular, stepped and solid.

Figure 26
Subject: **Revd. John Wesley**
Title: None
Height: 7¾ in (20 cm)
Colour: White, black and gilt.
Rarity: Av.
Description: Similar to *fig.* 25, but the base, although circular and solid, is not stepped.

Figure 27
Subject: **Revd. John Wesley**
Title: None
Height: 7¼ in (18.25 cm)
Colour: White, black and gilt.
Rarity: Av.
Description: Very similar to *fig.* 21 (J. Wesley) *pl.* D-9. Solid base.

Plate 11
Figure 28
Subject: **Revd. Charles Wesley**
Title: None
Height: 5¾ in (14.5 cm)
Colour: White, gilt and black.
Rarity: VR.
Description: Similar to *fig.* 23 (C. Wesley) *pl.* D-10. The right hand is raised in blessing; the left hand holds an open bible with *VII* on one page and *VIII* on the other page. Square solid base.
Observations: 1. See *observations fig.* 35 (C. Wesley) *pl.* D-15, for reasons for supposing that *fig.* 28 portrays Charles Wesley.
2. The open bibles in Wesley figures are occasionally found with the pages numbered, usually *VI*, *VII*, or *VIII*. One has been noted with 'St Luke' on one page and '*VII*' on the other. The significance of this is not known.

Plate 12
Figure 29
Subject: **? Revd. John Wesley**
Title: None
Height: 5¾ in (14.5 cm)
Colour: White, gilt and black.
Rarity: R.

Section D. Religious

Plate 11 (Left)
Fig. 28 Charles Wesley
By courtesy of Mr John Hall

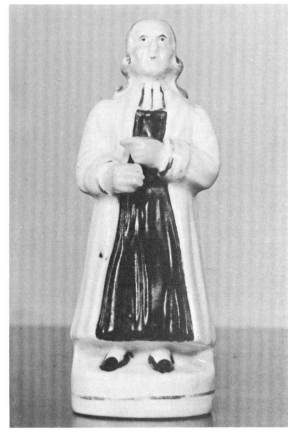

Plate 12 (Right)
Fig. 29 John Wesley

Description: Bare-headed with bands, sur-plice and cassock. He points to his right with his left hand. Solid circular base.
Observations: Generally assumed to be John Wesley. It is closer to the figure illustrated in Minton's first figure design book (no. 165) than any known figure, see *pl.* D-15.

Plate 12A
Figure 30
Subject: **Pere Moulaert**
Title: None
Date: *c.* 1850
Height: 3⅛ in (8 cm)
Colour: Black and white.
Rarity: VR.
Pair: *Fig.* 31 (Hallahan). Same series as *fig.* 31(*a*)(Unidentified nun).
Description: Similar to *fig.* 33 (Moulaert),

except that he wears a three-cornered hat and his hands are crossed on his chest with a book in his right hand.
Observations: See *fig.* 33 (Moulaert).

Figure 31
Subject: **Sister Hallahan**
Title: None
Date: *c.* 1850
Height: 3⅜ in (8.5 cm)
Colour: Black and white.
Rarity: VR.
Pair: *Fig.* 30 (Moulaert). Same series as *fig.* 31(*a*) (Unidentified nun).
Description: She stands, a hood over her head hanging below her knees behind. She wears a long-skirted dress, no scapular; her hands are folded over her breast and a rosary and cross hang from her left wrist.

Observations: See *fig.* 33 (Moulaert).

Figure 31(a)
Subject: **Unidentified nun**
Title: None
Date: *c.* 1850
Height: 3¼ in (8.25 cm)
Colour: Black and white.
Rarity: R.
Series: Same series as *fig.* 30 (Moulaert) and *fig.* 31 (Hallahan).
Description: She is standing, wearing a short hood, long bodice and an apron. Her arms hang down with the hands clasped, holding a cross on a long chain.
Observations: Her clothes suggest that she is of a lower standing than Sister Hallahan.

Fig. 30 Moulaert   *Fig.* 31 Hallahan   *Fig.* 31(a) Unidentified nun   *Fig.* 32 Hallahan   *Fig.* 33 Moulaert

Plate 16 (Left)
Fig. 36 John Fletcher
To the right of the figure is an engraving of the Revd. John Fletcher without doubt the source of the figure.

Plate 17 (Right)
Fig. 37 Charles Wesley
*By courtesy of
Mr and Mrs Eric Joyce*

Plate 16
Figure 36
Subject: **Revd. John Fletcher**
Title: John Fletcher (gilt script)
Height: 6¾ in (17 cm)
Colour: White, gilt and black.
Maker: Unknown
Rarity: VR. D.
Pair: A titled pair to this figure probably exists, see *fig.* 37 (C. Wesley) *pl.* D-17.
Description: Bare-headed, his hair is neither as long nor as curly as that of either Charles or John Wesley. He wears bands, cassock and gown, stockings and shoes. His right hand is across his chest and he holds a skull in his left hand.
Observations: 1. A striking resemblance between this figure and the engraving illustrated in the same plate will be noted.
2. Holy men are often depicted studying the skull, the symbol of mortality. It serves to remind people of the life hereafter and of the shortness of this life.

Plate 17
Figure 37
Subject: **Revd. Charles Wesley**
Title: None
Height: 6¾ in (17 cm)
Colour: White, gilt and black.
Maker: Unknown
Rarity: VR.
Pair: Probably a pair to *fig.* 36 (Fletcher) *pl.* D-16, although a titled version has not yet been recorded. I have however, heard of, although not personally seen, a matching pair of both figures, untitled.
Description: Similar in all respects, other than size, to *fig.* 35 (C. Wesley) *pl.* D-15.
Observations: Unfortunately I have never handled this figure, which was formerly in the collection of Mr and Mrs Eric Joyce. It appears that Wesley's right hand has been incorrectly restored.

D334

Plate 18
Figure 38
Subject: **Revd. Edward Goulburn**
Title: Coulburn (*sic*) (gilt script)
Height: 11½ in (29 cm)
Colour: Well coloured.
Rarity: R. D.
Description: He stands bare-headed, in a pulpit. His left hand rests on a bible; his right on a drape over the top of the pulpit. He wears a choker, low-cut waistcoat and jacket.
Observations: Balston stated that this surname with a 'C', could not be found in the *D.N.B.*, in the *B.M. Library Catalogue*, nor in the *London Telephone Directory* (1958). Moreover, the Librarian of the Evangelical Library could find no record of a minister of this name either. It seemed likely to Balston that the 'C' was a mistake for a 'G' and that the figure represented Dr E. M. Goulburn, Headmaster of Rugby School (1849–57) and Dean of Norwich (1866–97), a celebrated preacher and author of three popular devotional books. I have now seen five examples of this figure, and all are titled similarly. If the figure does represent Goulburn, it is the only known example of a figure of a contemporary Church of England clergyman; popular possibly because he started as an Evangelical, although later he became a High Churchman.

Figure 39
Subject: **Revd. Thomas Raffles**
Title: Dʳ Raffles (gilt script)
Height: 9½ in (24 cm)
Colour: Usually white, gilt and black.
Rarity: R. D. (titled); Av. (untitled).
Description: Standing bare-headed, in bands, cassock and gown. There is a pedestal to his right. His hands are crossed, his left hand clasping a bible, the lower edge of which is supported on the pedestal.

Observations: 1. An identical figure has been found titled 'Revd J. Fletcher' in gilt script (*fig.* 40).
2. See *observations* fig. 4 (Protestantism) *pl.* D-2 for auction price. In addition, an untitled figure fetched 32 gns at Christie's in 1969.

Figure 40
Subject: **? Revd. John Fletcher** (Raffles)
Title: Revᵈ J. Fletcher (gilt script)
Height: 9½ in (24 cm)
Colour: Usually white, gilt and black.
Rarity: VR. D. (titled); Av. (untitled).
Description: As for *fig.* 39 (Raffles).
Observations: Balston considered that this figure represented the *Revd. Joseph Fletcher* (1784–1843). Joseph Fletcher had a son, also called *Joseph* (1816–76). There is certainly no resemblance to the *Revd. John Fletcher*, see *fig.* 36, *pl.* D-16, although the potter may well have intended that the figure represent him. It is not known, in fact, whether *fig.* 40 is like either Dr Raffles, Joseph Fletcher the elder, or Joseph Fletcher the younger.

Plate 19
Figure 41
Subject: **? Revd. Thomas Raffles**
Title: None
Height: 9½ in (24 cm)
Colour: White, gilt and black.
Rarity: R.
Description: Identical in all respects to *figs.* 39 (Raffles) and 40 (? Fletcher), *pl.* D-18, except that his right forearm rests on the bible and he does not clasp it with his left hand.
Observations: 1. A titled version of this figure has not been recorded.
2. The minor differences in the positioning of the hands is a fact and not an error of restoration.

Section D. Religious

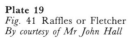

Plate 19
Fig. 41 Raffles or Fletcher
By courtesy of Mr John Hall

Plate 20
Fig. 42 Spurgeon

Plate 21
The Revd. Charles Spurgeon (1834-92)
The striking resemblance between this engraving and
the figures illustrated on *pls.* D-20 and 22 leaves little
doubt that this was their source.
By courtesy of Mr. John Hall

Plate 20
Figure 42
Subject: **Revd. Charles Haddon Spurgeon**
Title: C H Spurgeon (raised capitals)
Date: *c.* 1856
Height: 12½ in (31.75 cm)
Colour: Well coloured.
Rarity: VR. D. A.

Description: He stands bare-headed, his
right arm raised. He wears a frock-coat, bow-
tie, low-cut waistcoat and trousers. To his
left is a pedestal with three books on it.
Observations: The striking resemblance
between this figure and the engraving of
Spurgeon illustrated on *pl.* D-21, will be
noted.

Plate 21
Revd. Charles Haddon Spurgeon
This engraving, by an unknown artist, is
the source of *fig.* 42 (Spurgeon) *pl.* D-20.
The potter had to design the lower half of
the figure himself. The engraving is also the
source of *figs.* 43 and 44, *pl.* D-22.

D335

Plate 22 (Left)
Fig. 43 Spurgeon
Fig. 44 Spurgeon
In the collection of
Lt.-Col. A.C.W. Kimpton

Plate 23A (Right)
Revd. John Elias
(1774-1841)
Line-engraving by
Lowenstam, published by
William Mackenzie of
London, Caerleon and
Abertawe *(no date).*
By permission of the
National Museum of Wales

Plate 23
By courtesy of
Mr and Mrs Eric Joyce

Fig. 45 Elias   *Fig.* 46 Bryan   *Fig.* 47 Gurney   *Fig.* 48 Christmas Evans

Plate 22

Figure 43
Subject: **Revd. Charles Haddon Spurgeon**
Title: CH Spurgeon (raised capitals)
Date: *c.* 1856
Height: 11½ in (29 cm)
Colour: Usually white, gilt and black.
Rarity: C.
Description: Standing half-length, in pulpit.

D336

Dress and stance as in *fig.* 42, *pl.* D-20; an open bible in front of him.
Observations: 1. Based on the engraving of Spurgeon illustrated on *pl.* D-21.
2. A similar figure fetched 12 gns at Christie's in 1969.

Figure 44
Subject: **Revd. Charles Haddon Spurgeon**

Title: C H/Spurgeon (raised capitals)
Date: *c.* 1856
Height: 11¾ in (29.75 cm)
Colour: Usually white, gilt and black.
Rarity: C.
Description: Similar dress and stance to *fig.* 42, *pl.* D-20. He is standing, half-length, in a pulpit, the outlines of which are plain, instead of curved as in *fig.* 43. The base of

Colour Plate 39
Dwight Lynam Moody and Ira D. Sankey. *Figs.* 9 and 10, *pl.* D-4. See page 327.

Plate 22 continued
the pulpit is solid, instead of having two fenestrations.
Observations: 1. See *fig*. 14 (Wesley) *pl*. D-7 for auction prices.
2. Based on the engraving of Spurgeon illustrated on *pl*. D-21.

Plate 23
Figure 45
Subject: **Revd. John Elias**
Title: Rev. John Elies (*sic*) (raised capitals)
Height: 14 in (35.5 cm)
Colour: Well coloured.
Rarity: R.
Pair: Fig. 48 (Christmas Evans)
Description: He stands bare-headed, in frock-coat, breeches, stockings and shoes; a bible in his left hand, with his fingers between the leaves; his left elbow resting on a pedestal.
Observations: 1. Occasionally the title differs. For instance the following title in raised capitals has been seen on two occasions: 'Evg. John Blies'.
2. Based on a line-engraving by L. Lowenstam, published by William Mackenzie of London, Caerleon and Abertawe, see *pl*. D-23A.
3. A similar figure fetched £85 at Sotheby's in 1967.

Figure 46
Subject: **Revd. John Bryan**
Title: J. Bryan (raised capitals)
Height: 10½ in (26.5 cm)
Colour: Well coloured.
Rarity: Av.
Description: He stands bare-headed, in frock-coat, breeches, stockings and shoes.

He is very portly. His right hand rests on a bible lying on a pedestal.
Observations: 1. Identified from a lithograph of the Revd. John Bryan in the National Library of Wales, see *ch*. 3, *pl*. 25A.
2. A similar figure, together with *fig*. 32 (Wood) *pl*. G-16, fetched 62 gns at Christie's in 1965.

Figure 47
Subject: **Joseph John Gurney**
Title: J. J. Gurney (gilt script)
Height: 11¼ in (28.5 cm)
Colour: Well coloured.
Rarity: R.
Description: He stands bare-headed, in cut-away coat, waistcoat and trousers. His right hand is on his hip and his left hand supports a bible on a pedestal. His legs are crossed.
Observations: 1. There is a 10 in (25 cm) version of this figure which is identical except for an oval base.
2. A similar figure fetched 38 gns at Christie's in 1965.

Figure 48
Subject: **Revd. Christmas Evans**
Title: Rev Christmas Evans (raised capitals)
Height: 13½ in (34.25 cm)
Colour: Well coloured.
Rarity: R.
Pair: Fig. 45 (Elias)
Description: He stands bare-headed, in tailcoat, breeches, stockings and shoes. His right eye is closed. His left forearm rests on two bibles lying on a pedestal. He holds a bible in his right hand.

Observations: 1. Based on a line-engraving by E. Pick, published by William Mackenzie of London, Edinburgh and Glasgow, see *pl*. D-23B.
2. A similar figure, with *fig*. 16 (O'Connell) *pl*. B-2, fetched 40 gns at Christie's in 1963. Another, with *fig*. 39 (Raffles) *pl*. D-18 (untitled version) fetched 26 gns at Christie's in 1964.

Plate 23A
Revd. John Elias
Line-engraving by L. Lowenstam, published by William Mackenzie of London, Caerleon and Abertawe (n.d.). It is the source of *fig*. 45, *pl*. D-23.

Plate 23B
Revd. Christmas Evans
Line-engraving by E. Pick, published by William Mackenzie of London, Edinburgh and Glasgow (n.d.). It is the source of *fig*. 48, *pl*. D-23.

Plate 24
Figure 49
Subject: **? Revd. Robert Trogwy Evans**
Title: Mr Robert Evans (raised capitals)
Date: *c*. 1856
Height: 11½ in (29 cm)
Colour: Well coloured.
Rarity: VR.
Description: He stands bare-headed, in cravat, frock-coat, waistcoat and trousers. In his right hand he holds a scroll against his chest. His left arm rests on a fluted pedestal.
Observations: This figure bears a striking

Plate 23B
Revd. Christmas Evans (1766-1838)
Line-engraving by E. Pick, published by William Mackenzie of London, Edinburgh and Glasgow (no date).
By permission of the National Museum of Wales

Plate 24
Fig. 49 Robert Evans
Fig. 42 (section G) Palmer
Note the striking resemblance between the two figures.
By courtesy of Mr and Mrs Eric Joyce

Plate 24A
Fig. 50 Huntington

Plate 24B
William Huntington (1745-1813)
An ivory bust, c.1812
By courtesy of the Victoria and Albert Museum

Plate 24C
Edward Jenner (1749-1823)
This portrait by James Northcote (1803) should
also be compared with *fig.* 50, *pl.* D-24A.
By courtesy of the National Portrait Gallery

resemblance to *fig.* 42 (Palmer) *pl.* G-18A.
The fact that Palmer's title is on a plaque
suggests that *fig.* 49 preceded it. Nobody with
the name of Robert Evans was associated
with the trial of William Palmer. However,
when Palmer left school at the age of seven-
teen, his father apprenticed him to Messrs
Evans & Sons, the wholesale chemists of
Lord Street, Liverpool. He was sacked
a few months later, for stealing money
enclosed by customers in letters addressed to
the firm. This episode is described in Robert
Graves's *They Hanged my Saintly Billy*, a biography of William Palmer. The christian
names of Mr Evans Senior and Mr Evans
Junior are not given in this volume but in
any event it is extremely unlikely that the
figure portrays either. The scroll in the
right hand suggests either a political or
theatrical portrait. Balston put forward the
possibility that the figure represented the
Revd. Robert Trogwy Evans, whose name
appeared in the *Dictionary of Welsh Biography*
(1959). He was a man with a considerable
reputation and exactly of the same age
as the Rugeley poisoner. Balston discounted
his original suggestion that the figure
portrayed the Ven. Robert Wilson Evans,
Archdeacon of Westmorland who at the
time of the Rugeley murders was sixty-
seven. It seemed improbable that he would
have been portrayed so like Palmer, a robust
young man of thirty-two. My personal feeling is that the evidence of identification is
still inconclusive.

Plate 24A
Figure 50
Subject: **William Huntington**
Title: None
Height: $8\frac{1}{2}$ in (21.5 cm)

Colour: Well coloured.
Rarity: VR.
Description: He sits bare-headed, in an armchair, in coat, high-cut waistcoat, breeches
and stockings. His left hand grasps a book
which is resting on a pedestal.

Observations: 1. How this figure was identified
originally I do not know, but there is little
doubt that the identification is correct as is
evidenced by comparison of the figure with
a photograph of an ivory bust of Huntington
in the Victoria and Albert Museum, see next
plate.
2. He has been described as 'tall and strongly
built with irregular features and ruddy
complexion, ample forehead'.
3. Huntington wrote his own epitaph:

Here lies the coalheaver, who departed this life
July 1st, 1813, in the 69th year of his age, beloved of
his God, but abhorred of men. The omniscient Judge
at the grand assize shall ratify and confirm this to the
confusion of many thousands, for England and its
metropolis shall know that there hath been a prophet
among them.

Plate 24B
William Huntington
An ivory bust, *c.* 1812 [$4\frac{1}{2}$ in (11.5 cm)] in the
Victoria and Albert Museum. Comparison
with *fig.* 50, *pl.* D-24A leaves little room for
doubt that Balston was correct in his identification.

Plate 24C
Edward Jenner
Portrait (1803) by James Northcote in the
National Portrait Gallery. Note the similarity
between it and *fig.* 50, *pl.* B-24A. This figure
is catalogued in the Gloucester City Museum
as *Edward Jenner* (1749–1823), the discoverer
of vaccination. The museum acquired the
figure as part of a bequest. The Jenner
attribution was made by the owner now

dead. In 1840, an act of the English parliament provided for the payment of vaccination fees out of the rates. Vaccination was
first made compulsory in the United Kingdom in 1853. Whether the figure portrays
Huntington, Jenner or someone else will
never be known with certainty until the
discovery of an identical portrait which must
almost certainly exist.

Plate 25
Figure 51
Subject: **Father Theobald Mathew**
Title: Father Mathew (gilt script)
Date: *c.* 1843
Height: $6\frac{3}{4}$ in (17 cm)
Colour: Black, gilt and white.
Rarity: VR. D.
Description: He stands bare-headed, in stock,
long frock-coat and high boots. His right arm
is raised before him. His left hand hangs by
the side and grasps a top hat (*open end up*).
Observations: Very similar to, and probably
based on, the engraving of Father Mathew
administering the 'Temperance Pledge',
illustrated in *ch.* 3, *pl.* 25B.

Plate 26
Figure 52
Subject: **Father Theobald Mathew**
Title: None
Date: *c.* 1843
Height: $5\frac{1}{8}$ in (13 cm)
Colour: Black, gilt and white.
Rarity: VR.
Description: He stands bare-headed, in
stock, long frock-coat and high boots. His
right arm is raised and his left hand, with no
hat in it, rests on his thigh.
Observations: Identified from the engraving
of Father Mathew illustrated in *ch.* 3, *pl.*

Colour Plate 40
General Booth. *Fig.* 55, *pl.* D-28. See page 342.

Colour Plate 41
Revd. Charles Haddon Spurgeon. *Fig.* 43, *pl.* D-22. See page 336.

Section D. Religious

Plate 25 (Left)
Fig. 51 Mathew
This figure, largely decorated in underglaze black, exemplifies the tendency of the compound to show a brown or bluish tinge, particularly when sparingly applied.

Plate 26 (Right)
Fig. 52 Mathew
Fig. 53 Mathew

Plate 27 (Left)
Fig. 54 Evan Roberts
In the collection of
Mr D.P.M. Michael

Plate 27A (Right)
Evan Roberts (1878-1951)
A photograph taken at the time of the great religious revival in Wales, c.1905.
By courtesy of
Mrs E. Holden

THE GREAT REVIVAL IN WALES.   Mr. EVAN ROBERTS

Plate 26 continued

25B; also from engravings which appeared in *The Illustrated London News* of August 5th 1843.

Figure 53
Subject: **Father Theobald Mathew**
Title: None
Date: *c.* 1843
Height: 6 in (15.25 cm)
Colour: Black, gilt and white.
Rarity: VR.
Description: Standing, dressed similarly to *figs.* 51 and 52. His right arm is raised, and

his left arm hangs by his side with a top hat in his hand (*open end down*).
Observations: It is of interest to note that the identities of *figs.* 52 and 53 were established before the discovery of the 'titled' *fig.* 51. The identifications had been based on engravings such as that illustrated in *ch.* 3, *pl.* 25B.

Plate 27
Figure 54
Subject: **Evan Roberts**
Title: Evan Roberts (gilt script)
Date: *c.* 1905

Height: 13½ in (34.25 cm)
Colour: White, gilt and black.
Maker: In the style of Sampson Smith.
Rarity: VR.
Description: He stands bare-headed, his right arm raised, his left hand resting on a pedestal. He wears a frock-coat, waistcoat, trousers and shoes.
Observations: 1. A post-Victorian figure which, had it not been possible to accurately date, might well have been attributed to the late Victorian era.
2. It is interesting to note that the potter still managed to obtain a passable likeness of his subject, see *pl.* D-27A.

D341

Plate 28 *Fig.* 55 Booth   *Fig.* 56 Booth   **Plate 29** *Fig.* 57 Band of Hope

Plate 27A
Evan Roberts
A photograph taken at the time of the great religious revival in Wales, *c.* 1905. Compare with *fig.* 54, *pl.* D-27.

Plate 28
Figure 55
Subject: **General Booth**
Title: None
Date: *c.* 1900
Height: 14 in (35.5 cm)
Colour: Well coloured, underglaze blue
Maker: Unknown, see *observations*.
Rarity: R.
Description: A bust with no pedestal. He wears a Salvation Army cap and uniform and has a long flowing beard. The cap-band is inscribed 'THE SALVATION ARMY'. On his jersey is a crowned device inscribed 'BLOOD AND FIRE', and on his coat collar and shoulder straps are further crowned devices inscribed 'S', all in gold, probably hand-painted—a cast figure.
Observations: Balston described this bust as follows:

. . . one bright spot in this period (1880–1901) . . . The great white beard suggests that it was not made earlier than the nineties, since he was only born in 1829. Both in its size and in being a cast figure it differs from all other good portrait figures of the Victorian era, and it is the only portrait with underglaze blue which must be dated later than 1863.

There is however, considerable doubt about this figure in the minds of other collectors, both as regards its date and its provenance. Many do not attribute the figure to Staffordshire at all, and others think that it should be dated to later than the 90's, possibly *c.* 1912, the date of the general's death. Colonel Mary Booth, grand-daughter of General Booth, an enlarged copy of whose bust of the general modelled in 1904, may now be seen in Westminster Abbey, wrote to me:

It is quite likely that it was produced in 1912, when my grandfather died. Many copies of my bust have been made and it may have inspired the one who made this bust. Of course, there are many photographs that could have been used.

Figure 56
Subject: **General Booth**
Title: None
Date: *c.* 1900
D342

Height: 9¾ in (24.5 cm)
Colour: Well coloured.
Rarity: VR.
Description: Bust on pedestal which is attached. He is bare-headed and wears uniform of the Salvation Army. His beard is more shaped and less flowing than that of *fig.* 55. There is a raised 'S' on either side of his collar and 'SALV.' in indented capitals is visible on the shirt front. Hollow base.
Observations: More likely to emanate from Staffordshire than the preceding figure, and probably a little earlier.

Plate 29
Figure 57
Subject: **The Band of Hope**
Title: Band/of/Hope (raised capitals)
Date: *c.* 1847
Height: 6 in (15.25 cm)
Colour: Usually poorly coloured.
Rarity: Av.
Description: Two little girls in plumed hats and short skirts hold a scroll upon which is inscribed 'Band/of/Hope'.
Observations: The Band of Hope was the first temperance organization for children. It was founded in Leeds, in 1847, for children who had taken the pledge.

Plate 30
Figure 58
Subject: **The Band of Hope**
Title: Band/of/Hope (raised capitals)
Date: *c.*1847
Height: 10 in (25 cm)
Colour: Usually poorly coloured.
Rarity: Av.
Description: Two children stand, bare-headed, in short skirts, and a third sits between them in a long skirt. Above, is a watch-holder surmounted by two flags bearing the title 'Band/of/Hope'.
Observations: The Band of Hope was the first temperance organization for children. It was founded in Leeds, in 1847, for children who had taken the pledge.

Figure 59
Subject: **The Band of Hope**
Title: Band of Hope (raised capitals)
Date: *c.* 1847
Height: 14 in (35.5 cm)

Colour: Well coloured.
Rarity: Av.
Description: Hope stands bare-headed, with a shield over her left arm. To her right is a kilted child holding a square flag, and to her left a tree trunk with a serpent coiled round it.
Observations: See preceding figure.

Figure 60
Subject: **The Independent Order of Good Templars**
Title: I O G T (raised capitals)
Date: *c.* 1868
Height: 11¼ in (28.5 cm)
Colour: A 'porridge' school piece. Usually uncoloured, but well coloured examples turn up occasionally, see *pl.* D-30A.
Maker: Sampson Smith
Rarity: Av.
Description: Three officials of the Order sit at a table covered with a cloth inscribed 'I O G T'. The centre figure behind the table is a bearded man. On each side is a woman in a hat in the style of the early seventies (*cf.* Princess Louise, *pl.* A-77). All three wear scarves which are embossed as follows, from left to right: 'R.H.S.' 'W.G.T.' and 'L.H.S.' These initials may stand for 'Right Honorary Secretary', 'Worshipful Grand Templar' and 'Left Honorary Secretary'. The letters are not easily decipherable in the uncoloured versions.
Observations: The order was introduced into Great Britain in 1868.

Figure 61
Subject: **The Independent Order of Good Templars**
Title: None
Date: *c.* 1868
Height: 9½ in (24 cm)
Colour: Well coloured.
Rarity: VR.
Description: Similar to *fig.* 60, but the central figure has no beard and holds a book in his left hand. There is no title nor are the scarves inscribed with initials.
Observations: See preceding figure.

Plate 30
T: *Fig.* 58 Band of Hope
Fig. 60 Good Templars
Fig. 61 Good Templars

B: *Fig.* 59 Band of Hope
Fig. 62 Good Templars
Fig. 63 Fountain

Figure 62
Subject: **The Independent Order of Good Templars**
Title: Faith / Hope / and / Charity (*on the pedestal*); The Good Templars Motto (*on the base*), both in raised capitals.
Date: *c.* 1868
Height: 15½ in (39.25 cm)
Colour: Usually sparsely coloured.
Rarity: Av.
Description: Three women stand, bareheaded, in long dresses. The one in the centre holds an anchor which rests on a square pedestal. The woman on the right carries a child in her left arm, and the woman on the left holds an open book in her left hand.
Observations: See *fig.* 60. (IOGT).

Figure 63
Subject: **Fountain, 1861**
Title: Fountain/1861 (raised capitals)
Date: 1861
Height: 15 in (38 cm)
Colour: Usually sparsely coloured.
Rarity: R.
Description: A girl stands on a high pedestal, wearing a long dress and shawl. To her right, stands a young man with his legs crossed holding up a mug in his right hand into which she pours from a jug. To her left, stands a woman in a low plumed hat and long dress.
Observations: 1. The man is dressed identically to the man portrayed in *fig.* 218, *pl.* A-70. This has enabled that figure to be dated and constitutes part of the evidence for supposing it portrays Prince Louis of Hesse.
2. See *pl.* D-31 and *p.* 375.

Plate 30A
Fig. 60 Good Templars
One of the relatively rare examples of a
'porridge' piece well coloured. Compare with
the usual uncoloured version illustrated on
pl. D-30.
In the Thomas Balston collection

Plate 31
Fig. 64 Fountain
By courtesy of Miss M.M. Frame

Plate 30A
Figure 60
Subject: **The Independent Order of Good
Templars**
Observations: This figure has been dealt with
under *pl.* D-30. The example illustrated on
this plate is one of the relatively rare well
coloured pieces.

Plate 31
Figure 64
Subject: **Fountain**
Title: None
Date: *c.* 1861
Height: 12 in (30.5 cm)
Colour: Well coloured.
Rarity: Av.
Description: A young, bare-headed, kilted
man stands to the right of a fountain, with a
jug on his right shoulder. To the left of the
fountain, a young girl sits with her left arm
round a jug which rests on the ground be-
hind the fountain.
Observations: A number of similar figures are
known. They probably all relate to the
Temperance Societies which were very
active in 1861 both in spreading propaganda
and in installing public drinking fountains.

Section E
Theatre, Opera, Ballet and Circus
Biographies and Historical Notes

AFRICAN SALL (dates unknown), coloured good-time girl, otherwise known as 'BLACK SALL'.

For biography see **Waters, William** (?–1823).
See **pl. E**-36.

ALBERT, THERESE (dates unknown), French actress and dancer. Has been described as 'a versatile and accomplished Parisian darling, as delightful a songstress as actress'. She appeared at St. James's Theatre on April 24th, 1844, in the role of 'Madame de Folignac' in *Le Procès de la Polka*, this being a benefit performance for her. The music was directed by Jullien. During the performance she danced the *Royal Polka* with Mlle Eliza Forgeot.
See **pls. E**-71, 72.

ALBONI, MARIETTA (1823–94), Italian contralto opera singer, born at Città di Castello in Umbria. She was brought to London in 1847 as a rival attraction to Jenny Lind, and proved sensational. Played the title role in *La Cenerentola* at Covent Garden, in 1848. She sang at Rossini's funeral in 1868. Died near Versailles.
See **pls. E**-20, 21.

ALBRECHT, Jules Perrot (1800–92) in the role of (*pl.* E-68).
See **Giselle**.

ALI BABA and the FORTY THIEVES, an oriental tale usually regarded as one of the *Arabian Nights*.

Ali Baba and Kassim were two brothers living in Persia. One day, the former, whilst collecting wood in the forest, saw forty robbers gain access to a cave by saying 'Open Sesame!', whereupon a door in the rock opened. Ali Baba used the same password and on entering the cave, found it full of stolen treasure. He brought home some sacks full of gold. He later revealed his discovery to his brother, who in turn went into the cave but forgot the password after entering it, and so was unable to get out. When he was discovered by the robbers, they cut him into quarters which were strung up in the cave. Ali Baba, coming to seek him, conveyed the body home. To simulate a natural death he sent for an old cobbler to sew the quarters of the body together. Through this cobbler the thieves, determined to kill anyone who still knew their secret, traced the house of Ali Baba.

Their purpose was defeated by the ingenuity of Morgiana, Ali Baba's servant, who eventually destroyed them with boiling oil.

The story of Ali Baba has been dramatized on many occasions. One of the principal productions was at Covent Garden in 1815, when the title role was played by John Liston.
See **pls. E**-127, 130.

ALICE, Jenny Lind (1820–87) in the role of (*pls.* E-80, 84, 85, 85A, 87); Maria Malibran (1808–36) in the role of (*pls.* E-86, 87).
See **Robert le Diable**.

ALMANSOR, PRINCE, Mr Hemming in the role of (*pls.* E-78A, 78B, 80).
See **Elephant of Siam**.

ANATO, PALMYRE (dates unknown), French equestrian rider belonging to the Cirque National, who performed at Drury Lane in 1848.

The Illustrated London News for March 18th, 1848 included an engraving inscribed 'Franconi at Drury Lane.—Mlle Palmyre Anato in the circle'. Reporting the visit it said:

'. . . The *troupe* from the Cirque National—the amphitheatre in the Champs Elysées at Paris, made their first appearance before a London audience at Drury Lane, the false floor used for Promenade Concerts being covered with clay, sawdust, mould and other materials.'

The achievements of the female riders were regarded as most attractive, and among the most graceful feats was that of Mlle Palmyre Anato who is portrayed in the engraving leaping through two hoops. In the foreground is the trainer, M Adolpe Franconi, carrying his whip.
See **pls. E**-98, 100.

ANDROCLES, the hero of a story told by Aulus Gellius.

Androcles, a slave, ran away from his cruel master and concealed himself in a cave in Africa. There he was confronted by a lion who presented to him a swollen paw from which he extracted a thorn. Subsequently, Androcles was recaptured and sentenced to fight with a lion in the arena. Instead of the lion attacking him, it showed every sign of affection and gratitude. It transpired that the lion was none other than the one to whom Androcles had shown kindness. Both Androcles and the lion were released afterwards.

The story was a popular one in the circus world. Among the most famous 'Lion Kings' to play the part of 'Androcles' were Lorenzo and the negro, Macomo. The most celebrated lion was *Wallace*, a lion belonging to Fairgrieve's group of performing animals.
See **pls. E**-78, 100.

ANNA BOLENA, opera by Donizetti.
See **Anne Boleyn** (1507–36).

ANNE BOLEYN, second queen of Henry VIII (1507–36), daughter of Sir Thomas Boleyn. Became Henry VIII's mistress in 1527, and secretly married him in 1533, after Catherine of Arragon's marriage had been declared null. Her daughter, Princess Elizabeth, the future Elizabeth I, was born in September, 1533. Anne was charged by Henry with criminal intercourse with several persons, and condemned to death. Her marriage having been declared invalid, she was executed in 1536.

The story was the subject of an opera *Anna Bolena* by Gaetano Donizetti, first performed in Milan in 1830 and soon performed throughout Europe. The opera covers the period when the star of Anne Boleyn is on the wane and the King is in love with Lady Jane Seymour, the Queen's beautiful lady-in-waiting. Jane begs her royal lover to deal kindly with Anne, despite his assertion that the Queen had never truly loved him. However, Henry contrives a plot in which he recalls Lord Percy, earl of Northumberland, Anne's first love, from banishment and offers him a position in the Court. By this means, he creates a situation in which he is able to accuse the Queen of betraying her marriage vows and receiving a lover in her private apartments. A tribunal of peers is called and both Anne and Percy are condemned to the block. Anne meets her death bravely and with her full dignity as a queen. Cannons are fired and there is cheering in the distance as the new queen is proclaimed.
See **pls. E**-115, 116, 117, 118.

ARINETTE, Maria Foote (1797–1867) in the role of (*pl.* E-17).
See **Little Jockey**.

ARSACES, Mary Shaw (1814–?) in the role of (*pl.* E-91).
See **Semiramide**.

ARTAXERXES, opera by Thomas Augustine Arne (1710–78), composed in 1762. Arne provided his own English text, based on Metastasio. The opera held the stage until early in the 19th century.
See **pls. E**-140, 141.

BARTON, Mr (dates unknown), actor. Played the part of 'Giaffier' in *The Bride of Abydos* at Astley's in April, 1847.
See **pls. E**-26, 28.

BEN BACKSTAY, T. P. Cooke (1786–1864) in the role of (*pl.* E-108).
See **T. P. Cooke.**

BETTY, WILLIAM HENRY WEST (1791–1874), English child actor prodigy, known as the 'Young Roscius'. He took London by storm in the 1804–5 season, when he went to Covent Garden on December 1st. There, and at Drury Lane, he appeared in all the great tragic roles of Shakespeare, ousting even Mrs Siddons and Kemble from favour. After a brief and brilliant success opinion turned against him, and he was hissed off the stage when he attempted 'Richard III.' He went to Cambridge in 1808, and three years later again endeavoured to get on the stage, but without success. His father squandered his money, and the rest of his life was passed in complete obscurity.
See **pl.** E-134.

BLOOMER, AMELIA (1818–94), *née* Jenks, American champion of women's right to wear trousers. Born at Homer, New York. In 1840, she married a lawyer called Dexter C. Bloomer. She became the first woman to own, edit and publish a paper exclusively devoted to the interests of women. This was *The Lily: A Monthly Journal devoted to Temperance and Literature*. In the issue of May, 1851, she startled Victorians by advocating that women should adopt the form of dress first worn in America by Mrs Elizabeth Smith Miller, daughter of Gerrit Smith, the American abolitionist. Whilst on her honeymoon in Switzerland, Mrs Smith Miller had made for herself an all-purpose travelling costume, similar to that worn in sanatoria there 'by those recovering from the effects of tight-lacing and lack of physical exercise'. As soon as it was known that Mrs Bloomer was herself wearing the dress, letters poured in asking how to make it. Mrs Bloomer described the dress in *The Lily*:

We would have the skirt reaching down to a little below the knee, and not made quite so full as is the present fashion. Underneath this skirt, trousers made moderately full, in fair mild weather, coming down to the ankle (not instep) and there gathered in with an elastic band, or, what we think decidedly prettier, gathered three or four times, half an inch apart, and drawn up to just sufficient width to permit the foot to pass through. The shoes or slippers to suit the occasion.

Bloomerism provoked a world-wide sensation and brought unexpected notoriety to Mrs Bloomer—but she and her friends found the costume a useful gimmick to attract men into lecture halls to hear their arguments in favour of equal rights.

The Bloomer Costume; or, The Figure of Fun was produced at the Strand in September, 1851, and *Bloomerism; or, The Follies of the Day* ran at the Adelphi in October of that year. There were also *Bloomer polkas* and *quadrilles* and a song *I want to be a Bloomer*! A popular broadsheet of 1851, *I'll be a Bloomer*, ran:

Listen, females all
  No matter what your trade is,
  Old Nick is in the girls,
    The Devil's in the ladies!
Married men may weep,
  And tumble in the ditches,
Since women are resolved
    To wear the shirts and breeches.

Ladies do declare
  A change should have been sooner,
The women, one and all,
    Are going to join the Bloomers.
Prince Albert and the Queen
  Had such a jolly row, Sirs;
She threw off stays and put
    On waistcoat, coat and trousers.

A great deal of misunderstanding has been caused by writers alleging that Mrs Bloomer visited England. She never left America. A 'Mrs Dexter' came here from the United States to lecture. 'Dexter' was Mrs Bloomer's husband's christian name. This may have caused the confusion. All titled figures are inscribed 'Bloomers'—this refers to the costume or the cult, rather than to Mrs Bloomer herself.
See **pls. E**-63, 64, 65, 66, 67.

BRIDE OF ABYDOS, THE, a poem by Lord Byron published in 1813.
Zuleika, the daughter of Giaffier, the Pasha of Abydos is, on her father's instructions, to become the reluctant bride of the rich Bey of Karasman, whom she has never seen. She tells her beloved brother Selim of her unhappiness, and he reveals to her that he is not her brother at all but her cousin, the son of her father's brother, murdered by her father. Not only this, but he also confesses to being a pirate chief and asks Zuleika to share his lot. At this moment Giaffier, waving his sabre, comes upon them. He kills Selim, and Zuleika dies of grief.
The first dramatized version of the poem, by William Dimond, was produced at Drury Lane on February 5th, 1818. It was highly successful. It was revived both in London and the provinces until well into the nineteenth century (1858). The second London production was at Astley's Amphitheatre on April 5th, 1847. *The Illustrated London News* of April 17th, had this to say about it:

Astley's: Under the intelligent superintendence of Mr Broadfoot, a very effective Easterpiece has been produced at this house called 'The Bride of Abydos'. Our contemporaries have generally fallen into the mistake of noticing this piece itself as a new one. It is an equestrian version, if we may so term it, of Dimond's tragic play of the same name which was first produced at Drury Lane Theatre in 1818, the principal characters being sustained by Kean, H. Johnston, Pope, T. Cooke and Mrs Mardyn. Some liberties are taken with Byron's story and parts of 'The Corsair' are amalgamated with it, Selim killing Giaffier at the conclusion and winning Zuleika.

In the Astley's production the part of 'Selim' was taken by Mr Harwood, that of 'Zuleika' by Miss Rosa Henry and that of 'Giaffier' by Mr Barton.
See **pls. E**-26, 27, 28.

BRIGAND, THE, a romantic drama in two Acts by J. R. Planché, from the French. Produced at Drury Lane on November 18th, 1829, and revived at the Surrey Theatre on February 2nd, 1867. The chief character in the drama was 'Massaroni.'
See **pls. E**-56, 56A.

BRIGHT, ELLEN (1832–50), the third 'Lion Queen'. Niece of George Wombwell, the menagerist, and daughter of John Bright, a bugle player in the band. At 16, became 'Lion Queen' in one of Wombwell's menageries. Appeared before Queen Victoria at Windsor Castle. On January 11th, 1850, while performing at Chatham in a cage with a lion and tiger, the latter exhibited some waywardness, for which she imprudently struck it with a riding whip. The infuriated beast immediately sprang upon her with a hoarse roar, siezed her by the throat and killed her before she could be rescued. At the inquest the jury returned a verdict that the deceased was killed by a male tiger whilst exhibiting in its den, and expressed a strong opinion against the practice of allowing persons to perform in a den with animals. The affair led to the prohibition of such performances by women, but the leading menageries continued to have 'Lion Kings'.
See **pls. E**-79, 80.

BROOM GIRL, THE, a characterization made famous by Madame Vestris, in the 1820's, in the song called *The Bavarian girl's song*. She first sang it for Liston's benefit at the Haymarket on September 18th, 1826; then she introduced it to *The £100 Note*. Others who sang the song include John Liston and Miss Love.
See **pl.** E-61.

BRUTUS, MARCUS, one of the conspirators in Shakespeare's tragedy *Julius Caesar*.
See **pl.** E-121 and **Shakspearian characters.**

CASTELLAN, JEANNE ANAIS (1819–?), French soprano who appeared both at Her Majesty's Theatre and at Covent Garden. She sang as 'Leonore' in *Fidelio* at Covent Garden in 1850, the first performance being in the presence of the Queen. Of this it was said, 'She did her utmost to be womanly but she was neither sufficiently intense nor touching—and the music tore her voice, an organ that had never been altogether regulated'. She appeared as 'Lady Jane Seymour' with Luigi Lablache in the character of 'Henry VIII' in Donizetti's opera *Anna Bolena*.
See **pl.** E-116.

CATALANI, ANGELICA (1779–1849), dramatic soprano. Born in Italy, she received her education in Rome and made her operatic début in Venice in 1797. Her début in London, in 1806, was brilliant and her drawing power earned her a vast salary. In 1812, she appeared in the first performance in England of *The Marriage of Figaro*. She retired in 1828, and directed a singing school near Florence.
See **pl.** E-68.

CATARINA, OU LA FILLE DU BRIGAND, a ballet in three Acts and five Scenes, written by Jules Perrot, the music composed by Signor Pugni expressly for Her Majesty's Theatre and dedicated to Madame Michau. First performance March 3rd, 1846.
The story of Catarina, a beautiful girl, who on the death of her father became the leader of a band of robbers near Rome, and of her lieutenant, Diavolino, is said to be founded on an incident in the life of the Italian painter, Salvator Rosa (1615–73).
A contemporary account described the production as 'a true *ballet d'action*'. The first dance in the ballet, the *Pas Stratégique*, was executed by Lucille Grahn playing 'Catarina', accompanied by a troop of bandit damsels with muskets on the

shoulders. It was regarded as the most striking in the piece.
See **pls. E**-51, 52, 53, 54.

CHAPMAN, NELLIE (dates unknown), second 'Lion Queen'. Niece of George Wombwell (1778–1850), founder of Wombwell's menagerie which became the first travelling collection in England.

Polly Hilton had appeared in her father, Joseph Hilton's fairground menagerie as the first 'Lion Queen' in the 1840's. The attractiveness of the spectacle was tempting to proprietors of circuses, and Wombwell persuaded his niece to become the second 'Lady of the Lions'. She acted under the pseudonym of 'Pauline de Vere' until she became 'Lady George' Sanger in 1849. In 1847, she appeared before Queen Victoria at Windsor.
See **pl. E**-78.

CINDERELLA, a fairy tale by Charles Perrault (1628–1703), the subject of many operas, probably the finest of which was Rossini's *La Cenerentola.* This was produced at Covent Garden in 1848, with Marietta Alboni in the title role

Cinderella is a poor waif, cruelly treated by her step-mother and two step-sisters. When her household chores are done she sits in the corner of the hearth in the cinders, whence her name. When her sisters go to a ball, she remains at home, but her fairy-godmother arrives and equips her with beautiful clothes, a coach made out of a pumpkin, and six horses transformed from mice. She goes off to the ball, with the proviso that she returns before the stroke of twelve. The Prince falls in love with her, but she rushes off at midnight leaving one of her tiny glass slippers behind. She resumes her shabby clothes. Meanwhile the Prince announces that he will marry her whom the slipper fits. To the horror of her sisters the slipper is found to fit Cinderella and she marries the Prince.
See **pls. E**-20, 21, 22.

CLOWN, a complex figure of pantomime. The chief types include the simpleton or village idiot, the jester or professional fool and the knave. Among the more famous clowns of the past are Joseph Grimaldi (1779–1837) and Tom Mathews (1805–89).
See **pls. E**-100, 101.

COLLEEN BAWN; or, THE BRIDES OF GARRYOWEN, THE, a domestic drama in three Acts by Dion Boucicault, founded on Gerald Griffin's novel *The Collegians*, published in 1829. First produced in America in December, 1859, and in England at the Adelphi Theatre on September 10th, 1860. The term 'Colleen Bawn' is Anglo-Irish for 'Fair Girl'.

The novel is a sombre, yet sensational account of the injudicious secret marriage of Hardress Cregan with a girl of lower station than his own, which he soon repented when he discovered himself in love with a woman no less beautiful and of greater refinement. Under strong pressure from a domineering mother he allowed himself to become affianced to this lady and plotted the murder of his innocent young wife. He was arrested on the eve of his marriage with his second

love. The tragedy is relieved by some amusing scenes of Irish life.
See **pls. E**-15, 16.

COLUMBINE, the young girl of the English harlequinade. She is usually the daughter, ward or wife of the old man, Pantaloon, in love with Harlequin, with whom she eventually elopes. She is dressed in conventional ballet dress with a wreath of small roses in her hair.
See **pl. E**-126.

CONRAD, pirate chief, the hero of Byron's poem *The Corsair.*
See **pls. E**-139, 140.

COOKE, THOMAS POTTER (1786–1864), actor. Son of a London surgeon. In his youth, served in the Royal Navy. Initially played in the provinces. In 1829, appeared as 'William' in 400 consecutive performances of *Black-Eyed Susan*, at the Surrey Theatre. Nicknamed 'Tippy', he excelled at the hornpipe, which he was often called upon to perform, whether or not it formed an integral part of the play. Played 'Long Tom Coffin' in *The Pilot*, first produced at the Adelphi, 1825, and 'Dick Fid' in *The Red Rover*, first produced at the Adelphi, 1829. He was equally famous in the provinces as in London. He figures frequently in theatrical portraits and tinsel pictures of the time. Reputed 'the best sailor . . . . . that ever trod the stage'. Last appearance at Covent Garden in 1860.

A reporter for *The Illustrated London News*, when describing his career (October 15th, 1853), said of him:

He has always enjoyed a great advantage . . . he has had his speciality . . . The British public loves a specialist. For five and twenty years he has been the sailor of the British stage.

The nautical melodramas were produced for the most part in the so-called Minor theatres as opposed to the big Patent houses, licensed by the Lord Chamberlain for legitimate drama. On the whole the audiences of the 19th century found the 'Minors' more to their liking, as this jingle written by H. S. Leigh in 1874, indicates:

I gape in Covent Garden's walls,
I doze in Drury Lane;
I strive in the Lyceum's stalls
To keep-awake in vain.
There's naught in the dramatic way,
That I can quite abide;
Except the pieces that they play
Upon the Surrey side.

The Surrey side of the Thames was rich in Minor theatres: the Surrey itself, Astley's, and the Royal Coburg, which still exists as the Old Vic.

The British tar held very much the same position in the 19th century as the 'good' cowboy in a white hat in American 'Westerns' does today.

Although figures of sailors may have been propaganda pieces in memory of past victories or in praise of heroes in the Crimea, the potters were equally stimulated by the nautical melodramas of the years before.
See **pls. E**-58, 80, 91, 108, 109.

COOPER, THOMAS ABTHORPE (1776–1849), English actor. Son of a surgeon, he made his début at Edinburgh in 1792. First appeared in London at Covent Garden in 1795, where he played 'Hamlet', 'Richmond' and 'Macbeth'. In 1796, he went to Philadelphia and spent the rest of

his life in the United States, except for visits to Drury Lane in 1803 and 1827. He soon became a firm favourite with the American public, appearing in most of the tragic roles of Shakespeare, his best part being 'Macbeth'. He was one of the first of the leading English actors to become an American citizen.
See **pls. E**-13, 14.

COPPERFIELD, DAVID, the character from whom the tale by Dickens took its name. It is often regarded as a veiled autobiography. It has been dramatized on a number of occasions.
See **pls. E**-45, 46 and **Dickens, Charles.**

CORSAIR, THE, a poem by Byron, published in 1814, and subsequently dramatized.
See **pls. E**-139, 140.

CROCKETT (?–1870), 'Lion King'. Although originally a musician in the band of Sanger's circus, he was offered the appointment of 'Lion King', when prompted by the spirit of competition Sanger decided to introduce performing lions. He was chosen chiefly on account of his imposing appearance, being a tall, handsome man, with a full beard. He had had no previous experience with wild beasts. However, as he suffered from a chest complaint, which performing on a wind instrument aggravated, and as the salary was tempting, he accepted the appointment and followed the profession until the day of his death. He exhibited great heroism when the lions got loose at Astley's and one of the grooms was killed. He went amongst them alone, with only a switch in his hand, and in a few minutes he had safely caged the animals without receiving a scratch.
See **pl. E**-97.

CRUISER, an English thoroughbred stallion notorious for his ferocity, who was broken in by the American tamer, J. S. Rarey.
See **pl. E**-77.

CUSHMAN, CHARLOTTE SAUNDERS (1816–76), American actress, born at Boston. First appeared in opera in 1834, and as 'Lady Macbeth' in 1835. In 1844, she accompanied Macready on a tour through the northern states. In 1845, accompanied by her sister, **SUSAN** (1822–59), she appeared in London where she received a rapturous welcome, playing such characters as 'Lady Macbeth', 'Rosalind' and 'Meg Merrilies'. She was regarded as 'the most powerful actress America has produced'. On December 29th, 1845, she appeared at the Haymarket Theatre in the role of 'Romeo', with her sister as 'Juliet'. The two sisters later toured the provinces. They remained in England until 1849, but returned from 1852 to 1857. Charlotte Cushman retired from the stage in 1875.
See **pls. E**-1A, 3.

DANNY MAN, Edmund Falconer (1814–79) in the role of (*pls.* E-15, 16).
See **Colleen Bawn.**

DIAVOLINO, Jules Perrot (1800–92) in the role of (*pls.* E-51, 52, 53).
See **Catarina.**

DICKENS, CHARLES JOHN HUFFAM (1812–70), novelist. The son of a government clerk, he underwent in early life, as a result of his family's poverty, hardships similar to those depicted in *David Copperfield*. He received little education. He became a Commons reporter in 1833, and began writing articles for periodicals. *Pickwick Papers* (*The Posthumous Papers of the Pickwick Club*) was first issued in twenty monthly parts from April, 1836 to November, 1837, and as a volume, in 1837, when Dickens was only 25 years old. There followed *Oliver Twist* (1837–9), *Nicholas Nickleby* (1838–9), *Martin Chuzzlewit* (1843), *David Copperfield* (1849) and many others. He was intimately connected with the stage throughout his life, exerting an immense influence on it through the dramatization of his books. He began to give public readings in 1858. A number of plays, based on his novels, were performed *before* the books had finished appearing in fortnightly parts. W. T. Moncrieff and Edward Stirling were foremost in adapting his novels for the stage.

It is a curious thing, that although Dickens's works were read throughout Victoria's reign by nearly everyone who could read, no earthenware figures of him by Staffordshire potters have so far come to light. It is quite possible that most of the few figures known of characters appearing in his novels are, in fact, portraits of actors. *See* **pls. E**-38, 39, 40, 41, 42, 43, 44, 45, 46, 47.

DUCROW, ANDREW (1793–1842), equestrian performer, son of a Flemish 'strong man'. Became chief attraction at Astley's in 1824. In 1827, he introduced his great feat, then unparalleled, of riding six horses at the same time. He had a genius for inventing romantic plays on an equestrian basis and for what would now be called the 'All - Colour - Spectacular'. He introduced the legend of 'Mazeppa'—the soldier tied head downwards on a runaway horse as a punishment for adultery. Londoners raved at the daring spectacle. He took on the lease of Astley's Amphitheatre in 1830, in partnership with William West. In 1832, he performed before William IV in a temporary amphitheatre erected in the grounds of the Pavilion at Brighton. His first wife, companion in many triumphs, died in 1836; he subsequently married **MISS WOOLFORD**, the leading tight-rope performer of his establishment. Died in 1842, shortly after the amphitheatre had been destroyed by fire for the third time. *See* **pls. E**-68, 100, 146.

DULCAMARA, DR, Luigi Lablache (1794–1858) in the role of (*pl.* E-62). *See* **L'elisir d'amore**.

DUNDREARY, LORD, Edward Askew Sothern (1826–81) in the role of (*pl.* E-18). *See* **Our American Cousin**.

EDGARDO, Sims Reeves (1818–1900) in the role of (*pl.* E-62). *See* **Lucia di Lammermoor**.

EGERTON, SARAH (1782–1847), *née* Fisher, actress. She appeared at Bath, in 1803. As a tragedienne at Covent Garden, she was overshadowed by Mrs Siddons. She was the original 'Ravina' in Pocock's *Miller and his Men*, 1813. She relapsed into obscurity from which she eventually emerged perm-

anently in adaptations from the *Waverley Novels*. Thus, she appeared as 'Helen Macgregor', opposite Macready in the title role, in Pocock's *Rob Roy Macgregor; or, Auld Lang Syne* on March 12th, 1818, at Covent Garden. A third-rate actress in tragedy, she approached the front rank in melodrama. *See* **pls. E**-74, 75.

EILY O'CONNOR, Agnes Robertson (1833–1916) in the role of (*pls.* E-15, 16). *See* **Colleen Bawn**.

ELEPHANT OF SIAM, OR THE FIRE FIEND, an Indian dramatic spectacle. First produced at the Adelphi on December 3rd, 1829, with Mr Hemming in the role of 'Prince Almansor'. Said to be the first time that an elephant appeared on the English stage. *See* **pls. E**-78A, 78B, 80.

ELLA, MLLE (dates unknown), equestrian. Born in Louisiana of French parents, she first appeared at Drury Lane in 1853. While riding a horse at full gallop, she would leap over the Stars and Stripes nine feet wide. She reappeared with her own troupe in 1857. The finale of her act, whilst riding upright upon her horse, was an aerial vault through a floral garland onto a 'throne of fame'. There she was supported on either side by a dancer. Despite her shapely legs and tiny feet it became known that she was a husband and father. He had for years dressed with actresses in their rooms and been on terms of the greatest intimacy with the ladies! *See* **pls. E**-91, 98.

ELSSLER, THERESE (1808–78) and **FANNY** (1810–84), celebrated dancing sisters, born in Vienna. Their first success was at Berlin, in 1830. In 1841, after touring through Europe, they went to America and excited unwonted enthusiasm. Fanny retired, in 1851, and Thérèse married Prince Adalbert of Prussia, in 1850, and became a baroness. *See* **pls. E**-72, 122, 123.

ESMERALDA, LA, a ballet in three Acts and five Scenes. Written by Jules Perrot, it was based on Victor Hugo's novel *Notre Dame de Paris*. It was first produced at Her Majesty's Theatre, London on March 9th, 1844, with Mlle Carlotta Grisi in the title role, and Jules Perrot as 'Gringoire'. *See* **pls. E**-29, 30, 31, 32, 33, 34.

FALAHAA, Mr (dates unknown), thought to have been a Scottish music-hall artist, now forgotten. *See* **pl. E**-143.

FALCONER, EDMUND (1814–79), actor and dramatist, whose real name was Edmund O'Rourke. Author of *The Cagot; or, Heart for Heart*, a drama played at the Lyceum, in 1856. Manager of the Lyceum from 1858 to 1859, and from 1861 to 1862. In September, 1860, he played the part of 'Danny Man' in *The Colleen Bawn* at the Adelphi. His Irish drama *Peep o'Day* was produced at the Lyceum in November, 1861, and ran for over a year. Joint-lessee of Drury Lane from 1862 to 1866. Opened Her

Majesty's Theatre, Haymarket, with *Oonagh*, in 1866. *See* **pls. E**-15, 16.

FALSTAFF, James Henry Hackett (1800–71) in the role of (*pl.* E-1B); James Quin (1693–1766) in the role of (*pl.* E-11); Mr Newsome in the role of (*pls.* E-8, 9). *See* **pls. E**-7, 10 and **Shakspearian characters**.

FITZWILLIAM, FANNY ELIZABETH (1801–54), *née* Copeland, actress. Played as a child at Dover, where her father was manager. Appeared at the Haymarket, 1817, and at Drury Lane, 1821–2. In 1832, she leased Sadler's Wells. Played at the Adelphi, 1845–7. Appeared as 'Mistress Page' in *The Merry Wives of Windsor* at Sadler's Wells, 1847–8. Subsequently returned to the Haymarket. *See* **pl. E**-145.

FLORIZEL, Frederick Robinson (1830–1912) in the role of (*pl.* E-1A). *See* **Shakspearian characters**.

FOOTE, MARIA, fourth Countess of Harrington (1797–1867), actress. She appeared at Covent Garden as 'Amanthis' in *The Child of Nature*, in 1814, with immediate success, and continued to play at the same theatre until 1825. She frequently acted at Drury Lane and toured extensively throughout Great Britain and Ireland until 1831. In January, 1831, she appeared as 'Arinette' in *The Little Jockey*. In 1831, she married Charles Stanhope, fourth Earl of Harrington, after a previous intrigue with a Colonel Berkeley. She had also recovered damages for breach of promise from 'Pea Green' Haynes, winning much popular support. *See* **pl. E**-17.

FORGEOT, ELIZA (dates unknown), French actress and dancer. In 1842, the St James's theatre became established as the legitimate home of the French stage in London. It was called the 'French theatre'. whilst its notepaper was printed 'Théâtre Français, King Street, St James's, à Londres.' A permanent company was engaged with Mlle Eliza Forgeot as directrice. A succession of stars from Paris visited the theatre. Mlle Forgeot's charming supporting performances always earned her favourable notices. She danced the *Royal Polka* with Madame Albert at St James's Theatre on April 24th, 1844. The music was directed by Jullien. *See* **pls. E**-71, 72.

FOSTER, STEPHEN COLLINS (1826–64), American song-writer, born in Pittsburg. Of his 125 compositions, nearly a quarter are negro melodies, the best known being *The Old Folks at Home*, *Old Dog Tray*, *Old Kentucky Home* and *Oh, Susanna*. The airs and words are his own composition. Despite immense success, he died in poverty. *See* **pl. E**-119, **pls. I**-21, 21A.

FRA DIAVOLO, the popular name of an Italian brigand and renegade monk, Michele Pezza (1760–1806). The same name was given to an *opéra comique* in three

Acts by Daniel Auber, first produced in Paris, in 1830, and in English, adapted by R. Lacy, at Drury Lane on November 3rd, 1831. The opera has nothing in common with Fra Diavolo but its name.

Fra Diavolo, or 'Brother Devil', is a notorious bandit who, masquerading as the Marquis of San Marco, compromises an inn-keeper's daughter in the course of a jewel robbery. He is later betrayed by his henchmen and shot. When facing death he gallantly absolves the girl of wrong-doing and reunites her with her worthy young lover.
See pl. E-60.

GAMP, SAIREY, professional nurse, a character in *Martin Chuzzlewit*, a novel by Dickens, first published 1843. Disreputable and old, her large cotton umbrella has given rise to the term 'a gamp' for an umbrella, also for a midwife. She was a bosom-friend of 'Betsey Prig'.

In the dramatized version of *Martin Chuzzlewit*, these two parts were for a long time acted by men. Enormous popularity in the part of 'Gamp' was won by John Sleeper Clarke (1833–99), the American comedy actor. The novel was first dramatized at the Lyceum on August 8th, 1844, with Mr Keeley playing the part of Mrs Gamp.
See pl. E-43, Dickens, Charles and Martin Chuzzlewit.

GARRICK, DAVID (1717–79), English actor, manager and dramatist, born at Hereford. In 1736, he studied Latin and Greek under Samuel Johnson, and in 1737, went to London to study for the bar. However, his legal studies came to nothing and in 1738, he went into partnership with his brother, as a wine merchant. The partnership was dissolved in 1740. He now devoted his attention to preparing himself for the stage, and, in 1741, made a successful début at Ipswich as 'Aboan' in Southerne's *Oroonoko*. On October 19th, he appeared in London at Goodman's Fields, and his success as 'Richard III' was so tremendous that the two Patent Theatres were deserted, and crowds flocked to the unfashionable East End playhouse. However, the managers of Drury Lane and Covent Garden had Goodman's Fields closed, as it had no licence. Garrick played at both the Patent Theatres and ultimately settled at Drury Lane. Here he became joint-patentee, in 1747. During this period he played continually. He retired from the stage in 1776. He is regarded as the most versatile actor in the history of the British stage.
See pls. E-7, 13.

GENNARO, Guiseppe Mario (1810–83) in the role of (*pl.* E-23).
See Lucrezia Borgia.

GIAFFIER, Mr Barton in the role of (*pls.* E-26, 28).
See Bride of Abydos, The.

GILPIN, JOHN (dates unknown), the name of a real citizen of London owning land near Olney, where the poet William Cowper was living in 1785. The story of John Gilpin was told to Cowper by Lady Austen to divert him from melancholy. He laughed over it during the night and next day turned it into a ballad. This was first published anonymously in the *Public Advertiser*, but subsequently reprinted in chapbook form, and included in the same volume as *The Task* in 1785.

John Gilpin, 'a linen-draper bold' of Cheapside, and his wife, decided to celebrate their twentieth wedding anniversary by a trip to 'The Bell' at Edmonton. Gilpin rode a borrowed horse, and his wife, her sister and the children drove in a chaise and pair. As soon as John's horse began to trot he lost control, and the poem describes his headlong career to Edmonton, and ten miles beyond to Ware, and then back again:

> Nor stopped till where he had got up
> He did again get down

Harlequin and Johnny Gilpin's Ride was produced at Astley's in December, 1844, with Mr Wells, the equestrian, in the title role.
See pls. E-101, 102.

GISELLE OU LES WILIS, a fantastic ballet in two Acts by Vernoy de Saint-Georges, Gautier and Coralli, with music by Adolphe Adam. First produced in Paris on June 28th, 1841. The first London performance was at Her Majesty's Theatre, March 12th, 1842. On this occasion the title role was taken by Carlotta Grisi; the choreography being ascribed to Deshayes, and Jules Perrot, Grisi's husband and teacher. It is the only ballet with an unbroken tradition of performance since its first production, now covering a period of over one hundred years.

In the first Act, which takes place on the Rhine at vintage-time, Giselle, a peasant girl, falls in love with Albrecht, duke of Silesia, who is disguised as a peasant and calls himself Loys. They express their pleasure by dancing. Hilarion, a gamekeeper, mad with jealousy denounces Giselle's lover as an impostor, a nobleman in disguise. This disclosure leads Giselle first to try and kill herself with Albrecht's sword, and later to seek relief in a mad frenzied dance, at the termination of which she falls dead. In the second Act she issues forth from her tomb as a phantom or Wili.[1] She fills Albrecht with bitter-sweet rapture, since he pursues her only to grasp a wraith, but finally returns to her tomb, leaving him once more overwhelmed with grief.
See pl. E-68.

1. There is a Slav legend that Wilis are affianced maidens, who having died before their wedding day, cannot rest peacefully in their graves. There still remains that passion for dancing which they could not satisfy during life, and at midnight they rise up and gather in bands on the highway and woe betide the young man who meets them, for he must dance until he drops.

GLOVER, MARY (?–d.1860), actress. Played the part of 'Yourawkee' in *Peter Wilkins* at the Theatre Royal, Covent Garden, April 1827.
See pl. E-24.

GLYN, ISABELLA DALLAS (1823–89), *née* Gearns, actress. Played under her mother's name of Glyn. Made her début at Manchester as 'Constance' in *King John*, 1847. Appeared in Shakspearian parts on the York circuit, and at Sadler's Wells, from 1848 to 1851, and in 1859. First appeared at Drury Lane, 1851. Gave Shakspearian readings and lessons in England and America.
See pls. E-1B, 2.

GRAHN, LUCILLE (dates unknown), ballet dancer. Played the title role in the celebrated ballet *Catarina*, at Her Majesty's Theatre, March 1846.
See pls. E-51, 52, 54.

GRAS, JULIE DORUS (1805–96), French prima donna. Native of Valenciennes, daughter of M Dorus, leader of the orchestra in that town. She trained at the Paris conservatoire and began her career as a concert singer in various towns in France and Belgium. In November 1830, she made her début in Rossini's *Le Compte d'Ory* in Paris. She was supreme as 'Alice' in Meyerbeer's opera. Every vocalist, including Jenny Lind, who played the role subsequently adopted Dorus's model, such was her superiority in the part. For fifteen years she sustained the premier place in the Academie Royale. In 1833, she married M Gras, one of the first violins in the opera's orchestra. She had been known in London for some years as an opera singer of immense popularity when, in December 1847, she was asked by Jullien to take the part of 'Lucia' in Donizetti's opera *The Bride of Lammermoor*. This was Jullien's first operatic attempt and one in which a British tenor, Sims Reeves, taking the part of 'Edgardo', took London by storm.
See pl. E-62.

GRIMALDI, JOSEPH (1779–1837), actor and pantomimist. Acted both at Sadler's Wells and Drury Lane for many years. His greatest success was as a clown in *Mother Goose* at Covent Garden. He took his farewell benefit at Drury Lane on June 27th, 1828.
See pls. E-100, 101.

GRINGOIRE Jules Perrot (1880–92) in the role of (*pl.* E-29).
See pls. E-31, 32, 33 and Esmeralda.

GRISI, CARLOTTA (1821–99), ballet dancer, born in Austria. As a young dancer she met Jules Perrot who became her teacher, and subsequently her husband. She was the original 'Giselle' when it was produced in Paris in 1841, with Petipa as 'Albrecht'. In the following year she played the title role when the ballet was first produced at Her Majesty's Theatre with Perrot as 'Albrecht'. Although she appeared in numerous ballets, including *La Esmeralda*, *Giselle* is the one inseparably linked with her name.
See pls. E-29, 68, 70, 71.

GRISI, GIULIA (1811–69), Italian soprano. Sister of Guiditta and wife of the Italian tenor Guiseppe Mario. Born in Milan, she became renowned for her roles in Bellini's operas, particularly *I Puritani* which was written especially for her. With Mario as 'Gennaro', she played the title role in Donizetti's opera *Lucrezia Borgia* at Covent Garden in 1847.
See pl. E-23.

HACKETT, JAMES HENRY (1800–71), American character actor. Born in New York, he made his first appearance in 1826, and became famous for his portrayal of Yankee characters, many of which he introduced into new or existing plays. Many of the plays in which he appeared are now lost, for he objected to the printing of play manuscripts in case other actors should appropriate his parts. He was the first American

actor to appear in London as a star, which he did in 1833, playing 'Falstaff', one of his most famous parts, and several of his Yankee characterizations. He was a keen student of Shakespeare, and he also exerted an influence on the development of native drama in the United States, by offering prizes for new American plays.
See **pl. E-1B.**

HAMLET, John Philip Kemble (1757–1823) in the role of (*pls.* E-1A, 2, 4, 6, 7, 13, 13A).
See **Shakspearian characters.**

HARLEQUIN, the young lover of Columbine in the English harlequinade. Usually portrayed as a languishing, lackadaisical lover, foppishly dressed in a close-fitting suit of bright silk diamonds, often with a lace frill and ruffles. He wears a small, black, cat-faced mask.
See **pl. E-126.**

HEMMING, Mr (dates unknown), actor or possibly, elephant trainer. Played the role of 'Prince Almansor' in *The Elephant of Siam* at the Adelphi in 1829.
See **pls. E-78A, 78B, 80.**

HENRY V, King of England (1387–1422). Succeeded his father Henry IV, in 1413. He distinguished himself in the wars with France, his victory at the battle of Agincourt, in 1415, being his greatest triumph. His life was the subject of a play by Shakespeare.
See **pls. E-12,** 97 and **Shakspearian characters**—it was George Rignold's (1838–1912) most famous role.

HENRY VII, King of England (1457–1509). Born at Pembroke Castle, he was grandson of the Owen Tudor who married Queen Catherine, widow of Henry V. As Earl of Richmond, he defeated and slew Richard III at Bosworth Field in 1485, and was crowned. As monarch and founder of the Tudor dynasty, his policy was to restore peace and prosperity to a war-torn and impoverished land. The struggle between Richard III and the Earl of Richmond provided the story of Shakespeare's play *The Tragedy of Richard III.*
See **pls. E-13,** 14 and **Shakspearian characters.**

HENRY VIII, King of England (1491–1547). Succeeded his father Henry VII, in 1509, when he was 18 years of age. He was handsome, skilled in music and sports, and had a love of the sea and a deep interest in theology. He was married in all six times. His first wife, Catherine of Arragon and his fourth, Anne of Cleves were divorced. His second, Anne Boleyn and his fifth, Catherine Howard were beheaded for infidelity. His third, Jane Seymour died shortly after childbirth, and his sixth, Catherine Parr survived him. His reign saw the rise and fall of Cardinal Wolsey. His marriages, his quarrel with Rome and rejection of papal supremacy, and his suppression of the monasteries, made the reign one of the most crucial in English history. He was the first English monarch to have a navy, and he built the royal dockyards at Woolwich and Deptford. Though dubbed by some as an unnatural monster, he was from first to last extremely popular with the people.

The story of Henry VIII and Anne Boleyn was the subject of an opera, *Anna Bolena*, by

Gaetano Donizetti, first performed in Milan in 1822 and later throughout Europe.
See **pls. E-115, 116, 117** and **Anna Bolena.**

HERCULES, the most famous of the Greek heroes. He embarked on twelve labours imposed on him by Eurystheus, king of Argos. The first of these labours was to bring back the skin of the Nemean lion, an enormous creature which was devastating the valley of Nemea near Cleonæ. As the pelt could not be pierced by any weapon, Hercules strangled the lion with his hands.
See **pl. E-96.**

IAGO, character in Shakespeare's *Othello* (*pl.* E-13).
See **Shakspearian characters.**

ISAACS, REBECCA (1829–77), actress and vocalist. Famous for the song *I want to be a Bloomer!* sung in the music-halls throughout the land during the 'Bloomer' craze of 1851.
See **pls. E-65, 66.**

JAMES V OF SCOTLAND William Charles Macready (1793–1873) in the role of (*pls.* E-7, 62).
See **King of the Commons.**

JANE SEYMOUR, LADY (? 1509–37), later third queen of Henry VIII, Jeanne Anais Castellan (1819–?) in the role of (*pls.* E-116, 118).
See **Anna Bolena.**

JESSICA, character in Shakespeare's *Merchant of Venice.*
See **pl. E-13** and **Shakspearian characters.**

JIM CROW, Thomas Dartmouth Rice (1806–60) in the role of (*pl.* E-37).
See **Rice, Thomas Dartmouth.**

JOAN OF ARC, St (1412–31). A girl whose heroism inspired the French to drive the English out of Orleans, thus enabling Charles VII to be proclaimed King of Rheims. She was burned as a heretic at Rouen, being canonized at St Peter's, Rome in 1920. The story has been dramatized on many occasions.
See **pl. E-97.**

JOHN, King of England (1167–1216). Youngest son of Henry II. Attempted to seize the crown during King Richard's imprisonment in Austria, but was pardoned and nominated as successor by his brother on his death-bed. Crowned in May, 1199. In 1205, he entered on a quarrel with the church over the election to the Archbishopric of Canterbury. Excommunicated, 1209. A demand by the barons and clergy that John should keep his oath and restore the laws of Henry I was rejected. Thereupon, the army of the barons assembled at Stamford and marched on London. They met the King at Runnymede where, on June 15th, 1215, he was compelled to sign the Magna Carta, the basis of the English constitution.

The story of King John was the subject of a play by William Shakespeare.
See **pl. E-1** and **Shakspearian characters.**

JULIEN (JULLIEN), LOUIS ANTOINE (1812–60), French conductor and im-

presario. After some success in Paris, he came to England and gave summer concerts at Drury Lane, in 1840. He began a series of promenade concerts during the winter seasons from 1842 to 1859, when classical music was given by the best artists. He organized the opera season of 1847–8, when Sims Reeves made his début in *Lucia di Lammermoor*. He was an adventurer, a first class showman and advertiser, a dandy and something of a megalomaniac. He wooed popularity on the grand scale. Thus he habitually performed a quintet from *I Puritani* on 20 cornets, 20 trumpets, 20 trombones, 20 ophicleides and 20 serpents; and greeted the 1851 Exhibition with a grand quadrille for a gigantic orchestra of 207 instruments, some of them invented for the occasion. He was a mediocre composer of popular dance music. His appeal was as much visual as aural. His waistcoats, his gloves and his gestures were all part of the entertainment. The 'Proms' today owe something to Jullien—the *Fantasia on British Sea Songs* is pure Jullien, as is the horse-play on the last night. He became bankrupt in 1857, and retired to Paris, where he was imprisoned for debt, eventually dying in a lunatic asylum.
See **pl. E-81.**

JULIET, Susan Cushman (1822–59) in the role of (*pl.* E-1A); Charlotte Vandenhoff (1818–60) in the role of (*pl.* E-1C).
See **pls. E-3, 13** and **Shakspearian characters.**

JUMBO (1863–85), African elephant. Obtained in 1865 from the Jardin des Plantes, Paris by the London Zoo. He was then nearly two years old and already 4 feet tall. He rapidly became a national hero and the pride of Britain.

It is not clear whether *Jumbo* gave his name to all the stuffed nursery elephants that were similarly christened, or whether the name already had elephantine connotations. In 1881, he became dangerous. At that time he was 11 feet, 6 inches high and weighed over 6 tons. In 1882, he attracted the attention of the American showman, Phineas T. Barnum, who cabled a purchase offer of ten thousand dollars for what he subsequently described as 'the biggest brute walking the earth'. The Fellows of the Royal Zoological Society met and accepted the offer by a substantial majority, but the news caused a public outcry. Fortified by this, a handful of Fellows who had voted against selling *Jumbo* to the States, attempted to seek a High Court injunction, but the judge refused the application. Many songs were produced at the time, the most famous being:

Jumbo said to Alice 'I love you',
Alice said to Jumbo 'I don't believe you do;
for if you really love me, as you say you do
You would'nt go to Yankee-land and leave me at
the Zoo'.

When *Jumbo* was being led to the docks, it is said, he sat down and refused to budge. After two hours his agents cabled Barnum '*Jumbo* has sat down, what shall we do?' Barnum cabled back 'Let the brute remain there a week if he wants to. It is the best advertisement in the world'. Eventually the chill of evening drove *Jumbo* to give up his 'sit-down' strike, and he boarded the freighter *Assyrian Queen*, specially prepared to accommodate him.

His stay in America was short-lived, for in

September, 1885, Britain was cast into an abyss of grief to hear that *Jumbo*, whilst crossing a railway line at Ontario, had charged a train, throwing the locomotive on to its side and derailing the freight cars. It had cost him his life.

Barnum undaunted, selected *Alice*, his smallest female elephant, and billed her as 'The Great Jumbo's Widow'. For years thereafter, she remained a money-spinner. As Barnum said, 'Give 'em sentiment 'till it hurts—there's nothing like it for bringing 'em in'.[1]

Sir Garrard Tyrwhitt-Drake, in his *Staffordshire Pottery Animals* (*Country Life*: June 9th, 1955), stated that *Jumbo* was the only African elephant he had ever seen depicted in pottery. All the rest were Indian.
See **pls. E**-103, 104, 105, 106.

1. The Zoological Society of London have no record of an 'Alice', other than in the various songs and poems written at the time. These songs probably inspired Barnum to christen his smallest female elephant 'Alice'.

KEAN, CHARLES JOHN (1811–68), actor and manager. Second son of Edmund Kean. Educated at Eton with the idea of detaching him from the stage, but was engaged at Drury Lane at the time of his father's break with the theatre. He played 'Shylock' in *The Merchant of Venice* when it was performed, under his direction, at Windsor Castle before Queen Victoria on December 28th, 1848. With his wife Ellen Tree (1806–80), he rose to the head of his profession at the Princess's Theatre (1851–9), where he set his stamp upon a style of management which lasted for the rest of the century. Lavish spectacle embellished all types of drama. He played the part of 'Rolla' in *Pizarro* when it was revived at the Princess's Theatre, September 1st, 1856.
See **pls. E**-13, 78.

KEAN, EDMUND (1787–1833), actor. Appeared as a child at Her Majesty's Theatre and Drury Lane. Had an adventurous boyhood. Broke both his legs tumbling in Saunders's circus. Recited before George III at Windsor. Underwent hardship for a number of years. Attracted attention of Drury Lane stage-manager whilst acting at Dorchester, and was engaged by him for three years. In 1814, appeared as 'Shylock' with great success, and increased his reputation with 'Richard III'. He also played 'Hamlet', 'Othello' and 'Iago' and was invited to her house by Mrs Garrick. Played 'Rolla', the Inca chief, in *Pizarro*. Visited America, in 1820, and reappeared at Drury Lane as 'Richard III', in 1821. Taken ill at Covent Garden, March, 1833, whilst acting 'Othello' and died two months later. He was unrivalled as a tragedian, but ruined himself by drunkenness and ostentation. .
See **pls. E**-13, 14, 97, 139.

KEMBLE, ADELAIDE (1814–79), *afterwards* Mrs Sartoris, vocalist and author. Daughter of the actor Charles Kemble. First sang at the Ancient Concerts, 1835. She toured in Germany and was at Paris, 1837–8; appeared with success at Venice as 'Norma'. Sang in Italian operas, including *Semiramide*, at Covent Garden, 1841–2. Married Edward John Sartoris in 1843. Published *A Week in a French Country House* (1867).
See **pl. E**-91.

KEMBLE, FRANCES ANNE (1809–93),

usually known as FANNY, daughter of Charles and Maria Thérèsa Kemble. Charles was the youngest of the three Kemble brothers, the others being John Philip (1757–1823), and Stephen (1758–1822).

Said to have had no particular desire for a theatrical career, but appeared at Covent Garden as 'Juliet', in 1829, in order to save her father who was managing the theatre, from bankruptcy. She was an immediate success, and for three years filled the theatre, bringing prosperity to everyone connected with it. In addition to 'Juliet', she played 'Portia', 'Beatrice' and many other leading roles. She was equally at home in tragedy as in comedy. In 1832, she went to America where she was again a great success. In 1834, she married Pierce Butler of Philadelphia, but was divorced in 1848. In her youth she was a most beautiful girl, and in later life her face retained its beauty but with the added charm of a mature countenance.
See **pl. E**-110.

KEMBLE, JOHN PHILIP (1757–1823), actor. Eldest son of the actor and manager, Roger Kemble. Played, as a child, in his father's company, but was educated for the Roman Catholic priesthood. However, in 1781, he appeared in Dublin as 'Hamlet', gaining great success. During an engagement at Drury Lane Theatre, from 1783 to 1802, he presented over 120 characters including 'Hamlet'—played with Mrs Siddons (his sister), 'King John', 'Othello' and 'King Lear'. As manager, from 1788, he began to dress characters unconventionally. Re-opened Drury Lane with 'Macbeth' in 1794, having played meanwhile at the Haymarket. Manager at Covent Garden from 1803 until the theatre was burnt down in 1808, playing 'Hamlet', 'Antonio', 'Iago' etc. Re-opened Covent Garden in 1809. Died at Lausanne.
See **pls. E**-1A, 2, 4, 6, 7, 13, 13A, 60.

KING OF THE COMMONS, THE, play produced at the Princess's Theatre on May 23rd, 1846, with William Charles Macready in the role of 'James V of Scotland.'
See **pls. E**-7, 62.

LABLACHE, LUIGI (1794–1858), Italian operatic singer. Born and died in Naples. His father was a French émigré, his mother an Irish-woman. He made his London début, in 1830, in *Il matrimonio segreto* and the following year, he appeared for the first time in Paris, in the same opera. Thereafter, he alternated between London and Paris. He taught singing to Queen Victoria. His voice was a deep bass, and his acting almost as brilliant as his singing. He sung many times at Drury Lane with Jenny Lind, in 1848. Among the parts he played were those of 'Henry VIII' in Donizetti's opera *Anna Bolena*, 'Doctor Dulcamara' in Donizetti's *L'elisir d'amore* and 'Sergeant Sulpice' in Donizetti's *La figlia del reggimento*.
See **pls. E**-22, 62, 81, 83, 116.

LA FIGLIA DEL REGGIMENTO (*The Daughter of the Regiment*), *opéra-comique* in two Acts by Donizetti. First produced in Paris and in Milan in 1840, and in London at Her Majesty's Theatre, on May 27th, 1847, with Jenny Lind as 'Marie' and Luigi Lablache as 'Sergeant Sulpice'.

ACT I: Marie, whilst a tiny infant, had

been discovered on the battlefield by Sergeant Sulpice of the French 11th Regiment. As nobody had claimed her she had been adopted by the regiment and had won the hearts of all equally. As she grew up to womanhood she repaid her friends' kindness by serving them in the capacity of a vivandière (girl sutler). However, when Sulpice had discovered Marie on the battlefield, he had found pinned to her clothing a letter addressed to the Marchioness of Berkenfeld. One day this rich lady, whilst driving through the Tyrol, stopped at the camp. Sulpice felt bound to show her the letter. On the same day, too, Marie disclosed to him that she had fallen in love with a young Swiss named Tonio, who had recently saved her from great danger. Almost at the same time, Tonio was dragged into the camp by a party of Napoleon's soldiers, having been captured and apprehended as a spy. When Marie disclosed to all that she loved Tonio, they welcomed him as a friend and gave their consent to the marriage of their beloved 'daughter' to this youth, provided that he joined their ranks and served Napoleon in future. This he agreed to do. However the Marchioness, having read the document given her by Sulpice, declared the vivandière to be her own lost niece and insisted that she return with her to her château and be educated to fill the position to which she had been born.

ACT II: For the next year Marie was instructed in Berkenfeld Castle, by masters and teachers, in all the accomplishments considered necessary for the education of a young lady of high rank. She found the life cramping and irksome, and missed her friends in the camp. At the end of the year, the Marchioness arranged a marriage between Marie and the son of a duchess. About this time, Sergeant Sulpice was wounded and was allowed to convalesce at the château. Tonio, meanwhile, had become commanding officer of the regiment, having been rapidly promoted for gallantry on the battle-field. He announced that his new military rank rendered him a fit suitor for Marie. The Marchioness, in opposing the wishes of the lovers, revealed that she was, in fact, not the aunt but the mother of Marie. However, further pressure was placed upon her and she relented, giving her consent to the union of Marie and Tonio and breaking off the contract with the son of the duchess. The delighted soldiers raised cheers for the happiness of their beloved 'Daughter of the Regiment'.
See **pls. E**-80, 81, 82, 83, 90, 91, **pl. C**-87.

L'ELISIR D'AMORE (*The elixir of love*), opera in two Acts by Donizetti, based on Eugène Scribe's *Le philtre*. First produced in Milan, in 1832. First performed in London, at the Lyceum, in 1836.

ACT I: Nemorino, a peasant, is in love with the beautiful and wealthy Adina, the owner of a farm, but Adina is peeved over his lack of courage in coming to the point. Sergeant Belcore arrives at the village and seeks to win Adina's heart by storm. Nemorino is teased by the villagers about his rival, and for a ducat buys from a Dr Dulcamara, a travelling quack, a flask of cheap Bordeaux which he is assured is an elixir of love that within twenty-four hours will enable him to win Adina. Under the influence of Bordeaux, he vexes Adina even more, and she engages herself to marry

Sergeant Belcore that very day.

ACT II: While preparations for the wedding are taking place, Nemorino complains bitterly to Dulcamara of the ineffectiveness of his elixir. He is advised to buy a second bottle, and enlists under Belcore to pay for it. Adina realizing that he has joined the army for her, shows her preference to him, but he treats her with indifference. Villagers, learning that his rich uncle is dead, give him attention which he attributes to the elixir not knowing, as the villagers do, that his uncle has made a Will making him heir. Adina buys back from Sergeant Belcore her lover's enlistment paper, and having set him free, behaves so coyly that Nemorino threatens to seek death in battle, whereupon she faints right into his arms. Belcore bears this unlucky turn of affairs with the bravery of a soldier, while Dulcamara's fame becomes such that he can sell the villagers his entire stock of Bordeaux at a price that makes him rich.

See pl. E-62.

LIND, JOHANNA MARIA, known as **JENNY LIND** and afterwards as **Madame Jenny Lind-Goldschmidt** (1820–87), soprano. Born in Stockholm and known as the 'Swedish Nightingale'. By the age of 25 she had become a leading figure in the opera houses of Sweden, Germany and France, but it was not until 1847, that she paid her first professional visit to England, appearing in London as 'Alice' in Meyerbeer's opera *Robert le Diable*. She was an idol after her first appearance. During the next two years she appeared in many operas, including Donizetti's *La Figlia del Reggimento*, and at many concerts. She retired from the operatic stage in 1849, but continued to sing at concerts. She visited America from 1850 to 1852, making extensive concert tours under the management of P. T. Barnum. Married Mr Otto Goldschmidt, her concert conductor, in 1852, and lived at Dresden from 1852 to 1855. After touring Germany, Austria and Holland, 1854–5, she returned to Great Britain and toured there from 1855–6. She became a naturalized British subject in 1859. Her last public appearance was in 1883. Professor of singing at the Royal College of Music, 1883–6.

See pl. C-87,
pls. E-79A, 80, 81, 82, 83, 84, 85, 85A, 87, 88, 89, 90, 91, 132, 147.

LISTON, JOHN (1776–1846), English comedian. Started life as an usher in a provincial school. His first efforts as an actor were made in company with Stephen Kemble. Although in private life he was nervous and melancholic and much interested in the study of theology, he had only to appear on the stage to set the audience laughing. He excelled in farce. He played his first comic part at the Haymarket Theatre in 1805, appearing as 'Sheepface' in *The Village Lawyer*, and for the next thirty years was one of the leading players. His 'Paul Pry', dress and all, was imitated by many others. In 1815, he appeared as 'Ali Baba' in *The Forty Thieves* at the Covent Garden Theatre. He also appeared as 'Van Dunder' in *'Twould Puzzle a Conjurer* at the Haymarket in 1824 and as 'Sam Swipes' in *Exchange No Robbery* at the Haymarket in 1820, and again at Drury Lane in 1826. He was the first comic actor to command a salary greater than that of a tragedian. He retired in 1837.

See pls. E-48, 49, 127.

E352

LITTLE JOCKEY, comic opera drama by William Dimond, revived at the Olympic Theatre on January 3rd, 1831, with Maria Foote in the role of 'Arinette'.

See pl. E-17.

LITTLE RED RIDING HOOD, a tale translated from the French of Perrault by Robert Samber *c.* 1729.

Little Red Riding Hood, having been sent by her mother to take a cake and some butter to her sick grandmother, loiters on the way. She gets into conversation with a wolf whom she tells of her errand. He hurries on, devours the grandmother and taking the old lady's place in the bed pretends he is her, when Red Riding Hood arrives. Finally he devours the child.

The story has been dramatized on numerous occasions.

See pls. E-124, 125.

LONG TOM COFFIN, T. P. Cooke (1786–1864) in the role of (*pl.* E-109).
See **Pilot, The.**

LORENZO (dates unknown), 'Lion King'. Travelled with Fairgrieve's menagerie for several years preceding its dispersion in 1872. Following the death of Macomo in 1870, was recognized as the most successful performer with lions. He represented the story *Androcles and the lion* with a famous lion named *Wallace*.

See pls E-78, 100.

LORENZO, character in Shakespeare's *Merchant of Venice.*
See **pl. E-13** and **Shakspearian characters.**

LUCIA DI LAMMERMOOR, opera in three Acts by Donizetti based on the novel *The Bride of Lammermoor* by Sir W. Scott, published in 1819. The opera was first produced in Naples in 1835, and in London in 1838. In December 1847, it was produced at the Drury Lane Theatre with Mr Sims Reeves in the role of 'Edgardo' and Madame Dorus Gras as 'Lucia', this being Jullien's first operatic attempt. It was a resounding success, the British tenor, hitherto little known in this country, took London by storm.

ACT I: The story centres on the young Lord Edgar (Edgardo), Master of Ravenswood, the last in the line of an ancient Scottish family who dwelt in a crumbling castle in the wild hills of Lammermoor. Much of his land had fallen into the hands of the Ashton family, a less noble family that had gained considerable power which they used to taunt the Ravenswood family. The Ashton family, however, overreached itself, and Sir Henry Ashton on coming into the estates found himself ruined. In this desperate situation, he tried to arrange a marriage between his beautiful young sister Lucia, and Sir Arthur Bucklaw, a nobleman, who held high office and had great wealth. The latter was willing to exert influence if Lucia's hand were bestowed on him in marriage. Lucia had, however, fallen in love with the Master of Ravenswood who had rescued her from an attack by a wild bull. When her brother heard of this, he became furious and vowed vengeance on the pair. Edgar was compelled to leave the country on a secret mission to France, and his letters to Lucia were intercepted.

ACT II: By a process of deceit Sir Henry Ashton forced Lucia to sign a marriage contract with Sir Arthur Bucklaw, but no sooner had she done this than Edgar dashed into the room, having just returned from France. He was shown the signed marriage contract, and seeing that Lucia had broken her troth, fell into a passion of rage and grief. He snatched her ring from his finger and returned it to her, and rushing from the room returned to his castle.

ACT III: In the castle he was visited by Henry Ashton, and after passionate words passed between them, an agreement was reached that they should settle their differences by a duel next morning. Shortly after Henry Ashton had returned to his mansion, and the bride and bridegroom had been escorted to their chamber, shrieks were heard. It transpired that Lucia, in her anxiety and sorrow, had slain her newly-made husband. She herself became utterly demented and died a few hours later. When the sad news was brought to Edgar, who now understood that he had wronged her, since she had been cruelly deceived, he determined not to live without her and stabbed himself in the heart, falling dead.

See **pl. E-62.**

LUCREZIA BORGIA, opera by Donizetti, first produced in Milan in 1833, and in London at Covent Garden in 1847, with Giulia Grisi in the title role and Guiseppe Mario as 'Gennaro'.

Rodrigo Borgia (1431–1503), Pope Alexander VI, a Spaniard by birth, was elected to the pontificate in 1492. He was the father of at least two illegitimate children, Cesare Borgia (1476–1507), notorious for his violence and crime and Lucrezia Borgia (1480–1519). Donizetti's opera is based on the tradition that the Borgias possessed the secrets of a mysterious and deadly poison which they used against their enemies, although this has not been substantiated by historical research.

Lucrezia, the guilty heroine, discovered that her son, a child born of a secret amour of her early youth, was the trusted friend of the young Duke Orsini and other noblemen who detested and feared the powerful and cruel Borgia family who at that time held chief power in Italy. Her son, Gennaro, knew nothing of his parentage and had been brought up by an old fisherman. He was not only handsome and charming, but had already distinguished himself in recent warfare. Lucrezia and Gennaro developed an affection for each other that offended both Lucrezia's husband, the Duke Alphonso of Ferrara and Gennaro's friends, the young Duke Orsini and his companions. Lucrezia plotted to murder Duke Orsini and four of his companions by causing poison to be added to a flagon of wine at a banquet. When they had drunk the wine she told them what she had done and showed her five victims the coffins in which they would shortly lie. Unbeknown to her however, Gennaro was also at the banquet, and had also consumed the wine. He demanded a sixth coffin. Lucrezia revealed herself to him as his mother and begged him to take the antidote, but he refused and died; Lucrezia, in a paroxysm of grief, also drank the poisoned wine and fell dead beside him.

See **pl. E-23.**

MACBETH, William Charles Macready (1793–1873) in the role of (*pls.* E-1B, 2).
See **Shakspearian characters.**

MACBETH, LADY, Isabella Dallas Glyn (1823–89) in the role of (*pls.* E-1B, 2); Mrs Sarah Siddons (1755–1831) in the role of (*pls.* E-2, 4, 5, 6, 7).
See **Shakspearian characters.**

MACDONALD, ALEXANDER, *or* **MAC-IAN OF GLENCOE** (*d.* 1692) was the chief of his clan. He joined Claverhouse, taking part in the rising of the northern Highlands in 1689. He was bidden to take the oath of allegiance within a stipulated time. When that period had elapsed he made a vain effort to find a magistrate to administer the oath, and finally persuaded Sir Colin Campbell to do this five days later. His tardy action was ignored, and the clan was destroyed in their home in the valley of Glencoe in 1692. Although the massacre of Glencoe was condemned, none of the agents were brought to justice.
See **pl.** E-133.

MACGREGOR, HELEN, Sarah Egerton (1782–1847) in the role of (*pls.* E-74, 75).
See **Rob Roy.**

MACGREGOR, ROB ROY, William Charles Macready (1793–1873) in the role of (*pls.* E-74, 76 *and pl.* I-6).
See **Rob Roy.**

MACOMO (d. 1870), 'Lion King'. A negro sailor who, on returning from a voyage, sought employment at George Hilton's menagerie. He soon became famous, far and wide, for his daring which was without parallel. On one occasion he entered a cage where two tigers were engaged in furious conflict, and armed only with a whip, attempted to separate them. Both tigers turned their fury upon him and severely lacerated him, but he continued to belabour them, until they cowered before him and knew him for their master. With the assistance of keepers he then succeeded in getting one of the tigers into another cage. Like Van Amburgh and Crockett, he appeared to bear a charmed life and died a natural death in 1870. His name was derived from a Zulu chieftain who fought against the British.
See **pl.** E-100.

MACREADY, WILLIAM CHARLES (1793–1873), actor. Educated at Rugby. His first appearance was as 'Romeo', in Birmingham, in 1810. First appeared at Covent Garden in 1816. In 1818, appeared as 'Rob Roy Macgregor', one of his favourite parts, opposite Sarah Egerton as 'Helen Macgregor', in Pocock's *Rob Roy Macgregor; or, Auld Lang Syne.* In 1819, his 'Richard III' raised him to the head of his profession. In 1823, he began to play at Drury Lane following a quarrel with the management at Covent Garden. Appeared as 'Shylock' in *The Merchant of Venice*, at the Haymarket in September, 1839. Visited America in 1843. Appeared as 'James V of Scotland' in *The King of the Commons* at the Princess's Theatre in 1846. Retired from the stage after playing 'Macbeth' at Drury Lane on February 26th, 1851. Described by Talfourd as 'the most romantic of actors'.
See **pls.** E-1B, 2, 7, 62, 74, 76, **pl.** I-6.

MALIBRAN, MARIA FELICITA (1808–36), opera singer. Born in Paris, she was the daughter of the Spanish tenor Manuel Garcia. After studying in Naples, she had her official début in London at the King's Theatre on June 7th, 1825, as 'Rosina'. Subsequently, she went to New York, where for two years she appeared with the Manuel Garcia opera company in works by Rossini and Mozart. She went into temporary retirement in New York after marrying the French merchant Malibran, but they soon parted. On returning to Paris, she made her début, in 1828, at the Théâtre des Italiens. Her success was stupendous. She appeared later in most of the major cities of Italy and in London. Early in 1836, she married the violinist Charles de Bériot. However, a month later she fell from a horse and suffered head injuries that she never overcame. She appeared in only a few more concerts. Her death caused a furore and was dramatic in the extreme. After her last concert at Manchester, she received an ovation, but was unable to sing any encores having collapsed in her dressing-room. She died a week later, September 23rd, 1836, and was buried in Manchester, but was disinterred later, after great fuss, and taken to France.
See **pls.** A-2, 3,
pls. E-86, 87, 130, 148, 149.

MAN FRIDAY, character in *Robinson Crusoe.*
See **pl.** E-144 and **Robinson Crusoe.**

MARIE (*Maria*) Jenny Lind (1820–87) in the role of (*pls.* E-80, 81, 82, 83, 90, 91).
See **La Figlia del Reggimento.**

MARIO, GUISEPPE (1810–83), Italian tenor. Born in Sardinia to a noble family. His initial training was for the army. In 1836, he fled from Italy with a young ballet dancer. On reaching Paris, he began to study singing at the Paris conservatoire, making his début at the opera in *Robert le Diable.* In 1839, he made a sensational début in London in *Lucrezia Borgia.* Thereafter, he achieved a long series of operatic triumphs in Paris, London and America. He was strikingly handsome and endowed with a beautiful voice. He frequently appeared with the soprano Giulia Grisi, whom he married in 1844. His last appearance at Covent Garden was in 1871. He retired to Rome and lost his fortune through ill-advised speculations.
See **pls.** E-23, 81, 82.

MARSTON, JENNY (*c.* 1830–61), actress. Played the part of 'Perdita' in Phelps' revival of *The Winter's Tale* at Sadler's Wells in July, 1851.
See **pl.** E-1A.

MARTIN CHUZZLEWIT, a novel by Dickens, published from 1843 to 1844. A dramatized version of the novel was first produced at the Lyceum in 1844.
See **pl.** E-43; **Dickens, Charles; Gamp, Sairey; and Prig, Betsy.**

MASANIELLO (1623–47), properly TOMMASO ANIELLO, Neopolitan fisherman and patriot. Born in Amalfi, he led a successful revolt of the inhabitants of Naples against their Spanish rulers on July 7th, 1647. He was assassinated by Spanish agents nine days later.

Masaniello is the subject of an opera by Auber *La muette de Portici* (The dumb girl of Portici), first produced in Paris in February 1828.

In seventeenth century Naples, Fenella, the young and beautiful, but mute sister of Masaniello, is seduced, persecuted and imprisoned by Alfonso, son of the Spanish Viceroy of Naples, who is about to marry the Princess Elvira of Spain. Masaniello leads an insurrection against Alfonso, which proves successful, and he is given the crown of Naples. However, he is poisoned by a former friend, and goes mad. This enables Alfonso to quell the revolt. Masaniello is killed and Fenella commits suicide.
See **pls.** E-111, 134.

MASSARONI, chief character in a romantic drama by J. R. Planché.
See **Brigand, The.**

MATHEWS, CHARLES JAMES (1803–78), actor and dramatist. Son of Charles Mathews by his second wife. Trained as an architect, taking to the stage professionally in 1835, when he replaced his father in the management of the Adelphi. Was engaged by Madame Vestris during her tenancy of the Olympic Theatre. Wrote *A Song of Jenny Jones and Ned Morgan* which he included in his one-Act farce, *He would be an Actor,* produced at the Olympic in 1836, *see* section I. Married Madame Vestris in 1838. Subsequently, they took over the management of Covent Garden, where they staged some brilliant productions, including *London Assurance* with Mathews as 'Dazzle'. After the death of Madame Vestris, Mathews continued to act, and later married an actress named Lizzie Davenport.
See **pl.** E-134.

MAZEPPA, IVAN STEPANOVITCH (1644–1709), hetman (*military commander*) of the Cossacks. Born of a noble family, he became page to Casimir V, king of Poland. According to legend, a nobleman caught him in an intrigue with his wife. As a punishment, he was bound naked on the back of a wild Ukrainian horse, which was then lashed into madness. It galloped off through forest and river, never stopping till it reached the Ukraine, where it fell dead. Mazeppa was rescued by peasants and joined the Cossacks. He was elected hetman in 1687. Peter the Great made Mazeppa Prince of the Ukraine but later Mazeppa changed his allegiance, fighting on the side of Charles XII of Sweden at the battle of Pultowa, 1709. After their defeat he fled to Bender, where he died.

In 1819, Byron wrote a piece called *Mazeppa.* This poem was founded on a description of the ride in Voltaire's *Charles XII.* An equestrian drama by H. M. Milner, based on Byron's poem, was first produced at the Coburg, later the Old Vic, on November 3rd, 1823. It was revived by Ducrow at Astley's on April 4th, 1831.

Mazeppa proved to be the only enduring performance of the kind with which Astley's was for so many years associated, the majority owing their popularity to recent military events. The drama continued in popularity for the next fifty years, the fortunes of the daring youth immortalized by the genius of Byron and the headlong flight of the wild horse of the Ukraine, proving an unfailing source of attraction. It was the trump-card of every hippo-dramatic manager who possessed, or could borrow a white horse, or even on occasions a zebra, to enact the part of the 'fiery untamed steed' upon whose back the hero was borne.

See pls. E-107, 107A, 107B and **Menken, Adah Isaacs.**

MENKEN, ADAH ISAACS (1835–68), American equestrian actress of Jewish extraction. Orphaned at 13, she made her first appearance as a dancer at the opera-house at New Orleans, of which city she was a native. She later appeared at Havana, but subsequently abandoned the boards for the literary profession, publishing a volume of poems. In 1858, she made her début as an actress in New Orleans and later performed in the chief towns of the West.

In 1864, Mr Friend employed her as the chief attraction when Astley's reopened as a circus. The management pinned their faith in her powers of attraction, not upon her talent as an actress, but upon her beauty and grace, and her ability to play the part, without recourse to a double, for the fencing and riding. Enormous posters appeared everywhere, representing her, apparently in a nude state, on the back of a wild horse, and inviting the public to go to Astley's and see 'the beautiful Menken'. Girls dressed their hair *à la Menken*—like the frizzled crop of a negress. Although not the first woman to play the part, her name is inseparably linked with it.

'Wild was her look, wild was her air,
Back from her shoulders streamed her hair,
Her locks that wont her brow to shade,
Started erectly from her head;
Her figure seemed to rise more high—
From her pale lips a frantic cry
Rang sharply through the moon's pale light,
And life to her was endless night!'

In London, she published a volume of poems titled *Infelicia* which was dedicated to Dickens. In 1856, she married John Isaacs Menken, and retained this name through subsequent matrimonial adventures, including an illegal marriage to Heenan, the pugilist. She died in Paris.

See pls. E-107, 107B and **Mazeppa, Ivan Stepanovitch.**

NEWSOME, MR (dates unknown), equestrian rider at Astley's.
See pls. E-8, 9.

NICHOLAS NICKLEBY, a novel by Dickens, published from 1838 to 1839 in monthly numbers. The novel was an attack on the so-called 'Yorkshire schools', notorious in the 1830's as the distant prisons for the unwanted children of London couples. Young gentlemen were boarded, clothed and educated for about 20 gns per year each, with an assurance that there were 'no extras or vacations'. Dickens picked on Bowes Academy ('Dotheboys Hall') for background, as this school had been the subject of a public scandal some years previously and evidence of the state of the school and the manner in which the boys were treated was available in newspaper accounts. Nicholas Nickleby, a high spirited young man, who with his mother and sister had been left penniless on the death of his father, was sent by his uncle as usher to 'Dotheboys Hall' where Wackford Squeers (*q.v.*) starved and maltreated forty urchins under pretence of education.

A dramatized version of the novel in two

Acts by E. Stirling was first produced at the Adelphi in November 1838, *i.e.* prior to publication of the final instalment of the novel.

See pls. E-38, 39, 40, 41, 42 and **Dickens, Charles.**

NICKLEBY, KATE, character in Dickens' *Nicholas Nickleby*, first published in serial form, 1838–9. Sister of Nicholas, she married Frank Cheeryble.
See pls. E-38, 40, 42.

NICKLEBY, RALPH, character in Dickens' *Nicholas Nickleby*, first published in serial form, 1838–9. Uncle of Nicholas Nickleby, Ralph was a miser and a usurer.
See pls. E-39, 40, 41, 42.

NISBETT, LOUISA CRANSTOUN (1812–58), actress. Played in the provinces until 1829. Married John Alexander Nisbett in 1831, returning to the stage in 1832, after her husband's sudden death. She continued to act in various London theatres until 1844, when she married Sir William Boothby, but again returned to the stage after his death in 1846. She retired in 1851. Regarded as a charming actress in comedy.
See pl. E-131.

O'NEILL, ELIZA (1791–1872), English actress. First appeared on the stage in her birthplace, Drogheda, where her father was actor-manager of the local theatre. In 1814, she was engaged for Covent Garden, making her first appearance as 'Juliet'. For the following five years she had a career of unbroken triumph, both in comedy and tragedy. She retired, in 1819, to marry Mr (later Sir William) Becher.
See pl. E-91.

OPHELIA, character in Shakespeare's *Hamlet* (*pl.* E-1A).
See **Shakspearian characters.**

OTHELLO, character in Shakespeare's *Othello* (*pl.* E-13).
See **Shakspearian characters.**

OUR AMERICAN COUSIN, play first produced in New York in 1859, and at the Haymarket in 1861. Edward Sothern (1826–81) made his name in this play in the role of 'Lord Dundreary'.
See pl. E-18.

PAGE, MISTRESS, Fanny Elizabeth Fitzwilliam (1801–54) in the role of (*pl.* E-145).
See **Shakspearian characters.**

PANTALOON, the old man, Columbine's father, guardian or husband in the Harlequinade. He is the butt of Clowns' practical jokes.
See pl. E-100.

PAUL ET VIRGINIE, a romance by Bernardin de St Pierre, published in 1787. It was later the subject of various musical scores, lyrical dramas and operas.

The story is a simple one of a boy and girl, children of two mothers, who have sought refuge from their troubles in Mauritius. The children, having been brought up together far from civilization and the conventions of Europe, fall deeply in

love. Virginia is summoned to France for a few years by a rich relative, and her return is awaited by Paul with intense longing. When the ship arrives, it is wrecked by a hurricane within sight of the shore, and Paul's efforts to reach it fail. Virginia is seen on the poop being entreated by a naked sailor to take off her clothes and be saved, she refuses and drowns. Shortly after Paul dies of grief.

Paul and Virginia was first produced at Covent Garden in 1800, being adapted for the stage—with a happy ending—by James Cobb. It was revived on many occasions, the most successful production being that at Drury Lane in 1822, with Madame Vestris in the role of 'Paul'. It was one of her most famous 'breeches parts'.
See pl. C-73,
pls. E-112, 113, 114, 115.

PEGGOTTY, CLARA, a character in Dickens' novel *David Copperfield*, first published in 1849, and first dramatized in 1850.

Servant to Mrs Copperfield, and nurse and friend to her son David. After the death of her mistress, Peggotty married Mr Barkis, a carrier, but she never forgot her old love for David, whose housekeeper she finally became.
See pl. E-45.

PEGGOTTY, MR DANIEL, a character in Dickens' *David Copperfield*, first published in 1849, and first dramatized in 1850.

Mr Peggotty, brother to Clara Peggotty, is a rough, kind-hearted and noble-souled fisherman. His nephew Ham and his adopted niece Emily, both members of his household, were engaged to be married, but before the wedding day Emily eloped with Steerforth, a brilliant plausible fellow who had succeeded in winning her affections and seducing her.
See pl. E-46.

PEGGOTTY, HAM, a character in Dickens' novel *David Copperfield*, first published in 1849, and first dramatized in 1850.

Nephew of Daniel Peggotty, he was engaged to little Emily, but on the eve of their marriage, she eloped with Steerforth.
See pl. E-46.

PERDITA, Jenny Marston (1830–61) in the role of (*pl.* E-1A).
See **Shakspearian characters.**

PERROT, JULES JOSEPH (1800–92), ballet dancer. Born at Lyons, he spent his early years in a travelling show in which he played characters requiring unusual acrobatic ability. After studying under Vestris, he made his début at the Opéra, Paris in 1830, in *Le Rossignol*. In 1840, whilst visiting Naples, he fell in love with a young dancer, Mlle Carlotta Grisi. They married and later secured an engagement to dance together in *Le Zingaro*, in Paris. In 1842, Perrot appeared as 'Albrecht' in *Giselle* at Her Majesty's Theatre, the title role being taken by Grisi. In March 1844, he appeared as 'Gringoire' in *La Esmeralda* at Her Majesty's Theatre, the title role again being taken by Grisi. The following month they danced together in *The Opera Polka* at the same theatre. In 1846, he played 'Diavolino', in *Catarina* at Her Majesty's Theatre. This time the title role was taken by Mlle Lucille Grahn. In 1851, he received the official title of *Maître de ballet*, which he

retained until his retirement in 1860.
See **pls.** E-24, 29, 51, 52, 53, 60, 68, 69, 70, 71.

PETER WILKINS, a drama adapted from *The Life and Adventures of Peter Wilkins*, a romance by Robert Paltock (1697–1767), first produced at Covent Garden in April, 1827.

The story is similar to that of *Robinson Crusoe*, but not written with the same conviction as of Defoe. Peter Wilkins is shipwrecked in the Antarctic and reaches an island inhabited by a strange winged race of 'glums' and 'gawries' who are enveloped in an outer silk-like skin which, on spreading, enables them to fly. One of these, Yourawkee, who is particularly beautiful, falls by accident outside his hut. He takes her in, tends her and marries her, and in the course of time becomes a person of importance in the kingdom.
See **pls.** E-24, 25.

PICKWICK, SAMUEL, the leading character in Dickens' *The Pickwick Papers*, which was first issued in twenty monthly parts from April, 1836, to November, 1837, and first dramatized with the title *The Pickwickian*, in 1837.

Mr Pickwick is Chairman of the Pickwick Club, which he founded. His adventures and that of his associates are interspersed by incidental tales contributed by various characters. Samuel Weller, Pickwick's devoted servant, is generally regarded as the greatest character Dickens ever drew.
See **pl.** E-44 and **Dickens, Charles.**

PILOT, THE, a tale of adventure at sea by J. F. Cooper (1789–1851), first published in 1823. It was dramatized by E. Fitzball and first performed at the Adelphi on October 31st, 1825, and many times later. The part of 'Long Tom Coffin', the hero of the play, was made famous by T. P. Cooke and was performed by him no less than 562 times in the 25 years following the first production.
See **pl.** E-109.

PIZARRO, a tragedy in five Acts, adapted from Augustus von Kotzebue's drama *The Spaniard in Peru* by R. B. Sheridan, first produced at Drury Lane on May 24th, 1799. It was an immediate success, running for 31 nights. This success was not only due to the performance of John Philip Kemble as 'Rolla' and Mrs Siddons as 'Elvira', but also to the magnificence of the scenery, preparations for which caused the theatre to cancel the performance on the eve of the first night. Later actors to play 'Rolla' included Wallack, Young, Macready and Charles Kean.

Francisco Pizarro (1478–1541) the subject of the drama, was the Spanish conqueror of Peru. He was assassinated in Lima by followers of his former lieutenant and subsequent rival Almagro, who had been defeated and later beheaded in 1538.

The main characters in Sheridan's tragedy were as follows:

Ataliba,   *King of Quito.*
Rolla,   }
Alonzo,   } *Commanders of his Army.*
Pizarro,   *Leader of the Spaniards.*
Elvira,   *Pizarro's mistress.*
Cora,   *Alonzo's wife.*

The speech of Rolla, exulting the Peruvians to defend their king and country and their civil and religious institutions against a ferocious band of lawless invaders, was highly instrumental in the success of the piece. It is the only passage of the play to which Sheridan has an exclusive claim. The appeal to the people in support of their rights and national independence is bold and animating and is Sheridan the politician and orator, rather than Sheridan the dramatist.
See **pls.** E-78, 80.

PRIG, BETSEY, a nurse. She is a bosom-friend of Mrs Gamp. Both are characters in Dickens' novel *Martin Chuzzlewit*, first published in 1843.
See **pl.** E-43 and **Dickens, Charles and Martin Chuzzlewit.**

QUIN, JAMES (1693–1766), Irish actor. Born in London, he made his début at Dublin in 1712. In 1716, the sudden illness of a leading actor led to Quin being called upon to play 'Bajazet' in *Tamerlane* at Drury Lane. His success was immediate. In 1718, he went to Lincoln's Inn Fields Theatre where he remained for fourteen years appearing as 'Hotspur', 'Othello', 'Lear', 'Falstaff' and 'Buckingham', also as the 'Ghost' in *Hamlet*. In 1732, he went to Covent Garden and from there he returned to Drury Lane, where he remained for several years and was regarded as the first actor in England. He then became largely eclipsed by Garrick of whom he said, 'if the young fellow is right, I and the rest of the players have been all wrong'. In 1751, he retired to Bath, having spent the last years of his career in rivalry with Garrick.
See **pl.** E-11.

RAREY, JOHN SOLOMON (1827–66), American horse-tamer. Began giving lessons on horse training in 1852. Arrived in England in 1857, and exhibited before the Queen and Prince Albert at Windsor. Subsequently, he toured all over Europe teaching methods of horse training. In 1860, he returned to America with *Cruiser*, an English thoroughbred stallion notorious for his ferocity, until Rarey, in response to a public challenge in London, broke his spirit by leaving him all night with his forelegs tied and his hind legs drawn up and tied to a collar put over his head. Gave public exhibitions in the United States (1860–2). Author: *The Modern Art of Taming Wild Horses.*

The following extract from The Times of August 2nd, 1859 is of interest:

Summer Diversions
Mr. RAREY at the ALHAMBRA PALACE . . . Many inquiries having been made during the past week by noblemen and gentlemen as to when Mr. Rarey would give the next EXPOSITION of his system of subduing vicious horses, and of the proper manner of gentleing and teaching the horse for all practicable purposes, promises to be a good subject to test to the uttermost Mr. Rarey's skill in dealing with dangerous horses. Admission—reserved seats, £1 1s.; second seats, 15s.; third seats, 7s. 6d. Doors open at half-past 11. The exhibition to commence at 12. Tickets to be had at the box-office of the Alhambra Palace.
See **pls.** E-77, 80.

RED ROVER, THE, a tale of adventure at sea by J. F. Cooper (1789–1851), first published in 1828. It was dramatized by E. Fitzball and first produced at the Adelphi, in 1829, with T. P. Cooke in the part of 'Dick Fid'.
See **pl.** E-80.

REEVES, JOHN SIMS (1818–1900), tenor vocalist. Assumed name of Sims, *c.* 1847. He studied the pianoforte under Johann Baptist Cramer, singing under Tom Cooke and J. W. Hobbs; he first appeared publicly as a vocalist in 1839, at Newcastle. He sang at the Grecian Theatre, City Road, London, in 1842, and joined Macready's Drury Lane Company. He studied under Bordogni in Paris and Alberto Mazzucato in Milan. He was heard by Jullien when travelling in Italy in search of a company for the operatic establishment he had just formed at Drury Lane. An engagement was at once contracted. He made his début at Drury Lane on December 6th, 1847 in his favourite part of 'Edgardo'. He was an outstanding success, and thenceforth ranked as the premier English tenor.
See **pls.** E-62, 81.

RICE, THOMAS DARTMOUTH (1806–60), American vaudeville performer and negro impersonator, also known as 'JIM CROW'. In 1828, whilst playing in Ludlow and Smith's Southern Theatre in Louisville, Kentucky, he gave an intermission between the acts of a play based on a song and shuffling dance, done by an old negro, called 'Jim Crow', whilst grooming a horse. It was a tremendous success, being performed later in many parts of the United States. In 1833, Rice visited Washington and there had as a partner in his turn, four-year-old Joseph Jefferson (1829–1905). The miniature 'Jim Crow' dressed in a ragged nondescript costume with a white hat, his face blackened with burnt cork, was tumbled out of a sack at the conclusion of Rice's song, and performed a song and dance himself. Jefferson was to become one of America's most famous actors, the turning-point in his career being when he played the part of 'Asa Trenchard' in *Our American Cousin*, just as this play also proved the turning-point in the career of E. A. Sothern in the role of 'Lord Dundreary'. In 1836, Rice came to England and appeared at the Royal Surrey Theatre, London. The production started the enormous vogue of nigger minstrels in England, but despite this he himself never became part of a troupe, preferring to work alone.
See **pl.** E-37.

RICHARD III, King of England (1452–85), David Garrick (1717–79) in the role of (*pls.* E-7, 13); Edmund Kean (1787–1833) in the role of (*pls.* E-13, 14, 97, 139).
See **pl.** E-9, **Henry VII** and **Shakspearian characters.**

RICHMOND, EARL of, Thomas Cooper (1776–1849) in the role of (*pls.* E-13, 14).
See **Henry VII** and **Shakspearian characters.**

RIGNOLD, GEORGE (1838–1912), English actor. Started his stage career at Bath and Bristol theatres. He made a name

for himself in London as 'Sir John Bridges', in 1870. His most famous role was 'Henry V', which he first played in New York and later, at Drury Lane, in 1879. He twice visited Australia with success.
See **pl. E-**97.

ROB ROY (1671–1734), Scottish freebooter. Began life as a grazier at Balquhidder. His herds were so often plundered that he had to maintain a band of armed followers to protect both himself and those of his neighbours who paid him protection money. In 1694 he, supported by others loyal to the Jacobite cause, laid claim to be chief of the clan of Gregor. In 1712, he incurred losses in cattle speculations for which he had borrowed money from the Duke of Montrose. Because of this, his land was seized, his house plundered and his wife Helen Macgregor turned adrift with her children in midwinter. Rob Roy now gathered his clansmen together and, in 1716, the year after the Jacobite rebellion, made open war on the Duke. Many stories are told of his hairbreadth escapes and of his generosity to the poor whose wants he supplied at the expense of the rich, and in return for which he was supplied with information about his enemies, the Dukes of Montrose and Atholl. He enjoyed the protection of the Duke of Argyll and assumed the name of Campbell. He died in his own house at Balquhidder on December 28th, 1734. One of his sons, James was the notorious outlaw James Mohr and another, Robin was hanged at Edinburgh for abduction.

In 1817, Sir W. Scott published his novel *Rob Roy*. The tale covers the period immediately preceding the Jacobite rising of 1715.

The story of Rob Roy Macgregor and his wife Helen has been dramatized on many occasions. An operatic drama in three Acts by J. Pocock, titled *Rob Roy Macgregor; or, Auld Lang Syne*, was produced at Covent Garden on March 12th, 1818, and again at Drury Lane on July 3rd, 1831.
See **pls. E-**74, 75, 76, 97, **pl. I-**6.

ROBERT LE DIABLE (*Robert, the Devil*), opera in four Acts by Meyerbeer. First produced in Paris in 1831, and in London at Drury Lane on April 8th, 1833. Miss Jenny Lind made her début at Her Majesty's Theatre as 'Alice' on May 4th, 1847.

Robert the Devil was the sixth Duke of Normandy and father of William the Conqueror. Many legends are gathered about him in consequence of his violence and cruelty.

The scene of Meyerbeer's opera is set at Palermo where Robert falls in love with Princess Isabella, daughter of the Duke of Messina, and hopes to win her hand in a tournament. Other characters include Bertram, a sinister-looking knight who exerts an evil influence on Robert, and who is, unbeknown to Robert, in reality his 'fiend-father'; Raimbaud, a Norman minstrel, who sings the true story of the life of Robert; and Alice, his betrothed, a young village maiden who transpires to be Robert's foster-sister, with whom he had played as a child in Normandy. After a series of intrigues and counter-intrigues, Alice eventually overcomes the evil influence of Bertram on Robert, and the opera closes with Robert

E356

being led by Alice to join his waiting bride Isabella at the altar.
See **pls.** E-80, 84, 85, 85A, 87.

ROBERTSON, AGNES KELLY (1833–1916), actress. First seen on the stage in Scotland as a child, and in 1850, under the tuition of Charles Kean, made her début in London. Married actor and dramatist Dionysius Boucicault and accompanied her husband on his tours in America, where she was immensely popular. Although a Scotswoman by birth, she played the part of the Irish heroine 'Eily O'Connor' in *The Colleen Bawn* at the Adelphi Theatre, September, 1860 with great success. She was universally loved and respected.
See **pls.** E-15, 16.

ROBINSON CRUSOE, THE LIFE AND STRANGE SURPRISING ADVENTURES OF, a romance by Daniel Defoe first published in 1719. The work is based on the true-life story of Alexander Selkirk (1676–1721), son of a shoemaker of Largo, who ran away to sea. After a quarrel with his captain, he was, at his own request, put ashore on the uninhabited Pacific island of Juan Fernandez. He remained there from 1704 until his rescue in 1709. Defoe's romance has been dramatized on many occasions. The book details the methods by which Robinson Crusoe built himself a house, domesticated goats and made himself a boat; his anxieties when the island was visited by cannibals and his rescue of the poor savage Man Friday (*q.v.*) from death. Finally, the arrival of an English ship in a state of mutiny, the subduing of the mutineers and Crusoe's rescue are described.
See **pl.** E-144.

ROBINSON, FREDERICK (1830–1912), actor. Played the part of 'Florizel' in Phelps' revival of *The Winter's Tale* at Sadler's Wells in July, 1851.
See **pl.** E-1A.

ROLLA, a character in Sheridan's *Pizarro*. A commander of the army of Ataliba, king of Quito.
See **pls.** E-78, 80 and **Pizarro**.

ROMEO, Charlotte Cushman (1816–76) in the role of (*pl.* E-1A).
See **pls.** E-3, 13 and **Shakspearian characters**.

RUBINI (dates unknown), conjuror. Played at the St James's, St George's and Egyptian Halls, London. Included in his repertoire was an act called 'Beheading a Lady' which was described as a 'marvel of magic'.
See **pls.** E-92, 93.

SAM SWIPES, John Liston (1776–1846) in the role of (*pl.* E-48).
See **Liston, John**.

SAMSON AND THE LION. The story of Samson and the lion is told in Judges, Chapter XIV, verses 5 and 6.

5. Then Samson went down with his father and mother to Thamnatha. And when they were come to the vineyards of the town, behold a young lion met him raging and roaring.
6. And the Spirit of the Lord came upon Samson, and he tore the lion as he would have torn a kid in pieces, having nothing at all in his hand: and he would not tell this to his father and mother.

Figures of Samson and the lion are often erroneously identified as Van Amburgh, Crockett or Hercules.
See **pls.** E-94, 97

SELIM, Mr Harwood in the role of (*pls.* E-27, 28).
See **Bride of Abydos, The**.

SEMIRAMIDE (*Semiramis*), opera in two Acts by Rossini, based on Voltaire's tragedy. First produced in Venice in 1823, and in London, at the King's Theatre, on July 15th, 1824. First produced in English at the Theatre Royal, Covent Garden on October 1st, 1842, with Adelaide Kemble in the title role.

Semiramis, a mythical figure, the daughter of the fish-goddess Derceto, was a favourite heroine of the seventeenth and eighteenth centuries.

The opera is based on the events which follow the murder by Semiramis of her husband, King Ninus, with the help of her lover, Assur. Later, she falls in love with a handsome young warrior whom she believes to be a Scythian, but who is actually her son, Arsaces. When she discovers his identity, she saves his life by receiving Assur's dagger blow intended for him. Arsaces then kills Assur and ascends the throne.
See **pl.** E-91.

SHAKSPEARIAN CHARACTERS KNOWN OR SUSPECTED TO EXIST IN STAFFORDSHIRE POTTERY:

THE TRAGEDY OF KING RICHARD III (1592–4).
Richard, duke of Gloucester, *afterwards* King Richard III.
Henry, earl of Richmond, *afterwards* King Henry VII.

A MIDSUMMER-NIGHT'S DREAM (1594–6).
Titania, *Queen of the Fairies.*

ROMEO AND JULIET (1594–6).
Romeo, *son to Montague, head of one of the two Houses at variance with each other,* and Juliet, *daughter to Capulet, head of the other House.*

THE SECOND PART OF KING HENRY IV (1596–8).
Henry, *Prince of Wales; afterwards* King Henry V.
Sir John Falstaff, *a fat, witty, good-humoured old knight, loving jests, self-indulgent, and over-addicted to sack.*

THE LIFE AND DEATH OF KING JOHN (1596–8).
King John.

THE MERCHANT OF VENICE (1596–8).
Shylock, *a rich Jew.*
Lorenzo, *in love with Jessica.*
Jessica, *daughter to Shylock.*

JULIUS CAESAR (1598–1600).
Marcus Brutus, *conspirator against Julius Caesar.*

THE MERRY WIVES OF WINDSOR (1600–2).
Mistress Page.

Colour Plate 42
Giulia Grisi as 'Lucrezia' and Guiseppe Mario as 'Gennaro' (Left). *Fig.* 46, *pl.* E-28. See page 376. Romeo and Juliet (Right). *Fig.* 11, *pl.* E-3. See page 265.

Colour Plate 43
T.P. Cooke as 'Ben Backstay' (Left). *Fig.* 217, *pl.* E-108. See page 429. Charlotte Cushman as 'Romeo' and Susan Cushman as 'Juliet' (Right). *Fig.* 1, *pl.* E-1A. See page 361.

HAMLET, PRINCE OF DENMARK
(1600–2).
Hamlet, *son to the late, and nephew to the present king.*
Ophelia, *daughter to Polonius, Lord Chamberlain.*

OTHELLO, THE MOOR OF VENICE
(1604–6).
Othello, *a noble Moor; in the service of the Venetian State,* and
Iago, *his Ancient.*

MACBETH (1604–6).
Macbeth, *a general of the army of Duncan, King of Scotland,* and
Lady Macbeth.

THE WINTER'S TALE (1610–2).
Florizel, *son of Polixenes, King of Bohemia.*
Perdita, *daughter of Leontes, King of Sicilia and Queen Hermione.*

SHAW, MARY (1814–?), known as Mrs Alfred Shaw, opera singer. Born in Kent, she studied at the Royal Academy and later with Sir George Smart. Sung in Verdi's first opera *Oberto* at La Scala, 1839. She made her English début as 'Arsaces' in *Semiramide* at Covent Garden on October 1st, 1842, being a worthy partner for Adelaide Kemble who played the title role. *The Times* reported that 'she sustained the character of Arsaces with more than ordinary éclat'.
See **pl. E**-91.

SHYLOCK, William Charles Macready (1793–1873) in the role of (*pl.* E-1B); Charles Kean (1811–68) in the role of (*pl.* E-13).
See **Shakspearian characters.**

SIDDONS, MRS SARAH (1755–1831), actress. When very young acted in company with William Siddons, whom she married in 1773, against her parent's wishes. Engaged by Garrick at Drury Lane, 1775–6, opening with 'Portia' and ending with 'Lady Anne' (*Richard III*). First appeared as 'Lady Macbeth', in London, in 1785. Retired temporarily, 1789–91. Played the 'Queen' in *Richard II*, 1791, and in *Hamlet*, 1796. Played 'Elvira' in *Pizarro*, 1799. Acted at Covent Garden from 1806 to 1812, her farewell performance being in the role of 'Lady Macbeth'. Sister of John Philip Kemble.
See **pls. E**-2, 4, 5, 6, 7.

SOTHERN, EDWARD ASKEW (1826–81), actor. Played a few small parts in this country before going to America. There, in 1859, he appeared in New York in *Our American Cousin* as 'Lord Dundreary', an imbecile peer. This small, insignificant part was worked up by Sothern until at the end of the first month it was the equal to any other character. At the end of the run 'he was the whole play'. In 1861, the play was produced at the Haymarket and Sothern carried the part, though nearly a failure at first, through 496 nights. The caricature gradually grew into a series of monologues which became the talk of the town. There were many revivals at the same theatre with Sothern in this role up to 1878, and his son Edward Hugh (1859–1933) revived his father's old part on several occasions. Sothern was essentially an eccentric comedian, and it was in that line that he did his most memorable work, although he had ambitions towards the playing of romantic drama.
See **pl. E**-18.

SQUEERS, WACKFORD, Yorkshire schoolmaster, a character in Dickens' *Nicholas Nickleby.* The novel was published in serial form from 1838 to 1839. A dramatized version in two Acts by E. Stirling was first produced at the Adelphi in November 1838, *i.e.* prior to publication of final instalments of the novel.
Brutal, rapacious and ignorant Squeers, headmaster of 'Dotheboys Hall', starves and maltreats forty urchins under the pretence of education. Nicholas is sent as scholastic assistant to 'Dotheboys Hall' by his ruthless uncle Ralph Nickleby, when his mother is left penniless on the death of his father. He thrashes Squeers and escapes with one of the urchins, who becomes one of his devoted friends.
See **pls. E**-38, 40, 41 and **Dickens, Charles** and **Nicholas Nickleby**.

STRATTON, CHARLES SHERWOOD (1832–83), otherwise known as 'Tom Thumb', an American dwarf exhibited in England by Barnham in 1844 and 1857. Married Lavinia Warren, also a dwarf, in 1863. He appeared at the Princess's Theatre in February, 1844. His imitation of Napoleon in his manner, gait, taking snuff and several of his well-known attitudes was considered by the reporter for *The Illustrated London News* to be good, but he also stated that:
... the production of this little monster affords another melancholy proof of the low state legitimate drama has been reduced to.
When first exhibited at Barnham's old American museum in New York, he was visited by 30,000 people. In March 1844, accompanied by Mr Barnham, he attended at Buckingham Palace and afforded entertainment to the Queen. She was so delighted that he was asked to perform on two subsequent occasions. His miniature palace, furniture and equipage excited considerable curiosity.
See **pl. E**-50.

SWIVELLER, DICK, a character in Dickens' *The Old Curiosity Shop.*
A friend to Fred Trent and clerk to Sampson Brass. He conspired to marry Little Nell, and thus gain possession of the enormous wealth which it was supposed her grandfather was hoarding up for her.
See **pl. E**-47.

TAM O'SHANTER AND SOUTER JOHNNY, a poem by Robert Burns. A farmer named Douglas Graham was the original 'Tam o'Shanter'. Shanter itself was the name of a farm belonging to Graham not far from Kirkoswald. 'Souter Johnny' was a drinking crony.
The story runs that a farmer, Tam o'Shanter, whilst returning from Ayr late one night well primed with liquor, passed the Kirk of Alloway. Seeing lights, he stopped and looked in, and saw warlocks and witches dancing to the sound of bagpipes played by Old Nick. Impelled by the sight of one 'winsome wench' among the beldams, Tam shouted, 'Weel done, Cutty Sark!'[1] Immediately the lights went out and the witches made for Tam like so many bees. Tam leapt on to his grey mare *Meg* and spurred her forwards, but just as he reached the middle of the bridge over the Doon where he would be out of the power of 'Cutty Sark', she seized the mare's tail, which was still within her jurisdiction, and pulled it off.

'The carlin claught her by the rump,
And left poor Maggie scarce a stump!'

The pantomime *Harlequin Tam o'Shanter*, based on Burns' tale, was produced at Astley's in December, 1843.
See **pl. E**-102,
pls. H-19, 19A, 20.
1. A 'sark' is a chemise.

TELL, WILLIAM, fourteenth century Swiss patriot.
For biography see **section I.**
See **pl. A**-55,
pl. E-60,
pls. I-7, 8, 9, 10.

THAMES TUNNEL, THE, the first passenger tunnel under any river. Plans for constructing a double and capacious roadway under the River Thames between Rotherhithe and Wapping were first exhibited by the celebrated engineer Sir Marc Isambard Brunel (1769–1849), in 1823. Work was commenced the following year. There was a delay lasting 7 years when the river broke in and filled the tunnel. However, it was eventually completed and opened to the public as a thoroughfare for foot-passengers on March 25th, 1843, the carriageways being finished later. The Queen and Prince Albert honoured the tunnel with a visit on July 26th, 1843 and 'appeared highly gratified at viewing this "The Greatest Wonder of the World"'. It is known that there were booths either in, or in the vicinity of the tunnel, and that each had its own address, *viz.,* 43, Thames Tunnel. A figure, believed to portray Jenny Lind and Luigi Lablache is known, inscribed 'Present from the Thames Tunnel'. Considered Brunel's greatest triumph, the tunnel now carries the Underground's East London Line under the Thames.
See **pl. E**-83.

THE THREE GRACES . . . daughters of Zeus; Euphrosyne, Aglaia and Thalia by name. Goddesses of beauty and grace who distributed joy and gentleness.
There is a lithograph, after Lejeune, in the Print Room of the British Museum of 'The Three Graces'. The print represents Taglioni in *La Sylphide*, Fanny Elssler in *Le Diable Boiteux* and Grisi in *La Jolie Fille de Gand*.
See **pls. E**-122, 123.

TITANIA, character in Shakespeare's *A Midsummer Night's Dream* (*pl.* E-115).
See **Shakspearian characters.**

TOM THUMB (1832–83), American dwarf.
See **Stratton, Charles Sherwood.**
See **pls. E**-50, 134.

VAN AMBURGH, ISAAC (1811–70), American lion-tamer, born in Kentucky. Came to England and, in 1838, attracted considerable attention by his Drury Lane performances with a mixed cage of lions, leopards and a lamb. Queen Victoria attended three performances in a fortnight. The Duke of Wellington was likewise

impressed, and commissioned Landseer to paint 'The Brute tamer of Pompeii'—the 'billing' he received at Astley's. It is said that the Duke asked him 'Were you ever afraid?', to which Van Amburgh replied 'The first time I am afraid, Your Grace, or that I fancy that my pupils are no longer afraid of me, I shall retire from the wild beast line'. Van Amburgh's great professional rival was 'Manchester Jack', the 'Lion King' of Wombwell's menagerie. Van Amburgh visited England again in 1843 and 1848. In the latter year he added a black tiger as an additional attraction. It was introduced in the drama of *The Wandering Jew*, a story which was then creating a great sensation all over Europe. In this year, also, Landseer's famous portrait of Van Amburgh was first exhibited at the Royal Academy. Van Amburgh also started a travelling circus with his performing lions, tigers and leopards. He was always portrayed in gladiator's dress.
See **pls. E**-95, 99, 100.

VAN DUNDER, John Liston (1776–1846) in the role of (*pl.* E–49).
See **Liston, John**

VANDENHOFF, CHARLOTTE ELIZABETH (1818–60), actress. Daughter of the actor John Vandenhoff. She made her first appearance at Drury Lane as 'Juliet' on April 11th, 1836. She was a capable actress in parts in which delicacy of feeling, rather than strength and passion, were required. Appeared in many roles. Authoress of *Woman's Heart*, a comedy in which she played the heroine, produced at the Haymarket, in 1852. In 1856, she married the actor, Thomas Swinbourne, but sought to repudiate it one month later.
See **pl. E**-1C.

VESTRIS, LUCIA ELIZABETH (1797–1856), English actress *née* Bartolozzi and grand-daughter of the engraver. Born in London. At 16, she married the dancer Armand Vestris (1787–1825), a member of a Florentine family that gave to France a series of distinguished actors and ballet dancers. She left him in 1820. She was an excellent singer and could well have made a career in grand opera, but limited herself to lighter entertainment. She was at her best in burlesque or high comedy. Her first success was in the title-role of Moncrieff's *Giovanni in London*, a burlesque of Mozart's *Don Giovanni*. She had great success in Paris, and returned to London on her own terms, playing alternatively at Covent Garden and Drury Lane. Her 'Paul' in *Paul and Virginia* at Drury Lane, in 1822, was one of her most famous 'breeches parts'. She was also renowned for her rendering of *The Broom Girl!* which she first sang at the Haymarket in 1826. In 1830, she took over the Olympic, with a strong cast which included Liston, Maria Foote (later Countess of Harrington), the Glovers, the Blands and two members of the Vining family. The theatre opened with *Olympic Revels*; this was followed by a succession of farces and burlesques. During her tenancy of the Olympic she engaged Charles Mathews the younger, whom she married in 1838. She afterwards undertook the management of Covent Garden and the Lyceum.
See **pls. E**-61, 113, 114, 134.

VINING, MRS CHARLES WILLIAM (dates unknown), *née* Johannot, actress. Made her début at the Theatre Royal, Drury Lane, December 1812. Took the title role in *Peter Wilkins* at the Theatre Royal, Covent Garden, April 16th, 1827.
See **pls. E**-24, 25.

WALLACE, lion belonging to Fairgrieve's group of performing animals. Became famous in the representation of the story of *Androcles and the lion*, in which the part of 'Androcles' was taken by the 'Lion King' Lorenzo.
See **pls. E**-78, 100.

WATERS, WILLIAM (?–1823), also known as 'Billy Waters' and 'Black Billy', mendicant. A coloured beggar with a peg leg who earned his living playing a fiddle in London's West End.

In 1821, Pierce Egan wrote his famous book *Tom & Jerry: Life in London or The Day and Night Scenes of Jerry Hawthorn, Esq. and his elegant friend Corinthian Tom in their rambles and sprees through the Metropolis*. It contained illustrations from real life by Cruikshank. The volume was an account of the adventures of two fictional regency bucks in London. It contained a wealth of information on well-known characters of the day, including Billy Waters, a coloured good-time girl known as Black Sall or African Sall and Tom Cribb, the 'Champion of England'. Billy Waters appeared in an illustration by Cruikshank of a tavern scene.

The book was produced as an operatic extravaganza in three Acts by W. T. Moncrieff at the Adelphi Theatre on November 26th, 1821. It was an immediate success, having the longest run up to that time. It played for upwards of 300 nights and only gave over because the actors were tired out; the audience being 'as mad for it as ever'.

The Catnach Press produced a series of cartoons of Tom and Jerry. A copy of the tenth edition, price twopence, is held in the British Museum Library. Titled *The Death, Last Will—and Funeral of 'Black Billy', also the Tears for the death of Tom and Jerry*, it seems to have been produced following the final night at the Adelphi. It contains skits on the 'death' of Tom and Jerry and Black Billy. However, at the foot of the sheet in italics signed *J: C. Mar. 25, 1823* (J. C. = Jas Catnach) appears an apparently quasi-serious obituary (see below) on Billy Waters. It seems that the beggar himself died in poverty at the time that the show, in which he featured as a character, came to the end of its first run.

LIFE OF BILLY WATERS
On Friday at St. Giles Workhouse the famous Billy Waters. Billy endeavoured up to the time of his illness to obtain for a wife and two children what he termed an honest living by the scraping of cat-gut, by which he amassed a considerable portion of browns (halfpence) at the West end of the town, where his hat and feathers with his peculiar antics excited much mirth and attention. He was obliged prior to his death to part with his old friend the fiddle for a trifling sum at the pawnbrokers. His wooden-pin had twice saved him from the Tread-Mill. He lost his leg in His Majesty's service, for which he received a pension. Every child in London knew him. A short time before he died he was elected King of the Beggars . . . J. C. Mar 25, 1823.
See **pls. E**-35, 36.

WELLS, MR, equestrian at Astley's.
See **pls. E**-101, 102 and **Gilpin, John.**

WEST, junr., MR, equestrian at Astley's.
See **pls. E**-107, 107A, **Mazeppa** and **Menken, Adah Isaacs.**

WILLIAMS, BARNEY (1823–76), American actor. With his wife, the sister of Mrs W. J. Florence, he appeared extensively in the United States, particularly in Irish comedies. They arrived in London in 1855, remaining for four years. In July, 1856, they appeared at the Adelphi Theatre and were described in *The Illustrated London News* as:

The original Irish boy and Yankee gal—Mrs Williams being the first to introduce that particular line of character on the stage known as 'the down East Yankee help', Mr Williams being equally original in his line of Irish character.

Barney Williams made his first appearance in 1836 and his last in 1875, and to the end remained an entertainer rather than an actor, a much-loved, jovial, rollicking, drinking, stage Irishman both on and off the boards.
See **pl. E**-19.

WOOD, WILLIAM BURKE (1779–1861), American-born actor. The first to hold a high place in the American theatre. He kept a detailed diary from 1810 to 1831, whilst manager of the Chestnut Street Theatre, Philadelphia which contains much of interest concerning the history of the early American theatre. He had a predilection for English classics and was superb both at polished comedy and also the lighter parts of tragedy. He married Juliana Westray, who appeared for many years under her husband's name.
See **pl. E**-60.

WOOLFORD, LOUISA.
See **pls. E**-68, 100, 146 and **Ducrow, Andrew,** whose second wife she was.

YOUNG, CHARLES MAYNE (1777–1856), English actor, the son of a doctor. Made his début, in 1798, as 'Mr Green' at Liverpool. Became an intimate friend of Sir Walter Scott. In 1800, he married a young actress, who died in childbirth the following year. He first appeared in London in the role of 'Hamlet' at the Haymarket Theatre with great success. He retired from the stage in 1832. During his years in London theatres, he played with John Philip Kemble, Mrs Siddons, Macready and Miss O'Neill.
See **pl. E**-91.

YOURAWKEE, Mary Glover in the role of (*pl.* E-24).
See **Peter Wilkins.**

ZULEIKA, Miss Rosa Henry in the role of (*pls.* E-27, 28).
See **Bride of Abydos, The.**

Colour Plate 44
David Garrick as 'Richard III' (Left). *Fig.* 22, *pl.* E-7. See pages 66 and 368. Mazeppa on a horse (Right). *Fig.* 216, E-107. See page 427.

Colour Plate 45
Carlotta Grisi as 'Esmeralda' and Jules Perrot as 'Gringoire'. *Figs.* 62 and 63, *pl.* E-29. See page 380.

E360

Section E
Theatre, Opera, Ballet and Circus
Details of the Figures

Plate 1
Figure 1(*a*)
Subject: **King John**
Title: None
Height: 12½ in (31.75 cm)
Colour: White and gilt or well coloured.
Rarity: C.
Description: King John, crowned, is sitting in a tent with both hands on a document, presumably the Magna Carta. At each side a page is standing with a flag above and behind him.
Observations: 1. This figure is generally regarded as a theatrical piece. Victorian actor-managers if they considered the pace of a play to be too slow to satisfy the taste of their patrons, not uncommonly produced a procession or tableau to brighten things up. This group is thought to portray such an interpolation into Shakespeare's *King John*. It is not likely to represent a particular actor in the part, although this possibility cannot be excluded.
2. A similar figure fetched 16 gns at Christie's in 1966; and another, with an unimportant piece, 30 gns in 1969.

Plate 1A
Figure 1
Subject: **Charlotte Cushman as 'Romeo' and Susan Cushman as 'Juliet'**
Title: *Jul.* O think'st thou we shall ever meet again?
Rom. I doubt it not; and all these woes shall serve
For sweet discourses in our time to come.
(transfer: upper and lower case)
Date: *c.* 1852
Height: 10½ in (26.5 cm)
Colour: Well coloured in the manner of Thomas Parr. White and gilt versions are also found.
Maker: Thomas Parr
Rarity: Av. D. A.
Series: One of the series of seven Shakspearian figures based on engravings in Tallis' *Shakespeare Gallery* (1852–3), all of which are illustrated in *ch.* 3.
Description: 'Romeo' and 'Juliet' stand with their arms entwined. 'Juliet' wears a cotehardie with girdle and 'Romeo' wears a kilt and jerkin with hose. Beneath is the quotation from *Romeo and Juliet* cited above.
Observations: 1. After an engraving from Tallis' *Shakespeare Gallery* illustrated in *ch.* 3, *pl.* 26 which is inscribed *CHARLOTTE AND SUSAN CUSHMAN | AS | ROMEO AND JULIET | Act 3, Scene 5.*

2. This figure appears in all three Kent lists as follows:

KENT LIST A *Stock No.* (*c.* 1901)	KENT LIST B *Stock No.*	KENT LIST C *Ref. No.* (1955)
281	329	329

Both contemporary copies and reproductions are becoming scarce.
3. A similar figure fetched 24 gns at Christie's in 1964; and another, 35 gns in the same rooms in 1967.
4. Figures titled 'Romeo | & | Juliet' in gilt script are, I believe, invariably late reproductions.

Figure 2
Subject: **Jenny Marston as 'Perdita' and Frederick Robinson as 'Florizel'**
Title: Winter's Tale (indented capitals)
Date: *c.* 1852
Height: 11¾ in (29.75 cm)
Colour: Well coloured in the manner of Thomas Parr. White and gilt versions are also found.
Rarity: R. D. A.
Series: One of the series of seven Shakspearian figures based on engravings in Tallis' *Shakespeare Gallery* (1852–3), all of which are illustrated in *ch.* 3.
Description: 'Perdita' and 'Florizel', each bare-headed, stand in front of a tree trunk (spill-holder) holding hands. 'Perdita' wears a low-cut double-skirted dress with tie belt and garland of roses on the skirt. 'Florizel' is wearing a long belted tunic, hose and shoes.
Observations: 1. After the engraving from *Tallis' Shakespeare Gallery* illustrated in *ch.* 3, *pl.* 27 which is inscribed *MISS JENNY MARSTON AND MR. F. ROBINSON | AS FLORIZEL AND PERDITA | Act 4, Scene 3.*
2. No. 390 in *Kent List A* and no. 405 in *Kent List B* but deleted as a 'discontinued line'. No reproductions have been seen.
3. A white and gilt version of the figure fetched £38 at Sotheby's in 1969; and a similar figure 35 gns at Christie's, three months later.

Figure 5
Subject: **Ophelia**
Title: Ophelia (indented capitals)
Date: *c.* 1852
Height: 10¼ in (25.75 cm); there is a smaller

version 6¼ in (16 cm).
Colour: Well coloured in the manner of Thomas Parr. White and gilt versions are also found.
Maker: Thomas Parr
Rarity: VR. D. A.
Pair: Either *fig.* 6 (Kemble as 'Hamlet'), *fig.* 32 (Kemble as 'Hamlet') *pl.* E-13, or *fig.* 32(*a*) (Kemble as 'Hamlet') *pl.* E-13A.
Description: She stands, her hair braided with flowers, holding a small posy in her right hand. She wears a double-skirted dress with narrow sash and there is a garland of flowers on her skirt.
Observations: 1. 'Ophelia' does not occur as an engraving in Tallis' *Shakespeare Gallery*. The potter rectified this omission by using the figure of 'Perdita' (*Winter's Tale*) with minor modifications and titling the figure 'Ophelia'.
2. The smaller version *only* appears in all three Kent lists as follows:

KENT LIST A *Stock No.* (*c.* 1901)	KENT LIST B *Stock No.*	KENT LIST C *Ref. No.* (1955)
285	308	308

Both contemporary copies and reproductions are very rare.

Figure 6
Subject: **John Philip Kemble as 'Hamlet'**
Title: Alas Poor Yorick (transfer: upper and lower case—black or gilt)
Date: *c.* 1852
Height: 11¼ in (28.5 cm); a 6¾ in (17 cm) untitled version is also known.
Colour: Well coloured in the manner of Thomas Parr. White and gilt versions are also found.
Maker: Thomas Parr
Rarity: R. D. A.
Pair: Fig. 5 (Ophelia). One of the series of seven Shakspearian figures based on engravings in Tallis' *Shakespeare Gallery* (1852–3), all of which are illustrated in *ch.* 3.
Description: He stands in round hat with single plume, shirt, short trunks and hose. He wears a cloak over both shoulders and holds a skull in his left hand to which he points with his right index finger.
Observations: 1. Based on the engraving from Lawrence's portrait in Tallis' *Shakespeare Gallery* illustrated in *ch.* 3, *pl.* 28, which is inscribed *JOHN PHILIP KEMBLE AS HAMLET | 'Alas! Poor Yorick' | Act. 5, Scene 1.*

Plate 1
Fig. 1(a) King John

Plate 1A continued
Note in *fig.* 6 and in the engraving the cloak is over *both* shoulders. *Fig.* 32, *pl.* E-13 is identical except that the cloak is only over his left shoulder; although from the same factory it cannot be properly described as being based on this engraving. The same applies to *fig.* 32(*a*), *pl.* E-13A. The small 6¾ in (17 cm) untitled version has the cloak over both shoulders, but to date I have not seen a copy which was undoubtedly contemporary, see *pl.* E-4.

E362

3. The Kent lists contain the following entries:

	KENT LIST A Stock No. (c. 1901)	KENT LIST B Stock No.	KENT LIST C Ref. No. (1955)
Hamlet (*large*)	275	273	273
Hamlet (*small*)	276	274	274

It is not clear to which of the variants of the large version the lists refer. Those reproductions of the large version I have seen are all of *fig.* 32, pl. E-13.

Plate 1B
Figure 3
Subject: **James Henry Hackett as 'Falstaff'**
Title: Falstaff (indented capitals)
Date: *c.* 1852
Height: 9½ in (24 cm). There is, also, an identical 7¼ in (18.25 cm) version.
Colour: Well coloured in the manner of Thomas Parr. White and gilt versions are also found.
Maker: Thomas Parr

Section E. Theatre, Opera, Ballet and Circus

Plate 1A
Note:
1. The style of titling is characteristic of figures made by Thomas Parr. The same standard was never obtained in reproductions.
2. Ophelia does not occur as an engraving in Tallis' *Shakespeare Gallery*. The potter rectified this omission by using the figure of 'Perdita' (*The Winter's Tale*. After minor modifications the piece was titled 'Ophelia'.
In the Thomas Balston collection.

Fig. 6 Kemble ('Hamlet')   Fig. 1 Cushman sisters ('Romeo' and 'Juliet')   Fig. 2 Marston and Robinson ('Perdita' and 'Florizel')   Fig. 5 Ophelia

Plate 1B   Fig. 3 Hackett ('Falstaff')   Fig. 4 Macready ('Shylock')   Fig. 8 Macready ('Macbeth')   Fig. 7 Glyn ('Lady Macbeth')
In the Thomas Balston collection

Rarity: R. D. A.
Series: One of the series of seven Shakspearian figures based on engravings in *Tallis' Shakespeare Gallery* (1852–3), all of which are illustrated in *ch.* 3.
Description: Standing bearded, in broad-brimmed hat. He wears a coat with deep braided cuffs over a long waistcoat, with a sash and belt, and loose trousers.
Observations: 1. After an engraving in Tallis' *Shakespeare Gallery* illustrated in *ch.* 3, *pl.* 29A which is inscribed *MR HACKETT AS*

FALSTAFF | King Henry IV | Part 1, Act 4, Scene 2.
2. The Kent lists contain the following entries:

	KENT LIST A Stock No. (c. 1901)	KENT LIST B Stock No.	KENT LIST C Ref. No. (1955)
Falstaff (*large*)	273	215	215
Falstaff (*small*)	274	216	216

Reproductions of both the large and small

versions are very common. All contemporary figures are rare.
3. The figure illustrated on this plate is a contemporary copy of the large version and that in *ch.* 3, *pl.* 29, a reproduction of the small version. Their different qualities are easy to perceive even in black and white illustrations.

Figure 4
Subject: **William Charles Macready as 'Shylock'**

E363

Plate 1B continued

Title: Shylock (indented capitals)
Date: c. 1852
Height: 9¾ in (24.5 cm). There is, also, an identical 7 in (17.5 cm) version.
Colour: Well coloured in the manner of Thomas Parr. White and gilt versions are also found.
Maker: Thomas Parr
Rarity: VR. D. A.
Series: One of the series of seven Shakspearian figures based on engravings in Tallis' *Shakespeare Gallery* (1852–3), all of which are illustrated in *ch.* 3.
Description: He stands, bearded and long haired, with a staff in his right hand. He wears a long gown edged in ermine and belted at the waist. Oval-shaped hat.
Observations: 1. After an engraving in Tallis' *Shakespeare Gallery* illustrated in *ch.* 3, *pl.* 30 which is inscribed *MR MACREADY AS SHYLOCK | Merchant of Venice | Act 1, Scene 3*.
2. The Kent lists contain the following entries:

	KENT LIST A Stock No. (c. 1901)	KENT LIST B Stock No.	KENT LIST C Ref. No. (1955)
Shylock (*large*)	277	355	355
Shylock (*small*)	278	356	356

Contemporary copies of both the large and small versions are extremely rare but reproductions of the small version are not uncommon.

Figure 7
Subject: **Isabella Glyn as 'Lady Macbeth'**
Title: Lady Macbeth (indented capitals)
Date: c. 1852
Height: 10 in (25 cm). There is, also, an 8 in (20.5 cm) version, an example of which is illustrated on *pl.* E-2. It has minor differences.
Colour: Well coloured in the manner of Thomas Parr. A white and gilt version is also found.
Maker: Thomas Parr
Rarity: VR. D. A.
Pair: Fig. 8 (Macready as 'Macbeth'). One of the series of seven Shakspearian figures based on engravings in Tallis' *Shakespeare Gallery* (1852–3), all of which are illustrated in *ch.* 3.
Description: Standing bare-headed, in long dress, her left arm by her side, her right arm across her waist. She clutches a letter in her right hand. A small brooch is pinned to her dress over the middle of her chest.
Observations: 1. After an engraving in Tallis' *Shakespeare Gallery* illustrated in *ch.* 3, *pl.* 31 which is inscribed *MISS GLYN AS LADY MACBETH | Act 1, Scene 5*. It will be noted that the large version does not approximate so closely to the engraving as the small version.
2. The Kent lists contain the following entries:

	KENT LIST A Stock No. (c. 1901)	KENT LIST B Stock No.	KENT LIST C Ref. No. (1955)
Lady Macbeth [8 in (20.5 cm)]	280	303	303

The large version does not appear in the Kent lists. Contemporary copies of both large and small versions are extremely rare, but late reproductions of the small version are common. No reproductions of the large version have been noted.
3. A small version of this figure and its pair

E364

(both reproductions) fetched 18 gns at Christie's in 1966.

Figure 8
Subject: **William Charles Macready as 'Macbeth'**
Title: Macbeth (indented capitals)
Date: c. 1852
Height: 10½ in (26.5 cm). There is, also, an 8¼ in (21 cm) version, an example of which is illustrated on *pl.* E-2. It has minor differences.
Colour: Well coloured in the manner of Thomas Parr. White and gilt versions are also found.
Maker: Thomas Parr
Rarity: VR. D. A.
Pair: Fig. 7 (Glyn as 'Lady Macbeth'). One of the series of seven Shakspearian figures based on engravings in Tallis' *Shakespeare Gallery* (1852–3), all of which are illustrated in *ch.* 3.
Description: He stands wearing a cockaded cap, jerkin, kilt with dagger suspended from the belt, a plaid over his left shoulder, a bossed shield on his left arm, hose and sandals.
Observations: 1. After an engraving in Tallis' *Shakespeare Gallery* illustrated in *ch.* 3, *pl.* 32 which is inscribed *MR MACREADY AS MACBETH | Act 1, Scene 3*.

2. Macready gave his farewell performance as 'Macbeth' at Drury Lane in 1851. Possibly the potter, when searching for a suitable illustration of him in that role, found it in Tallis' *Shakespeare Gallery* and sensed that others of the illustrations might appeal to the public when 'converted' to figurines.
3. The Kent lists contain the following entries:

	KENT LIST A Stock No. (c. 1901)	KENT LIST B Stock No.	KENT LIST C Ref. No. (1955)
Macbeth [8¼ in (21 cm)]	279	302	302

The large version does not appear in the Kent lists. Contemporary copies of both large and small versions are extremely rare, but late reproductions of the small version are common. No reproductions of the large version have been noted.

Plate 1C
Charlotte Vandenhoff
Engraving from Tallis' *Shakespeare Gallery* of Miss Vandenhoff as 'Juliet'. It is the source of *fig.* 1(*b*), the details of which are as follows:
Figure 1(*b*)
Subject: **Charlotte Elizabeth Vandenhoff as 'Juliet'**
Title: None
Date: c. 1852
Height: 7¾ in (20 cm)
Colour: Well coloured.
Maker: Thomas Parr
Rarity: VR. D. A.
Pair: Unrecorded
Description: She stands bare-headed, with hair down to her shoulders, her left hand across her waist, her right hand by her side. She wears a bodice with pagoda sleeves, full-length skirt and overskirt.
Observations: 1. Based on the engraving from Tallis' *Shakespeare Gallery*, illustrated on this plate, which is inscribed:

MISS VANDENHOFF AS JULIET

Plate 1C
Engraving from Tallis' *Shakespeare Gallery* of Miss Vandenhoff as 'Juliet'. It is the source of *fig.* 1(b).

Jul: 'Give me my Romeo: and, when he shall die,
Take him and cut him out in little stars,
And he will make the face of heaven so fine
That all the world will be in love with night,
And pay no worship to the garish sun.—'
        ROMEO AND JULIET
        Act 3, Sc. 2.
Engraved by Hollis from a Daguerreotype by Paine of Islington.

2. Only one example of this figure has been reported and it is in America. It is decorated in the same way as the seven Shakspearian figures based on engravings in Tallis' *Shakespeare Gallery* (1852–3) recorded by Messrs Mander and Mitchenson, and differs from them only in being untitled (see *p.* 15). I understand from Mr John Hall, who has seen the figure, that it is identical to the engraving, except that Juliet's left arm is across her chest; a modification one might reasonably expect the potter to make.
3. The figure does not appear in any of the three Kent lists.
4. Miss Vandenhoff first played 'Juliet' in 1836 at Drury Lane. Daguerre published his invention in 1839. It was not until the late 1840's that photography was becoming big business. Clearly the daguerreotype by Paine of Islington is likely to date to the early 1850's when Tallis' *Shakespeare Gallery* was published.

Plate 2
Figure 7
Subject: **Isabella Glyn as 'Lady Macbeth'**
Title: Lady Macbeth (indented capitals)
Date: c. 1852
Height: 8 in (20.5 cm)
Observations: This is the small version of the figure. It is fully documented under *pl.* E-1B.

Fig. 8 Macready ('Macbeth') *Fig.* 7 Glyn ('Lady Macbeth') *Fig.* 10 ?Mrs Siddons ('Lady *Fig.* 9 Kemble ('Hamlet')
Macbeth')

Plate 3
Fig. 11 Romeo and Juliet

Figure 8
Subject: **William Charles Macready as 'Macbeth'**
Title: Macbeth (indented capitals)
Date: c. 1852
Height: 8¼ in (21 cm)
Observations: This is the small version of the figure. It is fully documented under *pl.* E-1B.

Figure 9
Subject: **John Philip Kemble as 'Hamlet'**
Title: None
Date: 184–
Height: 8½ in (21.5 cm)
Colour: Usually pastel shades.
Maker: Unknown
Rarity: R. A.
Pair: Fig. 10 (? Mrs Siddons as 'Lady Macbeth')
Description: Standing in round hat with two plumes, tunic, short trunks and hose, a cloak with no edging over both shoulders. A broad ribbon passes from his right shoulder across his tunic. In his left hand he holds a skull to which he points with his right index finger. Serpentine fronted base.
Observations: 1. After a painting by Sir Thomas Lawrence, titled *John Philip Kemble Esq. as Hamlet*, now in the National Portrait Gallery. The figure shows none of the characteristics of the Parr and Kent group, *i.e.* it is not a 'Tallis figure'. It can be assumed that the potter's source was not the engraving of Lawrence's painting to be found in Tallis' *Shakespeare Gallery*, but rather one such as that illustrated in *ch.* 3, *pl.* 33.
2. The pair to this figure—a woman standing, wearing a crown and with a cloak over both shoulders and clutching a handkerchief in her left hand—probably represents 'Lady Macbeth' and is quite possibly a portrait of Kemble's sister, Mrs Siddons. 'Hamlet' and 'Lady Macbeth' were considered the principal male and female characters of the Shakspearian drama of that era.

Figure 10
Subject: **?Mrs Siddons as 'Lady Macbeth'**
Title: None
Date: 184–
Height: 8 in (20.5 cm)
Colour: Usually pastel shades.
Maker: Unknown
Rarity: R. A.
Pair: Fig. 9 (Kemble as 'Hamlet')
Description: Standing, wearing a crown with a plume, long dress with puff sleeves, a cloak over both shoulders. Her right hand is across her waist and in her left hand she holds a handkerchief or cloth. Serpentine fronted base.
Observations: Generally thought to portray Kemble's sister Mrs Siddons in the role of 'Lady Macbeth', although no engraving has been found to correspond.

Plate 3
Figure 11
Subject: **Romeo and Juliet**
Title: None
Date: c. 1852
Height: 11¼ in (28.5 cm)
Colour: Well coloured in pastel shades.
Maker: Unknown
Rarity: VR. D. A.
Description: Very similar to *fig.* 1 (Charlotte and Susan Cushman as 'Romeo' and 'Juliet') *pl.* E-1A. The stance and dress are virtually identical, except that 'Romeo' is wearing a round hat with a solitary plume. The 'ermine' band around his neck in the figure illustrated is a contemporary covering to a firing crack.
Observations: No engraving has been found by which it is possible to make a positive identification, but the faces of 'Romeo' and 'Juliet' portrayed in *fig.* 1 are very similar to those portrayed in *fig.* 11. This adds weight to the view that the latter group is indeed, a portrayal of the Cushman sisters as 'Romeo' and 'Juliet'.

Plate 4
Fig. 12 ?Mrs Siddons and Kemble ('Lady Macbeth' and 'Hamlet')

Fig. 6 Kemble ('Hamlet') small untitled version
In the collection of Messrs Raymond Mander & Joe Mitchenson

Plate 6
Figure 15
Subject: **John Philip Kemble as 'Hamlet'**
Title: None
Date: 184–
Height: 12 in (30.5 cm)
Colour: White and gilt.
Maker: Unknown
Rarity: VR.
Pair: *Fig.* 16 (? Mrs Siddons as 'Lady Macbeth')
Description: Standing in round hat with one plume and cloak over both shoulders, breeches instead of short trunks, and stockings. In his left hand he holds a skull, to which he points with his right index finger.
Observations: The source of this figure is unknown, even so, there is little doubt that it portrays John Philip Kemble.

Figure 16
Subject: **?Mrs Siddons as 'Lady Macbeth'**
Title: None
Date: 184–
Height: 11⅛ in (28.25 cm)
Colour: White and gilt.
Maker: Unknown
Rarity: VR.
Pair: *Fig.* 15 (Kemble as 'Hamlet')
Description: She stands crowned, in a long cloak. The potter has mistakenly left a gap between the arms and the body! She wears a low-necked bodice and in her left hand she holds a handkerchief. Her right hand is raised to her breast.
Observations: Has been mistakenly identified as Victoria from time to time.

Plate 4
Figure 6
Subject: **John Philip Kemble as 'Hamlet'**
Title: None
Date: Only 'late' copies have been seen.
Height: 6¾ in (17 cm)
Observations: This is the small version of the figure. It is fully documented on *pl.* E-1A.

Figure 12
Subject: **?Mrs Siddons as 'Lady Macbeth' and John Philip Kemble as 'Hamlet'**
Title: None
Date: 184–
Height: 6½ in (16.5 cm)
Colour: White and gilt.
Rarity: VR.
Description: She stands on the left, crowned. She wears a cloak and long dress. He stands on the right, wearing a round hat with one plume, cloak over both shoulders, tunic, breeches instead of small trunks, and stockings. He holds a skull in his left hand. Between them is a pillar or tree stump.
Observations: Hamlet is wearing a dress similar to that portrayed in *fig.* 15, *pl.* E-6.

Plate 5
Figure 14
Subject: **?Mrs Siddons as 'Lady Macbeth'**
Title: None
Date: 184–
Height: 9¼ in (23.5 cm)
Colour: Well coloured.
Rarity: R.
Pair: The pair to this figure is likely to be John Philip Kemble as 'Hamlet', but the figure has not yet come to light. *Fig.* 13 has been reserved for it.
Description: Similar in most respects to *fig.* 10, *pl.* E-2, except that it is taller. Also, the cloak is edged with ermine and the shape of the base is slightly modified.

Plate 5
Fig. 14 ?Mrs Siddons ('Lady Macbeth')

Plate 6
Fig. 15 Kemble ('Hamlet')
Fig. 16 ?Mrs Siddons ('Lady Macbeth')
In the Thomas Balston collection

Section E. Theatre, Opera, Ballet and Circus

Fig. 23 Falstaff   Fig. 22 Garrick ('Richard III')   Fig. 20 Macready ('James V of Scotland')

Fig. 17 Kemble ('Hamlet')   Fig. 19 ?Mrs Siddons ('Lady Macbeth') and Kemble ('Hamlet')   Fig. 18 ?Mrs Siddons ('Lady Macbeth')

Plate 7
Figure 17
Subject: **John Philip Kemble as 'Hamlet'**
Title: None
Date: 184–
Height: 8½ in (21.5 cm)
Colour: Well coloured.
Maker: Unknown
Rarity: Av.
Pair: Fig. 18 (? Mrs Siddons as 'Lady Macbeth')
Description: He is standing in round hat with three plumes, tunic, short trunks and hose. There is a cloak over both shoulders which is edged with ermine. A broad ribbon passes from his right shoulder across his tunic. He holds a skull in his left hand, to which he points with his right index finger.

Observations: Based on Lawrence's painting *John Philip Kemble Esq. as Hamlet*, or from an engraving of it, see *ch. 3, pl.* 33.

Figure 18
Subject: **?Mrs Siddons as 'Lady Macbeth'**
Title: None
Date: 184–
Height: 8 in (20.5 cm)
Colour: Well coloured.
Maker: Unknown
Rarity: Av.
Pair: Fig. 17 (Kemble as 'Hamlet')
Description: She stands crowned, wearing an ermine-edged cloak over a long dress, a handkerchief or cloth in her left hand, her right hand over her right breast.
Observations: For the reasons for supposing

that this figure portrays Mrs Siddons, see *fig.* 9, *pl.* E-2.

Figure 19
Subject: **?Mrs Siddons as 'Lady Macbeth' and John Philip Kemble as 'Hamlet'**
Title: None
Date: 184–
Height: 8 in (20.5 cm)
Colour: Sometimes well coloured, usually sparsely coloured.
Maker: Unknown
Rarity: C.
Series: Forms the centrepiece to *figs.* 17 (Kemble as 'Hamlet') and 18 (? Mrs Siddons as 'Lady Macbeth').
Description: She stands on the left, dressed very similarly to *fig.* 18. He stands on the

Plate 7 continued

right, dressed very similarly to *fig.* 17, except that *1.* there is no broad ribbon passing from his right shoulder across his tunic and *2.* the cloak, which is ermine-edged, is only over his left shoulder. Between them is a clock-face.

Observations: 1. Seemingly that referred to as 'Hamlet and Ophelia' in all three Kent lists: no. 284 in *Kent List A*, and no. 272 in *Kent Lists B* and *C*.
2. A similar figure fetched 30 gns at Christie's in 1969.

Figure 20
Subject: **William Charles Macready as 'James V of Scotland'**
Title: Macready (gilt script)
Date: 1846
Height: 8 in (20.5 cm)
Colour: Well coloured, underglaze blue coat.
Maker: Unknown
Rarity: VR. (titled); R. (untitled).
Pair: There is no pair to the titled figure, but the untitled figure pairs *fig.* 21 (Unidentified actress) *pl.* E-62.
Description: He stands bare-headed and bearded, in long ermine-edged cloak, tunic, short trunks and stockings. To his left is a pedestal.
Observations: 1. Identified from an engraving in *The Illustrated London News* of May 23rd, 1846 depicting Macready as 'James V of Scotland' in the new play *The King of the Commons* at the Princess' Theatre, see *ch.* 3, *pl.* 34A. Although this engraving is not absolutely identical to the figure, others are known which deal with the same subject, and perusal of them all leaves little doubt as to the identification.
2. No titled figure is known to pair this figure, but in its untitled state it pairs *fig.* 21, *pl.* E-62 which is, for want of a better term, referred to as 'unidentified actress', see *p.* 29. It may be that this figure is, in fact, that of an actress, although so far it has defied identification. The alternative theory is that it does not portray anyone in particular, being produced simply to balance the figure of Macready.

Figure 22
Subject: **David Garrick as 'Richard III'**
Title: Richard the Third (gilt script)
Height: 9½ in (24 cm)
Colour: Well coloured.
Maker: Unknown
Rarity: VR. D. (titled); C. (untitled).
Description: Sitting bare-headed, on a low seat in a tent, his right hand raised. He wears an ermine-edged gown over a jerkin, doublet and hose. There is a garter below his left knee and he wears a chain and order round his neck.
Observations: 1. Based on Hogarth's painting of the 'nightmare' scene, *David Garrick as Richard III* (1745), now in the Walker Art Gallery, Liverpool, see *ch.* 3, *pl.* 35.
2. A similar figure fetched 22 gns at Christie's in 1964; another 12 gns in 1966; another £18 at Sotheby's in 1966, and another £12 in 1968. Yet another, 16 gns at Christie's in 1969.

Figure 23
Subject: **Sir John Falstaff**
Title: None
Height: 6¼ in (16 cm)
Colour: Well coloured.
Rarity: Av.

Description: Seated wearing a plumed bonnet, cloak, waistcoat, breeches and knee-boots, a mug in his right hand, a scroll in his left hand and his right foot on a stool.
Observations: A theatrical figure, but the actor has so far defied identification. It probably portrays Luigi Lablache, the opera singer, in the role of 'Falstaff'.

Plate 8
Figure 24
Subject: **Sir John Falstaff**
Title: None
Date: c. 1844
Height: 6¾ in (17 cm)
Colour: Sparsely coloured.
Rarity: VR. A.
Pair: A pair almost certainly exists, but so far has not turned up. *Fig.* 25 has been reserved for it.
Description: Seated on a horse facing right, bearded, in plumed round hat. He wears a doublet and hose and knee-boots. He bears a shield on his right forearm and holds the horse's reins in his left hand. He carries a sword.
Observations: The appearance is that of a circus figure and weight is added to this argument by the knowledge that Shakspearian equestrian acts were not infrequently put on at Astley's. The playbill illustrated on *pl.* E-9 advertises the programme at Astley's on Monday, January 29th, 1844. One item on the agenda is advertised as follows:

Mr. *NEWSOME*
The popular British Horseman, in his Novel Delineation on a Rapid Steed, of the Shakespearian Characters
Sir John FALSTAFF,
SHYLOCK, & RICHARD 3rd.

If this supposition is correct, a pair to this figure could be 'Shylock' or 'Richard III', and the discovery of one or other of these as equestrian figures would add weight to the hypothesis.

Plate 9
Astley's Playbill
Playbill advertising part of the programme for Astley's Royal Amphitheatre of Arts for Monday, January 29th, 1844.
Among the many items in this complex programme are scenes from the Battle of Waterloo; equestrian acts portraying Shakspearian characters, including 'Falstaff', 'Shylock' and 'Richard III' and an equestrian Christmas pantomime *Harlequin Tam o'Shanter and his steed Meg*. Each or every one of these could have inspired the potter to produce figures, see, also, *pl.* B-6.

Plate 10
Figure 26
Subject: **Sir John Falstaff**
Title: None
Height: 5½ in (14 cm)
Colour: Well coloured.
Rarity: R.
Pair: Not known
Description: Seated, in plumed round hat, a pistol in his left hand, and knee-boots.
Observations: Probably theatrical, almost certainly 'Falstaff', but the actual actor has so far defied identification.

Figure 27
Subject: **? Falstaff and another**
Title: None
Height: 6 in (15.25 cm)
Colour: Both well coloured and sparsely coloured versions exist.
Rarity: R.

Plate 8
Fig. 24 Falstaff
In the collection of Dr S.J. Howard

Plate 9
Part of a playbill advertising the programme for Astley's Royal Amphi-theatre of Arts for Monday, January 29th, 1844.
Note the item concerning Mr Newsome 'in his Novel Delineation, on a Rapid Steed, of the Shakespearian Characters Sir John Falstaff, Shylock, & Richard 3rd'.

Plate 10
Fig. 26 Falstaff
Fig. 27 ?Falstaff and
another
*In the collections of
Mr David Robinson and the
author*

Plate 11
L: *Fig.* 28 Quin ('Falstaff')
R: A Derby figure of Falstaff
Note Quin's right hand has been wrongly
restored. The sword hilt is omitted.
*In the collection of Messrs Raymond Mander and
Joe Mitchenson*

Description: Both men are seated at the foot of a tree trunk (spill-holder). The one on the left wears a plumed, round hat and is bearded. Although both arms are broken in the figure illustrated, it is known from another figure that he should be holding a mug. This man may well be 'Falstaff'. The one on the right wears a plumed hat, but has a moustache. He also carries a mug in his right hand. It has been suggested that this man is 'Pistol', but this is mere conjecture.

Plate 11
Figure 28
Subject: **James Quin as 'Sir John Falstaff'**
Title: Falstaff (raised capitals)
Date: *c.* 1850
Height: 17 in (42.5 cm)
Colour: White, black and gilt; one well coloured version with underglaze blue coat has been noted.
Rarity: R. D.
Description: He stands clean-shaven, with his left hand on his hip, wearing a long coat over a belted floral waistcoat, breeches and knee-boots. He has a small ruff around his neck and wears a broad-brimmed plumed hat on his head. In his right hand is a sword hilt but no sword. In the figure illustrated the right hand has been wrongly restored, omitting the sword hilt.
Observations: 1. Copied from the porcelain figure illustrated on the right of this plate. This figure is after an undated mezzotint of James Quin stated to be by and after

J. McArdell. It is undoubtedly Derby, being in light colours, 20 in (50 cm) in height, and on a rococo base. The figure is bearded and the hilt of the sword is modelled in porcelain, with a hole for the metal blade to be inserted. The first Derby figure probably dates from the death of the actor in 1766. Although the first figure was clean-shaven, subsequent figures were bearded; later, there was a reversion to the beardless type. By the 1850's, long after Quin was forgotten, the design had become the traditional representation of 'Falstaff'. In the Staffordshire figure the shield is omitted and the actor is beardless. It is the only one in the entire series to bear the name of the character.

That Quin played 'Falstaff' without a beard is borne out in *The Theatrical Steel-Yards of 1750*. A satirical print of theatrical conditions engraved by Patrick O'Brien published in April, 1751, includes a figure of Quin as 'Falstaff'. The mezzotint stated to be by and after J. McArdell shows 'Falstaff''s figure to be an exact copy of John Harper in the part, as illustrated in the *Stage Meeting* (1733), while the head is from the John Faber mezzotint of Thomas Hudson's portrait of Quin dated 1744.
2. Much of the research quoted above and elsewhere in section E is the work of Messrs Raymond Mander and Joe Mitchenson who have been most generous in supplying me with information.
3. A similar figure fetched 32 gns at Christie's in 1967.

Plate 12
Fig. 29 Henry V

To the right of the figure is
p. 197 from *The Illustrated London
News* of September 25th, 1847.
The engraving is of a painting
by John Calcott Horsley titled:
*Henry V, when Prince of Wales,
believing the King to be Dead, Takes
the Crown from the Cushion.*
In the collection of Dr S.J. Howard

Plate 12
Figure 29
Subject: **King Henry V**
Title: Henry V trying / on the crown (raised
capitals)
Date: *c.* 1847
Height: 13¾ in (35 cm)
Colour: Well coloured.
Rarity: R. D. A.
Description: He stands, in a long tunic, trying
on the crown. A hunting horn hangs from
his belt on his right side, and a sword hangs
from his belt on his left. To his left is a
pedestal upon which rests a cushion. The
sceptre, a rod symbolizing sovereignty, lies
on the cushion.
Observations: Based on a painting by John
Calcott Horsley titled *Henry V, when Prince
of Wales, believing the King to be Dead, Takes
the Crown from the Cushion.* As far as is known
the work was not a portrait of an actor in
the role. An engraving of the painting
appeared in *The Illustrated London News* of
September 25th, 1847 with the following
details:

'With Mr. Horsley's picture, for which he has
received one of the £200 Premiums, we conclude our
Series of Illustrations of the National Exhibition in
Westminster Hall. The painting is of a large gallery
size—height 14 feet, 3 inches and in width 10 feet,
and stands thus in the Catalogue:—"Henry V, when
Prince of Wales, believing the King to be Dead, Takes
the Crown from the Cushion . . . John Calcott Horsley."

Prince Henry . . .
". . . Thy due from me
Is tears and heavy sorrows of the blood,
Which nature, love, and filial tenderness
Shall, O dear father! pay thee plenteously:
My due from thee is this imperial crown,
Which, as immediate from thy place and blood,
Derives itself to me. Lo! here it sits,
Putting it on his head.
Which heaven shall guard; and put the world's
whole strength
Into one giant arm, it shall not force
This lineal honour from me. This from thee
Will I to mine leave, as 'tis left to me."
Exit.

King Henry IV., Part Second, Act IV., Scene 4.
In arrangement of colour, and in light and shade,
this is perhaps, the most successful picture in the
Exhibition. 'The mad wight', Prince Henry, is
represented as having just returned from the chase,
his horn still at his side, and spurs on his heels; he has
divested himself of one glove only, ere he lifts the
golden diadem to his brows; and, by the attitude in
which the Prince is standing, the artist has evidently

felt the proud defiance which Shakespeare intended
his Prince should feel when he makes him say:–
"And put the world's whole strength
Into one giant arm, it shall not force
This lineal honour from me."
The dying King is admirably expressed; and,
perhaps, indeed, this is the most beautiful portion of
the picture: the faint light glimmering on the forehead of the King, and the outstretched hand feebly
grasping the sceptre, as it rests on a faldstool by the
bedside, are exquisite ideas, most skilfully worked
out.'

Plate 13
Figure 30
Subject: **'Shylock'—? Charles Kean in
the role**
Title: None
Height: 12 in (30.5 cm)
Colour: White and gilt.
Rarity: VR. A.
Description: He stands bearded, wearing a
skull cap and a long coat over an even longer
robe. Round his waist he wears a sash from
which is suspended a pair of scales. His
right arm is across his chest and in his hand
he grasps a knife.
Observations: 'Shylock' in 'the trial scene' in
The Merchant of Venice, Act 4, Scene 1.

Shylock: 'The pound of flesh which I demand of him,
Is dearly bought; 'tis mine and I will have it'.

No positive identification has been made,
but it may well be a portrait of Mr Charles
Kean in the role, see *ch. 3, pl.* 36.

Figure 31
Subject: **Othello and Iago**
Title: Othello & Iago (raised capitals)
Date: *c.* 1858
Height: 12 in (30.5 cm)
Colour: Well coloured and pale versions exist.
Rarity: Av.
Description: 'Othello' stands on the left. He
wears a long gown over a long patterned
robe, sashed at the waist. Another sash
passes from his right shoulder to his left hip,
and on his head he wears a turban. 'Iago'
stands on the right. He holds a broad-
brimmed, plumed hat in his left hand by his
side, and his right hand is raised. He wears
a short cloak with an ermine cape over a
shirt, jerkin, doublet and hose. A striped

sash passes across his chest from right to left
and around his waist.
Observations: 1. Based on a water colour
Othello & Iago by S. A. Hart RA. The
original, in the Victoria and Albert, was
exhibited at the Royal Academy in 1858,
the year it was painted. An engraving of the
painting was published in the *National
Magazine* in 1858, see *ch.* 3, *pl.* 38.
2. A similar figure fetched 42 gns at Christie's
in 1966. Another, well coloured version,
fetched 190 gns at Christie's in 1969; whereas a white and gilt version fetched £80 at
Sotheby's six months later.

Figure 32
Subject: **John Philip Kemble as 'Hamlet'**
Title: Hamlet (indented capitals)
Date: *c.* 1852
Height: 11 in (28 cm)
Colour: Well coloured in the manner of
Thomas Parr. White and gilt versions are
also found.
Maker: Thomas Parr
Rarity: R. D. A.
Pair: Pair to *fig.* 5 (Ophelia) *pl.* E-1A.
Description: He stands in a round hat with
one plume, wearing a cloak draped over his
left shoulder only, tunic, short trunks and
hose. There is no broad ribbon across his
tunic. In his left hand he holds a skull to
which he points with his right index finger.
Observations: 1. In the colouring and style of
Thomas Parr. It is presumably based on the
engraving, after Lawrence's portrait, in
Tallis' *Shakespeare Gallery* inscribed *John
Philip Kemble as Hamlet.* However, it is not
as close to the portrait as *fig.* 6 (Kemble as
'Hamlet') *pl.* E-1A.
2. See *fig.* 6, *pl.* E-1A.

Figure 33
Subject: **Romeo and Juliet**
Title: None
Height: 12 in (30.5 cm)
Colour: Well coloured.
Rarity: R.
Description: 'Juliet' stands bare-headed, behind a brick wall which is waist high. Two
columns arising from the wall are joined by
a clock-face. 'Romeo' stands in front of the
wall wearing a plumed hat, jacket, breeches
and knee-boots. 'Juliet's' left arm is around
'Romeo's' neck and her right hand clasps
his right hand.
Observations: Undoubtedly portrays 'Romeo'
and 'Juliet', but has not yet been shown to
represent any particular actor or actress.

Figure 34
Subject: **Edmund Kean as 'Richard III'**
Title: None
Height: 9 in (23 cm) version illustrated here;
for 10 in (25 cm) version, see *pl.* E-14.
Colour: Well coloured; pale versions exist of
the larger figure.
Rarity: R.
Pair: Fig. 35 (? Cooper as 'Henry, Earl of
Richmond')
Description: Standing leaning to the right,
wearing a plumed round hat, long coat with
ermine edging, doublet and hose, knee-boots.
In the smaller version both arms are by the
side and he holds his sword in his right hand.
In the larger version the right hand holding
the sword remains by the side, but his left
arm is flexed at the elbow. The scabbard of
the sword may be seen between his legs, see
pl. E-14.
Observations: Based on a penny plain,
tuppence coloured theatrical 'combat' print

Section E. Theatre, Opera, Ballet and Circus

Plate 13
T: *Fig.* 30 Shylock
Fig. 31 Othello and Iago
Fig. 32 Kemble ('Hamlet')
Fig. 33 Romeo and Juliet

B: *Fig.* 34 Edmund Kean
('Richard III')
Fig. 35 ?Cooper
('Richmond')
Fig. 36 Unidentified man
and woman
Fig. 37 Garrick
('Richard III')
In the collection of
Mrs Constance Chiswell

inscribed *Mr. KEAN as RICHARD the THIRD*, see *ch.* 3, *pl.* 39.

Figure 35
Subject: **? T. A. Cooper as 'Henry, Earl of Richmond'**
Title: None
Height: 9 in (23 cm) version illustrated here; for 11⅛ in (28.25 cm) version, see *pl.* E-14.
Colour: Well coloured; pale versions exist of the larger figure.
Rarity: VR.
Pair: Fig. 34 (E. Kean as 'Richard III')
Description: Standing leaning to the left, in high plumed helmet, cuirass, breeches and knee-boots, a sword in his right hand. In the smaller version both hands are by the side, but in the larger version both arms are flexed at the elbows, see *pl.* E-14.
Observations: See preceding figure.

Figure 36
Subject: **Unidentified young man and woman**
Title: None
Height: 9½ in (24 cm)
Colour: Usually white and gilt, but coloured versions exist.
Maker: Thomas Parr
Rarity: Av.
Description: A young man and a girl are seated underneath an arch of boughs. The young man sits on the right and wears a round hat, jersey, breeches and stockings. He has his right arm round the girl's neck. The girl sits on the left and is bare-headed.
Observations: This figure has not yet been positively identified. It has been suggested that it portrays 'Lorenzo' and 'Jessica' from Shakespeare's *The Merchant of Venice*. I have heard of a painting by Daniel Maclise (1806–70) titled *How sweet the moonlight sleeps upon this bank!* ('Lorenzo' to 'Jessica'—Act. 5, Scene 1) which is supposed to be very similar, but I have never seen it myself. It has also been suggested that the figure represents 'Dolly Varden' and 'Joe Willet' from Dickens's *Barnaby Rudge*, but again I have no proof to offer.

Figure 37
Subject: **David Garrick as 'Richard III'**
Title: None
Height: 6¾ in (17 cm)
Colour: Well coloured.
Rarity: C.
Description: Very similar to *fig.* 22 (Garrick as 'Richard III') *pl.* E-7, except that it is much simplified, being made from one two-piece mould. He wears boots instead of shoes and there is no garter.
Observations: See *fig.* 22 (Garrick as 'Richard III') *pl.* E-7.

Plate 13A
Figure 32(a)
Subject: **John Philip Kemble as 'Hamlet'**
Title: Alas! poor Yorick (upper and lower case black script)
Date: *c.* 1852
Height: 11½ in (29 cm)
Colour: Well coloured in the manner of Thomas Parr.
Maker: Thomas Parr

Plate 13A
Fig. 32(a) Kemble ('Hamlet')

Rarity: VR. A.
Pair: Fig. 5 (Ophelia) *pl.* E-1A.
Description: Identical to *fig.* 32 (Kemble as 'Hamlet') *pl.* E-13, except that 1. the solitary plume is erect instead of horizontal and

Plate 14
Fig. 35 ?Cooper ('Richmond')   *Fig.* 34 Edmund Kean ('Richard III')

Plate 13A continued

2. the titling differs. In all other respects it is the same. In particular, note that the cloak is only over his left shoulder and there is no broad ribbon across his tunic. In *fig.* 6 (Kemble as 'Hamlet') *pl.* E-1A the cloak is over both shoulders and the titling, in upper and lower case gilt or black transfer, is obliquely placed.

Observations: 1. This third 'Tallis' Hamlet which first came to light in 1967 appears to be a variant of *fig.* 32, *pl.* E-13.
2. In the only recorded version, the solitary plume has been broken off and reapplied. It is possible that it has been incorrectly restored.
3. See *fig.* 6, *pl.* E-1A.

Plate 14
Figure 34
Subject: **Edmund Kean as 'Richard III'**
Title: None
Height: 10 in (25 cm)
Observations: This is the large version of the figure. It is fully documented under *pl.* E-13.

Figure 35
Subject: **? T. A. Cooper as 'Henry, Earl of Richmond'**
Title: None
Height: 11⅛ in (28.25 cm)
Observations: This is the large version of the figure. It is fully documented under *pl.* E-13.

Plate 15
Figure 38
Subject: **Edmund Falconer as 'Danny Man' and Agnes Robertson as 'Eily O'Connor'**
Title: None
Date: *c.* 1860
Height: 9 in (23 cm)
Colour: Well coloured.
Rarity: R. D.
Description: An archway of rocks which represents the entrance to a cave. Left: 'Danny Man' emerges from a boat wearing hat, coat, breeches and stockings. His left arm is outstretched. Right: 'Eily O'Connor', bare-headed and wearing a cloak, sits on a rock. Her hands are clasped in front of her and she appears to be about to swoon.
Observations: 1. *The Colleen Bawn*, a domestic drama in three Acts by Dion Boucicault, was first produced in England at the Adelphi Theatre on September 10th, 1860.
2. The source of *fig.* 38 is the coloured lithograph by John Brandard on the music-front to the *Colleen Bawn Waltz*. It portrays 'The

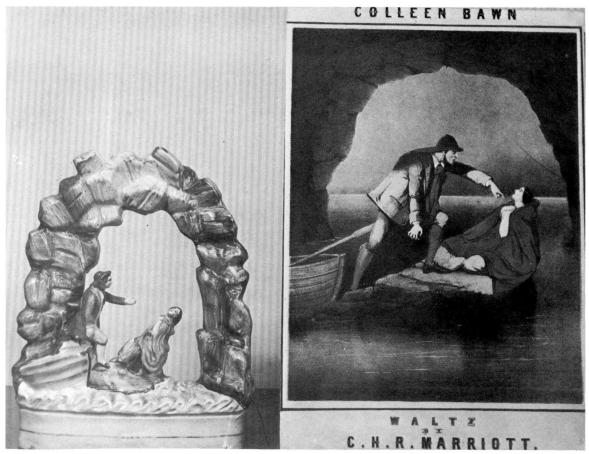

Plate 15 (Below right)
Fig. 38 Falconer and Robertson ('Danny Man' and 'Eily O'Connor')
To the right of the figure is the coloured lithograph music-front by John Brandard for the 'Colleen Bawn Waltz'.

Plate 16
Playbill for the Theatre Royal, New Adelphi advertising the '105th, 106th and 107th Nights of the Great Drama, *The Colleen Bawn.*'
Note 'Eily O'Connor' (the Colleen Bawn) was played by Miss Agnes Robertson (Mrs Dion Boucicault) and 'Danny Man' by Edmund Falconer.

Plate 17
Fig. 39 Foote ('Arinette')
Fig. 40 Foote ('Arinette')
Between the figures is the penny plain, tuppence coloured theatrical portrait no. 70, published by Orlando Hodgson, titled *Miss Foote as the Little Jockey.*
In the collection of Messrs Raymond Mander and Joe Mitchenson

Water Cave' (Act II) with Miss Agnes Robertson (Mrs D. Boucicault) as 'Eily O'Connor' (the Colleen Bawn) and Mr Edmund Falconer as 'Danny Man'.
3. A similar figure, together with *fig.* 156 (Hemming) *pl.* E-80, fetched 65 gns at Christie's in 1967.

Plate 16
The Colleen Bawn
Playbill for the Theatre Royal, New Adelphi dated Thursday, January 10th, 1861. It advertises the:
105th, 106th and 107th Nights of the Great Drama,
THE COLLEEN BAWN.

Plate 17
Figure 39
Subject: **Maria Foote as 'Arinette'**
Title: None
Date: 183–
Height: 6¼ in (16 cm)
Colour: Well coloured, underglaze blue coat.
Rarity: VR. D. A.
Description: She stands wearing a jockey's cap, long jacket, waistcoat, breeches and knee-boots. Her left hand is on her hip and her right hand is outstretched (*with a hole penetrating the hand for insertion of a whip*).

Observations: 1. A porcelain figure originally thought to be 'Rockingham' but now recognized as 'Staffordshire'.
2. Based on the penny plain, tuppence coloured theatrical portrait published by Orlando Hodgson, no. 70. It is inscribed *MISS FOOTE as the LITTLE JOCKEY.*
3. Maria Foote (1797–1867) played 'Arinette' in *The Little Jockey*, a comic opera drama by William Dimond, when it was revived at the Olympic Theatre on January 3rd, 1831.

Figure 40
Subject: **Maria Foote as 'Arinette'**
Title: None
Date: Uncertain
Height: 5½ in (14 cm)
Colour: Well coloured, underglaze blue coat.
Rarity: VR. D. A.
Description: She is standing wearing a jockey's cap, coat, waistcoat, breeches and knee-boots. Her right hand is on her hip and her left hand, in which she clutches a whip, is across her abdomen.
Observations: A pottery figure, unmistakably Staffordshire. It is a later and simplified version of *fig.* 39, possibly issued at the time of Miss Foote's death in 1867, although the style suggests a slightly earlier date.

Plate 18
Figure 41
Subject: **Edward Askew Sothern as 'Lord Dundreary'**
Title: None
Date: 1861
Height: 8½ in (21.5 cm)
Colour: Well coloured in the manner of Thomas Parr.
Maker: Thomas Parr
Rarity: VR.
Description: He stands bare-headed, with long whiskers and a monocle in his right eye. He wears an overcoat, waistcoat and strap-trousers. He is counting the number of his relations on the fingers of his left hand, with his right index finger.
Observations: 1. The wood-engraving illustrated on this plate is inscribed *MR. SOTHERN AS LORD DUNDREARY*. It is from a photograph, by Bassano of Regent Street, of the first production, in London at the Haymarket, on November 11th, 1861 of Tom Taylor's *Our American Cousin*, a drama in four Acts. There were revivals at the Haymarket in 1863, 1867 and on several occasions up to 1878, always with Sothern in the role of 'Lord Dundreary.' The world premier had been in New York in 1858, and it was in this production that Sothern practically created the part with which his

E373

Plate 18
Fig. 41 Sothern ('Lord Dundreary')
The wood-engraving illustrated to the right of the figure is titled *Mr Sothern as Lord Dundreary* and is from a photograph by Bassano of the first production in London at the Haymarket on November 11th, 1861 of Tom Taylor's *Our American Cousin*, a drama in four Acts.
In the collection of Messrs Raymond Mander and Joe Mitchenson

Plate 18 continued

name is always associated. It is said that at first he had so little opinion of the small part he had been offered by Laura Keene that he was quite forlorn, little dreaming that the character of the brainless peer would turn out to be the stepping-stone of his fortune.

The photograph from which this engraving is taken may be regarded as the source of the figure. The scene is the 'letter scene', Act 4, in which 'Brother Sam's' letter is read, 'Lord Dundreary' checking off his relations on his fingers. Dundreary whiskers and clothes became a fashion in the latter part of the nineteenth century.

2. The Kent lists contain the following entries:

KENT LIST A Stock No. (c. 1901)	KENT LIST B Stock No. (c. 1920)	KENT LIST C Ref. No. (1955)
282	290	—

(Deleted as *Discontinued Line*).

Both contemporary versions and reproductions are very rare. It will be noted that production ceased early in this century. Contemporary figures (produced *c.* 1861) have the typical colouring of figures made by Thomas Parr. Other figures are found in the dark maroon seen in Boer War figures emanating from the Kent factory. Maybe the majority were reproduced about 1890

when *Our American Cousin* was revived at the Novelty Theatre with Sothern's son, Edward Hugh (1859–1933) in the role.

Plate 19
Figure 42
Subject: **Mr and Mrs Barney Williams**
Title: None
Date: *c.* 1856
Height: 8 in (20.5 cm)
Colour: White, gilt and black.
Rarity: VR.
Description: He stands on the left, his left forearm resting on a wall, his legs crossed and his right hand pointing forwards. He wears a beaver hat with a pipe tucked into the hat band, neckerchief, long coat, waistcoat, breeches and stockings. She stands on the right, her right elbow resting on the wall and her left hand on her hip. She is bareheaded and wears a blouse with a sash and calf-length skirt.
Observations: Although no identical print has been found, there is little doubt that this figure portrays Mr and Mrs Barney Williams. Comparison with the engraving which appeared in *The Illustrated London News* on July 26th, 1856 inscribed *Mr and Mrs Barney Williams, Adelphi Theatre*:– *From a photograph by Mayall* strongly supports this theory. Mr Williams was appearing at the time in the character of 'Paddy O'Rafferty' in a revival

of the two-Act comedy *Born to Good Luck*.

Plate 20
Figure 43
Subject: **? Mlle Alboni as 'Cinderella'**
Title: None
Date: *c.* 1848
Height: 9 in (23 cm)
Colour: Well coloured and sparsely coloured versions exist.
Rarity: VR. A.
Description: Cinderella, wearing a plumed hat and ermine-edged gown, is seated in her 'pumpkin' coach, which is being drawn by a prancing horse plumed, and adorned with an ornate saddle-cloth.
Observations: The source of this figure is probably the 'Musical Bouquet' illustration (this plate), which is in turn derived from the coloured lithograph by John Brandard (*pl.* E-21). The Brandard original does not represent Rossini's *La Cenerentola* (an opera based on the story of Cinderella), although the 'Musical Bouquet' picture was used to illustrate the finale—*Now from fear no more I tremble*—sung by Mlle Alboni when the opera was played at Covent Garden in 1848. Whilst the figure is not therefore, strictly speaking, a portrait of Mlle Alboni, it may well have been intended as such. Note that the wheel-design in the Brandard lithograph is identical to that of the figure.

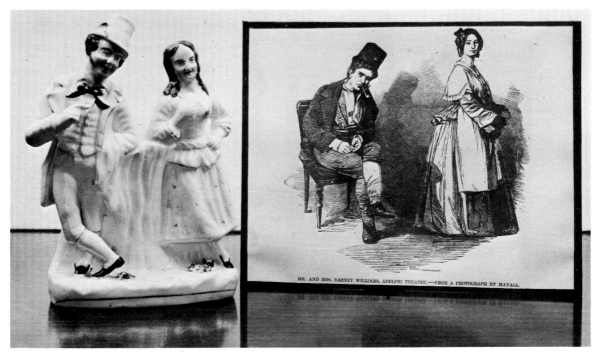

Plate 19
Fig. 42 Mr and Mrs Barney Williams
To the right of the figure is the engraving which appeared in *The Illustrated London News* on July 26th, 1856 captioned 'Mr and Mrs Barney Williams, Adelphi Theatre: From a photograph by Mayall'.

Plate 20
Fig. 43 ?Alboni ('Cinderella')
To the left of the figure is the *Musical Bouquet* engraving which was used to illustrate the finale sung by Mlle Alboni when the opera was played at Covent Garden in 1848.
By courtesy of Mr and Mrs Eric Joyce

Plate 21
Cinderella
A coloured lithograph by John Brandard. Its significance is discussed under the preceding plate.

Plate 22
Figure 44
Subject: **? Luigi Lablache as 'Prince Charming'**
Title: None
Height: 7 in (17.5 cm)
Colour: Well coloured.
Rarity: Av.
Pair: Fig. 45 (? Mrs Edwards as 'Cinderella')
Description: Standing half-right, bare-headed, in long ermine-edged cloak, military jacket and trousers. A sash passes from his left shoulder down to his right. There is a star on his left breast. Angled base.
Observations: I understand that there is some evidence that this figure portrays Luigi Lablache in the role of 'Prince Charming', but I have no first-hand information.

Figure 45
Subject: **? Mrs Edwards as 'Cinderella'**
Title: None
Height: 6¼ in (16 cm)
Colour: Well coloured.
Rarity: Av.
Pair: Fig. 44 (? Lablache as 'Prince Charming')
Description: She stands wearing a low feathered hat, with an ermine-edged cloak over a long double-skirted dress. Her right hand is on her hip, her left hand clutches the edge of her cloak. Angled base.
Observations: I have been unable to trace the evidence that this figure portrays Mrs Edwards as 'Cinderella', but I think it is quite possible.

Plate 23
Figure 46
Subject: **Giulia Grisi as 'Lucrezia' and Guiseppe Mario as 'Gennaro'**
E376

Title: None
Date: c. 1847
Height: 12¼ in (31 cm)
Colour: Well coloured.
Rarity: R. D. A.
Description: 'Gennaro' stands on the right, bare-headed and bearded, in long ermine cloak, blouse, kilt, long stockings and short

boots. He holds his left hand upwards towards his neck and his right hand outwards towards 'Lucrezia'. She stands to the left, bare-headed, with a scarf trailing to her right, in blouse and long skirt. She holds her left hand across her chest, and a mask in her right hand.

Plate 22   *Fig.* 44 ?Lablache ('Prince Charming')   *Fig.* 45 ?Mrs Edwards ('Cinderella')

Section E. Theatre, Opera, Ballet and Circus

Plate 24
T: *Fig.* 47 Glover
('Yourawkee')
Fig. 49 Glover and
Vining
Fig. 48 Vining ('Peter
Wilkins')

B: *Fig.* 50 Unidentified
male dancer
Fig. 51 Unidentified
female dancer
Fig. 52 Unidentified
female dancer
Fig. 54 Unidentified male
dancer
Fig. 55 Unidentified
female dancer
*By courtesy of Mr and Mrs
Eric Joyce*

Observations: 1. After a coloured lithograph by J. Brandard inscribed:
SCENE FROM LUCREZIA BORGIA
  Madame Grisi   *Signor Mario*
Luc: Tua madre—Oh mio Gennaro! tu l'ami!
Gen: Ah piu di me.
                                   Intro. Sc. 11
A music-front with the same lithograph is illustrated on this plate.
2. Donizetti's opera *Lucrezia Borgia* was produced at Covent Garden, in 1847, with Giulia Grisi in the title role and Guiseppe Mario as 'Gennaro'.

Plate 24
Figure 47
Subject: **? Mary Glover as 'Yourawkee'**
Title: None
Date: *c.* 1837
Height: 7½ in (19 cm)
Colour: Well coloured, underglaze blue cloak.
Rarity: R.
Pair: Fig. 48 (Vining as 'Peter Wilkins'); *fig.* 49 (Glover and Vining) forms a centrepiece.
Description: Standing bare-headed, in ermine-edged cloak, medium-length dress and pantaloons. She touches her head with

her right hand whilst her left hand rests on her hip. Hollow base.
Observations: See *fig.* 48 (Vining).

Figure 48
Subject: **Mrs Vining as 'Peter Wilkins'**
Title: None
Date: *c.* 1837
Height: 8 in (20.5 cm)
Colour: Well coloured, underglaze blue cloak.
Rarity: VR.
Pair: Fig. 47 (Glover as 'Yourawkee'); *fig.* 49 (Glover and Vining) forms a centrepiece.
Description: Standing bare-headed, in long coat buckled at the waist, and trousers. The hem of the coat is a distinctive feature. She touches her head with her left hand whilst her right hand rests on her hip. Hollow base.
Observations: 1. Based on an engraving, published by Thos. McLean, Haymarket, 1827, inscribed: *Mrs Vining in the Character of Peter Wilkins—The Castanet Dance—Act 1, Scene 5.*
2. *Peter Wilkins*; *or, The Flying Indians* was produced at the Theatre Royal, Covent Garden on April 16th, 1827.
3. The pair to this piece (*fig.* 47) is almost certainly Miss Mary Glover playing the part of 'Yourawkee'. 'Yourawkee' sings whilst

'Peter' dances. However, no print has been traced of Miss Glover in this character, so the figure could be just an imaginary one, see *p.* 35 and *ch.* 3, *pl.* 40.

Figure 49
Subject: **Miss Glover and Mrs Vining as 'Yourawkee' and 'Peter Wilkins'**
Title: None
Date: *c.* 1837
Height: 7¼ in (18.25 cm)
Colour: Well coloured.
Rarity: Av.
Series: Forms the centrepiece of the pair *fig.* 47 (Glover as 'Yourawkee') and *fig.* 48 (Vining as 'Peter Wilkins').
Description: Miss Glover stands on the left, dressed similarly to *fig.* 47. She touches her head with her right hand and links up with Mrs Vining with her left arm. Mrs Vining stands on the right, dressed similarly to *fig.* 48. She raises her left hand to her head. Solid base.
Observations: See *fig.* 48 (Vining as 'Peter Wilkins').

Figure 50
Subject: **Unidentified male dancer**
Title: None

E377

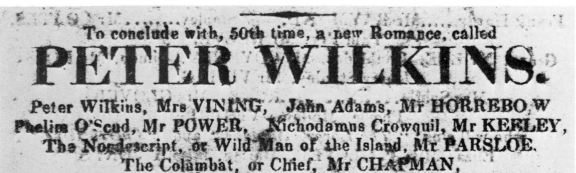

Plate 25
Peter Wilkins; or, *the Flying Indians*
Part of a playbill advertising the melo-romantic spectacle (*Easterpiece*) produced at the Theatre Royal, Covent Garden in April, 1827.
Note that the character of 'Peter Wilkins' is played by Mrs Vining, that of 'Yourawkee' by Miss M. Glover and that of 'Hallycarnie' by Miss J. Scott, in this case mis-spelt Sctt.

Plate 24 continued
Height: 9½ in (24 cm)
Colour: Well coloured.
Rarity: R.
Pair: *Fig*. 51 (Unidentified female dancer)
Description: Standing wearing an angled bonnet, long jacket, tights and knee-boots. His arms are crossed across his waist and he carries a flag in each hand. His left leg is crossed in front of his right leg.
Observations: Performing the 'Flag Polka'. It has been suggested that this figure portrays Jules Perrot, but there is no supporting evidence.

Figure 51
Subject: **Unidentified female dancer**
Title: None
Height: 9½ in (24 cm)
Colour: Well coloured.
Rarity: R.
Pair: *Fig*. 50 (Unidentified male dancer)
Description: Standing wearing an angled bonnet, low cut blouse, and short wide skirt with pantaloons and bootees. Her arms are crossed across her waist and she carries a flag in each hand.
Observations: Performing the 'Flag Polka'. Nothing is known of the identity of this dancer.

Figure 52
Subject: **Unidentified female dancer**
Title: None
Height: 7½ in (19 cm)
Colour: Well coloured.
Rarity: R.
Pair: No pair has been found so far, but undoubtedly one exists. *Fig*. 53 has been reserved for it.
Description: She stands wearing a four-cornered hat, blouse, skirt, modesty panties, stockings and shoes. Both hands are on her hips, and there is a scarf round her waist dangling over her forearms. A bag, or possibly a banjo, hangs from her waist.
Observations: There is some similarity between this dancer and each of the two dancers portrayed in *fig*. 138, *pl*. E-72.

Figure 54
Subject: **Unidentified male dancer**
Title: None
Height: 8 in (20.5 cm)
Colour: Well coloured with blue coat.
Rarity: Av.
Pair: *Fig*. 55 (Unidentified female dancer)
Description: He stands wearing a round hat, jacket edged with broad piping, and trousers. His right hand is on his hip and his left hand touches his hat.
Observations: This figure of a polka dancer is probably based on an engraving which has not come to light so far.

Figure 55
Subject: **Unidentified female dancer**
Title: None
Height: 7¾ in (20 cm)
Colour: Well coloured with blue coat.
Rarity: Av.
Pair: *Fig*. 54 (Unidentified male dancer)
Description: Wearing a round hat, jacket edged with broad piping, skirt and pantaloons. Her left hand is on her hip, her right hand touches the brim of her hat.
Observations: See *fig*. 54.

Plate 25
 Peter Wilkins; or, the Flying Indians
Part of a playbill advertising the 'melo-romantic spectacle (*Easterpiece*)' produced at the Theatre Royal, Covent Garden in April, 1827. Note that the character of 'Peter Wilkins' is played by Mrs Vining, that of 'Yourawkee' by Miss M. Glover and that of 'Hallycarnie' by Miss J. Scott, in this case mis-spelt Sctt.

Plate 26
Figure 57
Subject: **? Mr Barton as 'Giaffier'**
Title: None
Date: *c*. 1847
Height: 8 in (20.5 cm)
Colour: Well coloured.
Rarity: Av.
Pair: Not known
Description: Standing in turban, ermine-edged cloak, long coat, pantaloons and Turkish shoes. In his left hand he holds a firman (oriental sovereign's edict) to which he points with his right hand.
Observations: The figure portrays the same dramatic moment in Act 2, Scene 1 of Dimond's dramatized version of Byron's *The Bride of Abydos*, as that portrayed in West's Theatrical Portrait, No. 1, *Mr H. Johnston as Giaffier*, published February 24th, 1824. However, the costume is different; the figure must therefore portray another production, probably that at Astley's in 1847, when Mr Barton took the role.
2. See *general remarks* following *pl*. E-28.

Plate 27
Figure 58
Subject: **? Mr Harwood and Miss Rosa Henry as 'Selim' and 'Zuleika'**
Title: Bride of Abydos (gilt script)
Date: *c*. 1847
Height: 7⅛ in (18 cm)
Colour: Well coloured.
Rarity: VR. D. A.
Description: The example illustrated is the only one known. Unfortunately, the head of 'Selim' is missing. 'Selim' sits on the right, wearing a short jacket, pantaloons and Turkish slippers. His right arm encircles 'Zuleika's' waist. 'Zuleika' kneels on a cushion to his right. She wears a kerchief over her head, a blouse and long skirt.
Observations: 1. The figure portrays the dramatic moment in Act 1, Scene 2 of Dimond's dramatized version of Byron's *The Bride of Abydos*. The production was probably that at Astley's in 1847.
2. See *general remarks* following *pl*. E-28.

Plate 28
Figure 59
Subject: **? Mr Harwood and Miss Rosa Henry as 'Selim' and 'Zuleika'**
Title: None
Date: *c*. 1847
Height: 9¾ in (24.5 cm)
Colour: Well coloured.
Rarity: VR.
Description: 'Selim' stands on the left, wearing a turban, blouse with ermine-edged sleeves, skirt, pantaloons and Turkish slippers. There is a sash running from his left shoulder downwards and to his right. 'Zuleika' kneels on the right. She wears a tiara and veil, blouse with ermine-edged sleeves and long skirt with a sash round the waist. In her left hand she holds two roses and in the foreground, at their feet, is a violin.
Observations: 1. The figure portrays the highlight of Act 2, Scene 2 of Dimond's dramatized version of Byron's *The Bride of Abydos*. The production was probably that at Astley's in 1847.
2. See *general remarks* following this plate.

Figure 60
Subject: **? Mr Barton and Miss Rosa Henry as 'Giaffier' and 'Zuleika'**
Title: None
Date: *c*. 1847
Height: 12¾ in (32.25 cm)
Colour: Well coloured.

Section E. Theatre, Opera, Ballet and Circus

Plate 26
Fig. 57 ? Mr Barton
('Giaffier')
To the right of the figure
is West's *Theatrical Portrait
No.* 1 inscribed *Mr. H.
Johnston as Giaffier,*
published February 24th,
1824.
Note that the figure
portrays the same
'dramatic moment' in
Act 2, Scene 1 of
Dimond's dramatized
version of Byron's *The
Bride of Abydos* as the
West portrait, but the
costumes are different.
This means that the
figure portrays another
production, probably that
at Astley's in 1847 when
Mr Barton played
'Giaffier'.

Plate 27 (Right)
Fig. 58 Selim and Zuleika

Plate 28

Fig. 61 Selim and Zuleika   Fig. 60 Giaffier and Zuleika   Fig. 59 Selim and Zuleika

Rarity: VR.
Description: 'Giaffier' stands on the left. He wears a turban, blouse, skirt, pantaloons and Turkish slippers. In his right hand he holds a sword which rests against a pedestal. His left hand is clasped by 'Zuleika' who kneels to his left. She wears a blouse and long skirt and looks upwards at him as she pleads.
Observations: 1. The figure portrays a highlight in Act 1, Scene 3 of Dimond's dramatized version of Byron's *The Bride of Abydos.* The production was probably that at Astley's in 1847.
2. See *general remarks* following this plate.

Figure 61
Subject: **? Mr Harwood and Miss Rosa Henry as 'Selim' and 'Zuleika'**
Title: None
Date: *c.* 1847
Height: 11 in (28 cm)
Colour: Sparsely coloured; base coloured with 'combed' green and brown in the manner of Thomas Parr.
Maker: Thomas Parr
Rarity: VR.
Description: Selim stands on the right, wearing turban, long coat and gown. He wears a belt and carries a sword. 'Zuleika' kneels to his right. She wears a veil over her head and

a long dress and clasps his right hand in both of hers.
Observations: 1. The figure portrays a highlight in Act 2, Scene 2 of Dimond's dramatized version of Byron's *The Bride of Abydos.* The production was probably that at Astley's in 1847.
2. See *general remarks* following this plate.

THE BRIDE OF ABYDOS
GENERAL REMARKS

The large number of Staffordshire figures in Eastern costume has always presented difficulty in identification. Mr Anthony Oliver has done considerable research into

Plate 28 continued

this matter, and as a result it is now possible to positively identify five such figures as portraying highlights in William Dimond's dramatized version of Byron's *The Bride of Abydos*. A copy of the Dimond 1st edition is held in the library of the British Museum.

Giaffier (*fig*. 57, *pl*. E-26).

Although, clearly by no means the exact print, it seems a reasonable assumption that the West 'Theatrical Portrait' of Mr H. Johnston as 'Giaffier' represents the same scene in *The Bride of Abydos* as *fig*. 57. The costume of the figure is different, so it could not have been Mr Johnston who inspired the potter, nor the production in which Mr Johnston played, which incidentally, opened at Drury Lane on February 5th, 1818. Apart from provincial revivals, *The Bride of Abydos* was next produced in London at Astley's Amphitheatre on April 5th, 1847, slightly changed to suit the Astley audience but still keeping the same plot as in the Dimond version. In spite of careful research no illustrations of this production have been found. The next and last London production was at the Strand Theatre on May 31st, 1858. One of the costumes of this production can be seen in the Enthoven Collection at the Victoria and Albert Museum and it effectively rules out this as being the one portrayed by the potters. This leaves the production at Astley's in 1847, and it would seem not unreasonable to assume that the figure portrays Mr Barton as 'Giaffier'. In Act 2, Scene 1 (see *p*. 32 of the Dimond 1st edition) Giaffier, the Pasha of Abydos receives some disturbing news in the form of an ultimatum. He rants and raves about this, and pointing to it says in the course of his speech:

'Dares the ungrateful Amurath to me
Dispatch his vain Firman[1]'

There is another illustration of Mr. H. Johnston as 'Giaffier' in the same scene, drawn by Cruikshank. This can be seen in the Print Room of the British Museum. The above quotation also appears on it.

1. Firman is an oriental sovereign's edict.

Selim and Zuleika (*fig*. 58, *pl*. E-27).

This is the only known titled figure and unfortunately one head is missing. In Act 1, Scene 2 (see *p*. 10 of the Dimond 1st edition) Selim, Giaffier's supposed son—but in fact no blood son at all—leads his 'sister' Zuleika to a view overlooking the Hellespont. They are obviously in love with each other but at this point they think they are brother and sister. Thus, when later Giaffier arranges a political marriage for Zuleika to a very unattractive character called Osman Bey, hence, of course, the title of the play, Selim and Zuleika become upset. The quotation which matches this figure is:

Selim . . . 'Thus from this searching point at dawn to gaze
Encircling with free arm Zuleika's form'.

Selim and Zuleika (*fig*. 59, *pl*. E-28).

In Act 2, Scene 2 (see *p*. 36 of the Dimond 1st edition) female slaves have been playing musical instruments in Zuleika's apartment. They retire when Zuleika's supposed brother Selim enters. He has heard of the proposed marriage and is angry with her. She presents him with a rose to regain his favour and is rebuffed. Note, in this group, the musical instrument in the foreground. The quotation which matches this figure is:

E380

Zuleika. 'This rose a message from the Bulbul[1] bears.
Will Selim search for it? How! Reject my flower!'

1. Bulbul is an Eastern song-thrush.

Giaffier and Zuleika (*fig*. 60, *pl*. E-28).

In Act 1, Scene 3 (see *p*. 23 of the Dimond 1st edition) Selim has defied his supposed father Giaffier and rushed out in a temper. Giaffier is about to pronounce dire punishment, when Zuleika pleads for him. The figure shows Zuleika kneeling before her father, who rests his hand on his sword. The quotation for this figure is:

Zuleika (eagerly). 'For my sake, pardon him
I kneel to pray thee'.

Selim and Zuleika (*fig*. 61, *pl*. E-28).

In Act 2, Scene 2 (see *p*. 40 of the Dimond 1st edition) Zuleika kneels before her supposed brother Selim rejecting her proposed marriage as it upsets her 'brother' so much. The quotation for this figure is:

Zuleika. 'Enough!' (she kneels with sudden fervour)
'By Mecca's shrine behold me swear
An awful deep irrevocable vow
This hand shall n'er be clasped by Selim's foe'

It is Mr Anthony Oliver's view that each Staffordshire figure or group represents a dramatic highlight in the play, just as today the photographs outside the theatre do. Enlarging on this point he has written:

In many ways, of course, these figures performed a similar function, and although I have not been able, so far, to find any documentary proof, I believe that they would have been on sale at street traders' stalls outside the theatre. Had they actually been sold inside the theatre, I am sure someone would have mentioned it and I have never seen it referred to.

In conclusion it can be said of these five figures that the evidence of style supports the theory that they all portray characters in the 1847 production at Astley's.

Plate 29
Figure 62
Subject: **'Esmeralda'—? Carlotta Grisi in the role**
Title: None
Date: *c*. 1844
Height: 10¼ in (25.75 cm)
Colour: Well coloured.
Rarity: Av.
Pair: Fig. 63 (? Perrot as 'Gringoire'). The centrepiece to this pair is *fig*. 64 ('Esmeralda' and 'Gringoire').
Description: Bare-headed in open blouse and short skirt. She holds a tambourine up to her head with her left hand, while her right hand rests on the neck of a goat which is jumping up on her right side.
Observations: 1. *Notre Dame de Paris*, a picturesque historical romance by Victor Hugo, was first published in 1831. In it the author portrays Paris at the time of Louis XI. It was extremely popular in Victorian times, being transcribed into plays, ballets, burlesques and at least four operas.
2. *La Esmeralda*, a ballet in three Acts and five Scenes, written by Jules Perrot and based on Victor Hugo's novel, was first produced at Her Majesty's Theatre, London on March 9th, 1844. The part of 'Esmeralda' was played by Mlle Carlotta Grisi and that of the poet, 'Pierre Gringoire' by M Jules Perrot. The group of 'Esmeralda' with tambourine and goat (*fig*. 62) is based on the lithograph by John Brandard on the music-front titled *The Esmeralda Waltzes* illustrated on this plate. No dancer is named, but she may possibly be Carlotta Grisi. No print, in this costume, is known of the pair

to 'Esmeralda' (*fig*. 63), but likewise it may well be Perrot playing the part of 'Gringoire'. The centrepiece (*fig*. 64) portrays the two dancers together.
3. A goat accompanies 'Esmeralda' whilst she dances with a tambourine in Act 2, Scene 2 of the ballet.
4. The same music-front, with the head of 'Esmeralda' changed, was reissued in 1856 as the cover for a song *I am like a sportive fay* from the opera, *Esmeralda and the Hunchback of Notre Dame*, by Vincenzo Battista, when it was produced in English at Drury Lane on June 30th, 1856, with Lucy Escott in the title role, see *pl*. E-30. There is no doubt that *fig*. 62 is copied from the earlier version of the lithograph and does not portray Lucy Escott as previously thought. Likewise *fig*. 63 cannot represent Charles Manners who played 'Gringoire' in the opera.

Figure 63
Subject: **'Gringoire'—? Jules Perrot in the role**
Title: None
Date: *c*. 1844
Height: 9½ in (24 cm)
Colour: Well coloured.
Rarity: Av.
Pair: Fig. 62 (? Grisi as 'Esmeralda'). The centrepiece to this pair is *fig*. 64 ('Esmeralda' and 'Gringoire').
Description: Standing bare-headed, in half-length coat, jacket, breeches and stockings, a scarf around his neck. He holds a triangle in his left hand against his head, and a goat is jumping up on his left side.
Observations: See *fig*. 62 ('Esmeralda').

Figure 64
Subject: **'Esmeralda' and 'Gringoire'—? Carlotta Grisi and Jules Perrot in the roles**
Title: None
Date: *c*. 1844
Height: 6½ in (16.5 cm)
Colour: Well coloured.
Rarity: Av.
Pair: Forms the centrepiece to the pair *fig*. 62 ('Esmeralda') and *fig*. 63 ('Gringoire').
Description: 'Esmeralda' stands on the left, dressed as in *fig*. 62, holding a tambourine against her head with her left hand. 'Gringoire' stands on the right, dressed as in *fig*. 63, holding a triangle against his head with his left hand.
Observations: See *fig*. 62 ('Esmeralda').

Plate 30
Esmeralda
Music-front for the song, *I am like a sportive fay* from *Esmeralda and the Hunchback of Notre Dame*, an opera by Vincenzo Battista, see *fig*. 62 ('Esmeralda') *pl*. E-29.

Plate 31
Figure 65
Subject: **Esmeralda and Gringoire**
Title: None
Height: 7½ in (19 cm)
Colour: Well coloured.
Rarity: R.
Description: 'Esmeralda' stands on the left, wearing a short jacket and skirt. She holds a tambourine above her head in both hands. To the right, stands 'Gringoire' wearing round hat, short jacket, breeches and stockings. He faces to the right and holds a triangle in both hands. Between them a goat leaps up on to 'Esmeralda'.

Section E. Theatre, Opera, Ballet and Circus

Plate 29

In the background is a music-front titled *The Esmeralda Waltzes* with a lithograph by John Brandard of Esmeralda with tambourine. No dancer is named, but in all probability she was Carlotta Grisi (*see text*).

Fig. 63 ?Perrot ('Gringoire')   *Fig.* 64 Esmeralda and Gringoire   *Fig.* 62 ?Grisi ('Esmeralda')

Plate 30

The same music-front as that illustrated on the preceding plate was reissued in 1856 as a cover for the song *I am like a sportive fay* from *Esmeralda and the Hunchback of Notre Dame,* an opera by Vincenzo Battista, when it was produced in English at Drury Lane on June 30th, 1856 with Lucy Escott in the title role. The head of 'Esmeralda' had been changed. For the significance of this see 'observations' *fig.* 62, *pl.* E-29.
In the collection of Messrs Raymond Mander and Joe Mitchenson

Plate 31

Fig. 65 Esmeralda and Gringoire
In the collection of Messrs Raymond Mander and Joe Mitchenson

Observations: There is no evidence that this is a theatrical portrait although, of course, it may be.

E381

Plate 32 (Left)
Fig. 66 Esmeralda and Gringoire

Plate 33
Fig. 67 Gringoire and Esmeralda

Plate 34 (Left)
Fig. 68 Esmeralda

Plate 35
Fig. 70 Waters
To the right of the figure is a lithograph music-front inscribed: *A Portrait of Billy Waters, Progenitor of Promenade Concerts — He died about 20 years ago.*

Plate 32
Figure 66
Subject: **Esmeralda and Gringoire**
Title: None
Height: 10 in (25 cm)
Colour: White and gilt.
Rarity: R.
Description: 'Esmeralda' is seated on the left. She wears a five-cornered hat, blouse and skirt and holds a tambourine to her right.

'Gringoire' stands on the right, bareheaded, wearing jacket, waistcoat, breeches and stockings. He has his right hand on her shoulder and holds a bonnet in his left hand which is by his side. At their feet lies a goat.

Observations: There is no evidence that this is a theatrical portrait although, of course, it may be.

Plate 33
Figure 67
Subject: **Gringoire and Esmeralda**
Title: None
Height: 5½ in (14 cm)
Colour: Well coloured.
Rarity: VR.
Series: Same series as *fig.* 165 (Lind and Lablache as 'Marie' and 'Sergeant Sulpice') *pl.* E-83.

Section E. Theatre, Opera, Ballet and Circus

Description: 'Gringoire' stands to the left, leaning against a tree trunk (spill-holder). He wears a round hat, open jacket, breeches and stockings and holds a triangle in both hands. 'Esmeralda' stands to the right, wearing a round hat, blouse and skirt, a tambourine in her left hand. At the foot of the tree lies a goat.

Observations: Almost certainly theatrical, although the source is unknown.

Plate 34
Figure 68
Subject: **Esmeralda**
Title: None
Height: 12 in (30.5 cm)
Colour: White and gilt.
Rarity: R.
Pair: There must be a pair to this figure, although to date it has not been recorded. *Fig.* 69 has been reserved for it.
Description: She stands to the right of a pedestal, wearing a plumed hat, blouse and wide skirt. There is a sash round her waist loosely knotted at the front. In her left hand she carries a tambourine and her right hand rests on the neck of a goat which is perched on the pedestal.
Observations: Probably not a theatrical figure, although the possibility cannot be excluded.

Plate 35
Figure 70
Subject: **Billy Waters**
Title: None
Date: c. 1843
Height: 8½ in (21.5 cm)
Colour: Well coloured.
Rarity: VR. D. A.
Pair: No pair is known, but a figure of African Sall (see *pl.* E-36) may exist and *fig.* 71 has been reserved for it. Alternatively, if a pair does exist, it could be a peg-legged

Scotsman, playing the bag-pipes, see below.
Description: Standing playing a fiddle. He is wearing a plumed cocked hat athwartships. The fiddle is in his left hand and bow in his right. He wears a jacket, waistcoat, neckerchief and trousers. His left leg, which is a peg leg, is on the pavement and his right leg on the roadway.
Observations: 1. The coloured lithograph music-front illustrated on this plate is inscribed:

A PORTRAIT OF BILLY WATERS,
PROGENITOR OF PROMENADE
CONCERTS—HE DIED ABOUT
TWENTY YEARS AGO
by
W. H. Montgomery

Thou Child of Genius! who with wooden leg,
Wert doomed to stroll—to 'scrape thy way' & beg,
Hadst thou been spared to these enlightened days
Thy Triumph sure would be 'a perfect blaze'.

No more with fiddle—but with staff in hand
Thou would'st *Conduct* some Monstrous Monstre—Band
For tho' thy skill in music—was all 'stuff',
Thy *garb*—thy *antics* now would be enough.

Fig. 70 is based on this lithograph. As Billy Waters died in 1823, the lithograph can be dated to about 1843. Contemporary figures and engravings of Billy Waters are known, so it is interesting to speculate why this particular music-sheet was issued. Dramatized versions of *Tom and Jerry* (see *p.* 419) were produced at intervals up to the 1870's and the music-sheet may have appeared in connection with one of these revivals. Alternatively, the reference to Billy Waters as 'the progenitor of promenade concerts' on a music-sheet, whose date approximates to 1843, suggests the possibility that it was in some way connected with the introduction of these concerts by the French conductor Louis Antoine Jullien (1812–60). Promenade concerts, similar to those of today, were introduced by him to Covent

Garden and the English Opera House during the winter seasons from 1842 to 1859.
2. Charles Hindley in *The True History of Tom and Jerry*, recording that Billy Waters died in St Giles's workhouse, stated:

'Poor Billy endeavoured, up to the period of his last illness, to obtain for a wife and two children what he termed, "An honest living by scraping de cat-gut!" by which he originally collected considerable sums of money at the West-end of the town, where his ribbon-decked cocked hat and feathers, with the grin on his countenance, and sudden turn and kick out of his wooden limb, and other antics and efforts to please, excited much mirth and attention, and were well rewarded from the pockets of John Bull'.

3. The pair of Derby figures titled 'Billy Waters' and 'African Sall' illustrated on *pl.* E-36 are included to enable collectors to identify a Staffordshire figure of the latter should it appear. Of the half-dozen or so different pre-Victorian figures of Billy Waters I have noted, two have paired, not African Sall, but an unidentified Scottish mendicant with a peg leg, playing the bag-pipes [see also, *fig.* 301 (Mr Falahaa) *pl.* E-143]. If however, the Staffordshire figure of Billy Waters is connected with Jullien's arrival and not, for instance, with a revival of *Tom and Jerry*, it is unlikely that a pair to it exists.

Plate 36
Billy Waters and African Sall
These two Derby figures are illustrated to enable collectors to identify a Staffordshire figure of African Sall should it appear.

Between the figures is an engraving from *Life in London* by Pierce Egan inscribed *Tom & Jerry* '*Masquerading it*' *among the Cadgers in the* '*Back Slums*', *in the Holy Land*.

In the centre-background of the illustration (which was designed by I. R. & G. Cruikshank) Billy Waters may be seen playing his fiddle.

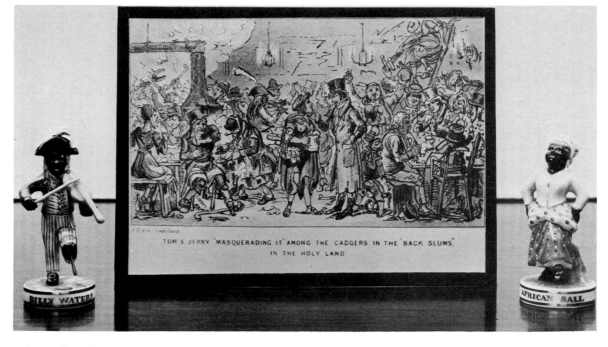

Plate 36
A pair of Derby figures.
L: Billy Waters
R: African Sall
These two figures are illustrated to enable collectors to identify a Victorian Staffordshire figure of African Sall should one exist. Between the figures is an engraving from *Life in London* by Pierce Egan inscribed "Tom & Jerry 'Masquerading it' among the Cadgers in the 'Back Slums', in the Holy Land". In the centre-background of the illustration (which was designed by I. R. & G. Cruikshank) Billy Waters can be seen playing his fiddle.
In the collection of Mr Bert Shevlov

Plate 37
Figure 72
Subject: **T. D. Rice as 'Jim Crow'**
Title: Jim Crow (gilt script)
Date: *c.* 1836
Height: 6 in (15.25 cm)
Colour: Well coloured.
Rarity: VR. D. A.
Description: A coloured man dressed in a round hat, jacket, waistcoat, neckerchief, trousers and shoes. His clothes are patched in many places.
Observations: The music-front illustrated on this plate is inscribed *JIM CROW* and refers to *THE CELEBRATED NIGGER SONG, sung by MR RICE with unbounded shouts of applause at the Royal Surrey Theatre.* Both *fig.* 72 and *fig.* 73 are likely to have been intended to portray T. D. Rice (1806–60) singing the refrain of his most famous song. Rice first appeared at the Surrey Theatre, London, in 1836, and started the enormous vogue of 'Nigger Minstrels' in England.

> 'Come listen all ye galls and boys,
> I'm just come from Tuckheo
> I'm goin' to sing a let . . . tel song
> My name him be Jim Crow. I was
> born in Ole Virging a long time a-go
> Ven Uncle Sam he made de in-e-my
> jump Jim Crow. Veel about and
> turn about and do jis so. Eb'ry
> time I veel about I jump Jim Crow'.

Figure 73
Subject: **T. D. Rice as 'Jim Crow'**
Title: None
Date: *c.* 1836
Height: 5¾ in (14.5 cm)
Colour: Well coloured.

Rarity: R.
Description: Very similar to *fig.* 72, but his posture is somewhat different and the base of the figure is circular instead of oval.
Observations: See preceding figure.

Plate 38
Figure 74
Subject: **'Wackford Squeers'**—? **Mr Wilkinson in the role**
Title: Wackford Squeers (transfer black capitals)
Date: 1839
Height: 8½ in (21.5 cm)
Colour: Well coloured.
Maker: Ridgway & Robey, Hanley
Rarity: VR.
Series: Same series as *fig.* 75 ('Kate Nickleby') and *fig.* 76 ('Ralph Nickleby'). Other characters from *Nicholas Nickleby* will doubtless turn up; *figs.* 77, 78 and 79 have been reserved for them.
Description: Standing bare-headed, in frockcoat, waistcoat, pantaloons and boots. In his right hand he carries a cane and in his left hand an open book.
Observations: The figures of characters from *Nicholas Nickleby* (*figs.* 74, 75 and 76) pose a problem as yet not entirely resolved. The novel *Nicholas Nickleby* by Charles Dickens was published in monthly numbers from 1838 to 1839. A dramatized version of the novel, a farce in two Acts by Edward Stirling, was first performed at the Royal Adelphi Theatre on November 19th, 1838.

Each figure has printed on the back 'PUBLISHED *June 15th, 1839,* / *BY* RIDGWAY & ROBEY / *HANLEY* / Staffordshire

Potteries', see ch. 2, *pl.* 5. Although only three figures have come to light, so far, there are likely to be others in the series. None of the figures 'match up' with any of the engravings by 'Phiz' in the original publication (see *pls.* E-41 and 42). As the figures are not based on 'Phiz' engravings, it has been thought that they might be based on engravings of the dramatized versions given at the Adelphi and elsewhere. If this were so it might be possible to identify them from illustrations (usually on the wrapper) of printed versions of such adaptations published by Webster, Lacey, and later by Dicks and others. Research in this direction has proved unproductive.

In the Webster publication the following information is given regarding the actors and their costume:
Ralph Nickleby—Dark green coat, blue spencer, dark grey pantaloons, Hessian boots, low-crowned broad-brimmed hat.—*Mr Cullenford.*
Squeers—Black coat, waistcoat, pantaloons, Hessian boots, dark great coat, comforter and gloves, black hat. 2nd dress. Drab morning gown.—*Mr Wilkinson.*
Kate Nickleby—Black dress, black bonnet and shawl. 2nd dress. Black. White veil over shoulders.—*Miss Cotterill.*

Part of the playbill for the original production is illustrated on *pl.* E-40.
Conclusion: Although these figures are not based on 'Phiz' engravings, there is still no conclusive evidence that they are theatrical portraits, though it seems likely that they are. The date on the figures suggests that if they are, in fact, portrait figures, they were issued in connection with the first production at the Adelphi on November 19th, 1838. If this is so, it could be that, in the course of time, the original engravings from

Plate 38
Fig. 74 Wackford Squeers
Fig. 75 Kate Nickleby
In the collection of
Mr Geoffrey A. Godden

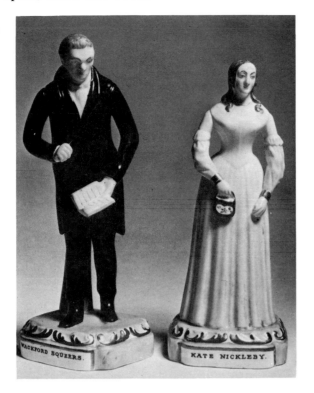

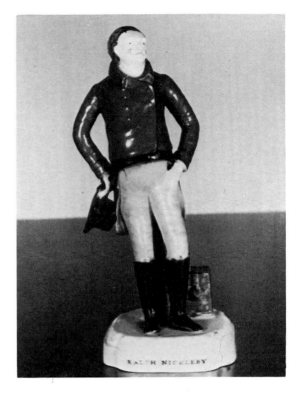

Plate 39 (Right)
Fig. 76 Ralph Nickleby

Afterwhich (for the Second Time,) with New Music, Extensive Scenery, Dresses, and Decorations, an entirely Original, Ironical, Local Burletta of Men and Manners, in Two Acts, founded on the celebrated, widely-diffused, extensively-circulated, and universally admired Papers by "BOZ;" written and adapted expressly for this Establishment, by Mr. E. STIRLING, called

NICHOLAS NICKLEBY

Or, Doings at Do-the-Boys Hall!

The SCENERY by Messrs. PITT & WILSON. The Dresses by Mr. GODFEE & Miss RAYNER.
The Properties by Mr. JAP. he Machinery by Mr. SAXBY.

☞ "It will be our aim, in the Life and Adventures of NICHOLAS NICKLEBY, to amuse by producing a rapid succession of characters and incidents, and describing them as cheerfully and pleasantly as in us lies; advancing thus much, he confidently hopes to enlist both their heartiest merriment and their kindliest sympathies."—Publisher's Prospectus.

Mr. Ralph Nickleby, Mr. CULLENFORD, Nicholas Nickleby, Mr. J. WEBSTER,
Newman Noggs, ... Mr. O. SMITH,
Squeers, Mr. WILKINSON, John Browdie, (a Yorkshireman) Mr. H. BEVERLY,
Monsieur Mantalini,........ (a Man Milliner) .... Mr. YATES,
Lord Verisopht, Mr. LANSDOWNE, .. Sir Melby Hawk, Mr. WILSON,
Smike,............(an Orphan)............ Mrs. KEELEY,
Mr. Pike, Mr. WELLINGTON, ... Mr. Pluck, Mr. SHAW,
Col. Chowser, Mr. ROBINSON, Scaley, Mr. SANDERS, Waiter, Mr. GEORGE,
Footman to Mons. Mantalini, Mr. UPSDELL, Guard, &c. Mr. DAVIS,
Mrs. Nickleby, Miss O'NEIL, ... Kate Nickleby, Miss COTTERILL,
Madame Mantalini, Miss SHAW, Miss Squeers, Miss GOWER,
Miss Price, Miss GROVE, ... Miss Knagg, Miss ENSCOE,
Mrs. Squeers, ... Mrs. FOSBROKE,

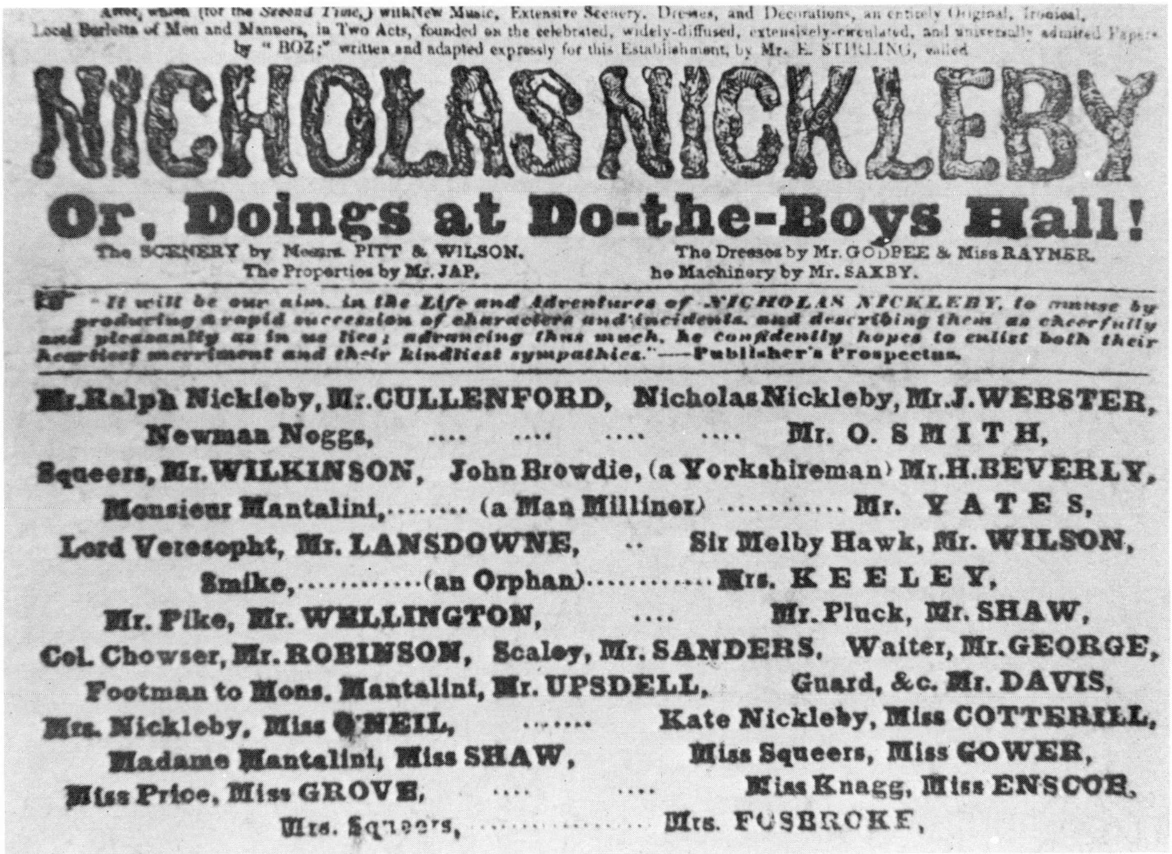

Plate 40
Part of a playbill advertising the first production of *Nicholas Nickleby or, Doings at Do-the-Boys Hall!* at the Theatre Royal Adelphi for Tuesday, 20th November, 1838 and during the week.
Note the novel, *Nicholas Nickleby* by Charles Dickens was published in monthly numbers from 1838 to 1839. It is not generally recognised that the novel was dramatized before publication of the final monthly number.

which the figures were made will come to light. However, the description of the costume worn by 'Kate Nickleby' in the original version does not tie up with the costume portrayed in the figure.

Figure 75
Subject: **'Kate Nickleby'—? Miss Cotterill in the role**
Title: Kate Nickleby (transfer black capitals)
Date: 1839
Height: 8 in (20.5 cm)
Colour: Well coloured.
Maker: Ridgway & Robey, Hanley
Rarity: VR.
Series: Same series as *fig.* 74 ('Wackford Squeers') and *fig.* 76 ('Ralph Nickleby')
Description: Standing bare-headed, in hour-glass bodice with ground-length skirt and long sleeves, a small handbag in her right hand.
Observations: See *fig.* 74 ('Wackford Squeers').

Plate 39
Figure 76
Subject: **'Ralph Nickleby'—? Mr Cullenford in the role**
Title: Ralph Nickleby (transfer black capitals)
Date: 1839
Height: $8\frac{1}{2}$ in (21.5 cm)
Colour: Well coloured.
Maker: Ridgway & Robey, Hanley
Rarity: VR.

Plate 41
The Yorkshire Schoolmaster at 'The Saracen's Head'. Original
'Phiz' engraving from *Nicholas Nickleby*. Ralph Nickleby is on
the left, with Nicholas clutching his hand. Wackford Squeers
is on the right. No engraving has been found in the
contemporary version of the novel to correspond with *figs.* 74,
75 and 76, *pls.* E-38 and 39.

Plate 42
Mr Ralph Nickleby's first visit to his poor relations. A 'Phiz'
engraving from a contemporary edition of *Nicholas Nickleby*.
L to R: Mrs Nickleby, Kate Nickleby, Nicholas Nickleby and
Ralph Nickleby.

Plate 43
Fig. 80 Sairey Gamp and Betsey Prig
To the right of the figure is the 'Phiz' engraving from the
contemporary edition of *Martin Chuzzlewit:* 'Mrs Gamp
proposes a toast.'
By courtesy of Mr and Mrs Eric Joyce

Plate 39 continued

Series: Same series as *fig.* 74 ('Wackford Squeers') and *fig.* 75 ('Kate Nickleby').
Description: He stands bare-headed, against a mounting block, wearing a spencer (short over-jacket) over a tailcoat, pantaloons and Hessian boots. He holds his low-crowned broad-brimmed hat in his right hand and his left hand is in his pocket.
Observations: 1. See *fig.* 74 ('Wackford Squeers') *pl.* E-38.
2. A similar figure fetched 26 gns at Christie's in 1966.

Plate 40
Nicholas Nickleby
Part of a playbill advertising the first production of *Nicholas Nickleby or, Doings at Do-the-Boys Hall!* at the Theatre Royal Adelphi for Tuesday, 20th November, 1838 and during the week.

Plate 41
Nicholas Nickleby
Original 'Phiz' engraving from *Nicholas Nickleby*. It is inscribed *The Yorkshire Schoolmaster at 'The Saracen's Head'*. Ralph Nickleby is on the left, with Nicholas clutching his hand. Wackford Squeers is on the right. No engraving has been found in the contemporary version of the novel to correspond with *figs.* 74, 75 and 76, *pls.* E-38 and 39.

Plate 42
Nicholas Nickleby
'Phiz' engraving from a contemporary edition of *Nicholas Nickleby*. It is inscribed *Mr Ralph Nickleby's first visit to his poor relations*. From left to right: Mrs Nickleby, Kate Nickleby, Nicholas and Ralph Nickleby.

Plate 43
Figure 80
Subject: **Sairey Gamp and Betsey Prig**
Title: None
Height: 7¼ in (18.25 cm)
Colour: Well coloured.
Rarity: VR. A.
Description: 'Sairey Gamp' is seated on the left holding an umbrella. She wears a bonnet, shawl and a coat over her long dress. 'Betsey Prig' sits on the right, similarly attired. Between them is a table on which is a teapot and a cup and saucer.
Observations: 1. The engraving illustrated to the right of the plate is by 'Phiz' (H. K. Browne, 1815–82). It is one of the illustrations which appeared in the first edition of Dickens' *Martin Chuzzlewit*. The scene portrayed is described in *ch.* 49:

'The temper of both parties was improved, for the time being, by the enjoyments of the table. When the meal came to a termination (which it was pretty long in doing), and Mrs Gamp having cleared away, produced the tea-pot from the top-shelf, simultaneously with a couple of wine-glasses, they were quite amiable.
"Betsey," said Mrs Gamp, filling her own glass, and passing the tea-pot, "I will now propoge a toast. My frequent pardner, Betsey Prig!"
"Which, altering the name to Sairah Gamp; I drink," said Mrs Prig, "with love and tenderness".'

Mrs Gamp's umbrella will be noted by the chimney-piece. *Fig.* 80 portrays the same scene. It seems likely to be theatrical. *Martin Chuzzlewit* was first dramatized in 1844 and was performed subsequently in various theatres on many occasions. In the dramatized version these two roles were, for a long time, acted by men. Enormous popularity in the part of 'Gamp' was won by John Sleeper Clarke (1833–99), the American comedy actor. It will be noted that in the figure the positions of Mrs Gamp and Betsey Prig are reversed. No theatrical print has been found which matches up with this figure, and it is therefore not possible at this stage to say with certainty whether or not it is theatrical, and if theatrical, which production it represents.
2. I have seen two small, late figures, one, untitled, of 'Sairey Gamp'; and the other, crudely titled in indented capitals, 'Betsey Prig'. This latter figure was probably a Kent production. I do not think either were theatrical.

Plate 44
Figure 81
Subject: **Mr Pickwick**
Title: Mr Pickwick (transfer black script)
Date: Late
Height: 7½ in (19 cm)
Colour: In the manner of William Kent.
Maker: William Kent
Rarity: Av.
Description: A toby jug. He stands, with his right arm raised in front of him, wearing a beaver hat, spectacles, long tailcoat, waistcoat, breeches and stockings.
Observations: 1. Almost certainly not a theatrical figure.
2. These figures are usually very late. Probably the majority were made in this century but I have seen one or two that appear to be a little earlier.
It appears in *Kent List C* as follows:

Ref. No.		Approx. Ht. in inches
391	Toby Jugs, Pickwick	7½

3. There is a Sampson Smith toby jug of 'Mr Pickwick' but I have never seen it. An example, with the following description, was sold at Christie's on March 18th, 1957:

'A Documentary Toby Jug in the form of Mr Pickwick, the old gentleman seated, with a benign expression, wearing a black hat, spectacles, yellow waistcoat, blue coat and pink breeches, the black and crabstock handle washed in tones of green and brown, 8½ in (21.5 cm), mark Sampson Smith / 1851 / Longton in raised capitals.'

Plate 45
Figure 82
Subject: **David Copperfield and Clara Peggotty**
Title: None
Height: 7¾ in (20 cm)
Colour: Well coloured.
Rarity: VR.
Description: 'David Copperfield' stands on the left, in peaked cap, jacket, waistcoat, trousers and shoes. He carries a basket over his right forearm. 'Clara Peggotty' stands on the right, wearing a bonnet, shawl and long dress. She carries a walking stick in her left hand.
Observations: Almost certainly represents 'David Copperfield' with 'Clara Peggotty', a servant to Mrs Copperfield who was nurse and friend to her son David:

'A girl with no shape at all and eyes so dark that they seemed to darken their whole neighbourhood in her face, and with cheeks and arms so hard and red that the birds might peck them in preference to apples'.

Plate 46
Figure 83
Subject: **Ham and Peggotty**
Title: None
Height: 9¼ in (23.5 cm)
Colour: Well coloured.
Rarity: R.
Description: 'Peggotty' sits on a wall mending his net. He is bare-headed, and his legs are crossed. 'Ham' stands on the right. He wears a fisherman's hat and has his jacket over his left arm. There is a basket of fish beside his left leg.

Plate 44
Fig. 81 Mr Pickwick

Plate 45
Fig. 82 David Copperfield and Clara Peggotty

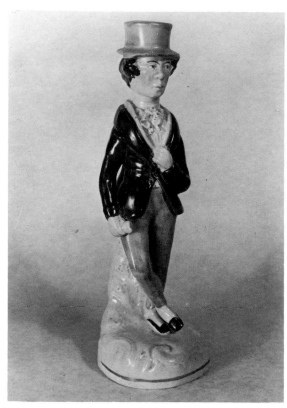

Plate 46 (Left)
Fig. 83 Ham and Peggotty

Plate 47
Fig. 84 Swiveller
*By permission of the Brighton
Art Gallery and Museum*

Plate 46 continued

Observations: This figure is generally re-garded as portraying 'Ham' and 'Peggotty' from Dickens' *David Copperfield*. This may well be so, although there is no conclusive evidence. There is nothing to suggest that it is theatrical.

Plate 47
Figure 84
Subject: **? Dick Swiveller**
Title: None
Height: 9 in (23 cm)
Colour: Well coloured.
Rarity: VR.
Pair: Unknown
Description: Standing 'propped up', with his right leg in front of his left. He is wearing a beaver hat several sizes too large for him, jacket, waistcoat and trousers. He holds a pair of gloves in his right hand.
Observations: No. 934 in the Willett Collec-tion and described as 'an actor'. It may well be theatrical. *The Old Curiosity Shop* was, of course, dramatized on many occasions.

Plate 48
Figure 85
Subject: **John Liston as 'Sam Swipes'**
Title: No! Am I a Gentleman? / Upon your Soul tho' Mother.
(black transfer: upper and lower case).
Date: *c.* 1827
Height: 6¼ in (16 cm)
Colour: Well coloured.
Maker: Enoch Wood & Sons
Rarity: R. D.
Pair: Same series as *fig.* 86 (Liston as 'Lubin Log') and others. See *observations*.
Description: He stands bare-headed, with his hands in his pockets, wearing a jacket, neckerchief, apron, breeches and striped stockings.

E388

Observations: 1. Based on a one and sixpenny plain, two shillings coloured lithograph by J. W. Gear inscribed:

> Polly Watts!
> *Written expressly for*
> MR. LISTON,
> *in the Character of*
> Sam Swipes
> in
> Exchange no Robbery,
> *adapted to the Air Isabel by*
> Peter Pigwiggin, the Younger
> *Author of 'Paul Pry'*

2. *Exchange no Robbery* was a comedy in three Acts by Theodore E. Hooke first produced at the Haymarket on August 12th, 1820, and again at Drury Lane on January 2nd, 1826.
3. John Liston was one of the most famous comedians of all time. In 1826, lithographs were produced of a number of his celebrated roles. They include the one illustrated on this plate. So far seven other figures based on these lithographs have come to light, and I am grateful to Mr John Hall for the following information:

Figures of John Liston based on lithographs of his celebrated characters issued in 1826
Fig. 85, *pl.* E-48.
'Sam Swipes' in *Exchange no Robbery*
Fig. 86, *pl.* E-49.
'Van Dunder' in *'Twould Puzzle a Conjuror*.
also
(*a*) 'Paul Pry' in *Paul Pry*
  Comedy in 3 Acts by J. Poole. First produced at the Haymarket on September 13th, 1825 and later at Drury Lane on June 13th, 1829.
(*b*) 'Moll Flaggon' in *The Lord of the Manor*.
  Comic opera in 3 Acts by John Burgoyne. First produced at Drury Lane in 1781. Music by Jackson. Revived at Drury Lane on December 20th. 1820, and the Lyceum on November 12th, 1834.
(*c*) 'Maw-Worm' in *The Hypocrite*.
  A comedy adapted from Cibber after Moliere's *Tartuff*. First produced at the Lyceum on July 27th, 1819—*in New form in five Acts with Music by Jolly*.
(*d*) 'Dominie Sampson' in *Guy Mannering*.
  An opera by Sir Henry Bishop. First produced at Covent Garden in March, 1816, and at the Lyceum on October 2nd, 1820.

(*e*) 'Lubin Log' in *Love, Law and Physic*, Farce in two Acts by James Kenney. First produced at Covent Garden in 1812, and later at Drury Lane on March 15th, 1823.
(*f*) 'Broom Girl'
  Madame Vestris played the 'Broom Girl' (see *fig.* 112, *pl.* E-61) for the first time for Liston's benefit at the Haymarket on September 18th, 1826; then she introduced it to *The £100 Note*. Mr Liston appeared as a 'Broom Girl' with Madame Vestris on November 6th, 1826, and with Madame Love on March 24th, 1828.

4. It may well be asked why *fig.* 87, and others of similar vintage, are included in this volume. There are at least two reasons. Firstly, they help to demonstrate the evolution of the typical Victorian figure. Secondly, there is some evidence to suggest that the manufacture of these figures continued into Victorian times. Liston retired in 1837 and died nine years later.
5. I am informed that this piece and others in the series have been found impressed 'ENOCH WOOD / & SONS / BURSLEM', but I have never seen a marked piece myself. Enoch Wood manufactured earthenwares etc. from 1818 to 1846.

Plate 49
Figure 86
Subject: **John Liston as 'Van Dunder'**
Title: Read it indeed! / That's very easily said, read it!!
(black transfer: upper and lower case)
Date: *c.* 1827
Height: 7¼ in (18.25 cm)
Colour: Well coloured.
Maker: Enoch Wood & Sons
Rarity: R. D.
Pair: Same series as *fig.* 85 (Liston as 'Sam Swipes') and others. See *observations*, *pl.* E-48.
Description: Standing wearing a steeple hat, large bow tie, pantaloons, stockings and shoes with rosettes. He holds a manuscript in both hands.
Observations: 1. No. 932 in the Willett Collection.

Plate 48
Fig. 85 Liston ('Sam Swipes')
To the right of the figure is a lithograph by J. W. Gear inscribed *Mr Liston in the Character of Sam Swipes in Exchange no Robbery*.

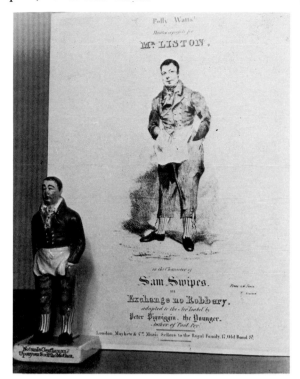

Plate 49 (Right)
Fig. 86 Liston ('Van Dunder')
By permission of the Brighton Art Gallery and Museum

Plate 50
Fig. 87 Stratton ('Tom Thumb')
To the left of the figure is a coloured engraving commomorating 'Genl. Tom Thumb's *MARRIAGE* at Grace Church N.Y. Feb. 10th 1863'. Beneath is a reference to Tom Thumb, his wife, best man and bridesmaid: 'Four wondrously formed & strangely beautiful ladies and gentlemen in miniatures, nature's smallest editions of her choicest works. *THE GREATEST WONDERS IN THE WORLD.* A married couple, a bachelor & a belle, all four weighing but 100 lbs. They are all perfect in development, educated & intelligent and fitted both intellectually and physically for all the duties & requirements of life. Robust health, beauty, grace, manly dignity and feminine sweetness are combined in them in the amplest manner. No Exhibition more Marvelously beautiful has ever been seen on earth'.

2. John Liston played 'Van Dunder' in *'Twould Puzzle a Conjuror*, a comic drama in two Acts by J. Poole at the Haymarket on September 11th, 1824.
3. See *observation* 5, *fig* 85, *pl.* E-48.

Plate 50
Figure 87
Subject: **Charles Sherwood Stratton, otherwise known as 'Tom Thumb'**
Title: None
Date: c. 1844

Height: 3 in (7.6 cm)
Colour: White and gilt.
Rarity: VR.
Description: He kneels on his left knee, bareheaded, in morning coat, waistcoat and trousers. His right hand is on his right knee and he holds the edge of his coat with his left hand. He appears to be 'taking a bow'. The height of the figure is small in proportion to the breadth of the base. This gives the impression that it is intended to portray a dwarf.

Observations: 1. There is little doubt that this figure represents 'Tom Thumb'. I have heard of an identical titled version, although I have never seen one myself. The important feature is that the size of the figure is small in proportion to the breadth of the base. *Fig.* 50 (Napoleon) *pl.* C-17 has also been called 'Tom Thumb'. This is unlikely to be so, for here the size of the figure is proportionate to the size of the tent.
2. 'Tom Thumb' was exhibited by Barnham in England in 1844, and again in 1857. He

Plate 51
Fig. 88 Perrot and Grahn ('Diavolino' and 'Catarina')
Fig. 89 Perrot ('Diavolino')
In the collection of Mrs Constance Chiswell

Plate 52 (Left)
CATARINA,
ou
LA FILLE DU BRIGAND
The Grand Ballet
By M. Perrot
Coloured lithograph music-front by John Brandard. It is the source of *fig.* 88, *pl.* E-51.
In the collection of Messrs Raymond Mander and Joe Mitchenson

Plate 53
Fig. 91 Perrot ('Diavolino')

Plate 50 continued
appeared at the Princess's Theatre in 1844.
3. A similar figure, together with three unimportant pieces, fetched 38 gns at Christie's in 1967.

Plate 51
Figure 88
Subject: **Jules Perrot as 'Diavolino' and Lucille Grahn as 'Catarina'**
Title: None
Date: *c.* 1846

Height: 8½ in (21.5 cm)
Colour: Well coloured.
Rarity: VR. D. A.
Pair: Forms the centrepiece of the pair *fig.* 89 (Perrot as 'Diavolino') and *fig.* 90 (Grahn as 'Catarina'). The latter has not been reported but must exist. The figure appears to be one of a series which includes *figs.* 93 and 94, *pl.* E-55, neither of which have been identified and each of which is likely to be a centrepiece.
Description: They dance the polka. Perrot

stands on the left, right hand on his hip, his left hand in Grahn's left hand. He wears a steeple hat with a long flowing ribbon and a medallion in the front, jacket, open shirt, pantaloons, socks and shoes. Grahn stands on the right, wearing a round hat and ribbon, her right hand to her hat, her left hand grasping his left hand. She is dressed in blouse and wide medium-length skirt.
Observations: The coloured lithograph music-front by John Brandard of Jules Perrot in the role of 'Diavolino' and Lucille Grahn as

Plate 54
Coloured lithograph by J. Brandard of Lucille Grahn in *Catarina*, Act I, Scene I.
The significance of this lithograph is that it suggests the existence of a pair to *fig.* 91 [Perrot ('Diavolino')] *pl.* E-53.

'Catarina' in Act 1, Scene 1 of *Catarina, ou la Fille du Brigand* is the source of this and other figures (see *pl.* E-52 and *ch.* 3, *pl.* 40B). This ballet, by Jules Perrot, was first performed at Her Majesty's Theatre in 1846.

Figure 89
Subject: **Jules Perrot as 'Diavolino'**
Title: None
Date: *c.* 1846
Height: 8½ in (21.5 cm)
Colour: Well coloured.
Rarity: VR. D. A.
Pair: Fig. 90 (Grahn as 'Catarina'; so far *not* recorded). Fig. 88 (Perrot and Grahn as 'Diavolino' and 'Catarina') forms the centrepiece of this pair.
Description: Dressed identically as in *fig.* 88, his right hand on his hip, his left hand touching the brim of his hat.
Observations: See *fig.* 88 (Perrot and Grahn as 'Diavolino' and 'Catarina').

Plate 52
Diavolino and Catarina
Coloured lithograph music-front by John Brandard inscribed:

CATARINA,
OU
LA FILLE DU BRIGAND
THE GRAND BALLET
BY M. PERROT
now performing with such great applause at
HER MAJESTY'S THEATRE.
The music composed by
SIGNOR PUGNI.

It is the source of *fig.* 88, *pl.* E-51.

Plate 53
Figure 91
Subject: **Jules Perrot as 'Diavolino'**
Title: None
Date: *c.* 1846
Height: 14½ in (36.75 cm)
Colour: Well coloured, paler versions are seen.
Rarity: VR.

Pair: This figure is almost certainly paired by Lucille Grahn in the role of 'Catarina'. Fig. 92 has been reserved for it. See *observations*.
Description: Standing wearing a steeple hat with long flowing ribbon and a medallion in the front. His right hand is on his hip and his left hand grasps the barrel of a rifle, the butt of which is resting on the ground beside him. He wears a cape, shirt, pantaloons and stockings. There are two pistols in his belt.
Observations: Comparison with the Brandard lithograph of Perrot in *Catarina* (*pl.* E-52) leaves little room for doubt about the identification of this figure. Note, in particular, the tall steeple hat with the sash and the medallion in the front; also, the belt with two pistols in it. Neither a pair to the figure nor an exact matching lithograph has been found, but there is a lithograph by J. Brandard of Lucille Grahn in *Catarina*, Act 1, Scene 1 (see *pl.* E-54), which suggests the existence both of a pair (Lucille Grahn) and a companion lithograph of Jules Perrot.

Plate 54
Lucille Grahn as 'Catarina'
Coloured lithograph by J. Brandard of Lucille Grahn in *Catarina*, Act 1, Scene 1. For the significance of this lithograph, see preceding figure.

Plate 55
Figure 93
Subject: **Pair of unidentified nautical dancers**
Title: None
Height: 9¾ in (24.5 cm)
Colour: Well coloured.
Rarity: R.
Series: Same series as *fig.* 88 (Perrot and Grahn) *pl.* E-51 and *fig.* 94 (Pair of unidentified Highland dancers).
Description: He stands on the right, in sailor's rig, his left hand touching his hat and his

Plate 55
Fig. 93 Pair of unidentified nautical dancers
Fig. 94 Pair of unidentified Highland dancers

Plate 56
Fig. 95 ?Massaroni

Plate 56A
Penny Plain, Tuppence Coloured Pollock Print:
*Characters and Scenes
in the Brigand*

Note there is a distinct similarity between 'Massaroni', as portrayed in the print (*see figure*) and the person portrayed in *fig.* 95, E-56, but the similarity is by no means clo enough for positive identification.

Plate 55 continued
right hand on his hip. She stands on the left, her left arm linked through his right arm. She wears a round plumed bonnet, jacket and medium-length wide skirt and has her right hand on her right hip.
Observations: Almost certainly a pair of single figures exist to match up with this figure, in much the same way as for *fig.* 88 (Perrot and Grahn); but they have not been identified so far. Likewise, it is very probable that the figure will turn out to be a theatrical portrait.

Figure 94
Subject: **Pair of unidentified Highland dancers**
Title: None
Height: 9¾ in (24.5 cm)
Colour: Well coloured.
Rarity: R.
Series: Same series as *fig.* 88 (Perrot and Grahn) *pl.* E-51 and *fig.* 93 (Pair of un-identified nautical dancers).
Description: He stands on the left, wearing a hat with long plume, jacket, shirt, kilt, sporran and socks. His right hand is on his hip and his left hand is held upwards and clasps her right hand. She stands on the right, with her left hand on her hip, holding a garland. She wears a round hat, bodice and medium-length wide skirt.
Observations: There is almost certainly a pair of single figures to match up with this figure, but so far they have not come to light. Likewise, also, it is quite probable that the figure will eventually be identified as a theatrical portrait.

Plate 56
Figure 95
Subject: **? Massaroni**
E392

Title: Brigand (gilt script)
Date: *c.* 1867
Height: 14¼ in (36.25 cm)
Colour: Well coloured.
Rarity: VR.
Description: He sits on a rock. To his right are two casks. He holds a mug in his right hand and the barrel of a rifle in his left. The rifle is between his legs with the butt on the ground. He wears a steeple hat with a long ribbon but no medallion, shirt, jacket, breeches, stockings and shoes.
Observations: 1. The general appearance is very similar to that of *fig.* 91 (Perrot) *pl.* E-53 but the essential factors that make it possible to identify that figure with relative certainty are missing from this figure. Thus, there is no medallion on the front of the hat, nor is he wearing a belt with two pistols attached. Nevertheless, it is just possible that the figure may portray Perrot in the role of 'Diavolino'.
2. Alternatively, the figure may portray an, as yet, unidentified actor in the role of 'Massaroni', a character in *The Brigand*, a romantic drama in 2 Acts by J. R. Planché, first produced at Drury Lane on November 18th, 1829 and revived at the Surrey Theatre on February 2nd, 1867. This seems a more plausible theory.

Plate 56A
Massaroni
Penny plain, tuppence coloured Pollock print:

POLLOCK'S
CHARACTERS & SCENES
IN THE
BRIGAND

Note that 'Massaroni' (top-left) is dressed very similarly to the brigand portrayed in *fig.* 95, *pl.* E-56. No doubt a print exists

which will eventually prove or disprove the tentative identification of the figure.

Plate 57
Figure 96
Subject: **Unidentified woman**
Title: None
Height: 6½ in (16.5 cm)
Colour: Well coloured in pastel shades.
Rarity: VR.
Pair: *Fig.* 97 (Unidentified man with shield)
Description: She stands wearing a plumed bonnet, bodice, skirt and pantaloons. In her left hand she carries a jug and in her right a garland. Beside her right foot is a dog or sheep.
Observations: Possibly theatrical.

Figure 97
Subject: **Unidentified man with shield**
Title: None
Height: 6¼ in (16 cm)
Colour: Well coloured in pastel shades.
Rarity: VR.
Pair: *Fig.* 96 (Unidentified woman)
Description: He stands bearded, and wearing a plumed bonnet, and tunic of chained mail. There is a sash over his right shoulder. In his right hand he carries a sword and in his left, a shield.
Observations: Possibly theatrical.

Figure 98
Subject: **Unidentified brigand**
Title: None
Height: 8¼ in (21 cm)
Colour: Well coloured.
Rarity: R.
Pair: See *observations*.
Description: He stands, apparently on rocks, with his right foot higher than his left. He

Plate 58
Fig. 100 Unidentified Highland soldier
Fig. 99 Unidentified sailor

wears a round plumed bonnet, open shirt, tunic and knee-boots, and holds a rifle across his chest in both hands.

Observations: Almost certainly theatrical and possibly belongs to the same series as *fig.* 99 (Unidentified sailor) *pl.* E-58.

Plate 58
Figure 99
Subject: **Unidentified sailor**
Title: None
Height: 7¾ in (20 cm)
Colour: Well coloured.
Rarity: VR.
Pair: See *observations*
Description: Standing, wearing a round straw hat, neckerchief, jacket, waistcoat, trousers and knee-boots. His left hand is on his hip and his right holds a pistol. There is another pistol in his belt.
Observations: May well be theatrical and is quite possibly a portrait figure of T. P. Cooke, although a corresponding engraving has not come to light so far. It may form part of a series of which *fig.* 98 (Unidentified brigand) *pl.* E-57 may be another.

Figure 100
Subject: **Unidentified Highland soldier**
Title: None
Height: 9¾ in (24.5 cm)
Colour: Well coloured.
Rarity: Av.
Pair: Unknown
Description: Standing bearded, wearing a plumed hat, and carrying a pistol in his right hand and a sword in his left. There is a sash over his right shoulder and he wears a kilt and sporran.
Observations: Probably theatrical; possibly military.

Plate 59
Fig. 102 Unidentified brigand and child

Fig. 101 Unidentified huntsman
By courtesy of Mr and Mrs Eric Joyce and in the collection of the author

Plate 59
Figure 101
Subject: **Unidentified huntsman**
Title: None
Height: 10¾ in (27 cm)
Colour: Well coloured.
Rarity: R.
Description: A huntsman is climbing a rock which is solid (*not* a spill-holder). He wears a plumed bonnet, shirt, breeches and stockings. There is a knife in his belt and at the foot of the rock lie a musket and a dead stag.
Observations: Included because it is possibly theatrical.

Figure 102
Subject: **Unidentified brigand and child**
Title: None
Height: 13¾ in (35 cm)
Colour: Well coloured.
Rarity: R.
Description: A man is kneeling on a rock, with his left knee flexed and his right leg straight. He wears a Tyrolese hat, jacket, shirt with neckerchief, breeches and stockings, and in his right hand he holds a rifle. Behind him, on a higher rock, stands a little girl wearing a plumed bonnet, jacket and skirt. She points forwards with her right hand.
Observations: Possibly theatrical, but so far unidentified. Is very similar to *fig.* 103 (Wood) *pl*. E-60 but cannot be connected with the opera *Fra Diavolo* for no child is mentioned in the script.

Plate 60
Figure 103
Subject: **William Burke Wood as 'Fra Diavolo'**
Title: None
Height: 8½ in (21.5 cm)
Colour: Well coloured.
Rarity: R.
Description: A man in a Tyrolese hat, jacket, shirt and neckerchief, waistcoat, breeches and knee-boots, crouches on a rock, peering round the edge, as if in the act of stalking. He holds a rifle in his right hand and his cape is draped over his left arm.
Observations: Based on a lithograph music-front by Endicott of New York illustrated in *ch*. 3, *pl*. 41. It is inscribed:

'*ON YONDER ROCK RECLINING*',
FROM AUBER'S GRAND OPERA
OF
FRA DIAVOLO
AS SUNG BY
MR. & MRS. WOOD

Fig. 104 Man sitting beside beach hut   Fig. 103 Wood ('Fra Diavolo')   Fig. 105 ?Tell

Plate 60

B: *Fig.* 106 Unidentified Moor
Fig. 107 Unidentified woman
Fig. 108 Unidentified male dancer
Fig. 109 Unidentified female dancer
Fig. 110 Unidentified man and woman with violin
Fig. 111 Unidentified male and female dancers
In the collection of Mrs Constance Chiswell

Section E. Theatre, Opera, Ballet and Circus

Figure 104
Subject: **Man sitting beside beach hut**
Title: None
Height: 6½ in (16.5 cm)
Colour: Sparsely coloured.
Rarity: R.
Description: A man dressed in a turban, jacket, shirt and trousers is sitting cross-legged, playing a violin, immediately to the left of what appears to be a beach hut, the window of which is open. A woman's face has appeared at the window.
Observations: This figure, as far as I am aware, has remained unexplained.

Figure 105
Subject: **? William Tell**
Title: None
Height: 9½ in (24 cm)
Colour: Well coloured.
Rarity: R.
Description: Standing, wearing a Tyrolese hat, gauntlets, knee-length coat with belt, and knee-boots. An Alpine horn hangs from his belt and he holds a cudgel in his left hand. There is a dog by his right leg.
Observations: It is generally thought to be William Tell, but I know of no evidence to confirm this. It is probably theatrical.

Figure 106
Subject: **Unidentified Moor**
Title: None
Height: 7½ in (19 cm)
Colour: Well coloured.
Rarity: R.
Description: Standing, in calf-length tunic, Turkish trousers and shoes. There is a scarf round his neck and a sash round his waist, and in his right hand he holds a scimitar (short curved Oriental sword).
Observations: This figure has been described in the literature as 'believed to be that of Kemble', but I know of nothing to support this identification.

Plate 60 continued

Figure 107
Subject: **Unidentified woman**
Title: None
Height: 9¼ in (23.5 cm)
Colour: Well coloured.
Rarity: R.
Pair: Not known, but one probably exists.
Description: Standing wearing a high hat, long ear-rings, bodice with leg-of-mutton sleeves and ankle-length skirt. Tassels hang down from a cord around her waist. She holds a handkerchief in her right hand. The base is decorated with flowers.
Observations: Almost certainly theatrical, but has defied identification so far.

Figure 108
Subject: **Unidentified male dancer**
Title: None
Height: 9¾ in (24.5 cm)
Colour: Well coloured.
Rarity: R.
Pair: Fig. 109 (Unidentified female dancer)
Description: Standing bare-headed, wearing a long coat, breeches and knee-boots. He holds a scarf in both hands, his left hand being held above his head and his right hand on his hip.
Observations: Possibly Jules Perrot, but there is no supporting evidence.

Figure 109
Subject: **Unidentified female dancer**
Title: None
Height: 9¾ in (24.5 cm)
Colour: Well coloured.
Rarity: R.
Pair: Fig. 108 (Unidentified male dancer)
Description: Standing bare-headed, in bodice, flounced knee-length skirt and modesty panties. She holds a scarf in both hands, her right hand being held above her head and her left hand on her hip.
Observations: Has defied identification.

Figure 110
Subject: **Unidentified man and woman with violin**
Title: None
Height: 7½ in (19 cm)
Colour: Well coloured.
Rarity: Av.
Description: The man stands on the right, with his right arm around the woman's neck, and his right leg crossed in front of his left leg. He has a military tunic with a belt round his waist, and a cross suspended from his neck. He holds his hat in his left hand and wears knee-boots. The woman, seated to his right, wears a bodice and full-length flounced skirt. She holds a violin in her left hand.
Observations: The identification of this figure is not known. There are several other similar figures. They are probably theatrical.

Figure 111
Subject: **Unidentified male and female dancers**
Title: None
Height: 7¼ in (18.25 cm)
Colour: Well coloured.
Rarity: R.
Description: He stands behind her with his arm round her waist, holding her left hand with his left hand, and her right hand with his right hand. He wears a plumed bonnet, doublet and hose. She is bare-headed, with a full-length dress displaying an inverted 'V' below the waist.

E396

Observations: This figure has defied identification so far.

Plate 61

Figure 112
Subject: **Madame Vestris as a 'Broom Girl'**
Title: None
Date: 184–
Height: 4¾ in (12.25 cm)
Colour: Sparsely coloured.
Rarity: R.
Description: Standing, wearing a bonnet and calf-length frock. Her left hand is in the small of her back, and in her right hand she holds a broom across her right shoulder.
Observations: 1. Based on a lithograph of Madame Vestris as a 'Broom Girl' by Richard J. Lane, published on November 24th, 1826 by J. Dickinson, New Bond Street.
2. Madame Vestris first played the 'Broom Girl' for Liston's benefit at the Haymarket on September 18th, 1826. Later, she introduced it to *The £100 Note*. She sung it at intervals throughout her life. This Staffordshire figure is almost certainly Victorian.
3. The lithograph illustrated in the frontispiece of this volume is of a street vendor selling Staffordshire images. Among the images may be recognized two of Madame Vestris as a 'Broom Girl'.

BAVARIAN GIRL'S SONG
Sung by Madame Vestris
Arranged and partly composed by Alexander Lee.

From Teutschland I come with my light wares
all laden,

To dear happy England in summer's gay bloom,
Then listen fair Lady and young pretty maiden,
Oh! Buy of the wand'ring Bavarian a Broom.
Buy a Broom. Buy a Broom.
Oh! Buy of the wand'ring Bavarian a Broom.

To brush away insects that sometimes annoy you,
You'll find it quite handy to use night and day,
And what better exercise pray can employ you,
Than to sweep all vexatious intruders away.
Buy a Broom. Buy a Broom.
And sweep all vexatious intruders away.

Ere winter comes on for sweet Home soon
departing,
My toils for your favor again I'll resume
And while gratitudes tear in my eyelid is starting,
Bless the time that in England I cried Buy a
Broom.
Buy a Broom. Buy a Broom.
Bless the time that in England I cried Buy a
Broom.
Spoken
Yes. I shall go back to my own Country and tell
them there
I sold all my wares in England.

Plate 62

Figure 20
Subject: **William Charles Macready**
Title: None
Date: c. 1846
Height: 8 in (20.5 cm)
Colour: Well coloured.
Rarity: R.
Pair: Fig. 21 (Unidentified actress)
Description: Identical to fig. 20 (Macready as 'James V of Scotland') pl. E-7, except that it is untitled. He stands bare-headed and bearded, in long ermine-edged cloak, tunic, short trunks and stockings. To his left is a pedestal,
Observations: See fig. 20, pl. E-7.

Figure 21
Subject: **Unidentified actress**
Title: None
Date: c. 1846
Height: 7¾ in (20 cm)

Colour: Well coloured.
Rarity: R.
Pair: Fig. 20 (Macready: untitled version)
Description: She stands bare-headed, wearing an ermine-edged coat, bodice and two-flounced calf-length skirt. Two tassels hang from her waist, and in her left hand she holds what appears to be a purse.
Observations: It may be that this figure does, in fact, portray an actress, although so far it has defied identification. Alternatively, it is purely fictional, having been made simply to 'balance' the figure of Macready.

Figure 113
Subject: **Luigi Lablache as 'Dr Dulcamara'**
Title: None
Date: c. 1848
Height: 8½ in (21.5 cm)
Colour: Well coloured.
Maker: Possibly Alpha factory
Rarity: VR.
Pair: Fig. 114 (Unidentified actress)
Description: He stands bare-headed, in stock and tailcoat, waistcoat and trousers, a manuscript in his right hand, his left arm by his side. The base of the figure is rococo.
Observations: 1. Based on a coloured lithograph music-front by John Brandard to *Operatic Celebrities* (a series of six selections), published in 1848, in which he holds a philtre (love-potion) instead of a piece of music, see ch. 3, pl. 42.
2. 'Dr Dulcamara' is the quack doctor in Donizetti's *L'elisir d'amore*.

Figure 114
Subject: **Unidentified actress**
Title: None
Date: c. 1848
Height: 8 in (20.5 cm)
Colour: Well coloured.
Maker: Possibly Alpha factory
Rarity: R.
Pair: Fig. 113 (Lablache as 'Dr Dulcamara')
Description: Standing bare-headed, with shoulder-length ringlets, wearing bodice and full-length skirt. She holds a scroll in her left hand and the base of the figure is rococo.
Observations: This figure is very similar to fig. 36, pl. H-10 titled 'Eliza Cook', but is reversed. Also, she wears no jacket over her bodice and in her left hand she holds a scroll instead of a book. The base is rococo. All this suggests that the figure does not, in fact, portray any particular person but is purely fictional; the potter seems to have 'borrowed' another figure in order to make a pair to 'balance' Lablache.

Figure 115
Subject: **Sims Reeves as 'Edgardo'**
Title: None
Date: c. 1847
Height: 10¼ in (25.75 cm)
Colour: Largely white, gilt and black.
Maker: Possibly Thomas Parr
Rarity: VR. D.
Pair: Fig. 116 (? Gras as 'Lucia'). Same series as figs. 117 (Unidentified girl in bloomers) and 118 (Unidentified man in bloomers), pl. E-63.
Description: He stands bare-headed, in thigh-length coat with cuffed sleeves, neckerchief, breeches and knee-boots. He holds a scroll in his right hand and his left hand is on his hip.
Observations: 1. Based on a coloured lithograph of Mr Sims Reeves as 'Edgardo' in

Section E. Theatre, Opera, Ballet and Circus

Plate 62
Note that the illustration is of three pairs of figures. In each instance the identity of the male figure is known with certainty: but, in each instance, also, the identity of the female figure is either not known or dubious. Maybe one or more of the female figures were made by the potters merely to 'balance' the male figures and with no particular person in mind.
In the collections of Miss Jean Anderson, Mr Robert Eddison and the author

Fig. 20 Macready ('James V of Scotland')   *Fig.* 115 Reeves ('Edgardo')   *Fig.* 113 Lablache ('Dr Dulcamara')

Fig. 21 Unidentified actress   *Fig.* 116 ?Gras ('Lucia')   *Fig.* 114 Unidentified actress

Plate 63
Fig. 119 A girl in bloomers
Fig. 120 Unidentified man
Fig. 117 Unidentified girl in bloomers
Fig. 118 Unidentified man in bloomers
Fig. 121 A girl in bloomers
Fig. 122 Unidentified man

Lucia di Lammermoor on a music-front for Popular Airs sung by Mr Sims Reeves, arranged for the piano-forte by C. W. Glover, see *ch.* 3, *pl.* 43.
2. Sims Reeves made his début at Drury Lane on December 6th, 1847 as 'Edgardo'. It was a triumph and he thenceforth ranked as the premier English tenor.

Figure 116
Subject: **? Madame Dorus Gras as 'Lucia'**
Title: None
Date: *c*. 1847
Height: 10¼ in (25.75 cm)
Colour: Largely white, gilt and black.
Maker: Possibly Thomas Parr
Rarity: VR. D.
Pair: Fig. 115 (Reeves as 'Edgardo'). Same series as *figs.* 117 (Unidentified girl in bloomers) and 118 (Unidentified man in bloomers), *pl.* E-63.
Description: She stands bare-headed, with long shoulder-length curls and a bun. She wears a hip-length jacket and a calf-length skirt. Her right hand is on her hip and in her left hand she holds a scroll.

Observations: This figure may well be intended to be Madame Dorus Gras in the character of 'Lucia' (see *p.* 36). There is, however, no proof of this, for the dress worn by Madame Gras as portrayed both in the music-front illustrated in *ch.* 3, *pl.* 43 and in the two engravings in *The Illustrated London News* of December 11th, 1847 is entirely different from the dress portrayed in the figure. Probably another engraving exists which will indicate whether this is, in fact, Madame Gras or someone else.

Plate 63
Figure 117
Subject: **Unidentified girl in bloomers**
Title: None
Date: *c*. 1851
Height: 10 in (25 cm)
Colour: Largely white, gilt and black.
Maker: Probably Thomas Parr
Rarity: VR.
Pair: Fig. 118 (Unidentified man in bloomers). Same series as *figs.* 115 (Reeves as 'Edgardo') and 116 (? Gras as 'Lucia'), *pl.* E-62.

Description: Standing, wearing a broad brimmed hat with no plume. Her shirt collar falls over the top of her jacket. There is no sash and her baggy trousers are tucked into calf-high boots. In her right hand she holds a flower in front of her waist, and her left hand is plunged into the pocket in the skirts of her coat. To her right is a tall vase with open top, standing on a two-tier pedestal.
Observations: Mr Balston identified this figure as Mrs Amelia Bloomer herself. However, the later discovery of the pair to the figure and the fact that it belongs to the same series as *fig.* 115 (Reeves as 'Edgardo') suggests that it may well be theatrical or operatic. So far it has defied positive identification. Incidentally, I do not believe that a portrait figure of Mrs Bloomer herself was even made. All figures known to me are either theatrical or were made simply to illustrate the 'Bloomer' costume.

Figure 118
Subject: **Unidentified man in bloomers**
Title: None

E397

Section E. Theatre, Opera, Ballet and Circus

Plate 63 continued

Date: *c.* 1851
Height: 10 in (25 cm)
Colour: Largely white, gilt and black.
Maker: Probably Thomas Parr
Rarity: VR.
Pair: *Fig.* 117 (Unidentified girl in bloomers).
Same series as *figs.* 115 (Reeves as 'Edgardo')
and 116 (? Gras as 'Lucia'), *pl.* E-62.
Description: Standing, wearing a broad-
brimmed hat, jacket, waistcoat and baggy
trousers tucked into his knee-boots. His
right hand is plunged into the pocket in the
skirts of his coat, and in his left hand he
holds a cigar. To his left is a tall vase with
open top, standing on a two-tier pedestal.
Observations: Has so far defied identification
but is probably theatrical. There is a strong
facial resemblance to Mr Sims Reeves,
compare with *fig.* 115, *pl.* E-62. See also
preceding figure.

Figure 119
Subject: **A girl in bloomers**
Title: None
Date: *c.* 1851
Height: 7¾ in (20 cm)
Colour: Well coloured in the tradition of
Thomas Parr.
Maker: Thomas Parr
Rarity: R.
Pair: *Fig.* 120 (Unidentified man)
Description: Standing bare-headed, wearing
jacket, sash round waist, calf-length skirt
and bloomers. She has a posy in her right
hand and a basket of flowers in her left.
Observations: A fine figure, which may be
theatrical, or alternatively, merely a decorative figure of a girl in bloomers. It is unlikely to be a portrait of Mrs Amelia Bloomer
herself. It will be observed that the figure is
a superior version of *fig.* 121, and it will also
be noted that the pair to the figure, *fig.* 120,
is quite unlike the pair to *fig.* 121, *fig.* 122.
This suggests that neither *fig.* 120 nor *fig.* 122
represent any particular person, but are
merely fictitious pairs for the 'girls in
bloomers', see *ch.* 3, *pl.* 44.

Figure 120
Subject: **Unidentified man**
Title: None
Date: *c.* 1851
Height: 8½ in (21.5 cm)
Colour: Well coloured in the tradition of
Thomas Parr.
Maker: Thomas Parr
Rarity: R.
Pair: *Fig.* 119 (A girl in bloomers)
Description: Standing bare-headed, in jacket,
shirt with neckerchief, waistcoat, breeches
with sash round waist, stockings and shoes.
His right hand is on his hip and his left hand
is raised to his head, and on it is perched a
bird.
Observations: Probably a decorative pair to
fig. 119.

Figure 121
Subject: **A girl in bloomers**
Title: None
Date: Late
Height: 8 in (20.5 cm)
Colour: Poorly coloured.
Maker: William Kent
Rarity: Av.
Pair: *Fig.* 122 (Unidentified man)
Description: Almost identical to *fig.* 119, but
it is a later and poorly moulded figure.
Observations: See *fig.* 119 (A girl in bloomers).

E398

Figure 122
Subject: **Unidentified man**
Title: None
Date: Late
Height: 8½ in (21.5 cm)
Colour: Poorly coloured.
Maker: William Kent
Rarity: Av.
Pair: *Fig.* 121 (A girl in bloomers)
Description: Standing bare-headed, with
open shirt and no neckerchief, jacket, waist-
coat, breeches and stockings. He holds a
basket of fruit on his head with his right
hand, and his left hand is on his hip.
Observations: A late, debased figure with
little resemblance to *fig.* 120 (Unidentified
man).

Plate 64

Amelia Bloomer

From an engraving which appeared in *The
Illustrated London News* of September 27th,
1851. This engraving was copied from *The
Lily* and came from a daguerreotype by T. W.
Brown of Auburn, New York State.

I am grateful to Mr Charles Neilson Gatty,
the authority on Bloomerism, for the information that this is *the only authentic picture of
Amelia Bloomer in her costume*. No figure has
yet been recorded which is based on this
daguerreotype. It appears that most 'Bloomer' figures simply illustrate the costume.
This is well demonstrated on *pl.* E-67. None
are likely to represent Amelia Bloomer herself, but at least two probably portray a
vocalist (Rebecca Isaacs) in one of the many
farces about Bloomerism which swept the
country in 1851, see *fig.* 123, *pl.* E-65.

Mrs Bloomer was the editor of a monthly
journal called *The Lily: A Monthly Journal
devoted to Temperance and Literature*. Of the
daguerreotype she wrote:

'We are not ambitious to show our face to our readers;
all we seek is to let them see what an "immodest"
dress we are wearing, and about which people have
made such an ado. We hope that our lady readers will
not be shocked at our "masculine" appearance, or
gentleman mistake us for one of their own sex.'

Plate 65
Figure 123
Subject: **? Rebecca Isaacs**
Title: None
Date: *c.* 1851
Height: 7½ in (19 cm)
Colour: Well coloured.
Rarity: VR. D.
Description: She stands, wearing a broad-
brimmed hat, with a coat over a knee-length
dress, Turkish trousers, socks and shoes.
There is a sash around her waist; one end
goes over her left shoulder and the other is
clasped in her left hand, which is against her
side. In her right hand, she holds a small
umbrella downwards against her side.
Observations: The coloured lithograph of a
girl in bloomers, carrying an umbrella in
her right hand, is by T. Coventry. It illustrates the music-front for the song *I want to
be a Bloomer!* sung by Miss Rebecca Isaacs,
the words by Henry Abrahams, the music by
W. H. Montgomery. It is the source of both
fig. 123, *pl.* E-65 and *fig.* 124, *pl.* E-66. The
lithograph *probably* portrays Miss Rebecca
Isaacs (1829–1877), actress and vocalist.
Miss Isaacs is known to have sung the song
in the music-halls of the period. Alternatively, the lithograph is simply one of 'a
girl in bloomers'. It is unlikely to be intended
to represent Amelia Bloomer herself, for
it bears no resemblance to the only authentic

portrait of her, which is illustrated on *pl.*
E-64.

> *I WANT TO BE A BLOOMER!*
> My heart is very sad Mother, I'm weary of my
> life . . .
> For Mother I'm now 18 . . . And yet I'm not a
> wife,
> I cannot sleep by night Mother, I cannot rest
> by day . . .
> For I want to be a Bloomer! Let me be a
> Bloomer! pray . . .
> For I want to be a Bloomer! Let me be a
> Bloomer! pray.
>
> I know I should look quite divine in that dear
> Bloomer dress . . .
> My feet, you know are very small, they could
> not well be less,
> And with those ducks of trowsers, And Paletot
> so gay,
> Oh! I should look quite enchanting, Let me be
> a Bloomer! pray
> Oh! I should look quite enchanting, Let me be
> a Bloomer! pray.
>
> I'm sure the Girls will all go mad, when e'er my
> dress they see . . .
> For when in the streets I'm walking, all their
> beaux will gaze on me,
> And then I shall be quite the rage, At Opera,
> Ball or Play . . .
> No other form but mine be seen, Let me be a
> Bloomer! pray . . .
> No other form but mine be seen, Let me be a
> Bloomer! pray.
>
> And then next day in the Papers, Long
> Paragraphs—so fine!
> Describing everything I wore, Oh! won't that
> be divine
> I'm certain then for lovers . . . I shall not wait a
> day . . .
> They will be dying at my feet, Let me be a
> Bloomer! pray . . .
> They will be dying at my feet, Let me be a
> Bloomer! pray.

Plate 66
Figure 119
Subject: **A girl in bloomers**
Observations: See *pl.* E-63.

Figure 124
Subject: **? Rebecca Isaacs**
Title: None
Date: *c.* 1851
Height: 8½ in (21.5 cm)
Colour: Well coloured in the manner of
Thomas Parr.
Maker: Thomas Parr
Rarity: VR. D.
Description: Similar to *fig.* 123, *pl.* E-65,
except for minor differences, particularly
with regard to the base and the height. The
hat is adorned with two feathers.
Observations: Based on a coloured lithograph
music-front by T. Coventry. See *pl.* E-65.

Figure 125
Subject: **A girl in bloomers**
Title: Bloomers (indented capitals)
Date: *c.* 1851
Height: 9½ in (24 cm)
Colour: Largely white, gilt and black.
Maker: Alpha factory
Rarity: R. D.
Series: Same series as *fig.* 127 (A girl in
bloomers)
Description: Standing, in a broad-brimmed
and plumed hat which is worn on the back
of her head, long coat buttoned at the neck
and Turkish trousers, *i.e.* bloomers. She
carries a closed book in her right hand and
a small umbrella in her left.
Observations: 1. This figure and the two
following figures were catalogued by Mr
Balston as portraits of Amelia Bloomer herself. There are two reasons why this is
unlikely to be so. Firstly, the very title

Plate 64
Amelia Bloomer (1818-1894)
An engraving which appeared in *The Illustrated London News* on September 27th, 1851. This engraving was copied from *The Lily* and came from a daguerreotype by T. W. Brown of Auburn, New York State. This is the only authentic picture of Amelia Bloomer in her costume. No Staffordshire portrait figure based on it has been recorded.

Plate 65
Fig. 123 ?Rebecca Isaacs
To the right of the figure is a coloured lithograph music-front by T. Coventry for the song *I want to be a Bloomer!* sung by Miss Rebecca Isaacs, the words by Henry Abrahams, the music by W. H. Montgomery. This lithograph is the source both of *fig.* 123 and *fig.* 124 and seems likely to be a portrait of Miss Isaacs in bloomer costume.

Plate 66
Fig. 119 A girl in bloomers
Fig. 125 A girl in bloomers
Fig. 126 A girl in bloomers
Fig. 127 A girl in bloomers
Fig. 124 ?Rebecca Isaacs
In the collections of Mrs Constance Chiswell and the author, and by courtesy of Mr and Mrs Eric Joyce

Plate 66 continued

'Bloomers' suggests no more than that the figures are of girls in bloomers. Secondly, none of the three figures show any close resemblance to the only known authentic portrait of Amelia Bloomer in the costume, see *pl.* E-64.

2. A similar figure, together with an example of *fig.* 127, fetched 62 gns at Christies in 1963. Another, together with another example of *fig.* 127, fetched £200 at Puttick and Simpson's in 1969. Another, by itself, fetched 100 gns at Christie's in 1969.

Figure 126
Subject: **A girl in bloomers**
Title: Bloomers (gilt script)
Date: c. 1851
Height: 10 in (25 cm)
Colour: Largely white, gilt and black.
Maker: Probably Alpha factory
Rarity: VR. D.
Description: Standing, in broad-brimmed hat, with no plume, placed on top of her head. She wears a man's collar and bow tie with a long coat and bloomers. There is a sash round her waist. Her right hand is by her side and in her left hand she holds a fan.
Observations: 1. Very similar to *fig.* 127 (A girl in bloomers) except for the manner of titling, the fact that her left elbow is slightly less flexed, and also that she holds a fan instead of a cigar in her left hand.
2. See *fig.* 125.

Figure 127
Subject: **A girl in bloomers**
Title: Bloomers (indented capitals)
Date: c. 1851
Height: 10 in (25 cm)
Colour: Largely white, gilt and black.
Maker: Alpha factory
Rarity: VR. D.
Series: Same series as *fig.* 125 (A girl in bloomers)
Description: Identical to *fig.* 126, except for the manner of titling, the fact that her left elbow is slightly more flexed, and also that she holds a cigar in her left hand rather than fan.
Observations: See *fig.* 125.

Plate 67
Figure 128
Subject: **A girl in bloomers**
Title: None
Date: c. 1851
Height: 9¾ in (24.5 cm)
Rarity: VR. D.
Description: Standing, wearing a broad-brimmed hat, knee-length coat, Turkish trousers and shoes. Her left hand is across her waist and her right hand, in which she holds a handkerchief, is by her side.
Observations: Both this figure and the smaller 7½ in (19 cm) version are based on a lithograph by N. Currier of *The Bloomer Costume*.

Plate 68
Figure 57
Subject: **? Mr Barton as 'Giaffier'**
Observations: See *pl.* E-26.

Figure 129
Subject: **Unidentified man with cloak**
Title: None
Height: 6½ in (16.5 cm)
Colour: Well coloured.
Rarity: VR.
Pair: *Fig.* 130 (Woman wearing trefoiled hat)

Description: He stands bare-headed, wearing an ermine-edged cloak, jacket, breeches, stockings and shoes. His right hand is on his hip and his left hand by his side clasping what is possibly a manuscript.
Observations: Probably an opera singer.

Figure 130
Subject: **Unidentified woman with trefoiled hat**
Title: None
Height: 6¾ in (17 cm)
Colour: Well coloured.
Rarity: VR.
Pair: *Fig.* 129 (Unidentified man with cloak)
Description: She stands, wearing a trefoiled hat, and gown with puffed sleeves showing a 'V' of underskirt.
Observations: It has been suggested that this figure is a portrait of Madame Angelica Catalani (1779–1849), but I do not know the evidence to support this claim.

Figure 131
Subject: **A pair of trick-riders on horseback**
Title: None
Date: 184–
Height: 8½ in (21.5 cm)
Colour: Well coloured.
Rarity: R.
Description: A man and a girl stand upon the saddle of a horse facing left; the man to the left and the girl to the right. They support a long 'flag'.
Observations: 1. It has been suggested that this figure represents Andrew Ducrow (1793–1842) and his second wife Louisa Woolford, the most famous of all trick-riders.
2. The term 'flag' is one used in the circus world to describe the long cloth held out for the horse to jump over.

Figure 132
Subject: **Jules Perrot as 'Albrecht'**
Title: None
Date: c. 1842
Height: 10 in (25 cm)
Colour: Well coloured.
Rarity: Av.
Pair: *Fig.* 133 (? Grisi)
Description: He stands bare-headed, other than for a ribbon round his forehead, wearing vest, jacket, pantaloons and stockings. There is a sash round his waist. His right arm is raised to his head and his left hand is on his hip.
Observations: 1. There are several versions of this figure. In the version illustrated the legs are from separate moulds. In another version [*fig.* 132(a)], the legs are incorporated in the column.
2. Identified as Jules Perrot playing 'Albrecht' in *Giselle* from a music-front in the 'Musical Bouquet' series no. 24 (see *ch.* 3, *pl.* 45) which shows him in the same costume. This engraving is a montage (combination of pictures) and the original source of the figure is so far untraced.
3. The first London performance of *Giselle* was at Her Majesty's Theatre on March 12th, 1842 with Carlotta Grisi in the title role and Perrot as 'Albrecht'.
4. An example of this figure, catalogued as 'Blondin', was sold at Sotheby's for £55 in 1969.

Figure 133
Subject: **? Carlotta Grisi**
Title: None

Date: c. 1842
Height: 9½ in (24 cm)
Colour: Well coloured.
Rarity: Av.
Pair: *Fig.* 132 (Perrot as 'Albrecht')
Description: Standing wearing a low hat, dress with short sleeves, skirt shortened to show modesty panties, stockings and shoes. Her right arm is across her waist and her left hand touches the back of her head.
Observations: 1. In the figure illustrated the legs are from separate moulds. In another version [*fig.* 133(a)], the legs are incorporated in the column.
2. This figure probably portrays Carlotta Grisi, Perrot's wife, but so far no picture has been found by which it can be identified, see *p.* 36.

Figure 134
Subject: **Jules Perrot as 'Albrecht'**
Title: None
Date: c. 1842
Height: 9 in (23 cm)
Colour: Poorly coloured.
Rarity: R.
Pair: *Fig.* 135 (? Grisi)
Description: A crude version of *fig.* 132 (Perrot as 'Albrecht'). In this figure his right arm is on his hip and his left arm raised to his head. A scarf is placed behind the hands, across the back of the figure.
Observations: See *fig.* 132 (Perrot as 'Albrecht') and also *ch.* 3, *pl.* 45.

Figure 135
Subject: **? Carlotta Grisi**
Title: None
Date: c. 1842
Height: 9 in (23 cm)
Colour: Poorly coloured.
Rarity: R.
Pair: *Fig.* 134 (Perrot as 'Albrecht')
Description: A debased version of *fig.* 133 (? Grisi). She wears no hat, her left hand is on her hip, her right hand is raised to her head, and the scarf is placed behind the hands, across the back of the figure.
Observations: See *fig.* 133 (? Grisi) and *p.* 36.

Plate 69
Figure 136
Subject: **? Jules Perrot**
Date: 184–
Height: 7¾ in (20 cm)
Colour: Well coloured, largely in underglaze blue.
Rarity: VR. A.
Pair: Unknown
Description: He stands bare-headed, wearing a narrow moustache. Dressed in vest, tunic with puffed sleeves, sporran and sword. He carries a plumed bonnet in his right hand which is by his side, and his left elbow is flexed with his hand beneath his mouth. He is standing on steps, left foot lower than the right. Ornate base.
Observations: General facial appearance is very similar to Jules Perrot and the figure is obviously ballet or operatic, although it has so far defied positive identification.

Plate 67
Fig. 128*(small version)* A girl in bloomers

In the centre is a lithograph by N. Currier of *The Bloomer Costume.* It is the source of both figures.

Fig. 128 A girl in bloomers

Plate 68
T: *Fig.* 129 Unidentified man with cloak
Fig. 130 Unidentified woman with trefoiled hat
Fig. 131 A pair of trick-riders on horseback
Fig. 57 ?Mr Barton ('Giaffier')

B: *Fig.* 132 Perrot ('Albrecht')
Fig. 133 ?Grisi
Fig. 134 Perrot ('Albrecht')
Fig. 135 ?Grisi
By courtesy of Mr and Mrs Eric Joyce

Plate 69
Fig. 136 ?Perrot

Plate 70 (Left)
fig. 137 La Polka
To the right of the figure
is the music-front for
No. 1 of Jullien's
*Celebrated Polkas — The
Original Polka.* It is the
source of *fig.* 137.
*In the collection of
Messrs Raymond Mander
and Joe Mitchenson*

Plate 71
Music-front for:
Jullien's *Original Polka
Quadrilles*
'The only edition in
which the original polka
is introduced'.
T, L to R
*The Original Polka, The
Queen & P. Albert Polka,
The Royal Polka.*
C, L to R
*Les Roses Polka, The
Camelras Polka.*
B, L to R
*The Drawing Room Polka,
The Opera Polka, The
Imperial Polka.*

Plate 72
T: *Fig.* 139 Unidentified female castanet
dancer
Fig. 140 Unidentified male castanet dancer
Fig. 141 A woman with two children
Fig. 142 Unidentified Turkish woman
Fig. 143 Unidentified Turk

B: *Fig.* 147 Macready ('Rob Roy
Macgregor')
Fig. 144 Unidentified girl playing a drum
Fig. 145 Unidentified brigand
Fig. 138 Madame Albert and Mlle Forgoet
In the collection of Mrs Constance Chiswell

Plate 73
The unidentified source of *fig.* 141, *pl.* E-72.
This engraving, undoubtedly the source of *fig.* 141,
pl. E-72, has unfortunately had the caption removed
and, to date, has defied positive identification.
By courtesy of Mr John Hall

Plate 70
Figure 137
Subject: **The Original Polka**
Title: La Polka (gilt script)
Date: *c.* 1844
Height: 8 in (20.5 cm)
Colour: Well coloured.
Rarity: VR. D. A. (titled); R. (untitled).
Description: The man stands on the left, bare-headed, wearing a cloak, ermine-edged coat, neckerchief, breeches and knee-boots. His left arm is round the lady's waist and he clasps her hands in his right hand. She stands on the right, wearing a four-cornered hat, ermine-edged coat, calf-length dress, pantaloons and bootees.
Observations: In 1844, Jullien published a series of *Celebrated Polkas*. *No. 1, The Original Polka*, said to be the first to be introduced into this country, was published *c.* April 6th, 1844. This date is known because the first edition of the quadrille (music for it) was advertised in *The Illustrated London News* for April 6th, 1844 and a second edition in the issue dated May 4th. In addition to the music, there was a description of the dance, by E. Coulon, and a coloured lithograph front by J. Brandard [see *pl.* E-70 and *pl.* E-71 (top-left)].

The lithograph of *The Original Polka* which is the source of *fig.* 137 ('La Polka') depicts two dancers in national costume, often said to be Perrot and Grisi. This identification is unlikely to be correct because the first time they danced the polka together in this country was on April 11th, 1844 at Her Majesty's Theatre. Here it is understood they danced *La Polka*, which incidentally was *The Opera Polka* and not *The Original Polka*. *The Opera Polka* is that illustrated in the middle of the bottom row of *pl.* E-71. An illustration similar to, but not identical to this, together with music was published by Jullien, although not in the series of *Celebrated Polkas*, and here the dancers (Perrot and Grisi) are named. No figure based on either of these illustrations is known.

Plate 71
Jullien's Original Polka Quadrilles
Top, left to right:
The Original Polka, The Queen & P. Albert Polka, The Royal Polka.
Centre, left to right:
Les Roses Polka, The Camelras Polka.
Bottom, left to right:
The Drawing Room Polka, The Opera Polka, The Imperial Polka.

Plate 72
Figure 138
Subject: **Madame Albert and Mlle Eliza Forgeot introducing The Royal Polka**
Title: None
Date: 1844
Height: 9 in (23 cm)
Colour: Well coloured.
Rarity: VR. D.
Description: Two female dancers, each wearing plumed bonnet, bodice, scarf, knee-length, wide-flounced skirt and bootees. The girl on the left clasps the left hand of the girl facing her with her right hand, and has her left hand on the girl's shoulder. The girl on the right has her right hand on her partner's shoulder.
Observations: In 1844, Jullien published a series of *Celebrated Polkas*. The coloured lithograph music-front by John Brandard for *No. 2, The Royal Polka* depicts two dancers

and is inscribed: '*Danced at the French play by Mlle. Forgeot and Madame Albert*'.
This lithograph is a possible source of *fig.* 138, although it is not identical. It is reproduced in miniature, top right, *pl.* E-71.
The following is an extract from the playbill:

'French Plays
Saint James Theatre King Street
*For the benefit of Mad*ᵉ *Albert and*
her last appearance but two
On Wednesday Evening, April 24th 1844
Le Proces de la Polka
Madame de Folignac—Madame Albert.
During the piece
Madame Albert and Madlle. Eliza Forgeot
Will, for the night only, introduce the popular
Polka dance
as danced at the Theatre des Variétés, Paris
and taught by Monsieur E. Coulon.
The music composed and on this occasion
directed by Monsieur Jullien'.

Figure 139
Subject: **Unidentified female castanet dancer**
Title: None
Height: 8 in (20.5 cm)
Colour: Well coloured.
Rarity: VR.
Pair: Fig. 140 (Unidentified male castanet dancer)
Description: She stands, wearing a round plumed hat, her left hand on her hip and her right hand held up towards her head touching a castanet. She wears a gown, bodice and skirt.
Observations: It has been suggested that this figure, together with its pair *fig.* 140, represent the two celebrated dancing sisters Thérèse and Fanny Elssler doing a castanet dance, but I do not know the evidence for this.

Figure 140
Subject: **Unidentified male castanet dancer**
Title: None
Height: 8 in (20.5 cm)
Colour: Well coloured.
Rarity: VR.
Pair: Fig. 139 (Unidentified female castanet dancer)
Description: Standing, wearing a plumed hat, jacket, vest and pantaloons, his right hand on his hip, his left hand raised to his head clutching a castanet. There is a violin beside his left leg.
Observations: See *fig.* 139.

Figure 141
Subject: **A woman with two children**
Title: None
Height: 11¾ in (29.75 cm)
Colour: Well coloured.
Rarity: VR.
Description: She stands bare-headed, except for a ribbon, wearing low bodice and ankle-length skirt with a sash round her waist. On either side of her is a bare-headed child. Each appears to be a girl. The child on her right, clutches her right hand with both hands. The child on her left, clutches her skirt with her left hand and her arm with her right. She herself is holding a floral hoop against her head with her left hand.
Observations: A tantalizing piece, for the engraving illustrated on *pl.*E-73 is undoubtedly the source of the figure. Unfortunately, if there was ever an inscription on the engraving, it has been destroyed. In spite of exhaustive enquires, I have failed to establish the identity of the work. On its back was a

pencilled note that it was of Josephine Bartolozzi (sister of Madame Vestris), after a painting by Romney. Josephine Bartolozzi, who was the wife of Joshua Anderson, was an actress who lived between 1807 and 1848. These dates preclude Romney as the artist, for he died in 1802. Although I have shown this illustration to many authorities, it has so far defied identification. It may not, of course, portray anyone in particular.

Figure 142
Subject: **Unidentified Turkish woman**
Title: None
Height: 8 in (20.5 cm)
Colour: Well coloured.
Rarity: Av.
Pair: Fig. 143 (Unidentified Turk)
Description: She stands, wearing Turkish head-dress, blouse, skirt and underskirt. She holds a pair of cymbals in her hands. There is a pedestal beside her right leg.
Observations: It has been suggested that this figure and its pair, *fig.* 143, are portraits of Fanny and Thérèse Elssler in Turkish dress, but I know of no evidence in support of this.

Figure 143
Subject: **Unidentified Turk**
Title: None
Height: 8 in (20.5 cm)
Colour: Well coloured.
Rarity: Av.
Pair: Fig. 142 (Unidentified Turkish woman)
Description: Standing in Turkish head-dress, long coat and Turkish trousers. To his left is a pedestal. He holds a scimitar in his left hand and an unidentified object in his right hand.
Observations: See preceding figure.

Figure 144
Subject: **Unidentified girl playing a drum**
Title: None
Height: 10½ in (26.5 cm)
Colour: Well coloured.
Rarity: R.
Pair: Unknown
Description: She is standing wearing a plumed hat, blouse with neckerchief and wide knee-length skirt with sash. Her right hand is raised to her head and her left hand is resting on a drum which is suspended from the left side of her waist.
Observations: It has been suggested that this figure represents Fanny Cerito in *La Vivandière*, but it bears no resemblance to the lithograph, thus titled, by Haguertal. Another suggestion, and one with more substance, is that it is Miss Poole as 'Marie' in *The Daughter of the Regiment. The Illustrated London News* of January 15th, 1848, contains an engraving of Miss Poole in this role, but it is not close enough to the figure for positive identification. In an article on Miss Poole accompanying the engraving, it is remarked that:

'Many of our readers will doubtless recollect the then popular song of the *Merry Little Drummer*, in the *Legion of Honour*, composed expressly for Miss Poole, by Alexander Lee, in which she played the drum to perfection, and sang it two hundred nights, to a nightly encore'.

Figure 145
Subject: **Unidentified brigand**
Title: None
Height: 9 in (23 cm)
Colour: Well coloured.
Rarity: R.
Description: He stands, wearing a round hat

Plate 79
*Death of the 'Lion Queen',
in Wombwell's Menagerie, at
Chatham.*
Engraving from
The Illustrated London News

DEATH OF THE "LION QUEEN," IN WOMBWELL'S MENAGERIE, AT CHATHAM.—(SEE NEXT PAGE.)

Plate 79

Ellen Bright

An engraving published in *The Illustrated London News* on January 19th, 1850. It is inscribed: *Death of the 'Lion Queen', in Wombwell's Menagerie, at Chatham.* The tragedy which shocked the whole of England had occurred eight days previously. Although one version of the figure, produced to record the event, portrays a leopard, there is no doubt that it was a *tiger* that killed Ellen Bright.

Plate 79A

Figure 157
Subject: **Woman in Tyrolese costume**
Title: None
Height: 8 in (20.5 cm)
Colour: Well coloured in the manner of Thomas Parr.
Maker: Thomas Parr
Rarity: VR.
Pair: Fig. 157(a) (Man in Tyrolese costume)
Description: Standing, wearing a wide-brimmed hat decorated with flowers, necklace, low-cut bodice and long skirt. She holds a hurdy-gurdy in her left hand and is turning the handle with her right hand.
Observations: It has often been suggested that this figure portrays Jenny Lind. It certainly looks very like her, but so far no lithograph has been found by which a positive identification can be made, nor is there any record of Jenny Lind playing the hurdy-gurdy. The recent discovery (1968) of the pair to this figure, a man in Tyrolese costume, suggests that both figures may portray members of one of the several Tyrolese groups touring the country in the thirties and forties. Thus, we may read of the 'Tyrolese ministrels', a group of four men and a girl, and of the 'Rainer family', a group known to have played at various royal functions.

Figure 157(a)
Subject: **Man in Tyrolese costume**
Title: None
Height: 8¼ in (21 cm)
Colour: Well coloured in the manner of Thomas Parr.
Rarity: VR.
Pair: Fig. 157 (Woman in Tyrolese costume)
Description: Standing, a tree-trunk to his right, and with his right leg crossed in front of his left. He wears a tall, plumed Tyrolese hat, jacket, waistcoat, breeches, stockings and shoes. He holds what appears to be a dagger in his left hand and pistol in his right.
Observations: See preceding figure.

Plate 80

Figure 149
Subject: **John Solomon Rarey and Cruiser** (facing left)
Observations: Untitled version. See *pl*. E-77.

Figure 153
Subject: **Rolla**
Title: Rolla (raised capitals)
Date: Uncertain
Height: 13¾ in (35 cm)
Colour: Well coloured.
Rarity: VR. D. A.
Description: Standing on a bridge over a river, in which there is a swan. He is wearing a tunic and sash. He holds a plumed bonnet above his head with his right hand and carries a small child on his left arm.
Observations: 1. 'Rolla' is a character in Sheridan's *Pizarro*. The moment portrayed is Act 5, Scene 2.
2. Probably a theatrical portrait, but its source has not yet come to light, so that the actor remains unidentified, see *ch*. 3, *pl*. 46.

Figure 154
Subject: **Ellen Bright**
Title: Death of the Lion Queen (gilt script)
Date: *c*. 1850
Height: 15 in (38 cm)
Colour: Well coloured.
Rarity: Av. A.
Description: She stands, wearing a plumed hat, jacket and calf-length skirt. A lion is lying behind her and to her right. To her left, is a leopard on its hind legs with its forelegs on her waist.
Observations: 1. Newspaper cuttings leave little room for doubt that the animal which actually killed Ellen Bright was a tiger. The large 'titled' version of the figure, an example of which is illustrated, invariably portrays the animal as a leopard; however, a small 'untitled' version, in which the animal is correctly portrayed as a tiger, was also made.
2. A similar figure fetched 24 gns at Christie's in 1964.

Figure 155
Subject: **T. P. Cooke—? as 'Dick Fid'**
Title: None
Height: 10½ in (26.5 cm)
Colour: Well coloured.
Rarity: R.
Description: A sailor is standing with his left hand on his hip, his right hand pointing forwards and his right leg in front of his left leg. He wears a straw hat, short jacket, neckerchief, belt and bell-bottom trousers. A pistol, presumably attached to his belt, is pressed against the right side of his chest.
Observations: This figure is certainly a portrait of T. P. Cooke, an actor specializing in sailor roles, who had been an authentic serving sailor. There is some evidence for supposing that it portrays him as 'Dick Fid' in *The Red Rover*, see *ch*. 3, *pls*. 47 and 47A.

Colour Plate 46
Nellie Chapman. *Fig.* 150, *pl.* E-78. See page 406.

Plate 79A
Fig. 157 Woman in Tyrolese
costume

Fig. 157(a) Man in Tyrolese
costume
By courtesy of Mr John Hall

Plate 80
T: *Fig.* 159 Lind ('Alice')
Fig. 156 Hemming ('Prince
Almansor')
Fig. 149 *(facing left: untitled)* Rarey
Fig. 155 T. P. Cooke

B: *Fig.* 154 Bright
Fig. 160 Lind ('Marie')
Fig. 158 Lind ('Alice')
Fig. 157 Woman in Tyrolese
costume
Fig. 153 'Rolla'

Plate 80 continued

Figure 156
Subject: **Mr Hemming as 'Prince Alman-
sor'**
Title: None
Height: 6½ in (16.5 cm)
Colour: Well coloured.
Rarity: Av. A.
Description: An elephant stands in front of a
castle with two turrets and a clock tower.
His trunk points upwards to a window
underneath the clock, through which a man
with a plumed bonnet is leaning. The bars
of the window have been wrenched sideways.
Observations: 1. *The Elephant of Siam; or, The
Fire Fiend*, an Indian dramatic spectacle was
first produced at the Adelphi on December
3rd, 1829. The playbill refers to the 'extraordinary sagacity evinced by her (the
elephant's) contrivance for the escape of the
Prince (Almansor)'. Mr Hemming played
the part of 'Prince Almansor'. This is said to
be the first time that an elephant appeared
on the English stage.

Characters in the play and scenes therefrom were reproduced in penny plain,
tuppence coloured juvenile drama sheets
published by J. L. Marks, 17 Artillery
Street, Bishopsgate and may be seen in the
Stone collection at the Victoria and Albert
Museum.

W. West also published sheets at his
Theatrical Print Warehouse opposite the
Olympic Theatre in the Strand. One such
sheet published on March 16th, 1830 (see
pl. E-78A) is inscribed *The Royal Elephant,
enabling Prince Almansor and his Attendants to
make their Escape*. The appropriate extract
from the stage directions is as follows:

The Elephant enters and wrenches the bars from the
Prince's window. The Prince's followers descend.—
Prince Almansor enters, and the Elephant bears him
off on her back . . .

Similar incidents in which elephants
were employed in rescues from upstairs
windows were used in numerous elephant
dramas up to the 1850's. The piece illustrated
(*fig.* 156) is generally accepted as portraying
Mr Hemming playing the part of 'Prince
Almansor'.

2. The figure is often incorrectly described
as 'Mr Hemming's Circus Act'. Mr Anthony
Oliver has offered an ingenious explanation
for the confusion. Maybe Mr Hemming,
who played the part of 'Prince Almansor'
was not a proper actor but merely the
elephant's trainer. Very possibly he toured
later as a solo act—'Mr Hemming's Circus
Act'. Confirmation of this theory is still
lacking.

3. The impressed mark 'JJ' has been found
on the base of one example, see *pl.* E-78B.

4. A similar figure fetched 45 gns at Christie's in 1967, and another, at the same sale,
together with *fig.* 38 (Colleen Bawn) *pl.* E-15
fetched 65 gns.

Figure 157
Subject: **Woman in Tyrolese costume**
Observations: See *pl.* E-79A.

Figure 158
Subject: **Jenny Lind as 'Alice'**
Title: Jenny Lind as Alice in Meyerbeer's
Opera (gilt script)
Date: c. 1847
Height: 13½ in (34.25 cm)
Colour: Well coloured.

Rarity: Av. D. A.
Description: Kneeling bare-headed, her arms
round the pedestal of a Celtic cross. The
pedestal is decorated with vine leaves and
the cross faces to the front. She wears a low
bodice, full-length broad skirt with a sash,
the ends of which very nearly touch the
ground. Ornate base.
Observations: 1. The lithograph shown in
ch. 3, *pl.* 48 is by and after T. Packer and is
of Jenny Lind as 'Alice' in Meyerbeer's
opera of *Robert the Devil*. It is the source of
fig. 158 and a number of similar figures. The
engraving illustrated on *pl.* E-85A is from
The Illustrated London News of May 8th, 1847.
The caption reads *Mdlle. Jenny Lind as 'Alice'
and Herr Staudigi as 'Bertram' in Meyerbeer's
opera of 'Roberto il Diavolo' at Her Majesty's
Theatre*. *Fig.* 171, *pl.* E-85A and possibly
others are derived from this engraving.
There are a number of figures, with similar
but not identical features, each of which
portray the same dramatic moment in the
opera.

2. Jenny Lind appeared in London as 'Alice'
in Meyerbeer's opera of *Robert the Devil* in
1847.

3. A similar figure fetched 48 gns at Christie's
in 1967.

4. It is remarkable how few examples of this
and similar figures exist in which the cross
has not been broken off. I know of no satisfactory explanation for this.

Figure 159
Subject: **Jenny Lind as 'Alice'**
Title: Jenny Lind (gilt script)
Date: c. 1847

Plate 81

Fig. 161 Unidentified male opera singer

Fig. 160 Lind ('Marie')

Fig. 162 Jullien
In the collections of Mr A. Guy Stringer and the author

Plate 82

Fig. 160 Lind ('Marie')
Photograph by M. L. Pecker

Fig. 163 Lind

Fig. 161 Unidentified male opera singer
In the collection of Mr David Robinson

Height: 9½ in (24 cm)
Colour: Well coloured.
Rarity: R.
Description: Similar to *fig.* 158, except that the pedestal faces half-right and her left hand touches the top of it. The base of the figure is plain and the ends of her sash fall only half way down her skirt.
Observations: 1. See preceding figure.
2. A similar figure fetched 55 gns at Christie's in 1966; and another, 65 gns at Christie's in 1969.

Figure 160
Subject: **Jenny Lind as 'Marie'**
Observations: See *pls*. E-81 and 82.

Plate 81
Figure 160
Subject: **Jenny Lind as 'Marie'**
Title: Jenny Lind (indented capitals)
Date: c. 1847
Height: 7¾ in (20 cm)
Colour: Well coloured
Maker: Alpha factory
Rarity: Av. D. A.
Pair: Certainly pairs *fig.* 162 (Jullien); in untitled state may pair *fig.* 161 (Unidentified male opera singer).
Description: She stands bare-headed, in necklace, bodice and flounced skirt, holding a piece of music in both hands.
Observations: The Daughter of the Regiment (*La Figlia del Reggimento*), a comic opera in

E411

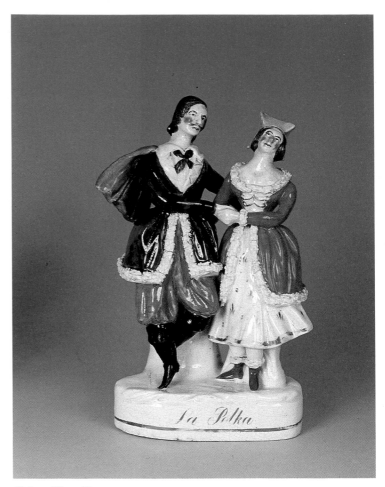

Colour Plate 47
Charles Keen as 'Rolla'. *Fig.* 152, *pl.* E-78. See page 406.

Colour Plate 48
The Original Polka. *Fig.* 137, *pl.* E-70. See page 403.

Colour Plate 49
John Philip Kemble as 'Hamlet'. *Fig.* 32 (a), *pl.* E-13A. See page 371.

Colour Plate 50
Henry VIII and Anne Boleyn. *Fig.* 231, *pl.* E-116. See page 433.

Plate 81 continued

three Acts by Donizetti, has proved to be the inspiration of several 'Jenny Lind' figures.

ACT I

The 'vivandière' scene in Act I of the opera, is performed in military costume. A music-front with a coloured lithograph by John Brandard is illustrated in *ch. 3, pl. 49*. It is from Jullien's *Celebrated Polkas, No. 16* and is inscribed *Mlle. Jenny Lind in the character of 'Maria' in Donizetti's opera 'La Figlia del Reggimento'. Fig. 164, pl.* E-83 whose source is this print, occurs in two sizes. The 8 in (20.5 cm) version may be found titled 'M. Lind' in indented capitals, or 'Mᵈ Lind' in gilt script; the 6¾ in (17 cm) version, which is that illustrated on *pl.* E-83, has only been found titled 'M. Lind' in indented capitals. No pair is known to either version. The music-front illustrated in *ch. 3, pl. 49A* is again by John Brandard. It shows Miss Jenny Lind in the role of 'Marie' and is titled *La Vivandiere Quadrille*. It is the undoubted source of *fig. 177, pl.* E-91. Moreover, it will be noted that the girl in military uniform portrayed on the left of *fig. 165, pl.* E-83 is also likely to be Miss Lind in the role of 'Marie', the costume being very similar. It may well be that the figure on the right is intended to be Luigi Lablache in the character of 'Sergeant Sulpice'.

On *pl.* E-90 there is an illustration of a music-front by John Brandard for *The songs in La Figlia del Reggimento*. It is the source of *fig. 176, pl.* E-90 which is titled in gilt script *Jenny Lind as Maria (sic)*. It is not certain to which Act this relates.

ACT II

Evening clothes are worn for the 'music lesson' scene in Act II. It seems probable that *fig. 160, pl.* E-81 portrays Miss Lind at that moment, although there is no proof of this. It will be noted that she is standing bare-headed, in the costume she wore in Act II, holding a piece of music in both hands. The 7¾ in (20 cm) version of the figure is titled 'Jenny Lind' in indented capitals; the 6¼ in (16 cm) version (*pl.* E-82) is untitled. The large version undoubtedly pairs *fig. 162* (Jullien). The small version undoubtedly pairs the small version of *fig. 161* (Unidentified opera singer), see *pl.* E-82. The large version of *fig. 161*, which has never been found titled, is believed to pair an untitled version of *fig. 160* (Lind).

Figure 161
Subject: **Unidentified male opera singer**
Title: None
Date: 184–
Height: 8¼ in (21 cm)
Colour: Well coloured.
Maker: Alpha factory
Rarity: VR.
Pair: Possibly a pair to *fig. 160* (Lind as 'Marie')—untitled version.
Description: Standing bare-headed, with moustache and fringed beard, cloak, tunic and knee-boots. He holds a piece of music in both hands.

The smaller version, *pl.* E-82, is probably meant to be the same person, but presents certain differences. There is no beard, the cloak only covers his left shoulder and he wears a neckerchief.
Observations: 1. See *fig. 160* (Lind as 'Marie').
2. This figure and its small version present certain difficulties. For what it is worth, the small version has been purchased together with the small Jenny Lind, and the large version has been purchased with a 'titled'

large Jenny Lind. Whereas, there is no doubt that both versions of the female portray Jenny Lind, it is possible that the large version of the male portrays a different person from the small version. The large version, in particular, bears a strong resemblance to Guiseppe Mario in the role of 'Gennaro', see *pl.* E-23. It has also been suggested that it portrays Luigi Lablache (who sang with Miss Lind); or alternatively, Sims Reeves. It is *not* Jullien, for although there is a facial similarity, the dress is quite wrong.
3. The large version may belong to the same series as *fig. 280, pl.* E-135.

Figure 162
Subject: **Louis Antoine Jullien**
Title: Jullien (indented capitals)
Date: *c.* 1847
Height: 8 in (20.5 cm)
Colour: Well coloured.
Maker: Alpha factory
Rarity: R.
Pair: Fig. 160 (Lind as 'Marie')—7¾ in (20 cm) version.
Description: Standing, bare-headed and bearded, in swallow-tailed coat, waistcoat and trousers. He holds a piece of music on a pedestal to his left and a scroll in his right hand.
Observations: 1. In some versions the open piece of music has definite notes inscribed on it.
2. A similar figure fetched 72 gns at Christie's in 1966.

Plate 82
Figure 160 (small version)
Subject: **Jenny Lind as 'Marie'**
Title: None
Date: *c.* 1847
Height: 6¼ in (16 cm)
Colour: Well coloured.
Maker: Alpha factory
Rarity: R.
Pair: Fig. 161 (Unidentified opera singer)—small version
Description and Observations: } See *pl.* E-81.

Figure 161 (small version)
Subject: **Unidentified male opera singer**
Title: None
Date: 184–
Height: 6½ in (16.5 cm)
Colour: Well coloured.
Maker: Alpha factory
Rarity: VR.
Pair: Fig. 160 (Lind as 'Marie')—small version
Description and Observations: } See *pl.* E-81.

Figure 163
Subject: **Jenny Lind as a concert singer**
Title: Jenny Lind (gilt script)
Height: 8⅛ in (20.75 cm)
Colour: Sparsely coloured.
Rarity: VR.
Description: Standing bare-headed, low-cut bodice with pagoda sleeves, flounced skirt with waist sash ending in two tassels, her left hand across her waist, her right arm apparently by her side. In the only figure known to me (that illustrated on this plate) the right arm has been broken off just below the elbow.
Observations: Portrays Jenny Lind as a concert singer.

Plate 83
Figure 164
Subject: **Jenny Lind as 'Marie'**
Title: M. Lind (indented capitals), or
M.ᵈ Lind (gilt script)
Date: c. 1847
Height: 8 in (20.5 cm); 6¾ in (17 cm) version illustrated.
Colour: Well coloured.
Maker: Alpha factory
Rarity: Av.
Description: Standing in low-crowned, broad-brimmed hat with her right hand raised to its brim, bodice with epaulettes, and wide ankle-length skirt.
Observations: 1. See *fig.* 160 (Lind as 'Marie') *pl.* E-81.
2. A similar figure (large version) fetched 48 gns at Christie's in 1965; another, 65 gns in 1966; another, 46 gns at the same sale.

Figure 165
Subject: **Jenny Lind and ? Luigi Lablache as 'Marie' and 'Sergeant Sulpice'**
Title: Present from the Thames Tunnel (gilt script)
Date: c. 1847
Height: 5 in (12.75 cm)
Colour: Well coloured.
Rarity: VR. (titled); Av. (untitled).
Series: Same series as *fig.* 67 ('Esmeralda' and 'Gringoire') *pl.* E-33.
Description: Jenny Lind stands on the left of a tree trunk (spill-holder) wearing a military hat, bodice and calf-length skirt. She carries a drum under her left arm and her right hand is at the salute. A soldier stands on the right of the tree trunk beating a drum. This may be Luigi Lablache in the role of 'Sergeant Sulpice'.

Plate 83
Fig. 164 Lind ('Marie')

Fig. 165 Lind and ?Lablache
('Marie' and 'Sergeant Sulpice')

Plate 84
Fig. 166 Lind
Fig. 167 Lind ('Alice')

Plate 85
Fig. 168 Lind
Fig. 169 Lind
Fig. 170 Lind ('Alice')
In the Thomas Balston collection

Section E. Theatre, Opera, Ballet and Circus

Plate 85A
Fig. 171 Lind ('Alice')
To the right of the photograph is an engraving of Mdlle. Jenny Lind as 'Alice'. It appeared in *The Illustrated London News* of May 8th, 1847.
In the collection of Mr D. P. M. Michael

Observations: 1. See *fig.* 160 (Lind as 'Marie') *pl.* E-81.
2. The two examples of this figure found inscribed 'Present from the Thames Tunnel', see *ch.* 4, *pl.* 9, were presumably purchased at one of the booths either in, or in the vicinity of the tunnel, which was opened in 1843.

Plate 84
Figure 166
Subject: **Jenny Lind as a concert singer**
Title: None
Height: 7¾ in (20 cm)
Colour: Sparsely coloured.
Rarity: VR.
Description: Very similar to *fig.* 163 (Lind) *pl.* E-82, except that it is untitled, and the modelling is not quite so fine. The figure illustrated, which is the only one known to me, has had the right arm restored.
Observations: Jenny Lind as a concert singer.

Figure 167
Subject: **Jenny Lind as 'Alice'**
Title: None
Date: *c.* 1847
Height: 11 in (28 cm)
Colour: Well coloured; dull green base.
Rarity: VR. D.
Description: Similar to *fig.* 158, *pl.* E-80 but her right arm is round the cross and her left hand on the front of the pedestal. The ends of her sash fall only halfway down her skirt. The base is ornate and decorated with a ribbon upon which it may have been intended to inscribe a title; but no titled version has ever been recorded.

Plate 85
Figure 168
Subject: **Jenny Lind as a concert singer**
Title: Jenny Lind (gilt script)
Height: 8 in (20.5 cm)
Colour: Well coloured.
Rarity: VR. D. A.
Pair: Not known
Description: Standing bare-headed, in bodice and wide flounced skirt. She holds both hands in front of her waist.

Figure 169
Subject: **Jenny Lind as a concert singer**
Title: Jenny Lind (gilt script)
Height: 11½ in (29 cm)
Colour: Well coloured.
Rarity: VR. D. A.
Description: Standing bare-headed, in peaked bodice (as in *fig.* 173, *pl.* E-87) and long skirt with broad trimming at the bottom. Her right hand, holding a reticule, hangs by her side, and her left hand touches the peak of the bodice.
Observations: A reticule is defined as a lady's netted or other bag carried as a substitute for a pocket.

Figure 170
Subject: **Jenny Lind as 'Alice'**
Title: Jenny Lind (gilt script)
Date: *c.* 1847
Height: 10 in (25 cm)
Colour: Well coloured.
Rarity: R.
Description: Standing bare-headed, in bodice and full-length skirt. To her right, is a pedestal surmounted by a Celtic cross. Her left

hand is on the top of the pedestal and her right hand on the side of the cross.
Observations: A similar figure fetched 82 gns at Christie's in 1966.

Plate 85A
Figure 171
Subject: **Jenny Lind as 'Alice'**
Title: None
Date: *c.* 1847
Height: 8 in (20.5 cm)
Colour: Well coloured.
Rarity: VR.
Description: Similar to *fig.* 158 (Lind as 'Alice') *pl.* E-80, except that both pedestal and cross are turned half-right and her head touches the pedestal.
Observations: 1. See *fig.* 158 (Lind as 'Alice') *pl.* E-80.
2. Based on an engraving from *The Illustrated London News* of May 8th, 1847 inscribed:
'Mdlle. Jenny Lind as "Alice" and **Herr Staudigi** as "Bertram" in Meyerbeer's opera of *Roberto il Diavolo* at Her Majesty's Theatre'.

Plate 87
Fig. 173 Lind
Fig. 172 ?Lind ('Alice')
By courtesy of
Mr and Mrs Eric Joyce

Plate 86

Maria Malibran

It has been suggested that the features of Maria Felicita Malibran (1808–36) portrayed on this music-front, inscribed *Gems à la Malibran de Beriot* are very similar to those of the actress portrayed in the role of 'Alice' in *Robert le Diable* (*fig.* 172, *pl.* E-87).
See observations under that figure.

Plate 87

Figure 172
Subject: **? Jenny Lind as 'Alice'**
Title: None
Height: 8½ in (21.5 cm)
Colour: Rather crudely coloured.
Rarity: VR. D.
Description: Kneeling bare-headed, her arms round the pedestal of a Celtic cross. The

pedestal is quite plain. She wears a bodice and long dress with no sash, necklace and long hair.

Observations: The facial features and hair style are unlike those of Jenny Lind, but very similar to those of Maria Felicita Malibran, see preceding plate. However, further research has shown that the figure is unlikely to portray Malibran for *Robert le Diable* is not among the thirty-five different operas she is recorded as having sung in, in her brief career of eleven years. This sort of thing shows how dangerous it can be to draw too hasty a conclusion in these matters. Other singers contemporary with Lind are known to have played 'Alice' and the identity of the figure must therefore remain in doubt although my feelings are that it is simply a poor portrait of Jenny Lind.

Figure 173
Subject: **Jenny Lind as a concert singer**
Title: Jenny Lind (gilt script)
Height: 8¼ in (21 cm)
Colour: Well coloured.
Rarity: Av. D. A.
Description: Standing bare-headed, in peaked bodice and long flounced skirt. Her right hand is at the peak of her bodice, and from it hangs a reticule. Her left arm is by her side.

Plate 88

Figure 174
Subject: **Jenny Lind as a concert singer**
Title: Jenny Lind (gilt script)
Height: 7½ in (19 cm)
Colour: Well coloured.
Rarity: VR. D. A.
Description: Very similar to *fig.* 173 (Lind) *pl.* E-87, but she carries a posy in her right hand and her reticule is apparently suspended from a sash round her waist. Two or three flowers lie at her feet.
Observations: A very fine figure.

Plate 88
Fig. 174 Lind
In the collection of Mrs H. de C. Hastings

Plate 89
Fig. 175 Lind
In the collection of M. Marc de Smedt

Plate 89
Figure 175
Subject: **Jenny Lind as a concert singer**

Plate 90
Fig. 176 Lind ('Maria')
To the right of the figure is the music-front, by John Brandard, for *The songs in La Figlia del Reggimento* inscribed, 'Madlle. Jenny Lind as Maria'.
In the collection of Messrs Raymond Mander and Joe Mitchenson

Plate 91
T: *Fig.* 178 Unidentified actress
Fig. 179 Unidentified actor
Fig. 180 ?Mlle Ella and two female dancers
Fig. 181 Kemble and Shaw ('Semiramide' and 'Arsaces')
Fig. 182 Unidentified fiddler

B: *Fig.* 177 Lind ('Marie')
Fig. 183 Unidentified female dancer
Fig. 184 Unidentified sailor
Fig. 185 Unidentified child actress
Fig. 186 Unidentified child actress
In the collection of Mrs Constance Chiswell

Title: None
Height: 5¾ in (14.5 cm)
Colour: Sparsely coloured.
Rarity: R.
Description: In long dress with puffed sleeves, a shawl over her right shoulder and her arms crossed in front.

Plate 90
Figure 176
Subject: **Jenny Lind as 'Marie'**
Title: Jenny Lind as Maria (*sic*) (gilt script)
Date: *c.* 1847
Height: 10½ in (26.5 cm)
Colour: Well coloured.
Rarity: VR. D. A.
Description: Standing in a low-crowned, broad-brimmed hat, jacket with epaulettes, bodice and ankle-length skirt with five flounces.
Observations: 1. Based on the music-front, by John Brandard, for *The songs in La Figlia del Reggimento*.
2. See *fig.* 160 (Lind as 'Marie') *pl.* E-81.

Plate 91
Figure 177
Subject: **Jenny Lind as 'Marie'**
Title: None
Date: *c.* 1847
Height: 8 in (20.5 cm)
Colour: Well coloured.
Rarity: VR. D. A.
Description: Standing, wearing a plumed round hat, military jacket, neckerchief,

waistcoat and ankle-length skirt. A drum which she is playing with a pair of drumsticks is suspended from her left side.
Observations: Based on the music-front by John Brandard *La Vivandiere Quadrille*, see ch. 3, *pl.* 49A. See also *fig.* 160 (Lind as 'Marie') *pl.* E-81.

Figure 178
Subject: **Unidentified actress**
Title: None
Height: 8¼ in (21 cm)
Colour: Well coloured.
Rarity: R.
Pair: *Fig.* 179 (Unidentified actor)
Description: She stands, wearing a plumed hat, bodice with leg-of-mutton sleeves and lace collar, flounced calf-length skirt, her right hand on her hip and a scroll in her left hand.
Observations: Has been said to be Eliza O'Neill in the character of 'Belvidera' in *Venice Preserved*, but I know of nothing to substantiate this theory.

Figure 179
Subject: **Unidentified actor**
Title: None
Height: 8¼ in (21 cm)
Colour: Well coloured.
Rarity: R.
Pair: *Fig.* 178 (Unidentified actress)
Description: Standing, wearing a round plumed hat, military tunic with epaulettes,

gauntlets and a medal, seal or star suspended from his neck. His left hand is on his hip, his right arm outstretched to his right.
Observations: Has been said to be Charles Mayne Young in the character of 'Jaffier' in *Venice Preserved*, but I know of nothing to substantiate this theory.

Figure 180
Subject: **? Mlle Ella and two female dancers**
Title: None
Date: *c.* 1857
Height: 9¾ in (24.5 cm)
Colour: Well coloured.
Rarity: R.
Description: Three steps lead up to a 'throne of fame' upon which Mlle Ella stands. She wears a plumed bonnet, bodice, wide knee-length skirt and modesty pantees. Each of her hands is clasped by a dancer who stands at either side at the foot of the 'throne'. Each of these dancers wears a round hat, bodice, knee-length wide skirt and modesty panties. A 'flag' connects all three dancers.
Observations: Has so far defied positive identification, but is likely to portray the equestrian Mlle Ella at the conclusion of her act, during which she somersaulted through a 'floral garland' (hoop) onto a 'throne of fame'. The term 'flag' is one used in the circus world to describe the long cloth held out for the horse to jump over.

E417

Plate 91 continued
Figure 181
Subject: **Miss Adelaide Kemble as 'Semiramide' and Mrs Alfred Shaw as 'Arsaces'.**
Title: None
Date: *c.* 1842
Height: 6 in (15.25 cm)
Colour: Well coloured.
Rarity: VR. D.
Description: 'Semiramide' stands on the left, bare-headed, with gown, bodice and flounced skirt. There is a sash round her waist, the end of which very nearly reaches the ground. 'Arsaces' stands on the right, wearing a crown, gown, tunic with sash and Turkish trousers.
Observations: Based on a lithograph music-front by John Brandard of Miss Adelaide Kemble and Mrs Alfred Shaw singing the duet *Thy smile is joy indeed!*, see ch. 3, *pl.* 50. It will be noted that the figure is a mirror-image of its source.

Figure 182
Subject: **Unidentified fiddler**
Title: None
Height: 8¼ in (21 cm)
Colour: Well coloured.
Rarity: R.
Description: Standing, wearing a round plumed hat, ornate shirt, pantaloons and stockings. He is playing the fiddle.
Observations: It has been suggested that this figure portrays Frederic Maccabe, the musician and ventriloquist, who retired from the stage in 1874. This identification has been based on a lithograph music-front by M. and N. Hanhart inscribed *Lady Rise Serenade*. It was written and composed by Frederic Maccabe and sung by him as the 'troubadour of the past' in his entertainment of varieties. Whilst this possibility cannot be excluded, the figure and the lithograph are not 'close enough' to justify dogmatism.

Figure 183
Subject: **Unidentified female dancer**
Title: None
Height: 7½ in (19 cm)
Colour: Well coloured.
Rarity: R.
Description: Standing, wearing a lace bonnet surmounted by a round hat, bodice and ankle-length skirt. Her left hand is on her hip and her right hand holds what appears to be an apron, or possibly a pleat of her skirt, outwards and to her right.
Observations: Has been said to be the dancer Jenny Dawson, but I do not know on what grounds.

Figure 184
Subject: **Unidentified sailor**
Title: None
Height: 7½ in (19 cm)
Colour: Well coloured.
Rarity: R.
Pair: Unknown
Description: Seated on a barrel, bare-headed with jacket, tunic, neckerchief and knee-boots. He carries a pistol in each hand.
Observations: It has been suggested that this figure is a representation of T. P. Cooke.

Figure 185
Subject: **Unidentified child actress**
Title: None
Height: 6¾ in (17 cm)
Colour: Well coloured.
Rarity: R.
Description: Standing, wearing a plumed hat, jacket, kilt and knee-boots. There is a sash across his left shoulder and he holds a scroll in his right hand. Hollow base.
Observations: It has been said that this figure represents Miss Davenport as 'Young Norval' in *Douglas*, but I know of nothing to substantiate this theory.

Plate 92 (Left)
Playbill advertising
Rubini! The Great and Famous Conjuror Beheading a Lady. May 1st 1869.
By courtesy of
Mr Robert Wood

Plate 93
Fig. 187 ?Rubini
In the collection of
Dr S. J. Howard

Plate 95
Van Amburgh at Vauxhall Gardens
This engraving appeared in *The Illustrated London News* of September 2nd, 1848. Although there is

a marked similarity between the engraving and *figs.* 188 and 189, there still is no doubt that the latter portray 'Sampson and the Lion'.
By courtesy of the Illustrated London News

Plate 94
Fig. 188 Samson and the Lion

Figure 186
Subject: **Unidentified child actress**
Title: None
Height: 7 in (17.5 cm)
Colour: Well coloured.
Rarity: R.
Description: Standing, wearing a round hat with a bow in the brim, bodice, knee-length skirt and pantaloons. She is holding her apron forwards from her skirt with both hands.
Observations: It has been said that this figure represents Miss Davenport in *Maid of all Work*, but I know of nothing to substantiate this.

Plate 92
Rubini
Playbill for New Theatre Royal, West Hartlepool, May 1st, 1869, advertising:

Rubini! The Great and Famous Conjuror,
Beheading a Lady,
Having just terminated a Brilliant Season
of nearly 200 *Representations at the*
St James's, St George's & *Egyptian Halls, London.*

The theme seems identical to that portrayed in *fig.* 187, *pl.* E-93, but the figure appears to belong to a decade or two earlier.

Plate 93
Figure 187
Subject: **? Rubini**
Title: None
Date: Uncertain
Height: 10¼ in (25.75 cm)
Colour: Well coloured in underglaze blue.
Rarity: VR. D. A.
Description: Standing bare-headed, with ankle-length, ermine-edged cloak fastened at the neck and open below as an inverted 'V', trousers and shoes. In his right hand he holds a dagger, and in his left he grasps the hair of a head or mask.
Observations: The theme of this figure seems identical to that of the playbill illustrated on the preceding plate. There is also some similarity in the facial features. The date of

the playbill is 1869, and the figure is certainly a decade or more earlier than this. I am grateful to Mr Robert Wood for the following note:

I cannot see any incompatability in the dates because of colouring, for coloured posters, in provincial towns, came into fashion after the 1851 Exhibition, and Rubini could well have been touring for ten years before he came to Hartlepool.

Again, there were other magicians before him, and from the style of gown worn by the figure I should have been more inclined to link it with earlier performances of the 1830's and 1840's.

Plate 94
Figure 188
Subject: **Samson and the lion**
Title: None
Height: 10 in (25 cm)
Colour: Well coloured.
Rarity: C.
Description: Standing bare-headed, with a short beard, tunic, and a scarf over his left shoulder. To his left is the lion on its hind legs. He is in the act of prizing open its jaw with both hands.
Observations: 1. Is almost certainly a small version of *fig.* 189, *pl.* E-97 and depicts the same person. There has been much argument about the identity of this person. The figure has been included in this section because it was at one time identified as Mr Isaac Van Amburgh, on the grounds that it resembled 'in reverse' the engraving *Van Amburgh at Vauxhall Gardens*, which appeared in *The Illustrated London News* of September 2nd, 1848, see *pl.* E-95. It has been argued against this that in neither figure is Van Amburgh wearing gladiatorial rig, which he always did when appearing with his animals. Stanley suggests that *fig.* 188 portrays Van Amburgh and mentions that *fig.* 189 is commonly regarded as 'Samson and the Lion', but himself gives preference to the 'Lion King' of Sanger's called Crockett, an extremely well-known personality who was described by Thomas Frost, in 1875, as being 'A tall, handsome man, with a full beard'.

His lion act included a wrestling episode similar to that depicted in the pottery group.

It has, also, been suggested that the figure represents Hercules, the most famous of the Greek heroes, who embarked on twelve labours imposed on him by Eurystheus, king of Argos. The first of these labours was to bring back the skin of the Nemean lion, an enormous creature which was devastating the valley of Nemea near Cleonæ. As the pelt could not be pierced by any weapon, Hercules strangled the lion with his hands. The marble statue illustrated on *pl.* E-96 of Hercules killing the Nemean lion is to be seen in the Ashmolean Museum, Oxford. It is attributed to Baccio Bandinelli (1493–1560), the Florentine sculptor. It will be noted that *figs.* 188 and 189 bear a close similarity to this statue.

Messrs Raymond Mander and Joe Mitchenson tell me that they have seen a magenta plate with an identical design to *fig.* 189 inscribed 'Samson and the Lion'. Unfortunately, this plate is no longer in their hands, so I have not had an opportunity to photograph it. I have also heard of one of the two figures being found titled 'Samson and the Lion', although again I have unfortunately not seen it myself. In the face of the evidence of such authorities as Messrs Raymond Mander and Joe Mitchenson, there is no room for doubting that both figures represent 'Samson and the Lion'.
2. A similar figure fetched 10 gns at Christie's in 1964.

Plate 95
Van Amburgh
The engraving illustrated inscribed: *Van Amburgh at Vauxhall Gardens* appeared in *The Illustrated London News* of September 2nd, 1848. The text accompanying the engraving referred to the events that had taken place at Vauxhall Gardens during the current season:

Plate 96
Hercules killing the Nemean lion
This marble statue is attributed to Baccio
Bandinelli (1493-1560), the Florentine sculptor.

Plate 95 continued

'Fireworks, lamps, fountains, and fancy fairs, have
all been in full swing; and now the wonderful performances of Van Amburgh, with his trained animals,
have been added to the programme of amusements.
With the nature of this extraordinary spectacle the
public is already acquainted. None of the brute-
tamers, from the "Lion King" himself to the itinerant
keeper who makes the leopards jump through the
hoops in the wild beast show, can come near Mr. Van
Amburgh. There is no appearance of "bullying" the
animals in his exhibition. He rolls about amongst and
upon the huge creatures of the desert and the jungle,
as a child would do with a large family dog on the
hearth-rug; and they seem in turn to regard him with
the same degree of affection.'

It will be noted that *fig.* 188, *pl.* E-94 and
fig. 189, *pl.* E-97 bear some resemblance to
this illustration, except that in neither is the
man portrayed dressed as a gladiator. Mr
Van Amburgh was always dressed in this
way, see *fig.* 200, *pl.* E-100.

Plate 96
Hercules
The marble statue of Hercules killing the
Nemean lion, illustrated on this plate, is
attributed to Baccio Bandinelli. It will be
noted that *fig.* 188, *pl.* E-94 and *fig.* 189, *pl.*
E-97 bear a close similarity to this statue.
See *fig.* 188, *pl.* E-94.

Plate 97
Figure 34
Subject: **Edmund Kean as 'Richard III'**
Observations: See *pl.* E-13.

Figure 189
Subject: **Samson and the lion**
Title: None
Height: 12¾ in (32.25 cm)
Colour: Well coloured.
Rarity: C.
Description: Standing bare-headed, with

E420

Note the close resemblance between it and
figs. 188 and 189, *pls.* E-94 and 97 which, even
so, almost certainly portray 'Samson and the
Lion'.
Ashmolean Museum, Oxford

long flowing beard, tunic, scarf over his left
shoulder and sandals. To his left, stands a
lion on its hind legs. He is attempting to
prize open its jaw with both hands.
Observations: 1. A larger version of *fig.* 188,
pl. E-94, but it has been separately illustrated because of the controversy surrounding
the identity of the person portrayed. The
figure almost certainly represents Samson and
the Lion, and *not* Van Amburgh, nor Hercules
and the Nemean Lion, nor Crockett.
2. See *fig.* 188, *pl.* E-94.

Figure 190
Subject: **George Rignold as 'Henry V'**
Title: None
Date: *c.* 1879
Height: 15½ in (39.25 cm)
Colour: Sparingly coloured.
Maker: Sampson Smith
Rarity: Av.
Description: Standing, in an open crown over
a chain-mail cap, wearing cuirass, gauntlets
and thigh plates. His left arm is round a tall
flag-pole with a large flag, and his right foot
is on a step. On the floor, between his legs,
is a heart-shaped shield with an unidentified
animal decorating it.
Observations: 1. Identified from a Parian
figure of similar design, which although
untitled is known from a contemporary
advertisement to be Rignold as 'Henry V':

France. Before Harfleur. K. Hen: 'Once more unto the
breach, dear friends, once more . . .'
Act 3, Scene 1.

2. There is an engraving of this figure in the
sample page from an old Sampson Smith
catalogue illustrated in *ch.* 2, *pl.* 11.
3. See *ch.* 3, *pl.* 52.
4. An example of this figure, together with
fig. 11 (Wallace) *pl.* I-6 fetched 20 gns at
Christie's in 1969.

Plate 97
T: *Fig.* 189 Samson and
the Lion
Fig. 190 Rignold
('Henry V')

B: *Fig.* 191 Rob Roy
Fig. 193 Joan of Arc
Fig. 34 Edmund Kean
('Richard III')

Figure 191
Subject: **Rob Roy Macgregor**
Title: None
Height: 11¼ in (28.5 cm)
Colour: Well coloured.
Rarity: R.
Pair: There may well be a pair to this figure,
Helen Macgregor. *Fig.* 192 has been set
aside for this possibility.
Description: Standing, much inclined to his
right, in full Scottish uniform, plaid over his
right shoulder, horn suspended from his
left shoulder, a round shield behind his left
forearm and dirk in his right hand. No
sporran.
Observations: Mr Anthony Oliver has re-

ported recently a striking resemblánce
between this figure and a penny plain
tuppence coloured combat print of T. P.
Cooke as 'Rhoderick Dhu' in *The Lady of the
Lake*. If this figure is indeed 'Rhoderick
Dhu' and not 'Rob Roy' then its pair may
well be 'James Fitz-James'.

Figure 193
Subject: **Joan of Arc**
Title: None
Height: 11¾ in (29.75 cm)
Colour: Sparsely coloured.
Rarity: R.
Description: Standing bare-headed, wearing

a cuirass and skirt. A scabbard hangs from
a diagonal belt over her left thigh. Her
hands are held in front. There is a perfora-
tion in her right hand for a sword, which is
probably intended to point downwards, and
not as illustrated in the plate. A helmet
stands on a tree stump to her right.
Observations: 1. Based on a coloured lithograph music-front by John Brandard for the
Joan of Arc Waltz by Chas. d'Albert, see *ch.*
3, *pl.* 53. This lithograph probably portrays
an actress in the role, but her identity is
unknown.
2. A similar figure fetched 28 gns at Christie's
in 1969.

FRANCONI AT DRURY-LANE.—MDLLE. PALMYRE ANATO IN THE CIRCLE.

Plate 98
*Franconi at Drury-Lane: —
Mdlle. Palmyre Anato in the
Circle.*
This engraving appeared
in *The Illustrated London
News* of March 18th, 1848.
It may have been the
inspiration for *fig. 196,
pl.* E-100.
The identical engraving
was used again in 1857
for a playbill for the
Theatre Royal, Drury
Lane, see *The Antique
Dealer and Collectors Guide:*
October, 1969. It
advertised the 'Inimitable
Miss Ella — Entirely new
and more wonderful
Flying Acts of
Equestration'. It is a
reminder of the danger of
assuming that an
engraving is necessarily
of the person named
under it.

MR. VAN AMBURGH
And his group of LIVING ANIMALS, entitled the
BRUTE TAMER
OF POMPEII!
With Appropriate Scenery, Costumes, &c.
Malerius............(The Roman Renegade)............Mr. VAN AMBURGH
Gladiators, and principal Characters by the Artistes of this Establishment.
The principal Events will Embody
THE OUTSKIRTS OF THE FOREST—ARRIVAL OF THE ROMAN RENEGADE.
TREACHERY OF HIS FRIEND.
THE WILD BEASTS' LAIR!
Imminent peril of Malerius.
TERRIFIC ATTACK
BY A ROYAL BENGAL TIGER.
Malerius' surprising Strength displayed—The Animal completely subdued.
Spacious Roman Arena, with the Assemblage of the whole of the
MATCHLESS COLLECTION OF LIONS, LEOPARDS, AND TIGERS.
In the last scene, MR. VAN AMBURGH will display his astonishing power over
THE LIONS, LEOPARDS, AND TIGERS,
AND WILL ENCOUNTER
THE LARGEST TIGER EVER EXHIBITED IN EUROPE.

Plate 99
Van Amburgh (1811-1870)
Part of a playbill for the
Theatre Royal, Drury
Lane for March 26th and
27th, 1841 introducing
Mr. Van Amburgh.
Van Amburgh always
appeared dressed as a
gladiator. See *fig.* 200,
pl. E-100.

Plate 98
Mdlle Palmyre Anato
This engraving appeared in *The Illustrated London News* of March 18th, 1848. It is inscribed: *Franconi at Drury-Lane:– Mdlle. Palmyre Anato in the Circle.* It may well have been the inspiration for *fig.* 196, *pl.* E-100. The accompanying report said:

We last week described the clever performances of the Cirque National troupe at Drury-Lane. The achievements of the female riders are by far the most attractive; and among one of the most graceful feats is that of Mdlle. Palmyre Anato, illustrated in our engraving.

We are glad to know that the performances of the troupe have attracted numerous and fashionable audiences.

Plate 99
Van Amburgh
Part of a playbill for the Theatre Royal, Drury Lane for March 26th and 27th, 1841, introducing 'Mr Van Amburgh and his group of LIVING ANIMALS, entitled the *BRUTE TAMER OF POMPEII!*'
Van Amburgh always appeared dressed as a gladiator, see *fig.* 200, *pl.* E-100.

Section E. Theatre, Opera, Ballet and Circus

Plate 100

Figure 194
Subject: **? Andrew Ducrow and Louisa Woolford**
Title: None
Height: 10 in (25 cm)
Colour: Well coloured.
Rarity: R.
Description: On a horse facing right; they are standing, side by side, on an ornate saddle and saddle-cloth. To the right, is Ducrow wearing a plumed hat, shirt, jacket, pantaloons and knee-boots; and to the left, his wife, wearing a plumed hat, bodice, knee-length skirt and bootees.
Observations: Commonly thought to be a representation of Andrew Ducrow, the equestrian and his second wife Miss Woolford, the tight-rope performer.

Figure 195
Subject: **Unidentified female equestrian**
Title: None
Height: 7¼ in (18.25 cm)
Colour: Well coloured.
Rarity: R.
Pair: Unknown
Description: On a horse facing left, wearing a plumed bonnet and veil and long riding habit. Decorated saddle-cloth.
Observations: Is generally regarded as a circus figure, and has been variously identified as Madame Klatt and Madame Caroline. I have not come across any illustration of either of these performers close enough to the figure to justify dogmatism.

Figure 196
Subject: **? Mlle Palmyre Anato**
Title: None

Date: *c.* 1848
Height: 9¾ in (24.5 cm)
Colour: Well coloured.
Rarity: VR. A.
Pair: Not known
Description: Seated side-saddle on her horse, facing left, holding a large floral garland (hoop). Her right hand is on the horse's mane and her left hand on her hip. She wears a bodice and knee-length skirt. Her feet are visible. The horse is dressed with an ornate saddle-cloth.
Observations: Probably inspired by an illustration which appeared in *The Illustrated London News* on March 18th, 1848 inscribed *Franconi at Drury-Lane:– Mdlle. Palmyre Anato in the Circle*, see *pl.* E-98.

Figure 197
Subject: **Androcles and the lion**
Title: None
Height: 8 in (20.5 cm)
Colour: Well coloured.
Rarity: Av.
Description: Androcles is seated on the right, bare-headed, bearded, with knee-length tunic and sandals. The lion is squatting on the left, his right front paw is on Androcles's right knee and his left front paw is held in Androcles's hand.
Observations: Has many similarities to *fig.* 151, *pl.* E-78, and may, likewise, portray the famous lion *Wallace* with which Lorenzo, the lion tamer represented the story of *Androcles and the lion*.

Figure 198
Subject: **Unidentified clown**
Title: None
Height: 6½ in (16.5 cm)
Colour: Well coloured.

Rarity: R.
Pair: *Fig.* 199 (Unidentified pantaloon)
Description: Dressed as a clown. He has a double ruff, and his eyebrows are picked out as inverted 'V's'. His right hand is on his hip and his left hand in his trouser pocket.
Observations: 1. Has been variously called Joseph Grimaldi (1779–1837) and Tom Mathews (1805–89) with no proof. The appearance of the head is very similar to that observed in portraits of Mathews.
2. Each clown had his own particular design of make-up. This was registered by being drawn on an egg and deposited with the 'union'.

Figure 199
Subject: **Unidentified pantaloon**
Title: None
Height: 6¾ in (17 cm)
Colour: Well coloured.
Rarity: R.
Pair: *Fig.* 198 (Unidentified clown)
Description: An old man dressed as pantaloon. He has normal eyebrows and a cane in his left hand. His right hand is tucked into his jacket.
Observations: Has defied identification.

Figure 200
Subject: **Van Amburgh**
Title: Mr, Van Amburgh (gilt script)
Date: *c.* 1839
Height: 6¼ in (16 cm)
Colour: Well coloured.
Rarity: R. D. A.
Description: Standing, bare-headed and bearded, in a short-skirted dress as worn by the gladiators. He is surrounded by his lions, including one on his left shoulder.

Section E. Theatre, Opera, Ballet and Circus

Plate 100 continued
Observations: 1. Van Amburgh invariably wore gladiatorial rig during public appearances with his lions.
2. A similar figure, badly damaged, fetched 70 gns at Christie's in 1965.

Figure 201
Subject: **Macomo as 'Androcles', and a lion**
Title: None
Height: 8 in (20.5 cm)
Colour: Well coloured.
Rarity: R. D. A.
Description: A negro kneels on the right, wearing turban and long tunic with sash. A lion stands on the left, in front of a tree trunk (spill-holder). His left forepaw is raised on the negro's lap. Rococo base.
Observations: There is every reason to suppose that this figure represents Macomo, the negro 'Lion King', who frequently performed the story of *Androcles and the lion*.

Plate 101
Figure 202
Subject: **Unidentified clown**
Title: None
Height: 4¼ in (10.75 cm)
Colour: Well coloured.
Rarity: R.
Pair: There is probably a pair to this figure —pantaloon.
Description: Very similar to *fig.* 198 (Unidentified clown) *pl.* E-100, except that he is sitting.
Observations: See *fig.* 198, *pl.* E-100.

Figure 202(a) (not illustrated)
Subject: **Three unidentified clowns**
Title: None
Date: 188–
Height: 13¼ in (33.5 cm)
Colour: Well coloured.
Maker: Probably Sampson Smith
Rarity: VR. A.
Description: A group of three clowns, standing in a row with linked arms, wearing brightly patterned and chequered circus clothes.

Observations: 1. This must surely be a portrait group, but the identities of the trio are, to date, unknown.
2. A similar group fetched £170 at Sotheby's in 1969.

Figure 203
Subject: **'John Gilpin'—? Mr Wells in the role**
Title: John Gilpin (indented capitals)
Date: c. 1845
Height: 5 in (12.75 cm)
Colour: Well coloured.
Rarity: VR.
Pair: Fig. 204 ('Gilpin')
Description: On a horse facing left, bareheaded, wearing cloak, riding jacket, breeches and knee-boots. He is holding the reins and the horse is about to jump a fence. His tricorn hat is on the ground.
Observations: See *fig.* 204 (Gilpin)

Figure 204
Subject: **'John Gilpin'—? Mr Wells in the role**
Title: John Gilpin (indented capitals)
Date: c. 1845
Height: 5¼ in (13.5 cm)
Colour: Well coloured.
Rarity: VR.
Pair: Fig. 203 ('Gilpin')
Description: On a horse facing right, bareheaded. He has lost his wig which lies on the ground. He has also lost control of the reins and has his arms around the horse's neck. He is wearing a riding jacket, breeches and knee-boots.
Observations: Note that in *fig.* 203, 'Gilpin' has lost his tricorn hat, but in *fig.* 204 the matter is carried a stage further—the wig, as well, has gone and he has lost control of the reins. *Harlequin and Johnny Gilpin's Ride* was produced at Astley's in December, 1844. *The Illustrated London News* of December 28th, 1844 included an engraving of the scene inscribed:

'The main incident is the celebrated citizen's ride; the role filled by the popular equestrian Mr Wells'.

This engraving is illustrated on the right of *pl.* E-102. It will be noted that 'Gilpin' is

portrayed hurtling forwards on his horse with both hat and wig in the air. *Figs.* 203 and 204 were probably intended to portray Mr Wells as 'John Gilpin.'

Plate 102
Figure 205
Subject: **'John Gilpin'—? Mr Wells in the role**
Title: None
Date: c. 1845
Height: 7¾ in (20 cm)
Colour: Well coloured.
Rarity: R.
Pair: Fig. 206 ('Gilpin')
Description: On a horse facing right, wearing tricorn hat, riding jacket, waistcoat, breeches and knee-boots, his right hand holding the reins.
Observations: Probably 'circus', see *fig.* 206 ('Gilpin').

Figure 206
Subject: **'John Gilpin'—? Mr Wells in the role**
Title: None
Date: c. 1845
Height: 7¼ in (18.25 cm)
Colour: Well coloured.
Rarity: R.
Pair: Fig. 205 ('Gilpin')
Description: On a horse facing left, bareheaded, wearing a riding coat, waistcoat, breeches and knee-boots. His hands are round the horse's neck, his tricorn hat has fallen off and is lying on the ground, and the horse is about to jump a wall.
Observations: This figure and its pair *fig.* 205, may well be 'circus'. *Harlequin and Johnny Gilpin's Ride* was staged at Astley's in December, 1844. The engraving from *The Illustrated London News* of December 28th, 1844, illustrated on the right of this plate, depicts an incident from the production which may well have been the inspiration of these figures, the role of 'John Gilpin' being filled by the popular equestrian of the day, Mr Wells.

Plate 101
Fig. 204 ?Wells ('Gilpin')
Fig. 202 Unidentified clown
Fig. 203 ?Wells ('Gilpin')
By courtesy of Mr and Mrs Eric Joyce

Plate 102
Fig. 209 Tam o'Shanter
Fig. 205 ?Wells ('Gilpin')
Fig. 206 ?Wells ('Gilpin')
Fig. 208 Gilpin
Background:
L: Scene from the pantomime of
Harlequin Tam o'Shanter, at Astley's. From
The Illustrated London News, January 6th,
1844.

Now do thy utmost speed, my Meg,
And win the keystone of the brig;
Then at them thou thy tail may toss —
A running stream they dare not cross.
Robert Burns
R: Scene from *Harlequin and Johnny
Gilpin's ride,* at Astley's. From *The
Illustrated London News,* December 28th,
1944.
Nor stopped till where he had got up
He did again get down.
William Cowper
*In the collections of Dr S. J. Howard and the
author*

Figure 208
Subject: **John Gilpin**
Title: John Gilpin (indented capitals)
Date: c. 1845
Height: 7 in (17.5 cm)
Colour: Well coloured.
Rarity: VR.
Pair or series: There is probably a pair to
this figure—'Gilpin'; *fig.* 207 has been reser-
ved for it, see *observations.* Same series as *fig.*
209 ('Tam o'Shanter') and its pair.
Description: On a horse facing left, bare-
headed, wearing riding jacket, waistcoat,
breeches and knee-boots. His arms are round
the horse's neck, his tricorn hat is on the
ground and his horse is about to leap a gate.
Rococo base.
Observations: 1. May be 'circus', see *fig.* 206.
2. It might well be thought that *fig.* 209
('Tam o'Shanter') is the pair to 'Gilpin'
but I have been assured by Mr John Hall
that he has seen an individual pair to each of
these figures. The pair to *fig.* 208 ('Gilpin')
portrays Gilpin wearing his tricorn hat and
holding the horse's reins.

Figure 209
Subject: **Tam o'Shanter**
Title: Tam o'Shanter (indented capitals)
Date: c. 1844
Height: 7¾ in (20 cm)
Colour: Well coloured.
Rarity: VR.

Pair or series: I am informed that there is a
pair to this figure—'Tam o'Shanter'. *Fig.*
210 has been reserved for it, see *observations.*
Same series as *fig.* 208 ('Gilpin') and its pair.
Description: On a horse facing right, crossing
a bridge. He wears a Scotch bonnet, riding
jacket, plaid, breeches and tartan stockings.
His right arm is raised and he holds a manuscript in his right hand.
Observations: 1. I am informed that the pair
to this figure is not *fig.* 208 ('Gilpin') as might
be supposed from perusal of *pl.* E-102, but
another portrait of 'Tam o'Shanter' on his
grey mare, *Meg.* This portrays events after
his steed's tail had been pulled off by the
witches as he reached the middle of the
bridge over the Doon. *Fig.* 210 has been
reserved for the piece.
2. Both figures may well be 'circus'. The
pantomime of *Harlequin Tam o'Shanter* was
put on at Astley's in December, 1843. A
scene from the pantomime captioned *Harlequin Tam o'Shanter and his Steed Meg* appeared in *The Illustrated London News* of January
6th, 1844, and is shown to the left of *pl.* E-
102. It depicts the flight of 'Tam o'Shanter'
through the storm on his grey mare, *Meg,*
followed by the witches pulling on the
horse's tail. This pair of figures may have
been inspired by the engraving of the
Astley's production in which incidentally,
'Clown' was played by King and 'Pantaloon' by Mathews.

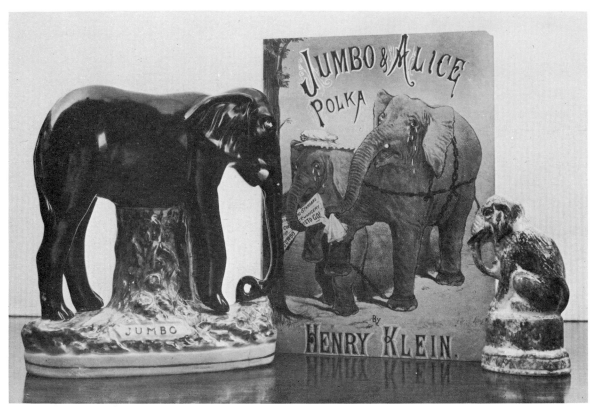

Plate 103
Fig. 211 Jumbo
Fig. 212 *(facing left)* Jumbo
Between these two figures is an example of one
of the several music-sheets of the period titled

Jumbo and Alice Polka by Henry Klein. The
special edition of the *Evening Standard* held in
Alice's trunk is headlined 'Jumbo is to GO'.

Plate 104
Fig. 212 *(facing right) Jumbo*
Behind and to the right is
an engraving which
appeared in *The Illustrated
London News* of April 1st,
1882 captioned 'Jumbo's
journey to the docks'.

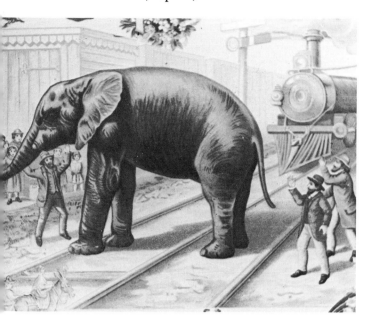

Plate 105
The scene as *Jumbo* was coaxed across the
railway line in Ontario in 1885.
*From a Victorian scrapbook in the possession of the
Hon. Mrs C. Wildman*

Plate 106
The death of *Jumbo*, Ontario, 1885.
*From a Victorian scrapbook in the possession of the
Hon. Mrs C. Wildman*

Plate 103
Figure 211
Subject: **Jumbo**
Title: Jumbo (raised capitals)
Date: *c.* 1882
Height: 10½ in (26.5 cm)
Colour: Rather crudely coloured. The
elephant may be fawn, grey, or jet black.
Maker: Parr and Kent group of potters
Rarity: R. D.
Description: An African elephant, standing,·
facing right, with no trappings and stunted
tusks. His trunk, the end of which is curled,
touches the ground. The belly is supported
on a tree trunk.
Observations: 1. Appears in *Kent List A* (*c.*
1901):

	Stock No.
Elephant (Jumbo)	60

It does not appear in *Kent List B* nor *C*.
It was presumably manufactured over a
twenty year period.
2. It has been suggested that the 'black'
figure was issued after *Jumbo* had died from
the effects of charging a train in 1885.
3. There is no known figure of *Alice*.
Incidentally, the only references to *Alice* in
the files on *Jumbo* in the possession of The
Zoological Society of London, are in the
various songs and poems written at the time.
4. African elephants have big ears, a hollow
along the spine of the back and a level
sloping forehead. Indian elephants, the
species most often found in zoos, have small
ears, a rounded back and a pronounced
hollow between the forehead and the crown.
African elephants are rare in Staffordshire
pottery, see *p.* 409.

Figure 212 (shown facing *left*)
Subject: **Jumbo**
Title: Jumbo (indented capitals *front* and
back)
Date: *c.* 1882
Height: 6½ in (16.5 cm)
Colour: Fawn
Rarity: VR. D.

Pair: This figure is titled on the front and
the back and may face right or left. It was
presumably sold in pairs.
Description: He squats on his hind legs on a
two-tiered pedestal. Medium size tusks.
Hollow base. A cast figure.

Plate 104
Figure 212 (shown facing *right*)
Subject: **Jumbo**
Observations: 1. See *pl.* E-103.
2. Behind and to right is an engraving which
appeared in *The Illustrated London News* of
April 1st, 1882 inscribed: *Jumbo's journey to
the docks.*

Plate 105
Jumbo
'Jumbo' being coaxed across the railway
line, Ontario, 1885.
From a Victorian scrap-book.

Plate 106
Jumbo
The death of 'Jumbo', Ontario, 1885.
From a Victorian scrap-book.

Plate 107
Figure 213
Subject: **Mazeppa on a horse**
Title: None
Date: *c.* 1864
Height: 9⅛ in (23.25 cm)
Colour: Well coloured.
Rarity: Av.
Description: Scantily clad and bound to the
back of a horse, facing right. Behind is a
tree trunk (spill-holder), and in front are
two wolves chasing the horse.
Observations: 1. Based on a woodcut first
used in 1838 to advertise *Mazeppa* at Astley's
with Mr West, jun. in the title role, see *pl.*
E-107A. The same woodcut was also used
to decorate a playbill advertising *Mazeppa*
with Miss Adah Isaacs Menken in the title
role, again at Astley's in October 1864, see
pl. E-107B. Because the figure was probably

intended by the potter to represent Miss Adah
Isaacs Menken in the role of 'Mazeppa',
although it is obviously based on the earlier
woodcut, some writers have described it as
a portrait of her. In the light of what has
been said, this is obviously incorrect and it
is best to regard the figure simply as a
representation of 'Mazeppa', although it
may be a portrait of Mr West.
2. A similar figure fetched 16 gns at Christie's
in 1964.

Figure 214
Subject: **Mazeppa on a zebra**
Title: None
Date: 186–
Height: 14 in (35.5 cm)
Colour: Well coloured.
Rarity: R. D.
Description: Bound, virtually naked, to the
back of a zebra, which is facing left. The
zebra is crossing a bridge. In the background
is a tree trunk (spill-holder), and in the foreground are three wolves.
Observations: *Mazeppa* was the trump-card
of every hippo-dramatic manager who
possessed, or could borrow a white horse,
or even on occasions a zebra, to enact the
part of the 'fiery, untamed steed' upon whose
back the hero was borne.

Figure 215
Subject: **Mazeppa on a horse**
Title: None
Date: *c.* 1864
Height: 5 in (12.75 cm)
Colour: Well coloured.
Rarity: Av.
Description: Bound, virtually naked, to the
back of a horse, facing left. There are no
wolves.
Observations: See *fig.* 213.

Figure 216
Subject: **Mazeppa on a horse**
Title: None
Date: *c.* 1864
Height: 8¼ in (21 cm)

Plate 107
Fig. 213 Mazeppa   *Fig.* 214 Mazeppa and zebra   *Fig.* 215 Mazeppa   *Fig.* 216 Mazeppa

Plate 107A (Left)
Playbill for July 23rd, 1838 advertising *Mazeppa* at Astley's with Mr West jun. in the title role.
In the collection of Messrs Raymond Mander and Joe Mitchenson

Plate 107B (Right)
Playbill for November 7th, 1864 advetising *Mazeppa* at Astley's with Miss Adah Isaacs Menken in the title role.
Note the same woodcut has been used as in the earlier playbill illustrated on the preceding plate. It cannot portray Mr West jun.
By courtesy of the Victoria and Albert Museum

Plate 107 continued
Colour: Well coloured.
Rarity: VR. D.
Description: Bound, virtually naked, to the back of a horse, facing left. Behind is a tree trunk (spill-holder), and in the foreground are three wolves.
Observations: See *fig.* 213.

E428

Plate 107A
Mazeppa
Playbill for July 23rd, 1838, advertising *Mazeppa* at Astley's with Mr West, jun. in the title role. See *fig.* 213, *pl.* E-107.

Plate 107B
Mazeppa
Playbill for November 7th, 1864, advertising *Mazeppa* at Astley's with Miss Adah Isaacs Menken in the title role. See *fig.* 213, *pl.* E-107.

Plate 108
Fig. 217(b) ?T. P. Cooke
('Ben Backstay')
Fig. 218(b) Unidentified
girl
Fig. 217(a) ?T. P. Cooke
('Ben Backstay')
Fig. 217 ?T. P. Cooke
('Ben Backstay')
To the right of this figure
is a lithograph of
Mr T. P. Cooke as 'Ben
Backstay'. Published
April 9th, 1823 by
Orlando Hodgson.
*In the collections of
Mr Anthony Oliver and the
author*

Plate 108
Figure 217
Subject: **? T. P. Cooke as 'Ben Backstay'**
Title: None
Date: 184–
Height: 10½ in (26.5 cm)
Colour: Well coloured.
Rarity: R. A.
Pair: *Fig.* 218 (Unidentified girl)
Description: A sailor, with fringed beard, stands bare-headed doing the hornpipe. His left hand, in which he holds a money-bag, is

raised to the left side of his head, and his right hand is on his hip. He wears a jacket, shirt, neckerchief, trousers and belt. Below his right forearm is his straw hat, and behind his legs is an anchor.
Observations: 1. Probably based on a lithograph of Mr T. P. Cooke as 'Ben Backstay', published April 9th, 1823 by Orlando Hodgson.
2. There are smaller and inferior versions of this figure, each of which has minor variations and each of which is paired by an un-

identified girl, see *figs.* 217(a) and 217(b).
3. Mr Anthony Oliver writing on this subject (*The Antique Dealer and Collectors Guide*: November, 1967) said:

'It is not always possible to be so definite about an identification and there are many figures which could represent five or six different actors in a dozen different nautical plays. This last statement is perhaps the explanation of their manufacture. If, as I suspect, some of the cruder, more durable figures, were hawked in the street outside the theatres, then a figure which represented a moment common to many different plays would save changing the stock too

Plate 109
Fig. 219 T. P. Cooke
('Tom Coffin')
To the left of the figure is
a penny plain print *West's
Characters in the Pilot*. Tom
Coffin may be seen, on
the right, standing on a
rock defying the
American sodiers as they
fire at him. He is about
to leap into the sea and
swim to his ship.
*In the collection of Mr
Anthony Oliver*

Plate 108 continued
often. Into this category come what I call the "Jack Ashore" figures.

'Almost a standard ingredient of the nautical play is the arrival of the sailor hero clutching his money-bag and dancing the hornpipe. I think it is possible that the many different versions of this figure do not portray a specific actor like Cooke but merely the sailor hero in triumph, a moment which would have been instantly recognisable to the public of the day.'

Figure 218 (not illustrated)
Subject: **Unidentified girl**
Title: None
Date: 184–
Height: 10¼ in (25.75 cm)
Colour: Well coloured.
Rarity: R. A.
Pair: Fig. 217 (? T. P. Cooke)
Description: Standing bare-headed, doing the hornpipe. Her right hand is raised to the right side of her head and in it she carries a money-bag. Her left hand is on her hip and in it she holds her straw hat. She is wearing a bodice and three-flounced dress, and at her feet and to the right is a basket, possibly of fruit.
Observations: 1. See preceding figure.
2. As for *fig.* 217, there are smaller and inferior versions of this figure, of which *fig.* 218 (*b*) is illustrated.
3. If *fig.* 217 does indeed portray T. P. Cooke, this figure is unlikely to be more than a 'balancing' pair.

Plate 109
Figure 219
Subject: **T. P. Cooke as 'Tom Coffin'**
Title: None
Date: 184–
Height: 8¼ in (21 cm)
Colour: Well coloured.
Rarity: VR. D. A.
Description: Standing bare-headed, on a rock bestrewn with shells. He wears a neckerchief, striped shirt, belt and trousers and in his right hand he holds a handkerchief.
Observations: *The Pilot*, a tale of adventure at sea by J. F. Cooper (1789–1851) was first published in 1823. It had enormous success as a novel. It was dramatized by E. Fitzball and first performed at the Adelphi Theatre on October 31st, 1825, and many times later at various theatres, including the Surrey. The part of 'Long Tom Coffin', the hero of the play, was made famous by Mr T. P. Cooke and was performed by him no less than 562 times in the 25 years following the first production. The figure portrays the highlight of Scene 3, at the end of Act 1, a moment before the curtain falls. Note the penny plain, tuppence coloured sheet *West's Characters in the Pilot, Plate 4th, Price 1d. Plain.* 'Tom Coffin' is the figure on the rocks, surrounded and being fired on by soldiers. This is the same moment as that portrayed by the figure. 'Tom' does indeed

throw himself into the sea whilst firing continues, but eventually swims to a ship and is rescued. Now turn to the figure. The potter could not have him standing on top of a rock, as in the print, so he built the piece up and suggested the seashore by means of shells. The rest of the figure, even to minute detail, is similar to the print. Note how his neckerchief blows out in the wind in an identical manner in both print and figure. It is the only example of a penny plain print known to me in which the print does more than *suggest*. In this instance it *identifies* the figure as 'Tom Coffin' beyond doubt. That being so, it is assuredly a portrait of T. P. Cooke, for it was he who made the part famous. The actual moment in the play (Act 1, Scene 3) is as follows:

Tom loses his harpoon and then his sword, finding himself surrounded by soldiers he runs up the rock (left), and they present their muskets to him.
Sergeant: Surrender.
Long Tom (coughing): My Commander taken, and you would secure Tom too. No, no. These waves are to me what the land is to you. I was born on them, and sooner than be captured by an inimy, I always meant that they should be my grave.
Colonel: Fire. (*They fire. Tom throws himself into the sea and disappears. They force Barnstaple off right*).

Plate 110 (Left)
Fig. 220 ?Fanny Kemble
To the right of the figure is a lithograph of Miss Fanny Kemble by Richard J. Lane, ARA, after a drawing by Sir Thomas Lawrence, PRA.

MASANIELLO

Plate 111
Fig. 221 Masaniello and Fenella

Plate 110
Figure 220
Subject: **? Fanny Kemble**
Title: None
Date: 184–
Height: 6½ in (16.5 cm)
Colour: Well coloured.
Rarity: R.
Pair: Not known
Description: Standing bare-headed, in bodice with off-the-shoulder neckline, and leg-of-

mutton sleeves. The overskirt is edged with ermine exposing an inverted 'V' of underskirt.
Observations: 1. The identification of this figure is based on its closeness to a drawing of Miss Fanny Kemble by Sir Thomas Lawrence PRA. This was Lawrence's last work, being completed in 1829.
2. Frederick White in *Actors of the Century* (1898) refers to Fanny Kemble's autobiography *Records of a girlhood* in which there is

a passage telling of Sir Thomas Lawrence's relations with her family, and of her own interviews with him while he was engaged upon her portrait:

'This portrait, 'tho a good likeness of her at her very best—"like those who love me have sometimes seen me" as she herself expressed it—gives a wrong impression of her as she was known to the public during the three years of her early stage career. In the first place, littleness her chief feature, has not been emphasized and secondly, she was slightly disfigured by smallpox'.

Section E. Theatre, Opera, Ballet and Circus

Plate 111

Figure 221

Subject: **Masaniello and Fenella**

Title: Masaniello (raised capitals)

Height: 11½ in (29 cm)

Colour: Sparsely coloured.

Rarity: R.

Description: 'Masaniello' stands on the right, wearing a fisherman's cap and smock. He holds a net over his left shoulder in which there is a solitary fish. His right hand rests on 'Fenella's' head. She wears a bonnet, bodice, skirt and apron. Her left hand is round 'Masaniello's' waist and her right hand supports a basket of fish.

Observations: 1. As 'Fenella', the dumb girl of Portici, is portrayed in addition to 'Masaniello' it is likely that this figure is theatrical rather than historical. It is probably based on Auber's opera *La Muette de Portici*. Nothing has been found, to date, to substantiate the view that it portrays actual actors in the role.
2. There is a close resemblance between this figure and *fig.* 277, *pl.* E-134.

Plate 112

Figure 222

Subject: **Paul and Virginia**

Title: Paul & Virginia (gilt script)

Height: 13½ in (34.25 cm)

Colour: Well coloured.

Rarity: R. (titled); Av. (untitled).

Description: Seated beside each other on a mound with flowers. 'Paul' sits on the right. He is bare-headed with a straw hat hung over his shoulders. He wears a shirt, and trousers rolled up above the knees. 'Virginia' sits on the left, bare-headed and wearing a long dress. Between them they hold a bird's nest in their hands. In the figure illustrated their hands have been broken and the restoration is incorrect.

Observations: 1. Probably not theatrical.
2. See also *fig.* 209, *pl.* C-73.

Plate 113

Figure 223

Subject: **Madame Vestris as 'Paul'**

Title: None

Height: 9½ in (24 cm)

Colour: Well coloured.

Rarity: R.

Description: Sitting on a rock with her hands at waist level held in prayer, bare-footed and legs crossed. She is wearing shirt, neckerchief and trousers. To her right, is her jacket and below are waves.

Observations: For the reasons for supposing this figure to be Madame Vestris, see *fig.* 226, *pl.* E-114.

Figure 224

Subject: **Madame Vestris as 'Paul'**

Title: None

Date: 185–

Height: 7 in (17.5 cm)

Colour: Well coloured.

Rarity: VR. D.

Description: Kneeling on her right knee with her hands (made from separate moulds) held together in prayer. She is bare-headed and bare-footed, wearing open shirt, jacket and trousers. The base is designed to look like the sea.

Observations: For the reasons for supposing this figure to be Madame Vestris, see *fig.* 226, *pl.* E-114.

Plate 114

Figure 225

Subject: **Madame Vestris as 'Paul'**

Title: None

Date: 185–

Height: 7 in (17.5 cm)

Colour: Well coloured.

Rarity: Av.

Description: Very similar to *fig.* 223 (Vestris as 'Paul') *pl.* E-113, except that it is smaller and her hands are held higher. She is more obviously in prayer.

Observations: See *fig.* 226.

Figure 226

Subject: **Madame Vestris as 'Paul'**

Title: None

Date: c. 1822

Height: 6¾ in (17 cm)

Colour: Well coloured.

Rarity: R. D. A.

Description: Very similar to *fig.* 224, *pl.* E-113 but it is porcelaneous, she kneels on her left instead of her right knee and the base is circular and shallow instead of oval and deep.

Observations: 1. *Paul and Virginia* was a very successful romance by Bernardin de St Pierre first published in 1787. The novel had a tragic ending—'Virginia' was drowned in a shipwreck and 'Paul' died of grief shortly after. It was adapted as a musical for the stage by James Cobb, being first produced at Covent Garden on May 1st, 1800. Cobb gave it a happy ending and the final curtain came down with 'Paul' giving thanks on his knees for 'Virginia's' deliverance from the shipwreck. It was revived with different casts at different theatres for the next 23 years. Mr Anthony Oliver, after careful research, finds that Madame Vestris was the only actress who played the part of 'Paul', and she played it only in 1822, at Drury Lane, it being one of her most famous breeches parts[1].

There is little doubt that *figs.* 223 and 224, *pl.* E-113, and *figs.* 225 and 226, *pl.* E-114 are of females. It follows that the scene portrayed is almost certainly Madame Vestris as she appeared at the final curtain playing 'Paul' in *Paul and Virginia*.

No original print has yet come to light of Madame Vestris kneeling in prayer in her

Plate 114
Fig. 225 Vestris ('Paul')
Fig. 226 Vestris ('Paul')
To the left of the figures
is a full-length engraving
inscribed 'Madame
Vestris as Paul in Paul
and Virginia'.
To the right of the figure
is a three-quarter-length
engraving by T. Woolnoth
date March 15th, 1823
and inscribed 'Madame
Vestris as Paul'.
It will be noted that in
both engravings the
actress is portrayed
dressed similarly to *figs.*
223 and 224. *pl.* E-113
and to *figs.* 225 and 226.
*In the collection of
Mr Anthony Oliver*

Plate 115
Fig. 229 ?Titania   *Fig.* 227 Paul   *Fig.* 228 Virginia   *Fig.* 230 Henry VIII and
                                                                                  Anne Boleyn

Plate 114 continued
'big scene', although there is little doubt that one exists. Contemporary copies of the novel, when illustrated, always include 'Paul' kneeling.

The costume and hair style in each of the portrait figures is similar to the two engravings of Madame Vestris as 'Paul' illustrated on this plate. That on the left is inscribed *Madame Vestris as Paul in Paul and Virginia*. It shows her as 'Paul', in full length, standing and dressed similarly to the four figures and indeed, as described in

E432

the stage directions for the printed play.

The engraving on the right by T. Woolnoth, published on March 15th, 1823, shows the actress three-quarter length and dressed in the same manner. It is inscribed *Madame Vestris as Paul*.

2. Comparison of *fig.* 224, *pl.* E-113 and *fig.* 226, *pl.* E-114 is of particular interest. The latter figure is porcelaneous and often offered as 'Rockingham'; whereas the former is obviously 'Staffordshire'. Current opinion is that the porcelain figure was also manufactured in Staffordshire, being followed,

probably some years later, by the cruder earthenware model. The porcelain figure, although coloured in underglaze blue and hitherto dated to the 1840's, probably dates to 1822 or thereabouts; the earthenware figure may date to the death of Vestris in 1856. Both dates are uncertain and subject to debate.

1. *Breeches parts* is the name given to roles written for men—usually handsome heroes—and played by women. Many actresses of the period were addicted to breeches parts.

Plate 116
C: *Fig.* 231 ?Henry VIII and Anne Boleyn
L: Music-front with coloured engraving by John Brandard inscribed 'First Book of Select Airs from Anne Boleyn'.
R: Lithograph music-front for *The March in 'Anna Bolena'* portraying *Madame Castellan as 'Lady Jane Seymour'* and *Signor Lablache as 'Henry 8th'*. (*See text for the arguments concerning the identity of fig.* 231)

Plate 115
Figure 227
Subject: **Paul**
Title: None
Date: Uncertain
Height: 8¼ in (21 cm)
Colour: In the manner of Thomas Parr.
Maker: Thomas Parr
Rarity: R.
Pair: *Fig.* 228 ('Virginia')
Description: Standing bare-headed, in jacket, shirt, neckerchief and trousers supported by a sash. His right hand is by his side and in it he holds his straw hat; in his left hand is a rose.
Observations: Probably not theatrical.

Figure 228
Subject: **Virginia**
Title: None
Date: Uncertain
Height: 8 in (20.5 cm)
Colour: In the manner of Thomas Parr.
Maker: Thomas Parr
Rarity: R.
Pair: *Fig.* 227 ('Paul')
Description: Standing bare-headed, in calf-length dress, a shawl over her shoulders, her right hand raised towards her chin and her left hand by her side. Her left leg is crossed in front of her right leg.
Observations: Probably not theatrical.

Figure 229
Subject: **? Titania**
Title: None
Date: Uncertain
Height: 8½ in (21.5 cm)
Colour: Largely white and gilt.
Maker: Thomas Parr
Rarity: VR.
Description: Standing with a garland of flowers round her head, her right hand by her side, holding what is possibly a wand; bodice and wide full-length skirt, a posy of flowers in her left hand which is held in front of her 'wasp' waist.
Observations: Almost certainly a theatrical figure. It has been suggested that it portrays

'Titania', Queen of the Fairies in Shakespeare's *A Mid-Summer Night's Dream*.

Figure 230
Subject: **? Henry VIII and Anne Boleyn**
Title: None
Date: Uncertain
Height: 9½ in (24 cm)
Colour: Well coloured.
Rarity: R.
Description: Seated, Henry to the left and Anne to the right, his left arm round her waist. Behind them is a tree trunk (spill-holder) and in front there appears to be a pump beneath which there is a bucket. Henry wears a plumed hat, short ermine-edged gown, doublet and hose. Anne is bare-headed with bodice and ankle-length skirt and apron. In her left hand she carries a basket.
Observations: There is some doubt about the identification of this figure. There is no evidence that it is theatrical.

Plate 116
Figure 231
Subject: **? Henry VIII and Anne Boleyn**
Title: None
Height: 10 in (25 cm)
Colour: Well coloured.
Rarity: R.
Pair: Possibly *fig.* 232 (? Anne Boleyn and Jane Seymour) *pl.* E-118.
Description: Henry is standing on the right and Anne on the left. He is holding her left hand with his right hand.
Observations: 1. The coloured engraving by John Brandard illustrated on *pl.* E-117 and inscribed *King Henry the Eighth presenting Anne Boleyn to his Court as Queen* seems to be the source of this piece. For this reason some collectors regard the figure simply as a portrait of Henry VIII and Anne Boleyn. The position is complicated by the existence of the two lithograph music-fronts illustrated on this plate. It will be noted that the engraving on the left is identical to that on *pl.* E-117. It is inscribed *First book of Select Airs from Anne Boleyn—Arranged by Charles*

W. Glover. That on the right is similar, although not identical. Many consider that it portrays the same characters. It is captioned *The March in 'Anna Bolena'* and below is inscribed:

Madame Castellan as Lady Jane Seymour
Signor Lablache as Henry 8th,
in Donizetti's opera
ANNA BOLENA
Arranged for the Piano Forte by Stephen Glover

On these grounds some collectors consider that *fig.* 231 portrays Signor Lablache and Madame Castellan in the characters of 'Henry VIII' and 'Jane Seymour'. Some weight is added to the argument that the piece is a theatre figure by the existence of a possible pair, see *pl.* E-118.
2. *Anna Bolena*, an opera by Donizetti, was first produced in Milan in 1830 and soon performed throughout Europe.

Plate 117
Henry VIII and Anne Boleyn
Coloured engraving by John Brandard inscribed *King Henry the Eighth presenting Anne Boleyn to his Court as Queen*. It is the source of *fig.* 231, *pl.* E-116.

Plate 118
Figure 232
Subject: **Two women and a stag**
Title: None
Height: 10½ in (26.5 cm)
Colour: Well coloured.
Rarity: VR.
Pair: Possibly *fig.* 231 (? Henry VIII and Anne Boleyn) *pl.* E-116.
Description: On the right, a woman stands. She wears a bonnet, bodice and full-length skirt. She rests her right forearm on a wall to her right and her left forearm and hand in front of her waist. To the left, a woman kneels. She is bare-headed, with bodice and ermine edging to the sleeves, and long skirt. She holds a posy in her right hand and caresses a fawn with her left.
Observations: The base of this figure is decorated in an identical manner to the base of *fig.* 231 (? Henry VIII and Anne

Plate 117 (Left)
Coloured engravings by John Brandard inscribed 'King Henry the Eighth presenting Anne Boleyn to his Court as Queen'. It is thought to be the source of *fig.* 231, *pl.* E-116, but see text. *In the collection of Messrs Raymond Mander and Joe Mitchenson*

Plate 118
Fig. 232 Two women and stag

Plate 118 continued
Boleyn) *pl.* E-116. This suggests that it is either a pair, or belongs to the same series, and adds weight to the theory that *fig.* 231 is a theatrical figure. It is possible, but by no means proven, that *fig.* 232 portrays Anne Boleyn and Jane Seymour in Windsor Park —a scene from Donizetti's opera *Anna Bolena*.

Plate 119
Figure 233
Subject: **Circus boy**
Title: None

Height: 7¼ in (18.25 cm)
Colour: Well coloured.
Rarity: R
Pair: Fig. 234 (Circus girl)
Description: Standing, wearing a four-cornered plumed hat, jacket and trousers. He grasps the neck of a cobra in his right hand and in his left he holds a horn.

Figure 234 (not illustrated)
Subject: **Circus girl**
Title: None
Height: 7 in (17.5 cm)
Colour: Well coloured.

Rarity: R.
Pair: Fig. 233 (Circus boy)
Description: Standing, wearing a four-cornered plumed hat, blouse, skirt and pantaloons. She holds a cobra in her left hand and a horn in her right hand.

Figure 235
Subject: **Stephen Collins Foster**
Title: None
Height: 8¼ in (21 cm)
Colour: Well coloured in the manner of Thomas Parr.
Maker: Thomas Parr.

Plate 119
Fig. 233 Circus boy

Fig. 235
Stephen Foster

Fig. 236 Scotsman
with harp and music

Fig. 237 Man
leaning on urn

Fig. 238 Woman
leaning on urn

In the collections of Dr S. J. Howard and the author

Plate 120
Fig. 239 Unidentified Roman woman

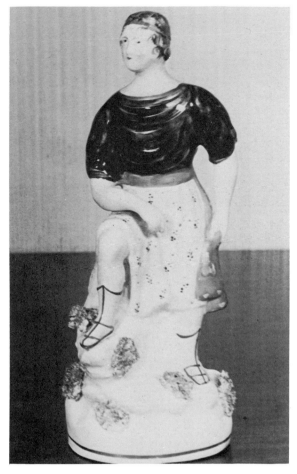

Plate 121
Fig. 240 ?Brutus

Rarity: VR.
Description: Sitting on a bank, holding a banjo in his left hand. He wears a felt hat, shirt with neckerchief, jacket and trousers. The base of the bank is inscribed obliquely in upper and lower case gilt transfer:

> I'm goin' to Alabama
> Wid my banjo on my knee;
> I come from Lousiana
> My true lub for to see
>   Oh Susanna

Observations: Almost certainly portrays Stephen Foster, the American song-writer who specialized in negro melodies.

Figure 236
Subject: **Scotsman with harp and music**
Title: None
Height: 10 in (25 cm)
Colour: Sparsely coloured.
Rarity: R.
Description: Wearing plumed bonnet, jacket with a plaid over his left shoulder, kilt and stockings. In his right hand, he holds a harp and in his left hand, some music.
Observations: Has so far defied identification.

Figure 237
Subject: **Man leaning on urn**
Title: None
Height: 7 in (17.5 cm)

Colour: Well coloured.
Rarity: R.
Pair: Fig. 238 (Woman leaning on urn)
Description: Standing bare-headed, facing half-left, in doublet and hose. He is leaning on an urn with his right elbow, and in his left hand he holds a manuscript.
Observations: Has so far defied identification.

Figure 238
Subject: **Woman leaning on urn**
Title: None
Height: 7¼ in (18.25 cm)
Colour: Well coloured.
Rarity: R.
Pair: Fig. 237 (Man leaning on urn)
Description: Standing bare-headed, in bodice and ankle-length skirt. She leans on an urn with her left elbow and in her right hand she holds what is possibly a manuscript.
Observations: Has so far defied identification.

Plate 120
Figure 239
Subject: **Unidentified Roman woman**
Title: None
Date: 185–
Height: 6½ in (16.5 cm)
Colour: Well coloured in the manner of

Thomas Parr.
Maker: Thomas Parr
Rarity: R.
Description: Standing bare-headed, her torso enclosed in a loose cloak similar to that worn by Roman ladies, *c*. 200 AD. Her arms are crossed in front of her chest, and her legs are bare.
Observations: Has so far defied identification.

Plate 121
Figure 240
Subject: **? Brutus**
Title: None
Height: 9 in (23 cm)
Colour: Well coloured.
Rarity: R.
Description: Standing, wearing a band of ribbon round his hair, tunic with a long sash round his waist and sandals of open leather work. His right foot is raised on a rock, his left arm is by his side, and his right elbow flexed at a right angle, with the forearm resting on the right knee.
Observations: It has been suggested that this figure is theatrical and portrays Mr Kean as 'Brutus' in *Julius Caesar*, I do not know the evidence in support of this claim.

E435

Plate 122
Fig. 241 The Three Graces
By courtesy of Miss M. M. Frame

Note in the foreground the ceramic watch which appears to belong to the figure. Occasional findings of this sort cast some doubt on the belief that watch-holders were intended to carry genuine watches.

Plate 123
Fig. 242 The Three Graces
By courtesy of Mr Joe Fairhurst

Plate 122
Figure 241
Subject: **The Three Graces**
Title: None
Height: 10 in (25 cm)
Colour: Well coloured.
Rarity: Av.
Description: The central theme is a watch-holder decorated in flowers. On either side it is supported by a bare-headed dancer in bodice and ankle-length skirt. In the centre a third dancer kneels with her right hand on top of her head.
Observations: There is a lithograph, after Lejeune, of 'The Three Graces' in the Print Room of the British Museum. The print represents Taglioni in *La Sylphide*, Fanny Elssler in *Le Diable Boiteux* and Grisi in *La Jolie Fille de Gând*. So far it has not been possible to positively identify the dancers portrayed in this figure.

Plate 123
Figure 242
Subject: **The Three Graces**
Title: None
Height: 9½ in (24 cm)
Colour: Well coloured.
Rarity: VR.
Description: There are three dancers in a row. Each of the two outer dancers wears a floral head-dress and calf-length dress. Each is bare-footed. The centre dancer is bare-headed but otherwise similarly dressed. Her hands are crossed across her waist and in each hand she holds a hand of one of the outer dancers. Each of their inner hands are held upwards and inwards supporting a floral garland over the head of the centre dancer.

E436

Observations: Exactly the same remarks apply here as for *fig.* 241, *pl.* E-122. This figure is very close to the lithograph after Lejeune and may well portray Taglioni, Fanny Elssler and Grisi.

Plate 124
Figure 243
Subject: **Little Red Riding Hood**
Title: None
Height: 10 in (25 cm)
Colour: Well coloured.
Rarity: C.
Description: 'Little Red Riding Hood' is seated on the right, and to her right is the wolf crouched on its two hind legs. Behind them is a tree trunk (spill-holder).
Observations: See *fig.* 246, *pl.* E-125.
Figure 244
Subject: **Little Red Riding Hood**
Title: None
Height: 7¼ in (18.25 cm)
Colour: Well coloured.
Rarity: VR.
Description: 'Little Red Riding Hood' stands on the right, in bonnet and long cloak, a basket over her left forearm. The wolf stands to her right.
Observations: 1. See *fig.* 246, *pl.* E-125.
2. This is a particularly fine piece and may well be theatrical.

Figure 245
Subject: **Little Red Riding Hood**
Title: None
Height: 15 in (38 cm); 9½ in (25 cm) version illustrated.
Colour: Contemporary copies of the large

version are well coloured. The smaller version tends to be crudely coloured.
Maker: Thomas Parr.
Rarity: VR. (large version); C. (small version).
Description: Standing wearing bonnet, cloak and long dress, a basket in her left hand, her right hand resting on the neck of a wolf.
Observations: 1. Contemporary copies of the large version are particularly fine. Copies of the small version are usually poorly modelled.
2. The large version appears in all three Kent lists as follows:

	KENT LIST A Stock No. (c. 1901)	KENT LIST B Stock No.	KENT LIST C Ref. No. (1955)
Red Riding Hood, No. 1	337	323	323

3. See *fig.* 246, *pl.* E-125.

Plate 125
Figure 246
Subject: **Little Red Riding Hood**
Title: None
Height: 9 in (23 cm)
Colour: Well coloured.
Rarity: VR.
Description: On a horse facing left, wearing cloak and ankle-length dress. She holds a basket in her left hand.
Observations: There is no horse in the story of *Little Red Riding Hood*. This suggests that the figure may be theatrical, probably circus. The story of *Little Red Riding Hood* has, of course, been dramatized on numerous occasions. It is unlikely that figures such as *fig.* 243 and *fig.* 245 are theatrical, but *fig.* 244, a particularly well executed figure, may well be so.

Plate 124
Fig. 243 Red Riding Hood
Fig. 244 Red Riding Hood
Fig. 245 Red Riding Hood
By courtesy of Miss M. M. Frame

Plate 125
Fig. 246 Red Riding Hood
By courtesy of Miss M. M. Frame

Plate 126
Fig. 247 A pair of Highland dancers
Fig. 248 Harlequin
Fig. 249 Columbine
Fig. 250 Unidentified male actor
Fig. 251 Unidentified pair of dancers

Figs. 248 and 249 are 'late'. Note the 'blotches' on the base instead of the fine 'combing' noted on contemporary figures emanating from the Thomas Parr factory.
In the collection of Messrs Raymond Mander and Joe Mitchenson

Plate 126
Figure 247
Subject: **A pair of Highland dancers**
Title: None
Height: 8 in (20.5 cm)
Colour: Well coloured.
Rarity: R.
Description: On the left is a Highlander wearing a tall plumed hat, plaid over his left shoulder, kilt and stockings. His left arm is round his partner's shoulder and he holds her left hand in his right hand. She stands to the right and is bare-headed, in bodice, knee-length skirt and bootees.
Observations: Has so far defied identification.

Figure 248
Subject: **Harlequin**
Title: None
Height: 7 in (17.5 cm)
Colour: Well coloured in the manner of Thomas Parr.
Maker: Thomas Parr
Rarity: VR. (contemporary); R. (late).
Pair: Fig. 249 (Columbine)
Description: Dressed in a close-fitting suit of bright silk diamonds, his left hand raised towards his head and his right hand on his hip.
Observations: This figure and its pair, *fig.* 249 (Columbine), are usually found in the 'late' state. Contemporary figures are extremely rare. Both appear in all three Kent lists:

	KENT LIST A Stock No. (c. 1901)	KENT LIST B Stock No.	KENT LIST C Ref. No. (1955)
Harlequin and Columbine	295	270	270

Figure 249
Subject: **Columbine**
Title: None
Height: 6¾ in (17 cm)
Colour: Well coloured in the manner of Thomas Parr.

Maker: Thomas Parr
Rarity: VR. (contemporary); R. (late).
Pair: Fig. 248 (Harlequin)
Description: Standing bare-headed, in bodice and knee-length flounced skirt. Her right hand touches her head and her left hand is held in front of her waist. Her right leg is crossed in front of her left.
Observations: See *fig.* 248 (Harlequin).

Figure 250
Subject: **Unidentified male actor**
Title: None
Height: 6½ in (16.5 cm)
Colour: Sparsely coloured.
Rarity: R.
Description: A slender figure, probably theatrical. He stands, wearing a plumed hat, long coat, shirt with neckerchief, breeches and stockings.
Observations: Has, so far, defied identification.

Figure 251
Subject: **Unidentified pair of dancers**
Title: None
Height: 6¾ in (17 cm)
Colour: Well coloured.
Rarity: R.
Description: She stands in front and to the left. She is bare headed, in bodice and skirt cut away to expose an inverted 'V' of underskirt. He stands behind and to the right. He wears a round hat, morning coat and trousers. His right hand is round her waist and her right hand is near it. Both their left arms are by the side with their hands entwined.
Observations: Nothing is known of the identity of this curious pair.

Plate 127
Figure 252
Subject: **Unidentified girl singer**
Title: None
Height: 6¾ in (17 cm)

Colour: Well coloured.
Rarity: R.
Description: Standing wearing a plumed hat, bodice, skirt, pantaloons and boots. Her left hand is on her hip and in her right hand she holds a scroll.
Observations: Probably operatic, but has so far defied identification.

Figure 253
Subject: **Woman with deer**
Title: None
Height: 8½ in (21.5 cm)
Colour: Well coloured.
Rarity: R.
Pair: Fig. 254 (Unidentified huntsman)
Description: Standing, wearing a plumed hat, bodice and flounced skirt. She holds what appears to be a dead deer underneath her right arm.
Observations: Bears a striking resemblance to *fig.* 259, *pl.* E-128. The pair may be decorative or theatrical.

Figure 254
Subject: **Unidentified huntsman**
Title: None
Height: 8¾ in (22 cm)
Colour: Well coloured.
Rarity: R.
Pair: Fig. 253 (Woman with deer)
Description: Standing, wearing a plumed bonnet, hunting jacket, waistcoat, neckerchief and trousers. He carries a bow in his right hand, and there is a horn in his belt. His left hand caresses the head of a dog.
Observations: See preceding figure.

Figure 255
Subject: **Unidentified banjo player**
Title: None
Height: 7¾ in (20 cm)
Colour: Well coloured.
Rarity: R.
Pair: Unknown

Plate 127
Fig. 252 Unidentified girl singer
Fig. 253 Woman with deer

Fig. 254 Unidentified huntsman
Fig. 255 Unidentified banjo player
Fig. 256 ?Liston (Ali Baba)

Description: Standing, wearing a tricorn hat, long coat, shirt, neckerchief, breeches and stockings, playing a banjo.
Observations: Has so far defied identification, but may well be theatrical.

Figure 256
Subject: **'Ali Baba'—? John Liston in the role**
Title: None
Date: Uncertain
Height: 7 in (17.5 cm)
Colour: Well coloured.
Rarity: R.
Pair: It is possible that a figure of 'Morgiani' will eventually turn up.
Description: Standing, wearing a turban, thigh-length robe, vest, pantaloons and Turkish shoes, a sash round his waist. His right hand is on his hip and his left hand is held forwards holding a goblet.
Observations: This figure has been identified as 'Ali Baba' in *Ali Baba and the Forty Thieves*. The principal productions were at Drury Lane (1806) with John Bannister as 'Ali Baba', and at Covent Garden (1815) with John Liston in the role.

The costume worn by 'Ali Baba' fits in very well with the description in Cumberland's *British Theatre*:

'Ali Baba's second dress, rich vest, long velvet robe trimmed with fur, white trousers, boots, turban, sash and handsomely trimmed'.

The moment portrayed is the high-spot of Scene VIII:

Hasarac (in an aside): This goblet is yet to be paid for.
Ali Baba: Come, fill it up Sir. Come, I will give you a toast that pretty near concerns me. I'll tell you why before we part. Here's confusion to the memory of the robbers in the cave. (*He says this to Hasarac, who in point of fact is a robber, but he is there under the pretence of an honest merchant. Hasarac drops dagger from sleeve in confusion at mention of robbers*).
Morgiana (aside seeing the dagger): A dagger in his sleeve! What can this mean? Allah protect us (*looking at him*). 'Tis the pretended merchant, the captain of the bandits. The dagger explains his purpose. Fairy of the lake inspire me. Ali Baba come, now for a

dance. (*Music, and Morgiana dances with a tambourine, in which imitating two or three of the passions, she prevents Hasarac's attempts to stab Ali Baba without her intention being discovered. Hasarac at length lifts up his dagger and is on the point of assassinating Ali Baba, when Morgiana seizes his arm, and in the scuffle forces the dagger into the breast of the robber, who falls and expires*).
Ali Baba: Merciful prophet, what have you done?
Morgiana: Preserved your life, destroyed the enemy. Look there, that dagger was aimed at you. Know you that face, the captain of the bandits, (*then Morgiana joyfully*) the last of all your foes.

It seems probable that this figure portrays John Liston in the 1815 production. Unfortunately, the exact print for the identification of the figure has not been found, although there are many penny plain, tuppence coloured prints of 'Ali Baba' holding up the cup. It will be recalled that 'Ali Baba' had stolen the cup by going to the cave and saying *Open Sesame*, having heard the robbers do the same thing. He then made himself into a very rich man, being finally tracked down by 'Hasarac', the captain of the bandits. It is this moment, when 'Ali Baba' lifts up the cup full of wine and gives a toast, which is the quote mentioned earlier. Figures are occasionally seen of ladies dancing with a tambourine; one might well turn out to be 'Morgiana'.

Plate 128
Figure 257
Subject: **Unidentified female dancer**
Title: None
Height: 9⅛ in (23.25 cm)
Colour: Well coloured.
Rarity: Av.
Pair: Fig. 258 (Unidentified male dancer)
Description: Standing, wearing a bonnet, bodice, knee-length skirt and pantaloons. She holds a scarf over her shoulders and in her right hand a bird. There is a cat on her left shoulder.
Observations: This figure and its pair have so far defied identification.

E439

Plate 128
Fig. 257 Unidentified female dancer
Fig. 258 Unidentified male dancer

Fig. 259 Unidentified woman
Fig. 260 Unidentified woman
Fig. 261 Unidentified brigand

Plate 128 continued
Figure 258
Subject: **Unidentified male dancer**
Title: None
Height: 9¾ in (24.5 cm)
Colour: Well coloured.
Rarity: Av.
Pair: Fig. 257 (Unidentified female dancer)
Description: Standing, wearing a plumed bonnet, vest, kilt and stockings. A scarf is draped over his shoulders, and in his left arm he holds a dog. There is a bird on his right shoulder.

Figure 259
Subject: **Unidentified woman**
Title: None
Height: 8¼ in (21 cm)
Colour: Well coloured.
Rarity: Av.
Pair: Unknown
Description: Standing, with plumed bonnet, bodice and full-length skirt, scarf over her shoulders. In her right hand, she holds a handbag and in her left, a basket of flowers.
Observations: There is a striking resemblance between this figure and *fig.* 253, *pl.* E-127. It has so far defied identification.

Figure 260
Subject: **Unidentified woman**
Title: None
Height: 9⅛ in (23.25 cm)
Colour: Well coloured.
Rarity: VR.
Pair: Unknown
Description: Standing, wearing a plumed hat, jacket, waist-sash and full-length skirt. Her left hand is by her side and in her right hand, which is held in front of her chest, she holds a rose.
Observations: Has some similarity to the lady depicted in a coloured lithograph music-front by John Brandard inscribed *Martha— Quadrille pas Chas. d'Albert*. The similarity is not close enough to be diagnostic.

Figure 261
Subject: **Unidentified brigand**
Title: None
Height: 9¼ in (23.5 cm)
Colour: Well coloured.
Rarity: R.
Description: Wearing a tall plumed hat, cloak, jacket, shirt, breeches and stockings. He holds a rifle by his side, the barrel being grasped in his left hand.
Observations: See *fig.* 265 (Unidentified brigand) *pl.* E-129.

Plate 129
Figure 262
Subject: **Pair of music-hall artists**
Title: None
Date: c. 1890
Height: 14½ in (36.75 cm)
Colour: Sparsely coloured.
Maker: In the style of Sampson Smith
Rarity: VR.
Series: It has been suggested that it forms the centrepiece for *fig.* 291 (Unidentified woman) *pl.* E-140, and its pair.
Description: They stand on a plinth decorated with a clock-face, grapes and vine leaves. The man stands on the right, wearing a bowler with low bell crown and curled brim, jacket, shirt with neckerchief, pantaloons and knee-boots. His left hand is on his hip and his right arm round her waist. The lady stands on the left, wearing a small hat, necklace, off-the-shoulder bodice, wide-flounced above-knee skirt and bootees. Her right hand is on her hip and her left arm round his waist.
Observations: A typical music-hall pair of the 1890's which has so far escaped positive identification.

Figure 263
Subject: **Unidentified polka dancers**
Title: None
Height: 14½ in (36.75 cm)

Colour: Sparsely coloured.
Rarity: R.
Description: The man stands on the left, wearing round hat, jacket, striped shirt, tunic and knee-boots. There is a sash round his waist into which are pushed two pistols. His right hand is raised to his hat and his left arm is round the lady's waist. She stands on the right, wearing a hat, bodice and wide skirt. Her left hand is raised to her head and holds a circular garland.
Observations: Has so far defied identification.

Figure 264
Subject: **Unidentified Highlander and woman**
Title: None
Height: 14½ in (36.75 cm)
Colour: Sparsely coloured.
Rarity: Av.
Description: The man stands on the left, bare-headed and holding a bonnet in his right hand. His left arm is round the lady's waist. He wears a jacket, shirt, sash round his waist, kilt and boots. She stands on the right, wearing a bodice and long flowing dress, her hands are crossed in front.
Observations: Probably theatrical, but has so far defied identification.

Figure 265
Subject: **Unidentified brigand**
Title: None
Height: 15½ in (39.25 cm)
Colour: Well coloured.
Rarity: Av.
Pair: Unknown
Description: He stands, wearing a plumed bonnet, cloak with ermine hood, jacket, tunic, sash round his waist with a pistol inserted therein, gartered stockings and shoes. His right hand is on his hip and he holds the muzzle of a rifle with his left hand.
Observations: Probably theatrical, but has so far defied identification. There is a marked

Plate 129
Fig. 262 Unidentified pair of music-hall artists
Fig. 263 Unidentified pair of polka dancers
Fig. 264 Unidentified Highlander and woman
Fig. 265 Unidentified brigand
In the collections of Messrs Raymond Mander and Joe Mitchenson and the author

resemblance between this figure and *fig.* 261, *pl.* E-128.

Plate 130
Figure 266
Subject: **Unidentified actress**
Title: None
Height: 11¾ in (29.75 cm)
Colour: Well coloured.
Maker: Possibly Alpha factory
Rarity: VR. A.
Pair: Unknown
Description: Standing bare-headed, in short jacket, calf-length dress with waist sash, Turkish trousers and slippers. Her left arm is by her side and she holds a helmet in her left hand. She clasps a posy of flowers in her right hand which she holds in front of her chest.
Observations: The head and shoulders of this figure closely resemble those of *fig.* 36 (Eliza Cook) *pl.* H-10, and the similar piece, *fig.* 114 (Unidentified actress) *pl.* E-62. The reason for this has, so far, not been determined.

The figure is probably theatrical, and may portray Maria Malibran, see *pl.* E-86, but so far no proof of this has been forthcoming.

Figure 267
Subject: **? Ali Baba**
Title: None
Height: 9¾ in (24.5 cm)
Colour: Well coloured.
Rarity: R.
Pair: Unknown
Description: Standing, wearing an oriental hat, tunic with waist-sash, pantaloons and slippers. His right hand is raised outwards, and his left arm is across his chest.
Observations: *Ali Baba and the Forty Thieves* was an extremely popular oriental tale frequently dramatized in Victorian times. This figure probably represents 'Ali Baba,'

Plate 130
Fig. 266 Unidentified actress
Fig. 267 ?Ali Baba
In the collection of Mr Ronald Shockledge

but so far the actor portraying the role, if this is in fact a portrait figure, has not been identified. See also *fig.* 256, *pl.* E-127.

Plate 131
Fig. 268 Unidentified actress
By courtesy of Mr and Mrs Eric Joyce

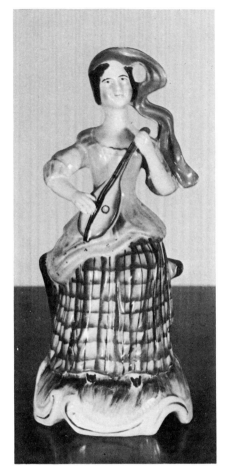

Plate 132
Fig. 269 Unidentified actress

Plate 131
Figure 268
Subject: **Unidentified actress**
Title: None
Height: 12½ in (31.75 cm)
Colour: Well coloured.
Rarity: Av.
Description: Standing, wearing a plumed hat, her hair draped down over her shoulders, scarf round her neck, short coat, blouse, waist sash and long skirt. She holds a riding crop in her left hand.
Observations: 1. This figure has been variously identified as Dorothy Vernon, 'La Zingara' and Louisa Nisbett as 'Constance' in *The Love Cause* by Sheridan Knowles. The latter seems the most probable, but is still not entirely convincing, see the engraving which appeared on *p*. 256 of *The Illustrated London News* of April 17th, 1847.
2. The one certain thing to be said is that the figure surely portrays someone. If this were not so, why are there at least two, and probably more, versions of the same figure? In the example illustrated, note that the collar of the blouse is clearly defined overlapping the scarf; in another version, the scarf appears to be in direct contact with the neck. These differences, and several others of a minor nature, are in the moulds.

Plate 132
Figure 269
Subject: **Unidentified actress**
Title: None
Height: 10½ in (26.5 cm)

Colour: Well coloured.
Rarity: R.
Pair: Not known
Description: A lady, with a flowing scarf around her head, is seated playing a banjo. She wears a blouse and tartan skirt.
Observations: Roy Johnson in *Precious Miscellany—Twopenny Ha'penny Treasures* which appeared in the *Woman's Journal* (*Antique Supplement*) stated that this figure may be 'Jenny Lind with a tartan compliment to Queen Victoria'.

However, there is no evidence that Jenny Lind ever played the banjo, and no print has come to light, to my knowledge, to support this view.

Plate 133
Figure 50
Subject: **Unidentified man, woman and child**
Title: None
Height: 9½ in (24 cm)
Colour: Well coloured.
Rarity: R.
Description: A young woman stands on the left and a young man on the right; between them they support a child on their shoulders. The woman is bare-headed, with bodice, skirt and pantaloons. The man is bare-headed with a long coat and trousers. The child, who has one hand on the girl's head and one hand on the man's head, is bare-headed with shirt and kilt, bare-legs and no pantaloons. There is little doubt it is a boy.
Observations: This figure is reminiscent of

those portraying Miss Glover and Mrs Vining (see *figs*. 47, 48 and 49, *pl*. E-24) but is unlikely to be related, for no male child appeared in *Peter Wilkins*.

Figure 270
Subject: **A group of the MacDonalds of Glencoe**
Title: None
Height: 10¼ in (25.75 cm)
Colour: Well coloured.
Rarity: Av.
Description: To the left, is a Highlander wearing bonnet, jacket, kilt and stockings. In his right hand he carries what appears to be a club, and his right arm is raised in the act of defence. By his right leg is a dog. To his left, is a woman wearing a bonnet, bodice and skirt and in her arms she carries a child.
Observations: 1. When this figure was sold at Christie's in October 1964, it was described as 'A group of the MacDonalds of Glencoe, MacIan defending his wife and child from the Campbells'. The lot, consisting of this figure and another unimportant piece, fetched 16 guineas.
2. The group is probably not theatrical.
3. There is said to be an engraving of this event upon which the figure is based, but I have not seen it.

Figure 271
Subject: **Unidentified girl and musician on couch**
Title: None
Height: 10¼ in (25.75 cm)
Colour: Well coloured.
Rarity: Av.
Pair: There is a 'matching' pair to this figure.
Description: He kneels on the right, wearing a plumed hat, jacket, coat, tunic and knee-boots. He holds a fiddle in his left hand and his right hand is round the waist of the girl, who sits to his right. She is bare-headed, wearing a bodice and skirt. A bird sits on the arm of the settee.
Observations: Almost certainly a theatrical piece, but it has so far defied identification.

Figure 272
Subject: **A pair of unidentified dancers**
Title: None
Height: 11½ in (29 cm)
Colour: Well coloured.
Rarity: Av.
Description: She stands on the left, and he on the right. She is bare-headed, wearing bodice and broad knee-length skirt, a scarf passes from the top of her head (being held there by her right hand), behind her back and to the front of her skirt (being held there by her left hand). He is bare-headed, with shirt, pantaloons and knee-boots; his right hand is in front of his right thigh and his left hand, holding a mask, is raised above his head.
Observations: Has so far defied identification.

Figure 273
Subject: **Pair of unidentified dancers**
Title: None
Height: 10½ in (26.5 cm)
Colour: Well coloured.
Rarity: R.
Description: He stands on the left, wearing a plumed steeple hat, ermine-edged cloak, jacket, breeches and stockings. She stands on the right, holding his left hand in her right hand, and with her left hand on her hip.

Section E. Theatre, Opera, Ballet and Circus

Plate 133
T: *Fig.* 270 A group of the MacDonalds of Glencoe
Fig. 271 Unidentified girl and musician on a couch
Fig. 272 Pair of unidentified dancers

B: *Fig.* 50 Unidentified man, woman and child
Fig. 273 Pair of unidentified dancers
Fig. 274 Unidentified man
Fig. 275 Unidentified man
By courtesy of
Mr and Mrs Eric Joyce

She wears a bodice and wide knee-length skirt.
Observations: This figure has so far defied identification.

Figure 274
Subject: **Unidentified man**
Title: None
Height: $11\frac{1}{4}$ in (28.5 cm)
Colour: Well coloured.
Rarity: Av.
Pair: Unknown
Description: Standing, wearing a plumed hat, ermine-edged cloak draped over his left shoulder, tunic, breeches and knee-boots. A dog, standing on its hind legs, is leaning against his right leg, and he strokes its head with his right hand.
Observations: Has so far defied identification.

Figure 275
Subject: **Unidentified man**
Title: None
Height: $11\frac{1}{4}$ in (28.5 cm)
Colour: Well coloured.
Rarity: Av.

Pair: Unknown
Description: Standing, wearing a plumed hat, jacket, breeches, stockings and knee-boots. To his left, is a spring issuing from a rock, beneath which is a jug. His left hand rests on a rock.
Observations: Has so far defied identification.

Plate 134
Figure 276
Subject: **Unidentified child actor**
Title: None
Height: 5 in (12.75 cm)
Colour: Well coloured.
Rarity: R.
Pair: Unknown
Description: Standing bare-headed, in Roman tunic, scabbard suspended from his waist, a shield in his left hand and a hole for a sword in his right hand.
Observations: It has been suggested that this figure portrays Master Betty (1791–1874). There are, however, numerous other possibilities, and the figure has so far defied positive identification. It might possibly be a child actor portraying 'Tom Thumb.'

E443

Plate 134 continued
Figure 277
Subject: **Masaniello and Fenella**
Title: None
Height: 8 in (20.5 cm)
Colour: Well coloured.
Rarity: R.
Description: 'Fenella' is seated on the left, her left hand is held out and there are coins in it. There are also coins on her lap. She is bare-headed, wearing bodice and long skirt. 'Masaniello' stands on the right, wearing a loose cap, short coat, shirt, neckerchief, tunic

and thigh-boots. There is a pistol in his belt and a barrel between his legs. His right hand is held facing backwards as in 'receiving a tip'. Inkwell.
Observations: There is little doubt that this figure portrays 'Fenella' and 'Masaniello', as will be appreciated by comparing it with the titled piece, *fig.* 221, *pl.* E-111.

Figure 278
Subject: **Unidentified actor**
Title: None
Height: 5½ in (14 cm)

Colour: Well coloured.
Rarity: R.
Pair: *Fig.* 279 (Unidentified actress)
Description: Standing bare-headed, wearing cravat, morning coat and trousers. His right hand is on a pedestal and his left hand on his hip.
Observations: It has been suggested that this figure portrays Charles Mathews the younger, husband of Madame Vestris. The only evidence of which I know, in support of this, is that it is a pair to *fig.* 279, which is thought to portray Madame Vestris.

Figure 279
Subject: **Unidentified actress**
Title: None
Height: 5½ in (14 cm)
Colour: Well coloured.
Rarity: R.
Pair: Fig. 278 (Unidentified actor)
Description: Standing bare-headed, in bodice and ankle-length skirt. Her right hand is held up towards her chest and her left arm is by her side. She holds a book in her left hand.
Observations: Has always been thought to portray Madame Vestris, although I do not know on what grounds. Because of this its pair, *fig.* 278, is considered likely to portray her husband, Charles Mathews the younger.
2. A similar pair of figures fetched 34 gns at Christie's in 1965.

Plate 135
Figure 280
Subject: **Unidentified brigand**
Title: None
Height: 8¼ in (21 cm)
Colour: Well coloured.
Rarity: R.
Pair: Appears to belong to the same series as *fig.* 161 (Unidentified male opera singer) *pl.* E-81.
Description: Standing, wearing plumed hat, cloak, coat, breeches and knee-boots. In his right hand he holds what appears to be a

scroll, but the hand has been restored and I have not seen an unrestored version.
Observations: As noted, this figure appears to belong to the same series as *fig.* 161, *pl.* E-81, but so far no pair has been found to it. It bears a striking resemblance, also, to *fig.* 287(*a*) (? 'Conrad') *pl.* E-140. It is almost certainly theatrical, but has so far defied positive identification.

Plate 136
Figure 281
Subject: **Unidentified actor**
Title: None
Height: 7¼ in (18.25 cm)
Colour: Well coloured.
Rarity: R.
Pair: Unknown
Description: Standing, wearing a plumed hat, cloak, gauntlets, breeches and knee-boots. Scroll in his right hand. Shaped base.
Observations: Clearly theatrical, but has so far defied identification.

Plate 137
Figure 282
Subject: **Unidentified girl**
Title: None
Height: 7 in (17.5 cm)
Colour: Well coloured.
Rarity: R.

Description: Standing, wearing bonnet, blouse, knee-length skirt and stockings, holding a skipping rope in both hands.
Observations: Probably a decorative figure only.

Figure 283
Subject: **Unidentified girl**
Title: None
Height: 6¼ in (16 cm)
Colour: Well coloured.
Rarity: R.
Pair: Unknown
Description: Standing, wearing a plumed bonnet, bodice, calf-length skirt; her left hand on her hip, her right hand held forwards. A dancing pose. Hollow base.
Observations: Has so far defied identification.

Figure 284
Subject: **Unidentified girl**
Title: None
Height: 6¾ in (17 cm)
Colour: Well coloured.
Rarity: R.
Pair: Unknown
Description: Standing, wearing a plumed hat, bodice and ankle-length skirt. There is a sash over her right shoulder and she holds what is possibly a manuscript in her left hand.
Observations: Has so far defied identification.

Plate 137
Fig. 282 Unidentified girl

Fig. 283 Unidentified girl

Fig. 284 Unidentified girl
By courtesy of Mr John Hall

Plate 138
Fig. 285 Unidentified pair of musicians

Fig. 286 Unidentified pair of musicians

Plate 138
Figure 285
Subject: **Unidentified pair of musicians**
Title: None
Height: 16½ in (41.5 cm)
Colour: Well coloured.
Rarity: Av.
Description: He stands on the left and she on the right. Both are dressed as gypsies. He holds a concertina above his head, and she holds an ornate harp to her left.
Observations: Almost certainly based on a print which has so far not come to light.

Figure 286
Subject: **Unidentified pair of musicians**
Title: None
Height: 15¼ in (38.5 cm)
Colour: Well coloured.
Rarity: Av.
Description: She stands on the left, and he stands on the right. Both are wearing gypsy costume. She holds an ornate harp to her left, it being balanced on a wall, and he holds an accordion to his left.
Observations: Almost certainly based on a print which has so far not come to light.

Plate 139
Figure 287
Subject: **? Conrad**
Title: None
Height: 9 in (23 cm). There are two smaller versions of this figure:
Fig. 287(*a*), *pl.* E-140: 7¼ in (18.25 cm);
fig. 287(*b*), *pl.* E-139: 6⅛ in (15.5 cm).
Colour: Well coloured.
Rarity: Fig. 287: VR. D. A.; *fig.* 287(*a*): C.; *fig.* 287(*b*): Av.

Description: Standing, facing to the right, with his head turned to his right. He is wearing a plumed hat (or turban), doublet and hose and calf-boots. His left arm points forward and he grasps a scroll in his left hand; his right hand is by his side and in it he grasps a cylindrical object, possibly a telescope or alternatively, a case for the scroll. His left knee is bent, with his foot resting on a rock. In both the smaller versions, the left arm is by his side.
Observations: Until very recently only the two smaller versions were recorded. They were generally thought to represent 'Conrad', a pirate chief in the Aegean Sea, the hero of Byron's poem *The Corsair*, first published in 1814 and subsequently dramatized. However, I do not know on what evidence this identification was based. The recently discovered large figure is of superb quality, and obviously portrays the same subject. Underneath the example illustrated was an old label which identified the piece as *Edmund Kean as Richard the Third after a print by Kennedy in the Brighton Theatre*. Enquiry at the Theatre Royal, Brighton disclosed that there was a print there of *Edmund Kean as Richard the Third*, published by M. & M. Skelt, 18 Swan Street, Minories, London. No. 31. This print has some resemblance, especially with regard to dress and the objects carried in the hands, but the pose is entirely different. The identification of all three figures really remains unsolved.

Plate 140
Figure 6(a), *pl.* D-3A
Subject: **Unidentified Quaker**
Observations: See section D.

Figure 287(a)
Subject: **? Conrad**
Observations: See *pl.* E-139.

Figure 288
Subject: **Unidentified man and woman**
Title: None
Height: 8 in (20.5 cm)
Colour: Well coloured.
Rarity: Av.
Description: He stands on the left, bareheaded, in thigh-length coat, breeches and knee-boots. In his right hand he holds a posy and his left arm is round her neck. She sits on the right, wearing bodice with long sleeves and full-length skirt. She holds some flowers in both hands.
Observations: Probably theatrical, but has not been identified to date.

Figure 289
Subject: **Unidentified man with mask**
Title: None
Height: 7½ in (19 cm)
Colour: Well coloured.
Rarity: R.
Pair: Unknown
Description: Standing, wearing a round hat, tunic, breeches and stockings. His left hand is on his hip and his right hand by his side. He holds a mask in his right hand, and his right leg is crossed in front of his left.
Observations: Almost certainly theatrical, but has so far defied identification.

Figure 290
Subject: **Unidentified man**
Title: None
Height: 7½ in (19 cm)
Colour: Largely white and gilt.

Plate 139
Fig. 287(b) ?Conrad   Fig. 287 ?Conrad

Plate 140
By courtesy of Mr and Mrs Eric Joyce

T: Fig. 288 Unidentified man and woman
Fig. 287(a) ?Conrad
Fig. 6(a) (section D) Unidentified quaker
Fig. 289 Unidentified man with mask
Fig. 290 Unidentified man
B: Fig. 291 Unidentified woman
Fig. 293 Female middle eastern musician
Fig. 294 Male middle eastern musician
Fig. 295 Unidentified man and woman

Rarity: VR.
Pair: Unknown
Description: Standing bare-headed, with long drooping moustache, morning coat, waistcoat and trousers. He holds a top hat in his right hand and his left hand rests on a pedestal.
Observations: Not likely to be theatrical. It is possibly a politician, but it has so far defied identification.

Figure 291
Subject: **Unidentified woman**
Title: None
Height: 14½ in (36.75 cm)
Colour: Sparsely coloured.
Rarity: R.
Pair: There is almost certainly a pair to this figure; *fig*. 292 has been reserved for it. It has been suggested that *fig*. 262, *pl*. E-129 forms a centrepiece, but I have no evidence to support this.
Description: Standing in front of a brick wall with a bridge and small stream. She wears a plumed hat, off-the-shoulder bodice, flounced knee-length skirt and bootees and is playing a fiddle.
Observations: Probably a music-hall star of the late Victorian era.

Figure 293
Subject: **Female Middle Eastern musician**
Title: None
Height: 11½ in (29 cm)
Colour: Well coloured.
Maker: Possibly John (& Rebecca) Lloyd, Shelton
Rarity: VR.
Pair: Fig. 294 (Male Middle Eastern musician)

Description: Standing, wearing oriental head-dress, full-length ermine-edged gown, calf-length skirt and pantaloons. There is a sash round her waist and a violin by her left side.
Observations: 1. This figure and its pair have been variously identified. They have been described (Christie's, 1965) as 'Mr Wood and Rebecca Paton as "Atabarnes" and "Mandane", in *Artaxerxes*'. Alternatively, it has been suggested that they portray Mr Sinclair and Rebecca Paton in the same opera. The former suggestion seems the more likely. Another suggestion is that they portray characters in *Ali Baba and the Forty Thieves*. Mr Bryan Latham (1955) thought that they portrayed the Inca prince 'Rolla' and the singing girl 'Elvira', from the drama *Pizarro* first produced at Drury Lane in 1799, with Kemble and Mrs Siddons in these parts.
2. There are a number of versions of this figure. Perhaps the best is *fig*. 296, *pl*. E-141, which is impressed 'Lloyd/Shelton'.

Figure 294
Subject: **Male Middle Eastern musician**
Title: None
Height: 12 in (30.5 cm)
Colour: Well coloured.
Maker: Possibly John (& Rebecca) Lloyd, Shelton
Rarity: VR.
Pair: Fig. 293 (Female Middle Eastern musician)
Description: Standing, wearing oriental head-dress, full-length ermine-edged cloak, tunic and pantaloons. There is a sash round his waist. His left arm is by his side and his right arm across his chest. There are holes in both the hands, presumably for supporting

Plate 141
Fig. 296 Female middle eastern musician
The base of the figure illustrated is impressed 'Lloyd/Shelton'.

E447

Plate 142
Fig. 298 Two middle eastern musicians

Fig. 299 Unidentified middle eastern gentleman
In the collection of Mr Ronald Shockledge

Plate 140 continued
some sort of musical instrument.
Observations: See preceding figure.

Figure 295
Subject: **Unidentified man and woman**
Title: None
Height: 14½ in (36.75 cm)
Colour: Sparsely coloured.
Rarity: Av.
Description: She stands on the left, and he on the right. He has his right arm round her waist. She is bare-headed, wears jacket and full-length dress, and holds a violin by her right side. He wears a coat, waistcoat, breeches and knee-boots and is also bare-headed.
Observations: Probably theatrical.

Plate 141
Figure 296
Subject: **Female Middle Eastern musician**
Title: None
Height: 13¼ in (33.5 cm)
Colour: Well coloured. The blue differs somewhat from the classical cobalt blue.
Maker: John (& Rebecca) Lloyd, Shelton
Rarity: VR. D. A.
Pair: There must be a pair to this figure, for which *fig.* 297 has been reserved, but I have not seen it.
Description: Identical in all respects to *fig.* 293, *pl.* E-140 except that it is taller (owing to minor differences in the base) and there is a hole in the top of the turban (presumably for a feather to be inserted). The base of the figure illustrated is impressed 'LLOYD / SHELTON', see ch. 2.
Observations: See *fig.* 293 (Female Middle Eastern musician) *pl.* E-140.

Plate 142
Figure 298
Subject: **Two Middle Eastern musicians**
Title: None
Height: 11¼ in (28.5 cm)

Colour: Well coloured.
Rarity: R.
Description: Two musicians dressed in Middle Eastern head-dress and robes are seated on a cushion at the entrance of what appears to be a tent. The tent is decorated with a clock-face. The musician on the right is playing a violin.
Observations: Probably theatrical.

Figure 299
Subject: **Unidentified Middle Eastern gentleman**
Title: None
Height: 10½ in (26.5 cm)
Rarity: R.
Pair: There is a pair to this figure, a lady in Middle Eastern costume (*fig.* 300).
Description: Standing, wearing a turban, full-length gown and tunic with Turkish slippers.
Observations: Probably theatrical, but may be religious.

Plate 143
Figure 301
Subject: **Mr Falahaa**
Title: Mr Falahaa (gilt capitals)
Height: 10 in (25 cm)
Colour: Well coloured.
Rarity: VR.
Description: Dancing the 'Highland fling'. He is wearing a plumed bonnet, shirt, plaid over his left shoulder, kilt and sporran. There is a medal on the left breast immediately below the cross sash. His left leg has been amputated and he is wearing a peg leg.
Observations: Many enquiries have been made about this figure and to date it remains unidentified. A Scottish mendicant, wearing a peg leg and playing bag-pipes is known to pair at least two untitled pre-Victorian versions of 'Billy Waters'. Other pre-Victorian figures of 'Billy Waters' pair 'African Sall', see *pl.* E-36. Although 'Billy

Waters' and 'African Sall' are referred to in Pierce Egan's *Tom & Jerry*, there is no mention of a 'Mr Falahaa' in this work. Enquiries have been made of the Royal Scottish Museum, Edinburgh; the National Museum of Antiquities, Scotland and the National Portrait Gallery. The general consensus of opinion is that the figure portrays a now forgotten Scottish music-hall star. I am grateful to Mr Jack House of Glasgow for the following note:

'There was a peg-legged beggar named "Hawkie", but he certainly didn't wear the kilt. There was also, around 1800–10, an idiot boy called "Feea", who did wear the kilt but had not a peg leg . . . If he (Mr Falahaa) existed, he might well be one of the itinerant Scots who went to England because the money was better there. The word "Falahaa" seems to me to be some kind of corruption of the Gaelic. I must say, though, that I have never come across any case of a man with a peg leg wearing the kilt and I feel that this is the kind of thing a Mr. Falahaa type might get away with in England but not in Scotland.'

Plate 144
Figure 302
Subject: **Robinson Crusoe**
Title: None
Height: 6 in (15.25 cm)
Colour: Well coloured.
Rarity: Av.
Pair: Fig. 303 ('Man Friday')
Description: Standing bearded, with his hands clasped in front of his waist, wearing goat-skin hat, long goat-skin coat, trousers and shoes. He wears a belt round his waist and has a strap over his left shoulder from which an axe is suspended over his back. There is a horn tucked under his left arm. A gun is propped up against a rock to his left and there is a dead bird on the ground to his right. Hollow base. Both porcelaneous and earthenware versions have been noted.
Observations: See next figure.

Plate 143
Fig. 301 Mr Falahaa
By courtesy of The Director, the Laing Art Gallery and Museum, Newcastle upon Tyne; formerly in the collection of the late Lady Lucy Wise

Plate 144
By courtesy of Oliver Sutton Antiques

Fig. 302 Robinson Crusoe

Fig. 303 Man Friday

Figure 303
Subject: **Man Friday**
Title: None
Height: 6 in (15.25 cm)
Colour: Well coloured.
Rarity: VR.
Pair: *Fig.* 302 ('Robinson Crusoe')
Description: A bare-footed black man standing, wearing a turban, goat-skin jacket, and knee-length pantaloons. A quiver containing arrows is suspended from a strap over his right shoulder and he holds a dead kid under his right arm. There is a bow on the ground to his right. Hollow base. Both porcelaneous and earthenware versions have been noted.
Observations: *The Life and strange surprising Adventures of Robinson Crusoe*, a romance by Daniel Defoe, first published in 1719, was based on the real-life story of Alexander Selkirk (1676–1721), son of a shoemaker of Largo, who ran away to sea and after a quarrel with his captain was, at his own request, put ashore on the uninhabited island of Juan Fernandez, in 1704. He remained there until rescued, in 1709. The story has been dramatized on many occasions but the figures have not been shown to be theatrical portraits so far, although they may well be so.

Plate 145
Figure 304
Subject: **Mrs F. E. Fitzwilliam as 'Mistress Page'**
Title: None
Height: $8\frac{5}{8}$ in (21.75 cm)
Colour: Well coloured.
Rarity: VR.
Description: Standing, wearing a round plumed hat decorated with a series of triangles under the brim, bodice, and overskirt revealing an inverted 'V' of underskirt, her right hand across her waist.

Plate 145
L: *Fig.* 304 Mrs Fitzwilliam ('Mrs Page')
R: Engraving from Tallis' *Shakespeare Gallery* of Mrs Fitzwilliam as 'Mrs Page'
Note: This is the only example of the figure known to me and unfortunately her left arm is missing. On the basis of the engraving it is assumed that the arm will be found to be outstretched with a letter grasped in her hand.
Figure: By courtesy of Paul and Dorothy Stockman
Engraving: By courtesy of the Librarian, Finsbury Public Library

Plate 145 continued

Observations: 1. Almost certainly based on the engraving by J. Sherratt from a daguerreotype by Mayall, published in Tallis' *Shakespeare Gallery* (1852–3), which is inscribed: *Mrs FITZWILLIAM as Mrs PAGE.*

'What! have I scap'd love-letters in the holiday time of my beauty and am I now a subject for them? Let me see'.

MERRY WIVES OF WINDSOR
Act 2 Sc 1

Note in particular the similarity of hat design.
2. The only recorded example of this figure is that illustrated. Unfortunately the left arm is missing. However, it may be assumed reasonably that in an undamaged version it will be found outstretched with a letter clasped in the hand, as in the Tallis engraving.
3. Although its source is Tallis' *Shakespeare Gallery*, or the original daguerreotype, the figure is not decorated in the manner of Thomas Parr. There is no clue in the decoration of the factory from which it emanated.

Plate 146
Figure 305
Subject: **Girl on a tight-rope—? Louisa Woolford**
Title: None
Height: 12 in (30.5 cm)
Colour: Well coloured.
Rarity: VR. A.
Description: She stands on a tight-rope with her legs crossed, a flag in her right hand and her left hand on her hip. She is wearing a bonnet, jacket, blouse, skirt and bootees. Behind the tight-rope is a brick wall and on either side, flags.
Observations: An attractive piece, almost certainly 'circus'. It may well portray Miss Louisa Woolford, Ducrow's second wife, and leading tight-rope performer. Brought up to be both wire-walker and trick-rider, she danced on the back of a horse as it circled, as confidently as if she had the power to float on air. She was the prototype of all equestrian *ballerine*. Dickens described the thrill of her.

Plate 147
Figure 306
Subject: **Unidentified man and woman**
Title: None
Height: 7½ in (19 cm)
Colour: Well coloured.
Rarity: VR.
Description: The girl stands on the left, bare-headed, wearing blouse and flounced skirt. The man stands behind and to the right, bare-headed, wearing coat, waistcoat, breeches, stockings and shoes.
2. This figure has been said to be based on a Baxter print (used as an illustration for music) portraying Jenny Lind in *The Daughter of the Regiment*.

I have only been able to find a record of one portrait by Baxter of Jenny Lind in this role, published July 19th, 1856. She is wearing a bright red skirt and blue jacket, and is marching, hat in hand, at the head of the troops. If the figure portrays Jenny Lind, then presumably, it portrays her as 'Marie' in Act II (music-room scene) and the man is the Duke of Crackenthorp whom she was being compelled to marry. However, the dress is not the same, as she wore in this scene (compare with *fig.* 160, *pl.* E-81).

Plate 148
Figure 307
Subject: **Maria Malibran**
Title: None
Date: c. 1836
Height: 7¼ in (18.25 cm)
Colour: Well coloured. None of the three examples known to me are decorated in underglaze blue. (cf. Balston's *Supplement* (1963), *p.* 5)
Rarity: VR. D. A.
Description: Sitting bare-headed, on a one-ended sofa. She wears a low-necked, full-sleeved, and full-skirted dress. In her right hand, she holds a small open book on her lap. Oblong base.

Observations: 1. Based on an engraving for the *Dramatic Magazine* after A. M. Huffam by J. Rogers inscribed MME *MALIBRAN GARCIA* (see *pl.* A-3).

2. This figure has been identified in the past as portraying the authoress Letitia Elizabeth Landon; and later, on the discovery of *fig.* 2, *pl.* A-2 as Queen Victoria herself. In 1968, Mr Anthony Oliver drew my attention to the engraving of Maria Malibran. This threw doubt on the earlier identifications. Confirmation that this figure is indeed a portrait of Maria Malibran came early in 1969 with the discovery of the titled figure (*fig.* 308).

Plate 149
Figure 308
Subject: **Maria Malibran**
Title: Malibran (indented capitals on plaque)
Date: c. 1836
Height: 9¼ in (23.5 cm)
Colour: Well coloured
Rarity: VR. D. A.
Description: Sitting bare-headed, on a one-ended sofa. She wears a low-necked, full-sleeved, and full-skirted dress. In her right hand, she holds a small open book on her lap. The base of the figure is in the style of Obadiah Sherratt.
Observations: 1. Based on an engraving for the *Dramatic Magazine* after A. M. Huffam by J. Rogers inscribed MME *MALIBRAN GARCIA* (see *pl.* A-3).
2. Maria Malibran died in 1836. Shortly after the accession of the young Queen on June 20th, 1837, the figure was modified (by the addition of a crown) and retitled 'Her Majesty, Queen Victoria,' (see *pl.* A-2).
3. This figure fetched 500 gns at Christie's in 1969.

Plate 146
Fig. 305 Girl on a tight-rope — ?Louisa Woolford
In the collection of Mr David Robinson

Plate 147
Fig. 306 Unidentified man and woman
By courtesy of Mr Geoffrey Godden

Plate 148
Fig. 307 Malibran

Plae 149
Fig. 308 Malibran
By courtesy of Messrs Christie, Manson and Woods

Section F
Sport
Biographies and Historical Notes

ARCHER, FREDERICK (1857–86), champion jockey. Apprenticed to Matthew Dawson the Newmarket trainer in 1867. He rode his first race in 1870. In a remarkable career which included winning the Derby five times, the Oaks four, the St. Leger six, the Two Thousand Guineas five and the One Thousand Guineas twice he had, in all 2,746 mounts. He was a big man and his great problem was weight reduction during the racing season. Whilst suffering from temporary insanity he shot himself at Newmarket.
See **pls. F-**7, 11, 13.

BOX, THOMAS (1809–76), cricketer. He played for Sussex, his native county and was a constant member of William Clarke's *All England XI*. He was the most celebrated wicket-keeper of his time.
See **pls. F-**1, 2, 3.

CAESAR, JULIUS (dates unknown), cricketer. He played for Surrey for many years, and also in William Clarke's *All England XI* from 1849 to 1857, and subsequently until 1867, under Parr. He was a renowned batsman and went with Parr's teams to America and Australia.
See **pls. F-**6, 7.

CAUNT, BENJAMIN (1815–61), champion prizefighter. The son of a servant of Lord Byron, at Newstead. After beating William Thompson, in 1838, was styled 'champion'. Became 'champion of England' after beating John Leechman ('Brassey'), in 1840. Visited the United States. Subsequently ran a public-house in London.
See **pl. F-**13.

CLARKE, WILLIAM (1798–1856), cricketer. Born at Nottingham, he originated, in 1846, the celebrated 'All England' matches and became captain of the renowned XI which used to tour the country playing against odds. Five feet, nine inches in height and weighing thirteen stone, eleven pounds, he was the greatest lob bowler of all time. In 1852, Felix published a little book entitled *How to Play Clarke, Being an Attempt to Unravel the Mysteries of the Ball and show what defence and hitting are to be employed against this Celebrated Bowler*. No other bowler has ever been paid such a compliment as this.
See **pls. F-**1, 3.

CRIBB, TOM (1781–1848), champion prizefighter. He was born at Bitton, Gloucestershire. His first public contest, in 1805, ended in victory after seventy-six rounds. He was subsequently taken in hand by the well-known sportsman Captain Barclay-Allardice. There followed a meteoric rise to pugilistic stardom. He twice defeated Jem Belcher, and the American negro Molineaux. He was 'champion of England' from 1808 to 1824, and retired unbeaten to be a London publican. He guarded the entrance to Westminster Abbey at the coronation of George IV.
See **pl. F-**12.

GRAPPLERS: In an ancient Scandinavian form of duel, known as *Baeltespaennare*, the combatants, who were usually motivated by jealousy, were stripped and bound together by a leather belt. They fought to the death with short-bladed knives. *The Grapplers*, a large statue in bronzed-zinc, modelled by J. P. Molin, was lent by Sweden to the London International Exhibition of 1862 and attracted considerable attention. The statue now stands in front of the National Museum in Stockholm.
See **pl. F-**7.

HEENAN, JOHN CARMEL (1835–73), American prizefighter, otherwise known as 'The Benicia Boy'. Born in New York State, he married Adah Menken in 1859. The marriage was dissolved two years later and appears in any event to have been illegal. On April 17th, 1860, he fought Tom Sayers at Farnborough, this being the most savage fisted battle of the nineteenth century. It ended in a draw, both fighters being awarded a champion's belt.

Upon the seventeenth day of April,
  All in the morning soon,
The Yankee and the champion Sayers
  Prepared to meet their doom.

They fought like lions in the ring,
  Both men did boldly stand,
They two hours and six minutes fought,
  And neither beat his man.

Tom hit at the Benicia boy
  Right well you may suppose,
Heenan returned the compliment
  Upon the champion's nose.

Like two game cocks they stood the test,
  And each to win did try,
'Erin-go-bragh', cried Heenan,
  'I will conquer, lads, or die'.

Cried Sayers, 'I will not give in,
  Nor to a Yankee yield,
The belt I mean to keep my boys,
  Or die upon the field'.

Two long hours and six minutes
  They fought, and the claret flew
Sayers proved himself a brick, so did
  Yankee doodle doo.

The bets did fly about, my boys,
  And numbers looked with joy
On Sayers, the British champion,
  And the bold Benicia boy.

At length bounced in the peelers,
  And around the ring did jog,
So those heroes were surrounded
  By a lot of Hampshire hogs.

Who caused them to cut their stick,
  And from the fight refrain,
That they were both determined
  In the ring to meet again.

And when two heroes fight again,
  For honour and for wealth,
He that's the best man in the ring,
  Shall carry off the belt.

See **pls. F-**7, 7A, 7B, **Menken, Adah Isaacs** (section E) and **Sayers, Tom**.

LILLYWHITE, FREDERICK WILLIAM (1792–1854), a Sussex bricklayer who in middle life became a professional cricketer. He first played at Lords in 1827 and became the foremost bowler in the round-arm style, legalised by the M.C.C. in 1828. He described cricket as 'Me bowling, Pilch batting and Box keeping wicket'. Was a member of William Clarke's *All England XI*. After more than twenty brilliant seasons in cricket, he died of cholera in 1854.
See **pls. F-**1, 2.

MASTER M'GRATH (c. 1866–71), a black greyhound, belonging to Lord Lurgan. Won the blue ribbon of the coursing world, the Waterloo Cup in 1868, 1869 and 1871. By this feat, which coursing writers unanimously pronounced him incapable of, *Master M'Grath* stamped himself as the most remarkable greyhound ever put into the slips. *The Illustrated London News* of March 11th, 1871 reported that 'His speed was terrific and his cleverness and killing powers equal to it; indeed, he never gave any of his opponents a chance'.
  His owner received the Queen's command to take him to Windsor for her inspection. He became 'the most famous dog that ever lived. His name was known in the humblest cottage, his deeds were celebrated in song and ballad, his picture was to be seen everywhere' (*Country Life*: February 9th, 1956).
See **pl. F-**7.

MOLINEAUX, TOM (1784–1818), American negro prizefighter. The son of a slave on a Virginian cotton plantation. Fought in England early in the nineteenth century.

On May 22nd, 1811, he knocked out Rimmer, but in the following September he was knocked out by Tom Cribb. In a return fight he again suffered defeat. He died penniless in Ireland.
See **pl.** F-12 (text only).

PARR, GEORGE (1826–91), cricketer. Born at Radcliffe, near Nottingham. Played for Nottinghamshire from 1846 to 1870. Captain of the *All England XI* from 1857 to 1870, having succeeded William Clarke. Followed Pilch as the greatest batsman of his age—'his name was on the lips of every player for twenty years'. Five feet, nine inches in height with fringe beard and square face.
See **pls.** F-6, 7.

PILCH, FULLER (1803–70), cricketer. A Norfolk man who played for Kent from 1836 to 1854. For a long period, he was regarded as the best batsman in the game. He was six feet in height, with a tremendous reach, which he further increased by designing a bat of regulation length but with a short handle and long blade.
See **pls.** F-1, 2, 3.

PRETENDER, a light brown greyhound belonging to Mr Punchard. Was defeated by *Master M'Grath* in the Waterloo Cup of 1871.
See **pl.** F-7.

SAYERS, TOM (1826–65), prizefighter. Born in Pimlico, he started life as a bricklayer. He fought his first fight in 1849, and was only beaten once thereafter. Champion of England in 1857. On April 17th, 1860, he partook in the most famous barefist fight of the nineteenth century. Although only a middle-weight, he was matched against John Carmel Heenan 'The Benicia Boy', the greatest American heavy-weight since Tom Molineaux. The fight, which took place at Farnborough, aroused intense public interest, being attended by over 12,000 spectators. Sayers, who scaled 10 stone, 10 pounds and stood 5 feet, 8 inches, gave 3 stone and was 6 inches shorter than Heenan. In the fourth round Sayers dislocated his right arm, which remained useless for the remainder of the fight. Although outclassed physically, he continued to hold his own against Heenan by superb courage and footwork. The fight lasted for two hours and six minutes and ended after thirty-seven rounds in a draw, by which time the American's face had been terribly savaged and he was virtually blind, and the Englishman had been knocked down on numerous occasions. The verdict was thought to be well merited, and the champion's belt was awarded to each contestant. Sayers retired after this fight and refused to accept Heenan's challenge. He died later from tuberculosis; the public subscribing £3,000 for his dependants.
See **pls.** F-7, 7A, 7B.

TRAVIS, ELIZABETH, the title on a greyhound which has proved an insolvable problem. A perusal of the appropriate registers has failed to reveal a greyhound of this name during the period in question. The title probably refers to the owner of the hound. Only one such figure is known.
See **pl.** F-10.

VOLUNTEER RIFLES.
For details see **section C.**
See **pl.** C-93,
pls. F-5, 5A.

WEBB, MATTHEW (1848–83), captain in the mercantile marine. On August 25th, 1875, he became the first man to swim the Channel without a life-jacket, accomplishing the feat from Dover to Calais in twenty-one hours, forty-five minutes. In 1883, he was drowned whilst attempting to swim the Niagara rapids.
See **pls.** F-7, 8, 9.

Section F
Sport

Details of the Figures

PORTRAIT OF LILLYWHITE.   PORTRAIT OF PILCH.   PORTRAIT OF BOX.

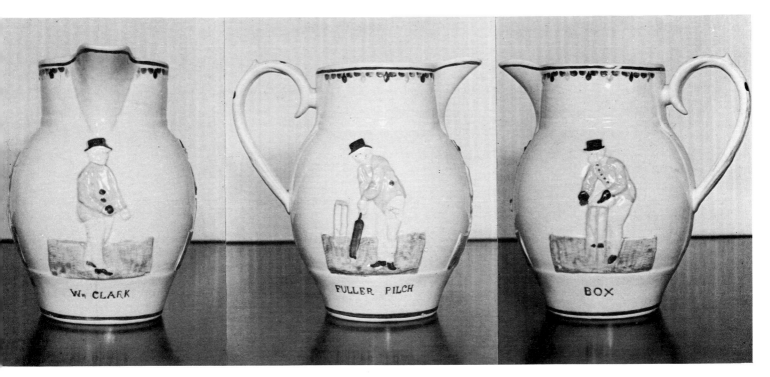

Plate 3
Staffordshire 'Pratt ware' jug. No factory mark.
L: Wm Clark (*sic*)
C: Fuller Pilch
R: Box

Both Pilch and Box were at one time members of William Clarke's All England XI, which for many years toured all over the country playing local sides.
In the collection of Mr I. N. R. Shield

Plate 1
Figure 1
Subject: **William Clarke or Frederick Lillywhite**
Title: None
Date: *c.* 1843
Height: 6½ in (16.5 cm)
Colour: Both well coloured and sparsely coloured versions exist.
Rarity: VR. D.
Series: Same series as *fig.* 2 (Pilch) and *fig.* 3 (Box)
Description: He stands facing half-right, with a cricket ball in his right hand. He wears beaver hat, tie, shirt, braces and trousers. His jacket is hung over the branch of a tree (spill-holder), the main trunk of which is behind him.
Observations: 1. For discussion about the identity of this figure, see *pl.* F-3.
2. A similar figure fetched 140 gns at Christie's in 1969.

Figure 2
Subject: **Fuller Pilch**
Title: None
Date: *c.* 1843
Height: 7½ in (19 cm)
Colour: Both well coloured and sparsely coloured versions exist.
Rarity: VR. D.
Series: Same series as *fig.* 1 (Clarke or Lillywhite) and *fig.* 3 (Box)
Description: He stands holding his bat; a wicket and a tree trunk (spill-holder) behind him. He wears a beaver hat, shirt and trousers.
Observations: For discussion about the identity of this figure, see *pl.* F-3.

Figure 3
Subject: **Thomas Box**
Title: None
Date: *c.* 1843
Height: 6½ in (16.5 cm)
Colour: Both well coloured and sparsely coloured versions exist.
Rarity: VR. D.
Series: Same series as *fig.* 1 (Clarke or Lillywhite) and *fig.* 2 (Pilch)
Description: He stands over the wicket, a tree trunk (spill-holder) behind him, his jacket over a branch. He wears a beaver hat, shirt, jacket and trousers.
Observations: For discussion about the identity of this figure, see *pl.* F-3.

Plate 2
Lillywhite, Pilch and Box
Left: Portrait of Lillywhite, from *The Illustrated London News* of July 22nd, 1843.
Centre: Portrait of Pilch, from *The Illustrated London News* of July 15th, 1843.
Right: Portrait of Box, from *The Illustrated London News* of July 15th, 1843.

Plate 3
Clarke, Pilch and Box
Staffordshire 'Pratt ware' jug, 6½ in (16.5 cm). No factory mark. The jug is decorated with portraits of (from *left* to *right*) Wm Clark (*sic*), Fuller Pilch and Box.
Observations: The three engravings illustrated on *pl.* F-2 appeared in *The Illustrated London News* in 1843. That on the left, of Lillywhite, appeared in the edition of July 22nd, in connection with a report of the *Marylebone Club* v. *All England* game. In this match Box and Pilch represented the *Marylebone Club* and Lillywhite played for *All England*. The centre engraving, of Pilch, and that on the right, of Box, appeared in the edition of

July 15th, in connection with the *Kent* v. *All England* match played at Lords. In this match Pilch played for *Kent* and Box and Lillywhite for *All England*. Clarke, the captain of *All England* is not recorded as having played in either of these two matches.

Three portraits decorating a 'Pratt ware' jug are illustrated on *pl.* F-3. They are inscribed 'Wm Clark' (*sic*), 'Fuller Pilch' and 'Box'. There is no factory mark on the piece illustrated. It is said that about twenty-four of these jugs were made and distributed to cricketers about 1840. Reproductions are known. One in the possession of Mr Anthony Baer is impressed on the base 'Leeds Pottery'. Apart from being obviously of later date, the only evident difference is that 'Wm Clark' has been changed to 'W. Clark' on the reproduction. Mr Baer, an authority on cricket history, tells me that no 'W. Clark' is recorded in Victorian times, so presumably the cricketer referred to is 'W. Clarke', the captain of *All England*.

Fig. 2 is based on the engraving of Pilch and *fig.* 3, likewise, is obviously Box. The difficulty arises with regard to *fig.* 1. Is it Lillywhite or is it Clarke? I have set forth the facts and the reader must now examine the photographs and make up his own mind. In favour of it being Lillywhite is the obvious similarity between the engraving and the figure. Note in particular the braces, a very important point. It is in fact, not uncommon to find a figure facing one way, and its source another. A telling point in favour of it being Clarke, is the evidence of the name inscribed on the jug. In the face of such conflicting evidence, the identification of this piece is likely to be a problem which will never be satisfactorily resolved.

Plate 4
Fig. 4 Unidentified bowler
Fig. 6 Unidentified batsman and wicket-keeper
Fig. 8 Tennis and cricket
Fig. 7 Unidentified batsman and bowler
Fig. 5 Unidentified batsman
*In the collection of
Mr Anthony Baer
Photograph by M. L. Pecker*

Plate 5 (Left)
Fig. 9 Unidentified batsman in military uniform
*In the collection of
Mr I. N. R. Shield*

Plate 5A (Right)
Fig. 10 Pair of unidentified batsmen in military uniform

Plate 4
Figure 4
Subject: **Unidentified bowler**
Title: None
Height: 5¾ in (14.5 cm)
Colour: Well coloured.
Rarity: R. D.
Pair: *Fig.* 5 (Unidentified batsman)
Description: He stands, a wicket to his right, a ball in his right hand. He wears a hat, open shirt, jacket and trousers.
Observations: Probably not a portrait.

Figure 5
Subject: **Unidentified batsman**
Title: None
Height: 5¾ in (14.5 cm)
Colour: Well coloured.
Rarity: R. D.

Pair: *Fig.* 4 (Unidentified bowler)
Description: He stands holding a bat, a wicket to his right. He wears a cap, open shirt, jacket and trousers.
Observations: 1. Probably not a portrait.
2. A similar figure, together with a 9 in (23 cm) version of *fig.* 18 (Unidentified jockey) *pl.* F-7, fetched 28 gns at Christie's in 1964.

Figure 6
Subject: **Unidentified batsman and wicket-keeper**
Title: None
Height: 6½ in (16.5 cm)
Colour: Well coloured.
Rarity: R. D.
Pair: *Fig.* 7 (Unidentified batsman and bowler)

Description: The batsman stands to the right. He wears a round hat, open shirt, jacket and trousers. The wicket-keeper is squatting behind the wicket. He is bare-headed and wears an open shirt, jacket and trousers.
Observations: Possibly a portrait group.

Figure 7
Subject: **Unidentified batsman and bowler**
Title: None
Height: 6½ in (16.5 cm)
Colour: Well coloured.
Rarity: R. D.
Pair: *Fig.* 6 (Unidentified batsman and wicket-keeper)
Description: The batsman stands to the left. He wears a cap, open shirt, jacket and trousers. His bat is in his right hand. He is poised

Colour Plate 51
Unidentified batsman.
Fig. 14, *pl.* F-7.
See page 458.
Unidentified bowler.
Fig. 13, *pl.*, F-7.
See page 459.

Colour Plate 52
A pair of unidentified
batsmen in military
uniform.
Fig. 10, *pl.* F-5A.
See page 458.

Plate 4 continued

to run. The bowler stands to the right, the ball in his right hand; he is in the act of making a delivery. He is bare-headed with open shirt, jacket and trousers.
Observations: Possibly a portrait group.

Figure 8
Subject: **Tennis and cricket**
Title: None
Date: c. 1895
Height: 10¼ in (25.75 cm)
Colour: Sparsely coloured.
Maker: William Kent
Rarity: Av.
Description: A girl stands on the left, a tennis racket in her right hand, a ball in her left, the net behind. A boy stands on the right, a bat in his left hand and ball in his right hand.
Observations: This figure, catalogued as 'Tennis and Cricket' appears in *Kent List A* (stock no. 378). It also appears in *Kent List B* (stock no. 359), but is deleted in red ink as a 'discontinued line'. It does not appear in *Kent List C*.

Plate 5
Figure 9
Subject: **Unidentified batsman in military uniform**
Title: None
Date: c. 1860
Height: 11¾ in (29.75 cm)
Colour: Sparsely coloured.
Rarity: VR. D. A.
Pair: No pair has been found to this figure, but one probably exists. *Fig. 10, pl.* F-5A could be the centrepiece of a pair.
Description: Standing with his bat in his right hand and his left hand on his waist. He is wearing an officer's uniform similar to that worn by officers of the Volunteer Rifles, see *pl.* C-93. There is a wicket, behind and to his right.
Observations: The identity of this figure has so far escaped discovery. It has been suggested that it is the Prince of Wales, but there is no evidence to support this. Maybe there is some connection with the revival of the Volunteers, in 1860, at the time of the Anglo-French war scare.

Plate 5A
Figure 10
Subject: **Pair of unidentified batsmen in military uniform**
Title: None
Date: c. 1860
Height: 9½ in (24 cm)
Colour: Well coloured, underglaze blue jackets.
Rarity: VR. D. A.
Series: See preceding figure.
Description: Two cricketers, each in uniform similar to that worn by officers of the Volunteer Rifles, stand, one on each side of a wicket. The one on the left, wears a moustache, pointed beard and carries his bat in his right hand; the one on the right, is a little shorter, wears a fringe beard, supports his bat against his side with his left hand and grasps a ball in his right hand.
Observations: See preceding figure.

Plate 6
Figure 11
Subject: **Unidentified bowler** (small version)
Title: None
Date: c. 1865
Height: 10⅛ in (25.4 cm)

Colour: Well coloured.
Maker: Probably Sampson Smith
Rarity: Av. D. A.
Pair: Fig. 12 (Unidentified batsman)
Description: Standing with a ball in his right hand and left arm across his chest. His jacket is to the left, and wicket and bat to the right. He wears a peaked cap, has a fringe beard except under his chin, blouse, neckerchief and trousers.
Observations: 1. This figure is regarded as the small version of *fig. 13, pl.* F-7. It is dealt with separately because forgeries of it are known, see *p.* 99, *ch.* 6.
2. The identity of the figure remains obscure. Balston suggested that it was George Parr and supported this identification by John C. Anderson's engraving of Parr in *Sketches at Lords* (1852), in which similar hair, fringe beard, and square face are depicted. It is common practice to indicate the captain in a cricket group by giving him both bat and ball. Parr was a renowned batsman and captain of the *All England XI* from 1857 to 1870, the period to which this figure belongs. The figure is illustrated in Mr Bryan Latham's book, but the title 'Alfred Mynn' has been added later. It is unlikely that the figure portrays Mynn as the potter would almost certainly have designed the figure to suggest his vast bulk—over six feet tall, and about nineteen stone in his heyday.

Figure 12
Subject: **Unidentified batsman** (small version)
Title: None
Date: c. 1865
Height: 10¼ in (25.75 cm)
Colour: Well coloured.
Maker: Probably Sampson Smith
Rarity: Av. D. A.
Pair: Fig. 11 (Unidentified bowler)
Description: Standing holding his bat in both hands, the wicket to his right, his jacket to his left. He wears a cap, blouse, neckerchief and trousers. He is clean-shaven, except for a moustache.

Observations: 1. This figure is regarded as the small version of *fig. 14, pl.* F-7. It is dealt with separately because forgeries of it are known, see *p.* 99, *ch.* 6.
2. The identity of the figure remains obscure. Balston supported the view that it portrayed Julius Caesar. He advanced this theory on the grounds that Caesar was a great batsman and played for the *All England XI* from 1849 to 1867. Mr Falcke, an antique dealer specializing in cricket prints and figures, once told Mr Balston that although neither of these figures had been seen with a title, there was the tradition that *fig.* 11 portrayed George Parr and *fig.* 12 portrayed Julius Caesar. Stanley, on the other hand, after comparing innumerable prints, considered Joseph Guy a more likely choice. As Guy played in the 1847 *All England XI*, my preference is for Julius Caesar, for the figure obviously belongs to the 1860's–70's and not earlier.

Plate 7
Figure 13
Subject: **Unidentified bowler** (large version)
Title: None
Date: c. 1865
Height: 14 in (35.5 cm)
Colour: Well coloured.
Maker: Probably Sampson Smith
Rarity: Av. D. A.
Pair: Fig. 14 (Unidentified batsman)
Description: Almost identical to *fig.* 11, *pl.* F-6 except that he wears a round-topped cap.
Observations: 1. This figure is generally regarded as the large version of *fig.* 11, *pl.* F-6. It is dealt with separately because, to date, no forgeries of it have been reported.
2. This figure possibly represents George Parr. See under *fig.* 11, *pl.* F-6.
3. A similar figure fetched 40 gns at Christie's in 1964, and another 40 gns in 1967. A lot, comprising a similar figure and its pair fetched £200 at Puttick and Simpson in 1968, and a similar lot, £200 at Sotheby's in 1969.

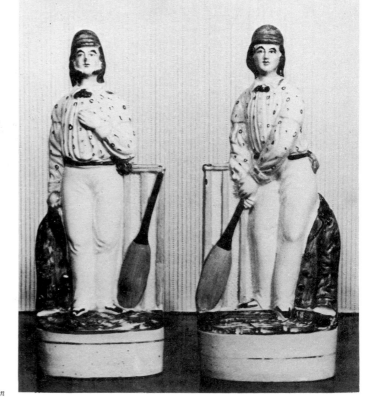

Plate 6
Fig. 11 Unidentified bowler *(small version)*
Fig. 12 Unidentified batsman *(small version)*
In the collection of Lt.-Col. A. C. W. Kimpton

Plate 7
T: *Fig.* 15 Heenan and Sayers
Fig. 17 Grapplers
Fig. 18 Unidentified jockey
Fig. 19 Webb

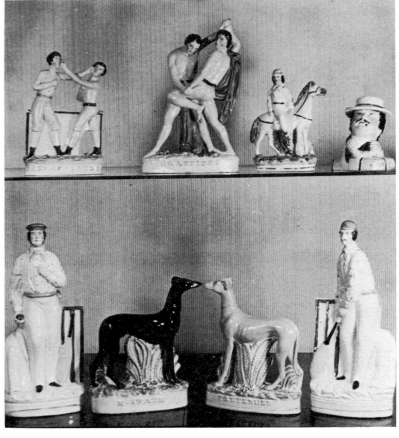

B: *Fig.* 13 Unidentified bowler *(large version)*
Fig. 20 M'Grath
Fig. 21 Pretender
Fig. 14 Unidentified batsman *(large version)*

Figure 14
Subject: **Unidentified batsman** (large version)
Title: None
Date: *c.* 1865
Height: 14 in (35.5 cm)
Colour: Well coloured.
Pair: *Fig.* 13 (Unidentified bowler)
Description: Almost the same as *fig.* 12, *pl.* F-6.
Observations: 1. This figure is generally regarded as the large version of *fig.* 12, *pl.* F-6. It is dealt with separately because, to date, no forgeries of it have been reported.
2. This figure possibly represents Julius Caesar. See under *fig.* 12, *pl.* F-6.
3. A lot comprising a similar figure and its pair fetched £200 at Puttick and Simpson in 1968; and a similar lot, £200 at Sotheby's in 1969. A similar figure, by itself, fetched 75 gns at Christie's in 1969.

Figure 15
Subject: **John Heenan and Tom Sayers**
Title: Heenan Sayers (raised capitals)
Date: *c.* 1860
Height: 9¾ in (24.5 cm)
Colour: Well coloured.
Rarity: Av. D. A.
Description: Heenan, the taller boxer, stands on the left. Both boxers are bare to the waist and each has his fist in the other's face. They wear breeches and long stockings. Two plain posts in the background.
Observations: A similar figure fetched 44 gns at Christie's in 1963, and another 44 gns at Christie's in 1964. A poor version fetched 42 gns in the same rooms in 1967. A fine group fetched 110 gns at Christie's in 1968; and another, 120 gns in the same rooms in 1969.

Figure 17
Subject: **The Grapplers**
Title: Grapplers (raised capitals)
Date: *c.* 1862
Height: 11½ in (29 cm)
Colour: Well coloured.
Rarity: Av. D. A.
Description: Two naked combatants are bound together by a belt round their waists. Each carries a short knife in his right hand. There is a drape over the right shoulder of the right combatant.
Observations: 1. Based on a group in bronzed-zinc modelled by J. P. Molin. An engraving of this group featured in a report on the International Exhibition which appeared in *The Illustrated London News* on November 1st, 1862. It is illustrated in *ch.* 3, *pl.* 54. The group attracted considerable attention, and elicited nearly unanimous admiration.
2. A fine example fetched 140 gns at Christie's in 1967; another, £320 at Sotheby's in 1969; and another, 350 gns at Christie's two months later. This is the highest recorded auction-room price for a single Victorian figure which, incidentally, is neither rare nor strictly speaking a portrait figure!

Figure 18
Subject: **Unidentified jockey**
Title: None
Date: *c.* 1880
Height: 7½ in (19 cm)
Colour: Well coloured.
Maker: Kent & Parr
Rarity: Av.
Pair: A matching pair does exist.
Description: On a horse facing right. The jockey wears cap, coloured shirt, knotted tie, breeches and boots.
Observations: 1. The identical figure, both

in size and appearance, is illustrated in *Kent List A*, being catalogued as:

Stock No.
82 ....Jockeys

It also appears in *Kent List B*. Here the illustration differs. The base is no longer white with a gold line, but is coloured all over. The entry is:

Stock No.
96 ....Jockeys

In *Kent List C* the figure is catalogued but not illustrated.
2. Stanley illustrates an 11½ in (29 cm) version and states that it has the Sampson Smith stamp beneath.
3. The master-mould of a similar figure was found, in 1948, in a disused part of the Sampson Smith factory. I understand the mould had no form of identification on it, although in a *Catalogue of original moulds of Sampson Smith figures and figurines* issued later by Barker Bros. Limited, the figure is listed as 'Champion Jockey'. As far as is known this title has never been found on the figure, and therefore it is not possible to confirm that the figure portrays the champion jockey, Fred Archer, although it may do so.
4. A lot comprising a pair of similar figures and a single similar figure, each 9 in (23 cm) in height, fetched 50 gns at Christie's in 1969.

Figure 19
Subject: **Captain Matthew Webb**
Title: None, but there are several marks which include a 'W' (or possibly 'M') and a 'C' (see *pl.* F-8).
Date: *c.* 1875
Height: 5¾ in (14.5 cm)
Colour: Well coloured.
Rarity: R. D.

Colour Plate 53
Unidentified jockeys. *Figs.* 23 and 24, *pl.* F-11. See page 463.

Colour Plate 55
Tom Cribb. *Fig.* 25, *pl.* F-12. See page 463.

Colour Plate 54
The Grapplers. *Fig.* 17, *pl.* F-7. See pages 78 and 459.

F460

Section F. Sport

Plate 7A (Left)
Fig. 15(a) Heenan and
Sayers
By courtesy of
Mr and Mrs R. Bonnett

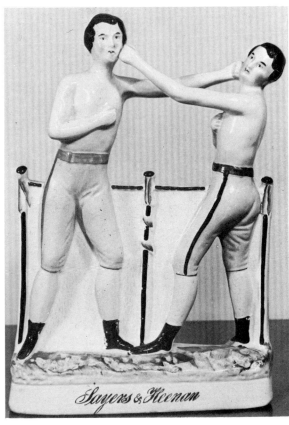

Plate 7B (Right)
Fig. 16 Heenan and
Sayers
In the Thomas Balston
collection

Plate 7 continued
Description: A caricature piece, the large head is out of all proportion to the size of his body. The straw hat is a detachable lid. He has a moustache and wears a striped shirt with a broad collar, knotted tie and trousers. His elbows rest on a flat corded bundle which may well represent a bale of corks roped together.
Observations: 1. The features strongly resemble those of Captain Webb, see *pl.* F-9. The identification is further supported by the nautical clothes, the bale of corks and the mark ←⊖→ which suggests that he is in transit.
2. See also *pls.* F-8 and F-9.

Figure 20
Subject: **Master M'Grath**
Title: M'Grath (raised capitals)
Date: *c.* 1871
Height: 10 in (25 cm)
Colour: Black and gilt.
Rarity: R.
Pair: Fig. 21 (*Pretender*)
Description: Black greyhound, facing right.
Observations: 1. See *ch.* 3, *pl.* 55 for illustration of engraving upon which this figure is probably based.
2. *Master M'Grath* won the Waterloo Cup three times. On the last occasion in 1871, he beat *Pretender*.
3. A similar figure and its pair fetched 45 gns at Christie's in 1966.

Figure 21
Subject: **Pretender**
Title: Pretender (raised capitals)
Date: *c.* 1871
Height: 10 in (25 cm)
Colour: Light-brown and gilt.
Rarity: R.

man, is on the left, bare to the waist; Sayers, *Description*: Light-brown greyhound, facing left.
Observations: A similar figure fetched 12 gns at Christie's in 1964.

Plate 7A
Figure 15(a)
Subject: **John Heenan and Tom Sayers**
Title: Sayers & Heenan (gilt script)
Date: Late
Height: 8¾ in (22 cm)
Colour: Well coloured.
Rarity: VR.
Description: Identical to *fig.* 15, *pl.* F-7, except for height and title.
Observations: This and *fig.* 16, *pl.* F-7B provide something of a mystery. Both were discovered in a reputable antique shop about fifteen years ago and were said to have come from a reputable source and to have 'age'. No further examples of either have been reported.
  This particular figure was stolen in May 1969, and is still missing. It is surprisingly heavy, the surface is coarse, and the base looks modern but the colouring is excellent. The title, in German gold, has been applied by hand, not as a transfer. The figure is late —how late is uncertain—probably this century.

Plate 7B
Figure 16
Subject: **John Heenan and Tom Sayers**
Title: Sayers & Heenan (gilt script)
Date: Late
Height: 13¼ in (33.5 cm)
Colour: Well coloured.
Rarity: VR.
Description: Heenan, the taller and heavier

Pair: Fig. 20 (*M'Grath*)
to the right, is attired similarly. Each has his fist in the other man's face. The design is almost the same as that of *fig.* 15, *pl.* F-7, except that there are three decorated posts in the background instead of two plain posts.
Observations: See preceding plate.

Plate 9
Captain Matthew Webb (1848-83)
The close similarity between the portrait of Webb on this match-box label and the facial features of *fig.* 19, *pl.* F-8 will be noted.

Plate 8
Fig. 19 Webb
The photograph illustrates some of the marks which are a constant finding on the corded bundle upon which his elbows rest.

Plate 10
Fig. 22 Elizabeth Travis
By courtesy of Mr and Mrs Eric Joyce

Plate 8
Figure 19
Subject: **Captain Matthew Webb**
Observations: This plate illustrates the various marks on the bale of corks which are a constant finding. They include a 'C', 'W' (or 'M'), the number '8997' and the sign ←⊖→ which may indicate that he is in transit. For details see under *fig.* 19, *pl.* F-7.

Plate 9
Captain Matthew Webb
Portrait of Captain Webb on a match-box top. It will be noted that the features are very similar to those portrayed in *fig.* 19, *pl.* F-7.

Plate 10
Figure 22
Subject: **Unidentified greyhound**

Title: Elizabeth Travis (gilt script)
Height: 11 in (28 cm)
Colour: Light-brown and gilt.
Maker: Probably Sampson Smith
Rarity: VR.
Pair: Unknown
Description: Greyhound facing left, a hare in its mouth.
Observations: Extensive enquiries through 'Stud Dog Charts' and 'Coursing Calendars'

Plate 11
Fig. 23 Unidentified jockey
Fig. 24 Unidentified jockey

Section F. Sport

Plate 12

Fig. 25 Cribb
To the left of the figure is an engraving by I. R. and G. Cruikshank which appeared in Pierce Egan's novel *Tom and Jerry,* first published in 1821.

Tom and Jerry call upon the 'Champion of England' to view his parlour and the silver cup presented to him from the sporting world, of the value of eighty guineas, as a tribute to the last memorable battle with Molineaux, at Thistleton Gap, Rutland on September 28th, 1811, after which the Champion did not fight again.

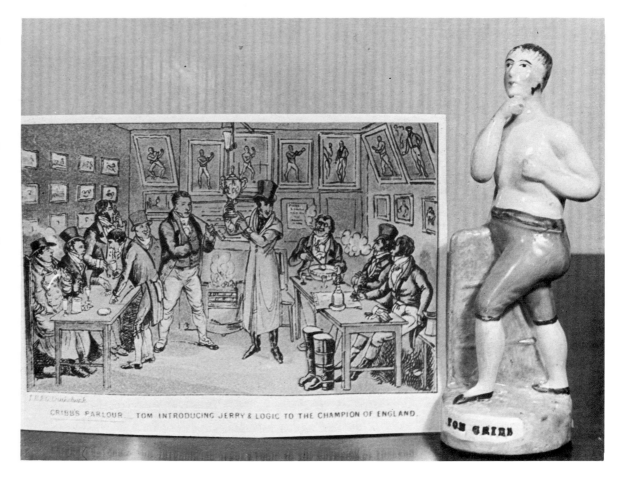

CRIBB'S PARLOUR — TOM INTRODUCING JERRY & LOGIC TO THE CHAMPION OF ENGLAND.

have been made but no trace found of a greyhound of this name. It has been suggested that it is the name of the owner either of the greyhound or of the figure, or of both.
2. I have seen a similar figure, with the hound facing right, inscribed 'A present from Blackpool' (gilt script). I have also heard of a matching pair of coursing hounds inscribed 'A present from Rhyl'.
3. This figure fetched 20 gns at Christie's in 1966.

Plate 11

Figure 23
Subject: **Unidentified jockey**
Title: None
Date: *c.* 1875
Height: 7¼ in (18.25 cm)
Colour: Well coloured.
Maker: In the style of John Parr
Rarity: VR. A.
Pair: *Fig.* 24 (Unidentified jockey)
Description: A jockey on horse, facing right; he wears cap, neckerchief, shirt, breeches and riding boots. His left hand is on the horse's mane and his right hand on his right thigh.
Observations: An 'action' piece reminiscent of engravings of the period, although so far unidentified.

Figure 24
Subject: **Unidentified jockey**
Title: None
Date: *c.* 1875
Height: 7¼ in (18.25 cm)
Colour: Well coloured.
Maker: In the style of John Parr
Rarity: VR. A.
Pair: *Fig.* 23 (Unidentified jockey)
Description: A jockey on horse, facing left. In all other respects similar to *fig.* 23.

Plate 12
Figure 25
Subject: **Tom Cribb**
Title: Tom Cribb (indented capitals)
Date: 184–
Height: 7¼ in (18.25 cm)
Colour: Well coloured.
Rarity: VR. D. A.
Pair: No pair has so far been found for this figure, but pre-Victorian figures are known which pair with Molineaux. *Fig.* 26 has been reserved for a possible pair.
Description: He stands facing left, a wall behind him. He is bare to the waist, wearing breeches, stockings and slippers. His right fist is under his chin and his left fist across his chest.
Observations: 1. Tom Cribb (1781–1848) was 'Champion of England' from 1808 to 1824. His last battle with the American negro Molineaux was on September 28th, 1811. Several different 'pairs' of Cribb and Molineaux are known but all have pre-Victorian characteristics. The colouring and appearance of this figure (with the solitary exception of the style of titling) are typically Victorian. That similar titling continued into the Victorian era is proved by *fig.* 2 (Victoria) *pl.* A-2. The probability is that the figure was produced *c.* 1848 as a memorial piece. In these circumstances it may or may not have had a pair (Molineaux).
2. It has been said that the potters did not often obtain a good likeness of their subject. I do not agree. Compare the likeness of this figure with the Cruikshank engraving illustrated on this plate.
3. See *ch.* 3, *pl.* 68.

Plate 13
Fig. 27 Caunt
By permission of the Brighton Art Gallery and Museum

Plate 13
Figure 27
Subject: **Ben Caunt**
Title: Ben. Caunt (raised capitals)
Date: 1844
Height: 15½ in (39.25 cm)
Colour: Well coloured.
Maker: Impressed on the back is 'BY H. BENTLEY + MODELED (*sic*) FROM LIFE + 1844' (indented capitals), see *ch.* 2, *pl.* 4. Little is known of H. Bentley, but he appears to have been both a designer and manufacturer from Hanley, see *p.* 11.
Rarity: VR. D.
Description: A bust on a pedestal in one piece. The bust is 11 in (28 cm) in height and the pedestal 4½ in (11.5 cm). He is bare-headed with fringe beard and wears a high collar, bow tie, coat and waistcoat. Underneath the title the following appears in indented capitals: 'Belt presented at Jem Burns May 1841'. This belt is modelled on the shelved part of the pedestal. Around the pedestal are details of his birth, height and weight and a list of the fights won or lost in three columns.
Observations: 1. No. 1030 in the Willett collection. Described as 'Coloured earthenware . . . Staffordshire'.
2. A 13¾ in (35 cm) version with identical modeller's mark and covered in a brown glaze, described as a 'Doulton stoneware figure', fetched 46 gns at Christie's in 1969.

Figure 28 (not illustrated).
Subject: **Fred Archer**
Title: Fred Archer (raised capitals)
Date: Late
Height: 8¼ in (21 cm)
Colour: Rather crude.
Rarity: VR.
Description: On a horse facing right, wearing cap, shirt, breeches and riding boots.
Observations: I have not seen this piece, only one copy of which has been reported. This example was very heavily crazed and the gold on the lettering looked 'new'. My informant, uncertain at first, hence its inclusion. has recently decided that it is a forgery.

Section G
Crime

Biographies and Historical Notes

BLACK BESS, the famous mare of Dick Turpin. Of her Eliza Cook wrote:

Right onward she went till she stagger'd and dropp'd;
But her limbs only fail'd when her heart pulse had
    stopp'd.
Her dare-devil rider lived on for a while,
And told of her work with a triumphing smile:
And the fame of Dick Turpin had been something
    less
If he'd ne'er rode to York on his bonnie Black Bess.
Though she saved him, and died to prove what she
    could do,
Yet *her* life was most precious by far of the two.

See **pls. G-**1, 3, 4, 5, 6, 8.

CHINA GOVERNESS, THE, novel by Margery Allingham. The following appears in the foreword to this work:

The title derives from a Staffordshire figure which, according to the author, was made in 1850 as part of the celebrated and now highly praised series of portrait groups of notorious scenes and characters of the period. These include the Murder Cottages, Maria Marten's Red Barn, James Rush and Potash Farm and many other examples of the grisly taste of the time.

The china governess was Thyrza Caleb, a young woman employed by the wealthy Kinnit family as a governess to two young cousins. She was tried in 1849 for the murder of their music-master who was alleged to be her lover, and although she was acquitted she committed suicide shortly after her release. The crime attracted considerable attention because of its peculiar nature, the victim having been stabbed from behind through the back of a chair. The Staffordshire figure showing the governess, the chair, and her two young charges was produced in the following year but was suppressed by the family to avoid perpetuating the scandal.

A number of collectors have enquired of me as to whether or not the foreword of this book was in part fact or entirely fictional. In response to my enquiry the late Miss Allingham informed me that she had made it all up.

COLLIER, WILLIAM (1831–66), tenant-farmer of Kingsley, near Froghall, North Staffordshire. He was found guilty at Stafford Assizes of the murder on July 5th, 1866, of Thomas Smith junr., a neighbouring farmer who had caught him in the act of poaching. Initially, he pleaded innocence but after being found guilty confessed that he left home with the twin barrels of his gun loaded. With one barrel he shot two rabbits and then encountered Thomas Smith. He fired at him, hitting him in the head, and when his victim tried to flee, struck him with the gun until the barrel broke. Collier's execution took place on August 7th, 1866, and was the last execution in public at Stafford Gaol. A great crowd watching were revolted when the execution was fumbled and subsequent murderers were dispatched in private.

See **pl. G-**27 and **Smith junr., Thomas.**

GARDINER, FRANK (1830–*c.* 90), Australian bushranger.[1] Born at Goulburn, New South Wales, his real name was probably Frank Christie. He began his criminal career in 1850, by stealing horses. He was apprehended and sentenced to five years imprisonment but escaped after five weeks. He was recaptured in 1854, when he was again arrested for horse-stealing. This time he was sentenced to seven years hard labour. He was released after four years and joined a band of bushrangers. In 1861, he was captured by the police after wounding two and being wounded himself. Handcuffed and left in charge of a policeman, he was rescued by other bushrangers. In June 1862, the gold escort from Forbes was stopped by the gang, some of the members of the escort were wounded, and the boxes of gold were stolen. £1000 reward was offered for the apprehension and conviction of the bush-rangers. The police succeeded in recovering much of the gold but Gardiner disappeared and was not arrested until February 1864, when he was found at Appis Creek, Queensland. In partnership with another man, he was conducting a public-house and store. He was tried in Sydney and sentenced to thirty-two years imprisonment. He was a model prisoner and in spite of public protest was released in July 1874, when he had served ten years, on the understanding that he would leave Australia. He went to San Francisco, where he lived an honest life. He differed from most of the notorious bush-rangers in that he came of a respectable family and was not actually guilty of murder. Even so, he was lucky to escape the fate of some of his associates who were executed.

See **pl. G-**10.

1. Robber in the Australian bush country.

GRECIAN AND DAUGHTER, THE.
See **Roman Charity, The.**

HUDSON, GEORGE (1800–71), the 'Railway King'. Born near York, the son of a prosperous yeoman, he started life as a linen-draper. In 1827, he was bequeathed £30,000 by a wealthy great-uncle in a deathbed Will and thereby became one of the richest men in York. He embarked on a career of company promotion and railway building, and was closely associated with George Stephenson and his son Robert. In 1844, he clashed with Gladstone, then President of the Board of Trade in the Peel administration, over the Railway Bill, melodramatically dubbed by *The Railway Times* as the 'Railway Plunder Bill'. In this

Bill the government set out to check monopoly and assert the right of public control over the railways. Hudson, on behalf of the railway managers, succeeded in driving a wedge between Peel and Gladstone and secured such a whittling away of the Bill as to render it innocuous.

He was three times Lord Mayor of York and was elected Member of Parliament for Sunderland, in 1845. He rapidly became a millionaire, establishing a network of railways which later became the Midland, the North-Eastern and the Great Western. His rise to power and prosperity was by questionable means and he was exposed at the time of the 'railway mania' (1847–8) and plunged into ruin. The committees of investigation set up by the shareholders of his companies, in 1849, showed that he had manipulated accounts, misappropriated shares and published false balance sheets, by which means, for many years, he was able to declare dividends not truly carried, arranging for their payment out of new or borrowed capital. He was never criminally prosecuted for his offences, for company law was still in its infancy. However, publication of his huge frauds led to his downfall and relegation to poverty and obscurity. Nevertheless, Sunderland continued to elect him, until 1859. He was known as 'Gumsher Hudson', a Yorkshire term for wisdom; also, as the 'Yorkshire Balloon' and the 'Railway Napoleon'. At the zenith of his career, when he controlled about one-third of the whole railway system of the British Isles, he gained the title of the 'Railway King'.

See **pls. G-**12, 13, 14.

KING, TOM (?–1735), highwayman associate of Turpin. Was accidentally shot and killed by Turpin near Epping Forest. *See* **pls. G-**1, 2, 3, 4, 5, 6, 7, 8, 9, and **Turpin, Dick.**

MANNING, FREDERICK GEORGE (1800–49), landlord of the White Hart Hotel, Taunton. In 1847, he married Marie de Roux, afterwards known as Maria Manning. In 1849, they came to live at 3, Miniver Place, Bermondsey. On August 9th, they were, together, involved in the murder of Patrick O'Connor, Maria's former lover. A hole was made in the kitchen floor and O'Connor was invited to supper. Manning killed him and, helped by his wife, buried the body in the hole that was waiting. Afterwards, Maria visited O'Connor's lodgings and stole both money and personal effects. The trial took place at the Old Bailey and the executions, by hanging, on the roof of Horsemonger Lane Gaol on November 13th, 1849. Charles Dickens, who had witnessed the executions from a house, where he had paid ten guineas for five tickets, wrote a letter of protestation against public executions to *The Times* but it was not until nineteen years later that the last execution in public took place.

See **pl. G**-18.

MANNING, MARIA (1821–49), formerly Marie de Roux, a native of Lausanne. She was maid to a daughter of the Duke of Sutherland at Stafford (now Lancaster) House. In 1847, she married Frederick George Manning (*q.v.*) and was involved with him in the murder of her former lover Patrick O'Connor. She was hanged on November 13th, 1849.

See **pl. G**-18.

NORWICH CASTLE: Built shortly after the Norman Conquest, the original structure was an earth mound surmounted by timber fortifications. About the middle of the twelfth century, most of the fortifications were replaced by a great stone keep, the fifth largest in Britain. The building, 70 feet high and nearly square, with walls 100 feet long, is now the only surviving portion of the castle. For much of its history, the castle served as the County Gaol. In 1849, James Rush was hanged there for the murder of Isaac Jermy, Recorder of Norwich, and his son, at Stanfield Hall. Rush was afterwards buried within the prison walls. In 1894, the building was re-roofed and fitted as a museum.

See **pls. G**-20, 22, 23.

O'BRIEN, LUCY (dates unknown), daughter of Joseph Gabbett of Limerick and wife of William Smith O'Brien (*q.v.*).

See **pl. G**-17.

O'BRIEN, WILLIAM SMITH (1803–64), Irish nationalist. Born in County Clare, he entered parliament, in 1826. He made repeated efforts to improve poor relief and education in Ireland. In October, 1843, he joined O'Connell's Repeal Association, but O'Connell's aversion to violence led to the development of a wide gulf between them. A sequel to this was that the Young Irelanders set up a Repeal League under O'Brien's leadership. In 1848, he led an abortive insurrection which ended ludicrously in a virtually bloodless battle in a cabbage-garden at Ballingarry. He was arrested on a charge of high treason and sentenced to be hanged, drawn and quartered. Later, his sentence was commuted to transportation for life. He was confined on Maria Island, Tasmania. In 1854, he was released on the condition that he did not return to Ireland and in 1856, he received a free pardon. He died in Bangor, North Wales.

See **pl. G**-17.

ORTON, ARTHUR (1834–98), the 'Tichborne Claimant'. The Tichborne family was a pre-Conquest Catholic family of Hampshire who received a baronetcy in 1626. In 1866, the eleventh baronet, Alfred Joseph Tichborne, died. A butcher from Wagga-Wagga in New South Wales, Thomas Castro, otherwise Arthur Orton of Wapping, who had emigrated to Australia in 1852, now claimed the title and returned to England at the invitation of Lady Tichborne,

widow of the tenth baronet. Lady Tichborne had been convinced by descriptions of him that he was her long-lost eldest son, presumed lost at sea off America, in 1854. She 'recognized' him on arrival and in 1871 supported him in a suit for ejectment against the twelfth baronet, a boy of five. His case collapsed in March 1872, after a trial lasting 103 days. He was arrested for perjury and brought to trial in 1873. The trial lasted 188 days and cost £55,315. He was found guilty and sentenced to fourteen years hard labour. He was released in 1884, and, in 1895, confessed the imposture. He died in poverty. The 'Claimant' is alleged to have said:

Some 'as money, and some 'as brains; God made one lot for the benefit of the other.

See **pl. G**-16.

PALMER, WILLIAM (1824–56), member of the Royal College of Surgeons and one time house surgeon at St. Bartholomew's Hospital. He eventually settled down as a general practitioner at Rugeley in Staffordshire. Was interested in the breeding of racehorses. He poisoned his wife in 1854, and his brother in August, 1855. When his best friend, John Parsons Cook died at the *Talbot Arms* in December, 1855, the latter's stepfather William Stevens became suspicious. His anxiety deepened when he found that Cook's betting book had disappeared and that Palmer was anxious to fasten up the coffin. He returned to London to consult his lawyer. Investigations took place, Palmer was arrested and eventually tried and convicted at the Old Bailey of the murder of Cook. He was hanged in June, 1856.

See **pl. G**-18A.

PALMER'S HOUSE: The home of William Palmer (1824–56), the Rugeley poisoner. A typical Georgian residence separated from the street by a narrow forecourt and railings.

See **pl. G**-18B.

PERA
See **Roman Charity, The**.

PESTAL, PAVEL IVANOVICH (1794–1826), Russian colonel and conspirator. It became apparent towards the end of the reign of Alexander I (1777–1825) that, in practice, he was becoming more and more reactionary. This led to the growth of opposition, particularly among young army officers who had imbibed liberalism in the west. After 1817, secret societies were formed in the army. The *Northern Society*, based at St Petersburg, favoured constitutional monarchy and the abolition of serfdom; the *Southern Society*, based on Kiev, favoured republicanism and advocated division of land among the peasants, etc. This southern group was led by Colonel Paul Pestal.

The uncertainty about the succession, following the death of Alexander I, led to a military revolt on December 26th, 1825. Started by the *Northern Society*, it was ill-planned and half-hearted and rapidly suppressed by Nicholas I. An uprising in the south, on the same day, was also crushed. Pestal was arrested and later executed.

A melody published in Victorian times was, allegedly, scratched by Pestal on the wall of his dungeon with a link of his chain, on the night previous to his execution, in 1826.

See **pl. G**-11.

POTASH FARM: The farmhouse occupied by James Rush and Emily Sandford. The following description of the farm appeared in *The Norfolk Chronicle and Norwich Gazette* on Wednesday April 4th, 1849:

POT-ASH FARM is situated at a distance of seven furlongs from Stanfield, and three miles from Wymondham. The land adjoins Ketteringham on the one side, and Stanfield-hall farm on the other; and the house, which has a south aspect, is a very neat looking brick building, being nearly opposite Stanfield hall. The land which lies between them is flat, and the road, which the assassin is supposed to have taken, lies nearly in a direct line across it. The farm-house stands close to a bye road, leading into the main road to Wymondham. It has a centre porch entrance, with apartments on each side; and has a neat garden in front, with numerous out-houses and offices in the rear. The house had many visitors during the first few weeks after the murders; and the peculiar construction of the interior, with the multiplicity of doors communicating with the exterior, excited much observation. The rooms are all small; the best sitting room, with Mr Rush's and Emily Sandford's room, and Jas. Rush junior's room, are papered; one on the ground-floor is painted; and the rest are whitewashed. Rush and Emily Sandford occupied apartments in the end of the building. These were originally one room, and are divided by a thin partition; whatever is said or done in one room, can be heard in the other. Rush chose the front door as the entrance to his apartments, and the family were compelled to use one of the back approaches from the farm-yard. All the doors to his own rooms were secured by extra bolts and locks. Rush and Emily Sandford's apartments were all situated for secrecy; being flanked by a short passage, and closed by a thick door with extra bolts and locks.

See **pls. G**-20, 21, 23.

ROMAN CHARITY, THE: A painting by Rubens in the Rijksmuseum, Amsterdam. It is based on the legend of Cimon who was imprisoned without food or water, and Pera his daughter, who fed him during fleeting daily visits and eventually saved his life. A Chelsea figure, the work of Willems, modeller for Chelsea *c.* 1758 and a Staffordshire figure, probably the work of Obadiah Sherratt, titled 'Grecian & Daughter', were inspired by the painting. The rather crude Victorian piece (*fig.* 55, *pl.* **G**-28) is based on either the Rubens painting or on one or other of the earlier figures already mentioned. *The Grecian & Daughter*, the story adapted for the stage by Murphy, was first performed in the latter part of the 18th century with Mrs Siddons in the title role.

See **pl. G**-28.

RUSH, JAMES BLOMFIELD (1800–49), West Norfolk farmer and land-agent; also, an appraiser and auctioneer. He was an illegitimate child, his reputed father being a gentleman farmer of good property, near Wymondham. His mother was Mary Blomfield, daughter of a Norfolk farmer. She married a Mr Rush of Felmingham, who permitted her son to take his name.

Rush owned Potash farm, near Wymondham. The farm was mortgaged for £5,000 to Isaac Jermy, Recorder of Norwich, who lived about one mile away at Stanfield Hall. Jermy gave notice to foreclose on November 30th, 1848, but at 8pm on the 28th, Rush entered the Hall and shot Jermy and his son dead and wounded his daughter-in-law and the housemaid, Eliza Chastney. His trial took place at Norwich and lasted six days. He refused legal aid and cross-examined witnesses at great length. He, himself, spoke for over fourteen hours. It was shown at the trial that he had forged Jermy's signature to a document by which Jermy gave him absolute ownership of the farm. Rush was found guilty. When passing sentence of death the Judge said:

'You commenced a system of fraud by endeavouring to cheat your landlord, and you followed that up by making the unfortunate girl whom you had seduced, the tool whereby you could commit a forgery; and having done that, you terminated your guilty career by the murder of the son and grandson of your friend and benefactor . . . there is no one that has witnessed your conduct during the trial, and heard the evidence disclosed against you, that will not feel with me, what I say, when I tell you, that you must quit this world by an ignominious death, an object of unmitigated abhorrence to every one'.

Rush was hanged on the bridge over the moat at Norwich Castle on April 21st, 1849. He was buried within the prison walls.
See **pls. G**-19, 23.

SANDFORD, EMILY (dates unknown), mistress of James Rush, the murderer (*q.v.*). She first met Rush about 1847, and became enamoured with him, leaving London for Potash Farm. There she was seduced by Rush who had promised to marry her if she bore him a child. Rush was convicted largely on her evidence of his words and movements. Referring to her evidence in his summing up the Judge said:

'It does not fix the prisoner with the guilt of the murder, but that something of an extraordinary nature had occurred'.

In passing sentence on Rush, he remarked:

'If you had performed your promise to that unfortunate girl to make her your wife, the policy of the law, that seals the lips of a wife in any proceeding against her husband, might have prevented the appearance of a material witness against you'.

See **pls. G**-19, 23, 24.

SMITH junr., THOMAS (1842–66), bachelor son of a wealthy farmer who owned 'Whiston Eaves', Kingsley, near Froghall, North Staffordshire. This was an extensive farm just beyond the slope of the Churnet Valley. In 1866, Thomas Smith was deliberately shot dead by a neighbouring smallholder named 'William Collier, whom he had caught in the act of poaching on his land. Collier was eventually hanged for the crime.
See **pl. G**-27 and **Collier, William**.

STANFIELD HALL: The house occupied by Isaac Jermy, Recorder of Norwich. The following description appeared in *The Norfolk Chronicle and Norwich Gazette* of Wednesday, April 4th, 1849:

STANFIELD HALL is a handsome building of the Elizabethan period; standing on one of the highest spots in the county of Norfolk, and the grounds being in the three parishes of Wymondham, Ketteringham and Hethel. It was built by the Reverend G. Preston; who, on coming into possession, pulled down the old edifice; and the large windows, divided by mullions, the clustered turretted chimneys, and the finials to the gables, give an admirable facsimile of the Tudor style of domestic architecture. The arms of the family are displayed upon the entrance porch. The Reverend George Preston spent £15,000 in the re-building of this mansion; and the Recorder had expended a large sum in furnishing the various rooms. The mansion stands on a fine lawn, and is surrounded by a park, which is enclosed by a large moat. This moat is crossed by a bridge directly in front of the house. Comfort and convenience have been studied in the construction of the edifice, of which we give a view; and also a plan of the ground-floor. The principal entrance is by the porch, which opens into a spacious hall. This hall opens into the "staircase-hall;" so called, as it contains the staircase to the principal upper-rooms. The drawing and dining-rooms are to the left of the entrance-hall and the staircase-hall, the doors from each being in the latter. A long passage runs along the right side of the entrance and staircase halls. On the right of this passage and opening into it, is the butler's pantry; and the servants' rooms lie to the right of the pantry. Between the housekeeper's rooms and the cook's pantry is a passage, to which access is gained by a glass-door from the lawn. By this door Rush used to enter; having access to the hall whenever he pleased. It was, also, by this door that the assassin, whoever he was, entered the house after Mr Jermy was shot; he appears, from the direction he was going, when he was seen by the butler, to have been making his way to the library, where Mr Jermy's deeds were deposited. The passage opens into a long corridor, on which the servants' rooms abut, and this corridor ends in the passage before referred to, as running to the right of the entrance hall. Opposite the entrance to the corridor a lamp is fixed, which gives light to the vicinity. Another lamp, between the drawing and dining-room doors, lights the staircase hall.

See **pls. G**-20, 23, 24, 25, 26.

TICHBORNE CLAIMANT (1834–98). *See* **Orton, Arthur**.

TURPIN, RICHARD (1706–39), highwayman. The son of an innkeeper at Hemp-

stead, Essex. He joined a gang of robbers and entered into partnership with the highwayman Tom King on the Cambridge road. In 1735, Turpin and King stole a horse in Epping Forest. A keeper was on the point of arresting King, when Turpin rode up and fired. He missed the keeper and killed King. Escaping to Yorkshire, he was arrested four years later for horse-stealing and hanged at York. The romances connected with the name of Turpin are legendary.

The story of Turpin, his famous mare *Black Bess* and Tom King was popularized in Harrison Ainsworth's novel *Rookwood* (1834). It was dramatized on many occasions subsequently, being a frequent attraction at Astley's.
See **pls. G**-1, 2, 3, 4, 5, 6, 8.

WOOD, JEMMY (1756–1836), a draper who kept a small shop in Westgate, Gloucester. On his death, he was found to have left £781,007. A Will, dated 1834, divided his estate between four executors but difficulties arose when a person whose identity was never discovered, sent a charred fragment of a Codicil to a Mr Helps. The Codicil left £200,000 to the City of Gloucester and Mr Helps himself also derived benefit from it. Legal proceedings, which ended in the House of Lords, lasted from 1837 to 1844. The Corporation of Gloucester, who spent nearly £8,000 on the proceedings, got nothing, because the money could only go to them as Trustees and the Codicil gave no indication of the purposes of the Trust. Intense public interest was aroused by the case because of the disclosure of many scandalous and ridiculous details of Jemmy Wood's conduct.
See **pls. G**-15, 16.

Plate 1

Dick Turpin and Black Bess

Part of a playbill advertising performances of *Rookwood or the exploits of Turpin and Black Bess* at the Theatre Royal for March 26th and 27th, 1841.

Figures of Dick Turpin and Tom King tend to be accepted as the potters' versions of famous criminals, and so indeed they are, but these highwaymen operated in the early part of the eighteenth century and it is unlikely that the potters would have thought of making them, had the theatres not reminded them of them. Turpin figures in Ainsworth's *Rookwood* (*c.* 1840) which gives an account of his famous ride to York on *Black Bess*. The novel was followed by a spate of theatrical productions. No doubt some of the figures of Turpin and King are theatrical portraits, although this has not yet been proved. Another source of highwaymen and murderers may have been the popular 'Penny Dreadfuls'.

Plate 2

Figure 1

Subject: **Dick Turpin**

Title: Dick · Turpin (raised capitals)

Height: 11 in (28 cm)

Colour: Well coloured.

Rarity: VR. D. A.

Pair: *Fig.* 2 (King)

Description: Standing, in cocked hat (athwartships), lace collar, long coat, breeches and knee-boots. In his right hand, he holds a mug against his chest and in his left hand, a whip.

Observations: 1. It is widely thought that this figure and its pair are theatrical, but this has never been proved.

2. A similar figure fetched 38 gns at Christie's in 1969.

Figure 2

Subject: **Tom King**

Title: Tom · King (raised capitals)

Height: 10½ in (26.5 cm)

Colour: Well coloured.

Rarity: VR. D. A.

Pair: *Fig.* 1 (Turpin)

Description: Standing, in tricorn hat, plain collar, long coat, breeches and knee-boots which are turned down. In his right hand, he holds a mug against his chest.

Observations: 1. Note 'restored' version of this figure which is illustrated on *pl.* G-4.

2. See preceding figure.

Plate 3

Figure 3

Subject: **Dick Turpin on Black Bess**

Title: D. Turpin (raised capitals)

Height: 10 in (25 cm)

Colour: Well coloured, black horse.

Rarity: Av.

Pair: *Fig.* 4 (King)

Description: On horse facing right, in tricorn hat, long coat with large ermine cuffs, breeches, and knee-boots. He carries a pistol in his right hand.

Observations: See following figure.

Figure 4

Subject: **Tom King**

Title: T. King (raised capitals)

Height: 10 in (25 cm)

Colour: Well coloured, brown horse.

Rarity: Av.

Pair: *Fig.* 3 (Turpin)

Description: On horse facing left, in tricorn hat, long coat with large ermine cuffs, breeches, and knee-boots.

Observations: A similar figure and its pair fetched 22 gns at Christie's in 1965; and another similar pair 40 gns at Christie's in 1969.

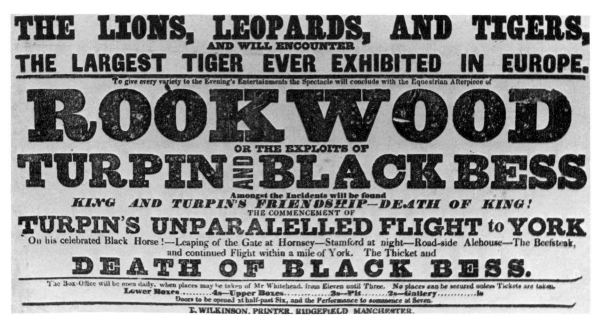

Plate 1

Rookwood or the exploits of Turpin and Black Bess. Part of a playbill advertising performances at the Theatre Royal for March 26th and 27th, 1841.

Ainsworth's novel *Rookwood* was followed by a spate of theatre productions; probably some figures of Turpin and King are 'theatrical portraits' although this has never been proved.

Plate 2
Fig. 1 Turpin
Fig. 2 King

Plate 3
T: *Fig.* 3 Turpin
Fig. 4 King
Fig. 5 Turpin
Fig. 6 King

B: *Fig.* 7 King
Fig. 8 Turpin
Fig. 9 Turpin
Fig. 10 King

Plate 3 continued
Figure 5
Subject: **Dick Turpin on Black Bess**
Title: Dick Turpin (raised capitals)
Height: 10½ in (26.5 cm)
Colour: Well coloured, black horse.
Maker: In the style of Sampson Smith
Rarity: Av.
Pair: Fig. 6 (King)
Description: On horse facing right, in tricorn hat, coat, breeches, and knee-boots. A pistol in his right hand. Long saddle-cloth.

Figure 6
Subject: **Tom King**
Title: Tom King (raised capitals)
Height: 10¾ in (27 cm)
Colour: Well coloured, brown horse.
Maker: In the style of Sampson Smith
Rarity: Av.
Pair: Fig. 5 (Turpin)
Description: On horse facing left, in high-crowned hat with turned-up brim, coat, stockings and high-low boots. A pistol in his right hand. Long saddle-cloth.

Figure 7
Subject: **Tom King**
Title: Tom King (raised capitals)
Height: 12 in (30.5 cm)
Colour: Sparsely coloured, white horse.
Maker: In the style of Sampson Smith
Rarity: Av.
Pair: Fig. 8 (Turpin)
Description: On horse facing right, in cocked hat (athwartships), cloak, coat, stockings and high-low boots. Long, square-cut saddle-cloth.

Figure 8
Subject: **Dick Turpin on Black Bess**
Title: Dick Turpin (raised capitals)
Height: 12 in (30.5 cm)
Colour: Well coloured, black horse.
Maker: In the style of Sampson Smith
Rarity: Av.
Pair: Fig. 7 (King)
Description: On horse facing left, in tricorn hat, cloak, coat, stockings and high-low boots. Long, square-cut saddle-cloth.

Figure 9
Subject: **Dick Turpin on Black Bess**
Title: Dick Turpin (raised capitals)
Height: 10¾ in (27 cm)
Colour: Well coloured, black horse.
Rarity: Av.
Pair: Fig. 10 (King)
Description: On horse facing right, in tricorn hat, long coat, breeches, and knee-boots. A pistol in his right hand.

Figure 10
Subject: **Tom King**
Title: Tom King (raised capitals)
Height: 10¾ in (27 cm)
Colour: Well coloured, white horse.
Rarity: Av.
Pair: Fig. 9 (Turpin)
Description: On horse facing left, in tricorn hat, long coat, breeches, and knee-boots.

Plate 4
Figure 2
Subject: **Tom King**

Title: Tom · King (raised capitals)
Observations: For full details see *pl.* G-2. This figure has been included as an illustration of restoration work which amounts to faking. Except for the head, the entire figure is genuine. From the neck upwards the figure has been totally restored from a mould probably made from the head of *fig.* 10, *pl.* G-3. If the illustration on *pl.* G-2 is re-examined, it will be seen that the faked head differs in minor respects from the genuine article.

Figure 11
Subject: **Dick Turpin on Black Bess**
Title: Dick/Turpin (raised capitals)
Date: c. 1870
Height: 8¾ in (22 cm)
Colour: Well coloured, black horse. Usually decorated with 'Bright Gold'.
Maker: Sampson Smith
Rarity: C.
Pair: Fig. 12 (King)
Description: On horse facing right, in tricorn hat, long coat, breeches and knee-boots, a pistol in his right hand.
Observations: 1. The same figure has been found inscribed 'Frank Gardiner' in gilt script, with the original title erased, see *pl.* G-10.
2. See next figure.

Figure 12
Subject: **Tom King**
Title: Tom/King (raised capitals)
Date: c. 1870
Height: 8¾ in (22 cm)

Section G. Crime

Colour: Well coloured. Usually decorated with 'Bright Gold'.
Maker: Sampson Smith
Rarity: C.
Pair: *Fig.* 11 (Turpin)
Description: On horse facing left, in tricorn hat, long coat, breeches and gaiters, a pistol in his right hand.
Observations: 1. The original Sampson Smith press-mould of this figure is in the possession of the author, see *ch.* 4, *pl.* 4.
2. A similar figure and its pair fetched 20 gns at Christie's in 1966.
3. This figure has been found with the following mark in relief on its base: ⊕

Figure 13
Subject: **Dick Turpin on Black Bess**
Title: D. Turpin (raised capitals)
Height: 9¾ in (24.5 cm)
Colour: Well coloured, black horse.
Rarity: C.
Pair: *Fig.* 14 (King)
Description: Almost the same design as *fig.* 3, *pl.* G-3, but the ermine cuffs are less prominent.

Figure 14
Subject: **Tom King**
Title: Tom King (raised capitals)
Height: 9¾ in (24.5 cm)
Colour: Well coloured.
Rarity: C.
Pair: *Fig.* 13 (Turpin)
Description: Almost the same design as *fig.* 4, *pl.* G-3, except for manner of titling.

Figure 15
Subject: **Dick Turpin on Black Bess**
Title: Dick Turpin (raised capitals)
Height: 11½ in (29 cm)
Colour: Well coloured, black horse.
Maker: Sampson Smith
Rarity: Av.
Pair: *Fig.* 16 (King)
Description: On horse facing right, in cocked hat (athwartships), long coat, breeches and knee-boots, a pistol in his right hand.
Observations: 1. This figure, together with its pair, have on rare occasions been found with the following maker's mark in relief on their bases:
'S. SMITH/LONGTON/1851.'
See *ch.* 2, *pl.* 8.
2. A similar figure and its pair fetched 24 gns at Christie's in 1964, another pair fetched 20 gns in the same rooms in 1966, and another pair fetched £34 at Sotheby's in 1966.

Figure 16
Subject: **Tom King**
Title: Tom King (raised capitals)
Height: 11½ in (29 cm)
Colour: Well coloured.
Maker: Sampson Smith
Rarity: Av.
Pair: *Fig.* 15 (Turpin)
Description: On horse facing left, in tricorn hat, long coat, breeches and gaiters, a pistol in his right hand.
Observations: See preceding figure.

Figure 17
Subject: **Dick Turpin on Black Bess**
Title: Dick Turpin (raised capitals)
Height: 11¾ in (29.75 cm)
Colour: Well coloured, black horse.
Rarity: R. A.
Pair: *Fig.* 18 (King) *pl.* G-5.
Description: On horse facing left, in cocked hat (athwartships), lace collar, long coat, breeches and knee-boots. There is a pistol in his left hand and holster with two pistols on the saddle.

Plate 5
Fig. 18 King
Fig. 19 Turpin
In the collections of Lady Ranfurly and the author

Plate 6
Fig. 21 Turpin
Fig. 22 King
By courtesy of Mr John Hall

Plate 5
Figure 18
Subject: **Tom King**
Title: Tom King (raised capitals)
Height: 12¼ in (31 cm)
Colour: Well coloured.
Rarity: R. A.
Pair: Fig. 17 (Turpin) *pl.* G-4.
Description: On horse facing right, in tricorn hat, long coat with lace collar, breeches, stockings and calf-boots with turn-overs.
Observations: This figure and its pair are very fine.

Figure 19
Subject: **Dick Turpin on Black Bess**
Title: Dick:Turpin (raised capitals)
Height: 13¼ in (33.5 cm)
Colour: Well coloured, black horse.
Rarity: VR. D. A.
Pair: The pair to this figure is unknown but probably exists. Fig. 20 has been reserved for it.
Description: On horse facing right, in tricorn hat, long coat, ermine cuffs, breeches and knee-boots. He holds a pistol in his right hand.
Observations: The largest and finest figure known of Turpin on *Black Bess*.

Plate 6
Figure 21
Subject: **Dick Turpin on Black Bess**
Title: None
Height: 8¼ in (21 cm)
Colour: Well coloured, black horse.
Rarity: Av.
Pair: Fig. 22 (King)
Description: On horse facing right, in tricorn hat, long coat with lace collar and ermine sleeves, breeches and knee-boots. He holds a pistol in his right hand.

Figure 22
Subject: **Tom King**
Title: None
Height: 8 in (20.5 cm)

Colour: Well coloured.
Rarity: Av.
Pair: Fig. 21 (Turpin)
Description: On horse facing left, in tricorn hat, long coat, breeches and knee-boots. He holds a pistol in his right hand.

Plate 7
Figure 24
Subject: **Tom King**
Title: Tom×King (raised capitals)
Height: 12 in (30.5 cm)
Colour: Poorly coloured.
Maker: In the style of Sampson Smith
Rarity: R.
Pair: There is almost certainly a pair to this figure, although it has not yet come to light. Fig. 23 has been reserved for it.
Description: On horse facing left, in cocked hat, cloak, coat and breeches. There is a pistol in his belt, and another in his left hand, which is by his side. A crude figure.

Plate 8
Figure 25
Subject: **Tom King**
Title: None
Height: 9 in (23 cm)
Colour: Well coloured.
Rarity: Av.
Pair: Fig. 26 (Turpin)
Description: On horse facing right, wearing plumed hat, cloak, coat, gauntlets, breeches and knee-boots. There is a pistol in his right hand, ornate saddle and saddle-cloth. Both the horse's forelegs are held straight.
Observations: 1. There has been much confusion in the past regarding the identity of this figure and its pair (*fig.* 26) because they bear a close similarity to certain penny plain, tuppence coloured portraits of highwaymen, other than Turpin and King. The matter has now been cleared up. A pre-Victorian Staffordshire figure inscribed 'Tom King &' is illustrated on *pl.* G-9. This figure is identical in all essential respects to *fig.* 25. It is now clear that *fig.* 25 portrays Tom King and *fig.* 26, Dick Turpin.

Plate 7
Fig. 24 King

2. In addition to the pair illustrated, there are two other pairs that are almost identical. In the pair illustrated, it will be noted that both the horse's forelegs are straight. In a second pair, the near-side front leg is flexed and in a third pair, the off-side front leg is flexed. Sometimes these figures are found wrongly paired. Separate catalogue numbers have not been given to the two additional pairs mentioned.

Colour Plate 56
Dick Turpin and Black Bess. *Fig.* 15, *pl.* G-4.
See page 471.

Colour Plate 57
Dick Turpin and Tom King. *Figs.* 1 and 2,
pl. G-2. See page 468.

Section G. Crime

Plate 8 continued

Figure 26
Subject: **Dick Turpin on Black Bess**
Title: None
Height: 9 in (23 cm)
Colour: Well coloured.
Rarity: Av.
Pair: *Fig.* 25 (King)
Description: On horse facing left, in beaver hat, cloak, neckerchief, long coat, waistcoat, gauntlets, breeches and knee-boots. He holds a pistol in his right hand. There is an ornate saddle and saddle-cloth and both the horse's forelegs are held straight.
Observations: 1. See preceding figure.
2. This is the only figure of Dick Turpin which I have seen, in which the horse is occasionally found coloured other than in black. However, the evidence in favour of the figure being Dick Turpin is such as to justify the assumption that this is just a 'potter's error'.

Plate 9

Tom King

The discovery of the pre-Victorian Staffordshire figure inscribed 'TOM KING &' illustrated on this plate enables us to identify, with confidence, similar untitled Victorian figures of both Turpin and King, such as those illustrated on *pl.* G-8.

Plate 10

Figure 27
Subject: **Frank Gardiner**
Title: Frank Gardiner (gilt script)
Date: c. 1874
Height: 9¼ in (23.5 cm)
Colour: Well coloured.
Maker: Sampson Smith
Rarity: VR.
Description: Identical in every way to *fig.* 11 (Turpin) *pl.* G-4, except that the title has been erased and the name 'Frank Gardiner'

Plate 8
Fig. 25 King

Fig. 26 Turpin
By courtesy of Mr and Mrs Eric Joyce

substituted, in gilt script. The figures vary slightly in size.
Observations: 1. Frank Gardiner's premature release, in 1874, after serving only 10 years of a 32-year sentence for gold robbery, caused a public outcry.
2. This is one of a number of figures which

are known with two titles. It is often possible to determine who was originally portrayed. In this case it was undoubtedly Turpin. When the demand arose, the potters were astute enough to erase his name and substitute that of Frank Gardiner, later reverting to the original title.

Plate 9 (Left)
Tom King
The discovery of this pre-Victorian Staffordshire figure inscribed 'TOM KING &' enables us to identify, with confidence, similar untitled Victorian figures of both Turpin and King, such as those illustrated on *pl.* G-8.
By courtesy of Messrs D. M. & P. Manheim

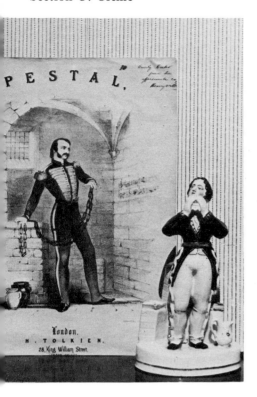

Plate 11
Fig. 28 Pestal
By courtesy of Mr and Mrs Eric Joyce

Plate 14
Off the rail
A cartoon by Leech published in *Punch* at the time of the fall of Hudson in 1849.

Plate 12
Fig. 29 Hudson
In the collection of Mr Geoffrey Allan

Plate 13
George Hudson, MP (1800-71)
This portrait of Hudson (c. 1848) by Francis Grant, RA hangs in the Mansion House, York.
By permission of York Corporation

Plate 11
Figure 28
Subject: **Colonel Paul Pestal**
Title: None
Date: 184–
Height: 8¼ in (21 cm)
Colour: Well coloured with blue coat.
Rarity: VR. D. A.
Description: Standing bare-headed, with whiskers but no moustache, in skirted coat with a belt and trousers. Both hands are raised in front of him. On each side, a heavy chain hangs against his legs from his belt to his ankles. To his left, there is a jug on the floor and a closed book on a low wall. To his right, there is an open book on the wall.
Observations: Probably based on the lithograph music-front, inscribed 'Pestal', by Stannard and Co., after a painting by J. McNevin, published by H. Tolkien, 28, King William Street, London Bridge. It shows him, bare-headed with moustache as well as side-whiskers, in different clothes (tunic with epaulettes, belt and trousers), with a heavy chain on both wrists, his right hand holding part of a loop of it hanging from a wall. There are two jugs on the ground in front of the wall. The cover is for a melody titled *Yes! The die is cast* written by John Melton and arranged by J. R. Ling. The music is prefaced by the following:

'The Martyrdom of Col. Pestal by the Russian Government has been rendered immortal by the exquisite melody he scratched on the wall of his dungeon with a link of his chain on the night previous to his execution. Mr Melton has attempted to pourtray (*sic*) the emotions by which the unfortunate patriot was actuated in his last hours when he composed this beautiful Air. The Publisher'

Plate 12
Figure 29
Subject: **George Hudson**
Title: Rail/Way/Bill (indented capitals)
Date: c. 1844
Height: 9½ in (24 cm)
Colour: Well coloured, underglaze blue coat.
Rarity: VR. D. A.

Colour Plate 58
Emily Sandford, Norwich Castle and James Blomfield Rush. *Figs.* 47, 49, and 48, *pl.* G-23. See page 483.

Colour Plate 59
William Palmer. *Fig.* 42, *pl.* G-18A. See page 479.

G476

Plate 12 continued

Description: Standing with both hands in trouser pockets. He wears a beaver hat, neckerchief, jacket, waistcoat and trousers. He has a sizeable paunch.

Observations: 1. I am grateful to Mr E. Atkinson, Archivist of British Transport Historical Records, who kindly looked into this matter for me. His conclusion, which was supported by the Curators of both the Castle and Yorkshire Museums at York, was that the figure portrays George Hudson, the 'Railway King'. It is known that a number of figures of him were made, although no Staffordshire figure has, to my knowledge, been recorded hitherto. A copy of an advertisement which appeared in *The Yorkshire Gazette* for November, 1847, is of some interest, although it refers to figures probably produced locally.

> GEORGE HUDSON, ESQ., M.P.
> B. Mitchell respectfully informs
> his Fellow-Citizens and the Gentry of the County
> that he has now on Sale
> an admirable Full Length Statue, in Composition, of
> the Hon. Member for Sunderland, executed from a
> Model by Mr. Bradley, of this City, Sculptor,
> which has been pronounced by competent judges as
> a most FAITHFUL LIKENESS of the Hon.
> Member.
> Size 17 Inches—Price 3s. 6d. each
> Stonegate, York. Nov. 18, 1847.

2. The title of the figure presumably refers to the Railway Bill introduced by Gladstone, when President of the Board of Trade, in 1844. Hudson got the Bill substantially whittled down. The most famous and popular of the clauses of the new Bill was the requirement that every company run at least one train a day over its lines conveying third-class passengers at 1d. a mile.

Plate 13
George Hudson
This portrait of Hudson by Francis Grant, RA which hangs in the Mansion House, York has the following inscription on a plaque underneath:

> This Portrait of GEORGE HUDSON M.P. Lord Mayor of the CITY of YORK for the years 1837, 1838 and 1847 is by permission of the Corporation placed in the Mansion House at the request of a number of his fellow citizens as a permanent memorial of their personal respect for him and their gratitude for the eminent services he has rendered for the CITY by the promotion of many important Public Works and Improvements, which have been highly conducive to the advantage and prosperity of its inhabitants.
> Francis Grant R.A. JAMES RICHARDSON, Esq.
>   Pinxit   Lord Mayor 1848

There is some similarity between *fig.* 29, *pl.* G-12 and this portrait.

Plate 14
George Hudson
A cartoon by Leech, inscribed *Off the Rail*, published in *Punch* at the time of the fall of Hudson in 1849.

Plate 15
Figure 30
Subject: **Jemmy Wood**
Title: Jemmy Wood (gilt script)
Date: *c.* 1845
Height: 8 in (20.5 cm)
Colour: Well coloured.
Rarity: VR.
Description: Half-sitting with both hands in waistcoat pockets, bare-headed, in tailcoat, waistcoat, breeches, stockings and pumps with gilt buckles. Enormous paunch.
Observations: See *fig.* 31, *pl.* G-16.

Plate 15
Fig. 30 Wood

Plate 16
Figure 31
Subject: **Jemmy Wood**
Title: None
Date: *c.* 1845
Height: 14⅜ in (36.5 cm)
Colour: Well coloured.

Plate 16
Fig. 31 Wood
Fig. 32 Wood
Fig. 33 Wood
Fig. 34 Orton
In the Thomas Balston collection

Section G. Crime

Plate 16 continued
Rarity: VR.
Description: Standing bare-headed, in coat, waistcoat, breeches, stockings and pumps. His left hand is in his waistcoat pocket and his right hand in his trouser pocket. Great paunch.
Observations: 1. *Figs.* 30–33 (inclusive) closely resemble the woodcut portrait in *Life and Anecdotes of Jemmy Wood* (Kent & Co. n.d.), published *c.* 1845, see *ch.* 3, *pl.* 55A. 2. There is also a mini-version of Jemmy Wood, see *ch.* 4, *pl.* 5.

Figure 32
Subject: **Jemmy Wood**
Title: Jemmy Wood (raised capitals)
Date: *c.* 1845
Height: 11 in (28 cm)
Colour: Well coloured.
Rarity: Av.
Description: Almost identical to *fig.* 31, but in addition, there is a pedestal to his left.
Observations: 1. A similar figure fetched 16 gns at Christie's in 1967; and another, together with *fig.* 34 (Orton), 50 gns in 1969. 2. See *fig.* 31 (Wood).

Figure 33
Subject: **Jemmy Wood**
Title: Jimmy, Wood (script capitals)
Date: *c.* 1845
Height: 7½ in (19 cm)
Colour: Well coloured.
Rarity: Av.
Description: Standing bare-headed, in tailcoat, waistcoat, breeches, stockings and pumps. His left hand is in his waistcoat pocket and right hand in his trouser pocket.
Observations: 1. A similar figure fetched 18 gns at Christie's in 1963; another, fetched 10 gns in the same rooms in 1964 and another, fetched 20 gns in the same rooms in 1966. 2. See *fig.* 31 (Wood).

Figure 34
Subject: **Arthur Orton**
Title: Sir. R. Tichborne (raised capitals)
Date: *c.* 1873
Height: 14¾ in (37.5 cm)
Colour: Usually sparsely coloured—a 'porridge' piece. Sometimes lavishly and garishly coloured.
Maker: Sampson Smith
Rarity: Av.
Description: Standing with a bird in his left hand, a gun in his right hand. He wears a beaver hat, overcoat, coat, cravat, trousers strapped under the instep and pumps.
Observations: A similar figure fetched 22 gns at Christie's in 1963; and another, together with *fig.* 32 (Wood), 50 gns in 1969.

Plate 17
Figure 35
Subject: **William Smith O'Brien**
Title: None
Date: *c.* 1848
Height: 9 in (23 cm)
Colour: Usually sparsely coloured.
Rarity: R.
Pair: No pair to this piece is known, but the possibility cannot be excluded.
Description: He stands bare-headed, in an open-neck shirt, short trousers and barefeet. He is handcuffed and his left forearm rests on a draped pedestal.
Observations: 1. The hair style is very similar to that of *fig.* 36, and this, together with the presence of handcuffs, makes it almost

G478

Plate 17   *Fig.* 35 O'Brien   *Fig.* 36 O'Brien   *Fig.* 37 Mrs O'Brien

In the Thomas Balston collection

certain that the figure represents O'Brien. 2. A similar figure fetched 16 guineas at Christie's in 1964.

Figure 36
Subject: **William Smith O'Brien**
Title: S. O'Brien (indented capitals)
Date: *c.* 1848
Height: 7 in (17.5 cm)
Colour: Well coloured.
Maker: Alpha factory
Rarity: R. D.
Pair: Fig. 37 (Mrs O'Brien)
Description: Sitting bare-headed, wearing long coat, jacket, trousers and shoes. Handcuffed.
Observations: 1. In 1848, O'Brien was convicted of high treason, and sentenced to be hanged, drawn and quartered, but was transported to Tasmania. 2. A similar figure and its pair fetched 115 gns at Christie's in 1963; and another pair, £150 at Sotheby's in 1968.

Figure 37
Subject: **Mrs O'Brien**
Title: Mrs. O'Brien (indented capitals)
Date: *c.* 1848
Height: 7½ in (19 cm)
Colour: Well coloured.
Maker: Alpha factory
Rarity: VR. D.
Pair: Fig. 36 (O'Brien)
Description: She is facing half-left, in the act of getting up from an armchair, she has a shawl over her head, lace collar, bell sleeves and wide flounced skirt.
Observations: See preceding figure.

Plate 18
Figure 38
Subject: **Frederick George Manning**
Title: Unknown

Date: *c.* 1849
Height: 8⅝ in (21.75 cm)
Colour: Well coloured.
Rarity: VR. D.
Pair: Fig. 39 (Maria Manning)
Description: Standing bare-headed, wearing cravat, coat and trousers. His left arm rests on a pedestal and he holds his top-hat (open end up) in his left hand.
Observations: The only known example of this figure is untitled, but colour, style and appearance leave no room for doubting that it is the pair to *fig.* 39 (Maria Manning) of which I have seen three examples, two titled and one untitled.

Figure 39
Subject: **Maria Manning**
Title: Mrs Manning (gilt script)
Date: *c.* 1849
Height: 8¾ in (21.25 cm)
Colour: Well coloured.
Rarity: VR. D.
Pair: Fig. 38 (Manning)
Description: Standing, in poke bonnet, Zouave jacket and wide skirt. She rests her right hand, in which she holds a handkerchief, on a pedestal.
Observations: See preceding figure.

Figure 40
Subject: **Frederick George Manning**
Title: F. G. Manning (gilt script)
Date: *c.* 1849
Height: 9½ in (24 cm)
Colour: Well coloured.
Rarity: R. D.
Pair: Fig. 41 (Maria Manning)
Description: Standing bare-headed, wearing cravat, coat and trousers. His left arm rests on a pedestal and he holds a manuscript, possibly his confession, in his left hand.

Plate 18 (Above and below)   Fig. 39 Mrs Manning
Fig. 38 (untitled version)
Manning

Fig. 40 Manning   *Fig.* 41 Mrs Manning

Plate 18A
Fig. 42 Palmer

Observations: The Mannings were executed in November, 1849 for the murder of Patrick O'Connor, Maria Manning's former lover.

Figure 41
Subject: **Maria Manning**
Title: Maria Manning (gilt script)
Date: *c.* 1849
Height: 9 in (23 cm)
Colour: Well coloured.
Rarity: R. D.
Pair: *Fig.* 40 (Manning)
Description: Similar to *fig.* 39, except that there is no pedestal. Her right hand, holding a handkerchief, rests by her side.
Observations: A similar figure and pair fetched 52 gns at Christie's in 1963.

Plate 18A
Figure 42
Subject: **William Palmer**
Title: William · Palmer (raised capitals on plaque)
Date: *c.* 1856
Height: 11¼ in (28.5 cm)
Colour: Well coloured.
Rarity: R. D.
Description: He stands bare-headed, wearing neckerchief, waistcoat and trousers. Fence to his left. Title occasionally mis-spelt.
Observations: 1. There is a close similarity between this figure and that titled 'Mr Robert Evans', see *fig.* 49, *pl.* D-24.
2. Palmer was executed in June, 1856, for the murder of his friend, John Parsons Cook, in December, 1855.

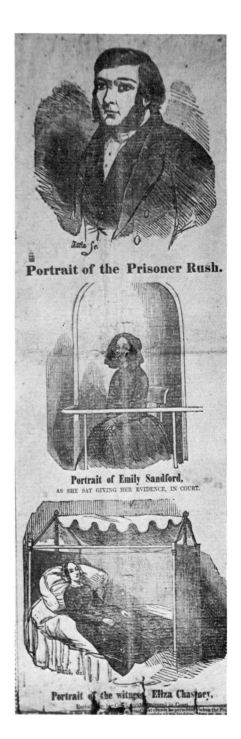

Plate 18B
T: *Fig.* 43 Palmer's House
B: An engraving of the 'Residence of William Palmer at Rugeley' which appeared in *The Illustrated London News* on May 24th, 1856.
By courtesy of Mr and Mrs Eric Joyce

Portrait of the Prisoner Rush.

Portrait of Emily Sandford,
AS SHE SAT GIVING HER EVIDENCE, IN COURT.

Portrait of the witness Eliza Chastney,

Plate 19
Portraits of Rush, Emily Sandford and Eliza Chastney which appeared in *The Norfolk Chronicle and Norwich Gazette* on April 4th, 1849.

Plate 18A continued
3. A similar figure fetched 68 gns at Christie's in 1965; and another, 160 gns in 1969.

Plate 18B
Figure 43
Subject: **Palmer's House**
Title: Palmers House (raised capitals)
Date: *c.* 1856
Height: 7¾ in (20 cm)
Colour: Well coloured.
Rarity: R. D.
Description: A typical Georgian residence, two-storied, with front door, five windows and two square chimneys.
Observations: 1. A similar figure, together with *fig.* 46(*a*) (Stanfield Hall) *pl.* G-20, fetched 30 gns at Christie's in 1967.
2. Very similar to an engraving inscribed *Residence of William Palmer at Rugeley* which appeared in *The Illustrated London News* on May 24th, 1856.

G480

Plate 19
Rush, Sandford and Chastney
Portraits of Rush, Emily Sandford and Eliza Chastney which appeared in *The Norfolk Chronicle and Norwich Gazette* on April 4th, 1849.
A figure of Eliza Chastney has so far not come to light, but it could well be that one was made.

Plate 20
Figure 44
Subject: **Potash Farm**
Title: Potash Farm (gilt script)
Date: *c.* 1849
Height: 8½ in (21.5 cm)
Colour: Well coloured.
Rarity: C. D.
Series: Same series as *fig.* 45 (Norwich Castle) and *fig.* 46 (Stanfield Hall).
Description: Three-storied farmhouse with

central porch, twelve windows and one chimney. An extension to the right has two storeys, doorway, three windows and one chimney.
Observations: 1. The home of James Blomfield Rush who murdered Isaac Jermy, Recorder of Norwich on November 28th, 1848.
2. A 5¼ in (13.5 cm) version of this figure with minor differences is known [44(*a*)]. Sometimes it is titled 'Stanfield Hall' [44(*b*)]. Occasionally it is untitled.

Figure 45
Subject: **Norwich Castle**
Title: Norwich Castle (gilt script)
Date: *c.* 1849
Height: 9 in (23 cm)
Colour: Well coloured.
Rarity: VR. D.
Series: Same series as *fig.* 44 (Potash Farm)

Section G. Crime

Plate 20
Fig. 44 Potash Farm
Fig. 45 Norwich Castle
Fig. 46 Stanfield Hall
*By courtesy of the Curator of
the Norwich Castle Museum*

Plate 20
Fig. 44 Potash Farm
Fig. 45 Norwich Castle
Fig. 46 Stanfield Hall
*By courtesy of the Curator of
the Norwich Castle Museum*

and *fig.* 46 (Stanfield Hall).
Description: Classical Norman keep, protected by a curtain wall strengthened with two towers, between which run steps leading to an ornate doorway, to the right of the keep.
Observations: 1. Rush was executed on the bridge over the moat at Norwich Castle on April 21st, 1849.
2. No small version of this figure has so far come to light.
3. It is most mysterious that only one example of this figure is known, whilst the others in the series are quite common. Incidentally, this unique figure is in the Norwich Castle Museum.

Figure 46
Subject: **Stanfield Hall**
Title: Stanfield Hall (gilt script)
Date: *c.* 1849
Height: 8 in (20.5 cm)
Colour: Well coloured.
Rarity: C. D.
Series: Same series as *fig.* 44 (Potash Farm) and *fig.* 45 (Norwich Castle).
Description: Three-storied house with central porch, twelve windows and two chimneys. A two-storied extension, to the right, has one doorway and six windows with no chimneys. There is a moat with a bridge, at the right end.

Observations: 1. The home of Isaac Jermy, Recorder of Norwich, who was murdered by James Rush on November 28th, 1848.
2. A 5¾ in (14.5 cm) version of this figure with minor differences is known [46(*a*)]. As in the case of *fig.* 44(*a*), this version is also found erroneously titled 'Potash Farm' [46(*b*)]. Occasionally it is untitled.
3. Unlike *figs.* 44 and 45, *fig.* 46 bears little resemblance to the building it is intended to portray. See *fig.* 52, *pl.* G-25.
4. One example of the large version has been seen erroneously titled 'Stanfield Farm' (gilt script).

Plate 21
*Potash Farm, near
Wymondham*
This engraving appeared
in *The Illustrated London
News* of March 31st, 1849.
It will be noted that *fig.* 44
(Potash Farm) bears a
close similarity to the
engraving.
*By courtesy of The Illustrated
London News*

Plate 23
Fig. 44(b) Potash Farm
(Stanfield Hall)
Fig. 47 Sandford
Fig. 49 Norwich Castle
Fig. 48 Rush
Fig. 44(a) Potash Farm

Plate 20 continued
5. A lot comprising *figs.* 44 and 46 fetched
22 gns at Christie's in 1966; and another,
40 gns in the same rooms in 1967.

Plate 21
Potash Farm
This engraving inscribed *Potash Farm, near
Wymondham* appeared in *The Illustrated
London News* of March 31st, 1849. When
compared with *fig.* 44, *pl.* G-20 it becomes
apparent that the potter obtained a reasonable likeness of his subject.

G482

Plate 22
Norwich Castle
This engraving appeared in *The Illustrated
London News* of August 14th, 1847. There is
a close similarity between it and *fig.* 45, *pl.*
G-20.

Plate 23
Figure 44(a)
Subject: **Potash Farm** (small version)
Observations: 1. Forgeries of this figure have
been noted occasionally during the last two

years; those of its pair are far commoner.
The gilding is particularly crude.
2. For details see *fig.* 44 (Potash Farm) *pl.*
G-20.

Figure 44(b)
Subject: **Potash Farm** (small version er-
roneously titled 'Stanfield Hall').
Observations: For details see *fig.* 44 (Potash
Farm) *pl.* G-20.

Plate 24
Fig. 46(a) Stanfield Hall
Fig. 50 ?Sandford
By courtesy of Mr Arthur Thornton

Figure 47
Subject: **Emily Sandford**
Title: Emily Sandford (gilt script)
Date: *c.* 1849
Height: 9½ in (24 cm)
Colour: Well coloured.
Rarity: Av. D.
Pair: *Fig.* 48 (Rush)
Description: Standing, wearing a shawl over her head, blouse with bell sleeves, lace collar and wide skirt. She holds a manuscript in her left hand. There is a pedestal to her right.
Observations: A similar figure and pair fetched 88 gns at Christie's in 1965, and another pair 80 gns in the same rooms in 1967.

Figure 48
Subject: **James Blomfield Rush**
Title: James B. Rush (gilt script)
Date: *c.* 1849
Height: 10 in (25 cm)
Colour: Well coloured.
Rarity: Av. D.
Pair: *Fig.* 47 (Sandford)
Description: Standing bare-headed, a speech in his right hand, a pedestal to his left. He wears frock-coat, cravat, waistcoat and trousers.
Observations: 1. Rush was found guilty of the murder of the Recorder of Norwich, Isaac Jermy and hanged at Norwich Castle in April, 1849.
2. See preceding figure.

Figure 49
Subject: **Norwich Castle**
Title: Norwich/Castle (raised capitals on blue plaque)
Height: 6 in (15.25 cm)
Colour: Well coloured.
Rarity: VR.
Description: Three castellated towers, the centre one being the largest. Nine barred windows and central door with plaque over.
Observations: 1. Unlike *fig.* 45, *pl.* G-20 it bears no resemblance to any part of Norwich Castle. The piece is probably a figment of the potter's imagination but there is a vague resemblance to the castle portrayed in the city's arms—a castle over a lion.
2. *Fig.* 49(a), *pl.* G-26 is very similar, except that the blue plaque has a royal coat-of-arms embossed on it, instead of the words 'Norwich Castle', and above the plaque is a clock-face. Before the discovery of *fig.* 45, *pl.* G-20 it, too, was held to represent Norwich Castle, particularly as Norwich Castle was originally a royal castle built at the expense of William I and held for him by a Constable. In the light of present knowledge however, this figure cannot be held to represent any particular castle.

Plate 24
Figure 46(a)
Subject: **Stanfield Hall** (small version)
Observations: 1. For details see *fig.* 46 (Stanfield Hall) *pl.* G-20.

2. Many forgeries of this figure have been noted during the last two years. They are apparent immediately, because of the inability of the forger to gild in the manner of the Victorian craftsmen. Forgeries of the small version of Potash Farm are far less common.
3. Crude, pasty yellow, untitled copies of the small version of this figure, and its pair, are seen occasionally. Rarely, an example is found impressed on the base 'LEEDS POTTERY'. These are probably relatively late copies.

Figure 50
Subject: **? Emily Sandford**
Title: None
Date: *c.* 1849
Height: 6¼ in (16 cm)
Colour: Well coloured.
Rarity: R.
Pair: No pair is known to this figure, but one probably exists. *Fig.* 51 has been reserved for it.
Description: Standing bare-headed, in short jacket, full skirt and apron, a duster in her right hand.
Observations: The face bears a striking resemblance to that of *fig.* 47, *pl.* G-23, and it is generally accepted that this figure, too, portrays Emily Sandford.

Section H
Authors, Poets, Composers et cetera
Biographies and Historical Notes

ANDERSON, JOHN, traditionally the Town Piper of Kelso. A character in a poem by Burns.
See **pl. H**-21.

ARMOUR, JEAN (1767–1834), daughter of a Mauchline mason. The poet Robert Burns became entangled with her and later wrote 'Never a man loved, or rather adored, a woman more than I did her'. In 1786, he gave her a written declaration of marriage, which her father subsequently destroyed, preferring his daughter's loss of reputation to the proposed match. The poem *The Rigs o' Barley* which appeared in Burns' first small volume of poems, published in 1786, is regarded as his own epithalamium, Annie being a blind for Jean Armour.
See **pl. H**-21.

AULD LANG SYNE, poem by Burns.

> Should auld acquaintance be forgot,
> And never brought to min'?
> Should auld acquaintance be forgot,
> And days o' lang syne?
> CHORUS
> For auld lang syne, my dear,
> For auld lang syne,
> We'll tak' a cup o' kindness yet,
> For auld lang syne?

An older song of the same name, but different both in melody and words, was familiar all over Scotland generations before the birth of Burns.
See **pl. H**-21.

BROWNING, ELIZABETH BARRETT (1806–61), English poetess. Between 1830 and 1860, she wrote many poems showing great intellectual grasp and imaginative fervour. In 1846, she married Robert Browning and, afterwards, lived mostly in Italy. At the age of fifteen she injured her spine in a fall, and in consequence was for many years compelled to lie on her back.
See **pls. H**-22, 23.

BROWNING, ROBERT (1812–89), English poet. His earlier poems and dramas were far from popular, largely because of a difficult style. From 1864 onwards, he published many works which were appreciated, some of which contained the finest poetry of this period. In 1846, he married Elizabeth Barrett and with her settled in Florence. When she died in 1861, he returned to London but frequently revisited Italy in later life.
See **pl. H**-22.

BURNS, ROBERT (1759–96), Scottish
H486

poet. Born at Alloway, the son of a cottar, he was educated by his father. In 1772, obtained work as a farm-labourer. His first small volume of poems, published in 1786 at Kilmarnock, startled the world and led to his subsequent recognition as Scotland's greatest poet. He bought a farm with the five hundred pounds derived from the sales of the book. In 1786, he gave Jean Armour, the daughter of a Mauchline mason, a written declaration of marriage. Trysted with Mary Campbell, a sailor's daughter from Argyllshire, to go with him as his wife to Jamaica, 1786. Renewed his relations with Jean Armour in 1787. Throughout his career he poured fourth song after song of emotional tenderness which made his name immortal. *Tam o' Shanter*, his most popular work, was written in one day in 1790. He died at Dumfries in 1796.
See **pls. H**-9, 10, 12, 13, 14, 15, 16, 17, 18, 18A.

BYRON, GEORGE GORDON, sixth Baron (1788–1824), poet. Born in London, the son of the irresponsible Captain John Byron. His first ten years were spent in his mother's lodgings in Aberdeen, her husband having squandered her fortune. He was lame from birth and the squalid surroundings and violent temper of his deserted mother produced a repression in him which explains many of his later actions. He succeeded to the title, in 1798, on the death of the notorious 'wicked lord', the fifth baron—his great-uncle. He received his education at Aberdeen Grammar School and Harrow School, proceeding to Trinity College, Cambridge, in 1805. Here he led a life of dissipation. During this period he produced a collection of poems under the title of *Hours of Idleness*. These poems, published in 1807, were critically reviewed. Byron replied with his powerful Popian satire *English Bards and Scotch Reviewers* (1809). He then set out on his grand tour, visiting Spain, Malta, Albania, Greece and the Aegean. During his visit to Athens, which lasted from December, 1809, to March, 1810, he met Theresa Macri, the eldest of three beautiful daughters of a British vice-consul, with whom he lodged. She is believed to have inspired *The Maid of Athens*, the most popular of his shorter poems. In 1813, he published the first of a series of oriental pieces titled *Giaour*. There followed *Lara*, in 1814 and the *Bride of Corinth*, in 1815. During this period he dramatized himself as a man of mystery and a gloomy romantic figure. He became the

darling of London society and there developed the concept of the 'Byronic hero'. In 1815, he married Anne Isabella Milbanke, who left him in 1816, following the birth of a daughter. He was suspected of something more than brotherly love for his half-sister, Augusta Leigh, and was ostracized. In 1817, he sold Newstead Abbey, the family home, although he had lived there but little during his nineteen years of ownership. He left for the continent. In Venice, he met the Countess Teresa Guiccioli, who became his mistress. Some of his best works belong to this period. He gave active help to the Italian revolutionaries. In 1823, he joined the Greek insurgents who had risen against the Turks. He died of marsh fever in Missolonghi. His body was brought back to England and is buried at Hucknall Torkard, near Nottingham.
See **pls. H**-7, 7A, 8, 9.

CAMPBELL, MARY (c.1768–86), otherwise known as 'Highland Mary'. The daughter of a Clyde sailor Archibald Campbell, from Argyllshire. In 1786, Burns tried to persuade her to go with him to Jamaica, as his wife. However, she died of malignant fever at Greenock, later that year. After her death, he composed some of his finest poems in her memory, *Will ye go to the Indies, my Mary?*; *To Mary in Heaven* (October, 1789) and *Highland Mary* (November, 1792).
See **pls. H**-9, 10, 12, 14, 18A.

CAUDLE, MR and MRS, characters in *Punch. Mrs Caudle's Curtain Lectures* by Douglas Jerrold appeared in *Punch* in 1845 and added greatly to the popularity of the periodical.
Mr Caudle was a 'toyman and doll-merchant' and his wife a voluble scold. Her lectures were addressed to him whenever he wanted to go to sleep, and were reproofs for his mildly convivial habits and exhortations to take the family to the seaside, or elaborate expositions on similar domestic subjects.
See **pl. H**-24.

COOK, ELIZA (1818–89), English poetess. The daughter of a London tradesman. She wrote for various magazines from a very early age and issued volumes of poetry in 1838, 1864 and 1865. She conducted *Eliza Cook's Journal* from 1849 to 1854, much of which was republished as *Jottings from my Journal*, 1860.
See **pls. H**-10, 11.

DON QUIXOTE, a satirical romance by Cervantes, published in 1605. The work is in the form of a burlesque of the romances of chivalry, which were already losing their popularity. The book was translated into English as early as 1612. The story has been reproduced on the stage in various forms on many occasions.

Don Quixote was an elderly Spanish gentleman whose head had been turned by reading old stories about knights. He made up his mind to be a knight himself, although he lived in an age when armed knights were unknown. He put on a suit of rusty armour, obtained an old sword and lance and rode from his house on the back of an aged horse called *Rosinante* to seek adventure and win fame. As the knights of old were always attended by squires, he persuaded a fat and lazy farm labourer called Sancho Panza to be his squire, promising to make him the governor of an island and a rich man. Sancho was delighted with the idea that he would become a wealthy man and, mounted on his ass he followed the crazy old gentleman. Don Quixote had many adventures, most of them foolish and many of them amusing. To his disordered imagination, the most commonplace objects assumed fearful or romantic forms.
See **pl. H**-26.

FLUSH, the dog belonging to Elizabeth Barrett Browning (1806–61), a gift of a friend Mary Mitford (1787–1855), the novelist.
See **pl. H**-22.

HATHAWAY, ANNE (1556–1623). Married William Shakespeare in 1582.
See **pl. H**-11.

HIGHLAND MARY.
See **Campbell, Mary** (*c.* 1768–86).

JOHN ANDERSON, MY JO, poem by Burns.

> John Anderson, my jo, John,
>   When we were first acquent;
> Your locks were like the raven,
>   Your bonnie brow was brent;
> But now your brow is beld, John,
>   Your locks are like the snaw;
> But blessings on your frosty pow,
>   John Anderson, my jo.

John Anderson, in the flesh, was traditionally the Town Piper of Kelso.
See **pl. H**-21.

JOHNSON, SAMUEL (1709–84), lexicographer and writer. Educated at Lichfield Grammar School and Pembroke College, Oxford. He attained eminence following the publication of several works, including *The Vanity of Human Wishes* (1749). He was, for many years, the most prominent literary man in England. He published his famous *English Dictionary* in 1755. He produced many other works and was greatly honoured during his life, enjoying a crown pension of £300 a year from 1762. His biography was written by James Boswell.
See **pl. H**-10.

LOCHINVAR, the hero of a ballad included in Sir Walter Scott's *Marmion*. Lochinvar's fair Ellen is about to be married to 'a laggard in love and a dastard in war', when Lochinvar arrives at the bridal feast and claims a dance with her. As they reach the hall door he swings the lady on to his horse and rides off with her.
See **pl. H**-27.

MACRI, THERESA (1795–1875), the 'Maid of Athens'. She was the eldest of three very beautiful daughters of the British vice-consul with whom Byron lodged on his visit to Athens from December, 1809, to March, 1810. She inspired *The Maid of Athens*, the most popular of Byron's shorter poems, subsequently set to music by Gounod. The poet's boat, the stern-board of which may still be seen at Newstead Abbey, was also named *The Maid of Athens*. Theresa Macri married the British consul at Missolonghi. After his death she became very poor and an appeal for her support was published in *The Times* of March 23rd, 1872.
See **pls. H**-7, 7A, 9.

MAID OF ATHENS.
See **Macri, Theresa** (1795–1875).

MAIDA, a favourite greyhound of Sir Walter Scott.
See **pl. H**-18.

MILTON, JOHN (1608–74), poet. Born at Cheapside, the son of a London scrivener. From St. Paul's School he went to Cambridge. His best-known work *Paradise Lost* was written between 1658 and 1663. It is regarded as the greatest poem of its kind in the language. In 1652, he became totally blind. He died in 1674 and was buried in St. Giles' Church, Cripplegate, London. A monument was erected to his memory in Westminster Abbey.
See **pls. H**-1, 2, 5, 6, 7, 9.

MOZART, WOLFGANG AMADEUS (1756–91), Austrian composer. Born at Salzburg, the youngest child of Leopold Mozart, he began studying the harpsichord when he was only four years old. He made his first professional tour through Europe at the age of six; other tours followed. When his first symphonies were performed in London, his harpsichord playing amazed the Queen's music master, Johann Christian Bach. Every branch of musical composition was enriched by his genius, particularly opera—*Don Giovanni*, *The Marriage of Figaro*, and *The Magic Flute* being milestones in the evolution of opera. He married Constanze Weber, cousin of the composer, who although a charming wife was a poor manager and debt and difficulties increased. In 1787, he was appointed 'Kammer-Musicus' to Joseph II, at a salary of £80 a year. In writing the noble Requiem Mass commissioned for Count Walsegg, he felt he was writing his own requiem. He caught typhus and died before the work was finished. In all he wrote over 600 compositions.
See **pl. H**-28.

MY NANNIE, O!, poem by Burns.

> Behind yon hills, where Lugar flows,
> 'Mang moors an' mosses many, O,
> The wintry sun the day has closed,
> And I'll awa' to Nannie, O.

Agnes Fleming, a servant at Calcothill, near Lochlea, was the one here sung of as Nannie.
See **pl. H**-21.

RIGS O' BARLEY, THE, poem by Burns. It appeared in his first small volume of poems published at Kilmarnock in 1786.

> Corn rigs, an' barley rigs,
>   An' corn rigs are bonnie:
> I'll ne'er forget that happy night,
>   Amang the rigs wi' Annie.

This is the poet's own epithalamium (nuptual poem). Annie is a blind for another

name, Jean Armour, of whom Burns wrote: 'Never a man loved, or rather adored, a woman more than I did her'. He married her subsequently.
See **pl. H**-21.

ROUSSEAU, JEAN-JACQUES (1712–78), French philospher, political writer and composer. He was born at Geneva. Contributed the musical section to Diderot's *Encyclopédie*. Studied social questions with great ardour and, in 1761, published his novel *Julie, ou la Nouvelle Héloïse*. This was followed, in 1762, by *Emile*. These works contained much at variance with convention and he was obliged to leave France for a time. Whilst in England he wrote *Confessions* and the celebrated *Le Contrat Social*.
See **pls. H**-10, 10A.

SANCHO PANZA, a character in *Don Quixote*, a satirical romance by Cervantes, published in 1605.
See **pl. H**-26 and **Don Quixote**.

SCOTT, SIR WALTER (1771–1832), Scottish novelist and poet. Born at Edinburgh and educated for the Bar. In 1814, he published *Waverley*, anonymously. It was an immediate success. Other stories followed; the Waverley novels and their author were everywhere the subject of discussion. Included in these novels were *Rob Roy* and the *Bride of Lammermoor*. Scott is often portrayed with his favourite hound *Maida*. The chief works of his latter years were *Woodstock*, *Life of Napoleon* and *Tales of a Grandfather*. He died at Abbotsford. He was created a baronet in 1820.
See **pls. H**-17, 18.

SHAKESPEARE, WILLIAM (1564–1616), dramatist and poet. Born about April 23rd, 1564 in Henley Street, Stratford-upon-Avon. The record of his baptism in the register of Holy Trinity Church states: *April 26: Gulielmus filius Johannes Shakspere*. At the time of his birth, his father John Shakespeare, was a prosperous, respected tradesman and his mother, the daughter of a yeoman farmer. He probably received his early education at the local grammar school and very possibly witnessed some of the plays produced by companies of travelling actors in Stratford during his boyhood. At the age of eighteen, he married Anne Hathaway, daughter of Richard Hathaway, who belonged to a well-respected yeoman family. The marriage took place in 1582, when Anne was aged twenty-six. Shakespeare had three children—Susanna and the twins Hamnet and Judith. He left Stratford about 1585, according to tradition to avoid prosecution for poaching deer. It is probable that he went to London to seek his fortune in a company of players. From 1592 onwards, he can be definitely traced, first as an actor and then as a reviser and writer of plays. His first narrative poem *Venus and Adonis* was published in 1593. He had associations with various companies of players and partnerships in certain theatrical ventures, and it was for his own company that many of his plays were written. At one stage he was one of the proprietors of the Globe theatre. The approximate dates of some of his plays are as follows:
Henry VI, three parts, 1590–2
Richard III, 1592–4
Romeo and Juliet and *A Midsummer-Night's Dream*, 1594–6
King John and *The Merchant of Venice*, 1596–8

Hamlet, 1600–2
Othello and *Macbeth,* 1604–6
Winter's Tale, 1610–2
Henry VIII, 1612–3
When his success as a playwright was assured, he resumed his connection with his native town. By 1610, he had ceased to work in London and settled permanently in Stratford. He died at the age of fifty-two and was buried in the local parish church.
See **pl. C**-96,
pls. H-1, 2, 3, 4, 5, 6, 7, 9, 11, 28.

SHAKESPEARE'S HOUSE: Reputed to be the birthplace. No record of the erection of the building survives, but the architectural features suggest that it was built in the late fifteenth, or early sixteenth centuries. The building consisted of a low foundation wall of stone, on which was erected a framing of oak beams, the spaces between the timbers being filled in with wattle and daub and the structure consolidated by a massive stone chimney stack in the centre and a raftered roof. Tradition assigns the western, or left hand portion of the building, as the poet's birthplace, and the eastern portion as a shop owned by Shakespeare's father and used in connection with his trade as glover and wool dealer. At one time, they were two separate buildings. The earliest extant representation of the birthplace (1769) shows the building with dormer windows and gable, a deep porch or penthouse and a projecting bay window. Subsequent drawings show that towards the end of the eighteenth century the dormer windows, bay window and porch were removed and the front (the living room of the house) fitted up as a butcher's shop. At the beginning of the nineteenth century the eastern portion also underwent a change, being refashioned at the front in red brick,

the original timber framing remaining behind undisturbed. The birthplace remained in the hands of descendants of Shakespeare until 1806, when it was sold to Thomas Court for £210. For over a century before that date the eastern part, formerly John Shakespeare's shop, had been in use as an inn, known first as *The Maidenhead* and afterwards as *The Swan and Maidenhead.* In 1847, a sale poster was displayed in Stratford-upon-Avon, London and elsewhere announcing the sale of:

Shakespeare's house—the truly heart-stirring relic of a most glorious period, and of England's immortal bard . . . the most honoured monument of the greatest genius that ever lived.

The sale took place at the Auction Mart, London on September 16th, 1847 and the house was purchased for £3,000 by committees set up in London and Stratford to raise funds to buy the property. The Stratford Birthplace Committee undertook the difficult and expensive task of retrieving the building from its state of disrepair, a careful plan of restoration being undertaken, in stages, from 1857 to 1864. The plan included the demolition of adjoining property to prevent fire risk, the removal of the brick front of the 'Maidenhead' portion, the restoration of the timber framing according to the earlier pattern, the replacement of the bay window and penthouse over the entrance and the restoration of the dormer windows.
See **pl. H**-7.

SYNTAX, Dr., a caricature of a clergyman and schoolmaster who sets out during the holidays on his old horse *Grizzle* to 'make a TOUR and WRITE IT' and meets with a series of amusing misfortunes. His adventures were the subject of a number of drawings by Rowlandson. The verses which accompany the drawings were written by

William Combe (1741–1823). The first of these works *Dr. Syntax in search of the Picturesque* was a parody of the popular books of picturesque travels of the day. It appeared in the *Poetical Magazine* in 1809. This was followed, in 1820, by *The Second Tour of Dr Syntax in search of Consolation* for the loss of his wife and, in 1821, by *The Third Tour of Dr Syntax in search of a Wife.*
See **pl. H**-25.

TAM O' SHANTER AND SOUTER JOHNNY, characters in a poem by Burns.
For details see **section E.**
See **pl. E**-102,
pls. H-19, 19A, 20.

THOM, JAMES (1802–50), sculptor. A self-taught artist who began life as an apprentice to a builder. He sculptured figures of 'Tam o'Shanter' and 'Souter Johnny' which were secured for the Burns monument at Ayr and attracted great interest in London.
See **pls. H**-19, 19A.

VOLTAIRE, FRANCOIS-MARIE AROUET de (1694–1778), French philosopher and writer. His first works offended the authorities and from 1726 to 1728 he lived in London. Here he wrote some of his dramas. On returning to France, he published his *Philosophical Letters* which aroused the enmity of the priesthood. For the next fifteen years he lived in a castle at Cirey where he wrote a great deal. From 1850 to 1853 he lived in Berlin at the invitation of Frederick the Great.
See **pl. H**-10B.

Section H
Authors, Poets, Composers et cetera
Details of the Figures

Plate 1
Figure 1 (not illustrated)
Subject: **John Milton**
Title: None
Date: 185–
Height: 18½ in (47.5 cm)
Colour: Well coloured, in the tradition of Thomas Parr.
Maker: Thomas Parr.
Rarity: VR. A.
Pair: Fig. 2 (Shakespeare)
Description: Standing bare-headed, in cloak, doublet, breeches and stockings. He rests his left hand, in which he holds a manuscript, on three books on a round pedestal. The manuscript is inscribed in upper and lower case transfer:

> Into the Heaven of Heavens,
> I have presum'd
> An earthly guest
> And drawn empyreal air.

He holds a corner of his cloak across himself with his right hand.
Observations: See next figure.

Figure 2
Subject: **William Shakespeare**
Title: None
Date: 185–
Height: 18½ in (47.5 cm)
Colour: Well coloured, in the tradition of Thomas Parr.
Maker: Thomas Parr
Rarity: VR. A.
Pair: Fig. 1 (Milton)
Description: Standing bare-headed, in cloak, doublet, breeches and stockings. His right elbow rests on four books which lie on a pedestal decorated with three heads, presumably those of, from *left* to *right*: Elizabeth I, Henry V and Richard III. His cheek rests on the knuckles of his right hand. He points to the writing on a manuscript hanging over the front of the pedestal, with the index finger of his left hand. In the figure illustrated the writing is indecipherable. His right leg is crossed over his left leg at the knee.
Observations: 1. Based on the monument designed by William Kent (1684–1748), with the statue by Peter Scheemakers (1691–1770), erected in Poet's Corner, Westminster Abbey, in 1741.
2. In the original statue the manuscript held by Shakespeare is inscribed with the following quotation from *The Tempest*, Act. 4, Scene 1:

> The Cloud cupt Tow'rs,
> The Gorgeous Palaces,
> The Solemn Temples,
> The Great Globe itself,
> Yea all which it Inherit,
> Shall Dissolve,
> And like the baseless fabrick of a Vision,
> Leave not a wreck behind.

3. The earliest copies of this figure and its pair are by Enoch Wood. They date to *c.* 1790. A pair may be seen in the Glaisher collection in the Fitzwilliam Museum at Cambridge. The figure illustrated is decorated in the manner of Thomas Parr and can be dated with confidence to the 1850's.

Plate 2
Figure 3
Subject: **William Shakespeare**
Title: Shakespeare (gilt script)
(The figure illustrated on this plate is an untitled version. For the titled version, see *pl.* H-3.)
Date: *c.* 1864
Height: 18½ in (47.5 cm)
Colour: Well coloured.
Maker: Sampson Smith
Rarity: Av.
Pair: Fig. 280 (Garibaldi) section C—the figure is illustrated on *pl.* H-2.
Description: Similar to *fig.* 2, *pl.* H-1, except that there are no heads decorating the pedestal, and his left hand is on his left thigh and clutches a book.
Observations: 1. The titled version of this figure (see *pl.* H-3) seems to pair *fig.* 280 (Garibaldi), although it will be noted that there are minor differences in the shape of the base. That they do pair is suggested by the fact that 1864 was the year that Garibaldi

Plate 1
Fig. 2 Shakespeare
To the left of the figure is a photograph of the monument designed by William Kent with a statue by Peter Scheemakers which was erected in Poet's Corner, Westminster Abbey in 1741.
Photograph by A.F. Kersting, FRPS

H489

Plate 2 continued
visited England, and also the year during which the tricentenary of the birth of Shakespeare was celebrated.
2. Another version of the same figure is illustrated on *pl.* H-4. The minor variants include:

(i) The title is in raised capitals and the spelling is 'Shakspeare'.

(ii) He is standing on a low wall.

I have given the number *fig.* 3(*a*) to this figure, for which no pair has yet been recorded.
3. A titled version of *fig.* 3 fetched 10 gns at Christie's in 1964, and another 9 gns in 1966.

Figure 4
Subject: **William Shakespeare** (see *pl.* C-96)
Title: Shakspeare (*sic*) (raised capitals)
Date: 1864
Height: 15 in (38 cm)
Colour: Well coloured.
Maker: Probably Sampson Smith
Rarity: R.
Pair: *Fig.* 281 (Garibaldi) *pl.* C-96.
Description: Standing bare-headed, in cloak, doublet, breeches and stockings. His right elbow rests on a pedestal with three books. He holds his left hand on his hip and does not carry a book in it. There is no paper on the pedestal and his legs are not crossed.
Observations: Probably produced in 1864, the year during which Garibaldi visited England and the tricentenary of the birth of Shakespeare was celebrated.

Figure 5
Subject: **John Milton**
Title: None
Height: 14½ in (36.75 cm)
Colour: Sparingly coloured.
Rarity: R.

H490

Pair: *Fig.* 6 (Shakespeare)
Description: Standing bare-headed, in cloak, doublet, breeches and stockings. His left arm rests on a pedestal decorated with S's and reversed S's. There are two books on the pedestal, and a manuscript hangs from its top. He holds an open book in his right hand.
Observations: The figure is of a slate-grey hue.

Figure 6
Subject: **William Shakespeare**
Title: None
Height: 14½ in (36.75 cm)
Colour: Sparingly coloured.
Rarity: R.
Pair: *Fig.* 5 (Milton)
Description: Standing bare-headed, in cloak, doublet, breeches and stockings. His right elbow rests on two books on a pedestal which is decorated with S's and reversed S's. A manuscript hangs from the front of the pedestal. He almost touches the pedestal with his left hand which is pointing to the manuscript.
Observations: 1. The figure is of a slate-grey hue.
2. A similar piece fetched 18 gns at Christie's in 1964.

Figure 280 (section C)
Subject: **Giuseppe Garibaldi**
Title: Garibaldi (gilt script)
Date: *c.* 1864
Height: 19 in (48 cm)
Colour: Well coloured, red shirt.
Maker: Sampson Smith
Pair: *Fig.* 3 (Shakespeare)
Description: See section C.

Plate 3
Figure 3
Subject: **William Shakespeare**
Observations: See *pl.* H-2.

Plate 3
Fig. 3 Shakespeare

Plate 4
Fig. 3(a) Shakespeare
By courtesy of Miss M.M. Frame

Plate 5
T: *Fig.* 7 Milton
Fig. 9 Milton
Fig. 15 Milton and Shakespeare
Fig. 10 Shakespeare
Fig. 8 Shakespeare

B: *Fig.* 11 Milton
Fig. 13 Shakespeare
Fig. 14 Shakespeare
Fig. 12 Shakespeare
By courtesy of Mr and Mrs Eric Joyce
and in the collection of the author

Plate 4
Figure 3(a)
Subject: **William Shakespeare**
Observations: See *pl.* H-2.

Plate 5
Figure 7
Subject: **John Milton**
Title: Milton (raised capitals)
Height: 11¼ in (28.5 cm)
Colour: Sparsely coloured.
Rarity: Av.
Pair: *Fig.* 8 (Shakespeare)
Description: Standing bare-headed, in doublet, breeches and stockings. His left elbow rests on three books lying on a round pedestal and in his left hand he holds a manuscript. His right hand holds up a corner of his cloak across him.
Observations: 1. A small and less elaborate version of *fig.* 1, *pl.* H-1.
2. A similar figure and its pair fetched 14 gns at Christie's in 1966; another and its pair, 32 gns at Christie's in 1969.

Figure 8
Subject: **William Shakespeare**
Title: Shakspere (*sic*) (raised capitals)
Height: 10¾ in (27 cm)
Colour: Sparsely coloured.
Rarity: Av.
Pair: *Fig.* 7 (Milton)
Description: He stands bare-headed, in cloak, doublet, breeches and stockings. His right elbow rests on four books lying on a

pedestal, the base of which is decorated with two heads. His right hand almost touches his right cheek. In his left hand he holds a scroll of paper. His right leg is crossed over his left at the knee.
Observations: Based on the statue by Peter Scheemakers in Poet's Corner, Westminster Abbey, see *fig.* 2, *pl.* H-1. This is a small and less elaborate version.

Figure 9
Subject: **John Milton**
Title: None
Height: 7½ in (19 cm)
Colour: Sparsely coloured.
Rarity: Av.
Pair: *Fig.* 10 (Shakespeare)
Description: Similar to *fig.* 7. He stands bare-headed, his left arm on a pedestal with three books. His cloak is draped around his left shoulder, waist and right leg.

Figure 10
Subject: **William Shakespeare**
Title: None
Height: 7½ in (19 cm)
Colour: Sparsely coloured.
Rarity: Av.
Pair: *Fig.* 9 (Milton)
Description: Similar to *fig.* 8. He stands bare-headed, with his right elbow on a pedestal with three books. A cloak is draped over his left shoulder and beside his left leg. His right leg is crossed in front of his left leg.

Figure 11
Subject: **John Milton**
Title: None
Height: 12 in (30.5 cm)
Colour: Well coloured.
Rarity: R. A.
Pair: *Fig.* 12 (Shakespeare)
Description: He stands bare-headed, a cloak over his right shoulder. He wears doublet, breeches and stockings. His right arm is outstretched and his hand supports a book against his thigh. His left elbow is on a pedestal and his left hand points outwards.

Figure 12
Subject: **William Shakespeare**
Title: None
Height: 12 in (30.5 cm)
Colour: Well coloured.
Rarity: R. A.
Pair: *Fig.* 11 (Milton)
Description: He stands bare-headed, in cloak, doublet, breeches and stockings. His left forearm rests on three books on a square pedestal. He holds a paper in his left hand to which he points with his right hand. His left leg is crossed in front of his right leg.

Figure 13
Subject: **William Shakespeare**
Title: None
Date: *c.* 1848
Height: 11 in (28 cm)
Colour: Well coloured.
Rarity: Av.

Section H. Authors, Poets, Composers et cetera

Plate 5 continued
Description: Shakespeare stands above a clock, bare-headed and wearing cloak, doublet, breeches and stockings. His left forearm rests on a book on a pedestal. To the left of the clock sits 'Tragedy' a scarf over her head, and to the right sits 'Comedy', bare-headed, a paper in her right hand.
Observations: 1. Based on *The Shakespeare Clock* designed and modelled by Bell and made in Parian by Minton. It was exhibited at the Society of Arts Exhibition of British Manufacturers in 1848, see *ch. 3, pl.* 56.
2. This figure, together with *figs*. 32 (Milton) and 33 (Shakespeare), *pl.* H-9 fetched 50 gns at Christie's in 1969.

Figure 14
Subject: **William Shakespeare**
Title: None
Height: 10½ in (26.5 cm)
Colour: Well coloured.
Rarity: Av.
Description: Shakespeare is standing above a clock, bare-headed, in cloak, doublet, breeches and stockings. His left forearm rests on three books on a pedestal. To the left of the clock sits 'Hamlet' wearing high plumed hat, doublet, breeches and stockings, a cloak over his right shoulder. To the right of the clock sits a lady, probably 'Lady Macbeth'. She wears a crown, a low-necked dress and cloak.
Observations: 1. Possibly portrays John Philip Kemble as 'Hamlet' and his sister, Mrs Siddons as 'Lady Macbeth', see *p.* 484. 'Hamlet' and 'Lady Macbeth' were considered the principal male and female characters of the Shakspearian dramas.
2. A similar figure fetched 15 gns at Christie's in 1964.

Figure 15
Subject: **John Milton and William Shakespeare**
Title: None
Height: 9 in (23 cm)
Colour: Well coloured.
Rarity: Av.
Description: Milton stands to the left of the clock, his left elbow resting on two books, his right arm holding a third against his right thigh. Shakespeare stands to the right of the clock, his right forearm resting on two books. He holds a manuscript in each hand. His right leg is crossed in front of his left leg.
Observations: A similar figure, together with *fig.* 31 (Shakespeare) *pl.* H-9, fetched 18 gns at Christie's in 1966.

Plate 6
Figure 16
Subject: **John Milton and William Shakespeare**
Title: None
Height: 9 in (23 cm)
Colour: Well coloured and sparsely coloured versions seen.
Rarity: Av.
Description: Identical to *fig.* 15, *pl.* H-5 except that it has been converted into a watch-holder.

Plate 7
Figure 17
Subject: **Lord Byron**
Title: L. Byron (indented capitals)
Date: c. 1848
Height: 7½ in (19 cm)
Colour: Well coloured with blue coat.
Maker: Alpha factory

H492

Rarity: Av.
Description: He sits bare-headed, in jacket and loose trousers. There is a cloak over his shoulders.
Observations: A similar figure, together with *fig.* 28 (Byron and 'Maid of Athens') *pl.* H-9, fetched 18 gns at Christie's in 1967.

Figure 18
Subject: **Lord Byron and Maid of Athens**
Title: Byron & Maid of Athens (gilt script)
Height: 13½ in (34.25 cm)
Colour: White, gilt and black.
Rarity: Av.
Description: He sits on the left, bare-headed, in open-necked shirt, jacket and breeches, his left arm round her shoulder. She sits on the right, wearing a cap and long dress. Her head rests on her left hand. Rococo base.

Figure 19
Subject: **Lord Byron**
Title: Byron (raised capitals)
Height: 16½ in (41.5 cm)
Colour: Well coloured.
Rarity: R.
Description: He stands bare-headed, in Grecian dress.
Observations: A similar figure fetched 25 gns at Christie's in 1966.

Figure 20
Subject: **Lord Byron**
Title: None
Height: 8 in (20.5 cm)
Colour: Well coloured and sparsely coloured versions noted.
Rarity: Av.
Pair: Fig. 21 ('Maid of Athens')
Description: He sits bare-headed, above a clock-face, wearing neckerchief and skirt, jacket, waistcoat and loose trousers, a cloak over his shoulders.
Observations: See next figure.

Figure 21
Subject: **Maid of Athens**
Title: None
Height: 8 in (20.5 cm)
Colour: Well coloured and sparsely coloured versions noted.
Rarity: Av.
Pair: Fig. 20 (Byron)
Description: She sits, with a kerchief over her hair, above a clock-face, wearing a low-necked bodice, long skirt with two flounces and a long scarf over her right shoulder. In her right hand, she holds a

Plate 6
Fig. 16 Milton and Shakespeare

Plate 7
T: *Fig.* 17 Byron
Fig. 18 Byron and Maid of Athens
Fig. 19 Byron
Fig. 20 Byron
Fig. 21 Maid of Athens

B: *Fig.* 23 Shakespeare's House
Fig. 24 Shakespeare
Fig. 25 Milton
Fig. 22 Shakespeare's House
Fig. 26 Shakespeare

Colour Plate 60
William Shakespeare and John Milton. *Figs.* 24 and 25, *pl.* H-7. See page 494.

Colour Plate 61
Robert Burns and Sir Walter Scott and Maida. *Figs.* 58 and 57, *pl.* H-18. See page 501.

Plate 7 continued
paper, possibly a poem, on her lap.
Observations: This figure and its pair, together with *fig.* 28 (Byron and 'Maid of Athens') *pl.* H-9, fetched 38 gns at Christie's in 1966.

Figure 22
Subject: **Shakespeare's House**
Title: Shakespere's House (*sic*) (gilt script)
Date: *c.* 1840
Height: 5 in (12.75 cm)
Colour: Well coloured.
Rarity: R.
Description: A two-storied, thatched cottage. There are two chimney stacks, three windows and one door.
Observations: 1. Bears a very close resemblance to the *birthplace* at Stratford-on-Avon prior to the restoration of 1857–64.
2. A similar figure fetched 20 gns at Christie's in 1964.

Figure 23
Subject: **Shakespeare's House**
Title: Shakspeare's House (*sic*) (raised capitals)
Date: *c.* 1864
Height: 10¼ in (25.75 cm)
Colour: Well coloured.
Rarity: R.
Description: A three-storied, half-timbered house with two doors, an oriel window in the first floor and three dormer windows in the second floor. The roof is thatched and there are two chimney stacks.
Observations: 1. Bears a close resemblance to the *birthplace* at Stratford-on-Avon following its restoration in 1864, see *ch.* 3, *pl.* 57.
2. A similar figure fetched 26 gns at Christie's in 1967.

Figure 24
Subject: **William Shakespeare**
Title: None
Height: 7½ in (19 cm)
Colour: Well coloured.
Rarity: Av.
Pair: Fig. 25 (Milton)
Description: Standing bare-headed, in cloak, doublet, breeches and stockings. His left forearm rests on two books lying on a pedestal. There is a paper in his left hand and his right hand points to it, but does not touch it. His left leg is crossed over the right.
Observations: See *ch.* 6, *pl.* 2A for an example of a similar figure apparently 'faked up' to represent a man with a peg leg playing a concertina.

Figure 25
Subject: **John Milton**
Title: None
Height: 7½ in (19 cm)
Colour: Well coloured.
Rarity: Av.
Pair: Fig. 24 (Shakespeare)
Description: He stands bare-headed, in doublet, breeches and stockings. His left elbow is on a pedestal, with his left hand pointing inwards. He holds a book against his leg with his right hand.

Figure 26
Subject: **William Shakespeare**
Title: Shaks-/peare (*sic*) (raised capitals)
Height: 14 in (35.5 cm)
Colour: Sparsely coloured.
Rarity: R.
Description: He stands bare-headed, in cloak, doublet, breeches and stockings. His right elbow rests on three books on a

H494

Plate 7A
Fig. 20 (a) ?Byron

Fig. 21 (a) ?Maid of Athens
By courtesy of Mr and Mrs R. Bonnett

Plate 8 (Right)
Fig. 27 Byron
In the collection of Mrs H. de C. Hastings

pedestal, a paper hangs from its top. His left hand is empty and points towards the paper. He is standing under an arch with a pointed canopy.
Observations: 1. Appears to be a crude representation of the monument designed by William Kent, erected in Poet's Corner, Westminster Abbey, in 1741, see *fig.* 2, *pl.* H-1.
2. A similar figure fetched 40 gns at Christie's in 1969.

Plate 7A
Figure 20(a)
Subject: **? Lord Byron**
Title: None
Height: 7⅛ in (18 cm)
Colour: Well coloured.
Rarity: VR.
Pair: Fig. 21(a) (? 'Maid of Athens')
Description: Sitting with round head-dress, wearing jacket, waistcoat, open shirt, breeches and calf-boots. There is a basket of flowers on his lap.
Observations: Has many features reminiscent of other figures of Byron.

Figure 21(a)
Subject: **? Maid of Athens**
Title: None
Height: 7⅛ in (18 cm)
Colour: Well coloured.
Rarity: VR.
Pair: Fig. 20(a) (? Byron)
Description: Sitting, with a garland round her hair, wearing low-necked bodice and full-length shirt. She has a long scarf over her left shoulder in one end of which she holds some flowers on her lap.
Observations: Has many features reminiscent of other figures of the 'Maid of Athens'.

Plate 8
Figure 27
Subject: **Lord Byron**
Title: Lord Byron (gilt script)
Height: 8½ in (21.5 cm)
Colour: Well coloured.
Rarity: VR.
Description: A bust. Bare-headed in open necked shirt, waistcoat and jacket, upon the lapel of which is a star.

Plate 9
T: *Fig.* 28 ?Byron and Maid of
Athens
Fig. 29 Burns with Highland
Mary
Fig. 30 Burns with Highland
Mary

B: *Fig.* 31 Shakespeare
Fig. 32 Milton
Fig. 33 Shakespeare
Fig. 34 Shakespeare
By courtesy of Mr and Mrs Eric Joyce

Plate 9
Figure 28
Subject: **? Lord Byron and Maid of
Athens**
Title: None
Height: 8¾ in (22 cm)
Colour: Well coloured.
Rarity: R.
Description: Byron sits on the left, on a low
ottoman, with his legs extended to his right.
He is bare-headed with long hair and wears
a collarless shirt which is buttoned up to the
neck, a long jacket with loose, short sleeves
and trousers held in place with a sash. The
'Maid' stands on the right, with her right
hand held in his left. She wears a scarf
wound over her hair which hangs down on
both sides, blouse, pleated skirt and
bloomers.
Observations: 1. Probably Byron and the
'Maid of Athens', although no other figures
portray the former with long hair or collarless shirt.
2. A similar figure, together with *figs.* 20
(Byron) and 21 ('Maid of Athens'), fetched
38 gns at Christie's in 1966.
Figure 29
Subject: **Robert Burns and Highland
Mary**
Title: None
Height: 13 in (33 cm)
Colour: Largely white and gilt.
Rarity: R.
Description: A spill-holder in the form of a
tree trunk. Burns stands to the left and in
front, wearing bonnet, jacket, breeches and
stockings, with a plaid over his left shoulder
and his left arm round Mary's shoulders.
Mary stands bare-headed and with bare
feet. His right foot and her left foot are on a
stick lying on the ground, and below them

in transfer gilt upper and lower case is the
following verse from *Highland Mary*:

Mony a vow and lock'd embrace
Our parting was fu' tender;
And, pledging aft to meet again,
We tore ourselves asunder.

Figure 30
Subject: **Robert Burns and Highland
Mary**
Title: Burns & his/Highland Mary (raised
capitals)
Height: 10½ in (26.5 cm)
Colour: Well coloured.
Rarity: Av.
Description: Burns stands on the left; Mary
on the right. Their right hands are clasped
and each wears Highland costume.
Observations: A similar figure fetched 38 gns
at Christie's in 1969.

Figure 31
Subject: **William Shakespeare**
Title: None
Height: 6¾ in (17 cm)
Colour: Well coloured.
Rarity: R.
Description: He is seated bare-headed, in
doublet, breeches and stockings. In his left
hand, he holds an open book on his lap, and
in his right hand, he holds a pen. A large jar
is standing to his left and his left foot is on a
closed book.
Observations: A similar figure, together with
fig. 15 (Milton and Shakespeare) *pl.* H-5,
fetched 18 gns at Christie's in 1966.

Figure 32
Subject: **John Milton**
Title: Milton (gilt script)
Height: 8¾ in (22 cm)
Colour: Sparsely coloured.

Rarity: R.
Pair: *Fig.* 33 (Shakespeare)
Description: He stands bare-headed, in
cloak, doublet, breeches and stockings. His
left elbow rests on a pedestal, and to the
right of the pedestal is a tree trunk decorated
with grapes and leaves. This tree trunk is
surmounted by a sloping watch-holder with
a clock-face at its bottom.

Figure 33
Subject: **William Shakespeare**
Title: Shakespeare (gilt script)
Height: 9½ in (24 cm)
Colour: Sparsely coloured.
Rarity: R.
Pair: *Fig.* 32 (Milton)
Description: He stands bare-headed, in
cloak, doublet, breeches and stockings. His
right forearm rests on a single book on a
pedestal, his left hand on his doublet. To
the left of the pedestal is a tree trunk
decorated with grapes and leaves and surmounted by a sloping watch-holder with a
clock-face at its bottom.
Observations: This figure and its pair,
together with *fig.* 13 (Shakespeare) *pl.* H-5,
fetched 50 gns at Christie's in 1969.

Figure 34
Subject: **William Shakespeare**
Title: None
Height: 8¼ in (21 cm)
Colour: Well coloured.
Rarity: R.
Pair: *Fig.* 35 (? Rousseau) *pl.* H-10.
Description: He stands bare-headed, in
cloak, open jacket, long waistcoat, breeches
and stockings. His right forearm rests on
two books on a square pedestal and his left
forearm is across his chest. His right leg,
from a separate mould, is crossed in front of
his left knee. Rococo base.

Plate 10
Figure 35
Subject: **? Rousseau**
Title: None
Height: 8¼ in (21 cm)
Colour: Well coloured.
Rarity: R.
Pair: *Fig.* 34 (Shakespeare) *pl.* H-9.
Description: Standing bare-headed, in doub-
let, waistcoat, breeches and stockings. His
left forearm rests on one book on a square
pedestal. His right arm is by his side.
Rococo base.
Observations: Various identifications have
been made, but the facial resemblance is so
close to that of portraits of Rousseau (see
pl. H-10A) that I am inclined to think there
is little doubt that this is who it is intended
to be. Among other suggestions have been
Dr Samuel Johnson; the head is certainly
similar to that in the painting by Sir Joshua
Reynolds in the National Portrait Gallery.
The figure is No. 977 in the Willett collection at Brighton and is catalogued as
Edward Gibbon (1737–94), the author of
The Decline and Fall of the Roman Empire.

Figure 36
Subject: **Eliza Cook**
Title: Eliza Cook (indented capitals)
Date: *c.* 1849
Height: 10¾ in (27 cm)
Colour: Well coloured.
Maker: Alpha factory
Rarity: R.
Description: She stands bare-headed, with
long ringlets. She wears a jacket, bodice and
long dress. In her right hand, she holds a

Colour Plate 62
Edward Morgan and Jenny Jones. *Figs.* 2, 3 and 4, *pl.* I-2. See page 515.

Plate 10 continued
closed book. Oval base.
Observations: 1. *Fig.* 114, *pl.* E-62 is somewhat similar and at first sight appears to be a mirror-image of Eliza Cook. However, this figure pairs *fig.* 113 (Lablache) *pl.* E-62. In any event the difference between the two figures is quite substantial. The woman portrayed in *fig.* 114 has no jacket, the object in her hand has been changed from a book to a scroll, and the base is rococo instead of plain. See *p.* 29 for further observations on this figure.
2. A similar figure fetched 22 gns in 1964, another 22 gns in 1965, and a third 30 gns in 1969, each at Christie's.

Figure 37
Subject: **Robert Burns**
Title: Rob! Burns (raised capitals)
Height: 13 in (33 cm)
Colour: Well coloured or crude green.
Rarity: C.
Pair: Fig. 38 ('Highland Mary').
Description: He stands bare-headed, in long coat, waistcoat, breeches and stockings. There is a plaid over his shoulders and he holds a bonnet in his left hand and an open book in his right hand.
Observations: 1. A late version of this figure has been found to pair a late version of *fig.* 38 ('Highland Mary'). Contemporary versions of 'Highland Mary' have only been found in the 17 in (42.5 cm) size and no pairing figure of Burns of this size has so far come to light.
2. A contemporary version, together with *fig.* 47 (Burns and Mary) *pl.* H-12, fetched 17 gns at Christie's in 1964; another, by itself, fetched 28 gns at Christie's in 1969; and another, 'late' and by itself, fetched 12 gns in the same rooms, in the same year.

Figure 38
Subject: **Highland Mary**
Title: Highland/Mary (raised capitals)
Height: 17 in (42.5 cm); 13 in (33 cm) late version illustrated.
Colour: The large, contemporary version is well coloured. The small, late version. is extremely crudely coloured with a rather unpleasant green.
Rarity: VR. (contemporary version); C. (late version).
Pair: See observations.
Description: Standing with bare feet, her plaid over her head and in a plain dress. There is a pedestal to her left and a book in her right hand.
Observations: The 17 in (42.5 cm) version of this figure is a fine piece, but curiously enough no pair has ever come to light. Conversely, the 13 in (33 cm) figure is remarkably poor and is paired by an equally poor version of *fig.* 37 (Burns).

Figure 39
Subject: **Robert Burns**
Title: Robert Burnes (*sic*) (raised capitals)
Height: 13 in (33 cm)
Colour: Well coloured.
Rarity: R.
Description: Almost the same as *fig.* 37 (Burns) except that the title is different, the book in his right hand is closed instead of open and there is a plough to his left, instead of a bonnet in his left hand.

Plate 10A
Rousseau
The facial characteristics will be noted to be remarkably similar to those of *fig.* 35, *pl.* H-10.

Plate 10
T: *Fig.* 36 Cook
Fig. 114 (section E) Unidentified actress
Fig. 74 (section B) Franklin
Fig. 35 ? Rousseau
B: *Fig.* 37 Burns
Fig. 38 Highland Mary
Fig. 39 Burns

Note:
(1) *Fig.* 114, *pl.* E-62 was formerly thought to portray Eliza Cook. It is now recognized as a 'theatre' figure, having as its pair, *fig.* 113 Lablache *pl.* E-62.
(2) *Fig.* 74, *pl.* B-25A was formerly identified as Voltaire. This is now recognized as incorrect and the figure is thought to portray Benjamin Franklin.
(3) The example of *fig.* 38 (Highland Mary) which is illustrated is the small 'late' version.

Plate 10A
Rousseau (1712-1778)
The portrait is very similar to
Fig. 35, *pl.* H-10.

Plate 10B
Fig. 40 Voltaire
In the Thomas Balston collection

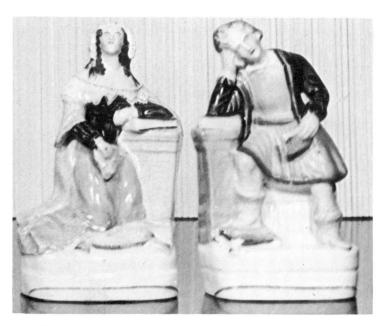

Plate 11
Fig. 41 ? Hathaway
Fig. 42 ? Shakespeare

Plate 12
T: *Fig.* 43 Burns
Fig. 45 Burns
Fig. 44 Highland Mary

B: *Fig.* 47 Burns and Mary
Fig. 48 Burns and Mary
Fig. 49 Burns and Mary
In the collection of Mr Ronald Shockledge

Plate 10B
Figure 40
Subject: **Voltaire**
Title: Voltaire (script capitals)
Height: 3½ in (9 cm)
Colour: Well coloured.
Rarity: VR.
Description: Head and neck, above an ink-well.

Plate 11
Figure 41
Subject: **? Anne Hathaway**
Title: None
Height: 6¾ in (17 cm)
Colour: Well coloured.
Rarity: R.
Pair: *Fig.* 42 (? Shakespeare)
Description: Seated, with bonnet and long dress. Her left elbow rests on a book on a pedestal, and she carries a handkerchief in her right hand.
Observations: The identification is based on the assumption that *fig.* 42 is Shakespeare. Nevertheless, it will be noted that the woman bears a striking resemblance to Eliza Cook, see *fig.* 36, *pl.* H-10.

Figure 42
Subject: **? William Shakespeare**
Title: None
Height: 6¾ in (17 cm)
Colour: Well coloured.
Rarity: R.
Pair: *Fig.* 41 (? Hathaway)
Description: Seated bare-headed, in jacket, tunic and boots. In his left hand he holds a book and his right elbow rests on another book on a pedestal, his right hand supporting his head.
Observations: Has been described as the 'young Shakespeare' for reasons unknown to me.

Plate 12
Figure 43
Subject: **Robert Burns**
Title: Burns (gilt script)
Height: 16 in (40.5 cm)
Colour: Sparsely coloured.
Rarity: R.
Pair: *Fig.* 44 ('Highland Mary')
Description: He stands in bonnet, jacket, waistcoat, breeches and stockings, a plaid over his left shoulder. His left hand grasps a book lying on a pedestal to his left and his right clasps his jacket.

Figure 44
Subject: **Highland Mary**
Title: Mary (gilt script)
Height: 16 in (40.5 cm)
Colour: Sparsely coloured.
Rarity: R.
Pair: *Fig.* 43 (Burns)
Description: She stands, with a scarf over her head, in jacket, overskirt which is lifted in her right hand and a short skirt. In her left hand, she holds a book in front of her.

Figure 45
Subject: **Robert Burns**
Title: None
Height: 8 in (20.5 cm)
Colour: Well coloured, with underglaze blue coat.
Rarity: R.
Pair: Unknown, but probably exists. *Fig.* 46 has been reserved for it.
Description: Standing bare-headed, in long coat, waistcoat, breeches, stockings and shoes. His left elbow rests on a book lying

on a fluted pedestal to his left. In his left hand he clasps a scroll. His right hand is on his hip. Hollow base.
Observations: Probably Burns, but not proven to be so.

Figure 47
Subject: **Robert Burns and Highland Mary**
Title: Burns/and his/Mary (raised capitals)
Height: 12 in (30.5 cm)
Colour: Usually sparsely coloured.
Maker: Sampson Smith
Rarity: C.
Description: He stands bare-headed, with his left arm round Mary's shoulders. There is a tree trunk (spill-holder) behind him.
Observations: 1. Occasionally copies are found marked in relief on the base:

S. SMITH
LONGTON
1851

2. A few reproductions were made from the original press-mould found in a disused part of the Sampson Smith factory in 1948, see *ch.* 6, *pl.* 3.
3. An example of this figure with the factory mark in relief on the base, together with *fig.* 66 (Rigs o'Barley) *pl.* H-21, fetched 22 gns at Christie's in 1963. Another (unmarked), together with *fig.* 49 (Burns and Mary), fetched £16 at Sotheby's in 1966.

Figure 48
Subject: **Robert Burns and Highland Mary**
Title: Burns & H^d Mary (raised capitals)
Height: 12 in (30.5 cm)
Colour: Usually well coloured.
Rarity: C.
Description: They are seated underneath an arch of bare boughs, Burns to the right and Mary to the left. Burns wears a bonnet, plaid, long coat and breeches and Mary is bare-headed. In the foreground is a stream with a swan in it.
Observations: An example of this figure, together with *fig.* 67 (O Nanny Gang wee me) *pl.* H-21 fetched 12 gns at Christie's in 1966.

Figure 49
Subject: **Robert Burns and Highland Mary**
Title: None
Height: 12 in (30.5 cm)
Colour: Well coloured.
Maker: Thomas Parr
Rarity: Av.
Description: Both sit in front of a tree trunk (spill-holder). On the left is Burns, dressed in bonnet, coat and trousers. On the right Mary sits, bare-headed. Eight lines of poetry, in black transfer upper and lower case letters, are inscribed on the base:

> How sweetly bloomed the gay green birk,
>   How rich the hawthorn's blossom!
> As, underneath their fragrant shade,
>   I clasped her to my bosom!
> The golden hours, on angel wings,
>   Flew o'er me and my dearie:
> For dear to me as light and life
>   Was my sweet Highland Mary.

Observations: 1. The inscription on the base is the second verse of *Highland Mary*, a poem written by Burns in November, 1792. Copies of the figure have been noted inscribed with other verses.
2. An example of this figure fetched 22 gns at Christie's in 1963. Another, together with

Plate 13
Fig. 50 Burns

Plate 14
Fig. 51 Burns and Mary

fig. 47 (Burns and Mary) fetched £16 at Sotheby's in 1966.
3. Appears in all three Kent lists.

Plate 13
Figure 50
Subject: **Robert Burns**
Title: None
Height: 13¾ in (35 cm)
Colour: Well coloured.
Rarity: R.
Description: Standing in bonnet, long coat, waistcoat, breeches and stockings, his left hand on his hip and his right arm encircling part of a brick wall. Against the wall is a flower pot with a flower growing up the wall. At his feet is a waterfall and against the wall, also, is a spade.
Observations: Almost certainly Burns.

Plate 14
Figure 51
Subject: **Robert Burns and Highland Mary**
Title: Burns & Highland Mary (gilt script)
Height: 7 in (17.5 cm)
Colour: Well coloured.
Rarity: R.
Description: Mary sits on the left, bare-headed and Burns sits on the right. His right arm is round her shoulder and his left hand clasps her right hand. He wears a bonnet, long coat, plaid over his left shoulder, breeches and stockings.

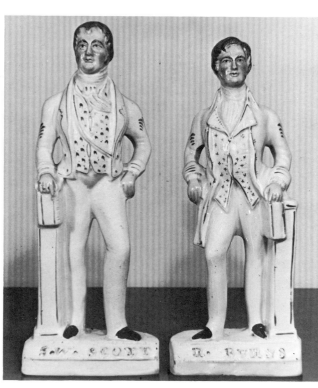

Plate 15 (Left)
Fig. 52 Burns

Plate 17 (Right)
Fig. 54 Scott
Fig. 55 Burns
In the Thomas Balston collection

Plate 15
Figure 52
Subject: **Robert Burns**
Title: R. Burns/Born January 25/1759/Died July 21/1796 (gilt script)
Date: c. 1882
Height: 15¾ in (39.75 cm)
Colour: Sparsely coloured.
Maker: Sampson Smith
Rarity: VR. D.
Description: He stands in bonnet, long coat,
H500

waistcoat, breeches and stockings. His right arm rests on a pedestal and his left arm on his hip. The whole is mounted on a high round pedestal composed of 'bricks'.
Observations: 1. The only example of this figure which I have seen is inscribed under its base 'Sampson Smith/Longton, Staff/England/1882' in indented upper and lower case letters. The inscription is very shallow and difficult to decipher. There is some doubt as to whether the date is 1882 or 1892.

2. This figure fetched 65 gns at Christie's in 1966.
3. See *fig.* 53, *pl.* H-16.

Plate 16
Figure 53
Subject: **Robert Burns** (Press-mould *only* illustrated)

Plate 18
Fig. 56 Burns
Fig. 57 Scott
Fig. 58 Burns

Title: R. Burns/B.Jan.25/1759/D.Jul.21/
1796 (raised capitals)
Date: *c.* 1892
Height: 15¾ in (39.75 cm)
Maker: Sampson Smith
Description: He stands in bonnet, long coat,
waistcoat, breeches and stockings, his left
hand on his hip and his right hand by his
side resting on a wall. The whole is mounted
on a high square pedestal inscribed as above.
Observations: 1. The press-mould of this figure was found in 1948 in a disused part of
the old Sampson Smith factory. The front of
the mould is inscribed:

B
May the
2
1892

The letter B has been found on a number of
old moulds and probably signifies an original 'block-mould', see *ch.* 4, *pls.* 2 and 3.
2. No contemporary version of the figure has
yet been recorded and no reproductions
were made from the mould which, incidentally, is now in the author's collection.

Plate 17
Figure 54
Subject: **Sir Walter Scott**
Title: S. W. Scott (raised capitals)
Height: 12 in (30.5 cm)
Colour: Well coloured and sparsely coloured
versions exist.
Rarity: VR. A.
Pair: *Fig.* 55 (Burns)
Description: He stands bare-headed, in
swallow-tailed coat, waistcoat and trousers,
his left hand on his hip and his right hand
on a pedestal to his right.

Figure 55
Subject: **Robert Burns**
Title: R. Burns (raised capitals)
Height: 11½ in (29 cm)

Colour: Well coloured and sparsely coloured
versions exist.
Rarity: VR. A.
Pair: *Fig.* 54 (Scott)
Description: He stands bare-headed, in long
coat and trousers, his right hand on his hip,
his left hand on a pedestal to his left.

Plate 18
Figure 56
Subject: **Robert Burns**
Title: None
Date: *c.* 1848
Height: 7½ in (19 cm)
Colour: Well coloured, with blue coat.
Maker: Alpha factory
Rarity: R.
Description: He is sitting bare-headed, in
long coat, long waistcoat, breeches and
stockings. He holds a snuff-box in his right
hand and is taking a pinch of snuff with his
left.
Observations: 1. Has all the characteristics of
the Alpha factory and can therefore be
dated with confidence to *c.* 1848.
2. The clothes are not those of a contemporary, but both they and the head closely
resemble known figures of Burns.

Figure 57
Subject: **Sir Walter Scott and Maida**
Title: Sir Walter Scott (gilt script)
Height: 14¾ in (37.5 cm); 10¾ in (27 cm)
version illustrated.
Colour: Well coloured.
Rarity: R.
Pair: *Fig.* 58 (Burns). No pair has been
found to the 14¾ in (37.5 cm) version of
Scott.
Description: Standing bare-headed, in swal-
low-tailed coat and trousers, a plaid over his
left shoulder, a hound to his right.
Observations: 1. As already noted, this figure

occurs in titled form as a 14¾ in (37.5 cm)
version to which no pair has been found,
and as a 10¾ in (27 cm) version which pairs
fig. 58 (Burns). Both figures are of earthenware and have closed bottoms. A third
figure exists which is 14 in (35.5 cm) in
height and porcelaneous with an open
bottom. It is never titled and no pair is
known for it. It is very similar, but not
identical, to the titled version. The dog, in
particular, exhibits minor differences.
2. An example of the large earthenware
version of this figure fetched 20 gns at
Christie's in 1967, and another of the
porcelaneous version, 28 gns at the same
sale. An example of the small version and its
pair fetched 55 gns at Christie's in 1969.

Figure 58
Subject: **Robert Burns**
Title: R. Burn (*sic*) (gilt script)
Height: 10½ in (26.5 cm)
Colour: Well coloured.
Rarity: R.
Pair: *Fig.* 57 (Scott) [10¾ in (27 cm) version]
Description: He stands bare-headed, in long
coat, breeches and gaiters, a plaid over his
left shoulder. He reads a book which he
holds in his left hand, and to his right are
various farming implements.
Observations: An example of this figure and
its pair fetched 55 gns at Christie's in 1969.

Plate 18A
Figure 59
Subject: **Robert Burns**
Title: None
Date: *c.* 1844
Height: 9¾ in (24.5 cm)
Colour: Well coloured.
Rarity: R.
Description: He stands bare-headed, in coat,

Plate 18A
Fig. 59 Burns

Fig. 60 Burns and Mary

Plate 19
Fig. 61 Tam o'Shanter

Fig. 62 Souter Johnnie
In the collection of Mr H.T. Appleton

Plate 18A continued
breeches and stockings, a plaid over his left shoulder and draped across him. He holds a scroll in his left hand and a flower in his right.
Observations: 1. This figure is based on an engraving which appeared in *The Illustrated London News* of August 10th, 1844 in connection with the Burns Festival at Ayr on August 6th of that year, see *ch.* 3, *pl.* 58. 2. An example of this figure fetched 42 gns at Christie's in 1969.

Figure 60
Subject: **Robert Burns and Highland Mary**
Title: Highland Mary (gilt script)
Height: 9 in (23 cm)
Colour: Well coloured.
Rarity: R.
Description: Burns is seated on the left with 'Highland Mary' on the right. Behind the poet is a tree trunk (spill-holder). He is bareheaded with coat, breeches and stockings and she wears a plumed bonnet.

Plate 19
Figure 61
Subject: **Tam o' Shanter**
Title: Tam o Shanter (indented capitals)
Height: 8¾ in (22 cm)
Colour: Well coloured.
Rarity: Av.
Pair: Fig. 62 ('Souter Johnny')
Description: Seated wearing a hat, jacket, waistcoat, breeches and stockings, a mug in his right hand, his left hand on the arm of a chair.
Observations: See next figure.

Figure 62
Subject: **Souter Johnny**
Title: Souter Johnnie (*sic*) (indented capitals)
Height: 8¼ in (21 cm)
Colour: Well coloured.

Rarity: Av.
Pair: Fig. 61 ('Tam o' Shanter')
Description: Seated wearing a kerchief round his head, jacket, apron, breeches and stockings. A jug in his right hand.
Observations: 1. This figure and its pair are based on the figures sculptured by James Thom (1802–50) which were secured for the Burns monument, Ayr, see *pl.* H-19A. Thom was a self-taught artist.
2. Souter = *shoemaker*.
3. A similar figure and its pair fetched 28 gns at Christie's in 1966. A very fine 13½ in (34.25 cm) version of the figure and its pair fetched £100 at Sotheby's in 1969.

Plate 19A
 Tam o' Shanter and Souter Johnny
Lithograph music-front for *Tam o'Shanter and Souter Johnny, a Song of mony Counsels sweet*. The engraving incorporates the celebrated figures sculptured by James Thom and later secured for the Burns monument at Ayr. *Figs.* 61 and 62, *pl.* H-19 are based on them.

Plate 20
Figure 63
Subject: **Tam o'Shanter and Souter Johnny**
Title: Tam o Shanter & Sooter Johnny (*sic*) (raised capitals)
Date: *c.* 1892
Height: 12¾ in (32.25 cm)
Colour: Well coloured.
Maker: Sampson Smith
Rarity: Av.
Description: 'Tam o'Shanter' is seated on the left, wearing hat, jacket, waistcoat, breeches and stockings. In his right hand, he holds a mug. 'Souter Johnny' is seated on the right separated by a barrel from 'Tam o'Shanter'. He wears a kerchief, long coat, apron, breeches and stockings and in his right hand he holds a jug.

Observations: 1. This figure may be found with two different factory marks in relief on the base:
Either

SAMPSON SMITH
1851
LONGTON
or

SAMPSON SMITH
LONGTON, STAFF
ENGLAND
1892

The year 1851 possibly refers to the year of *establishment*; the year 1892 may refer to the year of *manufacture*.
2. There are a number of engravings, such as that illustrated, all of which are similar to the group but none of which are identical.
3. The figure appears in the page from the Sampson Smith catalogue illustrated in *ch.* 2, *pl.* 11, the title differing slightly.

Figure 64
Subject: **Tam o'Shanter and Souter Johnny**
Title: Tam O Shanter & Souter Johney (*sic*) (gilt script)
Height: 10¼ in (25.75 cm)
Colour: Both well coloured and white and gilt versions are known.
Rarity: R.
Pair: Fig. 65 (John Anderson) *pl.* H-21.
Description: 'Tam o'Shanter' is seated on the left, in bonnet, jacket, waistcoat, breeches and stockings, a plaid over his left shoulder and a cup in his right hand. 'Souter Johnny' is seated on the right and between them is a table with a jug on it. 'Souter Johnny' wears a kerchief, coat, apron, breeches and stockings and in his right hand he has a cup.

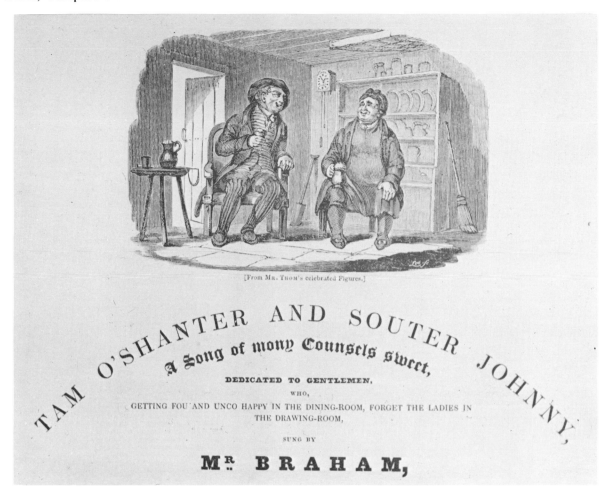

Plate 19A
Lithograph music-front for *Tam o'Shanter and Souter Johnny, a Song of mony Counsels sweet*. The engraving incorporates the celebrated figures sculptured by James Thom and later secured by the Burns monument at Ayr. *Figs.* 61 and 62, *pl*, H-19 are based on them.
By courtesy of Mr John Hall

Plate 20
Fig. 63 Tam o'Shanter and Souter Johnny
Fig. 64 Tam o'Shanter and Souter Johnny
Between these two figures is an engraving entitled *Tam o'Shanter and Souter Johnny*.

Plate 21
T: *Fig.* 66 Rigs o'Barley
Fig. 67 O Nanny Gang wee me

B: *Fig.* 68 Auld Lang Syne
Fig. 65 John Anderson, my jo
*By courtesy of Mr and Mrs Eric Joyce
and in the collection of the author*

Plate 21
Figure 65
Subject: **John Anderson and his wife**
Title: John Anderson, my jo (gilt script)
Height: 10¼ in (25.75 cm)
Colour: Both well coloured and white and gilt versions are known.
Rarity: Av.
Pair: Fig. 64 ('Tam o'Shanter' and 'Souter Johnny') *pl.* H-20.
Description: An old lady sits on a high backed armchair. To her left an old gentleman sits on a similar chair. She has her left hand on his shoulder and both his hands rest on a cane.
Observations: 1. After the poem of the same name by Robert Burns. John Anderson, in the flesh, was traditionally the Town Piper of Kelso.
2. A similar figure, together with *fig.* 68 (Auld Lang Syne) fetched 28 gns at Christie's in 1966.
H504

Figure 66
Subject: **Robert Burns and Jean Armour**
Title: Rigs o'Barley (gilt script)
Height: 7¼ in (18.25 cm)
Colour: Well coloured.
Rarity: R.
Description: Burns is seated on the left, in bonnet, jacket, waistcoat, breeches and stockings. To his left, Jean Armour sits, in jacket and long dress. On either side is a sheaf of barley.
Observations: 1. The song *The Rigs o'Barley* which appeared in Burns' first small volume of poems published in Kilmarnock, in 1786, is regarded as his own epithalamium, Annie being a blind for Jean Armour, see *p.* 571.
2. For auction price see *fig.* 47, *pl.* H-12.

Figure 67
Subject: **Robert Burns and Agnes Fleming**
Title: Large version: O. Nannie. Wilt. Thou/

Gang. Wi. Me (raised capitals)
Small version (illustrated): O Nanny Gang wee me (gilt script)
Height: Large version: 11¾ in (29.75 cm)
      Small version: 8 in (20.5 cm)
Colour: Well coloured.
Rarity: VR. (large version); R. (small version)
Description: Both figures are similar but by no means identical. Burns stands to the left, in Highland rig with plumed bonnet, plaid over his left shoulder and sporran. Annie is on the right, bare-headed in three-quarter length Scottish dress.
Observations: 1. Agnes Fleming, a servant at Calcothill, near Lochlea, was the one sung of as Nannie in Burns' *My Nannie, O!*, see *p.* 571. I have failed to find the title line in any of the poetical works of Robert Burns.
2. For auction price, see *fig.* 48, *pl.* H-12.

Plate 22
Fig. 69 ? Elizabeth
Barrett Browning
Fig. 70 ? Robert Browning
In the collection of
Dr. S.J. Howard

Plate 23
Fig. 71 ? Elizabeth
Barrett Browning
Fig. 72 ? Elizabeth
Barrett Browning

Figure 68
Subject: **Three Highland gentlemen**
Title: Auld Lang Syne (gilt script)
Height: 7½ in (19 cm)
Colour: Well coloured.
Rarity: Av.
Description: Three gentlemen, all wearing bonnets, are seated round a table drinking. The one on the left, wears a jacket and trousers and the one on the right, a jacket, plaid, sporran and kilt.
Observations: 1. The older song of the same name, but different both in melody and

words, was familiar all over Scotland generations before the birth of Burns.
2. A similar figure together with *fig.* 65 (John Anderson) fetched 28 gns at Christie's in 1966.

Plate 22
Figure 69
Subject: **? Elizabeth Barrett Browning and Flush**
Title: None
Height: 5¼ in (13.5 cm)
Colour: Well coloured.

Rarity: R.
Pair: Fig. 70 (? Robert Browning)
Description: Seated, bare-headed, on a couch. She wears a bodice and long skirt, open in front to display some underskirt. She has a small flower in her hair. Her right forearm rests on the arm of the couch and she carries a handkerchief in her right hand. A small dog sits beside her, on her left.
Observations: No contemporary print has been found to prove the identity of this person, but the general consensus of opinion is that it is Elizabeth Barrett Browning.

H505

Plate 22 continued
Figure 70
Subject: **? Robert Browning**
Title: None
Height: 6 in (15.25 cm)
Colour: Well coloured.
Rarity: R.
Pair: *Fig.* 69 (? Elizabeth Barrett Browning)
Description: Seated, bare-headed, on a couch, wearing coat, waistcoat and trousers. His left elbow is on the arm of the couch and he carries a manuscript in his left hand. To his right, also seated on the couch, is a small dog.
Observations: The identification of this figure is based on the assumption that its pair is Elizabeth Barrett Browning.

Plate 23
Figure 71
Subject: **? Elizabeth Barrett Browning**
Title: None
Height: 6¼ in (16 cm)
Colour: Well coloured.
Rarity: R.
Pair: Unknown
Description: Bare-headed in jacket, blouse and bloomers, a book in her left hand. It seems possible that a quill has been broken from her right hand.
Observations: This figure is suggestive of an authoress and the face is very similar to other figures which are thought to portray Elizabeth Barrett Browning.

Figure 72
Subject: **? Elizabeth Barrett Browning and Flush**
Title: None
Height: 5¾ in (14.5 cm)
Colour: Well coloured.
Rarity: VR.
Description: A bare-headed woman is reclining on a couch, her head to the right. She is stroking a small dog.
Observations: This figure may well portray Elizabeth Barrett Browning who, for many years, was compelled to lie on her back, see *p*. 569.

Plate 24
Figure 73
Subject: **Mr and Mrs Caudle**
Title: Mr & Mrs Caudle (gilt script)
Date: *c.* 1845
Height: 6 in (15.25 cm)
Colour: Well coloured.
Rarity: Av.
Description: Both seated, he to the left and she to the right. He is wearing a hat, jacket, waistcoat and trousers and she a bonnet and long length dress. She has hold of the brim of his hat as if to pull it off.
Observations: See following figure.

Figure 74
Subject: **Mr and Mrs Caudle**
Title: Mr & Mrs Caudle (gilt script)
Date: *c.* 1845
Height: 7 in (17.5 cm)
Colour: Well coloured.
Rarity: Av.
Description: They both stand in front of chairs; she on the left and he on the right. She is wearing a bonnet, shawl and long dress and he is wearing a top hat, jacket, waistcoat and trousers. His head lolls over to the right as if he is drunk and she has hold of the brim of his hat as if to pull it off.
Observations: 1. *Mrs Caudle's Curtain Lectures* by Jerrold were a popular feature of *Punch* during the year 1845.

H506

Plate 24
Fig. 73 Mr and Mrs Caudle

Fig. 74 Mr and Mrs Caudle
By courtesy of Mr and Mrs Eric Joyce

2. A similar figure and another unimportant piece fetched 13 gns at Christie's in 1964. The same figure, by itself, fetched 16 gns at Christie's in 1969.

Plate 25
Figure 75
Subject: **Dr Syntax**
Title: None
Date: 185–
Height: 5½ in (14 cm)
Colour: Well coloured, in the manner of Thomas Parr.
Maker: Thomas Parr
Rarity: R.
Description: Leaning backwards against a tree trunk. He wears a tricorn hat, long coat, breeches and stockings and he holds a T-handled stick in his left hand.
Observations: Figures of 'Dr Syntax' are usually of an earlier period but this version has the style and colouring typical of pieces manufactured by Thomas Parr.

Plate 26
Figure 76
Subject: **Sancho Panza on an ass**
Title: Sancho Panza (indented capitals)
Date: 185–
Height: 8 in (20.5 cm)
Colour: Well coloured in the manner of Thomas Parr.
Maker: Thomas Parr
Rarity: Av.
Pair: *Fig.* 77 ('Don Quixote')
Description: On an ass facing right, wearing hat, jacket, breeches and stockings.

Plate 25
Fig. 75 Dr Syntax
By courtesy of Mr John Hall

Plate 26
Fig. 76 Sancho Panza
Fig. 77 Don Quixote
In the collection of
Mr Geoffrey

Observations: 1. The story of 'Don Quixote' and his 'squire' 'Sancho Panza' has been dramatized in various forms on many occasions. It is therefore possible, although unlikely, that this figure and its pair *fig.* 77 ('Don Quixote') are theatrical.

2. Both figures appear in all three **Kent** lists as follows:

	KENT LIST A Stock No. (c. 1901)	KENT LIST B Stock No.	KENT LIST C Ref. No. (1955)
Don Quixote	243	210	210
Sancho Panza	354	347	347

Reproductions are rare.

Figure 77
Subject: **Don Quixote on Rosinante**
Title: Don Quixote (indented capitals)
Date: 185–
Height: 9¾ in (24.5 cm)
Colour: Well coloured in the manner of Thomas Parr.
Maker: Thomas Parr
Rarity: Av.
Pair: *Fig.* 76 ('Sancho Panza')
Description: Dressed as a knight on a horse facing left, with helmet, shield and sword.
Observations: See *fig.* 76 ('Sancho Panza').

Plate 27
Fig. 78 Lochinvar
In the collection of Lady Ranfurly

Plate 27
Figure 78
Subject: **Lochinvar and Ellen**
Title: The Flight (indented capitals)
Height: 10 in (25 cm)
Colour: Well coloured.
Rarity: R.
Description: 'Lochinvar' wearing a round hat, cloak, coat and knee-boots, with a pistol in his right hand, is astride a horse, facing right. 'Ellen' sits on his lap with her right arm round his neck. She wears a plumed hat and long dress.
Observations: 'Lochinvar' was the hero of a ballad included in the fifth canto of Scott's *Marmion*. Although not positively identified the figure probably portrays 'Lochinvar' in flight with his 'fair Ellen'.

Plate 28
Fig. 79 Mozart
To the right of the figure is its source
— an engraving of a statue of Mozart
by A.H. Payne, published by Brain
& Payne, 12, Paternoster Row,
London. Although the potters have
made a superb copy of the engraving
— the engraving is a poor copy of
the statue, which, executed by
Ludwig Schwanthaler in 1842, stands
in Mozart-Platz, Salzburg.
Figure: In the collection of
Dr. S.J. Howard
Engraving: By courtesy of Mr John Hall

Plate 28
Figure 79
Subject: **Wolfgang Amadeus Mozart**
Title: None
Date: *c.* 1842
Height: 11¼ in (28.5 cm)
Colour: Well coloured and enriched with
elaborate gilding.
Rarity: VR. D. A.
Pair: Unknown
Description: Standing bare-headed, with his
left leg slightly flexed. His right arm is
partially outstretched and he holds a scroll
of music in his left hand. The top three
buttons of his jacket are undone and the
frilled cuff of his shirt protrudes from his
right sleeve. He is wearing a cravat and
shoes with buckles. Hexagonal base.
Observations: 1. Identical in almost every
detail to an engraving by A. H. Payne of a
statue of Mozart by Von Ludwig Schwanthaler. This engraving was published by
Brain & Payne, 12, Paternoster Row, London.
2. I am grateful to Dr Hans Schurich,
Honorary Curator of the Mozart Museum,
Salzburg for the following information:

... The monument stands in Mozart-Platz in Salzburg
and was unveiled on 4 September, 1842.
The engraving is a poor quality representation of
the monument and I presume it to be a copy of another
engraving which featured on the memorial programme
given to the guests of honour on the day of the un-
veiling.

The original engravings of the monument may be
found in *W. A. Mozarts Söhne* by Dr Walter Hummel,
Bärenreiter-Verlag, Kassel-London.

3. Von Ludwig Schwanthaler (1802–48)
was an eminent German sculptor, born in
Munich. He held the office of professor of
sculpture in the Munich academy from
1835. Among his works, other than that
of Mozart, are the colossal statue of Bavaria,
and statues of Goethe and Jean Paul
Richter.

Figure 80 (not illustrated)
Subject: **William Shakespeare**
Title: None
Height: 11¾ in (29.75 cm)
Colour: Well coloured.
Rarity: VR.
Pair: Unrecorded but almost certainly
Milton, for which *fig.* 81 has been reserved.
Description: He stands bare-headed in cloak,
doublet, breeches and stockings, his right
hand pointing to the right, his left leg
crossed infront of his right leg. He is leaning
against a rococo clock-face, on the top of
which he supports an open book with his
left hand, and at the base of which there is a
putto.
Observations: Illustrated in Christie's catalogue for the sale of '19th Century Popular
Ceramics' held on November 3rd, 1969 at
which it fetched 50 gns.

Section I
Miscellaneous
Biographies and Historical Notes

ALPHINGTON PONIES, THE (dates unknown). Two sisters, by name Durnford, came from Alphington early in the 1830's and settled in Lavender Cottage, Avenue Road, Torquay where they lived for many years. The tale behind this was that their father had run away with their governess; meanwhile they themselves had been engaged to two brothers, one of whom accidentally shot and killed the other at a shooting party and died soon afterwards himself.

They became eccentrics and their costume was peculiar. Their shoes were generally green but sometimes red. They were by no means bad-looking girls when young, but they were so berouged as to present the appearance of painted dolls. Their brown hair, worn in curls, was fastened with blue ribbon, and they wore felt or straw hats, usually tall in the crown and curled up at the sides. About their throats they had very broad, frilled or lace collars that fell down over their backs and breasts a long way. But in summer their necks were bare, and adorned with chains of coral or bead. Their gowns were short, so short indeed as to display about the ankles a great more than was necessary of certain heavily-frilled cotton investitures of their lower limbs. In winter over their gowns were worn check jackets of a 'loud' pattern reaching to their knees, and of a different colour from their gowns, and with lace cuffs. They were never seen, winter or summer, without their sunshades.

The sisters dressed exactly alike and were so much alike in face as to appear to be twins. They were remarkably good walkers, kept perfectly in step, were always arm-in-arm, and spoke to no one but each other. They lived with their mother and kept no servant.

When first they came to Torquay, they drove a pair of pretty ponies they had brought with them from Alphington; but their allowance being reduced, and being in straitened circumstances, they had to dispose of the ponies and carriage. By an easy transfer the name 'Alphington Ponies' passed from the beasts to their former owners. Some years later, probably in the early fifties, they moved to Exeter. Their story was related in some detail by S. Baring-Gould in *Devonshire Characters* from which work, much of this biography has been culled.
See **pl. I**-18.

BAILIFF'S DAUGHTER OF ISLINGTON, THE. The title of an old ballad included in Percy's *Reliques of Ancient English Poetry* (1765)

There was a youth, and a well-beloved youth,
And he was a squire's son.
He loved the bailiff's daughter dear,
That lived in Islington.

But she was coy, and never would
On him her heart bestow,
Till he was sent to London Town
Because he loved her so.

When seven years had passed away,
She put on mean attire,
And straight to London she would go
About him to enquire.
And as she went along the road,
Through weather hot and dry
She rested on a grassy load,
And her love came riding by.

'Give me a penny, thou 'prentice good,
Relieve a maid forlorn;'
'Before I give you a penny, sweetheart,
Pray tell me where you were born?'

'Oh, I was born at Islington'.
'Then tell me if you know
The bailiff's daughter of that place?'
'She died, sir, long ago'.

'If she be dead, than take my horse,
My saddle and bridle also,
For I will to some distant land,
Where no man shall me know'.

'Oh, stay! oh, stay! thou goodly youth,
She standeth by thy side,
She's here alive, she is not dead,
But ready to be thy bride'.

See **pl. I**-3.

BEAUMARIS CASTLE, founded in 1295 by Edward I to guard the Menai Strait on the Anglesey shore. It is now mostly in ruins. It stands on level ground by the sea and was defended regularly all round. It consists of two lines of fortifications forming an inner and outer bailey and except at one point, where the sea entered to form a small dock, is surrounded by a moat. It has been claimed as the culminating point of British medieval military architecture; and its geometric pattern became a model for builders of smaller castles in England in the 14th century.
See **pl. I**-49.

BILLY (*c.* 1827), terrier. Famous as the 'champion rat killer'. His record—established in London's candlelit Westminster Pit—was 100 in $5\frac{1}{2}$ minutes! Rat killing furnished the poor man's sport in the 1820's, as bear-baiting did for the wealthy. The winning terrier was the one that killed the most rats in the shortest time.
See **pl. I**-19A.

BLUE COAT BOY.
See **Christ's Hospital.**

BRAIDWOOD, JAMES (1800–61), Superintendent of the London Fire-engine Establishment. Born in Edinburgh, he was educated at the High School. After acquiring a knowledge of the building trade, which qualified him for his future profession, he was appointed 'Superintendent of the Fire-engines' in Edinburgh. In 1830, he published a work *On the Construction of Fire-engines and Apparatus*. This drew the attention of the London insurance companies to the great advantage of union and organization in their arrangements for extinguishing fires and, in 1832, they appointed Braidwood as Superintendent of the London Fire-engine Establishment. Braidwood applied scientific methods to fire-fighting and the success of the Establishment was such that the Government saw no reason for taking over the responsibility, though often urged to do so by insurance companies. The Superintendent was a popular figure with the public, and was cheered as he rode with his men to the scene of a fire standing on the horse-drawn engine. His ability to deal with the majority, if not all conflagrations, received mention in a music-hall song:

'My heart's on fire
Not all the Fire Brigade could
Subdue the flames
Though led by Mr Braidwood'.

Braidwood met his death at the Great Fire of Tooley Street, London Bridge—London's most disastrous peacetime fire since the Great Fire of 1666. The fire broke out at Cotton's Wharf on Saturday afternoon, June 22nd, 1861. The cause was thought to be spontaneous combustion of hemp. The extent of the fire was such that Braidwood ordered out all his available force. The circumstances of his death were described in *The Illustrated London News* of June 29th, 1861:

. . . Mr Braidwood proceeded down one of the approaches to the river from Tooley-street, between the east and west parts of the wharf, and stopped halfway down to give some direction to a body of firemen who were there, when the wall of one of the warehouses, bulging out in the middle, fell a heap of ruins into the roadway, burying beneath the débris Mr Braidwood and Mr Scott, of the firm of O'Connor & Scott. Braidwood's body was dug out from the burning ruins two days later, much mutilated. The gallant fellow, it was proved, was giving brandy to sustain his men at the moment the wall gave way and buried him beneath its ruins. The fall of the wall was shown to have been caused by the weight and expansion of bales of cotton, which, to the number of 1600, were stored in the warehouse.

The Times correspondent had this to say of the appearance of the fire:

At about ten o'clock the fire seemed at its worst. Probably between eight and nine there was a greater body of flame than at any subsequent period, but the broad light of a summer's evening drowned its hideous glare. It was not 'til night fell that the tremendous terrors of the spectacle could be appreciated in all their horrid grandeur. Never since the fire of 1666 had such a scene been witnessed. The whole south bank of the river from London-bridge to below the Custom House seemed one stupendous pile of fire, glowing at its core with an intensity that made it painful to look at, and casting a ruddy glare above on everything far and near.

The fire caused damage estimated at £2 million. After renewed pressure from the insurance companies Parliament passed an Act which resulted in the establishment of the Metropolitan Fire Brigade in 1866. From that date, insurance companies ceased to protect the city from fire.
See **pl. I**-1.

BRIGHT, JOHN (1811–89), statesman and orator. The son of a miller, he was one of the leaders of the Reform movement which led to the introduction of Free Trade.
See **pl. I**-23.

BRUCE, ROBERT (1274–1329), King of Scotland. In 1296, he paid homage to Edward I, but a year later led a rebellion. He defeated Edward II at Bannockburn in 1314, but made peace, in 1328, with Edward III. Robert Bruce was the subject of an opera by Rossini, first produced in Paris on December 30th, 1846. A drama titled *Wallace and Bruce* by Robe was produced at the Coatbridge Adelphi on November 27th, 1869.
See **pl. I**-6.

BUNKER, CHANG and ENG (1811–74), the original Siamese twins born of Chinese parents in Siam. They were joined by a ligament at the lower part of the breast bone (*xiphopagus*), but although at first compelled to be always face to face, the ligament stretched as they grew so that eventually they were able to stand side by side, and even back to back. Their father was a fisherman and the twins soon became famous swimmers. The peculiarity of their movements in the water attracted the attention of a Scottish merchant, Mr Robert Hunter, and finally led to their leaving their native country in quest of a fortune. Removed to North America, they were shown in his circus by Barnum, appeared at Sadler's Wells in 1831, married English sisters, and settled down as farmers in North Carolina.

Chang, whose name was derived from the Siamese word for 'left', was the left of the pair and was much smaller and more feeble than his brother Eng, whose name signified 'right'. Their habits were very active. During the latter part of their lives they and their families lived in two houses about a mile and a half apart, and it was an inflexible rule that they should pass three nights alternately in each house. They raised large families of children, Chang being the father of ten, Eng of nine. Eng was very good natured, Chang cross and irritable. Chang drank heavily and was often drunk, but Eng never felt any influence from the debauch of his brother, a fact that suggests there was no free interchange in their circulations. They often had bitter quarrels, but as in the case of most other conjoined twins, when the one (Chang) died, the other refused separation and died shortly after.
See **pls. I**-23, 24.

CAERNARVON CASTLE, founded in 1283, by Edward I. A superb example of that type of castle whose whole united strength is provided by the single circuit of its towered walls. It is combined with a

fortified tower attached to it and built at the same time. In plan it resembles an hour-glass, narrow in the middle and bulbous at both ends. The towers are all polygonal in shape. It was the castle in which the first Prince of Wales, later Edward II, was born (1284) and presented to the people. Edward VIII was proclaimed Prince of Wales there in 1911, and Prince Charles in 1969. Generally regarded as the finest example in existence of military architecture of the middle ages.
See **pls. I**-49, 51.

CAMPBELL, THOMAS (1777–1844), poet. Son of a Glasgow merchant, educated at Glasgow University. He published *Pleasures of Hope*, in 1799. Amongst his most popular poems were *The Harper*, probably written during or after his visit to Ireland in the mid-1830's, which featured the dog *Tray*, and *The Soldier's Dream*, one of the war songs for which he is principally remembered.
See **pls. C**-72, 73,
pls. I-21, 21A.

CHRIST'S HOSPITAL: Founded in London by Edward VI in 1553, as an independent school for the sons of those who were in need of assistance towards the cost of educating and maintaining their children. Removed from London to Horsham, Sussex, in 1902. Also known as the Blue Coat School on account of the school uniform.
See **pl. I**-16.

COLIN. Has defied identification.
See **pl. I**-34 and **Flora** (*fig.* 69, *pl.* I-33).

COLSTON, EDWARD (1636–1721), philanthropist. Educated at Christ's Hospital, London. In 1683, he resided at Bristol, trading with the West Indies. Member of Parliament for Bristol from 1710 to 1713. Between 1690 and 1712, he founded and endowed alms-houses and schools at Bristol; the most important of these, Colston's Hospital, was opened in July, 1710. The boys wore uniform not unlike Christ's Hospital uniform. One of the most illustrious pupils was Thomas Chatterton (1752–1770), the poet. In 1861, the school was moved to Stapleton on the outskirts of Bristol.
See **pl. I**-18.

COLSTON BOY.
See **Colston, Edward** (1636–1721).

DARBY AND JOAN, a humorous title for an attached husband and wife, especially in advanced years and humble life. The *Gentleman's Magazine* of 1735, **5,** 153 has, under the title *The joys of love never forget : a song,* a second-rate copy of verses containing a reference to 'Old Darby, with Joan by his side', who 'are never happy asunder'. This is usually regarded as the source of the names, but both the identity of the author as well as the identity of 'Darby' and 'Joan' remain obscure.
See **pl. I**-38.

DARLING, GRACE HORSLEY (1815–42), English heroine. In 1838, accompanied by her father, she put off in a small coble from the lighthouse on the Farne Islands, off the Northumberland coast, of which her father was the keeper, and saved four men and a woman from the wreck of

the steamer *Forfarshire*. She died, four years later, of consumption.
See **pl. I**-18.

DOG TRAY, achieved popularity after the publication of Thomas Campbell's (1777–1844) poem *The Harper*. The relevant verse is:

On the green banks of Shannon, when Sheelah was nigh,
No blithe Irish lad was so happy as I;
No harp like my own could so cheerily play,
And wherever I went was my poor dog Tray.

Campbell's first poem was published in 1799, but there is no record regarding the date of *The Harper*.

Stephen Foster (1826–64), the American song-writer, composed *Old Dog Tray*, a melody very popular in Victorian times.
See **pls. I**-21, 21A.

DRAKE, SIR FRANCIS (1540–96), circumnavigator and Elizabethan admiral. Made many voyages of discovery. Was a leading figure, under Lord Howard, in the attack upon and destruction of the Spanish Armada in 1588.
See **pl. I**-15.

DUDLEY CASTLE, dates to the eighth century. It is mentioned in the Domesday survey, before the Conquest. In 1265, Roger II who had fought for Henry III against the barons began to refortify the castle. In 1272, the first year of Edward I, Roger II died and it was his grandson, John Somery, who finished the castle which his grandfather had begun. Whilst most of the best Edwardian castles were royal strongholds built to bridle Wales, Dudley is as good an English example as exists. A great fire occurred there in 1750. Apparently, coiners took possession of the vaults and whilst carrying on their nefarious trade set the old building on fire. There are extensive caverns under the castle which were very popular in Victorian times, and the scanty ruins of a priory. The extensive remains of the ancient castle are surrounded by beautiful grounds, opened as a zoo in 1937.
See **pl. I**-53.

EUSTON STATION was opened in 1838. The first train to be seen in London was in 1836. It ran from London Bridge to Deptford, the line being the beginning of the South-Eastern Railway. Euston was the second station to be opened in the capital. The massive Doric arch remained, until its demolition in 1963, the most impressive entrance to a London terminus. Queen Victoria first travelled in a train in June, 1842. The first express train in the Scottish service ran between Euston and Edinburgh—Glasgow on February 29th, 1848. Leaving Euston at 10 a.m., it reached Princess Street by 1.40 a.m. the following day (*1st class only*).
See **pl. I**-49.

FLORA, the goddess of flowers and spring of the ancient Romans, but see under 'observations' *fig.* 69, *pl.* I-33.
See **pl. I**-33.

GELERT, the name of a hound given by King John to Prince Llewelyn. Beddgelert, a village at the foot of Snowdon, means 'grave of Gelert'. At the site of *Gelert's* 'grave' is a plaque with the following inscription:

In the 13th century, Llewelyn, Prince of North Wales, had a palace at Beddgelert. One day he went hunting without Gelert 'The Faithful Hound' who was unaccountably absent. On Llewelyn's return, the truant stained and smeared with blood, joyfully sprang to meet his master. The Prince alarmed hastened to find his son, and saw the infant's cot empty, the bedclothes and floor covered with blood. The frantic father plunged his sword into the hound's side thinking it had killed his heir. The dog's dying yell was answered by a child's cry. Llewelyn searched and discovered his boy unharmed; but nearby lay the body of a mighty wolf which Gelert had slain. The Prince filled with remorse is said never to have smiled again.

> He buried Gelert here
> The spot is called
> BEDDGELERT

Similar stories are found in other places and Baring-Gould traced their origin to Indian sources. As far as Beddgelert is concerned, the myth is locally of modern growth —not older than 19th century.
See **pls. I**-20A, 21.

GILES, ROGER (dates unknown), a Devonshire schoolmaster. Little is known of him, but S. Baring-Gould wrote in *The Vicar of Morwenstow* (1876):

The people of Wellcombe were very ignorant. Indeed, a good deal of ignorance lingered late in the West of England. The schoolmaster had not thrown a great blaze of light on the Cornish mind in the first half of the present century.

I give a specimen of English composition by a schoolmaster of the old style in Devonshire; and it may be guessed that the Cornish fared not better for teachers than their Wessex neighbours.

This is an advertisement, said to have been written over a little shop:

> ROGER GILES,
> SURGIN, PARISH CLARK & SKULEMASTER,
> GROSER & HUNDERTAKER.

Respectably informs ladys and gentleman that he drors teef without wateing a minit, applies laches every hour, blisters on the lowest tarms, and vizicks for a penny a peace. He sells God-father's kordales, kuts korns, bunyons, doctersh osses, clips donkies wance a month, and undertakes to luke arter every bodies nayls by the ear. Joesharps, penny wissels, brass kanelsticks, frying pans, and other moozikal hinstrumints hat grately redooced figers. Young ladys and gentlemen larns their grammur, and langeudge in the purtiest mannar, also grate care taken off their morrels and spellin. Also zarm-zinging, tayching the base vial, and oll other zorts of fancy work, squadrils, pokers, weazels, and all country dances tort at home and abroad at perfekshun. Perfumery and snuff, in all its brancies. Astimes is cruel bad I beg to tell ee that i has just beginned to sell all sorts of stashonary ware, cox, hens, vouls, pigs, and all other kinds of poultry. Blackin-brishes, herrins, coles, scrubbin-brishes, traykel and godily bukes and bibles, mise-traps, brick-dist, whisker-seeds, morrel pokkerankerchers, and all zorts of swatemaits, including taters, sassages and other garden stuff, bakky, zizars, lamp oyle, tay kittles, and other intozzilkatin likkers, a dale of fruit, hats, zongs, hare oyle, pattins, bukkits, grindin stones and other aitables, korn and bunyon zalve and all hardware, I as laid in a large azzortment of trype, dogs mate, lolipops, ginger beer, matches and other pikkles, such as hepsom salts, hoysters, Winzer sope, anzetrar— old rags bort and zold here and nowhere else, newlayde heggs by me Roger Giles; zinging burdes keeped, sich as howles, donkies, paycox, lobsters, crickets, also a stock of a celebrated brayder.

P.S.—I tayches gography, rithmetic, cowsticks, jimnasticks, and other chynees tricks.

Baring-Gould concluded:

I should have held this to be an invention inspired by Caleb Quotem, in George Colman's play 'The Review', but that Mr Burton of the Curiosity Shop, Falmouth, has shown me old signboards almost as absurd.

Mr Burton, otherwise known as 'Honest John Burton', was himself a well-known Cornish character. He was still in business in 1926. In spite of his nickname there are many stories concerning his 'unending supply of signboards'.
See **pl. I**-18.

1. The version given by Baring-Gould omits the reference to *newlayde heggs by me Roger Giles* which I have added as it is the subject of *fig. 46, pl. I*-18.

GIRAFFE, THE NUBIAN (1826–9), the first giraffe to be seen in England.

Originally regarded as a compromise between the camel and the leopard and known as a *camelopard*.

In 1826, troops of Mehemet Ali, Pasha of Egypt shot a mother giraffe in the Sudan and captured her two calves. They were strapped to the backs of camels and taken to Cairo. The Pasha decided to give them as presents for the rulers of the two countries most concerned with Egyptian affairs, Charles X of France and George IV of England. They were despatched to Alexandria accompanied by an escort of Arabic and Moorish attendants belonging to the royal stables. Lots were drawn and France was allocated the larger specimen. His arrival in Paris caused a furore of excitement. The smaller giraffe travelled from Egypt to Malta, where he stayed for six months and then continued his journey to England, arriving at Waterloo Bridge on August 11th, 1827, accompanied by two Egyptian cows acting as wet nurses, two Arab keepers and an interpreter. They were conveyed to Windsor in a special caravan drawn by four horses. The King, who had returned to Windsor from Brighton, satisfied his yearning for the unusual by having a special building made to house the camelopard and provided it with a spacious paddock in the menagerie. He also commissioned two paintings, the most attractive being by Jacques-Laurent Agasse (1780–1849), the distinguished French animal painter. The King's attachment to the giraffe provided the caricaturists of the day with an opportunity for satire. One caricature appeared showing the King and the weighty Lady Conyngham, under whose influence he had fallen, riding on the giraffe. It was titled *The Camelopard, or a new Hobby*. The giraffe never recovered from the effects of the 45 day camel ride from the Sudan to Cairo. Its legs were seriously weakened and an elaborate pulley was made to enable it to stand up. It died in October, 1829.

The next giraffes, four in number, arrived in the Zoological Gardens on May 24th, 1836 and were accompanied by their Nubian attendants. A foal was born in 1840.
See **pl. I**-18.

GORDON-CUMMING, ROUALEYN GEORGE (1820–66), big-game hunter. Second son of Sir William Gordon-Cumming, bart. Educated at Eton, he served in the Madras cavalry from 1838 to 1840. In 1843, he took up a sportsman's life in South Africa. In 1850, he published the notes of his rough diary under the title of *Five Years of a Hunter's Life in the Far Interior of South Africa*. He exhibited his trophies in the Great Exhibition of 1851 and afterwards toured the country lecturing and exhibiting his lion skins. In 1855, a series of pictures of the hunter's travels by Harrison Weir, the great animal painter, were added to the exhibition as a diorama. In 1858, he settled at Fort Augustus, where his museum became a great attraction. After the death of Gordon-Cumming, the exhibition was purchased by Barnum and destroyed in his great fire. The exploits of Gordon-Cumming are legendary and he had many hair-raising escapes from death, particularly in encounters with lions. Amongst his other extraordinary experiences, he narrowly avoided being bitten by a puff adder; he 'danced' a waltz of life and death holding on to the tail of a hippopotamus; and it was only by the greatest presence of mind that he avoided being attacked and devoured by a tremen-

dous herd of wild dogs. Even after his return from South Africa, he narrowly escaped being gored to death by a fierce Highland bull.
See **pls. I**-4, 5.

JOHN BULL, the typical Englishman. In 1712, John Arbuthnot (1667–1735), issued a collection of pamphlets under the title *The History of John Bull*. These pamphlets were later rearranged and republished in Pope and Swift's *Miscellanies* of 1727. The pamphlets were designed to advocate, in the form of amusing allegories, the termination of the war with France; the various parties concerned being designated under the names of John Bull, Nicholas Frog (the Dutch), Lewis Baboon (the French king), Lord Strutt (Philip of Spain). Bull and Frog are engaged in a law-suit with Baboon and their case is put in the hands of Humphrey Hocus, an attorney (the Duke of Marlborough), and won. This work was the origin of John Bull, the typical Englishman. He is described as 'an honest plain-dealing fellow, choleric, bold, and of a very inconstant temper . . . '.
See **pl. C**-140,
pl. I-27.

JONES, JENNY (dates unknown), a dairymaid at Pontblyddin Farm, near Llangollen. She married a ploughman at the farm, Edward Morgan, a former sailor: They had been childhood sweethearts.
See **pl. I**-2 and **Morgan, Edward**.

LAMB and FLAG: Originally represented the Holy Lamb. It was also the coat-of-arms of the Templars, a medieval military religious order founded to protect the Holy Sepulchre and Christian pilgrims. The Paschal Lamb was the ancient badge of the *Queen's Royal Regiment (West Surrey)* and was conferred to the regiment in the Royal Warrant of July 1st, 1751. The reason for the adoption of the Paschal Lamb for the regimental badge has not been precisely established. *The Lamb and Flag*, a public house at Canon's Town, near Penzance, derives its name from the tin-stamp of the Bolitho family used as a mark of purity on ingots of tin. The building is Elizabethan and the old smelting-house is still standing next door. The inn-sign portrays a lamb with a halo over its head carrying a flag.
See **pl. I**-22.

LAMBTON, CHARLES WILLIAM (1818–31), eldest son of John George Lambton (1792–1840), first Earl of Durham. Master Lambton was painted by Sir Thomas Lawrence (1769–1830) in 1825, and the portrait, still in the hands of the Durham family, and variously known as *Day Dreams* and *The Red Boy* is regarded as one of Lawrence's masterpieces. The potters probably used engravings of the portrait as their source as all known figures have a blue coat.
See **pl. I**-17.

LION SLAYER, THE
See **Gordon-Cumming, Roualeyn George** (1820–66).

MACREADY, WILLIAM CHARLES (1793–1873).
For biography see **section E**.
See **pls. E**-1B, 2, 7, 62, 74, 76,
pl. I-6.

MONKEY PLUCK: The following is an extract from a recent edition of Mrs Beeton's *Household Management*:

Section I. Miscellaneous

Chinese Green Tea

'*Cloud Mist*' *Tea*: This tea is the most expensive kind. It is rarely exported as there is only enough for home consumption. It has an exquisite fragrance and is drunk in small cups as one would drink a liqueur. It grows high up on rocks and monkeys are trained to pick the leaves. It is also called '*Monkey Pluck*'.

See **pl. I-**18.

MORGAN, EDWARD (b.179–?), plough-man at Pontblyddin Farm, near Llangollen. Morgan returned to the farm after twenty years in the navy to marry his childhood sweetheart, Jenny Jones, a dairy-maid at the farm.

In 1825, Charles James Mathews (1803–78), then an architect with the Welsh Iron & Coal Co. of Coed Talwn, went to live at Pontblyddin Farm and there found 'a pretty little Welsh dairymaid and a simple ploughman called Edward Morgan'. Mathews had lately heard what he thought was an old Welsh air, *Cader Idris*, and to it he composed the *Song of Jenny Jones and Ned Morgan*.

My name is Ned Morgan,—I live at Llangollen,
The vale of St. David, the flow'r of North Wales;
My father and mother, too, live at Llangollen,—
Good truth, I was born in the sweetest of vales;
Yes, indeed, and all countries and foreign and beauti-
That little vale I prize far above,   ful,
For indeed in my heart I do love that Llangollen,
And sweet Jenny Jones, too, in truth I do love.

For twenty long years I've ploughed the salt ocean
And served my whole time on a man-o'-war ship;
And 'deed, Goodness knows, we had bloodshed
                                           engagements,
And many a dark storm on the pitiless deep:
And I've seen all the lands that are famous in story,
And many fair damsels to gain me have strove;
But I said 'In my heart I do love that Llangollen,
And sweet Jenny Jones, too, in truth I do love.'

I've seen good King George and Lord May'r of
                                           London,
With kings of far countries and many a queen;
The great Pope of Rome, and Duchess of Angouleme,
Up from King George to Sir Watkin I've seen;—
But no princesses, kings, dukes, nor commissioners,
No, goodness knows it, my envy could move;
For indeed in my heart I do love that Llangollen,
And sweet Jenny Jones in truth I do love.

I parted a lad from the vale of my fathers,
And left Jenny Jones a coquette young lass;
And now I'm returned a storm-beaten old mariner,—
Jenny from Jones into Morgan shall pass.
And we'll live on our cheese and our ale in content-
                                           ment,
And long through our dear native valley we'll rove;
For indeed in our hearts we both love that Llangollen,
And sweet Jenny Morgan in truth I do love.

Some time afterwards Mathews sang this song in a private gathering, and John Parry (1776–1851) 'an old gentleman in a volumi-nous white choker and a shiny suit of black' told him that he had written the air and won a prize with it at the Eisteddfod of 1804.

Later Mathews became an actor, and introduced his song into his one-act farce *He would be an actor*, produced at the Olympic Theatre in 1836. For the next twenty years the song was immensely popular and was 'whistled about the streets' (see *The Life of Charles James Mathews*, by Charles Dickens,

MULLER, GEORGE (1805–98), preacher and philanthropist. Born in Germany, he came to London in 1829. Initially he was the Nonconformist preacher at Teignmouth. In 1830, he adopted the principle that trust in God is sufficient for all purposes, both temporal and spiritual. Thenceforth he de-pended for support entirely on free-will offerings. From 1832 until his death, he lived

at Bristol, where he conducted philanthropic work, concentrating mainly on the care of orphan children. In 1836, he founded an Orphan House at Ashleydown, Bristol. His work grew until the number of children under his care exceeded two thousand. In 1845, he published *The Lord's Dealings with George Müller*.

See **pl. I-**18.

PARR, THOMAS (1483?–1635), known as 'Old Parr'. In 1635 John Taylor, the 'water-poet', published a pamphlet *The Olde, Olde, very Olde Man; or the Age and Long Life of Thomas Parr, the sonne of John Parr of Winnington, in the parish of Alberbury, in the county of Salopp (or Shropshire), who was born in the reign of Edward IV and is now living in the Strand, being aged 152 years and odd months. His manner of life and conversation in so long a pil-grimage; his marriages, and his bringing up to London about the end of September last, 1635.* This scarce book is the only work of authen-ticity that contains any particulars concern-ing this venerable old man. Sir George Cor-newall Lewis and others have regarded the story of his extraordinary age as unsupported by any trustworthy evidence.

Taylor records that he was born in 1483, went into service in 1500, and of his issue that 'he hath had two children by his first wife, a son and a daughter, the boy's name was John and lived but ten weeks and the girl's name was Joan and she lived but three weeks'. The story of an intrigue, for which old Thomas was chastised by the Church is thus versified by Taylor:

. . . In's first wife's time,
He frailly, foully fell into a crime,
Which richer, poorer, older men, and younger,
More base, more noble, weaker men, and stronger,
Hath fall'n into, . . .
For from the emperor to the russet clown,
All states, each sex, from the cottage to the crown,
Have in all ages since the first creation,
Been foil'd and overthrown with love's temptation:
So was Old Thomas, for he chanced to spy
A beauty, and love entered at his eye;
Whose powerful motion drew on sweet consent,
Consent drew action, action drew content:
But when the period of these years were passed,
Those sweet delights were sourly sauced at last.
Fair Katharin Milton was this beauty bright,
(Fair like an angel, but in weight too light),
Whose fervent feature did inflame so far,
The ardent fervor of Old Thomas Parr,
That for law's satisfaction, 'twas thought meet,
He should be purged, by standing in a sheet;
Which aged (he) one hundred and five year,
In Alberbury's Parish Church did the wear.
Should all that so offend such pennaunce do,
Oh, what a price would linen rise unto!
All would be turned to sheets; our skirts and smocks,
Our table linen, very porter's frocks,
Would hardly scape transforming.

'Old Parr' was brought to London by the Earl of Arundel in 1635 and carried to Court, where he was introduced to King Charles I. He did not long survive his removal to the metropolis, where he died on November 15th, 1635. He was buried in Westminster Abbey.

'Parr's Life Pills' were much in vogue in mid-Victorian times, and it may be that the figures of 'Old Parr' were made for the purpose of advertising the pills. An ad-vertisement from *The Graphic* of October 5th, 1878 reads:

*Important testimonial
in favour of*
Parr's Life Pills
Tong Lane,
Whitworth,
near Rochdale.
15th June, 1878.
*Dear Sirs,
I received the box of pills you sent by post safely. This medicine has been of the greatest use to me and my family*

without the aid of any doctors at all. No other medicine has been used but yours. I cannot fully detail to you how much good they have done our household, etc. etc.
                        (*Signed*) John Wormwell,
                              Weslyan Local Preacher
Messrs. Roberts & Co.
  The above letter ought to convince the most sceptical of the amazing curative powers of 'Parr's Life Pills'.

See **pl. I-**18.

PAXTON, SIR JOSEPH (1801–65), English gardener and architect. Born near Woburn, was a working gardener to the Duke of Devonshire at Chiswick and Chatsworth. He redesigned the gardens and looked after the Duke's Derbyshire estates. He formulated a plan of a building for the Great Exhibition of 1851. This structure was afterwards re-erected at Sydenham as the Crystal Palace. The Palace was destroyed by fire in 1936. He wrote on gardening and was Liberal Member of Parliament for Coventry from 1854.

See **pls. I-**23, 25.

QUEEN'S ROYAL REGIMENT (West Surrey): The old 2*nd Foot* raised in 1661 for service in Tangier. Battle honours include the Peninsular War, 1808–14; South Africa, 1851–3; China, 1860; Burma, 1885–7 and South Africa, 1899–1902. Granted naval buttons in commemoration of services in Lord Howe's fleet on the 'Glorious First of June', 1794. Now incorporated in the *Home Counties Brigade*. The 'Lamb and Flag' emblem was embodied in the badge of the *Queen's Royal Regiment*.

See **pl. I-**22.

RED MAIDS' SCHOOL, Bristol. Founded in 1634, in accordance with the terms of the Will of John Whitsun, an alderman of the City and County of Bristol. It is one of the oldest girls' schools in the country. Today, it provides grammar school education for girls aged 11 to 18. The traditional school uniform which consists of straw-bonnets with white linen tippets and aprons over red dresses is still worn by boarders on special occasions. In a short history of the school by Walter Adam Sampson, reference is made to the school clothing and a quotation included in which instructions are given for the appointment of 'one grave, painful and modest woman of good life and honest conversation whether married or unmarried', who was to have charge of the 'forty poor women children' for whom the Red Maids' School was originally founded, and also, this woman 'shall cause every one of the said women children to go and be apparelled in red cloth'.

See **pl. I-**17.

ROB ROY.
For biography see **section E.**
See pls. **E-**74, 75, 76, 97,
pl. I-6.

ROBIN HOOD, a legendary figure of the middle ages. A gallant and generous outlaw who roamed in Sherwood Forest, where he spent his time gaily 'under the greenwood tree' with Little John, Friar Tuck and his merry men. He was skilled with the bow and arrow and robbed proud abbots and rich knights, but gave generously to the poor. Tradition has made the outlaw into a politi-cal personage, a deposed 'Earl of Hunting-don'. In Scott's *Ivanhoe* he is represented as a Saxon holding out against the Normans. Nevertheless, there is no evidence that he was anything other than a figure of popular imagination. The story of Robin Hood has

been dramatized on numerous occasions.
See **pl. I**-13.

ROCH, St (c. 1295–1327), born at Montpellier. Patron of the plague-smitten. In art it is customary to portray him accompanied by a dog.
See **pl. I**-50.

SCARBOROUGH CASTLE: A twelfth century castle on the 'Scaur', a peninsula which divides Scarborough into two parts, the north bay and south bay. It is protected on the landward side by a moat. Built in the reign of Stephen, Scarborough was a great fortress forming part of the fiefs of William of Crumale, earl of York which was surrendered to Henry II after his accession. The castle was later besieged by Oliver Cromwell. Today, it forms a majestic ruin situated on the summit of the headland where it towers above the castle dykes and old town and harbour. Nearby, the graveyard of St Mary's Parish Church contains the burial place of Anne Brontë.
See **pl. I**-54.

SIAMESE TWINS
See **Bunker, Chang and Eng** (1811–74).

STANHOPE, LADY HESTER LUCY (1776–1839), eccentric. Eldest daughter of Charles, third Earl Stanhope. In 1803, resided with her uncle, William Pitt, and as mistress of his establishment, had full scope for her queenly instincts. She was given a pension of £1,200 by George III when Pitt died in 1806. The change from the excitements of public life was irksome to her, and in 1810, she left England and wandered in the Levant. She visited Jerusalem, camped with Bedouins in Palmyra and, in 1814, settled on Mount Lebanon. She adopted Eastern manners and dress, interfered in Eastern politics and had an astounding ascendency over the tribes around her, who came to regard her as a sort of prophetess. She was accompanied on her journeys by Dr C. L. Meryon (1783–1877) who acted as her physician, see section C. Her last years were poverty-stricken.
See **pl. A**-40,
pl. C-95A,
pls. I-36, 37.

TALBOT, MARY ANNE (1778–1808), female sailor, later dubbed 'British Amazon'; also known as **JOHN TAYLOR**. She was the youngest of sixteen natural children. Little is known of her mother, but her father is reputed to have been the Earl of Talbot. She was born in London, but spent the first five years of her life at a village near Shrewsbury. She was then removed by some friends of Lord Talbot who was then dead, to Mrs Tapley's boarding-school, near Chester and came under the eye of her only surviving sister.

On the death of her sister, a Mr Sucker of Newport, Shropshire assumed the authority of a guardian over her and took her from the school and placed her in his own family, where she was treated with great severity. He introduced her to a Captain Essex Bowen of the 82nd regiment of foot, who escorted her to London and put her up at the Salopian Coffee-house, Charing Cross. Before long he effected her seduction, and thereafter compelled her to dress as a footboy and accompany him first to St Domingo and then to Flanders. In 1792, her tyrant was killed in the capture of Valenciennes and she herself was wounded twice.

From the dread of her sex being discovered, she concealed her wounds, the cure of which she effected by the assistance of a little basilicon, lint and Dutch drops.

Though relieved of her oppressor, she was left friendless in a strange country. She threw away her drummer's dress and assumed that of a sailor boy. After a long overland journey, she joined what she took to be a French trader, but soon found it to be a privateer. This vessel fell in with the British fleet, then in the Channel under the command of Lord Howe. Mary Anne was taken prisoner. She was interrogated by Lord Howe, who accepted her story, which did not, of course, disclose her sex, and arranged for her to be stationed on board the *Brunswick* commanded by Captain Harvey. As a powder-monkey, she took part in the spirited action on June 1st, in which Captain Harvey was mortally wounded and in which she herself received a severe wound above the left ankle by a grape-shot which struck on the aftermost brace of the gun, and rebounding on the deck, lodged in her leg. The shattered bone penetrated the skin. Later, a musket ball perforated her thigh a little above the knee of the same leg. She lay in this crippled state until the action was over, when she was conveyed to the cockpit, but though she was subjected to the most excruciating pain, the grape-shot could not be extracted through fear of injuring the tendons amongst which it lay. On the arrival of the *Brunswick* at Spithead, she was conveyed to the *Royal Hospital*, Haslar from which, after four month's attendance as an out-patient, having experienced a partial cure, she was discharged. It appears that the naval surgeons were not the only ones to be hoodwinked by the 'British Amazon'. It is recorded that from time to time she entered other hospitals for treatment to her leg. She was an in-patient at both the *Middlesex Hospital* and *St Bartholomew's*. On one occasion her leg was prepared for amputation, but she took her own discharge.

She joined the *Vesuvius* which belonged to Sir Sidney Smith's Squadron and experienced further adventures which included imprisonment for a year and a half at Dunkirk. Her true sex was not discovered until soon afterwards she was seized by a press-gang in Wapping. After her discharge from the navy, she made numerous applications to the Navy Pay Office at Somerset House for money due to her for service on board the *Brunswick* and *Vesuvius*. She eventually received a pension of 12s 0d a week in the name of John Taylor and was placed in a lodging, the keeper of which was strictly enjoined to break her, if possible, of her masculine habits. However, this proved impossible. At one stage, she fell in with Haines, the notorious highwayman, who later atoned for his crimes by swinging in chains upon Hounslow Heath. He persuaded her to join him in 'an excursion upon the road' and actually furnished her with money to equip herself with a pair of buckskin breeches and boots and a brace of pistols, her sailor's habit not being thought suitable for the purpose. However, at the last moment she declined the enterprise.

She became a household servant to Robert Kirby, a London publisher, who described her life in his *Wonderful Museum*, 2nd volume, 1804, from which much of this biography has been culled.
See **pl. I**-4.

TAYLOR, MARY
See **Talbot, Mary Anne** (1778–1808).

TELL, WILLIAM, fourteenth century Swiss patriot, the hero of the liberation of Switzerland from Austria, probably legendary. He is represented as a skilful marksman who refused to do honour to the hat of Gessler, the Austrian bailiff of Uri, which had been placed on a pole. Because of this he was arrested and required to hit with an arrow an apple placed on the head of his little son. He successfully accomplished this feat, and later shot Gessler dead with a second arrow. He led a successful rebellion against the oppression. Although these events are placed in the fourteenth century, Swiss historians have shown that there is no evidence for the existence of a real William Tell. The story has been dramatized on many occasions.
See **pl. A**-55,
pl. E-60,
pls. I-7, 8, 9, 10.

TOM BROWN'S SCHOOLDAYS, a story by Thomas Hughes (1822–96) of an ordinary schoolboy at Rugby under Dr Arnold's headmastership. In the book, he publicised schoolboy cruelties and loyalties and thereby considerably influenced ideas on English public schools.
See **pl. I**-26.

TRINITY COLLEGE, CAMBRIDGE: Founded in 1546, by incorporating various small halls and hostels. The Great Gate is of the sixteenth century.
See **pl. I**-51.

WALLACE, WILLIAM (1272–1305), Scottish hero and chief champion of Scotland's independence. In 1297, he drove the English out of Scotland after winning the great battle of Stirling Bridge. On his return, he was elected Governor of Scotland. In 1298, Edward I invaded Scotland and defeated Wallace at Falkirk. His whereabouts thereafter are uncertain until his arrest near Glasgow on August 3rd, 1305. He was taken to London and tried in Westminster Hall. He was condemned to be hanged, drawn, beheaded and quartered, the quarters to be sent to Newcastle, Berwick, Stirling and Perth.

The story of Wallace has been dramatized on a number of occasions. A play in five Acts by C. Waddie titled *Wallace; or, the Battle of Stirling Bridge* was produced at Stirling town hall on September 3rd, 1898. A drama by Robe titled *Wallace and Bruce* was produced at the Coatbridge Adelphi on November 27th, 1869.
See **pl. I**-6.

WHITTINGTON, RICHARD (1359–1423), mayor of London. The younger son of Sir William Whittington, a Gloucestershire knight. Went to London at an early age to learn the merchant's trade. By the age of twenty was already a successful merchant. Married Alice Fitzwaryn, the daughter of a rich knight. At the age of forty he was appointed Mayor of London (or Lord Mayor, as the title officially became some years later) by Richard II. Although installed in the Mayor's office at first by an edict of the king, he was sufficiently popular for his fellow merchants to elect him mayor on three later occasions. He survived Richard II's fall from power in 1399, and won the support of the usurping Henry IV and his son Henry V, to each of whom he made substantial loans. His greatness lay in the success with which he organized the financial resources of the City in support of the European foreign policy of the House of Lancaster. He left the bulk of his great fortune to build and endow public edifices.

Two centuries after his death an Elizabethan story-teller immortalized his career by introducing the old Mediterranean folk-tale of the poor merchant who makes his fortune by selling his cat in a kingdom overrun with rats and mice, where cats are unknown. This tale was soon the favourite of the English middle-class. It has been dramatized on many occasions and over the past 150 years has shared with *Cinderella* the distinction of being the most popular pantomime.
See **pl. I**-4.

WILBERFORCE, WILLIAM (1759–1833), philanthropist. Son of a Hull merchant, he was educated at Cambridge, entering parliament in 1780. In 1788, he began a nineteen year crusade for the abolition of the slave-trade. His Bill was eventually passed and received the royal assent in 1807. Thereafter, he sought to secure the abolition of the slave-trade abroad and the total abolition of slavery itself, but declining health forced him to retire from parliament in 1825.
See **pl. I**-23.

WILL WATCH.
For biography see **section C**.
See **pl. C**-3,
pls. I-14, 14A, 15.

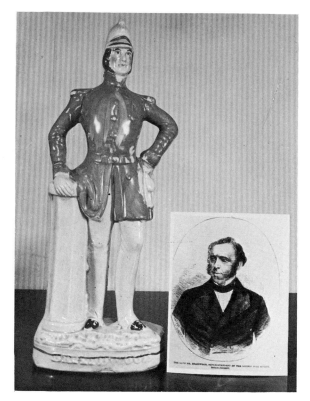

Plate 1
Fig. 1 Braidwood
In the collection of Lady Sneddon

Plate 2
Fig. 3 Jones

Fig. 4 Morgan and Jones

Fig. 2 Morgan
In the Thomas Balston collection

Section I
Miscellaneous
Details of the Figures

Plate 1
Figure 1
Subject: **James Braidwood**
Title: Braidwood (raised capitals)
Date: *c.* 1861
Height: 15 in (38 cm)
Colour: Specimens differ, none are particularly well coloured.
Rarity: R. D.
Description: Standing, wearing a fireman's helmet, coat, epaulettes and trousers. His left hand is on his hip and his right hand rests on a fluted pedestal.
Observations: Braidwood was killed in June 1861, but he was a well-known public figure for many years before that. Nevertheless, the style of the figure suggests that it was issued to commemorate his death—an event which caused great public sorrow. At his funeral the bells of every City church tolled throughout the day, every shop was closed and the procession was over a mile and a half long.

Plate 2
Figure 2
Subject: **Edward Morgan**
Title: Edward Morgan (gilt script)
Date: *c.* 1836
Height: 11½ in (29 cm)
Colour: Well coloured.
Rarity: R. D. A.
Pair: Fig. 3 (Jones); *fig.* 4 (Morgan and Jones) forms a centrepiece.
Description: Standing, in sailor's rig; in his left hand he holds a jug on a stool, and in his right hand a mug above his head.
Observations: 1. Based on an undated lithograph by E. Walker and J. C. Rowland published by T. Catherall of Chester and inscribed *Edward Morgan*, see *ch.* 3, *pl.* 59.
2. Edward Morgan, a ploughman at Pontblyddin Farm, near Llangollen was the subject of a song sung by Charles James Mathews at the Olympic Theatre, in 1836. This is the earliest period to which the figure could date. The song was extremely popular for the next twenty years. The figure and its pair are similar to pieces known to have been produced during the Crimean War, and may have been issued for the first time then, although of course, Morgan's sea-time dates to the Napoleonic wars.
3. A similar figure fetched 50 gns at Christie's in 1966.

Figure 3
Subject: **Jenny Jones**
Title: Jenny Jones (gilt script)
Date: *c.* 1836
Height: 10¼ in (25.75 cm)
Colour: Well coloured.
Rarity: R. D. A.
Pair: Fig. 2 (Morgan); *fig.* 4 (Morgan and Jones) forms a centrepiece.
Description: Standing, in a steeple hat over a frilled bonnet. She wears a shawl over both shoulders and an apron (*ffedod*) over two underskirts (*pais*). A can hangs from her right forearm and she holds a piece of knitting, two needles and a ball of wool in both hands. There is a low fence against her left leg.
Observations: 1. Based on a lithograph by E. Walker and J. C. Rowland published by T. Catherall of Chester and inscribed *Jenny Jones*, see *ch.* 3, *pl.* 60.
2. See preceding figure.
3. A similar figure fetched 90 gns at Christie's in 1966.

Figure 4
Subject: **Edward Morgan and Jenny Jones**
Title: Langolen/I/Mile (raised capitals)
Date: *c.* 1836
Height: 10⅝ in (26.75 cm)
Colour: Well coloured.
Rarity: R. D. A.
Series: Forms a centrepiece for the pair, *fig.* 2 (Morgan) and *fig.* 3 (Jones).
Description: In the centre of the figure is a milestone inscribed Langolen/I/Mile (*sic*). To the left of the milestone, Morgan stands bare-headed, wearing jacket, waistcoat, shirt, neckerchief and trousers. His left forearm rests on the milestone. To the right of the milestone, stands Jenny Jones wearing a steeple hat. Her right forearm rests on a tub of ? cheese which stands on top of the stone.
Observations: 1. There can be no doubt about the identity of these two figures, for it will be noted that the lithograph of Jenny Jones illustrated in *ch.* 3, *pl.* 60 depicts a milestone also inscribed *Langolen/I/Mile*.
2. A similar figure fetched 70 gns at Christie's in 1969.

Plate 3
Figure 5
Subject: **Unidentified youth and girl**
Title: London / 30 / Miles (raised capitals)
Height: 11 in (28 cm)
Colour: Usually sparsely coloured.
Rarity: Av.
Description: A youth stands to the left of a milestone inscribed 'London / 30 / Miles'. He is bare-headed, wearing a jacket, shirt, neckerchief, breeches and knee-boots. There is a bag over his right arm, and his left hand in which he holds his hat, rests on the top of the milestone. Behind the stone is a tree trunk (spill-holder) and to the right of the stone the girl sits wearing a broad-brimmed hat, bodice and ankle-length skirt.

Plate 3
Fig. 3 Unidentified youth and girl

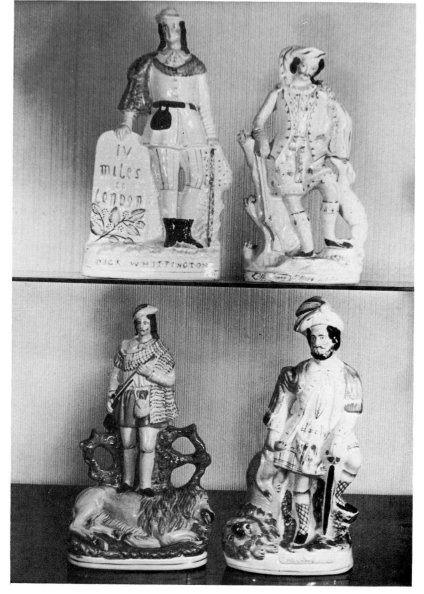

Plate 4
T: *Fig.* 6 Whittington
Fig. 7 Talbot

B: *Fig.* 8 Gordon-Cumming
Fig. 9 Gordon-Cumming

Plate 3 continued
Observations: 1. When this figure was sold at Christie's it was described as *A group of 'The Bailiff's Daughter of Islington'*. This is the title of an old ballad, included in Percy's *Reliques*. A squire's son loves the bailiff's daughter of Islington (Norfolk), but his friends send him to London bound as an apprentice. After seven years, the lovers meet again and are united. Although this reunion may well have taken place at a point '30 miles from London' and not at Islington, the attribution must remain in doubt, for the daughter was wearing 'mean attire' and the youth 'came riding by', see *p.* 606.
2. A similar figure, together with *fig.* 18 (Tell) *pl.* I-7 fetched 26 gns at Christie's in 1964.

Plate 4
Figure 6
Subject: **Richard Whittington**
Title: Dick Whittington (raised capitals)
Height: 17 in (42.5 cm)
Colour: Well coloured.
Rarity: Av.
Description: Standing, wearing a hat, cape, coat, breeches, stockings and boots. There is a belt round his waist with a wallet attached. He carries a bundle and stick in his left hand, and his right hand rests on a

milestone inscribed 'IV / miles / to / London' (raised upper and lower case).
Observations: 1. The significance of the inscription on the milestone is unknown to me. The source of the figure is almost certainly a print; possibly theatrical.
2. A similar figure, together with *fig.* 17 (Tell) *pl.* I-7, fetched 15 gns at Christie's in 1963. Another, by itself, fetched 22 gns at Christie's in 1969; and another, together with *fig.* 58 (Chang and Eng Bunker) *pl.* I-23, fetched 30 gns at Christie's five months later.

Figure 7
Subject: **Mary Anne Talbot, otherwise John Taylor**
Title: Sportsman: Mary Taylor (gilt script)
Height: 14 in (35.5 cm)
Colour: Usually mainly white and gilt but two superb coloured examples with underglaze blue coats have been recorded.
Rarity: VR. (titled); Av. (untitled).
Description: She leans against a tree trunk on her right, wearing a moustache, plumed hat, cloak, jacket, tunic and stockings (*probably Highland dress*). A dog, standing on its hind legs, rests one paw against her left knee. Her right hand (*gloved*) is on the muzzle of a rifle resting against the tree.

Observations: 1. This is not an uncommon figure, but only in the one instance (that illustrated) has it been found titled. It is usually in the pale state, although Mr Bonnett tells me that one very fine example in underglaze blue has passed through his hands. The piece illustrated is a fairly late figure and the writing is in 'Bright Gold'. It has been argued that the title has been applied to the figure later, but after careful examination I am certain this is not so. The title appears to derive from Mary Anne Talbot's real name and her male pseudonym, 'John Taylor'. There is no 'Mary Taylor' to be found in any of the usual books of reference and it was only by accident that this identification was made. I have been unable to find any portrait of Mary Anne Talbot identical to the figure, but most collectors who have examined the piece agree with me that it has feminine characteristics inspite of the moustache. The bust is certainly more like that of a woman than of a man. Mary Anne Talbot was at one time in league with highwaymen, particularly the notorious Haines. She is also known to have gone on the stage and this could account for the unexpected costume which may well be theatrical. Certainly it bears no relation to any conventional costume worn by sportsmen in her lifetime.

Section I. Miscellaneous

Moreover, it is unlikely that with the best will in the world she would have been able to grow such a moustache! Curiously enough, of the parts she quotes as having played, only one seems to have been male *i.e.* 'Jack Hawser' in *Banian Day*, produced at the Haymarket, in 1796. The facial features of Mary Anne as portrayed in a contemporary engraving (see *ch. 3, pl.* 61A) are not unlike those of the figure. Her story was revived on a number of occasions in Victorian times and may well have inspired a figure.

2. An untitled version, together with *figs.* 11 (Wallace) and 13 (Bruce), *pl.* I-6 fetched 44 gns at Christie's in 1963.

Figure 8
Subject: **Roualeyn George Gordon-Cumming**
Title: None
Date: 185–
Height: 16 in (40.5 cm)
Colour: Well coloured.
Rarity: Av.
Description: Standing on the back of a dead lion, wearing a plumed bonnet, shirt and short kilt over breeches and stockings. There is a plaid around him which is draped over his left shoulder. He is holding up a gun. His right hand is on the stock and his left hand on the barrel.
Observations: 1. I have heard of, but not seen, a similar figure, 14 in (35.5 cm), titled 'Cumming'.
2. See next figure.

Figure 9
Subject: **Roualeyn George Gordon-Cumming**
Title: The lion slayer (raised capitals on plaque)
Date: 185–
Height: 16¾ in (42.25 cm)
Colour: Well coloured.
Maker: Sampson Smith
Rarity: Av.
Description: Standing with left foot on a rock, wearing plumed bonnet, short jacket, kilt and a scarf over both shoulders. In his right hand, he holds up the hind paw of a lion, whose head is on the ground. His left hand rests on the hilt of his sword.
Observations: 1. This figure appears in the page from the old Sampson Smith catalogue illustrated in *ch. 2, pl.* 11.
2. A similar figure, together with *fig.* 8 (Gordon-Cumming), fetched £24 at Sotheby's in 1966; a similar lot, together with a third unimportant piece, fetched 20 gns at Christie's in 1967. Another lot, the same as the first, fetched 12 gns at Christie's in 1969.

Plate 5
Figure 10
Subject: **Roualeyn George Gordon-Cumming**
Title: None
Date: 185–
Height: 13¾ in (35 cm)
Colour: Usually sparsely.
Rarity: Av.
Description: Standing, wearing a round hat, a scarf over his shoulders, jacket, belt with a shooting bag attached, breeches and knee-boots. He holds the stock of a rifle in his right hand and the barrel in his left, and by his left side stands a dog.
Observations: Generally regarded as being a portrait of 'The lion slayer'.

Plate 5
Fig. 10 Gordon-Cumming
In the collection of
Mr F.J. Stephens

Plate 6
Figure 11
Subject: **William Wallace**
Title: Wallace (raised capitals)
Height: 17½ in (43.5 cm)
Colour: Well coloured.
Rarity: Av.
Description: Standing, leaning somewhat to his left, in plumed bonnet, a plaid over his left shoulder, kilt, sporran and stockings. He holds a round shield on his left arm and a sword in his right hand which is by his side.
Observations: A similar figure, together with *fig.* 7 (Talbot) *pl.* I-4 and *fig.* 13 (Bruce) fetched 44 gns at Christie's in 1963. Another, together with *fig.* 190 (Rignold) *pl.* E-97, fetched 20 gns at Christie's in 1969.

Figure 12
Subject: **William Wallace**
Title: Wallace (gilt script)
Height: 15½ in (39.25 cm)
Colour: Well coloured.
Rarity: Av.
Description: Standing in full Scottish uniform, a plaid over both shoulders and sword in his right hand.
Observations: 1. The identical figure has been used for *fig.* 13 (Bruce) with the title changed.
2. *Fig.* 261 (Prince Charles) *pl.* A-97 is in a

similar style.
3. A similar figure and *fig.* 13 (Bruce) together fetched 16 gns at Christie's in 1966.

Figure 13
Subject: **Robert Bruce**
Title: Bruce (gilt script)
Height: 15½ in (39.25 cm)
Colour: Well coloured.
Rarity: Av.
Description: Standing in full Scottish uniform, a plaid over both shoulders and his sword in his right hand.
Observations: 1. The same figure has been used for *fig.* 12 (Wallace) with the title changed.
2. A similar figure and *fig.* 12 (Wallace) together fetched 16 gns at Christie's in 1966.

Figure 14
Subject: **William Charles Macready as 'Rob Roy Macgregor'**
Title: Rob Roy (raised capitals)
Height: 13½ in (34.25 cm)
Colour: Well coloured.
Rarity: R.
Pair: Unknown
Description: Standing, much inclined to his right, wearing plumed bonnet, plaid over his right shoulder, kilt, sporran and stock-

I517

Plate 6
T: *Fig.* 11 Wallace
Fig. 16 Rob Roy
Fig. 14 Macready
('Rob Roy')

B: *Fig.* 12 Wallace
Fig. 15 Rob Roy
Fig. 13 Bruce

Plate 6 continued

ings. There is a round shield behind his left forearm and a halberd (combined spear and battle-axe) in his right hand which passes behind his right leg.

Observations: Almost certainly Mr Macready as 'Rob Roy Macgregor'. It is probably based on a tinsel portrait of Mr Macready published by A. Park, see *pl.* E-76. Although the shield is reversed, in all other respects *e.g.* sporran and halberd, the figure is identical. However, it is not such a good likeness as *fig.* 147, *pl.* E-74. Conversely, *fig.* 191, *pl.* E-97 is not sufficiently near to the tinsel

portrait to justify dogmatism, although it too, probably represents Mr Macready as 'Rob Roy Macgregor'. In this figure Rob Roy holds a dirk instead of a halberd and does not wear a sporran.

Figure 15
Subject: **Rob Roy Macgregor**
Title: Rob Roy (gilt transfer capitals)
Height: 18½ in (47.5 cm)
Colour: Sparsely coloured.
Maker: In the style of Sampson Smith
Rarity: Av.

Description: Standing, wearing a plumed bonnet, a long beard, plaid over his left shoulder, kilt, sporran and stockings. His right hand is on his hip and there is a round shield in front of his left forearm.

Figure 16
Subject: **Rob Roy Macgregor**
Title: Rob Roy (raised capitals; gilt transfer capitals illustrated)
Height: 19 in (48 cm)
Colour: Sparsely coloured.
Maker: In the style of Sampson Smith

Section I. Miscellaneous

Plate 7
Fig. 18 Tell and Son

Fig. 17 Tell

Fig. 19 Tell and son

Plate 8
Fig. 20 Tell

Fig. 21 Tell and son
In the collection of Mrs Constance Chiswell

Rarity: Av.
Pair: Fig. 17 (Tell) *pl.* I-7.
Description: Standing, wearing a plumed bonnet, short beard, plaid over his left shoulder, kilt, sporran and stockings. His right hand is on his hip and there is an octagonal shield, decorated with thistles, on his left arm.

Plate 7
Figure 17
Subject: **William Tell**
Title: Wᵐ Tell (raised capitals)
Height: 18¾ in (47.75 cm)
Colour: Sparsely coloured.
Maker: In the style of Sampson Smith
Rarity: Av.
Pair: Fig. 16 (Rob Roy) *pl.* I-6.
Description: Standing, in plumed bonnet, short-skirted dress and calf-high boots. His left hand is on his hip and his right hand supports his bow.
Observations: A similar figure, together with *fig.* 6 (Whittington) *pl.* I-4, fetched 15 gns at Christie's in 1963.

Figure 18
Subject: **William Tell and Son**
Title: William Tell (gilt script)
Height: 10¼ in (25.75 cm)
Colour: Well coloured.
Rarity: Av.

Description: Standing, wearing a high-plumed bonnet, short-skirted tunic and a cape over both shoulders which is fastened at the neck. To his right, stands a small boy holding an apple.
Observations: 1. May well be theatrical, although this has never been proven. It has been alleged that it portrays Macready.
2. See also *fig.* 18(a), *pl.* I-10.
3. A similar figure, together with *fig.* 5 (Unidentified youth and girl) *pl.* I-3, fetched 26 gns at Christie's in 1964; and another, together with *fig.* 63 (John Bull) *pl.* I-27, fetched 35 gns at Christie's in 1969.

Figure 19
Subject: **William Tell and Son**
Title: W. Tell (raised capitals on blue plaque)
Height: 8¼ in (21 cm)
Colour: Well coloured.
Rarity: VR.
Description: Standing, wearing a plumed bonnet and short-skirted tunic. He holds his bow by his right side and his left arm is round a young boy's shoulder. The boy, who is on the right, holds an apple pierced by an arrow in his left hand.
Observations: This figure, which is titled with a blue plaque, emanates from the same factory as *fig.* 49 (Norwich Castle) *pl.* G-23 and *fig.* 100 (Trinity College) *pl.* I-51.

Plate 8
Figure 20
Subject: **William Tell**
Title: None
Height: 14 in (35.5 cm)
Colour: Well coloured.
Rarity: Av.
Description: Standing, wearing a plumed bonnet, a cape over both shoulders, tunic, breeches and sandals with leather thongs. He supports his bow with his left hand against his side and in his right hand he holds an apple.

Figure 21
Subject: **William Tell and Son**
Title: None
Height: 7 in (17.5 cm)
Colour: Well coloured.
Rarity: VR. D. A.
Description: William Tell stands on the left, firing an arrow from a crossbow. His quiver lies on the ground in front. A boy stands on the right, blind-folded, with an apple on his head. He is bound to one of the two tree trunks (spill-holders), which form the background of the piece.
Observations: A very fine group which may well be theatrical.

Plate 9
Fig. 22 Tell
By courtesy of Mr and Mrs Eric Joyce

Plate 10
Fig. 22(a) Tell   *Fig.* 18(a) Tell and Son

Plate 9
Figure 22
Subject: **William Tell**
Title: Wm Tell (gilt script)
Height: 9 in (23 cm)
Colour: Well coloured.
Rarity: VR.
Description: Standing, in plumed bonnet, short-skirted tunic, a cape over both shoulders fastened at his neck. He holds his bow in his left hand.
Observations: 1. Very similar to *fig.* 18 (Tell) *pl.* I-7, except that there is no child. Both figures may well prove to be theatrical. It has been suggested that they portray Macready, but there is no supporting evidence.
2. See also *fig.* 22(*a*), *pl.* I-10.

Plate 10
Figure 18(a)
Subject: **William Tell and Son**
Title: William Tell (gilt script)
Height: 9¾ in (24.5 cm)
Colour: Well coloured.
Rarity: VR.
Description: Identical to *fig.* 18, *pl.* I-7, except that the apple is on the boy's head and not in his hands.
Observations: See *fig.* 18, *pl.* I-7.

Figure 22(a)
Subject: **William Tell**
Title: None
Height: 9 in (23 cm)
Colour: Well coloured.
Rarity: VR.
Description: Standing, wearing an angled bonnet, short-skirted tunic with belt, and cape over both shoulders fastened at his neck. He holds his bow in his left hand.
I520

Circular base with a step.
Observations: 1. Virtually identical to *fig.* 22 (Tell) *pl.* I-9, except that the bonnet is angled, the cloak does not extend behind his right leg, there is no title and the base is stepped. Nevertheless, the similarity is close enough to confirm the identification.
2. The fact that two similar figures have been produced, makes it almost certain that they are theatrical figures based on an engraving which has so far escaped discovery.

Plate 11
Figure 23
Subject: **Unidentified forester**
Title: OR (gilt transfer capitals)
Height: 17½ in (43.5 cm)
Colour: Usually largely white and gilt.
Rarity: Av.
Description: Standing, wearing a plumed hat, cloak, jacket, breeches and knee-boots. To his right is a tree trunk (spill-holder) and in his right hand he holds what appears to be a staff. There is a dog by his right foot.
Observations: This figure has been the subject of much discussion. It is usually found titled in the manner illustrated on this plate, *i.e.* with 'OR' centrally placed; although sometimes the 'OR' is to one or other side. Occasionally it is found with no title at all and very rarely there is evidence that there have been other letters as well as the 'OR'. I once saw two such figures in the same shop. The titling was extremely difficult to decipher, and I made a note that it could be 'Coris', 'Soris' or 'Goris'. Hunts through every conceivable reference book took me no further. 'OR' has been noted in raised capitals, I am told.

Mr Balston once told me that for many years he owned a 20½ in (51.25 cm) version of this figure. It was titled 'Forister' (*sic*) in gilt script. It was so beautifully designed and moulded that he kept it for years although he did not consider it a portrait figure. He could not imagine in what circumstances the rest of the word was omitted. It seems unlikely that 'OR' would be central if 'FORISTER' was intended.

Mr Stanley records the figure as 'Orlando', the lover of 'Rosalind', in Shakespeare's *As you like it*. Again, one would not expect the 'OR' to be central if this was so. There is a character in *As you like it* called 'Corin' who was a shepherd, and it is just conceivable that this figure portrays him, particularly having regard to the staff and the dog. Nevertheless, this does not explain, why, apart from rare instances, it is usually titled 'OR' only, usually with no evidence that any other letters had ever been present. The matter remains a mystery.

Plate 12
Figure 24
Subject: **Unidentified forester**
Title: None
Height: 11¼ in (28.5 cm)
Colour: Well coloured in the manner of Thomas Parr.
Maker: Thomas Parr
Rarity: R.
Pair: *Fig.* 25 (Unidentified forester)
Description: Standing, wearing a plumed hat, tunic and belt, together with calf-length boots. There is a hunting horn suspended by a chain around his neck. Both his hands are gauntleted and in his left hand he holds an arrow, whilst his right hand supports a bow.

Section I. Miscellaneous

Plate 11 (Left)
Fig. 23 Unidentified forester
In the collection of
Mr F.J. Stephens

Plate 12 (Right)
Fig. 24 Unidentified forester
Fig. 25 Unidentified forester
In the collection of
Miss E.M. Groves

Plate 13 (Left)
Fig. 26 Robin Hood
By courtesy of
Miss M.M. Frame

Plate 14A (Right)
Fig. 29(a) Will Watch

Observations: This figure, together with its pair, *fig.* 25, are thought to be symbolic of *The Ancient Order of Foresters*. They certainly bear a close resemblance to the coat-of-arms of this Order.

Figure 25
Subject: **Unidentified forester**
Title: None
Height: 11 in (28 cm)

Colour: Well coloured in the manner of Thomas Parr.
Maker: Thomas Parr
Rarity: R.
Pair: *Fig.* 24 (Unidentified forester)
Description: Standing, wearing a plumed hat, tunic and belt, together with calf-length boots. A hunting horn is suspended from a chain round his neck. Both hands are gauntleted and in his left he holds a cudgel by his side. His right hand is on his hip and

to his right stands a dog.
Observations: See preceding figure.

Plate 13
Figure 26
Subject: **Robin Hood and Little John**
Title: Robin Hood (raised capitals)
Height: 15¼ in (38.5 cm)
Colour: Usually white, gilt and black.
Rarity: C.

Plate 14
Fig.27 Unidentified male dancer   *Fig.28* Sailor and girl and boat   *Fig.29* Watch

In the collection of Mrs Constance Chiswell

Plate 13 continued
Description: 'Robin Hood' sits on the left, wearing plumed bonnet, tunic and belt and calf-length boots. To his right, is a dog and to his left, stands 'Little John', also wearing a plumed bonnet, tunic, belt and calf-length boots. He carries a cudgel in his left hand and his right hand is raised. Behind them is a tree trunk (spill-holder).
Observations: There are several figures of 'Robin Hood', who is generally regarded as a legendary outlaw. The story has been dramatized on numerous occasions. None of the figures appear to be theatrical, although this possibility cannot be excluded.

Plate 14A
Figure 29(a)
Subject: 'Will Watch'
Title: Will Watch (raised capitals)
Height: 15 in (38 cm)
Colour: Well coloured.
Rarity: Av.
Description: Standing, leaning slightly over to the right, wearing a wide-brimmed hat, long coat, tunic, sash round his waist, breeches and calf-boots. There are two corded packages between his legs and two barrels to his left, upon which he rests the stock of his blunderbuss, whilst he supports the muzzle with his left hand. He holds a pistol in his right hand and there is a knife in his belt.
Observations: See under *fig.* 29 ('Will Watch') *pl.* I-14.

Plate 14
Figure 27
Subject: **Unidentified male dancer**
Title: None
Height: 12¼ in (31 cm)
Colour: Well coloured.
Rarity: Av.
Pair: Unknown
I522

Description: Standing, with his right hand raised to his hat and his left hand on his hip, as if performing the hornpipe. He wears a plumed hat, ermine-edged cloak, decorated jacket, breeches and knee-boots. Tassels from his waist sash extend to his knees.
Observations: Almost certainly theatrical. It has been suggested that it portrays Mr Kean in the character of 'Iago', but I do not know upon what grounds this theory is based.

Figure 28
Subject: **A sailor and girl and boat**
Title: None
Height: 10½ in (26.5 cm)
Colour: Well coloured.
Rarity: R.
Description: The sailor stands on the left, wearing a plumed hat, jacket and trousers. He has a pistol in his right hand and a dagger in his left. The girl stands on the right, wearing a plumed hat, bodice and wide knee-length skirt. She carries a sword in her right hand and a shield in her left. In front of them is a boat on which is a barrel and an upturned jug and glass.
Observations: Almost certainly theatrical, but has so far eluded identification.

Figure 29
Subject: **Will Watch**
Title: Will Watch (raised capitals on plaque)
Height: 14 in (35.5 cm)
Colour: Well coloured.
Rarity: Av.
Description: Standing, leaning to his left, wearing a low plumed hat, jacket, shirt, sash round his waist, breeches, gauntlets and knee-boots. He holds a pistol in his right hand and the barrel of a blunderbuss in his left. To his left are two barrels.
Observations: 1. 'Will Watch' was the legendary hero of many ballads and melodramas. 2. See his biography (section C) and *fig.* 2 (Bart) *pl.* C-2.

Plate 15
Figure 30
Subject: **Will Watch**
Title: Will Watch (raised capitals on plaque)
Height: 12¾ in (32.25 cm)
Colour: Well coloured and sparsely coloured versions have been seen.
Rarity: Av.
Description: Sitting on a tree trunk, wearing a wide-brimmed, plumed hat turned up in front, a long coat, shirt, sash round his waist with a pistol, breeches and calf-boots. His left hand is on his hip and his right hand by his side. In it he holds a pistol, the muzzle of which he rests on a barrel.
Observations: See under *fig.* 29 (Will Watch) *pl.* I-14.

Figure 31
Subject: **Unidentified man with horn**
Title: None
Height: 13½ in (34.25 cm)
Colour: Well coloured.
Rarity: R.
Pair: Unknown
Description: Standing, inclined to his left, a scarf round his head and neck, cloak, doublet and hose, and calf-boots. His left hand is on his hip and his right hand holds, what appears to be a horn, to his ear. A dog, standing on its hind legs, has its front paws on his right leg.
Observations: Reputed to be a theatrical figure. It is said to portray an unidentified actor in the role of 'Richard II', in Shakespeare's tragedy. I have not been able to confirm this. Another suggestion, that it portrays 'Launce', the clown in Shakespeare's *The Two Gentlemen of Verona* and his dog *Crab*, likewise lacks confirmation.

Figure 32
Subject: **? Sir Francis Drake**
Title: None
Height: 19 in (48 cm)
Colour: Sparsely coloured.

Plate 15

Fig. 31 Unidentified man with horn

Fig. 32 ?Drake

Fig. 30 Watch

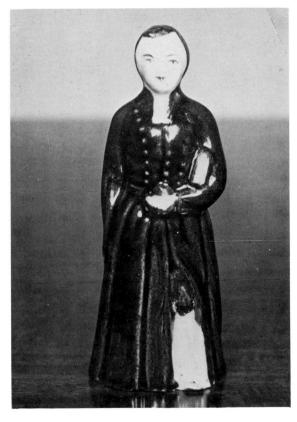

Plate 16
Fig. 33 Blue coat boy
By courtesy of Mr and Mrs Eric Joyce

Rarity: R.
Description: Standing, wearing a tall hat with a cross on it, doublet and hose. There is a cross suspended from his neck and his right hand is on his hip, whilst his left hand holds the stock of a blunderbuss which rests on his left shoulder.
Observations: 1. Generally regarded as representing Sir Francis Drake. It probably does, although I have not been able to confirm this.
2. A similar figure, catalogued as 'a Conquistador, possibly Pizarro', fetched 20 gns at Christie's in 1969.

Plate 16
Figure 33
Subject: **Blue coat boy**
Title: None
Height: 3½ in (9 cm)
Colour: Well coloured.
Rarity: R.
Description: Standing bare-headed, wearing the coat of a Blue coat boy. His right arm is by his side, there is a book underneath his left arm and he holds his left hand in front of his waist. Hollow base.
Observations: A similar, but not identical, boy from Christ's Hospital was illustrated in *The Illustrated London News* of September 24th, 1842.

I523

Section I. Miscellaneous

Plate 17
Figure 34
Subject: **Rabbi at entrance to synagogue**
Title: None
Height: 7½ in (19 cm)
Colour: Well coloured.
Rarity: VR.
Description: A domed building with a central door reached by steps and two smaller side doors. A man dressed as a rabbi stands in the central doorway.

Observations: Has so far defied identification. It has been suggested that it portrays 'Shylock'.

Figure 35
Subject: **Charles William Lambton**
Title: None
Height: 4¼ in (10.75 cm)
Colour: Well coloured, underglaze blue jacket.
Rarity: R. A.

Description: Sitting on a rock, bare-headed, wearing a short jacket, open shirt with frilled collar, breeches, stockings and shoes. He supports his head with his left hand, his left elbow resting on a ledge. His right hand rests on another ledge. His right leg is bent up and under his left thigh.
Observations: 1. After a painting of *Master Lambton* by Sir Thomas Lawrence PRA executed in 1825, see *ch. 3, pl.* 62.
2. The 5⅛ in (13 cm) version to which *fig.*

I524

Section I. Miscellaneous

35(a) has been allotted, is from a slightly different mould. It has been made as an inkwell, see ch. 3, pl. 62.

3. Lawrence's painting is famed as *The Red Boy* but the figure has only been found with the jacket in underglaze blue.

Figure 36
Subject: **A girl in the uniform of Red Maids' School, Bristol**
Title: Red Maid. Bristol (indented capitals)
Date: c. 1880
Height: 5¼ in (13.5 cm)
Colour: In the tradition of the Parr and Kent group of potters. The title is in black or 'Bright Gold'.
Maker: Kent and Parr
Rarity: R.
Pair: Fig. 37 (Colston schoolboy) pl. I-18.
Fig. 38 (Müller's orphans) pl. I-18 forms a centrepiece.
Description: Standing, wearing a poke bonnet, white tippet, white apron and red dress. She holds a basket in her left hand.
Observations: 1. The Red Maids' School was founded in 1634. The figure appears to date to the 1880's. Maybe, it was produced in 1884 in connection with the 250th anniversary of the foundation; alternatively, it was produced to raise funds for the school.
2. A lot consisting of figs. 36, 37 and 38 fetched 36 gns at Christie's in 1963.

Plate 18
Figure 37
Subject: **A Colston's Hospital schoolboy**
Title: Colston Boy. Bristol (indented capitals)
Date: c. 1880
Height: 5½ in (14 cm)
Colour: In the tradition of the Parr and Kent group of potters. The title is in black or 'Bright Gold'.
Maker: Kent and Parr
Rarity: R.
Pair: Fig. 36 (Red Maids' schoolgirl) pl. I-17.
Fig. 38 (Müller's orphans) forms a centre-piece.
Description: Standing, wearing a round cap, gown with bands and belt, stockings and shoes, a bible in his left hand.
Observations: 1. Possibly sold to raise funds for the school.
2. The uniform is not unlike that of Christ's Hospital, see fig. 33, pl. I-16. Edward Colston, who founded the school in 1710, was educated at Christ's Hospital, London. The style of the figure suggests manufacture in the 1880's.
3. A lot consisting of figs. 36, 37 and 38 fetched 36 gns at Christie's in 1963.

Figure 38
Subject: **A boy and girl from George Muller's orphanage**
Title: George. Mullers. Orphans. Bristol. (indented capitals)
Date: c. 1880
Height: 5¾ in (14.5 cm)
Colour: In the tradition of the Parr and Kent group of potters. The title is in black or 'Bright Gold'.
Maker: Kent and Parr
Rarity: R.
Pair: Forms the centrepiece for the pair fig. 36 (Red Maids' schoolgirl) pl. I-17 and fig. 37 (Colston schoolboy).
Description: A boy and girl in Victorian orphanage dress. The boy wears a peaked cap, short jacket, waistcoat and pantaloons and carries a bag in his right hand. The girl wears a poke bonnet, short cape, muslin dress and shoes and carries a bag in her left hand.

Observations: 1. Possibly sold to raise funds for the Orphan House founded by George Müller at Bristol, in 1836. The style of the figure suggests its manufacture in the 1880's.
2. A lot consisting of figs. 36, 37 and 38 fetched 36 gns at Christie's in 1963.

Figure 39
Subject: **Grace Darling**
Title: Grace Darling (gilt script)
Date: c. 1838
Height: 7 in (17.5 cm)
Colour: Well coloured.
Rarity: VR.
Description: Grace and her father are in a small boat, both facing right. Grace kneels in the bows with her hands raised and clasped. Her father sits in the stern. Behind them is a rocky coast, with a lighthouse in the centre and a cottage to the left. The cottage has one door on the ground floor and two windows on the first floor with a straight roof edge above them.
Observations: Grace Darling and her father, the lighthouse keeper on the Farne Islands, rescued four men and a woman from the wreck of the steamer *Forfarshire*, in 1838.

Figure 40
Subject: **Grace Darling**
Title: Grace Darling (gilt script; untitled version illustrated)
Date: c. 1838
Height: 6½ in (16.5 cm)
Colour: Well coloured.
Rarity: R.
Description: Grace and her father sit in a small boat facing each other. Behind them is a rocky coast, with a lighthouse in the centre and a cottage to the left. The cottage has both a door and window on the ground floor and a single window above, with a curved roof over it.
Observations: 1. A titled version of this figure fetched 26 gns at Christie's in 1964; and another 60 gns in the same rooms in 1969.
2. A crude reproduction of the figure is known, 5½ in (14 cm) in height. There are minor differences in modelling, the number '18' is impressed on the bottom, it is untitled and the base is painted all over in green. In general it is a poor sort of figure, and the collector should have no difficulty in recognizing it.

Figure 41
Subject: **The Alphington Ponies**
Title: A Present from Torquay (gilt script)
Date: 184–
Height: 4½ in (11.5 cm)
Colour: Well coloured.
Rarity: VR. (titled); R. (untitled)
Description: The two sisters are standing arm-in-arm. They wear small hats, tall in the crown and curled up at the sides, long jackets, short skirts and pantalettes and each carries an umbrella.
Observations: Accounts of the 'Alphington Ponies' can be found in Ellis' *Historical Survey of Torquay*, pp. 341–2, and in S. Baring-Gould's *Devonshire Characters*, pp. 16–21. A lithograph by P. Gauci reproduced on p. 20 of Baring-Gould's book confirm that this group portrays the 'Alphington Ponies'. If further proof is needed the reader is referred to ch. 3, pl. 63 where the two sisters are illustrated on a music-front inscribed *Torquay Polka*.

Figure 42
Subject: **Thomas Parr**
Title: Old Parr (gilt script)
Height: 9½ in (24 cm)

Colour: Well coloured.
Rarity: Av.
Description: Standing bare-headed and bearded, in cloak, jacket, breeches and stockings. He holds a basket of vegetables in his left hand.
Observations: 1. Parr's *Life Pills* were much advertised in Victorian times, and it may well be that the figures of 'Old Parr' were used for advertising purposes.
2. The potter has obtained a good likeness of 'Old Parr'. Comparison with the engraving by R. Page, illustrated in ch. 3, pl. 64, confirms this. The likeness was taken by Rubens who saw Thomas Parr when he was alleged to be 'about 140 years of age', and painted him.
3. A similar figure fetched 24 gns in 1964; another, 46 gns in 1966; another, 24 gns in 1967; and another, 48 gns in 1969—all at Christie's.

Figure 43
Subject: **Monkey porter**
Title: None
Height: 8 in (20.5 cm)
Colour: Well coloured.
Rarity: VR.
Description: A monkey squats on a tree stump. To his left, is a tea-barrel standing on a coil of rope. The barrel has no lid. The monkey carries a basket on his back held by thongs to both wrists.
Observations: See p. 601, for discussion on 'Monkey Pluck' tea. Both basket and barrel may have held samples of tea.

Figure 44
Subject: **Giraffe and keeper** (facing right)
Title: None
Height: 9½ in (24 cm)
Colour: Well coloured.
Rarity: R.
Pair: Fig. 45 [Giraffe and keeper (L); see ch. 3, pl. 65]
Description: A baby giraffe stands in front of a tree trunk (spill-holder). To the right, is his keeper wearing a plumed head-dress, cloak with ermine-edge, tunic and calf-boots. In his right hand he holds a bucket with which to feed the animal.
Observations: May well have been inspired by the painting of the first giraffe to be seen in England, together with his two Arab keepers, by Laurent Agasse, see ch. 3, pl. 66.

Figure 45
Subject: **Giraffe and keeper** (facing left; see ch. 3, pl. 65)
Title: None
Height: 9½ in (24 cm)
Colour: Well coloured.
Rarity: R.
Pair: Fig. 44 [Giraffe and keeper (R)]
Description: Apart from minor differences, a mirror-image of fig. 44 [Giraffe and keeper (R)].
Observations: See under fig. 44 [Giraffe and keeper (R)].

Figure 46
Subject: **Roger Giles**
Title: Roger/Giles (indented capitals)
Height: 5 in (12.75 cm)
Colour: Well coloured.
Rarity: R.
Description: Squatting, in round hat, jacket, breeches, stockings and shoes. His backside is laid bare.
Observations: 1. See details of the signboard attributed to Roger Giles which appear on p. 599. *Newlayde heggs by me Roger Giles* is the subject of this risqué figure.

Section I. Miscellaneous

Plate 18 continued

2. Victorian copies of the figure are rare, although I have seen one pre-Victorian 'Pratt ware' version, identical except that it was untitled and made as a pepper-pot. Most copies appear to be relatively late, having been sold as souvenirs by Mr Burton of the *Curiosity Shop*, Falmouth, at least until 1926.

Figure 47
Subject: **A rescue dog**
Title: None
Height: 8 in (20.5 cm)
Colour: Well coloured.
Rarity: Av.
Description: A dog stands in front of a tree trunk (spill-holder), dragging a baby from the river by his vest.
Observations: 1. There were a number of famous 'rescue dogs' in Victorian times, but I have failed to identify this particular animal. There is a plate, decorated with a similar scene, inscribed *Man's faithful hound*.
2. A play by Frederick Reynolds, called *The Caravan; or, The Driver and his Dog*, which was produced at Drury Lane in 1803, had a scene in which a dog called *Carlos* rescued a child from drowning. No connection between this dog and the figure has been found so far.

Plate 19
Figure 48
Subject: **Dog protecting child from snake**
Title: None
Height: 11 in (28 cm)
Colour: Sparsely coloured.
Rarity: R.
Description: A child is sleeping at the foot of a tree (spill-holder). Entwined in the branch of the tree is a snake and below the tree looking up at the snake is a dog.
Observations: Another 'rescue dog' figure. I have so far been unable to pin down the story, but it probably records an event in India, in Victorian times.

Plate 19A
Figure 48(a)
Subject: **? Billy the rat catcher**
Title: None
Date: c. 1840
Height: $7\frac{3}{8}$ in (18.75 cm)
Colour: Well coloured.
Rarity: R.
Description: A terrier facing left, with a large solitary dead rat at its feet.
Observations: 1. *Billy* the rat catcher was a terrier famous as the 'champion rat killer'. His record, gained in London's *Westminster Pit*, was 100 rats in $5\frac{1}{2}$ minutes. Rat killing was the poor man's sport of the 1820's, much as bear-baiting was that of the wealthy.
2. This figure certainly portrays a rat catcher; it may well be intended to portray the illustrious *Billy*.

Figure 48(b)
Subject: **? Billy the rat catcher**
Title: None
Date: c. 1840
Height: 6 in (15.25 cm)
Colour: Well coloured.
Rarity: R.
Pair: The same figure is found facing *both* left and right.
Description: A terrier with two dead rats at its feet.
Observations: See preceding figure.

Plate 19B
Figure 48(c)
Subject: **Child, dog and snake**
Title: None
Height: $6\frac{1}{4}$ in (16 cm)
Colour: Well coloured.
Rarity: R.
Pair: Fig. 48(d) (Child, dog and snake with head bitten off)
Description: A naked child lies on the ground to the right, and a dog, probably a Newfoundland, stands to the left. In the foreground, a snake is slithering to the right.
Observations: See next figure.

Plate 19
Fig. 48 Dog protecting child from snake
In the collection of Mr H. T. Appleton

Plate 19A
Fig. 48(a) ? 'Billy' the rat catcher
In the collection of Mrs P. Stockman

Section I. Miscellaneous

Plate 19B
Fig. 48(d) Child, dog and
snake with head bitten off
Fig. 48(c) Child, dog and
snake
*In the collection of
Dr. S.J. Howard*

Plate 19C (Left)
Fig. 49 Eagle and child

Plate 20 (Right)
A Child rescued by its
Mother from an Eagle's
nest.
Painting by
George Dawe RA
(1781-1829),
the inspiration of
Fig. 49, *pl.* 1-19C.
*By courtesy of
Mr H.R.H. Woolford*

Figure 48(d)
Subject: **Child, dog and snake with head
bitten off**
Title: None
Height: 7 in (17.5 cm)
Colour: Well coloured.
Rarity: R.
Pair: Fig. 48(c) (Child, dog and snake)
Description: A naked child is sitting on a dog,
probably a Newfoundland, squatting facing
left. At the dog's feet lies a snake with its
head bitten off.
Observations: A plate engraved with the
same subject is in the possession of Dr. S. J.
Howard. It is inscribed:

> *The Deliverer*
> *1851*
> *Exhibition*

There is no indication given as to who is
portrayed, nor, so far as I am aware, are
dogs known to bite snakes heads off.
It has been suggested that the dog is
Bashaw, a Newfoundland who belonged to
the Earl of Dudley (*c*. 1831). This dog is the
subject of a statue by M. C. Wyatt (1777–
1862) now in the Victoria and Albert
Museum. I know of nothing to substantiate
this.

Plate 19C
Figure 49
Subject: **A child rescued by its mother
from an eagle's nest**
Title: None
Date: *c*. 1860
Height: 16 in (40.5 cm)

Colour: Well coloured.
Rarity: R.
Description: A mother is rescuing a child
from an eagle's nest in which, in addition to
the child, there are two eaglets. The angry
eagle is perched above.
Observations: 1. Based on *A Child rescued by its
Mother from an Eagle's nest*, a painting by
George Dawe RA (1781–1829), exhibited
at the Royal Academy, in 1813. It rivalled
Wilkie's *Blind Man's Buff* as the picture of
the year.
2. The following explanatory note is to be
found in the catalogue of the 1813 exhibition:

> It is within the memory of some of the oldest
> inhabitants of a mountainous district of Scotland
> that, impelled by a maternal solicitude to recover her
> infant which an eagle had borne away to its nest, a
> mother climbed to the very topmost crag of a cliff

I527

so steep and terrific that the hardiest bird-catchers in that region had hitherto pronounced it inaccessible. She succeeded in bringing off her child before it had received any material injury, the bird hovering round her during the attempt but not offering in any way to molest her.

3. Mr Anthony Oliver, to whom I am grateful for much of the research on this subject, has suggested that the figure was produced when the story was dramatized. *The Eagle and Child; or, A Mother's Courage* opened at

the Britannia Theatre, Hoxton on October 10th, 1859.

4. I have seen two other figures apparently portraying the same story; also a pair of eagles, 10 in (25 cm) in height, one (facing right) clutches a child and the other (facing left) clutches a lamb. See also *fig.* 49(*a*), *pl.* I-21A.

5. An example of this figure, and another unimportant figure, fetched 14 gns at Christie's in 1964. The same figure, by itself, fetched 12 gns at Christie's in 1969.

Section I. Miscellaneous

Plate 21A
Fig. 51(a) Dog Tray
Fig. 49(a) Eagle, dog and child
In the collection of
Mr A. Guy Stringer

Plate 20A
Figure 50
Subject: **Gelert and Prince Llewelyn's son**
Title: None
Height: 8⅝ in (21.75 cm)
Colour: Largely white and gilt.
Rarity: VR.
Description: A bare-headed child sits on the left. On the right squats a hound, facing left. Both are on a couch at the foot of which lies a dead wolf, facing left.
Observations: 1. Based on an engraving by W. H. Mote after Daniel Maclise (1806–70). This engraving which is inscribed *Faithful Gelert* is the frontispiece of *The People's Gallery of Engravings*, edited by Mrs Milner (second series, vol IV).
2. The figure is a mirror-image of the engraving. Very possibly a pair to the figure will be found which is identical to the engraving.

Plate 21
Figure 50(a)
Subject: **Gelert and Prince Llewelyn's son**
Title: None
Height: 10½ in (26.5 cm)
Colour: Well coloured.
Rarity: R.
Description: A watch-stand consisting of a child in a cradle, protected by a dog to the right. At the foot of the cradle is a dead wolf and above the cradle is a cherub.
Observations: A similar figure, and another unimportant piece, fetched 15 gns at Christie's in 1964.

Figure 51
Subject: **Dog Tray**
Title: Dog Tray (raised capitals)

Height: 13 in (33 cm)
Colour: Generally sparsely coloured.
Rarity: C.
Description: *Tray* is squatting on the left and a man is seated on the right. He wears a low hat, cloak, jacket, breeches, stockings and shoes. Behind them is a tree trunk (spill-holder).
Observations: The dog *Tray* achieved popularity after the publication of Thomas Campbell's poem *The Harper* (c. 1836):

When at last I was forced from my Sheelah to part,
She said (while the sorrow was big at her heart),
'Oh! remember your Sheelah when far, far away;
And be kind, my dear Pat, to our poor dog Tray'.

Stephen Foster, the American song-writer, composed *Old Dog Tray*, also very popular in Victorian times:

> Old Dog Tray's ever faithful,
> Grief cannot drive him away,
> He's gentle, he is kind,
> I'll never, never find
> A better friend than Old Dog Tray.

Plate 21A
Figure 49(a)
Subject: **Eagle, dog and child**
Title: None
Height: 8 in (20.5 cm)
Colour: Well coloured.
Rarity: R.
Description: An eagle is perched on top of some rocks overlooking a child, asleep. To the left of the child is a dog whose right front paw is raised as if in the act of protecting the child from the eagle.
Observations: Probably based on an actual incident, although I have been unable to track it down.

Figure 51(a)
Subject: **Dog Tray**
Title: Dog Tray (raised capitals)
Height: 10 in (25 cm)
Colour: White, gilt and black.
Rarity: Av.
Description: On the left, a young lad lies asleep at the foot of a tree. To his right is a hoop and a stick. *Tray* sits on a rock, above and to the right.
Observations: See under *fig.* 51, *pl.* I-21.

Section I. Miscellaneous

Plate 22
Fig. 52 Lamb and flag

Plate 22
Figure 52
Subject: **Lamb and flag**
Title: None
Height: 3 in (7.6 cm)
Colour: Sparsely coloured.
Rarity: R.
Description: A lamb is lying down, facing right. Behind is a flag.

Plate 23
Figure 53
Subject: **Train group**
Title: None
Date: 184–
Height: 9 in (23 cm)
Colour: Well coloured.
Rarity: R.
Description: A boy and a girl, possibly the Prince of Wales and Princess Royal, with a dog between them, are seated before a tree stump (spill-holder) with a train emerging from a tunnel below.
Observations: This figure, together with *fig.* 91 (? Euston station) *pl.* I-49, and another unimportant piece, fetched 18 gns in Christie's in 1966.

Plate 23
T: *Fig.* 53 Train group
Fig. 54 Woman and parakeet
Fig. 56 Unidentified man
Fig. 55 Man and parakeet
Fig. 57 Unidentified soldier

B: *Fig.* 58 Siamese twins
Fig. 60 Unidentified gardener and girl
Fig. 59 Unidentified man and child
Note: Fig. 59 is damaged and has been incorrectly restored, see text.

Section I. Miscellaneous

Plate 24
Chang and Eng Bunker (1811-1874)
Lithograph by W. Day, published by
R. Ackermann & Co., 96, Strand, London on
December 1st, 1829. It is inscribed 'The
Siamese Youths (*AGED 18*)'.
Fig. 58, *pl.* 1-23 is thought to portray the twins
whilst on show at Barnum's circus.
*By courtesy of The Librarian
Finsbury Public Library*

Figure 54
Subject: **Woman and parakeet**
Title: None
Height: 8 in (20.5 cm)
Colour: Well coloured.
Rarity: R.
Pair: Fig. 55 (Man and parakeet)
Description: A lady is seated on a high-backed
chair wearing a bodice and long skirt. A
parakeet is perched on her right arm.
Observations: Has so far defied identification.

Figure 55
Subject: **Man and parakeet**
Title: None
Height: 8 in (20.5 cm)
Colour: Well coloured.
Rarity: R.
Pair: Fig. 54 (Woman and parakeet)
Description: A man bare-headed, dressed in
jacket, waistcoat, breeches and knee-boots,
is seated in a high backed chair. A parakeet
is perched on his left arm.
Observations: Has so far defied identification.

Figure 56
Subject: **Unidentified man**
Title: None
Date: Probably *c.* 1870
Height: 5½ in (14 cm)
Colour: Well coloured.
Rarity: Av.
Description: A fat man is seated on a wall
holding his right hand towards his right eye.
He wears a short jacket, neckerchief, waistcoat, trousers and shoes. His left hand is
plunged into his waistcoat pocket.
Observations: A fairly late figure. It has been
suggested that it portrays John Bright
(1811–89), but I know of no evidence to
substantiate this claim. In the trade, the
figure is sometimes referred to as 'The snuff-
taker'. I have heard of a figure of a man
standing in frock-coat, 3¾ in (9.5 cm) titled
'Bright' in indented capitals, but I have
never seen it.

Figure 57
Subject: **Unidentified soldier**
Title: None
Height: 10 in (25 cm)
Colour: Well coloured.
Rarity: C.
Description: A fairly stout man with a fringe
beard, standing with his head tilted slightly
to his left, plumed hat, ermine-edged cloak
tied in front of his neck, short jacket, sash
over his right shoulder, belt, trousers and
knee-boots. He holds his sword in his left
hand by his side.
Observations: This figure has been given
many different identifications, but none are
convincing. There is a similarity between
the figure and *fig.* 100 (Unidentified Highland soldier) *pl.* E-58.

Figure 58
Subject: **Chang and Eng Bunker**
Title: None
Height: 11¾ in (29.75 cm)
Colour: Well coloured.
Rarity: R.
Description: A man in Highland dress is
seated on the left, playing a musical instrument. On the right sit Siamese twins, each
wearing a plumed bonnet. All are seated
under a decorated arch.
Observations: 1. A circus piece. The twins
were removed to North America and subsequently shown in his circus by Barnum,
see *pl.* I-24.

2. This group is sometimes found with the
faces of both the musician and the twins
coloured black.
3. A similar figure fetched 30 gns at Christie's in 1969; and another, together with
fig. 6 (Whittington) *pl.* I-4, fetched 30 gns
in the same rooms, five months later.

Figure 59
Subject: **Unidentified man and child**
Title: None
Height: 10½ in (26.5 cm)
Colour: Pale and well coloured versions are
known.
Rarity: R.
Description: A man is standing bare-headed,
wearing a long coat, breeches, stockings and
shoes. He is dressed in eighteenth century
costume. His left arm is round the shoulders
of a small girl wearing a cloak, blouse,
skirt, stockings and shoes. His right forearm
rests on what appears to be a chimney-
stack surmounted by a pot and cowl
Alternatively, it is a lamp. In front is a spade,
pick and an object which has been identified
as a 'coal harness'.
Observations: 1. I am grateful to Mr and Mrs
Eric Joyce for letting me know that as a
result of their research they are confident
that the apparatus portrayed is connected
with coal mining. The theme of the figure is
probably something to do with the employment of children in the mines. It was at one
time suggested that the person portrayed
was the Earl of Shaftesbury, but the
costume is of an earlier period. More
recently, the idea has been put forward that
the figure portrays William Wilberforce,
the English philanthropist, whose Bill for
the abolition of the slave-trade was eventually passed, receiving the royal assent in
1807. This seems quite feasible.
2. The chimney-stack, if such it is, has been
wrongly restored in the figure illustrated.
3. A similar figure described as 'a group of
Paxton, standing beside a pedestal, moulded
with agricultural trophies . . .' fetched 55
gns at Christie's in 1969.

Figure 60
Subject: **Unidentified gardener and girl**
Title: None
Height: 11¾ in (29.75 cm)
Colour: Both well coloured and sparsely
coloured versions known.
Rarity: Av.
Description: An elderly gentleman with a
bald head and side-boards is standing to the
left of a small girl. He is wearing a jacket,
waistcoat, breeches and stockings. In his
right hand he holds a spade and from his
left arm there hangs a basket. The child
clutches his coat with her right hand.
Observations: Generally supposed to portray
Sir Joseph Paxton (1801–65), gardener and
architect who designed the Crystal Palace.
It may well be that this is so, but I know of no
evidence to support this claim.

Plate 24
Chang and Eng Bunker
This lithograph by W. Day, published by
W. Ackermann in 1829, is of the original
Siamese twins at the age of eighteen.
They were born of Chinese parents in
Siam. Their father was a fisherman and
they soon became famous swimmers. The
peculiarity of their movements in the water
attracted the attention of a Scottish
merchant, and finally led to their leaving
their native country in quest of fortune. *Fig.*
58, *pl.* I-23 is thought to portray the twins
whilst 'on show' at Barnum's circus.

Section I. Miscellaneous

Plate 25 (Left)
Fig. 61 Unidentified
gardener and girl
In the collection of
Mr Geoffrey Allen

Plate 26 (Right)
Fig. 62 Two schoolboys

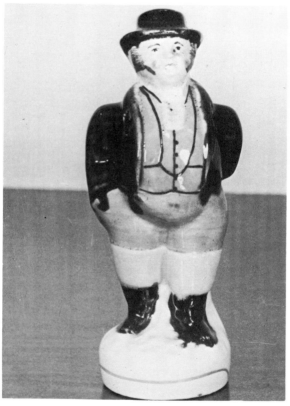

Plate 27 (Left)
Fig. 63 John Bull
By courtesy of
Mr and Mrs Eric Joyce

Plate 28 (Right)
Fig. 64 Unidentified man
and woman and another
man

Plate 25
Figure 61
Subject: **Unidentified gardener and girl**
Title: None
Height: 10 in (25 cm)
Colour: Well coloured.
Rarity: R.
Description: He stands on the right, wearing a tricorn hat, long coat, breeches and calf-

boots. He holds a spade in his left hand and a basket of apples in his right. To his right, stands a small girl wearing a plumed bonnet, blouse and skirt, with an apple in her right hand.
Observations: Is somewhat similar to *fig.* 60, *pl.* I-23. It may portray Sir Joseph Paxton, but I know of no evidence to substantiate this.

Plate 26
Figure 62
Subject: **Two schoolboys**
Title: None
Height: 10 in (25 cm)
Colour: Well coloured.
Rarity: Av.
Description: Two schoolboys stand in front of a tree trunk (spill-holder). Both are

Plate 29
Fig. 65 The rescue
In the collection of Mr Anthony Oliver

Plate 30
Fig. 66 Smuggler quarrel

bare-headed and wear short jackets, ties, waistcoats and trousers. The one on the left appears to be bullying the one on the right —he has grabbed him by the lapel of his coat. The one on the right has raised his right arm in self-defence. There is one slate on the ground in front of the boy on the left, and another to the right of the boy on the right.
Observations: Thought to portray a scene in *Tom Brown's Schooldays*.

Plate 27
Figure 63
Subject: **John Bull**
Title: None
Height: 7½ in (19 cm)
Colour: Well coloured.
Rarity: Av.
Description: Standing, wearing a 'low' top hat, short jacket, waistcoat, trousers and knee-boots, his right hand in his trouser pockets.
Observations: 1. John Bull—the typical Englishman, see *p.* 600. There is no evidence known to me to support the contention that this is a portrait of William Ball, commonly known as 'John Bull'. It bears no real resemblance to the portrait of this worthy that appeared in *The Illustrated London News* on June 12th, 1851.
2. The same figure, together with *fig.* 18 (Tell) *pl.* I-7, fetched 35 gns at Christie's in 1969.

Plate 28
Figure 64
Subject: **Unidentified man and woman and another man**

Title: None
Height: 7¾ in (20 cm)
Colour: Well coloured.
Rarity: R.
Description: A man stands on the right, bare-headed, wearing jacket, waistcoat, breeches, stockings and shoes. His left hand is in his pocket and his right arm round the neck of a girl standing to his right. She is bare-headed with a bun and wears a bodice and ankle-length skirt. She has a handbag in her right hand. Immediately to the right of the man's left leg there protrudes the head of a man, which is not unlike that of the first man.
Observations: This figure, which incidentally is No. C. 434—1928 in the collection in the Victoria and Albert Museum, has so far defied identification. It was at one time identified as the brothers Grimm, but I know of no reason for this and I am unable to throw any light on its correctness or otherwise. At a guess the figure looks far more like crime, possibly 'theatre crime'.

Plate 29
Figure 65
Subject: **Unidentified soldier, sailor and girl**
Title: The rescue (raised capitals)
Height: 11½ in (29 cm)
Colour: Well coloured.
Rarity: R.
Description: On the right, a sailor stands with his left arm round the waist of a girl on his left. He is bare-headed and wears a jacket, neckerchief, vest, trousers and belt. The girl is also bare-headed, and wears a bodice and full-length skirt. She holds her left arm by

her side, clutching her hat in her hand. The sailor's right hand rests on the left shoulder of a soldier standing to the left. He wears a peaked cap, military jacket, belt with a sash and trousers. His arms are crossed in front of him, and his legs are crossed, also. Between the soldier and the sailor is a barrel.
Observations: Almost certainly theatrical, but has so far defied identification.

Plate 30
Figure 66
Subject: **Two smugglers and girl**
Title: Smuggler quarrel (raised capitals on plaques)
Height: 11⅛ in (28.25 cm)
Colour: Well coloured.
Rarity: R.
Description: A bare-headed smuggler is seated on a barrel in the centre of a boat. He is wearing a jacket, shirt, neckerchief, breeches and thigh-boots. He is trying to push away with his right hand another smuggler on his right, and he is being supported in this endeavour by a girl on his left. The attacking smuggler is wearing a round hat, jacket, neckerchief, shirt and trousers and has his left foot on a crate. His right hand is raised and in it he clasps a knife. He grasps his opponent's shoulder with his left hand. The girl stands wearing a round hat, jacket and calf-length skirt. She tries to push away the attacking smuggler with her right hand and holds the left hand of the attacked smuggler in her left hand.
Observations: Almost certainly literary or theatrical, but has so far defied identification.

Plate 31 (Left)
Fig. 67 Girl in prayer

Plate 32 (Right)
Fig. 68 Girl and deer
In the collection of
Mr F. J. Stephens

Plate 31
Figure 67
Subject: **Girl in prayer**
Title: None
Height: 10½ in (26.5 cm)
Colour: Well coloured.
Rarity: R.
Description: A bare-headed girl with long hair is kneeling on her right knee with her hands raised in prayer. She is scantily dressed with both breasts exposed. The base is decorated with edging and three tassels.
Observations: This figure is, also, in the Glaisher collection at Cambridge. There it is catalogued as 'St. Mary Magdalene'. I do not know the evidence for this, and on the whole, the general appearance of the figure is theatrical.

Plate 32
Figure 68
Subject: **Girl and deer**
Title: None
Height: 11 in (28 cm)
Colour: Well coloured.
Rarity: R.
Pair: Unknown
Description: She is squatting bare-headed, wearing a blouse, long skirt and a sash round her waist. She clasps on her lap a small deer who looks up at her.
Observations: Has so far defied identification. Possibly theatrical.

Plate 33
Figure 69
Subject: **Flora**
Title: Flora (gilt script)
Height: 6½ in (16.5 cm)
Colour: Well coloured.
Maker: Possibly the Parr and Kent group of potters.
Rarity: R. A.
Pair: Fig. 70 (Colin) *pl*. I-34.
I534

Description: Sitting on a bank with her legs crossed, bare-headed, with a bonnet slung from her neck. She holds a flower in her right hand and a basket hangs from her right wrist. She wears a tartan bodice and calf-length skirt. A porcelaneous figure.
Observations: 1. The pair to this piece is *fig.* 70 (Colin) *pl*. I-34 but the situation is rendered confusing by the following entry in *Kent List C* (1955):

Ref. No.		*Approx. Ht. in inches*
530	Figure, Colleen	6
531	Figure, Flora	6

These figures cannot be traced either in *Kent List B* (which carries the same reference numbers as *Kent List C* but only goes to no. 419), or in *Kent List A*. On the available evidence 'Colleen' would appear to be a mistake for 'Colin'. The figures are not typical of those produced by the Parr and Kent group of potters. Maybe the moulds were purchased by Kent from another firm. This might explain their omission from *Kent Lists A* and *B* and also the error in *Kent List C*.
2. I have been unable to find out who 'Flora' and 'Colin' were. In the piece illustrated 'Flora' is wearing a tartan bodice. It has been suggested that the figure portrays Flora Macdonald (1722–90), the Jacobite heroine who helped Prince Charles to reach Skye. However, she was married to Allan Macdonald, and I know of no 'Colin' in her story.
3. 'Flora' is, of course, the goddess of flowers and spring of the ancient Romans. She was often portrayed in stage extravaganzas, especially at the Olympic Theatre in the Strand. There is a print of Mrs Stirling as the 'Goddess Flora'. However, this does not explain why the pair to the figure should be 'Colin.'

Plate 33
Fig. 69 Flora

Plate 34
Fig. 70 Colin
Unfortunately the engraving illustrated on the
right, which is attributed to Fairburn, carries no
indication as to whom Colin was. In the figure
illustrated, the flute has been broken off and the
neck damaged.
In the collection of Dr S.J. Howard

Plate 34
Figure 70
Subject: **Colin**
Title: Colin (gilt script)
Height: 6½ in (16.5 cm)
Colour: Well coloured.
Maker: Possibly the Parr and Kent group
of potters.
Rarity: VR. A.
Pair: *Fig.* 69 (Flora) *pl.* I-33.
Description: Sitting on a bank with his legs
crossed, wearing a bonnet and Highland
dress. He is playing a flute. A porcelaneous
figure.
Observations: 1. Based on an engraving
entitled *Colin*. Unfortunately there is nothing
on the engraving to indicate who 'Colin' was.
2. See also *fig.* 69 (Flora) *pl.* I-33.

Plate 35
Figure 71
Subject: **Sweep on mule**
Title: None
Height: 9 in (23 cm)
Colour: Well coloured.
Rarity: R.
Pair: Unknown
Description: Bare-footed, on a mule or
donkey, facing left. He is bare-headed, with
jacket, open shirt, and trousers rolled up
to the knees. He holds the reins by his side
in his left hand and brandishes a brush
above his head in his right hand.
Observations: Apparently the figure portrays
a sweep. What the significance of this is,
remains obscure.

Plate 35
Fig. 71 Sweep on mule
In the collection of Lt. Col. A.C.W. Kimpton

Section I. Miscellaneous

Plate 36
Fig. 72 ?Stanhope

Plate 37
Fig. 73 Woman and parrot
By courtesy of Miss M.M. Frame

Plate 38
Fig. 74 Darby and Joan
In the collection of Mr H.T. Appleton

Plate 39
Fig. 75 Unidentified man and girl
By courtesy of Miss M.M. Frame

Section I. Miscellaneous

Plate 40
Fig. 76 Two unidentified men
In the collection of Mr P. Redmayne

Plate 36
Figure 72
Subject: **? Lady Hester Stanhope and Dr Meryon**
Title: None
Height: 7¾ in (20 cm)
Colour: Well coloured.
Rarity: R.
Description: A lady is seated on top of a bridge wearing a broad-brimmed hat, bodice and long dress. Behind the bridge is a tree trunk (spill-holder). To the left is a bearded man dressed as an Arab. He proffers a mug, held in his left hand, to the lady.
Observations: The style of colouring of this figure is identical to *fig.* 279(*a*), *pl.* C-95A. The theme, too, is similar. It is obviously from the same factory. It has defied positive identification, but may well be Lady Hester Stanhope (1776–1839), who in 1810, made a pilgrimage to Jerusalem and, crossing the desert, camped with Bedouins amid the ruins of Palmyra. She was accompanied on this journey by Dr C. L. Meryon (1783–1877) who acted as her physician and dressed as an Arab, see section C. There is yet another figure of the same basic design. This time the woman sits on a branch of a tree (spill-holder); underneath is a gate and a basket of grapes. The Arab is handing her a bunch of grapes. The height of this figure is 10½ in (26.5 cm). Incidentally, *fig.* 113, *pl.* A-40 is said to have been found titled 'Lady Hester Stanhope'.

Plate 37
Figure 73
Subject: **Woman and parrot**
Title: None
Height: 9 in (23 cm)
Colour: Well coloured.
Rarity: Av.
Pair: Unknown
Description: A woman stands wearing a plumed head-dress, bodice, knee-length skirt, Turkish trousers and shoes. To her right, is a pedestal upon which stands a cage. On the top of the cage a parrot is perched.
Observations: This figure has been alleged to represent Lady Hester Stanhope, but I know of no evidence to support this idea.

Plate 38
Figure 74
Subject: **Darby and Joan**
Title: Darby & Joan (raised capitals)
Height: 11 in (28 cm)
Colour: Sparsely coloured.
Rarity: Av.
Description: 'Darby' stands on the right, wearing a frilled hat, short jacket, waistcoat, breeches, stockings and shoes. 'Joan' stands on the left, wearing a plumed bonnet, calf-length coat, muff and ankle-length skirt.
Observations: A similar group fetched 20 gns at Christie's in 1966.

Plate 39
Figure 75
Subject: **Unidentified man and girl**

Title: None
Height: 8¾ in (22 cm)
Colour: Well coloured.
Rarity: Av.
Description: The man stands on the right, wearing a plumed bonnet, ermine-edged cape, jacket with a sash over his left shoulder, breeches and knee-boots. Behind him is a tree trunk (spill-holder). His right hand rests on the bare head of a girl kneeling to his right. She wears a bodice and full-length skirt and holds a basket in both hands. A dog is clambering up the left leg of the man, and at his feet lie an axe and a saw.
Observations: Almost certainly a theatrical piece, but the significance of the axe and the saw have so far escaped elucidation.

Plate 40
Figure 76
Subject: **Two unidentified men**
Title: None
Height: 6¼ in (16 cm)
Colour: Well coloured.
Rarity: R.
Description: Two men, each of whom is bare-headed, sit on either side of a table. The man on the left, wears a long jacket, waistcoat, breeches, stockings and shoes and in his right hand he holds a pipe. The rather older man on the right, wears a jacket, waistcoat, trousers and shoes and in his left hand he holds a mug. They hold hands across the table and on the table top is another pipe and a jug.
Observations: Has so far defied identification.

Plate 41
Fig. 77 Unidentified officer equestrian

Fig. 78 Unidentified female equestrian
In the collection of Mrs Terence Richards

Plate 41
Figure 77
Subject: **Unidentified officer equestrian**
Title: None
Height: 7 in (17.5 cm)
Colour: Well coloured, underglaze blue coat.
Rarity: R.
Pair: *Fig.* 78 (Unidentified female equestrian)
Description: On a horse facing right, wearing helmet, military tailcoat with epaulettes, breeches and knee-boots.
Observations: Has so far defied identification. It is possible that this pair portrays Sir R. and Lady Sale, see *figs.* 66 and 67, *pl.* C-26, but there is nothing to substantiate this theory.

Figure 78
Subject: **Unidentified female equestrian**
Title: None
Height: 6½ in (16.5 cm)
Colour: Well coloured, underglaze blue coat.
Rarity: R.
Pair: *Fig.* 77 (Unidentified officer equestrian)
Description: On a horse facing left, in round hat and riding habit.
Observations: See preceding figure.

Plate 42
Figure 79
Subject: **Unidentified officer equestrian with flag**
Title: None
Height: 12½ in (31.75 cm)
Colour: Sparsely coloured.
Maker: In the style of Sampson Smith
Rarity: R.

Pair: There is almost certainly a pair to this figure for which *fig.* 80 has been reserved.
Description: On a horse facing right, standing on a plinth decorated with a clock-face, grapes and vine leaves. He is wearing a cocked hat athwartships, military uniform with epaulettes and carrying a flag in his left hand.
Observations: Has so far defied identification.

Plate 43
Figure 81
Subject: **Unidentified officer equestrian with flag**
Title: None
Height: 12¼ in (31 cm)
Colour: Sparsely coloured.
Rarity: R.
Pair: Probably a pair exists
Description: On a prancing horse facing right, in tall plumed helmet and military uniform and bearing a flag in his right hand.
Observations: Has so far defied identification.

Figure 82
Subject: **Unidentified soldier equestrian with flag**
Title: None
Height: 11½ in (29 cm)
Colour: Sparsely coloured.
Rarity: R.
Pair: Probably a pair exists
Description: On a prancing horse facing right, in tall plumed helmet and military uniform with knee-boots. He bears a flag in his right hand.
Observations: Has so far defied identification.

Section I. Miscellaneous

Plate 42 (Left)
Fig. 79 Unidentified
equestrian officer with flag
In the collection of
Lady Ranfurly

Plate 43A (Right)
Fig. 82(a) Unidentified
soldier on horseback
By courtesy of Mr John Hall

Plate 43
Fig. 81 Unidentified
equestrian officer with flag
Fig. 82 Unidentified
equestrian soldier with flag
In the collection of
Lady Ranfurly

Plate 43A
Figure 82(a)
Subject: **Unidentified equestrian soldier**
Title: None
Height: 10¼ in (25.75 cm)
Colour: Well coloured.
Rarity: R.
Description: On a horse facing right, wearing helmet, military uniform and knee-boots. He carries a shield with the cross of St

George in his left hand and holds the hilt of his sword in his right. Watch-holder.
Observations: It has been suggested that this is a circus piece portraying Philip Astley (1742–1814), the equestrian performer who opened Astley's Royal Amphitheatre in 1798. Prior to this, he had joined General Elliott's light horse (1759), rising to the rank of sergeant-major. There is, however, no concrete evidence to support this theory.

Plate 44
Fig. 83 Man with girl on pony
By courtesy of Mr J. Fairhurst

Plate 45
Fig. 85 Male musician on couch
Fig. 86 Female musician on couch
By courtesy of Miss M.M. Frame

Plate 44
Figure 83
Subject: **Man with girl on pony**
Title: None
Height: 10 in (25 cm)
Colour: Well coloured.
Rarity: R.
Pair: There is almost certainly a pair to this figure, for which *fig.* 84 has been reserved.
Description: A small girl is riding on a pony, facing left, crossing a bridge. There is a swan in the river under the bridge, and to the right of the bridge a man is sitting. He wears a plumed hat, jacket, sash over his left shoulder, breeches, stockings and shoes and his right arm rests on the pony's rump.
Observations: Possibly circus, but has so far defied identification.

Plate 45
Figure 85
Subject: **Male musician on couch**
Title: None
Height: 9 in (23 cm)
Colour: Well coloured.
Rarity: Av.
Pair: *Fig.* 86 (Female musician on couch)
Description: On a couch facing right, bareheaded with floral jacket, breeches, stockings and boots. His right elbow is on the arm of the couch, and in his left hand he holds a violin.
Observations: Possibly theatrical, but has so far defied identification.

Figure 86
Subject: **Female musician on couch**
Title: None
Height: 9 in (23 cm)
Colour: Well coloured.
Rarity: Av.
Pair: *Fig.* 85 (Male musician on couch)
Description: On couch facing left, bareheaded with necklace and long dress. Her left elbow is on the arm of the couch, and she holds an open book in her left hand. She clutches a violin in her right hand.
Observations: Has so far defied identification.

Plate 46
Fig. 87 Charity girl

Plate 47
Fig. 88 *(facing left)* Girl, with helmet, sword and shield

Plate 48
Fig. 90 Unidentified man

Plate 46
Figure 87
Subject: **Charity girl**
Title: None
Date: *c.* 1880
Height: 7½ in (19 cm)
Colour: Coloured in the tradition of the Parr and Kent group of potters.
Maker: Kent & Parr
Rarity: R.
Pair: There may well be a 'pairing' boy.
Description: Standing, wearing bonnet, cape, calf-length dress with sash round her waist, stockings and shoes. She holds a manuscript in each hand.
Observations: Almost certainly a charity girl, and may well be from a charity school in the Bristol area, for it comes from the same factory as *figs.* 36, 37 and 38, *pls.* I-17 and 18.

Plate 47
Figure 88
Subject: **Girl with helmet, sword and shield** (facing left)
Title: None
Height: 7 in (17.5 cm)
Colour: Well coloured.
Rarity: R.
Pair: *Fig.* 89 [Girl with helmet, sword and shield (*R*)]
Description: Seated, facing left, wearing a helmet, bodice, knee-length skirt, stockings and shoes. In her left hand she holds a shield and in her right hand a manuscript. In front of her lies a sword.
Observations: Said to represent 'France'.

It has also been postulated that it portrays Joan of Arc.

Figure 89 (not illustrated)
Subject: **Girl with helmet, sword and shield** (facing right)
Title: None
Height: 7 in (17.5 cm)
Colour: Well coloured.
Rarity: R.
Pair: *Fig.* 88 [Girl with helmet, sword and shield (*L*)]
Description: A mirror-image of *fig.* 88:
Observations: See preceding figure.

Plate 48
Figure 90
Subject: **Unidentified man**
Title: None
Height: 9¼ in (23.5 cm)
Colour: Well coloured.
Rarity: VR.
Pair: It is very likely that a pair exists, but it is, as yet, unrecorded.
Description: Standing, bare-headed and bearded. He wears a knee-length coat with white collar, belt with tassel and calf-boots. He holds a bonnet in his left hand. To his right, is a square, fluted pedestal upon which he rests his right elbow. His right hand is in front of his waist and is empty.
Observations: Has, to date, defied identification. Is probably theatrical, but could well be a political figure.

Plate 49
T: *Fig.* 94 Unidentified building
Fig. 95 Unidentified building

B: *Fig.* 92 Beaumaris Castle
Fig. 91 ?Euston Station
Fig. 93 Caernarvon Castle
By courtesy of Mr and Mrs Eric Joyce

Plate 50
Fig. 96 Unidentified ecclesiastical building inscribed 'St Roch'
In the collection of Dr S.J. Howard

Plate 49
Figure 91
Subject: **? Euston station**
Title: None
Date: c. 1848
Height: 10½ in (26.5 cm)
Colour: Well coloured.
Rarity: R.
Description: There are two girls in Highland dress standing on either side of a tall arch surmounted by a clock-face. Above the clock-face is a railway train facing to the left.
Observations: A similar figure was sold at Christie's in 1966, with the description:

A group commemorating the opening of Euston Station in 1848 (*sic*), with two figures of girls on either side of a clock face, with a railway train above . . .

In addition to *fig.* 91 the lot consisted of *fig.* 53 (Train group) *pl.* I-23 and another unimportant group. It fetched 18 gns.

Euston Station was opened in 1838 and the Doric arch remained, until its demolition in 1963, the most impressive entrance to a London terminus. In 1848, there was an important acceleration in the Scottish service with the introduction of the first express trains running between London (Euston) and Edinburgh (1st class only—13 hours). Both this figure and *fig.* 53, may commemorate the latter event.

Figure 92
Subject: **Beaumaris Castle**
Title: Beaumaris Castle (raised capitals on plaque)
Height: 6¼ in (16 cm)
Colour: Well coloured.
Rarity: VR.
Description: To the left is a circular tower, in the centre a gate and to the right two smaller towers.

Observations: 1. This figure is a fairly accurate portrayal of 'The Gate next the Sea' at Beaumaris Castle. Today, a modern bridge of wood has superseded the original drawbridge which, when raised, barred the gate. Beside it is the small dock for ships, on which the castle depended for news of the outside world, or for supplies in times of siege. By 1296, a fully laden vessel of 40 tons could sail up to the main gate when the tide served. The boats were made fast to a ring fixed in a buttress which contained the castle mill.
2. A similar figure fetched 18 gns at Christie's in 1964.

Figure 93
Subject: **Caernarvon Castle**
Title: Caernarvon Castle (raised capitals on plaque)
Height: 7½ in (19 cm)
Colour: Well coloured.
Rarity: VR.
Description: On the right is a gateway with a very high narrow arch surmounted by a round turret. In the centre is a square tower with a slender hexagonal turret, and on the left a hexagonal tower.

Figure 94
Subject: **Unidentified building**
Title: None
Height: 8 in (20.5 cm)
Colour: Well coloured.
Rarity: R.
Description: A two-storied building with a central triangular frieze surmounted by a clock-face and supported on either side by a square tower.
Observations: Has defied positive identification. It has been suggested that it

represents the old Theatre Royal at Drury Lane, which was destroyed by fire on February 24th, 1809. It was the theatre in which such famous actors as David Garrick, John Philip Kemble and Mrs Siddons made their names. I do not know the evidence for this theory. It has also been suggested that it portrays the east front of St Paul's Cathedral, but this I have confirmed is certainly not so. It is not dissimilar to the fronts of certain Wesleyan and Baptist chapels in Wales and the source may eventually be traced there.

Figure 95
Subject: **Unidentified building**
Title: None
Height: 7¼ in (18.25 cm)
Colour: Well coloured.
Rarity: R.
Description: An ecclesiastical building with a central triangular frieze surmounted by a figure of a holy man with shepherd's crook and dog. Hitherto this was thought to represent 'The Good Shepherd'. However, since the discovery of *fig.* 96, *pl.* I-50 it seems likely to portray 'St. Roche'. On either side of the building are two conical pediments.
Observations: At one time was regarded as possibly representing the City Temple.

Plate 50
Figure 96
Subject: **Unidentified ecclesiastical building dedicated to St Roch**
Title: St Roch (gilt script)
Height: 9¾ in (24.5 cm)
Colour: Well coloured.
Rarity: VR.
Description: An ecclesiastical building with a central triangular frieze surmounted by a

Plate 51
T: *Fig.* 97 Unidentified castle
Fig. 98 Unidentified castle dated 1851

B: *Fig.* 99 Unidentified castle
Fig. 100 Trinity College, Cambridge
Fig. 101 Unidentified school

saint with a crook in his right hand and a dog clambering up his left side. At his feet is a plaque inscribed 'St. Roch'. On either side are two conical pediments.
Observations: In spite of intensive enquiries, I have been unable to identify this ecclesiastical building. A high authority in the Roman Catholic church has not been able to obtain any information as to the whereabouts of any church dedicated to St. Roch. In fact, his whole feeling is that the church of Rome do not have one in this country.

Plate 51
Figure 97
Subject: **Unidentified castle**
Title: None
Height: $5\frac{1}{2}$ in (14 cm)
Colour: Well coloured.
Rarity: Av.
Description: On the left, is a round tower surmounted by a smaller tower. In the centre, a small gateway and to the right, another round tower.
Observations: Bears some resemblance to the Queen's Gate, Caernarvon Castle. Has been said to be Beaumaris Castle, but it differs in many respects from the titled version and I have been unable to identify it from the castle itself. It may represent Conway Castle but I cannot confirm this.

Figure 98
Subject: **Unidentified castle**
Title: None
Date: 1851
Height: $5\frac{3}{4}$ in (14.5 cm)
Colour: Well coloured.
Rarity: R.
Description: A central round tower with gateway, clock-face and plaque inscribed '1851' and two smaller flanking towers.

Observations: The date suggests that it may commemorate the Great Exhibition. However, many other dates are found inscribed on similar castles. They range from 1840–1859 and their significance remains obscure. There is a close similarity between this figure and *fig.* 49 (Norwich Castle) *pl.* G-23 and also *fig.* 49(a) (A royal castle) *pl.* G-26.

Figure 99
Subject: **Unidentified castle**
Title: None
Height: $7\frac{1}{2}$ in (19 cm)
Colour: Well coloured.
Rarity: Av.
Description: A complex structure of pinnacles and turrets with a central stairway leading up to two main doors. On the right of the structure stands a drummer boy.
Observations: Has been said to represent Cortachy Castle, Angus, but it bears no resemblance to such illustrations of the castle that I have seen.

Figure 100
Subject: **The Great Gate, Trinity College, Cambridge**
Title: Trinity College (raised capitals on blue plaques)
Height: 8 in (20.5 cm)
Colour: Well coloured.
Rarity: Av.
Description: A central flight of steps leads upwards to a Gothic doorway, flanked by two smaller doors; two storeys, a clock-face and battlements above. On each side is a hexagonal tower.
Observations: 1. Roughly based on the east front of the Great Gate at Trinity College, see *ch.* 3, *pl.* 67.
2. This figure is titled in raised capitals on

blue plaques. Other figures titled in a similar manner include: *fig.* 19 (Tell) *pl.* I-7; *fig.* 49 (Norwich Castle) *pl.* G-23 and *fig.* 49(a) (A Royal Castle) *pl.* G-26. Presumably, all emanate from the same factory.
3. A similar figure, together with two less important figures, fetched 32 gns at Christie's in 1963. Another, together with three less important figures, fetched £28 at Sotheby's in 1966.

Figure 101
Subject: **Unidentified school**
Title: School (raised capitals)
Height: $7\frac{1}{4}$ in (18.25 cm)
Colour: Well coloured.
Rarity: R.
Description: A two-storied house with three doors, five windows and two chimneys.
Observations: Has so far escaped positive identification.

Plate 52
Fig. 102 Brunswick School

Plate 52
Figure 102
Subject: **Brunswick school**
Title: Brunswick/school (indented capitals)
Height: 3½ in (9 cm)
Colour: Well coloured.
Rarity: VR.
Description: A single-storied building with a central doorway with a small door to the right. There are four windows, a plaque with the school's name over the doorway and two chimney-stacks. In front is a garden. A pastille-burner.
Observations: 1. Porcelaneous, probably Staffordshire, but this is not certain.
2. It seemed that this piece might be a representation of *Brunswick Wesleyan School*, Leek, Staffordshire, which was closed sometime between August, 1913 and July, 1914. The school is listed in the Board of Education's *Voluntary Schools, Trusts and Tenure, 1906* and its deed is dated 1827. According to the minutes of the Committee of Council on Education (1860-1) the school had been accepted for Government aid from August 31st, 1860. However, the Librarian at Leek Public Library, whose advice was sought on this matter wrote that:

'the original building was enlarged to its present size and not rebuilt, and the present building certainly bears no relationship to the figure'.

3. Likewise, it seemed that this school might be *Brunswick School*, Dutton Homestall near East Grinstead. This school was founded in 1866 by two sisters Kate and Charlotte Thompson. It was sited at Luxworth House, 29–30 Brunswick Road, Hove and moved to its present site, in 1896. A plaque on the original building describes it as *Formerly*

The Misses Thompson's Preparatory School and notes that Sir Winston Churchill was educated there from 1883 to 1885. The sisters are reputed to have said that they did their best to turn the boys out as gentlemen and Winston was the one case in which they had failed. Once again, however, the piece bears no resemblance to this building.

Plate 53
Figure 103
Subject: **The Keep at Dudley Castle**
Title: Dudley Castle (gilt script)
Height: 6¼ (16 cm)
Colour: Well coloured.
Maker: In the style of Sampson Smith
Rarity: VR. A.
Description: There is a central gate surmounted by battlements. On either side is a ruined tower. In front of the castle are two sheep.
Observations: An excellent representation of the Keep at Dudley Castle.

Plate 54
Figure 104
Subject: **Scarborough Castle**
Title: Scarboro' Castle (gilt script)
Height: 5¼ in (13.5 cm)
Colour: Well coloured.
Rarity: VR. A.
Description: A ruined castle on top of a mound.
Observations: Bears such a close similarity to the ruin of Scarborough Castle that identification would have been possible even in the absence of the title.

Plate 53
Fig. 103 Dudley Castle
To the right of the figure is an Edwardian
postcard of the Keep at Dudley Castle. It will
be noted that the figure closely resembles its
source.

Plate 54
Fig. 104 Scarborough Castle
To the right of the castle is an Edwardian
postcard illustrating Scarborough Castle. It will
be noted that the representation is reasonably
accurate.

Plate 55
Fig. 105 Unidentified house — 'A present from Scarborough'
The chimney stack on the right has been broken off.

Plate 56
Fig. 106 Courting under difficulties.
By courtesy of Mr and Mrs Eric Joyce

APPENDIX
SECTION B
Plate 1A
Fig. 6(a) Cobden

Plate 55
Figure 105
Subject: **Unidentified house**
Title: A present / from / Scarborough (gilt script)
Height: $4\frac{5}{8}$ in (12 cm)
Colour: Well coloured.
Rarity: VR.
Description: A three-storied gabled house with two doorways, each of which is entered by a flight of steps. That on the left leads to a penthouse. There are two windows on the ground floor, two on the first floor, and one dormer window. There are two chimney-stacks. In the figure illustrated the stack on the right has been broken off. Money-box.
Observations: May represent a building in Scarborough, although I have not, as yet, had an opportunity to identify it. A pair of matching swans, each inscribed 'A present from Scarborough', has been noted.

Plate 56
Figure 106
Subject: **Courting under difficulties**
Title: None
Date: c. 1850
Height: $12\frac{1}{4}$ in (31 cm)
Colour: Well coloured.
Rarity: R.
Description: A girl is looking out of the dormer window of a thatched house. She has her arms round the waist of a sailor who has one foot on the porch and another on a large water-butt. A farmer with a pitch-fork is about to prod the sailor in the rump.
Observations: 1. No. 1658 in the Willett Collection at Brighton.
2. This figure is referred to in *Courtship and*

Matrimony in Staffordshire Pottery Figures by G. Woolliscroft Rhead (*Connoisseur*: April, 1915):

In 'courtship under difficulties' the ardent lover, with the friendly help of the rain-tub, mounts to the bedroom window, clasps as well as may be his inamorata to his bosom, while the irate parent steals round the corner armed with a pitch-fork! The piece in question is a late example, about 1830[1].

Nevertheless, it is, in the broadest sense, a piece of true art, since it mirrors in a most graphic and convincing manner the lights and shadows of human experience, and the transient nature of earthly bliss—light and bliss being represented by the caresses of the loved one, shadow by the pitch-fork and the fell intent of the aforesaid parent.

[1]. Today this figure would generally be regarded as being of rather later date c. 1850.

3. A similar figure fetched 60 gns at Christie's in 1969; and another, 28 gns a few months later.

APPENDIX
SECTION B
Plate 1A
Figure 6(a)
Subject: **Richard Cobden**
Title: R. Cobden. W. P. (*sic*) (raised capitals)
Date: c. 1846
Height: $9\frac{1}{2}$ in (24 cm)
Colour: Well coloured.
Rarity: VR.
Description: He stands bare-headed, in frock-coat, waistcoat and trousers.

SECTION C
Plate 25
Figure 65 (not illustrated)
Subject: **Napoleon**
Observations: See section C for details of this figure, a contemporary version of which has now been recorded.

Appendix
Selected Auction Prices
1978-80 and 1985-86

All prices are for figures sold at Christie's South Kensington except where otherwise stated and have been selected to show a representative range rather than record prices. (S) = Sotheby's; (P) = Phillips.

Plate	Figure	1978-80 Price (£)	1985-86 Price (£)
A—British and Foreign Royalty			
1	1	120	150
7	8 with 9	400	300
19	54	90	120
20	56 with 57	180	220
27	73	90	110
32	87	140	140
34	92	80	100
37	99	95	120
47	143	240	180
48	139 with 140	100	100
49	144	240	170
51	148	480	500
54	158 with 159	130	130
55	169	95	110
57	175	85	150
58	184	55	150
62	192 with 193	650	450
68	210 with 211	320	300
69	214 with 215	320	350
70	217	85	120
—	218	300	200
72	219	55	80
—	—	100 (S)	—
84	240 with 241	140	130
87	248	160 (S)	150
92	253	280	350
102	271	85	70
B—Statesmen and Politicians			
1	2 with 5	100	250
—	4	120	280
—	7 with 8	100	220
—	13	120	150
2	14	150	120
—	16	280	320
—	—	280	—
—	17	200	100
—	19	85	200
3	20	90	120
—	21	600	750
—	23	95	300
4	25	70	200
5	29	190	120
7	31	220	—
—	—	220	—
—	—	220	—
10	34	80	150
14	45 and 46	85	150
—	48	95	130
16	51	220	200
—	—	220	—
—	52 with 53	340 (S)	370
—	54 with 55, and 56	150	300
17a	58	60	120
19	61	85	95
20	64	90	90
21	66	160	200
—	—	340	—
—	67	190	250
25	72 with 73	200	200
—	73	140	130
25a	74	110	130
27	85	50	100
C—Naval, Military and Exploration			
5	4	400	700
6	5	90	120
—	—	120	—
9	8	300	280
11	19	75	70
—	20	120	130
—	21	65	110
—	22	120	80
—	22 with 23	100	180
—	26	50	50
12	38	80	70
—	39	55	65
13	32	95	80
14a	42a	80	50
31	73	55	80
32	74	360 (S)	400
—	75	60	200
35	82	60	100
—	86 with 87	90	100
—	—	110	—
38	94	160	150
—	96	110	70
—	97	100	200
42	102 with 103	300	400
43	107	650	900
44	109	240	650
—	111	450	700
46	114 with 115	130	550
47	117 with 118	550	800
50	124	75	350
51a	127	140	900
54	135	680	850
—	139	220	400
55	142	80	300
—	143	100	250
56	146	170	180
—	150	190	300
—	151	75	350
58	153	60	200
59	157 with 158	120	350
67	173	160	300
—	—	260	—
68	179	260	650
69	181	70	300
—	183 with 184	130	300
—	186	65	250
—	187	70	250
70a	191	160	450
—	—	400 (S)	200
71	193	140	200
—	194	110	250

Plate	Figure	_1978-80_ Price (£)	_1985-86_ Price (£)	Plate	Figure	_1978-80_ Price (£)	_1985-86_ Price (£)
—	195	85	200	13	31	320	400
—	196	95	250	24	49	60	90
—	197	240	300	35	70	160	250
—	198	190	200	—	—	130	—
—	199	180	250	77	148	50	120
72	201	90	80	80	154	320	380
—	204	100	75	—	156	100	200
73	210	85	150	133	270	90	150
—	212	160	200				
74	214	110	180				
76	221 with 222	200	350	**F—Sport**			
77	223	75	200				
—	224	190	250	4	5	130	200
—	225	120	220	—	7	320	400
—	—	220	—	6	11 with 12	400	400
—	—	160	—	7	13 with 14	600 (S)	700
79	231	65	150	—	15	260	350
80	232	380	600				
89	147	130	150				
—	266	80	350	**G—Crime**			
90	267	80	200				
92b	274	260	500	8	26	90	130
93	276	140	250	16	32	55	100
	277	110	150	—	34	140	250
97	282	80	150	17	36 with 37	850	500
100	289	100	300	18a	42	220	1,200
—	290	110	250				
101	294 with 295	90	250				
102	296	120	150	**H—Authors, Poets, Composers, et cetera**			
—	299	90	150				
—	300	320	300	7	20 with 21	110	—
103	302 with 303	100	600	—	25	35	50
106	304 with 305	150	250	9	31	140	—
113	322 with 323	120	220	10	35	85	110
114	326 with 327	95	250	18	56	85	100
118	332 with 333	85	120	—	—	170 (S)	—
119	339	95	150				

D—Religious

Plate	Figure	_1978-80_ Price (£)	_1985-86_ Price (£)
20	42	480	750
23	46	70	130
—	47	400	500

I—Miscellaneous

Plate	Figure	_1978-80_ Price (£)	_1985-86_ Price (£)
2	4	110	130
18	40	75	120
—	42	60	75
19a	48b	140 (S)	—
23	53	65	80
—	58	80	200
35	71	120	—
40	76	55	—
51	100	60	130
56	106	190	300

E—Theatre, Opera, Ballet and Circus

Plate	Figure	_1978-80_ Price (£)	_1985-86_ Price (£)
1	1a	72 (P)	90
1a	2	100	150
12	29	1,300 (S)	1,300

Bibliography and References

Balston, Thomas

1951   Victorian Staffordshire Portraits. *Country Life Annual*, p. 57.

1958   *Staffordshire Portrait Figures of the Victorian Age.* London: Faber and Faber Limited.

1963   *Supplement to Staffordshire Portrait Figures of the Victorian Age.* London: John Hall.

1963   *The Thomas Balston Collection of Staffordshire Portrait Figures of the Victorian Age.* At Stapleford Park, Melton Mowbray: National Trust.

Bedford, John

1964   *Staffordshire Pottery Figures.* London: Cassell.

Blacker, J. F.

c. 1910   *The ABC of English Ceramic Art (Nineteenth Century).* London: Stanley Paul & Co.

Bruce, George

1964   Staffordshire Pottery. *The Ideal Home,* **Dec.,** p. 105.

Causey, Andrew

1967   Art Form of the Victorian Masses. *The Illustrated London News,* **250,** 24.

Coxe, Anthony Hippisley

1957   The Circus in Ceramics. *The Tatler and Bystander,* **226,** 14.

Fleischman, Theo

1966   Popularité de Napoléon en Angleterre. *Bulletin de Société Belge d'Etudes Napoléoniennes,* **54,** 5.

Godden, Geoffrey A.

1963   Victorian Portrait Figures. *The Pottery Gazette and Glass Trade Review,* **May,** p. 555.

1963   *British Pottery & Porcelain 1780–1850.* London: Arthur Barker Limited.

1964   *Encyclopaedia of British Pottery and Porcelain Marks.* London: Herbert Jenkins. [Reprinted by Barrie and Jenkins.]

1965   Victorian Earthenware Chimney-Ornaments. *Apollo,* **82,** 45.

1966   *Antique China and Glass under £5.* London: Arthur Barker Limited.

1966   *An Illustrated Encyclopaedia of British Pottery and Porcelain.* London: Herbert Jenkins. [Second edition Barrie and Jenkins.]

Guth, Paul

1956   Le Staffordshire tel qu'on le collectionne en France. *Connaissance des Arts,* **51,** 62.

Haggar, R. G.

1955   *Staffordshire Chimney Ornaments.* London: Phoenix House.

Hall, C. Douglas

1955   *The story of 'Old Staffordshire' Pottery by Kent of Burslem.* Burslem: William Kent (Porcelains) Ltd. (Referred to in text as *Kent List C.*)

Joyce, Day

1956   American Portrait Figures in Staffordshire Pottery of the 19th Century. *The Antiques Journal, formerly The American Antiques Journal,* **vol. 11,** no. 2, p. 34.

1957   Staffordshire Portrait Pottery. Tracing History through Clay Figures. *The Antique Dealer and Collectors Guide,* **vol. 12,** no. 2, p. 24.

1957   Historical Staffordshire Pottery. Royalty, Politicians & Divines. *The Antique Dealer and Collectors Guide,* **vol. 12,** no. 3, p. 27.

1957   War Heroes in Pottery. The Folk Art of Staffordshire. *The Antique Dealer and Collectors Guide,* **vol. 12,** no. 4, p. 28.

1957   Headline Personalities. The News in Staffordshire Pottery. *The Antique Dealer and Collectors Guide,* **vol. 12,** no. 5, p. 25.

1958   Undying Fame in Pottery. International, Literary and Theatre Personalities. *The Antique Dealer and Collectors Guide,* **vol. 12,** no. 6, p. 31.

1958   Last Great British Folk Art. Popular Sentiment expressed in Pottery. *The Antique Dealer and Collectors Guide,* **vol. 12,** no. 7, p. 28.

Joyce, Day and Eric

1957   History Recorded in Pottery: Staffordshire Figures of Personalities of the Crimean War. *The Illustrated London News,* **231,** 611.

1959   Sportsmen in Staffordshire Pottery. *Country Life,* **125,** 1376.

Kennedy, J. D.

1928   Old Staffordshire Pottery. Cottage Ornaments that are of Particular Interest to the Modest Collector. *Homes and Gardens,* **10,** 114.

Kent, William

c. 1901–02   *Price List, William Kent, Manufacturer of Novelties in Earthenware, etc., Novelty Works, Wellington Street, Burslem, Staffs.* (Referred to in text as *Kent List A.*)

c. 1920   *Price List, William Kent, Manufacturer of Earthenware Figures, etc., including Reproductions of Old Staffordshire Ware. Novelty Works, Wellington Street, Burslem, Stoke-on-Trent.* (Referred to in text as *Kent List B.*)

Latham, Bryan

1953   *Victorian Staffordshire Portrait Figures for the Small Collector.* London: Alec Tiranti Ltd.

1953   Staffordshire Portrait Figures. *The Lady,* **138,** 851.

1954   Collecting Victorian Staffordshire Portrait Figures. *Homes and Gardens,* **vol. 35,** no. 12, p. 64.

1954   Soldiers of the Queen. *The Lady,* **140,** 388.

1955   Staffordshire Theatre Figures—Starting a Collection. *The Lady,* **141,** 560.

1955   The British Army in Pottery. *Army Quarterly and Defence Journal,* **70,** 237.

1956   Victorian Staffordshire Portrait Figures. *Antiques* (New York).

1968   A Collector at Home. *Homes and Gardens,* **vol. 49,** no. 9, p. 100.

Latham, Jean

1965   A Zoo of Staffordshire Animals. *The Antique Dealer and Collectors Guide*, **vol. 20**.

1966   Collecting Castles, Cottages and Criminals. *The Antique Dealer and Collectors Guide*, **vol. 20**, no. 9, p. 58.

Lee, Albert

1935   Staffordshire Figures in America. *Connoisseur*, **Nov.**, p. 262.

Lewis, Griselda

1956   *A Picture History of English Pottery*. London: Hulton Press.

Littledale, M.

1954   A Friar and Nun believed to be Père Moulert and Sister Hallahan. *The Antique Dealer and Collectors Guide*, **Jan.**

Oliver, Anthony

1967   Solving Puzzles in Staffordshire Naval Figures. *The Antique Dealer and Collectors Guide*, **vol. 22**, no. 4, p. 48.

1967   The Naval Figure in Staffordshire Pottery. *The Port of London Authority Monthly*, **42**, 269.

1969   Collecting Victorian Staffordshire Figures, Part I: A Re-appraisal. *The Antique Dealer and Collectors Guide*, **Aug.**, p. 69.

1969   Collecting Victorian Staffordshire Figures, Part II: Some Practical Hints. *The Antique Dealer and Collectors Guide*, **Sept.**, p. 66.

1969   Collecting Victorian Staffordshire Figures, Part III: Identification. *The Antique Dealer and Collectors Guide*, **Oct.**, p. 73.

Addenda, 1981:

1970   Farewell to my Legless Mother. *The Antique Dealer and Collectors Guide*, **May**, p. 69.

1971   Victorian Staffordshire Pottery Animals. *The Antique Dealer and Collectors Guide*, **Jan.**, p. 82.

1971   A Panorama of Portrait Figures. *The Antique Dealer and Collectors Guide*, **April**, p. 94.

1971   *The Victorian Staffordshire Figure*. London: Heinemann.

1973   Staffordshire Portraits of a Boxing Scandal. *The Antique Dealer and Collectors Guide*, **May**, p. 68.

1973   Staffordshire Figures. Heroes and Heroines, Villains and Victims. *Art and Antiques Weekly*, **June**, p. 28.

1973   Theatrical Staffordshire Figures. Staffordshire Stage. *Art and Antiques Weekly*, **Dec.**, p. 27.

1974   Sporting Staffordshire Figures. *Art and Antiques Weekly*, **June**, p. 18.

1975   Crime in Staffordshire Pottery. Those Villainous Victorians. *Art and Antiques Weekly*, **July**, p. 24.

1976   Staffordshire Celebrities. They came to London to see the Queen. *The Antique Dealer and Collectors Guide*, **June**, p. 114.

1976   The Coursing Greyhound in Staffordshire Pottery. Chapter in: Coursing. The Pursuit of Game with Gazehounds (The Standfast Sporting Library), p. 254.

1976   Chapter on Staffordshire Figures in: Discovering Antiques. The Story of World Antiques, p. 1613. London: B.P.C. Publishing.

1979   Toys from the Fair. *The Antique Dealer and Collectors Guide*, **April**, p. 106.

1981   *Staffordshire Pottery. The Tribal Art of England*. London: Heinemann.

Read, Herbert

1929   *Staffordshire Pottery Figures*. London: Duckworth.

Rhead, G. W. and F. A.

1906   *Staffordshire Pots and Potters*. London: Hutchinson and Co.

Rowed, Charles

1926   Pottery Inspirations —Anecdotal notes on familiar names. *The Ideal Home*, **Jan.**, p. 37.

S. C. J.

1926   Little Figures of Other Days. Bygone Fancies portrayed in Earthenware and Porcelain. *Homes and Gardens*, **7**, 289.

Stanley, Louis T.

1963   *Collecting Staffordshire Pottery*. London: W. H. Allen.

'The Sunday Times' Colour Magazine

1964   *Matter of Fact—The Thomas Balston Collection of Staffordshire Portrait Figures*. June 14th, p. 30.

'The Times'

1963   *Some Eminent Victorians. Staffordshire Portrait Figures from the Thomas Balston Collection*. May 9th, p. 26.

1965   *Cavalcade of Earthenware Figures*. July 3rd, p. 11.

Troubetzkoy, Simone

1956   Prenez goût au Staffordshire. *Femina—Illustration*, **24**, 80.

Tyrwhitt-Drake, Sir Garrard

1955   Staffordshire Pottery Animals. *Country Life*, **117**, 1490.

Willett, Henry

1899   *Catalogue of a Collection of Pottery and Porcelain Illustrating Popular British History*. London: Her Majesty's Stationery Office.

General Index

General Index

Index of Figure Subjects

Index of Figure Subjects

555

Index of Figure Subjects

Index of Figure Subjects